Tutorial on
Software Design
Techniques
FOURTH EDITION

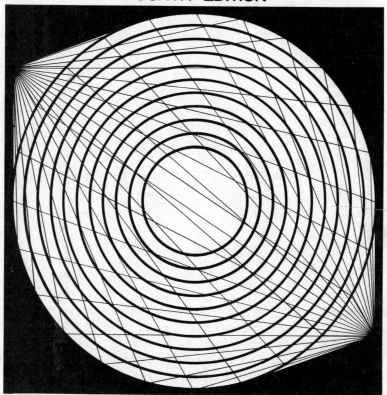

Peter Freeman
Anthony I. Wasserman

IEEE CATALOG NUMBER EHO205-5
LIBRARY OF CONGRESS NUMBER 83-81873
IEEE COMPUTER SOCIETY ORDER NUMBER 514
ISBN 0-8186-0514-6

 IEEE COMPUTER SOCIETY

1884 · 1984
A CENTURY OF ELECTRICAL PROGRESS

IEEE
COMPUTER
SOCIETY
PRESS

Dedication

To the many people who have used the first three editions of this book, especially those who have taken the trouble to tell us about their experience with these ideas.

Published by IEEE Computer Society Press
1109 Spring Street
Suite 300
Silver Spring, MD 20910

IEEE Catalog Number EHO205-5
Library of Congress Number 83-81873
IEEE Computer Society Order Number 514
ISBN 0-8186-0514-6 (Paper)
ISBN 0-8186-4514-8 (Microfiche)

Order from: IEEE Computer Society
Post Office Box 80452
Worldway Postal Center
Los Angeles, CA 90080

IEEE Service Center
445 Hoes Lane
Piscataway, NJ 08854

The Institute of Electrical and Electronics Engineers, Inc.

Acknowledgments

We would like to express our deepest appreciation to the authors of the papers in this volume who have graciously consented to having their work reprinted. Without their help, this book would literally not exist. We are also pleased to publicly thank Margaret Brown and Chip Stockton of the IEEE Computer Society for their work in producing this edition on an extremely tight schedule.

To the Reader

This book is intended for both beginning and experienced designers, analysts, and managers needing a broad introduction to software engineering methods. The focus throughout is on the leading edge of practical software technology, with a few papers selected to show important research developments that are likely to affect practice within the next few years.

Along with a number of "classics", this volume includes several original papers, and others that are not easily available elsewhere. Taken together, these papers explain important concepts and techniques and provide illustrative examples. Each Part begins with an overview to tie the papers together, and to provide some insight into why these papers were chosen.

This fourth edition has been revised and expanded to reflect the latest ideas in the field and to incorporate new material found to be of high interest to a number of audiences, including university and professional development classes in software engineering. Nearly half of the papers did not appear in the third edition of the book.

During the three years since the publication of the third edition, the field of software specification and design has grown in several dimensions. These changes are reflected in this edition by an increased emphasis on software development methodology, by efforts to integrate process design and data design, and by advances in techniques for analyzing and modeling distributed and concurrent systems.

We have largely retained the structure of the previous edition, which follows a traditional life cycle. We note, however, that these distinctions are being blurred by increasing integration of ideas, and by the use of prototyping approaches, which address several phases of the development process at once.

We believe that this new edition provides a good introduction to concepts of software design and outlines current research and development activities in the field. We continue to be grateful to all who have used the previous editions of the book, especially those who have taken the trouble to think about the issues and argue with us about them.

Peter Freeman

Anthony I. Wasserman

August, 1983

Table of Contents

Part I

Introduction

Five papers are included in this Part to provide an introduction to the study of design techniques. The first, "Fundamentals of Design," was prepared especially for this fourth edition. It describes the place of design in the total life cycle of software development and provides perspective on the nature of design. It also identifies several fundamental operations of design that can be observed in many design techniques.

The next two papers are reprinted here because of their historical perspective. Both were written not only before modern specification and design techniques were in use but also before many techniques existed. Indeed, the development situations described in these two papers even predate the use of modern high level languages and structured programming techniques.

The paper by Boehm, "Software and its Impact", is a summary of a widely cited report on the costs of software development for the Air Force. The article by Brooks, "The Mythical Man-Month", is excerpted from his book of the same title. Both papers provide the views of experienced managers of large-scale software development and provide

many insights into the problems encountered in such developments.

The causes of the difficulties cited by Boehm and Brooks were not in the programming task itself but rather were in knowing *what* to program, reducing the need for evolution (maintenance) and properly managing the entire effort. Both Boehm and Brooks were extremely influential in efforts to introduce modern software development practices.

Wasserman's paper provides an introduction to the subjects covered in the remainder of the book. It describes the life cycle, defines its phases, outlines some of the major concepts underlying much of current software technology, and introduces many of the techniques described in more detail by the papers reprinted in this volume.

Finally, Freeman's paper describes the state-of-the-art in the emerging area of reusability. The concept of "reusable software engineering" implies that many different products of the software development process can be reused, not just code. Freeman points out how specifications and designs can be reused and observes that major savings in development costs and maintenance can be achieved through such reuse.

EHO205-5/83/0000/0001$01.00 © 1983 IEEE

FUNDAMENTALS OF DESIGN

Peter Freeman

University of California, Irvine

This paper addresses several important questions that arise when one attempts to understand software design: What is the basic nature of any design activity? In what context does software design take place? What are the underlying intellectual operations that are performed in software design? What are the most critical factors in design? What is the nature and the role of various current topics in software design?

As we attempt to answer these questions, we take a perspective that focuses on fundamentals. This will provide a framework and reference baseline that will facilitate your comprehension of the other papers in this volume as well as of other works on design. While many of the concepts discussed here come from or are applicable to design in a number of fields, our focus is on software design.

Because this paper attempts to do a number of different things, it runs the same risk that many software systems face -- that of turning into a disorganized collection of topics, without much overall coherence! As in a good design, we have tried to combat that risk by organizing the paper into well-structured parts. We begin with a discussion of the philosophy of design in general and then move on to place software design in a context of system development. The core of the paper discusses a number of design concepts, including basic operations, important factors, and particular approaches. A short section surveys some research issues in design and the final section discusses some of the motivations for actually doing design in software development.

Again, keep in mind that the purpose of this paper is to provide a conceptual framework for the study and practice of software design.

THE NATURE OF DESIGN

It is essential that one have a conceptual understanding of a complex activity in order to master its intricacies. Without such a framework, one has only isolated facts and techniques whose interrelationships may be obscured. Without an understanding of broad classes of phenomena, one is condemned to understand each new instance by itself.

Design of complex objects such as large information systems is such an activity. The number of techniques, tools, pieces of information, and caveats from experience with which one must deal are numerous. The time taken to master large-scale design is measured in years of full-time activity -- if it can be mastered at all! One can be taught to take square roots or to integrate simple equations without knowing much of the philosophy of mathematics, but it is doubtful that one can acquire even modest skill in system design without having a firm grasp of the philosophy of design.

There is no single philosophy of design, however -- neither now or ever (for the more complex forms of it, at least). What we have is a large number of similar, but differing, views as to the nature of design and as to its basic concepts. As a result, it is impossible to train designers in a short time or even to introduce all of the writings on the philosophy of design.

We will briefly describe what others have said about the nature of design and present our viewpoint in order to clarify some of the presentations of this tutorial. Acquisition of a more complete understanding of the nature of design -- and, indeed, development of an individual viewpoint -- will require additional study and reflection.

Views of Designing

Designing is one of those interesting human activities that is all around us, in which everyone engages in one form or another, and that eludes precise characterization because of its many forms and its complexity. Design in other fields such as architecture and mechanical engineering is an old and well-established activity. While designing software has its own characteristics, it also shares much with design in other fields. As a prelude to the study of some of the more detailed ideas currently prevalent in the design of software, it is instructive of consider what others have written about the general nature of design. (Indeed, for a number of years, Jones has taught a "mind-expanding" seminar for the designers of a major computer manufacturer.)

J. Christopher Jones (1981) in his book *Design Methods* describes a number of the new design methods that have been developed for architectural, urban, and industrial design. Some of these are of quite general applicability (and consequently are not very powerful) and may be of use in some software design situations.

In his introduction, he pulls out one-line definitions of design from a number of design philosophers (*i.e.*, people who have given serious thought to the nature of design and its underlying, generalizable concepts). These descriptions of designing are quite varied, but they do share the common theme of addressing the process of design, not the results:

"Finding the right physical components of a physical structure."

"Decision making, in the face of uncertainty, with high penalties for error."

"A goal-directed problem-solving activity."

"Simulating what we want to make (or do) before we make (or do) it as many times as may be necessary to feel confident in the final result."

"The conditioning factor for those parts of the product which come into contact with people."

"Engineering design is the use of scientific principles, technical information and imagination in the definition of a mechanical structure, machine or system to perform prespecified functions with the maximum economy and efficiency."

"Relating product with situation to give satisfaction."

"The performing of a very complicated act of faith."

"The optimum solution to the sum of the true needs of a particular set of circumstances."

"The imaginative jump from present facts to future possibilities."

"A creative activity -- it involves bringing into being something new and useful that has not existed previously."

Simon's (1981) interesting lectures, *The Sciences of the Artificial*, should be read by anyone concerned with design and computing. In them, he states simply that "design is concerned with devising artifacts to attain goals." Included in his lectures are brief descriptions of the areas in which a designer must be knowledgeable and of the fundamental aspects of design. Of special note is his emphasis on the concepts of hierarchy, allocation of the designer's resources during design, and satisficing* rather than optimizing in complex design situations -- all concepts that should be familiar to the software designer.

One of the standard works on traditional engineering design is the book by Asimow (1962). The opening sentence of the book provides a succinct view: "Engineering design is a purposeful activity directed toward the goal of fulfilling human needs, particularly those which can be met by the technological factors of our culture." The remainder of his book describes a set of steps that can be followed to achieve that objective.

The innovative thinker on architectural design, Christopher Alexander (1964), who is often quoted by those concerned with software design, stresses the desired result of design:

(...) every design problem begins with an effort to achieve fitness between two entities: the form in question and its context. The form is the solution to the problem; the context defines the problem. In other words, when we speak of design, the real object of discussion is not the form alone, but the ensemble comprising the form and its context. Good fit is a desired property of this ensemble into form and context.

Lucas (1974), in introducing a new approach to the design of information systems for organizations, focuses on a particular aspect of the design environment which he has deemed to be of paramount importance: "Creative design tech-

---

*"Satisficing" is a term introduced by Simon to describe the common situation in which we will accept a solution that meets all our constraints, even though it may not be an optimal solution. In most design situations, the complexity makes it difficult, if not impossible, to find optimal solutions.

niques are focused on solutions to organization behavior problems in systems design."

This focus on one part of the problem is typical of most attempts to improve actual design practice and can be seen, for example, in the ideas of Mumford (1981) whose concern is user-centeredness. This is not surprising since, as one goes down to more detail from the philosophical statements quoted above, the drive to be operational forces one to select particular elements of the problem on which to concentrate.

Mayall (1979), in a general-readership book written about product design, identifies ten principles of design that he has observed in a wide variety of situations. An interesting exercise is to apply his principles of time, value, synthesis, and so on to software design and to draw out specific prescriptions for action. His underlying message, though, is expressed in his first principle:

> *The Principle of Totality*: All design requirements are always interrelated and must always be treated as such throughout a design task.

As he notes, ". . . design is the great integrator; a subject in its own right and certainly not, now or ever, a derivative of art and science in whatever terms these themselves may be defined."

Although one can philosophize about the nature of design indefinitely, beyond a certain point it will not have much practical impact on what we do. As you begin to delve more deeply into the nature of what you do (in this case, design), this philosophizing can be quite valuable in generating a substantive and productive understanding. The next section begins the process of focusing this pragmatic software design.

Design As A Goal-driven Activity

It is clear that design is an activity with a definite goal in view -- creation of an artifact that meets certain goals. The obvious goal in most design situations is to create a system that provides certain functions. All too often, in software design, this seems to be the only goal to which much attention is paid.

There are other very important goals for many systems, however, such as reliability, user-centeredness, maintainability, efficiency, and security. Increasingly, these other goals are at least as important as the goal of providing certain functions.

It is a fundamental characteristic of designing that we are permitted the opportunity to achieve any set of desired goals. If we want a system to be very user-centered, we have the opportunity to design it that way (or, at least to emphasize that goal within other existing constraints). On the other hand, if we do not pay attention to all of our goals during design, there is usually little that can be done later to incorporate them into the system. If we have devised an artifact without paying attention to whether it possesses certain qualities or not, then it should be no surprise that it doesn't have them!

The primary way in which objectives enter into the design process is their use in making decisions. If we are seeking a highly reliable system, then each design decision should be evaluated as to whether it will have a significant impact on the system reliability or not. If it does, then we can make the decision on the basis of which alternative contributes most to reliability. In most design situations, we have a number of objectives which must be balanced. Not all will be equally applicable to every decision, but for those that do apply to a given decision we must consider their interactions and relative importance if they interact in a negative way.

Finally, all of the major objectives of a design effort should serve as guidelines for choice of an overall system structure that fits the structure of the problem situation. One of the determining factors of the problem environment is precisely the conditions we place on possible solutions -- *i.e.*, the objectives of the design.

The Purpose of Technical Design

Most of the view of design quoted above rightfully emphasized the larger purpose of most design activities -- creating artifacts to attain goals in a social context. The matrix of activities germane to any design activity is quite involved and extensive. One must consider organizational and behavioral factors that lie in the domain of the social sciences, managerial concerns that are addressed by organizational theory, aesthetic concerns (yes! even in software!) and the technical information and techniques peculiar to the technology being used.

Our concern here is primarily limited to the technical aspects of design, not because they are necessarily the most important, but because without a solid understanding of them, the other concerns have little meaning. If one steps back from the particular design techniques discussed in this volume, three basic purposes of design can be discerned (remember, hereafter we are focusing on the technical domain only):

- discovery of problem structure;

- creation of the outlines (architecture, logical structure) of a solution for the problem;

- review of the results to ascertain if they meet the stated goals.

There is nothing magical or immutable about these objectives of design and, indeed, others might characterize things differently. This is simply one way of abstracting from the details of multiple design techniques.

Good designers understand intuitively that a successful design is one that matches the structure of the problem for which the designed object is a solution. What is often difficult to understand for beginning designers is that most design situations are incredibly complex and that the structure of the problem that seems to be obvious at first glance may not accurately reflect the actual situation. The first purpose of design, then, must be to discover enough of the structure of the problem so that there is a reasonable chance of devising an appropriate solution. This is the analysis activity that must precede the synthesis of new structures.

An an example, consider a small but quickly growing company. As the organization grows, the old manual accounting procedures become too slow and inadequate for meeting the demands of a growing company needing more frequent and current information on its operations. A simple-minded approach would be to automate the functions now performed by hand. But would that be sufficient? Probably not.

Some of the other aspects of the problem that must be considered in this situation include the following: how to convert easily from existing systems, how to train personnel in use of the new system, how to design interfaces so that current personnel can use the new system without extensive training, how to provide backup and security of critical files, how to provide for expansion of the system in the future as the company continues to grow in ways and amounts that are unpredictable because of the nature of the company's business base, what are the economies of various possible implementations, and how to interface with other planned and existing systems of the company (inventory, billing, project management).

The point is that there are many possible factors that will impact the eventual success of the system being designed. While one in general cannot consider all possible factors, the most significant must be identified, and their influence must be taken into account. Discovering the structure of the problem means understanding the interactions between these factors and the desired functional characteristics of the system.

Once we think we understand the problem, the next major step is to develop the outlines of the solution. This is the creative aspect of design in the strict sense of the word, although developing an accurate understanding of the problem requires just as much creativity in many cases.

The major activity is the establishment of the architecture of the system. That is, we engage in a combination of spelling out in general terms how the artifact will look to the user -- the functions it will perform -- and how it will be built -- the major algorithms and data representations it will use.

Some parts of this process of spelling out the overall structure may require that we extend the design to a very detailed level in order to determine the feasibility of performing certain functions. But, in general, we are establishing the major pieces of the system, their relationships, interfaces to other systems and the outside world, and carefully specifying *what* must be done along with rough indications of *how* it is to be done.

The third purpose of design is to review repeatedly what has been done so far, to compare it to what is desired, and thus to evaluate progress. Review takes place at all stages of the development cycle, of course, but it is most central to the design phase. Review of code production is intended to determine that what has been implemented is what was specified; review of test results is meant to confirm that a sufficient set of tests have been run; review of specifications seeks to determine if the loosely stated requirements of the customer have been captured in operational terms. Review at the design phase, though, goes beyond just determining if something that has been previously spelled out has indeed been done -- it is an integral part of the process of discovering the nature of the problem and the proper structure of the solution.

Before we look at some of the basic concepts of software design, it will be useful to place the design activity more accurately in the larger context of systems development. The next section does this.

THE CONTEXT OF SOFTWARE DESIGN

The design process should be viewed as the central, unifying activity of software engineering. If one is doing a requirements analysis to support a planned software development, careful concern of design constraints must take place; if the detailed technical specification of a system is being done, then one is working directly with design features; and if one is helping an existing software system evolve, then the design rationale on which it is based must be understood. In all of these software engineering activities, one is either directly designing or is forced to deal with various aspects of design. Thus, the underlying assumption is that the design process is, indeed, a central aspect of software engineering.

The Software Lifecycle

Although there are many models of the system development process with different properties (see, for example, Kerola and Freeman (1981)), we believe the following five-stage cycle provides a good basis for our discussions:

1) *Analysis* - The eventual user or purchaser discovers a need for which an information system seems to be the answer, the nature of the need is analyzed, the requirements for a system that would satisfy these needs are established. This may be a formal stage in the process, or it may occur concurrently with the functional specification stage.

2) *Functional Specification* - Descriptions of the system are developed, along with constraints on its structure and resource usage; these constitute the external design of the system. Economic constraints on the development process itself are stated. This stage is often combined with the analysis and in some instances is blended into the internal design stages in an iterative sequence that goes back and forth between statement of specifications and refinement of the design.

3) *Architectural Design* - Working from the functional specifications, the underlying structure of the problem for which this system will be a solution is sought out. When this structure becomes clear, an internal design of the system is devised. This design is necessarily at a gross level of detail. The parts of the system and their relationships, the basic algorithms that the system will use, and the major data representations and organizations that will be needed are all primary elements of the design at this stage.

4) *Detailed Design* - The major parts of the design are now made more detailed. Precise algorithms and data structures are spelled out. Interfaces between parts are detailed. If not already done at the architectural stage, decisions as to which will be hardware are made. Detailed design (as well as architectural design) may require several levels of refinement. This stage stops short of spelling out all programming details (*e.g.*, housekeeping and local data structures).

5) *Implementation* - Producing a physical realization of the design includes programming, testing of individual pieces, integration of pieces into subassemblies, system testing, performance evaluation and acceptance testing. (If we were investigating all parts of the cycle, not just design, then this stage should be broken into at least three stages: programming, testing, and system integration.)

6) *Evolution* - Everything that happens after the system is "finished" is often termed maintenance. In fact, it is much more than "maintenance": repair of problems, adaptation to new conditions, and enhancement with new functions all take place over the lifetime of a system.

It is important to recognize two things that so far have been left implicit. First, the stages we have outlined here are temporal stages. Although they are named by the dominant *activity* of each stage, as we will see below, many activities may occur at each stage. Thus, for example, design may occur during evolutionary activity consisting of the addition of a new function.

Second, we have not clearly differentiated between software design and total system (*i.e.*, hardware, software, and other components) design. This was intentional. In some situations, there is little or no choice of hardware nor of which functions will be in hardware and which will be in software. In such cases, most of the stages outlined above deal primarily with software design. In other cases, the choice of hardware may be open, and the focus of the design effort down to a relatively low level may be on the logical design of the total system, with decisions between hardware and software implementation delayed as long as possible.

The overall structure of the development process in either case is nearly the same, even though the nature of the decisions made varies.

Thus, for our purposes here we have not made a careful distinction.

Activities At Each Stage

In order to understand better what must be done to create a system, an informal analysis of the development process itself will be helpful. For each stage, we will list the primary inputs (I), outputs (O), and major operations (OP). There are, of course, some inputs (such as the general knowledge of the people involved) that are present at all stages, but we will not list these explicitly.

Analysis

I: primitive needs, system context, user problems

O: requirements definition

OP: identification of major functions, information sets, and constraints

Functional Specification

I: requirements, system analysis of context

O: specifications of system functions, data collections, design constraints, and objectives (external design of system)

OP: conversion of needs into explicit functions, selection of constraints that are operational, shaping of user interfaces

Architectural Design

I: specifications, general context of desired system, knowledge of similar systems

O: structural description of inside of system (definition of modules and their interfaces)

OP: discovery of problem structure, identification of major pieces of system, establishment of relationships between parts, abstraction, decomposition

Detailed Design

I: architectural description, programming environment details

O: blueprints for programs

OP: abstraction, elaboration, choice of alternatives

Implementation

I: blueprints

O: program code, data and file layouts, working system

OP: encoding of algorithms and data representations, testing, debugging

Evolution

I: system, documentation, operational requirements, change requests

O: improved system

OP: debugging redesign, reprogramming, enhancement (in many cases, all of the stages above)

The most important point to be gained from this informal analysis is that "design" takes place during many different stages of the development cycle. While it is important to identify some stages as being design-intensive, the application of design techniques may take place at many points.

Design *versus* Analysis

The word design is used in a number of different ways, as you may have noticed! In some textbooks you will find a discussion of the design activity that has nothing to do with establishing the modularity of a system; in others you will see design discussed without any mention of providing a set of functions that meet the user's needs. The problem is that *external* design (specifying the functions that a system is to provide) has not been differentiated from *internal* design (specifying the structure of the software that will provide the functions). Many of the same concepts (such as abstraction and consistency) apply to both types of design, but they obviously have rather different objectives: external design is trying to satisfy externally-posed objectives that relate to the world of the user, while internal design is trying to satisfy internal objectives that relate to the technology and constraints of the machine.

There are also two ways of going about the process of understanding the problem (analysis) and creating a solution (design). In one, the ideal is to understand the problem first (*i.e.* do the analysis) and then to design a solution. In the second, the concept is that analysis of the problem and design of the solution go forward together. In fact, of course, neither "pure" model can be followed.

However, the selection of one or the other will imply what "workproducts" are to be produced. Further, we believe that the model being followed will also materially affect your ability to arrive at appropriate solutions. In particular, on complex design problems careful analysis of the problem before beginning design of the solution is indicated. On simpler problems, a more combined approach may be appropriate. Although, since the tendency of most designers is to jump ahead to possible solutions, delay of that activity as long as possible may be beneficial to the final result.

Lifecycle Models

We noted above that there are numerous models of the "lifecycle" of a system. Some of these models are descriptive (*i.e.*, they describe what exists), some are prescriptive (*i.e.*, they prescribe what steps should be taken), and some are normative (*i.e.*, they establish a standard -- for example, some of the DoD regulations that set out specific development phases that must be followed).

As concern for the software engineering process has increased almost exponentially, so has concern for having the "right" lifecycle model. This concern has some very positive aspects and some that are counterproductive in some instances. On the positive side, the backbone of any systematic, visible software engineering process must be a clear set of workproduct definitions and an indication of what steps should be taken to create those workproducts; this is precisely what a lifecycle model in intended to do -- and can do if used properly. Also, since most software is still developed today without the aid of any very well-defined lifecycle, almost any lifecycle, properly used, is better than none.

The negative side of this concern over having the "right" lifecycle is that a lot of effort can be expended for little or no gain. It must be remembered that we are discussing *models*, not reality. Models, by definition, are an abstraction of reality. They can help us shape reality by helping us see the relationships between different aspects of development more clearly, and thus it is important that they be relatively accurate. However, since they are always simpler than reality (or should be!), we should not become too impatient when they seem not to capture everything we see in practice.

What appears to be happening is that as people in a wide variety of situations realize the importance of the lifecycle that is being followed, they are trying to find better descriptions than the traditional ones. This is all to the good, but it means that our collective understanding of the characteristics of software lifecycles is changing rather rapidly. In such a situation, we must be prepared to cope with models that always seem inadequate; eventually the rate of change of our understanding will slow down, and then we will be able more easily to prescribe appropriate lifecycle models. (Fifteen years ago, great concern was expressed that we did not have adequate descriptive means to handle the large collections of on-line data that were just starting to grow; while we certainly do not have the last word yet, the situation with respect to data models is not nearly so fluid now as it was then.)

One of the factors that has led to a great deal of discontent with current lifecycle models is the fact that they tend to be very sequential and imply that development must extend over long periods of time. Extended development periods lead to real problems in a world in which the requirements for a system may change several times before the system is completed. This concern for foreshortening the development cycle (and the models that describe it), along with other factors, has led to the development of various system prototyping concepts and tools.

Prototyping is one of the underlying design concepts that we discuss in the next section. More generally, we will try to explicate some fundamental intellectual operations and concepts that are incorporated in many design situations and techniques.

DESIGN CONCEPTS

In understanding complex physical situations, it is necessary to have a solid grasp of underlying principles such as the laws of motion. While the basic concepts of design are not so well understood as the laws of physics, we have found the concepts discussed below very useful in helping us understand the design process.

Designing *versus* Programming

Because so much software development has been done in the past without the benefit of much logical design, that people sometimes confuse programming with design. (Indeed, the development of small programs often does not require much design, further confusing people involved in large-scale projects.) While there is a close interaction between the two activities, they do differ.

If we characterize the activities in software design and development in a general way, it is clear that programming is only part of the total process. First, consider the several activities involved in programming at the lowest level (coding):

-devising local and concrete data representations for information;

-forming precise algorithms for doing necessary processing;

-taking care of housekeeping details necessitated by the particular programming system used (language plus run-time environment);

-choosing names, forming syntactically correct language statements, and making the program letter perfect.

By contrast, design, especially at the higher levels, is concerned with somewhat different activities:

-abstracting the operations and data of the task situation so that they may be represented in the system;

-determining precisely what is to be done by the software under design;

-establishing an overall structure of the system;

-establishing interfaces and definite control and data linkages between parts of the system and between the system and other systems;

-choosing between major design alternatives;

-making trade-offs dictated by global constraints and conditions in order to meet varied requirements such as reliability, generality, and user-centeredness.

There is an easy way of distinguishing betwen the two activities. When programming, we are constructing programs (often in some higher-level language). We must bind data representations and control sequences so that the program will execute properly. When designing, we are devising *representations* of programs, not actual programs. Clearly, we will be doing some of the same things in both activities --*e.g.*, we may choose some definite control sequences during design-- and detailed design often comes arbitrarily close to producing complete programs (especially when using a metacode).

Another way of emphasizing the difference between programming and design is to consider what is actually produced --*i.e.*, what is on the pieces of paper produced by a programmer or a designer. A programmer produces programs and documentation of those programs. the documentation is needed to make the programs understandable to humans, but it is not a necessary condition of existence. That is, the programs exist without the documentation, and indeed we often instruct someone studying a program to "go to the code" for the final word on program content.

By contrast, when designing, we produce representations of programs. These representations may be very high-level in detail (*e.g.*, an overall black-box diagram representing major control-flow) or very near to actual programs (*e.g.*, a metacode description of a program that is complete except for minor housekeeping details).

Thus, design is an activity concerned with making major decisions, often of a structural nature. It shares with programming a concern for abstracting information representation and processing sequences, but the level of detail is quite different at the extremes. Design builds coherent, well-planned representations of programs that concentrate on the interrelationships of parts at the higher levels and on the logical operations involved at the lower levels. Programming is then the process of turning such a representation into a program that will execute on a specific machine.

Fundamental Design Activities [*]

Understanding of the design activity is not sufficient to build a complete model that will accurately describe all of the activities observed in designing. We can, however, describe a framework of concepts that will aid our perception of practical design work.

First, it is important to differentiate between the *stages* or steps of the typical lifecycle (as described above) and the *activities* that are carried out. The stages are often named with a term that represents the dominant activity that occurs at that time in the development sequence, but it is clear that many different activities may occur during a particular stage. >From this perspective, the stages of development can best be viewed as relating to managerial concerns (schedules, budgets, deliverable workproducts) while the activities can best be viewed as relating to the technical work being performed (creation, checking, and modification of representations).

[*]This section reflects considerable contribution by Professor Arndt von Staa, through our joint work on a forthcoming paper that explores the fundamental processes of design more deeply.

Next, it is useful to characterize the intellectual activities that take place in design as operations that convert one representation (the input) of a piece of software (*e.g.*, a functional specification) into another (output) representation (*e.g.*, an architectural design). This view of the fundamental role of representation, and thus the operations on it, is further discussed in a later section.

Focusing now just on the intellectual activities, we perceive an hierarchy of operations:

Construction activities

  Creation activities

     decomposition
     translation
     abstraction
     elaboration
     evaluation
     decision-making

  Reflection activities

     search
     reconstruction
     change detection
     scouting

Control activities

  Verification activities

     comparison
     corruption identification
     representation quality control

  Validation activities

     prediction
     control
     extraction

The difference should be clear between constructive activities that build new representations and control activities that provide information about the technical work that permit us to control it. Creation activities are the most obvious elements of the design process since they are involved in producing new designs. *Reflection* refers to the common situation in which we are "walking backwards" in the development process by deriving from a given representation (*e.g.*, a program) the representation from which it was derived (*e.g.*, a specification).

Verification processes evaluate the degree of imprecision of a particular representation due to errors introduced in producing it from its predecessor representation (*e.g.*, the errors in a program that were introduced in creating it from the specification that preceded it in the development process). *Validation* evaluates the degree to which the overall goals for the system will be achieved, given the current representation of the system (*e.g.*, determining that a particular detailed design, if implemented without error, will meet the goals established for the system). These connotations are in agreement with the common usage of these terms.

The remainder of this part of the paper will briefly discuss each of these elemental design actions. Bear in mind that our purpose here is to explain the *core* meaning of important design processes, not to define them unambiguously.

Decomposition

Decomposition is used in numerous ways in design. We decompose the overall problem to be solved into pieces so that we may understand each more readily, we decompose a system into subsystems and the subsystems into modules in order to control the interactions among parts, and we decompose a task such as designing a particular facility into subtasks so that several people may work on it simultaneously; almost every design problem we have to solve involves some decomposition into subproblems.

Because we use decomposition in so many ways in ordinary activities, it is easy to overlook it as a specific technique. In so doing, we may fail to focus on its characteristics. When decomposing something, we must be concerned with the boundaries along which we make the decomposition, how many pieces to break it into, and to what level of detail to carry the decomposition. Some design techniques help us address these issues specifically; others do so only implicitly.

The result of decomposition of a system, as well as the process used to carry it out, is important. Indeed, it is crucial since it is precisely the all-important structure of a system that decomposition will help establish. There are few measures of the "goodness" of decomposition, so that most of the judgements that must be made involve a lot of designer's intuition; the objective of some design techniques, however, is to make the results of decomposition more reliably "good."

Translation

During development we often must convert a representation written in some language into another representation written in a different language, maintaining, however, the same meaning in the output representation as is in the input representation; we commonly call this process *translation*. The purpose of performing a translation is usually to obtain a new representation of the system that has some desired properties. For example, we may have represented the modular structure of a system using structure charts in order to gain the advantage of a graphical representation; at some later time, we may then need to translate the connections shown on the chart and the accompanying interface definitions into statements in a module interconnection language being used to build the physical system.

The process of translation in design is usually a manual one (except at the programming language level) and, thus, is very prone to error. Consequently, it is a design action that must be very carefully applied.

Abstraction

Abstraction is the operation of generalizing, of throwing away irrelevant details, of separating the essentials of a situation from the inessential, of considering something as a general quality unrelated to any particular concrete object. We abstract in many situations in order to see the overall structure of something. Theorems in mathematics, physical laws, and generalizations of all kinds are abstractions that permit us to better understand individual situations by relating them to other situations having similar characteristics. Abstraction has long been used in programming through the use of subroutines in which we abstract a set of operations into a single name. The value of this type of abstraction is extremely important at the level of design as well.

Examples of abstraction in design are abundant. When we start to work on a design, we are working with the concepts of the end user, stated in the language of the problem domain. For example, we may need to deal with accounts receivable, billing ledgers, order books, posting, balancing, billing, and so on. While each of these concepts will eventually have a realization in the machine in terms of variables and operations in some programming language or in hardware, they are not tied down at the initial stage --*i.e.*, they are more abstract.

There is another dimension in which abstraction or generalization is valuable. Suppose we are presented with the requirements for a data management system in which there are demands to enter data, change them, list them out for checking, delete them, change their ordering, select subsets of them for printing in any of several different formats, produce backup tapes of the data base, produce output tapes for distribution, and so on. This list of requirements (even in the partial form presented here) is somewhat bewildering. By abstracting and noting that we have editing functions, output functions, and maintenance functions, however, we can get a clearer picture of the problem situation. This in turn will help us to devise an appropriate system design.

Elaboration

Although not an exact complement, elaboration is in many ways the opposite of abstraction. To elaborate something means to make it more detailed, to add features, to work it out to perfection. Top-down design procedures make heavy use of elaboration, but other approaches and aspects of design involve elaboration as well. If we are following a most-critical-component-first design approach, then, after devising the critical components, we elaborate our design by adding additional less-critical parts. When we take a general set of functions and list the particular functions implied, we are elaborating. When we take a gross representation of control flow and add the housekeeping details we are elaborating.

When we take abstractions and convert them into equivalent functions and representations expressed in other terms, it is a form of elaboration, but it is not precisely the same as adding detail. In this case we are really carrying one set of abstractions into another set. They *may* be more detailed, but need not be. For example, we may have started our design dealing with abstract data types such as sales orders, then converted these into blocks and lists, next taken these abstractions into arrrays and pointers, and finally taken the representation into a form directly implementable in the memory structures of an actual machine. This refinement process is essential to the use of abstractions.

Evaluation

Generally, to evaluate is to ascertain the properties of something. Many times in the development process we must determine that something meets some set of expectations. More specifically, evaluation has come to mean the process of determining that a specific workproduct meets the specifications from which it was derived. For example, we may evaluate an architectural design to make sure it fulfills the functional specifications or that a set of detailed module designs conforms to the architectural design.

Evaluation is close to verification and validation. The main difference, in our view, is that evaluation connotes a dynamic process that takes place continuously and at a micro level during the design process, whereas verification and validation, as often practiced, are discrete activities applied to a final (or near-final) workproduct.

Decision-making

In the last analysis, decision-making is what design is all about. We first identify what decision must be made, then generate alternatives among which to decide, next evaluate these alternatives to form the basis for a rational decision, and finally choose one alternative. This process is interrelated with and uses all the other fundamental operations of design. As we discuss below, the order and form of decision-making is determined by the method.

Search

The action of searching for something is, of course, a fundamental mental activity that is used consequently. In the context of a reflection activity in which we are producing representations from which some already existing representations were derived, however, searching means to look for those specific representations that could have generated the target.

Reconstruction

The actual production of the input representations found by the search process during reflection is called reconstruction. This activity shares some of the basic creation actions discussed above, but differs because it is tightly constrained by knowing what the output representation is. We believe that this makes it a different mental activity when viewed from the perspective of trying to understand what is going on in the designer's mind.

Change Identification

A more constrained form of search as described above is the generation of specific proposals for changing a given input representation in order that it can accurately be mapped into a given output representation. The most common form of this action is the reflection of changes in a workproduct (e.g., the specifications from which the code was produced).

Comparison

When we examine the verification processes that occur during design, one of the most important is comparison. By this term, we mean the examination of the consistency of meaning between two or more representations to make sure that they form a consistent whole (e.g., data and process specifications).

Corruption Detection

We use the term *corruption* to denote the difference in meaning between two representations that are supposed to have the same meaning. For example, a program specification may indicate parameters A, B, and C in that order; the actual implementation of the program may erroneously list the parameters in order A, C, B. This would be a corruption. *Corruption detection*, then, is the activity of examining two representations (or sets of representations) to find corruptions in the output representation as compared to the input representation.

Representation Quality Control

A representation, just as any other object, can be compared to a set of external quality criteria. An important action is this evaluation process to determine, and thus control, the quality of the representations produced.

Prediction

Prediction is another fundamental mental activity that is used in many ways. Here we use it to indicate an action that is central to the validation process -- the determination of whether a specification, if eventually implemented without error, describes a system which will meet the current goals for the system.

Control

This is the action in validation that is used to determine if an actual system (or component thereof) satisfies the current goals.

Extraction

It sometimes occurs in validation that the system as built (or predicted) is not consistent with the stated goals, but is nonetheless acceptable. The action of obtaining the revised goals from the actual system we call extraction.

As we noted above, the actions described here do not form a complete and consistent model of the design process. However, they do assist in understanding the more complex design methods that are the primary subject of this volume.

Methods and Methodologies

What is a method? Simply, it is a way of doing things -- in this case, designing. A method for finding the roots of a polynomial or for balancing a general ledger is usually well specified with little or no room for alternative courses of action. A method for solving urban social problems will not be so well-defined and will leave much (usually too much) room for different paths to be taken by the person following the method. This range of constraints on problem-solving methods -- from precise algorithms on the one hand to loose collections of heuristics on the other -- is true of design methods as well. While precise software design methods can be constructed (*e.g.*, steps to follow in designing a symbol table system), the design methods usually considered for medium to large-scale software systems tend toward the neuristic end of the scale.

For our purposes, a design method specifies three things: 1) what decisions are to be made, 2) how to make them, and 3) in what order they should be made. A particular method may ignore or leave implicit one of these elements, and in most cases the statement of the method overall is done informally (far from an algorithmic representation)! Let us look briefly at several commonly encountered design methods.

The best-known method is called *top-down* design. Let us look at the three paramenters of this method. The decisions to be made at any point in time are those that affect the greatest possible amount of the total design. The order then follows: if we have grouped decisions into classes or levels, we make decisions at the highest level first and then iteratively make decisions at the lower levels. Decisions within levels are usually made randomly or, more correctly, according to some other method. The level of a decision is often defined in terms of its distance away from actual implementation concerns. Thus, deciding on the form of a functon is high-level while deciding on the format of a symbol table is low-level. Various means of making decisions may be specified, but a general caveat in top-down design is to make decisions that take into account as many as possible of the relevant design goals and constraints and that restrict as little as possible the set of alternatives for lower-level decisions.

A closely related method is called the *outside-in* method. Basically it is the same as top-down, only the sense of direction is defined in terms of the outside of the system (what the user sees) *versus* the inside (the implementation). Obviously this may correspond to top-down if one defines top-level decisions as those that deal with the functions of the system. However, if one defines top-level as those decisions dealing with the overall structure of the implementation, then the two methods will specify different orders of making decisions. In fact, the outside-in approach has been developed largely to counteract the tendency of some designers even when using a top-down approach to pay insufficient attention to the needs of the end users.

The obvious corollary of outside-in design is the *inside-out* design method. When using this approach, one makes decisions relating to the implementation of the system first before making decisions concerning the external functions of the system. Of course, one must have a clear concept of what is needed on the outside before internal decisions can be made. This method tends to define less closely what decisions are to be made, in contrast to the top-down and outside-in methods. The latter broaden the class of decisions to be made to include those that affect the functional architecture of the system. The criteria for making decisions is also more oriented toward satisfying design objectives relating to the implementation of a system. The techniques for making these decisions can thus be more rigorous since one is dealing with time-space trade-offs which can be quantified as opposed to qualitative measures of user satisfaction (in the case of external functions).

Another method often discussed is the *bottom-up* approach. In this method, one makes the lowest-level decisions first and gradually builds the capabilities of the system. The decisions to be made are determined by where one is in the process, starting with decisions concerning basic building blocks and internal functions of the system and proceeding up to decisions concerning external functions. The decision rules used also depend on the point in the process: the low-level decisions tend to concentrate more on internal criteria, of course; the later decisions are more influenced by what is available from the lower levels of design.

Yet another method is the *most-critical-component-first* attack. In this approach, one first designs those parts of the system whose operation is most constrained (*e.g.*, a real-time processing module in a command and control system). The criteria for making decisions is to make them so that the desired critical parameters are satisfied. Once the critical components are designed, decisions can be made according to some other method.

It is important to stress that none of these "definitions" should be taken as being hard and fast. Further, rarely are they ever followed precisely. A strict top-down approach usually will only work in examples in which a prior design effort has already determined what is possible at the lower levels. A real design effort using top-down approach will normally be mixed with bottom-up and/or most-critical-component-first design approaches. Thus, the descriptions of these methods should be taken as conceptual models, not as rigorous prescriptions.

One often hears the term "design methodology." It is important to understand the distinction between a method and a methodology -- especially since the distinction is not always carefully maintained. In essence, a methodology is a collection of methods, chosen to complement one another, along with rules for applying them. Thus, a comprehensive design methodology would spell out several methods (*e.g.*, top-down and critical-component) and provide rules for when to use one and when to switch to another. More generally, a design methodology includes management techniques, documentation procedures, tools to aid the designer, standards for specifications that serve as the input to the design process, and standards for the output of the process which must serve as the input to the implementation procedures. DoD (1982) discusses this issue in detail.

The important point made in this section is that there are different approaches to design -- different methods -- and that isolated methods must be coupled with other methods and rules for applying them in the form of methodologies. We have not discussed how one chooses particular methods nor how one puts together methods to form a methodology. These topics, while extremely important, are beyond the scope of our consideration here.

Prototyping

Building a model of a complex artifact before building the final version -- prototyping -- is a well-established technique in traditional engineering. Recently, a great deal of interest has arisen in using prototyping in software development. While hardly a new idea, concern over the problems often encountered in traditional systems development coupled with the widespread acceptance of different modes of computing (interactive) and the emergence of some new tools (program generators, data base query systems) has sparked this new interest.

Prototyping is, indeed, a valuable tool for the software designer. Unfortunately, it must be used properly or it can lead to many of the same problems of loss of project control and of systems that are difficult to maintain. There is a good bit of confusion in the current literature on what prototyping really is, stemming from the desire of some to jump on a bandwagon and claim that their particular language or tool or method is the thing that everyone has been looking for! While we cannot provide a complete guide to prototyping here, it will be useful to discuss briefly the relationship of prototyping to the design process.

Simply, we see three ways in which a prototyping activity can be productively used in software development:

Traditional prototyping. In this mode, one builds a functioning system that is substantially like the desired one. It is placed into service, studied, and then replaced by the final system. Typically, the " prototype" does not have a full complement of functions and error checks, may be implemented in an efficient manner, and is used only by "understanding" users. The switchover to a full, well-built system that is based on the experience with the prototype is done on a definite schedule. An example is a quick and inefficient implementation of a compiler for a new language; once the language design is frozen an efficient compiler can be built.

Concurrent prototyping can be used to bring up a limited version of a system quickly while a traditional development process is employed to build the full system. Experience with the prototype may be used in the full system, although the emphasis is more on getting results to the customer quickly via the prototype and less on collecting information that will be relevant to the system design effort. For example, a management support system can be quickly put together using existing packages to provide needed information even though the report formats may be inconsistent and some features may be missing; while the prototype is supplying the essential information, a refined and complete implementation can be built.

Decision prototyping can be used at *each* stage of development where needed to help make decisions. Thus, at the functional specification stage, one might build a prototype of the user interface in order to get feedback from potential users on proposed specification; at the design stage, one might prototype several different architectures to study which provides the most efficient implementation; during implementation one could prototype alternative algorithms to study their execution properties.

As better tools for prototyping are developed and as our understanding of how to use them improves, prototyping should become an integral part of many software development efforts.

Critical Parameters

There are three parameters of the design process that are expecially critical to its success:

the representation used, the experience of the designer, and the information available. We will briefly discuss the nature of each of these parameters and illustrate their importance to design.

Representation

One way of characterizing design is that it is a process of building a representation of the object to be created. We take it as self evident that some representation of a piece of software exists from inception until a binary image is loaded into memory for execution.

There are several reasons why design representation is so important: Representations are needed so that the information involved can be communicated to others, the limited capacity of the human mind for technical detail must be augmented (representations of current software systems often run to hundreds or even thousands of printed pages), the form of the representation may greatly affect the performance of various design tasks (review, backup, prediction of results), and the representation of information affects our success or failure in producing more refined representations that are closer to the desired final result.

A *design* is a representation of an object. Fundamentally, a design is a collection of information that tells us something about the object we want to create. Thus, the *design process* can be viewed as an information-gathering process that continually expands the design by putting more and more information into the representation until a termination point is reached. Typically, we terminate a design when we have enough information to implement the object. Figure 1 illustrates this informational view of design.

It follows then that design is a process of deciding what information to include in the design and what information not to include. This has led us in an earlier paper (Freeman, 1975) to propose that it is primarily the decisions made in the course of design that must be represented.

It is important to distinguish representations from documentation. The current use of the word "documentation" usually denotes information describing an object such as a program, an operating procedure, or the results of a design process. It may also connote specifications that "document" a set of needs. This word has the further connotation in many instances, expecially in design where the object does not yet exist, of representing everything we know about the object.

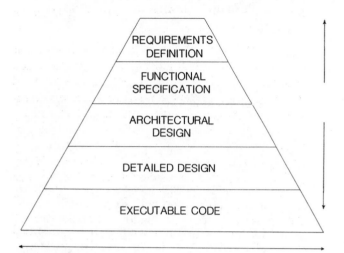

Figure 1: An informational view of design

It is precisely this connotative use of the word "documentation," however, that we believe has prevented clear thinking about design representation. In the case of a program that exists, it is understood that the documentation *augments* the actual object and that we must go to the object itself as the final authority on questions of substance. (This in fact is a standard maxim given to those attempting to understand a program.) In the case of a program *design*, however, the "documentation" *is all that exists.* Thus, it is more than information about an object (*i.e.*, documentation); it is a representation of the object being created.

The failure to be clear about what the flowcharts, lists, diagrams, and voluminous prose generated during design really constitute has prevented us from thinking clearly about the role of these *representational forms.* Of course, everyone recognizes that the stacks of paper generated during a design process contain (in theory) all the information we have available about the object (usually, there is additional, unrecorded information). Yet, few people have specifically treated such *ad hoc* collections of information as a representation in the same way that an architect views graphical representations of a building or an engineer views mathematical representations of a physical process. Just as other design professions have carefully evolved (and in many cases consciously created) the representational forms they use, so must we do the same for software design.

Recently there has been increased concern taken with software design. Some of this work has explicitly addressed the issue of representation. Structure charts (Stevens, *et al*, 1974) and program description languages (Caine, *et al*, 1975; Van Leer, 1976) are both forms for representing program designs and have been used with some success. Peters (1981) surveys a number of design representation schemes in his book.

Our own work (Freeman, 1975) on software design rationalizations[*] provided another form for representing a design; while typically requiring too much effort to carry out in the full format proposed earlier, its ability to capture the decisions being made during design led to one of the representational forms discussed by Freeman (1978).

Knowledge

The role of knowledge in design is fairly obvious. Since the objective of design is to make rational choices among alternatives in order to fulfill a set of requirements, there is a need for information on which to base decisions. We need knowledge of two types: preexisting and developed.

Preexisting knowledge includes information

---

[*] Software design rationalization is a technique for capturing not only the design decisions, but the reasoning that led to them. Specifically, one is instructed for each deision, to list a set of alternative choices, an evaluation for each alternative, and the reason for the one actually chosen. While it is clear that this provides a great amount of information not normally found in a design, which may be very useful to later attempts to understand the design, it is not clear that the added effort of producing this detailed "rationalization" is cost-effective. The decision statement representation discussed below appears to be a more natural representation for actual design situations.

about the equipment and other systems to which the new systems must interface, knowledge of the operational requirements of the system, and knowledge of alternative structures. For example, in the design of a text-processing system, the designer should know about alternative ways of representing text, of searching for occurrences of strings, and so on.

Software designers do not have handbooks that parallel those available to designers in other fields. Even if there existed, for example, information on a variety of software structures, there would still be a need for other important classes of information. During design, expecially if it deals with a new situation, many needs for information arise. In the design of a terminal interface language, for example, we may need to know the preference of potential users for alternative forms of commands. Or in the design of a symbol table, we may need to know the expected usage density for the particular situation at hand. This type of information must be developed by small experiments or analyses carried out during design. This is where decision prototyping can be used.

There is a limit to the amount of information that can be used effectively in the design process, however. If one has too much information to process in making a design decision, the effort expended in evaluating it may exceed the gains from making a slightly more rational decision. Evaluating this type of trade-off requires experience.

Experience

The experience that a designer must have, just as the information he or she should possess, is of several types: experience at designing, experience with similar design situations, and experience with the technologies that must interface to the design process.

As we have noted, designing is a complex process that cannot be captured in the form of a set of explicit instructions. One must learn how to design by doing it. But, beyond this elementary stage, many of the operations of designing require a large amount of intuition and decision-making that cannot be expressed entirely as rational decisions. For example, knowing how many alternatives to consider, which one to look at first, which ones to reject out of hand, and so on, are decisions that generally are made well only if one has made them before and learned from the experi-

ence. Allocating the resources of the design team requires experience with what types of activity will pay off best. Since such decisions come up repeatedly and in many different forms, one must be prepared to make them quickly.

Experience with previous designs of a similar nature is critical. Many decisions cannot be made entirely rationally either because of lack of hard information on the alternatives or because the interactions between a large number of factors cannot be clearly discerned. Further, knowledge of similar designs provides one with a prototype on which to base the current design. This type of experience is more than just simple knowledge, since often the prototype serves more as a guide to decision-making than as a template.

The third type of experience that is essential is with the technologies to which design interfaces. If a designer has no personal knowledge of programming, it will be difficult for him or her to specify feasible structures that can be easily programmed. Knowledge of the limits and possibilities of hardware are essential to the software designer. Experience with creating new system organizations can be a great aid. Experience with managing both the design process and the implementation procedures again provides the designer necessary insights to some of the factors that may influence the eventual success of the design.

Reusability

The information generated during the development of a system, both about the system and about the process used to create it, may often be relevant in a specific way to some future development activity. Making it possible to capture and reuse this information, and thus to reduce significantly the cost of the new development and improve its quality, has been called reusable software engineering (Freeman, 1980a). At the core of this concept is the need for representations that not only hold the information we may be interested in sometime in the future, but also that can be effectively modified and reused.

A viable approach in many situations, even with today's inadequate design representations, is to go about a design task by first trying to reuse and modify an existing design. At the external design level, this would consist of taking the functional specification of a system and modifying it to meet the stated requirements. At the architectural

17

design level, one could use subsystems and modify the modular structure of an existing design to arrive at an appropriate design for the new system.

The reuse of designs is heavily employed in other engineering fields as a routine course of action. With improved representations and procedures, we may be able to do this in software as well. Freeman (1982) discusses reusability in more detail.

While there is obviously much more that could be said about the concepts underlying the practice of software design, those presented here form a sufficient set to aid your understanding of the field. Because this is a still-expanding field, current research efforts are underway that will expand our understanding significantly. The next section provides one perspective on what is needed in this area.

DESIGN RESEARCH[*]

Given the important role that design plays in software engineering, there should be little argument that, if possible, we should try to improve it through appropriate research. Our central thesis is that such improvement is possible if we have a solid scientific understanding of design on which to build a viable (software) engineering design methodology.

Essentially, we must have a body of teachable knowledge about design. It should be intellectually rigorous, analytic, formalized where appropriate, and based on empirical studies where possible. It is this kind of scientific understanding of physical phenomena that makes engineering in other disciplines possible. The "artificial" nature of software highlights the processes that create it, and it is this situation that increases the importance of the design process in software engineering.

This central thesis is based on the ideas of H.A. Simon (1981). Professor Simon argues that our modern world has several very important undertakings that are wholly "artificial" (in the sense of being created by human beings) but that can be studied in a scientific manner. Computing is one of these. In this context, he argues for the creation of a science of design that would include seven components. In the context of software engineering, we have modified his list to include the following topics:

[*] This section is based on (Freeman, 1980b).

- generation and selection of design alternatives;
- design representations;
- solution procedures for design problems;
- how people design;
- design structures.

These are the categories in which we believe research can be profitably undertaken. The following descriptions are not intended to be exhaustive nor explained in full detail. Our purpose here is only to indicate directions for design research.

Generation and Selection of Alternatives

Design is sometimes conceptualized as a process of choosing among alternative structures (both gross and detailed) that go to make up the artifact being designed. This model of design implies that alternatives must be generated first, then evaluated, and finally one of them chosen. Some of the questions of interest for software design include the following:

- How can spaces of alternatives be characterized in a well-defined way so that alternatives can be easily generated?
- How do we measure the quality of a design so that competing choices can be evaluated?
- How does the order in which design decisions are made limit or expand our options?
- Given a specific design problem, how can we allocate our resources in order to achieve a satisfactory design?

Currently there is very little research that touches on this area. A few studies of software quality (e.g., Boehm, et al, 1973) and work on design complexity (e.g., McCabe, 1976) provide us some design metrics, but there is almost no work on spaces of alternatives or on design strategies.

Some design methods (e.g., structured design) explicitly address some of the evaluation questions suggested above. Most design methods, of course, are intended to be improved means of generating and selecting alternatives. The problem, however, is that they are not based on any scientific understanding of either the design process or the artifacts being designed. Thus, any improvements over intuitive design that they may offer will come about through the natural perceptiveness of their inventors. While in fact many advances do come about this way, in the long run, a science-based technology must depend on a solid basis of systematic knowledge.

Design Representations

We discussed above the importance of representation to the design process. Some of the questions that need answers are these:

- What information is necessary to each stage of design?

- How can the information be represented to make it easy to determine properties of the design (*e.g.*, completeness, quality, consistency)?

- How can the representation be used to help determine ramifications of the design?

There is quite a bit of work on design representation in the sense of creating new forms (*e.g.*, Peters, 1981) and, of course, most design methods are intimately coupled with representation. A few explicit studies (*e.g.*, Freeman, 1978) of design representation have been made, and there is an increasing amount of psychological research aimed at some aspects of designing. Overall, however, there is very little work being done explicitly on design representations. As with design methods, eventually a firmer scientific basis must be established.

Solution of Design Problems

A third area in which some underlying scientific theory is needed to support our practical endeavors is the understanding of the logical or intellectual nature of design problem-solving. People solve design problems all the time even though they may not have a clear understanding of how it is done; but people also fail at design problem-solving.

We can characterize the components of design solutions and back up from this to derive the intellectual operations necessary (*e.g.*, establish a framework, generate alternatives, select an appropriate one, etc.) to arrive at an acceptable design solution. (Obviously, the operations listed above are at a very gross level of explanation.)

The following are some of the questions we would like answered:

- What are the intellectual operations (at a detailed as well as at a macro level) necessary to design?

- Can we differentiate in terms of design operations between varying design situations (such as design of a real-time control system and design of a data base)?

- What are the larger phases of the design process, and are they the same for all types of problems?

Questions in this area are based on an informational view of design --*i.e.*, that design is an information-processing activity and as such can be studied in information-processing terms (information objects and the operations on them necessary to achieve new informational states).

There has been a good deal of work in other fields (and some in computer science) on models of design in an attempt to answer these questions. (See, for example, Freeman and Newell, 1971 and Bazjanac, 1974). For the most part, this work can be described as thought-provoking but not conclusive. New research in this area should build on the earlier work and make it specific to the area of software design. Software, while being purely symbolic, results in physical events (outputs of the computer). Further, while it is a static artifact, it represents and results in highly dynamic behavior. These facts lead us to believe that such theoretical studies of design have not yet been carried far enough in the field of software.

Psychology of Design

It is also clear that we can learn from studying how people actually design. There are two main subareas of investigation here:

- cognitive psychology studies of people designing;

- human factor studies of the languages, tools, etc. used by designers.

The first type of study typically results in a model of the observed behavior that is consistent with already established knowledge about cognitive behavior. (See Levin, 1976, for example.) As our understanding of how people design is deepened through such models, we will be able to augment more intelligently what they can do.

Human factors are used here to describe studies ranging from the impact of using linear *versus* graphical languages through the effect of physical working environment to the identification of the factors of group dynamics. We have lumped together a number of investigations in which psychological studies or studies based on and consistent with psychology will result in knowledge that guides us to a deeper understanding of design and how to carry it out.

Design Structures

The final research area that identified as potentially contributing to software design is what we shall call "design structures." The other areas mentioned deal primarily with the design process; this area deals with the artifacts being designed. Much of computer science, of course, deals with the nature of software artifacts. An area that is not dealt with systematically, however, is the study of the characteristics of classes of designs *qua* designs. Questions of interest center around properties of the designs and include the following:

- What are the characterizing distinctions between designs?

- How can designs be cataloged and retrieved?

- Are there meaningful groups of design components that appear in different classes?

- Can necessary and sufficient sets of design structures be identified to build up entire classes of applications?•

Work that attempts to categorize all the algorithms of a particular type (*e.g.*, sorting) is similar to what we have in mind here. However, the study of algorithms doesn't go far enough because it doesn't take into account the practical matters of actual designs. What we are referring to is closer to studies in biology or archeology that take existing organisms or artifacts and classify and study them.

All of the topics introduced above will involve research of a long-term nature (even though some short-term results may ensue). While we might be able to use the results today, the objective is to establish a body of scientifically produced and verifiable knowledge about design on which a variety of undertakings can be based.

Current Design Research

Current work that falls in the design area is largely focused on program design (or on system design in a very general and abstract sense). The literature, contains papers on several subjects:

- *Project experience*: Typically, the theme is "We did the following in our project, and this is what we think we observed." Such studies are useful but are obviously limited in what they can teach us.

- *Design representations*: As noted above, current work in this area is almost entirely devoted to developing new representations. Experience with them will give us some information, but such experience is expensive to obtain and is often inconclusive.

- *Design methods*: In the past ten years many people have realized that the methods followed in the design of software can have a large impact on the quality of the final product as well as on their ability to control the design activity. This has led to a proliferation of design methods. Such methods are often either highly intuitive or very formal, depending on the inclinations of their inventors. Evaluating them runs into the same problems noted with respect to design representations. Further, they tend to concentrate on detailed program design which increasingly is not where the problems lie.

- *Tools*: At present there appears to be an upsurge of interest in tools for the design process. These tools usually support a given method or, worse, are not built consistent with any one coherent method. Tools add several dimensions of complexity to the task of augmenting or improving what designers do, and we suspect that in many cases the efforts to build design tools (when such efforts are not based on a solid understanding of design) will fail.

- *Evaluation techniques*: As noted above, there is some rudimentary work on evaluating designs along different dimensions. Some of this work looks promising, but there is still a long way to go.

This brief overview of design research in no way serves as a survey of the field; indeed, the contents of this tutorial volume only partially address that objective. What we have tried to do, however, is to provide a structure for design research that will aid you in sorting out and comprehending the increasing number of papers that are appearing. In addition, it might provide you the impetus to contribute to our understanding!

Why Design?

Over the past few years, the need for systematic software design has received increasingly widespread acceptance. Therefore, it is unnecessary to go to great lengths to motivate the study of design techniques. However, a brief discussion of a few major factors will help to place design in context.

Perhaps the most important reason to design is that the creation of complex systems involves a very large amount of detail and complexity (*i.e.*, relationships of many sorts between many parts). If this complexity is not controlled, then the desired results will rarely be achieved. Design is the primary tool for controlling and dealing with this mass of detail and its attendant complexity. The regularity and structure of design methods and techniques serve to guide us through complex chains of reasoning where we might otherwise become lost.

A second important reason to design is to aid in the discovery of the underlying structure of the problem situation. An artifact created for any purpose must fit itself to the environment in which it will exist if it is to be successful. In simple situations, the nature of the environment and the necessary structure of the artifact may be more or less obvious and/or prescribed. In complex situations this is rarely the case and this structure must be discovered through design.

A third and increasingly important reason for design is its impact on system quality. We want systems that are reliable, user-centered, efficient, portable, and so on. These are all properties of a system that are global in nature and which demand global design decisions.

During design, we are working with logical properties and the overall structure of the system. There is not yet a huge investment in code and detailed decisions that cannot be changed when an evaluation indicates the desired system properties are not being met. If reliability, useful user functions, modularity, and so on are not planned for before programming is begun, then generally they will be unobtainable. Design at a logical level provides the flexibility to make the global decisions needed to achieve desired system quality.

CONCLUSION

We certainly have not presented all there is to say about the nature of design -- that was not our purpose. We have presented enough of the conceptual aspects of design, however, to permit you to go beyond the simple study of design techniques. Studying the philosophy of design may not translate immediately into improved design performance, nor may it ever be directly identifiable as a precise cause of improved performance. But, as with most activities, a deeper understanding of the design process will eventually pay off. It is for this reason that we have introduced you to this aspect of the study of software design.

The design problems you face, the organizational context in which you work, and your personal skills will vary in some respects from those that we have described here. This introduction, coupled with the other material and references in this volume, should provide you a global view that will assist in the improvement of your design skills.

ACKNOWLEDGEMENT

Numerous and continuing discussions with Tony Wasserman have served to improve significantly my understanding of design. His contribution is gratefully acknowledged.

REFERENCES

Alexander, Christopher. *Notes on the Synthesis of Form.* Harvard University Press, 1964.

Asimow, Morris. *Introduction to Design.* Prentice-Hall, 1962.

Bazjanac, Vladimir. "Architectural Design Theory: Models of the Design Process," in W. R. Spillers (ed.) *Basic Questions of Design Theory*, North-Holland/American Elsevier, 1974.

Boehm, B.W., *et al.* "Characteristics of Software Quality," Technical Report TRW-SS-73-09, TRW Systems Group, Redondo Beach, CA, 1973.

Caine, Stephen H. and E. Kent Gordon. "PDL - A Tool for Software Design," *Proc. AFIPS 1975 NCC.* (Reprinted in this volume.)

DoD. "Ada Methodologies: Concepts and Requirements." Ada Joint Program Office, U.S. Department of Defense, 1982. (Reprinted in this volume.)

Freeman, Peter. "Reusable Software Engineering: Concepts and Research Directions," *Proc.*

ITT Workshop on Reusability in Programming, Newport, R.I., 1983. (Reprinted in this volume.)

Freeman, Peter. "Reusable Software Engineering: A Statement of Long- Range Research Objectives," Technical Report #159, ICS Department, University of California, Irvine, 1980a.

Freeman, Peter. "The Central Role of Design: Implications for Research," *Software Engineering: Research Directions*, Academic Press, pp. 121-132, 1980b.

Freeman, Peter. "Software Design Representation: Analysis and Improvements," *Software Practice and Experience*, Vol. 8, pp. 513-528, 1978.

Freeman, Peter. "Toward Improved Review of Software Designs," *Proc. AFIPS 1975 NCC.*

Freeman, Peter and Allen Newell. "A Model for Functional Reasoning in Design," *Proc. 2nd International Joint Conference on Artificial Intelligence*, 1971.

Jones, J. Christopher. *Design Methods: Seeds of Human Futures.* 2nd Edition, John Wiley and Sons, 1981.

Kerola, P. and Peter Freeman. "A Comparison of Lifecycle Models," *Proc. 5th International Conference on Software Engineering*, pp. 90-99, 1981.

Levin, Steven. *Problem Selection in Computer Program Design.* Ph.D. Thesis, University of California, Irvine, CA, 1976.

Lucas, H. *Toward Creative Systems Design.* Columbia University Press, 1974.

Mayall, W.H. *Principles in Design.* Heinemann Educational Books, Ltd., London, 1979.

McCabe, T.J. "A Complexity Measure," *Transactions Software Engineering*, SE-2,4 (Dec.), p. 308, 1976.

Mumford, E. "Participative Systems Design: Structure and Method," *Systems, Objectives, Solutions*, (1,1), 1981.

Peters, L.J. *Software Design: Methods and Techniques.* Yourden Press, 1981.

Simon, H.A. *The Sciences of the Artificial.* 2nd. Edition, MIT Press, 1981.

Stevens, W.P., G.J. Myers and L.L. Constantine. "Structured Design," *IBM Systems Journal*, 13,2 (1974). (Reprinted in this volume.)

Van Leer, P. "Top-Down Development Using a Program Design Language," *IBM Systems Journal*, 15,2 (1976).

Software and Its Impact: A Quantitative Assessment

by Barry W. Boehm

"You software guys are too much like the weavers in the story about the Emperor and his new clothes. When I go out to check on a software development the answers I get sound like, 'We're fantastically busy weaving this magic cloth. Just wait a while and it'll look terrific.' But there's nothing I can see or touch, no numbers I can relate to, no way to pick up signals that things aren't really all that great. And there are too many people I know who have come out at the end wearing a bunch of expensive rags or nothing at all."

—An Air Force decisionmaker

•
•
•
•

Recently, the Air Force Systems Command* completed a study, "Information Processing/Data Automation Implications of Air Force Command and Control Requirements in the 1980s," or CCIP-85 for short. The study projected future Air Force command and control information processing requirements and likely future information processing capabilities into the 1980s, and developed an Air Force R&D plan to correct the mismatches found between likely capabilities and needs.

Although many of the CCIP-85 conclusions are specific to the Air Force, there are a number of points which hold at least as well elsewhere. This article summarizes those transferable facts and conclusions.

Basically, the study showed that for almost all applications, software (as opposed to computer hardware, displays, architecture, etc.) was "the tall pole in the tent"—the major source of difficult future problems and operational performance penalties. However, we found it difficult to convince people outside the software business of this. This was primarily because of the scarcity of solid quantitative data to demonstrate the impact of software on

operational performance or to provide perspective on R&D priorities.

The study did find and develop some data which helped illuminate the problems and convince people that the problems were significant. Surprisingly, though, we found that these data are almost unknown even to software practitioners. (You can test this assertion via the Software Quiz, p. 51.) The main purpose of this article is to make these scanty but important data and their implications better known, and to convince people to collect more of it.

Before reading further, though, please try the Software Quiz. It's intended to help you better appreciate the software issues which the article goes on to discuss.

Software is big business

One convincing impact of software is directly on the pocketbook. For the Air Force, the estimated dollars for FY 1972 are in Fig. 5; an annual expenditure on software of between $1 billion and $1.5 billion, about three times the annual expenditure on computer hardware and about 4 to 5% of the total Air Force budget. Similar figures hold elsewhere. The recent World Wide Military Command and Control System (WWMCCS) computer procurement was estimated to involve expenditures of $50 to $100 million for hardware and $722 million for software.[1] A recent estimate for NASA was an annual expenditure of $100 million for hardware, and $200 million for software—about 6% of the annual NASA budget.

For some individual projects, here are some overall software costs:

IBM OS/360	$ 200,000,000[2]
SAGE	250,000,000[3]
Manned Space Program, 1960-70	1,000,000,000[3]

Overall software costs in the U.S. are probably over $10 billion per year, over 1% of the gross national product.

If the software-hardware cost ratio appears lopsided now, consider what will happen in the years ahead, as hardware gets cheaper and software (people) costs go up and up. Fig. 6 shows the estimate for software expenditures in the Air Force going to over 90% of total adp system costs by 1985; this trend is probably characteristic of other organizations, also.

*The views in this article do not necessarily reflect those of the United States Air Force.
[1] *Datamation*, March 1, 1971, p. 41.
[2] Alexander, T., "Computers Can't Solve Everything," *Fortune*, May 1969.
[3] Boehm, B. W., "System Design," in *Planning Community Information Utilities*, (eds.) H. Sackman and B. W. Boehm, AFIPS Press, 1972.

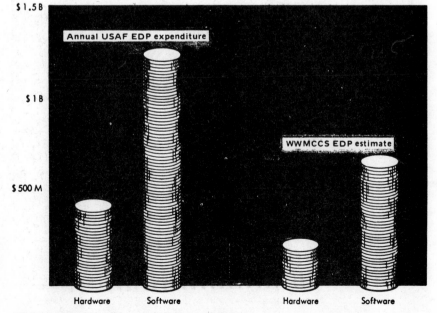

Fig. 5. USAF software is big business.

One would expect that current information-processing research and development projects would be strongly oriented toward where the future problems are. However, according to recent Congressional testimony by Dr. Ruth Davis of the National Bureau of Standards (NBS) on federally-funded computing R&D projects:

... 21% of the projects were concerned with hardware design, 40% were concerned with the needs of special interest communities such as natural sciences, engineering, social and behavioral sciences, humanities, and real-time systems, 14% were in the long-range payoff areas of metatheory, while only 9% were oriented to the highly agonizing software problems identified by most customers as their major concern."[4]

One result of the CCIP-85 study has been to begin to reorient Air Force information processing R&D much more toward software. Similar R&D trends are evident at DOD's Advanced Research Projects Agency (ARPA), National Science Foundation, and the National Bureau of Standards. But much remains to be done.

Indirect costs even bigger

Big as the direct costs of software are, the indirect costs are even bigger, because software generally is on the critical path in overall system development. That is, any slippages in the software schedule translate directly into slippages in the overall delivery schedule of the system.

Let's see what this meant in a recent software development for a large defense system. It was planned to have an operational lifetime of seven years and a total cost of about $1.4 billion—or about $200 million a year worth of capability. However, a six-month software delay caused a six-month delay in making the system available to the user, who thus lost about $100 million worth of needed capability—about 50 times the direct cost of $2 million for the additional software effort. Moreover, in order to keep the software from causing further delays, several important functions were not provided in the initial delivery to the user.

Again, similar situations develop in domestic applications. IBM's OS/360 software was over a year late.[2] The U.S. air traffic control system currently operates much more expensively and less effectively because of slippages of years in software (and also hardware, in this case) development, which have escalated direct software costs to over $100 million.[5] Often, organizations compensate for software development slippages by switching to a new system before the software is adequately tested, leading to such social costs as undelivered welfare checks to families with dependent children, bad credit reports, and even people losing their lives because of errors in medical software.

Getting software off the critical path

Once software starts slipping along the critical path, there are several more or less unattractive options. One option is to add more people in hopes that a human wave of programmers will quickly subdue the problem. However, Brooks' excellent article[6] effectively shows that software is virtually incompressible with respect to elapsed time, and that such measures more often make things worse rather than better. Some other unhappy options are to skimp on testing, integration, or documentation. These usually cost much more in the long run. Another is just to scrap the new system and make do with the old one. Generally, the most attractive option is to reduce the system to an austere but expandable initial capability.

For the future, however, several opportunities exist for reducing software delays and getting software off the critical path. These fall into three main categories:

1. Increasing each individual's software productivity.

2. Improving project organization and management.

3. Initiating software development earlier in the system development cycle.

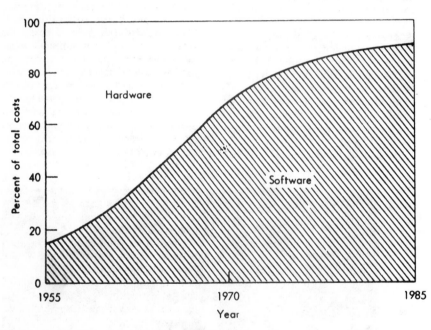

Fig. 6. Hardware/software cost trends.

4 "Government Bureau Takes on Role of Public Protector Against Computer Misuse." *ACM Communications*, November 1972, p. 1018.
5 Hirsch, P., "What's Wrong With the Air Traffic Control System?" *Datamation*, August 1972, pp. 48-53.
6 Brooks, F., "Why Is The Software Late?" *Data Management*, August 1971.

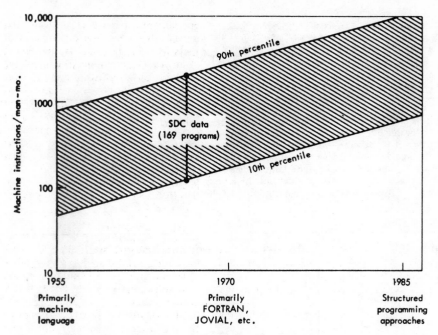

Fig. 7. Technology forecast: software productivity.

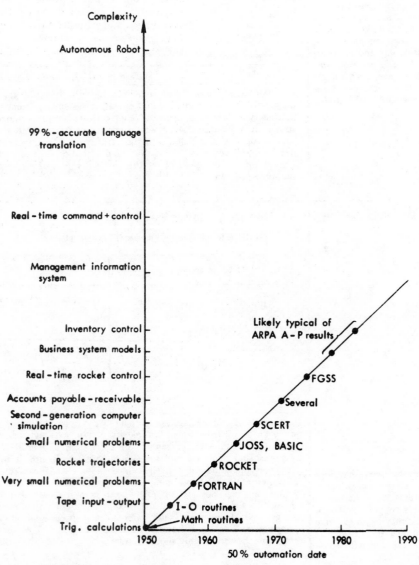

Fig. 8. Growth of automatic programming

Software Impact

Increasing software productivity: definitions

Fig. 7 shows a simplistic view of likely future trends in software productivity. It is probably realistic in maintaining at least a factor-of-10 spread between the 10th and 90th percentiles of software productivity, but it begs a few important questions.

One is, "What is software?" Even the courts and the Internal Revenue Service have not been able to define its metes and bounds precisely. The figures above include computer program documentation, but exclude operating procedures and broad system analysis. Clearly, a different definition would affect software productivity figures significantly.

Another important question is, "What constitutes software production?" As early as the mid-1950s there were general-purpose trajectory analysis systems with which an analyst could put together a modular, 10,000-word applications program in about 10 minutes. Was this "software production?" With time, more and more such general-purpose packages as ICES (MIT's Integrated Civil Engineering System), Programming-by-Questionnaire, RPG, MARK IV, and SCERT have made the creation of significant software capabilities so easy that they tend to be eliminated from the category of "software productivity," which continues to refer to those portions of the software directly resulting from handwritten strings of assembly or FORTRAN-level language statements. Fig. 8 is an attempt to characterize this trend in terms of a "50% automation date": the year in which most of the incoming problems in an area could be "programmed" in less than an hour by a user knowledgeable in his field, with one day of specialized training.

Thus, if we want to speak objectively about software productivity, we are faced with the dilemma of:

1. Either redefining it in terms of source instructions rather than object instructions—thereby further debasing the unit of production (which isn't completely objective even using object instructions as a base)—or

2. Continuing to narrow the range of definition of "software productivity" to the more and more difficult programs which can't be put together more or less automatically.

The eventual result of ARPA's major "automatic programming" effort will be to narrow this latter range even further.[7]

[7] Balzer, Robert M., *Automatic Programming*, Institute Technical Memorandum, University of Southern California, Information Sciences Institute, September 1972.

A Software Quiz

Very little in the way of quantitative data has been collected about software. But there is some which deserves to be better known than it is. Because, otherwise, we have nothing but our intuition to guide us in making critical decisions about software, and often our intuition can be quite fallible. The four questions below give you a chance to test how infallible your software intuition is. **Answers to the quiz appear on the following two pages.**

1A. Where Does the Software Effort Go?

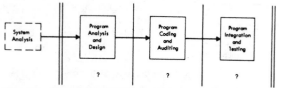

If you're involved in planning, staffing, scheduling or integrating a large software effort, you should have a good idea of how much of the effort will be spent on analysis and design (after the functional specification for the system has been completed), on coding and auditing (including desk checking and software module unit testing), and on checkout and test. See how well you do in estimating the effort on a percentage basis for the three phases. The results for such different large systems as SAGE, OS/360, and the Gemini space shots have been strikingly similar.

3A. Where Are Software Errors Made?

	Batch (all errors)	Real-time (final validation phase only)
Computation and assingment	?	?
Sequencing and control	?	?
Input – output	?	?
Declarations	?	?
Punctuation	?	Not available
Correction to errors	Not available	?
Total	100 %	100 %

If you're setting test plan schedules and priorities, designing diagnostic aids for compilers and operating systems, or contemplating new language features (e.g., GOTO-free) to eliminate sources of software errors, it would be very useful to know how such errors are distributed over the various software functions. See how well you do in estimating the distribution of errors for typical batch programs and for the final validation of a critical real-time program.

2A. How Do Hardware Constraints Affect Software Productivity?

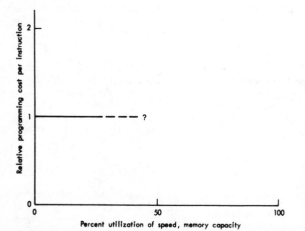

Another useful factor to know in planning software development is the extent to which hardware constraints affect software productivity. As you approach complete utilization of hardware speed and memory capacity, what happens to your software costs? Do they stay relatively constant or do they begin to bulge upward somewhat? The data here represent 34 software projects at North American Rockwell's Autonetics Division with some corroborative data points determined at Mitre.

4A. How Do Compilers Spend Their Time?

(Knuth study: 440 Lockheed programs: 250,000 statements)

Number of operands	%
1 (A = B)	?
2 (A = B ⊕ C)	?
3 (A = B ⊕ C ⊕ D)	?
>3	?

Recently, Donald Knuth and others at Stanford performed a study on the distribution of complexity of FORTRAN statements. Try to estimate what percentage of their sample of 250,000 FORTRAN statements were of the simple form A=B, how many had two operands on the right-hand side, etc. If you're a compiler designer, this should be very important, because it would tell you how to optimize your compiler—whether it should do simple things well or whether it should do complex things well. Here the results refer to aerospace application programs at Lockheed; however, a sample of Stanford student programs showed roughly similar results.

1B. Where Does the Software Effort Go?

	Analysis and Design	Coding and Auditing	Checkout and Test
SAGE	39%	14%	47%
NTDS	30	20	50
GEMINI	36	17	47
SATURN V	32	24	44
OS/360	33	17	50
TRW Survey	46	20	34

How close did you come to that large 45-50% for checkout? Whatever you estimated, it was probably better than the planning done on one recent multimillion dollar, multiyear (nondefense) software project by a major software contractor which allowed two weeks for acceptance testing and six weeks for operational testing, preceded by a two-man-month test plan effort. Fortunately, this project was scrapped in midstream before the testing inadequacies could show up. But similar schedules have been established for other projects, generally leading to expensive slippages in phasing over to new systems, and prematurely delivered, bug-ridden software.

Another major mismatch appears when you compare the relative amount of effort that goes into the three phases with the relative magnitude of R&D expenditures on techniques to improve effectiveness in each of the phases. Relatively little R&D support has been going toward improving software analysis, design, and validation capabilities.

The difference in the later TRW data probably reflects another insight: that more thorough analysis and design more than pays for itself in reduced testing costs.

(Refs.: Boehm, B.W., "Some Information Processing Implications of Air Force Space Missions: 1970-1980," *Astronautics and Aeronautics*, January 1971. Wolverton, R., *The Cost of Developing Large-Scale Software*, TRW Paper, March 1972.)

Answers to A Software Quiz

2B. How Do Hardware Constraints Affect Software Productivity?

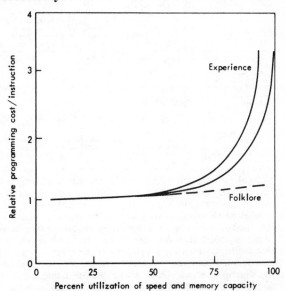

Hopefully, your estimate was closer to the "experience" curve than the "folklore" one. Yet, particularly in hardware procurements, people make decisions as if the folklore curve were true. Typically, after a software job is sized, hardware is procured with only about 15% extra capacity over that determined by the sizing, presenting the software developers with an 85% saturated machine just to begin with. How uneconomic this is will be explained by Fig. 11 in the text.

Those data also make an attractive case for virtual memory systems as ways to reduce software costs by eliminating memory constraints. However, the strength of this case is reduced to the extent that virtual memory system inefficiencies tighten speed constraints.

(Ref.: Williman, A. O., and C. O'Donnell, "Through the Central 'Multiprocessor' Avionics Enters the Computer Era," *Astronautics and Aeronautics*, July 1970.)

Software Impact

Increasing software productivity: factors

However, the fact remains that software needs to be constructed, that various factors significantly influence the speed and effectiveness of producing it, and that we have at least some measure of control over these factors. Thus, the more we know about those factors, the more our decisions will lead to improved rather than degraded software productivity. What are the important factors?

One is computer system response time. Studies by Sackman and others[8] comparing batch versus on-line programming have shown median im-

provements of 20% in programming efficiency using on-line systems.

However, in these same studies, *variations between individuals* accounted for differences in productivity of factors up to 26:1. Clearly, selecting the right people provides more leverage than anything else in improving software productivity. But this isn't so easy. Reinstedt[9] and others have shown that none of the selection tests developed so far have an operationally-dependable correlation with programmer performance. Weinberg, in his excellent book,[10] illustrates the complexity of the issue by citing two programmer attributes for each letter of the alphabet (from age and agility through

zygosity and zodiacal sign), each of which might be a plausible determinant of programmer performance. Still, the potential payoffs are so large that further work in the areas of personnel selection, training, and evaluation should be closely followed. For example, the Berger Test of Programming Proficiency has proved fairly reliable in assessing the programming capability of experienced programmers.

Other factors such as *programming languages* have made significant differences in software productivity. Rubey's PL/I study showed differences of up to 2:1 in development time for the same program written in two different languages. In a related effort, Kosy obtained a 3.5:1 productivity improvement over one of the Rubey examples by using ECSS, a special-purpose lan-

[8] Sackman, H., *Man-Computer Problem Solving*, Auerbach Publishers, Inc., 1970.

[9] Reinstedt, R. N., "Results of a Programmer Performance Prediction Study," *IEEE Trans. Engineering Management*, December 1967, pp. 183-187.

[10] Weinberg, G., *The Psychology of Computer Programming*, Van Nostrand Reinhold, 1971.

Answers to A Software Quiz (cont'd.)

3B. Where Are Software Errors Made?

	7 batch programs (all errors)		Benchmark space booster control (all errors)	On-board space booster control (final validation phase only)
	PL/I	2 COBOL 2 JOVIAL 3 FORTRAN		
Computation and assignment	9%	25%	28%	20%
Sequencing and control	20	17	27	51
Input-output	8	8	7	6
Declarations	32	35	38	16
Punctuation	31	15	n. a.	n. a.
Corrections to errors	n. a.	n. a.	n. a.	7
Total (%)	100%	100%	100%	100%
Errors (No.)	214	140	313	87

Several points seem fairly clear from the data. One is that GOTO-free programming is not a panacea for software errors, as it will eliminate only some fraction of sequence and control errors. However, as Column 4 shows, the sequence and control errors are the most important ones to eliminate, as they currently tend to persist until the later, more difficult stages of validation on critical real-time programs. Another point is that language features can make a difference, as seen by comparing error sources and totals in PL/I with the other languages (FORTRAN, COBOL, and JOVIAL), although in this case an additional factor of less programmer familiarity with PL/I also influences the results.

(Refs.: Rubey, R. J., et al, *Comparative Evaluation of PL/I*, United States Air Force Report, ESD-TR-68-150, April 1968. Rubey, R.J., *Study of Software Quantitative Aspects*, United States Air Force Report, CS-7150-R0840, October 1971.)

4B. How Do Compilers Spend Their Time?

NUMBER OF OPERANDS IN FORTRAN STATEMENTS
(Knuth study: 440 Lockheed Programs, 250,000 statements)

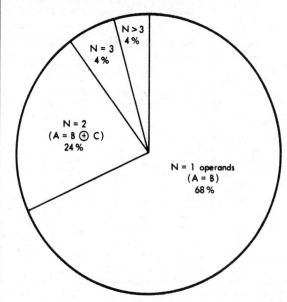

It's evident from the data that most FORTRAN statements used in practice are quite simple in form. For example, 68% of these 250,000 statements were of the simple form A=B. When Knuth saw this and similar distributions on the dimensionality of arrays (58% unindexed, 30.5% with one index), the length of DO loops (39% with just one statement), and the nesting of DO loops (53.5% of depth 1, 23% of depth 2), here was his reaction:

"The author once found . . . great significance in the fact that a certain complicated method was able to translate the statement
$$C(I*N+J):=((A+X)*Y) +2.768((L-M)*(-K))/Z$$
into only 19 machine instructions compared with the 21 instructions obtained by a previously published method. . . . The fact that arithmetic expressions usually have an average length of only two operands, in practice, would have been a great shock to the author at that time."

Thus, evidence indicates that batch compilers generally do very simple things and one should really be optimizing batch compilers to do simple things. This could be similarly the case with compilers and interpreters for on-line systems; however, nobody has collected the data for those.

(Ref.: Knuth, D.E., "An Empirical Study of FORTRAN Programs," *Software Practice and Experience*, Vol. 1, 1971, p. 105.)

---

guage for simulating computer systems.

Weinberg has also shown[10,11] that the choice of *software development criteria* exerts a significant influence on software productivity. In one set of experiments, programmers were given the same program specification, but were told either (Group P) to finish the job as promptly as possible or (Group E) to produce as efficient a program as possible. The results were that Group E finished the job with an average of over twice as many runs to completion, but with programs running an average of six times faster.

Another important factor is the software *learning curve*. The table in the next column shows the estimated and actual programming effort involved in producing three successive FORTRAN compilers by the same group.[12]

Compiler Effort No.	Man-Months	
	Estimated	Actual
1	36	72
2	24	36
3	12	14

Clearly, software estimation accuracy has a learning curve, also.

But other factors in the programming environment make at least as large a contribution on any given project. The most exhaustive quantitative analysis done so far on the factors influencing software development was an SDC study done for the Air Force Electronic Systems Division in 1965,[13] which collected data on nearly 100 factors over 169 software projects and performed extensive statistical analysis on the results. The best fit to the data involved 13 factors, including stability of program design, percent mathematical instructions, number of subprograms, concurrent hardware development, and number of man-trips—but even that estimate had a standard deviation (62 man-months) larger than the mean (40 man-months).

Increasing software productivity: prescriptions

Does all this complexity mean that the prospect of increasing software productivity is hopeless? Not at all. In

[11] Weinberg, G. M., "The Psychology of Improved Programming Performance," *Datamation*, November 1972.

[12] McClure, R. M., "Projection vs Performance in Software Production," in *Software Engineering*, (eds.) P. Naur, and B. Randell, NATO, January 1969.

[13] Nelson, E. A., *Management Handbook for the Estimation of Computer Programming Costs*, SDC, TM-3224, Oct. 31, 1966.

Software Impact

fact, some of the data provide good clues toward avenues of improvement. For example, if you accurately answered question 1 on the Software Quiz, you can see that only 15% of a typical software effort goes into coding. Clearly, then, there is more potential payoff in improving the efficiency of your analysis and validation efforts than in speeding up your coding.

Significant opportunities exist for doing this. The main one comes when each of us as individual programmers becomes aware of where his time is really going, and begins to design, develop and use thoughtful test plans for the software he produces, beginning in the earliest analysis phases. Suppose that by doing so, we could save an average of one man-day per man-month of testing effort. This would save about 2.5% of our total expenditure on software. · Gilchrist and Weber[14] estimate about 360,000 software practitioners in the U.S.; even at a somewhat conservative total cost quotation of $30,000 per man-year, this is about $10.8 billion annually spent on software, yielding a testing savings above of about $270 million per year.

Another opportunity lies in the area of programming languages. Except for a few experiments such as Floyd's "Verifying Compiler," programming languages have been designed for people to express programs with a minimum of redundancy, which tends to expedite the coding process, but makes the testing phase more difficult. Appropriate additional redundancy in a program language, requiring a programmer to specify such items as allowable limits on variables, inadmissible states and relations between variables,[15] would allow a compiler or operating system to provide much more help in diagnosing programming errors and reducing the time-consuming validation phase. For example, of the 93 errors detected during execution in Rubey's PL/I study, 52 could have been caught during compilation with a validation-oriented programming language containing features such as those above.

Another avenue to reducing the validation effort lies in providing tools and techniques which get validation done more efficiently during the analysis phase. This is the approach taken in *structured programming*. This term

has been used to describe a variety of on-line programming tool boxes, programming systems, and innovative structurings of the software production effort. An example of the first is the Flexible Guidance Software System, currently being developed for the Air Force Space and Missile Systems Organization. The second is exemplified by the Technische Hogeschool Eindhoven (THE)[16] and automated engineering design (AED) systems, while innovative structuring may be seen in experiments such as the IBM chief programmer team (CPT) effort.[17] Although they are somewhat different, each concept represents an attempt to bring to software production a "top-down" approach and to minimize logical errors and inconsistencies through structural simplification of the development process. In the case of the THE system, this is reinforced by requiring system coding free of discontinuous program control ("GO-TO free"). In the chief programmer approach, it is accomplished by choosing a single individual to do the majority of actual design and programming and tailoring a support staff around his function and talents.

As yet, none of the systems or concepts described has been rigorously tested. Initial indications are, however, that the structured approach can shorten the software development process significantly, at least for some

struction system for the *New York Times*) cut expected project costs by 50% and reduced development time to 25% of the initial estimate.

The validation statistics on this project were particularly impressive. After only a week's worth of system integration, the software went through five weeks of acceptance testing by *Times* personnel. Only 21 errors were found, all of which were fixed in one day. Since then during over a year's worth of operational experience, only 25 additional errors have been found in the 83,000-instruction package.[18]

At this point, it's still not clear to what extent this remarkable performance was a function of using remarkably skilled programming talent, and to what extent the performance gains could be matched by making a typical programming team into a Chief Programmer Team. Yet the potential gains were so large that further research, experimentation and training in structured programming concepts was one of the top priority recommendations of the CCIP-85 study.

Improving software management

Even though an individual's software productivity is important, the CCIP-85 study found that the problems of software productivity on medium or large projects are largely problems of management: of thorough organiza-

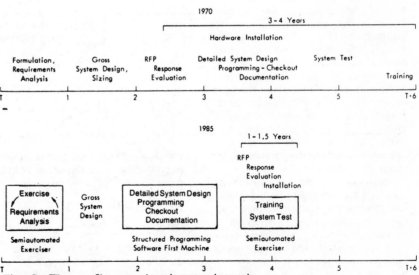

Fig. 9. The software development cycle.

classes of programs and programmers. In one case, the use of AED reduced the man-effort of a small system from an envisioned six man-months to three man-weeks. A major experiment using the CPT concept (on an 83,000-in-

tion, good contingency planning, thoughtful establishment of measurable project milestones, continuous monitoring on whether the milestones are properly passed, and prompt investigation and corrective action in case they are not. In the software management area, one of the major difficulties

[14] Gilchrist, B., and K. E. Weber, "Employment of Trained Computer Personnel—A Quantitative Survey," *Proceedings, 1972 SJCC*, p. 641-648.

[15] Kosy, D. W., *Approaches to Improved Program Validation Through Programming Language Design*, The Rand Corporation, P-4865, July 1972.

[16] Dijkstra, E. W., "The Structure of the 'THE' Multiprogramming System," *ACM Communications*, May 1968.

[17] Baker, F. T., "Chief Programmer Team," *IBM Systems Journal*, Vol. 11, No. 1, 1972, pp. 56-73.

[18] Baker, F. T., "System Quality Through Structured Programming," *Proceedings, 1972 FJCC*, pp. 339-344.

is the transfer of experience from one project to the next. For example, many of the lessons learned as far back as SAGE are often ignored in today's software developments, although they were published over 10 years ago in Hosier's excellent 1961 article on the value of milestones, test plans, precise interface specifications, integrated measurement capabilities, formatted debugging aids, early prototypes, concurrent system development and performance analysis, etc.[19]

Beyond this, it is difficult to say anything concise about software management that doesn't sound like motherhood. Therefore, this article will simply cite some good references in which the subject is explored in some detail.[20,21,22]

Getting an earlier start: the software-first machine

Even if software productivity never gets tremendously efficient, many of the most serious software agonies would be alleviated if we could get software off the critical path within an overall system development. In looking at the current typical history of a large software project (Fig. 9) you can see that the year (or often more) spent on hardware procurement pushes software farther out onto the critical path, since often the software effort has to wait at least until the hardware source selection is completed.

One of the concepts developed in the CCIP-85 study for getting software more off the critical path was that of a "software-first machine." This is a highly generalized computer, capable of simulating the behavior of a wide range of hardware configurations. Fig. 10 provides a rough plan of such a software-first machine. It would have the capability of configuring and exercising through its microprogrammed control, a range of computers, and could also simultaneously provide some additional hardware aids to developing and testing software.

Suppose a large organization such as the Air Force owned such a machine. The following events could then take place: a contractor who is trying to develop software for an airborne computer could start with a need for a machine which is basically the IBM 4PI, but with a faster memory and different interrupt structure. This software contractor could develop, exercise, store, and recall his software based on the

microprogrammed model of the machine. When it turned out that this architecture was hampering the software developers, they could do some hardware/software tradeoffs rather easily by changing the microprogrammed machine representation; and when they were finished or essentially finished with the software development, they would have detailed design specifications for the hardware that could be produced through competitive procurement in industry. Similarly, another contractor could be developing software for interface message processors for communications systems, based on variants of the Honeywell DDP 516; another could be improving a real-time data processing capability based on an upgrade of a CDC 3800 computer on another virtual machine.

The software-first machine could be of considerable value in shortening the time from conception to implementation of an integrated hardware/software system. In the usual procurement process (Fig. 9), the hardware is chosen first, and software development must await delivery of the hardware.

With the software-first machine, software development can avoid this wait, as hardware procurement can be done during the system test phase: the necessary hardware fabrication will start from a detailed design and, with future fabrication technology, should not introduce delays. This saving translates also into increased system operating life, as the hardware installed in the field is based on more up-to-date technology.

However, the software-first machine concept has some potential drawbacks. For example, it might produce a "centrifugal tendency" in hardware development. Allowing designers to tailor hardware to software might result in the proliferation of a variety of similar although critically different computers, each used for a special purpose.

A final question concerning the software-first machine remains moot: Can it be built, at any rate, at a "reasonable" cost? Architectures such as the CDC STAR, ILLIAC IV, and Goodyear STARAN IV would be virtually impossible to accommodate in a single machine. Thus, it is more likely that vari-

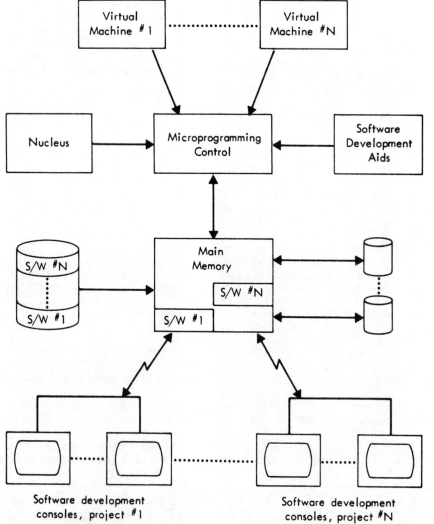

Fig. 10. Software-first machine concept.

[19] Hosier, W. A., "Pitfalls and Safeguards in Real-Time Digital Systems with Emphasis on Programming," IRE Transactions on Engineering Management, Vol. EM-8, June 1961, pp. 99-115.
[20] Naur, P. and B. Randell (eds.) Software Engineering, NATO Science Committee, January 1969.
[21] Buxton, J. N. and B. Randell, (eds.) Software Engineering Techniques, NATO Science Committee, April 1970.
[22] Weinwurm, G., (ed.) On the Management of Computer Programming, Auerbach, 1970.

Software Impact

ous subsets of the software-first machine characteristics will be developed for various ranges of applications.

One such variant is under way already. One Air Force organization, wishing to upgrade without a simultaneous hardware and software discontinuity, acquired some Meta 4 microprogrammed machines which will originally be installed to emulate the existing second-generation hardware. Once the new hardware is in operation, they will proceed to upgrade the system software using a different microprogrammed base. In this way they can upgrade the system with a considerably reduced risk of system downtime.

Another existing approach is that of the microprogrammed Burroughs B1700, which provides a number of the above characteristics plus capabilities to support "direct" execution of higher-level-language programs.

Other hardware-software tradeoffs

In addition, there are numerous other ways in which cheaper hardware can be traded off to save on more expensive software development costs.

A most significant one stems from the striking difference between "folklore" and "experience" in the hardware-software curves shown in Fig. 2B of the Software Quiz. This tradeoff opportunity involves buying enough hardware capacity to keep away from the steep rise in software costs occurring at about the 85% saturation point of cpu and memory capacity.

Thus, suppose that one has sized a data-processing task and determined that a computer of one-unit capacity (with respect to central processing unit speed and size) is required. Fig. 11 shows how the total data-processing system cost varies with the amount of excess cpu capacity procured for various estimates of the ratio of ideal software-to-hardware costs for the system. ("Ideal software" costs are those that would be incurred without any consideration of straining hardware capacity.) The calculations are based on the previous curve of programming costs and two models of hardware cost: the linear model assumes that cost increases linearly with increases in cpu capacity; the "Grosch's Law" model assumes that cost increases as the square root of cpu capacity. Sharpe's data[23] indicates that most applications fall somewhere between these models.

It should be remembered that the curves are based on imprecise observations; they clearly cannot be used in "cookbook" fashion by system designers. But even their general trends make the following points quite evident:

1. Overall system cost is generally minimized by procuring computer hardware with at least 50% to 100% more capacity than is absolutely necessary.

2. The more the ratio of software-to-hardware cost increases (as it will markedly during the seventies), the more excess computing capacity one should procure to minimize the total cost.

3. It is far more risky to err by procuring a computer that is too small than one that is too large. This is especially important, since one's initial sizing of the data-processing job often tends to underestimate its magnitude.

Of course, buying extra hardware does not eliminate the need for good software engineering thereafter. Careful configuration control must be maintained to realize properly the benefits of having extra hardware capability, as there are always strong Parkinsonian tendencies to absorb excess capacity with marginally useful tasks.

Software responsiveness

Another difficulty with software is its frequent unresponsiveness to the actual needs of the organization it was developed for. For example, the hospital information system field has several current examples of "wallflower" systems which were developed without adequately consulting and analyzing the information requirements of doctors, nurses, and hospital administrators. After trying to live with these systems for a while, several hospital administrators have reluctantly but firmly phased them out with such comments as, "We know that computers are supposed to be the way to go for the future, but this system just doesn't provide us any help," or, "Usage of the system began at a very low level—and dropped off from there."

The main difficulties stem from a lack of easily transferable procedures to aid in the software requirements analysis process. This process bears an all-too-striking resemblance to the class of folk tales in which a genie comes up to a man and tells him he has three wishes and can ask for anything in the world. Typically, he spends his first two wishes asking for something like a golden castle and a princess, and then when he discovers the operations, maintenance, and compatibility implications of his new acquisitions, he is happy to spend the third wish getting back to where he started.

Similarly, the computer is a sort of genie which says, "I'll give you any

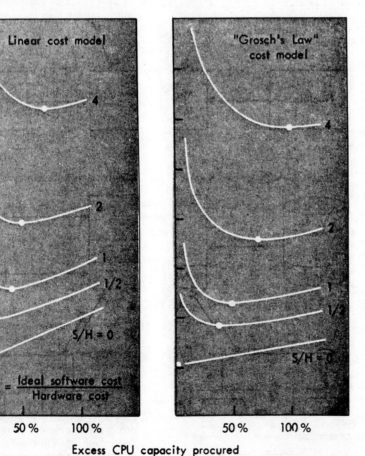

Fig. 11. Hardware-software systems costs.

23 Sharpe, W. F., *The Economics of Computers*, Columbia University Press, 1969.

23 Sharpe, W. F., *The Economics of Computers*, Columbia University Press, 1969.

processed information you want. All you need to do is ask—by writing the software to process it." Often, though, we go the man in the folk tale one better by canvassing a number of users (or nonusers) and putting their combined wish lists into a software requirements analysis. But our technology base for assessing the operations, maintenance, and compatibility implications of the resulting software system is just as inadequate. Thus, large airline reservations software developments (Univac / United, Burroughs / TWA) have reached the point that the customer preferred to wish them out of existence rather than continue them— but only after the investment of tens of millions of dollars. In other cases, where no alternative was available, software rewrites of up to 67% (and in one very large system, 95%) have taken place—*after* the "final" software package had been delivered—in order to meet the user's operational needs.

Considering the major needs for better requirements analysis techniques, the relative lack of available techniques, and the added fact (from Fig. 1B of the Software Quiz) that about 35% of the total software effort goes into analysis and design, it is not surprising that the top-priority R&D recommendation made by the CCIP-85 study was for better techniques for performing and validating information system requirements analyses, and for generating and verifying the resulting information system designs.

The recent DATAMATION articles on automated system design[24,25] indicated some promising initial developments in this area such as Teichroew's ISDOS project, FOREM, and IBM's TAG (Time-Automated Grid) system. Other significant aids are being developed in the area of special languages and packages such as SCERT, CASE, CSS, SAM, and ECSS to accelerate the process of design verification by simulating information-processing systems. Also, ARPA's major research effort in automatic programming is focused strongly on automating the analysis and design processes.

Software reliability and certification

Another major area in which the CCIP-85 study identified a serious mismatch between future needs and likely software capabilities was in the area of software certification: of providing guarantees that the software will do what it is supposed to do. (Other significant problem or opportunity areas identified by CCIP-85 included, in order, data security, airborne computing power, multisource data fusion, data communications, source data automation, image processing, performance analysis, parallel processing, and software transferability.)

This is a significant concern right now, but it becomes even more pressing when one extrapolates current trends toward more complex software tasks and toward more and more automated aids to decision making. Just consider the trends implicit in the results of the recent AFIPS/Time Survey[26] which indicated that currently *30% of the labor force must deal with computers in their daily work, but only 15% of the labor force is required to have any understanding of computers.* Extrapolating this trend into the 1980s, as is done in Fig. 12, indicates that perhaps 40% of the labor force will be trusting implicitly in the results produced by computer software.

Software reliability: problem symptoms

Will software be deserving of such trust? Not on its past record. For example, some of the most thoroughly tested software in the world is that of the Apollo manned spaceflight efforts. Yet on Apollo 8, an unforeseen sequence of astronaut actions destroyed the contents of a word in the computer's erasable memory—fortunately, not a critical error in this case. And on Apollo 11, the data flow from the rendezvous radar was not diverted during the critical lunar landing sequence, causing a computer overload that required astronaut Armstrong to divert his attention from the process of landing the spacecraft—fortunately again, without serious consequences. And during the 10-day flight of Apollo 14, there were 18 discrepancies found in the software—again fortunately, without serious consequences.

Other space missions haven't been so fortunate. Recently a software error aboard a French meteorological satellite caused it to "emergency destruct" 72 out of 141 high-altitude weather balloons, instead of interrogating them. An early U.S. Mariner interplanetary mission was lost due to a software error. And the Soviet Union has had missions fail because of software errors.

Down on earth, software reliability isn't any better. Each new release of os/360 contains roughly 1,000 new software errors. On one large real-time system containing about 2,700,000 instructions and undergoing continuous modifications, an average of one software error per day is discovered. Errors in medical software have caused people to lose their lives. And software errors cause a constant stream of social dislocations due to false arrests, incor-

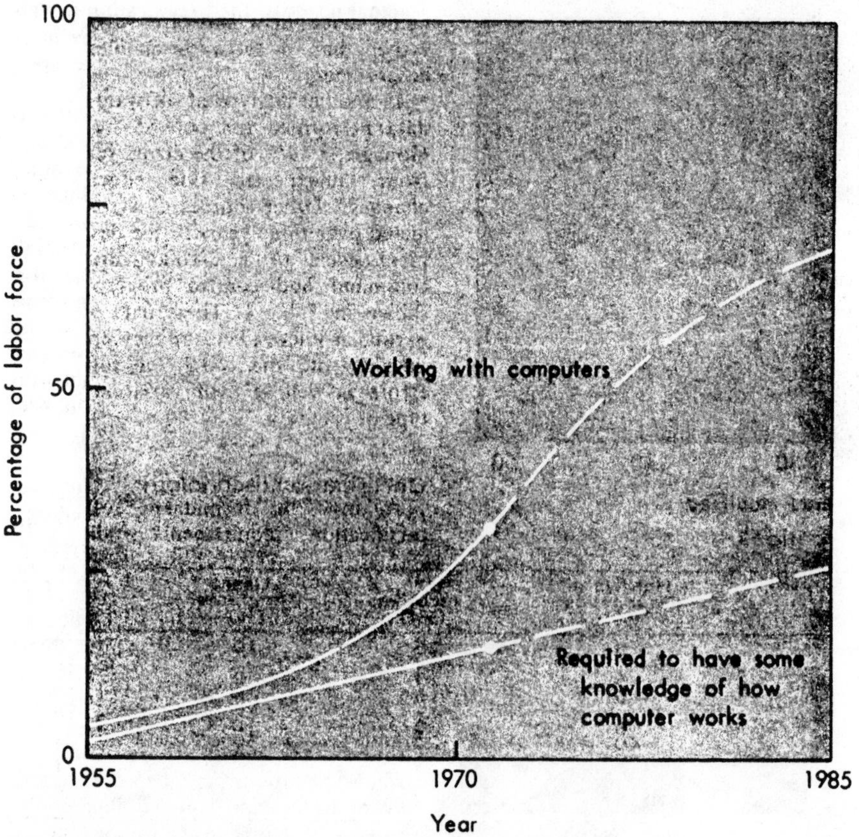

Fig. 12. Growth of trust in computers and software.

[24] Teichroew, D., and H. Sayari, "Automation of System Building," *Datamation*, August 15, 1971, pp. 25-30.

[25] Head, R. V., "Automated System Analysis," *Datamation*, August 15, 1971, pp. 23-24.

[26] *A National Survey of the Public's Attitudes Toward Computers*, AFIPS and Time, Inc., November 1971.

Software Impact

rect bank balances or credit records, lost travel reservations, or long-delayed payments to needy families or small businesses. Also, lack of certification capabilities makes it virtually impossible to provide strong guarantees on the security or privacy of sensitive or personal information.

Software reliability: technical problems

As the examples above should indicate, software certification is not easy. Ideally, it means checking all possible logical paths through a program; there may be a great many of these. For example, Fig. 13 shows a rather simple program flowchart. Before looking at the accompanying text, try to estimate how many different possible paths through the flowchart exist.

Even through this simple flowchart, the number of different paths is about ten to the twentieth. If one had a computer that could check out one path per nanosecond (10^{-9} sec), and had started to check out the program at the beginning of the Christian era (1 A.D.), the job would be about half done at the present time.

So how does one certify a complex computer program that has incredibly more possible paths than this simple example? Fortunately, almost all of the probability mass in most programs goes into a relatively small number of paths that can be checked out.

But the unchecked paths still have some probability of occurring. And, furthermore, each time the software is modified, some portion of the testing must be repeated.

Fig. 14 shows that, even for small software modifications, one should not expect error-free performance thereafter. The data indicate that small modifications have a better chance of working successfully than do large ones. However, even after a small modification the chance of a successful first run is, at best, about 50%. In fact, there seems to be a sort of complacency factor operating that makes a successful first run less probable on modifications involving a single statement than on those involving approximately five statements—at least for this sample.

At this point, it's not clear how representative this sample is of other situations. One roughly comparable data point is in Fig. 3B of the Software Quiz, in which only 7% of the errors detected were those made in trying to correct previous errors. The difference in error rates is best explained by both the criticality of the application and the fact that the modifications were being made in a software validation rather than a software maintenance environment.

In another analysis of software error data performed for CCIP-85 by McGonagle,[27] 19% of the errors resulted from "unexpected side effects to changes." Other sources of errors detected over three years of the development cycle of a 24,000-instruction command and control program are shown in Table 1. These data are of particular interest because they provide insights into the *causes* of software errors as well as their variation with type of program.

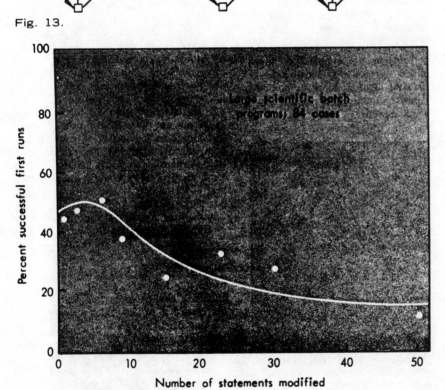

Fig. 13.

Fig. 14. Reliability of software modifications.

Certification technology

Against the formidable software certification requirements indicated

	Hardware Diagnostics (%)	Executive (%)	User Programs (%)	Total (%)
Unexpected side effects to changes	5	25	10	19
Logical flaws in the design				
Original design	5	10	2	8
Changes	5	15	8	12
Inconsistencies between design and implementation	5	30	10	22
Clerical errors	40	20	50	28
Inconsistencies in hardware	40	—	20	11
	100	100	100	100
Total errors detected, 3-year sample	36	108	18	162
Number of instructions	4K	10K	10K	24K

Table 1. Distribution of software error causes.

[27] McGonagle, J. D., *A Study of a Software Development Project*, James P. Anderson and Co., September 21, 1971.

above, the achievements of current technology leave a great deal to be desired. One organization paid $750,-000 to test an 8,000-instruction program, and even then couldn't be guaranteed that the software was perfect, because testing can only determine the *presence* of errors, not their *absence*. The largest program that has been mathematically proved correct was a 433-statement ALGOL program to perform error-bounded arithmetic; the proof required 46 pages of mathematical reasoning.[28]

However, there are several encouraging trends. One is the impressive reduction of errors achieved in the structured programming activities discussed earlier in this article. Another is the potential contribution of appropriately redundant programming languages, also discussed earlier. A third trend is the likely development of significant automated aids to the program-proving process, currently an extremely tedious manual process. Another is the evolutionary development and dissemination of better software test procedures and techniques and the trend toward capitalizing on economies of scale in validating similar software items, as in the DOD COBOL Compiler Validation System. But even with these trends, it will take a great deal of time, effort, and research support to achieve commonly usable solutions to such issues as the time and cost of analytic proof procedures, the level of expertise required to use them, the difficulty of providing a valid program specification to serve as a certification standard, and the extent to which one can get software efficiency and validability in the same package.

Where's the software engineering data base?

One of the major problems the CCIP-85 study found was the dearth of hard data available on software efforts which would allow us to analyze the nature of software problems, to convince people unfamiliar with software that the problems were significant, or to get clues on how best to improve the situation. Not having such a data base forces us to rely on intuition when making crucial decisions on software, and I expect, for many readers, your success on the Software Quiz was sufficiently poor to convince you that software phenomena often tend to be counterintuitive. Given the magnitude of the risks of basing major software decisions on fallible intuition, and the opportunities for ensuring more responsive software by providing designers with usage data, it is surprising how little effort has gone into endeavors to collect and analyze such data. Only after a decade of R&D on heuristic compilers, optimizing compilers, self-compiling compilers and the like, has there been an R&D effort to develop a *usage-measuring* compiler. Similar usage-measuring tools could be developed for keeping track of error rates and other software phenomena.

One of the reasons progress has been slow is that it's just plain difficult to collect good software data—as we found on three contract efforts to do so for the CCIP-85 study. These difficulties included:

1. Deciding which of the thousands of possibilities to measure.

2. Establishing standard definitions for "error," "test phase," etc.

3. Establishing what had been the development performance criteria.

4. Assessing subjective inputs such as "degree of difficulty," "programmer expertise," etc.

5. Assessing the accuracy of *post facto* data.

6. Reconciling sets of data collected in differently defined categories.

Clearly, more work on these factors is necessary to insure that future software data collection efforts produce at least roughly comparable results. However, because the data collection problem is difficult doesn't mean we should avoid it. Until we establish a firm data base, the phrase "software engineering" will be largely a contradiction in terms. And the software components of what is now called "computer science" will remain far from Lord Kelvin's standard:

"When you can measure what you are apeaking about, and express it in numbers, you know something about it; but when you cannot measure it, when you cannot express it in numbers, your knowledge is of a meager and unsatisfactory kind: it may be the beginning of knowledge, but you have scarcely, in your thoughts, advanced to the stage of *science*."

But, in closing, I'd like to suggest that people should collect data on their software efforts because it's really in their direct best interest. Currently, the general unavailability of such software data means that whoever first provides system designers with quantitative software characteristics will find that the resulting system design tends to be oriented around his characteristics.

For example, part of the initial design sizing of the ARPA Network was based on two statistical samples of user response, on Rand's JOSS system and on MIT's Project MAC. This was not because these were thought to be particularly representative of future network users; rather, they were simply the only relevant data the ARPA working group could find.

Another example involves the small CCIP-85 study contracts to gather quantitative software data. Since their completion, several local software designers and managers have expressed a marked interest in the data. Simply having a set of well-defined distributions of program and data module sizes is useful for designers of compilers and operating systems, and chronological distributions of software errors are useful for software management perspective. Knuth's FORTRAN data, excerpted in Fig. 4B of the Software Quiz, have also attracted considerable designer interest.

Thus, if you're among the first to measure and disseminate your own software usage characteristics, you're more likely to get next-generation software that's more responsive to your needs. Also, in the process, there's a good chance that you'll pick up some additional clues which begin to help you produce software better and faster right away.

Acknowledgements. Hundreds of people provided useful inputs to CCIP-85 and this extension of it; I regret my inability to properly individualize and acknowledge their valuable contributions. Among those providing exceptionally valuable stimulation and information were Generals L. Paschall, K. Chapman, and R. Lukeman; Colonels G. Fernandez and R. Hansen; Lieutenant Colonel A. Haile, and Captain B. Engelbach of the United States Air Force; R. Rubey of Logicon; R. Wolverton and W. Hetrick of TRW; J. Aron of IBM; A. Williams of NAR/Autonetics; D. McGonagle of Anderson, Inc.; R. Hatter of Lulejian Associates; W. Ware of Rand; and B. Sine. Most valuable of all have been the never-ending discussions with John Farquhar and particularly Don Kosy of Rand. □

Dr. Boehm is head of the information sciences and mathematics department at the Rand Corp. He has also been a lecturer and instructor at UCLA and was study director of the project discussed in this article. He is a member of many scientific organizations, serves on several government advisory panels, and has published a wide selection of scientific papers. He has a PhD in mathematics from UCLA.

[28] Good, D. I., and R. L. London, "Computer Interval Arithmetic: Definition and Proof of Correct Implementation," *ACM Journal*, October 1970, pp. 603-612.

THE MYTHICAL MAN-MONTH

Extracted from *The Mythical Man-Month*, published (1975) by Addison-Wesley. The extract was prepared by the editors of *Datamation*, and published in the December 1974 issue.

HOW DOES A PROJECT GET TO BE A YEAR LATE? . . . . . . ONE DAY AT A TIME.

By Frederick P. Brooks, Jr.

Dr. Brooks was part of the management team charged with developing the hardware for the IBM 360 system. In 1964 he became the manager of the Operating System/360 project; this trial by fire convinced him that managing a large software project is more like managing any other large undertaking than programmers believe and less like it than professional managers expect.

About his OS/360 project, he says: "Managing OS/360 development was a very educational experience, albeit a very frustrating one. The team, including F. M. Trapnell who succeeded me as manager, has much to be proud of. The system contains many excellences in design and execution, and it has been successful in achieving widespread use. Certain ideas, most noticeably device-independent input/output and external library management, were technical innovations now widely copied. It is now quite reliable, reasonably efficient, and very versatile.

The effort cannot be called wholly successful, however. Any OS/360 user is quickly aware of how much better it should be. The flaws in design and execution pervade especially the control program, as distinguished from language compilers. Most of the flaws date from the 1964-1965 design period and hence must be laid to my charge. Furthermore, the product was late, it took more memory than planned, the costs were several times the estimate, and it did not perform very well until several releases after the first."

Analyzing the OS/360 experiences for management and technical lessons, Dr. Brooks put his thoughts into book form. Addison-Wesley Publishing Company (Reading, Mass.) will offer "The Mythical Man-Month: Essays on Software Engineering", from which this article is taken, sometime next month.

NO SCENE FROM PREHISTORY is quite so vivid as that of the mortal struggles of great beasts in the tar pits. In the mind's eye one sees dinosaurs, mammoths, and saber-toothed tigers struggling against the grip of the tar. The fiercer the struggle, the more entangling the tar, and no beast is so strong or so skillful but that he ultimately sinks.

Large-system programming has over the past decade been such a tar pit, and many great and powerful beasts have thrashed violently in it. Most have emerged with running systems—few have met goals, schedules, and budgets. Large and small, massive or wiry, team after team has become entangled in the tar. No one thing seems to cause the difficulty—any particular paw can be pulled away. But the accumulation of simultaneous and interacting factors brings slower and slower motion. Everyone seems to have been surprised by the stickiness of the problem, and it is hard to discern the nature of it. But we must try to understand it if we are to solve it.

More software projects have gone awry for lack of calendar time than for all other causes combined. Why is this case of disaster so common?

First, our techniques of estimating are poorly developed. More seriously, they reflect an unvoiced assumption which is quite untrue, i.e., that all will go well.

Second, our estimating techniques fallaciously confuse effort with progress, hiding the assumption that men and months are interchangeable.

Third, because we are uncertain of our estimates, software managers often

lack the courteous stubbornness required to make people wait for a good product.

Fourth, schedule progress is poorly monitored. Techniques proven and routine in other engineering disciplines are considered radical innovations in software engineering.

Fifth, when schedule slippage is recognized, the natural (and traditional) response is to add manpower. Like dousing a fire with gasoline, this makes matters worse, much worse. More fire requires more gasoline and thus begins a regenerative cycle which ends in disaster.

Schedule monitoring will be covered later. Let us now consider other aspects of the problem in more detail.

Optimism

All programmers are optimists. Perhaps this modern sorcery especially attracts those who believe in happy endings and fairy godmothers. Perhaps the hundreds of nitty frustrations drive away all but those who habitually focus on the end goal. Perhaps it is merely that computers are young, programmers are younger, and the young are always optimists. But however the selection process works, the result is indisputable: "This time it will surely run," or "I just found the last bug."

So the first false assumption that underlies the scheduling of systems programming is that *all will go well*, i.e., that *each task will take only as long as it "ought" to take.*

The pervasiveness of optimism among programmers deserves more than a flip analysis. Dorothy Sayers, in her excellent book, *The Mind of the*

Maker, divides creative activity into three stages: the idea, the implementation, and the interaction. A book, then, or a computer, or a program comes into existence first as an ideal construct, built outside time and space but complete in the mind of the author. It is realized in time and space by pen, ink, and paper, or by wire, silicon, and ferrite. The creation is complete when someone reads the book, uses the computer or runs the program, thereby interacting with the mind of the maker.

This description, which Miss Sayers uses to illuminate not only human creative activity but also the Christian doctrine of the Trinity, will help us in our present task. For the human makers of things, the incompletenesses and inconsistencies of our ideas become clear only during implementation. Thus it is that writing, experimentation, "working out" are essential disciplines for the theoretician.

In many creative activities the medium of execution is intractable. Lumber splits; paints smear; electrical circuits ring. These physical limitations of the medium constrain the ideas that may be expressed, and they also create unexpected difficulties in the implementation.

Implementation, then, takes time and sweat both because of the physical media and because of the inadequacies of the underlying ideas. We tend to blame the physical media for most of our implementation difficulties; for the media are not "ours" in the way the ideas are, and our pride colors our judgment.

Computer programming, however, creates with an exceedingly tractable medium. The programmer builds from pure thought-stuff: concepts and very flexible representations thereof. Because the medium is tractable, we expect few difficulties in implementation; hence our pervasive optimism. Because our ideas are faulty, we have bugs; hence our optimism is unjustified.

In a single task, the assumption that all will go well has a probabilistic effect on the schedule. It might indeed go as planned, for there is a probability distribution for the delay that will be encountered, and "no delay" has a finite probability. A large programming effort, however, consists of many tasks, some chained end-to-end. The probability that each will go well becomes vanishingly small.

The mythical man-month

The second fallacious thought mode is expressed in the very unit of effort used in estimating and scheduling: the man-month. Cost does indeed vary as the product of the number of men and the number of months. Progress does not. *Hence the man-month as a unit for measuring the size of a job is a dangerous and deceptive myth.* It implies that men and months are interchangeable.

Men and months are interchangeable commodities only when a task can be partitioned among many workers *with no communication among them* (Fig. 1). This is true of reaping wheat or picking cotton; it is not even approximately true of systems programming.

When a task cannot be partitioned

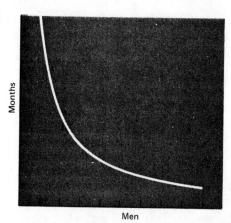

Fig. 1. The term "man-month" implies that if one man takes 10 months to do a job, 10 men can do it in one month. This may be true of picking cotton.

because of sequential constraints, the application of more effort has no effect on the schedule. The bearing of a child takes nine months, no matter how many women are assigned. Many software tasks have this characteristic because of the sequential nature of debugging.

In tasks that can be partitioned but which require communication among the subtasks, the effort of communication must be added to the amount of work to be done. Therefore the best that can be done is somewhat poorer than an even trade of men for months (Fig. 2).

The added burden of communication is made up of two parts, training and intercommunication. Each worker must be trained in the technology, the goals of the effort, the overall strategy, and the plan of work. This training cannot be partitioned, so this part of the added effort varies linearly with the number of workers.

V. S. Vyssotsky of Bell Telephone Laboratories estimates that a large project can sustain a manpower build-up of 30% per year. More than that strains and even inhibits the evolution of the essential informal structure and its communication pathways. F. J.

Corbató of MIT points out that a long project must anticipate a turnover of 20% per year, and new people must be both technically trained and integrated into the formal structure.

Intercommunication is worse. If each part of the task must be separately coordinated with each other part, the effort increases as $n(n-1)/2$. Three workers require three times as much pairwise intercommunication as two; four require six times as much as two. If, moreover, there need to be conferences among three, four, etc., workers to resolve things jointly, matters get worse yet. The added effort of communicating may fully counteract the division of the original task and bring us back to the situation of Fig. 3.

Since software construction is inherently a systems effort—an exercise in complex interrelationships—communication effort is great, and it quickly

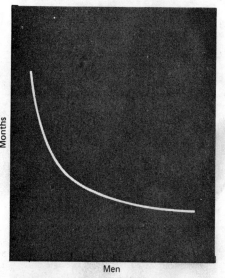

Fig. 2. Even on tasks that can be nicely partitioned among people, the additional communication required adds to the total work, increasing the schedule.

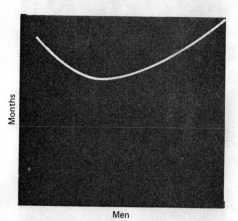

Fig. 3. Since software construction is complex, the communications overhead is great. Adding more men can lengthen, rather than shorten, the schedule.

Extracted from *The Mythical Man-Month*, published (1975) by Addison-Wesley. The extract was prepared by the editors of *Datamation*, and published in the December 1974 issue.

dominates the decrease in individual task time brought about by partitioning. Adding more men then lengthens, not shortens, the schedule.

Systems test

No parts of the schedule are so thoroughly affected by sequential constraints as component debugging and system test. Furthermore, the time required depends on the number and subtlety of the errors encountered. Theoretically this number should be zero. Because of optimism, we usually expect the number of bugs to be smaller than it turns out to be. Therefore testing is usually the most mis-scheduled part of programming.

For some years I have been successfully using the following rule of thumb for scheduling a software task:

⅓ planning

⅙ coding

¼ component test and early system test

¼ system test, all components in hand.

This differs from conventional scheduling in several important ways:

1. The fraction devoted to planning is larger than normal. Even so, it is barely enough to produce a detailed and solid specification, and not enough to include research or exploration of totally new techniques.

2. The *half* of the schedule devoted to debugging of completed code is much larger than normal.

3. The part that is easy to estimate, i.e., coding, is given only one-sixth of the schedule.

In examining conventionally scheduled projects, I have found that few allowed one-half of the projected schedule for testing, but that most did indeed spend half of the actual schedule for that purpose. Many of these were on schedule until and except in system testing.

Failure to allow enough time for system test, in particular, is peculiarly disastrous. Since the delay comes at the end of the schedule, no one is aware of schedule trouble until almost the delivery date. Bad news, late and without warning, is unsettling to customers and to managers.

Furthermore, delay at this point has unusually severe financial, as well as psychological, repercussions. The project is fully staffed, and cost-per-day is maximum. More seriously, the software is to support other business effort (shipping of computers, operation of new facilities, etc.) and the secondary costs of delaying these are very high, for it is almost time for software shipment. Indeed, these secondary costs may far outweigh all others. It is therefore very important to allow enough system test time in the original schedule.

Gutless estimating

Observe that for the programmer, as for the chef, the urgency of the patron may govern the scheduled completion of the task, but it cannot govern the actual completion. An omelette, promised in ten minutes, may appear to be progressing nicely. But when it has not set in ten minutes, the customer has two choices—wait or eat it raw. Software customers have had the same choices.

The cook has another choice; he can turn up the heat. The result is often an omelette nothing can save—burned in one part, raw in another.

Now I do not think software managers have less inherent courage and firmness than chefs, nor than other engineering managers. But false scheduling to match the patron's desired date is much more common in our discipline than elsewhere in engineering. It is very difficult to make a vigorous, plausible, and job-risking defense of an estimate that is derived by no quantitative method, supported by little data, and certified chiefly by the hunches of the managers.

Clearly two solutions are needed. We need to develop and publicize productivity figures, bug-incidence figures, estimating rules, and so on. The whole profession can only profit from sharing such data.

Until estimating is on a sounder basis, individual managers will need to stiffen their backbones, and defend their estimates with the assurance that their poor hunches are better than wish-derived estimates.

Regenerative disaster

What does one do when an essential software project is behind schedule? Add manpower, naturally. As Figs. 1 through 3 suggest, this may or may not help.

Let us consider an example. Suppose a task is estimated at 12 man-months and assigned to three men for four months, and that there are measurable mileposts A, B, C, D, which are scheduled to fall at the end of each month.

Now suppose the first milepost is not reached until two months have elapsed. What are the alternatives facing the manager?

1. Assume that the task must be done on time. Assume that only the first part of the task was misestimated. Then 9 man-months of effort remain, and two months, so 4½ men will be needed. Add 2 men to the 3 assigned.

2. Assume that the task must be done on time. Assume that the whole estimate was uniformly low. Then 18 man-months of effort remain, and two months, so 9 men will be needed. Add 6 men to the 3 assigned.

3. Reschedule. In this case, I like the advice given by an experienced hardware engineer, "Take no small slips." That is, allow enough time in the new schedule to ensure that the work can be carefully and

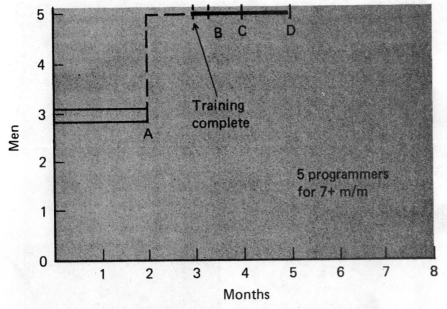

Fig. 4. Adding manpower to a project which is late may not help. In this case, suppose three men on a 12 man-month project were a month late. If it takes one of the three an extra month to train two new men, the project will be just as late as if no one was added.

Extracted from *The Mythical Man-Month*, published (1975) by Addison-Wesley. The extract was prepared by the editors of *Datamation*, and published in the December 1974 issue.

thoroughly done, and that rescheduling will not have to be done again.

4. Trim the task. In practice this tends to happen anyway, once the team observes schedule slippage. Where the secondary costs of delay are very high, this is the only feasible action. The manager's only alternatives are to trim it formally and carefully, to reschedule, or to watch the task get silently trimmed by hasty design and incomplete testing.

In the first two cases, insisting that the unaltered task be completed in four months is disastrous. Consider the regenerative effects, for example, for the first alternative (Fig. 4 preceding page). The two new men, however competent and however quickly recruited, will require training in the task by one of the experienced men. If this takes a month, *3 man-months will have been devoted to work not in the original estimate.* Furthermore, the task, originally partitioned three ways, must be repartitioned into five parts, hence some work already done will be lost and system testing must be lengthened. So at the end of the third month, substantially more than 7 man-months of effort remain, and 5 trained people and one month are available. As Fig. 4 suggests, the product is just as late as if no one had been added.

To hope to get done in four months, considering only training time and not repartitioning and extra systems test, would require adding 4 men, not 2, at the end of the second month. To cover repartitioning and system test effects, one would have to add still other men. Now, however, one has at least a 7-man team, not a 3-man one; thus such aspects as team organization and task division are different in kind, not merely in degree.

Notice that by the end of the third month things look very black. The March 1 milestone has not been reached in spite of all the managerial effort. The temptation is very strong to repeat the cycle, adding yet more manpower. Therein lies madness.

The foregoing assumed that only the first milestone was misestimated. If on March 1 one makes the conservative assumption that the whole schedule was optimistic one wants to add 6 men just to the original task. Calculation of the training, repartitioning, system testing effects is left as an exercise for the reader. Without a doubt, the regenerative disaster will yield a poorer product later, than would rescheduling with the original three men, unaugmented.

Oversimplifying outrageously, we

state Brooks' Law:

Adding manpower to a late software project makes it later.

This then is the demythologizing of the man-month. The number of months of a project depends upon its sequential constraints. The maximum number of men depends upon the number of independent subtasks. From these two quantities one can derive schedules using fewer men and more months. (The only risk is product obsolescence.) One cannot, however, get workable schedules using more men and fewer months. More software projects have gone awry for lack of calendar time than for all other causes combined.

Calling the shot

How long will a system programming job take? How much effort will be required? How does one estimate?

I have earlier suggested ratios that seem to apply to planning time, coding, component test, and system test. First, one must say that one does *not* estimate the entire task by estimating the coding portion only and then applying the ratios. The coding is only

one-sixth or so of the problem, and errors in its estimate or in the ratios could lead to ridiculous results.

Second, one must say that data for building isolated small programs are not applicable to programming systems products. For a program averaging about 3,200 words, for example, Sackman, Erikson, and Grant report an average code-plus-debug time of about 178 hours for a single programmer, a figure which would extrapolate to give an annual productivity of 35,800 statements per year. A program half that size took less than one-fourth as long, and extrapolated productivity is almost 80,000 statements per year.[1]. Planning, documentation, testing, system integration, and training times must be added. The linear extrapolation of such spring figures is meaningless. Extrapolation of times for the hundred-yard dash shows that a man can run a mile in under three minutes.

Before dismissing them, however, let us note that these numbers, although not for strictly comparable problems, suggest that effort goes as a power of size *even* when no communication is involved except that of a man with his memories.

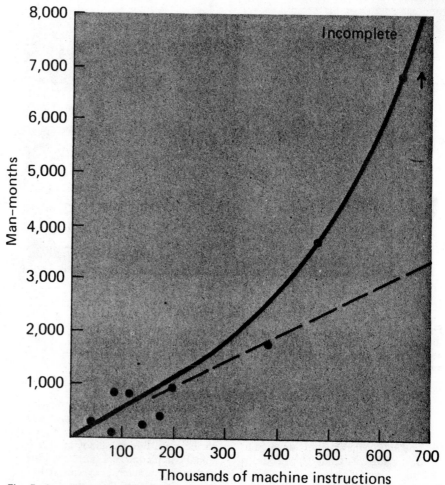

Fig. 5. As a project's complexity increases, the number of man-months required to complete it goes up exponentially.

Extracted from *The Mythical Man-Month*, published (1975) by Addison-Wesley. The extract was prepared by the editors of *Datamation*, and published in the December 1974 issue.

Fig. 5 tells the sad story. It illustrates results reported from a study done by Nanus and Farr[2] at System Development Corp. This shows an exponent of 1.5; that is,

effort = (constant)×(number of instructions)$^{1.5}$

Another SDC study reported by Weinwurm[3] also shows an exponent near 1.5.

A few studies on programmer productivity have been made, and several estimating techniques have been proposed. Morin has prepared a survey of the published data.[4] Here I shall give only a few items that seem especially illuminating.

Portman's data

Charles Portman, manager of ICL's Software Div., Computer Equipment Organization (Northwest) at Manchester, offers another useful personal insight.

He found his programming teams missing schedules by about one-half—each job was taking approximately twice as long as estimated. The estimates were very careful, done by experienced teams estimating man-hours for several hundred subtasks on a PERT chart. When the slippage pattern appeared, he asked them to keep careful daily logs of time usage. These showed that the estimating error could be entirely accounted for by the fact that his teams were only realizing 50% of the working week as actual programming and debugging time. Machine downtime, higher-priority short unrelated jobs, meetings, paperwork, company business, sickness, personal time, etc. accounted for the rest. In short, the estimates made an unrealistic assumption about the number of technical work hours per man-year. My own experience quite confirms his conclusion.

An unpublished 1964 study by E. F. Bardain shows programmers realizing only 27% productive time.[5]

	Prog. units	Number of programmers	Years	Man-years	Program words	Words/man-yr.
Operational	50	83	4	101	52,000	515
Maintenance	36	60	4	81	51,000	630
Compiler	13	9	2¼	17	38,000	2230
Translator (Data assembler)	15	13	2½	11	25,000	2270

Table 1. Data from Bell Labs indicates productivity differences between complex problems (the first two are basically control programs with many modules) and less complex ones. No one is certain how much of the difference is due to complexity, how much to the number of people involved.

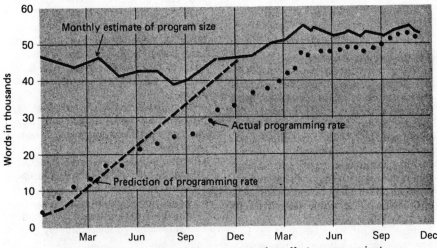

Fig. 6. Bell Labs' experience in predicting programming effort on one project.

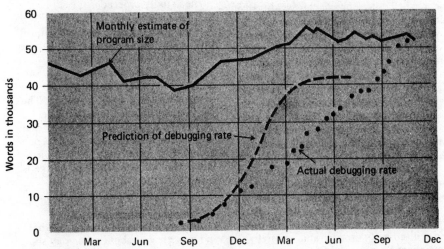

Fig. 7. Bell's predictions for debugging rates on a single project, contrasted with actual figures.

Aron's data

Joel Aron, manager of Systems Technology at IBM in Gaithersburg, Maryland, has studied programmer productivity when working on nine large systems (briefly, *large* means more than 25 programmers and 30,000 deliverable instructions). He divides such systems according to interactions among programmers (and system parts) and finds productivities as follows:

Very few interactions	10,000 instructions per man-year
Some interactions	5,000
Many interactions	1,500

The man-years do not include support and system test activities, only design and programming. When these figures are diluted by a factor of two to cover system test, they closely match Harr's data.

Harr's data

John Harr, manager of programming for the Bell Telephone Laboratories' Electronic Switching System, reported his and others' experience in a paper at the 1969 Spring Joint Computer Conference.[6] These data are shown in Table 1 and Figs. 6 and 7 .

Of these, Fig. 6 is the most detailed and the most useful. The first two jobs are basically control programs; the second two are basically language translators. Productivity is stated in terms of debugged words per man-year. This includes programming, component test, and system test. It is not clear how much of the planning effort, or effort in machine support, writing, and the

Extracted from *The Mythical Man-Month*, published (1975) by Addison-Wesley. The extract was prepared by the editors of *Datamation*, and published in the December 1974 issue.

like, is included.

The productivities likewise fall into two classifications: those for control programs are about 600 words per man-year; those for translators are about 2,200 words per man-year. Note that all four programs are of similar size—the variation is in size of the work groups, length of time, and number of modules. Which is cause and which is effect? Did the control programs require more people because they were more complicated? Or did they require more modules and more man-months because they were assigned more people? Did they take longer because of the greater complexity, or because more people were assigned? One can't be sure. The control programs were surely more complex. These uncertainties aside, the numbers describe the real productivities achieved on a large system, using present-day programming techniques. As such they are a real contribution.

Figs. 6 and 7 show some interesting data on programming and debugging rates as compared to predicted rates.

OS/360 data

IBM OS/360 experience, while not available in the detail of Harr's data, confirms it. Productivities in range of 600-800 debugged instructions per man-year were experienced by control program groups. Productivities in the 2,000-3,000 debugged instructions per man-year were achieved by language translator groups. These include planning done by the group, coding component test, system test, and some support activities. They are comparable to Harr's data, so far as I can tell.

Aron's data, Harr's data, and the OS/360 data all confirm striking differences in productivity related to the complexity and difficulty of the task itself. My guideline in the morass of estimating complexity is that compilers are three times as bad as normal batch application programs, and operating systems are three times as bad as compilers.

Corbató's data

Both Harr's data and OS/360 data are for assembly language programming. Little data seem to have been published on system programming productivity using higher-level languages. Corbató of MIT's Project MAC reports, however, a mean productivity of 1,200 lines of debugged PL/I statements per man-year on the MULTICS system (between 1 and 2 million words).[7]

This number is very exciting. Like the other projects, MULTICS includes control programs and language transla-

tors. Like the others, it is producing a system programming product, tested and documented. The data seem to be comparable in terms of kind of effort included. And the productivity number is a good average between the control program and translator productivities of other projects.

But Corbató's number is *lines* per man-year, not *words!* Each statement in his system corresponds to about three-to-five words of handwritten code! This suggests two important conclusions:

- Productivity seems constant in terms of elementary statements, a conclusion that is reasonable in terms of the thought a statement requires and the errors it may include.
- Programming productivity may be increased as much as five times when a suitable high-level language is used. To back up these conclusions, W. M. Taliaffero also reports a constant productivity of 2,400 statements/year in Assembler, FORTRAN, and COBOL.[8] E. A. Nelson has shown a 3-to-1 productivity improvement for high-level language, although his standard deviations are wide.[9]

Hatching a catastrophe

When one hears of disastrous schedule slippage in a project, he imagines that a series of major calamities must have befallen it. Usually, however, the disaster is due to termites, not tornadoes; and the schedule has slipped imperceptibly but inexorably. Indeed, major calamities are easier to handle; one responds with major force, radical reorganization, the invention of new approaches. The whole team rises to the occasion.

But the day-by-day slippage is harder to recognize, harder to prevent, harder to make up. Yesterday a key man was sick, and a meeting couldn't be held. Today the machines are all down, because lightning struck the building's power transformer. Tomorrow the disc routines won't start testing, because the first disc is a week late from the factory. Snow, jury duty, family problems, emergency meetings with customers, executive audits—the list goes on and on. Each one only postpones some activity by a half-day or a day. And the schedule slips, one day at a time.

How does one control a big project on a tight schedule? The first step is to *have* a schedule. Each of a list of events, called milestones, has a date. Picking the dates is an estimating problem, discussed already and crucially dependent on experience.

For picking the milestones there is

only one relevant rule. Milestones must be concrete, specific, measurable events, defined with knife-edge sharpness. Coding, for a counterexample, is "90% finished" for half of the total coding time. Debugging is "99% complete" most of the time. "Planning complete" is an event one can proclaim almost at will.[10]

Concrete milestones, on the other hand, are 100% events. "Specifications signed by architects and implementers," "source coding 100% complete, keypunched, entered into disc library," "debugged version passes all test cases." These concrete milestones demark the vague phases of planning, coding, debugging.

It is more important that milestones be sharp-edged and unambiguous than that they be easily verifiable by the boss. Rarely will a man lie about mile-

> None love
> the bearer of bad news.
> *Sophocles*

stone progress, *if* the milestone is so sharp that he can't deceive himself. But if the milestone is fuzzy, the boss often understands a different report from that which the man gives. To supplement Sophocles, no one enjoys bearing bad news, either, so it gets softened without any real intent to deceive.

Two interesting studies of estimating behavior by government contractors on large-scale development projects show that:

1. Estimates of the length of an activity made and revised carefully every two weeks before the activity starts do not significantly change as the start time draws near, no matter how wrong they ultimately turn out to be.
2. *During* the activity, *over*estimates of duration come steadily down as the activity proceeds.
3. *Underestimates* do not change significantly during the activity until about three weeks before the scheduled completion.[11]

Sharp milestones are in fact a service to the team, and one they can properly expect from a manager. The fuzzy milestone is the harder burden to live with. It is in fact a millstone that grinds down morale, for it deceives one about lost time until it is irremediable. And chronic schedule slippage is a morale-killer.

"The other piece is late"

A schedule slips a day; so what? Who gets excited about a one-day slip? We can make it up later. And the other piece ours fits into is late anyway.

Extracted from *The Mythical Man-Month*, published (1975) by Addison-Wesley. The extract was prepared by the editors of *Datamation*, and published in the December 1974 issue.

A baseball manager recognizes a nonphysical talent, *hustle*, as an essential gift of great players and great teams. It is the characteristic of running faster than necessary, moving sooner than necessary, trying harder than necessary. It is essential for great programming teams, too. Hustle provides the cushion, the reserve capacity, that enables a team to cope with routine mishaps, to anticipate and forfend minor calamities. The calculated response, the measured effort, are the wet blankets that dampen hustle. As we have seen, one *must* get excited about a one-day slip. Such are the elements of catastrophe.

But not all one-day slips are equally disastrous. So some calculation of response is necessary, though hustle be dampened. How does one tell which slips matter? There is no substitute for a PERT chart or a critical-path schedule. Such a network shows who waits for what. It shows who is on the critical path, where any slip moves the end date. It also shows how much an activity can slip before it moves into the critical path.

The PERT technique, strictly speaking, is an elaboration of critical-path scheduling in which one estimates three times for every event, times corresponding to different probabilities of meeting the estimated dates. I do not find this refinement to be worth the extra effort, but for brevity I will call any critical path network a PERT chart.

The preparation of a PERT chart is the most valuable part of its use. Laying out the network, identifying the dependencies, and estimating the legs all force a great deal of very specific planning very early in a project. The first chart is always terrible, and one invents and invents in making the second one.

As the project proceeds, the PERT chart provides the answer to the demoralizing excuse, "The other piece is late anyhow." It shows how hustle is needed to keep one's own part off the critical path, and it suggests ways to make up the lost time in the other part.

Under the rug

When a first-line manager sees his small team slipping behind, he is rarely inclined to run to the boss with this woe. The team might be able to make it up, or he should be able to invent or reorganize to solve the problem. Then why worry the boss with it? So far, so good. Solving such problems is exactly what the first-line manager is there for. And the boss does have enough real worries demanding his action that he doesn't seek others. So all the dirt gets swept under the rug.

But every boss needs two kinds of information, exceptions for action and a status picture for education.[12] For that purpose he needs to know the status of all his teams. Getting a true picture of that status is hard.

The first-line manager's interests and those of the boss have an inherent conflict here. The first-line manager fears that if he reports his problem, the boss will act on it. Then his action will preempt the manager's function, diminish his authority, foul up his other plans. So as long as the manager thinks he can solve it alone, he doesn't tell the boss.

Two rug-lifting techniques are open to the boss. Both must be used. The first is to reduce the role conflict and inspire sharing of status. The other is to yank the rug back.

Reducing the role conflict

The boss must first distinguish between action information and status information. He must discipline himself *not* to act on problems his managers can solve, and *never* to act on problems when he is explicitly reviewing status. I once knew a boss who invariably picked up the phone to give orders before the end of the first para-

Fig. 8. A report showing milestones and status is a key document in project control. This one shows some problems in OS development: specifications approval is late on some items (those without "A"); documentation (SRL) approval is overdue on another; and one (2250 support) is late coming out of alpha test.

Extracted from *The Mythical Man-Month*, published (1975) by Addison-Wesley. The extract was prepared by the editors of *Datamation*, and published in the December 1974 issue.

graph in a status report. That response is guaranteed to squelch full disclosure.

Conversely, when the manager knows his boss will accept status reports without panic or preemption, he comes to give honest appraisals.

This whole process is helped if the boss labels meetings, reviews, conferences, as *status-review* meetings versus *problem-action* meetings, and controls himself accordingly. Obviously one may call a problem-action meeting as a consequence of a status meeting, if he believes a problem is out of hand. But at least everybody knows what the score is, and the boss thinks twice before grabbing the ball.

Yanking the rug off

Nevertheless, it is necessary to have review techniques by which the true status is made known, whether cooperatively or not. The PERT chart with its frequent sharp milestones is the basis for such review. On a large project one may want to review some part of it each week, making the rounds once a month or so.

A report showing milestones and actual completions is the key document. Fig. 8 (preceding page), shows an excerpt from such a report. This report shows some troubles. Specifications approval is overdue on several components. Manual (SRL) approval is overdue on another, and one is late getting out of the first state (ALPHA) of the independently conducted product test. So such a report serves as an agenda for the meeting of 1 February. Everyone knows the questions, and the component manager should be prepared to explain why it's late, when it will be finished, what steps he's taking, and what help, if any, he needs from the boss or collateral groups.

V. Vyssotsky of Bell Telephone Laboratories adds the following observation:

I have found it handy to carry both "scheduled" and "estimated" dates in the milestone report. The scheduled dates are the property of the project manager and represent a consistent work plan for the project as a whole, and one which is a priori a reasonable plan. The estimated dates are the property of the lowest level manager who has cognizance over the piece of work in question, and represents his best judgment as to when it will actually happen, given the resources he has available and when he received (or has commitments for delivery of) his prerequisite inputs. The project manager has to keep his fingers off the estimated dates, and put the emphasis on getting accurate, unbiased estimates rather than palatable optimistic estimates or self-protective conservative ones. Once this is clearly established in everyone's mind, the project manager can see quite a ways into the future where he is going to be in trouble if he doesn't do something.

The preparation of the PERT chart is a function of the boss and the managers reporting to him. Its updating, revision, and reporting requires the attention of a small (one-to-three-man) staff group which serves as an extension of the boss. Such a "Plans and Controls" team is invaluable for a large project. It has no authority except to ask all the line managers when they will have set or changed milestones, and whether milestones have been met. Since the Plans and Controls group handles all the paperwork, the burden on the line managers is reduced to the essentials—making the decisions.

We had a skilled, enthusiastic, and diplomatic Plans and Controls group on the OS/360 project, run by A. M. Pietrasanta, who devoted considerable inventive talent to devising effective but unobtrusive control methods. As a result, I found his group to be widely respected and more than tolerated. For a group whose role is inherently that of an irritant, this is quite an accomplishment.

The investment of a modest amount of skilled effort in a Plans and Controls function is very rewarding. It makes far more difference in project accomplishment than if these people worked directly on building the product programs. For the Plans and Controls group is the watchdog who renders the imperceptible delays visible and who points up the critical elements. It is the early warning system against losing a year, one day at a time.

Epilogue

The tar pit of software engineering will continue to be sticky for a long time to come. One can expect the human race to continue attempting systems just within or just beyond our reach; and software systems are perhaps the most intricate and complex of man's handiworks. The management of this complex craft will demand our best use of new languages and systems, our best adaptation of proven engineering management methods, liberal doses of common sense, and a God-given humility to recognize our fallibility and limitations.

References

1. Sackman, H., W. J. Erikson, and E. E. Grant, "Exploratory Experimentation Studies Comparing Online and Offline Programming Performance," *Communications of the ACM*, 11 (1968), 3-11.

2. Nanus, B., and L. Farr, "Some Cost Contributors to Large-Scale Programs," *AFIPS Proceedings, SJCC*, 25 (1964), 239-248.

3. Weinwurm, G. F., *Research in the Management of Computer Programming*. Report SP-2059, 1965, System Development Corp., Santa Monica.

4. Morin, L. H., *Estimation of Resources for Computer Programming Projects*, M. S. thesis, Univ. of North Carolina, Chapel Hill, 1974.

5. Quoted by D. B. Mayer and A. W. Stalnaker, "Selection and Evaluation of Computer Personnel," *Proceedings 23 ACM Conference*, 1968, 661.

6. Paper given at a panel session and not included in the *AFIPS Proceedings*.

7. Corbató, F. J., *Sensitive Issues in the Design of Multi-Use Systems*. Lecture at the opening of the Honeywell EDP Technology Center, 1968.

8. Taliaffero, W. M., "Modularity the Key to System Growth Potential," *Software*, 1 (1971), 245-257.

9. Nelson, E. A., *Management Handbook for the Estimation of Computer Programming Costs*. Report TM-3225, System Development Corp., Santa Monica, pp. 66-67.

10. Reynolds, C. H., "What's Wrong with Computer Programming Management?" in *On the Management of Computer Programming*. Ed. G. F. Weinwurm. Philadelphia: Auerbach, 1971, pp. 35-42.

11. King, W. R., and T. A. Wilson, "Subjective Time Estimates in Critical Path Planning—a Preliminary Analysis," *Management Sciences*, 13 (1967), 307-320, and sequel, W. R. King, D. M. Witterrongel, and K. D. Hezel, "On the Analysis of Critical Path Time Estimating Behavior," *Management Sciences*, 14 (1967), 79-84.

12. Brooks, F. P., and K. E. Iverson, *Automatic Data Processing, System/360 Edition*. New York: Wiley, 1969, pp. 428-430.

Dr. Brooks is presently a professor at the Univ. of North Carolina at Chapel Hill, and chairman of the computer science department there. He is best known as "the father of the IBM System/360," having served as project manager for the hardware development and as manager of the Operating System/360 project during its design phase. Earlier he was an architect of the IBM Stretch and Harvest computers.

At Chapel Hill he has participated in establishing and guiding the Triangle Universities Computation Center and the North Carolina Educational Computing Service. He is the author of two editions of "Automatic Data Processing" and "The Mythical Man-Month: Essays on Software Engineering" (Addison-Wesley), from which this excerpt is taken.

Extracted from *The Mythical Man-Month*, published (1975) by Addison-Wesley. The extract was prepared by the editors of *Datamation*, and published in the December 1974 issue.

Information System Design Methodology*

Anthony I. Wasserman

Medical Information Science, University of California at San Francisco, San Francisco, CA 94143

There is a great need for a systematic approach to the specification, design, and development of information systems. This article describes the motivating reasons for such an approach and surveys some of the techniques that have been developed to assist the software specification and design activity. A methodology is seen as a combination of tools and techniques employed within an organizational and managerial framework that can be consistently applied to successive information system development projects. The ways that information system development organizations can create and use such methodologies are emphasized.

Introduction and Historical Background

In the 1960s, software developers attempted to design and implement increasingly complex systems, often seeking to make innovative use of computers and information technology. Sophisticated applications, including airline and hotel reservation systems, on-line medical record systems, data base management systems, and manufacturing process control systems, were undertaken.

A significant percentage of these systems was unsuccessful, with the developer failing to construct a system that was satisfactory for the envisioned application. Other systems were successfully completed, but were extremely late, far over their budgets, inordinately expensive in terms of resource utilization, and/or poorly suited for the intended users of the system. Many different reasons can be cited for the failure of these projects, including the following:

(1) The intellectual complexity of the application itself was so great that either the analyst(s) could not understand the problem completely or could not convey the problem to the implementers.

(2) The developers didn't orient the system to the end users, who then rejected the system as being difficult to learn or difficult to use.

(3) The analyst(s) didn't take the organizational environment into account in specifying the system, thereby leading to an unusable system.

*Invited paper given at the 1979 Benjamin Franklin Colloquium on Information Science, Philadelphia, Pennsylvania, May 11, 1979.

Received July 11, 1979.

(4) Analysts and developers were overly optimistic about the development time, development cost, and/or operational cost of the system.

(5) There were no intermediate steps during the project at which project management and customer could review progress and determine the system status.

(6) The application demanded the use of highly advanced technology, which was often not generally available.

(7) There was little or no effective communication between the user community and the development organization.

The result of this multiplicity of problems was a "software crisis." The entire software and system development process was out of control. It was often impossible to distinguish the successful projects from the unsuccessful projects until very late in the project cycle. Project management could not provide accurate estimates of the development times or costs. Even worse, projects that had gone off in the wrong direction were nearly impossible to salvage, due to time constraints and prohibitive costs. Every piece of software for every information system was a "custom design," with no consistent pattern to follow and little experience from previous efforts.

The proliferation of these "disasters" made it apparent that a major cause of difficulty was the lack of a systematic approach to information system design and development. The concept of "software engineering" emerged, based upon the notion that an engineeringlike form of discipline could be applied to building software systems. Two meetings sponsored by NATO in 1968 and 1969 [1] served to identify the problem more clearly and to provide some initial approaches to the solution.

During the late 1960s and early 1970s, software engineering was largely a research activity with little impact on day-to-day software development practices. From this foundation, though, came some of the most important notions of modern software development techniques, including top-down design, stepwise refinement [2], modularity [3,4], and structured programming [5,6]. The relationship between programming languages, problem solving, and high-quality software was also recognized at this time, leading to the design of a number of programming languages, most notably Pascal [7].

Although there were a few tentative steps at putting some of the ideas together, such as the work of Mills and Baker with Chief Programmer Teams [8], the primary focus was on individual techniques, intended to address specific software development problems, with relatively little attention given to integration of the various techniques.

The first of these concepts to have a widespread impact was "structured programming," although in a somewhat different sense than that originally intended by Dijkstra. The emphasis was on code production and the development of good programming style (program comprehensibility), rather than on the entire problem-solving/programming activity.

The Life Cycle

A more significant impetus came from the manufacturing concept of a "life cycle," in which products are first conceived, specified in detail, designed, and then built and maintained until they are no longer usable. By using the concept of a "software life cycle," it becomes possible to invent a framework to bring together all of the different techniques for software production *with* appropriate management techniques.

The importance of this concept may be seen by analogy with the steps involved in developing a custom-built house. At first, the customer presents the architect with some general idea of the requirements: size of available lot, number of rooms, cost constraints, style of house (Victorian, colonial, ultramodern, etc.), and other such requirements or wishes.

Once these requirements are established, the designer/architect may take one of several steps. First, the architect may offer pictures of previously designed and built houses, in the hope of simplifying the design activity and thereby saving money for the customer. Next, the architect may produce some original drawings to present the customer with some design alternatives, or to help the customer gain a more accurate understanding of what is desired.

Having done this, the architect will proceed with more detailed design of the house, including placement of the rooms, decisions concerning their size, layout on the property, and so on. The architect will also integrate the constraints concerning the placement of electrical wiring, plumbing, and other necessities for conforming to the building codes of a given location.

When this is done, the architect will have produced not only an artistic rendering of the house, but also a *blueprint* that represents the design in a precise way. With this blueprint, the customer may consult one or more architects to review the work of the first architect and may then, when fully satisfied, select a builder to construct the house according to the blueprint.

The blueprint is a precise and *standard* engineering notation that can be understood and followed by other architects and by contractors. Different builders, given the same blueprint, will build the same house, with only minor differences in their selections of fixtures, landscaping, and miscellaneous features. However, the overall structure will be identical and the contractor will make use of (to the greatest extent possible) standard components, such as appliances and bathtubs, in creating a realization of the architect's design.

This explicit architectural design activity is valuable, since it permits careful study of the design problems and revision of the specifications in the absence of a real house. It is clear that the problems of redesign are greatly complicated if the builder had already made substantial progress on the construction when the customer decided upon fundamental changes in the design.

Although the specification and design phases make it less likely that there will be significant changes in the basic structure once construction is begun, the builder still has some challenging problems. First, it is important to be able to accommodate relatively small requests on the part of the customer without having to make major modifications to what has already been done. Second, the builder must manage time and resources carefully, since the price for building the house has been negotiated previously. Thus, for example, phases of the construction process have to be carried out in a certain schedule, using a critical path method or a similar process.

The home-building analogy is an excellent one for software development, since many of the same specification, design, and implementation problems arise in both domains. In particular, the notion of the life cycle carries over to the home-building area, even including evolution, such as the adding of new rooms, renovation of the kitchen, and rewiring of the entire house.

With respect to software, then, the life cycle provides a framework for the type of engineering process being sought. The various steps of the engineering process then serve to delineate the activities of software development. These stages include, but are not limited to, requirements analysis and definition, design, manufacture, quality assurance, and maintenance/enhancement. Throughout the entire process, there are aspects of management and communication, including documentation, budgeting, personnel deployment, project review, scheduling, and configuration management, that serve to tie the stages together and provide the organizational environment in which the technical procedures can be made effective. The combination of the modern technical procedures with the management techniques creates a synergistic effect in which the resulting process provides significantly greater improvement in the software production process than would be provided by either the technical or the management innovations alone.

In the remainder of this article, the primary focus will be on some of the methods that have been developed and used during one or more stages of the software life cycle, and on some efforts that have been made to integrate a collection of techniques into coherent methodologies. It will be apparent that the state of the art is not very advanced. There are few complete methodologies in existence, and very little in the way of objective data to justify the use of such methodologies.

Instead, much of the present work and a large portion of the current trend to systematic software development practices are based on recognition of the *ineffectiveness* of previous practices and on the inherent appeal of following a systematic approach rather than an *ad hoc* one. Furthermore, the data that has been made available overwhelmingly substantiates the value of the engineering approach.

Information Systems

Systematic software development practices are applicable to virtually any class of computer-based system which will have a lifetime considerably longer than its development time and which requires more than a single person to carry out the design and development. The concern in this article, however, will be upon "information systems" as a subset of all possible systems.

There are a large number of definitions and models of an information system. For present purposes, though, there are only a handful of salient characteristics that bear specific mention:

(1) They are to be used by persons who are unfamiliar with the technical aspects of computer hardware and software so that the underlying operating system, language processor(s), and hardware should be made as invisible and unobtrusive as possible.

(2) The way in which they are used and integrated into an organizational environment is at least as significant as the way that they are constructed.

(3) Information systems frequently involve access to and modification of large volumes of data, possibly stored as data bases.

(4) The way in which humans interact with the system is of great importance and affects selection and placement of terminals, hard versus soft copy, and volume, speed, and noise level of output devices, as well as input media.

These notions, when interpreted broadly, introduce a large variety of considerations into the system design and development process. Among these considerations are:

(a) *reliability*—whether the system is available and working properly when the user wants to use it,

(b) *simplicity*—the nature of the user interaction should be simple and easy to use; users should not have to conform to a rigid syntax,

(c) *invisibility*—the underlying characteristics of the computer, its operating system, and the programming language used for writing the system should be hidden from the user to the greatest extent possible,

(d) *user friendliness*—the system should provide meaningful error messages, should not terminate unexpectedly, and should enable the user to work with familiar terms and concepts; interactive information systems should provide on-line assistance and other similar features,

(e) *economy*—the system should be cost effective or cost justifiable in terms of both development and operational costs,

(f) *evolvability*—the system should be easily adaptable to conform to changing user requirements or to new execution environments, i.e., new hardware or operating systems.

While it is hard to quarrel with these objectives for information systems, they are hard to achieve in practice. Furthermore, some are less important than others for particular projects and must be balanced and traded off against one another. The importance of such a tradeoff analysis illustrates the necessity of obtaining a thorough understanding of the problem, the operational environment, and the overall requirements before proceeding with system development.

This need becomes even more apparent when one considers the balancing of objectives in traditional engineering endeavors. In the design of an automobile, for example, the manufacturer must balance the choice of exterior and interior dimensions against the cost of raw materials and the intended weight of the vehicle, which in turn must be balanced against the size and type of engine required to give satisfactory performance and to meet fuel economy standards. These choices must then be weighed against marketing considerations that determine the competitive position of the product in the market, balanced against corporate goals of profitability.

Even without adding in the requirements imposed by regulatory agencies and the technological innovations in various components, the complexity of the design and production process becomes staggering, and far exceeds the intellectual grasp of all but a handful of experts.

Much the same situation exists with information systems. Most information systems are *extremely* complex, far more so than one would believe at first glance. Methods and tools for information system design and development should be based upon a small number of underlying concepts. Six of them may be seen as recurring themes throughout the remainder of this article.

(1) *Modularizaton*—the problem-solving notion of "divide-and-conquer" permits one to subdivide a difficult problem into subproblems and then to subdivide those problems repeatedly until the resulting problems become intellectually manageable.

(2) *Abstraction*—the psychological notion of "abstraction" permits one to concentrate on a problem at some level of generalization without regard to irrelevant low-level details; use of abstraction also permits one to work with concepts and terms that are familiar in the problem environment without having to transform them to an unfamiliar structure.

(3) *Written and oral communication*—communication of knowledge and concepts among all of the persons involved in the design and development of an information system is critical; this information must be *represented* in such a way that it can be effectively communicated.

(4) *Commitment of development organization to software engineering*—the environment in which the development organization works has a strong impact on the ease of

communication, the quality of the final product that can be developed, and the productivity of the developers.

(5) *Availability of appropriate tools*—tools are a major component of an environment and must be usable and well integrated with one another; as with any engineering activity, the quality of the final product is largely determined by the quality of the tools used to specify, design, model, build, test, and describe it.

(6) *Phased approach to software quality*—the quality of the product is determined from the start. Failure to identify the problem or the user needs will result in a poor specification, which will be reflected in an inadequate system, requiring extensive modifications and enhancements that lead to uncontrollable maintenance costs and user dissatisfaction. This reason, above all, provides the best justification for use of a systematic methodology for information systems design.

The following sections describe the various stages of the software life cycle. Each stage is then described in general terms, followed by a discussion of one or more methods that have been used to assist the development process during that stage. The conclusion returns to the concept of the need for a methodology and the way in which management procedures can effectively implement these techniques within organizations.

Requirements Analysis and Definition

In this article, the term "requirements analysis and definition" (RA & D) will be used to encompass the traditional notion of "systems analysis" and the activity of producing a system specification. In its common usage, RA & D implies more of a concern with software structure (*not* detail) than is normally within the realm of systems analysis.

The product of RA & D is a requirements specification, a clear statement of the user requirements and any related or implied system constraints. Desirable properties of a specification include completeness, consistency, comprehensibility, traceability to the requirements, unambiguity (hence testability), modifiability, and writeability. The effort to achieve these properties in a specification has important implications for the RA & D activity.

Before proceeding, it should be noted that the requirements specification may be seen as being just a part of an overall system specification, which may include life cycle constraints such as expected system lifetime and hardware/software specifications—target machines, programming languages, or software interfaces. One can draw a distinction between requirements definition and specification by noting that the requirements definition focuses on what the user needs while the specification addresses what will be built.

Ross [9], Freeman [10], and others have noted that the primary purpose of RA & D is to understand and to communicate that understanding to others. Many of the techniques that have been developed are aimed directly at that need for understanding.

However, it is important to observe that there are several audiences for a specification, each of which has a somewhat different perspective and need. The terminology, emphasis, and perspective of each is normally quite different. This diversity of readership has been explored elsewhere [11,12].

Essentially, the specification must serve the needs of the end user, the customer (not necessarily the same), the system designer(s), and the system validation organization. End users are concerned with the usability of the system and its external features; an appropriate specification is relatively informal and emphasizes the ways in which the user interacts with the system, the nature of the data stored in the system, and the format of various outputs. In general, a mathematical formalization is unnecessary and may be counterproductive, since most users are unwilling to authorize the development of a system whose specification is incomprehensible.

At the same time, however, the formalization can be extremely useful to the validation organization, since it provides a precise, unambiguous statement of the behavior of the system. It is therefore an objective basis against which tests can be performed.

A third perspective is needed by the designers and developers, whose primary consideration is in identifying the *structure* of the problem so that it can be reflected in the structure of the software system. While they are concerned with external input and output, they must be equally concerned with internal data flows and usage. Clearly, the internal software structure is of little interest to the end user.

Thus, there is often the need for more than one kind of specification. This difficulty is rarely recognized and most of the existing methods of system specification are clearly addressed to one, or at most two, classes of readers. As noted in [11], specification techniques must take greater recognition of the different necessary views and provide appropriate mechanisms for communication, making certain to tie the different views together in such a way that they can be seen to be equivalent.

Methods for Requirements Analysis and Specification

A large number of techniques have been devised, developed, and used for assisting in the requirements analysis and/or specification phases of the software life cycle. Five such methods, representative of the entire set of such techniques, are Structured Systems Analysis (SSA), Structured Analysis and Design Technique (SADT)*, Problem Statement Language (PSL), Software Requirements Engineering Methodology (SREM), and the USE Specification Method. In this section, we shall briefly examine each of these, not so much with the intent of providing detailed information, but rather to see how they address the various concerns about software quality and how they fit into the notions of information systems design methodology.

---

*SADT is a trademark of SofTech, Inc.

46

Structured Systems Analysis (SSA)

Structured Systems Analysis [13,14] is a technique that is intended to be used with Structured Design (see below) as a way to tie together the specification and design phases of software development. It incorporates four separate concepts that are used together to create the specification:

(i) Data Flow Diagrams show the flow of data between various processing units along with the processes to be carried out and the stores of data that are created, accessed, and modified throughout the system. A process is described in nonprocedural terms within the box. Each box may be "exploded" into another level of detail (or multiple levels) showing additional data flow, error conditions, and similar items.

(ii) A Data Dictionary records information about all of the various data items and constraints upon them.

(iii) Immediate Access Analysis is based upon a relational data base design to show the data base and the types of operations that will be performed.

(iv) Program Design Language ("Structured English") or Decision Tables are used to show the process logic for each process box.

SSA can be seen as a design specification approach, since it produces a specification that reflects some of the architectural design of the system.

The SSA technique, while successfully blending process design and data design, has a few shortcomings. First, the use of SSA requires four different notations rather than one or two. Second, the data flow diagrams can become unwieldy if one is not careful to minimize the number of crossing lines and duplication of boxes. Finally, SSA dwells upon the technical aspects of the system analysis without providing for the management procedures that are essential to the effective use of such a tool.

Structured Analysis and Design Technique (SADT)

SADT [9,15] is a technique that was developed by Douglas Ross as a method for modeling complex problems and systems. It is a general-modeling tool whose use is applicable not only to data processing problems, but also to a general class of problems. In attempting to understand a problem and communicate that understanding, one builds models, perhaps more than one, taking on different vantage points and attempting to model differing aspects of a system.

An SADT diagram may model processes or data. In a process model (called an "actigram"), data flow and constraints are shown with arrows. An arrow entering a process box from the left is input; an arrow entering from above is a constraint (which is typically left unchanged by the process); arrows exiting from the right are output from the process (and perhaps serve as input or constraint for another box); finally, arrows entering from below denote mechanisms for carrying out the process.

The arrows serve to bound the context of a process. Each process may then be expanded through hierarchical decomposition into any number of successive levels of detail, until the model is completed. In much the same way, one can begin with abstract data objects, and model the data by showing the processes that create and use the data, proceeding through successive levels of data definition and decomposition.

One of the significant contributions of SADT is that it truly aims to be a *methodology* for requirements analysis and definition. SADT includes management procedures to be used in conjunction with the modeling aspects. Two points are critical: all diagrams go through an "author–reader" cycle, in which diagrams are reviewed by one or more people familiar with the problem being modeled and/or the SADT notation, and all comments must be received in written form, thereby establishing effective communication during requirements analysis.

SADT also has some discernible weaknesses. First, the models built in SADT often do not lend themselves to immediate transformation into designs or implementations. The modeling technique and notation is quite general, and is not specifically aimed at the transformation from problem analysis to software construction. Second, it takes considerable training and experience to become a skilled SADT author. Use of SADT requires a change in individual problem-solving and thinking strategies as well as understanding of the notation and modeling technique. At this time, there is no automated support for SADT but work is underway to develop such support.

Problem Statement Language (PSL)

PSL [16] is a technique developed by Daniel Teichroew of the University of Michigan as part of a larger project called ISDOS (Information System Design and Optimization System). PSL is a formal language for statement of a problem, supported by an analyzer called PSA (Problem Statement Analyzer). PSA accepts PSL as input and is used to produce a number of reports describing internal and external data flows, management information, and other related system data. PSA checks for inconsistencies in naming and data flow and reports these inconsistencies to the user.

PSL is based upon the definition of objects and their relationships, providing for more than 20 kinds of objects and more than 50 kinds of relationships. In addition to the formal checking that can be performed by PSA, PSL serves as an effective documentation tool by permitting the analyst or designer to specify the actions to be taken within a procedure and to show the hierarchical decomposition of the system. Estimates of frequency of use of a procedure, along with scheduling information can also be included to support other necessary system design and development activities.

PSL's major weaknesses appear to be the complexity of the syntax, with the need to remember a large number of reserved words and syntactic structures, along with the expense of installing and operating PSA, which runs predominantly on large-scale systems.

Software Requirements Engineering Methodology (SREM)

SREM [17] is a requirements methodology developed as part of the U.S. Army Ballistic Missile Defense software by TRW, Inc. SREM is a very large methodology, including a notation for describing concurrency of operations (R-nets), the processes themselves (RSL [18], similar to PSL), and automated tools to support the creation and checking of requirements documents.

Although the methodology was developed for real-time systems in which the system model is one of stimulus/response, a similar model can be devised for interactive information systems, since an asynchronous user input from the terminal may be treated as a stimulus, with the appropriate system action forming the response.

The developers of SREM have tried to cover all of the issues associated with the systematic development of requirements. In developing their methodology and tools, however, they have created a facility that is presently only feasible for very large software systems and apparently non-cost effective for small- and medium-size projects.

USE Specification Aid

The USE Specification Method [11] is part of the User Software Engineering methodology under development by this author [19]. It is directed toward the specification of interactive information systems, which are seen to consist of three parts: a user interface, a data base, and the operations mapped from the user onto the data base. Each of these parts is represented in a different way, with transition diagrams showing the user interface and identifying the semantic actions that are to be carried out upon recognition of the associated syntactic unit. The data base is defined using relational data base design (as with SSA). Finally, a variety of notations, ranging from English to highly formal algebralike specifications, may be used to define the semantics of the operations.

Like SSA, there is a strong attempt to blend data base definition and use with the information system processes. The technique is effective for relatively simple systems, but it has several drawbacks. First, it requires the use of three different notations to specify a system. Second, nothing is provided in the way of management procedures to creating and reviewing the specification. Finally, the transition diagrams can become quite complex as one tries to provide additional error-handling and diagnostic messages for users. At some points, the diagrams may become quite difficult to understand.

Other Approaches

There are, of course, many other techniques that can be used (and have been used) for this phase of the system development process. Among these are HIPO (see below), Higher Order Software (HOS) [20], and algebraic specifications [21,22]. Algebraic specifications are a mathematical formalization that describes the functional properties of operations upon data types and provides a set of axioms that formally describe the behavioral properties of the operations and their interactions with one another. The value of these algebraic specifications is that they are precise, representation-independent, and lend themselves to the use of program verification techniques. On the other hand, these algebraic specifications are, at present, quite limited in the kinds of objects and operations that can be specified. With respect to information systems, there is relatively little experience with them, although there have been a few attempts to extend the ideas of data abstractions to the data base environment [23-25].

Algebraic specifications have been reflected in a number of specification languages, including SPECIAL [26], part of the SRI Hierarchical Design Methodology [27,28], AXES [29], which is part of HOS, and SSL [30], developed by Science Applications, Inc. Finally, Gypsy [31] has been designed and implemented as both a specification language and a programming language.

In short, there are a wide variety of notations and approaches to requirements analysis and definition, and to the description of that analysis in a specification. The orientation of the specification varies from rather informal, problem-oriented forms to highly formal notations oriented to the design and/or verification aspects of system construction. The common theme of all of these approaches is to get away from the traditional system analysis methods, which provide only a lengthy narrative with little or no structure, and little emphasis on the system development process itself.

It is becoming increasingly clear that more than one form of requirements definition and specification is needed to satisfy the needs of all of the different purposes to which the requirements statement must be put. Furthermore, the importance of the requirements definition is becoming more and more apparent for its role in getting the system properties accurately defined at an early stage, resulting in savings in maintenance costs later on.

Architectural and Detailed Design

While the requirements and specification activity is used to determine *what* is to be done in a software system and the constraints that must be met in the construction of that system, the design phase is used to determine *how* to do it. Design involves the analysis of various design alternatives, including tradeoffs among a number of possible solutions based on the existing constraints.

These constraints may include such things as machine resources (time, main memory, secondary storage), development time or costs, interfaces to existing subsystems, use of specific hardware or programming languages, operational costs, or the necessity of software portability, just to name a few possibilities.

The design activity may be divided into two distinct phases, termed architectural and detailed design. During architectural design, the emphasis is on determining the structure of the system, decomposing the system into modules, and precisely specifying the interfaces between the modules. During detailed design, the emphasis is on the selection and evaluation of algorithms to carry out the logical steps specified for the individual modules.

Design may be treated as an implicit part of the specification process or may be treated as an explicit phase of the overall system development process [10]. On larger projects, at least, there is a definite trend toward making design an explicit activity so that one does not confuse the problem definition and understanding activity with the attempt to define system structures.

It should be noted, though, that there is a close interrelationship between the specification and design phases whether or not they are made explicit. Typically, early attempts to define a system architecture result in identification of problem areas—incompleteness, inconsistency, infeasibility—in the specification. The attempt to design a system meeting the specification highlights the problems and forces a revision of the specification. Such iteration is common throughout the system life cycle: when one is working primarily upon a specific phase of system development, there is continually the need to look back to the prior phase(s) to be certain that the new work is consistent with the previous work and to identify and correct any errors that may have been made at the previous stage. Similarly, one must anticipate some of the activities that will occur at succeeding phase(s) of system development and to provide information that will simplify that work as well as permitting the checking of that work against the current phase.

One can then envision a moving "window" covering more than one software development phase, making clear that no aspect of the system development activity is carried out in isolation. Instead, each phase continually ties down additional aspects of the system, proceeding from its function through its structure through its realization. As a result, increased constraints are placed at each phase of the process, with the most highly creative activities coming at the early stages.

The steps of architectural and detailed design, then, serve to tighten up any loose points in the specification, and to define for the programmer the steps to be included in the implementation of each module.

The end result of the design activity is to produce a *representation* of the system in a form that can be easily constructed by the implementor. It is important to recognize that the representation of the design, as captured in a "software blueprint," can provide a comprehensible and unambiguous statement for the implementer.

In the following discussion of techniques for architectural and detailed design, it is important to stress the extent to which the methods can aid the software developer in producing a blueprint for a program, one that can be built in a straightforward way directly from the detailed design. Finally, it should be seen that the architectural design lays out the overall structure of the system, but that it must be used in conjunction with one of the detailed design aids to produce the design representation. This point illustrates the difficulties in trying to construct a system directly from the specification without analyzing the design possibilities and producing a validated design.

Techniques for Architectural and Detailed Design

There are many tools and techniques being used to support the software designer. Historically, the flowchart has served as the primary tool for this task. However, traditional flowcharts have now been largely discredited [32] and have been replaced with a variety of more sophisticated and more comprehensible aids. In this section, we shall present a few such tools and techniques, beginning with an architectural design method and proceeding through detailed design aids.

Structured Design

The design technique that has received the most attention and use is Structured Design [33,34], as originally developed by Constantine and advanced by Yourdon and Myers. Structured Design is concerned with the development of well-structured systems, the ability to compare alternative designs and determine their relative quality, and the transformation of data flow diagrams into programs structures.

One of the key issues in Structured Design is *modularity*. In creating a design, major emphasis is given to the effectiveness of the modular decomposition. Modularity is measured by two yardsticks: *cohesion* and *coupling*. Cohesion refers to the extent to which the components of a module (typically statements, but alternatively data) are conceptually related. Coupling refers to the way in which modules are related to one another and the forms of interconnections that are used in the design, primarily the way(s) in which data are communicated among modules.

Ideally, each module should carry out a single, well-defined function, where the action of the function can be described in a sentence or two. Such modules may be described as having a high degree of cohesiveness, particularly in contrast with modules that simply contain a collection of unrelated statements.

Similarly, each module should be coupled to other modules through explicit data passing in order to make the input to and the output from each module as visible as possible. The use of common data areas or global variables provides a greater degree of coupling and is therefore less desirable. At the worst extreme, it is possible to create modules that make explicit use of data objects or program segments contained within another module. This is the worst form of coupling, since changes to a single module may have an indirect impact upon other modules.

In summary, then, the goal of structured design is to create system structures in which the modules have high cohesion and low coupling. Structured Design also provides some other metrics for evaluating the quality of a design. Myers [34] has even suggested a technique for "scoring" a design, but experienced designers seldom need to utilize this objective measure and can simply examine alternative designs and select the best one using these criteria.

Structured design is a highly useful aid to architectural design and provides the designer with a high-level system architecture. By using bubble charts based on data flow and transforming them into Structure Charts, it is possible to obtain a number of alternative architectural designs quickly. The emphasis on modularization is valuable for a development team and for making certain that subsystem interfaces are properly established at an early stage of the development. The major weakness of Structured Design is that it addresses a relatively small portion of the system life cycle, providing little or no help with specification or with detailed design and implementation. However, some work has been done to tie Structured Systems Analysis [13,14] to Structured Design to cover a larger portion of the life cycle.

HIPO

Another technique that has been heavily used for design is HIPO [35,36] (Hierarchical-Input-Process-Output), developed by IBM primarily as a documentation aid, but used for the description of both specifications and designs. HIPO consists of a collection of hierarchically organized diagrams in which each processing box (module) has explicit input and output items. In this way, the notion of modular decomposition is achieved within HIPO.

A HIPO process box may contain either a nonprocedural description of the steps that may be performed within the process or a more detailed, procedurelike sequence of steps that shows the actual process logic. Accordingly, there is some applicability of the technique for various steps of the software development process for specification, architectural, and detailed design. Indeed, the same HIPO tool can be used repeatedly throughout a single development activity, with gradual refinements made to the diagrams as additional steps are taken.

HIPO is in widespread use, primarily for its value as a documentation aid. It has the advantage of being very easy to learn and use and can be applied to both specification and design. With care, it can be an effective tool, since the hierarchy supports abstraction and the input-process-output notion supports modularity. The tendency in practice, though, seems to be somewhat informal, without the checking of interfaces and control of decomposition that are needed for proper use.

Jackson Design Method

The Jackson Design Method [37], developed by Michael Jackson in England, relies upon three fundamental observations:

(1) The program structure should be closely related to the problem structure.

(2) For many systems, the problem can be reduced to the creation of a mapping from the input structure to the output structure.

(3) A design method, in order to gain wide acceptance, should be easily teachable and readily usable by a large number of *average* designers.

Jackson's method is aimed at all of these points and directed primarily at commercially oriented data processing systems, although it has been used with success for control-oriented programs as well. Essentially, one builds up a program structure based on the structure of the input and the structure of the output, joining the two structures at the appropriate point(s). One then lists the various operations that must be performed within the system and allocates them within the resulting structure. Given this structure, it becomes possible to create directly the program structure and construct an implementation.

Of course, in practice, the situation is rarely that simple. In particular, the input structure and the output structure don't always neatly fit together, creating what Jackson calls a "structure clash." There are several ways to resolve such a clash, with the most effective one being to create an intermediate structure that can successfully interface with both the input structure and the output structure.

The idea behind Jackson's method is to create a workable design, not *necessarily* the best design, but one that a large number of designers would independently create and is satisfactory for the problem at hand. Unlike some of the techniques previously mentioned, Jackson's method gives little or no assistance in the process of requirements analysis and specification. One must have previously determined the input and output structures before using this tool. Furthermore, it appears that the method and hence the resulting program structures are quite sensitive to major changes in the input and output structures.

Jackson is working on expansion of the method and on techniques to tie the design method to other phases of software development. One recent advance has been to automatically generate COBOL programs from the process logic and a separately prepared data description.

Jackson's method has been heavily used and has been adopted on a companywide basis by several organizations that develop large software systems; these organizations have begun to work on additional automated tools to show the program structure and transform the resulting processing notation into executable code.

DREAM

DREAM (Design Realization, Evaluation, and Modeling) [38,39] is a method under development by Bill Riddle and colleagues at the University of Colorado. DREAM was developed to address the problems of designing operating systems and other systems with a high degree of concurrency. The method involves the description of the system in a design notion (DDN).

The notion of a model is important in the use of DREAM, since one wishes to build an object about which one can ask questions. With such a model, it becomes possible to evaluate designs against one another. Like several of the methods described above. DREAM is still very much in a research and development environment.

Structured Flowcharts

It was noted above that traditional flowcharts were no longer favored as a method of representing a design. There are several reasons for this situation, including:

(a) The notation used in flowcharts is inconsistent with notations used in both specification and implementation, making the transitions between phases unnecessarily complicated.

(b) Traditional flowcharts are difficult to read due to their nonlinearity; the number of paths on the chart grows rapidly as the complexity of the program logic increases.

(c) There is very little automated support for flowcharts, especially in comparison with program design languages.

(d) There is no effective way to control the level of detail contained within each box of a flowchart; some boxes show an operation at a high level of abstraction, while others specify a low-level detail, such as "$i := i + 1$."

As a result, alternative schemes for representing the detailed design of programs and their modules have been devised. One of these schemes is termed structured flowcharts, or Nassi-Shneiderman charts, after their inventors [40].

A structured flowchart is a large box containing the logic for a processing unit. As with traditional flowcharts, there is a well-defined notation for the various logical steps, including sequential composition of statements, if-then-else branching, calls to subprograms, and so on. There are some major differences, though. First, the types of control structures are limited to sequential composition of statements, subprogram/function calls, if-then-else branches, and iteration through a while-do condition, consistent with the basic flow of control statements used in structured coding. Next, the box structure serves to contain the various statements and places a constraint upon the way in which one may draw a structured flowchart.

As a result, a structured flowchart is considerably more readable than is a traditional flowchart, due largely to the almost linear nature of the chart. Also, structured flowcharts can be drawn much more compactly than traditional flowcharts, so that the design can be shown in a smaller amount of space.

Structured flowcharts are strictly limited to detailed design activities and provide little or no assistance in creating the specification or deciding on the gross program structure. However, they have been used in a large number of settings and have been found valuable by many of their users [41].

Program Design Languages

Program design languages [42], alternatively called "Structured English" or "metacode" or "pseudocode," may be viewed as very-high-level programming languages. They are intended to express the logic of a program module in narrative form, following a format that makes them readable.

A program design language (PDL) may be either informal or formal. Formal PDLs impose a programming languagelike syntax upon their users, making it possible to use automated tools to check the validity of the syntax. Less formal PDLs are not subject to the same kind of automated checking.

In either event, a PDL is used to describe the algorithm used to carry out the required steps within a program module. It contains a specification of the interfaces (input and output) between the given module and other modules to which it is linked during program execution, a brief statement (one or two sentences) of the function performed by the module, and then a description of the logic used in realizing that function.

A PDL is a detailed design tool and is therefore an appropriate way to illustrate the precise algorithms being used within a module. Because the architectural design has delineated the module structure, each piece of PDL reflects only a small part of the overall project logic. If one uses the rule of thumb that a program unit should contain no more than 50 program statements, then the PDL for a module should contain no more than 10–15 statements. In general, the PDL description for a given program is approximately 20–25% of the overall program length.

Program design languages have been seen to be extremely effective replacements for flowcharts. There are several apparent reasons for this:

(1) They are machine-processable, using the text-editing facilities available in the software development environment.

(2) They can be easily read, so that a group of designers can easily review the PDL of a given designer to determine the quality of the design.

(3) They are read in a top-to-bottom manner and provide a more accurate reflection of the program structure than do flowcharts at a later stage in software development.

It seems safe to conclude that traditional flowcharts will soon be replaced almost entirely by either structured flowcharts or by program design languages.

Other Methods

Many other design techniques have been developed and used. Warnier's Logical Construction of Programs [43], which predates Jackson's Design Method, is similar in approach, with the main difference being that Warnier limits his effort by beginning with the format of the output and works backward from there, rather than attempting to match an input and an output structure. In addition, there are methods based on finite state automata and their transitions, decision tables, and specification/design blends, such as the Unified Design Specification System [44].

For the most part, there are few quantitative measures that assist the designer in evaluating the quality of designs.

As a result, much of the current work may be viewed as producing an *adequate* design, rather than an *optimal* design. This situation is to be expected, since relatively little work has been done at capturing performance or other similar constraints and effectively capturing them in the design activity. However, the experience gained by such efforts is essential to the creation of a "science of design." Typically, such constraints remain separate until the implementation phase, when failure to achieve them becomes critical. There is clearly a need to develop ways to integrate design constraints into the design process more effectively.

Implementation and Coding

The actual production of code, originally thought to be the major activity of software development, takes up no more than 20% of the total development time. However, its importance cannot be overemphasized, simply because it is the part of the software development process that is most visible during testing, maintenance, and operation. The most elegant designs and the best goals of the developers can be lost with inadequate code.

Code production has received considerable attention from those concerned with programming methodology. In addition to its high visibility, this attention has been intensified for several reasons:

(i) The task of writing code is closely tied to the problem solving and overall system development process.

(ii) The areas of programming language design and compiler construction have long been major research topics in computer science. Programming language design and development is an extremely popular activity.

(iii) The *style* employed in the coding process has a significant impact on the program's testability, maintainability, and comprehensibility.

In every software development project, it is necessary to make the decision concerning the programming language that is to be used to implement the system under development. As often as not, this decision is constrained by "outside forces," such as availability of compilers, compatibility with other subsystems, contractor-imposed requirements, availability of processors for a variety of target machines, programmer experience, and/or a "popularity contest" among the members of the development team. It is indeed rare that the system developer has the freedom to select a language that is well suited for the problem at hand.

Such a situation, while far from ideal, is not entirely negative. After all, engineering involves the construction of artifacts under constraints, and an inadequate programming language is just another constraint. Furthermore, it is generally possible to write well-structured, comprehensible programs in the "worst" programming languages, and ill-structured, poorly documented, inefficient programs in the "good" programming languages.

Nonetheless, the vast body of work in the areas of programming language design [45-49] and programming methodology [50-55] during the past decade has shown that there is a strong relationship between the host programming language, the quality of the resulting software, and the productivity of the programmers using given languages.

In treating the area of coding and implementation, it is important to separate the discussion into three separate areas: the role of coding in the software development process, the issues of proper programming style, and the development of new programming languages and extensions to older languages to enhance their support for a systematic approach to programming.

As noted above, coding occupies a rather odd position in the software life cycle. Most of the major decisions concerning the functions of the system and the design approach to be taken have already been made, yet the programmer can make or break the system by succeeding or failing to implement the system according to the existing specification and documentation.

One of the strongest negative tendencies is for the programmer to engage in premature coding before the design (or even the specification) has been written and approved. In some cases, such a parallel activity is fruitful; in the large majority of the cases, though, most, if not all, of the early programming work will have to be thrown away once the design is made final.

It is very hard for programmers to suppress the urge to write code—after all, that is their primary job function. In addition, they are often pressured by higher-level management that does not recognize the importance of the specification and design phases and only recognizes code as a measure of project progress.

There is at least one exception where early coding is valuable. When one is undertaking a large, innovative, or complex system, it is frequently useful to build a "throwaway" system, in much the same way that engineers build breadboards. The idea behind such a prototype system is to use the prototype as a model, identify some major characteristics of the system, and give the users the chance to work with and suggest modifications to the prototype system. Such systems are often extremely valuable and are built on a very-short-term basis, often capturing only a portion of the specifications and ignoring the design phase almost completely. Such systems are typically built by a single individual, who is able to build the system without the need for the communication and documentation required for projects requiring more than a few people.

Techniques for Coding and Implementation

This section covers a number of topics related to the quality of programs that are produced during the coding and implementation phases of information system design and development. These topics include the techniques to be used for writing high-quality code, the interrelationship between programming and testing strategies, the attempt to make use of existing code and software systems, and the features of various programming languages. Some of these coding techniques have been shown to have a favorable effect upon program quality and/or programmer productivity.

Guidelines for Programming Style

There are a number of guidelines intended to enhance programming style. Although more comprehensive lists can be found in several books, such as ref. 56, the following list covers many of the most critical aspects of programming style:

(1) Modularize the system—construct modules that are small in size, hide a single design decision or carry out a single function, and have clearly defined interfaces, passing data explicitly wherever possible. These steps aid comprehensibility of the system, permit testing and verification of small program units, and support team development of software systems.

(2) Strive for program readability—use mnemonic names for variables, procedures, functions, data types, and other program objects; annotate the code with comprehensive comments, making such that they agree with the specification; use consistent indentation practices so that code groupings can be easily seen; construct programs so that control flow within each program unit is linear; provide sufficient external documentation in the form of cross-reference tables, calling diagrams, and design representations to assist the reader.

(3) Avoid programming tricks—side effects and aliasing can be used to produce unexpected results, causing programs to do the unexpected and complicating the validation effort; machine-dependent code, particularly at the instruction level of the host computer, should be avoided wherever possible.

(4) Restrict use of global data—data should be explicitly passed between program units wherever possible; the number of parameters may be minimized by judicious use of structured objects such as arrays and records. Excessive use of global variables permits more units to access and/or modify those variables, complicating the problem of identifying faulty program units when a global variable obtains an incorrect value.

(5) Use data abstraction concepts—construct functions and procedures (or abstract data types [57] for those languages providing them) for commonly used classes of objects and define the necessary operations upon those objects. This step restricts access to the representation of objects, thereby simplifying modification of the program and alteration of representation decisions. It also permits the data types with their operations to be separately validated and the relatively small size of the code effecting the operation simplifies the validation process.

(6) Minimize the number of paths through programs—both testing and verification strategies rely on coverage of the different paths of control flow through a program. Deeply nested "if-then-else-end if" statements, for example, cause exponential growth in the number of such paths. Simple control paths also reduce the complexity of verification conditions that must be proved at different program points; elimination of the "goto" and similar constructs can assure a linear flow of control.

(7) Give preference to static data structures—data objects based on fixed storage allocation not only eliminate some of the execution time overhead, but minimize the likelihood of errors caused by lack of available storage or by references to nonexistent objects.

These points are important not only in support of the testing and verification activities that must follow the coding, but also for the eventual maintenance of the program. It should be noted that data design and implementation issues figure just as significantly as program structure issues in this list and that there is a need to balance attention between these aspects of program construction.

Implementation Strategies

There are many alternative strategies for proceeding with the implementation of the program. A program that is designed in a top-down fashion need not be implemented that way, nor must a program that is designed in a top-down way be implemented that way. There are instead as many strategies for implementation as there are for specification and design.

In general, the implementation strategy to be followed should be based on the criticality of certain program regions and the procedure for testing to be followed. If the performance of certain program units is of paramount importance, then that module and those related to it should be implemented first so that performance data can be gathered and extra time can be left to determine the correctness of the implementation.

Another possibility is to combine a top-down implementation strategy with top-down testing, constructing program "stubs" to fill in for the unimplemented routines. In this way, the high levels of the program structure are developed, with successively lower levels constructed as necessary.

Alternatively, the low-level routines can be implemented, with driver programs built to test out the performance and the correctness of those routines. Unlike stubs, however, which can be expanded to fill out the remainder of a program function, drivers must typically be discarded after use. In general, a top-down implementation/testing strategy is the most productive approach.

Despite the relatively low cost of the coding phase, the cost of the testing phase is extremely high. Thus, it is important to try, wherever possible, to use software components that have been thoroughly designed, tested, and used in earlier systems. This presents the obvious savings in development and testing cost.

Reusable Software

The notion of reusable software is a critical idea in software engineering, although it has not been successfully exploited in the past. There are several reasons for this lack of use of existing software, including the following:

(1) The programmer as "prima donna"—programmers have been unwilling to accept and use any nontrivial routines that they did not write. Anything more complicated than a square-root routine or perhaps a sorting routine is simply not used outright.

(2) Poor quality of software modules—there has been little or no assurance that software modules met certain performance, space utilization, or correctness constraints. Unless the code was superbly documented, accompanied by test data and test results, and was compatible with the

execution environment of the program, it simply wasn't accepted.

(3) The difficulty of extracting useful "software components" from other systems—much software is so deeply embedded into its original execution environment that it is hard to extract and use elsewhere.

While this is not an exhaustive list of the difficulties of reusing software, it is indicative of the problems faced in making significant use of such software. Yet, reuse of products is an important characteristic of engineering disciplines, in much the same way as are standard components. Clearly, if one is able to use software pieces from other systems, then less time must be spent on system design and redesign. Similarly, successful designs can be reused in order to simplify the problems of redesigning systems having similar properties.

There has been some, albeit limited, experience with the reuse of software. The first, and most significant, such experience is with mathematical software. There exist libraries of algorithms and source programs to execute a broad range of mathematically oriented procedures. Such mathematical packages, along with some widely used statistical packages, are thoroughly documented, widely tested and used, and provide explicit information concerning the nature of the algorithm(s) used. The application user can make use of these routines with confidence.

A second class of reusable software is used for data base management. Data base management systems have been built on top of file systems for a large number of computer systems and interfaced to several programming languages, particularly COBOL. The DBMS provides high-level access to information stored on secondary storage devices and prevents the programmer from having to rewrite the low-level file access routines.

Finally, a growing number of software tools [58] are being developed to be reused for a number of software development projects. At this stage of development, tools are widely dispersed, and only a few systems possess integrated sets of tools. There is a need to examine tools much further, identify those which are truly beneficial, and determine those that need to be built to increase the productivity of system developers still further.

In all of these cases, the tool can be beneficial in saving programmer time, either by providing an automated aid for performing the task more effectively or by eliminating the need to write code that others have written. However, the existence of such software does not take away from the need to adopt and use effective system development methodologies. The mere existence of a data base management system may in fact place constraints upon the development and design activities and make certain design approaches more attractive than others, but it does *not* take away from the basic need to understand the problem and communicate that understanding before going ahead with an implementation that uses the data base management system.

Programming Languages

In the final analysis, the programming language used for the construction of the information system may be the single most important determinant of software quality once the specification and design have been completed. Certainly, the extent to which the primitive data objects and control structures of the language conform to the primitives of the problem is a major consideration in the ease of transforming the design to the program, in minimizing the number of errors that occur during this transformation, and in enhancing the comprehensibility of the resulting code.

Despite the great effort in designing a vast number of programming languages over the past five years, most everyday programming is done with a handful of languages, all of which have very serious shortcomings from the standpoint of modern programming language design. This is particularly true of information systems design, since few languages have adequate features for dealing with exceptional conditions during execution, embedding the data base operations of the information system with the procedural steps of the programming language, dealing with strings, and truly assisting the programmer achieve the above-mentioned goals of abstraction, modularization, and program readability.

A few trends can be seen in programming languages, however:

(1) There is decreased reliance on highly machine-dependent programs, particularly those written in assembly language. Part of this shift is due to the sharply lower cost of hardware and the availability of high-level language processors for a variety of small computers.

(2) There is considerable experimentation with new languages, particularly Pascal, not only within the academic community, but also within the industrial and personal computing communities. The lessons of structured programming have been assimilated and it is apparent that many of the features of Pascal contribute to better programming style and to higher programmer productivity. Despite its shortcomings with respect to input/output and other features critical for information systems, Pascal has attained a wide following and has become available on virtually every computer system available.

(3) There is considerable interest in the efforts of the Department of Defense to develop a new language, Ada [59,60]. Although the language is directed to computer programs that will be embedded in rockets and other kinds of specialized systems, the language is seen as having a major impact on future software development, due to the strength of its sponsorship. Ada is of particular interest because it attempts to incorporate a number of state-of-the-art programming language design concepts into a practical tool. However, it is still too early to determine if the language implementation will be successful and how widely Ada will be adopted and used.

It seems clear that most information system development organizations will examine the programming language(s) they are presently using and will give consideration to some more modern language(s) for their development activities, despite the added expense that they are likely to incur in training and software conversion. There is clearly a need for additional work in the area of programming languages to support information systems, since there are only a few languages, such as PLAIN [61], that presently address this need.

Many people believe that the present concept of an application programmer is rapidly becoming obsolete and that such persons will be replaced by a large number of turnkey systems and "end-user" programming, thereby obviating the need for systematic software development methodologies [62]. However, this does not seem likely to happen in the foreseeable future, for several reasons:

(1) While there will be an increasing number of "very-high-level languages" that can indeed be used effectively by persons with little or no programming experience, there will remain the need for persons to define those languages and to build processors for them.

(2) The tendency in computing continues toward the design and development of increasingly sophisticated applications involving greater complexity. Software engineering skills will certainly play a role in helping the developers understand these new problems and to develop workable solutions. The growing use of distributed systems and distributed data bases is simply one instance of such applications.

(3) There will be a need for persons with an interdisciplinary background, combining their knowledge of some application area, such as medicine, transportation, or personnel, with computer science in order to help design and develop the required systems in those disciplines.

(4) Computer science and software engineering are still in very primitive stages as technical disciplines. There is *much* more to be learned and understood before the technical specialists are able to devise the tools and the application systems that can permit end users to define their own applications.

In summary, even though coding and implementation is by far the best understood of the phases of information system design and development, there is still a great deal of room for improvement and innovation. In addition, there is a need to gain a better understanding of the way that programmers write code and the extent to which the features of a given language (or even the language itself) affect the quality of the software that is written and the speed with which it can be correctly written.

Quality Assurance: Testing and Verification

According to most measurements, approximately half(!) of the development effort on a software system takes place after the code has been written. A system must undergo successive rounds of testing prior to being acceptable for release to its customers.

First, there is unit testing, in which individual program modules are tested for correctness, to see that they meet their specifications. Next, there is integration testing, in which two or more modules are joined and tested together, to see if they work properly together and to make certain that the interfaces mesh. Finally, there is acceptance testing in which the user (or the user's designated agent) determines whether the system conforms to the specification for the system.

Each of these steps is time-consuming and frequently requires modification to the code, design, or specification. In general, errors found during unit testing are caused by routine programming errors—uninitialized variables, improperly checked array bounds, poorly formatted output. Errors found during integration testing reflect design errors, in which the module boundaries were not correctly drawn or where different implementers disagreed over the interface specifications. Finally, errors found during acceptance testing usually reflect specification errors—incomplete, inconsistent, incorrect, or ambiguous statements of what the system was supposed to do.

The most serious aspect of this situation is that the errors that were made first are detected last! An error in the requirements definition or its translation into the system specification may not be caught until the entire system has been constructed and many of its components have been thoroughly tested. Such an error, in some circumstances, may require massive changes in the system design, with resulting reconstruction of large parts of the system and repetition of the testing process.

It is for this reason that analysis and design errors are the most expensive kind of error. Not only do such errors remain undetected for the longest time, but they also require greater modifications to the system (with the resultant possibility of introducing new errors). Furthermore, it often takes a long time to identify such errors in the first place, since their detection requires the participation of the user to find the error and to agree upon the correct function of the system.

One can clearly see, then, that improved methods of error detection, combined with more effective testing procedures, are a key to reduced costs in information system development. By finding and correcting problem areas at an early stage, too, the costs of maintenance and enhancement of the system throughout its lifetime can also be reduced. These savings are the payoff for improved practices of software design and development.

At present, much of the existing software was developed without the use of any such formal techniques. It was simply made to work by an extensive process of trial-and-error, with continuing patches and modifications [63]. As a result, many systems are plagued by infrequent, but nonetheless annoying, aberrant behavior, where the program suddenly fails or loses data for no apparent reason. After a period of time, the code loses any structure that it may once have had, and it becomes increasingly difficult to modify without causing additional errors [64].

Another related problem is that these errors are not detected until very late in the software development cycle. A project may appear to be making normal progress on all fronts, only to be interminably delayed by the need to fix specification and design errors after the code is written.

Many such systems fail to ever reach their original goal and end up in an unfinished state or go unused by their intended user community. Thus, it is essential to incorporate procedures that permit an early evaluation of software quality and correctness as part of the system development methodology.

Attempts to assess the correctness of programs may be divided into two separate categories: testing and verification. Verification is a formal, mathematical proof that the program is in conformity with its specifications. Testing, by contrast, is a series of controlled experiments that seek to provide empirical evidence that a program behaves properly (and provides the desired results for broad classes of anticipated inputs). Although testing and verification may be viewed as distinct activities, there is some overlap between them, particularly with symbolic execution systems [65,66], and it has been predicted that the eventual approach to determination of program correctness will be a blend of testing and verification techniques.

At present, neither testing nor verification are well advanced. Verification, for the most part, is limited to small, mathematically oriented programs in which it is possible to provide a precise specification; these constraints automatically rule out verification for information systems, which typically involve exceptional conditions (such as arithmetic overflow), data bases, user interaction, and other such complications.

Furthermore, the cost of verification is quite high. There are only a small number of people with the ability to construct program proofs and progress toward automated verification aids has been quite slow, although a few have been successfully developed [67,68]. Given this situation, researchers in program verification anticipate that formal proof techniques will only be applied to the most critical sections of critical programs, until (and if) more powerful means of verification and more powerful automated tools are devised and verified.

While greater progress has been made in the area of testing, it, too, is far from being a well-understood activity. Various kinds of tools have been constructed, but they have a tendency to work for only a single language in a single execution environment. A program analyzer for FORTRAN, for example, can identify variables that have not been initialized and can detect sections of code that cannot be reached through the specified program flow, but cannot generate the test data that makes it possible to certify the correctness of the program.

There is a large flurry of activity toward building testing tools [69-71], along with a more gradual activity toward developing a theory of testing and test data selection [72, 73]. There is a need to integrate the existing tools so that someone hoping to conduct extensive tests on a given program can have all of the necessary tools available within a single environment for the program. Because of space considerations and this article's emphasis on design, further discussion of testing techniques is omitted here; the interested reader is directed to ref. 51 for further information.

System Evolution

Evolution of information systems, including maintenance and enhancement, is not strictly part of an information system design methodology, so it will not be treated in any extensive detail here. However, their importance should not be overlooked, since they typically account for two or four times the original development costs on average systems, and *far more* on systems with long lifetimes or systems that have been replicated a large number of times. (One can imagine the maintenance cost associated with fixing an error in a piece of software placed in microcomputer read-only memory in an automobile or a toy.)

A large share of the cost of maintenance and enhancement comes as a result of failure to understand the user's problem in the first place, with the resulting need to fix the operational system. Of course, there will always be the need for some maintenance costs as users identify additional desired capabilities or as new hardware and/or operating systems are introduced. However, an information system development methodology must attempt to minimize such costs.

There are several effective measures for reducing maintenance. The first, and the most obvious, is to get it right the first time. While this statement may appear facetious, it is completely serious. Many errors arise because system developers are in too much of a rush to review the user requirements and to help the users come to a good understanding of their problems and the way in which the information system should be properly integrated into their organization. Furthermore, too little attention is given to review of the project throughout its development to make certain that the system under development remains in conformity with the user requirements.

Other effective measures for reducing maintenance are to maintain close contact with end users and customers, involve them in the review of the requirements and specification documents, and give one or more of their representatives the opportunity to participate in the development and review of user documentation, as well as to experiment with the system prior to its official release. In general, a large number of problems arise because the system development organization isolates itself from the user community and creates a series of difficulties that must only be resolved at a later date, including misinterpretation of the requirements and improper design of interfaces.

Maintenance and enhancement is particularly difficult with poorly designed and poorly written systems. It is virtually impossible to impose good structure where there was none before, short of rewriting large portions of the entire system. Effort placed into such an activity is often worthless and would have been more usefully placed into redesign and recoding. The high turnover of personnel in this field serves to reinforce this point, since poorly built systems are nearly incomprehensible for others to read, understand, and modify without introducing additional problems.

The best approach, then, is to anticipate the need for enhancement and to create systems that are modifiable. Modularization of the system seems to be the key to this approach, since existing modules may be replaced with better versions of the same module and since new modules may be added to the system with minimal disruption to the existing modules.

Good documentation of the specification and design is also valuable for maintenance, since that reduces the need of the maintainer to "go to the code." It should be noted, however, that good maintenance practices require modification to the specification and design documents as well as to the code, so that no inconsistencies will arise. Above all, the maintenance organization must be cautioned against the "quick fix" that is often employed to get a system back into operation without a thorough analysis of the cause(s) of the problem and a study of alternative strategies to prevent the reoccurrence of the same problem or a secondary effect of that problem.

In conclusion, then, anticipation of maintenance and enhancement aspects of a system are essential components of the design and development activities if there is any expectation that the implemented system will be used for a long period of time or in multiple settings. Failure to plan for this evolutionary phase can result in excessive maintenance costs and/or inability to make the desired changes.

The Programming Environment

Still another consideration for the system development organization is the environment in which software design and development is performed. Although it is rarely considered a part of an information system development methodology, the programming environment has a critical role within an organization's selection and adoption of a methodology. If the programmers and designers cannot make good use of the computing resources that are available to them in their development environment, then the organization will not gain the full measure of benefit out of an information system development methodology.

While some of the environmental factors are noise levels, privacy, and the nature of the workspace, other factors are more directly related to the facilities of the computer system and support personnel for software development. An ideal programming environment should enhance the productivity of the development personnel and provide a set of tools that simplifies the process of software production and permits problems with the system to be identified and repaired. The programming environment should contain both facilities for the individual member of a development group and for the overall management of the project.

The constituents of the programming environment include the operating system and its utility programs, the programming language to be used along with its translator (compiler and/or interpreter) and run-time support (debugging aids and execution profilers), text and program preparation and documentation aids, and management tools including automated facilities for configuration manage-ment, scheduling, budgeting, and related tasks. The various tools in the environment should work together in harmony and have the ability to construct new tools upon existing tools.

A programming environment can be batch-oriented or interactive. Although each of them has certain advantages, an interactive development environment is becoming increasingly more attractive. There are a number of reasons for this advantage:

(1) For many, the period of time between the submission of a batch job and the receipt of the run is largely unproductive, particularly when the batch turnaround time is highly variable. If the turnaround time is high, then there is a sharp loss in productivity if a programmer has made a minor error in the program or in the instructions to the operating system.

(2) The availability of a shared development environment makes it possible to store virtually all of the documentation related to a specific project on line where it may be accessed by all members of the development team. The "mail" system available on many time-sharing systems is an effective scheme for transmitting memos and for making others aware of modifications to software or documentation.

(3) The developer is able to maintain a relatively uninterrupted stream of thought through working at the terminal, without the sequence of steps related to preparation and submission of batch jobs.

Of course, these advantages may be offset by a number of disadvantages, which can actually outweigh the advantages in some settings. Among these disadvantages are the potentially higher cost of hardware and/or software to support the interactive environment, the increased tendency of the programmer to write code, and the tendency to make the "quick fix" and try it out in the interactive environment. With proper management procedures and the greatly reduced cost of hardware and terminals, though, the interactive environment offers many attractive characteristics.

The discussion of programming environments is highly complex and there is no room to cover the topic in any detail here. In summary, though, it is important to give attention to the programming environment, including batch versus interactive development, the physical environment available for the development team members, the programming language(s), the tools for documentation, design, and testing, and automated support for the software design techniques and management procedures that comprise the methodology.

Management Procedures

As noted at the beginning of this article, a software development methodology is actually a blend between a collection of technical procedures and a set of management techniques that can result in effective deployment of project personnel, predictability of project schedule, budget, and outcome, accurate estimation of software properties, and the final result of a high-quality system that meets the needs of its users throughout the lifetime of the system.

From the standpoint of an information system development methodology, there are several key issues to be addressed:

(1) linkage of the various stages of the life cycle,

(2) evaluation of individual and project progress,

(3) appropriate team organization and individual assignments,

(4) deciding when a system is ready to be released and controlling the means by which it is released and modified,

(5) evaluation and integration of new technical procedures.

Although this is only a small subset of the total range of management considerations, the following discussion will be largely limited to this set, with the interested reader referred to other sources on project management [74,75].

Linkage of Project Phases

The distinction between a collection of methods and a *methodology* is the extent to which the methods are unified and coherently managed. The job of the software project manager is to guide the project through the different phases—determine when a project is ready to progress from one phase to the next and when it is necessary to back up to a previous phase to do further work.

At each stage, there is a need for documentation and review of the work, for continuing feasibility analysis, and for a check to make certain that the different phases are consistent with one another. As noted before, if there is no easy transition among the project phases (in both the forward and backward directions), then it is likely that errors will be introduced as a result of the transition. The manager must develop procedures to ease this transition, choosing compatible development tools at each stage. For example, SSA and Structured Design were intended to be used with one another, so that the transition from specification to design with those methods is likely to be easier than it would be with some other collection of techniques.

The intent of the linkage is to preserve effective communication of system progress throughout development and to maintain documents that show the status of a system throughout the different phases. Many organizations presently have satisfactory linkage along a small portion of the total project life cycle but have not extended their development methodology to cover the entire development cycle.

Evaluation of Progress

One of the most serious shortcomings of traditional approaches to information system development was that it was often difficult to determine whether satisfactory progress was being made and whether the project was likely to be completed successfully within time and budget constraints. The problem was that there were few, if any, intermediate milestones or products.

Thus, it was hard for a manager to see how well either individuals or the entire team was progressing. Programmers worked independently and only gave subjective estimates of their progress; their code and documentation were kept as "private property" rather than shared among the members of the group. The lack of communication among programmers frequently led to difficulties in interfacing various segments of code, as well as to widely disparate styles of programming, thereby complicating the testing and maintenance stages.

The intended effect of a system development methodology is to formalize the review procedures, to establish teamwork within a group with sharing of preliminary designs and code, and to make the intermediate products of the design process more visible. In this way, the manager can obtain an earlier evaluation of system quality, can identify any trouble areas, and gain a better idea of the progress of the project against its schedule.

Each of the technical procedures discussed above has some form of associated documentation or representation. A well-written specification or a comprehensible design representation is an excellent measure of progress. Best of all, they can be reviewed and evaluated.

Review and evaluation of project progress can be conducted either formally or informally, and may take place at one or more points during the system development activity. In any event, the objective of the review is to identify errors, locate potential problem areas, and measure progress against objectives.

Different techniques are appropriate at different stages. During the requirements analysis and definition stage, evaluation can be performed by the customers against the developer's preliminary functional specification. Similarly, the SADT author–reader cycle provides a mechanism for evaluating the accuracy of an SADT model and recommending changes. During the design stage, it is common to conduct design reviews and structured walkthroughs [76-78] to locate errors. During implementation, code inspections are useful to locate instances of poor programming style or incorrect logic. These manual techniques can serve as a valuable check against both major and minor errors in system specification, design, and implementation.

One other particularly useful management technique for controlling project progress is the appointment of a production program librarian, as incorporated in the Chief Programmer Team (CPT) approach to programming developed by IBM [79]. A program librarian has the responsibility of keeping track of all documents associated with a project and making sure that all members of the project team have access to those documents as needed. The librarian can also perform a variety of important clerical tasks, ranging from entering programs or documentation to typing manuals and reports. Experience seems to indicate that a person with a clerical background is more likely to perform well in this job than is a person with an information systems background, especially because this position represents an upward step in the career path of someone with clerical experience.

Personnel Deployment

Within any given information system development organization, the management must determine how to structure the organization and what assignments should be given to the individuals in that organization. Historically, most organizations have had similar structures, with project teams consisting of five to ten persons. The patterns of promotion have typically been from programmer to analyst to successive levels of management.

The traditional approach has suffered from several flaws. First, a person who is a good programmer is not necessarily a good analyst or a good manager. The types of individual trails and specific skills required for the different job roles are quite different. A programmer who is conversant with all of the low-level details of a specific machine and with the characteristics of a given language processor is often happiest when permitted to continue with nuts-and-bolts tasks; when given a job that involves working with people or dealing with nontechnical issues, the programmer does poorly. Similarly, persons with good managerial skills or problem-solving abilities are frequently unable to follow through with the task of constructing a correctly functioning program.

Thus, a system development methodology must provide alternative roles for individuals and find ways to use them appropriately on different projects. In addition, organizations must create career paths for persons who do not wish to switch between the technical and managerial sides of projects. A person with a very specific set of skills can be valuable to a large number of projects over time, and can be most valuable to the organization by continuing to use those skills on successively more challenging projects.

In addition to the Chief Programmer team organization, several other kinds of organizations have been used in conjunction with system development methodologies. The best of these are based on a "teams-of-specialists" approach. Rather than have a single project team go through all phases of system development, it is possible to pass a project from a requirements analysis team to a design team to an implementation team, and to make use of an independent quality-assurance team. In smaller organizations, many of the individuals may belong to more than one of the teams associated with a given project, but the idea is to make a sharp distinction between the phases by assigning responsibility for each phase to a different team. It is not necessary to use a completely different set of people in each phase; indeed, some continuity is often helpful if the particular individuals are able to "change hats" with each successive new phase.

Release Control

The development of a medium-to-large-sized information system involves the coordination of a large number of items, including user requirements, life cycle requirements, budgets, schedules, formal specifications, contracts, design documents, program code, test data and test results, user documentation, change requests, and so on. Even if a single individual is responsible for all of these items and even if all of these documents are stored on-line in compatible format, it is very easy to become overwhelmed by the volume of documentation and by the complexity of the system.

The situation becomes even more complex when a given system is intended to run in more than one execution environment and when the system is being modified during its lifetime. In such a situation, the assemblage of documentation and code representing a specific release of the system is a significant task, as is the decision concerning when to release new program modules or a new system to replace existing versions.

Effective management of this problem requires some form of *configuration management* [80], a formalized procedure that identifies every item associated with the project and keeps track of it. The configuration management process makes it practical to keep track of multiple versions of a system and to maintain project control that gives explicit authorization for each modification to the "current" system. Thus, in addition to managing the people within an organization and managing the structure of the organization, it is necessary to manage the software products of the organization, from their original conception through their final release at the end of their useful lifetime.

New Technical Procedures

In addition to running the individual projects, the management of an information system development organization must continually evaluate technical methods and management procedures. Once a methodology has been selected, it must be continually monitored to see if the techniques are working properly and if the individuals are satisfied with the methodology. It is often the case that specific methods, such as those described above, will have to be adapted for use on a given class of applications or wthin the structure of a given organization. The management is also responsible for training people in use of these techniques and making sure that they are used properly.

The selection and use of a methodology is not a one-time decision. The state of the art is highly volatile, with a large number of new techniques being introduced and used. Almost every conference and journal brings new ideas on programming methodology or system development techniques. Data in support of various ideas are just beginning to appear, so that one can base decisions concerning the use of specific techniques on the experience of others. (However, to this point, it does not appear that these experiences are directly transferable.)

The role of the management, then, is not only to select the methodology, but also to modify it over time, either by modifying techniques presently in use, or by introducing new techniques that seem to be more effective. In any case, change should proceed gradually, with ideas tried out on small, noncritical pilot projects, using persons who are motivated to try the innovative techniques and to assess them [81]. In that way, the information system development methodology for an organization can evolve and the organization can use current techniques that are well suited for their people and their applications.

Conclusion

This article has covered a broad spectrum of topics associated with the need for systematic procedures for the analysis, design, and implementation of information systems. These topics have included not only some of the successful technical methods that have been employed at each stage of the system life cycle, but also some of the underlying management concepts.

Because many of the ideas are new and largely untested, it is impossible to be prescriptive about many of the steps that should be taken to initiate and incorporate a system development methodology within an organization. It *is* clear, though, that previous methods for information system development were unreliable and that some more orderly approach to the development process is essential.

What is important now is for organizations to move toward such methodologies, try out new methods, and establish an openness to change, gradually integrating those techniques that seem effective and gradually extending their efforts to cover more of the system development life cycle. It is equally important for organizations to report on their experience with these techniques and with their collection into methodologies, so that improvements can be made in existing methods and new, more effective methods can be devised.

The payoffs of methodologies for information system design are considerable, including higher-quality systems, lower costs for testing and maintenance, greater personnel satisfaction, and better management control. With the rapidly increasing role of information systems in society, it is essential to utilize development techniques that will make it possible to build reliable and cost-effective systems that will properly serve their users.

Acknowledgments

Computing support was provided by National Institutes of Health grant RR-1081 to the University of California, San Francisco, Computer Graphics Laboratory; Principal Investigator, Dr. Robert Langridge.

The author gratefully acknowledges the cooperation of many developers and users of the techniques described here through informal discussions describing experiences. The author also wishes to thank the Benjamin Franklin Colloquium on Information Science, which encouraged him to write this article. Special thanks are due to Peter Freeman for many hours of discussion and Susan Stinson for her careful reading and detailed comments on an earlier version of this article.

References

1. Buxton, J.M.; Naur, P.; Randell, B., Eds. *Software Engineering Concepts and Techniques.* New York: Petrocelli/Chapter; 1976.
2. Wirth, N. "Program Development by Stepwise Refinement." *Communications of the ACM.* 14(4):221-227; 1971.
3. Parnas, D. "On the Criteria to be Used in Decomposing Systems into Modules." *Communications of the ACM.* 15(12): 1053-1058; 1972.
4. Liskov, B. "A Design Methodology for Reliable Software Systems." *Proceedings of the AFIPS 1972 FJCC.* 41 (part 1): 191-200; 1972.
5. Dahl, O.-J.; Dijkstra, E.W.; Hoare, C.A.R. *Structured Programming.* London: Academic; 1972.
6. Mills, H.D. "Mathematical Foundations for Structured Programming." Technical Report FSC 72-6012. Gaithersburg, MD: IBM Federal Systems Division; 1972.
7. Wirth, N. "The Programming Language Pascal." *Acta Informatica.* 1(1): 35-63; 1971.
8. Baker, F.T. "Chief Programmer Team Management of Production Programming." *IBM Systems Journal.* 11(1): 56-73; 1972.
9. Ross, D.T. "Structured Analysis (SA): a Language for Communicating Ideas." *IEEE Transactions on Software Engineering.* SE-3(1): 16-33; 1977.
10. Freeman, P. "A Perspective on Requirements Analysis and Specification." *Proceedings of the IBM Design '79 Symposium,* Monterey, CA; 1979.
11. Wasserman, A.I.; Stinson, S.K. "A Specification Method for Interactive Information Systems." *Proceedings: Specifications of Reliable Software.* IEEE Computer Society; 1979: 68-79.
12. Hamilton, M.; Zeldin, S. "Properties of User Requirements." In: Schneider, H.-J., Ed. *Formal Models and Practical Tools for Information Systems Design.* Amsterdam: North-Holland; 1979.
13. Gane, C.; Sarson, T. *Structured Systems Analysis.* Englewood Cliffs, NJ: Prentice-Hall; 1979.
14. DeMarco, T. *Structured Analysis and System Specification.* New York: Yourdon; 1978.
15. Ross, D.T.; Schoman, Jr., K.E. "Structured Analysis for Requirements Definition." *IEEE Transactions on Software Engineering.* SE-3(1): 6-15; 1977.
16. Teichroew, D.; Hershey III, E.A. "PSL/PSA: a Computer-Aided Technique for Structured Documentation and Analysis of Information Processing Systems." *IEEE Transactions on Software Engineering.* SE-3(1): 41-48; 1977.
17. Alford, M.W. "A Requirements Engineering Methodology for Real-Time Processing Requirements." *IEEE Transactions on Software Engineering.* SE-3(1): 60-69; 1977.
18. Bell, T.E.; Bixler, D.C.; Dyer, M.E. "An Extendable Approach to Computer-Aided Software Requirements Engineering." *IEEE Transactions on Software Engineering.* SE-3(1): 49-60; 1977.
19. Wasserman, A.I. "USE: a Methodology for the Design and Development of Interactive Information Systems." In: Schneider, H.-J., Ed. *Formal Models and Practical Tools for Information Systems Design.* Amsterdam: North-Holland; 1979.
20. Hamilton, M.; Zeldin, S. "Higher Order Software–a Methodology for Defining Software." *IEEE Transactions on Software Engineering.* SE-2(1): 9-32; 1976.
21. Guttag, J.V.; Horning, J.J. "The Algebraic Specification of Abstract Data Types." *Acta Informatica.* 10(1): 27-52; 1978.
22. Goguen, J.; Tardo, J.J. "An Introduction to OBJ: a Language for Writing and Testing Formal Algebraic Program Specifications." *Proceedings: Specifications of Reliable Software.* IEEE Computer Society; 1979: 170-189.
23. Lockemann, P.; Mayr, H.C.; Weil, W.H.; Wohlleber, W.H. "Data Abstractions for Database Systems." *ACM Transactions on Database Systems.* 4(1): 60-75; 1979.
24. Weber, H.J. "Modularity in Data Base System Design: a Soft-

ware Engineering View of Data Base Systems." In: Weber, H.J.; Wasserman, A.I., Eds. *Issues in Database Management.* Amsterdam: North-Holland; 1979: 65-91.

25. Wasserman, A.I. "The Extension of Abstract Data Types to Data Base Management." In preparation.

26. Roubine, O.; Robinson, L. "SPECIAL Reference Manual." Technical Report CSG-45. Menlo Park, CA: SRI International; 1976.

27. Robinson, L.; Levitt, K.N.; Neumann, P.G.; Saxena, A.R. "A Formal Methodology for the Design of Operating System Software." In: Yeh, R.T., Ed. *Current Trends in Programming Methodology.* Englewood Cliffs, NJ: Prentice-Hall; 1977: 61-110.

28. Spitzen, J.M. "An Example of Hierarchical Design and Proof." *Communications of the ACM.* 21(12): 1064-1075; 1978.

29. Hamilton, M.; Zeldin, S. "AXES Syntax Description." Technical Report TR-4. Cambridge, MA: Higher Order Software, Inc.; 1976.

30. Austin, S.L.; Buckles, B.P.; Ryan, J.P. "SSL—a Software Specification Language." Technical Report SAI-77-537-HU. Science Applications, Inc.; 1976.

31. Good, D.I.; et al. "Report on the Language Gypsy—Version 2.0." Certifiable Minicomputer Project, University of Texas at Austin, Report ICSCA—CMP—10, Revision 1, 1978.

32. Shneiderman, B.; Mayer, R.; McKay, D.; Heller, P. "Experimental Investigations of the Utility of Detailed Flowcharts in Programming." *Communications of the ACM.* 20(6): 373-381; 1977.

33. Yourdon, E.; Constantine, L.L. *Structured Design.* Englewood Cliffs, NJ: Prentice-Hall; 1979.

34. Myers, G.J. *Composite/Structured Design.* New York: Van Nostrand Reinhold; 1978.

35. Stay, J.F. "HIPO and Integrated Program Design." *IBM Systems Journal.* 15(2): 143-154; 1976.

36. *HIPO—a Design Aid and Documentation Technique.* White Plains, NY: Data Processing Division, IBM Corporation. Document GC20-1851.

37. Jackson, M.A. *Principles of Program Design.* London: Academic; 1975.

38. Riddle, W.; et al. "DREAM—a Software Design Aid System." In: Moneta, J., Ed. *Information Technology, Proceedings of the 3rd Jerusalem Conference on Information Technology.* Amsterdam: North-Holland; 1978.

39. Riddle, W. "An Event-Based Design Methodology Supported by DREAM." In: Schneider, H.-J., Ed. *Formal Models and Practical Tools for Information System Design.* Amsterdam: North-Holland; 1979.

40. Nassi, I.; Shneiderman, B. "Flowcharting Techniques for Structured Programming." *ACM SIGPLAN Notices.* 8(8): 12-26; 1973.

41. Yoder, C.M.; Schrag, M.L. "Nassi-Shneiderman Charts: an Alternative to Flowcharts for Design." *Proceedings of the Software Quality and Assurance Workshop. Software Engineering Notes.* 3(5): 79-86; 1978.

42. Caine, S.H.; Gordon, E.K. "PDL—a Tool for Software Design." *Proceedings of the AFIPS 1975 NCC.* 44: 271-276; 1975.

43. Warnier, J.D. *Logical Construction of Programs.* New York: Van Nostrand Reinhold; 1974.

44. Biggerstaff, T.J. "The Unified Design Specification System (UDS²)." *Proceedings: Specifications of Reliable Software.* IEEE Computer Society; 1979: 104-118.

45. Liskov, B.; Snyder, A.; Atkinson, R.; Schaffert, C. "Abstraction Mechanisms in CLU." *Communications of the ACM.* 20(8): 564-576; 1977.

46. Wulf, W.A.; et al., Eds. "An Informal Description of Alphard (preliminary)." Technical Report CMU-CS-78-105. Department of Computer Science, Carnegie-Mellon University; 1978.

47. Lampson, B.W.; et al. "Report on the Programming Language

Euclid." *ACM SIGPLAN Notices.* 12(2): 1-79; 1977.

48. Department of Defense Advanced Research Projects Agency. "Requirements for High Order Computer Programming Languages—'Steelman'." June 1978.

49. Wasserman, A.I., Handa, E.F.; Sherertz, D.D. "Report on the Programming Language PLAIN." Technical Report No. 34. Laboratory of Medical Information Science, University of California, San Francisco; 1978.

50. Freeman, P.; Wasserman, A.I.; Eds. *Tutorial on Software Design Techniques, 2nd ed.* Long Beach, CA: IEEE Computer Society; 1977.

51. Miller, Jr., E.F.; Howden, W.E., Eds. *Tutorial: Software Testing and Validation Techniques.* Long Beach, CA: IEEE Computer Society; 1978.

52. Yeh, R.T., Ed. *Current Trends in Programming Methodology.* 4 Vols. Englewood Cliffs, NJ: Prentice-Hall; 1977, 1978.

53. Turski, W.M. *Computer Programming Methodology.* Philadelphia: Heyden & Son; 1978.

54. *Proceedings of the 3rd International Conference on Software Engineering.* Long Beach, CA: IEEE Computer Society; 1978.

55. Bates, D., Ed. *Software Engineering Techniques.* 2 Vols. Maidenhead, England: Infotech International; 1977.

56. Kernighan, B.; Plauger, P.J. *The Elements of Programming Style, 2nd ed.* New York: McGraw-Hill; 1978.

57. Liskov, B.; Zilles, S.N. "Programming with Abstract Data Types." *ACM SIGPLAN Notices.* 9(4): 50-59; 1974.

58. Kernighan, B.; Plauger, P.J. *Software Tools.* Reading, MA: Addison-Wesley, 1976.

59. Fisher, D.A. "DoD's Common Programming Language Effort." *Computer.* 11(3): 24-33; 1978.

60. Ichbiah, J.D., Ed. "Preliminary Ada Reference Manual." *ACM SIGPLAN Notices.* 14(6); June 1979.

61. Wasserman, A.I. "The Data Management Facilities of PLAIN." *Proceedings of the ACM 1979 SIGMOD Conference.* 60-70; 1979.

62. McCracken, D.D. "The Changing Face of Applications Programming." *Datamation.* 24(12): 24-30; 1979.

63. Miller, Jr., E.F. "Program Testing Technology in the 1980's." *The Oregon Report: Proceedings of the Conference on Computing in the 1980's.* Long Beach, CA: IEEE Computer Society; 1978: 72-79.

64. Belady, L.A.; Lehman, M.M. "Characteristics of Large Systems." In: Wegner, P., Ed. *Research Directions in Software Technology.* Cambridge, MA: MIT Press; 1979: 106-138.

65. King, J.C. "Symbolic Execution and Program Testing." *Communications of the ACM.* 19(7): 385-394; 1976.

66. Howden, W.E. "Symbolic Testing and the Dissect Symbolic Evaluation System." *IEEE Transactions on Software Engineering.* SE-3(4): 266-278; 1977.

67. Suzuki, N. "Verifying Programs by Algebraic and Logical Reduction." *Proceedings of the 1975 International Conference on Reliable Software.* Long Beach, CA: IEEE Computer Society; 1975: 473-481. *ACM SIGPLAN Notices.* 10(6):473-481; 1975.

68. Musser, D.R. "Abstract Data Type Specification in the Affirm System." *Proceedings: Specifications of Reliable Software.* Long Beach, CA: IEEE Computer Society; 47-57.

69. Stucki, L. "New Directions in Automated Tools for Improving Software Quality." In: Yeh, R.T., Ed. *Current Trends in Programming Methodology, Vol. 2, Program Validation.* Englewood Cliffs, NJ: Prentice-Hall; 1977: 80-111.

70. Ramamoorthy, C.V.; Ho, S.F. "Testing Large Software with Automated Software Evaluation Systems." *IEEE Transactions on Software Engineering.* SE-1(1): 46-58; 1975.

71. Myers, G.J. *The Art of Software Testing.* New York: Wiley-Interscience; 1979.

72. Goodenough, J.B.; Gerhart, S.L. "Toward a Theory of Testing: Data Selection Criteria." In: Yeh, R.T., Ed. *Current Trends in Programming Methodology, Vol. 2, Program Validation.*

Englewood Cliffs, NJ: Prentice-Hall; 1977: 44-79.

73. Howden, W. "Theoretical and Empirical Studies of Program Testing." *IEEE Transactions on Software Engineering.* SE-4(4): 293-298; 1978.

74. Reifer, D.J., Ed. *Tutorial: Software Management.* Long Beach, CA: IEEE Computer Society; 1979.

75. *Second Software Life Cycle Management Workshop.* Publication 78CH1390-4C. Long Beach, CA: IEEE Computer Society; 1978.

76. Waldstein, N.S. "The Walk-Thru–a Method of Specification, Design, and Review." Technical Report TR 00.2536. IBM Data Processing Division, Poughkeepsie, NY; 1974.

77. Fagan, M.E. "Design and Code Inspections to Reduce Errors in Program Development." *IBM Systems Journal.* 15(3): 182-211; 1976.

78. Myers, G.J. "A Controlled Experiment in Program Testing and Code Walkthroughs/Inspections." *Communications of the ACM.* 21(9): 760-768; 1978.

79. Baker, F.T. "Structured Programming in a Production Programming Environment." *IEEE Transactions on Software Engineering.* SE-1(2): 241-252; 1975.

80. Bersoff, E.H.; Henderson, V.D.; Siegel, S.G. "Software Configuration Management: a Tutorial." *Computer.* 12(1): 6-14; 1979.

81. Wasserman, A.I. "Practical Strategies for Improving Software Development." In: Hosier, J., Ed. *Structured Analysis and Design.* Maidenhead, England: Infotech International; 1978: 357-368 (reprinted in ref. 50).

They who have written the books of science cease not to teach, though dead.

DeBury, *Philobiblon*

Indexers' Dreams

Far forward we reach
Arranging conversations;
Single-sided silent speech,
Fragile, groping, inchoate.

Inside one quiet pattern
Fitting an ideal dream,
Certainty escapes the net,
Yet yields: a time machine.

Karl F. Heumann

REUSABLE SOFTWARE ENGINEERING: CONCEPTS AND RESEARCH DIRECTIONS*

Peter Freeman

University of California
Irvine, California 92717

NOTE

This paper was presented at a research workshop and should be read with that in mind. It is included in *Tutorial: Software Design Techniques* because it treats in a broad manner a theme that is expected by many to become highly significant in the next five years. We have placed it in the introductory part of the book to emphasize the critical role of techniques and representations at all stages of development to enable effective reuse of software engineering results. PF.

ABSTRACT

The objective of reusable software engineering is to enable the broad reuse of all types of information found in development situations. This paper defines classes of information to be reused, discusses the processes and conditions surrounding reuse, and suggests research tasks that will improve our ability to practice reuse.

INTRODUCTION

The reuse of program code alone has almost no value. It is entirely inconsistent to exhort developers to put more effort into the analysis and design activities and not attempt to reuse the information generated there. While the reuse of a piece of code implicitly involves the reuse of analysis and design, great opportunity is missed by not being able to reuse *explicitly* the associated design and analysis information. This view underlies and motivates our interest in the reuse of *all* information generated in the course of development -- *reusable software engineering*.

Although the idea of reusing programs is quite old and has become an important aspect of the practical field of computer utilization, the current popular revival of the idea has yet to produce any significant agreement on the meaning of the term "reusability." Indeed, the range of topics selected for this workshop is a good indication of this! Our focus in this paper is on basic concepts of reusability and research needed to strengthen them and their application.

We assume readers of this paper are members of the research and advanced development community. While others may profit from what we have to say, we will not waste words on motivation or tutorial explanation.

Our purpose here, then, is threefold: To advance a particular view of reusability that guides our research; to provide a conceptual framework that will help organize and place in perspective other concepts and developments; and to suggest lines of research that flow from the conceptual framework.

This paper is organized into four major sections. Following this introduction, we discuss basic concepts and present our model of reusability. Then five major research areas with direct impact on reusability are outlined and illustrated with specific tasks that should be undertaken. We conclude the paper with a brief summary of reusable software engineering.

---
*This research supported by the National Science Foundation under grant MCS 81-03718 with the cooperation of the Air Force Office of Scientific Research

BASIC CONCEPTS OF REUSABILITY†

We consider three topics: What is being reused? How should it be reused? What is needed to enable successful reuse?

Reusable Information

Two observations lead us to a broad definition of what is being reused in software engineering. First, most of the economic motivations for reusability in programming relate to a reduction in the labor component necessary to bring into existence a new software system. Second, it is generally agreed that programming, narrowly defined, is only a small portion of the cost of creating a system. This leads us to define the *object* of reusability to be *any information which a developer may need in the process of creating software.*

We are *not* interested in the very important reuse of programs by multiple end-users upon multiple occasions (e.g., when an operating system is used on many different machines or a stress analysis program is used over and over for different calculations). Thus, the focus is on the information needed by the *developer* (or, the maintainer that is adding to an existing system).

This definition is far too broad to help us understand and push forward specific research, however. To narrow our scope of interest, Figure 1 presents a hierarchy of types of information that software developers typically need. These types will be explained below; while their definitions can be debated, they provide a concrete context in which to think about reusability.

The hierarchy in Figure 1 is not necessarily a strict ordering, nor have we shown all possible relations. The basic ordering principle is that if B falls below A in the graph then B cannot be realized (or, pragmatically, *should* not be realized!) without A; while the ordering is transitive, some redundant edges are included to emphasize the close connection of certain types of information (e.g., between application-area knowledge and functional architecture).

The labels on the right side of Figure 1 indicate levels of information. These group-

---

† This draws upon and extends our earlier work, including Freeman (1976, 1980, 1981).

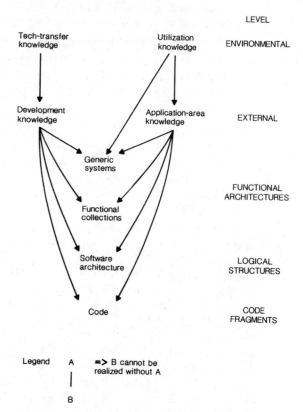

Figure 1 Hierarchy of Software Development Information

ings are not absolute, but they provide a useful set of abstractions that aid our understanding. In the following we will define each layer and the types of information contained within it.

Code Fragments. Executable code is often viewed as the primary product of the programmer and its effective reuse is one of the oldest objectives of software technology. Subroutines permit the reuse of code and this is apparently what most people mean by "reusability." Preserving the code product in a form that can be used again in new situations (by providing large, structured libraries of subroutines) is a current goal of several organizations.

The essential characteristics of this area of reusability are:

(a) the item being reused is a piece of executable code;

(b) the definition of the piece of code is often organization- or system-specific (e.g. uses a specific chart of accounts or assumes it will run under a particular operating system);

(c) the operational focus is on reducing the number of lines of code that a programmer must create in order to build a new application;

(d) Any single piece of code in the collection that can be reused probably has little or no operational meaning without being coupled with other pieces of code (hence, we use the term "fragments").

While there are obvious pragmatic differences, we do not differentiate here between PDL, higher-level language, or directly executable forms of "code." We include internal data structures in the definition of code. It should also be noted that the definition above concentrates on libraries of small pieces of code; larger pieces are often reused, including entire subsystems that are reused as an adjunct to some new system. This form of reuse is, of course, quite valuable so that our definition may over-emphasize the fragmentation aspect. The central issue, however, is the level of description of the information being reused, not its size.

Logical Structures. This level of information normally consists of both the process and data architectures of software. These architectures are characterized by their identification of the parts (modules, data collections) and the relationships between them (calling, parameter passing, inclusion). The parts are characterized functionally or semantically but not tied to any specific implementation. This is often called the *internal design* of a system.

Functional architectures. The external design of a system includes those aspects seen by the user or others that are not familiar with its internal structure. This level of information is normally a specification of functions and data objects -- a description of these entities without the details of how they are realized. We perceive two types of functional architectures that specifically relate to reusability objectives: functional collections and generic systems.

A *reusable functional collection* is a set of application functions that:

(a) are packaged as a unit;

(b) all pertain to a given application area;

(c) substantially cover the area;

(d) may be used separately.

Mathematical subroutine packages and SPSS are examples of reusable functional collections. The processing of statistical data or a set of standardized tests can often be handled by the application of a collection of functions to the data.

Other tasks -- for example, control of a complex manufacturing process -- may demand a more integrated system of functions. In this situation, a *generic system* may suffice for a given application and thus obviate the need for new development. A generic system is characterized by:

(a) consisting of a number of subsidiary functions;

(b) being organized so that the functions taken together all apply to a single, major function;

(c) being applicable to a number of different situations without modification of the code.

A primary difference in these two functional architectures is that a collection leaves out the order of application of functions while a generic system includes it.

External knowledge. The next level of information that may be reused is "external" because it is information that pertains to things outside the technical composition of the software itself. There are two rather different types of information here: application-area knowledge and development knowledge.

Application-area knowledge is whatever is known about a substantive area in which we are using a computer. For example, scientific laws, mathematical systems, and rules of accounting are all instances of application-area knowledge. In well-understood and mature areas (such as mathematics), our supply of application-area knowledge may be extensive, well-recorded, and easily reused. In other areas (such as hotel-management), the supply of knowledge may be largely informal, unrecorded, and consequently difficult to reuse.

Development knowledge is the information that we have regarding the process of developing a software system. This may include lifecycle models, workproduct definitions, test plans, and quality assurance checklists. We often do not think about reusing this information, but as we formalize our development processes there will increasingly be opportunities in which such items can be reused.

While seemingly disparate, these two types of information come together in the context of a development activity. Viewed abstractly, application-area knowledge provides the information necessary for making design decisions and development knowledge structures the sequence of those decisions.

Environment-level information. The highest level of information also consists of two rather different types of information that share a commonality -- they both deal with the relationship of all the lower levels of information to even broader categories of information that have nothing specific to do with software.

Utilization knowledge consists of what we know about how a software system is used in practice. For example, information about the way in which a hotel-management system fits into the overall operation of a hotel and knowledge about the way in which a particular mathematical theory is used in some branch of engineering are both instances of utilization knowledge. The distinction between this and application-area knowledge may be more one of orientation than any fundamental difference. However, in most situations we can distinguish the two by factoring out of the application-area knowledge information that describes the relationship between the application and the environment in which it is used. The two types of information, of course, must be used together, but for purposes of understanding and capturing them it is useful to separate them.

Technology-transfer knowledge is what we know about transferring new software technology to those people and situations involved with the development of software. It is, in effect, the utilization knowledge relating to the development knowledge.

We observe that communication among those interested in reusability would be greatly improved by having a common set of terms. We suggest that terms based on the type of information primarily being reused would be a useful scheme. Thus, we could talk about *code reuse, design reuse, specification reuse, test plan reuse, application model reuse* and so on.

Now that we have described *what* we wish to reuse, let us consider *how* it is to be reused.

Reusable Software Engineering

The previous section stresses the variety of information present in a development context. If our objective is to make development more efficient by reusing information, then clearly we must consider ways to reuse this entire spectrum of information.

It is this perspective that originally led us to propose (Freeman, 1980) the term *reusable software engineering* to denote software engineering activities that would both utilize existing information (reuse it) as well as produce, as a side-effect, information that could readily be reused in the future. Using SADT^{TM} notation, Figure 2 shows a simple model of reusable software engineering.

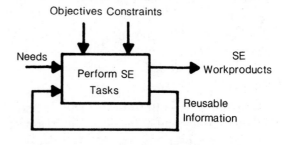

Figure 2. Simple Model of Reusable Software Engineering

The duality of this definition must be emphasized. On the one hand, the task before us is to modify existing software

---

^{TM}SADT is a trademark of SofTech, Inc.

engineering practices so that they take advantage of reusable information. On the other, we need to modify or augment these procedures so that they also produce information that can be reused in the future.

Figure 2 shows two distinct outputs. In practice, however, the reusable information and workproducts will often be the same as the end-result workproducts. Thus, for example, an architectural design that could be reused would not differ from a well-documented design that was produced without reusability in mind. (As will be discussed further below, this implies that the core of the reusability problem is to make sure that our systems are properly represented.) However, there may be additional information that is specifically intended for facilitating reuse. For example, a design rationalization (Freeman, 1975) that explains the design choices made and alternatives rejected could be of great value during reuse of a design but might have only limited use as part of the end product.

Finally, *reuse* has the connotation that one may use a workproduct in a situation other than the original one for which it was created with less effort than would be required to create a new workproduct. Modification of the workproduct in order to make it usable in the new situation is included in this connotation. We have not defined in how many new situations a workproduct must be usable in order to qualify as a reusable item. Informally, the cost of making a workproduct reusable should be amortized over some number of reuse instances; if it cannot be then the cost of reusing it (now including the amortized original development cost) will exceed the cost of developing the item *de novo*.

As a side note, it is important to observe the similarity between the levels of information and the concept of reusable software engineering on the one hand and the activities that go on during the evolutionary (maintenance) phase of a system's life on the other. We have not yet attempted a precise correlation, but informally we see a very close correspondence between the concepts presented here and those presented by Zvegintzov (1982). Intuitively, the "maintenance problem" appears to be a strict subset of the problem of reusing workproducts in original development; the primary restriction in the maintenance area is that the problem specification is usually better defined and the workproduct does not have to be located.

Having characterized what it is that we wish to reuse and indicated how the information is to be reused, we will now consider the third topic: What is needed to enable successful reuse?

Characterization of the Reusability Problem

In this section we provide an analysis of the problem of reusing software engineering information. This analysis, by decomposing the overall problem into pieces, structures and delineates some of the research results that are needed to make reusable software engineering possible.

We have previously (1976, 1980) characterized the reusability problem in terms of four questions and will follow that outline here. Our continued work in this area, however, has convinced us that we had "assumed away" one of the more critical aspects of reusability -- locating an appropriate set of information to reuse. Hence, what follows takes a somewhat broader view.

We assume a model of development that includes the following aspects:

(a)   a situation exists in which there is:

- a set of needs which potentially can be filled by a software system;

- a software professional attempting to meet those needs by creating the needed software;

- a supply of workproducts from previous development situations;

(b)   there is some defined sequence of steps that will be taken to create the needed software (that is, the overall task has been, or can be, decomposed into some reasonably well-defined set of tasks) and the results of these tasks (the work-products) form a chain of representations of the resulting software;

(c) at various points in the development, a need for certain creative results, expressed as a software engineering workproduct (such as a design, a functional specification, or a test plan), may arise.

At any such point, we can characterize the problem of software engineering reusability as the problem of successfully answering the following five *reusability questions:*

(a) Does there exist a workproduct that may be considered for reuse at this point in the development process?

(b) In what ways does an existing workproduct not meet our specific needs?

(c) In what ways can the workproduct be changed so that it does meet our needs?

(d) What side-effects (unintended changes in the workproduct characteristics) will these changes induce?

(e) What effects will these changes have on the workproducts that are derived later in the development chain from this workproduct?

These reusability questions capture the essence of the reuse problem. There are many ramifications, variations, and implications of these questions and their underlying assumptions, but we will not attempt an explication of them here. However, we must stress the centrality of the underlying assumption that software development is based on a decomposable process whose intermediate results can be represented as well-defined workproducts.

Indeed, the explication of these questions requires a deeper understanding of forming and manipulating representations of software than now exists. Our desire to answer these pragmatic questions leads in a natural way to certain research topics. The next section describes these.

RESEARCH IN REUSABILITY

We now focus on identifying research and advanced development topics that are relevant to reusability. For topics in each of the five information levels we have identified typical (but by no means the only or even the highest priority) projects of

three different expected payoff periods. Table 1 summarizes twenty-four topics that will contribute to reusable software engineering (as well as other areas). The suggested projects are labeled short-term (results available within 1 year); mid-term (1-5 years needed); and long-term (more than 5 years). Bear in mind that the objective of this paper is to identify *some* topics for further exploration; it is not intended to be a thorough characterization nor a complete survey.

Code Fragments

Transfer the Raytheon experience (short-term). A number of organizations could benefit immediately from carrying out reusability programs as Raytheon (Lanergan and Poynton, 1979) has done. To do so, they need to know about it, have clean descriptions of what to do, how it is done, how to develop such a program, and be able to share experiences in some systematic way. A guidebook for *reusable-software* engineering is needed.

Develop program description schemes (mid-term). One of the essential problems in reusing code fragments is to be able to locate an appropriate piece of code that is stored in a large collection of fragments. A standard descriptive system for classifying code fragments as to function, operational characteristics, error actions, and other parameters would permit the easy location and exchange of reusable code. Development of such a classification scheme is an iterative task since it will influence the nature of the supply of reusable code and in turn should be influenced by what exists. An initial attempt at this is underway at Irvine (Prieto-Diaz, 1983).

Develop component technology (long-term). A mature technology employing reusable code fragments would utilize consistent classification schemes for different areas, uniform packaging and quality assurance standards, and well-developed delivery mechanisms. Some of these elements exist and others don't. A long-term project to

Information level	Short-term	Mid-term	Long-term
Code Fragments	Transfer Raytheon-like experience	Develop program description schemes	Develop component technology
Logical Structures	Publish existing architectures	Develop inter-connection technology	Provide architecture visualization
Functional Architectures collections	Transfer SPSS experience	Improve system interfaces	Develop domain analysis methodology
generic systems	Document existing systems & failures	Develop specific generic designs	Develop system generation technology
External Knowledge applications	Study & describe current practice	Identify important factors by area	Formalize domains of knowledge
development	Publish workproduct definitions	Develop modifiable development guides	Integrate different approaches
Environment Knowledge utilization	Survey current utilization	Identify critical success factors	Identify long-range structural changes
technology transfer	Develop generalized reuse training	Study actual reuse situations	Understand developer reactions

TABLE 1: REPRESENTATIVE R & D PROJECTS

pull together and develop a coherent component technology is needed to demonstrate the economic and technical feasibility of this approach.

Logical Structures

This level of information is primarily concerned with the logical structure of systems of programs and data. The projects suggested deal with our ability to describe software and understand existing architectures.

Publish existing architectures (short-term). There are many application systems as well as operating systems that are widely used and that could serve as models for future systems -- in short that could be reused. Few systems are well-described architecturally even by the organizations that built them. Almost none are publicly described. The problems of retaining proprietary advantages may restrict public dissemination although systems in the public domain could be described), but there is no reason that large organizations could not do this on an internal basis. Valuable logical structure information exists now, just waiting to be put into a form that can be reused.

Develop interconnection technology (mid-term). The idea of programming-in-the-large (De Remer and Kron, 1976) is fundamental to the success of all types of code reusability and the creation of logical structures. Research on module interconnection languages (MIL's) should be continued because of its importance to reusability as well as original development. There should be a close tie between work on MIL's and efforts to standardize module packaging and descriptions. Prieto-Diaz and Neighbors (1982) survey the current state of the art in MIL's.

Provide architecture visualization (long-term). Logical structure information is valuable because it helps us understand the nature of the parts of a system and their interconnection without becoming bogged down in details. Simple graphical representations for the structure of a system are widely recognized as useful, although they are not so widely utilized. A significant extension of these descriptive capabilities into new dimensions could possibly provide us with powerful new understandings of system architectures, just as non-visible spectrum photographs of the earth provide us invaluable information about geological structures.

Functional Architectures

The reuse of code fragments or logical structures is pertinent when one is building a new system. If the end-user's task is well-defined and frequently encountered, then the reuse of software to support or automate an entire application task is appropriate. This situation can be divided into:

- reusable functional collections;

- generic systems.

We will treat generic systems in the next section. Some representative projects that would extend our ability to reuse functional collections are:

Transfer SPSS experience (short-term). SPSS [Klecka, Nie, and Hall, 1975] (and similar, competing packages) serves as an indispensable tool in the social sciences. Its

existence and usefulness clearly negates the need for writing many thousands of lines of code.

Why has it been successful? What are its characteristics? What was the history of its development? Answers to such questions, properly published, might aid the development of other widely used functional collections in areas of business (*e.g.*, market forecasting) or science (*e.g.*, differential equations).

Improve system interfaces (mid-term). Informal observation indicates that in many routine development environments, a major block to the effective reuse of existing functional packages is the difficulty or impossibility of employing a package as a subsystem to another system. There are a range of mechanisms needed here: better MIL's are a part of it; better inter-language connection capability within the context of a given language; better execution control environments. More advanced operating systems often include such capabilities (or at least rudimentary forms of them). Making those capabilities more widely available without having to completely change operating systems would be most valuable.

Develop domain analysis methodology (long-term). Domain analysis [Neighbors, 1980, 1983] is a generalization of systems analysis in which the objective is to identify the operations and objects needed to specify information processing in a particular application domain. The ultimate purpose is the creation of domain-specific languages that permit specifications to be written in terms meaningful in the domain.

In addition to their usefulness to system generation, tools such as Draco [Neighbors, 1980, 1983] and a domain analysis methodology will permit the easier identification of the elements of a reusable functional collection. For example, the basis of a functional collection for processing standardized tests is reported in [Gonzalez, 1981] and for real-time tactical displays in [Sundfor, 1983]. While domain analysis is possible with our current tools and understanding, our experience to date indicates the strong need for a better methodology. Development of it will not be rapid since it entails improving or adapting existing analysis tools and gaining experience with their application.

The following show promise for improving our ability to reuse generic systems.

Document existing systems (short-term). Generic systems exist today in a number of different areas (operating systems probably being the most ubiquitous). As the range and extent of computer applications rapidly increases, a simple way to facilitate their construction is by providing some well-documented models of existing generic systems. Special emphasis should be placed on the design and construction features that make the system generic (successes and failures).

Develop specific generic designs (mid-term). Although generic systems exist, we are unaware of generally-available designs (not code) that could be used to drive the construction of generic systems. Development of generic designs (and the resulting systems) for existing areas (*e.g.*, operating systems) or new applications would directly provide a greater stock of generic systems.

In the main, development of generic systems and other specific pieces of technology takes place in response to market opportunities. What we suggest in this case, however, is that generic development of particular systems could meet immediate demands of governmental bodies for lower software costs and at the same time provide leadership in showing others how to develop such systems.

Develop system generation technology (long-term). The next step beyond generic systems is to be able to generate similar systems rapidly, either automatically or with computer assistance. The power of program generation tools needs to be greatly increased. Draco is an example of work that will contribute directly to generation capability and indirectly to our understanding of the nature of generic systems.

External Knowledge Level

The first level of information "outside" a system is knowledge about the application area and about the development process itself. Knowledge about application areas includes almost all knowledge -- clearly more than we can cope with!! However, several specific projects would help us more readily reuse information from the applications-knowledge level.

Study and describe current practice (short-term). One of the simplest forms of application knowledge that should be reused is basic understanding of what goes on in specific applications. For example, how are customer enquiries processed in a service industry, how are payrolls processed in a firm, how are inventory levels managed in a warehouse? There are, of course, entire textbooks on some of these application areas, but they often contain too much information. The seemingly trivial step of providing clear, simple models of the flow and use of information in specific application areas could provide application developers a source of information that would be useful and readily reusable.

Identify important factors by area (mid-term). More difficult than simply describing what goes on in an application area is the task of determining what the critical operational factors are (in an information-processing sense). For example, knowing that it is the change in inventory levels, not the absolute magnitudes, that is the crucial factor in a particular application would be a piece of information that could be very important to an application developer. In essence, we are suggesting that in areas where the application level knowledge can be often reused that it would be worth identifying and empirically validating the key factors from an applications perspective.

Formalize domains of knowledge (long-term). If what goes on in an application area is understood and the key parameters have been identified, then an attempt can be made to formalize that knowledge. There are ways of capturing and representing application domain knowledge other than the domain analysis approach discussed above. For example, building models, devising sets of assertions, and preparing decision rules are all ways of capturing domain knowledge. It is the general form of this activity that we are suggesting here.

Also "external" to actual systems, but equally crucial, is knowledge about the development process. This knowledge, too, needs to be reused. The following are tasks which we believe would help us reuse development knowledge more readily.

Publish workproduct definitions (short-term). In order to reuse a specification or a design it is necessary to have a formal workproduct thaown definitions but inhibits reuse of their efforts.

While sethe publication of suggested workproduct definitions (along with examples) for a variety of development situations would have an immediate and beneficial impact. The objective is not to standardize workproducts but to upgrade the formality of typical workproducts as a first step toward encouraging reuse.

Devise modifiable development guidelines (mid-term). A pressing need in many organizations today is for a set of combined management/technical development guidelines that combine workproduct definitions, quality guidelines, and management review procedures. For an organization to reuse effectively the various workproducts it produces, it is essential that it follow a relatively formal set of guidelines. (See the Methodman report [DoD, 1982] for more discussion of this.)

Several commercial guidelines exist and a number of organizations have developed their own. Yet, most organizations do not have a set of guidelines in use and when faced with adopting a set, often find they must modify them. With a reasonable amount of effort a modifiable set of guidelines could be produced. The modification could be guided by an interactive program and the guidelines generated automatically. The resulting facility would permit an organization to put a set of guidelines into place much more readily than at

present. In turn, this would greatly facilitate the reuse of development efforts within an organization.

Integrate different approaches (long-term). Most of the techniques discussed so far could probably be magnified in impact if they were integrated with one another and with other aspects of software technology in appropriate ways. Research directed at developing integrated reuse methodologies, perhaps incorporating development perspectives other than traditional software engineering world-views [Kerola and Freeman, 1981] is needed. An important aspect of such work will be the choice of and experimentation with specific techniques to shed more light on their effectiveness. It should be noted that this type of integration, but aimed at *de novo* development methods, is one of the primary foci of the STARS Program [DoD, 1983].

Environmental Knowledge

The distinction between external and environmental level knowledge may be somewhat arbitrary. However, a distinction can be drawn between knowledge that is used directly in the construction of a system (*e.g.*, standard workproduct definitions or information about keyboard operator reaction times) and knowledge that relates more to the surrounding environment.

In the latter category, we distinguish two types of information: that which relates to the transfer of any of the types of knowledge we have been discussing and that which relates to the utilization of the systems we build. Utilization knowledge is the province of economics, organizational studies, and other fields that describe situations in which the utilization of computing systems has an impact. Our concern here is to find ways to extract useful information from those types of studies and make it readily reusable by those trying to build new systems. We suggest three things:

Survey current utilization (short-range). The systematic study of how computers are used is still in its infancy. More studies of this type, reported in a way that will help developers (in the broad sense) use the knowledge gained, should lead to improved systems.

Identify critical success factors (mid-range). This is analogous to the task suggested above under applications-area knowledge, only applied to the entire environment in which a system is utilized. Here the question is not what is the important factor within the substantive application area (*e.g.* inventory management), but rather what were the important factors for success in the environment in which the application was applied (e.g. an organization that centers its business on distribution of goods).

Identify structural changes (long-range). In the long-run, computer applications will have important structural changes on most organizations and the relationships of people within them. Identifying these changes and helping us understand cause and effect relationships will provide invaluable information that can be used in the future to help guide the creation of systems.

Technology transfer is only one of many types of environmental knowledge, but is one that has particular importance to software development. The core of the issue here is to be able to reuse knowledge about how to transfer new knowledge of all types to those that are specifically concerned with the reuse of software engineering results. We have identified three specific projects:

Develop generalized reuse training courses (short-term). Teaching programmers to build or use reusable workproducts is different from teaching someone to program. Generalized courses that are independent of organization and application areas can certainly be developed and could then be used by specific organizations in setting up their own reuse programs.

Study actual reuse situations (mid-term). The adoption of reusability strategies by an organization constitutes a major innovation in their way of doing business. Actual reuse situations need to be studied to determine the economic payoffs and the human/organizational impacts.

The need for and use of the economic aspect of the study is clear. The human/organizational aspects are critical in the long run because acceptance of the new procedures is the key. Because it involves innovation and change of a fairly radical nature in the work pattern of individuals, we need to understand as clearly as possible what the relevant factors are and how people react to them.

Understand programmer's reactions (long-term). We can identify factors and record people's reactions in a moderate amount of time. To understand *why* they react the way they do is a more ambitious and long-range effort. As with most of the longer-term projects outlined in this report, the payoffs would be directly to reusability and indirectly to the larger question of innovation in computing [cf. Kling and Scacchi, 1980].

Relationship To Other R&D Areas

It should be clear that reusability is an approach or way of looking at the software development problem. In that sense it is not a completely separate area of work (such as compiler theory or language design) which can be precisely compared to other areas. As with most software engineering research, there is a high degree of overlap with other, more narrow, research areas.

One way of looking at reusability is to consider it as an end-use focus for many other, more specific, research areas. For example, work on development lifecycle models has existed for some time. In the context of reusability, research aimed at understanding and explicating the properties of a particular lifecycle model might still be roughly the same but could be directed toward the explicit goal of evaluating the usefulness of that particular model for enhancing our ability to reuse software engineering workproducts.

There is a very strong underpinning of representational concerns in reusability.

Thus, most research aimed at languages, especially for expressing designs, is fundamental to reusability.

Similarly, work on methods for transforming representations and/or determining properties of specific instances using a representation is central to the concerns of reusability. This means, for example, that the work on representations in artificial intelligence is quite relevant to this area.

Portability and transferability of programs has long been a sought after goal and one even addressed by a few explicit research projects. Obviously the techniques for portability that have been developed apply, as would any future work. However, the emphasis in reusable software engineering, in our opinion, should be more on the reusability of designs and analysis information so that some of the work in other areas (such as AI) is more relevant

CONCLUSION

In order to be able to reuse software engineering results, we must:

(1) Have *complete representations* of the information that makes up any particular workproduct. If part of a design is stored only in the designer's head, we cannot reliably reuse it at arbitrary times in the future.

(2) Possess *modification procedures* that permit us to change a given workproduct in predictable ways in order to meet new constraints. These procedures may be as simple as changing the source of an input file in a detailed (PDL) design or as complex as altering the timing constraints in a specification.

(3) *Be able to locate* needed workproducts in a reasonable amount of time. An underlying premise of reusability is that many of the workproducts needed in everyday software development already exist; as is well understood, one of the primary problems is that it is difficult to locate the appropriate one in less time than it takes to create a new one.

(4) Have some *standardization of lifecycles and workproducts.* Reusability within an organization is certainly the place to start, but, eventually we must be able to reuse workproducts across the entire industry. This obviously requires some coherency on the major phases of development and the definition of the workproducts produced in each.

(5) *Educate* technical people and managers differently. One of the major blocks to reusability is the "not invented here" syndrome; yet, in other fields, standard parts and designs are often used.

The R&D directions suggested above are intended to address these desired conditions.

In closing, we would note two things: First, in defining areas for R&D exploration the emphasis should be on the expected results of the work. If this is done, then the relationship of an existing effort (similarly described) can be readily determined. Second, reusable software engineering is not the only approach to improving our ability to create software, of course, but it does hold the promise of significant gains in quality and productivity.

ACKNOWLEDGEMENT

The appreciable contribution of Jim Neighbors to these ideas is gratefully acknowledged. It is a pleasure to thank Sue Rose, Dennis Volper, and, most especially, Pat Harris for producing the typeset copy.

BIOGRAPHY

Peter Freeman is an Associate Professor of Information and Computer Science at the University of California, Irvine, and Director, Reuse Project.

Dr. Freeman's research activities have been concentrated in software design and analysis techniques and their application to the development process. His current research focuses on reusable software engineering. He is active in professional organizations, serves on several editorial boards, and has lectured widely on software engineering. He serves as a consultant to numerous industrial and governmental organizations and is President of Software Environments, Inc.

Dr. Freeman is Consulting Editor, McGraw-Hill Series in Software Engineering and Technology, and Academic Review Board Member, IBM Systems Research Institute. He has published numerous technical papers and is the author of *Software Systems Principles* (SRA, 1975). In addition, he has jointly edited (with Professor A. I. Wasserman) two books: *Software Engineering Education* (Springer-Verlag, 1976) and *Tutorial on Software Design Techniques, 4th Edition* (IEEE Computer Society, in press). He received his Ph.D. in computer science from Carnegie-Mellon University in 1970.

Mailing address: Information and Computer Science Department, University of California, Irvine, CA, 92717.

Telephone: 714-856-6064 or 714-856-7403.

Arpanet: Freeman@USC-ECLB.

REFERENCES

De Remer, F., and Kron, H. Programming-in-the-large versus Programming-in-the-small. IEEE Transactions on Software Engineering, 1976, SE - 2(2), 80-86.

DoD. Software Technology for Adaptable, Reliable Systems (STARS) Program Strategy. Department of Defense, 1983.

DoD. Ada Methodologies: Concepts and Requirements. Ada Joint Program Office, U.S. Department of Defense, 1982.

Freeman, P. Towards Improved Review of Software Designs. In the proceedings of 1975 National Computer Conference. Anaheim, CA: AFIPS, 1975.

Freeman, P. Reusable Software (Research proposal) Irvine, CA: University of California, ICS Dept., 1976.

Freeman, P. Reusable Software Engineering: A Statement of Long-Range Research Objectives (Tech. Rep. TR-159). Irvine, CA: University of California, ICS Dept., 1980.

Freeman, P. Research Directions in Reusable Software Engineering (Tech. Rep.). Irvine, CA: University of California, ICS Dept., 1981.

Gonzalez, L. A Domain Language for Processing Standardized Tests (MS Thesis). Irvine, CA: University of California, ICS Dept., 1981.

Kerola, P., and Freeman, P. Comparison of Lifecycle Models. In the proceedings of the 5th International Conference on Software Engineering. San Diego, CA: 1981.

Klecka, W.R., Nie, N.H., and Hull, C.H. Statistical Package for the Social Sciences Primer. New York: McGraw-Hill, 1975.

Kling, R., and Scacchi, W. Computing as Social Action: The Social Dynamics of Computing in Complex Organizations. Advances in Computing, 1980, 19, 250-327.

Lanergan, R.G. and Poynton, B.A. Reusable Code--The Application Development Technique of the Future. In the proceedings of IBM SHARE/GUIDE Software Symposium. Monterey, CA: 1979.

McIlroy, M.D. Mass-Produced Software Components. In Buxton, et al (Eds.) Software Engineering Concepts and Techniques. Petrocelli/Charter, 1976, 88-98.

Neighbors, J. Software Construction Using Components (Ph.D. Thesis and Tech. Rep. TR-160). Irvine, CA: University of California, ICS Dept., 1980.

Neighbors, J. The Draco Approach to Constructing Software from Reusable Components. Workshop on Reusability in Programming. Newport, RI: ITT, 1983.

Prieto-Diaz, R. A Software Classification Scheme (Ph.D. Thesis, in progress). Irvine, CA: University of California, ICS Dept., 1983.

Prieto-Diaz, R. and Neighbors, J. Module Interconnection Languages: A Survey (Tech. Rep. TR-189). Irvine, CA: University of California, ICS Dept., 1982.

Sundfor, S. Draco Domain Analysis for a Real Time Application: The Analysis (Tech. Rep. RTP 015). Irvine, CA: University of California, 1983a.

Sundfor, S. Draco Domain Analysis for a Real Time Application: Discussion of the Results (Tech. Rep. RTP 016). Irvine, CA: University of California, 1983b.

Zvegintzov, N. What life? What cycle? In the proceedings of AFIPS 1982 National Computer Conference. Houston, TX: AFIPS, 1982, 561-568.

Part II

Analysis Techniques

Before the technical process of design can occur, one must understand the problem to be solved and have a clear picture of what is to be designed and built. While this statement seems intuitively obvious, failure to understand requirements and constraints is a fundamental cause of problems with software projects.

We prefer to distinguish analysis from specification, which is the subject of Part III. Analysis is the process of understanding a problem and its context, along with identifying the requirements for a solution. Specification, or more accurately *functional specification*, is a description of the functions that are to be performed by a system (along with the data to be processed). While the activities of analysis and functional specification often overlap significantly, it should be clear that they serve different purposes, so that we can separately discuss methods for each.

Modern approaches to requirements analysis may be process-oriented, data-oriented, or user-oriented. In the first case, a system is analyzed in terms of the activities that are performed; in the second case, a system is analyzed in terms of the data that are used; in the last case, a system is analyzed in terms of what the user can do.

As we shall see, many of the techniques are hybrid, providing two or more of these approaches. It should be noted, though, that a thorough job of analysis demands that all these aspects of a system be addressed. In evaluating an analysis method, then, one can see the relative strengths and weaknesses of that method for analyzing processes, data, and the user interface to the system.

The first paper, by Freeman, describes some of the current trends and concepts in this area and introduces several of the techniques described in other papers. The next two papers provide an overview of SADT^{TM}, as developed by Doug Ross and his associates. The paper by Ross and Schoman discusses the nature of requirements definition and provides an excellent discussion of the concepts that must underlie the requirements

---

TM_{SADT} is a trademark of SofTech, Inc.

analysis and specification processes. Ross' "Structured Analysis" paper describes the philosophy behind and some of the details of the SADT nomenclature, presenting part of an SADT model that rationalizes the features of SADT. This latter paper is occasionally difficult to read, but it is the only publicly available paper providing detailed information about SADT.

Structured Systems Analysis (SSA) was developed to provide an analysis tool to be used together with Structured Design (see Part V). Two variants of SSA have emerged, one created by Tom DeMarco of Yourdon, Inc. (see DeMarco, *Structured Analysis and System Specification*, Prentice-Hall, 1979), and the other developed by Chris Gane and Trish Sarson. Both have become relatively popular in the past five years and are widely used, particularly on commercial applications.

Gane's paper on Structured Systems Analysis illustrates the SSA notation and shows how SSA supports a joint approach to program and data development, based on the development of data flow diagrams incorporating data stores. It serves as a brief summary of the ideas presented in the books on SSA. Gane strongly advocates the use of data dictionary facilities with SSA in order to maintain information on data stores, data elements, and processes.

While there are some notational and philosophical differences between the DeMarco approach and the Gane/Sarson approach to Structured Systems Analysis, Gane's paper illustrates the basic concepts that underlie both approaches.

A third method for analysis is ISAC (Information Systems work and Analysis of Changes), developed by Mats Lundeberg and colleagues in Sweden, beginning in the early 1970's. ISAC uses an activity modelling technique known as A-graphs as the first step of a methodology for information systems development. Lundeberg's paper gives on overview of A-graphs and the emphasis that ISAC gives to user involvement in the analysis and development effort.

The reader will note similarities among SADT activity diagrams, SSA dataflow diagrams, and ISAC

A-graphs. Indeed, these notations (and others), all employ some form of boxes and arrows to show activities, data flows, data objects, inputs, and outputs. All these methods are essentially modeling activities, and there are a limited number of concepts to be modeled.

All three of these methods (SSA, SADT, and ISAC) are *predominantly* process-oriented, in the sense that their users focus on activity modelling and that there is no conceptual data model associated with the activity model. (One might claim that the relational data model used in SSA serves that purpose, though.)

Bubenko, by contrast, proposes a data-oriented approach to analysis, using a conceptual data model. He views a conceptual database model and a conceptual processing model as being developed in parallel from a conceptual information model. The conceptual information model is created from a set of data types, entities, and events that are stated in a predicate calculus-like language. Bubenko's events are, in some ways, similar to the activities analyzed in the other approaches.

There is a growing tendency to examine systems from more than one perspective during the analysis phase, and the work of database mdoelling is becoming increasingly influential in information system development methodologies, if not over the entire range of software development methodologies. The increasing discussion of "object-oriented" approaches to software development (see, for example, Booch's paper in Part VI) is a reflection of the complementarity of processes and objects.

In short, as soon as one analyzes the operations (processes) in a system, one must identify the objects upon which they operate. Conversely, data objects are not static, so any analysis of the objects must also lead to identification of the meaningful operations upon those objects.

Interest in user-oriented design is growing rapidly, but it is not yet widely reflected in formal analysis techniques. Some of the techniques described in Part IV for external design address this subject to some extent, as does the User Software Engineering approach, described by Wasserman in Part IX.

REQUIREMENTS ANALYSIS AND SPECIFICATION: THE FIRST STEP

P. Freeman
University of California
Irvine, California

ABSTRACT

A multidimensional revolution has been taking
place in computing that is having an increasing impact
on the way in which computing systems and their applications are developed. This paper will outline the
state of the art of defining objectives for software
development. A set of trends are first identified.
Then several currently used techniques are briefly
described.

WHAT IS REQUIREMENTS ANALYSIS? WHAT IS SPECIFICATION?

The characteristics of the software revolution are
well-known: the cost of hardware is dropping while its
power continues to increase dramatically, the complexity of software[1] (especially in applications areas) is
increasing at highly non-linear rates, and the cost of
producing software (both in relative and absolute terms)
is soaring. A less well-understood aspect of the revolution is the increasing difficulty (and hence cost)
of "maintaining" software after it has been initially
developed.

Software engineering is an emerging field of academic and practical activity that provides the tools,
techniques, and methods necessary to apply the knowledge of computer science and other areas in a systematic way to achieve desired development objectives. An
important part of software engineering, as with traditional engineering disciplines, is concerned with defining objectives and establishing constraints on the
nature of the solution to be developed in later design
and construction activities. This "front-end" activity is our focus here.

To be more specific:

> Requirements analysis is the process of un-
> derstanding and recording in a clear form the
> requirements or needs to be met by the de-
> sign and construction of a system. A re-
> quirements analysis results in a require-
> ments definition (a specific workproduct).

> Specification is the process of describing
> the external or functional nature of a sys-
> tem proposed to meet some set of require-
> ments. A specification process results in a
> functional specification (also sometimes
> called a design spec).

While we have tried to be as specific as possible here
to aid your understanding, you must be warned that
these terms are used in many conflicting and imprecise
ways in practice. The underlying concepts must be
clearly understood and referred to in order to under-

stand properly any specific instance of their usage:
Requirements refer to the needs of people and organizations and specifications are descriptions (of systems)
that describe what but not how.

Another way of differentiating the two is to recognize that requirements analysis has essentially the
same objectives as systems analysis (but uses different
techniques and prescribes different standards for the
workproduct produced). Similarly, specification is an
activity that has been practiced for some time by designers and programmers, but the thing that is new is
the perception of how to do it significantly better
than in the past.

The objective of this paper, then, is twofold:
First, we will identify some general trends that will
help you understand better what is happening in this
area of software engineering. Second, we will survey
some of the tools and methods currently in use for requirements analysis and specification.

We will assume you are a programmer, system designer, analyst, applications engineer, or manager who
has some knowledge about software development and is
seeking an update. This paper is not intended for the
sophisticate who is trying to develop new methods or
tools.

SOME TRENDS AFFECTING REQUIREMENTS ANALYSIS AND
SPECIFICATION

In this section we will briefly discuss five
trends that will help you better understand the specific tools and techniques discussed later.

Life-cycle Awareness

The nature of early computing applications (scientific and engineering calculations), the rapid
growth of the technology, and the professional background of many of the early people in computing combined to obscure a fact that is now obvious: Software,
like any engineered artifact, goes through a life-cycle
of birth, growth, maturation, and death. In the case
of software, the terms analysis, design, construction,
and evolution (operation coupled with repair, adaptation, and enhancement) are typically used to describe
the phases of this life-cycle. (See [1] for further
discussion.)

The trend that is affecting what we do in development is the awareness that what we do in early phases
of the life-cycle may have tremendous impacts on the
cost and the quality of later phases. Specifically,
there often seems to be an inverse-law operating that
prevents the detection of errors introduced early until
very late in the life-cycle. This fact (which is due
to the technical characteristics of most development
activities), coupled with the greatly increased cost of
fixing problems in a running system over fixing them
before the design is committed to executable code,
places a great premium on doing the front-end activities correctly and in a way that will permit the early
detection of errors.

---

[1]We use "software" to refer to any collection of
two or more programs (system programs or applications).
Since good design demands that programs be small, this
definition covers most efforts involving programming.

Understanding and Communication

The primary purpose of the first stages of development must be to understand the problem and to communicate that understanding. Before requirements can be accurately stated or an effective design proposed, it is necessary to understand the problem.

Understanding means more than just giving a superficial classification of a problem. It means determining the various parts of the problem, not only in technical terms, but in human and organizational terms. It means identifying constraints that any eventual design must meet and determining contract conditions that will permit one to develop a pragmatic and economic solution.

Having developed a thorough understanding of the problem and the potential solutions, this understanding must be communicated to others. It must be communicated to the customer who has commissioned the system in the first place to make sure that the problem is correctly understood. It must also be communicated to the system designer, to analysts working on other parts of the system, and to management.

Realization of these basic purposes of requirements analysis and specification has led people to provide increased support for them through appropriate methods and tools. Reference [2] contains a good discussion of this trend.

Non-procedural Statements

Programming, of course, is concerned with procedures or sequences of actions. As we understand more about the types of systems we build, however, it is clear that in many instances the early consideration of sequencing leads to poorly structured systems that are hard to test and even harder to adapt and enhance over the lifetime of the system.

The positive way to look at this is to note that the emphasis in the early stages of development should be on the structure of a system, not on the detailed flow of control. This objective is showing up in the technology for requirements analysis and specification in the form of techniques that force you to pay attention to structure and to data flow (not control flow) and in languages that permit you to describe system components functionally without describing how those functions are carried out.

Support for Technical Concepts

Software development, while still chaotic in many respects, has matured to the point of being able to identify important technical concepts whose usage will help us achieve better quality systems. Three of those concepts are modularity, interfaces, and data abstraction.

The concept of modularity in software is to break a total system up into small units that can be specified, designed, and programmed in isolation from the rest of the system. More correctly, we say that such units can be built knowing only their function and their explicit connections to the rest of the system.

Interfaces are, of course, the defined connections between system parts. While the concept is old, the new realization is that such interfaces must be designed just as carefully as the units they connect. Indeed, in some cases, the design of the interfaces may be more critical than the design of the units themselves.

Data abstraction, simply put, is the concept of separating the representation of a data object by programs. A simple example is the storage of lists of information. An application program may need to create and manipulate lists. To operate on lists, it should not need to know how those lists are actually represented in memory.

The importance of these and other concepts (see [3] for further discussion) necessitates that software engineering tools and methods provide support for them. Thus, for example, specification languages are usually designed very carefully to make sure that one can express desired modularity and interfacing between system components.

Automation

The last trend discussed here is toward increased automation or automated support of requirements analysis and specification. There is no question that automated support can be valuable in the case of very large requirements definitions or specifications. Such support is essential for helping determine consistency and completeness of a large workproduct. It is also clear that the rigor of expressing one's thoughts in a language that can be processed by machine is useful.

On the other hand, machine processable languages are not able to express everything that needs to be said about a set of requirements. More importantly, highly formal languages are very poor for communicating with people, especially non-technical people. Since this is one of the more important aspects of requirements analysis, usage of such languages may detract from the overall goal of establishing a viable set of requirements. Thus, this trend toward automation has to be viewed as a two-edged sword.

Other Trends

In general, the intellectual understanding of requirements analysis and specification is not high. It is an activity that is often performed poorly and, until recently, not in any great amount in the software area. The trends we have identified here (see [4] for discussion of some other concepts) should be viewed merely as the current state of our understanding.

A BRIEF SURVEY OF REQUIREMENTS ANALYSIS AND SPECIFICATION TECHNIQUES[2]

The techniques presented here are adequately described elsewhere. Our objective is simply to introduce them.

Structured Analysis and Design Technique (SADT)[TM]

SADT is a methodology developed by Douglas T. Ross [5] that is useful for requirements analysis as well as for design [6]. It is a general-purpose modeling technique that is applicable to a wide range of problems, not just computer applications. It has been in use since 1974 by several organizations and is relatively well-known in the software engineering field.

SADT consists of three things: a set of methods that assist the analyst in understanding a complex subject, a graphical language for communicating that understanding, and a set of management and human-factors considerations for guiding and controlling the use of the methods and the language.

The methods of SADT are based on several concepts: Top-down decomposition is used to break complex topics up into small pieces which can be understood more readily. Model building provides both a way of communicating and a way of understanding through abstraction from the real world. Establishing and using explicit

---

[2] A part of this section is taken from [4].

[TM] SADT is a trademark of SofTech, Inc.

viewpoints and purposes for each model will help to control and limit the information in a model. Review and iteration are used to insure the quality of the model. Complementary analysis approaches are used to build on the activity/object duality of most situations.

The graphical language of SADT uses boxes and arrows coupled together in a simple syntax. The basic unit in the language is a box that indicates an activity (in an actigram) or an object (in a datagram): the arrows indicate flows of data between activities (actigrams) of the activities that operate on data (datagrams). An SADT diagram is drawn on a standard, single-page form to communicate the analyst's message about a particular subject; a diagram must contain between three and six boxes and their interconnecting arrows. Figure 1 is an example of an SADT activity diagram.

SSA is a partial methodology, some of whose components bear a strong resemblance to SADT. There are two similar versions [8], [9], which are sometimes referred to simply as structured analysis; we prefer the term structured systems analysis, however, to differentiate them from SADT and to indicate their cultural background. They are recent in origin, but are beginning to be employed widely in traditional data processing environments.

SSA uses many of the same concepts as SADT, including top-down problem decomposition, use of graphical language, and model building as a means of communicating with users. In addition, it incorporates some important data base concepts. We have labeled SSA a partial methodology because its components are not as well integrated as they might be and because it does

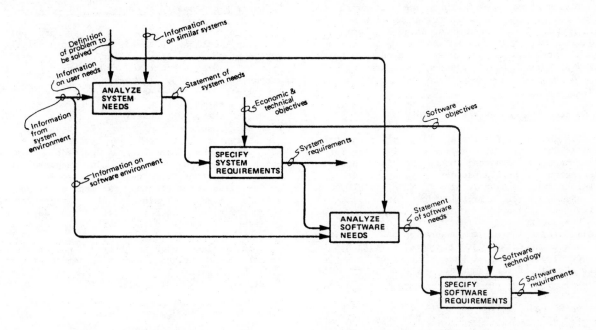

Figure 1: SADT Actigram showing the process of producing software requirements

An SADT model is an ordered collection of diagrams. The diagrams are related in a precise manner so that they fit together to form a coherent model of the subject. The number of diagrams in a model is determined by the breadth and depth of analysis that is required for the purpose of that particular model.

The management techniques of SADT have been chosen to coordinate and obtain the best results from the technical methods and tools. Included are document control procedures to keep track of the various stages of a model, review and approval standards for individual diagrams, and project estimation guidelines.

The graphical language of SADT and the procedures for using it are similar to an engineering drawing system, making it natural to use in traditional engineering situations (it's developer was instrumental in the development of numerically-controlled machine tools). The analysis and modelling techniques of SADT are geared to large and/or complex systems and it has been successfully used on a variety of projects (not just software). Its primary value in requirements analysis is that it provides a methodology for understanding complex requirements and recording that knowledge in a clear and precise form

Further information on SADT may be found in [7].

Structured Systems Analysis (SSA)

not presently include much in the way of management guidelines.

There are four features in SSA: data flow diagrams, data dictionaries, process logic representations, and data-store structuring techniques. SSA's data flow diagrams are very similar to SADT actigrams, although there are some important differences. In particular, the decomposition appears to be used rather loosely and a more complicated graphical notation is used that includes showing data stores directly on the data flow diagram.

SSA treats data in a much different manner than does SADT. One is encouraged to use a standard data dictionary system to record and define the data elements that appear during the analysis and definition of a system. These are the data elements that appear on the data flow arrows of the diagrams which are produced as the first step in SSA. Once data stores have been defined through the analysis process, SSA suggests organizing the data stores immediately; structuring techniques based on the relational model of data are prescribed to obtain efficiently designed stores.

In the decomposition process, one eventually reaches a level at which specific algorithms must be described. SSA suggest the use of a process logic representation such as decision tables, metacode, decision trees, or structured English for this. Different representations are suggested for different situations, but all have the advantage of being understandable by humans while still capturing accurately the intended sequencing.

The emphasis on data base design and some of the recommended uses of the data flow diagrams in SSA (e.g., for preliminary design) clearly indicate its assumption of an approach for the system analyst/designer to use in a process that begins with understanding the problem and ends with a specification of the software; this is what we have called implicit design. SSA methods provide strong support for problem understanding through the use of decomposition and modeling. Likewise, the representations of SSA serve as effective communication vehicles both to the user and to the programmer.

SSA is presented as a traditional systems analysis approach that has been strengthened by adding the four features listed above. The features are well-suited to specifying more accurately the requirements for a software system while their recommended usage in the implicit design pattern is well-suited to the manner in which many system analyst/designers are used to working. If applied properly, this strengthening of traditional DP system development should produce significant improvement.

Problem Statement Language/Analyzer(PSL/PSA)

PSL/PSA is a tool for the description and analysis of system definitions. It consists of a language for expressing specifications and an analyzer for processing the descriptions. PSL/PSA was developed by Professor Daniel Teichroew of the University of Michigan [10] and has been used by numerous organizations for approximately five years on a range of projects.

PSL/PSA incorporates three important concepts: First, all information about the developing system is to be kept in a computerized, development-information data base. Second, processing of this information is to be done with the aid of the computer to the extent possible. Third, specifications are to be given in "what" terms, not "how" terms.

The automated analyzer, PSA, operates on the data base of development information that has been built up out of PSL inputs. It can provide reports indicating changes to the development data base, listing subsets of the information, and producing summary reports. More importantly, it is able to perform some analyses of the information in the data base to indicate such things as gaps in the specified system information flow, unused data objects, and the dynamic behavior of the proposed system. Figure 2 shows the PSL/PSA system structure.

This approach primarily assists in the communication aspect of requirements analysis and specification. It does not incorporate any specific method to lead one to a better understanding of the problem being worked on. However, the act of formally specifying all development information and the analysis reports produced by PSA can both aid the analysts' understanding of the problem.

It was created at least partly in response to the tendency of analyst/designers to describe a system in programming-level details that are useless for communication with the non-technical user. At the same time, it provides sufficient rigor to make it useful for design specification. It has been used to advantage in situations ranging from commercial DP to air-defense systems.

Software Requirements Engineering Methodology(SREM)

SREM includes tools, methods, and procedures for their application. SREM was developed under the direction of the U.S. Army Ballistic Missile Defense program by several subcontractors and has been described extensively [11,12]. Its usage to date, however, has been limited to the specification of large missile-defense systems.

SREM shares the underlying concepts of PSL/PSA with some important additions. It focuses on techniques applicable to real-time systems through some generalizations of the PSL/PSA approach. In particular, it incorporates a "stimulus-response" model of real-time systems. It includes a graphical language and utilizes sophisticated graphical displays. It extends the PSA analysis concept by incorporating automated simulation facilities to provide the analyst additional feedback on the characteristics of the system being specified.

The language used for stating requirements in SREM is called RSL for Requirements Statement Language; it also has a graphical form called R-nets, illustrated in Figure 3. These languages permit one to express

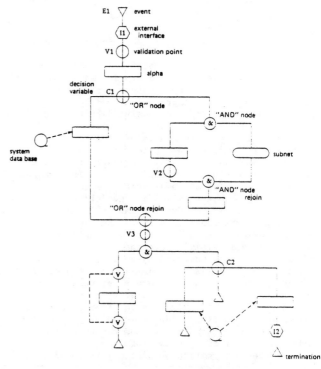

Figure 3: R-Net Terminology

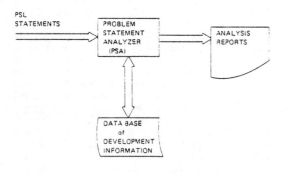

Figure 2: PSL/PSA System Structure

parallel operation, specify explicit interfaces to other subsystems, and tie validation assertions to particular points in the specification.

SREM was developed to expand traditional technical methods to permit more effective communication with those "outside" the technical system details. It results in a set of specifications for a software subsystem for which a more explicit design activity may then be invoked.

The strength of SREM for very large systems appears to be in its communication aspects. As with PSL/PSA, its usage will aid understanding, but there is not the explicit emphasis on problem-solving that exists, for

instance, in SADT. The concepts developed for SREM are important and will likely turn up in other requirements techniques.

Hierarchy-Input-Process-Output(HIPO)

HIPO is a documentation technique developed by IBM and used in a number of different situations. It is useful for design documentation as well as stating requirements and specifications before beginning design. It is based on two concepts: The input-process-output model of information processing and functional hierarchies.

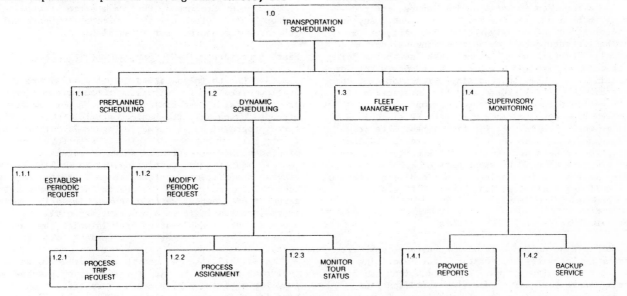

Figure 4: Functional Hierarchy Chart (Simplified)

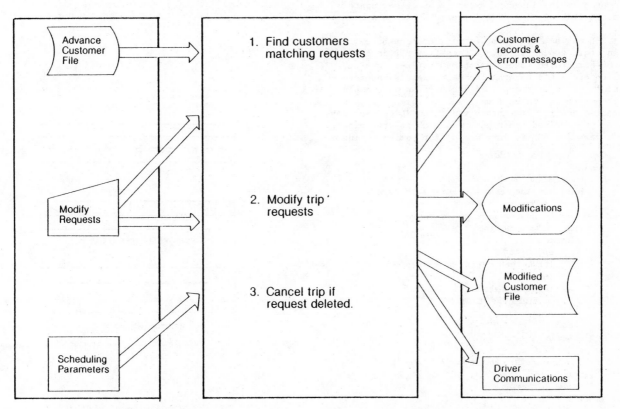

Figure 5: Simplified Process Chart for Function 1.1.2 (Modify Periodic Request)

HIPO is basically a graphical notation, consisting of hierarchy charts and process charts. Figure 4 shows an example of a hierarchy chart in which functions to be performed are broken down into ever greater detail by subfunctions. This is often a good way of describing a set of functions to be performed since it permits checking for completeness in a systematic way. This representation is not sufficient for describing all of a design, however, since there are usually cross-connections between functions which cannot be shown in this type of chart.

The second part of the HIPO notation, process charts, are illustrated in Figure 5. They are used to describe a function in terms of its inputs, the processing to be done, and the outputs produced. Any of the information, especially the process part, may be described in more detail by accompanying textual material. Sometimes a PDL description (see below) of the process is given. This notation is convenient for describing the operation of a single function, but does not permit one to describe easily the interaction of inputs and outputs of different functions.

HIPO has been used in a number of DP situations and some more complex specification tasks. Its drawbacks, especially with respect to interfaces and the description of data are limiting its acceptance. However, its ease of use and simplicity do make it a viable alternative for defining functional requirements and specifying individual functions. HIPO and its usage are described in [13].

Program Description Languages (PDL's)

PDL's (also called metacodes or pseudocodes) are programming language-like notations for describing the detailed design of programs. In applications (such as process control) requiring detailed specifications, they can also be used to specify the logic of processes to be automated. A PDL is a linear notation that looks like a programming language except that it may contain statements that are not directly executable on a computer.

A PDL may be free-form, formal, or somewhere in-between these two extremes. A free-form PDL is composed of structured control statements (if-then-else, do-while, etc.) and natural language expressions for conditions and operations. Figure 6 shows an example of a free-form PDL taken from [14]. A formal PDL also has precise control statements and in addition uses keywords or pre-defined functions to a much greater extent.

A free-form PDL is very useful for communicating

the logic of a process to a human-being and for checking of interfaces and other conditions, but is less expressive.

The concept of a PDL was introduced widely in the early 1970's with structured programming and has become quite popular in a wide range of software development situations. Its usage for specification or requirements definition is not as widely used thus far but should increase as more people attempt to make their program specifications precise. This is especially true in engineering applications in which the "user" wishes to have a computer programmed to carry out some well-defined control process. Because they don't have to be machine-processed, PDL's are often created on an ad hoc basis; reference [15] describes one particular PDL for which a processor is available.

Nassi-Schneiderman(N-S) Charts

N-S Charts (also called Chapin charts) are a form of flowcharts for use with structured programming. They are graphical like ordinary flowcharts but are constructed using only the basic control forms of structured programming, as shown in Figure 7. These basic forms, following the principles of structured programming, can then be nested as shown in Figure 8.

In addition to restricting one to well-structured program descriptions, this notation is quite compact compared to traditional flowcharts. For these reasons, a number of groups have found them quite valuable for expressing the logic of a program, especially in the process control application area in which the "user" wishes to carefully inspect the logic before it is coded.

As with PDL's, N-S charts are a detailed design tool that can also be used for specifying precise program logic at the requirements or specification phase. More information can be found in [16] and [17].

```
logical description of OPEN
begin
    get owner directory
    if not found then exitwith ('owner does not exist')
        check parameters for opening
        if not valid then return appropriate code
    else if buffer needed then
        begin
            allocate buffer
            if none then return ('no buffer space')
            create FCB
            if no space then begin release buffer
                return ('no FCBspace')
            end
        end
    else begin
        create FCB
        if no space then return ('no FCB space')
    end
    release directory
end
```

Figure 6: Free-Form PDL

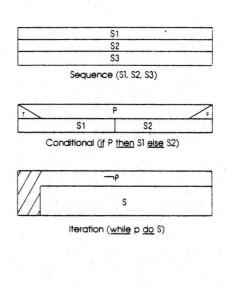

Sequence (S1, S2, S3)

Conditional (if P then S1 else S2)

Iteration (while p do S)

Figure 7: N-S Basic Forms

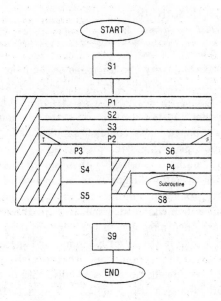

Figure 8: N-S Composite Diagram

CONCLUSION

This survey of the state-of-the-art in requirements analysis and specification for software has only
briefly described those techniques currently in use and
has not dealt at all with research developments that
may lead to even more powerful techniques in the future.
It should, however, provide you with enough overview
and references to learn more about those techniques
that are most appropriate for your situation.

There are four steps you can take to improve your
requirements analysis and specification activities:

1. Commit to doing a better job of understanding the requirements for each
development task and to communicating
that understanding to user and developer
alike.

2. Determine your needs for requirements
analysis and specification techniques.

3. Choose one or more of the techniques
discussed here.

4. Try them out on a real project, learn from
the experience, and refine and repeat
these steps.

There is no guarantee that this will permit you
to develop better systems in a more cost-effective
manner. The experience of your colleagues in many
situations, however, indicates it will.

REFERENCES

1 Teichroew, D., "Improvements in the System Life
Cycle," Proc. IFIP Congress 1974, North-Holland
Publishing Co.

2 Ross, D.T., "Structured Analysis for Requirements Definition," IEEE Trans. Sfw. Eng., January, 1977.

3 Ross, D.T., Goodenough, J.B., and Irvine, C.A.,
"Software Engineering: Process, Principles, and Goals,"

Computer, May, 1975.

4 Freeman, P., "A Perspective on Requirements
Analysis and Specification," in Structured Software
Development, Infotech International, Maidenhead,
England, 1979.

5 Ross, D.T., "Structured Analysis: A Language
for Communicating Ideas," IEEE Trans. Sfw. Eng.,
January, 1977.

6 Dickover, M.E., McGowan, C.L., and Ross, D.T.,
"Software Design Using SADT," Proc. 1977 ACM
National Conference, Association for Computing
Machinery, New York.

7 "Introduction to SADT," Technical Report
9022-78R, SofTech, Inc., Waltham, MA., 1976.

8 DeMarco, T., Structured Analysis and System
Specification, Yourdon Press, New York, 1978.

9 Gane, C., and Sarson, T., Structured Systems
Analysis: Tools and Techniques, IST Databooks,
New York, 1977.

10 Teichroew, D., and Hershey, E., "PSL/PSA: A
Computer-Aided Technique for Structured Documentation
and Analysis of Information Processing Systems,"
IEEE Trans. Sfw. Eng., January, 1977.

11 Davis, C., and Vick, C., " The Software
Development System," IEEE Trans. Sfw. Eng.,
January 1977.

12 Bell, T., Bixler, D., and Dyer, M., "An
Extendable Approach to Computer-aided Software
Requirements Engineering," IEEE Trans. Sfw. Eng.,
January, 1977.

13 Katzan, H., Systems Design and Documentation,
Van Nostrand, 1976.

14 Freeman, P., "Software Design Representation:
A Case Study," Sfw. Prac. & Exper., Vol.8, 501-511,
1978.

15 Caine, S.H., and Gordon, E.K., " PDL- A Tool
for Software Design," Proc.1975 AFIPS National
Computer Conference.

16 Nassi, I., and Shneiderman, B., "Flowchart
Techniques for Structured Programming," SIG PLAN
Notices, 8,8, 1973.

17 Chapin, N., "New Format for Flowcharts",
Sfw. Prac. & Exper., Vol.4, 341-358, 1974.

Structured Analysis for Requirements Definition

DOUGLAS T. ROSS AND KENNETH E. SCHOMAN, JR.

Reprinted from *IEEE Transactions on Software Engineering*, Volume SE-3, Number 1, January 1977, pages 69–84. Copyright © 1977 by The Institute of Electrical and Electronics Engineers, Inc.

Abstract—Requirements definition encompasses all aspects of system development prior to actual system design. We see the lack of an adequate approach to requirements definition as the source of major difficulties in current systems work. This paper examines the needs for requirements definition, and proposes meeting those objectives with three interrelated subjects: context analysis, functional specification, and design constraints. Requirements definition replaces the widely used, but never well-defined, term "requirements analysis."

The purpose of this paper is to present, in a comprehensive manner, concepts that apply throughout requirements definition (and, by implication, to all of system development). The paper discusses the functional architecture of systems, the characteristics of good requirements documentation, the personnel involved in the process of analysis, and management guidelines that are effective even in complex environments.

The paper then outlines a systematic methodology that incorporates, in both notation and technique, the concepts previously introduced. Reference is made to actual requirements definition experience and to practicable automated support tools that may be used with the methodology.

Index Terms—Functional specification, requirements analysis, structured analysis, requirements definition.

I. The Problem

THE obvious assertion that "a problem unstated is a problem unsolved" seems to have escaped many builders of large computer application systems. All too often, design and implementation begin before the real needs and system functions are fully known. The results are skyrocketing costs, missed schedules, waste and duplication, disgruntled users, and an endless series of patches and repairs euphemistically called "system maintenance." Compared to other phases of system development, these symptoms reflect, by a large margin, the lack of an adequate approach to requirements definition.

Given the wide range of computer hardware now available and the emergence of software engineering as a discipline, most problems in system development are becoming less traceable to either the machinery or the programming [1]. Methods for handling the hardware and software components of systems are highly sophisticated, but address only part of the job. For example, even the best structured programming code will not help if the programmer has been told to solve the wrong problem, or, worse yet, has been given a correct description, but has not understood it. The results of requirements definition must be both complete and understandable.

In efforts to deal with these needs, the expressions "system architecture," "system design," "system analysis," and "system engineering" seem to be accepted terminology. But in truth, there is no widely practiced methodology for systems

Manuscript received June 14, 1976; revised September 16, 1976.
The authors are with SofTech, Inc., Waltham, MA 02154.

work that has the clarity and discipline of the more classical techniques used in construction and manufacturing enterprises. In manufacturing, for example, a succession of blueprints, drawings, and specifications captures all of the relevant requirements for a product. This complete problem definition and implementation plan allows the product to be made almost routinely, by "business as usual," with no surprises. In a good manufacturing operation, major troubles are avoided because even the first production run does not create an item for the first time. The item was created and the steps of forming and assembly were done mentally, in the minds of designers and engineers, long before the set of blueprints and specifications ever arrived at the production shop. That simulation is made possible only because the notations and discipline of the blueprinting methodology are so complete and so consistent with the desired item that its abstract representation contains all the information needed for its imaginary preconstruction.

Software system designers attempt to do the same of course, but being faced with greater complexity and less exacting methods, their successes form the surprises, rather than their failures!

Experience has taught us that system problems are complex and ill-defined. The complexity of large systems is an inherent fact of life with which one must cope. Faulty definition, however, is an artifact of inadequate methods. It can be eliminated by the introduction of well-thought-out techniques and means of expression. That is the subject of this paper. Systems can be manufactured, like other things, if the right approach is used. That approach must start at the beginning.

Requirements Definition

Requirements definition includes, but is not limited to, the problem analysis that yields a functional specification. It is much more than that. Requirements definition must encompass everything necessary to lay the groundwork for subsequent stages in system development (Fig. 1). Within the total process, which consists largely of steps in a solution to a problem, only once is the problem itself stated and the solution justified—in requirements definition.

Requirements definition is a careful assessment of the needs that a system is to fulfill. It must say *why* a system is needed, based on current or foreseen conditions, which may be internal operations or an external market. It must say *what* system features will serve and satisfy this context. And it must say *how* the system is to be constructed. Thus, requirements definition must deal with three subjects.

1) *Context analysis*: The reasons *why* the system is to be created and why certain technical, operational, and economic feasibilities are the criteria which form *boundary conditions* for the system.

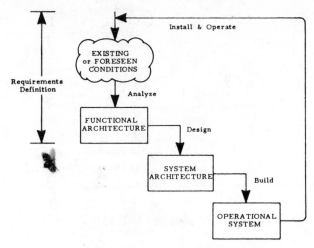

Fig. 1. Simplified view of development cycle.

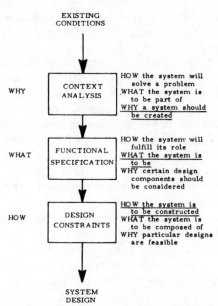

Fig. 2. Each subject has a fundamental purpose.

2) *Functional specification*: A description of *what* the system is to be, in terms of the functions it must accomplish. Since this is part of the problem statement, it must only present *boundary conditions* for considerations later to be taken up in system design.

3) *Design constraints*: A summary of conditions specifying *how* the required system is to be constructed and implemented. This does not necessarily specify which things will be in the system. Rather it identifies *boundary conditions* by which those things may later be selected or created.

Each of these subjects must be fully documented during requirements definition. But note that these are subjects, not documents. The contents of resulting documents will vary according to the needs of the development organization. In any case, they must be reference documents which justify all aspects of the required system, not design or detailed specification documents.

Each of the subjects has a specific and limited role in justifying the required system. Collectively, they capture on paper, at the appropriate time, all relevant knowledge about the system problem in a complete, concise, comprehensive form. Taken together, these subjects define the whole need. Separately, they say *what* the system is to be part of, *what* the system is to be, and of *what* the system is to be composed (Fig. 2). The process known as "analysis" must apply to all three.

Descriptions of these subjects just frame the problem; they do not solve it. Details are postponed, and no binding implementation decisions are yet made. Even detailed budget and schedule commitments are put off, except those for the next phase, system design, because they depend on the results of that design. Requirements definition only (but completely) provides *boundary conditions* for the subsequent design and implementation stages. A problem well-stated is well on its way to a sound solution.

The Problem Revisited

The question still remains: why is requirements definition not a standard part of every system project, especially since not doing it well has such disastrously high costs [2]? Why is project start-up something one muddles through and why does it seem that requirements are never completely stated? What goes wrong?

The answer seems to be that just about everything goes wrong. Stated requirements are often excessive, incomplete, and inconsistent. Communication and documentation are roadblocks, too. Because they speak with different vocabularies, users and developers find it difficult to completely understand each other. Analysts are often drawn from the development organization, and are unable to document user requirements without simultaneously stating a design approach.

Good requirements are complete, consistent, testable, traceable, feasible, and flexible. By just stating necessary boundary conditions, they leave room for tradeoffs during system design. Thus, a good set of requirements documents can, in effect, serve as a user–developer contract. To attain these attributes, simply proposing a table of contents for requirements documentation is not enough. To do the job, one must emphasize the *means* of defining requirements, rather than prescribe the contents of documentation (which would, in any case, be impossible to do in a generic way).

Even in organizations which do stipulate some document or another, the process of defining requirements remains laborious and inconclusive. Lacking a complete definition of the job to be done, the effect of a contract is lacking, and the designers will make the missing assumptions and decisions because they must, in order to get the job done. Even when the value of requirements definition is recognized, it takes more than determination to have an effective approach. To define requirements, one must understand: 1) the nature of that which is to be described; 2) the form of the description; and 3) the process of analysis.

Many remedies to these problems have been proposed. Each project management, analysis, or specification scheme, whether "structured" or not, has its own adherents. Most do indeed offer some improvements, for any positive steps are better than none. But a significant impact has not been achieved, because each partial solution omits enough of the essential ingredients to be vulnerable.

The key to successful requirements definition lies in remembering that people define requirements. Thus, any useful discussion of requirements definition must combine: 1) a generic understanding of systems which is scientifically sound; 2) a notation and structure of documenting specific system knowledge in a rigorous, easy-to-read form; 3) a process for doing analysis which includes definition of people roles and interpersonal procedures; and 4) a way to technically manage the work, which enables allocation of requirements and postponement of design.

Academic approaches won't do. A pragmatic methodology must itself be: 1) technically feasible, i.e., consistent with the systems to be developed; 2) operationally feasible, i.e., people will use it to do the job well; and 3) economically feasible, i.e., noticeably improve the system development cycle.

This paper sketches such an approach, which has been successful in bringing order and direction to a wide range of system contexts. In even the most trying of circumstances, something can be done to address the need for requirements definition.

II. The Process of Requirements Definition

The Nature of Systems

One fundamental weakness in current approaches to requirements definition is an inability to see clearly what the problem is, much less measure it, envision workable solutions, or apply any sort of assessment.

It is common practice to think of system architecture in terms of devices, languages, transmission links, and record formats. Overview charts of computer systems typically contain references to programs, files, terminals, and processors. At the appropriate time in system development, this is quite proper. But as an initial basis for system thinking, it is premature and it blocks from view precisely the key idea that is essential to successful requirements definition—the algorithmic nature of all systems. This important concept can best be envisioned by giving it a new name, the *functional architecture*, as distinct from the system architecture.

Systems consist of things that perform activities that interact with other things, each such interaction constituting a happening. A functional architecture is a rigorous layout of the activities performed by a system (temporarily disregarding who or what does them) and the things with which those activities interact. Given this, a design process will create a system architecture which implements, in good order, the functions of the functional architecture. Requirements definition is founded on showing what the functional architecture is (Fig. 3), also showing why it is what it is, and constraining how the system architecture is to realize it in more concrete form.

The concepts of functional architecture are universally applicable, to manual as well as automated systems, and are perfectly suited to the multiple needs of context analysis, functional specification, and design constraints found in requirements definition. Suppose, for example, that an operation, currently being performed manually is to be automated. The manual operation has a system architecture, composed of

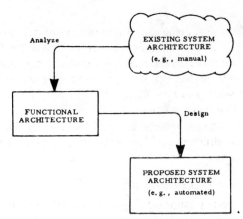

Fig. 3. Functional architecture is extracted by analysis.

people, organizations, forms, procedures, and incentives, even though no computer is involved. It also has a functional architecture outlining the purposes for which the system exists. An automated system will implement the functional architecture with a different system architecture. In requirements definition, we must be able to extract the functional architecture (functional specification), and link it both to the boundary conditions for the manual operation (context analysis) and to the boundary conditions for the automated system (design constraints).

Functional architecture is founded on a generic universe of *things* and *happenings*:

objects	operations
data	activities
nouns	verbs
information	processing
substances	events
passive	active

Things and happenings are so intimately related that they can only exist together. A functional architecture always has a very strong structure making explicit these relationships. Functional architecture is, perhaps surprisingly, both abstract and precise.

Precision in functional architecture is best achieved by emphasizing only one primary structural relationship over and over—that of parts and wholes. Parts are related by interfaces to constitute wholes which, in turn, are parts of still larger wholes. It is always valid to express a functional architecture from the generic view that systems are made of components (parts and interfaces) and yet are themselves components.

So like all other architectures, the structure of functional architecture is both modular and hierarchic (even draftsmen and watchmakers use "top-down" methods). Like other architectures, it can be seen from different viewpoints (even the construction trades use distinct structural, electrical, heating, and plumbing blueprints). And like other architectures, it may not necessarily be charted as a physical system would be (even a circuit diagram does not show the actual layout of components, but every important electrical characteristic is represented).

This universal way to view any system is the key to successful requirements definition. From our experience, people do not tend to do this naturally, and not in an organized fashion. In fact, we find that the most basic problem in requirements definition is the fact that most people do not even realize that such universality exists! When it is explained, the usual reaction is, "that is just common sense." But, as has been remarked for ages, common sense is an uncommon commodity. The need is to structure such concepts within a discipline which can be learned.

The Form of Documentation

To adequately define requirements, one must certainly realize that functional architecture exists, can be measured, and can be evaluated. But to describe it, one needs a communication medium corresponding to the blueprints and specifications that allow manufacturing to function smoothly. In fact, the form of documentation is the key to achieving communication. "Form" includes paging, paragraphing, use of graphics, document organization, and so forth. Because the distinction between form and content is so poorly understood, many adequate system descriptions are unreadable, simply because they are so hard to follow. When Marshall McLuhan said, "The medium is the message," he was apparently ignored by most system analysts.

Analysis of functional architecture (and design of system architecture) cannot be expressed both concisely and unambiguously in natural language. But by imbedding natural language in a blueprint-like graphic framework, all necessary relationships can be shown compactly and rigorously. Well-chosen graphic components permit representation of all aspects of the architecture in an artificial language which is natural for the specific function of communicating that architecture.

The universal nature of systems being both wholes and parts can be expressed by a graphic structure which is both modular and hierarchic (Fig. 4). Because parts are constrained to be wholes, interfaces must be shown explicitly. Interface notation must allow one to distinguish input from output from control (the concept of "control" will not be defended here). Most important, the notation itself must distinguish the things with which activities interact from the things which perform the activities. And because the graphics are a framework for the descriptive abilities of natural language, one must be able to name everything.

To achieve communication, the form of the diagram in which graphic symbols appear is also important. They must be bounded—to a single page or pair of facing pages—so that a reader can see at once everything which can be said about something. Each topic must be carefully delineated so a reader can grasp the whole message. A reader must be able to mentally walk through the architectural structure which is portrayed, just as blueprints enable a manufacturer to "see" the parts working together. And finally, everything must be indexed so that the whole set of diagrams will form a complete model of the architecture.

This appears to be a tall order, but when done elegantly, it yields documentation that is clear, complete, concise, consistent, and convincing. In addition, the hierarchic structure of the documentation can be exploited both to do and to manage

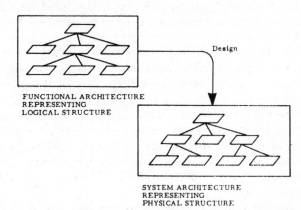

FUNCTIONAL ARCHITECTURE
REPRESENTING
LOGICAL STRUCTURE

SYSTEM ARCHITECTURE
REPRESENTING
PHYSICAL STRUCTURE

Fig. 4. Physical structure is seldom identical to logical structure.

the process of analysis. By reviewing the emergent documentation incrementally, for example, while requirements are being delineated, all interested parties can have a voice in directing the process. This is one of the features that results in the standardized, business-as-usual, "no surprises" approach found in manufacturing.

The Analysis Team

When thinking about why requirements are neither well-structured nor well-documented, one must not forget that any proposed methodology must be people-oriented. Technical matters matter very much, but it is the wishes, ideas, needs, concerns, and skills of people that determine the outcome. Technical aspects can only be addressed through the interaction of all people who have an interest in the system. One of the current difficulties in requirements definition, remember, is that system developers are often charged with documenting requirements. Their design background leads them (however well-intentioned they may be) to think of system architecture rather than functional architecture, and to define requirements in terms of solutions.

Consider a typical set of people who must actively participate in requirements definition. The *customer* is an organization with a need for a system. That customer authorizes a *commissioner* to acquire a system which will be operated by *users*. The commissioner, although perhaps technically oriented, probably knows less about system technology than the *developers* who will construct the system. These four parties may or may not be within one organization. For each administrative structure, there is a *management* group. Requirements definition must be understood by all these parties, answer the questions they have about the system, and serve as the basis for a development contract.

Each of these parties is a partisan whose conflicting, and often vague, desires must be amalgamated through requirements definition. There is a need at the center for trained, professional *analysts* who act as a catalyst to get the assorted information on paper and to structure from it adequate requirements documentation. The mental facility to comprehend abstraction, the ability to communicate it with personal tact, along with the ability to accept and deliver valid criticism, are all hallmarks of a professional analyst.

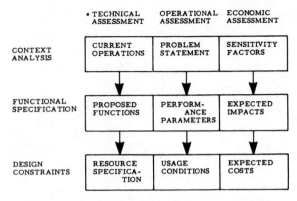

Fig. 5. Multiple viewpoints of requirements definition.

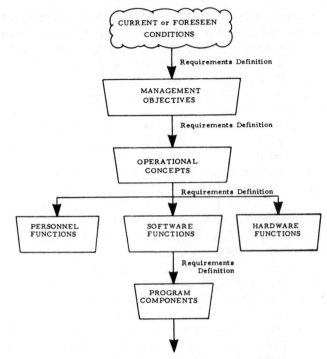

Fig. 6. Analysis is repetitive in a complex environment.

Analysts, many of whom may be only part-time, are not expected to supply expertise in all aspects of the problem area. As professionals, they are expected to seek out requirements from experts among the other parties concerned. To succeed, the task of analysis must be properly managed and coordinated, and the requirements definition effort must embody multiple viewpoints. These viewpoints may be overlapping and, occasionally, contradictory.

Managing the Analysis

Because many interests are involved, requirements definition must serve multiple purposes. Each subject—context analysis, functional specification, and design constraints—must be examined from at least three points of view: technical, operational, and economic. Technical assessment or feasibility concerns the architecture of a system. Operational assessment concerns the performance of that system in a working environment. Economic feasibility concerns the costs and impacts of system implementation and use. The point is simply that a wide variety of topics must be considered in requirements definition (Fig. 5). Without a plan for assembling the pieces into coherent requirements, it is easy for the analysis team to lose their sense of direction and overstep their responsibility.

Requirements definition, like all system development stages, should be an orderly progression. Each task is a logical successor to what has come before and is completed before proceeding to what comes after. Throughout, one must be able to answer the same three questions. 1) What are we doing? 2) Why are we doing it? 3) How do we proceed from here? Adequate management comes from asking these questions, iteratively, at every point in the development process. And if management is not to be a chameleon-like art, the same body of procedural knowledge should be applicable every time, although the subject at hand will differ.

It is precisely the lack of guidance about the process of analysis that makes requirements definition such a "hot item" today. People need to think about truly analyzing problems ("divide and conquer"), secure in the knowledge that postponed decisions will dovetail because the process they use enforces consistency. Analysis is an art of considering everything relevant at a given point, and nothing more. Adequate requirements will be complete, without over-specification, and will postpone certain decisions to later stages in the system devel-

opment process without artifice. This is especially important in the development of those complex systems where requirements are imposed by higher level considerations (Fig. 6). Decisions must be *allocated* (i.e., postponed) because too many things interrelate in too many complicated ways for people to understand, all at once, what is and is not being said.

Controlling a system development project is nearly impossible without reviews, walk-throughs, and configuration management. Such techniques become workable when the need for synthesis is recognized. Quite simply, system architectures and allocated requirements must be justifiable in light of previously stated requirements. One may choose, by plan or by default, not to enforce such traceability. However, validation and verification of subsequent project stages must not be precluded by ill-structured and unfathomable requirements.

Obviously, decisions on paper are the only ones that count. Knowing that an alternative was considered and rejected, and why, may often be as important as the final requirement. Full documentation becomes doubly necessary when the many parties involved are geographically separated and when staff turnover or expansion may occur before the project is completed.

The features just discussed at length—functional architecture, documentation, analysis teamwork, and the orderly process of analyzing and synthesizing multiple viewpoints—all must be integrated when prescribing a methodology for requirements definition.

III. STRUCTURED ANALYSIS

Outline of the Approach

For several years, the senior author and his colleagues at SofTech have been developing, applying, and improving a general, but practical approach to handling complex system problems. The method is called Structured Analysis and Design Technique (SADT [TM]) [3]. It has been used successfully on a wide range of problems by both SofTech and clients. This paper has presented some of the reasons why SADT works so well, when properly applied.

SADT evolved naturally from earlier work on the foundations of software engineering. It consists of both techniques for performing system analysis and design, and a process for applying these techniques in requirements definition and system development. Both features significantly increase the productivity and effectiveness of teams of people involved in a system project. Specifically, SADT provides methods for: 1) thinking in a structured way about large and complex problems; 2) working as a team with effective division and coordination of effort and roles; 3) communicating interview, analysis, and design results in clear, precise notation; 4) documenting current results and decisions in a way which provides a complete audit of history; 5) controlling accuracy, completeness, and quality through frequent review and approval procedure; and 6) planning, managing, and assessing progress of the team effort. Two aspects of SADT deserve special mention: the graphic techniques and the definition of personnel roles.

Graphic Techniques

The SADT graphic language provides a limited set of primitive constructs from which analysts and designers can compose orderly structures of any required size. The notation is quite simple—just boxes and arrows. *Boxes* represent parts of a whole in a precise manner. *Arrows* represent interfaces between parts. *Diagrams* represent wholes and are composed of boxes, arrows, natural language names, and certain other notations. The same graphics are applicable to both activities and data.

An SADT model is an organized sequence of diagrams, each with concise supporting text. A high-level overview diagram represents the whole subject. Each lower level diagram shows a limited amount of detail about a well-constrained topic. Further, each lower level diagram connects exactly into higher level portions of the model, thus preserving the logical relationship of each component to the total system (Fig. 7).

An SADT model is a graphic representation of the hierarchic structure of a system, decomposed with a firm purpose in mind. A model is structured so that it gradually exposes more and more detail. But its depth is bounded by the restriction of its vantage point and its content is bounded by its viewpoint. The priorities dictated by its purpose determine the layering of the top-down decomposition. Multiple models accommodate both multiple viewpoints and the various stages of system realization.

The arrow structure on an SADT diagram represents a constraint relationship among the boxes. It does not represent flow of control or sequence, as for example, on a flowchart for a computer program. Constraint arrows show necessary conditions imposed on a box.

Most arrows represent interfaces between boxes, whether in the same or different models. Some arrows represent noninter-

[TM] Trademark of SofTech, Inc.

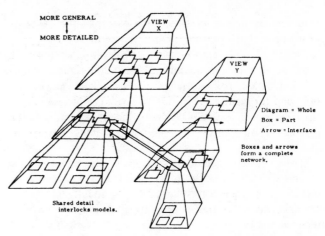

Fig. 7. SADT provides practical, rigorous decomposition.

Name	Function
Authors	Personnel who study requirements and constraints, analyze system functions and represent them by models based on SADT diagrams.
Commenters	Usually authors, who must review and comment in writing on the work of other authors.
Readers	Personnel who read SADT diagrams for information but are not expected to make written comments.
Experts	Persons from whom authors obtain specialized information about requirements and constraints by means of interviews.
Technical Committee	A group of senior technical personnel assigned to review the analysis at every major level of decomposition. They either resolve technical issues or recommend a decision to the project management.
Project Librarian	A person assigned the responsibility of maintaining a centralized file of all project documents, making copies, distributing reader kits, keeping records, etc.
Project Manager	The member of the project who has the final technical responsibility for carrying out the system analysis and design.
Monitor (or Chief Analyst)	A person fluent in SADT who assists and advises project personnel in the use and application of SADT.
Instructor	A person fluent in SADT, who trains Authors and Commenters using SADT for the first time.

Fig. 8. Personnel roles for SADT.

face interlocking between models. Together, these concepts achieve both overlapping of multiple viewpoints and the desirable attributes of good analysis and design projects (e.g., modularity, flexibility, and so forth [4]). The interface structure, particularly, passes through several levels of diagrams, creating a web that integrates all parts of the decomposition and shows the whole system's environmental interfaces with the topmost box.

Process Overview

Clearly, requirements definition requires cooperative team work from many people. This in turn demands a clear definition of the kinds of interactions which should occur between the personnel involved. SADT anticipates this need by establishing titles and functions of appropriate roles (Fig. 8). In a requirements definition effort, for example, the "authors" would be analysts, trained and experienced in SADT.

The SADT process, in which these roles interact, meets the needs of requirements definition for continuous and effective communication, for understandable and current documentation, and for regular and critical review. The process exploits the structure of an SADT model so that decisions can be seen in context and can be challenged while alternatives are still viable.

Throughout a project, draft versions of diagrams in evolving models are distributed to project members for review. Commenters make their suggestions in writing directly on copies of the diagrams. Written records of decisions and alternatives are retained as they unfold. As changes and corrections are made, all versions are entered in the project files. A project librarian provides filing, distribution, and record-keeping support, and, not so incidentally, also ensures configuration control.

This process documents all decisions and the reasons why decisions were made. When commenters and authors reach an understanding, the work is reviewed by a committee of senior technical and management personnel. During the process, incorrect or unacceptable results are usually spotted early, and oversights or errors are detected before they can cause major disruptions. Since everything is on record, future enhancement and system maintenance can reference previous analysis and design decisions.

When documentation is produced as the model evolves, the status of the project becomes highly visible. Management can study the requirements (or the design) in a "top-down" manner, beginning with an overview and continuing to any relevant level of detail. Although presentations to upper management usually follow standard summary and walk-through methods, even senior executives sometimes become direct readers, for the blueprint language of SADT is easily learned.

Implementing the Approach

How the ideas discussed in this paper are employed will vary according to organization needs and the kinds of systems under consideration. The methodology which has been described is not just a theory, however, and has been applied to a wide range of complex problems from real-time communications to process control to commercial EDP to organization planning. It is, in fact, a total systems methodology, and not merely a software technique. ITT Europe, for example, has used SADT since early 1974 for analysis and design of both hardware/software systems (telephonic and telegraphic switches) and nonsoftware people-oriented problems (project management and customer engineering). Other users exhibit similar diversity, from manufacturing (AFCAM [5]) to military training (TRAIDEX [6]). Users report that it is a communications vehicle which focuses attention on well-defined topics, that it increases management control through visibility and standardization, that it creates a systematic work breakdown structure for project teams, and that it minimizes errors through disciplined flexibility.

There is no set pattern among different organizations for the contents of requirements documentation. In each case, the needs of the users, the commissioner, and the development organization must be accommodated. Government agencies tend to have fixed standards, while other organizations encourage flexibility. In a numerical control application, almost 40 models were generated in requirements definition (SINTEF, University of Trondheim, Norway). At least one supplier of large-scale computer-based systems mandates consideration of system, hardware, software, commercial, and administrative constraints. Among all distinct viewpoints, the only common ground lies in the vantage points of context analysis, functional specification, and design constraints. Experience has shown that use of well-structured models together with a well-defined process of analysis, when properly carried out, does provide a strong foundation for actual system design [7].

Because local needs are diverse, implementation of the approach discussed in this paper cannot be accomplished solely by the publication of policy or standards. It is very much a "learn by doing" experience in which project personnel acquire ways of understanding the generic nature of systems. One must recognize that a common sense approach to system manufacturing is not now widely appreciated. A change in the ways that people think about systems and about the systems work that they themselves perform cannot be taught or disseminated in a short period of time.

Further Developments

In manufacturing enterprises, blueprinting and specification methods evolved long before design support tools. In contrast to that analogy, a number of current efforts have produced systems for automating requirements information, independent of the definition and verification methodology provided by SADT. To date, SADT applications have been successfully carried out manually, but in large projects, where many analysts are involved and frequent changes do occur, the question is not whether or how to automate but simply what to automate.

Existing computer tools which wholly or partly apply to requirements [8] are characterized by a specification (or a design) database which, once input, may be manipulated. All such attempts, however, begin with user requirements recorded in a machine-readable form. Two impediments immediately become evident. The first is that requirements stated in prose texts cannot be translated in a straightforward manner to interface with an automated problem language. The second is that no computer tool will ever perform the process of requirements definition. Defining and verifying requirements is a task done by users and analysts [9].

Given the right kind of information, however, computer tools can provide capabilities to insure consistency, traceability, and allocation of requirements. A good example of this match to SADT is PSL/PSA, a system resulting from several years' effort in the ISDOS Project at the University of Michigan [10], [11]. The PSL database can represent almost every relationship which appears on SADT diagrams, and the input process from diagrams to database can be done by a project librarian. Not only does SADT enhance human communication (between user and analyst and between analyst and designer), but the diagrams become machine-readable in a very straightforward manner.

Fig. 9. System development is a chain of overlapping questions, documented at each step.

The PSA data analyzer and report generator is useful for summarizing database contents and can provide a means of controlling revisions. If the database has been derived by SADT, enhancements to existing PSA capabilities are possible to further exploit the structure of SADT models. For example, SADT diagrams are not flow diagrams, but the interface constraints are directed. These precedence relations, systematically pursued in SADT to specify quantities (volumes and rates) and sequences, permit any desired degree of simulation of a model (whether performed mentally or otherwise).

Computer aids are created as support tools. SADT provides a total context, within which certain automated procedures can play a complementary role. The result will be a complete, systematized approach which both suits the needs of the people involved and enables automation to be used in and extended beyond requirements definition. Such comprehensive methods will enable arbitrary systems work to attain the fulfillment that blueprint techniques deliver in traditional manufacturing.

IV. CONCLUSION

Requirements definition is an important source of costly oversights in present-day system innovation, but something can be done about it. None of the thoughts presented here are mere speculation. All have produced real achievements. The methods described have been successfully applied to a wide range of planning, analysis and design problems involving men, machines, software, hardware, databases, communications, procedures, and finances. The significance of the methods seems to be that a well-structured approach to documenting what someone thinks about a problem or a system can materially aid both that person's thinking and his ability to convey his understanding to others. Properly channeled, the mind of man is indeed formidable. But only by considering all aspects of the task ahead can teamwork be more productive and management be more effective. Communication with nontechnical readers, an understanding of the nature and structure of systems [12], and indeed a thorough knowledge of the process of analysis itself are the essential ingredients of successful requirements definition.

APPENDIX

Asking the Right Questions

The basic difficulty in requirements definition is not one of seeing the woods instead of the trees. The real need is for a methodology which, in any given circumstance, will enable an analyst to distinguish one from the other. It is always more important to ask the right questions than it is to assert possibly wrong answers. It is said that when a famous rabbi was asked, "Rabbi, why does a rabbi always answer a question with a question?" he replied, "Is there a better way?" This is the famous dialectic method used by Socrates to lead his students to understanding. Answering questions with questions leaves options open, and has the nature of breaking big questions into a top-down structure of smaller questions, easier and easier to address. The answers, when they are ultimately supplied, are each less critical and more tractable, and their relations with other small answers are well-structured.

This is the focus of requirement definition. The appropriate questions—*why, what, how*—applied systematically, will distinguish that which must be considered from that which must be postponed. A sequence of such questions, on a global, system-wide scale, will break the complexity of various aspects of the system into simpler, related questions which can be analyzed, developed, and documented. The context analysis, functional specification, and design constraints subjects which are part of requirements definition are merely parts of an overlapping chain of responses to the appropriate why, what, how questions (Fig. 9). In different circumstances, the subjects may differ, but the chaining of questions will remain the same. *Why* some feature is needed molds *what* it has to be, which in turn molds *how* it is to be achieved.

These questions form an overlapping repetition of a common pattern. Each time, the various aspects of the system are partitioned, and the understanding which is developed must be documented in a form consistent with the pattern. It is not sufficient merely to break big problems into little problems by shattering them. "Decompose" is the inverse of "compose"; at every step, the parts being considered must reassemble to make the whole context within which one is working.

The English word "cleave" captures the concept exactly. It is one of those rare words that has antithetical meanings. It means both to separate and to cling to! Thus, in the orderly process of top-down decomposition which describes the desired system, multiple views must intersect in order to supply the whole context for the next stage of system development (Fig. 10).

And Finding the Right Answers

Probably the most important aspect of this paper is its emphasis on a common approach to all phases of system development, starting with requirements definition. Knowing how postponed decisions will be handled in later phases (by the same methods) allows their essence to be established by boundary conditions, while details are left open (Fig. 11). The

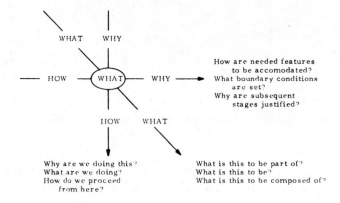

WHAT   WHY

HOW   WHAT   WHY

HOW   WHAT

How are needed features
to be accomodated?
What boundary conditions
are set?
Why are subsequent
stages justified?

Why are we doing this?
What are we doing?
How do we proceed
from here?

What is this to be part of?
What is this to be?
What is this to be composed of?

(This pattern occurs repeatedly in Fig. 9 and
constitutes its primary structure.)

Fig. 10. Right questions occur within a context and form a context as
well.

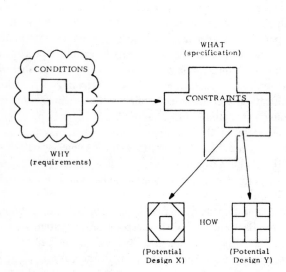

Fig. 11. Postponed decisions occur within a prior framework.

PURPOSE

Why have we
chosen these
decompositions?

VIEWPOINT

How do we look at it?

TECHNICAL   OPERA-   ECONOMIC
             TIONAL

VANTAGE POINT
What system do we see

Strategic

Tactical

Software

Program

DELINEATION OF PURPOSE
Why do we decompose
this subject as we do?

Fig. 12. Subjects are decomposed according to viewpoint, vantage
point, and purpose.

knowledge that all requirements must ultimately be implemented somehow (again by the same methods) allows their
completeness and consistency to be verified. Finally, an orderly sequence of questions enforces gradual exposition of
detail. All information is presented in well-structured documentation which allows first-hand participation by users and
commissioners in requirements definition.

The way to achieve such coherence is to seek the right kind
of answers to every set of why, what, how questions. By this
is meant to establish the viewpoint, vantage point, and purpose
of the immediate task before writing any document or con-
ducting any analysis.

The initial *purpose* of the system development effort is established by context analysis. Proper cleaving of subjects and
descriptions then takes two different forms, the exact nature
of which are governed by the overall project purpose. One
cleaving creates partial but overlapping delineations according

to *viewpoint*—viewpoint makes clear what aspects are considered relevant to achieving some component of the overall purpose. The other cleaving creates rigorous functional architectures according to *vantage point*—vantage point is a level of
abstraction that relates the viewpoints and component purposes
which together describe a given whole subject (Fig. 12).

Depending on the system, any number of viewpoints may be
important in requirements definition and may continue to
be relevant as the vantage point shifts to designing, building,
and finally using the system. Any single viewpoint always highlights some aspects of a subject, while other aspects will be lost
from view. For example, the same system may be considered
from separate viewpoints which emphasize physical characteristics, functional characteristics, operation, management, performance, maintenance, construction cost, and so forth.

Picking a vantage point always abstracts a functional architecture, while muting implementation-defined aspects of the

system architecture. The placement of a vantage point within a viewpoint establishes an all-important *bounded context*—a subset of purpose which then governs the decomposition and exposition of a particular subject regarding the system.

Can Give the Right Results

Requirements definition, beginning with context analysis, can occur whenever there is a need to define, redefine, or further delineate purpose. Context analysis treats the most important, highest level questions first, setting the conditions for further questioning each part in turn. Each subsequent question is asked within the bounded context of a prior response. Strict discipline ensures that each aspect of any question is covered by exactly one further question. Getting started is difficult, but having done so successfully, one is introduced to a "top-down" hierarchy of leading questions, properly sequenced, completely decomposed, and successively answered.

Whether explicitly stated or not, vantage points, viewpoints, and purposes guide the activities of *any* analysis team which approaches a requirements definition task. With the global understanding offered by the above discussion, analysts should realize that a place can be found for every item of information gathered. Structuring this mass of information still must be done, on paper, in a way that ensures completeness and correctness, without overspecification and confusion. That is the role of SADT.

ACKNOWLEDGMENT

The authors would like to thank J. W. Brackett and J. B. Goodenough of SofTech, Inc., Waltham, MA, who made several helpful suggestions incorporated into the presentation of these ideas. Many people at SofTech have, of course, contributed to the development and use of SADT.

REFERENCES

[1] B. W. Boehm, "Software and its impact: A quantitative assessment," *Datamation*, pp. 48–59, May 1973.
[2] P. Hirsch, "GAO hits Wimmix hard: FY'72 funding prospects fading fast," *Datamation*, p. 41, Mar. 1, 1971.
[3] *An Introduction to SADT*TM, SofTech, Inc., Waltham, MA, document 9022-78, Feb. 1976.
[4] D. T. Ross, J. B. Goodenough, and C. A. Irvine, "Software engineering: Process, principles, and goals," *Computer*, pp. 17–27, May 1975.
[5] Air Force Materials Laboratory, *Air Force Computer-Aided Manufacturing (AFCAM) Master Plan*, vol. II, app. A, and vol. III, AFSC, Wright Patterson Air Force Base, OH, rep. AFML-TR-74-104 (available from DDC as AD 922-041L and 922-171L), July 1974.
[6] *TRAIDEX Needs and Implementation Study*, SofTech, Inc., Waltham, MA, Final rep., DARPA Contract MDA903-75-C-0224 (to be available through NTIS), May 1976.
[7] B. W. Boehm, "Software design and structure," in *Practical Strategies for Developing Large Software Systems*, E. Horowitz, Ed. Reading, MA: Addison-Wesley, 1975, pp. 115–122.
[8] R. V. Head, "Automated system analysis," *Datamation*, pp. 22–24, Aug. 15, 1971.
[9] J. T. Rigo, "How to prepare functional specifications," *Datamation*, pp. 78–80, May 1974.
[10] D. Teichroew and H. Sayani "Automation of system building," *Datamation*, pp. 25–30, Aug. 15, 1971.
[11] D. Teichroew and E. A. Hershey, "PSL/PSA: A computer-aided technique for structured documentation and analysis of information processing systems," this issue, pp. 41–48.
[12] F. M. Haney, "What it takes to make MAC, MIS, and ABM fly," *Datamation*, pp. 168–169, June 1974.

Kenneth E. Schoman, Jr., received degrees in management and electrical engineering from the Massachusetts Institute of Technology, Cambridge.

He has been active in systems and policy analysis for over seven years. He taught for three years and was an Administrative Staff Member at the Massachusetts Institute of Technology. He is currently Manager of Systems Definition and Engineering at SofTech, Inc., Waltham, MA. As project leader for the functional and data analysis of complex systems, he has worked in areas as diverse as telecommunications, manufacturing job control, software development, and configuration management. His earlier work was in problem solving methods and factors affecting student and teacher performance. He has written one book.

Structured Analysis (SA): A Language for Communicating Ideas

DOUGLAS T. ROSS

Reprinted from *IEEE Transactions on Software Engineering*, Volume SE-3, Number 1, January 1977, pages 16–34. Copyright © 1977 by The Institute of Electrical and Electronics Engineers, Inc.

Abstract—Structured analysis (SA) combines blueprint-like graphic language with the nouns and verbs of any other language to provide a hierarchic, top-down, gradual exposition of detail in the form of an SA model. The things and happenings of a subject are expressed in a data decomposition and an activity decomposition, both of which employ the same graphic building block, the SA box, to represent a part of a whole. SA arrows, representing input, output, control, and mechanism, express the relation of each part to the whole. The paper describes the rationalization behind some 40 features of the SA language, and shows how they enable rigorous communication which results from disciplined, recursive application of the SA maxim: "Everything worth saying about anything worth saying something about must be expressed in six or fewer pieces."

Index Terms—Graphic language, hierarchic, requirements analysis, requirements definition, structured analysis (SA), structured programming, system analysis, system design, top-down.

I. BLUEPRINT LANGUAGE

NEITHER Watt's steam engine nor Whitney's standardized parts really started the Industrial Revolution, although each has been awarded that claim, in the past. The real start was the awakening of scientific and technological thoughts during the Renaissance, with the idea that the lawful behavior of nature can be understood, analyzed, and manipulated to accomplish useful ends. That idea itself, alone, was not enough, however, for not until the creation and evolution of blueprints was it possible to express exactly how power and parts were to be combined for each specific task at hand.

Mechanical drawings and blueprints are not mere pictures, but a complete and rich language. In blueprint language, scientific, mathematical, and geometric formulations, notations, mensurations, and naming do not merely describe an object or process, they actually model it. Because of broad differences in subject, purpose, roles, and the needs of the people who use them, many forms of blueprint have evolved, but all rigorously present well structured information in understandable form.

Failure to develop such a communication capability for data processing is due not merely to the diversity and complexity of the problems we tackle, but to the newness of our field. It has naturally taken time for us to escape from naive "programming by priesthood" to the more mature approaches, such as structured programming, language and database design, and software production methods. Still missing from this expanding repertoire of evidence of maturity, however, is the common thread that will allow all of the pieces to be tied together into a predictable and dependable approach.

Manuscript received June 21, 1976; revised September 16, 1976.
The author is with SofTech, Inc., Waltham, MA 02154.

II. STRUCTURED ANALYSIS (SA) LANGUAGE

It is the thesis of this paper that the language of structured analysis (SA), a new disciplined way of putting together old ideas, provides the evolutionary natural language appropriate to the needs of the computer field. SA is deceptively simple in its mechanics, which are few in number and have high mnemonic value, making the language easy and natural to use. Anybody can learn to read SA language with very little practice and will be able to understand the actual information content being conveyed by the graphical notation and the words of the language with ease and precision. But being a language with rigorously defined semantics, SA is a tough taskmaster. Not only do well conceived and well phrased thoughts come across concisely and with precision, but poorly conceived and poorly expressed thoughts also are recognized as such. This simply *has* to be a fact for any language whose primary accomplishment is valid communication of understanding. If both the bad and the good were *not* equally recognizable, the understanding itself would be incomplete.

SA does the same for any problem chosen for analysis, for every natural language and every formal language are, by definition, included in SA. *The only function of SA is to bind up, structure, and communicate units of thought expressed in any other chosen language.* Synthesis is composition, analysis is decomposition. *SA is structured decomposition, to enable structured synthesis to achieve a given end.* The actual building-block elements of analysis or synthesis may be of any sort whatsoever. Pictures, words, expressions of any sort may be incorporated into and made a part of the structure.

The facts about Structured Analysis are as follows.

1) It incorporates any other language; its scope is universal and unrestricted.

2) It is concerned only with the orderly and well-structured decomposition of the subject matter.

3) The decomposed units are sized to suit the modes of thinking and understanding of the intended audience.

4) Those units of understanding are expressed in a way that rigorously and precisely represents their interrelation.

5) This structured decomposition may be carried out to any required degree of depth, breadth, and scope while still maintaining all of the above properties.

6) Therefore, SA greatly increases both the quantity and quality of understanding that can be effectively and precisely communicated well beyond the limitations inherently imposed by the imbedded natural or formal language used to address the chosen subject matter.

The universality and precision of SA makes it particularly effective for requirements definition for arbitrary systems problems, a subject treated in some detail in a companion paper (see [5]). Requirements definition encompasses all aspects of system development prior to actual system design, and hence is concerned with the discovery of real user needs and communicating those requirements to those who must produce an effective system solution. Structured Analysis and Design Technique (SADT™) is the name of SofTech's proprietary methodology based on SA. The method has been applied to a wide range of planning, analysis, and design problems involving men, machines, software, hardware, database, communications procedures, and finances over the last two years, and several are cited in that paper. It is recommended that that paper (see [5]) be read prior to this paper to provide motivation and insight into the features of SA language described here.

SA is not limited to requirements definition nor even problems that are easily recognized as system problems. The end product of an SA analysis is a working model of a well-structured understanding, and that can be beneficial even on a uniquely personal level—just to "think things through." Social, artistic, scientific, legal, societal, political, and even philosophic subjects, all are subject to analysis, and the resulting models can effectively communicate the ideas to others. The same methods, approach, and discipline can be used to model the problem environment, requirements, and proposed solution, as well as the project organization, operation, budget, schedule, and action plan. Man thinks with language. Man communicates with language. SA structures language for communicating ideas more effectively. *The human mind can accommodate any amount of complexity as long as it is presented in easy-to-grasp chunks that are structured together to make the whole.*

III. Outline of the Demonstration

Five years ago I said in an editorial regarding software [1]: "Tell me *why* it works, not *that* it works." That is the approach taken in this paper. This paper does not present a formal grammar for the SA language—that will come later, elsewhere. This paper also is not a user manual for either authors or readers of the language—a simple "how to" exposition. Instead, we concentrate here on the motivation *behind* the features of SA in an attempt to convey directly an appreciation for its features and power even beyond that acquired through use by most SA practitioners. SA has been heavily developed, applied, taught, and used for almost three years already, but the design rationale behind it is first set down here.

SA (both the language and the discipline of thought) derives from the way our minds work, and from the way we understand real-world situations and problems. Therefore, we start out with a summary of principles of exposition—good storytelling. This turns out to yield the familiar top-down decomposition, a key component of SA. But more than that results, for consideration of how we view our space-time world shows that we always understand anything and everything in terms of *both* things *and* happenings. This is why all of our languages have *both* nouns *and* verbs—and this, in turn, yields the means

by which SA language is universal, and can absorb any other language as a component part.

SA supplies rigorous structural connections to any language whose nouns and verbs it absorbs in order to talk about things and happenings, and we will spend some time covering the basics carefully, so that the fundamentals are solid. We do this by presenting, in tabular form, some 40 basic features, and then analyzing them bit by bit, using SA diagrams as figures to guide and illustrate the discussion.

Once the basics have thus been introduced, certain important topics that would have been obscure earlier are covered in some depth because their combinations are at the heart of SA's effectiveness. These topics concern constraints, boundaries, necessity, and dominance between modular portions of subject matter being analyzed. It turns out that constraints based on purpose and viewpoint actually *make* the structure. The depth of treatment gives insight into how we understand things.

The actual output of SA is a hierarchically organized structure of separate diagrams, each of which exposes only a limited part of the subject to view, so that even very complex subjects can be understood. The structured collection of diagrams is called an *SA model*. The demonstration here concludes with several special notations to clarify presentation and facilitate the orderly organization of the material. Since actual SA diagrams (some good, some illustrating poor style) are used, as figure illustrations, the reader is exposed here to the style of SA even though the SA model represented by the collection of figures is not complete enough to be understandable by itself. Later papers will treat more advanced topics and present complete examples of SA use and practice in a wide variety of applications.

IV. Principles of Good Storytelling

There are certain basic, known principles about how people's minds go about the business of understanding, and communicating understanding by means of language, which have been known and used for many centuries. No matter how these principles are addressed, they always end up with hierarchic decomposition as being the heart of good storytelling. Perhaps the most relevant formulation is the familiar: "Tell 'em whatcha gonna tell 'em. Tell 'em. Tell 'em whatcha told 'em." This is a pattern of communication almost as universal and well-entrenched as Newton's laws of motion. It is the pattern found in all effective forms of communication and in all analyses of why such communication is effective. Artistic and scientific fields, in addition to journalism, all follow the same sequence, for that is the way our minds work.

Only something so obvious as not to be worth saying can be conveyed in a single stage of the communication process, however. In any worthwhile subject matter, Stage Two ("Tell 'em") requires the parallel introduction of several more instances of the same pattern starting again with Stage One. Usually a story establishes several such levels of telling, and weaves back and forth between them as the need arises, to convey understanding, staying clear of excesses in either detail (boredom) or abstraction (confusion).

™Trademark of SofTech, Inc.

V. The SA Maxim

This weaving together of parts with whole is the heart of SA. The natural law of good communications takes the following, quite different, form in SA:

"Everything worth saying
about anything worth saying something about
must be expressed in six or fewer pieces."

Let us analyze this maxim and see how and why it, too, yields hierarchically structured storytelling.

First of all, there must be something (anything) that is "worth saying something about." We must have some subject matter that has some value to us. We must have an interest in some aspect of it. This is called establishing the *viewpoint* for the model, in SA terminology. Then we must have in mind some audience we want to communicate with. That audience will determine what is (and is not) "worth saying" about the subject from that viewpoint. This is called establishing the *purpose* for the model, in SA terminology. As we will see, every subject has many aspects of interest to many audiences, so that there can be many viewpoints and purposes. But each SA model must have only one of each, to bound and structure its subject matter. We also will see that each model also has an established *vantage point* within the purpose-structured context of some other model's viewpoint, and this is how multiple models are interrelated so that they collectively cover the whole subject matter. But a single SA model considers only worthy thoughts about a single worthy subject.

The clincher, however, is that *every* worthy thought about that worthy subject must be included. The first word of the maxim is *everything*, and that means exactly that—absolutely nothing that fits the purpose and viewpoint can be left out. The reason is simple. By definition everything is the subject itself, for otherwise it would not *be* that subject—it would be a *lesser* subject. Then, if the subject is to be broken into six or fewer pieces, every single thing must go into exactly one of those (nonoverlapping) pieces. Only in this way can we ensure that the subject stays the same, and does not degenerate into some lesser subject as we decompose it. Also, if overlapping pieces were allowed, conflicts and confusions might arise.

A "piece" can be anything we choose it to be—the maxim merely requires that the single piece of thought about the subject be broken into several (not too few, and not too many[1]) pieces. Now, certainly if the original single piece of thought about the subject is worthy, it is very unlikely that the mere breaking of it into six-or-fewer pieces exhausts that worth. The maxim still applies so that every one of them must similarly be expressed in six-or-fewer *more* pieces—again and again—until the number of pieces has grown to suit the

---

[1] Many people have urged me to relate the magic number "six" to various psychological studies about the characteristics of the human mind. I won't. It's neither scientific nor "magic." It is simply the *right* number. (Readers who doubt my judgement are invited to read for themselves the primary source [6].) The only proper reference would be to the little bear in the Goldilocks story. His portions always were "just right," too!

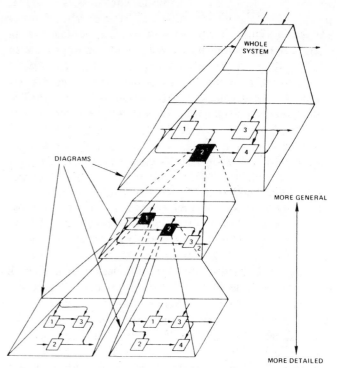

Fig. 1. Structured decomposition.

total worthiness. At a fine enough level of decomposition, it is not worth continuing. No further decomposition is required for completely clear understanding. Thus we see that the SA maxim must be interpreted *recursively*, and yields top-down hierarchic decomposition. The SA language allows this hierarchic structure to be expressed (see Fig. 1).

VI. Expression

In the maxim, the word "express" covers both the rigorous grammar of SA language itself, as well as the grammar (however well or ill formed) of the natural language chosen to address the subject matter. By definition, SA language includes all other languages, and regardless of what language is embedded, the decomposition discipline (expressed by the SA language component of the combined language) ensures that at each stage, the natural language (whatever it may be) is used to address and express only every worthy thought about a more and more restricted piece of the worthy subject matter. Because of this orderly zeroing-in, SA certainly cannot decrease the effectiveness of that chosen language. In effect, the SA maxim is valid by definition, for whenever the subject matter has already been broken down to such a fine level that the SA decomposition would add nothing to what already would be done (as, for example, in jokes or some poetry) the chosen language stands by itself, not decreased in effectiveness.

Most of the time the conscious practice of Structured Analysis and its thought discipline improves people's ability to think clearly and find solutions. In the cases where this does not happen, however, Structured Analysis still "works," in the sense that the bad portions stand out more clearly and are understood to be bad and needing further attention. For the next step in our demonstration we consider thoughts, and the expression of thoughts in language.

VII. THINGS AND HAPPENINGS

We live in a space-time world. Numerous philosophical and scientific studies, as well as the innate experience of every person, shows that we never have any understanding of any subject matter except in terms of our own mental constructs of "things" and "happenings" of that subject matter. It seems to be impossible for us to think about anything without having that subject automatically be bounded in our minds by a population of parts or pieces (concrete or abstract—but in any case "nominal" things, i.e., literally things to which we give names or nouns) which provide the basis for our even conceiving of the subject matter as a separate subject. Immediately, however, once we are aware of the things, we are aware of the happenings—the relationships, changes, and transformations which take place between and among those things and make the subject matter meaningful or interesting (the "verbial" things, to which we give action words or verbs).

The universality of things and happenings provides the next basic step of decomposition (after the still more fundamental decomposition of recognizing and isolating the purpose and viewpoint which established the "worth" of possible things to say about the "worth" of the subject matter). Every one of our languages, whether natural or artificial, formal or informal, has those two complementary aspects—nouns and verbs, operators and operands, etc.—to permit the expression of thoughts about the subject matter. Thus the means is provided to incorporate any other language into SA. The incorporation of other languages into SA is not forced, nor awkward.

SA language provides the same graphic notation for both the things and the happenings aspects of any subject. Every SA model has two dual aspects—a *thing* aspect, called the *data decomposition*, and a *happening* aspect, called the *activity decomposition*. The model is incomplete without both decompositions.

VIII. BOUNDED SUBJECT MATTER

So we have now established the starting premises. The SA maxim forces gradual, top-down decomposition, leaving nothing out at any stage, and matching good storytelling exposition. The things and happenings (*data* and *activities*, in SA technical terms) match the nominal and verbial construction of any chosen language for directly addressing the subject, so we will never be "at a loss for words." Now we are ready to address the specifics—how SA language (mostly graphical, using boxes and arrows) actually allows well structured expression of well structured thought. We do this in stages: 1) we dump the entire body of the subject matter all at once into a table of some 40 separate items of notation and conventions—just to bound the subject itself; 2) we then start to pick our way through these topics, starting with those that define the basics of boxes and arrows; and 3) then we will use those basic expository capabilities to complete the consideration of the list.

In a prior, companion paper [2], which had its roots in the same background that led to the development of SA, we described and illustrated a univeral, standard pattern or process which appears to permeate all of software engineering and problem-solving in general. Since that pattern is so close to the natural phenomena of understanding which we are discussing here with respect to SA itself, we will use it to motivate, clarify, and structure the presentation. The idea of the pattern is captured in five words: 1) purpose; 2) concept; 3) mechanism; 4) notation; and 5) usage. Any systematic approach to a problem requires a concise purpose or objective that specifies which aspect of the problem is of concern. Within that purpose we formulate a valid conceptual structure (both things and happenings) in terms of which the problem can be analyzed and approached. We then seek out (or work out) the designs (mechanisms—concrete or abstract, but always including both data and activity aspects) which are capable of implementing the relevant concepts and of working together to achieve the stated purpose. (This combines three of the five words together.) Now, purpose, concepts, and mechanism, being a systematic approach to a *class* of problems, require a notation for expressing the capabilities of the mechanism and invoking its use for a particular problem in the class. Finally, usage rules are spelled out, explicitly or by example, to guide the use of the notation to invoke the implementation to realize the concept to achieve the specified purpose for the problem. The cited paper [2] gives numerous carefully drawn examples showing how the pattern arises over and over again throughout systematic problem solving, at both abstract and concrete levels, and with numerous hierarchic and cross-linked interconnections.

IX. THE FEATURES OF SA LANGUAGE

Fig. 2 is a tabulation of some 40 features or aspects of SA which constitute the basic core of the language for communication. For each feature, the purpose, concept, mechanism, and notation are shown. Usages (for the purposes of this paper) are covered only informally by the examples which follow. The reader should scan down the "purpose" column of Fig. 2 at this time, because the collection of entries there set the objectives for the bounded subject matter which we are about to consider. Note also the heavy use of pictures in the "notation" column. These are components of graphic language. But notice that most entries mix *both* English *and* graphic language into a "phrase" of SA notation. Clearly, any other spoken language such as French, German, or Sanskrit could be translated and substituted for the English terms, for they merely aid the understanding the syntax and semantics of SA language itself.

In Fig. 2, the *name* and *label* portions of the "notation" column for rows 1 and 2, and the corresponding *noun* and *verb* indications in rows 6 and 7 are precisely the places where SA language absorbs other natural or formal languages in the sense of the preceding discussion. As the preceding sections have tried to make clear, *any* language, whether informal and natural or formal and artificial, has things and happenings aspects in the nominal and verbial components of its vocabulary. These are to be related to the *names of boxes* and *labels on arrows* in order to absorb those "foreign" languages into SA language.

Notice that it is not merely the nouns and verbs which are absorbed. Whatever richness the "foreign" language may possess, the full richness of the nominal and verbial expressions, including modifiers, is available in the naming and labeling por-

Fig. 2. SA language features.

#	PURPOSE	CONCEPT		MECHANISM	NOTATION		NODE
1	BOUND CONTEXT	INSIDE/OUTSIDE		SA BOX	NAME		A11
2	RELATE/CONNECT	FROM/TO		SA ARROW	LABEL		A12
3	SHOW TRANSFORMATION	INPUT-OUTPUT		SA INTERFACE	INPUT / OUTPUT		A13
4	SHOW CIRCUMSTANCE	CONTROL		SA INTERFACE	CONTROL		A14
5	SHOW MEANS	SUPPORT		SA MECHANISM	MECHANISM		A15
6	NAME APTLY	ACTIVITY HAPPENINGS	DATA THINGS	SA NAMES	ACTIVITY VERB	DATA NOUN	A211
7	LABEL APTLY	THINGS	HAPPENINGS	SA LABELS	NOUN	VERB	A212
8	SHOW NECESSITY	I-O	C-O	PATH			A213
9	SHOW DOMINANCE	C	I	CONSTRAINT			A214
10	SHOW RELEVANCE	ICO	ICO	ALL INTERFACES			A215
11	OMIT OBVIOUS	C-O	I-O	OMITTED ARROW			A216
12	BE EXPLICIT WITHOUT CLUTTER	PIPELINES, CONDUITS, WIRES		BRANCH			A221
13				JOIN			A221
14	BE CONCISE AND CLEAR	CABLES, MULTI-WIRES		BUNDLE			A222
15				SPREAD			A222
16	SHOW EXCLUSIVES	EXPLICIT ALTERNATIVES		OR BRANCH			A223
17				OR JOIN			A223
18	SHOW INTERFACES TO PARENT DIAGRAM	ARROWS PENETRATE		SA BOUNDARY ARROWS (ON CHILD)	NO BOX SHOWN		A231
19	SHOW EXPLICIT PARENT CONNECTION	NUMBER CONVENTION FOR PARENT, WRITE ICOM CODE ON CHILD BOUNDARY ARROWS			(ON CHILD)		A232
20	SHOW UNIQUE DECOMPOSITION	DETAIL REFERENCE EXPRESSION (DRE)		C-NUMBER OR PAGE NUMBER OF DETAIL DIAGRAM	BOX DRE		A233
21	SHOW SHARED OR VARIABLE DECOMPOSITION	DRE WITH (MODEL NAME)		SA CALL ON SUPPORT	BOX STUB DRE		A234

#	PURPOSE	CONCEPT	MECHANISM	NOTATION	NODE
22	SHOW COOPERATION	INTERCHANGE OF SHARED RESPONSIBILITY	SA 2-WAY ARROWS		A311
23	SUPPRESS INTERCHANGE DETAILS	ALLOW 2-WAY WITHIN 1-WAY PIPELINES	2-WAY TO 1-WAY BUTTING ARROWS		A312
24	SUPPRESS "PASS-THROUGH" CLUTTER	ALLOW ARROWS TO GO OUTSIDE DIAGRAMS	SA "TUNNELING" (WITH REFERENCES)	PARENT OFFSPRING	A313
25	SUPPRESS NEEDED-ARROW CLUTTER	ALLOW TAGGED JUMPS WITHIN DIAGRAM	TO ALL or FROM ALL	TO ALL	A314
26	SHOW NEEDED ANNOTATION	ALLOW WORDS IN DIAGRAM	SA NOTE	NOTE:	A32
27	OVERCOME CRAMPED SPACE	ALLOW REMOTE LOCATION OF WORDS IN DIAGRAM	SA FOOTNOTE	(n=integer)	A32
28	SHOW COMMENTS ABOUT DIAGRAM	ALLOW WORDS ON (NOT IN) DIAGRAM	SA META-NOTE	(n=integer)	A32
29	ENSURE PROPER ASSOCIATION OF WORDS	TIE WORDS TO INTENDED SUBJECT	SA "SQUIGGLE"	(TOUCH REFERENT)	A32
30	UNIQUE SHEET REFERENCE	CHRONOLOGICAL CREATION	SA C-NUMBER	AUTHOR INITS INTEGER	A41
31	UNIQUE BOX REFERENCE	PATH DOWN TREE FROM BOX NUMBERS	SA NODE NUMBER (BOX NUMBERS)	A, D, OR M ∈ PARENT # ∈ BOX #	A42
32	SAME FOR MULTI-MODELS	PRECEDE BY MODEL NAME	SA MODEL NAME	MODEL NAME/NODE#	A42
33	UNIQUE INTERFACE REFERENCE	ICOM WITH BOX NUMBER	SA BOX ICOM	BOX# ICOM CODE	A43
34	UNIQUE ARROW REFERENCE	FROM - TO	PAIR OF BOX ICOMs	BOX ICOM$_1$ BOX ICOM$_2$	A44
35	SHOW CONTEXT REFERENCE	SPECIFY A REFERENCE POINT	SA REF.EXP. "DOT"	A122.411 "WHICH SEE"	A45
36	ASSIST CORRECT INTERPRETATION	SHOW DOMINANCE GEOMETRICALLY (ASSIST PARSE)	STAIRCASE LAYOUT	DOMINANCE	A5
37	ASSIST UNDERSTANDING	PROSE SUMMARY OF MESSAGE	SA TEXT	NODE# ∈ T ∈ INTEGER	A5
38	HIGHLIGHT FEATURES	SPECIAL EFFECTS FOR EXPOSITION ONLY	SA FEOs	NODE# ∈ F ∈ INTEGER	A5
39	DEFINE TERMS	GLOSSARY WITH WORDS & PICTURES	SA GLOSSARY	MODEL NAME ∈ G ∈ INTEGER	A5
40	ORGANIZE PAGES	PROVIDE TABLE OF CONTENTS	SA NODE INDEX	NODE# ORDER	A5

tions of SA language. As we shall see, however, normally these capabilities for richness are purposely suppressed, for simplicity and immediacy of understanding normally require brevity and conciseness.

Fig. 2 has introduced our subject and has served to point out the precise way in which SA absorbs other languages, but this mode of discourse would make a long and rambling story. I therefore proceed to use SA itself to communicate the intended understanding of Fig. 2. This will not, however, be a perfect, or even a good example of SA communication in action, for the intent of this paper is to guide the reader to an understanding of SA, not to teach how to fully exploit SA diagrams and modeling. The SA diagrams presented here only as figures are incomplete and exhibit both good *and* bad examples of SA expressiveness, as well as showing all the language constructs. Our subject is too complex to treat in a small model, but the figures at least present the reader with some measure of the flexibility of the language.

The reader is forewarned that there is more information in the diagrams than is actually referenced here in text which uses them as "figures." After the paper has been read, the total model can be studied for review and for additional understanding. Everything said here about the SA language and notations applies to each diagram, and most features are illustrated more than once, frequently before they are described in the text. Therefore, on first reading, please ignore any features and notations not explicitly referenced. Non-SA "first-reading" aids are isolated by a bold outline, in the diagrams.

In practical use of SofTech's SADT, a "reader/author cycle" is rigorously adhered to in which (similar to the code-reading phase of egoless structured programming) authors, experts, and management-level personnel read and critique the efforts of each individual SADT author to achieve a fully-acceptable quality of result. (It is in fact this rigorous adherence to quality control which enables production SA models to be relied upon. So far as possible *everything* worthy has been done to make sure that *everything* worthy has been expressed to the level required by the intended readership.)

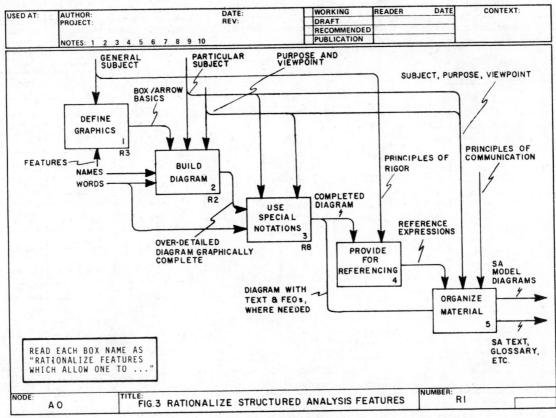

SADT DIAGRAM FORM ST098 9/75
Form © 1975 SofTech, inc., 460 Totten Pond Road, Waltham, Mass. 02154, USA

Fig. 3. Rationalize SA features.

X. PURPOSE AND VIEWPOINT

Fig. 3 is an SA diagram[2] and, by definition, it is a meaningful expression in SA language. It consists of box and arrow graphical notation mixed with words and numbers. Consonant with the tutorial purpose of this paper, I will not, here, try to teach how to *read* a diagram. My tutorial approach aims only to lead to an understanding of what is *in* a diagram.

So we will just begin to examine Fig. 3. Start with the title, "Rationalize structured analysis features"—an adequate match to our understanding of the purpose and viewpoint of this whole paper. We seek to make rational the reasons behind those features. Next read the content of each of the boxes: "Define graphics; build diagram; use special notations; provide for referencing; organize material." These must be the six-or-fewer "parts" into which the titled subject matter is being broken. In this case there are five of them, and sure enough this aspect of SA follows exactly the time-tested outline approach to subject matter. Because our purpose is to have a graphics-based language (like blueprints), once we have decided upon some basics of graphic definition we will use that to build a diagram for some particular subject, adding special notations (presumably to improve clarity), and then because (as with blueprints) we know that a whole collection will be required

to convey complex understanding in easy-to-understand pieces, we must provide for a way of referencing the various pieces and organizing the resulting material into what we see as an understandable whole.

Now, I have tried to compose the preceding long sentence about Fig. 3 using natural language constructs which, if not an exact match, are very close to terms which appear directly in Fig. 3. In fact, the reader should be able to find an exact correspondence between things which show in the figure and every important syntactic and semantic point in each part of the last sentence of the preceding paragraph, although the diagram has more to it than the sentence. Please reread that sentence now and check out this correspondence for yourself. In the process you will notice that considerable (though not exhaustive) use is made of information which is not *inside* the boxes, but instead is associated with the word-and-arrow structure of the diagram *outside* the boxes. This begins to show why, although SA in its basic backbone does follow the standard outline pattern of presentation, the box-and-arrow structure conveys a great deal more information than a simple topic outline (only the box *contents*) could possibly convey.

XI. THE FIRST DETAIL VIEW

Fig. 4 is another SA diagram. Simpler in structure than the diagram of Fig. 3, but nonetheless with much the same "look."

[2]The SADT diagram form itself is © 1975, SofTech, Inc., and has various fields used in the practice of SADT methodology.

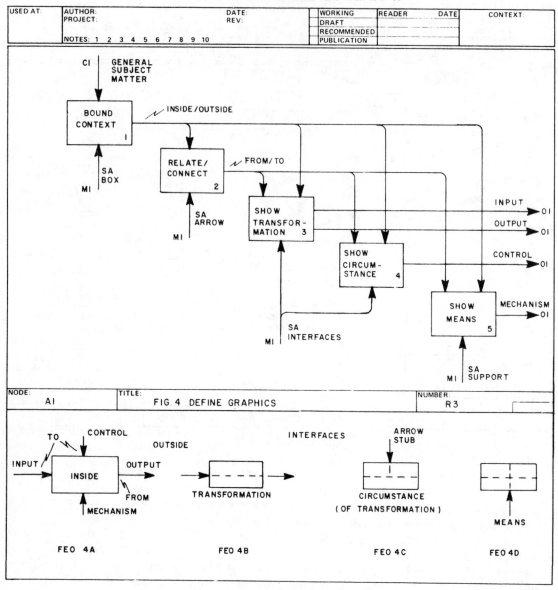

SADT DIAGRAM FORM ST098 9/75
Form © 1975 SofTech. Inc. 460 Totten Pond Road. Waltham, Mass. 02154 USA

Fig. 4. Define graphics.

The title, "Define graphics," is identical to the name inside the first box of Fig. 3, which is here being broken into five component worthy pieces, called the *nested factors* in SA terminology. Again the words written inside the boxes are legible, but are they understandable? How can "Bound context; relate/connect; show transformation; show circumstance; show means," be considered parts of "Define graphics?" It is not very clear, is it? It would seem that something must be wrong with SA for the touted understandability turns out to be, in fact, quite obscure!

Look at Fig. 4 again and see if you don't agree that we have a problem—and see if you can supply the answer to the problem.

The problem is not with SA at all, but with our too-glib approach to it. SA is a rigorous language and thereby is unforgiving in many ways. In order for the communication of un-derstanding to take place we ourselves must understand and conform to the rules of that rigor. The apparent obscurity should disappear in a twinkling once the following factor is pointed out: namely, *always be sure to do your understanding in the proper context*. In this case, the proper context was established by the title of Fig. 3, "Rationalize structured analysis features," and the purpose, to define graphical concepts and notations for the purpose of representing and conveying understanding of subject matters. Now, if we have all of that firmly implanted in our mind, then surely the name in Box 1 of Fig. 4 should be amply clear. Read, now, Box 4. 1[3] for yourself, and see if that clarity and communication of intended understanding does not take place.

[3] To shorten references to figures, "Box 4. 1" will mean "Box 1 of Fig. 4," etc. in the following discussion.

You see, according to the diagram, the first feature of defining graphics is to "Bound the context"—precisely the subject we have just been discussing and precisely the source of the apparent obscurity which made SA initially appear to be on shaky ground. To aid first reading of the figures, a suggested paraphrasing of the intended context is given in a bold box on each of the other diagrams (see Fig. 3).

As we can see from the section of Fig. 4 labeled FEO 4A[4] the general subject matter is isolated from the rest of all subject matter by means of the SA box which has an inside and an outside (look at the box). The only thing we are supposed to consider is the portion of that subject matter which is *inside* the box—so the boundary of the box does bound the context in which we are to consider the subject.

XII. THE SA BOX AS BUILDING BLOCK

We lack the background (at this point) to continue an actual reading of Fig. 4, because it itself defines the basic graphic notations used in it. Instead, consider only the sequence of illustrations (4A-4D) labeled FEO. FEO 4A shows that the fundamental building block of SA language notation is a box with four sides called INPUT, CONTROL, OUTPUT, and MECHANISM. As we have seen above, the bounded piece of subject matter is *inside* the box, and, as we will see, the actual boundary of the box is made by the collection of *arrow stubs* entering and leaving the box. The bounded pieces are related and connected (Box 4.2) by SA arrows which go *from* an OUTPUT of one box *to* the INPUT or CONTROL of another box, i.e., such arrow connections make the *interfaces* between subjects. The names INPUT and OUTPUT are chosen to convey the idea that (see FEO 4B and Box 4.3) the box represents a *transformation* from a "before" to an "after" state of affairs. The CONTROL interface (see FEO 4C and Box 4.4) interacts and constrains the transformation to ensure that it applies only under the appropriate circumstances. The combination of INPUT, OUTPUT, and CONTROL fully specifies the bounded piece of subject, and the interfaces relate it to the other pieces. Finally, the MECHANISM *support* (not interface, see FEO 4D and Box 4.5) provide means for realizing the complete piece represented by the box.

We will see shortly why Fig. 4 contains no INPUT arrows at all, but except for that anomaly, this description should make Fig. 4 itself reasonably understandable. (Remember the context—"Rationalize the features of SA language which allow one to define graphic notation for....") The diagram (with FEO's and discussion) is the desired rationalization. It fits quite well with the idea of following the maxim. We don't mind breaking *everything* about a bounded piece of subject matter into pieces as long as we are sure we can express completely how all those pieces go back together to constitute the whole. Input, output, control, and mechanism provide that capability. As long as the right mechanism is provided, and the right control is applied, whatever is inside the box can be a valid transformation of input to output. We now must see

[4]This notation refers to the sequence of imbedded illustrations in Fig. 4 which are "For exposition only" (FEO).

how to use the "foreign" language names and labels of boxes and arrows. Then we can start putting SA to work.

XIII. USING THE BASICS FOR UNDERSTANDING

Fig. 4, and especially FEO 4A, now that we have digested the meaning of the diagram itself, has presented the basic box-and-arrow-stubs-making-useful-interfaces-for-a-bounded-piece-of-subject-matter building block of SA. We now can start to use the input, output, control, and mechanism concepts to further our understanding. Knowing even this much, the power of expression of SA diagrams beyond that of simple outlining will start to become evident.

Fig. 5, entitled "Build diagram," details Box 3.2. Referring back to Fig. 3 and recalling the opening discussion of its meaning (which we should do in order to establish in our mind the proper context for reading Fig. 5) we recall that the story line of Fig. 3 said that after Box 3.1 had defined the arrow and box basics, then we would build an actual diagram with words and names for a particular subject in accordance with a purpose and viewpoint chosen to convey the appropriate understanding. Looking at Box 3.2 in the light of what we have just learned about the box/arrow basics in Fig. 4, we can see that indeed the inputs are words and names, which will be transformed into a diagram (an over-detailed, but graphically complete diagram, evidently). Even though the mechanism is not specified, it is shown that this diagramming process will be controlled by (i.e., constrained by) the graphic conventions, subject, and viewpoint. Now refer to Fig. 5 with this established context and consider its three boxes:—"Build box structure; build arrow structure; build diagram structure." That matches our understanding that a diagram is a structure of boxes and arrows (with appropriate names and labels, of course). Study Fig. 5 yourself briefly keeping in mind the points we have discussed so far. You should find little difficulty, and you will find that a number of the technical terms that were pure jargon in the tabulated form in Fig. 2 now start to take on some useful meaning. (Remember to ignore terms such as "ICOM" and "DRE," to be described later.)

If you have taken a moment or so to study Fig. 5 on your own, you probably have the impression things are working all right, but you are still not really sure that you are acquiring the intended level of understanding of Fig. 5. It seems to have too many loose ends semantically, even though it makes partial sense. If this is your reaction, you are quite right. For more detail and information is needed to make all the words and relationships take on full meaning. Fig 5 does indeed tell *everything* about "Build diagram" in its three boxes, which are themselves reasonably understandable. But we need more information for many of the labels to really snap into place. This we will find in the further detailing of the three boxes. Context *orients* for understanding (*only* orients!); details *enable* understanding (and strengthen context).

Fig. 6 provides the detailing for Box 5.1. Especially for this diagram, it is important to keep in mind the appropriate context for reading. It is not "*Draw* an SA diagram," but to motivate the *features* of SA. Thus, when we read the title, "Build

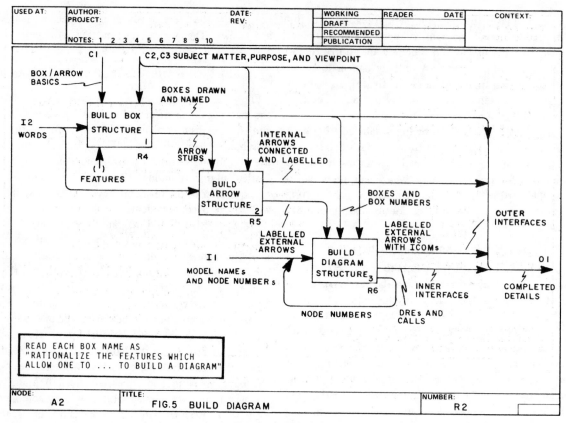

Fig. 5. Build diagram.

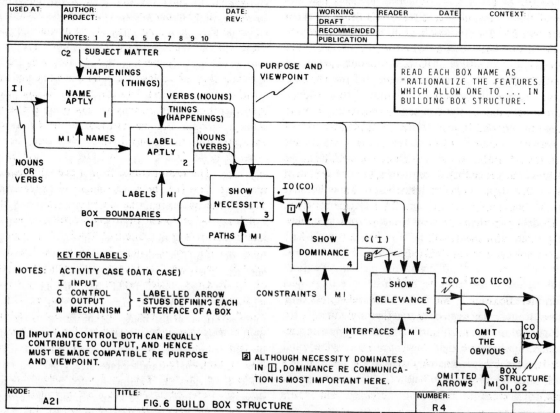

Fig. 6. Build box structure.

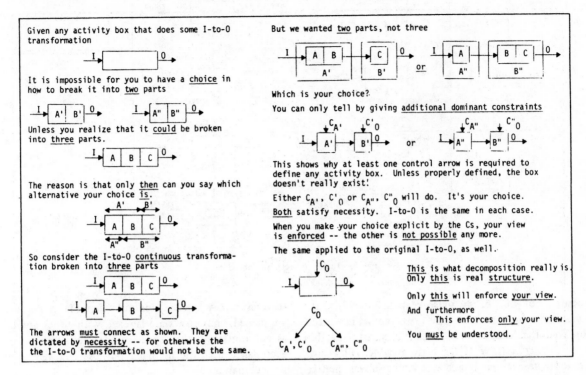

Fig. 8. Dominance and necessity.

Fig. 8 tells the story in concise form. Please read it now. Then please read it again, for all experience with SA shows that this simple argument seems to be very subtle and difficult for most people to grasp correctly. The reason is that the *everything* of the SA maxim makes the I-to-O *necessity* chain the *weakest possible structure*—akin to *no structure at all*. It merely states a fact that *must be true* for every SA box, because of the maxim. Therefore *dominant constraints*, expressed by the control arrows for activity boxes are, in fact, the *only* way possible, to impose structure. Furthermore, that enforcement of structure is unique and compelling—no other structure can be (mis-) understood in place of that intended by the SA author. This is, of course, all mediated by the effectiveness with which the SA author wields the chosen non-SA language used for names of boxes and labels on arrows, but the argument presented in this paper holds, nonetheless. This is because whenever the imprecision of the non-SA language intrudes, more SA modeling (perhaps even with new purpose and viewpoint for greater refinement, still, of objectives) is forced by the reader/author cycle of the SADT discipline.

XVI. THE RULE OF OMISSION

Now consider Boxes 6.5 and 6.6 "Show relevance" and "Omit the obvious." These two ideas follow right along with the above discussion. Namely, in the case of activity diagramming, *if inputs are relevant* (i.e., if they make a strong contribution to understandability) *then they are drawn*. But on the other hand, since the important thing is the structure imposed by the control dominance and output necessity, and inputs *must* be supplied in any case for those outputs to result, *obvious inputs can and should be omitted from* the box struc-

ture of SA *activity diagramming*. In other words, whenever an obvious input is omitted in an activity diagram, the reader knows that (because of the SA maxim) whatever is needed will be supplied in order that the control and output which *are* drawn can happen correctly. Omitting the obvious makes the understandability and meaning of the diagram much stronger, because inputs when they *are* drawn are known to be important and nonobvious. Remember that SA diagrams are not wiring diagrams, they are vehicles for communicating understanding.

Although activity and data are dual in SA and use the same four-sided box notation, they are not quite the same, for the concept of dominance and constraint in the *data* aspect centers on *input* rather than control. In the data case, the weak chain of necessity is C-O-C-O-⋯ not I-O-I-O-⋯ as it is in the activity case. The reason comes from a deep difference between space and time (i.e., between things and happenings). In the case of the happening, the dominant feature is the control which says when to cut the transformation to yield a desired intermediate result, because the "freedom" of happenings is in time. In the case of things, however, the "freedom" which must be constrained and dominated concerns which version of the thing (i.e., which part of the data box) is the one that is to exist, regardless of time. The input activity for a data box "creates" that thing in that form and therefore it is the dominant constraint to be specified for a data box. An unimportant control activity will happen whenever needed, and may be omitted from the diagram.

Therefore, the rule regarding the obvious in SA is that *controls may never be omitted from activity diagrams and inputs may never be omitted from data diagrams*. Fig. 6 summarizes all of this discussion.

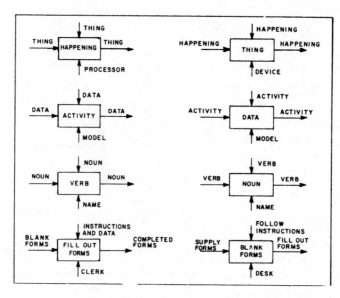

Fig. 7. Duality of activities and data.

box structure," of Fig. 6, we must keep in mind that the worthy piece of subject matter is not *how* to build box structure, nor even the features which *create* box structure, but motivation for *explanation* of the features which allow box structure to represent the bounded context subject matter. This actually is a very sophisticated subject and normally we would only be diagramming it after we had already prepared rather complete models of the "how to" of SA so that many of the terms and ideas would already be familiar. In this paper, however, the opening discussion must serve instead. The next four sections discuss Fig. 6.

XIV. DUALITY OF DATA AND ACTIVITIES

Recall that a complete SA model has to consider both the things and happenings of the subject being modeled. Happenings are represented by an activity decomposition consisting of activity diagrams and things are represented by data decomposition consisting of data diagrams. The neat thing about SA language is that both of these complementary but radically different aspects are diagrammed using exactly the same four-sided box notation. Fig. 7 illustrates this fact. The happening/activity and thing/data domains are completely dual in SA. (Think of an INPUT activity on a data box as one that creates the data thing, and of OUTPUT as one that uses or references it.) Notice that mechanism is different in interpretation, but the role is the same. For a happening it is the *processor*, machine, computer, person, etc., which makes the happening happen. For a thing it is the *device*, for storage, representation, implementation, etc. (of the thing).

A quick check of Fig. 4 shows that mechanism's purpose is to show the means of realization, and that it is *not an interface* but is instead something called "support" in SA (described later in Section XXIII). For either activity or data modeling, a support mechanism is *a complete model*, with both data and activity aspects. As Fig. 7 shows, that complete "real thing" is *known by its name*, whereas things and happenings are identified by nouns and verbs (really nominal expressions and verbial expressions). With this in mind, we can see that the first two boxes in Fig. 6 motivate the naming and labeling

features of SA to do or permit what Fig. 7 requires—boxes are named, and arrows are labeled, with either nouns or verbs as appropriate to the aspect of the model, and of course, in accordance with the intended purpose and viewpoint of the subject matter.

XV. CONSTRAINTS

We will consider next Boxes 6.3 and 6.4 together, and with some care, for this is one of the more subtle aspects of SA—the concept of a *constraint*—the key to well structured thought and well structured diagrams. The word *constraint* conjures up visions of opposing forces at play. *Something can be constrained only if there is something stronger upon which the constraining force can be based.* It might seem that from the ideas of SA presented so far, that that strong base will be provided by the rigorously defined bounded context of a box. Given a strong boundary, it is easy to envision forces saying either to stay inside the boundary or to stay outside the boundary. It is a pleasing thought indeed, and would certainly make strong structure in both our thinking and our diagrams. The only trouble is it does not work that way (or at least not immediately), but in fact it is just the opposite! In SA thinking *it is the constraints that make the boundaries, not the other way around.* This is a tricky point so we will approach it slowly. It is still true that a constraint, to be a constraint, has to have something to push against. If it is not the bounded-context boundary, then what is it?

The subtle answer is that *the purpose and viewpoint of the model provide the basis for all constraints* which in turn provide the strength and rigidity for all the boundaries which in turn create the inescapable structure which forces correct understanding to be communicated. This comes about through the concepts of *necessity* and *dominance*, which are the subjects of Boxes 6.3 and 6.4. Dominance sounds much like constraint, and we will not be surprised to find it being the purveyor of constraint. But "necessity" has its own subtle twist in this, the very heart of SA. Therefore we must approach it, too, with some deliberation.

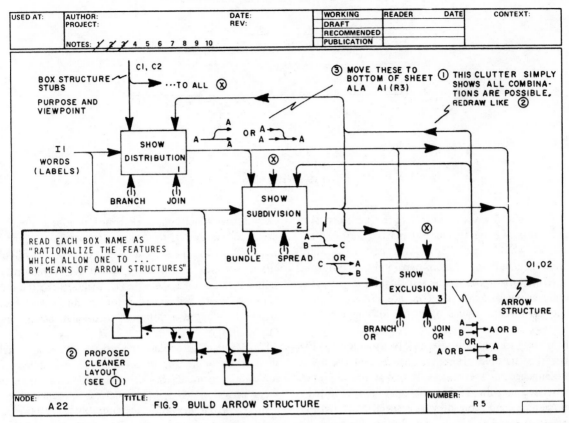

Fig. 9. Build arrow structure.

XVII. STRENGTHENING OF BOUNDARIES

Recall that a constraint does need something to push on. What is that? The answer is the one originally proposed, but rejected. *Constraints are based on the boundary of a bounded context—but of the single box of the parent diagram which the current diagram details.* (A parenthesized hint that this would turn out to be the case *does* appear in the original rejection of the view that boundaries provide the base for constraints, above.) In other words, the constraints represented by the arrows on a diagram are *not* formed by the several boundaries of the boxes of *that* diagram, but all are based on the single boundary of the corresponding box in the *parent* diagram. As was stated above in Section XV, the constraints form the box boundary interfaces and define the boxes, not the other way around. The strength of those constraints comes from the corresponding "push" passed through from the parent. As the last "C_O" portion of Fig. 8 indicates, this hierarchic cascading of constraints is based entirely on the *purpose* of the model as a whole (further constrained in spread by the limited *viewpoint* of the model) as it is successively decomposed in the hierarchic layering forced by the six-or-fewer rule of the SA maxim.

All of this is a direct consequence of the *everything* of the SA maxim, and may be inferred by considering Fig. 8 recursively. The boundary of the top-most box of the analysis is determined entirely by the subject matter, purpose, and viewpoint of the agreed-upon outset understanding. ("Tell 'em whatcha gonna tell 'em.") Then each of the subsequent constraints derives its footing only insofar as it continues to reflect that subject, purpose, and viewpoint. And, each, in turn, provides the same basis for the next subdivision, etc. Inconsistencies in an original high-level interpretation are ironed out and are replaced by greater and greater precision of specific meaning.

Even though the basis for all of the constraint structure is the (perhaps ill-conceived, ambiguous, ill-defined) *outer* boundary, that boundary and the *innermost* boundary, composed of the collective class of all the boundaries of the finest subdivision taken together, are merely two representations of the *same* boundary—so that *strengthening of the inner boundary through extensive decomposition automatically strengthens the outer boundary*. It is as though the structured analyst (and each of his readers as well) were saying continually "My outermost understanding of the problem as a whole can only make sense, now that I see all this detail, if I refine my interpretation of it in this, this, and this precise way." This is the hidden power of SA at work. This is how SA greatly amplifies the precision and understandability of any natural or formal language whose nouns and verbs are imbedded in its box and arrow structure.

XVIII. ARROW CONNECTIONS

Fig. 6, which led to this discussion, detailed Box 5.1 "Build box structure"; Fig. 9 decomposes Box 5.2, "Build arrow

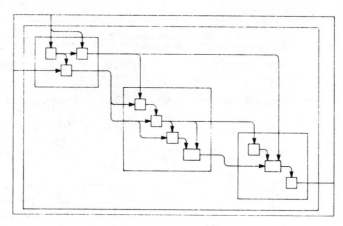

Fig. 10. Nested factors.

structure." From Fig. 5 we see that the controlling constraints that dominate Box 5.2 are the subject matter, purpose, and viewpoint, as we would expect, along with the "arrow stubs" which resulted from building each box separately. The outputs are to be internal arrows connected and labeled, as well as labeled external arrows. A relevant (i.e., nonobvious) input is the collection of words—nouns or verbs—for making those labels.

With this context in mind, we are now ready to look at Fig. 9, "Build arrow structure." Here is an example of the use of non-English language to label arrows. Small graphical phrases show the intended meaning of "branch" and "join" for distribution, and "bundle" and "spread" with respect to subdivision, as well as two forms of logical OR for exclusion. We have seen many examples of these in use in the diagrams already considered, so that the ideas should be quite transparent.

The little pictures as labels show how the labels attach to arrows to convey the appropriate meaning. In most good SA diagramming the OR's are used very sparingly—only when they materially assist understanding. In most circumstances, the fact that arrows represent constraints either of dominance or necessity supplies the required understanding in clearer form merely by topological connection. This also is the reason why there is no graphical provision for the other logical functions such as AND, for they are really out of place at the level of communication of basic SA language. In order for them to have an appropriate role, the total context of interpretation of an SA model must have been drawn down very precisely to some mathematical or logical domain at which point a language more appropriate to that domain should be chosen. Then logical terms in the nominal and verbial expressions in labels can convey the conditions. This is preferable to distorting the SA language into a detailed communication role it was not designed or intended to fulfill.

XIX. Boundaries

Fig. 12, "Build diagram structure," will provide detailing for the third and last box of Fig. 5. It is needed as a separate consideration of this motivation model because the building of box structure (Box 5.1, detailed in Fig. 6) and arrow structure (Box 5.2, detailed in Fig. 9) only cover arrows between boxes in a single diagram—the *internal* arrows. Box 4.2 requires that

every arrow which relates or connects bounded contexts must participate in both a *from* and a *to* interface. Every *external* arrow (shown as the second output of Box 5.2) will be missing either its source (from) or its destination (to) because the relevant boxes do not appear on this diagram. As the relationship between Boxes 5.2 and 5.3 in Fig. 5 shows, these labeled arrows are indeed a dominant constraint controlling Box 3, "Build diagram structure."

Fig. 10 helps to explain the story. This is a partial view of three levels of nesting of SA boxes, one within the other, in some model (not an SA diagram). Except for three arrows, every arrow drawn is a complete from/to connection. The middle, second-level box has four fine-level boxes within it, and it in turn is contained within the largest box drawn in the figure. If we consider the arrows in the middle, second-level box, we note that only two of them are internal arrows, all of the others being external. But notice also that every one of those external arrows (with respect to that middle-level box) are in fact *internal* with respect to the model as a whole. Each of those arrows does go from one box to another box— a lowest-level box in each case. In completing the connection, *the arrows penetrate the boundaries of the middle-level boxes* as though those boundaries were not there at all. In fact, there are only two real boundaries in all of Fig. 10—the two boundaries characteristic of every SA decomposition. These are 1) the *outer boundary* which is the outermost edge of Fig. 10, itself, and 2) the *inner boundary* which is the entire set of edges of all of the lowest-level boxes drawn in Fig. 10, considered as a single boundary. As was stated above, the SA maxim requires that the outer boundary and the inner boundary must be understood to be *exactly the same* so that the subject is merely decomposed, not altered in any way.

XX. Parents and Children

To understand how the structuring of Fig. 10 is expressed in SA terms we must be clear about the relationship between boundaries and interfaces, boxes and diagrams, and the parent/child relationship. Fig. 11 lays all of this out. In the upper right appears the diagram for the largest box drawn in Fig. 10, and in the lower left appears the diagram for the central middle-level box which we were discussing. The first thing to notice is that the diagrams are here drawn as though they were

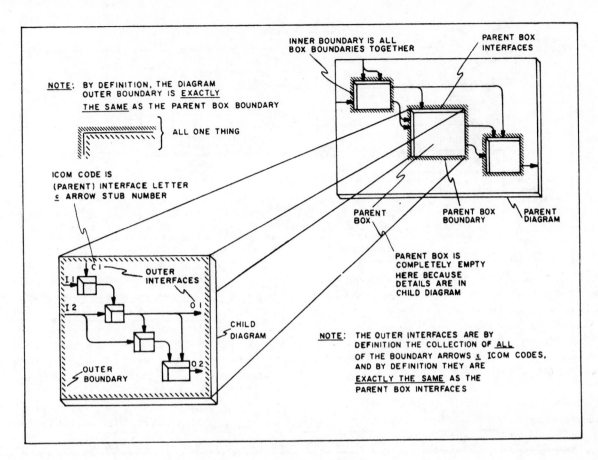

Fig. 11. Boundaries and interfaces.

punched out of Fig. 10, (like cutting cookies from a sheet of cookie dough). Although the dimensions are distorted, the note in the upper left points out that, by definition, *the diagram outer boundary is actually the same as the parent box boundary* (i. e., the current child diagram is the "cookie" removed from the sheet of dough and placed to one side).

Fig. 11 also points out that, just as for the hierarchic decomposition as a whole, the *inner boundary of the parent diagram is the collection of all its child box boundaries considered as a single entity*. Notice the terminology—with respect to the current child diagram, one of the boxes in the parent diagram is called the *parent box* of the child diagram. By definition of Fig. 4, that *parent box boundary* is the collection of *parent box interfaces and support* which compose it. Since we have just established that the outer boundary of the current diagram is the same as the corresponding parent box boundary, the parent box edges (interfaces *or* support) which compose the parent box boundary must somehow match the outer edges of the child diagram. This is the connection which we seek to establish rigorously.

By Fig. 10 we know that the external arrows of the child diagram penetrate through the outer boundary and are, in fact, the *same* arrows as are the stubs of the interfaces and support which compose the parent box boundary. Therefore, the connection which has to be made is clear from the definition. But for flexibility of graphic representation, *the external arrows of the current diagram need not have the same geometric layout, relationship, or labeling* as the corresponding stubs on the par-

ent diagram, which are drawn on a completely different (parent) diagram.

In order to allow this flexibility, we construct a special code-naming scheme called *ICOM codes* as follows: An ICOM code begins with one of the letters I-C-O-M (standing for INPUT, CONTROL, OUTPUT, MECHANISM) concatenated with an integer which is obtained by considering that the stubs of the corresponding parent box edge are numbered consecutively from top to bottom or from left to right, as the case may be. With the corresponding ICOM code written beside the unattached end of the arrow in the current diagram, that arrow is no longer called "external," but is called a *boundary arrow*. Then *the four outer edges of the child diagram are, by definition, the four collections of ICOM boundary arrows* which are, by definition, exactly the same as the corresponding parent box edges, as defined by Fig. 4 and shown in Fig. 11. Thus even though the geometric layout may be radically different, the rigor of interconnection of child and parent diagrams is complete, and the arrows are continuous and unbroken, as required. Every diagram in this paper has ICOM codes properly assigned.

The above presentation is summarized in the first two boxes of Fig. 12 and should be clear without further discussion. Boxes 12.3 and 12.4 concern the SA language notations for establishing the relationships between the child and parent diagram cookies by means of a *detail reference expression* (DRE) or an SA *call*. We will consider these shortly. For now it is sufficient to note that the topics we have considered here

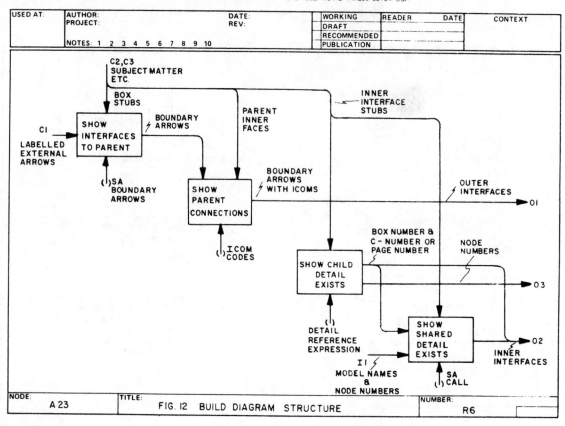

Fig. 12. Build diagram structure.

complete the detailing of Fig. 5, "Build diagram"—how the box structure and arrow structure for individual diagrams are built, and then how the whole collection of diagrams is linked together in a single whole so that *everything* of the top-most cookie (treated as a cookie sheet from which other cookies are cut with zero width cuts) is completely understandable. Each individual diagram itself is only a portion of the cookie dough with an outer boundary and an inner boundary formed by the decomposition operation. Nothing is either gained or lost in the process—so that the SA maxim is rigorously realized. Everything can indeed be covered for the stated purpose and viewpoint. We now complete our presentation of the remaining items in the 40 features of Fig. 2, which exploit further refinements of notation and provide orderly organization for the mass of information in a complete SA model.

XXI. Word Notes

In SA language, not everything is said in graphical terms. Both words and pictures are also used. If the diagram construction notations we have considered so far were to be used exclusively and exhaustively, very cluttered and nonunderstandable diagrams would result. Therefore SA language includes further simplifying graphic notations (which also increase the expressive power of the language), as well as allowing nongraphic additional information to be incorporated into SA diagrams. This is the function of Fig. 13 which details Box 3.3. Fig. 13 points out that the (potentially) cluttered diagram is only graphically complete so that special *word* notations are needed. Furthermore, special arrow notations can supply more clarity, to result in a complete *and* understandable diagram.

We will not further detail Box 13.2. We merely point out that its output consists of three forms of verbal additions to the diagram. The first two—NOTES and [n] footnotes—are actual parts of the diagram. The diagrams we have been examining have examples of each. The third category, (n) metanotes, are *not* parts of the diagram themselves, but are instead notes *about* the diagram. The (n) metanotes have only an observational or referential relation to the actual information content of these diagrams and therefore they do not in any way alter or affect the actual representational function of the SA language, either graphical or verbal. There is no way that information in (n) metanotes can participate in the information content of the diagrams, and therefore they should not be used in an attempt to affect the interpretation of the diagrams themselves, but only for mechanical operations regarding the diagram's physical format or expression. Examples are comments from a reader to an author of a diagram suggesting an improved layout for greater understandability. A few examples are included on the diagrams in this paper. The [n] footnotes are used exclusively for allowing large verbal expressions to be concisely located with respect to tight geometric layout, in addition to the normal footnoting function commonly found in textual information.

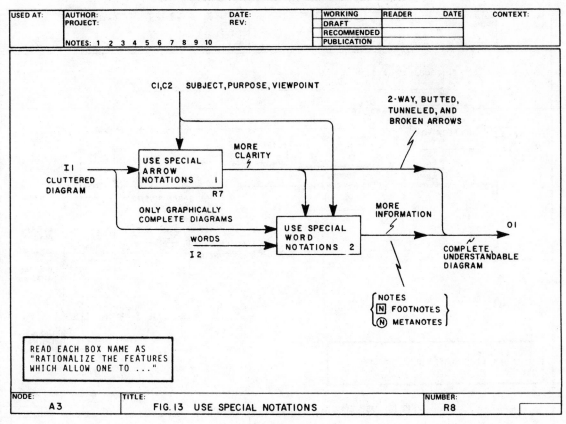

Fig. 13. Use special notations.

XXII. SPECIAL GRAPHIC NOTATIONS

Fig. 14 provides the motivation for four very simple additions to the graphic notation to improve the understandability of diagrams. With respect to a specific aspect of the subject matter, two boxes sometimes really act as one box inasmuch as each of them shares one portion of a well-defined aspect of the subject matter. In this case, arrowheads with dots above, below, or to the right of the arrowhead are added instead of drawing two separate arrows as shown in FEO 14A. Two-way arrows are a form of bundling, however, *not* a mere shorthand notation for the two separate arrows. If the subject matters represented by the two separate arrows are not sufficiently similar, they should *not* be bundled into a two-way arrow, but should be drawn separately. Many times, however, the two-way arrow *is* the appropriate semantics for the relationship between two boxes. Notice that if other considerations of diagrams are sufficiently strong, the awkward, nonstandard two-way arrow notations shown also may be used to still indicate dominance in the two-way interaction.

SA arrows should always be thought of as conduits or pipelines containing multistranded cables, each strand of which is another pipeline. Then the branching and joining is like the cabling of a telephone exchange, including trunk lines. Box 14.2 is related to both two-way arrows and pipelines, and points out that a one-way pipeline stub at the parent level may be shown as a two-way boundary arrow in the child. This is

appropriate since, with respect to the communication of understanding at the parent level, the relationship between boxes is one-way, whereas when details are examined, two-way cooperation between the two sets of detailing boxes may be required. An example is the boss-worker relation. The boss (at parent level) provides one-way command, but (at the child diagram level) a two-way interchange between worker and boss may be needed to clarify details.

Box 14.3 motivates an additional and very useful version of Box 6.6 ("Omit the obvious"). In this case, instead of omitting the obvious, we only postpone consideration of necessary detail until the appropriate level is reached. This is done by putting parentheses around the unattached end of an external arrow, or at the interface end of a parent box stub. The notation is intended to convey the image of an arrow "tunneling" out of view as it crosses a parent box inner boundary only to emerge later, some number of levels deeper in a child's outer interface, when that information is actually required. These are known as "tunneled" or "parenthesized" boundary arrows when the sources or destinations are somewhere within the SA model, and as (proper) *external* arrows when the missing source or destination is unspecified (i.e., when the model would need to be imbedded in some context larger than the total model for the appropriate connection to be made).

Finally, Box 14.4 is a seldom-used notation which allows internal arrows themselves to be broken by an ad hoc labeling scheme merely to suppress clutter. Its use is discouraged be-

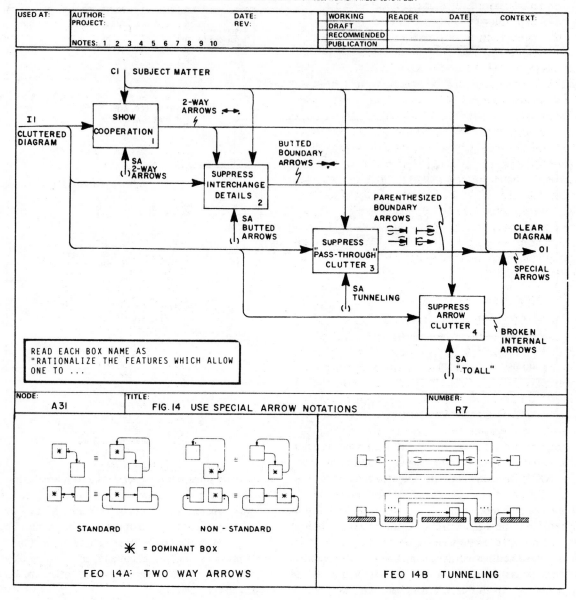

Fig. 14. Use special arrow notations.

cause of its lack of geometric continuity and because its use is forced only by a diagram containing so much information already that it is likely not be be clearly understood and should be redrawn. Examples occur in Fig. 9 just for illustration.

XXIII. The Reference Language

Returning to Fig. 3, we now have considered all of the aspects of basic SA language which go into the creation of diagrams themselves, with the single exception of the detail reference expressions and SA call notation of Fig. 12, which were saved until this point since they relate so closely to Box 3.4, "Provide for referencing."

A complete and unique SA reference language derives very nicely from the hierarchically nested factors imposed by the SA maxim. Diagrams, boxes, interfaces, arrows, and complete contexts can be referenced by a combination of model names,

node numbers (starting with A for activity or D for data, and derived directly from the box numbers), and ICOM codes. The insertion of a dot, meaning "which see" (i. e. "find the diagram and look at it"), can specify exactly which diagram is to be kept particularly in mind to provide the context for interpreting the SA language. Thus "A122. 4I1" means "in diagram A122, the first input of box 4"; "A1224. I1" means "in diagram A1224, the boundary arrow I4"; "A1224I1" means "the first input interface of node A1224." The SA language rules also allow such reference expressions to degenerate naturally to the minimum needed to be understandable. Thus, for example, the mechanism for showing that the child detailing exists is merely to write the corresponding chronological creation number (called a C-number) under the lower right-hand corner of a box on the diagram, as a DRE. (A C-number is the author's intials, concatenated with a sequential integer—

assigned as the first step whenever a new diagram sheet is begun.) When a model is formally published, the corresponding detail reference expression is normally converted into the page number of the appropriate detail diagram. The omission of a detail reference expression indicates that the box is not further detailed in this model. (For all the diagrams considered in this paper, the DRE's have been left in C-number form.)

The *SA call* notation consists of a detail reference expression preceded by a downward pointing arrow stub, and allows sharing of details among diagrams. It will not be covered in this paper beyond the illustration in Fig. 15, which is included here more to illustrate why mechanism support is not an interface (as has repeatedly been pointed out) than to adequately describe the SA call scheme. That will be the subject of a future paper, and is merely cited here for completeness. The SA call mechanism (see also [2]) corresponds very closely to the subroutine call concept of programming languages, and is a key concept in combining multiple purposes and viewpoints into a single model of models.

XXIV. Organizing the Model

The final box of Fig. 3, Box 3.5, "Organize material," is not detailed in this model. Instead, we refer the reader back to the tabulation of Fig. 2 where the corresponding items are listed. In final publication form each diagram is normally accompanied by brief, carefully-structured *SA text* which, according to the reading rules, is intended to be read *after* the diagram itself has been read and understood. The SA text supplements but does not replace the information content of the diagram. Its purpose is to "tell 'em whatcha told 'em" by giving a walk-through through the salient features of the diagram, pointing out, by using the reference language, how the story line may be seen in the diagram. Published models also include glossaries of terms used, and are preceded by a *node index*, which consists of the node-numbered box names in indented form in node number sequence. Fig. 16 is the node index for the model presented in this paper, and normally would be published at the beginning to act as a table of contents.

XXV. Conclusion

The principle of good storytelling style (see Section IV) has been followed repeatedly in this paper. We have provided motivations for each of the 40 SA language features of structured analysis by relating each one to a need for clear and explicit exposition with no loss from an original bounded context. (The "node" column of Fig. 2 maps each feature to a diagram box in the other figures.) In the process, we have seen how the successive levels of refinement strengthen the original statement of purpose and viewpoint, to enforce unambiguous understanding. The best "tell 'em whatcha told 'em" for the paper as a whole is to restudy the SA model in the figures. (Space precludes even sketching the corresponding data decomposition.) The diagrams not only summarize and integrate the ideas covered in the paper, but provide further information, as well.

There are more advanced features of the SA language which will be covered in subsequent papers in the context of applications. In practice, SA turns out to depend heavily on the

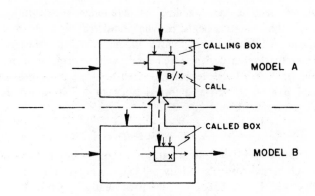

Fig. 15. SA "call" for detailing.

```
RATIONALIZE SA FEATURES
A1   DEFINE GRAPHICS
     A11   Bound Context
     A12   Relate/Connect
     A13   Show Transformation
     A14   Show Circumstance
     A15   Show Means

A2   BUILD DIAGRAM
     A21   Build Box Structure
           A211   Name Aptly
           A212   Label Aptly
           A213   Show Necessity
           A214   Show Dominance
           A215   Show Relevance
           A216   Omit the Obvious

     A22   Build Arrow Structure
           A221   Show Distribution
           A222   Show Subdivision
           A223   Show Exclusion

     A23   Build Diagram Structure
           A231   Show Interfaces to Parent
           A232   Show Parent Connections
           A233   Show Child Detail Exists
           A234   Show Shared Detail Exists

A3   USE SPECIAL NOTATIONS
     A31   Use Special Arrow Notations
           A311   Show Cooperation
           A312   Supress Interchange Details
           A313   Supress "Pass-Through" Clutter
           A314   Supress Arrow Clutter

     A32   Use Special Word Notations

A4   PROVIDE FOR (UNIQUE) REFERENCING
     ( A41   Sheet Reference)
     ( A42   Box Reference)
     ( A43   Interface Reference)
     ( A44   Arrow Reference)
     ( A45   Context Reference)

A5   ORGANIZE MATERIAL
```

Fig. 16. Node index.

disciplined thought processes that lead to well-structured analyses expressed in well-structured diagrams. Additional rules and supporting methodology organize the work flow, support the mechanics of the methods, and permit teams of people to work and interact as one mind attacking complex problems. These are covered in SofTech's SADT methodology. The fact that SA incorporates by definition any and all languages within its framework permits a wide variety of natural and artificial languages to be used to accomplish specific goals with respect to understanding the requirements for solution. Then those requirements can be translated, in a rigorous, organized, efficient, and, above all, understandable fashion, into actual system design, system implementation, maintenance, and training. These topics also must of necessity appear in later papers, as well as a formal language definition for the ideas unfolded here.

Acknowledgment

The four-sided box notation was originally inspired by the match between Hori's activity cell [3] and my own notions of Plex [4]. I have, of course, benefitted greatly from interaction with my colleagues at SofTech. J. W. Brackett, J. E. Rodriguez, and particularly J. B. Goodenough gave helpful suggestions for this paper, and C. G. Feldmann worked closely with me on early developments. Some of these ideas have earlier been presented at meetings of the IFIP Work Group 2. 3 on Programming Methodology.

References

[1] D. T. Ross, "It's time to ask why?" *Software Practise Experience*, vol. 1, pp. 103-104, Jan.-Mar. 1971.

[2] D. T. Ross, J. B. Goodenough, C. A. Irvine, "Software engineering: Process, principles, and goals," *Computer*, pp. 17-27, May 1975.

[3] S. Hori, "Human-directed activity cell model," in *CAM-J* long-range planning final rep., CAM-I, Inc., 1972.

[4] D. T. Ross, "A generalized technique for symbol manipulation and numerical calculation," *Commun. Ass. Comput. Mach.*, vol. 4, pp. 147-150, Mar. 1961.

[5] D. T. Ross and K. E. Schoman, Jr., "Structured analysis for requirements definition," this issue, pp. 6-15.

[6] G. A. Miller, "The magical number seven, plus or minus two: Some limits on our capacity for processing information," *Psychol. Rev.*, vol. 63, pp. 81-97, Mar. 1956.

C P Gane

ImpSysTech SA

Reprinted with permission from *Infotech State of the Art Report on Data Design*, 1980. Copyright © 1979 by Chris P. Gane.

C P GANE is Directeur of ImpSysTech SA, Geneva and President of Improved System Technologies Inc, New York, where he has developed techniques of Structured Systems Analysis that have been widely accepted. Prior to founding IST, he was Vice-President for Development at Yourdon Inc. His 12 years in data processing includes experience with IBM in London, where he worked on foreign exchange, banking and brokerage systems, as well as consulting assignments with Olivetti, Control Data and Sanders Data Systems. Since settling in New York, in 1973, he has worked extensively on Structured Analysis, Structured Design, and Structured Programming, consulting, writing, developing and presenting seminars to both management and technical audiences throughout the US, and more recently in Europe. His publications include Structured systems analysis: tools and techniques *(with T Sarson) and* Learning to program in structured COBOL *(with E Yourdon and T Sarson).* He has also written a number of papers, most recently Structured analysis for distributed systems, *presented at GUIDE 45, November 1977.*

INTRODUCTION

This paper presents a successful, practical, approach to the definition of requirements
for a commercial data processing system, with particular reference to the definition
of data requirements, and indicates how this type of requirements statement lends
itself to the definition of physical subsystems and the design of each subsystem.

The key to successful Structured Analysis, it now appears, is the building of a
graphical, logical (in the sense of 'not-physical') model of the required system.
Such a logical model, plus a statement of systems objectives and system constraints,
constitutes an adequate requirements statement, which has two virtues. Firstly it
expresses 'what' the system is required to do, while not making any commitment as to
'how' the system should physically be implemented. Thus a systems analyst can use
the logical model to express system requirements without having any detailed current
knowledge of DP techniques, and present the model to the systems designer, leaving
the designer in no doubt as to what the system should do, but giving him the greatest
possible freedom to devise a physical design which does it most cost-effectively.
Secondly, the logical model turns out to be a very good way of showing non-technical
users what the nature of the system is going to be, and how the various parts will
fit together.

What does such a logical model look like? Let us consider one of the simplest of all
businesses, Joe's Auto Parts (slogan: 'If you want it, we'll get it'). Joe holds no
inventory, but takes orders for spares from his customers, promising future delivery.
When he has enough orders for spares from a given car firm to earn a bulk discount,
he sends the firm a bulk order, and on receiving the bulk order, gives each customer
what they want, charging them the full retail price.

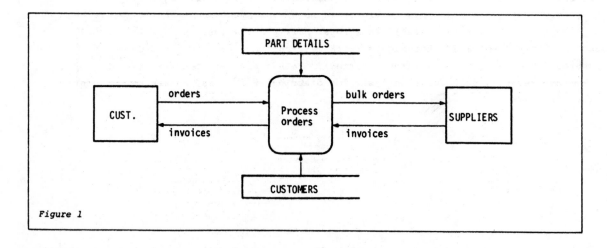

Figure 1

Figure 1 shows a very general picture of the data flow in Joe's business. Customers send in orders, and the single process block processes them, using a store of data (in some form) about Parts Details - price, delivery and so on - and a store of data about customers - whether they are in good credit standing, and so on.

This very crude *data flow diagram* (DFD) uses just four symbols, as shown in Figure 2.

1 An *external entity* symbol (square): a source and/or destination of data outside the system.

2 A *data flow* symbol (arrow): a pathway along which data moves into, around, and out of the system.

3 A *process* symbol (rounded rectangle): some function which transforms data.

4 A *data store* symbol (open-ended rectangle): a place in the system where data is stored in some way.

It turns out that these four simple symbols are the *minimum* required to model a commercial system, and that these same symbols can be used to model at any level of detail. For instance, Figure 1 is clearly rather trivial - let us expand 'Process Orders' to see more detail.

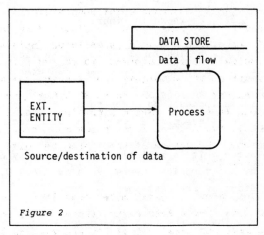

Figure 2

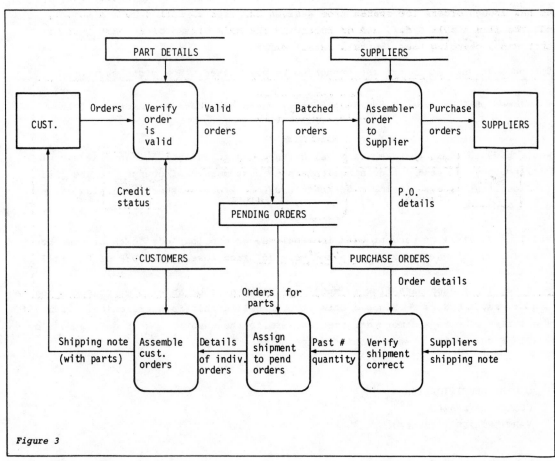

Figure 3

117

Figure 3 shows orders coming from customers into a more detailed process 'Verify order is valid'. This process needs data about parts (to check the part exists and is available) and data about customers (to check credit). Out of the process come valid orders - one important simplification is that in high-level DFDs we omit error paths and exception handling. The valid orders are stored in a data store of 'Pending Orders' which may be a spike on the office wall, or may be an IMS database (we do not care at this stage). We just note that there is a logical requirement to store valid orders until they can be batched to make a bulk order.

The lower stream of data in Figure 3 shows the data describing the bulk shipment from the suppliers being verified (note there are no error paths shown), assigned to individual orders and delivered to customers.

Clearly, there must be some financial flows. We must bill our customers, and pay our suppliers, as shown in Figure 4.

Figure 4 - a high-level logical data flow for transaction processing at Joe's Auto Parts - has several interesting features as follows:

1 It is logical, so makes no distinction between manual processes, computer processes, tape files, disk files or any such technicality.

2 Because it is logical, and uses a very simple symbology, it is readily understood by non-technical users, such as Joe. Users' managers commonly say, when such diagrams are explained to them:

   'That's the first thing you computer people have ever shown me that I have understood!' or:

   'Now I know what that system does!'

3 Though abstract, it is precise enough to be criticised. Joe might say:

   'I see what happens to payments from my customers, but what happens if they *don't* pay?'

We would have to admit that we are missing functions to analyse Accounts Receivable for delinquency and send out dunning letters to customers. Of course, we are glad to find out that we are missing a desired function *before* we start to design and program.

If still more detail of each process is required, we can 'explode' each process box in Figure 4, as shown for example in the more detailed lower-level DFD of Figure 5.

If more detail of each data flow is required, we need to be able to express the logical nature of, say, 'Orders'. Since a data structure like this is hierarchical, we may give a series of more and more detailed answers to the question 'What do you mean by Orders?' First we may name the chief components:

```
ORDER
    ORDER-IDENTIFICATION
    CUSTOMER-DETAILS
    PART-DETAILS (iterated)
```

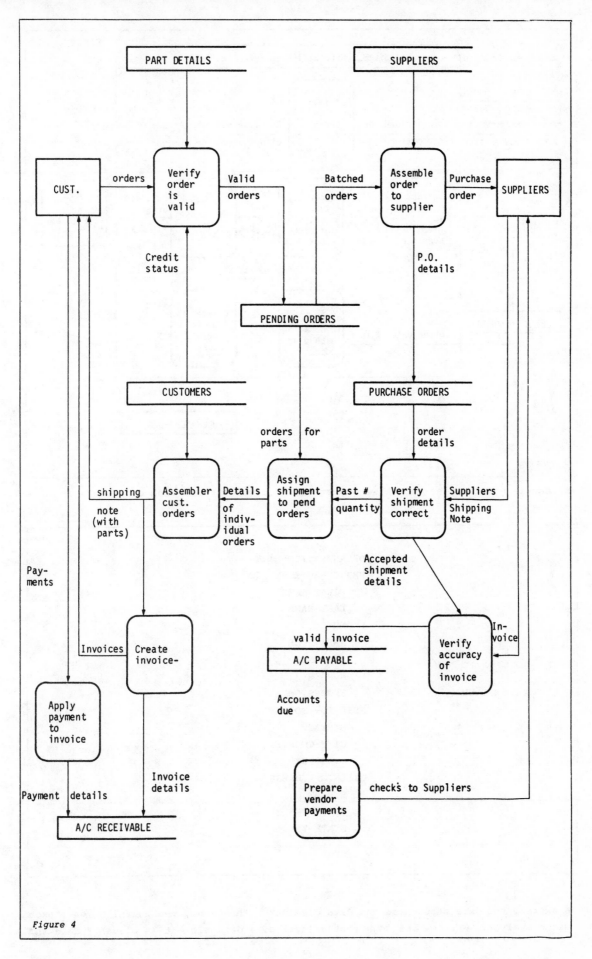

Figure 4

119

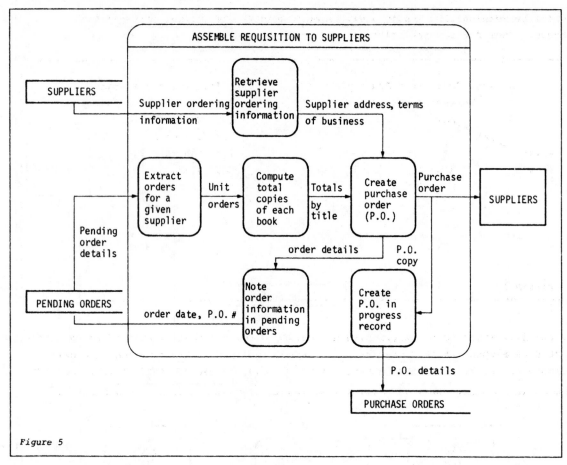

Figure 5

If that is not detailed enough we may state the components of each component, as follows:

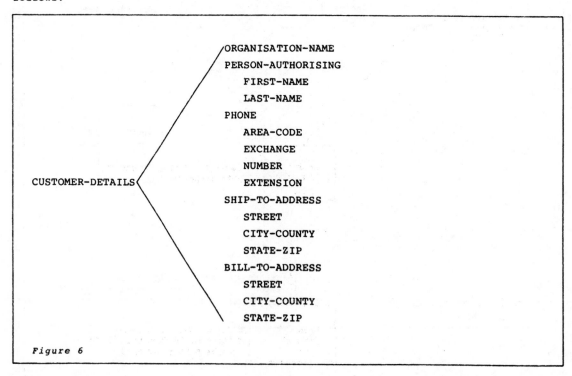

Figure 6

We express the data structures and data elements with honest, meaningful names chosen by the analyst. When we get down to the level of a data element (a piece of data that

120

cannot be meaningfully subdivided), we must specify its logical (not-physical) nature.   Thus for a North American area-code we might have:

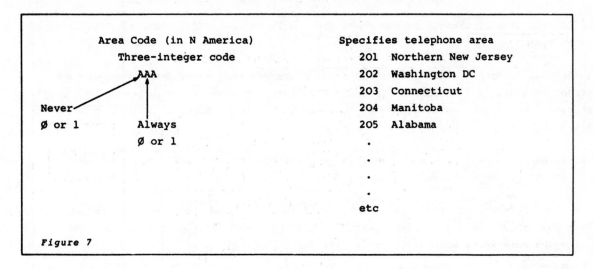

Figure 7

If all data structures are composed ultimately of data elements, then if we can define each data element in this way, state the way in which they are combined into data structures, state which data structures move along the various data flows in our DFD,

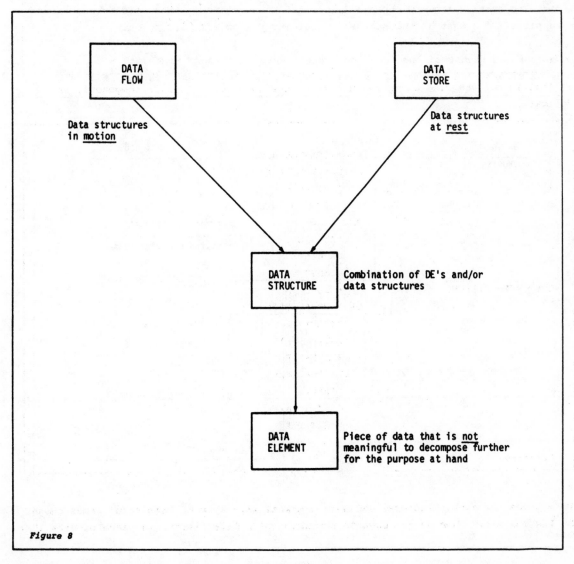

Figure 8

121

and are to be found at rest in our data stores, then we have defined all the *data objects* required for a *logical data dictionary*, related in Figure 8.

The logical data dictionary is the place where all detailed definitions of data objects are stored.

Now we have to consider the definition of data stores. For every data store we must define its contents (in terms of the data structures defined in the data dictionary). For some data stores, we will have to show the immediate accesses that have to be made to it.

The definition of data store contents is in principle very simple. What comes out must go in; no more, no less.

So we look at the data flows coming into the data store, compare them with the data flows coming out, make sure that nothing is missing, that nothing is redundant, and derive the data store contents accordingly.

Suppose we had detailed data flows for Joe's Auto Parts, and the complete flows in and out of 'Pending Orders' were as shown in Figure 9. Assume that the detailed contents of each flow have already been defined in the data dictionary. We have some non-immediate accesses to data (batched orders, orders for a given part), and some potentially immediate accesses which may physically be on-line enquiries: 'What orders are there for supplier X?', 'What is the status of customer Y's order?' and so on.

What must the contents of the 'Pending Orders' data store be? Since it is fed by a stream of orders, and streams of orders come out, it surely must contain records of

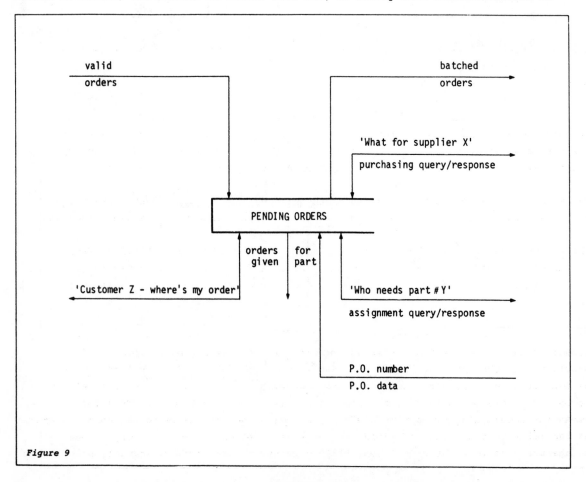

Figure 9

the data structure 'Orders', defined as in the list below. Is that enough? Inspection
shows us that it would be. Of course with a more complex data store, with say ten
inflows and twenty outflows, the derivation of contents is far from being so easy,
and the detailed logical components of each flow must be compared. It is valuable
to reduce the contents of each data store to several tables, or relations, in third
normal form, thus removing redundant data and getting the structures as simple as
possible.

```
ORDER

    ORDER-IDENTIFICATION
        CUSTOMER-ORDER-NUM
        CUSTOMER-ORDER-DATE
        PURCHASE-ORDER-NUM
        PURCHASE-ORDER-DATE

    CUSTOMER-DETAILS
        CUSTOMER-NAME
        PERSON-AUTHORISING
        PHONE
        SHIP-TO-ADDRESS
        BILL-TO-ADDRESS

    PART-DETAILS
        PART-NUMBER
        QUANTITY
        SUPPLIER
        PRICE
```

Having defined the necessary and sufficient contents for the data store, we now have
to investigate the immediate accesses required. An *immediate* access may be defined
as one which is required faster than it is possible to search or sort the entire
data store. For example, since the supplier of each part is held as a data element
in the data store, the question 'What orders do we have for supplier X?' can always
be answered given time, by scanning every record: if the question must be answered
while someone is on the phone, however, we must provide for some special secondary
access path (an index, a logical pointer, or the equivalent).

We use an Immediate Access Diagram as shown in Figure 10 to get a consolidated view
of the various immediate accesses required by different members of the user community.

The arrows connecting the boxes 'Customer-Name', 'Part-Number' and 'Supplier-Name'
to the box representing the data store are not data flow arrows - they merely represent
the necessity for immediate access to a record or records given Customer-Name and so
on.

When an immediate access diagram has been drawn up, with volumes, file sizes, frequency
of access and so on, we can use it as a database/file design planning tool. If
providing all the immediate accesses required presents no technical problem, and can
be done at acceptable cost, then so be it. However, if the cost of providing all the
secondary access paths is unacceptable, then something has got to go. Then the
immediate access diagram is very useful as a tool to get the users to put some valuation
on the relative importance of immediate accesses - obviously if it is very valuable
to the business to be able to access Pending Orders by part-number, and only nice-to-have

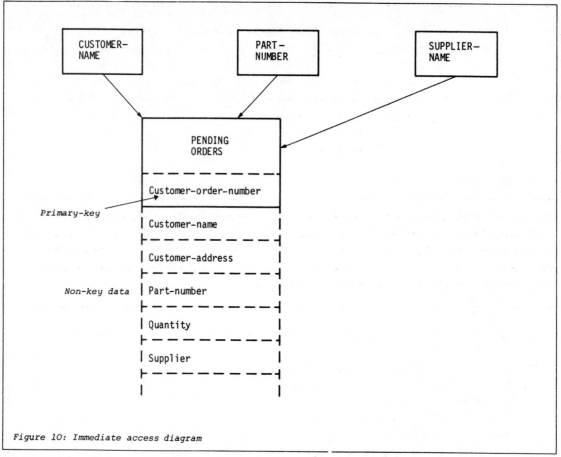

Figure 10: Immediate access diagram

to access by Customer-Name, then in a pinch we shall do away with the Customer-Name access.

The last tool of Structured Analysis we need to consider is for the expression of detailed logic. We have an overall DFD for the system, with typically 20 to 50 processes in it. Each process is exploded into a detailed DFD (as shown in Figure 5) with 10 to 20 processes in it. The logic of each of these detailed processes should be expressible in one or two pages - but one or two pages of what?

Normally we write logic out in natural English. For instance, suppose we exploded 'Apply payment to invoice' in Figure 4, and found that one of the detailed processes was 'Verify discount is correct'. Upon enquiring as to the detailed logic of this process, we are given a memo as shown below:

LOGIC IN NATURAL ENGLISH

'....Trade discount (to car dealers) is 20%. For private customers, 5% discount is allowed on orders for 6 items or more, 10% on orders for 20 items or more, and 15% on orders for 50 or more. Trade orders for 20 items and over receive the 10% discount over and above the trade discount.'

This is fairly clear as memos go: however carefully it is written, though, we must read *all* of it to process any one case. Thus, how long does it take to answer the question 'What discount for a trade customer with a 21 item order?'.

We need a more graphical method of displaying the structure of detailed logic, such as a decision tree:

124

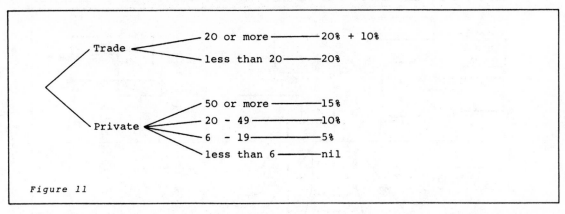

```
              ┌─── 20 or more ────── 20% + 10%
      Trade ──┤
              └─── less than 20 ──── 20%


              ┌─── 50 or more ────── 15%
              ├─── 20 - 49 ───────── 10%
    Private ──┤
              ├─── 6  - 19 ───────── 5%
              └─── less than 6 ───── nil
```

Figure 11

How long does it take you to answer the above question now? The decision tree is an
ideal tool for representing the detailed logic of processes which are mainly decisions.
In many cases, though, long sequences of actions must be carried out, sometimes
repeatedly; then the decision-tree cannot be used. We must use our second logic
tool, Structured English, as shown in Figure 12:

```
    Add up the total number of items on the order (in the quantity column)

    IF    the order is from a trade customer
      and-IF      the order calls for 20 or more
          THEN   discount is 30%
        ELSE      (order is for less than 20)
            SO   discount is 20%
    ELSE  (order is from a private customer)
      so-IF       the order calls for 50 or more
                 discount is 15%
        ELSE IF the order is for 20 to 49
                 discount is 10%
        ELSE IF the order is for 6 to 19
                 discount is 5%
        ELSE      (the order is for less than 6)
            SO no discount is given.
```

Figure 12: 'Structured English': discount-policy

This is a perfectly general strict dialect of English, using sequence, decision, and
repetition structures to express the detailed logic of any policy at all.

Figure 13 shows how these various tools fit together to make a logical model either
of an existing or a proposed system.

For more details of each of these tools, see (001).

Once the logical model has been developed by the analyst, and the user community
agree that it *does* meet their requirements, we can begin system design from a firm
foundation. Our first concern is strategic design, sometimes known as 'subsystem
packaging'. What will the subsystems be? What parts of the system function will be
automated, and what remain manual?

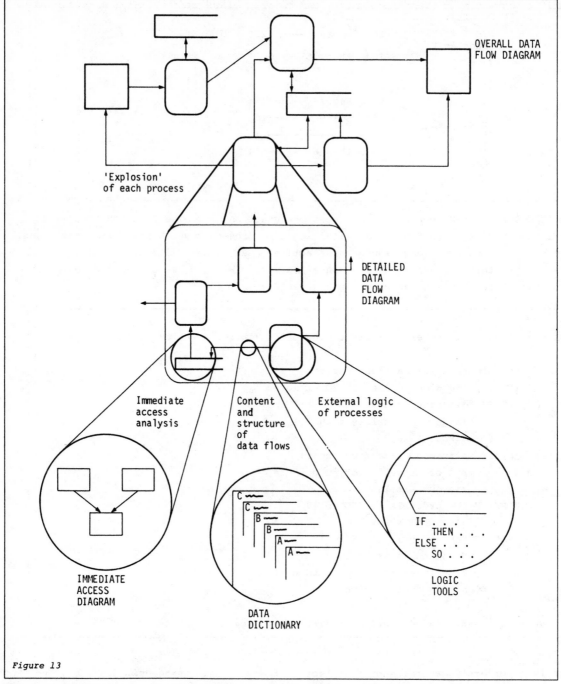

OVERALL DATA
FLOW DIAGRAM

'Explosion'
of each process

DETAILED
DATA
FLOW
DIAGRAM

Immediate
access
analysis

Content
and
structure
of
data flows

External logic
of processes

IMMEDIATE
ACCESS
DIAGRAM

DATA
DICTIONARY

IF . . .
    THEN . . .
ELSE . . .
    SO . . .

LOGIC
TOOLS

Figure 13

The overall DFD is an excellent tool for this. Figure 14 shows the way in which we might define subsystem boundaries. One alternative is to automate just order-entry; the area within the heavy dotted line. We should consider a batch solution, or an on-line solution, depending on the system objectives.

Alternatively, we might consider an integrated order entry/accounts receivable system, shown by the larger area within the dotted line. In each case we can read off from the DFD the functions and data stores that will be automated, and see the inputs to and outputs from our chosen solution.

When we have decided on the automation boundary and carved the computer system up into subsystems (creating the minimum number of intermediate files in the process), we have to design the software within each subsystem. Obviously we want a design that works, **and also we want a design that is** *changeable*; a modular piece of software whose modules

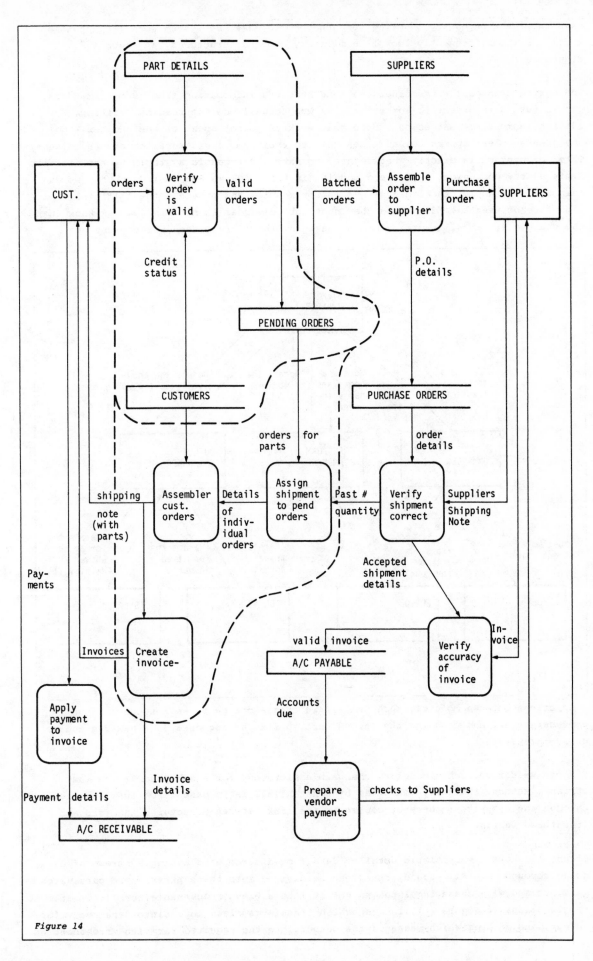

Figure 14

127

have the least necessary coupling between them to make the system work. Changeable modular systems frequently look like military command structures, as shown in Figure 15.

The system commander gives orders to, and receives information from, sub-commanders, who in turn give orders to worker modules who actually do the reading, writing, editing, computing, and so on. Note that workers do not speak to one another - no one speaks unless spoken to, and then only to their immediate superior or subordinate. This, of course, is exactly what we need to make a changeable system: by artificially limiting the communication between modules in this way, we are confident that we can change, for example, the logic of the Editor module, and provided the 'official' interface between the Editor and the Input Sub-Commander is not damaged, we know that the changed system will work. In many designs, there are hidden, or non-obvious

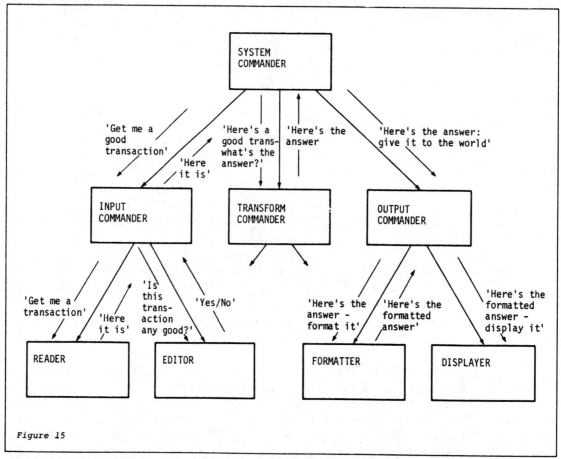

Figure 15

connections between modules, such that if we change one part, we introduce a bug somewhere else, and changing the second part to fix the bug creates a new bug and so on *ad infinitum*.

How can we derive such a modular, changeable hierarchy for a subsystem? The most reliable method, initially conceived by Constantine, is to base it on the *data flow* through the subsystem; here of course is the link between Structured Analysis and Structured Design.

Figure 16 shows a *very* simple detailed data flow diagram with a single stream of data going through it. All such diagrams can be divided into three parts - one part which is concerned with massaging input to get it into a clean processable form (the leftmost two functions in Figure 16), an area which transforms clean input into data ready for output, and an area which massages the output into the required form (the rightmost

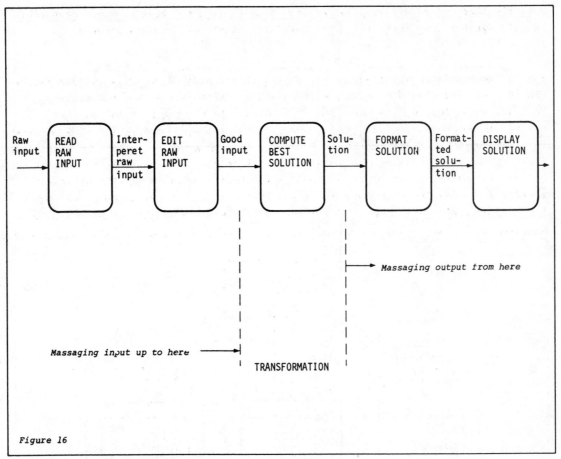

Figure 16

two functions in Figure 16).

Once we've identified these three areas, we can transform the data flow diagram into a structure chart as in Figure 17, where the large arrows show invocation, the small arrows with white-circle tails represent the data passed between modules, and the small arrows with black-circle tails represent control information such as a flag or a switch.

The structure chart tells us that 'Produce Best Solution' invokes 'Get Good Input'. In turn 'Get Good Input' invokes 'Read Input' which returns with some Raw Input data. 'Get Good Input' then invokes 'Edit Input' passing it the Raw Input data and receiving in return a flag (set to 'Good' or 'Bad' appropriately). If the input is good, 'Get Good Input' returns Control to 'Produce Best Solution' along with the Good Input Data, and so on. Note that each function on the detailed data flow diagram appears on the structure chart as a worker module at the bottom of the hierarchy.

The simple structure chart shown in Figure 17 is a prototype for systems with a single stream of data in the DFD - Constantine called this a 'transform-centred' structure (002).

If, as in many systems, we have a DFD more like Figure 18, with several alternate paths through the data flow, we need a different model for our structure chart.

In this multiple transaction case, we need a structure which gets a transaction, analyses it to determine what type of processing it receives, and then dispatches the transaction to a transaction-specific manager which invokes everything necessary for the transaction, as shown in Figure 19. Such a structure is 'transaction-centred'.

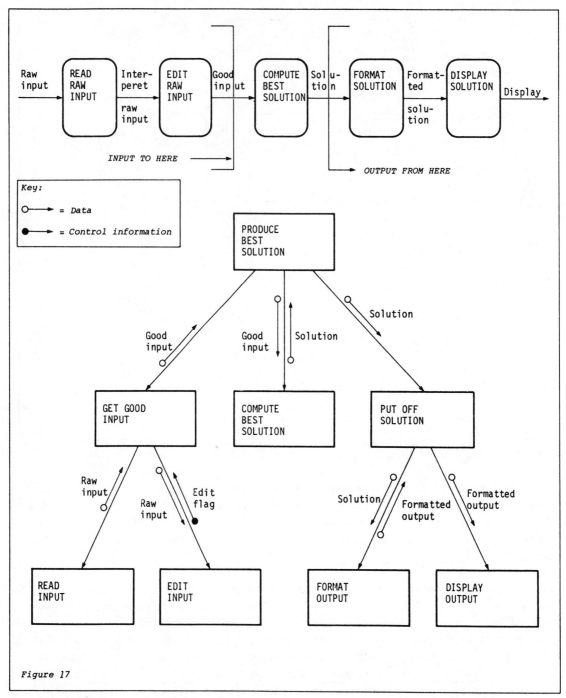

Figure 17

By examining the detailed data flow diagram, we can always use one of these two model structures, or a combination of them, to derive a hierarchical design. By marking the data and control interfaces on the structure chart, we can see very clearly, on one sheet of paper, all the significant aspects of the design, so that we can review it and see if there is any way it can be made more changeable.

We can summarise the steps of the Structured Analysis/Structured Design process, therefore, as in Figure 20.

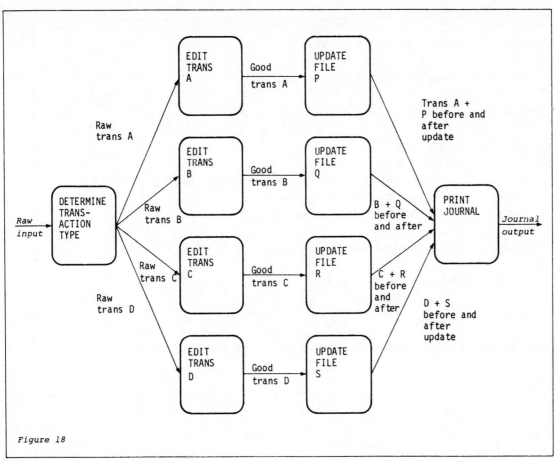

Figure 18

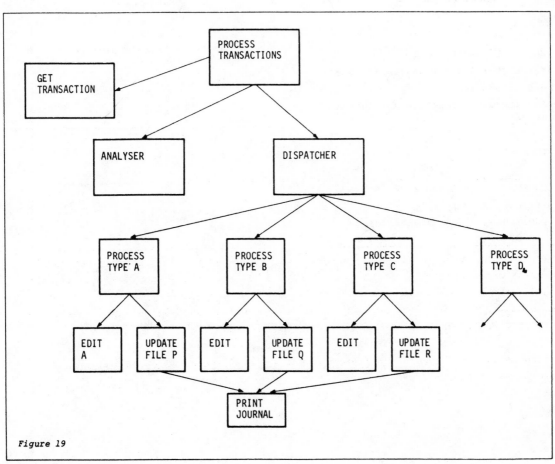

Figure 19

131

- Build logical model of current system

- Define objectives/constraints for new system

- Devise logical model for new system

  - overall and detailed DFDs
  - all data objects in logical data dictionary
  - detailed processes defined by decision trees/Struc Eng
  - logical contents of data stores expressed in 3rd normal form
  - immediate access diagrams where implied by objectives

- Design physical files/database from model

- Use DFD to define subsystem boundaries

- Produce detailed physical DFD for each subsystem

- Derive hierarchical modular software design from physical DFD

Figure 20

REFERENCES

001   GANE C P and SARSON T
      Structured Systems Analysis: tools
      and techniques
      Published by Prentice-Hall Inc
      (1979)

002   CONSTANTINE L L and YOURDON E
      Structured Design
      Published by Prentice-Hall Inc
      (1978)

Formal Models and Practical Tools
for Information Systems Design
H.-J. Schneider, Editor
North-Holland Publishing Company
© IFIP, 1979

AN APPROACH FOR INVOLVING THE USERS
IN THE SPECIFICATION OF INFORMATION SYSTEMS

Mats Lundeberg
Department of Administrative Information Processing,
University of Stockholm, Sweden

Abstract: This paper has two messages:

1   The users can control the specification of information systems by themselves - given suitable circumstances

2   The effectiveness of the specification process can be improved if it is performed on three levels (change analysis, activity studies, information analysis) instead of only on one level (information analysis)

The paper describes an approach for involving the users in the specification of information systems on the three levels change analysis, activity studies, and information analysis. The practical experience of using these three levels of specification is that it is much more work effective than starting with information analysis at once.

1   INTRODUCTION

1.1   THE SIGNIFICANCE OF THE PAPER

Two important messages of this paper are:

1   *The users can control the specification of information systems by themselves - given suitable circumstances*

2   *The effectiveness of the specification process can be improved if it is performed on three levels (change analysis, activity studies, information analysis) instead of only on one level (information analysis)*

Information systems shall only be developed if they can support human beings in facilitating or improving some of their activities. The development of information systems can thus be seen as part of the development of the activities in organizations. The persons responsible for the activities - the users - should also control the development of these activities. They should therefore also control the development of information systems to support the activities. In order to be able to do this, aids in form of working methods and description techniques are needed. Our experience is that the users can control the specification of information systems by themselves - given such aids and other suitable circumstances.

This paper describes an approach for involving the users in the specification of information systems on three levels:

1   *Change analysis* (in order to ensure that information systems are developed only when there really is a need for them)

2   *Activity studies* (in order to ensure that only such information systems are developed that give positive contributions to the activities of the organization in some way)

3   *Information analysis* (in order to ensure that information systems are developed in such a manner that the users understand what they contain and perform)

The practical experiences of using these three levels of specification are that it is much more work effective than starting with information analysis at once.

1.2   PURPOSE AND OUTLINE

The purpose of the paper is to describe the ISAC approach to information systems specification in an introductory manner. ISAC (Information Systems work and Analysis of Changes) is a research group at the department of Administrative Information Processing at the Royal Institute of Technology and the University of Stockholm, Sweden. Since 1971 research has been performed in the ISAC group around a new approach to information systems development with special emphasis on analysis and design of information systems. This work has been conducted in close contact with practical applications in different business companies and other organizations. The ISAC approach to information systems development has been described in [4], [5], [6], and [7]. This paper builds on these works and focuses on the specification part of information systems development.

The ISAC approach to information systems specification is described by:

- discussing some common problems in information systems specification in practice

- giving a short outline of the ISAC approach to information systems specification

- presenting parts of a case study of information systems specification

- summarizing the relations between the three levels change analysis, activity studies, and information analysis

- summarizing some experiences and possibilities in connection with the ISAC approach to information systems specification

2   SOME COMMON PROBLEMS IN INFORMATION SYSTEMS SPECIFICATION IN PRACTICE

Specifying information systems is an activity where many persons experience problems. In fact, empirical evidence suggests that the specification process is the bottle-neck in developing information systems in some cases. Examples of typical problems that are experienced in business companies and other organizations in Scandinavia in connection with specifying information systems are:

1   The communication between the different human beings that are involved does not work

2   Individual and varying specification methods are used

3   Poor and fast specifications sometimes result in other information systems being developed than those that are needed the most by the users

4   The specification process takes much more time than planned

5   Documentation from the specification process is missing or is incomplete or is not possible to understand

Some of these problems are typical not only for specification of information systems but for information systems development work in general. The discussion will however be concentrated to the information systems specification viewpoint. The problems are not independent of each other. The two first problems, for example, highly influence also the later problems.

The communication problems in the specification process exist mainly between users and systems analysts. Some of these communication problems may depend on the fact that these categories of people "speak different languages". Usually a number of other factors also contribute to the communication problems -- e.g., uncertainty concerning the problems that are to be solved and uncertainty about what the future will look like.

A concrete example of people not talking the same language is that common work methods often are missing in information systems development. The lack of generally accepted work methods increases the uncertainty about the development. The circumstance that individual and varying methods are used enhances the communication problems.

If the communication between the users and systems analysts does not work it may lead to poor specifications or that the specification process is hurried over too fast. Poor specifications may in turn result in the development of other information systems than those that the users really wanted. Instead, more or less conscious professional goals of the systems analysts can lead to the development of systems that are too ambitious in comparison with the users' needs. Another consequence of failing communication is that work takes longer a time than it should. A common example is that one has to start all over again because of missing guidelines the first time. Work is therefore delayed.

One result of information systems specification is by definition a documented specification. Despite this, parts of the documentation are often missing in practice. Information systems specification is found to be more abstract and hence more difficult than e.g. programming.

The examples of problems mentioned above indicate some of the difficulties in specifying information systems. *In summary, information systems specification is a difficult but essential work task in the development of information systems.* Two important needs in the specification process are:

1   *On the human side*, human beings need knowledge of how to clarify and specify problems and of how to communicate during this specification process

2   *On the subject matter side*, aids in form of working methods and description techniques for the specification process are needed

The ISAC approach to information systems specification is an approach which provides working methods and description techniques for the specification process. These working methods and description techniques help human beings to clarify and specify problems and facilitate the communication during the specification process. If you use the ISAC approach in your organization, you do not automatically solve all problems mentioned earlier. However, you may thereby take a significant step towards reducing some of them.

3   A SHORT OUTLINE OF THE ISAC APPROACH TO INFORMATION SYSTEMS SPECIFICATION

The ISAC approach to information systems specification consists of a work methodology from the needs, problems, and ideas experienced by the users to information analysis models. The information analysis models are the specifications for the subsequent data system design work. Methodology here refers to a number of manageable and coherent work steps including rules for what types of models and other documentation that are produced during these work steps. The documentation should be a natural part of the work and not something that is done afterwards.

Figure 3.1[1]) illustrates the relations between activities in an organization and the development of these activities. In the activities different problems and needs for changes constantly arise. Some of these you try to solve by developing the activities in the organization in various ways. When different development

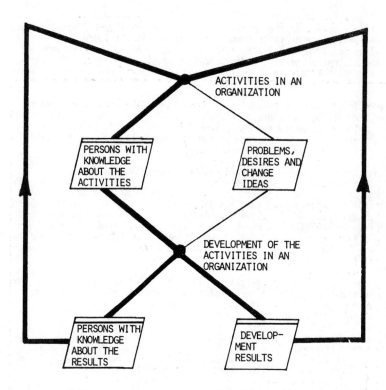

Figure 3.1 The relations between activities in an organization and the development of these activities

results have been implemented, new problems and needs for changes arise and so on. Figure 3.1 can be seen as a description of the learning cycle of an organization - a constant circulation between performing activities in the organization and developing these activities. The figure is very partial. The relations between the organization and its environment are, for example, lacking completely. One aspect is however stressed. The persons working with performing the activities in the organization learn much about these. This knowledge is an important resource when developing the activities in the organization. In the same way, the persons who participate in the development learn much in connection with this work. This knowledge is also an important resource when implementing the development results.

Figure 3.2[2)] illustrates information systems specification as part of the development of activities in an organization. The figure shows that we distinguish between change analysis and proper development as parts of the development of activities in the organization. The aim of change analysis is to clarify what kind of changes of the activities in an organization one should aim at. If the change analysis leads to the conclusion that the needs and problems of the users are of a different kind than the information systems kind, other development is performed instead.

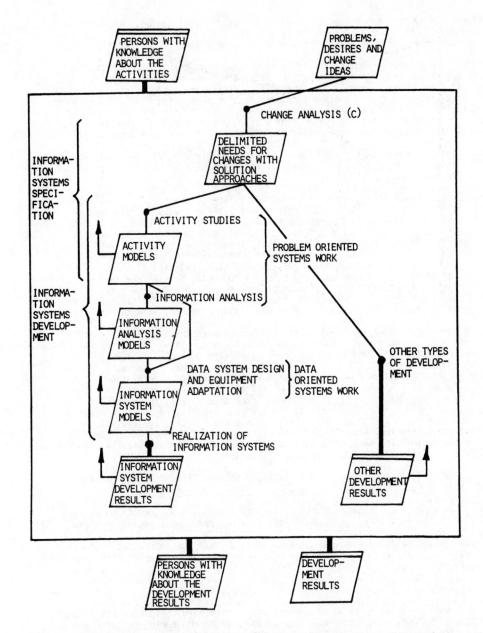

Figure 3.2 Information systems specification (change analysis, activity studies and information analysis) as part of the development of activities in an organization

Information systems specification is according to the ISAC approach performed on three levels: Change analysis, activity studies, and information analysis. A short presentation of these different areas will be given below.

The purpose of change analysis is to study the types of changes (improvements) that are needed in order to do something about the problems experienced in the activities of an organization. It is important to try and find the reasons behind the problems and not only the symptoms. The results from change analysis are a combination of development measures in order to cope with the defined needs for changes. Information systems development should be considered a suitable development measure only if the change analysis indicates that there are problems and needs in the information systems area. In this way, change analysis results in information systems specifications on a first, crude level. This level defines why information systems and not other measures are considered as solutions to existing problems and needs.

The purpose of activity studies is to delimit future information systems in the activities of the organization. The information systems should be delimited in such a way that they contribute to the solving of the problems of the different interest groups involved. In order to delimit information systems, one usually has to describe the activities in more detail than in the change analysis. Delimitation of future information systems should be made from the specific problems and needs that the users have and not using existing technical aids as a basis. The delimitation means that the input and output information sets of the information systems are defined, including relevant properties of the information sets. In this way, activity studies result in information systems specifications on a second, intermediate level. This level defines and delimits potential information systems.

The purpose of information analysis is to describe what the thus delimited future information systems shall contain and perform. The description is used in two different connections. On one hand it represents a means of communication for the affected interest groups in their discussion of the information contents. On the other hand it constitutes an exact basis for the succeeding data system design. The information analysis starts from the desired results from the information system. One then studies what is needed in order to arrive at these results. The structure of the information sets is also studied. Finally, necessary processes in the information system are described. In this way, information analysis results in information systems specifications on a third, detailed level. This level defines the information needs in detail and corresponds to what is usually referred to as a detailed information systems specification.

4 PARTS OF A CASE STUDY OF AN INFORMATION SYSTEMS SPECIFICATION PERFORMED ON THREE LEVELS

In [5] an example which goes through all the main chapters is used in order to illustrate the work steps in the different areas of the ISAC approach. The example is based on reality and taken from a dairy corporation (called Dairco). Parts of the Dairco case will be used here as well to illustrate the three levels of information systems specification. For a more comprehensive case description see [5].

4.1 CHANGE ANALYSIS

Dairco has a need for a revision of their order processing, invoicing and distribution activities. Dairco was formed by a number of merges during the past few years. This has lead to a situation where these activities are performed differently in different regions. What type of development should be chosen in order to develop these activities?

In Dairco a decision is made to set up a project group in order to find an answer to this question. The project group is put together with representatives and one systems analyst. Among the users in the project group there are "direct" users and "inbetween" users. The direct users come from different specialist functions at the central office. The inbetween users also come from the central office but represent the "end" users at the dairies indirectly.

None of these persons have performed change analysis earlier. It is therefore decided to have a learning program around change analysis, now that the project group has been established. Only the project group participates in the learning program, which takes place during three days and in a residential form. During these three days the basics of change analysis are treated. This includes method steps and description techniques. The project group then applies these methods and techniques to the problems in their own project. The learning program also turns out to be the real start of the project, now that work in the project group really begins.

The work then continues at Dairco until the following results are obtained:

1   An evaluation of the current situation

2   A chosen change alternative to be implemented in the future

3   A combination of development measures to implement the change alternative

The results of the evaluation of the current situation are the following needs for changes:

N1   Better order procedures
N2   Better distribution basis
N3   More effective order office work
N4   Common order system
N5   Better order entry equipment
N6   Better production planning basis

Three main change alternatives are discussed:

A0   *No change* (zero alternative), i.e. orders are brought to the office by the truck drivers

A1   Implement a *telephone order system*, where either the order personnel call the customers or the other way around

A2   Implement a *purchase proposal system*, where purchase proposals are sent to the customers

The project group proposes that Dairco continues to work with the purchase proposal idea. An overview of the relations between dairy, customer, and consumer in the purchase proposal system is given in figure 4.2 in the form of a so called A-graph (activity graph). Rules for how to interpret the different symbols in A-graphs are presented in figure 4.1. It should be noted that figure 4.2 has been drawn by the users themselves with the aid of the systems analyst in the project group.

The project group can now define necessary development measures in order to implement a purchase proposal system:

DM1   Information systems development
DM2   Continued organizational development

Information systems will be needed for the preparation and distribution of purchase proposals. Continued organizational development will be needed so that the personnel know how to work with the order processing activities in the future.

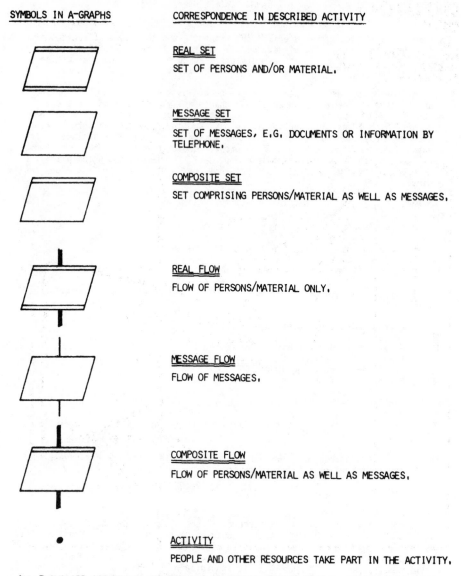

SYMBOLS IN A-GRAPHS

CORRESPONDENCE IN DESCRIBED ACTIVITY

REAL SET

SET OF PERSONS AND/OR MATERIAL.

MESSAGE SET

SET OF MESSAGES, E.G. DOCUMENTS OR INFORMATION BY TELEPHONE.

COMPOSITE SET

SET COMPRISING PERSONS/MATERIAL AS WELL AS MESSAGES.

REAL FLOW

FLOW OF PERSONS/MATERIAL ONLY.

MESSAGE FLOW

FLOW OF MESSAGES.

COMPOSITE FLOW

FLOW OF PERSONS/MATERIAL AS WELL AS MESSAGES.

ACTIVITY

PEOPLE AND OTHER RESOURCES TAKE PART IN THE ACTIVITY.

ALL FLOWS ARE ASSUMED TO GO FROM TOP TO BOTTOM ON THE GRAPHS. ARROWS ARE NEEDED ON UPWARD AND (POSSIBLY) HORIZONTAL FLOWS ONLY.

Figure 4.1 Explanation of symbols used in A-graphs

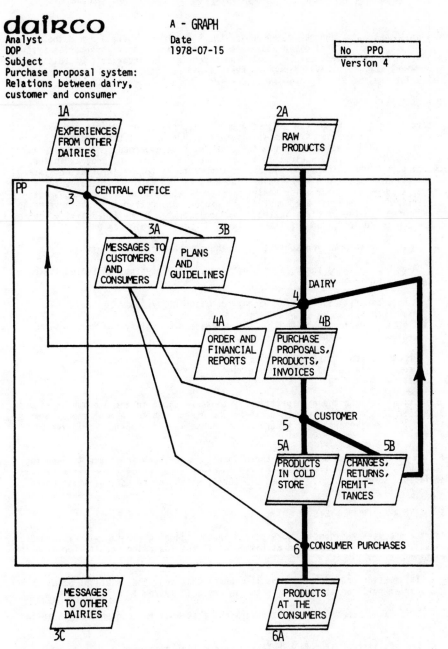

dairco
Analyst
DOP
Subject
Purchase proposal system:
Relations between dairy,
customer and consumer

A - GRAPH
Date
1978-07-15

No PPO
Version 4

Figure 4.2 Relations between dairy, customer and consumer in the purchase
proposal system (A-graph PPO)

The list of needs for changes given above, the A-graph in figure 4.2 and the defined development measures given above are concrete examples of information systems specifications on a first, crude level. The essential characteristic of this level is to define where and why information systems and not other measures are considered as solutions to existing problems and needs.

4.2   ACTIVITY STUDIES

In Dairco, the proposal of the project group is accepted. The project group thus continues with information systems development as one part of their work. The project group is satisfied with the way the learning program around change analysis was carried through. They would like to continue with a learning program in the same way during the information systems development. As to the information systems specification parts, a one week residential work period each is scheduled for activity studies and information analysis respectively. As before, method steps and description techniques are treated. The project group then applies these methods and techniques to the problems in their own project. The work with activity studies is then continued at Dairco until the following results are obtained:

1   A list of information subsystems of the purchase proposal system

2   A-graphs defining the relations between these subsystems including their inputs and outputs

3   A cost/benefit calculus for each information subsystem

The list of information subsystems of the purchase proposal system includes the following subsystems of order processing:

-1   Prognosis processing
-2   Order receiving and order summarizing
-3   Return processing

The relations between these information systems are shown in the A-graph in figure 4.3. Again, this A-graph has been drawn by the users with the aid of the systems analyst. The cost/benefit calculi are not included in this short description of the case.

The list of information subsystems shown above, the A-graph in figure 4.3 and the cost/benefit calculi (not shown here) are concrete examples of information systems specifications on a second, intermediate level, which defines and delimits potential information systems.

4.3   INFORMATION ANALYSIS

After the one week residential work period in the learning program with information analysis, this work is continued at Dairco until the following results for each information system:

1   Information precedence graphs (I-graphs) that show the relations among the different information sets in the information system

2   Information component graphs (C-graphs) that show the contents of these information sets

3   Process lists that define relevant information processes

4   Process tables that describe each process separately

An example of an I-graph is found in figure 4.5. The rules for interpretation of I-graphs are found in figure 4.4. Examples of C-graphs are found in figure 4.7.

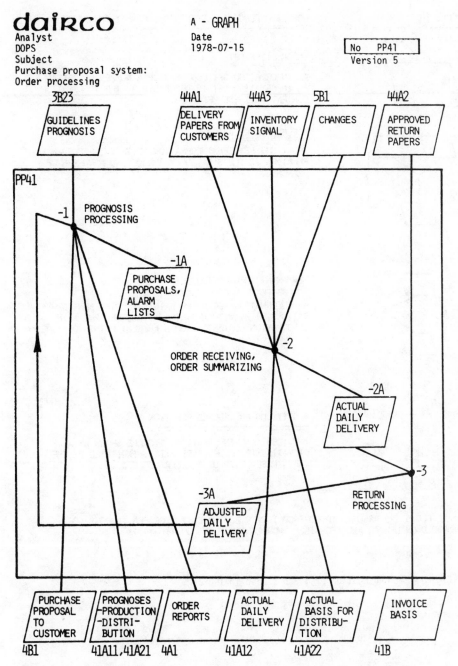

dairco
Analyst
DOPS
Subject
Purchase proposal system:
Order processing

A - GRAPH
Date
1978-07-15

No   PP41
Version 5

Figure 4.3 Order processing in a purchase proposal system (A-graph PP41)

SYMBOLS IN I-GRAPHS   CORRESPONDENCE IN DESCRIBED INFORMATION SYSTEM

INFORMATION SET

AN INFORMATION SET CONSISTS OF A NUMBER OF MESSAGES.
AN INFORMATION SET IS DESCRIBED BY THE INFORMATION
CONTENT IN THESE MESSAGES.

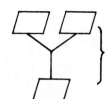

PRECEDENCE RELATION

RELATIONS BETWEEN INFORMATION SETS. THE PRECEDENCE
RELATION IS ILLUSTRATED BY A NODE AND A NUMBER OF
BRANCHES.

PERMANENT INFORMATION SET

AN INFORMATION SET WHICH EXISTS IN DIFFERENT GENE-
RATIONS, I.E. WITH A SIMILAR STRUCTURE BUT WITH
INFORMATION CONTENTS FROM DIFFERENT POINTS OF TIME.

FICTITIOUS PRECEDENCE RELATION

TWO IDENTICAL INFORMATION SETS ARE SHOWN BY A
FICTITIOUS PRECEDENCE RELATION, INDICATED BY THE
PARENTHESES WITHOUT A REFERENCE CODE.

ALL FLOWS ARE ASSUMED TO GO FROM TOP TO BOTTOM ON THE GRAPHS. ARROWS ARE
NEEDED ON UPWARD AND (POSSIBLE) HORIZONTAL FLOWS ONLY.

Figure 4.4 Explanation of symbols used in I-graphs

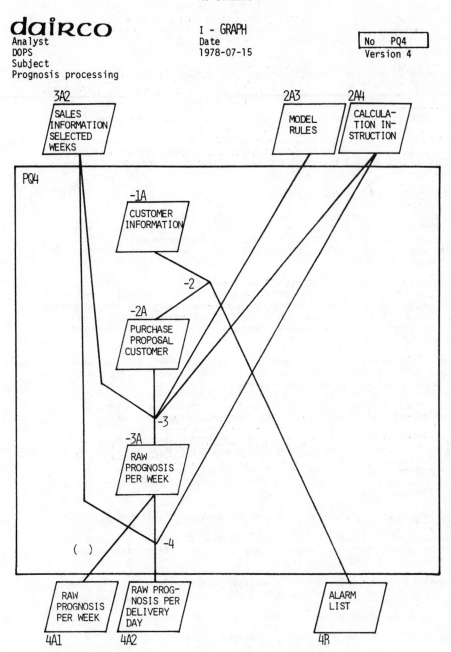

dairco
Analyst
DOPS
Subject
Prognosis processing

I - GRAPH
Date
1978-07-15

No PQ4
Version 4

Figure 4.5 I-graph PQ4

The rules for interpretation of C-graphs are found in figure 4.6. From figure 4.5 the following processes can be defined:

-2 Selection of purchase proposal customers and production of alarm list
-3 Calculation of raw prognosis per week
-4 Spreading of raw prognosis to delivery days

A process table describing the first of these processes in the form of a decision table is found in figure 4.8.

Together with the list of processes above the I-graph, C-graphs and process table in figures 4.5, 4.7, and 4.8 represent a concrete illustration of a detailed information systems specification.

4.4   SOME EXPERIENCES FROM THE DAIRCO CASE

In general terms, the Dairco case can be said to be a successful project. The users controlled the project and arrived at specifications which clearly expressed their intentions. The number of iterations in drawing the graphs was less than in other cases where only information analysis had been performed without change analysis and activity studies.

However, to illustrate the difficulties in specifying information systems, an unsuccessful episode from this project will also be introduced here. At a certain stage, the project group felt a little uncertain about how realizable one information system was and how the end users would react. After some discussion it was decided to implement a prototype system at one site. The idea was to gain experience for the real information system later on.

The project group had to make a large number of decisions about practical details in connection with the coming test period. One felt a great need to start the prototype test soon. Lack of time and stress came into the picture. This lead to a situation where parts of earlier produced documentation were overlooked in writing the computer programs for the prototype. Certain parts of the reports were omitted, a number of incorrect calculation rules were used in the programming etc.

What happened to the prototype? One started the test activities on time. But the prototype did not work as intended. After some time the prototype was taken out of use in order to adapt it to the users' specifications. The "new" prototype then worked as intended. A user reaction: "If we had looked at the ISAC drawings a little more into detail, our first test would have worked out from the beginning." The experiences from this episode underline:

-   The importance of performing sufficient information systems specifications

-   Time pressed and carelessly performed specification work leads to poor information systems that either have to be redone to a large extent or that are not used by the persons affected

5   SUMMARY OF THE RESULTS FROM CHANGE ANALYSIS, ACTIVITY STUDIES, AND INFORMATION ANALYSIS AND THE RELATIONS BETWEEN THESE

The results from change analysis can be summarized in three parts:

1   Evaluated activity model of the current situation with

-   A-graphs

-   Text pages with more detailed descriptions of the different parts of A-graphs

SYMBOLS IN C-GRAPHS	CORRESPONDENCE IN DESCRIBED INFORMATION SYSTEM

INFORMATION SET

INFORMATION SET OR INFORMATION SUBSET. IT IS GIVEN AN INFORMATION SET NAME FOLLOWED BY AN IDENTIFICATION TERM IN PARENTHESES. A TERM CAN CONSIST OF SEVERAL SUBTERMS. AN INFORMATION SUBSET IS IDENTIFIED BY THE IDENTIFICATION TERMS WITHIN PARENTHESES AND BY THE IDENTIFICATION TERMS "HIGHER" UP IN THE TREE STRUCTURE OF THE C-GRAPH.

ITERATION

REPETITION OF SEVERAL MESSAGES WITH THE SAME IDENTIFICATION OR PROPERTY TERM BUT WITH DIFFERENT VALUES OF THIS TERM. THE ASTERISK (*) INDICATES THE TERM THAT HAS REPEATED OCCURENCES.

ELEMENTARY INFORMATION SET

AN INFORMATION SET WITH ONLY ONE PROPERTY TERM. THE IDENTIFICATION TERMS ARE GIVEN BY INFORMATION SETS "HIGHER" UP IN THE STRUCTURE.

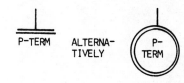

ALMOST-ELEMENTARY INFORMATION SET

AN INFORMATION SET THAT CONSISTS OF A NUMBER OF ELEMENTARY INFORMATION SETS WITH COMMON IDENTIFICATION TERMS. IDENTIFICATION TERMS ARE GIVEN BY INFORMATION SETS "HIGHER" UP IN THE STRUCTURE.

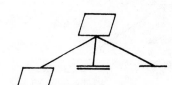

COMPONENT RELATION

DIVISION OF INFORMATION SET IN INFORMATION SUBSETS. TYPES OF COMPONENT RELATIONS (THE MESSAGE TYPES OF INFORMATION SETS AND THE TERMS OF MESSAGE TYPES) ARE INDICATED IMPLICITLY IN THE C-GRAPH.

Figure 4.6 Explanation of symbols used in C-graphs

dairco
Analyst
DOPS
Subject
Prognosis processing

C - GRAPH
Date
1978-07-15

No 2A4,41A,42A,4B
Version 3

INPUT INFORMATION SETS TO PROCESS PQ42

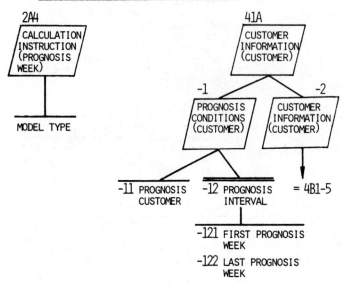

2A4
CALCULATION
INSTRUCTION
(PROGNOSIS
WEEK)

MODEL TYPE

41A
CUSTOMER
INFORMATION
(CUSTOMER)

-1 PROGNOSIS
CONDITIONS
(CUSTOMER)

-2 CUSTOMER
INFORMATION
(CUSTOMER)

-11 PROGNOSIS
CUSTOMER

-12 PROGNOSIS
INTERVAL

= 4B1-5

-121 FIRST PROGNOSIS
WEEK

-122 LAST PROGNOSIS
WEEK

OUTPUT INFORMATION SETS FROM PROCESS PQ42

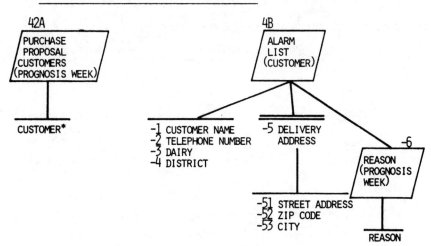

42A
PURCHASE
PROPOSAL
CUSTOMERS
(PROGNOSIS WEEK)

CUSTOMER*

4B
ALARM
LIST
(CUSTOMER)

-1 CUSTOMER NAME
-2 TELEPHONE NUMBER
-3 DAIRY
-4 DISTRICT

-5 DELIVERY
ADDRESS

-6 REASON
(PROGNOSIS
WEEK)

-51 STREET ADDRESS
-52 ZIP CODE
-53 CITY

REASON

Figure 4.7   C-graphs of input and output information sets to process PQ42

dairco

Analyst
DOPS
Subject
Prognosis processing

PROCESS TABLE
Date
1978-07-15

No   PQ42
Version 2

PREREQUISITES
FIND A MESSAGE IN 2A4.
FIND MESSAGES IN 41A FOR THE SAME CUSTOMER.

CALCULATIONS	1	2	3
PROGNOSIS CUSTOMER IN 41A11?	N	Y	Y
FIRST PROGNOSIS WEEK (41A121) ≤ ≤ PROGNOSIS WEEK (2A4) ≤ ≤ LAST PROGNOSIS WEEK (41A122)		N	Y
4B1-5 := 41A2	X	X	
PROGNOSIS WEEK (4B6) := PROGNOSIS WEEK (2A4)	X	X	
REASON (4B6) := "NOT PROGNOSIS CUSTOMER"	X		
REASON (4B6) := "OUTSIDE PROGNOSIS INTERVAL"		X	
PROGNOSIS WEEK (42A) := PROGNOSIS WEEK (2A4)			X
CUSTOMER (42A) := CUSTOMER (41A)			X

Figure 4.8 Process table for process PQ42

- Property tables with descriptions of relevant properties in connection with the different parts of A-graphs
- Tables with needs for changes
- List of interest groups

2 Evaluated activity model of chosen change alternative with
- A-graphs
- Text pages to A-graphs
- Property tables
- Tables with needs for changes
- List of interest groups

3 Plans for chosen change approach with
- Chosen development measures
- Outline of relations between development measures
- Time schedules
- Resource plans

The results from activity studies can be summarized in two parts:

1 Activity models of information subsystems with
- A-graphs
- Text pages to A-graphs
- Property tables
- List of information systems
- Cost/benefit calculus for each information subsystem

2 Plans of information subsystems with
- Chosen information subsystems for continued development
- Outlines of relations between the development of different subsystems
- Time plans
- Resource plans

The results from information analysis are detailed information analysis models for each information subsystem analyzed. Such models consist of
- I-graphs
- C-graphs
- Text pages to I-graphs
- Term catalogues
- Process lists
- Process tables
- Property tables

The transition from change analysis to activity studies is indicated in figure 5.1. Figure 5.2 shows the transition from activity studies to information analysis.

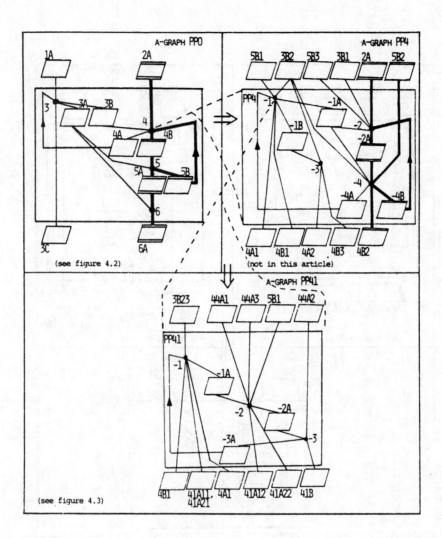

Figure 5.1   Transition from change analysis to activity studies: Preparation
of detailed activity models

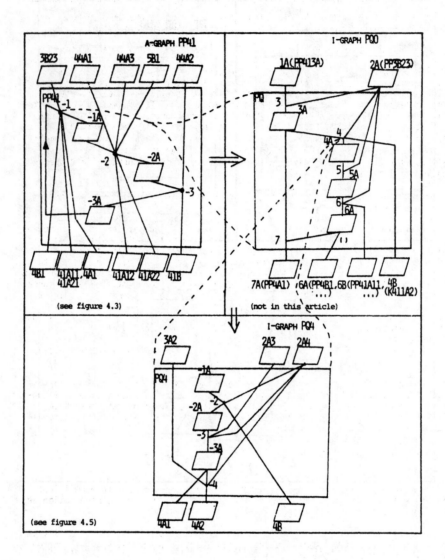

Figure 5.2   Transition from activity studies to information analysis: Preparation
of detailed information analysis models

6   SOME POSSIBILITIES THAT THE ISAC APPROACH TO INFORMATION SYSTEMS SPECIFICATION OFFERS

Our *experience*[3] shows that the following possibilities of the ISAC approach are essential in practical work with specifying information systems today:

The users can control the specification of information systems by themselves

The ISAC approach contains such structuring possibilities that the users themselves can describe and analyze their own activities, thereby understanding them better. After they have described and analyzed the activities, the next step is to describe possible future information systems that can facilitate or improve the activities. In doing this, you also give the information contents of the future information systems, thus specifying what the information systems shall do. The users have the best knowledge of the facts also in this case. No technical background or knowledge is needed in order to describe what the information systems shall do. The ISAC approach gives the users possibilities to perform this specification of information contents.

Information systems specification can be performed in a number of small, manageable and connected steps

To specify information systems is a difficult task. The subject area is comprehensive. Many complex problems have to be solved in connection with information systems specification. We think that the only way to solve complex problems is to divide them into subproblems until they become manageable. A requirement for this to work is that the solution to the subproblems gives the solution for the problem as a whole -- i.e., that the division in subproblems is coherent. The ISAC approach to information systems specification uses a partitioning in three levels. In each of these three levels there then is a number of steps that are performed, with each step using the results from the preceding steps. Together the chain of steps forms an integrated methodology for information systems specification.

It is possible to achieve good cooperation between different professional categories in the specification process

Good cooperation and good communication among human beings is an important prerequisite for successful information systems specification. The existence of a continuous chain of steps gives a clear picture of what everybody can contribute. This fosters a working collaboration between different interest and professional categories in the specification process, such as

- users
- problem oriented systems analysts

There are especially large possibilities of obtaining a good cooperation between different interest and professional groups in the specification process if in parallel with the ISAC approach one also works actively with the communication and learning process during information systems specification.

The advantages discussed here can have many important consequences for the way in which an organization specifies information systems in practice. We would therefore like to point out some of these:

Specification of information systems can become a natural part of the normal activities of the users

It often happens that many users are unfamiliar with their information systems. Some users do not understand completely what the information systems do. Others may think that the systems analysts bring up conditions and circumstances that have nothing to do with specification of information systems. With the ISAC approach, in which users can describe and analyze their own activities and specify the information systems by themselves, specification of information systems can become a natural part of the normal activities of the users and not something strange.

The problem oriented systems analyst can come to work as a catalyst

What is the role of the systems analyst in the ISAC approach? Will he or she no longer be needed when the users describe and analyze their own activities and specify the information systems by themselves? The systems analyst has in the ISAC approach the possibility to work as a catalyst -- i.e., a person who gives methods support when needed --, instead of an expert who knows best and who specifies the end results. Working as a catalyst is a very demanding task that calls for great skill, but it is also very stimulating and rewarding.

REFERENCES:

[1] Aamodt, M., Sørsveen, A., Mennesker, kommunikasjon og konsekvenser (NORCOL, Oslo, 1977) (in Norwegian).

[2] Gunnerblad, G., Holmqvist, H., Possne, K., Organisk utbildning. Bakgrund, program, metoder (PA-rådet, Stockholm, 1974) (in Swedish).

[3] Langefors, B., Theoretical Analysis of Information Systems (Studentlitteratur, Lund, 1966, third edition 1973).

[4] Lundeberg, M., Goldkuhl, G., Nilsson, A., Information Systems Development - A First Introduction to a Systematic Approach, draft available from research group ISAC, Department of Administrative Information Processing, University of Stockholm, 106 91 Stockholm, Sweden (1978).

[5] Lundeberg, M., Goldkuhl, G., Nilsson, A., Information Systems Development - A Systematic Approach, draft available from research group ISAC, Department of Administrative Information Processing, University of Stockholm, 106 91 Stockholm, Sweden (1978).

[6] Lundeberg, M., Goldkuhl, G., Nilsson, A., A Systematic Approach to Information Systems Development - Part I: Introduction, Information Systems, Vol 4 (1979) no 1.

[7] Lundeberg, M., Goldkuhl, G., Nilsson, A., A Systematic Approach to Information Systems Development - Part II: Problem and Data Oriented Methodology, Information Systems, Vol 4 (1979), no 2.

[8] Nissen, H.-E., Andersen, E.S., Systemering - Verksamhetsbeskrivning (Studentlitteratur, Lund, 1978) (in Swedish, English translation with the title "Information Systems Development - Description of Activities" is planned).

[9] Rogers, C.R., Freedom to learn (Charles E. Merrill Publishing Co., Columbus, Ohio, 1969).

---

1) In this and later figures of development activities we describe different activities and the results from these. We also illustrate that persons participate in the activities. The activities are described with small filled circles, the results with rhomboids and persons with rhomboids with double lines on top. In such cases when the results include real objects (e.g. machines) these are also illustrated with double lines on top.

2) That some of the sets outside the frame in figure 2.4.2 only go to/from the frame and not to any special activity should be interpreted as if they go to/

from all activities inside the frame. The iteration arrows (⌐⌐) shall in the same way be interpreted as if they go to all activities inside the frame. By having persons in this figure we once again emphasize that enterprise development including change analysis and information systems development should be considered as a communication and learning process.

3) This section deals with experiences from practical applications of the ISAC approach. They are formulated as possibilities since the achievement of these results in practical applications depends on how you use the methods. Methods must not be applied mechanically.

INFORMATION PROCESSING 80, S.H. Lavington (ed.)
North-Holland Publishing Company
© IFIP, 1980

Invited Paper

INFORMATION MODELING IN THE CONTEXT OF SYSTEM DEVELOPMENT

Janis A. BUBENKO, Jr.

Chalmers University of Technology
S-412 96 Goteborg, Sweden

The concepts of an information system and of information requirements are examined. An appraisal of significant results in the areas of information system specification and of data modeling is presented. A framework for specification of goal-oriented information requirements for an information system is outlined. It is argued that a total requirement specification must include an abstract model of the enterprise. The model should view the application in an extended time perspective. The main part of this paper is concerned with concepts useful for specification of such a model.

1. INTRODUCTION

The major characteristics of an information system, can be grouped into

a. technological, which concern the system's performance and reliability characteristics seen from a hardware point of view

b. functional and semantic, which concern the questions whether the system does the right things in a correct way and whether it can adapt to changing requirements

c. economical, which emphasize the total system's cost effectiveness and contribution to the objectives of the enterprise

d. social, which converge with those characteristics of the system which have an impact on the work environment of the enterprise or on or parts of society.

Clearly, these areas are not mutually independent. It is, however, essential that all these characteristics are explicitly considered in order to direct the system development process to a satisfactory outcome.

While much research work has been devoted to all these traits, only the technological area has, so far, been able to report substantial and revolutionary results. Progress in the other areas is, at best, evolutionary, and there is normally a time lag of ten years or more between initial research results and a wider practical use of them. This is particularly true for (b) - funtional and semantic characteristics of a system. Important contributions to improve parts of the system life cycle (see (44) for an overview) have been reported. In the area of software technology (50) including problem and requirement statement languages and tools, program design, program specification and verification and data abstraction, the number and variety of exploratory approaches is impressive. In the field of data modeling for data bases, likewise, a never ending stream of new ideas and concepts (see (24) and (27) for a survey and comparative analysis) all have as their objective the cap-

turing by the data base more 'semantics' of the application discourse. Pioneering work in the area of formal specification of information systems was carried out already during the sixties with a similar objective (53, 16, 25).

In spite of these notable efforts, the situation in practice still is that we have immense difficulties in designing systems which fully conform to expectations, satisfy stated requirements and which demonstrate a satisfactory reliabilty and maintainability. One of the major reasons for this imperfect situation can be found, we believe, in the very early phases of the system's life cycle. It is here that a 'model' of the application 'reality' is designed by the use of abstraction and negotiations between users. This model then forms the semantic basis for the contents of the information system.

In practically none of the reported approaches to system and software design is the application model defined explicitly but rather implicitly in terms of computer and data processing concepts, such as procedures, data structures, data sets, system flow diagrams and that like. Using this technique requirements for an information system are, when they are formally defined, not specified in WHAT-oriented, but rather in HOW-oriented, or solution-oriented terms. Such a specification hides semantics and basic assumptions about the application in procedures and stored information and, furthermore, drastically restricts the solution space of feasible designs. The proper, "goal-oriented" requirements of the information system are then normally found embedded in the informally stated 'initial specifications' or similar documents, of the system's objectives and scope. As the name indicates, a specification of WHAT- or goal-oriented requirements should include all required external properties of a system, and it should also include a complete model of the application. This model should be as free as possible from data processing and efficiency considerations. This paper is concerned with the formal specifications of goal-oriented system requirements and argues that they too should be strictly defined. It is postulated that, in order to precisely define them, a formal model, which depicts abstraction, assumptions and constraints of the selected parts of the application environment is needed. A new phase or level in the system development life cycle is thereby introduced.

The objective of this development phase is to define formally the WHAT-oriented requirements including the model. We believe that this model-building will, when performed in non-computer processing terms, enhance user understanding of the application. Therefore we call it the 'understanding level'.

As an introduction to the problems encountered in modeling at this level, we examine the concepts of information systems and information requirements in section 2.

Section 3 reviews the development and some significant work in the areas of information system methodology and data modeling. Achievements in both these fields constitue the basis for developing a framework for goal-oriented modeling. The framework and a set of associated modeling concepts are presented in sections 4 and 5. As will be shown, 'time' is the most essential concept in this approach, because it permits us to define model behaviour in non-procedural terms.

2. REQUIREMENTS, MODELS AND SYSTEMS

Intuitively we may say that an information requirement is "a requirement for knowledge of something". An information requirement is always associated with a 'consumer' or a set of consumers. A requirement may be associated with a person, who occasionally or periodically needs this additional knowledge in order to perform some task, or it can be associated with a mechanical, automated process, for instance, a computing process or a production process. We will not, in this paper, discuss whether the knowledge is adequate to the consumer or not, or whether there is alternative knowledge, which might serve the consumer better. This is, however, one of the major concerns of the part of system's life cycle, which deals with Corporate Requirement Analysis.

What do we mean then by 'knowledge of something'? This 'something' is apparently a part of the consumer's 'environment'. There is no need to consider this environment as something physical or static. It need not be restricted to a warehouse inventory, a production process or a traffic system. It can very well include abstract constructs like a set of laws of physics, a mathematical theory, a behavioural model of some organization or a set of laws for some system or country. Or it can be knowledge of knowledge of..... something. Whatever it is, we will restrict ourselves to cases that are within reach of our mental and abstractional capacity to create in our minds a "model" of this something. We will perceive, select and classify individual phenomena into classes of sufficiently similar phenomena and generelize relationships between individual phenomena into relations on sets of phenomena. We will also assume that these phenomena obey a

set of rules or that their behaviour is constrained in some way. By doing this we create a simplified, partial "model" of the environment in our minds.

If we accept this concept of a 'model', then two kinds of knowledge can be distinguished

a. knowledge of the model of some environment

b. knowledge of the 'state of affairs' or relationships of individual phenomena or of sets of phenomena represented by the concepts in the 'model', i. e. knowledge of an instance of the model.

According to researchers in Artificial Intelligence (37, 52) we may consider (a) as "abstract knowledge" and (b) as "concrete knowledge".

Concrete knowledge is seen as facts, statements concerning individual phenomena, entities or relationships in the model of the environment. The sentence "Supplier S supplies parts of type P to project J" is an example of a concrete fact and it also reveals a local view, where some phenomena of the reality are classified in the entity sets PROJECTS, SUPPLIERS and PARTS.

By abstract knowledge we denote such information which augments our interpretation of concrete information and by which we can draw inferences, conclusions of other facts. We include here also constraints, which delimit the number of different facts that can be part of the model. These constraints assure that the model behaves within limits of what is feasible in the application environment and that new facts added to the model are consistent with other information. Abstract knowledge does not, normally, concern individual phenomena, but rather classes and/or populations of such phenomena. Clearly, the border-line is not sharp.

Examples of knowledge which may aid our deductive capability are

- "every employee is a person"

- "every day is a part of a month"

- " a trucker is an employee who is currently assigned a transport of goods".

Examples of abstract knowledge of the 'constraint' type are

- "on a particular day an employee may be assigned to one and only one project"

- "every supplier supplies at least two parts to every project"

- "employees working on project x may not perform job type y more than z hours per month"

- "the monthly salary budget of the company is the sum of the salary budgets of its departments".

We have observed that in order to express abstract or concrete knowledge of some discourse, we must abstract the perceived structure of the application environment. We have classified individual entities into entity classes - possibly overlapping - and individual relationships into relationship classes.

The next problem concerns the representation of knowledge. It is obvious that concrete knowledge, i. e. facts, can easily be represented by some kind of data structure. The structure can be modified when new facts arrive, and it can be searched when one wants to retrieve some concrete information. But how can we represent abstract knowledge? Clearly, certain kind of abstract knowledge can easily be represented by 'structure'. For example, the asssertion "every truck is a vehicle", can be represented by connecting every 'truck' - entity with a 'vehicle' - entity by a relation of a particular meaning, thereby creating an ISA-hierarchy (51, 36). However, other kinds of abstract knowledge might be more difficult to represent structurally such as, for instance, "every supplier supplies at least two parts to every project". To deal with this kind of knowledge, basically two extreme approaches exist: i) the declarative approach and ii) the procedural approach. In a purely declarative approach we could represent our concrete, as well as abstract, knowledge by assertions and formulae using some mathematical - logical notation, such as predicate calculus. Queries against this knowledge base will then involve deduction procedures to generate an answer. Adding of new knowledge will imply proof procedures to check whether the new knowledge is consistent with the existing one.

In a purely procedural approach abstract knowledge would not be explicitly formulated, but rather built into procedures, which dealt with modifying the 'knowledge base' and answering queries. Using a procedural representation the same (kind of) knowledge might be represented in several different procedures. Representing this kind of knowledge procedurally depends therefore very much on how we intend to use our knowledge base (52). It is in contrast to the purely declarative approach where knowledge representation can be made - at least theoretically - usage-independent.

As pointed out in (51), few knowledge representation systems are purely of the declarative (WHAT) or of the procedural (hHOW) type. It seems that the declarative approach is more general and modular than the procedural approach. Possibilities of answering unanticipated queries and to insert new knowledge seem to be more pronounced in declarative models. As knowledge of some phenomena in these models is represented at 'one place' only, they should also be easier to overview and understand. The main problem with this approach, however, is its lack of efficient implementations.

The above discussion reveals our view of an information system as "a system which maintains knowledge of a model of some application environment". The model is technically made to reasonably correctly reflect the application reality by accepting "new knowledge" in terms of various kinds of transactions, which correspond to and describe events such as observations and decisions in the environment.

If we now look at 'requirements' from this point of view, we agree with (35) that a "requirement's definition must encompass everything necessary to lay the groundwork for subsequent stages in system development". Similar objectives have been expressed in (42) and (43). We believe, however, that requirements initially should be goal-oriented and express WHAT properties the system should have and not HOW the system is to be constructed (i. e. which information sets and processes it should include). A set of goal-oriented requirements then would have a semantic part which specifies -in terms of a conceptual information model - what knowledge is to be embodied by the system, and an operation part which specifies the 'boundary conditions' of the system in terms of system-environment interaction, representation of information, performance requirements, reliability requirements and the like. These parts together, then represent a complete basis and a set of constraints for the subsequent design stage, where a process-oriented, abstract specification of a system is constructed. Clearly, the transition from goal-oriented requirements to a process-oriented form is a critical step (3). We believe, however, that a sound formalism for specification of goal-oriented requirements will make this transition less critical. Before we outline a framework for specification of goal-oriented requirements, an appraisal of approaches to information system and data modeling is given in section 3.

3. APPROACHES TO INFORMATION SYSTEM AND DATA MODELING

The objective of an information system model is a high-level, computer implementation-independent description of the contents and processing subsystem of an information system. The objective of a data model is to define the 'semantics' and contents of an information system's data base. Both models have similar objectives. The difference lies in their scope in that the information system modeling field considers the system as a whole, while data modeling normally delimits itself to the structure and contents of the information system's stored information. In the following, we will survey developments in both fields and point out some significant achievements.

3.1 Information System Modeling

The information system view on modeling has derived from the designing of systems for processing documents, represented by file records or even punched cards, and maintenance of standing files. The typical view taken here is a set of subsystems with input-output relations to other subsystems. Early approaches to formal description of data processing systems thus focused on abstract description of file - or document - contents and on a description of the associated processing procedures and rules (53, 16).

In 1966 a theory of information systems analysis was presented (25), which included, among other issues, the concepts of an elementary message and an elementary process. The elementary message carries information of a real-world situation and contains references (26) to an object (or an object aggregate), a property type (or a relationship type) and a point - or interval- in time, when this information was observed. Works within the ISDOS project (44) and the design of tools for formal specification, design and optimization systems (32) have been inspired by this concept. Except for the unique time attribute, we can also compare the idea of an e-message with recent ideas in the area of relational data modeling, such as "semantically irreducible sentences" (7) and the use of "surrogates" (21, 18).

Further work on information system modeling nd specification, can be divided into three directions: i) specification languages and ools for large software systems, ii) high level implementation tools and iii) theoretical concepts for modeling.

The specification language approaches employ, in general, a hierarchical, top-down system decomposition philosophy and discipline. The PSL/PSA-technique (45), the Software Requirements Engineering Methodology - SREM (4, 19) and Structured Analysis (35) use the principle of stepwise decomposition of systems of processes, flow of control and associated data. Practical experience with high level system specification languages is still limited. There is, however, reason to believe that a disciplined application of these techniques will significantly improve the quality of the software produced.

High level implementation languages can also be seen as tools for specification of an information system. These languages normally assume an underlying data base according to some high level data model. The objective of these approaches is to provide the user/designer with a powerful set of tools by which systems can be incrementally and easily constructed. Examples of such approaches are USE (48), which uses a relational data model, and CS4 (6), where a binary, associative data model is employed. Very high level domain-specific languages, such as the System for Business Automation - SBA (54) and the use of abstract data types in system design e.g. (49) also belong to this field.

Conceptual developments in the field of information system modeling during the last years have headed in the direction of data modeling. For instance, in (20), abstract models are defined for both information and processes and in (34) the information system is specified by an integrated representation of collections of object classes, operation classes, event classes and associations between these categories.

3.2 Data modeling

A data model is a set of concepts and constructs by which the contents of and relationships within a data base can be described. The description is then called the schema, and the actual contents of the data base is called the extension of a corresponding schema. A schema describes both which kinds of concrete facts are contained in the data base and which constraints and rules they must conform to.

During the 70s several new concepts for data modeling have been suggested and efforts towards standardization are being made (40, 46). They all have a common objective: to better describe the semantics of the data and to specify a schema in high-level conceptual, application oriented terms. Data modeling approaches can be characterized along several dimensions (24, 12). In this paper two major classes of data modeling will be distinguished depending on which view of the application reality they take and which modeling concepts they employ.

The first class of models focusses on the types of sentences of the application to be included in the schema. The relational model (17) is a typical member of this class. Concrete information about some application is represented by a set of time - varying relations defined on a set of attributes. Abstract information is supplied mainly in terms of dependencies, which are defined on attribute sets within the relations. Normalization theory of relational data bases (5) deals with the problem of designing a "good" relational schema. Without going into the various methods of synthesis or decomposition, we might say that the objective of a schema design process is in general to arrive at a set of relations, which are non-redundant and which are in an elementary, irreducible form. The resulting relational schema will, in this way, 'more naturally' reflect the underlying reality.

The other class of data modeling approaches, which we may call structural, takes quite another starting point. Instead of examining attribute collections and their dependencies, the structural models focus directly on the structure and organization of the underlying application. While relations and dependencies were the basic constructs used in the relational model to represent knowledge, structural models employ several more modeling concepts and constructs. The most common of these concepts are the entity (or object) and the association (or relationship). The basic view these models take is that knowledge of a piece of some application reality at each point in time is represented by a set of entities (of various types) and a set of relationships between them. Entities and relationships possess properties, which may change with time. The application model thus represents a state of the reality. This state is changed by inserting or deleting entities and relationships or by changing their properties corresponding to the changing real world situation. Typical for this class of models is also that they use a graphical representation technique.

Most structural models make a more or less explicit distinction between entities and the names by which we refer to entities (39). This implies that we can distinguish two levels of the conceptual schema: one "ontological", where we focus on the "substance" of the application model (i e which kinds of entities and relationships to include in it) and one "significational", where a decision is made as to which names to use to refer to entities. Sets of names, as well as sets of entities are part of the model. This makes it possible to include an explicit definition of name assignment in the schema.

One issue, on which there are different views is distinction between and representation of entities, relationships and properties. We can here distinguish between at least three main views.

The binary view (1, 8, 6, 39) uses only two kinds of representational concepts: entities and labeled binary relations. This implies that relationships of higher order than two will be modeled as entities. As there is no "property" concept in this view, something that we perceive as a property will be modeled as a binary relation between one entity set and another entity set representing property values.

The entity-association view (e.g. 10, 31) is similar to the binary view, as also here properties are considered as entity relationships. The difference is, however, that relationships can be of any order and that they are distinguished from entities (or objects). The semantic constraint, that relationships cannot exist without the existence of the participating entities, is thereby included in the structure of the model.

In agreement with the entity-association view, the entity-association-property view (e.g. 15, 33, 38, 47) also distinguishes between entities and associations (or relationships). In addition to this, a distinction is made between entities and properties. The latter are seen as constructs, which characterize entities or associations and which have no independent existence of their own.

The ability of a data model to support different, local user views and information requirements, requires that it be possible to define and handle subsets and constructs of subsets of an entity set. Furthermore, certain relationships or properties may not generally hold for all members of an entity set, but only for a subset of it. Many works on data modeling somehow by-pass this problem, but there are exceptions (e.g. 22, 33, 36, 41). Some of them also emphasize a distinction between a generic object, the set of entities and individual members of an entity set.

The distinction, made in data models of the structural kind, between entities, relationships and properties and the possibility of defining subsets of entity sets embodies certain abstract knowledge in terms of semantic 'rules' or constraints. In general, however, the set of rules, which defines consistency or derivability between different 'facts' or which restrict the number of facts that can be embodied by an application model is large and varied. Only a few 'general' ones can be

represented by the structure of the model. More complex rules and constraints will normally require that they are described by declarative or procedural techniques (e.g. 10) as a supplement to the structural description.

3.3 Discussion

Information system (IS) and data modeling approaches outlined in this section deserve some comments from the requirement specification point-of-view. A characteristic of the IS modeling approaches is that they present a formal HOW-oriented solution to some goal-oriented requirements which are not explicitly stated. Decisions have already been made about how to (conceptually) process data, which data to store etc. From a knowledge representation point of view, we may say that IS-models represent all abstract application knowledge in a procedural form. While most data models, on the other hand, provide some concepts by which abstract knowledge (semantic rules, constraints) can be represented as part of the schema, they have a weak side with respect to requirements analysis. This weakness lies in the fact that most data models focus entirely on the stored information of a data base. If transactions, representing events in application environment which affect the state of the model, are not made an integral part of it, then it becomes extremely hard to define the real meaning of the data. This reflection will be elaborated in the following sections. Most data modeling issues surveyed in this section, will be encountered there also, but with an extra 'dimension' - time. We intend to show that this extra dimension provides a link by which powerful concepts from the fields of information system and data modeling can be integrated.

4. A FRAMEWORK FOR CONCEPTUAL INFORMATION MODELING AND REQUIREMENTS ANALYSIS

We will assume that our starting point is a set of unstructured, informally stated requirements for (output) information together with requirements concerning output format, performance, reliability and the like. We will focus on the information part of the requirements - the semantic part. Starting from this and the users' and/or designers unstructured knowledge of the application the task will be to build an abstract model of the application. At this stage the model will have nothing to do with data processing. Instead its objective is explicitly to specify abstractions made about the reality and to display all other assumptions made in terms of rules and constraints. We argue that the information output requirements and the operation requirements can be given a precise meaning only when considered together with the abstract model of the enterprise - here called the Conceptual Information Model. Our objective is also that the requirements together with the model constitute a total goal-oriented requirement specification, which provides a complete basis for design and specification of computer processing oriented system specifications.

The basic concepts for the conceptual information modeling approach will be outlined in section 5. This section gives an overall framework of the approach, including its assumptions and objectives.

A fundamental assumption is that every requirement is specified with respect to the specifier's (user's) perseption, i e model, of the part of the enterprise, which is relevant to the requirement. We will assume that the semantic part of an information requirement specifies

WHAT: I e which "phenomena" of the model the user is interested in and which time points or intervals of the reality this information should be associated with.

WHEN: Here the user indicates time points or intervals when the information is required.

The other part of a requirement concerns operative system properties such as actuality, performance and reliability. For instance, an actuality requirement might give a specification of the maximum allowable "age" of the requested information with respect to WHEN. In addition to these rather "local" requirements, a total specification will also include global system requirements concerning performance, reliability, security, flexibility, maintainability and the like. As these requirements will have no effect on the conceptual information model, we will not discuss them further.

The WHAT-part can be more or less complex and concern various time points and intervals relative to the time specifications in the WHEN-part. Examples:

a. The balance of a savings account

b. The sales volume of all inventory items for March and April this year and also for the corresponding months last year.

c. The optimum flight route from Copenhagen to New York for a particular scheduled flight and day.

The WHEN-part of the requirement defines a condition when the information must be supplied. It can refer to external conditions with respect to the information system (we exemplify with the WHAT-statement (a) such as

- at the end of every week

- upon terminal-operator request

- on the last day of every month, at 3 PM

and/or it can refer to internal conditions in the model. such as, for instance

- when the balance drops below $ 500.00

- when more than $ 1000.00 have been withdrawn during a year.

A partial examplification of the operation-part of a requirement could be an actuality requirement (see a.) that the retrieved balance of a particular savings-account should never be

"older" than, say, two hours. This provides a requirement on the design of a transaction processing strategy and choice of processing periodicity.

The above examples show a typical "goal-oriented" information requirement specification. No processing considerations are made. It illustrates our objective that requirements specifications should be as "design-free" as possible with respect to data structure, storage and processing issues, and put a minimum of restrictions on the technical part of the information system design.

Similar assumptions and objectives hold for developing the conceptual information model (CIM) for an enterprise:

1. A CIM should include a total model of those parts of the enterprise, which are relevant to existing and anticipated requirements. This contrasts with most conceptual models for data bases, which restrict the model to definition of stored (possibly virtually) information only.

2. A CIM should be as free as possible from technical (structure, storage, processing) decisions. (Note: the design of a particular CIM will require many assumptions and design decisions to be made. These decisions, however, will concern reality abstraction and generalization issues including the design of semantic rules and constraints).

3. As a consequence of 2), a CIM should impose as few restrictions as possible concerning feasible technical designs.

4. Concepts for designing a CIM, and a CIM itself, should posses all the well-known, desirable properties of a conceptual data model (e g (31)) such as

    - expressiveness

    - ease of formulation and reading

    - formality

    - ease in changing and

    - ease in transforming.

5. In addition to these, we would like to stress the desirability of incorporating the following features into a conceptual information modeling approach:
    - it should enhance user understanding and force active participation by stimulating and generating questions as to how the reality is abstracted, and which assumtions are made.

    - it should force the users/designers to state explicitly their assumtions and to arrive at a model which is as complete as possible. One criterion for completeness is that all required information can be produced (i e there are no "missing transactions"). The model should also employ concepts

and formalism, which makes consistency verification possible.

- it should make incremental introduction and integration of new requirements easy and natural in the sense
  that new requirments should require
  as few changes in an existing model
  as possible.

In our view, the information output requirements play a fundamental role in designing a
CIM. They define that part of the CIM which
corresponds to the "output" information. The
rest of the conceptual information model is
designed by a systematic procedure, where -
starting from the part of CIM which is defined
by the output requirments - for each kind of
information we ask questions of the following
kind:

- is this kind of information <u>initial</u> or can
  it be <u>derived</u> from other information? If
  assumed derivable, then a derivation rule
  must be defined.

- is this kind of event external or does it
  depend on certain conditions within the
  model? If not assumed external, then an
  occurence rule must be defined.

- which other particular constraints or
  rules hold for this construct?

Answers to these questions are not theoretically decidable, but lie in our decisions where
to draw the <u>external</u> <u>boundary</u> of the model and
which other assumptions about it to make.

During the design process, the scope of the
model is incrementally enlarged by introduction
of new kinds of information, about which the
same questions are asked. The process continues until all derivation and event occurence
rules are defined both for non-initial
information and for all endogenous (internal)
events respectively.

In order to be able to define a model with the
characteristics outlined above, <u>time</u> is introduced as one of its most essential components.
Entity existence rules, attribute and predicate
derivation rules, event occurence rules etc are
all expressed in terms of a suitably chosen
time argument. As a consequence of this full
"time-perspective" there is no concept of
"updating" at the CIM-level. Also concepts like
"insertion" and "deletion" will obtain a different meaning here. They will correspond to
existence and occurrence rules for entities and
relationships of the enterprise.

Figure 1 illustrates the role of a CIM in a
conceptual schema, or conceptual data base
model (CDBM) design process. The CIM design is
a strongly iterative process, where knowledge
and assumtions of the application environment
are successively incorporated and integrated in
the model. During the subsequent Conceptual
Information System Design stage many complex,
efficiency-oriented decisions are made such as:
which information about which time periods to
store in the data base, how to structure
processes on data, which transaction processing
and updating strategy to apply etc. All these

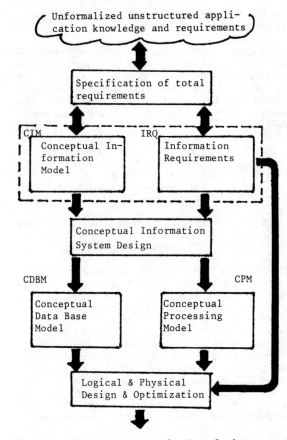

Figure 1. The role of CIM in the design process.

decisions must conform to and satisfy the
specified operative requirements in IRQ.

We have shown elsewhere (14) that the choice of
a CDBM-structure is intimately related to and
dependent on the choice of a conceptual processing model. This is avoided at the CIM/IRQ
- level. We therefore feel that this level can
provide the CDBM/CPM - designer with a better
"understanding" of the application and the
requirements than processing-oriented requirement specifications. Some concepts, found adequate for modeling at this "understanding
level", will be discussed in the following
section.

5. MODELING CONCEPTS

The concept of time is essential in our
approach. We need it to define event
occurrence conditions, to define existence criteria for entities, to define function and
predicate value variations and to define various dynamic constraints. We must also be able
to refer to certain time points or intervals -
or sets of these - using various referencing
expressions such as for example:

1. The set of first days every month during a
   summer season.

2. Since 1975 your salary is transferred to
   your ckeccking account every month on the
   26:th, between 12.00 and 13.15.

3. The set of days in March, 1975, when John Smith's car was taken in for repair (if any).

4. The week in year 1980, when the total of hours-worked was maximum.

Before going into declaration of entity, event and data types and specification of various kinds of constraints we will, therefore, present a model for dealing with time.

5.1 A time model

Obviously there is a need for a "calendar system" (10), but we need also to deal with time in much the same way as with the other concepts of our approach. In order to achieve this, we introduce a "time-model" consisting of an infinite set of time points T and a set of time interval <u>types</u> TI $= \{ TI_1, \ldots, TI_i, \ldots, TI_N \}$.

A particular time interval ti_i^j belongs to one and only one type TI_i. The set TI is partially ordered according to a total function with the semantic "part-of". Thus, "part-of: $TI_i \rightarrow TI_k$ implies that every interval in TI_i is a "part-of" an interval in TI_k. The set of time points, T, of course, functionally determines in this sense all intervals.

We will find it convenient to consider all individual intervals and time points as <u>events</u>. An event has the property that it has one and only one occurrence and that it thereafter has a, conceptually, unlimited existence in our model discourse. Taking this view, we can now assert that if "part-of:$TI_i \rightarrow TI_k$", then a time interval event in TI_k occurs after an integral number of occurrences in TI_i.

The kind of time model one may need for a <u>particular</u> application may vary, depending on which time intervals are found relevant in defining CIM. As an example, we will illustrate a time model, which in addition to the set of (real-) time points T, includes the interval types S (seconds), H (hours), D(days), W (weeks), M (months) and Y (years). Given a particular time point $t \in T$ we can now determine the second $s \in S$ it is a part of by referring "part-of (t)". Likewise, the day associated with $t \in T$ is " part-of (part-of (part-of (t))) ".

$$T \rightarrow S \rightarrow H \rightarrow D \begin{smallmatrix} \nearrow W \\ \searrow M \rightarrow Y \end{smallmatrix}$$

Figure 2. The 'part-of' functional relation defined on T and a time interval set {S,H,D,W,M,Y}

However, instead of this rather hard to read notation we introduce "part-of"- functions

```
second: T -> S
hour:   S -> H
day:    H -> D
week:   D -> W
month:  D -> M
year:   M -> Y
```

We will also use the notation, for instance,

<u>month</u> (t) month (day (hour (second (t)))), $\forall t \in T$.

In order to be able to refer to time points and intervals by names, we introduce the following simple data types:

```
SECOND#  : (0.0.. 3599.9)
HOUR#    : (0..23)
DAY#     : (1..31)
WEEK#    : (1..52)
YEAR#    : (0...)
MONTH    : ("Jan", "Feb",..., "Dec")
MONTH#   : (1..12)
```

and name-functions:

```
second#  : T -> SECOND
hour#    : H -> HOUR
day#     : D -> DAY
week#    : W -> WEEK
month-name: M -> MONTH
month#   : M -> MONTH
year#    : Y -> YEAR
```

We can see that each time point or interval is uniquely identified by its name-function and its part-of-function.

We will follow the shorthand notation shown earlier and use, for instance, $\forall t \in T$, week (t) instead of week (week (day (hour (second (t))))).

Thus, if we have two time interval types X and Y and the function "part-of: X --> Y" holds, then X "inherits" all functions defined for Y.

We can now illustrate the time referencing expressions (1) and (2) shown above.

"The set of first days in months during a summer season (in Sweden)" can be expressed as:

1. $\{X : X \in D \wedge \underline{day\#} (X) = 1 \wedge$
    $\underline{month\#} (X) > 5 \wedge \underline{month\#} (X) < 9\}$

"The 26:th every month since 1975 between noon and 1.15 PM" will be written as:

2. $\{t : t \in T \wedge \underline{day\#} (t) = 26 \wedge$
    $\underline{year\#} (t) \geq 1975 \wedge (\underline{hour\#} (t) = 12 \vee$
    $\underline{hour\#} (t) = 13 \wedge \underline{second\#} (t) < 900)) \}$

The expressions (3) and (4) above requires us to introduce other concepts of this approach in order to describe the various entities, events and relationships, which determine the time intervals.

5.2 Entities, types and events

The basic constituents of this modeling approach are - as in most other approaches - entities, which are phenomena about which we wish to make assertions and which have an independent existence. In order to characterize phenomena in a model, we need sets of values and for this purpose we need <u>data types</u> Data values have, in principle, no independent existence and they are meaningful only as long as they are used to characterize entities, events or relationships between entities. It is therefore possible to <u>first</u> define the information model on an "ontological level" (see 3.2) and then, in a subsequent phase, decide names to be used by introducing data types. In order to define the dynamic properties and/or behaviour of phenomena in our model, we use the concept of <u>event</u>. An event is assumed to have an indefinite existence <u>after</u> and <u>including</u> the time point or interval of its occurrence. We will in the following illustrate and discuss these and associated concepts. The illustrations are designed in the context of a small auto repair-shop example.

(i) Data types

Our model includes suitably chosen base types and interpreted types. The latter may be simple or aggregate. We will use a notation similar to (11) for declaration of interpreted data types. In figure 3 the "hierarchical" declaration of a aggregate data type ADDRESS is illustrated. If x is an individual address object, then we can reference its, say, "street-name" by "street-name (street-addr (x)" and its country-code by "country-code (postal-code (x))".

As pointed out above, the sole purpose of data types is to describe individual phenomena (in our model) and their "existence" is otherwise of no relevance to us.

```
data  ADDRESS:
      Street-addr : STRADDR;
      postal-code : ZIP;
      city:        string [1..*] of char;
      state:       string [1..20] of char;
      country:     string [1..25] of char;
      identifier:  (street-addr, postal-code),
                   (street-addr , city, state,
                   country);
data  STRADDR;
      street#:     (1..10000);
      street-name: string [1..30] of char;
      identifier street#, street-name;

data  ZIP;
      country-code: (S, DK, N, CH, USA,..., X);
      zip#:         string [1..10] of char;
      identifier    country-code, zip #;
```

Figure 3. Declaration of data types. An alternative way of declaring, say, 'city' would be to introduce a well defined set of city names.

(ii) Entities and entity types

Every entity in a CIM is an application relevant phenomenon - real or abstract - which has a limited existence and about which we wish to make assertions. No general and strict rules, as to which phenomena to consider as entities and which not to, can be given. Every entity belongs to at least one <u>entity type</u>. Members of an entity type have at least one common characteristic or property.

The set of entities, which at a particular point t in time exists and belongs to an

entity type E, constitutes the <u>entity population</u> of type E at time t ∈ T. This population will be denoted E(t). Each entity population has an associated predicate E(x,t), which is true if an entity x is a member of E(t). We can now define other membership predicates, e g EY(x,y), which we define as <u>true</u> if the entity x has, for some time point t during a year y ∈ Y, been a member of the population E(t). Formally

$$\forall x \ \forall y \ (Y(y) \wedge \exists t \ (E(x,t) \wedge \underline{year}(t) = y) \rightarrow EY(x,y))$$

where the predicate Y(y) tests if y is a "year-object" and where <u>year</u> is a time-model function defined in 5.1.

In our conceptual framework, entities may have multiple existence periods. We also postulate that, from the application point-of-view, <u>meaningful events</u> or criteria in a CIM must be specified; these define the start and the end of entity existence periods. For instance, an employee "exists" in an enterprise between consecutive "hiring" and "firing" events. This particular employee may, however, be <u>relevant</u> to our conceptual model for a considerably longer period of time. Supppose that we need to define and produce a yearly statistic, which is computed on data of all employees who are at some time during the last 10 years, been employed by the enterprise. The relevance period, which dictates the conceptual data base model and the processing model design, is in this case 10 years.

The types of things we wish to assert about individual entities of a certain type during their existence, their attributes, will be specified by <u>attribute functions</u>. The functions have the entity type and possibly a time point or interval type as arguments and an entity type, an event type or a data type as range. The populations that these functions are defined on depend on the time scope of the function's time-argument. This will be discussed later.

(iii) Events

This concept has already been discussed in connection with the time-model in section 5.1. An event "exists" indefinitely in our conceptual model from the time point or interval when it occurred. We will use the event concept to model phenomena in our reality, the duration which is of no relevance to the model or if the behaviour of the phenomena is irrelevant for our modeling purpose, e g observations, signals, messages or decisions. Events are classified in <u>event types</u> and each event type is functionally associated with a time event type, which defines its <u>time of occurrence</u>. In addition to this, functions can be defined from an event type to other entity, event, data or time event types which characterize the event. A subset of these functions, including the occurrence time function, is required to identify the event uniquely. These functions are <u>not</u> time dependent, though most of the attribute functions of entity types often will be. The occurrence time interval type associated

164

with an event type is entirely dependent on our abstraction of reality. In observing the process in a nuclear reactor, we may need a millisecond time resolution, while in talking about presidental elections, a time resolution of years might be sufficient.

(iv) Entity and event type specifications

In order to define an entity type completely, we need the following specifications:

- entity type name

- entity existence specification

- generalization specification

- attribute function specification

- identifier specification

The existence specification defines a criterion for considering an entity member of the entity population. This specification may require references to events, function values, time etc. The generalization specification defines the generalization structure, e g if an instance of the entity population E_1 also is an instance of some other entity population E_2. The usual "inheritance rules" (41) apply to generic structures, i e if for an entity x we can assert $E_1(x,t)$ and $E_2(x,t)$ and $E_1(x,t) \subseteq E_2(x,t)$ then E_1 inherits all functions, identifiers and generalizations specified for E_2. Existence is, however, not inherited.

Concerning attribute functions we may specify

- whether they are total (tf) or partial (pf)

- whether they are onto or into (relevant if the range is an entity or event type)

- their derivation rule(s): for a time-dependent function its "value" derivation rule must be specified (note that the "value" may be conceptual and refer to an entity or an event). In some cases alternative rules may be specified. Non-derivable functions must be initially assigned values when the entity starts an existence period in the model.

In figure 4, the PERSON entity type specification is examplified. The existence criterion states that persons do exist if employees or customers exist. The generalization specification is empty here as PERSON is not considered a subtype of any other entity type. The attribute functions "name", "pnumber" and "paddress" are total, i e are defined for each member of all populations of the type PERSON. The discrete attribute function "paddress" can be written

paddress: PERSON, D -> ADDRESS
and it is declared as (potentially) daily varying and derivable. The assumed derivation rule for this function is that the address value corresponds to that person's latest address-message event (see ADDR-MSG specification in fig 8).

```
entity PERSON;
existence ∀x ∀t ((EMPLOYEE(x,t) ∨
  CUSTOMER (x,t)) → PERSON (x,t));
generics;
attribute functions
tf name: PNAME;
tf pnumber: SOC-SEC#;
tf paddress (D). ADDRESS;
  derivation rule { a person's address at
  a particular day corresponds to this
  person's latest address-message (ADDR-MSG)
  event }
∀t∀p∀d ∃x (PERSON (p,t) ∧D(d) ∧
  day (t) = d ∧ ADDR_MSG(x) ∧
  person (x) = p ∧ day (x) ≤ d ∧
  ∄y(ADDR-MSG(y) ∧ person (y) = p ∧
  day (y) > day (x)) →
  paddress (p,d) = address (x))
tf birthdate : D;
identifier pnumber, (name, birthdate) ;
end ;
```

Figure 4. Specification of the entity type PERSON

We see that the requirement to define the derivation rule forces us to examine other parts of the model in order to see if some other information is relevant and can be used for this derivation purpose. If not, then our model must be extended by new entity or event types.

Examining the specifications of entity types EMPLOYEE, CUSTOMER and JOB in fig 5 - 7, we observe that also entity existence rules, and often also generic rules, are in general defined by use of other information. The membership of an entity population is by no means static. We could, for instance,

```
entity EMPLOYEE ;
existence {an employee exists at t if there
exists a latest HIRE-event, which is more
recent than the latest FIRE-event, if any}
∀ t ∀ x,(EMPLOYEE (x,t) ∧ ∃y (HIRE (y) ∧
employee (y) = x ∧ hdate (y) ≤ day (t) ∧
∃z (FIRE (z) ∧ employee (z) = x ∧ fdate (z) ≥
hdate (y) ∧ fdate (z) ≤ day (t) ))) ;

generics ∀x ∀t (EMPLOYEE (x,t)→ PERSON (x,t));

attribute functions
tf esalary (M) : MONEY ;
  derivation rule {an employee's monthly
  salary is the sum of all his/hers earnings
  on jobs performed (according to JOBREPORT
  events) that month}

∀m∀e∀z∀y∃t (M(m) ∧ month (t) = m ∧
EMPLOYEE (e,t) ∧ JOB (z,t) ∧ JOBREPORT (y) →
esalary (e,m) = SUM (hoursworked (y)*
payrate (z,m) : employee (y) = e ∧
worktype (y) = z ∧
month (date (y)) = m ∧ worktype (y) = z )) ;

identifier {inherited from PERSON} ;
end ;
```

Figure 5. Specification of the entity type EMPLOYEE

```
entity CUSTOMER ;
existence {a repair event introduces a
customer in the model. A customer ceases to
exist if he has not had any repairs during a
calender year (not defined formally here)} ;
generics ∀ x ∀t (CUSTOMER (x,t) → PERSON (x,t));

attribute functions
tf creditrating (Y) : CRCODE ;
    derivation rule {assigned on a yearly basis,
    dependent on payment performance (not de-
    fined formally here)}
tf unpaidamount (D) : MONEY ;
    derivation rule {total amount billed and
    not paid at day D (not shown formally here)}
identifier {inherited from PERSON};
end ;
```

Figure 6. A partial specification of entity
type CUSTOMER

```
entity JOB ;
existence........;
generics.........;
tf payrate (M) : MONEY ;
    derivation rule.....;
tf jobname : JOBCODE ;
...
end ;
```

Figure 7. A partial specification of entity
type JOB

define the entity type NEWYORKEMPLOYEE (an
employee, whose state in address (see fig 3) is
"New York") as

$$∀t∀e \ (EMPLOYEE \ (e,t)∧∃d(D \ (d)∧ \ \underline{day} \ (t) = d \ ∧$$
$$state \ (paddress(e,d) = 'NEW \ YORK') →$$
$$NEWYORKEMPLOYEE \ (e,t))$$

We have seen that events play a fundamental
role in specifying entity "behaviour", generics
and existence rules. Some event type specifications are shown in figures 8 and 9. Each
event type must be given an event occurrence
condition. If its occurrence cannot be fully
defined in terms of other events or conditions
in the model, then it is specified as external.
Sometimes a "mixed" condition can be specified,
e g an "internal condition" must hold in addition to an external event (see the occurrence
condition for REP in figure 9). In other cases
it may not be possible to define formally an
occurrence condition, only part of the information which is used to trigger it. This is, for
example, often the case in high level management decision making.

5.3 Relationship functions

Attribute functions were defined in one or two
domains, of which one was an entity or event
type. We will sometimes find it convenient to
define functions in more than two domains. One
of them will normally be a time domain. Take,
as an example, that we had a daily information

```
event ADDR-MSG ; {address message}
  person : PERSON ;
  address: ADDRESS;
  day : D;
  identifier  person, day ;
  occurence . condition  external ;
  end ;
```

```
event HIRE ; {hiring of an employee}
  employee : EMPLOYEE ;
  hdate : D ;
  identifier employee, day ;
  occurence condition  external ;
  end ;
```

```
event FIRE ; {firing of an employee}
  employee : EMPLOYEE
  fdate : D
  identifier  employee, day ;
  occurence condition  external ;
  end ;
```

```
event JOBREPORT ;
  employee : EMPLOYEE ;
  worktype : JOB ;
  repair   : REP ;
  date    : D ;
  hoursworked : QUANT ;
  identifier  employee, worktype, repair,date;
  occurence condition  external ;
  end ;
```

Figure 8. Event type specifications

```
event REP ;{the repair of a car}
  rcar : CAR ;
  rdate : D ;{start of repair}
  identifier  rcar, rdate ;
  occurence condition {if a repair request
  has been made and there is enough capacity
  in the repair-shop, then the request is
  granted and the event REP will occur}
  end ;
```

```
entity CAR ;
attribute functions
  tf serial : CARNUMBER ;
  pf owner (D) : CUSTOMER into ;
  tf make : CARMAKE ;
existence......;
generics......;
identifier  serial, make ;
end ;
```

Figure 9. Specification of entity type CAR and
of event type REP.

requirement which requested a list, for all
employees and for all jobs, of how many hours
that employee had worked on that job that particular day. Clearly, we could model this
situation in several ways.

One way would be to see it as a "relationship entity" of type EMPJOB defined on tuples (e,j), where EMPLOYEE (e,t) and JOB (j,t). Then we could specify a function, say, "hrsperday : EMPJOB,D—>QUANT" and define a derivation rule for it. The "independent existence" of entities of the EMPJOB type is, however, somewhat unnatural. We would also have to specify an "existence" criterion for it. In this case it is not easy to decide on meaningful birth and death events for an existence period.

A second way of dealing with this problem would be to consider it as a set of events, which includes one member for each employee, job and day combination. This would be defined by an event type say, JOBMESSAGE. The number of hours worked would then be defined as a derivable, one argument function of this event type. The occurrence rule could be that, if an employee during a particular day has performed work of a particular job type, then an event of type JOBMESSAGE will occur.

In our modeling framework, we will permit specification of multiargument functions, which in some cases will make definition of complex relationships more "natural" and more easy to read and reference. The situation we have been discussing above will then be specified as follows:

```
function empjobdayhours ;
domain emp: EMPLOYEE ;
       job: JOB ;
       day: D ,
range  QUANT ;
def    empjobdayhours (emp, job, day)
     = SUM (hoursworked (x) :
       JOBREPORT (x) ∧ employee (x) = emp ∧
       worktype (x) = job ∧ date (x) = day )
```

The domains are naturally bounded by the function's time argument - in this case it concerns employees and jobs, which have existed during the particular day.

Using the above function it is now easy to define other functions, e g the number of hours worked per employee, per year.

```
function emphrsyear ;
domain e : EMPLOYEE ;
       j : JOB ;
       y : Y ;
range  QUANT ;
def    emphrsyear (e, j, y) =
       SUM (empjobdayhours (emp, job, day) :
       emp = e ∧ year (day) = y ∧ job = j)
```

In a similar way we can define predicates as Boolean functions. As an example we take hasworkedonjob (e, j, y), which we define true if employee e sometime during a year y has worked on job j

```
function hasworkedonjob ;
domain e : EMPLOYEE ;
       j : JOB ;
       y : Y ;
range Boolean ;
def   ∀t∀e∀j∀y  ( EMPLOYEE (e,t)∧
      JOB (j,t)∧ Y (y) ∧ ∃r (JOBREPORT (r) ∧
      year (date (r) ) = y ∧
      worktype (r) = j ∧ employee (r) = e) →
      hasworkedonjob (e,j,y) )
```

5.4 Constraints

Specification of constraints constitutes an important part of the knowledge built into a conceptual information model. So far, however, only a few authors (11, 9), have given this topic a more thorough investigation. A constraint is a closed form predicate formula, which asserts that certain conditions must hold for specified time slices and instances of a CIM. Certain types of assertions were already introduced "locally" in connection with specification of entity types, event types and relationship functions. They were:

in entity type specifications

- existence assertion

- generalization assertion

- attribute function derivation rule specification and function characteristics (total, partial, into, onto)

- identifier assertion

in event type specification

- event occurrence assertion

- identifier assertion

in relationship function specification

- derivation rule specification

In addition to these types of constraints, there may exist other types, some of which have more of a "global" character.

In general, we may wish to include in our model also assertions, which

. specify cardinality constraints concerning

- entity populations

- event occurrences in time intervals

- various relationships

. specify permissible values for

- attribute functions and

- relationship functions

An example of a cardinality type constraint could be: "The number of repairs that can be started each day is twice the number of employees except in the summer season (June-August), when it is 1.5 times the number of employees". Semiformally:

```
∀t∀d∀r∀e  (T(t) ∧ D(d) ∧ REP (r) ∧
CARD (r : rdate (r) = d) ≤
(if month (d) > 5 ∧ month (d) < 9 then
1.5 else 2.0)*
CARD (e : EMPLOYEE (e,t) ∧ day (t) = d)
```

167

The standard example of a dynamic constraint, which asserts that "an employee's monthly salary must not decrease" can now be formulated as

$$\forall m \forall e \; (\forall t(\text{EMPLOYEE } (e,t) \wedge \underline{\text{month}} \; (t) = m) \wedge$$
$$\forall t \; (\text{EMPLOYEE } (e,t) \wedge \underline{\text{month}} \; (t) = m-1) \wedge$$
$$\text{esalary } (e,m) \geq \text{esalary } (e,m-1) \;)$$

where we have added the condition that the employee also must be fully employed for two consecutive months for this assertion to hold. These examples should demonstrate that this time-oriented conceptual modeling approach also can deal with time-varying constraint specifications.

In general the number of different kinds of constraints that may be specified for a particular application discourse is very large. Except for constraints, which in a more or less natural fashion can be specified locally as parts of entity, event and function specifications there is to date - as far as we know - no systematic and formal procedure on how to arrive at a complete set of global constraints (from the user and application point-of-view). In the relational model context, however, a procedure for complete and consistent declaration of dependencies has been suggested (29). Another large problem in constraint modeling is to prove that the set of assertions specified is consistent, i e does not contain contradictions. Important work on this topic is reported in (11). Much more research is, however, needed to prove completely the consistency of constraint assertions, especially when the model includes a time-perspective.

5.5 Design principles

It is beyond the scope of this paper to discuss the CIM design method in detail. Some basic principles should, however, be mentioned.

The first principle is that the scope and content of a CIM is determined by known or anticipated information requirements. It is assumed that they are at first more or less informally stated. Let $IRQ_I = \{IQ_1, IQ_2, \ldots, IQ_n\}$ be the set of informal requirements. The semantic part of each requirement IQ_i corresponds to a view W_i of those parts of the enterprise, which are relevant to IQ_i. As a next step, the view W_i is formally specified, using the basic concepts of this modeling approach (entity and event types, attribute and relationship functions).

An integration of two views implies that we may have to resolve various conflicts, inconsistencies and detect equalities as well as inequalities. View integration often implies synthesis in the sense that new types can be created by generalization or by aggregation of other types. It may also imply decomposition i e the creation of new, "lower level" types. Work on this problem for time constrained data models has been reported by (41, 11, 30, 2). General principles for how to perform view integration are, however, still lacking, and this task is therefore to a large extent still human art-work.

The changes made to the model, when two views

are integrated, may cause a respecification of the information requirements. It is also an open question whether to specify all "local" views first, and then integrate them into a "global" view or to perform incrementally, view by view, the integration and create the global model.

In order to examplify integration consider two requirements:

(IQ$_1$) WHAT: For each employee:name, number and last month's salary
WHEN: The first day of each month at 8 PM

(IQ$_2$) WHAT: For a customer: name and credit rating
WHEN: The day when a repair of that customer's car starts.

Two views that these requirements may assume are shown in figure 10. Integration now implies, among other things, that the types EMPLOYEE and CUSTOMER are generalized into PERSON and that certain attribute functions are "moved up" to this higher level type (see figures 4 to 9). It is now also possible, by using the formal model, to define more precisely and unambigously the information requirements. IQ above could now be formulated as:

$$\underline{\text{at}} \; \{ti : \text{day } (ti) = 1 \wedge \text{hour } (ti) = 8\}$$
$$\underline{\text{for each}} \; \{e : \text{EMPLOYEE } (e,t) \wedge \underline{\text{month}} \; (t)$$
$$= \underline{\text{month}} \; (ti) - 1\}$$
$$\underline{\text{display}} \; \text{name } (e), \; \text{pnumber } (e),$$
$$\text{esalary } (e, \underline{\text{month}} \; (ti) - 1) \; ;$$

where ti denotes a time interval. Note that IQ$_1$ lacks precision, at least concerning the set of employees this request refers to.

view (IQ$_1$)

```
entity EMPLOYEE ;
tf ename: NAME ;
tf enumber: SSN;
tf esalary (M) : MONEY ;
. . .
```

view (IQ$_2$)

```
entity CUSTOMER ;
tf name: CNAME ;
tf creditrating (Y) ; CRCODE ;
. . .

entity CAR ;
tf owner (D) : CUSTOMER ;
. . .

event REP
tf rcar : CAR ;
tf rdate : D ;
. . .
```

Figure 10. Formal specification of views corresponding to requirements IQ and IQ$_2$.

When all local views have been integrated, then we have obtained a global view of the part of the enterprise, which directly corresponds to the information output requirements. The CIM design process is, however, by no means finished.

The next logical step is to examine all the types and functions, so far introduced, and to determine their constraints. In particular, the specification of the various constraints, including derivation rules for functions and occurrence rules for endogenous events, will force us to examine the whole model in order to find information (about entities and/or events), which can be used in specifying the constraint. If such information is not found, then the model must be extended and new types of entities or events or new functions defined. This can be seen as a pure application of the "information precedence analysis principle" (25). In fact, the new types and functions introduced in this way, correspond to views embodied in the constraint definitions, which now act as new requirements on the model. The process continues until all function derivation and event occurrence rules are defined. This will give us a complete set of initial information in terms of external event types (see also (13)). They correspond to transaction types required to satisfy all information requirements.

Concepts used in this modeling approach avoid problems of normalization and multivalued dependencies (7, 28) in relational models. The main reason is probably that this approach, as most structural approaches, focusses on the underlying reality and not on idiosynchracies of attribute collections and tables (23). Another reason is our use of the "surrogate" concept (21) and a clear distinction between entities and names (39). Finally, the requirement, put on the analyst, to specify constraints in detail - and derivation rules in particular - forces him to be particularly attentive to constructs, which involve non-full dependence, transitivity and many-to-many mappings.

5.6 Discussion

We believe that the approach outlined here, covers most modeling problems discussed in the literature on data modeling. There is, however, one representation issue, which we have not yet paid attention to. It is the problem of representing sets of entities - possibly of different types - where attributes (or relationships) of the sets as such are of relevance. We may, for instance, consider sets of type CAR-POOL, which may include cars as well as persons as members. Individual sets (i e individual car-pools) of this type may have attribute functions such as "number of cars in pool on week W" or "the total mileage in month m".
In (22, 11, 18) special concepts are introduced to deal with this problem. We feel that this is not necessary. Set types can be naturally modeled as entity types and existence rules, membership functions or predicates can be conveniently defined for the entity types, which are their members. The same holds for set - subset specifications.

In conclusion, we would like to emphasize the following properties of the CIM approach

. the scope of the model is the total information system. It therefore integrates the power of information system specification models with the power of data models to specify complex entity/relationship structures. By introducing time, the application model can now be specified in a declarative fashion.

. as a consequence of the scope, there exist no updating, deletion and insertion concepts as we do not employ abstract machine concepts in this approach. For the same reason, the model is free from operations on data. The behaviour of the model is entirely defined in terms of constraints and of derivation and occurrence rules.

. a pure hierarchical "top-down" and stepwise refinement design approach is not applicable here, as such an approach presumes a processing-system oriented view.

. the CIM approach guides the users and designers to a complete model in the sense that all initial information needed to derive information specified in the requirements is defined. It can, however, not be guaranteed that we have arrived at a complete set of semantic rules and constraints.

The major utility of this kind of model is the understanding and knowledge of the application discourse it forces its users to specify explicitly. Note that this not only concerns the entity-relationship structure, but also the total relevant behaviour of the application. It seems reasonable to claim that making assumptions and rules of the environment formal and explicit, instead of embedding them in procedures, will eventually lead to systems, which conform better to the real requirements.

As indicated in section 4, we assume the CIM and the requirements IRQ as a basis for a subsequent design phase "Conceptual Information System Design" where a time-restricted, snapshot-type model of the data base and associated processing procedures is constructed. The utility of CIM and problems in designing a Conceptual Data Base Model (CDBM) without first defining CIM are discussed in (1).

Designing a CDBM/CPM from CIM/IRQ requires many performance and efficiency oriented decisions. We have to decide which time-slices of information to maintain in database, where to use accumulated values, which information to store explicitly and which to derive when requested etc. A large number of processing strategies are possible, which may all satisfy operative requirements. Therefore, the number of alternative implementations of a CIM is theoretically infinite and at present we know of no systematic procedure leading to a non-intuitively attained CDBM/CPM solution. Until we know more about this process, the utility of a CIM lies in increased understanding of the application and in the possibility of reasoning about the validity and correctness of a CDBM/CPM solution.

6. CONCLUDING REMARKS

The main message in this paper is that it is important to recognize specification of goal-oriented requirements as a vital part of the system life-cycle, where a deeper understanding and a detailed formal model of the application is developed. The model must focus on the application problem and its environment. It should not be restricted by decisions on how to organize data processing and storage. This view is similar to the way systems are designed in the field of engineering. Few engineers would consider designing, for instance, a computer program to perform stress calculations on a complex structure or developing a system to control a nuclear power plant, before a complete and correct mathematical model of the target system had been constructed. Unfortunately this is the rule rather than the exception in system design for administrative applications.

We have outlined a framework and a set of concepts for specification and design of a conceptual information model which is both time-unrestricted and completely processing-independent. Such a model should, we argue, constitute an essential part of a goal-oriented requirement specification. We do not, however, claim that the approach is complete in every respect. Much work remains to be done, in particular concerning the validation and verification of an application model. The ideas presented here should, therefore, be seen as a starting point for research in this direction.

Finally, some remarks on this modeling philosophy should be made from the point of view of a user or a designer. It is quite obvious that requirements analysis and the design of a conceptual information model requires the same detailed and hard work as detailed data design and programming. The difference lies in the way one reasons about the application problem. The reasoning required for conceptual information modeling is `axiomatic` rather than procedural in that we wish to specify explicitly and in a declarative fashion all our views, assumptions and rules about the reality. These will later be embedded in procedural solutions. This kind of reasoning is not common in practice today. It may therefore take some time until models of this kind gain practical acceptance, since they seemingly introduce hard and detailed work in an early phase of the system life cycle. It may be felt that this work is superfluous, as detailed specifications have to be developed anyway in the programming phase. Our rationale for advocating this approach is that it will enhance a better understanding of the problem and thereby most likely reduce the number of logical errors, which are passed over to the logical design; programming, implementation design and operation phases of the system's life cycle. It is well known that the cost of fixing logical errors and other inadequacies drastically increases with the progression of the system development process.

ACKNOWLEDGEMENT

The author wishes to thank Dennis Tsichritzis, University of Toronto, Eva Lindencrona-Ohlin, University of Stockholm, Bengt Lundberg, University of Lund and his colleagues Roland Dahl, Mats R Gustafsson, Hans-Uno Hansson, Terttu Karlsson and Anita Sandin for constructive criticism and suggestions.

The author is also gratefully indebted to the Editor for many valuable corrections and suggestions for improvement.

REFERENCES

[1] J.R Abrial, Data Semantics, in Data Management Systems, Kimbie & Koffeman (eds), North Holland 1974.

[2] C. Baldissera, S. Ceri, G. Pelegatti and G. Bracchi, Interactive Specification and Formal Verification of User`s Views in Data Base Design, Proc 5th Intntl Conf on Very Large Data Bases Rio de Janeiro, October 1979.

[3] R. Balzer, N. Goodman and D. Wile, Informality in Program Specifications, IEEE Trans Softw Eng No 2 March 1978.

[4] T.E. Bell, D.C. Bipler, M.E. Dyer, An Extendable Approach to Computer-Aided Software Requirements Engineering, IEEE Trans S.E., Vol SE 3, January 1977.

[5] C. Beeri, P.A. Bernstein and N. Goodman, A Sophisticates Introduction to Data Base Normalization Theory, Proc 4th VLDB, Berlin 1978.

[6] S. Berild and S. Nachmens, CS4 - A Tool for Data Base Design by Infologic Simulation, Proc 3rd Int Conf on VLDB, Tokyo 1977.

[7] H. Biller, On the Notation of Irreducible Relations, proc IFIP TC-2 Working Conference on Data Base Arcgitecture, Venice 1979.

[8] G. Bracchi, P. Paolini and G. Pelegatti, Binary Logical Associations in Data Modeling, Proc IFIP-TC-2 WC, Freudenstadt, W Germany 1976.

[9] G. Bracchi, A. Furtado and G. Pelegatti, Constraint Specification in Evolutionary Data Base Design, Proc IFIP Working Conf on Formal Information System Design", (H-J Schneider ed), North Holland 1979.

[10] B. Breutmann, E. Falkenberg and R. Mauer, CSL: A Language for Defining Conceptual Schemas, Proc IFIP TC 2.6 Working Conf on Data Base Architecture, Venice 1979.

[11] L.M. Brodie, Specification and verification of data base semantic integrity, Ph D Thesis, Computer Systems Research Group, Univ of Toronto, 1978.

[12] J.A Bubenko jr, Validity and Verification Aspects of Information Modeling. Proc 3rd VLDB, Tokyo, October 1977.

[13] J.A. Bubenko jr, IAM: Inferential Abstract Modeling – an approach to design of information models for large shared databases, IBM T.J. Watson Research Center, RC 6343., January 1977.

[14] J.A. Bubenko jr, On the Role of `Understanding Models` in Conceptual Schema Design, Proceedings 5th Int Conf on Very Large Data Bases, Rio de Janeiro, October 1979.

[15] P.P.S. Chen, The Entity-Relationship Model: Toward a Unified view of Data, ACM Tods, March 1976.

[16] Codasyl Development Committee, An Information Algebra, Communications of ACM, 1962.

[17] E.F. Codd, A Relational Model of Data for Large Shared Data Banks, CACM, 13,6, June 1970.

[18] E.F Codd, Extending the Database Relational Model to Capture More Meaning, ACM Tods, December 1979.

[19] C.G. Davis and C.R. Vick, The Software Development System, IEEE Trans on SE, Vol SE-3, January 1973.

[20] F. Grotenhius and J. van den Brock, A Conceptual Model for Information Processing, G.M. Nijssen (ed), Modeling in Data Base Management Systems, North Holland, 1976, pp 149-179.

[21] P.Hall, J.Owlett and S.Todd, Relations and Entities, in G.M.Nijssen (ed), Modeling in data Base Management Systems, North Holland, Amsterdam, 1976 pp 141-148.

[22] M.M. Hammer and D.J. McLeod, The Semantic Data Model, Proc ACM SIGMOD Conf, Austin, Texas, May 31-June 2, 1978.

[23] W. Kent, Limitations of Record-Based Information Models, ACM Tods, Vol 4, No 1, March 1979.

[24] L. Kerschberg, A. Klug and D. Tsichritzis, A Taxonomy of Data Models in Lockmann & Neuhold (eds) "System for Large Data Bases", North Holland Publ Co, Amsterdam, 1976.

[25] B. Langefors, Theoretical Analysis of Information Systems AStudentlitteratur (and Auerbach) Lund, Sweden 1973. (First edition, 1966).

[26] B. Langefors, Theoretical Aspects of Information Systems, IFIP Congress 1974, North Holland, 1974, pp 937-945.

[27] E. Lindencrona-Ohlin, A Study on Conceptual Data Modeling, Ph D Thesis, Chalmers Univ of Technology, Glteborg, May 1979.

[28] B. Lundberg, On the Declaration of Dependencies for a Universal Relation, Dept of Computer Science, Univ of Lund, Sweden, 1979 (to be published).

[29] B. Lundberg, On Complete and Consistent Declaration of Dependencies for Relations, Dept of Computer Science, Univ of Lund, 1980 (to be published).

[30] S.B. Navathe and M. Scholnick, View Representation in Logical Data Base Design, Proc ACM SIGMOD Conf, June 1978.

[31] G.M.Nijssen, On the Gross Architecture for the Next Generation Database Management System, Information Processing 77, B. Gilchrist, Editor, North Holland, 1977, pp 327-335.

[32] J.F. Nunamaker j and B.R. Konsynski jr, Computer-Aided Analysis and Design of Information Systems, CACM, December 1976.

[33] A. Pirotte, The Entity-Property-Association Model: An Information Oriented Data Base Model, Proc ICS-77, (eds Morlet and Ribbens), North Holland Publ Co, 1977.

[34] C. Rolland, O. Foucat and G. Benci, A Conceptual Model for the Design of Formal Information Systems, Centre de Recherche en Informatiqu de nancy, France, 1978.

[35] D.T. Ross and K.E. Schoman, Structured Analysis for Requirements Definition, IEEE Trans on SE, Vol SE 3, January 1977.

[36] N.D. Roussopoulos, CSDL: A Conceptual Schema Definition Language for the Design of Data Base Applications, Dept of Comp Sciences, Univ of Texas at Austin, April 1978.

[37] R. Schank and K. Colby, Computer Models of Thought and Language, Freeman, 1973.

[38] H.A. Schmid, A Comparative Study of Concepts for Conceptual Schema Design, Lecture notes, Nordic Research Course on "Conceptual Information Modeling for Data Bases", Ystad, Sweden, August 1979.

[39] M.E. Senko, Conceptual Schemas, Abstract Data Structures Enterprise Description, in Morlet and Ribbens (eds), International Computing Synposium, North Holland, Amsterdam, 1977, pp 85-101.

[40] E.H. Sibley, Standardization and Database Systems, Proc 3rd Int Conf on Very Large Data Bases, Tokyo, October 1977.

[41] J.M. Smith and D.C.P Smith, Database Abstractions: Aggregation and Generalization, ACM Trans on Database Systems, Vol 2, No 2, June 1977, pp 105-133.

[42] R.K. Stamper, Towards a Semantic Normal Form, in Bracchi, Nijssen (eds), Proc IFIP TC 2 Work Conf on Data Base Architecture, Venice 1979.

[43] A Silvberg, Software Requirement Defini-
      tion and Data Models, Proc 5th Int Conf
      on VLDB, Rio de Janeiro, 1979.

[44] D. Teichroew, Improvements in the System
      Life Cycle, Information processing 74,
      North Holland, 1974, pp 972-978.

[45] D. Teichroew and E.A. Herschey III,
      PSL/PSA: A Computer-Aided Technique for
      Structured Documentation and Analysis of
      Information Processing System, IEEE Trans
      on SE, Vol SE 3, January 1977.

[46] D. Tsichritzis and A. Klug (eds): The
      ANSI/X3/SPARC DBMS Framework, Tech Note
      12, Computer Systems Research Group, Univ
      of Toronto, July 1977.

[47] D.C. Tsichritzis and F.H. Lochovsky,
      Designing the Data Base, DATAMATION,
      August 1978.

[48] A.I. Wasserman, USE: A Methodology for
      the Design and Development of Interactive
      Information Systems, IFIP WG 8.1 Working
      Conf on Formal Models and Practical Tools
      for Information System Design, Oxford,
      England, April 1979.

[49] H. Weber, A Software Engineering View of
      Data Base Systems, Proc 4th VLDB, Berlin
      1978.

[50] P. Wegner, Research Directions in
      Software Technology, The MIT Press, Cam-
      bridge, Mass., 1979.

[51] T. Winograd, Five Lectures on Artifical
      Intelligence, Stanford AI Lab, AIM No
      246, 1974.

[52] K.K.T. Wong and J. Mylopulos, Two views
      of Data Semantics: A Survey of Data
      Models in Artifical Intelligence and
      Database Management, INFOR, Vol 15, No 3,
      October 1977.

[53] J.W. Young and H.K. Kent, Abstract Formu-
      lation of Data Processing Problems, Jour-
      nal of Industrial Engineering, Nov-Dec,
      1958, pp 471-479.

[54] M.M. Zloof and R.S de Jong, The System
      for Business Automation (SBA): Program-
      ming Language, Comm of the ACM, Vol 20,
      No 6, June 1977, pp 385-396.

Part III

Specification Methods

In many respects, the functional specifications of a system are the key to the success or failure of a development project. They are used by developers, customers, end users, management, and other interested parties as the definitive statement of the expected behavior of the system.

For most medium and large systems, extensive analysis has occurred by the time one is able to write such a specification. Requirements have been identified and stated, including not only the functional requirements (as seen by one or more different interest groups) but also the operational requirements for security, cost, installation, normal usage, and so on.

Thorough requirements analysis not only identifies needed objects and operations but also usually includes some structuring of these items as well. As we have seen in Part II, this structuring may be through data flow, hierarchical decomposition of functions, information modeling, or other related means. Thus, requirements analysis typically serves to illuminate the problem structure, the context(s) in which the system will be used, and the constraints on development and operation.

The purpose of a functional specification, then, is to record this information as a basis for subsequent development. Ideally, a functional specification should be

(1) comprehensible to all of those who must use it;

(2) complete in its description of system functions, inputs/outputs, and data;

(3) unambiguous in describing these system aspects;

(4) consistent in level of detail, use of names, and overall goals;

(5) easy to write and modify.

Unfortunately, these goals are often mutually conflicting, as the desire for non-ambiguity suggests the use of a formal notation that may be incomprehensible to those without a mathematical background. Formal notations are often difficult to write as well. Because achieving completeness in specifications is extremely difficult, much of the effort of system evolution is devoted to adding functions that went unspecified and unimplemented in previous versions of a system.

With the growing number of microprocessor-based systems, in which programs are part of an embedded system or where programs are stored in read-only memory, system failures become extremely critical, and evolution becomes prohibitively expensive, if not impossible. Thus, the need for improved specification methods becomes evident.

Clearly, there is a need for a variety of different specification methods, ranging from the informal through the highly formal. Small, noncritical systems can be successfully developed with an informal method, while highly complex and/or critical systems require the greater precision provided by a formal method.

Traditionally, the "informal" approach to specifications has been, at best, narrative text, perhaps divided into sections and paragraphs, which is fundamentally dependent on the inherent ambiguity of natural language. Often, the informal approach was no specification at all, simply an implemented system that was documented after the fact.

The distinction here between "informal" and "formal" is that an informal method cannot be subjected to automatic analysis tools or to mathematical proof techniques. However, even informal methods have a structuring mechanism, often a pictorial representation, and a standard notation for describing the behavior of a system, including its functions, inputs, outputs, and data.

Formal specification methods take many forms, of which three are notable:

(1) *Mathematically based schemes*, often based on the concept of formally specifying the properties of the data types used in the system (see Part VI). Other mathematically based schemes can be found in formal descriptions of programming languages, such as denotational semantics, but these have not as yet been widely used for broader classes of applications.

173

(2) *Machine processable, but nonexecutable, languages* for describing the properties of a system. These languages allow the specification of system functions and data, their interrelationships, the inputs and outputs, and other system aspects in a well-defined language, not unlike a programming language. These "formal specification languages" are typically accompanied by tools that check a specification written in that language for proper use of the language syntax and for consistent use of names. These tools also generate reports of data names, functions, interconnections, and similar information.

(3) *Machine processable, executable, languages* for describing the desired behavior of a system *and* for realizing it. These languages, which include program generators, automatic programming tools, some rapid prototyping systems, and many nonprocedural database query languages, are aimed at a new paradigm of software development in a high-level description of desired behavior independent of the implementation details. With such an approach, the specification language *is* the programming language, and many of the traditional concerns of design and implementation disappear. Indeed, the entire development effort focuses on producing the specification. (Of course, many such systems provide access to lower level information, thus allowing some tuning.)

The trend in formal specification methods is clearly toward the latter techniques, with increased use of analysis methods, such as those described in Part II, to understand the problem for which a system is needed. Many of the traditional concerns about detailed design and programming may diminish sharply as these executable languages emerge and assist in the efficient development of broader classes of systems.

The notion of a functional specification implies a description of the functions to be performed by a system. There are, however, several ways in which this functional description can be structured:

(1) *by functions* (tasks) to be performed by the system, irrespective of the interface to those functions by users or other systems; the functional specification may even show possible distribution and/or parallel operation of the functions;

(2) *by user-visible functions*, such as transactions or commands (see Part IV);

(3) *by data objects* manipulated by the system, with the functions arranged around the data objects.

Each of these alternatives is a viable approach to a functional specification. Traditionally, functional specifications have followed the first of these three approaches, and the papers in this Part reflect that tendency. The papers in Part VI reflect the data-oriented approach to a larger extent.

The papers in this Part (plus some in Parts VI and IX) emphasize the informal methods over the formal. This is due in part not only to the fact that much more is known and written on the informal methods but also to the fact that some form of informal method is useful in working with a formal specification. The informal method is particularly useful to customers, end users, and others who may not be able to comprehend the mathematically based formal method.

HIPO (Hierarchy plus Input-Process-Output) was developed within IBM more as a documentation tool than anything else. It has been used successfully both for stating specifications and for describing either the architecture or the detailed design of a system. It has the distinct advantages of being easy to learn and easy to use. Successive refinements of HIPO diagrams may be used to proceed from specifications through detailed design of a system. The paper by Stay explains HIPO and suggests how it can be used in a design method.

Heninger's paper describes a method for specifying requirements developed for an embedded software system on the A-7 aircraft. The method is based on sets of goals and design principles for requirements documentation. The requirements document is structured into chapters, two of which are "Hardware Interfaces" and "Software Functions." The description of hardware interfaces is organized by data item, one for each input or output that changes value independently of other inputs and outputs. There is a standard "template" for naming and describing each data item.

The description of software functions is organized by functions associated with output data items. The basic approach is to identify functions by working backward from output data items, which works well in this case because of the specialized nature of the outputs for the A-7 system. Some information on control flow is provided by tables of conditions and events.

The philosophy of the paper is that a disciplined approach to documentation and its structure is of great value in producing a precise, concise, unambiguous specification which is easy to check for completeness and consistency. While the specific method would seem to be less suitable for conversational systems or database applications, the paper includes some important observations that are useful in developing specification documents for systems other than embedded systems.

Michael Jackson's approach to program design is among the best known and widely used methods for software design, and his book *Principles of Program Design* (Academic Press, 1975) was important in calling attention to the need for systematic program design methods. (Jackson's paper in Part VII gives an overview of this design method.) At the same time, though, Jackson recognized that his approach failed to address adequately the important early steps of analysis and specification.

Accordingly, much of his subsequent work, in collaboration with John Cameron, has sought to provide a modelling tool that was both compatible with Jackson's design ideas and applicable to a large class of practical systems. In short, the goal was to expand a method for software and program design into a complete methodology (Jackson System Design, or JSD) for system development.

The paper by John Cameron gives a brief sketch of the modelling approach and the complete methodology. Modelling in JSD is based on the concept of long-running sequential processes connected by data streams, where no process is ever blocked for output. A process that is the target of a data stream may communicate with a connected process either by reading its output or by examining its state vector. This approach to modelling allows a very broad class of systems to be modelled and specified. Cameron's paper shows how the JSD approach works on two small problems.

Teichroew and Hershey's paper describes PSL/PSA, a problem statement language and associated analyzer that are central to the ISDOS approach to information systems development. PSL is a formal language that is suitable for the description of system properties. As a formal language, it is also suitable for machine processing, and PSA can be used both to check the consistency of a PSL description and to produce any of a number of reports describing the problem statement.

PSL is important as a forerunner of many of the formal specification languages. Yet Teichroew and Hershey's concern was not with verification of the system correctness, but rather with having a well-defined language in which to describe system properties. The PSL language allows the description not only of the structural properties of a problem, but also of some of the managerial aspects as well, such as system size.

The paper by Bell, Bixler, and Dyer describes the techniques used to define the requirements for the US Army Ballistic Missile Defense System. These authors focus on the Software Requirements Engineering Methodology (SREM), describing the Requirements Engineering and Validation System (REVS) and its major segments. The modelling process used in SREM is called R-nets and is based on Petri nets, to allow the modelling of concurrent processes. The Petri net concept has been extended to show software-related issues, such as validation points and data sharing.

The language of SREM is RSL (Requirements Statement Language), which draws heavily from PSL. While PSL is based on objects and relationships, RSL adds attributes for objects and the idea of R-nets, while reducing the descriptive project management information. RSL is supported by a set of tools, which includes the graphic display of R-nets. The role of SREM in the overall Software Development System used for the Ballistic Missile Defense system can be seen in the paper by Davis and Vick reprinted in Part IX.

The paper by Greenspan, Mylopoulos, and Borgida, by contrast, addresses a broader class of information systems and is one of a series of papers describing the TAXIS research project for developing interactive information systems. Whereas the other methods described in this Part have seen considerable practical application on systems of significant size, this approach is still being developed and is experimental. However, as a synthesis of ideas from different areas, it is worthy of study and investigation.

The authors attempt to unify concepts of semantic data modeling with those of software engineering. Their framework, called RMF, organizes the specification by data objects (entities), including not only the functions (activities) performed on those entities but also the "real world knowledge" about the objects (modeled as assertions).

They begin with a set of abstraction mechanisms (aggregation, classification, and generalization), following the ideas of Smith and Smith (see their paper in Part VI). These abstraction mechanisms support the creation of classification levels of objects, with the ability to associate properties of objects at each level.

Having defined objects and object classes, one can then define activities and activity classes. The RMF approach to activity classes draws on ideas from program verification (preconditions and postconditions) and from SADT (input, control, and output), as well as defines the components of the activity or activity class. Finally, one may define assertions and assertion classes. This approach leads to a specification whose structure may be examined according to either data organization or activity organization. The paper shows a large portion of a formal language that is used to provide the requirements definition, as well as comparing RMF with other approaches.

Discussed is a procedure of hierarchical functional design by which programming projects can be analyzed into system, program, and module levels. It is shown that program design is made more efficient by applying Hierarchy plus Input-Process-Output (HIPO) techniques at each level to form an integrated view of all levels.

Reprinted with permission from *IBM Systems Journal*, Volume 15, Number 2, 1976, pages 143–154. Copyright © 1976 by International Business Machines Corporation.

HIPO and integrated program design

by J. F. Stay

By the mid-1970s, programming appears to be reaching a stage of refinement and cost-effectiveness such that regular business management and control methods can be applied to it. Top-down development, structured programming, chief programmer teams, structured walk throughs, Hierarchy plus Input-Process-Output (HIPO), and structured design have taken us a long way toward transforming "a private art into a public practice."[1] As a result, a body of programming knowledge and methods that are teachable and practicable has been building. This paper discusses the integration of several programming methods by means of an example.

Most of the change in system development has been directed toward the programming effort. Although programming errors are the direct cause of many rework costs, perhaps one third of the rework ultimately can be traced back to errors in the analysis and design phases of a project.[2] Since maintenance can account for as much as seventy precent of all programming costs, more emphasis must be placed on the quality of analysis and design. Structured design and HIPO are useful techniques for organizing the application design process. This article describes how these two methods can be integrated to create a hierarchical functional design. This integrated method allows an application system to be specified from the highest functional level of a conceptual design to the lowest detailed level in a coded routine, using a single method and format. Both the concepts and the techniques of hierarchical functional design can be employed effectively throughout a development cycle in the following phases:

hierarchical functional design

Figure 1 HIPO: Hierarchy plus Input Process Output (A) Schematic diagram of a hierarchy chart (B) Schematic diagram of an input-process-output chart

- Requirement definition.
- System analysis.
- System design.
- Program design.
- Detailed module design.
- System and program documentation.

This paper presents a basis for the thought processes involved in designing a system through the use of these techniques. Although this paper does not explain the design techniques in detail, the references provide practical help.

Two techniques for achieving functional design are the following:

- Hierarchy plus Input-Process-Output (HIPO)
- Structured design

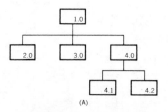

(A)

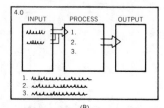

(B)

HIPO, a technique for use in the top-down design of systems, was developed originally as a documentation tool. HIPO charts continue to serve as the final programming documentation. HIPO consists of two basic components: a hierarchy chart, which shows how each function is divided into subfunctions; and input-process-output charts, which express each function in the hierarchy in terms of its input and output. These two types of charts are illustrated in Figure 1.

example

The HIPO design process is an iterative top-down activity in which it is essential that the hierarchy chart and the input-process-output charts be developed concurrently, so as to create a functional breakdown. The example of COMPUTE PAYABLE AMOUNT is followed through its development process as part of an accounts payable system.

The first step is to describe a given function as a series of steps, in terms of their inputs and outputs. The input-process-output chart for the example of COMPUTE PAYABLE AMOUNT is shown in Figure 2.

Having completed the input-process-chart, it is possible to move to the next level of the hierarchy. The COMPUTE PAYABLE AMOUNT hierarchy now appears as shown in Figure 3. It is now possible to develop an input-process-output chart for each of the boxes at the level shown in Figure 3. If additional definitions are required, the recommended approach is to make each line on the input-process-output chart a box on the next level of the hierarchy. This process causes the developer to focus on the level of function that is being defined.

Figure 2 HIPO chart for COMPUTE PAYABLE AMOUNT function

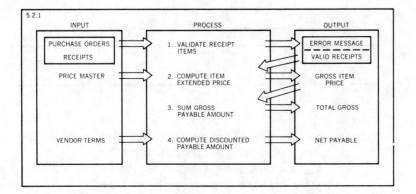

Structured design

The hierarchy plus input-process-output charting is that part of the hierarchical functional design process by which a problem description is made. The other component is structured design. Structured design[3] is a set of techniques for converting from a problem description to a functional, modular program structure. Myers[4] uses the term composite design in reference to the "structure attribute of a program, in terms of module, data, and task structure and module interfaces." This goes beyond the concept of modular design and addresses how a program module is designed, the proper scope of function of a module, and the appropriate communication between modules.

Two concepts of structured design are *module strength* (relationships within a module) and *module coupling* (relationship between modules). The way in which functions are grouped within modules determines the strength of the modules. A module may consist of a group of related functions, such as all editing functions, functions grouped according to the procedure of the problem, or all functions related to a data set.

Functional strength is the grouping of all steps to perform a single function. Although any application may contain modules that have some or all of these strengths, the objective is to produce modules that have functional strength. Functional strength does not apply only to the lowest modular level. A module may call other modules to perform subordinate functions, but if the upper-level module performs a single function and performs it completely, the module probably has functional strength. For example, the module COMPUTE PAYABLE AMOUNT might consist of the following statements (in pseudo-code):

Figure 3 COMPUTE PAYABLE AMOUNT function hierarchy

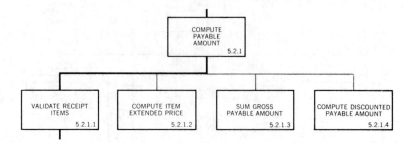

```
COMPUTE-PAY-AMT (RECEIPT, PAYABLE, RETURN-CODE);
    DO WHILE MORE-ITEMS; GET PRICE-MASTER;
        CALL VALIDATE-ITEM (RECEIPT-ITEM);
        CALL EXTEND-PRICE (RECEIPT-ITEM, PRICE);
        CALL SUM-AMOUNT (PRICE, TOTAL-PRICE);
        CALL COMPUTE-DISCOUNTED (TOTAL-PRICE,
        DISCOUNT-RATE, PAYABLE);
    END DO;
END;
```

This module performs very few functions by itself. However, it transforms one input (RECEIPT) into one output (PAYABLE) completely; at the same time it does no unrelated processing. Therefore, this module is said to have functional strength.

Interactions between modules, termed *module coupling*, may be as varied as interactions within a module. The extreme of module coupling exists when one module directly modifies an instruction in another module.

The preferred relationship between modules is *data coupling*. In data coupling, each module simply passes application data, usually as parameters to the next lower-level module. Use of artificial switches and indicators is avoided. When a calling module passes switches, indicators, or other control information to another module, these items must only communicate the status of the calling program. The calling program should not assume that it knows what the called program will do, based on this control information. A serious problem in program maintenance results when a simple change to a module changes the meaning of an item of control that has an unsuspected effect on the logic flow of one or more other modules.

This paper does not treat structured design in depth but only with sufficient detail to carry the concepts of functional strength and data coupling into earlier stages of the design process. The reader may find References 3 and 4 to be of valuable assistance in module design.

Hierarchical functional design

Hierarchical functional design addresses mental processes that may be applied to the application analysis and design tasks. Hierarchical functional design applies the design concepts of functional strength and data coupling to the functional decomposition and graphic techniques of HIPO to provide a single methodology that allows an application design to develop in an orderly manner from a clear statement of the requirement to an intelligible, well constructed set of application functions. A system that is designed through the use of hierarchical functional design is implemented in a top-down manner. Modules should have a single entry point and a single exit point; they should be small; and they should use the SEQUENCE, IF-THEN-ELSE, and DO-WHILE concepts of structured programming. Hierarchical functional design can be used in all phases of the development cycle, and thereby provide a visable system that is suitable for a design walk through. The chief programmer team concept is also supported, since functional breakdown with clearly defined interfaces allows modules to be delegated to developers or to other teams, with the common understanding that is required for programs to integrate properly.

Hierarchical functional design employs the following three design concepts:

- A functional design in which the computer solution is structured in terms of the user's function.
- An iterative process in which each level of design is validated against the level above it.
- Conceptual levels of design, in which each level emphasizes a particular aspect of the problem solution.

A computer system can be viewed as a single function that can be divided (or decomposed) into a hierarchy of sets of successively lower-level functions until the elemental functions are described. An understanding of the meaning of the term "function" is necessary for further discussion. *Function* can be defined as an action upon an object, or, for our purposes, the transformation of some input data to some return data.[3] A statement of function describes what is done rather than how it is done. Since a function is also singular, it is defined with a simple declarative statement that consists of only one verb and one object. Both the verb and the object may be conditional.

functional design

A function should also have the characteristics that are defined for structured design. A function should be completely defined in one place, and relationships among functions should be primarily data relationships. Thus the concepts of structured design are valid for designing systems as well as modules. Functional design, then, consists of stating what is to be done in terms of data in and out. A high-level functional statement is reduced to a set of more detailed low-level statements, in a verb-object format. The set of lower-level statements must equal the function of the higher-level statement. In the accounts payable example that is used in this paper, the high-level function is COMPUTE PAYABLE AMOUNT. This function is stated in terms of its input data (purchase receipt) and its output (net payable amount). In this case, the output may simply be passed to another function. The function COMPUTE PAYABLE AMOUNT is then reduced to the following four functional statements:

VALIDATE RECEIPT ITEMS
COMPUTE ITEM EXTENDED PRICE
SUM GROSS PAYABLE AMOUNT
COMPUTE DISCOUNTED PAYABLE AMOUNT

Each of these statements can then be expressed in terms of its input and output data. This set is an explicit statement of the steps required to perform the function COMPUTE PAYABLE AMOUNT.

This is only one example of the way in which a function may be subdivided. The structuring of subfunctions requires analytical skill and imagination, and each analyst may define the subcomponents of a function slightly differently. It is important, however, that the definition of a function determine the functions that are subordinate to it. The function COMPUTE PAYABLE AMOUNT could not legitimately have a subordinate function that, for example, updates the inventory balance.

iterative process The design of an application should be an orderly growth process from inception to implementation. During development, frequent reviews should be conducted so that a given design always meets its objective. Design has usually been done at least twice before a system is complete and running. First, a functional design has been made to provide an understanding between the user and the programming department. Then a logic design has been made, from which programming could proceed. With hierarchical functional design, the function is the logic, and redundant effort may thus be avoided.

Hierarchical functional design is an evolving, top-down process. The first step is a translation of a statement of need into a functional statement of system objectives. As information about a required system is gathered, that information is organized according to the functional structure. The first statement should contain display screen formats, report layouts, perhaps a two-level hierarchy chart, and a single level of HIPO charts. The analyst should walk through these charts with the customer to verify that this level of design conforms with the requirement. As the process of design moves to areas such as file access methods, record layout, and message traffic, definitions in successively lower levels the hierarchy may cause upper levels to change. This is typical of the program development process and is the reason for continuing discussion with the customer. This is the iterative process—the refining of the higher levels of design as the more detailed levels are developed. As the iteration of detail progresses downward, the impact on the top-level design should become minimal. Because of the successive iterations of assessing the upward impact of design decisions, the result is a stable, intelligible, and maintainable design.

Levels of the design hierarchy

As an application is divided into functions and each function in turn is subdivided, the hierarchy proceeds toward greater detail. All levels of the system are described as functions, and can be grouped into three categories, proceeding from the broadest to the finest level of detail, as follows:

- System
- Program
- Module

These three levels are conceptual, and are not a physical part of the design. Each conceptual level may represent multiple levels on the hierarchy chart, and any given box on a chart may be both the bottom of one conceptual level and the top of the next level.

The system level of the hierarchy contains the major component **system** parts of the application, and is the view that a department man- **level** ager might have of the application. A system might contain multiple system levels: Accounts payable is a component of a material control system, and in turn, the subsystems of accounts payable itself would be contained within the system level. This level of hierarchy is started by structuring the original statement of requirement for an application. The analysis phase of a project may result in a system-level hierarchy such as that in the example in Figure 4. Each box in Figure 4 can be stated in functional terms, and can be represented by a HIPO chart. Although the terms of the user may differ somewhat from those on the chart, the functional statement should be used because it is more explicit than the common term. For example, the term ACCOUNTS PAYABLE may be simply a subset of the general ledger, or it may be a complete system for managing the payment of vendor accounts. The functional term MANAGE VENDOR ACCOUNTS makes the objective of this application more clear.

Figure 4 System level of the accounts payable application

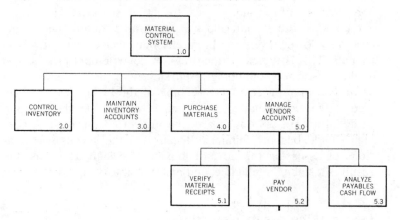

The system level normally does not include the representation of any executable computer instructions, but rather it provides a conceptual view of the application. Input and output are defined in terms of forms, files, and reports, which are a user's view of the data. If it appears that the user manager's view of the structure of an application does not provide the basis for program design, it should be mentioned that one of the primary objectives of functional design is to have a single view of the application that represents both the user's requirement and the program design. Although functions defined at the top level may be grouped differently for program design, they should all still exist with the same basic relationships in the computer implementation. This is the key to building systems that can be readily maintained and enhanced.

program level

The program level of the hierarchy shows the highest level of segmenting of the computer system. The program level may also be characterized as the end-user level, and represents the level of tasks initiated by a terminal operator in an interactive application, or batch programs in a batch application.

In the accounts payable application, consider the boxes below MANAGE VENDOR ACCOUNTS as tasks or programs. An example program level (one of the boxes in the accounts payable application) is shown in Figure 5. The program or task level is a result of the general design phase of a development project. Input and output for this level are usually defined as records or groups of records, messages, and report lines. Since this level normally represents executable computer instructions, it is recommended that program and module names be assigned to the boxes.

module level

Detailed program design occurs at the module level. Since design is an iterative process, detailed module design may expose

Figure 5 Program level of the accounts payable application

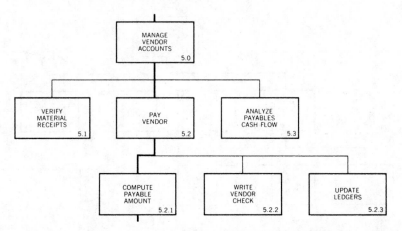

flaws or required restructuring of the more general design. It is essential that the upper-level HIPO charts be revised and revalidated before continuing with the design process. Design modification may be required when a low-level change causes the higher-level design to do something different from that which the user requires.

The module level represents an executable segment of program code that is usually compiled as a unit. This unit of code is typically called an "object module" to distinguish it from a "load module," which may be created by linking several functional modules together. At the module level of the hierarchy, the design is sufficiently detailed that program code can be written directly from the design. In the accounts payable application, two levels of modules are shown in Figure 6 below COMPUTE PAYABLE AMOUNT, which can be related to the program level in Figure 5.

The module level is the product of the specification phase of development. Input and output at this level are fields of data or parameters from or to other modules. The module level should represent a functional statement that can be completely grasped within a normal attention span. When translated into executable code, a module should usually contain fewer than fifty lines of structured high-level language statements. The HIPO chart at the module level may contain structured English (pseudo-code) statements to explain complex logic. In addition, where necessary, the extended description section of the HIPO chart may provide implementation notes as discussed in Reference 5.

The purpose of these conceptual levels is to reflect the objectives of users of the documents. The system level must be stated in terms that are relevant to user management. The module level is organized in such a way as to allow the programmer to write

Figure 6 Module level of the accounts payable application

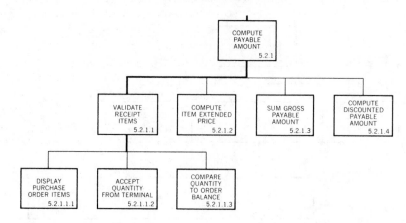

code. The program level provides the vehicle of communication between the system level and the module level by giving detail to the user and a higher-level view to the programmer.

Hierarchical functional design in a virtual system

The discussion thus far has considered the structure of an application as an aid in the design of an intelligible, maintainable system. A current major concern in system design is that of providing efficient performance of interactive applications in a virtual system environment. Performance tuning in a virtual system is a complex science that involves relationships among hardware, system software, and application design.[6, 7] Optimizing the performance of the application programs alone does not result in an efficient system. A conscious effort of tuning all the components that affect performance is required because programmers, for example, often attempt to write efficient—sometimes complex—code without regard for the way in which the modules may ultimately affect performance.

When viewing the structured design of an application, one can see readily that functional decomposition does not reflect the performance requirements of a transaction-driven application. Hunter,[5] for example, makes clear the issue of the compounded effect of excessive paging. He defines the working set as the twenty percent of the code that does eighty percent of the work, and advises that the "working set should become the focus of application tuning." The design process, if correctly executed, can produce modules each of which requires less than a single 4K byte page of storage. On that basis, the task of application tuning becomes an effort of identifying the most active modules, rewriting those modules for efficiency (if necessary), combining modules into logically related pages, and fixing active pages in main storage.

Performance tuning may, in extreme circumstances, require the radical modification of a few critical modules. Such modifications may include changing a CALL (transfer of control) to a COPY (compile-time inclusion) or even the integration and restructuring of modules. It must be clearly understood that only a very few modules ever seriously affect the performance of most systems. Thus, if an application is structured, the necessary tuning can be done consciously with proper control. With this perspective, even extreme coding techniques may be justified for those few modules that must be efficient to avoid performance degradation.

Concluding remarks

The improvement of the system development process requires innovation in two areas: the development of a discipline that involves a set of structured techniques, and an understanding of the theories on which that discipline is based.

Significant progress has been made in developing a discipline that, in time, should make program design and implementation an engineering skill. Structured programming provides basic building blocks for code development, much as electronic circuit development can be based on a set of predesigned, basic electronic components. HIPO and structured design are first steps in bringing that type of discipline to the design stage of application development.

It has been the intention of this article to address the following mental processes:

- Identification of function.
- Functional decomposition.
- Iterative design.
- Module relationship.
- Delayed performance optimization.

By applying the concepts of hierarchical functional design to the disciplines of HIPO and structured design throughout the analysis and design process, several of the following possible benefits are typically realized:

- User understanding and agreement on functional content are made easier.
- Missing or inconsistent information is identified early.
- Functions are discrete and are therefore more easily documented and, if necessary, modified.
- Documentation is accomplished with a single effort rather than multiple efforts at different stages of development.

- Module interfaces are simple and therefore reduce the probability of logic errors.
- The resultant design supports structured, top-down coding.
- Maintenance and enhancement are more transferable because the system can be easily understood at all levels.

Since these processes are ways of thinking about the design activity, it is often difficult to measure objectively the effect of using this knowledge. By applying these principles to a development project, however, one becomes aware of their value.

CITED REFERENCES

1. H. D. Mills and F. T. Baker, "Chief programmer teams," *Datamation* **19**, No. 12 (December 1973).
2. P. Moody and R. Perry, "Application development cycle problems," *Proceedings of Guide 40*, Miami Beach, May 18–23 (1975).
3. W. P. Stevens, G. J. Myers, and L. L. Constantine, "Structured design," *IBM Systems Journal* **13**, No. 2, 115–139 (1974).
4. G. J. Myers, *Reliable Software Through Composite Design*, Mason/Charter Publishers, New York, New York (1975).
5. John J. Hunter, "Rethinking application programs, key to VS success," *Computerworld*, March 25, 1975.
6. J. G. Rogers, "Structured programming for virtual storage systems," *IBM Systems Journal* **14**, No. 4, 385–406 (1975).
7. H. A. Anderson, Jr., M. Reiser, and G. L. Galati, "Tuning a virtual storage system," *IBM Systems Journal* **14**, No. 3, 246–263 (1975).

GENERAL REFERENCES

1. *HIPO—A Design Aid and Documentation Technique*, Order No. GC20-1851, IBM Corporation, Data Processing Division, White Plains, New York 10504.

2. *Structured Programming Independent Study Program*, Order No. SR20-7149, IBM Corporation, Data Processing Division, White Plains, New York 10504.

3. J. D. Aron, *The Program Development Process, Part 1, The Individual Programmer*, Addison-Wesley Publishing Company, Reading, Massachusetts, 31–36 (1974).

Reprint Order No. G321-5031.

Specifying Software Requirements for Complex Systems: New Techniques and Their Application

KATHRYN L. HENINGER

Abstract—This paper concerns new techniques for making requirements specifications precise, concise, unambiguous, and easy to check for completeness and consistency. The techniques are well-suited for complex real-time software systems; they were developed to document the requirements of existing flight software for the Navy's A-7 aircraft. The paper outlines the information that belongs in a requirements document and discusses the objectives behind the techniques. Each technique is described and illustrated with examples from the A-7 document. The purpose of the paper is to introduce the A-7 document as a model of a disciplined approach to requirements specification; the document is available to anyone who wishes to see a fully worked-out example of the approach.

Index Terms—Documentation techniques, functional specifications, real-time software, requirements, requirements definition, software requirements, specifications.

I. INTRODUCTION

MUCH software is difficult to understand, change, and maintain. Several software engineering techniques have been suggested to ameliorate this situation, among them modularity and information hiding [11], [12], formal specifications [4], [9], [10], [13], [16], [20], abstract interfaces [15], cooperating sequential processes [2], [18], [21], process synchronization routines [2], [8], and resource monitors [1], [6], [7]. System developers are reluctant to use these techniques both because their usefulness has not been proven for programs with stringent resource limitations and because there are no fully worked-out examples of some of them. In order to demonstrate feasibility and to provide a useful model, the Naval Research Laboratory and the Naval Weapons Center are using the techniques listed above to redesign and rebuild the operational flight program for the A-7 aircraft. The new program will undergo the acceptance tests established for the current program, and the two programs will be compared both for resource utilization and for ease of change.

The new program must be functionally identical to the existing program. That is to say, the new program must meet the same requirements as the old program. Unfortunately, when the project started there existed no requirements documentation for the old program; procurement specifications, which were originally sketchy, are now out-of-date. Our first step was to produce a complete description of the A-7 pro-

gram requirements in a form that would facilitate the development of the new program and that could be updated easily as the requirements continue to change.

Writing down the requirements turned out to be surprisingly difficult in spite of the availability of a working program and experienced maintenance personnel. None of the available documents were entirely accurate; no single person knew the answers to all our questions; some questions were answered differently by different people; and some questions could not be answered without experimentation with the existing system. We found it necessary to develop new techniques based on the same principles as the software design techniques listed above to organize and document software requirements. The techniques suggested questions, uncovered ambiguities, and supported crosschecking for completeness and consistency. The techniques allowed us to present the information relatively concisely, condensing several shelves of documentation into a single, 500-page document.

This paper shares some of the insights we gained from developing and applying these techniques. Our approach can be useful for other projects, both to document unrecorded requirements for existing systems and to guide software procurers as they define requirements for new systems. This paper introduces the techniques and illustrates them with simple examples. We invite anyone interested in more detail to look at the requirements document itself as a complete example of the way the techniques work for a substantial system [5].

First this paper addresses the objectives a requirements document ought to meet. Second it outlines the general design principles that guided us as we developed techniques; the principles helped us achieve the objectives. Finally it presents the specific techniques, showing how they allowed us to achieve completeness, precision, and clarity.

II. A-7 PROGRAM CHARACTERISTICS

The A-7 flight program is an operational Navy program with tight memory and time constraints. The code is about 12 000 assembler language instructions and runs on an IBM System 4 PI model TC-2 computer with 16K bytes of memory. We chose this program because we wanted to demonstrate that the run-time overhead incurred by using software engineering principles is not prohibitive for real-time programs and because

Manuscript received February 12, 1979; revised March 12, 1979.

The author is with the Naval Research Laboratory, Washington, DC 20375.

the maintenance personnel feel that the current program is difficult to change.

The A-7 flight program is part of the Navigation/Weapon Delivery System on the A-7 aircraft. It receives input data from sensors, cockpit switches, and a panel with which the pilot keys in data. It controls several display devices in the cockpit and positions several sensors. Twenty-two devices are connected to the computer; examples include an inertial measurement set providing velocity data and a head-up display device. The head-up display projects symbols into the pilot's field of view, so that he sees them overlaying the world ahead of the aircraft. The program calculates navigation information, such as present position, speed, and heading; it also controls weapon delivery, giving the pilot steering cues and calculating when to release weapons.

III. REQUIREMENTS DOCUMENT OBJECTIVES

For documentation to be useful and coherent, explicit decisions must be made about the purposes it should serve. Decisions about the following questions affect its scope, organization, and style: 1) What kinds of questions should it answer? 2) Who are the readers? 3) How will it be used? 4) What background knowledge does a reader need? Considering these questions, we derived the following six objectives for our requirements document.

1) *Specify external behavior only.* A requirements document should specify only the external behavior of a system, without implying a particular implementation. The user or his representative defines requirements using his knowledge of the application area, in this case aircraft navigation and weapons delivery. The software designer creates the implementation, using his knowledge of software engineering. When requirements are expressed in terms of a possible implementation, they restrict the software designer too much, sometimes preventing him from using the most effective algorithms and data structures. In our project the requirements document must be equally valid for two quite different implementations: the program we build and the current program. For our purposes it serves as a problem statement, outlining what the new program must do to pass acceptance tests. For those maintaining the current program, it fills a serious gap in their documentation: they have no other source that states exactly what the program must do. They have pilot manuals, which supply user-level documentation for the entire avionics system, of which the program is only a small part. Unfortunately, the pilot manuals make it difficult to separate the activities performed by the computer program from those performed by other devices and to distinguish between advice to the pilot and restrictions enforced by the program. The maintainers also have implementation documentation for the current program: mathematical algorithm analyses, flowcharts, and 12 000 lines of sparsely commented assembler code. But the implementation documents do not distinguish between the aspects that are dictated by the requirements and those that the software designer is free to change.

2) *Specify constraints on the implementation.* In addition to defining correct program behavior, the document should describe the constraints placed on the implementation, especially the details of the hardware interfaces. As is usually the case with embedded systems,[1] we are not free to define the interfaces to the system, but must accept them as given for the problem. A complete requirements description should therefore include the facts about the hardware devices that can affect the correctness of the program.

3) *Be easy to change.* Because requirements change, requirements documentation should be easy to change. If the documentation is not maintained during the system life cycle, control is lost over the software evolution; it becomes difficult to coordinate program changes introduced by maintenance personnel.

4) *Serve as a reference tool.* The primary function of the document is to answer specific questions quickly, rather than to explain in general what the program does. We expect the document to serve experienced programmers who already have a general idea about the purpose of the program. Precision and conciseness are valued. Indispensable reference aids include a glossary, detailed table of contents, and various indices. Since tutorial material has different characteristics, such as a narrative style, it should be developed separately if it is needed.

5) *Record forethought about the life cycle of the system.* During the requirements definition stage, we believe it is sensible to exercise forethought about the life cycle of the program. What types of changes are likely to occur [22]? What functions would maintainers like to be able to remove easily [17]? For any software product some changes are easier to make than others; some guidance in the requirements will help the software designer assure that the easy changes correspond to the most likely changes.

6) *Characterize acceptable responses to undesired events.* Undesired events [14], such as hardware failures and user errors, should be anticipated during requirements definition. Since the user knows the application area, he knows more than the software designer about acceptable responses. For example, a pilot knows better than a programmer whether a particular response to a sensor failure will decrease or increase his difficulties. Responses to undesired events should be stated in the requirements document; they should not be left for the programmer to invent.

IV. REQUIREMENTS DOCUMENT DESIGN PRINCIPLES

Our approach to requirements documentation can be summarized by the three principles discussed below. These principles form the basis of all the techniques we developed.

1) *State questions before trying to answer them.* At every stage of writing the requirements, we concentrated first on formulating the questions that should be answered. If this is not done, the available material prejudices the requirements investigation so that only the easily answered questions are asked. First we formulated the table of contents in Fig. 1 in order to characterize the general classes of questions that should be answered. We wrote it before we looked at the A-7

---

[1] An embedded system functions as a component of a significantly larger system. Parnas [15] has a discussion of embedded system characteristics.

Chapter		Contents
0	Introduction	Organization principles; abstracts for other sections; notation guide
1	Computer Characteristics	If the computer is predetermined, a general description with particular attention to its idiosyncrasies; otherwise a summary of its required characteristics
2	Hardware Interfaces	Concise description of information received or transmitted by the computer
3	Software Functions	What the software must do to meet its requirements, in various situations and in response to various events
4	Timing Constraints	How often and how fast each function must be performed. This section is separate from section 3 since "what" and "when" can change independently.
5	Accuracy Constraints	How close output values must be to ideal values to be acceptable
6	Response to Undesired Events	What the software must do if sensors go down, the pilot keys in invalid data, etc.
7	Subsets	What parts of the program should be easy to remove
8	Fundamental Assumptions	The characteristics of the program that will stay the same, no matter what changes are made
9	Changes	The types of changes that have been made or are expected
10	Glossary	Most documentation is fraught with acronyms and technical terms. At first we prepared this guide for ourselves; as we learned the language, we retained it for newcomers.
11	Sources	Annotated list of documentation and personnel, indicating the types of questions each can answer

Fig. 1. A-7 Requirements table of contents.

at all, basing it on our experience with other software. Then we generated questions for the individual sections. Like any design effort, formulating questions requires iteration: we generated questions from common sense, organized them into forms, generated more questions by trying to fill in the blanks, and revised the forms.

2) *Separate concerns.* We used the principle of "separation of concerns" [3] to organize the document so that each project member could concentrate on a well-defined set of questions. This principle also serves the objective of making the document easy to change, since it causes changes to be well-confined. For example, hardware interfaces are described without making any assumptions about the purpose of the program; the hardware section would remain unchanged if the behavior of the program changed. The software behavior is described without any references to the details of the hardware devices; the software section would remain unchanged if data were received in different formats or over different channels.

3) *Be as formal as possible.* We avoided prose and developed formal ways to present information in order to be precise, concise, consistent, and complete.

The next two sections of the paper show how these principles are applied to describe the hardware interfaces and the software behavior.

V. Techniques for Describing Hardware Interfaces

Organization by Data Item

To organize the hardware interfaces description, we have a separate unit, called a *data item*, for each input or output that changes value independently of other inputs or outputs. Examples of input data items include barometric altitude, radar-measured distance to a point on the ground, the setting of the inertial platform mode switch, and the inertial platform ready signal. Examples of output data items include coordinates for the flight path marker on the head-up display, radar antenna steering commands, and the signal that turns on and off the computer-failed light. The A-7 computer receives 70 input data items and transmits 95 output data items.

In order to have a consistent approach, we designed a form to be completed for each data item. We started with an initial set of questions that occurred to us as we read about the interfaces. How does the program read or write these data? What is the bit representation of the value? Can the computer tell whether a sensor value is valid? As we worked on specific data items, new questions occurred to us. We added these questions to the form, so that they would be addressed for all data items. The form is illustrated in Figs. 2 and 3 at the end of this section.

191

Symbolic Names for Data Items and Values

The hardware section captures two kinds of information about data items: *arbitrary details* that might change if a device were replaced with a similar device, and *essential characteristics* that would be shared by similar devices. The bit representation of a value is an arbitrary detail; the semantics of the value is an essential characteristic. For example, any barometric altitude sensor provides a reading from which barometric altitude can be calculated—this information is essential. But the resolution, representation, accuracy, and timing might differ between two types of barometric altitude sensors—this information is arbitrary.

Essential information must be expressed in such a way that the rest of the document can use it without referencing the arbitrary details. For example, each data item is given a mnemonic name, so that it can be identified unambiguously in the rest of the document without reference to instruction sequences or channel numbers. If a data item is not numerical and takes on a fixed set of possible values, the values are given mnemonic names so that they can be used without reference to bit encodings. For example, a switch might be able to take the values "on" and "off." The physical representation of the two values is arbitrary information that is not mentioned in the rest of the document in case it changes. The names allow the readers and writers of the rest of the document to ignore the physical details of input and output, and are more visually meaningful than the details they represent.

We bracket every mnemonic name in symbols indicating the item type, for example /input-data-items/, //output-data-items//, and $nonnumeric-values$. These brackets reduce confusion by identifying the item type unambiguously, so that the reader knows where to find the precise definition. Moreover, the brackets facilitate systematic cross referencing, either by people or computers.

Templates for Value Descriptions

The values of the numerical data items belong to a small set of value types, such as angles and distances. At first we described each data item in an ad hoc fashion, usually imitating the descriptions in the documents we referenced. But these documents were not consistent with each other and the descriptions were not always complete. We made great progress when we developed informal templates for the value descriptions, with blanks to be completed for specific data items. For example, the template for angles might read:

> angle (?) is measured from line (?) to line (?) in the (?) direction, looking (?)

For example, magnetic heading is measured from the line from the aircraft to magnetic north to the horizontal component of the aircraft X axis, in the clockwise direction looking down.

Although templates were not used as hard-and-fast rules, their existence made values easier to describe, made the descriptions consistent with each other, and helped us apply the same standards of completeness to all items of the same type.

Input Data Items Described as Resources, Independent of Software Use

When describing input data items, we refrain from mentioning how or when the data is used by the software, to avoid making any assumptions about the software function. Instead, we describe the input data items as if taking inventory of the resources available to solve a problem. We define numerical values in terms of what they measure. For example, the value of the input data item called /RADALT/ is defined as the distance above local terrain as determined by the radar altimeter. Many nonnumerical inputs indicate switch positions; these are described without reference to the response the pilot expects when he changes the switch, since the response is accomplished by the software. For example, when the pilot changes the scale switch on the projected map display, he expects the map scale to change. Since the response is achieved by the software, it is not mentioned in the input data item description, which reads, *"/PMSCAL/ indicates the position of a two-position toggle switch on the projected map panel. This switch has no hardware effect on the projected map display."*

Example of an Input Data Item Description

Fig. 2 shows the completed form for a nonnumerical input data item. The underlined words are the form headings. Value encoding shows how the mnemonic value names used in the rest of the document are mapped into specific bit representations. "Switch nomenclature" indicates the names of the switch positions as seen by the pilot in the cockpit. Instruction sequence gives the TC-2 assembler language instructions that cause the data to be transmitted to or from the computer. We are not usurping the programmer's job by including the instruction sequence because there is no other way to read in this data item—the instruction sequence is not an implementation decision for the programmer. The channel number is a cross reference to the computer chapter where the general characteristics of the eight channels are described. Data representation shows the location of the value in the 16-bit input word. Notice how the Comments section defines the value assumed by the switch while the pilot is changing it. This is an example of a question we asked about all switches, once it had occurred to us about this one.

Output Data Items Described in Terms of Effects on External Hardware

Most output data items are described in terms of their effects on the associated devices. For example, the description of the output data items called //STEERAZ// and //STEEREL// shows how they are used to communicate the direction to point the antenna of the radar. This section does not explain how the software chooses the direction. For other output data items we define the value the peripheral device must receive in order to function correctly. For example, the description of the output data item called //FPANGL// shows that the radar assumes the value will be a certain angle which

```
Input Data Item:  IMS Mode Switch

Acronym:  /IMSMODE/

Hardware:  Inertial Measurement Set

Description:  /IMSMODE/ indicates the position of a six-position rotary switch
              on the IMS control panel.

              Switch nomenclature: OFF; GND ALIGN; NORM; INERTIAL; MAG SL;
              GRID

Characteristics of Values
    Value Encoding:    $Offnone$       (00000)
                       $Gndal$         (10000)
                       $Norm$          (01000)
                       $Iner$          (00100)
                       $Grid$          (00010)
                       $Magsl$         (00001)

Instruction Sequence:  READ 24   (Channel 0)

Data Representation:  Bits 3-7

Comments:    /IMSMODE/ = $Offnone$ when the switch is between two positions.
```

Fig. 2. Completed input data item form.

```
Output Data Item:  Steering Error

Acronym:  //STERROR//

Hardware:  Attitude Direction Indicator (ADI)

Description:  //STERROR// controls the position of the vertical needle on the
             ADI.  A positive value moves the pointer to the right when
             looking at the display.  A value of zero centers the needle.

Characteristics of Values

    Unit:  Degrees

    Range:  -2.5 to +2.5

    Accuracy:  + .1

    Resolution:  .00122

Instruction Sequence:  WRITE 229   (Channel 7)
                       Test Carry Bit = 0 for request acknowledged
                       If not, restart

Data Representation:  11-bit two's complement number, bit 0 and bits 3-12
                      scale  = 512/1.25 = 409.6
                      offset = 0
```

```
( )            (        INDICATED VALUE              )
   Not used                                       0   0   0
___ ___ ___ ___ ___ ___ ___ ___ ___ ___ ___ ___ ___ ___ ___
 0   1   2   3   4   5   6   7   8   9  10  11  12  13  14  15
BIT
```

```
Timing Characteristics: Digital to DC voltage conversion.  See Section 1.5.7.

Comments:    The pointer hits a mechanical stop at + 2.5 degrees.
```

Fig. 3. Completed output data item form.

it uses to determine the climb or dive angle the aircraft should use during terrain following. We avoid giving any meaning to an output value that is not a characteristic of the hardware.

Example of an Output Data Item Description

Fig. 3 shows the completed form for a numerical output data item. Notice how the value is described in terms of its effect on a needle in a display, rather than in terms of what the needle is supposed to communicate to the pilot. The value is characterized by a standard set of parameters, such as range and resolution, which are used for all numerical data items. For Data representation, we show how the 16-bit output word is constructed, including which bits must be zero, which bits are ignored by the device, and which bits encode the out-

put value. Since the actual output value is not in any standard units of measurement, we also show how it can be derived from a value in standard units, in this case degrees. The relation between output values and values in standard units is given by the equation

$$\text{output value} = \text{scale} \times (\text{standard value} + \text{offset})$$

Since the same equation is used for all numerical data items, we need only provide the scale and offset values for a particular data item. Thus the output value for the data item //STERROR// in Fig. 3 is derived from a value in degrees by the following expression:

$$\text{output value} = 409.6 \times (\text{standard value} + 0)$$

193

The Timing considerations section contains a pointer to another section; since many output data items have the same timing characteristics, we describe them once, and include cross references. The comment shows a physical limit of the device.

VI. TECHNIQUES FOR DESCRIBING SOFTWARE FUNCTIONS

Organization by Functions

We describe the software as a set of functions associated with output data items: each function determines the values for one or more output data items and each output data item is given values by exactly one function. Thus every function can be described in terms of externally visible effects. For example, the function calculating values for the output data item //STERROR// is described in terms of its effects on a needle in a display. The meaning conveyed to the pilot by the needle is expressed here.

This approach, identifying functions by working backward from output data items, works well because most A-7 outputs are specialized; most output data items are used for only a small set of purposes. The approach breaks down somewhat for a general-purpose device, such as a terminal, where the same data items are used to express many different types of information. We have one general-purpose device, the computer panel, where the same set of thirteen seven-segment displays can display many types of information, including present position, wind speed, and sensor status. We handled this situation by acting as if each type of information had its own panel, each controlled by a separate function. Thus, we have forty-eight panel functions, each described as if it always controlled a panel, and a set of rules to determine which function controls the real panel at any given moment. This approach, creating *virtual panels*, allows us to separate decisions about what the values are from decisions about when they are displayed. It also causes the description to be less dependent on the characteristics of the particular panel device than it otherwise would be.

Software functions are classified as either demand or periodic. A *demand function* must be requested by the occurrence of some event every time it is performed. For example, the computer-failed light is turned on by a demand function when a computer malfunction is detected. A *periodic function* is performed repeatedly without being requested each time. For example, the coordinates of symbols on the head-up display are updated by periodic functions. If a periodic function need not be performed all the time, it is started and stopped by specific events. For example, a symbol may be removed from the head-up display when a certain event occurs.

This distinction is useful because different performance and timing information is required for demand and periodic functions. To describe a demand function one must give the events that cause it to occur; an appropriate timing question is *"What is the maximum delay that can be tolerated between request and action?"* To describe a periodic function, one must give the events that cause it to start and stop and the conditions that affect how it is performed after it is started; an appropriate timing question is *"What are the minimum and maximum repetition rates for this function?"*

Output Values as Functions of Conditions and Events

Originally we thought we would describe each output as a mathematical function of input values. This turned out to be a naive approach. We found we could seldom describe output values directly in terms of input values; instead we had to define intermediate values that the current program calculated, but that did not correspond to any output values. These in turn had to be described in terms of other intermediate values. By the time we reached input values, we would have described an implementation.

Instead, we expressed requirements by giving output values as functions of aircraft operating conditions. For example, the output data item named //LATGT70// should change value when the aircraft crosses 70° latitude; how the program detects this event is left to the implementation. In order to describe outputs in terms of aircraft operating conditions, we defined a simple language of conditions and events. *Conditions* are predicates that characterize some aspect of the system for a measurable period of time. For example, /IMSMODE/ = $Gndal$ is a condition that is true when the IMS mode switch in the cockpit is set to the GND ALIGN position (see Fig. 2). If a pilot expects a certain display whenever the switch is in this position, the function controlling the display is affected by the value of /IMSMODE/. An *event* occurs when the value of a condition changes from true to false or vice versa. Events therefore specify instants of time, whereas conditions specify intervals of time. Events start and stop periodic functions, and they trigger demand functions. Events provide a convenient way to describe functions where something is done when a button is first pushed, but not if the pilot continues to hold it down. Before we distinguished clearly between events and conditions, situations of this sort were very difficult to describe simply.

Consistent Notation for Aircraft Operating Conditions

Text Macros: To keep the function descriptions concise, we introduced over two hundred terms that serve as text macros. The terms are bracketed in exclamation points and defined in an alphabetical dictionary. A text macro can define a quantity that affects an output value, but that cannot be directly obtained from an input. An example is "!ground track angle!", defined as "the angle measured from the line from the aircraft to true north to !ground track!, measured clockwise looking down." Although the derivation of such values is left to the implementation, text macros provide a consistent, encapsulated means to refer to them while specifying function values.

Text macros also serve as abbreviations for compound conditions that are frequently used or very detailed. For example, !Desig! is a condition that is true when the pilot has performed a sequence of actions that designates a target to the computer. The list of events defining !Desig! appears only in the dictionary; while writing or reading the rest of the document, these events need not be considered. If designation procedures change, only the definition in the dictionary changes. Another example of a text macro for a compound condition is !IMS Reasonable!,[2] which represents the following bulky, specific condition:

!IMS total velocity! ≤ 1440 fps AND
change of !IMS total velocity! from .2 seconds
ago ≤ 50 fps

Even though this term is used many times in the function descriptions, only one place in the document need be changed if the reasonableness criteria change for the sensor.

The use of text macros is an application of stepwise refinement: while describing functions, we give names to complicated operating conditions or values, postponing the precise definitions. As the examples above show, we continue introducing new terms in the definitions themselves. This allows us to limit the amount of detail we deal with at one time. Furthermore, like the use of /, //, and $ brackets in the hardware descriptions, the use of ! brackets for text macros indicates to the reader that reference is being made to something that is defined precisely elsewhere. This reduces the risk of ambiguity that usually accompanies prose descriptions (e.g., !Desig! versus designated).

Conditions: We represent these predicates as expressions on input data items, for example, /IMSMODE/=$Gndal$, or expressions on quantities represented by text macros, for example, !ground track angle! = 30°. A condition can also be represented by a text macro, such as !IMS Reasonable!. Compound conditions can be composed by connecting simple conditions with the logical operators AND, OR, and NOT. For example, (!IMS Reasonable! AND /IMSMODE/=$Gndal$) is true only when both the component conditions are true.

Events: We use the notation @T(condition 1) to denote the occurrence of condition 1 becoming *true* and @F(condition 2) to denote the occurrence of condition 2 becoming *false*.

For example, the event @T(!ground track angle! < 30°) occurs when the !ground track angle! value crosses the 30° threshold from a larger value. The event @T(!ground track angle!=30°) occurs when the value reaches the 30° threshold from either direction. The event @T(/IMSMODE/ = $Gndal$) occurs when the pilot moves the switch to the GND ALIGN position. In some cases, an event only occurs if one condition changes when another condition is true, denoted by

@T(condition 3) WHEN (condition 4).

Thus, @T(/ACAIRB/=Yes) WHEN (/IMSMODE/=$Gndal$) refers to the event of the aircraft becoming airborne while the IMS mode switch is in the GND ALIGN position, while @T(/IMSMODE/=$Gndal$) WHEN (/ACAIRB/=Yes) refers to the event of the IMS mode being switched to GND ALIGN while the airplane is airborne.

[2]This text macro represents the condition that the values read from the inertial measurement set are reasonable; i.e., the magnitude of the aircraft velocity vector, calculated from inertial measurement set inputs, is less than or equal to 1440 feet per second and has changed less than 50 feet per second from the magnitude 0.2 seconds ago.

Using Modes to Organize and Simplify

Although each function is affected by only a small subset of the total set of conditions, we still need to organize conditions into groups in order to keep the function descriptions simple. To do this, we define *modes* or classes of system states. Because the functions differ more between modes than they do within a single mode, a mode-by-mode description is simpler than a general description. For example, by setting three switches, deselecting guns, and keying a single digit on the panel, the pilot can enter what is called the visual navigation update mode. In this mode, several displays and the radar are dedicated to helping him get a new position estimate by sighting off a local landmark. Thus the mode affects the correct behavior of the functions associated with these displays. The use of modes has an additional advantage: if something goes wrong during a flight, the pilot is much more likely when he makes the trouble report to remember the mode than the values of various conditions.

Each mode is given a short mnemonic name enclosed in asterisks, for example, *DIG* for Doppler-inertial-gyrocompassing navigation mode. The mode name is used in the rest of the document as an abbreviation for the conditions that are true whenever the system is in that mode.

The current mode is defined by the history of events that have occurred in the program. The document shows this by giving the initial mode and the set of events that cause transitions between any pair of modes. For example, the transition list includes the entry

DIG TO *DI*
@T(!latitude! > 70°)
@(/IMSMODE/=$Iner$) WHEN (!Doppler coupled!)

Thus the system will move from *DIG* mode to Doppler-inertial (*DI*) mode either if the aircraft goes above 70° latitude or if the inertial platform mode switch is changed to INERTIAL while the Doppler Radar is in use.

The table in Fig. 4 summarizes conditions that are true whenever the system is in a particular navigation mode. Thus in *DIG* mode the inertial platform mode switch is set to NORM, the aircraft is airborne, the latitude is less than 70°, and both the Doppler Radar and the inertial platform are functioning correctly. "X" table entries mean the value of that condition does not matter in that mode.

The mode condition tables are redundant because the information can be derived from the mode transition lists. However, the mode condition tables present the information in a more convenient form. Since the mode condition tables do not contain all the mode transition information, they do not uniquely define the current mode.

Special Tables for Precision and Completeness

In an early version of the document, function characteristics were described in prose; this was unsatisfactory because it was difficult to find answers to specific questions and because gaps and inconsistencies did not show up. We invented two types of tables that helped us express information precisely and completely.

MODE	/IMSMODE/	/ACAIRB/	!latitude!	Other
DIG	$Norm$	Yes	<70o	!IMS Up! AND !Doppler Up!
DI	$Norm$ OR $Iner$	Yes	<80o	!IMS Up! AND !Doppler Up! AND !Doppler Coupled!
I	$Iner$	X	<80o	!IMS Up!
IMS fail	X	X	X	!IMS Down!

Fig. 4. Section from the navigation mode condition table.

Condition Table: Magnetic heading (//MAGHDGH//) output values

MODES	CONDITIONS	
DIG, *DI*, *I* *Mag sl*,*Grid*	Always	X
IMS fail	(NOT /IMSMODE/=$Offnone$)	/IMSMODE/=$Offnone$
//MAGHDGH// value	angle defined by /MAGHCOS/ and /MAGHSIN/	0 (North)

Fig. 5. Example of a condition table.

Condition tables are used to define some aspect of an output value that is determined by an active mode and a condition that occurs within that mode. Fig. 5 gives an example of a condition table. Each row corresponds to a group of one or more modes in which this function acts alike. The rows are mutually exclusive; only one mode affects the function at a time. In each row are a set of mutually exclusive conditions; exactly one should be true whenever the program is in the modes denoted by the row. At the bottom of the column is the information appropriate for the interval identified by the mode-condition intersection. Thus to find the information appropriate for a given mode and given condition, first find the row corresponding to the mode, find the condition within the row, and follow that column to the bottom of the table. An "X" instead of a condition indicates that information at the bottom of the column is never appropriate for that mode.

In Fig. 5, the magnetic heading value is 0 when the system is in mode *IMS fail* and the condition (/IMSMODE/=$Offnone$) is true. Whenever the system is in *IMS fail* mode, the following condition is true, showing that the row is complete,

(/IMSMODE/=$Offnone$ OR(NOT /IMSMODE/=$Offnone$))

and the following statement is false, showing the row entries are mutually exclusive.

(/IMSMODE/=$Offnone$ AND(NOT/IMSMODE/=$Offnone$))

Condition tables are used in the descriptions of periodic functions. Periodic functions are performed differently in differ-

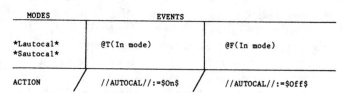

Event table : When AUTOCAL Light Switched on/off

MODES	EVENTS	
Lautocal *Sautocal*	@T(In mode)	@F(In mode)
ACTION	//AUTOCAL//:=On	//AUTOCAL//:=Off

Fig. 6. Example of an event table.

ent time intervals; the appropriate time interval is determined by the prevailing mode and conditions. Each row in the table completely characterizes the intervals within a mode that are meaningful for that function. The conditions must be mutually exclusive, and together they must describe the entire time the program is within the mode. These characteristics ensure that condition tables be complete, that is, all relevant intervals are indicated. They also ensure that condition tables be unambiguous, that is, given the aircraft operating conditions, the correct interval can be determined.

Event tables show when demand functions should be performed or when periodic functions should be started or stopped. Each row in an event table corresponds to a mode or group of modes. Table entries are events that cause an action to be taken when the system is in a mode associated with the row. The action to be taken is given at the bottom of the column.

The event table in Fig. 6 specifies that the autocalibration light controlled by output data item //AUTOCAL// be turned

Demand Function Name: Change scale factor

Modes in which function required:
    Lautocal, *Sautocal*, *Landaln*, *SINSaln*, *HUDaln*, *Airaln*

Output data item: //IMSSCAL//

Function Request and Output Description:

Event Table: When the Scale Factor Is Changed

MODES	EVENTS	
Lautocal *Landaln*	@T(In mode) WHEN (//IMSSCAL//=$Coarse$)	X
HUDaln	@T(In mode) WHEN (/IMSMODE/ = $Gndal$ AND //IMSSCAL//=$Coarse$)	@T(In mode) WHEN (NOT (/IMSMODE/=$Gndal$) AND //IMSSCAL//=$Fine$)
Sautocal *SINSaln* *Airaln*	X	@T(In mode) WHEN (//IMSSCAL//=$Fine$)
ACTION	//IMSSCAL//:=$Fine$	//IMSSCAL//:=$Coarse$

Fig. 7. Completed demand function form.

Periodic function name: Update Flight Path Marker coordinates

Modes in which function required:
    DIG, *DI*, *I*, *Mag Sl*, *Grid*, *IMS fail*

Output Data Items: //FPMAZ//, //FPMEL//

Initiation and Termination Events:
    Start: @T(//HUDVEL// = On)
    Stop: @T(//HUDVEL// = Off)

Output description:

The Flight Path Marker (FPM) symbol on the head-up display shows the direction of the aircraft velocity vector. If the aircraft is moving straight ahead from the nose of the aircraft, the FPM is centered on the display. The horizontal displacement from display center shows the lateral velocity component and elevation displacement shows the vertical velocity component.

Although the means for deriving Flight Path Marker position varies as shown in the table below, the position is usually derived from the current !System velocities!. The velocities are first resolved into forward, lateral, and vertical components. Then FPM coordinates are derived in the following manner:

//FPMAZ// shows $\dfrac{\text{Lateral velocity}}{\text{Forward velocity}}$ //FPMEL// shows $\dfrac{\text{Vertical velocity}}{\text{Forward velocity}}$

Condition Table: Coordinates of the Flight Path Marker

MODES	CONDITIONS		
DIG, *DI*	X	Always	X
I	/ACAIRB/ = No	/ACAIRB/ = Yes	X
Mag sl, *Grid*	/ACAIRB/=No	!ADC Up! AND /ACAIRB/=Yes	!ADC Down! AND /ACAIRB/=Yes
IMS fail	/ACAIRB/=No	X	/ACAIRB/=Yes
FPM COORDINATES	//FPMAZ//:= 0 //FPMEL//:= 0	based on !System velocities!	//FPMAZ//:= 0 //FPMEL//:=/AOA/

Fig. 8. Completed periodic function form.

on when the two listed modes are entered and off when they are exited. We use the symbol ":=" to denote assignment. The event @T(In mode) occurs when all the conditions represented by the mode become true, i.e., when the mode is entered. @F(In mode) occurs when any one of the conditions represented by the mode becomes false, i.e., when the system changes to a different mode.

Function Description Examples

Figs. 7 and 8 illustrate the forms we created for demand and periodic functions, respectively. All function descriptions indicate the associated output data items, thereby providing a cross reference to the hardware description. The list of modes gives the reader an overview of when the function is performed; the overview is refined in the rest of the description.

The event table in Fig. 7 shows both the events that request the function and the values output by the function at different times. For example, if the //IMSSCAL// value is $Coarse$ when the *Landaln* mode is entered, the function assigns it the value $Fine$. Notice how the table uses the symbolic names introduced in the hardware section for data items and data item values.

In Fig. 8 the initiation and termination section gives the events that cause this periodic function to start and stop. This function starts when another output data item, //HUDVEL//, is assigned the value On, and stops when //HUDVEL// is assigned the value Off. The function positions a symbol on a display device. The position of the symbol usually represents the direction of the aircraft velocity vector, but under some conditions the output data items are given other values. The output description consists of two parts: a brief prose description of the usual meaning of the symbol and a condition table that shows what will happen under different conditions. Notice that every mode in the mode list is accounted for in the table. The relevant conditions for this function are !ADC Up! or !ADC Down!, (the operating status of the air data computer sensor which provides a measurement of true airspeed) and /ACAIRB/= Yes and /ACAIRB/=No (whether the aircraft is airborne). Thus, if the system is in the inertial mode (*I*) and the aircraft is not airborne (/ACAIRB/=No is true), both coordinates of the symbol are set to zero.

VII. TECHNIQUES FOR SPECIFYING UNDESIRED EVENTS

Lists of Undesired Events

In order to characterize the desired response of the system when undesired events occur, we started with a list of undesired events and interviewed pilots and maintenance programmers to find out both what they would like to have happen and what they considered feasible. The key was the list of possible undesired events. To derive this list, we used the classification scheme shown in Fig. 9 as a guide.

For example, in the class "Resource failure—temporary," we include the malfunctioning of each sensor since the sensors tend to resume correct functioning; in the class "Resource failure—permanent," we include the loss of areas of memory.

VIII. TECHNIQUES FOR CHARACTERIZING TYPES OF CHANGES

In order to characterize types of changes, we looked through a file of change requests and interviewed the maintainers. To define requirements for a new system, we would have looked at change requests for similar systems. We also made a long list of fundamental assumptions that we thought would always be true about the system, no matter what. In a meeting with several maintenance system engineers and programmers, all but four of the fundamental assumptions were rejected; each rejected assumption was moved to the list of possible changes! For example, the following assumption is true about the cur-

```
1 Resource Failure
    1.1 Temporary
    1.2 Permanent
2 Incorrect input data
    2.1 Detected by examining input only
    2.2 Detected by comparison with internal data
    2.3 Detected by user realizing he made a mistake
    2.4 Detected by user from incorrect output
3 Incorrect internal data
    3.1 Detected by internal inconsistency
    3.2 Detected by comparison with input data
    3.3 Detected by user from incorrect output
```

Fig. 9. Undesired event classification derived from Parnas [19].

rent program, but may change in the future: "The computer will perform weapon release calculations for only one target at a time. When a target is designated, the previously designated target is forgotten." By writing two complementary lists—possible changes and fundamental assumptions—we thought about the problem from two directions, and we detected many misunderstandings. Producing a list of fundamental assumptions forced us to voice some implicit assumptions, so that we discovered possible changes we would have omitted otherwise. One reason for the success of this procedure is that it is much easier for a reviewer to recognize an error than an omission.

Listed below are examples of feasible changes.

1) Assignment of devices to channels may be changed.

2) The rate of symbol movement on the display in response to joystick displacement might be changed.

3) New sensors may be added. (This has occurred already in the history of the program.)

4) Future weapons may require computer control after release.

5) Computer self-test might be required in the air (at present it is only required on the ground).

6) It may be necessary to cease certain lower priority functions to free resources for higher priority functions during stress moments. (At present the program halts if it does not have sufficient time to perform all functions, assuming a program error.)

IX. DISCUSSION

We expect the document to be kept up-to-date as the program evolves because it is useful in many ways that are independent of our project. The maintainers of the current program plan to use it to train new maintenance personnel, since it presents the program's purpose in a consistent, systematic way. It is the only complete, up-to-date description of their hardware interfaces. One of the problems they now face when making changes is that they cannot tell easily if there are other places in the code that should be changed to preserve consistency. For example, they changed the code in one place to turn on a display when the target is twenty-two nautical miles away; in another place, the display is still turned on when the target is twenty nautical miles away. The unintended two-nautical-mile difference causes no major problems, but it adds unnecessary complexity for the pilot and the programmer. Inconsistencies such as this show up conspicuously in the function tables in our document. Besides using the document to check the implications of small changes, the maintenance staff want to modify it to document the next version of the program. They expect major benefits as they prepare system tests, since the document provides a description of acceptable program behavior that is independent of the program. In the past, testers have had to infer what the program is supposed to do by looking at the code. Finally they also intend to derive test cases systematically from the tables and mode transition charts.

The usefulness of these ideas is not limited to existing programs. They could be used during the requirements definition phase for a new product in order to record decisions for easy retrieval, to check new decisions for consistency with previously made decisions, and to suggest questions that ought to be considered. However, a requirements document for a new system would not be as specific as our document. We can describe acceptable behavior exactly because all the decisions about the external interfaces have been made. For a new program a requirements document describes a set of possible behaviors, giving the characteristics that distinguish acceptable from unacceptable behavior. The system designer chooses the exact behavior for the new product. The questions are the same for a new system; the answers are less restrictive. For example, where we give a specific number for the accuracy of an input, there might be a range of acceptable accuracy values for a new program.

X. Conclusions

The requirements document for the A-7 program demonstrates that a substantial system can be described in terms of its external stimuli and its externally visible behavior. The techniques discussed in this paper guided us in obtaining information, helped us to control its complexity, and allowed us to avoid dealing with implementation details. The document gives a headstart on the design phase of our project. Many questions are answered precisely that usually would be left to programmers to decide or to discover as they build the code. Since the information is expressed systematically, we can plan for it systematically, instead of working each detail into the program in an ad hoc fashion.

All of the techniques described in this paper are based on three principles: formulate questions before trying to answer them, separate concerns, and use precise notation. From these principles we developed a disciplined approach including the following techniques:

symbolic names for data items and values
special brackets to indicate type of name
templates for value descriptions
standard forms
inputs described as resources
outputs described in terms of effects
demand versus periodic functions
output values given as functions of conditions and events
consistent notation for conditions and events
modes for describing equivalence classes of system states
special tables for consistency and completeness checking
undesired event classification
complementary lists of changes and fundamental assumptions.

This paper is only an introduction to the ideas that are illustrated in the requirements document [5]. The document is a fully worked-out example; no details have been left out to simplify the problem. Developing and applying the techniques required approximately seventeen man-months of effort. The document is available to anyone interested in pursuing the ideas. Most engineering is accomplished by emulating models. We believe that our document is a good model of requirements documentation.

Acknowledgment

The techniques described in this paper were developed by the author together with D. Parnas, J. Shore, and J. Kallander. The author thanks E. Britton, H. S. Elovitz, D. Parnas, J. Shore, and D. Weiss for their careful and constructive reviews of the manuscript.

References

[1] P. Brinch Hansen, *Operating Systems Principles*. Englewood Cliffs, NJ: Prentice-Hall, 1973.
[2] E. W. Dijkstra, "Co-operating sequential processes," in *Programming Languages*, F. Genuys, Ed. New York: Academic, 1968, pp. 43-112.
[3] —, *A Discipline of Programming*. Englewood Cliffs, NJ: Prentice-Hall, 1977.
[4] J. V. Guttag, "Abstract data types and the development of data structures," *Commun. Ass. Comput. Mach.*, vol. 20, pp. 396-404, June 1976.
[5] K. Heninger, J. Kallander, D. L. Parnas, and J. Shore, *Software Requirements for the A-7E Aircraft*, Naval Res. Lab., Washington, DC, Memo Rep. 3876, Nov. 27, 1978.
[6] C. A. R. Hoare, "Monitors: An operating system structuring concept," *Commun. Ass. Comput. Mach.*, vol. 17, pp. 549-557, Oct. 1974.
[7] J. Howard, "Proving monitors," *Commun. Ass. Comput. Mach.*, vol. 19, pp. 273-279, May 1976.
[8] R. Lipton, *On Synchronization Primitive Systems*, Ph.D. dissertation, Carnegie-Mellon Univ., Pittsburgh, PA, 1973.
[9] B. Liskov and S. Zilles, "Specification techniques for data abstractions," *IEEE Trans. Software Eng.*, vol. SE-1, pp. 7-19, Mar. 1975.
[10] B. Liskov and V. Berzins, "An appraisal of program specifications," in *Proc. Conf. on Research Directions in Software Technology*, Oct. 10-12, 1977, pp. 13.1-13.24.
[11] D. L. Parnas, "Information distribution aspects of design methodology," in *Proc. Int. Fed. Inform. Processing Congr.*, Aug. 1971, vol. TA-3.
[12] —, "On the criteria to be used in decomposing systems into modules," *Commun. Ass. Comput. Mach.*, vol. 15, pp. 1053-1058, Dec. 1972.
[13] D. L. Parnas and G. Handzel, *More on Specification Techniques for Software Modules*, Fachbereich Informatik, Technische Hochschule Darmstadt, Darmstadt, W. Germany, 1975.
[14] D. L. Parnas and H. Wurges, "Response to undesired events in software systems," in *Proc. 2nd Int. Conf. Software Eng.*, 1976, pp. 437-446.
[15] D. L. Parnas, *Use of Abstract Interfaces in the Development of Software for Embedded Computer Systems*, Naval Res. Lab., Washington, DC, Rep. 8047, 1977.
[16] —, "The use of precise specifications in the development of software," in *Proc. Int. Fed. Inform. Processing Congr.*, 1977.
[17] —, "Designing software for ease of extension and contraction," in *Proc. 3rd Int. Conf. Software Eng.*, May 1978.
[18] D. L. Parnas and K. Heninger, "Implementing processes in HAS," in *Software Engineering Principles*, Naval Res. Lab., Washington, DC, course notes, 1978, Document HAS.9.

[19] D. L. Parnas, "Desired system behavior in undesired situations," in *Software Engineering Principles*, Naval Res. Lab., Washington, DC, course notes, 1978, Document UE.1.

[20] O. Roubine and L. Robinson, *SPECIAL Reference Manual*, Stanford Res. Inst., Menlo Park, CA, SRI Tech. Rep. CSL-45, SRI project 4828, 3rd ed., 1977.

[21] A. C. Shaw, *The Logical Design of Operating Systems*. Englewood Cliffs, NJ: Prentice-Hall, 1974.

[22] D. M. Weiss, *The MUDD Report: A Case Study of Navy Software Development Practices*, Naval Res. Lab., Washington, DC, Rep. 7909, 1975.

Kathryn L. Heninger received the B.A. degree in English from Stanford University, Stanford, CA, in 1972, the M.S.L.S. degree in library science in 1975 and the M.S. degree in computer science in 1977, both from the University of North Carolina, Chapel Hill.

She is presently a Computer Scientist for the Information Systems Staff at the Naval Research Laboratory, Washington, DC. Her research interests include program design methodologies and parallel processing.

TWO PAIRS OF EXAMPLES IN THE

JACKSON APPROACH TO SYSTEM DEVELOPMENT

J R Cameron

Michael Jackson Systems Ltd
21 Old Devonshire Rd
London SW12 9RD England

Abstract

The Jackson System Development method (JSD) develops formal system specifications
in a number of distinct steps. The specifications are written in terms of sequential processes; the early steps made a description or model of the relevant
external reality; the later steps add the functional requirement; the specifications are implemented in a series of mechanisable transformations. The method
is illustrated by two pairs of examples, each pair having rather similar
specifications, but different likely implementations.

1. INTRODUCTION

Conventional system development emphasises an
early definition of requirements, and the early
decomposition of a problem into subproblems. This
approach has at least the following disadvantages.

(1) The user is usually unable to state the
system requirements.

(2) Demonstrating that an implementation meets
the requirements is difficult.

(3) The decomposition into subproblems is
usually based on machine oriented
considerations.

(4) The decomposition is usually imprecisely
formulated and is only made precise by
further decomposition. This often comes
too late to change a poor initial decision.

JSD aims to make improvements by rearranging the
order decisions are made in a development, and by
making the consequences of each decision more
explicit.

In particular, before system requirements are
directly addressed, there is a significant modelling phase in which an abstraction of the relevant
external world is agreed with the user. This

model is realised as a set of long running sequential processes (conceptually each having its own
dedicated processor). Note that neither of the 2
JSD uses of model - the abstraction in the external
world and the realisation of the abstraction as
computer processes - are equivalent to 'model' as
used by some other writers. Model is often used
to describe an abstraction of the system itself
for the purposes of development or of performance
evaluation.

The requirements or system function is then specified by constructing new long running sequential
processes, which access information through their
connections with the model processes.

The finished specification is formally stated, is
in principle directly compilable, but not into an
efficient system. The usual implementation phase
consists of:

(1) transformations of the texts of the model and
function processes which make up the specification

(2) construction of special purpose scheduling
programs to run the specification processes.

Program inversion (ref 1,2) is the prototypical

example of a JSD transformation. (The transformation is from a process to a procedure by including a suspend and resume mechanism at each relevant I/O operation.) The separation of state vectors (the textpointer and local variables of a process) to allow one text and many state vectors to implement many identical processes is another. These transformations can be mechanised.

Above all JSD decomposes the development in a way other than merely by decomposing the system. In this sense it can properly claim to be a method.

The main JSD phases are model, function and implementation. These phases are further subdivided but these further divisions are not considered in this paper, either in general or in the solutions to the examples.

2. MAJOR JSD PHASES AND NOTATIONS

2.1 MODELLING

We are going to view the finished system as an information system about the real world which is described by the model.

The JSD model describes the evolution of the external entities of interest. The time varying behaviour of entities is central to JSD. (Contrast data models built out of data analysis, which do not describe the evolution of entities, only their permissible states.)

The model description covers the complete period during which the entity is of interest. If a mortgage lasts for 25 years, then the model of the mortgage covers all 25 years. An aircraft in an air traffic control system may be of interest for 3 hours; the model of the aircraft spans this complete period.

JSD models are running models. At build time we specify what can happen to an entity. As the system runs, input from the external world tells us what did happen, and the model is co-ordinated with the reality.

A JSD model has no outputs, nor is it concerned with system outputs. It merely records and reflects - models - a set of interesting external events.

Why modelling is so important.

(1) By including an explicit modelling phase we aim to avoid the mutual misunderstandings between user and designer which dog traditional system development.

(2) The model is the user's world (part of it anyway) and that is a good place to start. Moreover users naturally describe things in terms of events, and the order they can happen, so it is reasonable to start by formalising his view of these processes.

(3) The model is indirectly equivalent to a range of functions and it is easier to specify this range than the particular outputs required.

(4) The model defines the terms needed to describe system requirements.

Modelling notations. A diagrammatic and an equivalent textual notation are both used to specify the model processes and the later function processes and scheduling programs.

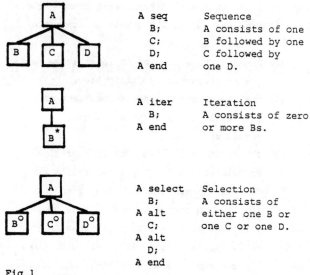

A seq	Sequence
B;	A consists of one
C;	B followed by one
D;	C followed by
A end	one D.
A iter	Iteration
B;	A consists of zero
A end	or more Bs.
A select	Selection
B;	A consists of
A alt	either one B or
C;	one C or one D.
A alt	
D;	
A end	

Fig 1

There is also a textual posit ... quit construct for problems requiring backtracking (ref 1,2).

In JSD an entity is an object or person who performs or suffers a number of time ordered actions (events). The model consists of 1 or more diagrams; each diagram has an entity as the root and the actions as leaves; together they describe the real world time constraints on the actions.

2.2 FUNCTION

<u>Extra function notations.</u> Fig 2 illustrates the notations used in the system specification diagram which shows the connections between model and function processes.

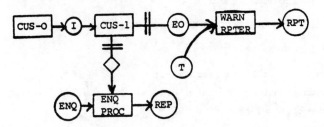

<u>Fig 2</u>

The rectangles are processes. The circles are data streams (unbounded FIFO queues). The diamonds are state vector connection: the process at the arrowhead may examine the state vector of the process to which it is connected.

In this example the model consisted of CUS-O, I and CUS-1. The suffix -O denotes the real world entity, the real CUStomer; the suffix -1 denotes the computer realisation of the same abstraction. The input I comes into the system to synchronise and coordinate the actions of CUS-1 with those of CUS-O.

The double bars denote relative multiplicity of processes: many CUS-1 for one ENQPROC; many CUS-1 for one WARNRPTER.

In this example ENQPROC and WARNRPTER were function processes. ENQPROC answered ad hoc enquiries about the CUStomer by examining the appropriate CUS-1's state. WARNRPTER produced periodic reports based on information written by I/O operations directly embedded in the model. The arrival of a record on the T data stream defines the end of a period. Note that both ENQPROC and WARNRPTER are also long running processes: ENQPROC answers all the ENQuiries; WARNRPTER produces all the reports.

CUS-1 will lag behind CUS-O, perhaps only by a fraction of a second, perhaps considerably if it is scheduled unfavourably. The exact amount of lag is not part of the JSD specification.

Because the result of an enquiry to ENQPROC is based on the current state of CUS-1, not CUS-O, there is a looseness in the specification. The answer depends on how up to date is CUS-1. This looseness is a deliberate part of JSD.

The arrangement of the arrows from EO and T indicates that WARNRPTER consumes a single data stream. The implied merge process is not exactly specified. Again there is a deliberate looseness in the specification. Cumulatively WARNRPTER consumes all EO but the division into periods is to some extent arbitrary.

This looseness can be avoided in JSD specifications but the possibility of including a degree of indeterminacy allows a considerable simplification. Ad hoc enquiries about the balance of a bank account give out of date replies, out of date to an extent which is unclear. And noone minds if a cheque is missing from the bottom of a monthly statement, provided it appears at the top of the next.

In each of these cases the exact operation of a process B depends on the scheduling of a process A. In JSD this relationship is never reciprocal.

2.3 IMPLEMENTATION

How do we assure ourselves that an implementation meets a requirements specification? Traditionally by testing, though the disadvantages of testing are well known. Mathematical proof has possibilities, but they have not been realised. Moving from specification to implementation in a series of transformations is an attractive 3rd possibility. Each transformation can be proved correct in general; an implementor can choose any succession of the standard transformations and know that the implementation is correct. Since the main transformations can be mechanised, he may even be sure that they have been correctly carried out.

Of course this presupposes that we have a suitable specification language to start with. We assert here that the networks of long running processes outlined above are such a suitable language.

In fact, for DP systems at least, some element of

transformation is necessary in any approach which separates problem oriented issues from machine oriented issues. Systems are about large numbers of entities (10^3-10^8 processes) which perform actions over a long period (10^4 days) at infrequent intervals (10^{-1} per day). Systems are run in target environments which have few processors (maybe 1), which run for short periods (maybe less than 1 day) but which can handle many transactions. This mismatch between problem structure and target machine structure can only be bridged by some type of transformation.

Approaches based only on the successive refinement of a single system structure (top down design, structured analysis and design, stepwise refinement) must, whether it is admitted or not, be refining the machine oriented structure. They start by considering the implementation.

Implementation notations

Q has been inverted with respect to 2 of its data streams to become a subroutine of P. (n+1 lines imply inversion with respect to n data streams.)

Fig 3

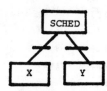

The components X and Y are invoked by SCHED (perhaps many times, order unspecified), but each runs to completion on each invocation.

Fig 4

When invoked, an inverted process partially executes. For our long running processes, partial execution on invocation is very much the norm. However as we near a final implementation, the notation in fig 4 allows the description of jobs, runs and procedures which do execute completely on invocation.

Subscripts on process names indicate that the process has been cut into pieces and we are referring to one of the parts.

Fig 5

Separate implementation of different parts of a

process - program dismemberment - is an important transformation, especially for function processes and scheduling processes.

Traditional DP symbols for e.g. tapes and disks are also sometimes used.

3. THE CAR RALLY AND GOLDEN HANDSHAKE EXAMPLES

3.1 THE CAR RALLY

In a car rally, drivers start from either checkpoint-1 or checkpoint-2 and drive the course in fig 6 without stopping. At each checkpoint there is a remote terminal. As each driver passes (or starts or finishes), an operator keys in the car-id;

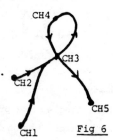

Fig 6

this causes a record to be sent to a single queue at a central computer; the record contains the car-id, the time and the checkpoint-id. A driver scores $A(t_1)+C(t_2)+D(t_3)+E(t_4)$ points or $B(t_1)+C(t_2)+D(t_3)+E(t_4)$ points (where t_j is the time taken for the jth section of the course and A,B,C,D,E are given functions) according to whether he started at CH-1 or CH-2. The program has to calculate each driver's total score and output it to a device which will display it on a scoreboard opposite the main grandstand. Assume all the drivers finish the course correctly.

3.2 THE GOLDEN HANDSHAKE SYSTEM

A company gives each employee a golden handshake when they retire; the amount depends on the length of time he or she has worked at the various jobs in the company. The career path of all employees is: start as office boy or messenger; promoted to clerk; promoted to manager; demoted to clerk (usually some other title); retires. When an employee starts, is promoted, demoted or retires, a record containing his employee-id, the date and a code discribing his new position (OB, ME, CL, MA, RE) is created and sent to the DP department. A program is required to compute the golden handshakes so that the cheques can be presented at the official retirement party. The golden handshake is $\$(A(t_1)+C(t_2)+D(t_3)+E(t_4))$ or $\$(B(t_1)+C(t_2)+D(t_3)+E(t_4))$ according to whether he started as an office boy or a messenger (where

t_j is the number of days spent in the jth company
job and A,B,C,D,E are given functions). Assume
that all employees follow this career path exactly.

3.3 COMPARISON OF THE TWO SYSTEMS

The specifications are identical in almost every
respect. The career path of an employee is the
same as the route of the rally. In each case the
input is a merged serial stream of records each of
which has 3 fields, the car-id/employee-id, the
ch-id/job-code, and the time/date. The same calculation produces the output. Each problem even
has a scheduling constraint - output must be produced quickly enough for the scoreboard/retirement
party. The Golden Handshake system just runs more
slowly. The comparison emphasises the abstraction
of the time dimension in the long running processes
used in JSD models and specifications. (In the GH
system a single process may run for 40 years.)

3.4 MODELLING PHASE

A misleading point. JSD does not normally start
from a description as detailed and precise as 3.1
and 3.2.

CAR is the only entity. The actions are to start
and end the various sections of the course. For
convenience in fig 7 the actions are identified by
the appropriate checkpoint-ids.

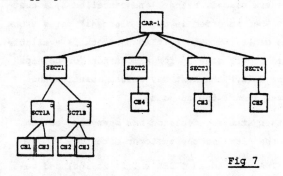

Fig 7

The decisions made at this stage are precise; no
later steps are needed to remove ambiguity.

The implications are also clear. From here we may
only develop systems which supply information about
cars driving the sections of this course in this
way. The model supports a defined range of functions; we have not yet considered which ones we

actually want.

Decisions about the abstraction of the user's world
are here made in considerable detail, ideally by
the user with some help from someone familiar with
the formal diagrammatic language. Traditionally
many of these decisions are made very late in the
programming phase by whoever finally builds the
'update' program.

3.5 FUNCTION PHASE

Reporting on the car's total mark can be done by
direct embedding in the CAR-1 processes. Unusually,
no extra process is needed.

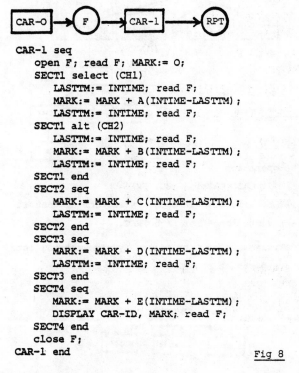

```
CAR-1 seq
    open F; read F; MARK:= 0;
    SECT1 select (CH1)
        LASTTM:= INTIME; read F;
        MARK:= MARK + A(INTIME-LASTTM);
        LASTTM:= INTIME; read F;
    SECT1 alt (CH2)
        LASTTM:= INTIME; read F;
        MARK:= MARK + B(INTIME-LASTTM);
        LASTTM:= INTIME; read F;
    SECT1 end
    SECT2 seq
        MARK:= MARK + C(INTIME-LASTTM);
        LASTTM:= INTIME; read F;
    SECT2 end
    SECT3 seq
        MARK:= MARK + D(INTIME-LASTTM);
        LASTTM:= INTIME; read F;
    SECT3 end
    SECT4 seq
        MARK:= MARK + E(INTIME-LASTTM);
        DISPLAY CAR-ID, MARK; read F;
    SECT4 end
    close F;
CAR-1 end
```

Fig 8

There are as many instances of CAR-1 as there are
cars in the rally.

3.6 IMPLEMENTATION

Almost all implementations of this system will
start with 2 basic transformations.
    (1) Invert CAR-1 with respect to its input F.
    (2) Separate the state vectors of the CAR-1
        processes.

For an on-line implementation the operation
        CALL CAR-1 (FREC, SV)
must be executed as soon as an FREC is available.

The operation will probably be part of a module (along with the SV accessing) under the control of a teleprocessing monitor.

We concentrate here on a batch implementation with monthly update, with the state vectors stored on a serially accessible medium. (Unless the cars are very slow this had better be the Golden Handshake system.) We design a special purpose SCHEDuler to consume the merged input stream of all the Fs and marker records which show the month ends.

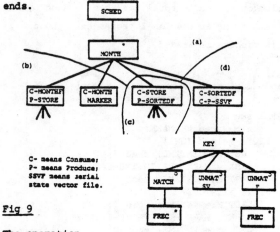

C- means Consume;
P- means Produce;
SSVF means serial
state vector file.

Fig 9

The operation

CALL CAR-1 (FREC, SV)

will be allocated into this structure so that it is executed once for each FREC.

SCHEDuler can be implemented by dismembering into the 4 parts as shown.

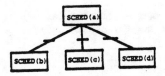

Fig 10

SCHED(a) will almost certainly be implemented by operator instructions: 'each month run SCHED(b) until the month marker (2nd Thursday of month) and then run the SORT ...'.

SCHED(b) could be operator instructions - 'keep input cards on this tray' - or a data entry program. SCHED(c) is a standard SORT. SCHED(d), the only part which invokes the specified processes, is the monthly job which runs the system.

Notice that the SCHEDuler contains a significant

portion of the finished system, including the SORT, but also that schedulers follow rather standard patterns.

The finished system consists of a monthly job and a combination of software and operator instructions to prepare the input. The code in the monthly job comes partly from the scheduler (the upper level collate), partly from the model (the structure of the inverted subroutine), and partly from the function (the embedded operations).

4. TWO ORDER PROCESSING SYSTEMS

4.1 MODEL OF VERSION (1)

In a simple order processing system ORDER and STOCK ITEM were chosen as entities; PLACE, AMEND, DELAY, ALLOCATE and CANCEL were the actions of an ORDER; INTRODUCE, ISSUE, RECEIVE and WRITE OFF were the actions of STOCK ITEM.

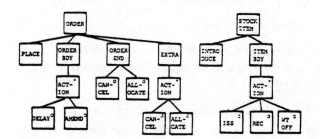

Fig 11

Orders are placed, amended and cancelled by a customer. When an order is due a clerk allocates stock to the order, or delays it if no stock is available. Delayed orders come up for allocation (or perhaps another delay) the next day unless meantime the customer amends the due date.

In this system the decision has been made not to model the clerk or the customer directly.

The EXTRA part in an ORDER's life is included because the clerk and the customer are not well enough coordinated to prevent a CANCEL after an ALLOCATE or vice versa.

This model could support functions such as: ad hoc enquiries about particular orders, or about stock levels; apology notes to customers whose orders have been delayed; warnings about low stock levels; periodic reports about outstanding orders analysed

relative to the current stock level; lists of allocated orders from which picking lists can be made
etc.

4.2 AUTOMATION OF ORDER ALLOCATION

In this version 2 of the system we replace the
clerk by a computer process which will delay and
allocate orders. The model is reduced; less happens in the world external to the system. Fig 12
shows the structure of ORDER without the actions
DELAY and ALLOCATE.

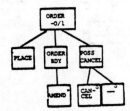

Fig 12

In the function phase, 2 new processes must be
added, ALLOCATOR which is the direct replacement
of the clerk, and ORDER-2 which is a functionally
oriented view of an order and which may well have
the same structure as the modelled ORDER in
version 1.

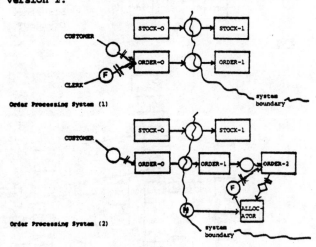

Order Processing System (1)

Order Processing System (2)

Fig 13.

Fig 13 shows the system specification diagrams for
the realised model in version 1, for the realised
model + allocator function in version 2, both with
an informal indication of what is happening outside the system boundary. The records on F,
supplied by the clerk in version 1, are supplied

by the ALLOCATOR in version 2 (though possibly by
following a different algorithm). ALLOCATOR is of
course a long running process; it performs all the
allocations in the system's life; arrival of a
record on H triggers one round of allocation.

This type of function is called an interactive
function in JSD. Interactive functions are closely
connected with automation. They are specified
before other types of function, immediately after
the modelling phase. Since the extent of the required automation is often not clear at the outset,
the subphase dealing with interactive functions
gives an opportunity to reconsider what will happen
externally in the real world, and perhaps as a
result to redefine the model of that external real
world.

Neither of these systems are developed further here.

5. A SIMPLE LIFT SYSTEM

N.B. An elevator in the USA is a lift in England.

5.1 MODELLING PHASE

Our system must control a lift which operates in a
building with 4 floors (0(=ground), 1, 2 and 3).
At first we assume there are only 4 request buttons
all inside the lift. Pressing button j means a
user wants to go to floor j. Later we will add 6
request buttons - up buttons on floors 0,1,2 and
down buttons on floors 1,2,3.

The model turns out to have 2 entities: LIFT with
actions ARRIVE FLOOR(j) and LEAVE FLOOR(j), and
BUTTON with action be PRESSed.

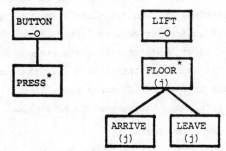

Fig 14

(Fig 14 assumes the lift starts between floors.)

The system specification diagram of the realised
model (fig 15) implies that a record can be input
to BUTTON-1 when the real BUTTON-0 is PRESSed.

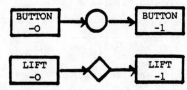

Fig 15

The connection LIFT-O to LIFT-1 is via sensors on each floor. Sensor(j) sets a value 1 (directly accessible by our system) if the lift is within 6" of its home position at floor j and sets a value 0 otherwise. The sensors do not generate records. They must be examined by LIFT-1 (actually continually) on LIFT-1's initiative - hence the state connection between LIFT-O and LIFT-1 in fig 15.

LIFT-1 therefore needs a more elaborate structure than LIFT-O, simply to realise in a computer process the same actions.

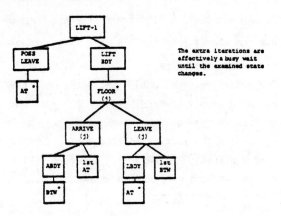

The extra iterations are effectively a busy wait until the examined state changes.

Fig 16

The model of LIFT contains very little. Actions like STOP and START are excluded because they are not needed, and would, in any case, need an extra set of sensors to realise. No decisions have been taken about the controlling algorithm. The model of LIFT expresses little more than the constraints of the lift shaft; it describes what can happen to the lift, not what we want to make happen.

5.2 FUNCTION PHASE

In the specification below, the lift only waits at the ground floor; when it moves, it goes all the way to the top, stopping to service requests on the way, and then back down, also servicing requests on the way. The lamp is switched on when

there is an outstanding request - defined as a PRESS received since LIFTCONTROL last told the lift to stop at that floor.

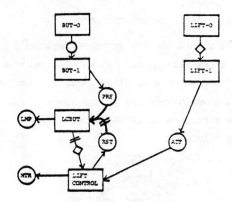

Fig 17

System
Specification
Diagram

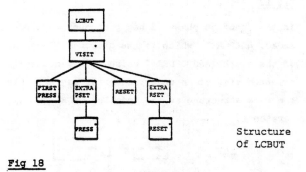

Fig 18

Structure
Of LCBUT

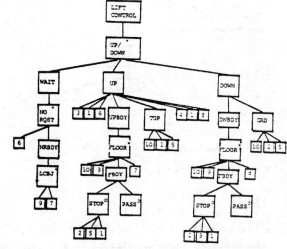

1. MOTOR:= ON
2. MOTOR:= OFF
3. POLARITY:= UP
4. POLARITY:= DOWN
5. write RST(K)
6. K:= 1
7. K:= K+1
8. K:= K-1
9. get SV of LCBUT(K)
10. read ATF

Fig 19

Structure of
LIFTCONTROL
With Operations
Allocated

```
LIFTCONTROL iter
  UPDOWN seq
    WAIT iter
      NORQST seq
        K:= 1;
        NRBDY iter while (K LE 3)
          get SV of LCBUT(K)
      WAIT quit (LCBUT(K) is PRESSed)
          K:= K+1;
        NRBDY end
      NORQST end
    WAIT end
    UP seq
      POLARITY:= UP;
      MOTOR:= ON;
      K:= 1;
      UPBDY iter while (K LE 2)
        FLOOR seq
          read ATF;
          get SV of LCBUT(K)
          FBDY select (LCBUT(K) IS PRESSed)
            MOTOR:= OFF;
            write RST(K);
            MOTOR:= ON;
          FBDY alt (LCBUT(K) NOT PRESSed)
          FBDY end
          K:= K+1;
        FLOOR end
      UPBDY end
      TOP seq
        read ATF; MOTOR:= OFF; write RST(K);
      TOP end
    UP end
    DOWN seq
      POLARITY:= DOWN; MOTOR:= ON; K:= K+1;
      DNBDY iter while (K GE 1)
        FLOOR seq
          read ATF;
          get SV of LCBUT (K);
          FBDY select (LCBUT(K) is PRESSed)
            MOTOR:= OFF; write RST(K); MOTOR:= ON;
          FBDY alt (LCBUT(K) NOT PRESSed)
          FBDY end
          K:= K-1;
        FLOOR end
      DNBDY end
      GRD seq
        read ATF; MOTOR:= OFF; write RST(K);
      GRD end
    DOWN end
  UPDOWN and
LIFTCONTROL end
```

Complete
Structure
Text of
LIFTCONTROL

Fig 20

LIFT-1 outputs an ATF record when it arrives at a floor. When travelling LIFTCONTROL is usually hung up waiting to read the next ATF record. When waiting at floor.0; LIFTCONTROL continually examines the SVs of LCBUT(j) for j=1,2,3.

To complete the specification: write the text of BUT-1 and LIFT-1 with their embedded output operations; write the text of LCBUT with the embedded **SWITCH ON** and **SWITCH OFF** operations.

A different algorithm. To change the service algorithm, simply replace LIFTCONTROL. We may, for example, want the lift only to travel up as far as the highest request, and down as far as the

lowest, returning to wait at floor 0 when there are no outstanding requests at all.

Ten buttons, 3 up buttons, 3 down buttons, 4 in the lift itself. Remarkably few changes are needed. LIFT-0 and LIFT-1 are unchanged. BUT-0, BUT-1 and LCBUT are also unchanged except of course now there are 10 of them. (Think about this; the buttons have different meanings, as the original 4 did, one from another, but they are still only PRESSed and in LCBUT RESET.) The only real change is that the conditions in LIFTCONTROL are much more complex.

Implementation. A full implementation is not developed here. We only remark that BUT-1 only copies its input to output; that there are 6 other processes in the original version; that a simple implementation on one microprocessor can be based on a round robin scheduler.

5.3 COMPARISON OF LIFT SYSTEM AND ORDER PROCESSING SYSTEM(2)

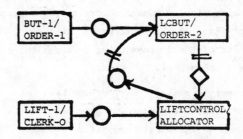

Fig 21

The patterns of processes in the system specification diagrams for these 2 systems are identical. (Of course the internal structures and texts do differ.)

LIFTCONTROL is an allocator of the single resource, the lift, between the competing claims of the outstanding request. LIFTCONTROL can be regarded as the replacement of the manual lift operator in the same way that the ALLOCATOR replaced the clerk, but in the lift problem, there was no ambiguity about what external world had to be modelled.

The near identity of these problems throughout the modelling and function phases is a sign of our success at separating specification from implementation. Many approaches to system development, (particularly those based on successive decompositions of the system function, as has already been suggested) have specification decisions and implementation decisions hopelessly entangled. The design question is posed: 'how to decompose the system?'. But often the design question is not much more than: 'knowing as little as I do know about the problem, what implementation decision now is least likely to prove embarrassing later?'.

6. SUMMING UP

The order of decision making in JSD differs considerably from that of the traditional approach. Many traditional requirements decisions belong in the JSD function phase; many traditional design decisions belong in JSD implementation; many JSD detailed modelling decisions are made very late by a programmer.

The method promises considerable advantages: better communication with the user; deferral of implementation decisions; the clarity provided by that separation of concerns forced by a genuine decomposition of the development task; the avoidance of the disadvantages referred to in the introduction.

The principle phases (only) of JSD have been outlined and some simple examples partially developed to illustrate and motivate them.

The method has important implications in a number of other areas not explored here. For example:-
System maintenance using JSD. The model is more robust than the functional requirement; this is another important reason for basing the development on an agreed model. System maintenance is viewed in JSD as the modification of processes part way through their execution.

Project organisation. The analyst/programmer division is meaningless in JSD. Instead there is a distinction between user oriented people who work closely with the user developing specifications and machine oriented people who transform processes, write special purpose schedulers, organise SV access paths on databases etc.

Background. JSD has developed out of JSP, a programming method. JSP is described in ref (1), (2). The development can be traced in chapter 11 of (1) and in (3).

Acknowledgements. Many of the ideas presented here are due to Michael Jackson. Our numerous discussions have meant that even ideas I think are mine are actually partly his.
Richard Beck of STL Ltd gave me the Lift problem.

References

(1) Jackson M A; Principles of Program Design; Academic Press, 1975.

(2) JSP: A Practical Method of Program Design; Leif Ingevaldsson; Chartwell Bratt, London 1979. Also in Swedish, Studentlitteratur.

(3) Information Systems: Modelling, Sequencing and Transformations; M A Jackson; in Proceedings of the 3rd International Conference on Software Engineering; ACM/IEEE.

PSL/PSA: A Computer-Aided Technique for Structured Documentation and Analysis of Information Processing Systems

DANIEL TEICHROEW AND ERNEST A. HERSHEY, III

Abstract—PSL/PSA is a computer-aided structured documentation and analysis technique that was developed for, and is being used for, analysis and documentation of requirements and preparation of functional specifications for information processing systems. The present status of requirements definition is outlined as the basis for describing the problem which PSL/PSA is intended to solve. The basic concepts of the Problem Statement Language are introduced and the content and use of a number of standard reports that can be produced by the Problem Statement Analyzer are briefly described.

The experience to date indicates that computer-aided methods can be used to aid system development during the requirements definition stage and that the main factors holding back such use are not so much related to the particular characteristics and capabilities of PSL/PSA as they are to organizational considerations involved in any change in methodology and procedure.

Index Terms—Computer-aided documentation, problem statement analysis, PSL/PSA, requirements analysis.

I. INTRODUCTION

ORGANIZATIONS now depend on computer-based information processing systems for many of the tasks involving data (recording, storing, retrieving, processing, etc.). Such systems are man-made, the process consists of a number of activities: perceiving a need for a system, determining what it should do for the organization, designing it, constructing and assembling the components, and finally testing the system prior to installing it. The process requires a great deal of effort, usually over a considerable period of time.

Throughout the life of a system it exists in several different "forms." Initially, the system exists as a concept or a proposal at a very high level of abstraction. At the point where it becomes operational it exists as a collection of rules and executable object programs in a particular computing environment. This environment consists of hardware and hard software such as the operating system, plus other components such as procedures which are carried out manually. In between the system exists in various intermediary forms.

The process by which the initial concept evolves into an operational system consists of a number of activities each of which makes the concept more concrete. Each activity takes the results of some of the previous activities and produces new results so that the progression eventually results in an operational system. Most of the activities are data processing activities, in that they use data and information to produce other data and information. Each activity can be regarded as receiving specifications or requirements from preceding activities and producing data which are regarded as specifications or requirements by one or more succeeding activities.

Since many individuals may be involved in the system development process over considerable periods of time and these or other individuals have to maintain the system once it is operating, it is necessary to record descriptions of the system as it evolves. This is usually referred to as "documentation."

In practice, the emphasis in documentation is on describing the system in the final form so that it can be maintained. Ideally, however, each activity should be documented so that the results it produces become the specification for succeeding activities. This does not happen in practice because the communications from one activity to succeeding activities is accomplished either by having the same person carrying out the activities, by oral communication among individuals in a project, or by notes which are discarded after their initial use.

This results in projects which proceed without any real possibility for management review and control. The systems are not ready when promised, do not perform the function the users expected, and cost more than budgeted.

Most organizations, therefore, mandate that the system development process be divided into phases and that certain documentation be produced by the end of each phase so that progress can be monitored and corrections made when necessary. These attempts, however, leave much to be desired and most organizations are attempting to improve the methods by which they manage their system development [20], [6].

This paper is concerned with one approach to improving systems development. The approach is based on three premises. The first is that more effort and attention should be devoted to the front end of the process where a proposed system is being described from the user's point of view [2], [14], [3]. The second premise is that the computer should be used in the development process since systems development involves large amounts of information processing. The third premise is that a computer-aided approach to systems development must start with "documentation."

This paper describes a computer-aided technique for documentation which consists of the following:

1) The results of each of the activities in the system development process are recorded in computer processible form as they are produced.

2) A computerized data base is used to maintain all the basic data about the system.

3) The computer is used to produce hard copy documentation when required.

Manuscript received June 29, 1976; revised September 20, 1976.

The authors are with the Department of Industrial and Operations Engineering, University of Michigan, Ann Arbor, MI 48109.

Reprinted from *IEEE Transactions on Software Engineering*, Volume SE-3, Number 1, January 1977, pages 41–48. Copyright © 1977 by The Institute of Electrical and Electronics Engineers, Inc.

The part of the technique which is now operational is known as PSL/PSA. Section II is devoted to a brief description of system development as a framework in which to compare manual and computer-aided documentation methods. The Problem Statement Language (PSL) is described in Section III. The reports which can be produced by the Problem Statement Analyzer (PSA) are described in Section IV. The status of the system, results of experience to date, and planned developments are outlined in Section V.

II. Logical Systems Design

The computer-aided documentation system described in Sections III and IV of this paper is designed to play an integral role during the initial stages in the system development process. A generalized model of the whole system development process is given in Section II-A. The final result of the initial stages is a document which here will be called the System Definition Report. The desired contents of this document are discussed in Section II-B. The activities required to produce this document manually are described in Section II-C and the changes possible through the use of computer-aided methods are outlined in Section II-D.

A. A Model of the System Development Process

The basic steps in the life cycle of information systems (initiation, analysis, design, construction, test, installation, operation, and termination) appeared in the earliest applications of computers to organizational problems (see for example, [17], [1], [4], and [7]). The need for more formal and comprehensive procedures for carrying out the life cycle was recognized; early examples are the IBM SOP publications [5], the Philips ARDI method [8], and the SDC method [23]. In the last few years, a large number of books and papers on this subject have been published [11], [19].

Examination of these and many other publications indicate that there is no general agreement on what phases the development process should be divided into, what documentation should be produced at each phase, what it should contain, or what form it should be presented in. Each organization develops its own methods and standards.

In this section a generalized system development process will be described as it might be conducted in an organization which has a Systems Department responsible for developing, operating, and maintaining computer based information processing systems. The System Department belongs to some higher unit in the organization and itself has some subunits, each with certain functions (see for example, [24]). The System Department has a system development standard procedure which includes a project management system and documentation standards.

A request for a new system is initiated by some unit in the organization or the system may be proposed by the System Department. An initial document is prepared which contains information about why a new system is needed and outlines its major functions. This document is reviewed and, if approved, a senior analyst is assigned to prepare a more detailed document. The analyst collects data by interviewing users and studying the present system. He then produces a report describing his proposed system and showing how it will satisfy the requirements. The report will also contain the implementation plan, benefit/cost analysis, and his recommendations. The report is reviewed by the various organizational units involved. If it passes this review it is then included with other requests for the resources of the System Department and given a priority. Up to this point the investment in the proposed system is relatively small.

At some point a project team is formed, a project leader and team members are assigned, and given authority to proceed with the development of the system. A steering group may also be formed. The project is assigned a schedule in accordance with the project management system and given a budget. The schedule will include one or more target dates. The final target date will be the date the system (or its first part if it is being done in parts) is to be operational. There may also be additional target dates such as beginning of system test, beginning of programming, etc.

B. Logical System Design Documentation

In this paper, it is assumed that the system development procedure requires that the proposed system be reviewed before a major investment is made in system construction. There will therefore be another target date at which the "logical" design of the proposed system is reviewed. On the basis of this review the decision may be to proceed with the physical design and construction, to revise the proposed system, or to terminate the project.

The review is usually based on a document prepared by the project team. Sometimes it may consist of more than one separate document; for example, in the systems development methodology used by the U. S. Department of Defense [21] for non-weapons systems, development of the life cycle is divided into phases. Two documents are produced at the end of the Definition subphase of the Development phase: a Functional Description, and a Data Requirements Document.

Examination of these and many documentation requirements show that a Systems Definition Report contains five major types of information:

1) a description of the organization and where the proposed system will fit; showing how the proposed system will improve the functioning of the organization or otherwise meet the needs which lead to the project;

2) a description of the operation of the proposed system in sufficient detail to allow the users to verify that it will in fact accomplish its objectives, and to serve as the specification for the design and construction of the proposed system if the project continuation is authorized;

3) a description of its proposed system implementation in sufficient detail to estimate the time and cost required;

4) the implementation plan in sufficient detail to estimate the cost of the proposed system and the time it will be available;

5) a benefit/cost analysis and recommendations.

In addition, the report usually also contains other miscellaneous information such as glossaries, etc.

C. Current Logical System Design Process

During the initial stages of the project the efforts of the team are directed towards producing the Systems Definition Report. Since the major item this report contains is the description of the proposed system from the user or logical point of view, the activities required to produce the report are called the logical system design process. The project team will start with the information already available and then perform a set of activities. These may be grouped into five major categories.

1) Data collection. Information about the information flow in the present system, user desires for new information, potential new system organization, etc., is collected and recorded.

2) Analysis. The data that have been collected are summarized and analyzed. Errors, omissions, and ambiguities are identified and corrected. Redundancies are identified. The results are prepared for review by appropriate groups.

3) Logical Design. Functions to be performed by the system are selected. Alternatives for a new system or modification of the present system are developed and examined. The "new" system is described.

4) Evaluation. The benefits and costs of the proposed system are determined to a suitable level of accuracy. The operational and functional feasibility of the system are examined and evaluated.

5) Improvements. Usually as a result of the evaluation a number of deficiencies in the proposed system will be discovered. Alternatives for improvement are identified and evaluated until further possible improvements are not judged to be worth additional effort. If major changes are made, the evaluation step may be repeated; further data collection and analysis may also be necessary.

In practice the type of activities outlined above may not be clearly distinguished and may be carried out in parallel or iteratively with increasing level of detail. Throughout the process, however it is carried out, results are recorded and documented.

It is widely accepted that documentation is a weak link in system development in general and in logical system design in particular. The representation in the documentation that is produced with present manual methods is limited to:

1) text in a natural language;
2) lists, tables, arrays, cross references;
3) graphical representation, figures, flowcharts.

Analysis of two reports showed the following number of pages for each type of information.

Form	Report A	Report B
text	90	117
lists and tables	207	165
charts and figures	28	54
total	335	336

The systems being documented are very complex and these methods of representation are not capable of adequately describing all the necessary aspects of a system for all those who must, or should, use the documentation. Consequently, documentation is

1) ambiguous: natural languages are not precise enough to describe systems and different readers may interpret a sentence in different ways;

2) inconsistent: since systems are large the documentation is large and it is very difficult to ensure that the documentation is consistent;

3) incomplete: there is usually not a sufficient amount of time to devote to documentation and with a large complex system it is difficult to determine what information is missing.

The deficiencies of manual documentation are compounded by the fact that systems are continually changing and it is very difficult to keep the documentation up-to-date.

Recently there have been attempts to improve manual documentation by developing more formal methodologies [16], [12], [13], [22], [15], [25]. These methods, even though they are designed to be used manually, have a formal language or representation scheme that is designed to alleviate the difficulties listed above. To make the documentation more useful for human beings, many of these methods use a graphical language.

D. Computer-Aided Logical System Design Process

In computer-aided logical system design the objective, as in the manual process, is to produce the System Definition Report and the process followed is essentially similar to that described above. The computer-aided design system has the following capabilities:

1) capability to describe information systems, whether manual or computerized, whether existing or proposed, regardless of application area;

2) ability to record such description in a computerized data base;

3) ability to incrementally add to, modify, or delete from the description in the data base;

4) ability to produce "hard copy" documentation for use by the analyst or the other users.

The capability to describe systems in computer processible form results from the use of the system description language called PSL. The ability to record such description in a data base, incrementally modify it, and on demand perform analysis and produce reports comes from the software package called the Problem Statement Analyzer (PSA). The Analyzer is controlled by a Command Language which is described in detail in [9] (Fig. 1).

The Problem Statement Language is outlined in Section III and described in detail in [10]. The use of PSL/PSA in computer-aided logical system design is described in detail in [18].

The use of PSL/PSA does not depend on any particular structure of the system development process or any standards on the format and content of hard copy documentation. It is therefore fully compatible with current procedures in most organizations that are developing and maintaining systems.

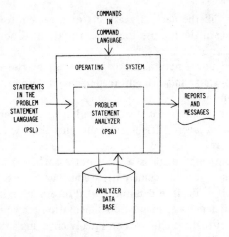

Fig. 1. The Problem Statement Analyzer.

Using this system, the data collected or developed during all five of the activities are recorded in machine-readable form and entered into the computer as it is collected. A data base is built during the process. These data can be analyzed by computer programs and intermediate documentation prepared on request. The Systems Definition Report then includes a large amount of material produced automatically from the data base.

The activities in logical system design are modified when PSL/PSA is used as follows:

1) Data collection: since most of the data must be obtained through personal contact, interviews will still be required. The data collected are recorded in machine-readable form. The intermediate outputs of PSA also provide convenient checklists for deciding what additional information is needed and for recording it for input.

2) Analysis: a number of different kinds of analysis can be performed on demand by PSA, and therefore need no longer be done manually.

3) Design: design is essentially a creative process and cannot be automated. However, PSA can make more data available to the designer and allow him to manipulate it more extensively. The results of his decisions are also entered into the data base.

4) Evaluation: PSA provides some rudimentary facilities for computing volume or work measures from the data in the problem statement.

5) Improvements: identification of areas for possible improvements is also a creative task; however, PSA output, particularly from the evaluation phase, may be useful to the analyst.

The System Definition Report will contain the same material as that described since the documentation must serve the same purpose. Furthermore, the same general format and representation is desirable.

1) Narrative information is necessary for human readability. This is stored as part of the data but is not analyzed by the computer program. However, the fact that it is displayed next to, or in conjunction with, the final description improves the ability of the analyst to detect discrepancies and inconsistencies.

2) Lists, tables, arrays, matrices. These representations are prepared from the data base. They are up-to-date and can be more easily rearranged in any desired order.

3) Diagrams and charts. The information from the data base can be represented in various graphical forms to display the relationships between objects.

III. PSL, A PROBLEM STATEMENT LANGUAGE

PSL is a language for describing systems. Since it is intended to be used to describe "proposed" systems it was called a Problem Statement Language because the description of a proposed system can be considered a "problem" to be solved by the system designers and implementors.

PSL is intended to be used in situations in which analysts now describe systems. The descriptions of systems produced using PSL are used for the same purpose as that produced manually. PSL may be used both in batch and interactive environments, and therefore only "basic" information about the system need to be stated in PSL. All "derived" information can be produced in hard copy form as required.

The model on which PSL is based is described in Section III-A. A general description of the system and semantics of PSL is then given in Section III-B to illustrate the broad scope of system aspects that can be described using PSL. The detailed syntax of PSL is given in [10].

A. Model of Information Systems

The Problem Statement Language is based first on a model of a general system, and secondly on the specialization of the model to a particular class of systems, namely information systems.

The model of a general system is relatively simple. It merely states that a system consists of things which are called OBJECTS. These objects may have PROPERTIES and each of these PROPERTIES may have PROPERTY VALUES. The objects may be connected or interrelated in various ways. These connections are called RELATIONSHIPS.

The general model is specialized for an information system by allowing the use of only a limited number of predefined objects, properties, and relationships.

B. An Overview of the Problem Statement Language Syntax and Semantics

The objective of PSL is to be able to express in syntatically analyzable form as much of the information which commonly appears in System Definition Reports as possible.

System Descriptions may be divided into eight major aspects:
1) System Input/Output Flow,
2) System Structure,
3) Data Structure,
4) Data Derivation,
5) System Size and Volume,
6) System Dynamics,
7) System Properties,
8) Project Management.

PSL contains a number of types of objects and relationships which permit these different aspects to be described.

```
Parameters:  DB=-EXRDB  NAME=hourly-employee-processing  NOINDEX  NOPUNCHED-NAMES  PRINT  EMPTY
         NOPUNCH  SMARG=5  NMARG=20  AMARG=10  BMARG=25  RNMARG=70  CMARG=1  HMARG=60  NODESIGNATE
         SEVERAL-PER-LINE  DEFINE  COMMENT  NONEW-PAGE  NONEW-LINE  NOALL-STATEMENTS
         COMPLEMENTARY-STATEMENTS  LINE-NUMBERS  PRINTEOF  DLC-COMMENT

 1  PROCESS                                                         hourly-employee-processing;
 2      /*  DATE OF LAST CHANGE - JUN 26, 1976, 13:56:44 */
 3  DESCRIPTION;
 4          this process performs those actions needed to interpret
 5          time cards to produce a pay statement for each hourly
 6          employee.;
 7  KEYWORDS:        independent;
 8  ATTRIBUTES ARE:
 9          complexity-level
10                      high;
11  GENERATES:       pay-statement, error-listing,
12                   hourly-employee-report;
13  RECEIVES:        time-card;
14  SUBPARTS ARE:    hourly-paycheck-validation, hourly-emp-update,
15                   h-report-entry-generation,
16                   hourly-paycheck-production;
17  PART OF:         payroll-processing;
18  DERIVES:         pay-statement
19      USING:       time-card, hourly-employee-record;
20  DERIVES:         hourly-employee-report
21      USING:       time-card, hourly-employee-record;
22  DERIVES:         error-listing
23      USING:       time-card, hourly-employee-record;
24  PROCEDURE;
25          1. compute gross pay from time card data.
26          2. compute tax from gross pay.
27          3. subtract tax from gross pay to obtain net pay.
28          4. update hourly employee record accordingly.
29          5. update department record accordingly.
30          6. generate paycheck.
31          note: if status code specifies that the employee did not work
32             this week, no processing will be done for this employee.;
33  HAPPENS:
34          number-of-payments TIMES-PER pay-period;
35  TRIGGERED BY:  hourly-emp-processing-event;
36  TERMINATION-CAUSES:
37                   new-employee-processing-event;
38  SECURITY IS:   company-only;
39
40  EOF EOF EOF EOF EOF
```

Fig. 2. Example of a FORMATTED PROBLEM STATEMENT for one PROCESS.

The *System Input/Output Flow* aspect of the system deals with the interaction between the target system and its environment.

System Structure is concerned with the hierarchies among objects in a system. Structures may also be introduced to facilitate a particular design approach such as "top down." All information may initially be grouped together and called by one name at the highest level, and then successively subdivided. System structures can represent high-level hierarchies which may not actually exist in the system, as well as those that do.

The *Data Structure* aspect of system description includes all the relationships which exist among data used and/or manipulated by the system as seen by the "users" of the system.

The *Data Derivation* aspect of the system description specifies which data objects are involved in particular PROCESSES in the system. It is concerned with what information is used, updated, and/or derived, how this is done, and by which processes.

Data Derivation relationships are internal in the system, while System Input/Output Flow relationships describe the system boundaries. As with other PSL facilities System Input/Output Flow need not be used. A system can be considered as having no boundary.

The *System Size and Volume* aspect is concerned with the size of the system and those factors which influence the volume of processing which will be required.

The *System Dynamics* aspect of system description presents the manner in which the target system "behaves" over time.

All objects (of a particular type) used to describe the target system have characteristics which distinguish them from other objects of the same type. Therefore, the PROPERTIES of particular objects in the system must be described. The PROPERTIES themselves are objects and given unique names.

The *Project Management* aspect requires that, in addition to the description of the target system being designed, documentation of the project designing (or documenting) the target system be given. This involves identification of people involved and their responsibilities. schedules, etc.

IV. REPORTS

As information about a particular system is obtained, it is expressed in PSL and entered into a data base using the Problem Statement Analyzer. At any time standard outputs or reports may be produced on request. The various reports can be classified on the basis of the purposes which they serve.

1) *Data Base Modification Reports:* These constitute a record of changes that have been made, together with diagnostics and warnings. They constitute a record of changes for error correction and recovery.

2) *Reference Reports:* These present the information in the data base in various formats. For example, the Name List Report presents all the objects in the data base with their type and date of last change. The Formatted Problem Statement Report shows all properties and relationships for a particular object (Fig. 2). The Dictionary Report gives only data dictionary type information.

3) *Summary Reports:* These present collections of information in summary from, or gathered from several different relationships. For example, the Data Base Summary Report provides project management information by showing the totals of various types of objects and how much has been said about them. The Structure Report shows complete or partial hierarchies. The Extended Picture Report shows the data flows in a graphical form.

4) *Analysis Reports:* These provide various types of analysis of the information in the data base. For example, the Contents Comparision Report analyzes similarity of Inputs and Outputs. The Data Process Interaction Report (Fig. 3) can be used to detect gaps in the information flow, or unused data objects. The Process Chain Report shows the dynamic behavior of the system (Fig. 4).

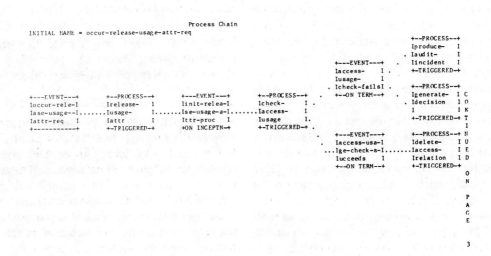

```
                                     111111111122222222223333
                                1234567890123456789012345678901 2
                                +----+----+----+----+----+----+----+--+
                        1  :D   :        :        :        :        :   :
                        2  : FDF FR      :        :        :        :   :
                        3  :    :D   :        :        :        :   :
                        4  :    : R  :        :        :        :   :
                        5  +----+----R---+----+----+----+----+----+--+
                        6  :        R    :        :        :        :   :
                        7  :        :DR R :        :        :        :   :
                        8  :        :D   :        :        :        :   :
                        9  :    F  :  D: :        :        :   :
                        10 +---+----+--F--+----+----+----+----+--+
                        11 :    :,  :   R   :        :        :   :
                        12 :        :   DR  :        :        :   :
                        13 :        :   : DR :        :        :   :
                        14 :    D  :   : R F: :        :        :   :
                        15 +R---+----+----+----+----+----+----+--+
                        16 :   FFR   :        :   D    :        :   :
                        17 :D   :        :        :        :        :   :
                        18 :    : F  :        :   :FDF FR      :   :
                        19 :        :        :   RD: :        :        :   :
                        20 +----+-F-+----+----+----+--FDR---+--+
                        21 :    FD   :        : P:      :        :   :
                        22 : FR  :        :        :  :F  F:D  :   :
                        23 :        :   :R F :        :   : D  :   :
                        24 :        : F:  :        :        :   D  :   :
                        25 :        :        :        :        :   : FF   :
                                +----+----+----+----+----+----+----+--+
```

Fig. 3. Example of part of a **Data Process Interaction Report.**

Fig. 4. Example of a **Process Chain Report.**

After the requirements have been completed, the final documentation required by the organization can be produced semiautomatically to a presented format, e.g., the format required for the Functional Description and Data Requirements in [21].

V. Concluding Remarks

The current status of PSL/PSA is described briefly in Section V-A. The benefits that should accrue to users of PSL/PSA are discussed in Section V-B. The information on benefits actually obtained by users is given in Section V-C. Planned extensions are outlined in Section V-D. Some conclusions reached as a result of the developments to date are given in Section V-E.

A. Current Status

The PSL/PSA system described in this paper is operational on most larger computing environments which support interactive use, including IBM 370 series (OS/VS/TSO/CMS), Univac 1100 series (EXEC-8), CDC 6000/7000 series (SCOPE,

TSS), Honeywell 600/6000 series (MULTICS, GCOS), AMDAHL 470/VS (MTS), and PDP-10 (TOPS 10). Portability is achieved at a relatively high level; almost all of the system is written in ANSI Fortran.

PSL/PSA is currently being used by a number of organizations including AT&T Long Lines, Chase Manhattan Bank, Mobil Oil, British Railways, Petroleos Mexicanos, TRW Inc., the U.S. Air Force and others for documenting systems. It is also being used by academic institutions for education and research.

B. Benefit/Cost Analysis of Computer-Aided Documentation

The major benefits claimed for computer-aided documentation are that the "quality" of the documentation is improved and that the cost of design, implementation, and maintenance will be reduced. The "quality" of the documentation, measured in terms of preciseness, consistency, and completeness is increased because the analysts must be more precise, the software performs checking, and the output reports can be reviewed for remaining ambiguities, inconsistencies, and omissions. While completeness can never be fully guaranteed, one important feature of the computer-aided method is that all the documentation that "exists" is the data base, and therefore the gaps and omissions are more obvious. Consequently, the organization knows what data it has, and does not have to depend on individuals who may not be available when a specific item of data about a system is needed. Any analysis performed and reports produced are up-to-date as of the time it is performed. The coordination among analysts is greatly simplified since each can work in his own area and still have the system specifications be consistent.

Development will take less time and cost less because errors, which usually are not discovered until programming or testing, have been minimized. It is recognized that one reason for the high cost of systems development is the fact that errors, inconsistencies, and omissions in specifications are frequently not detected until later stages of development: in design, programming, systems tests, or even operation. The use of PSL/PSA during the specification stage reduces the number of errors which will have to be corrected later. Maintenance costs are considerably reduced because the effect of a proposed change can easily be isolated, thereby reducing the probability that one correction will cause other errors.

The cost of using a computer-aided method during logical system design must be compared with the cost of performing the operations manually. In practice the cost of the various analyst functions of interviewing, recording, analyzing, etc., are not recorded separately. However, it can be argued that direct cost of documenting specifications for a proposed system using PSL/PSA should be approximately equal to the cost of producing the documentation manually. The cost of typing manual documentation is roughly equal to the cost of entering PSL statements into the computer. The computer cost of using PSA should not be more than the cost of analyst time in carrying out the analyses manually. (Computer costs, however, are much more visible than analysts costs.) Even though the total cost of logical system design is not reduced by using computer-aided methods, the elapsed time should be reduced because the computer can perform clerical tasks in a shorter time than analysts require.

C. Benefits/Costs Evaluation in Practice

Ideally the adoption of a new methodology such as that represented by PSL/PSA should be based on quantitative evaluation of the benefits and costs. In practice this is seldom possible; PSL/PSA is no exception.

Very little quantitative information about the experience in using PSL/PSA, especially concerning manpower requirements and system development costs, is available. One reason for this lack of data is that the project has been concerned with developing the methodology and has not felt it necessary or worthwhile to invest resources in carrying out controlled experiments which would attempt to quantify the benefits. Furthermore, commercial and government organizations which have investigated PSL/PSA have, in some cases, started to use it without a formal evaluation; in other cases, they have started with an evaluation project. However, once the evaluation project is completed and the decision is made to use the PSL/PSA, there is little time or motivation to document the reasons in detail.

Organizations carrying out evaluations normally do not have the comparable data for present methods available and so far none have felt it necessary to run controlled experiments with both methods being used in parallel. Even when evaluations are made, the results have not been made available to the project, because the organizations regard the data as proprietary.

The evidence that the PSL/PSA is worthwhile is that almost without exception the organizations which have seriously considered using it have decided to adopt it either with or without an evaluation. Furthermore, practically all organizations which started to use PSL/PSA are continuing their use (the exceptions have been caused by factors other than PSL/PSA itself) and in organizations which have adopted it, usage has increased.

D. Planned Developments

PSL as a system description language was intended to be "complete" in that the logical view of a proposed information system could be described, i.e., all the information necessary for functional requirements and specifications could be stated. On the other hand, the language should not be so complicated that it would be difficult for analysts to use. Also, deliberately omitted from the language was any ability to provide procedural "code" so that analysts would be encouraged to concentrate on the requirements rather than on low-level flow charts. It is clear, however, that PSL must be extended to include more precise statements about logical and procedural information.

Probably the most important improvement in PSA is to make it easier to use. This includes providing more effective and simple data entry and modification commands and providing more help to the users. A second major consideration is performance. As the data base grows in size and the number of users increases, performance becomes more important. Performance is very heavily influenced by factors in the computing environment which are outside the control of PSA development. Nevertheless, there are improvements that can be made.

PSL/PSA is clearly only one step in using computer-aided methods in developing, operating, and maintaining information processing systems. The results achieved to date support the premise that the same general approach can successfully be applied to the rest of the system life cycle and that the data base concept can be used to document the results of the other activities in the system life cycle. The resulting data bases can be the basis for development of methodology, generalized systems, education, and research.

E. Conclusions

The conclusions reached from the development of PSL/PSA to date and from the effort in having it used operationally may be grouped into five major categories.

1) The determination and documentation of requirements and functional specifications can be improved by making use

of the computer for recording and analyzing the collected data and statements about the proposed system.

2) Computer-aided documentation is itself a system of which the software is only a part. If the system is to be used, adequate attention must be given to the whole methodology, including: user documentation, logistics and mechanics of use, training, methodological support, and management encouragement.

3) The basic structure of PSL and PSA is correct. A system description language should be of the relational type in which a description consists of identifying and naming objects and relationships among them. The software system should be data-base oriented, i.e., the data entry and modification procedures should be separated from the output report and analysis facilities.

4) The approach followed in the ISDOS project has succeeded in bringing PSL/PSA into operational use. The same approach can be applied to the rest of the system life cycle. A particularly important part of this approach is to concentrate first on the documentation and then on the methodology.

5) The decision to use a computer-aided documentation method is only partly influenced by the capabilities of the system. Much more important are factors relating to the organization itself and system development procedures. Therefore, even though computer-aided documentation is operational in some organizations, that does not mean that all organizations are ready to immediately adopt it as part of their system life cycle methodology.

REFERENCES

[1] T. Aiken, "Initiating an electronics program," in *Proc. 7th Annu. Meeting, Systems and Procedures Assoc.*, 1954.

[2] B. W. Boehm, "Software and its impact: A quantitative assessment," *Datamation*, pp. 48–59, May 1973.

[3] ——, "Some steps toward formal and automated aids to software requirements analysis and design," *Inform. Process.*, pp. 192–197, 1974.

[4] R. G. Canning, *Electronic Data Processing for Business and Industry*. New York: Wiley, 1956.

[5] T. B. Glans, B. Grad, D. Holstein, W. E. Meyers, and R. N. Schmidt, *Management Systems*. New York: Holt, Rinehart, and Winston, 1968, 340 pp. (Based on IBM's study Organization Plan, 1961.)

[6] J. Goldberg, Ed., "The high cost of software," in the proceedings of a symposium held in Monterey, CA, Sept. 17-19, 1973, sponsored by the U.S. Air Force Office of Scientific Research, U.S. Army Research Office, Office of Naval Research. Menlo Park, CA: Stanford Research Institute, 1973.

[7] R. H. Gregory and R. L. Van Horn, *Automatic Data Processing Systems*. Belmont, CA: Wadsworth Publishing Co., 1960.

[8] W. Hartman, H. Matthes, and A. Proeme, *Management Information Systems Handbook*, (ARDI). New York: McGraw-Hill, 1968.

[9] E. A. Hershey and M. Bastarache, "PSA–Command Descriptions," ISDOS Working Paper no. 91, 1975.

[10] E. A. Hershey, E. W. Winters, D. L. Berg, A. F. Dickey, and B. L. Kahn, *Problem Statement Language–Language Reference Manual*, ISDOS Working Paper no. 68, 1975.

[11] G. F. Hice, W. S. Turner, and L. F. Cashwell, *System Development Methodology*. Amsterdam, The Netherlands: North-Holland Publishing Co., 1974, 370 pp.

[12] IBM Corporation, Data Processing Division, White Plains, NY, "Hipo–A design aid and documentation technique," Order no. GC-20-1851, 1974.

[13] M. N. Jones, "HIPO for developing specifications," *Datamation*, pp. 112-125, Mar. 1976.

[14] G. H. Larsen, "Software: Man in the middle," *Datamation*, pp. 61-66, Nov. 1973.

[15] G. J. Meyers, *Reliable Software Through Composite Design*. New York: Mason Charter Publishers, Inc., 1975.

[16] D. T. Ross and K. E. Schoman, Jr., "Structured analysis for requirements definition," in *Proc. 2nd Int. Conf. Software Eng.*, San Francisco, CA, Oct. 13-15, 1976.

[17] H. W. Schrimpf and C. W. Compton, "The first business feasibility study in the computer field," *Computers and Automation*, Jan. 1969.

[18] D. Teichroew and M. Bastarache, *PSL User's Manual*, ISDOS Working Paper no. 98, 1975.

[19] TRW Systems Group, *Software Development and Configuration Management Manual*, TRW-55-73-07, Dec. 1973.

[20] U.S. Air Force, "Support of Air Force automatic data processing requirements through the 1980's," Electronics Systems Division, L. G. Hanscom Field, Rep. SADPR-85, June 1974.

[21] U.S. Department of Defense, *Automated Data Systems Documentation Standards Manual*, Manual 4120.17M, Dec. 1972.

[22] J. D. Warnier and B. Flanagan, *Entrainment de la Construction des Programs D'Informatique*, vol. I and II. Paris: Editions d'Organization, 1972.

[23] N. E. Willworth, Ed., *System Programming Management*, System Development Corporation, TM 1578/000/00, Mar, 13, 1964.

[24] F. G. Withington, *The Organization of the Data Processing Function*, Wiley Business Data Processing Library, 1972.

[25] E. Yourdon and L. Constantine, *Structured Design*. New York: Yourdon, Inc., 1975.

Daniel Teichroew was born in Canada in 1925. He received the B.S. and M.A. degrees in mathematics from the University of Toronto, Toronto, Ont., Canada, in 1948 and 1949, respectively, and the Ph.D. degree in experimental statistics from the Institute of Statistics, North Carolina State College, Raleigh, NC.

From 1952 to 1955 he worked for the National Bureau of Standards, Washington, DC. In 1955 he was the Senior Electronics Application Specialist for the National Cash Register Company. From 1955 to 1956 he was Special Representative of Product Development and from 1956 to 1957 was Head of Business Systems Analysis for the National Cash Register Company. He was Associate Professor of Management and Professor of Management at the Stanford University Graduate School of Business from 1957 to 1962 and from 1962 to 1964, respectively. From 1964 to 1968 he was Professor and Head of the Division of Organizational Sciences at Case Institute of Technology. Since 1968 he has been Professor of Industrial and Operations Engineering, University of Michigan, Ann Arbor, and served as Chairman of that department from 1968 to 1973. He is also Director of the ISDOS Project.

Dr. Teichroew is President of the Society for Management Information Systems.

Ernest A. Hershey, III was born in Indiana in 1949. He received the B.S. degree in computer and communications science in 1971 and the M.S. degree in industrial and operations engineering in 1973 from the University of Michigan, Ann Arbor. He is presently working on the Ph.D. degree in industrial and operations engineering at the University of Michigan.

From 1969 to 1970 he worked for the IBM Corporation, New York, on their Internal Teleprocessing System Operations. From 1971 to 1973 he did counseling at the University of Michigan Computer Center. From 1971 to the present he has been a Research Associate on the ISDOS Project, University of Michigan.

An Extendable Approach to Computer-Aided Software Requirements Engineering

THOMAS E. BELL, MEMBER, IEEE, DAVID C. BIXLER, AND MARGARET E. DYER

Reprinted from *IEEE Transactions on Software Engineering*, Volume SE-3, Number 1, January 1977, pages 6–15. Copyright © 1977 by The Institute of Electrical and Electronics Engineers, Inc.

Abstract–The development of system requirements has been recognized as one of the major problems in the process of developing data processing system software. We have developed a computer-aided system for maintaining and analyzing such requirements. This system includes the Requirements Statement Language (RSL), a flow-oriented language for the expression of software requirements, and the Requirements Engineering and Validation System (REVS), a software package which includes a translator for RSL, a data base for maintaining the description of system requirements, and a collection of tools to analyze the information in the data base. The system emphasizes a balance between the use of the creativity of human thought processes and the rigor and thoroughness of computer analysis. To maintain this balance, two key design principles–extensibility and disciplined thinking–were followed throughout the system. Both the language and the software are easily user-extended, but adequate locks are placed on extensions, and limitations are imposed on use, so that discipline is augmented rather than decreased.

Index Terms–Automated simulation generation, automated tools, requirements language, REVS, RSL, simulation, software engineering, software requirements, software requirements engineering, SREM, SREP.

I. INTRODUCTION

THE development of data processing systems has too often resulted in cost overruns, schedule slippages, or failures to produce a system which satisfies the original requirements [1]. As Boehm stated, "Software (as opposed to computer hardware, displays, architecture, etc.) is 'the tall pole in the tent'–the major source of difficult future problems and operational performance penalties" [2]. His Air Force study showed that the annual expenditures by the Air Force and NASA for software are twice the expenditures for hardware. This indicates the tremendous impact that problems in developing software can have on the budgets of the services or on the cost of any large software-based system that is being developed.

A number of studies have identified the symptoms and suspected root causes of problems in software development. Among these are the McGonagle [3] study for the Air Force, studies by Bartlett *et. al.* [4], studies on software problems by Thayer *et. al.* [5], [6], and a study by Bell and Thayer [7]. In addition, studies by The MITRE Corporation [8] and the Applied Physics Laboratory of The Johns Hopkins University

[9] concentrated on how software is managed. Foremost among the problems in software development identified in these studies is the generally undisciplined approach which is usually taken.

The Ballistic Missile Defense Advanced Technology Center (BMDATC) is sponsoring an integrated software development research program [10] to improve the techniques for developing correct, reliable BMD software. Reflecting the critical importance of requirements in the development process, the Software Requirements Engineering Program has been undertaken as a part of this program by TRW Defense and Space Systems Group[1] to improve the quality of requirements specifications. The product of this program (the Software Requirements Engineering Methodology, SREM) includes techniques and procedures for requirements decomposition and for managing the requirements development process. In addition, SREM includes the Requirements Statement Language (RSL), a machine-processable language for stating requirements, and the Requirements Engineering and Validation System (REVS), an integrated set of tools to support the development of requirements in RSL. SREM was designed to bring the computer's aid to the requirements engineering phase of software development in order to reduce the number and severity of problems encountered there. The purpose of this paper is to describe the type of automated system SREM needed to be, the characteristics of SREM that we chose to meet these needs, and how we have checked our work to be sure that both human creativity and computer-imposed discipline are achieved.

II. SREM NEEDS FOR AUTOMATION

Developing software requirements is generally a difficult intellectual job, and the job begins to look nearly impossible when it involves large data processing systems like those in a Ballistic Missile Defense (BND) system. The requirements document for the current BMD system (the System Technology Program, Site Defense Project) contains 8248 requirement and support paragraphs in a 2500-page specification. Manually checking each paragraph against all others is an enormous task, and generating them initially is even harder; automated techniques are clearly needed. However, these automated techniques should not force the engineer to spend large amounts of mental energy dealing with simulators and control languages; he should be able to state the requirements in a reasonable, natural language and then have the automated techniques keep track of the changes, ensure consistency, and report the interactive effects of his statements.

Manuscript received July 22, 1976; revised September 14, 1976.

T. E. Bell was with the TRW Defense and Space Systems Group, Redondo Beach, CA. He is now with the Management Consulting Department, Peat, Marwick, Mitchell & Copartners, New York, NY.

D. C. Bixler is with the TRW Defense and Space Systems Group, Redondo Beach, CA 90278.

M. E. Dyer is with the TRW Defense and Space Systems Group, Huntsville, AL 35805.

[1] Under Contract DASG60-75-C-0022.

In order to allow the requirements engineer to use his creativity, the system should be natural and flexible; it should allow him to express requirements in terms of concepts which are familiar to him. If severe restrictions are built into the system, such as highly constrained syntax rules or a paucity of concepts, the engineer would spend more time trying to "work the system" and less time working the requirements development problem. In addition, the technologies involved in a BMD system are so extensive and advance so rapidly that no predefined set of concepts could ever be expected to satisfy the specific needs of all future projects. Therefore, such a system should be extensible at the concept level so that a particular project with an application requiring a new concept may add it to the system.

A computer-aided system should enforce some measure of discipline on the creativity of the engineer so that the development process always moves in the direction of reduced ambiguity and increased consistency. For example, the computer could perform static checking of the requirements to illuminate inconsistencies such as conflicting names, improper sequences of processing steps, and conflicting uses of items of information which must be present in the system. With a flow orientation, the computer could additionally check the dynamic consistency of the system through the use of a simulation.

The Software Requirements Engineering Program has produced a computer-aided system for the development of requirements which fulfills the needs described above. The following four sections of this paper provide an overview of that system, followed by descriptions of the Requirements Statement Language, the Abstract System Semantic Model (the central repository for requirements), and the tools that provide automated aid for the engineer.

III. OVERVIEW

The Requirements Engineering and Validation System (REVS) consists of three major segments:

1) a translator for the Requirements Statement Language (RSL),

2) a centralized data base, the Abstract System Semantic Model (ASSM), and

3) a set of automated tools for processing the information in the ASSM.

A diagram of the system is shown in Fig. 1.

Central to REVS is the ASSM, a relational data base similar in concept to the system used in the ISDOS Problem Statement Language/Problem Statement Analyzer (PSL/PSA) system [11], [12]. However, our need for extensibility and configuration management, as well as the flow approach needed for simulation, have necessitated many differences from the concepts used in PSL/PSA, and therefore differences in data base design.

The design of the ASSM provides a decoupling between the input language, RSL, and the analysis tools. This decoupling permits extending RSL without having to consider issues such as controlling the tools, interfacing with the host operating system, and doing other things which would compromise the naturalness needed in RSL. The decoupling has also permitted us to exercise great freedom in the design of RSL; we were

free to develop the most natural way of expressing requirements without making concessions to control languages or problems of configuration management.

RSL is designed to be a means for stating requirements naturally while still being rigorous enough for machine interpretation. We pursued this goal, in part, by orienting the design around the specification of flow graphs of required processing steps. These flow graphs are expressed in RSL in terms of "structures," which are the products of a mapping of the two-dimensional graph (e.g., Fig. 2) onto a one-dimensional stream suitable for computer input (e.g., Fig. 3). Structures are built from primitive flow specification blocks much as the control flow of a computer program is built from control specification primitives. The types of structure primitives available in RSL are fixed in order to provide discipline by precluding the formation of structures whose meaning may be unclear. The specification of the processing steps themselves, and of other information related to these processing steps (e.g., the data items which they use), is done in a much more flexible manner. In fact, the concepts which may be expressed in this nonprocedural segment of RSL are not necessarily fixed. The language is extensible at the concept level in order to respond to situation-specific needs and new, unanticipated needs for stating requirements. The structures and the nonprocedural statements of RSL are input to REVS through a translator which analyzes them to ensure individual correctness. The meaning of the statements is then abstracted and entered into the ASSM; no executable code is generated, only entries in the data base that can be used by the tools.

The tools' designers are freed from the syntax of RSL; they work with the abstracted information in the ASSM. Thus, a syntax change in RSL does not usually compromise any of the tools; tools may be added or modified as the Software Requirements Engineering Methodology (SREM) evolves, or as the application of REVS changes. The tools merely access the ASSM and in no way are dependent on RSL syntax.

The information available in the ASSM will support a wide variety of analysis tools. We have implemented a baseline set of widely applicable tools which perform analyses primarily related to flow properties of the information in the specification. Our analysis of requirements problems [7] indicated that these capabilities are very important in a methodology like SREM [13] for generating consistent, correct requirements and enforcing the desired discipline on the requirements generation process. Among these tools are an interactive graphics package to aid in the specification of the flow paths, static consistency checkers which primarily check for consistency in the use of information throughout the system, and an automated simulator generator and execution package which aids in the study of dynamic interactions of the various requirements. Situation-specific reports and analyses which a particular user may need in order to augment the information given by the baseline tools are generated through the use of a generalized extraction and reporting system. This system is independent of the extensions to RSL so that new concepts added to the language may be included in queries to the data base.

A unifying concept throughout the SREM, including RSL and REVS, is the specification of requirements for software in

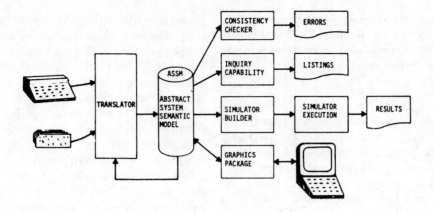

Fig. 1. Information flows in REVS.

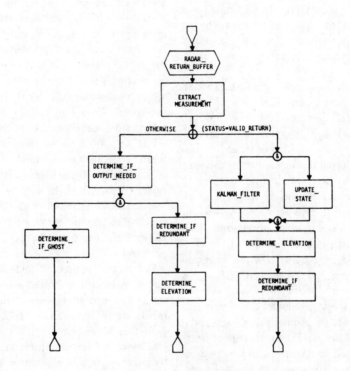

Fig. 2. Flow graph of a sample R_NET.

```
R_NET:  PROCESS_RADAR_RETURN.
    STRUCTURE:
        INPUT_INTERFACE RADAR_RETURN_BUFFER
        EXTRACT_MEASUREMENT
        DO (STATUS = VALID_RETURN)
            DO  UPDATE_STATE AND KALMAN_FILTER  END
            DETERMINE_ELEVATION
            DETERMINE_IF_REDUNDANT
            TERMINATE
        OTHERWISE
            DETERMINE_IF_OUTPUT_NEEDED
            DO  DETERMINE_IF_REDUNDANT
                DETERMINE_ELEVATION
                TERMINATE
            AND DETERMINE_IF_GHOST
                TERMINATE
            END
        END
    END.
```

Fig. 3. Sample R_NET in RSL.

221

terms of flows through the system [14]. The use of these flows helps to bring about a disciplined approach to the development of software requirements, much as structured programming has done for the implementation of software.

IV. RSL

Current software requirements documents are typically written in natural English and provide information about relatively isolated portions of the data processing system. Some of these pieces of information are very nebulous, and some are in such great detail that they represent an implementation—an implementation that may have been chosen without consideration of the remainder of the data processing system. The unevenness alone is annoying, and the probability is high that some parts of the system will be left without any written requirements. The largest deficiency of such documents, however, is that they often fail to provide critical information about how the pieces of the system will fit together. The implementor is then left without adequate information, and the requirements engineer cannot be certain the various pieces are consistent; often they are not, and no discipline is applied to make them consistent.

Our approach involves writing requirements in RSL [15], an artificial language. RSL provides information on how pieces of the system will fit together through use of the flow approach to defining the requirements. With this approach, the connectivity information is central to the development, and consistency may be easily checked, often through automated means. Another benefit of using an artificial language is the ability to define precisely the meaning of concepts in the language. With a natural language such as English, each person has a different idea about the connotation of a particular phrase and these differing ideas lead to ambiguities in interpretation of the specification. When an artificial language is used, the precise meaning of each concept may be fixed and documented. This leads to unambiguous interpretation of specifications using this language. Finally, an artificial language enables the designer to constrain the semantics (and thus the requirements statements) to a single, appropriate level of detail. Therefore, requirements in RSL can be (and are) limited to statements of true requirements that are testable in the software and are not overconstraining.

RSL is the primary means that a requirements engineer uses to communicate with REVS, so its characteristics can easily spell the success or failure of SREM. Therefore, we devoted considerable effort to RSL design and provide some of the important details of that design below.

Flows

The most obvious way to state system requirements for software is to describe the operations that each software module shall perform; these requirements differ little from program specifications. This type of "requirements specification" contains little information about the truly required sequence of processing, or even about communication between designed modules. Stating the requirements (even if they are at the correct level) without indicating the required sequence invites

problems in BMD systems and most other process control systems. The basic approach therefore must be statement of required operations as flows through the system. This orientation is facilitated by the stimulus-response nature of process control systems; each flow originates with a stimulus and continues to the final response. Specifying requirements in this fashion makes explicit the sequences of processing required. It also provides for direct testability of the requirements; the software may be tested to see if it provides the responses which were specified when given the associated stimulus.

Flows through the system are specified in RSL as requirements networks, also called R_NET's. In addition to enabling conditions, information requirements, and other material in R_NET's, they have flow structures consisting of nodes, which specify processing operations, and the arcs which connect them. The basic nodes include ALPHA's, which are the specifications of functional processing steps, and SUBNET's, which are specifications of processing flows at a lower level in the hierarchy. In essence, the SUBNET is an ALPHA which has been expanded to include internal details of the processing. All of the basic nodes are single-entry, single-exit. In addition to the simple sequential flow which may be represented by connecting this type of node, more complex flow situations are expressible in RSL by the use of structured nodes which fan-in and fan-out to specify different processing paths; the structured nodes are the AND, OR, and FOR EACH.

The AND node is the first of three structured nodes. The meaning of an AND structure, which contains several paths, is that these paths are mutually order-independent. The processes on parallel paths may be executed in any order, or even in parallel. The fan-in at the end of the AND structure is a synchronization point; all of the parallel paths must be completed before any of the processes following the rejoin are performed.

The second structured node, the OR node, also has several paths. A condition is attached to each path at an OR-type fan-out. The one path with a true condition is processed; the others are ignored. Each OR node must have an OTHERWISE path that is processed if none of the conditions are true. In case more than one condition is true, the first path (as indicated by either implicit or explicit ordering) is processed.

The final structure type is the FOR EACH. This structure contains only one path; this path is processed once for each element of a set of data-processing system entities that is currently present. For example, a requirement might state that proximity of interceptors be determined FOR EACH eentry object. The FOR EACH, therefore, specifies that a particular process or set of processes is to be iterated upon without sequential implications.

The syntax of the structures in R_NET's makes the basic nodes and the several types of fan-out nodes explicit. The fan-in nodes and all of the arcs are visible only by implication. An example of such a structure is the one shown in Fig. 2 and the syntax to represent it is shown in Fig. 3.

The syntax of structures in R_NET's is similar to the syntax of many structured programming languages and is designed to achieve the same effect; that is, enforcing a discipline on the user. Through the use of a fixed set of flow primitives, flow structures which are ambiguous or unclear are precluded from appearing on R_NET's. This helps the requirements engineer himself see where he is vague or ambiguous, aids in the communication of requirements between requirements engineers, and permits a highly automated analysis of the requirements by the tools.

Extensions

RSL is an extensible language in order to permit the inclusion of new concepts that may be needed for future requirements. Typically, BMD software must perform guidance (largely an analytical problem), must allocate resources (a heuristic problem), and must interact with all other parts of the BMD system (a coordination problem). The processing demands of such systems are so large that the state of the art (in hardware, software, algorithm concepts, etc.) is regularly stretched by the design of the data processing system, and the art advances quite rapidly. Combined with these difficulties for providing a language to state data processing requirements is our inability to know about future potential developments in other parts of a BMD system (radar, kill mechanism, etc.) which may require special interfaces or processing techniques. Any language with fixed concepts would quickly become inappropriate for stating such requirements because it would lack at least one needed concept. Therefore, RSL needed to be extensible.

To facilitate the implementation of extensibility at the concept level and to provide a clear framework for the concepts, the underlying architecture of RSL has been kept very simple. There are four primitives, outlined below, which form the foundation of the language.

1) *Elements*: Elements in RSL correspond roughly to nouns in English. The element types are simply standard prototypes which are used to describe the properties possessed by each element of the type. Some examples of standard element types in RSL are ALPHA (the class of functional processing steps), DATA (the class of conceptual pieces of data necessary in the system), and R_NET (the class of processing flow specifications).

2) *Relationships*: The relation (or relationship) in RSL may be compared with an English verb. More properly, it corresponds to the mathematical definition of a binary relation, a statement of an association of some type between two elements. The RSL relation is noncommutative; it has a subject element and an object which are distinct. However, there exists a complementary relationship for each specified relationship which is the converse of that specified relationship. DATA being INPUT TO an ALPHA is one of the relationships in RSL; the complementary relationship says that the ALPHA INPUTS the DATA.

3) *Attributes*: Attributes are modifiers of elements somewhat in the manner of adjectives in English; they formalize important properties of the elements. Each attribute has associated with it a set of values which may be mnemonic names, numbers, or text strings. Each particular element may have only one of these values for any attribute. An attribute may pertain to all element types or may be restricted to be used with only a certain set of types. An example of an attribute is INITIAL_VALUE which is applicable to elements of type DATA. It has values which specify what the initial value for

the data item must be in the implemented software and for simulations.

4) *Structures*: The final RSL primitive is the structure, the RSL representation of the flow model mentioned earlier. It is a mapping of a two-dimensional graph structure into a one-dimensional stream of computer input. It models the flows through the functional processing steps (ALPHA's) or the flows between places where accuracy or timing requirements are stated (VALIDATION_POINT's).

All concepts in RSL are expressed in terms of these four primitives. The structures are not extensible; this preserves the necessary discipline for flow descriptions. On the other hand, new types of elements, relationships, and attributes may be added to the language at will to express new concepts. In fact, all concepts (both new and old) are defined as extensions.

As an example of using the extension capability, a requirement often involves information entering the data processing system from outside hardware (radars, operator consoles, etc.). The port into the data processing system is embodied in a type of element called an INPUT_INTERFACE. The complex of information which it handles is called a MESSAGE; the INPUT_INTERFACE then PASSES the MESSAGE into the data processing system. The definitions of these two types of elements and their connecting relationship in RSL are as follows:

DEFINE ELEMENT_TYPE: INPUT_INTERFACE
> (*A port between the data processing system and the rest of the system which accepts data from another part of the system*).

DEFINE ELEMENT_TYPE: MESSAGE
> (*An aggregation of DATA and FILES that PASS through an interface as a logical unit*).

DEFINE RELATIONSHIP: PASSES
> (*An INPUT_INTERFACE "PASSES" a logical aggregation of data called a MESSAGE from the outside system into the data processing system*).

COMPLEMENTARY RELATIONSHIP: PASSED ("BY").

SUBJECT: INPUT_INTERFACE.

OBJECT: MESSAGE.

After these definitions are processed by the RSL translator and entered into the ASSM, they are available for use by any requirements engineer working with that data base. Of course, to make these particular definitions useful, additional relationships must be defined; of particular importance is the relationship which associates particular items of DATA with the MESSAGE.

With an extension mechanism this powerful, it would be a tempting proposition to provide only this mechanism so that the requirements engineer would have a means to provide his own concepts. This, however, would demand that the engineer design his own language for requirements statement as well as engineering the requirements themselves. Therefore, we have provided a core set of concepts that appears to be needed with great regularity, and have also provided the mechanism for extending the concepts as needed in particular problems. The examples of extensions given above are a part of this core set along with 19 other element types, 20 relationships, and 20 attributes.

Core Concepts

The following examples show the use of the core concepts to define requirements. They include the definitions of two required processing steps (ALPHA's), of a required item of information (DATA) which is to be OUTPUT FROM one of the ALPHA's, and of a statement from another document which necessitates the inclusion of several items in the requirements (ORIGINATING_REQUIREMENT).

    ALPHA: EXTRACT_MEASUREMENT.
        INPUTS: CORRELATED_RETURN.
        OUTPUTS: VALID_RETURN, MEASUREMENT.
        DESCRIPTION: "DOES RANGE SELECTION PER CISS
            REFERENCE 2 - 7".
        ENTERED_BY: "M. RICHTER".

    ALPHA: DETERMINE_IF_REDUNDANT.
        INPUTS: CORRELATED_RETURN.
        OUTPUTS: REDUNDANT_IMAGE.
        DESCRIPTION: "THE IMAGE OF THE RADAR RETURN
            IS ANALYZED TO DETERMINE IF IT IS REDUN-
            DANT WITH ANOTHER IMAGE".
        ENTERED_BY: "F. BURNS".

    DATA: MEASUREMENT.
        INCLUDES: RANGE_MARK_TIME, AMPLITUDE,
            RANGE_VARIANCE, RD_VARIANCE,
            R_AND_RD_CORRELATION.
        OUTPUT FROM: ALPHA EXTRACT_MEASUREMENT.
        DESCRIPTION: "THIS IS THE ESSENCE OF THE INFOR-
            MATION IN THE RETURN".
        ENTERED_BY: "F. BURNS".

    ORIGINATING_REQUIREMENT:
        DPSPR_3_2_2_A_FUNCTIONAL.
        DESCRIPTION: "ACTION: SEND RADAR ORDER IN-
            FORMATION: INFORMATION: RADAR ORDER,
            IMAGE (REDUNDANT)".
        TRACES TO: ALPHA COMMAND_PULSES
            ALPHA DETERMINE_IF_REDUNDANT
            MESSAGE RADAR_ORDER_MESSAGE
            DATA REDUNDANT_IMAGE
            ENTITY_CLASS IMAGE.
        ENTERED_BY: "T. E. BELL".

The Translator

The RSL translator is a component of REVS; its purpose is to analyze the RSL statements which are input to it and to make entries in the ASSM corresponding to the meaning of the statements. It does this by extracting the RSL primitives (elements, relationships, attributes, and structures) which exist in the input statements, and by mapping them to constructs in the ASSM. The translator also processes modifications and de-

letions from the data base which are commanded by RSL statements specifying changes to already-existing instances in the ASSM. This is done in a manner similar to that used in processing the additions to the ASSM; that is, the primitives are extracted and the referenced construct is modified or deleted. For all types of input processing, the translator references the ASSM to do simple consistency checks on the input. This prevents the occurrence of disastrous errors such as the introduction of an element with the same name as a previously existing element or an instance of a relationship which is tied to an illegal type of element. Besides providing a measure of protection for the data base, this type of checking catches, at an early stage, some of the simple types of inconsistencies that are often found in requirements specifications.

In addition to processing requirements statements given in terms of the core set of extensions, the translator accepts further extensions and enters them into the ASSM. Obviously, the extensions must be treated with even more care than the requirements statements since the deletion of, say, a previously legal element type may invalidate a large segment of the requirements. On the other hand, adding new concepts in response to each individual's desires is a pernicious practice. For these reasons, a lock mechanism has been built into the translator to enable it to reject any extensions while locked. This allows the management of a project to control the use of the extensions in their project and to enforce a disciplined use of the power of RSL.

The translator has been implemented using a compiler writing system [16]; this adds additional flexibility to the language. Changes to the syntax or the primitives of the language, which would be unthinkably expensive with a hand-built translator, may be accomplished with relatively small changes to the inputs of the compiler writing system. Thus, for example, if evolutions in the Software Requirements Engineering Methodology introduce a type of flow structure which does not currently exist in the language, the structure portion of RSL may be changed through the use of the compiler writing system. Of course, the impact of changes of this magnitude on the ASSM and tools are significant. Therefore, the use of this final level of flexibility is tightly controlled.

V. The Abstract System Semantic Model

The RSL statements that an engineer inputs to the Requirements Engineering and Validation System (REVS) are analyzed, and a representation of the information is put into a special data base. This data base is called the "Abstract System Semantic Model" (ASSM) because it maintains information about the required data processing system (RSL semantics) in an abstract, relational model. Each statement is checked for syntactic and elementary semantic correctness prior to being put into the ASSM. Therefore, a number of different tools can easily access the data without the need to check for these types of correctness with each access.

In addition to maintaining information about the requirements, the ASSM maintains the concepts used to express the requirements. This means that all extensions, both the core concepts and the additions and modifications of specific projects, are in the ASSM. This allows the RSL translator to process extensions in a manner similar to that in which it processes the requirements statements. The modified concepts are then available for use as soon as they are entered.

The information in the ASSM is not simply a collection of text. Instead of this, it exists as a relational model of the information contained in the RSL statements. In this model, elements are represented by nodes (records) in the data base, and relationships are represented as connections between the nodes. Attributes and their values then consist of a node for the value and a connection to the element node with which the attribute is associated. The structures are expanded to the graph which they represent. This type of representation facilitates retrieval of information from the data base in terms of queries about the relationships between elements; complex combinations of relationships can be traced simply by following the proper connections in the ASSM. In order to support extensions of the language, another level of model exists. At this level prototypes for each type of element, relationship, or attribute may legally be represented. Adding concepts then translates to adding new prototypes to the model. Each instance of an element, relationship, or attribute is linked to its prototype. This facilitates concept-oriented retrieval operations such as "Find all elements of type DATA which are not INPUT TO anything" as well as facilitating extensibility.

In addition to providing a means to enhance the efficiency of processing, the ASSM provides a central repository for all information about the system data processing requirements. In the environment of a large BMD system, this type of centralization is necessary since many individuals are continually adding, deleting, and changing information about requirements for the data processing system. The ASSM provides a means for all of them to work with the same base of current information; they can find out about the effects of their work on other requirements engineers, the characteristics of parts of the system that other people are defining, and the current status of their own work. The centralization allows both the requirements engineers and the analysis tools to work from a common baseline and enables implementation of management controls on changes to this baseline.

The function of the ASSM as a central repository for all information is crucial to both the extensibility and disciplined approach aspects of SREP. Extensibility of the language at the level of adding, deleting, or modifying concepts would be nearly impossible if those concepts were spread throughout the system. In addition, the residence of all information about both the software requirements and the concepts used for describing them in the ASSM makes it possible to take a modular and extendable approach to the tools. It also permits the imposition of configuration management controls in an efficient manner since blocking of modifications to the ASSM freezes the configuration. Finally, the analysis tools can easily scan through the data base to check for consistency, a task which would be extremely difficult without access to the description of the entire system at once.

VI. Automated Tools

For a large software system, many people develop requirements for different segments of the system; using SREM, each person develops RSL descriptions of the requirements for his particular part of the system. REVS assists in this activity, and also provides mechanisms for imposing discipline and control on the requirements and the requirements engineering process. This is accomplished by the third segment of REVS, the automated tools. The requirements engineer uses the tools to identify those areas which need further resolution, to aid him in resolving problems, and to evaluate his inputs. At various milestones in the development, the tools are also used to evaluate the entire system. Typical requirements engineering efforts will have several iterations of this type, with the tools being used at each stage to show areas which need further work.

The baseline set of tools in REVS contains flow-oriented analysis and validation aids for verifying the completeness, consistency, and correctness of the specified requirements. A generalized extraction and reporting system provides additional analysis and status information. While the flow-oriented analysis aids are not easily extensible, the flexible extraction system is a powerful extension capability adaptable both by the engineer to evaluate his requirements, and by management to maintain visibility and control.

Flow Orientation

The stating of requirements in RSL is based on identifying and relating other requirements information to specified functional flows of processing steps. In REVS, we have implemented tools to provide graphics input/output, to perform static analysis, and to create simulators based on this flow approach. These tools aid the engineer in developing the flows and in validating the consistency, completeness, and correctness of the specified flow structures and their related requirements.

Interactive Graphics: The interactive R_NET generation tool provides graphics capabilities for users of REVS. Through this facility, the requirements engineer may input, modify, or display R_NET's. It also provides an alternative to the RSL translator for specification of the flow portion of the requirements. Using this tool, the user may even develop a graphic representation of an R_NET previously entered in RSL. These flow diagrams (Fig. 2) are inherently two dimensional, so their display on a graphics system provides a more-easily understood representation than the (one-dimensional) language (Fig. 3). Through the use of the ASSM, the user may work with either the graphic or RSL language representation of R_NET's; they are completely interchangeable.

The interactive R_NET generation facility possesses full editing capabilities. The user may input an R_NET "from scratch" or he may modify one previously entered. At the conclusion of the editing session, the new R_NET replaces the old one (if any) in the ASSM. An alphanumeric keyboard and a trackball-driven cursor are the means by which the user communicates with the graphics system. He can select any of a series of functions from a menu of available functions. The editing functions provide means to position, connect, and delete nodes, to move them, to disconnect them from other nodes, and to enter or change their associated names and commentary. Menu selection and screen positioning are done using the trackball; names and commentary are entered through the keyboard. The size of an R_NET is not limited by the screen; zoom-in, zoom-out, and scroll functions are provided.

Simulation: The most thorough automated test of the consistency, completeness, and validity of requirements is often performed through simulation. For a large software system, the building of simulators must be automatic to preclude divergence of the requirements from the simulation and to allow rapid response and analysis of change.

The automatic simulator generation in REVS takes the ASSM representation of the requirements of a data processing system and generates from it simulators of the system. These simulators are of the discrete event type and are driven by externally generated stimuli. The baseline system generates simulators to be driven by a System Environment and Threat Simulation (SETS) Program [10], [17] which models the threat, the system environment, and the components of a BMD system which are external to the data processing system.

Two distinct types of simulators may be generated by REVS. The first is a simulator which uses functional models of the processing steps. These models may employ shortcuts to simulate the required processing, including the use of "artificial" data (those which are not required to appear in the ultimate real-time software). However, REVS recognizes such data only if they are declared as artificial. The discipline of requiring these declarations reduces the proliferation of data that might (or might not) be required in the ultimate software. This type of simulation serves as a means to validate the overall required flow of processing against higher level system requirements.

The other type of simulator uses analytic models, i.e., models that use algorithms similar to those which will appear in the software to perform complex computations. This type of simulation may be used to define a set of algorithms for the system which have the desired accuracy and stability. This does not establish feasibility of the set for any particular implementation; instead it provides an existence proof of an analytic solution to the problem. Both types of simulator are used to check dynamic system interactions, a type of analysis that is necessary for the dynamic, nonlinear, closed-loop control problems occurring in BMD systems.

The simulator generator transforms the ASSM representation of the requirements into simulator code in the programming language Pascal [18]. The same technique is used to generate both types of simulator. The flow structure of each R_NET is used to develop a Pascal procedure whose control flow implements that of the R_NET structure. Each processing step (ALPHA) reference on the R_NET becomes a call to a procedure consisting of the model or algorithm for the ALPHA. The models or algorithms are written by the requirements engineer in Pascal and are entered into the ASSM as textual attributes of the ALPHA's. The data definitions and structures and the data management procedures for the simulator are synthesized from the required data elements, their relationships, and their attributes in the ASSM. The code generated from the ASSM is automatically combined with standard simulation management procedures and SETS to form a complete simulator.

By automatically generating simulators in this manner from the ASSM, we ensure that the simulations match and trace to the requirements. New simulators can be generated as often as requirements change, but discipline is enforced by precluding direct change to simulator code; all changes are made to the requirements statements themselves.

Static Analysis: Of course, many requirements inconsistencies do not require the dynamics and cost of a simulation for detection. Therefore, a group of tools are included in REVS to statically (without simulation) check for completeness and consistency in the requirements specification. These tools detect deficiencies in the flow of processing and data manipulation stated in the requirements. Three classes of static analysis tools are included in REVS for this type of detection.

The first class of these tools checks the structure of the R_NET's entered interactively for correctness prior to permanent entry in the ASSM; this includes such things as checking for one and only one start node, proper branching and rejoining of paths, and proper termination of all paths. These checks ensure complete interchangeability between the graphic representation and the RSL form of the R_NET. Additional checks are performed on R_NET's in the ASSM to ensure proper branching and rejoining of paths which include SUBNET's.

The second class of analyzers deals with data flow through the R_NET's. They operate using the R_NET structure in much the same manner that data flow analyzers for programming languages use the control flow of the program [19], but are complicated by the concurrency of path specifications allowed in RSL. These tools detect definite and potential errors in data use (such as local data being used before it is set, and data being set in more than one of a set of parallel paths). Other reports concerning the lifetime and use of data may be generated from the information gathered through these data flow analyzers.

The third class of analysis tools checks for proper hierarchy in the specification. This means that definitions must be specified for all SUBNET's used in R_NET's, that SUBNET's must not make reference to each other in a recursive manner, and that all ALPHA's and SUBNET's must appear on at least one R_NET. A similar analysis is performed on data hierarchies specified in the requirements.

Extensions

The interactive graphics, flow analysis aids, and generalized query system provide the REVS user with a powerful set of automated tools. He may, however, want to have tools specialized to a particular application. The architecture of REVS and the flexibility of the extractor system facilitate such extensions at two levels—addition of completely new tools and creation of special reports by using the extractor.

Addition of Tools: REVS consists of layers of software surrounding the ASSM; the innermost layers contain the ASSM itself and a set of ASSM access routines, and the outermost layer is composed of the REVS executive. Between these reside the RSL translator and the automated tools which operate on data extracted from the ASSM, as shown in Fig. 4. By using the access routines to isolate the ASSM and by centralizing the control of REVS, the layered structure facilitates extensions to REVS and minimizes the impact on the software of extensions to RSL. Communicating in terms of RSL primitives, the ASSM access routines are unaffected by extensions

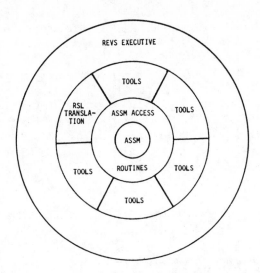

Fig. 4. REVS layered design.

to RSL and insulate the tools from the detailed organization of the data base. The ASSM can be physically restructured without impacting the tools.

The REVS executive invokes the automated tools based on command from the user. A new tool may be easily incorporated into REVS as an integral part by modifying the executive to recognize a new command and invoke the added tool.

Special Reports: The structure of REVS easily accommodates extensions to the baseline tools. However, adding a new tool each time a requirements engineer needs a special report or analysis is costly and does not allow timely responsiveness to needs. REVS alleviates this problem by providing the requirements engineer an extensible tool (the extractor) to produce specialized reports. The user completely controls the scope of the analysis and content of his reports; he is not burdened with the details of specifying the format nor with looking at tabular forms to extract needed information.

This flexibility of extraction from the data base is provided by the generalized extractor system. Using this system, the user can subset the elements in the ASSM based on some condition (or combination of conditions) and display the elements of the subset with any appended information he selects. Output is in a standardized form compatible with the RSL input form. Prepositions and additional punctuation are added so that a formal documentation of the requirements can be generated in an order standardized to the needs of a particular application. Being standardized RSL, outputs of the extractor can be easily correlated with the RSL inputs and the engineer has to deal with only one requirements format.

Information to be retrieved is identified in terms of RSL concepts. For example, if the user wants a report listing all DATA elements which are not INPUT TO any ALPHA (processing step), he enters the following commands.

    SET A = DATA THAT IS NOT INPUT.
    LIST A.

By combining sets in various ways, he can detect the absence and presence of data, trace references on the structures, and analyze interrelationships established in the ASSM. In ana-

lyzing user requests and extracting information from the ASSM, the extractor system uses the definition of the concepts contained in the ASSM. Thus, as RSL is extended, the extensions and their use in the requirements are immediately available.

The extractor system can be used both for *ad hoc* inquiries and for routinely generated extractor special reports. Both the requirements engineer and management may pre-define reports and enter the requests to the extractor as needed. This allows the requirements engineer to establish a repertoire of situation-specific consistency and completeness checks, and to perform automatic regressive testing. Managers can periodically request reports on the status of the ASSM to impose standards and control the development of requirements. For example, RSL supports the traceability of software requirements to system requirements to permit rapid, economical, and comprehensive change control. Using the generalized extractor system, a report can be produced at any time to show, for example, which requirements have no documented traceability and are therefore suspect.

VII. CONCLUSIONS

The REVS software is now operational on the Texas Instruments Advanced Scientific Computer at the BMDATC Advanced Research Center in Huntsville, AL. The software executes in the manner described in this paper. This fact, though comforting, is hardly adequate for a justification of the effort to produce the system. If we were to conclude this paper with nothing more than the proud assurance that the system does not abnormally terminate, we would fall into a category of system builders that B. Boehm has called "computer basket weavers."

Referring to people in this category, Boehm stated "A basket weaver has a very difficult job. He must plan his basket very carefully and he puts a lot of loving care into it; he builds it, studies it from various angles, discusses it with other basket weavers, and then goes off to build another basket. Very rarely though does he go out and sample users to find out whether they are interested in baskets with handles or with several compartments rather than one compartment, and the like. And, unless something changes considerably in computing, it will remain a kind of computer basket weaving" [20]. Boehm is criticizing computer science researchers for not doing adequate requirements analyses and for not checking the degree to which the systems fulfill the requirements after their implementation. A system purporting to improve requirements engineering certainly has a special responsibility to identify its requirements and then to check the degree of fulfillment.

The central nature of RSL led us to concentrate on its requirements in our early development—and to document the requirements so that we could track our progress. The material in Section II of this paper is a summary of that document after we had expanded our requirements to include the software in REVS. Merely having some set of requirements, of course, does not prove anything; how well does the system actually satisfy the users' needs?

Some of the test cases used to evaluate requirement satisfac-

```
OUTPUT_INTERFACE:  RADAR_ORDERS_BUFFER.
   ABBREVIATED BY:  ROB.
   CONNECTS TO:  RADAR.
   RECEIVES FROM:  DPS.
   PASSES:  RADAR_ORDER.
   ENTERED BY:  "MIKE RICHTER".

MESSAGE:  RADAR_ORDER.
   MADE BY:  RADAR_COMMAND.

DATA:  STARTUP.
   INCLUDES:  RO_ORDER_ID
              STARTUP_TIME.

DATA:  SHUTDOWN.
   INCLUDES:  RO_ORDER_ID.

DATA:  TRANSMIT_RECEIVE.
   INCLUDES:  RO_ORDER_ID
              RO_IMAGE_ID
              ALPHA_PHASE_TAPER
              BETA_PHASE_TAPER
              TRANSMIT_INFORMATION
              RECEIVE_INFORMATION
              NUMBER_OF_RANGE_GATES
              RANGE_GATE_INFORMATION.

ALPHA:  INITIATE_STATE_VAL_DATA.
   ARTIFICIALITY:  VALIDATION.
   INPUTS:  HANDOVER_DATA, HANDOVER_TIME.
   OUTPUTS:  UPDATE_STATE_VALIDATION_DATA.
   DESCRIPTION:  "THE REFERENCE ALGORITHM, KALMAN FILTER, IS
                 INITIALIZED.  HANDOVER_DATA IS COPIED INTO
                 UPDATE_STATE_VALIDATION_DATA WITH PLACE_IN_
                 TRACK_TIME SET TO HANDOVER_TIME.".

ALPHA:  INITIATE_TRACK_ON_IMAGE.
   INPUTS:  HANDOVER_DATA.
   OUTPUTS:  HOIQ, STATE_DATA, IMAGE_ID.
   CREATES:  IMAGE.
   SETS:  IMAGE_IN_TRACK.
   DESCRIPTION:  "A REQUEST FOR PULSES IS MADE BY ENTERING A
                 FORMAL RECORD REQUEST INTO THE HOIQ WHICH
                 FEEDS THE PULSE SENDING PROCEDURES.".
```

Fig. 5. RSL from BMD track loop.

tion using SREM are noted in Alford's paper [13]. Most of those, however, involved other parts of SREM than RSL and REVS. The cases noted below were particularly important in finding out whether users were interested in the "basket" that we had woven with RSL and REVS.

One of our first test cases involved restating into RSL a particularly involved part of the requirements for a medical information system. We hoped that the RSL statements would be clear enough that the user (a professional data processing specialist deeply involved in medical systems) would find graphical representations superfluous. Instead, we found that the graphics were really necessary for him to understand the flows through his system. When he used both RSL and graphics, he found five critical problems in the English requirements statements. One of these problems, for example, involved requiring a physician to check the same medical record five times when a single check would have sufficed. Implementing this system would have required changes in (and wastage of) physicians' time—if they had used the system at all! Clearly, our software system needs graphical output if it is to handle situations like this.

We were particularly interested in the medical system for this evaluation because its flows were far shorter than in a BMD system. Therefore, any indication of confusion in the absence of graphics would be magnified in the BMD situation. With the results described above, we were certain that graphics was required for our "basket" to satisfy the users' needs.

A later test case involved having BMD data processing engineers develop the requirements for an actual BMD function (tracking). In this case the RSL translator was implemented to the point that we could input the RSL statements and have them checked for consistency. Our experience in this case indicated that some of the concepts in the core set of RSL were inappropriately conceived; they were unambiguous, but they were not sufficient to express all of the requirements.

This BMD case resulted in revisions to RSL concepts that were incorporated into the baseline version of the language description. We found that the extensibility features of RSL worked, and we were able to revise the language without changing the translator. Thus, we found that we needed some features of our "basket" revised (the core concepts) but that other features were solid (the extensibility).

After the revisions to the core concepts, another BMD data processing engineer (one new to the project and not particularly sympathetic to many of its conclusions) started over on track-loop (the tracking function) using the revised RSL. He found a few further revisions that he desired in a concept area not fully explored previously. Again, concept changes were handled with the extension capability. The "basket" seemed to be getting quite close to the users' needs for stating requirements.

One type of user is the person writing the requirements in RSL, but another is the person reading the resultant statements. The information needed by the reader must be in the RSL statements written by the requirements engineer or the system is, at least, severely crippled. RSL text is rather cryptic, and readers expressed concern about whether adequate information existed in its easily written form. We performed another test case to evaluate whether our "basket" fulfilled the readers' information needs.

The RSL from the track-loop test case had given readers the impression that inadequate information existed there, so we used the actual RSL from that test case (an extract appears in Fig. 5). Then we modified the RSL with phrases that substituted for the standard RSL element, relationship, and attribute names. Finally, we had the material typed in a conventional

3.2.2.1 RADAR ORDERS BUFFER There shall be an output interface from the data processing system called RADAR ORDERS BUFFER. The data processing system shall communicate through this interface with RADAR. Across this interface shall be passed RADAR ORDER.

It is abbreviated by ROB. It was entered by MIKE RICHTER.

3.2.2.2 RADAR ORDER When transmitted across an interface the software shall handle the message RADAR ORDER. This message is made up of RADAR COMMAND.

3.2.2.3 STARTUP Information shall be maintained about STARTUP. This information shall include RO ORDER ID and STARTUP TIME.

3.2.2.4 SHUTDOWN Information shall be maintained about SHUTDOWN. This information shall include RO ORDER ID.

3.2.2.5 TRANSMIT RECEIVE Information shall be maintained about TRANSMIT RECEIVE. This information shall include:

```
RO ORDER ID
RO IMAGE ID
ALPHA PHASE TAPER
BETA PHASE TAPER
TRANSMIT INFORMATION
RECEIVE INFORMATION
NUMBER OF RANGE GATES
RANGE GATE INFORMATION.
```

4.1.3.1 INITIATE STATE VAL DATA Logical processing shall be done to INITIATE STATE VAL DATA. This shall have as input HANDOVER DATA and HANDOVER TIME. This shall have as output UPDATE STATE VALIDATION DATA.

NOTE: The reference algorithm, Kalman filter, is initialized. HANDOVER DATA is copied into UPDATE STATE VALIDATION DATA with PLACE IN TRACK TIME set to HANDOVER TIME.

In interpreting this requirement, note that the degree of artificiality in its statement is VALIDATION.

4.1.3.2 INITIATE TRACK ON IMAGE Logical processing shall be done to INITIATE TRACK ON IMAGE. This shall have as input HANDOVER DATA. This shall have as output HOIQ, STATE DATA, and IMAGE ID. This logical processing shall, when appropriate, identify a new instance of IMAGE. This logical processing, when appropriate, shall identify the type of entity instance as being IMAGE IN TRACK.

NOTE: A request for pulses is made by entering a formal record into the HOIQ which feeds the pulse-sending procedures.

Fig. 6. "Conventional" format for track loop.

format and added the usual paragraph numbers. All of this added no new information; all the changes could easily have been done by a computer; in fact, we documented our algorithms to be sure that we exercised no discretion in making the changes.

We tested the sufficiency of the RSL that we had put into a familiar format (with lots of redundant material) by presenting it to readers unaware of its origin. Without exception they thought the text (an extract is shown in Fig. 6) was from a real, normal specification. In fact they sometimes needed to see the original RSL to be convinced that it was merely the same material reformatted. The needed information, at least at the paragraph level, is contained in RSL statements; perhaps an automated capability to produce more familiar-looking output should be included in future versions of REVS to make our "basket" as useful as possible.

Our evaluation of RSL and REVS is clearly not yet complete since users have not yet employed the final versions of the software. We will continue our evaluation of SREM utility to ensure that we have actually produced an extensible system that encourages disciplined thinking in engineering correct, complete, meaningful software requirements. Our evaluations to date give every indication that RSL and REVS actually satisfy a critical need in furthering the development of large-scale software.

REFERENCES

[1] J. Goldberg, Ed., *Proc. Symp. on the High Cost of Software*, Naval Postgrad. School, Monterey, CA, Sept. 17–19, 1973.

[2] B. W. Boehm, "Software and its impact: A quantitative assessment," *Datamation*, vol. 19, pp. 48–59, May 1973.

[3] J. D. McGonagle, "A study of a software development project," James P. Anderson & Co., Fort Washington, PA, Sept. 1971.

[4] J. C. Bartlett *et al.*, "Software validation study," LOGICON Rep. DS-72210-R1370, NTIS Doc. AD-759 263, LOGICON, Inc., San Pedro, CA, Mar. 1973.

[5] T. A. Thayer, "Understanding software through empirical reliability analysis," in *Proc. 1975 Nat. Comput. Conf.*, June 1975, pp. 335–341.

[6] T. A. Thayer *et al.*, "Software reliability study: Final technical report," study performed by TRW Defense and Space Systems Group for the Air Force Systems Command's Rome Air Development Center, Griffiss Air Base, Rome, NY, Feb. 27, 1976.

[7] T. E. Bell and T. A. Thayer, "Software requirements: Are they really a problem?," in *Proc. 2nd Int. Software Eng. Conf.*, Oct. 1976.

[8] A. Asch, D. W. Kelliher, J. P. Locher, III, and T. Connors, "DOD weapon system software acquisition and management study, volume I, MITRE findings and recommendations," MITRE Tech. Rep. MTR-6908, The MITRE Corp., McLean, VA, May 1975.

[9] A. Kossiakoff, T. P. Sleight, E. C. Prettyman, J. M. Park, and P. L. Hazan, "DOD weapon systems software management study," APL/JHU SR 75-3, The Johns Hopkins Univ. Appl. Phys. Lab., Silver Spring, MD, June 1975.

[10] BMD Advanced Technology Center, "BMDATC software development system," vol. I and II, Ballistic Missile Defense Advanced Technology Center, Huntsville, AL, July 1975.

[11] D. Teichroew, E. A. Hershey, and M. J. Bastarache, "An introduction to PSL/PSA," ISDOS Working Paper 86, Univ. Michigan, Ann Arbor, Mar. 1974.

[12] E. A. Hershey, "A data base management system for PSA based on DBTG 71," ISDOS Working Paper 88, Univ. Michigan, Ann Arbor, Sept. 1973.

[13] M. W. Alford, "A requirements engineering methodology for real-time processing requirements," this issue, pp. 60–69.

[14] M. W. Alford and I. F. Burns, "R-nets: A graph model for real-time software requirements," in *Proc. Symp. on Comput. Software Eng., MRI Symp. Ser.*, vol. XXIV. Brooklyn, NY: Polytechnic Press, to be published.

[15] T. E. Bell and D. C. Bixler, "A flow-oriented requirements statement language," in *Proc. Symp. on Comput. Software Eng., MRI Symp. Ser.*, vol. XXIV. Brooklyn, NY: Polytechnic Press, to be published. (Also in TRW Software Series, TRW-SS-70-01.)

[16] O. Lecarme and G. V. Bochmann, "A (truly) usable and portable translator writing system," in J. L. Rosenfeld, Ed., *Information Processing 74*. Amsterdam: North-Holland, 1974.

[17] F. J. Mullin, "Software test tools," in *Proc. TRW Symp. on Reliable, Cost Effective, Secure Software*, TRW Software Ser. Rep. TRW-SS-74-14, pp. 6-47–6-48, Mar. 1974.

[18] K. Jensen and N. Wirth, "PASCAL: User manual and report," *Lecture Notes in Computer Science*, vol. 18. Berlin: Springer-Verlag, 1974.

[19] F. E. Allen and J. Cocke, "A program data flow analysis procedure," *Commun. Ass. Comput. Mach.*, vol. 19, pp. 137–147, Mar. 1976.

[20] B. W. Boehm, "Command/control requirements for future Air Force systems," in *Multi-Access Computing: Modern Research and Requirements*. Rochelle Park, NJ: Hayden, 1974, pp. 17–29.

Thomas E. Bell (S'62–M'63) was born in Phoenix, AZ, in 1940. After attending Harvey Mudd College, Claremont, CA, for 2½ years, he received the B.S. degree in applied physics from the University of California, Los Angeles, in 1963. His M.B.A. and Ph.D. degrees were from UCLA's Graduate School of Business in 1964 and 1968, respectively.

He was a member of the Rand Corporation's professional staff from 1967 through 1974. During this time he performed research into appropriate techniques to use computer graphics (both interactive and off-line) in human problem solving. However, his main emphasis was on the development of techniques for computer performance evaluation. In recognition of his contributions both during this period and subsequently, he was awarded the A. A. Michaelson Award in 1975 for outstanding personal contributions to computer performance evaluation. In 1974 he joined the Software Research and Technology Staff of TRW. His efforts were devoted to improving the development of software, both through research and application, in the environment of large, complex systems. Analysis of empirical data, development of new techniques, and design of a new software requirements statement language were emphasized. He is currently a Manager at Peat, Marwick, Mitchell & Copartners, in the Management Consulting Department. He is responsible for practice development and application in the area of productivity enhancement techniques for computers and the humans using and operating them.

Dr. Bell is a member of the Association for Computing Machinery, the IEEE Computer Society, the Institute for Management Sciences, and the Computer Measurement Group. He is the author of over 30 papers in computer science.

David C. Bixler was born in Youngstown, OH, on August 1, 1949. He received the B.S. degree in chemical engineering in 1971 and the M.S. degree in computer science in 1973, both from Michigan State University, East Lansing.

Since 1973 he has been associated with the Applied Software Laboratory of TRW Defense and Space Systems Group, Redondo Beach, CA, where he has worked in the areas of software requirements engineering, computer description languages, and computer emulations. His primary areas of interest are the semantics of programming languages and verification techniques for computer programs.

Mr. Bixler is a member of Tau Beta Pi and the Association for Computing Machinery.

Margaret E. Dyer received the B.S. and M.S. degrees in mathematics in 1964 and 1965, respectively, from the University of Michigan, Ann Arbor.

From 1965 to 1973 she was associated with Teledyne Brown Engineering where her primary responsibilities were the development of a conversational language processor, the development and application of simulations, and the comparative evaluation of fourth generation data processors. In 1973 she became a member of the Technical Staff of the MITRE Corporation. At MITRE and, subsequently, with TRW Defense and Space Systems Group, she has been involved with the development of advanced techniques for the development of software for large-scale, real-time control systems. Since joining TRW in 1974 she has concentrated on research and development of advanced software requirements engineering languages and automated tools. As Manager of the REVS Software and Language Development at the TRW Huntsville Facility, she is responsible for the design and development of the Requirements Engineering and Validation System.

CAPTURING MORE WORLD KNOWLEDGE IN THE REQUIREMENTS SPECIFICATION

Sol J. Greenspan and John Mylopoulos
Department of Computer Science
University of Toronto
Toronto, Ontario, CANADA

Alex Borgida
Department of Computer Science
Rutgers University
New Brunswick, New Jersey, USA

"The real problem is the mass of detailed requirements; and the only solution is the discovery or invention of general rules and abstractions which cover the many thousands of cases with as few exceptions as possible."

- C. A. R. Hoare

Abstract

The view is adopted that software requirements involve the representation (modeling) of considerable real-world knowledge, not just functional specifications. A framework (RMF) for requirements models is presented and its main features are illustrated. RMF allows information about three types of conceptual entities (objects, activities, and assertions) to be recorded uniformly using the notion of properties. By grouping all entities into classes or metaclasses, and by organizing classes into generalization (specialization) hierarchies, RMF supports three abstraction principles (classification, aggregation, and generalization) which appear to be of universal importance in the development and organization of complex descriptions. Finally, by providing a mathematical model underlying our terminology, we achieve both unambiguity and the potential to verify consistency of the model.

1. INTRODUCTION

Requirements definition is the task of gathering all of the relevant information to be used in understanding a problem situation prior to system development. The documentation of this information is called the requirements specification. The form and content of the requirements specification can have a tremendous impact on the task of software throughout its lifetime.

Experience over the last decade has led to some important observations that point to the need for improved requirements specification languages. First, it appears that more attention to requirements, including a better understanding of the problem situation, pays off in reduced total life-cycle effort and cost [3]. Secondly, it has been learned that it is difficult, indeed, to "get the requirements right"; some common problems are ill-defined terms, inconsistencies, ambiguities, and the tendency to mix requirements with design decisions [1].

Much of requirements definition involves such tasks as: defining terms in the domain of discourse, stating, clarifying and agreeing on assumptions and constraints, and discussing and negotiating the needs and objectives of an organization (business, government, industry). Whatever the application "world" (e.g. airline reservations, manufacturing, hospital administration, etc.) there is a body of "knowledge" used to interpret and understand that world.

For example, in considering the development of a variety of information systems for a large hospital in Toronto, we have found it necessary to become intimately familiar with a wide range of subject matters: medical knowledge, hospital procedures and policies, available therapies (drugs, surgery, etc.), legal responsibilities to government, and so on. We believe that this kind of real world knowledge needs to be captured in a formal requirements specification. The ability to efficiently design appropriate computer systems and enable them to evolve over their lifetime depends on the extent to which this knowledge can be captured.

Most current requirements languages concentrate primarily on functional specifications, which give a high-level target system description in terms of the functions to be performed by the ultimate system (with an emphasis on what the system is supposed to do but not how). In functional specification approaches, the world knowledge, whose importance we have been discussing, is often not an explicit part of the requirements specification. The knowledge is, at least initially, scattered throughout documents and the minds of people across the organization.

Reprinted from *Proceedings of the Sixth International Conference on Software Engineering*, 1982, pages 225–234. Copyright © 1982 by The Institute of Electrical and Electronics Engineers, Inc.

Our research addresses the development of languages and tools for requirements modeling, a specification approach directed toward high-level specifications which capture world knowledge directly and naturally in the specification. In this paper we present a framework for requirements modeling called RMF. An RMF model describes some "slice of reality". RMF guides the information gathering job of requirements definition. The resultant description should be useful in determining what the problem situation is and what solutions are possible. The design of RMF emphasizes the need for structuring the description to ease the task of finding answers to questions during system design and implementation and in the face of changing requirements.

Section 2 of the paper introduces our modeling approach and discusses the central theme, abstraction mechanisms. Section 3 is the core of the paper, presenting the main features of RMF along with illustrative examples. Section 4 discusses related work and fills in some background material. Finally, Section 5 discusses some interesting aspects of the framework and of our ongoing research.

2. MODELING AND ABSTRACTION

2.1 A modeling approach

The major goal of RMF is to form a synthesis of some modeling principles which we believe are essential to the requirements modeling task; but we stop short of providing a specific language incorporating them. We apply these principles to answer two key questions about requirements modeling: (1) What kind of information should be captured in a requirements model? (2) How should a requirements model be structured?

We have chosen a representation method in which a requirements model consists of a collection of conceptual entities (or simply entities) defined by their inter-relationships with other entities. Thus, the first question above is answered by (i) choosing appropriate specification units, or entity categories, and (ii) deciding what kinds of relationships are allowed within and between entities of each entity category; later on in the presentation we shall call the relationships properties and the types of relationships property categories.

RMF offers three kinds of specification units: object, activity, and assertion. As discussed in Section 4, these entity categories have been used successfully, in one form or another, across a wide range of modeling endeavors.

For a long time it has been asserted that abstraction is the best tool we have toward the intellectual manageability of complex descriptions [11,14]. The framework is based on the premise that effective structuring of large descriptions such as requirements models depends on the use of good abstractions. Below we introduce the abstraction mechanisms used in the framework.

2.2 Abstraction mechanisms

An abstraction mechanism is any descriptive facility that allows certain kinds of information to be included while precluding other, "lower-level" or "less important" details. In Software Engineering, abstraction is usually equated with the suppression of design decisions or implementation details. In this sense a requirements model should be "very abstract"; indeed, it is proposed as the "most abstract" specification for use in Software Engineering.

In RMF we propose the use of a set of complementary abstraction mechanisms for descriptive purposes. A first abstraction mechanism, aggregation, allows an entity to be viewed as a collection of components, or parts. A second abstraction mechanism is classification, which allows a new entity, the class, to capture common characteristics shared by a group of entities. A third abstraction, generalization, captures the common characteristics of several classes.

Classification allows one to consider only the characteristics shared by the instances of a class and to ignore individual differences. Aggregation allows one to consider an entity while ignoring further detail about the components. Generalization allows one to consider only those properties that a collection of classes have in common without considering the classes' individual differences.

A principal design goal of our RMF is to apply the abstraction mechanisms uniformly over all the entity categories. That is to say, there are, in an RMF model, classes for object, activity, and assertion entities; entities of all categories can have component parts; and classes of each entity category are organized according to their generality/specificity.

We feel that a specification language exhibiting such uniformity will be much easier to formalize, understand and use.

3. THE FEATURES OF RMF

We first show in terms of objects how the abstraction mechanisms work, and then we extend the presentation to activities and assertions as well.

3.1 Tokens, classes, and metaclasses

Entities are stratified into classification levels according to whether they are considered "individuals", called tokens, collections of tokens called classes, classes of classes called metaclasses, and so on. The tokens of a class are called its instances; similarly, a class is said to be an instance of a metaclass.

Simple examples of object tokens are john-smith (representing a particular person) and 7 (representing the number 7). PERSON is an example of a class, whose instances are tokens such as john-smith, while INTEGER is a class whose instances would include 7.

An example of a metaclass is PERSON_CLASS, whose instances are classes of persons, such as PERSON, PATIENT, PHYSICIAN, NURSE.

In addition to its instances, a class bears additional information, but for this we need the notion of properties.

For the remainder of the paper we will use lower case letters and digits for token identifiers and upper case letters for class and metaclass identifiers. The suffix "_CLASS" will be use for metaclass identifiers.

3.2 Properties -- factual and definitional

Entities can be related to other entities by participating in properties. Properties consist of three items of information: a subject, an attribute (or property name), and a value. To express the property of the token john-smith that his age is 23, we could write

<john-smith, age, 23>

where the subject, attribute, and value are john-smith, age (an identifier), and 23, respectively. This property expresses "factual" information about the subject and thus is termed a factual property.

Factual information alone is clearly not adequate for requirements modeling. We have introduced classes (and metaclasses) for the purpose of defining and describing collections of entities that, presumably, are grouped together because some uniform conditions hold over all of them. What is needed is a facility for specifying generic information that pertains to each of the instances of a class (or metaclass). For example, we may want to specify for the class PERSON that each person has an age which is an AGE_VALUE. The RMF feature used for this is called a definitional property. The triple

(PERSON, age, AGE_VALUE)

is used for now to represent the above information. The three components are again called subject, attribute, and value. (Note that we have used angular brackets and parentheses to distinguish the two kinds of properties.)

It may be helpful to think of a definitional property as defining a function, e.g.,

age: PERSON --> AGE_VALUE

whose domain is the property subject and whose range in the property value. Evaluation of the function for an instance of the domain results in a corresponding factual property, e.g.

age(john-smith) = 23.

The most important point to notice here is that 23 is, and must be, an instance of AGE_VALUE. In general, for a class C with definitional property (C,a,V), for every instance x of C, it must be the case that a(x) is an instance of V. The close correspondence between definitional and factual properties is called the property induction principle. The principle requires as well that every factual property of an object be induced by a definitional property of some containing class.

It is useful to be able to associate factual properties to classes as well as to tokens. For example, the information

"the average age of persons is 21"
"the number of nurses is 200"

should be considered factual rather than definitional, that is

<PERSON, average-age, 21>
<NURSE, cardinality, 200>

since the information pertains directly to the subjects rather than to their instances.

The inclusion of metaclasses in the framework allows the property induction principle to be extended. In order to allow the specification of the above two factual properties, it would be necessary to have also specified definitional properties that induce them, such as

(PERSON_CLASS, average-age, AGE_VALUE)
(PERSON_CLASS, cardinality, NUMBER).

At this point in the paper, we have described how two abstraction principles, classification and aggregation, are incorporated into the framework. The classification abstraction is supported by the "instance of" relationship between tokens and classes and between classes and metaclasses; we consider the three levels to be adequate for most modeling purposes. The grouping of all the properties of an entity relates the entity to other entities which may in turn be the subjects of other properties; this supports the aggregation abstraction. The property induction principle relates these two dimensions in a coherent way.

3.3 Objects, activities, assertions

As implied by the examples above, objects represent the "things" in the world, such as persons, numbers, equipment, documents, etc.

```
PERSON_CLASS PATIENT
    association ward: HOSPITAL_WARD,
                primary-physician: PHYSICIAN,
                consulting-physician: PHYSICIAN,
    inserted-by register: ADMIT_PATIENT,
    initially phys-ward?:
        primary-physician.specialty ≠ ward
        => consulting-physician.specialty = ward,
    updated-by transfer:
                TRANSFER(self,new-ward:WARD),
    removed-by release: RELEASE(self),
end {PATIENT}
```

Figure 1

Figure 1 is a description of the object class PATIENT, giving general information about patients for a particular hospital. The class is defined to be an instance of the metaclass PERSON_CLASS and has a number of definitional properties consisting of

<attribute> : <value>

pairs and grouped into property categories such as association, inserted-by, and initially.

The properties of PATIENT relate each patient to a ward and two physicians, one primary and the other consulting. Patients are "created" through an ADMIT_PATIENT activity, updated through a TRANSFER activity and removed through a RELEASE activity. When a patient is first created, it must be the case that if the ward to which a patient is assigned is not the specialty of his/her primary (care) physician, then it must be the specialty of the consulting physician.

```
ACTIVITY_CLASS ADMIT_PATIENT
      input p: PERSON,
      control w: WARD,
              phys, consulting-phys: PHYSICIAN,
      output pt: PATIENT,
      triggered-by a1: ARRIVAL(p),
      precondition already-in?: NOT INST(p,PATIENT),
           room-left?:
                      PATIENT.cardinality <
                            PATIENT_MAX,
      postcondition admitted?: IN_HOSPITAL(p),
      part check-id: CHECK_ID(p),
           put: CHOOSE_WARD(w,phys,consulting-phys),
           admit: INSERT(p,PATIENT),
           increment: INCREMENT(PATIENT.cardinality),
           urinalysis: PERFORM_URINALYSIS(p),
           blood-count: PERFORM_BLOOD_COUNT(p),
           blood-pressure: PERFORM_BLOOD_PRESSURE(p),
           temp: TAKE_TEMP(p),
end {ADMIT_PATIENT}
```

Figure 2

In Figure 2, we present a definition of the activity class ADMIT_PATIENT. It consists of one input property, a person, and one output property, a patient; also, it has three control properties, a ward and two physicians. The activity is triggered by instances of the assertion class, ARRIVAL, which is instantiated each time a person arrives at the hospital for admission.

ADMIT_PATIENT also includes two preconditions (already-in? and room-left?) and a postcondition (admitted?) that must be true before and after the activity, respectively. The preconditions assert that the person must not be already a patient of the hospital, and also that the number of patients (PATIENT.cardinality) is less than the hospital capacity (PATIENT_MAX). The postcondition asserts that the person has indeed been admitted once the ADMIT_PATIENT activity is over.

Finally, the "body" of ADMIT_PATIENT is defined by several part properties which specify the components of an ADMIT_PATIENT activity. The components involve checking the person's ID, choosing a ward and assigning a primary care and a consulting physician, inserting the person into the PATIENT class and incrementing the cardinality property of PATIENT; also, some tests are performed (urinalysis, blood-count, blood-pressure, and temperature).

We present an example of an assertion class in Figure 3 to underscore the uniform treatment of the entity categories. The assertion class IN_HOSPITAL has one argument, a patient, and asserts through its part property that the person is now physically

```
ASSERTION_CLASS IN_HOSPITAL
      argument p: PERSON,
      part patient?: INST(p,PATIENT),
           present?: PHYSICALLY_PRESENT(p),
end {IN_HOSPITAL}
```

Figure 3

present at the hospital.

We close this section by giving a definition of the metaclass PERSON_CLASS, in Figure 4. As stated in the previous section, PATIENT is entitled to a cardinality property only because it is an instance of this metaclass. Note that METACLASS is a built-in metametaclass that has all metaclasses as instances. Two other built-in metametaclasses have been found useful because they allow references to all entities and to all generic entities, respectively: (i) ENTITY, which has as instances all entities in a specification, including itself, and (ii) CLASS, which has as instances all classes, metaclasses, and the three built-in metametaclasses METACLASS, CLASS, and ENTITY.

```
METACLASS PERSON_CLASS
      association average-age: AGE_VALUE,
                  cardinality: NUMBER,
      end {PERSON_CLASS}
```

Figure 4

3.4 Generalization

To support the generalization abstraction mechanism, a new relationship, subclass, is offered which can be declared between two classes or two metaclasses. For example, suppose PERSON has been defined as shown in Figure 5. (Note: The part properties of a data class instance do not change values, while the association properties do.) Then, changing the first line of the definition of PATIENT (Figure 1) to
      PERSON_CLASS PATIENT subclass of PERSON
makes PATIENT a subclass or specialization of PERSON and PERSON a generalization of PATIENT.

```
PERSON_CLASS PERSON
      part name: PERSON_NAME,
           sin: SOCIAL_INSURANCE_#,
           ohip: ONTARIO_INS_#,
      association address: ADDRESS,
                  age: AGE_VALUE,
      end {PERSON}
```

Figure 5

What does it mean to say that PATIENT is a specialization of PERSON? Well, for one thing we expect that every instance of PATIENT is, under all circumstances, also an instance of PERSON. Indeed, the semantics of becoming an instance of a class include becoming an instance of all of the generalizations of the class. Conversely, when an object ceases to be an instance of a class, it also ceases to be an instance of its specializations.

Another aspect of specialization concerns the definitional properties of the two classes involved. All definitional properties of PERSON are inherited by PATIENT; so, by virtue of being declared a specialization of PERSON, PATIENT has, in addition to the properties specified in Figure 1, also a name, a social insurance number, an address, etc.

Property inheritance allows for economy of expression in a specification because a definitional property need only be mentioned once for the most general class to which it is applicable. Inheritance also serves as a memory aid, since knowing that a class is a subclass of another allows one to concentrate on the additional information needed to describe the subclass.

```
PERSON_CLASS CHILD subclass of PERSON
      association age: CHILD_AGE_VALUE,
                  guardian: PERSON,
      invariant guardian.age > 30,
end {CHILD}

PERSON_CLASS SURGICAL_PATIENT subclass of PATIENT
      association blood-type: BLOOD_TYPE,
                  surgery: SURGERY_TYPE,
end {SURGICAL_PATIENT}

PERSON_CLASS TRANSPLANT_SURGERY_PATIENT
                  subclass of SURGICAL_PATIENT
      association donor: PERSON,
end {TRANSPLANT_SURGERY_PATIENT}

PERSON_CLASS CHILD_PATIENT
                  subclass of CHILD, PATIENT
      association nurse: NURSE,
end {CHILD_PATIENT}
```

Figure 6

To illustrate the importance of generalization, suppose we have already defined the class PERSON and its specialization PATIENT. A number of other object classes are also relevant for our hospital example. CHILD specializes PERSON by restricting its age property to allow only values in CHILD_AGE_VALUE. SURGICAL_PATIENT as well as TRANSPLANT_SURGERY_PATIENT are specializations of PATIENT. CHILD_PATIENT gives an example of a class that has more than one immediate generalization. Figure 6 includes the definitions of all these object classes while Figure 7 summarizes the subclass relation for the object classes defined so far.

Specialization opens the door to a form of stepwise refinement that is based on the introduction of detail for special cases. Moreover, this form of refinement is not applicable only to object classes. Consider, for example, some specializations of ADMIT_PATIENT, as shown in Figure 8. The first, ADMIT_CHILD_PATIENT, simply

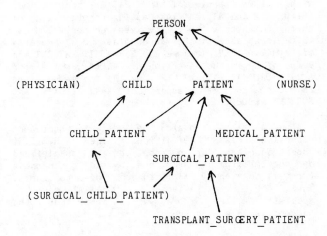

(The classes in parentheses have not been defined.)

Figure 7

assigns a nurse to the child patient in addition to all the things done for other patients. The second specializes ADMIT_PATIENT for surgical patients where a blood test is done for possible transfusion. ADMIT_SURGICAL_CHILD_PATIENT, the third, is a specialization of the previous two activities and therefore inherits all their definitional properties; in addition, it has a definitional property of its own which obtains permission for surgery from the child's guardian.

```
ACTIVITY_CLASS ADMIT_CHILD_PATIENT
                  subclass of ADMIT_PATIENT
      input p: CHILD,
      control n: NURSE,
      output pt: CHILD_PATIENT,
      part find-nurse: FIND_NURSE(n,w),
            admit: INSERT(P,CHILD_PATIENT),
end {ADMIT_CHILD_PATIENT}

ACTIVITY_CLASS ADMIT_SURGICAL_PATIENT
                  subclass of ADMIT_PATIENT
      output pt: SURGICAL_PATIENT,
      triggered-by a1: ARRIVAL(p)
                  AND SURGERY_NEEDED(p),
      part blood-typing: PERFORM_BLOOD_TYPING,
end {ADMIT_SURGICAL_PATIENT}

ACTIVITY_CLASS ADMIT_SURGICAL_CHILD_PATIENT
      subclass of ADMIT_CHILD_PATIENT,
                  ADMIT_SURGICAL_PATIENT
      part obtain-permission:
            OBTAIN_PERMISSION(p,p.guardian),
end {ADMIT_SURGICAL_CHILD_PATIENT}
```

Figure 8

Note that redefinitions of definitional properties must be consistent with the properties they replace. For example, the value of the age property of child, CHILD_AGE_VALUE, must be a specialization of AGE_VALUE (Figures 5 and 6). Similarly, the redefinitions of properties such as

p and pt in ADMIT_CHILD_PATIENT are all consistent
with the properties of ADMIT_PATIENT they replace
(Figures 2 and 8). An interesting application of
this consistency rule involves properties whose
value is an assertion class such as the a1 property
of ADMIT_PATIENT (Figure 2). For ADMIT_PATIENT the
value of a1 is the assertion ARRIVAL(p), while for
ADMIT_SURGICAL_PATIENT (Figure 8) the value of a1
is the stronger assertion ARRIVAL(p) AND
SURGERY_NEEDED(p).

Specialization can also be used to structure
assertion class definitions. The IN_HOSPITAL
assertion class, for instance, can be specialized
by specializing its arguments, by adding conjuncts
(parts), or even by redefining some of its parts.
Thus, for child patients, IN_HOSPITAL might be
specialized (see Figure 9) to check that the
patient is in a ward accompanied by a nurse.

ASSERTION_CLASS CHILD_IN_HOSPITAL
                        subclass of IN_HOSPITAL
        argument p: CHILD
        part in-ward?: IN_WARD(p),
             with-nurse?: WITH_NURSE(p),
end {CHILD_IN_HOSPITAL}

Figure 9

We close this section by pointing out that
metaclasses (and metametaclasses) are also
organized into specialization hierarchies, as
suggested in Figure 10.

4. RELATED WORK

In this section we argue the advantages and
utility of the requirements modeling framework. We
justify our choices of specification concepts
(namely, the entity categories, property
categories, and abstraction mechanisms) by
demonstrating that they are based on a consensus
over a wide variety of specification and modeling
experience. Moreover, our framework subsumes the
features of important requirements languages.

4.1 Related requirements languages

The achievement of a highly uniform framework is
a goal partly inspired by Softech's SADT [22]. SADT
offers data and activity concepts and uses the same
graphical box and arrow notation for describing
both. A data concept is defined (decomposed) in a
diagram showing the data subparts as boxes
interconnected by arrows representing activities.
Activity objects are defined by a "dual" kind of
diagram in which activity boxes are interconnected
by data arrows.

RMF's "object" and "activity" correspond to
SADT's data and activity, and RMF adds a third,
complementary specification unit, assertions, to
facilitate the explicit specification of
information which in an SADT model would usually be
specified in accompanying natural language text. In
addition, RMF makes explicit the use of abstraction
principles, which we believe the modeler tends to

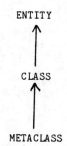

ENTITY

CLASS

METACLASS

Generalization hierarchy for metametaclasses

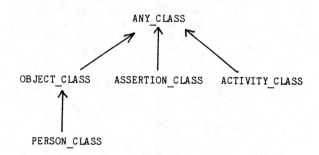

Generalization hierarchy for metaclasses

Figure 10

use implicitly during requirements modeling to
interpret an SADT model.

By way of analogy with SADT's three arrow types
(Input/Control/Output) between data and activity,
we have considered various kinds of relationships
between RMF's three entity categories as candidate
property categories. RMF property categories offer
some explicit interpretations for the relationships
represented by the SADT arrows.

A second language which supports requirements
specifications is PSL (Problem Statement Language)
[26] which was the first automated facility for
storing and managing "problem statements". A
problem statement is a functional specification in
the form of a data-oriented target-system
description. Such a functional specification
differs from a requirements model by making design
decisions that determine system boundaries. "System
structures" are distinguished from internal process
and data structures that are used to capture
characteristics of the target system.

PSL does offer a number of useful relationship
types which support our choice of property
categories. These relationship types fall into
several groups, some of which are roughly as
follows: (i) System Flow -- a process may receive
input data and generate output data; (ii) Data
Derivation -- a process may use data to derive or
update data; (iii) System Dynamics -- events occur
when a condition becomes true/false or upon
inception/termination of a process, and an event

may trigger a process. (Most of the words used in (i)-(iii) above stem from the PSL vocabulary of keywords.) Many of the RMF property categories coincide with these useful PSL relationships, and all PSL statements can be expressed in RMF. Moreover, by applying the notions of symmetry inspired by SADT, we discovered other useful relationships. The resultant symmetry among RMF relationships is what permits a rather concise formalization of RMF.

RSL (the Requirement Statement Language) is part of perhaps the most comprehensive project to date to examine and improve the state of the art [2]. The language itself is a functional specification language oriented to real-time systems such as command and control systems. It offers a set of relationships similar to but somewhat more concise than PSL, with the major differences being due to its real-time-system orientation. RSL allows members of an "entity-class" to be members of one subordinate "entity-type". However, there is no enforced relationship between data associated with an entity-class and data associated with its entity-types. This is a simple form of a kind of subclass relationship and an example of where RMF attempts to provide a more general modeling facility.

RSL also offers a general graphical control flow specification feature called an Rnet. The Rnets describe partial ordering among processes, have a "subnet" notation for suppressing details, and provide for control flow events to "trigger" other events. Thus, Rnets provide a formal structure for specifying information about events and conditions. RMF uses its assertion objects in several roles (property categories) to express these kinds of information.

4.2 Semantic database modeling and knowledge representation

As illustrated by a recent workshop [9], researchers in several areas of Computer Science, notably in Artificial Intelligence (AI) and Data Base Management, have independently concluded that real-world modeling is of paramount importance for building computer systems, albeit each of these areas has goals and perspectives that differ somewhat from those of Software Engineering.

One of the central themes of AI is the Representation of Knowledge [8], which has been found indispensable for simulating human behavior (e.g., natural language understanding) and for building "expert" systems. Semantic Networks (see [7] for a review) have been used in AI for over a decade as ways of representing and especially organizing world knowledge through the notions of "nodes" (for entities) and "links" of various types (indicating types of relationships). The abstraction principles used in RMF are directly supported by many versions of semantic networks. Generalization, under the heading of "IS-A hierarchies", has received considerable attention in AI. The basic organization of RMF, modulo the assertion classes, has been directly influenced by this AI research, especially PSN [15]. The

popularity of semantic networks in AI provides independent motivation to our work and further confidence in its appropriateness.

In the field of Data Bases, semantic or conceptual models (see [17] for an overview) have gained increasing popularity as ways of describing database schemata which enhance comprehensibility, and hence facilitate database design and maintenance. In fact, the terms "aggregation" and "generalization" were introduced in [24] in the context of database design. Semantic data models, however, concentrate by and large on the specification of objects (i.e. "data"). Increasing attention is being given to specification of constraints on the validity of data, and to a lesser extent to specification of activities. As discussed in [18], extending current modeling capabilities with respect to logical information and activities is essential to improving on current semantic models.

The Taxis model [19] is one of the few semantic data models that extends the use of abstraction facilities beyond data. In fact, Taxis uses aggregation, generalization, and classification for organizing relations, transactions, exceptions, and "scripts" for user interfaces [5]. Our current work on requirements modeling has been carried out within the framework of Taxis, with the purpose of providing a higher-level specification language that would be appropriate for expressing, as a special case of requirements specification, Corporate Requirements, the need for which is described in [16]. We expect, as well, that the use of the same abstraction principles in the RMF as in Taxis will enhance the utility of the RMF for information system design using Taxis.

Our approach is consistent with views in [29] that strongly advocate the use of semantic modeling in Software Engineering. Among other semantic modeling work relevant to requirements modeling, we note the work reported in [10],[23], and [25], which similarly emphasize the importance of modeling real-world phenomena as a system analysis approach. [23] presents a conceptual modeling approach based on semantic networks and uses an IS-A hierarchy for organizing concepts. Another language similar in spirit to RMF is presented in [27]; it is based on variations of the same abstraction principles provided by RMF.

We point out that although RMF has its roots in previous work in AI and Data Bases, it provides novel capabilities. These include assertions as another category of entities, property categories for defining (abbreviating) pertinent information types, and the uniform application of the abstraction principles to all object categories.

Of course, any descriptive framework based on classes must acknowledge Simula as a precursor. We also acknowledge Smalltalk (see Byte magazine, August 1981) as having influenced our basic framework; both RMF and Smalltalk are "object-oriented" (this is a different sense of the word "object" than used elsewhere in this paper) in that each specification unit encapsulates the description of some conceptual entity. Just how the ideas of these (as well as of certain other) programming languages compare to our framework is quite interesting, but such a discussion is beyond the scope of this paper.

5. AN ASSESSMENT OF RMF

5.1 Concerning methodology

At the heart of many software development methodologies lies one or more abstraction mechanisms, which allow us to ignore details at some level, plus a refinement principle which provides for the guided and gradual reintroduction of details across the abstraction dimension. The aggregation abstraction forms the core of software design methodologies such as "stepwise refinement" (e.g., [28]). Similarly, the "implementation" dimension is the basis for the abstract machine and abstract data type related methodologies (e.g., [20]). The generalization abstraction has not been exploited in Software Engineering as have the other dimensions. Yet, it is our contention that it is an invaluable organizational tool for system description in general, and for requirements modeling in particular.

The main idea of specification guided by generalization is that a model can be constructed by modeling first the most general classes, and then proceeding to more specialized classes. For example, in modeling a hospital world, one might consider first the concepts of patient, doctor, admission, treatment, etc. Later, the modeler can differentiate between child patients, heart patients, internists and surgeons, surgical and medical treatments, etc. At each step, only the information (properties) appropriate to that level are specified. (We do not rule out the need to iterate, i.e. to go back to revise previous level.)

Generalization is the appropriate principle to exploit when the difficulty of modeling is due to a large number of details rather than due to the complexity of the system/world; a hierarchy of classes organized along this dimension provides a convenient structure for distributing information (expressed uniformly as properties in RMF) and associating it where it most naturally belongs. Such stepwise refinement by specialization [6] is orthogonal and complementary to the more usual "stepwise refinement by aggregation", whose main effect is to decompose complex situations into a number of less complex ones. Both kinds of refinement are orthogonal and complementary to a third dimension, the progression from "world-oriented" specifications to specifications of a more and more completely implemented system.

5.2 An underlying model for RMF

Since descriptive languages are notoriously ambiguous, we are working on a detailed formal definition of a language based on RMF. We limit our discussion to an outline of the underlying formalism and the advantages of such a definition. (For a detailed presentation, see [13].)

The underlying model is based on a logic involving time, in which we can make assertions about the properties that any entity has with respect to special time entities called "situations". At any moment in time (i.e., in any situation), the "world" being described is characterized essentially by knowledge of what entities are instances of what classes (metaclasses,etc). Object classes have as instances those entities that are deemed to exist (i.e. to be relevant) at that time; an activity class has as instances activities that are occurring, or active, at that time; an assertion class is considered to have as instances assertions that are true at that moment.

Each period when an entity belongs to a class is characterized by an initial (insertion) time and a final (removal) time. During this period, the object is expected to have the factual properties induced by the definitional properties of the class. Thus, a description can, in fact, be expressed in the form of axioms defining the meaning of the "instance-of" and "subclass-of" relations.

Property categories can now be explained as designating axiom schemata, which provide templates for the axioms that represent properties in the respective property categories. For example, an initial condition for an object class expresses a condition that is true for each object that enters the class at its time of entry. This is captured in our logic by an axiom defining the property category initially as a predicate over properties of objects, involving the object, an assertion, and the insertion time (situation).

The axiom schemata give precise meaning to property categories, so that property categories can now be seen as abbreviations for commonly encountered restrictions on properties. The way is open for users of RMF to extend the list of property categories as dictated by the exigencies of special domains of discourse.

Such an underlying model relates an RMF description to formal semantics which will be useful for developing theoretical and pragmatic tools supporting the consistency of descriptions.

The big advantage of descriptions based on logic with time is that the descriptions are quite declarative. One has a view of the entire time-line (more precisely, over all relevant situations). Information that is typically represented by control flow specifications in other models is subsumed here by logical formulae involving situations plus information about the relationships between situations, which impose a partial (time) ordering on situations.

5.3 Uniformity

There are several senses in which the framework exhibits high uniformity. Given the "instance-of" relation and initial/final situations, it is straight-forward to define primitive insert/remove actions which add and delete entities from classes.

These actions are intuitive for objects. Applying the same ideas to assertions and activities, we model activation/termination of activities, and becoming true/false for assertions as the insertion/removal of entities of the respective categories.

The imposition of generalization hierarchies on each object category results in an interesting perspective as well. For objects, one can view an entity as starting out in a particular class and moving around on the hierarchy throughout its lifetime. For example, a person could become a child patient, later (by virtue of growing older) an adult patient, and so on. An activity's behavior can be viewed at several levels of generalization depending on what aspects of its participants (inputs, outputs, controls) its effects (preconditions, postconditions, and conditions it maintains), and components (parts) are associated at each level. For assertions, the imposition of a generalization hierarchy is particularly novel and interesting. Assertions viewed as entities are propositions whose (semantic) interpretation (i.e. specification of under what circumstances they are true) depends on the classes in which they reside. Clearly, in RMF, one assertion class is a specialization of another only if the former logically implies the latter. Property inheritance ensures consistency between assertion classes. Thus, the generalization abstraction organizes assertions according to both their arguments and their assertional import.

Concerning property categories, it turns out that most of those we have found useful can be defined in terms of a small number of items of information. There are many forms of uniformity (symmetry, duality) present. Many of the axiom schemata for the property categories are virtually identical except for, e.g., the entity category of the property subject or value, whether the insert vs. remove time is mentioned, the order of binding through quantifiers over classes and time, etc. As a simple example, initially, precondition, and inserted-by property categories all assert something about the insert time of the property subject, while postcondition and removed-by property categories all assert something about the remove time of the property subject. Parts and constraints are examples of property categories of objects that pertain to the entire instance interval and, in fact, their schemata are identical except for the fact that a part associates an object while a constraint associates an assertion.

5.4 Conclusion

We do not claim to have invented the abstraction mechanisms combined in the framework; rather, we have argued that they are independently motivated by several modeling endeavors. What we HAVE done is to combine them in a simple, constructive way, and we have explained some principles of interaction and their appropriateness for requirements specification.

When we say RMF "captures more world knowledge" than other specification techniques, we are referring to the semantic information that is conveyed by the three concept types, the kinds of relationships provided, and the use of assertions in roles where English is used in other techniques. More specifically, we mean that RMF captures world knowledge more formally (in the same sense that Predicate Calculus is more formal than English), and without resorting to more implementation oriented concepts.

We wish to stress that successful modeling depends not just on how one represents knowledge but on how one structures or organizes it. For example, Predicate Calculus would be adequate, from the point of view of expressibility, for representing knowledge; however, it does not provide good structuring facilities. We have argued in this paper that structuring/organizing a model should be based on useful abstraction mechanisms such as those offered by RMF.

In this paper we have bypassed discussing the important task of how the relevant terms of the domain of discourse are initially identified and recorded. We propose that this task should be done separately and thoroughly prior to RMF modeling. We intend to use an SADT-like technique to set up an initial ("structured") lexicon of the terms whose semantic relationships are of importance to the model. Our current research [13] investigates the connection between such a lexicon and the RMF model: how to proceed from the former to the latter and how to maintain consistency between them.

A common problem with using abstractions is that humans often over-abstract in an effort to establish regularity in their environment; thus, although at first sight all patients admitted to the hospital must have blood-pressure taken, some subclasses such as AMPUTEE may not, and even the most heartless hospital will not reject a patient because he doesn't know his health insurance number. One aspect of our current research concerns appropriate responses to such exceptional situations and how exception specifications serve as yet another abstraction principle in organizing large, detailed descriptions [4].

We also believe (calendar, clock) time to be essential to requirements modeling, since many requirements involve expressing things about time. The time model proposed in [10] would be appropriate and fits directly into our framework as object modeling; we would extend it to activity and assertion entities within RMF.

Finally, within the Taxis Project at the University of Toronto, we are applying the same general principles to different phases of Software Engineering, and we believe they will be a key factor in developing a unified approach to Software Engineering.

Acknowledgments: The authors wish to thank Brian Nixon for technical assistance during preparation of the manuscript, Theresa Miao for typing help, and, finally, the members of the Taxis Group for their constant support.

6. REFERENCES

[1] Bell, T. E., and T. A. Thayer, "Software Requirements: Are They Really a Problem?", Proceedings of the Second International Conference on Software Engineering, San Francisco, October 1976, pp. 61-68.

[2] Bell, T. E., D. C. Bixler, and M. E. Dyer, "An Extendible Approach to Computer-Aided Software Requirements Engineering," in [21], pp. 49-60.

[3] Boehm, B., "Software Engineering: R&D Trends and Defense Needs," in Wegner, P. (editor), Research Directions in Software Technology, MIT Press, 1979.

[4] Borgida, A., "Flexible handling of exceptions: a prospectus for research," Dept. of Computer Science, Rutgers Univ., Feb. 1982.

[5] Borgida, A., J. Mylopoulos, J., and H. K. T. Wong, "Methodological and Computer Aids for Interactive Information System Design," in Automated Tools for Information System Design,, H.-J. Schneider and A. Wasserman (editors), IFIP, North-Holland, 1982.

[6] Borgida, A., J. Mylopoulos, and H. K. T. Wong, "Taxonomic Software Specifications," in M. Brodie, J. Mylopoulos, and J. Schmidt (Eds.), Perspectives on Conceptual Modelling, Springer-Verlag, 1982.

[7] Brachman, R. J., "On the Epistemological Status of Semantic Networks," in [12].

[8] Brachman, R. and B. Smith (editors), Special Issue on Knowledge Representation, SIGART No. 50, February 1980.

[9] Brodie, M. L., and S. N. Zilles (eds.), Proceedings of the Workshop on Data Abstraction, Databases and Conceptual Modelling, Pingree Park, CO, 23-26 June 1980, SIGPLAN Notices, Volume 16, No. 1, Jan.1981.

[10] Bubenko, J. A., "Information Modeling in the Context of System Development," IFIP 80.

[11] Dijkstra, E. W., "Notes on Structured Programming," Structured Programming, Academic Press, 1972.

[12] Findler, N. (Editor), Associative Networks, Academic Press, 1979.

[13] Greenspan, S. J., Ph. D. Thesis on Requirements Modeling, Dept. of Computer Science, University of Toronto (forthcoming).

[14] Hoare, C. A. R., "Notes on Data Structuring," in Structured Programming, Academic Press, 1972.

[15] Levesque, H. J., and J. Mylopoulos, "A Procedural Approach to Semantic Networks," in [12], pp. 93-120.

[16] Lum, V., et al., 1978 New Orleans Data Base Design Workshop Report, IBM Research Report RJ2554, San Jose, July 1979.

[17] McLeod, D. and R. King, "Semantic Database Models," in Principles of Database Design, S. B. Yao (editor), Prentice Hall, 1981.

[18] McLeod, D., and J. Smith, "Abstraction in Databases," in [9].

[19] Mylopoulos, M., P. A. Bernstein, and H. K. T. Wong, "A Language Facility for Designing Interactive Database-Intensive Application," ACM Transactions on Database Systems, Volume 5, Number 2, June 1980, pp. 185-207.

[20] Parnas, D., "On the Criteria to be Used in Decomposing Systems Into Modules," Comm. ACM, Vol 15, No. 12, December 1972, pp. 1053-1058.

[21] Ross, D. T. (guest editor) Special Issue on Requirements Analysis," IEEE Transactions on Software Engineering, Vol. SE-3, No. 1, January 1977.

[22] Ross, D. T., "Structured Analysis(SA): A Language for Communicating Ideas," in [21], pp. 16-34.

[23] Roussopoulos, N., "CSDL: A Conceptual Schema Definition Language for the Design of Data Base Applications," IEEE Transactions on Software Engineering, Volume SE-5, Number 5, September 1979, pp. 481-496.

[24] Smith, J., and D. Smith, "Database Abstractions: Aggregation and Generalization," TODS, Vol. 2, No. 2, 1977, pp.105-133.

[25] Solvberg, A., "A Contribution to the Definition of Concepts for Expressing Users' Information Systems Requirements," Proc. International Conf. on Entity-Relationship Approach to Systems Analysis and Design, December 10-12,1979, pp. 359-380.

[26] Teichroew, D. and E. Hershey, III, "PSL/PSA: A Computer-Aided Technique for Structured Documentation and Analysis of Information Processing Systems," in [21], pp.41-48.

[27] Wilson, M., "A Semantics-Based Approach to Requirements Analysis and System Design," Proc. COMPSAC 79, Nov. 1979, pp.107-112.

[28] Wirth, N., "Program Development by Stepwise Refinement," Comm ACM, April 1971.

[29] Yeh, R. et al., "Software Requirement Engineering: A Perspective," Dept. of Computer Science, Univ. of Texas, Austin, 1979.

Part IV

External Design

The word "design" has been used to describe many different aspects of creating a software system, including the choice of functions for a system and the internal structure of the software. We find it useful to separate the design activity into categories. One such category is termed *external design*, denoting those activities and concepts related to designing the functional (or external) aspect of a system.

Despite all of the work in software engineering and its related disciplines of programming methodology, it is important for the designer to remember that the average user is totally unconcerned about the internal structure of a program, the programming language used to write that program, or the number of "goto" statements, if any, that appear in the code.

From the user's perspective, the only important issues are whether the program does what it should do, is available when needed, performs reliably and correctly, and whether it is easy to use. A beautifully structured program that ignores the user interface will almost certainly be rejected in favor of a more hospitable user interface. The validity of this observation may best be seen by examining the market for home computers and their software. Most of the best external designs are to be found there, especially in video games.

Thus, the software designer must be concerned with the external design of the system as well as with the architectural structure and the detailed algorithms. In many respects, this aspect of design is really an analysis and specification issue, so we take up this subject prior to discussing other aspects of system design. This Part includes four papers that address various aspects of the external design process.

The first paper, by Williamson and Rohlfs, "The User Interface Design Process," presents a methodology for interface design. Their methodology has well identified stages, beginning with goal setting based on requirements and concluding with finalization of the interaction language, with scenarios of use as an important

intermediate stage. The authors illustrate their methodology with a message system for an organization.

The paper by Wasserman and Stinson, "A Specification Method for Interactive Information Systems," describes part of the User Software Engineering methodology (see Part IX). Design of the user interface is a critical early step in the methodology, and this paper describes the use of transition diagrams for specifying the inputs, the system messages, and the associated operations. While the underlying ideas of this method have not changed since this paper was published in 1979, they have since been extended to be more flexible in handling different kinds of user input and in allowing input strings to be saved, thereby augmenting the basic notion of transition diagrams.

The remaining papers in this Part address the broader issues of user participation in the design process. It is now well understood that systems may have a significant impact on the organizations in which they are used and that one cannot successfuly impose a system on most user communities.

Enid Mumford has coined the term "Participative Systems Design" and her paper describes that concept, ·showing how these ideas were applied in the design of an interactive system. Participative systems design means "handing responsibility for the design of a new work system to the employees who eventually will have to operate it." Mumford divides Participative Systems Design into three approaches: "consultative" design, "representative" design, and "consensus" design, each of which demands a successively higher degree of user participation. Mumford's paper introduces a set of social, psychological, and organizational issues that have not received much recognition in the software engineering community, yet which are crucial to the operational success of computer-based systems in organizations.

The final paper, by Rudawitz and Freeman, describes "Client-Centered Design," using an approach that Mumford would term "consultative."

The guidelines presented in this paper include both user-oriented considerations, including user interfaces and organizational impact, and software engineering considerations, such as modular programs using good programming style.

It is clear from the papers in this Part that the process of design is much broader than the technical measures of system structure and selection of logical data structures. This observation holds true in other disciplines as well -- an architecture for a building may be attractive and economically feasible, but the proposed structure and use may be totally inappropriate in a specific environment. Just as architects must address environmental aspects when making a design, so should software designers be aware of the environment for which the software is being designed.

THE USER INTERFACE DESIGN PROCESS

Hilary Williamson
Sabine Rohlfs

Messaging Systems Department
Bell-Northern Research Ltd.
Ottawa, Ontario
Canada

This paper describes a pragmatic approach to user-oriented systems design. General phases in the design of a user interface are presented. Design phases and design justification are illustrated by examples from an organizational messaging system.

1. INTRODUCTION

The success of new office products and value-added network sevices will depend not only on their functionality, but also on their ease of use and user acceptance of them. To a great extent, these determine the efficiency and effectiveness gains — and therefore the success — of a system. This implies serious attention to the user interface.

User interface design traditionally refers to that subset of the system design process which deals with the layer of functionality driving the user – system interaction. Historically this was done by computer scientists as one component of an overall system design. This led to a computer-oriented design. More recently, there has been a growing interest from ergonomics and psychology in making the design more user-oriented.

When the user interface designer delves into the existing literature he finds: description of hardware such as lightpen or softkey and how they can be used to facilitate user – system dialogue [1]; general guidelines for system behaviour and the role of user and system in a dialogue [2], [3]; do's and don'ts for special purpose systems such as data entry systems [4], and classification schemes by task, type of problem solving activity, type of terminal, and so on [5], [6], [7].

What he does not find is a methodology that combines traditional systems analysis with the more recent guidelines from other disciplines. This makes it particularly difficult to design a system such as an office system, where there is a divergent user population with different user and organizational requirements, and where neither the technology nor its impacts are well understood.

This paper suggests a pragmatic aproach, based on a methodology for user-oriented design. This approach is based on the authors' experience in various projects, and some evidence from the literature. The paper does not cover all aspects of system design, nor does it consider the implementation phases.

Section 2 of the paper examines the user interface designer's position within the organization responsible for the product. An electronic messaging system is introduced in section 3. Phases in the design process are presented and illustrated by examples from the messaging system in section 4. The paper concludes with some general recommendations.

2. THE DESIGNER'S DILEMMA

During the design process the designer often finds himself in the position of having to find a compromise between the contradictory requirements of different users - one user's "must have" is another one's "not needed". Traditionally, designer and user have been described as a sort of Odd Couple (see for example [8]).

Taking a broader look, there are a variety of groups with influence on system design: for example, an organization might involve its marketing group, engineering and product control in addition to the designer's own management, and a steering committee. With this perspective, the Odd Couple expands into an Odd Quintuple:

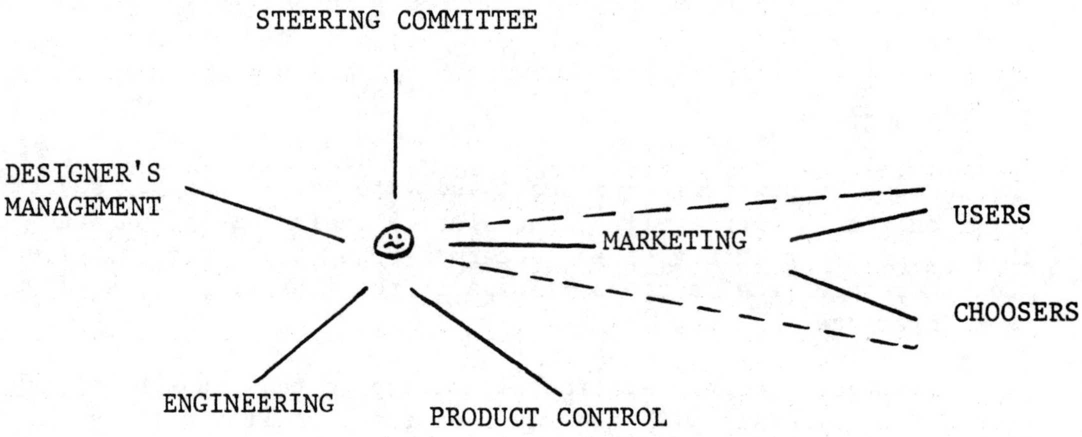

Figure I: The Odd Quintuple

The groups involved will vary from one organization to another, depending on organization structure, and the type of project and product management involved [9]. The picture becomes more complex when the design is for a product rather than an in-house system. In the case of a product it is sometimes difficult to identify future users, and hence participative design techniques (as described in [10]) are not directly applicable. The figure above illustrates both cases. In the in-house situation the designer has direct contact with users. In the case of a product, marketing often represents the end user, and are the designer's customer.

Each group in the example has a different perspective on the system, and different measurements of reward in their own positions. As a result, they often pull the design in different directions.

Marketing's view of the system is oriented towards the needs of their current and anticipated customer base, potential revenue and competitive position. Their view is in turn influenced to a large extent by the organizational requirements of the potential buyers, and less by the needs of the individual user. The choosers make the decision to purchase, but are rarely users themselves [11].

The product control group is interested in overall product integrity and in administration. Their bias is towards ease of support and maintenance, extensibility and release control. The emphasis is on administrative tools and interfaces, which become their measure of success.

Engineering are interested in a design that facilitates development, and helps them to control cost and schedule. Their aim is often ease of implementation, which does not necessarily imply ease of use. They are prone to resist changes in the design, particularly ongoing ones.

The designer's management is often interested in proving that they are on top of state-of-the-art developments in the field. This is their measure of success.

The mandate of the steering committee is to ensure design compatibility with company policy, judge the quality of the work, and arbitrate conflicts [12]. But it is hard to judge design quality [13], and experience shows that committee members are often influenced by their own background and positions.

Thus, the designer is caught between conflicting goals. This results in a bargaining situation, with the designer striving to hold together a consistent design, and to keep everyone happy. This often results in a design that satisfies no one.

The designer must understand these conflicting demands and pressures, and try to generate cooperation and consensus. The steering committee takes on this role for high-level decisions, but the designer himself must negotiate towards consensus on the myriad of detail decisions that determine a user-oriented design. He has to work as an educator, facilitator, consultant, and advisor, without taking the role of an arbitrator [14]. The designer must face the fact that design is as much a political as a conceptual process. "Unfortunately, 'politics' have been equated with evil, ... but politics are the process of getting commitment, or building support, or creating momentum for change." [12].

The intent of the remainder of this paper is to provide some guidelines for the conceptual side of the design process, and some techniques for justification of design that can aid the designer in consensus generation.

3. OVERVIEW OF A MESSAGING DESIGN

The following discusses design considerations for an organizational messaging system, and introduces an organizational messaging model. This is then used as a basis for presentation of phases in the user interface design process.

3.1 Organizational Messaging and Its Implications for Design

Today's perspective on messaging has emerged out of two very different backgrounds. The earlier public message switching services cater to the point-to-point transmission of textual information, and are used for the exchange of such information as stock lists or pricing updates. They are mainly used by the business community for "administrative" messaging purposes.

The later electronic message and conferencing systems, such as MSG [15], HERMES

[16], FORUM [17], EIES [18], were initially developed and used by a select scientific community as a replacement for certain types of phone calls, letters and face-to-face meetings. These systems are largely used for communication of "personal" messages between individuals.

Not only do these existing message systems come from historically different backgrounds, but they also serve very different user needs.

A system for general use within an organization should support both personal and administrative messaging features. In some respects, administrative and personal messaging represent extremes of usage:

> Administrative messaging is more formal. Communication paths tend to be fixed and related to the structure of an organization. Communication events are driven by organizational procedures. An example would be daily price updates from a head office to all branch offices, prepared by managers and entered by teletype operators.

> Personal messaging tends to be informal. Communication paths are more dynamic, from individual to individual. Communication events are based on need, which varies from day to day. As an example, John Smith asks Ann Dupont about her personal opinion of the outcome of a meeting.

Organizational messaging incorporates both administrative and personal usage. As an example, a manager sends monthly status reports, and also communicates with various people on a day-to-day problem solving basis. These two extremes in the spectrum of usage lead to design emphasis on flexibility in the basic functions.

3.2 Overview of an Organizational Messaging User Interface

A messaging user is an individual (or a group with the same job function), with a single user identity. A messaging user accesses the system interactively to read and send messages. This is the most common form of access for personal messaging use.

Another form of access, that originated in administrative systems, is provided by the auto-delivery station. This is a terminal that can accept delivery of messages in unattended mode, on behalf of one or more messaging users. For administrative messaging, this provides an alternative to signing on to read mail. In personal messaging, it might be used simply to provide a printed record of mail, or a general delivery facility.

An organization is a named set of messaging users and auto-delivery stations. An organization has an organization coordinator. This is a messaging user who has additional capabilities to administer the users of an organization.

Every messaging user has a basic environment that resembles his desk-top:

> an in-basket for his incoming messages with a tabular overview in an in-list,

> an out-basket containing certain outgoing messages with an overview in an out-list,

> a message sheet for message composition,

246

a note-file as a private filing area, with an overview in the note-list,

a personal profile.

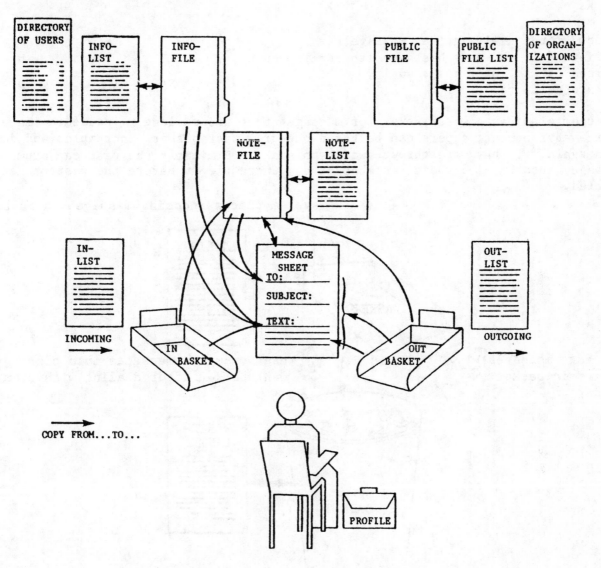

Figure II: User Environment

The elements of a user's messaging environment and their inter-relationships are described in the following.

The in-basket is a repository for all user's incoming messages and serves the same purpose as the in-basket on the desk-top. The in-list contains an overview with one entry per message, in order of arrival. Each entry is referenced by its temporary sequence number, a tag provided for ease of issuing commands. In addition, the system assigns a unique, system-wide message identification to every message when it is sent.   This global identification can be used in dialogue between users.

Each in-list entry contains two flags. The delivery flag highlights special cases in message delivery, such as that the message is urgent, or has been automatically

247

forwarded to this user.

The status flag tells the recipient how much he already knows about the message, in order to facilitate use of the in-list as a "to-do" list. For example, the flag can be:

 -"new" for a newly arrived message,
 -"listed" if the user has seen its in-list entry,
 -"read" if the user has read it,
 -"auto-delivered".

The user also has a wastebasket for messages that are no longer needed. In the office environment, papers can be taken out of a wastebasket, uncrumpled and dealt with again, if they were thrown away by mistake. Similarly the user can crumple a message into an electronic wastebasket and uncrumple it before the wastebasket is emptied.

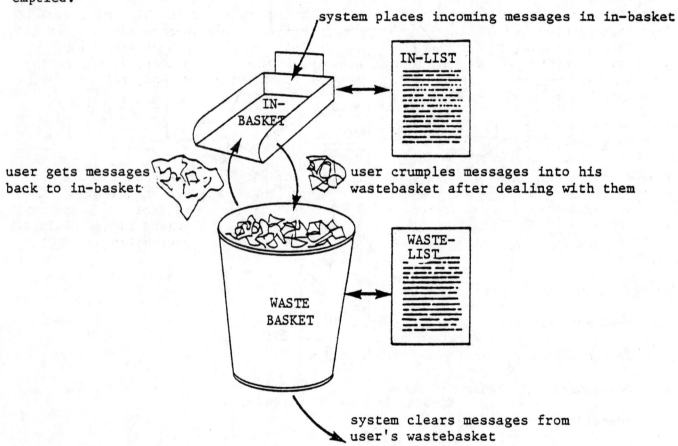

system places incoming messages in in-basket

IN-LIST

user gets messages back to in-basket

user crumples messages into his wastebasket after dealing with them

WASTE-LIST

system clears messages from user's wastebasket

Figure III: Wastebasket

In the standard office environment, the out-basket is a holding area for outgoing mail. This does not apply to the electronic out-basket since the system dispatches messages immediately. Instead, this out-basket can be used as a holding area for messages being "tracked", and the out-list becomes a "to-follow-up" list.

Tracking of delivery is critical for administrative messaging use when there is a time limit on important information, as for sensitive pricing data. It is also useful in personal messaging, for example in setting up an urgent meeting. This is discussed in more detail in section 4.3.1.

Message composition is based on the message sheet, which is like a sheet of formatted stationary always available on the desk-top. Its fields (including the recipient list) can be entered in any order, and the message sheet edited as a whole, just as for a conventional letter.

A user can compose a message by issuing commands to fill the specific fields of the message sheet, or he can be prompted to enter them by the system. He can copy a distribution list to the To: field and then insert more addresses. He can copy items from a private file folder into the contents field. He can copy entire messages from the in-basket or out-basket and insert comments, in order to annotate and then forward the information.

A user's personal profile provides a means of tailoring usage to his own needs. The organization coordinator sets initial profile values when he adds a user to the system, and only he can change certain profile permissions that are under organizational control. The user himself can change any other profile values at any time. A user need not bother with his profile but, with experience, he may wish to adjust his mode of interaction.

4. USER INTERFACE DESIGN PHASES

The following discusses phases in a user-oriented design, in the context of the organizational messaging system described above. This presents the authors' own view of the design process, based on the messaging design above and on previous work ([19], [20], [21]). It does not attempt to cover all phases in the product cycle from market research to implementation, but only the user-oriented design aspects.

Stages in the design are:

    Goal setting based on requirements.

    Design of a functional model.

    Development of scenarios of use.

    Identification of dimensions of use.

    Design of feature sets.

    Personalization of features.

    User documentation.

    Finalization of the interaction language.

As in any other design effort, these stages are iterative - the diagram below only reflects major iterations. The designer must communicate his design, and the focus for that communication changes throughout the design process towards different groups in the organization.

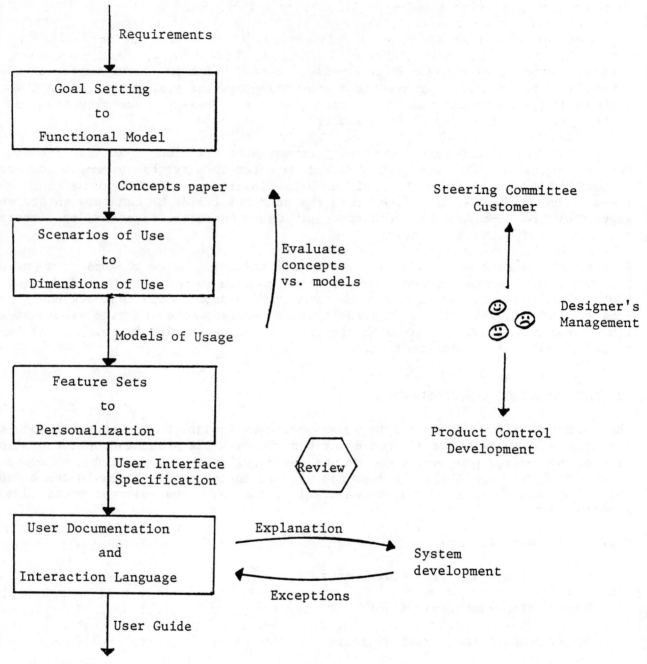

Figure IV: Phases of User Interface Design

4.1 Phase I: Goal Setting to Functional Model

The design process usually starts with some sort of requirements document, preceded by negotiations amongst various groups in the organization. Requirements are usually expressed as specific features or ways in which the system should behave. Dialogue is necessary in order for the designer to determine the intent behind the requirements as written.

4.1.1 The importance of clearly identified goals

The designer should not attempt the design process without working out a clear and agreed upon set of objectives with all groups involved. As noted in [22], "A system developed without specific, agreed objectives is rather like the old adage of Christopher Columbus' voyage of discovery: 'That he set out not really knowing where he was going, arrived not really knowing where he was, and came back not really knowing where he'd been.'" If early agreement on objectives cannot be reached, "no level of technical sophistication nor inspired project management can rescue the situation." [14].

The primary goal, in the case in question was to design an organizational messaging system. The designer starts by working out sub-goals, i.e. the implications of an "organizational" system. That is, it must include both administrative and personal messaging features. It requires flexibility in the basic functions in order to support a wide variety of users, and it must satisfy the needs of the organization in terms of administration and control.

Next, the designer lists the basic functions by asking some general questions. One such question is "How should the user perceive the system?". The answer chosen in the messaging design was that the user's working environment in the system should be analogous to his existing mail capabilities in the office and in particular on his desk-top, but only where this makes sense. It is neither useful nor desirable to transfer every existing feature into the electronic environment [22].

4.1.2 Developing the Functional Model

This approach leads to an in-basket analogous to the existing one. The in-list provides the overview that a person obtains by rummaging through the office in-basket and glancing at the cover page of each document in it. Direct transfer of the existing out-basket concept did not seem appropriate since it is mainly a dispatch holding area, and messages are dispatched immediately in the electronic environment. Instead the electronic out-basket was conceived as analogous to the electronic in-basket. The in-list is often used as a "to-do" list. The out-list would be used as a "to-follow-up" list and the out-basket becomes a holding area for messages being tracked.

At this point, the designer is building a model. The model must be tested and if necessary revised, based on participative design and on real use. In the case of a product, participative design techniques are not directly applicable, but in-house or pilot customer prototype systems can be used to provide some of the necessary feedback.

Another question for the designer is "How does the user perceive his organization in the system?". This leads to the concept of an organization coordinator/ombudsman, a shared organization file space, and a directory of all users in that organization (analogous to the office phone directory). The question "What control over usage costs will the organization deem essential?" leads to the concept of the coordinator allocating private file space to users in the same way that an office administrator allocates pencil and paper, or secretarial support.

Another key question "What does it mean to a user to read a message?" leads to a comparison between the standard use of the verb "read" and its meaning in the electronic context. In natural language "read" implies an understanding of content. In a computer activity, it only implies the presentation of information to the user on a screen or paper. One result of this is that if a message system tells a sender that a message has been 'read', the sender is likely to assume 'read and understood', which may or may not be true [20].

These are only samples of a long list of questions that the designer asks at this stage. The resulting answers and the analogies to the existing environment are important to the design, but are also very useful for discussion with users and in writing user documentation.

4.1.3 Some Guidelines

At this stage, the designer usually investigates other similar systems, in order to find out the issues in provision of the basic functions. For example, existing message systems support different feature sets; have different understandings of the same feature, e.g. the out-basket; or features work in different ways, e.g. in-list resequencing.

It is also important at this stage to review the general principles of human - computer system communication ([2], [6]), and to establish a set of specific guidelines which are particularly relevant to the current design. Those key to the messaging design were:

1.   The system is to be individually adjustable,
                              and
      it should appear simple to users with simple needs.

2.   The user has control if he so desires,
                              but
      in some areas the organization requires overall control.

3.   Things that are the same should look the same,
                              and
      things that are not, should not.

4.1.4 Results

The result of this phase of the design is a concepts paper giving a framework for the system, within which specific features can be defined and can evolve. The designer must be able to prove to the satisfaction of his customer that this framework addresses their very specific requirements and constraints. There are many discussions starting "But what if...?" in which the designer finds that he did not completely understand the requirements, and the customer discovers a technical possibility that enhances the functionality. This results in iteration, and some compromise as well as improvement to the initial design. It is critical that a satisfactory functional model be agreed upon at this stage. It is not only essential to further design, but also to later system evolution.

4.2 Phase II: Scenarios of Use to Dimensions of Use

In order to translate the functional model into a detailed feature set, the designer must understand who the users are. It is very dangerous to assume an average user since there is no average user, and "building a system to satisfy the average user is likely to result in a system that does not really meet any user's needs." [8].

Thus, the next step in the design process requires development of scenarios of use for different classes of users. Ideally this is done with the users themselves in the participative design approach [10]. In the case of product design, users might be represented indirectly by marketing, or designers could have direct contact with interested customers, or the users of a prototype system.

4.2.1 Examples of Scenarios of Use

Some of the scenarios of use identified in the organizational messaging design are summarized below:

 - A specially trained clerk works full-time in a teletype room. This
   person accepts handwritten or typed messages from all over the
   organization and enters them into the system on behalf of their
   originators.

 - A select group service with a secretary sending and receiving messages
   on behalf of one or more managers. The secretary may or may not deal
   directly with message content.

 - A manager interacts directly with the system on his own behalf.

For each class of users, the designer must examine each of the basic functions, in order to determine if it is useful for that class, and if so, how it should be adapted to their use.

For example, in the teletype room scenario, it seems most useful to have all messages auto-delivered, and to have the in-basket automatically cleared once delivery is complete. This class of user may not want to be aware of the existence of the electronic in-basket. They are unlikely to use private files.

In the case of the select group service, the secretary may peruse incoming mail and take action on the manager's behalf. The mode of use would vary according to the responsibility delegated by the manager. It is likely that the manager would use the in-list as a "to-do" list and to retain complete control over clearing it (as would the secretary to whom he has delegated complete messaging responsibility). He would probably use private files.

As can be seen from the above descriptions, there is no distinct boundary between different sorts of users, and indeed there is room for a great deal of individual variation in any of these cases. In developing these scenarios, the designer should consider the organizational impact of the system, that is implied changes in the user's job content, responsibility, autonomy, and job satisfaction. Of course, he cannot fully do this, as it is essentially an organizational issue that must be solved within the organization. Participative design or design by prototype will help the designer in developing scenarios of current and anticipated use and in analyzing their impacts.

4.2.2 Determining Dimensions of Use

At this stage, the designer is attempting to map the two-dimensional average user versus basic function view of the system, into the more general one of a variety of users versus features tailored to suit their preferred mode of interaction and organizational perspective.

In order to determine the dimensions of the mapping, it is important to find out what distinguishes the requirements of the different classes of users. The following lists some examples of dimensions of use that emerged during the organizational messaging design process.

a) Direct or Mediated Use:

Use of the system is considered to be direct if a person interacts with it to deal with message content, for example to read a message and compose a reply online. Use is mediated if a person interacts with the system on behalf of someone else. That is, the user is an intermediary who deals with the message but is not responsible for its content. This dimension affects such features as mode of message composition and use of filing.

b) Frequency of Use:

Whether a person is a casual or a full-time user determines to a large extent the degree of experience he has with the system, and therefore how much guidance he should receive.

c) Active or Automatic Mode of Interaction:

Use of features is defined to be active if the user takes responsibility himself for functions, such as deleting messages he no longer needs. Use is automatic if the user has the system do it for him, for example by having it always clear messages from the in-basket under fixed conditions.

Whether a user prefers an active or automatic mode of interaction depends on his job responsibilities as well as personality - some users show a tendency to follow the human principle of least effort. Also full-time users with a high volume of messages might choose an automatic mode to help in coping with information overload.

d) Message Trafffic and Message Flow:

This refers to the number of messages dealt with in a certain time period and whether they are mostly sent, mostly received, or balanced between the two. Automatic delivery can assist users with high incoming message traffic and selection options help a user to find messages in a full in-basket or out-basket.

e) Message Broadcast Patterns:

This is determined by the number of recipients on the address list of a message. In administrative messaging, messages are often sent to the same recipients on a more or less regular basis. Features like pre-defined distribution lists help to support this.

f) Terminal and Line Speed:

Finally, the user community can have a wide set of existing terminal types and different line speeds. These have an impact on the editing capabilities to be provided and on the general form of the interface.

4.2.3 Dimensions of Use Related to Classes of Users

In the examples above, use by the teletype room class would tend to be full-time, mediated and automatic, with high outgoing message traffic. They might have a limited use of the note-file for distribution lists. Messages could be automatically cleared from their in-baskets after auto-delivery.

The secretary class would use the note-file to a greater extent, for example to save the message sheet when asked to compose an urgent message. They could have all read messages automatically cleared from their in-baskets at the end of a session. They might want to receive notifications of new incoming messages during a session. Their use is also mediated.

The manager class are direct users, with a tendency to casual usage and a lower volume of mail. They might be expected to use the note-file extensively, for example to compose a message over a long period of time or to save incoming messages for later action. They would probably want to clear messages from in-baskets and to resequence, by command.

Note that in the first two examples users need not be aware of unused features like the wastebasket, but the feature is still available. This continuity of features between classes means that a user can naturally change his mode of interaction as his use evolves or his sophistication of usage increases.

In terms of the dimensions of use, administrative messaging tends to be mediated, full-time, and with high message traffic. Personal messaging is usually direct, more casual and with lower message traffic.

4.2.4 Results

The result of this phase of the design is a document on models of usage: identification of classes of users and of the dimensions of their use. Classes of users and the scenarios of their use are key for communication with marketing or the steering committee, with system choosers and with the users themselves. Dimensions of use are key to the next stages of design, to design justification and to consensus generation.   Both are important for iteration back to verify the functional model

4.3 Phase III: Feature Sets and Their Personalization

Having identified classes of users and dimensions of their use, the designer can now attempt a detailed mapping of their requirements into feature sets, keeping the guiding principles in mind. This along with consideration of interaction style, will determine feature personalization.

At this stage, the designer also defines the type of dialogue as well as the amount of system assistance to the user [5]. The form of the dialogue, e.g. command syntax, is defined here, but the exact vocabulary is usually not finalized until software development is underway, and a full set of exception situations have been identified.

It is also important to consider how much organizational control to build into the system, in order to satisfy both system choosers and users, who naturally have different points of view on this [14]. In order to support both organizational and user control in the messaging system, a user's profile was divided into a set of options and a set of permissions. Only the organization coordinator could modify permissions, such as allocation of private filing space, and only the user himself could modify options, such as the language of interaction.

The decision as to what should be a permission and what should be an option requires careful thought, consultation with the customers, and some understanding of the psychology and social dynamics of people in an organization.

4.3.1 An Example

The issue of tracking of messages is one controversial example of an area of potential conflict between organizational control and the individual. Tracking of delivery is essential from the organizational point of view, particularly in its administrative messaging applications. However many individuals consider tracking of messages into their electronic environment a serious invasion of privacy.

This led to a specification of tracking such that the sender can tell the system to track delivery of a message, but the recipient has full control of when delivery confirmation occurs. This can be active or automatic. The system informs the recipient that the message is being tracked by use of an in-list flag and also a prompt when the message is read. The recipient can acknowledge delivery by entering a simple command, analogous to signing for a registered letter. Alternatively he can specify the confirmation condition as a profile option for automatic confirmation. He can also choose to ignore the tracking request.

When the sender receives confirmation of delivery, all he knows is that the recipient has been made aware of the existence of his message, and not that he has either read or understood the content. The latter is not under the system's control. The system provides a tool for tracking - how it is used will be influenced by organization policies, but ultimately is under the control of individual users.

4.3.2 Implications of Analysis of User Classes on Personalization

It is important that the analysis of user classes be used to allow the system to be adjustable for individual users and not to enforce specific modes of use. A profile and feature package can be recommended for a particular class of users, but any user can set his own individual options.

When user classes were identified in the messaging design, it became apparent that both automatic clearing of the in-basket, and active clearing by user command, were desirable. This led to options in the user's profile to specify either that the user actively crumples in-basket messages or that the system should clear it automatically under certain circumstances. The wastebasket is available, but unobtrusive in automatic use.

There are a variety of profile options for in-basket and out-basket management (clutter management), resequencing, tracking, and so on. Analysis of classes of use leads naturally to personalization, by identifying how a feature should be provided according to different dimensions of use. There are additional options relating to general interaction style, for example language of interaction and verbosity of system prompts.

We hypothesize that full-time, direct, active, high volume, experienced users will tend to use the most general form of features. If the simpler forms are then defined within this context, usage can evolve naturally. In the example above, a user with the automatic clearing option need not be aware of the wastebasket, how to investigate its contents, and how to uncrumple messages from it. However it is there and he can look into it at any time. At some point, as his mode of usage changes, he may decide to reset his profile option to crumple by command.

4.3.3 Caveats for the Designer

Most of the detailed user interface design falls into this phase.   The following are some general caveats for the designer:

1. There is a tendency to avoid user interface decisions by providing an excess of options that confuse the concepts and become a source of inconsistencies.

2. The ongoing design effort is usually underestimated.

3. Difficulties in the design are often overlooked and only seen at the detailed level. Exceptions are to be expected in all design phases.

4. The designer's previous experience will, consciously or subconsciously influence his current work [22]. A design team with different backgrounds, and good review help balance this.

5. The law of routine ignorance [23], that is "the more often we do something, the more we tend to forget how we do it.".

4.3.4 Results

The result of this phase of design is a detailed user interface specification. This is an important review point. During the initial phases, the designer's focus for communication moves slowly from the customer and steering committee to developers and users. All should be included in the review process. This is the point at which development can start, and there will be iteration of the user interface design based on input from developers.

4.4 Phase IV: User Documentation and Finalization of the Interaction Language

The user interface specification is one basis for software design and development (other specifications define operational interfaces, administration and so on). This results in dialogue between the user interface designer and the developers, and iterations on feature design. Once this has stabilized, user documentation can be completed.

4.4.1 User Documentation

The content of user documentation is similar to that of the interface specification, but its perspective and its structure should be very different. Unfortunately, writing user documentation is often considered to be a very minor part of the design and development cycle, and the right resources are not assigned to the task.

Good user documentation requires, in addition to sound writing skills, the ability to understand the point of view of users, and a knowledge of the design concepts and the implementation. The latter is important in order to explain to the users how to deal with error situations and the quirks of the system, that is "what to do if...". In addition, interesting analogies and illustrations help make documentation palatable to the user. The analogies used to develop the functional model can now prove useful in explanation to the user.

Thus, user documentation should be produced as a joint effort between writer, designer, programmer and psychologist. If possible, it should be discussed with users to ensure their understanding. In the product situation, this becomes more difficult, and care must be taken not to bias the documentation towards one class of user.

It is desirable that the documentation team include one person, usually the writer, who is new to the system, in order to introduce a fresh perspective. With familiarity, user interface and software designers become comfortable with their own jargon and can lose track of what will be hard for the user to understand [22].

User documentation is very often poorly structured and forces a user to read an entire document in order to gain an understanding of the 10% of features, in which he is initially interested. Structure becomes even more important when the documentation must communicate with a variety of classes of users, with different dimensions of use. User documentation can be prefaced by a short list of questions, aimed at identifying dimensions of use. The answers are then linked to a recommended "reading list" of sections, needed by that person to start using the system. The intent behind this is to present a system with inherent flexibility, while minimizing complexity for an individual user.

Online documentation or help should remind the user of what he has read in a user guide, using the same style and terminology. In general, online documentation should be short and succinct (although extensive computer-aided learning modules might be used as a training tool). A maximum of a screenful of information, or a few lines on a teletype, seems reasonable for a help request from the user. A user frequently requests help when he is in doubt about a specific thing, for example the exact syntax of a command, or a particular command verb. To find out how to perform a sequence of actions, he would be more likely to consult the user guide, or his ombudsman.

4.4.2 Finalization of the interaction language

When the user guide is near completion, and before system implementation is finished, it is important to fix the language of interaction between user and system. The language syntax must be defined before development can start, but the exact wording of commands and the language and style of system messages, menu or help information can be finalized later. Guidelines on this and common pitfalls are well documented in the literature ([24], [20]).

4.5 Evolution

Design and development is iterative, and changes will occur after documentation is complete. It is very important that user documentation, epecially online documentation, be kept up-to-date during system evolution.

Implementation into the users' working environment will not be covered here, but the user interface designer should be involved at that time, both to explain the intent of the concepts and features and to learn by feedback from implementation and usage problems [8]. This will lead to a better understanding of the users and their requirements. Participative re-design with users can then occur on the basis of initial use, and this will be key to further iteration of the design.

The functional model is very important in system evolution. Design integrity must be monitored. The ad hoc addition of extra features without consideration of the model and classes of users can undo a good user interface, just as it can destroy a good system design.

The dimensions of use can be valuable in the evaluation of feature extensions and their justification. As stated in [14], "When criteria for success are ambiguous and lack a simple measure, decisions concerning system extensions will appear arbitrary from the perspective of some of the interested parties."

In addition to monitoring design integrity, it is also important to continually evaluate its applicability. Use evolves over time [25], and the dynamics of an individual's job must be reflected in a system whose intent is to make the person more effective in doing that job [14]. Thus we postulate that if a design is useful, it will soon have to be changed.

5. CONCLUSION

In a comparison of software design to engineering design, Malhotra et al. state that it is "very difficult, in fact, to ascertain whether the design is complete, is consistent, or whether it meets the functional requirements. This seems equivalent to not being able to tell if a building will stand up!" [13]. The user-oriented design approach described, and in particular the dimensions of use, can help in justification of design.

Identification of dimensions of use can be carried much further for various types of office products and value-added services. Continuation of existing research into understanding office procedures ([26], [27], [28]) can provide insight into scenarios of use, that lead to dimensions of use. This research also provides a base of understanding that is important to all phases of user-oriented design, and key to implementation. The approach described here can also be applied to the design of administrative user interfaces to a system. This area is very important to successful system implementation, but usually receives much less attention than the general user interface.

User interface design is a discipline that requires special knowledge and skills, just as compiler writing, data base design, or architecture do. A designer or design team should have, in addition to a grounding in computer science: some basics of user interface specific knowledge from psychology, such as on response time or memory span; from linguistics an understanding of the syntactic and semantic principles of language; and some background in sociology and organization theory, relevant to issues of job design and organizational control.

Currently, good user-oriented designers are rare. There is a need to educate computer scientists in the skills and knowledge outlined above. Psychologists and linguists with a good understanding of computer science are also a rare breed, and there is a need to educate them also. Since it may be difficult to find these skills in one individual, the designer must be a good teamworker. Guidelines exist already for design of some more or less standard user interfaces, such as data entry or reservation systems ([1], [5]). However, the designer who deals with a new sort of system must develop a new approach.

REFERENCES

[1] J. Martin; Design of man - computer dialogues; Englewood Cliffs, NJ,1973.

[2] W. Dehning, H. Essig, S. Maass; The adaptation of virtual man - computer interfaces to user requirements in dialogue; Report of the Department of Informatics, University of Hamburg, W-Germany, July 1980.

[3] B. Shneiderman; Human factors in designing interactive systems; Computer, December 1979.

[4] J. Gilb, G.M. Weinberg; Humanized input - techniques for reliable keyed input; Cambridge, MA, 1977.

[5] K.D. Eason; Dialogue design implications of task allocation between man and computer; Ergonomics, vol. 23, no. 9, September 1980.

[6] B. Shackel (ed.); Man - computer communication, vol. 1, summary report; Infotech State of the Art Report, Maidenhead, England, 1979.

[7] S.L. Smith; Requirements definition and design guidelines for the man - machine interface in C3 system aquisition; Mitre report no. M80-10, April 1980.

[8] M.J. Ginzberg; Steps towards more effective implementation of MS and MIS; Interfaces, vol. 8, no. 3, May 1978.

[9] F.G. Withington; Coping with computer proliferation; Harvard Business Review, vol. 58, May-June 1980.

[10] E. Mumford, F. Land, J. Hawgood; A participative approach to the design of computer systems; Impact of Science on Society, vol. 28, 1978.

[11] J. Bair; Avoiding working non-solutions to office communications system design; Proc. of COMPCON Spring 1980.

[12] P.G.W. Keen; Information systems and organizational change; Communications of the ACM, vol. 24, no. 1, January 1981.

[13] A. Malhotra, J.C. Thomas, J.M. Carroll, L.A. Miller; Cognitive processes in design; International Journal of Man-Machine Studies, vol. 12, 1980.

[14] P.G.W Keen, E.M. Gerson; The politics of software design; Datamation, November 1977.

[15] J. Vittal; MSG - a simple message system; Proc. of the International Symposium on Computer Message Systems; Ottawa, April 1981.

[16] T.H. Myer, C.D. Mooers; HERMES message system user's guide; Bolt Beranek & Newman, Boston, January 1977.

[17] J. Vallee, H.M. Lipinski, R.H. Miller; Group communication through
computers, vol. 1 (Design and use of the FORUM system); Institute for the Future report no. R-32, Menlo Park, CA, 1974.

[18] M. Turoff, S.R. Hiltz; Development and field testing of an electronic
information exchange system: final report on the EIES development project;
NJIT Computerized Conferencing and Communications Research report no. 9,
1978.

[19] S. Rohlfs; User interface requirements, Infotech State of the Art
Report on 'Convergence: Computers, Communication, and Office Automation',
Maidenhead, England, 1979.

[20] S. Rohlfs, Linguistic considerations for user interface design,
Proc. of the Workshop on Integrated Office Systems, Rocquencourt, France, November 1979.

[21] G. Millard, H. Williamson; How people react to computer conferencing;
Telesis (3), 1976.

[22] K.R. London; The people side of systems; New York, 1976.

[23] A.H. Konstam; The user - designer conflict and its resolution; Proc. of
the 7th Annual Computer Personnel Research Conference, Miami, 1980.

[24] T. Stewart; Communicating with dialogues; Ergonomics, vol. 23, no. 9,
September 1980.

[25] S.R. Hiltz, M. Turoff; The evolution of user behaviour in computerized
communication systems; Proc. of the International Communication Association
Conference, Acapulco, Mexico, 1980.

[26] C.A. Ellis, G.J. Nutt; Office information systems and computer science;
Computing Surveys, vol. 12, no. 1, 1980.

[27] L.A. Suchman; Office procedures as practical action: organization
theory and system design; Proc. of the 5th International Conference on Computer Communication, Atlanta, Georgia, October 1980.

[28] E.H. Wynn; Computer message systems as a unique medium of communication;
Proc. of the 5th International Conference on Computer Comunication, Atlanta,
Georgia, October 1980.

A Specification Method for Interactive Information Systems

Anthony I. Wasserman
Susan K. Stinson

Medical Information Science
University of California, San Francisco
San Francisco, CA 94143

An approach for developing specifications for interactive information systems is discussed. An interactive information system (IIS) is one that provides the computer-naive user with a means for conversational access to data stored within the system, typically through a predetermined set of operations. The system structure may be viewed as a user interface, a data base, and a set of operations upon the data base.

Three logical components of the system specification are identified: a user view, a design view, and a correctness view. Each of these components links the specification with a different view of the software life cycle.

This paper describes the different views of a specification and a method of specifying the system structure for an IIS. This specification method, being developed as part of the USE methodology, combines an informal specification with a more formal approach using transition diagrams for the user interface, logical data base design methods for the data, and a data manipulation language for describing the operations.

Introduction

Efforts to build sophisticated, reliable computer systems have focused attention on the need for good specifications and for tools to support their production and modification. This recognition has come for a number of reasons:

1 Many systems failed to meet the requirements of their users owing to the inadequacy of the original system specification.

2 Analysis and specification activities occupy a larger percentage of the software life cycle than does coding [1].

3 Testing and verification are virtually impossible in the absence of an accurate description of what the system is supposed to do.

4 Thorough understanding of the problem structure gained in producing a specification aids in developing the program structure.

5 Errors at the specification and design stage are the most common kinds of errors in software development [2], and are often not found until the acceptance testing stage, making them the most expensive form of error as well.

As the first detailed statement of system function, specifications play a critical role in the development activity, providing a foundation for future work and a link between the user's concept of the system and its actual implementation. The importance of the specification can be seen from Figure 1, which shows the interrelationships between the specification and other phases of the system development life cycle. This figure shows four different functions for a specification.

1 The specification is a means for precisely stating the system requirements. At this stage, the user's concept of the system is documented in as much detail as possible. The specification can be compared against the requirements definition to ascertain the correspondence between the specification and the user's needs.

2 The specification provides insight into the system structure and is used during the design phase as a checkpoint against which to validate the design. Typically, there will be an iteration between specification and design, as insight into some of the system construction problems helps to clarify the specification.

3 The specification is the basis against which testing and verification are performed. Clearly, one cannot prove that a program is correct in the absence of a clear understanding of the program's behavioral characteristics. Similarly, although certain kinds of testing can locate clerical errors and other low-level problems, system testing and acceptance testing require comparison of the system against an objective specification.

4 Modifications and enhancements to a system throughout its operational lifetime require an understanding of the system functions, as documented in the specification. During this phase, the specification can help to locate those system functions that must be changed, and can then be revised accordingly.

The implication of this multifaceted role for specifications is that a specification must be able to serve (to a greater or lesser extent) each of these four different functions. These considerations and others suggest some desirable goals for specifications:

1 completeness -- capturing all of the features of the system

2 comprehensibility -- ensuring that the specification can be understood by those who must approve it and work with it

3 testability -- attempting to quantify system requirements and to be sufficiently precise so that the correctness of the implemented system can be tested and/or verified

4 traceability -- ensuring that the system specification fulfills the requirements set forth for the system

Reprinted from *Proceedings of the Symposium on Specifications of Reliable Software*, April 1979, pages 68–79. Copyright © 1979 by The Institute of Electrical and Electronics Engineers, Inc.

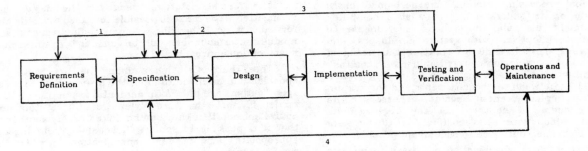

Paths 1: Matching the specification against the requirements
2: Creating the system structure from the problem structure
3: Determining that the implemented system conforms to
the specification
4: Modifying the specification and then the system as
operational needs change

Figure 1 --   Functions of a Specification in the
System Development Life Cycle

5   implementability -- determining that the system
can be feasibly implemented

6   consistency -- determining that different parts of
the system description do not impose inherently
conflicting requirements, and that consistent
nomenclature is used in the description

7   unambiguity -- assuring that the system description
has a unique interpretation in order to eliminate
confusion as to system requirements

8   writeability -- providing a scheme that simplifies the
problem of expressing the specification

9   modifiability -- structuring the specification so that
the system functions can be changed to fit changing
user requirements

Achievement of these goals, particularly those of
testability, consistency, and unambiguity, entail a
greater degree of formalism than is present in most
specifications. On the other hand, the formalism of an
algebraic specification or similar approach is often not
conducive to comprehensibility. Accordingly, we seek an
approach for specifications that is satisfactory for the
needs of different classes of users.

The above list contains many of the criteria for
specifications described by Liskov and Zilles [3].
However, we have placed somewhat more emphasis upon
the relationship of specifications to other phases of the
software life cycle, have replaced their concept of
"extensibility" with "modifiability", and are willing to
sacrifice "minimality" in order to achieve
comprehensibility for several classes of specification
users, e.g., end users, system designers, and quality
assurance groups. Similarly, we are willing to give up a
degree of generality to develop a specification technique
that is particularly effective for a certain common class
of systems.

Three Views of a Specification

Our approach to specification, then, consists of
three parts: a user view, a design view, and a verification
view. Each of these views accommodates at least one of
the functions of the specifications, and is intended to

address one or more of the goals for specifications listed
above. The model, depicted in Figure 2, emphasizes that
all of these functions must be addressed early in the
software development process.

The first step in system development is the system
concept, which is the image in the user's mind of the
system. This image is not static, but continues to evolve
during the development process. Many of the changes
are attributable to the user's increased understanding of
the system requirements and of the potential uses of an

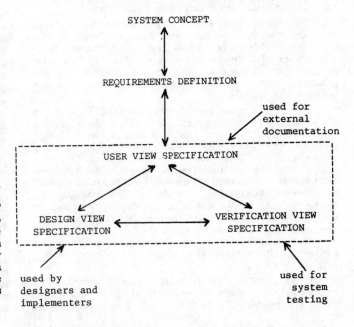

Figure 2 --   Specification Model

263

information processing system. Inexperienced users have little or no understanding of what a computer system might be able to do, and are unable to communicate effectively with system developers, who often have a difficult time interpreting the needs of users and in becoming sufficiently familiar with the task area. The system concept may also be modified when compromises between the requirements and the system design or implementation become necessary. The system concept is captured in the *requirements definition*, which must be modified as the system concept is changed during the development process.

The *user view* specification is based upon the requirements definition and is a detailed, but informal, description of the system function formulated by the developer working closely with the user. This informal description can serve as a contract between developer and user, and can also serve as the starting point for more formal specifications. It is often the case that more than one class of user will have access to a given information system, frequently with different privileges and operations. In such a case, it would be necessary to specify a separate view for each user class.

The user view specification is aimed at meeting the specification goals of comprehensibility for the reader and completeness of the system description. It is written using the terminology of the task environment, reflecting the user's view of the problem. This system model is intended for a user who is knowledgeable concerning the proposed system function, but is not familiar with the technical aspects of designing and programming it. (It should be noted that this characterization fits the large majority of end users and persons who contract for software development; not many are familiar with computer terminology, specification languages, or related topics.)

Historically, specifications (if they were written at all) were limited to this user view. However, the multiple uses of a specification require other views as well.

The *design view* specification serves as the link between the specification and design stages of the development life cycle, and may be considered as a form of architectural design. This view defines a high level program structure, identifies program modules to the greatest extent possible, and shows the logical data flow between the modules.

The design view specification is used to aid the software designer in implementing the system, easing the transition between the specification and design phases of the software life cycle. Typically, the functions of the module will be described in behavioral, i.e., non-procedural, terms; the detailed design stage will then evaluate and produce a procedural (algorithmic) version that can be shown to be equivalent to the specification. Similarly, data design will be at the logical level rather than at the physical level, except insofar as outside constraints or interfaces require the binding of low-level representational information. The design view primarily addresses the specification goals of implementability and consistency.

Finally, the *verification view* specification concentrates on correctness issues of the specification, making it possible to establish testing and verification procedures for the implemented system. The verification view uses a formal notation and defines the conditions that must be met by the implementation. Some of the recent work in specification languages [4,5,6] seeks to provide a single tool that can serve both the design view and the verification view of a specification.

The formal notations used for the design and verification views make it possible to utilize machine aids for consistency checking. Names, value ranges, and module interfaces can all be checked from such a specification approach.

Thus, there is a balance among the three views of a specification, intended to meet the diverse uses to which specifications are put. A fundamental assumption in this model is that the three views of the system are equivalent and that they can be linked to one another so that it is possible to achieve "traceability", linking the appropriate part of each specification view to the requirements.

Interactive Information Systems

In this paper, we wish to consider the application of these notions to the specification of an interactive information system (IIS). Such a system may be characterized as involving conversational access to data bases by computer naive users. Examples of such systems include airline reservation systems, hospital patient information systems, and some natural language dialogue systems.

These systems usually have a large data design component and a relatively simple control structure, in contrast to operating systems and other kinds of process-oriented software systems. Specification of the data elements is therefore equally as important as design of the program structure. Accordingly, the specification relies on both database design concepts and more traditional program specification notions.

An interactive information system may be seen as consisting of three major components: the user interface, the operations upon the data objects, and the data base (or files). As a general rule, the operations analyze the user input, frequently in a command language, produce any necessary diagnostic messages, and then invoke a procedure to carry out the user request, commonly involving access to, modification of, or addition to the data base. The database notion of a *transaction* is useful here -- a single logical process is carried out, possibly by a sequence of detailed steps.

In the remainder of this paper, we will develop and assess a specification method for an IIS, addressing the varying needs of different specification users and covering each component of the IIS. The technique described here is part of a methodology for IIS design and development being created at the University of California, San Francisco (see below).

Although three views of a specification have been identified, we will combine the design view and the verification view into a single unit, with the end result being an informal specification (user view) and a formalizable specification (information system engineering view). This simplification reduces the potential difficulties of writing three different specifications and then needing to demonstrate their equivalence. In this approach, we will adopt two notations, one corresponding to the user view and another corresponding to the information system engineering view. The first notation will be informal natural language, while the second will be more formal. Although the informal notation of the user view will preclude a formal proof of equivalence between the two views, it will be possible to explicitly link them and informally demonstrate their equivalence.

The User Interface

The IIS user interface provides the user with a language for communicating with the system. The interface can take many forms, including multiple choice (menu selection), a command language, a database query language, or natural language-like input. In all cases, however, the normal action of the program is determined by user input, and the program may respond in a variety of ways, including results, requests for additional input, error messages, or assistance in the use of the IIS.

The critical observation, though, is that the semantics of the IIS, i.e., its actions, are driven by raw or transformed user input. As with programming languages, the user language in its runtime context determines the semantic actions to be performed; the resemblance between such a user language and an interpreted programming language is quite strong.

Accordingly, an effective specification technique for programming languages can be used effectively for specifying user interfaces. The recognition of a syntactic unit (a token) can be tied to a semantic action. A variety of language definition techniques are applicable in this setting. For example, the entire set of legal inputs could be specified, showing the "subconversations" that may occur upon recognition of a given input. One could then axiomatize the semantics of each of the various constructs or sequences in the dialogue. Such an approach could lead to the use of verification techniques after implementation, since the user language would be formally specified.

Because these languages are interpreted rather than compiled and because user errors and requests for assistance cause many interruptions in the "normal" dialogue, the most formal approaches are somewhat impractical. Semiformal approaches are sufficiently practical for testing and verification of the IIS and are more flexible when the user input or program output must be changed. They also make the inclusion of error diagnostics, online assistance, and exception-handling more visible. This difference is particularly significant when it is necessary to repeat parts of a dialogue or perform other kinds of "backtracking" as a result of user errors in a partially completed subconversation.

Two techniques are equally useful for this step, and preference for one over the other is best determined by the presence of available automated tools and by individual taste. The first of these is language specification as it might be presented to a translator writing system such as YACC [7]. For a given syntactic construct, one may associate code to be invoked upon recognition of that construct. Although YACC was originally designed to aid in compiler construction, it has been successfully used in many applications systems as well.

An alternative approach (and the one we shall follow here) is to use transition diagrams [8], as used in the definition of American National Standard MUMPS [9]. Such an approach has also been suggested by Parnas [10].

A transition diagram is a network of nodes and directed paths. Each path may contain a token, corresponding to a character string in the primitive alphabet (such as ASCII), or the name of another diagram. If the path is blank, it will be traversed as a default case, i.e., if all other paths leaving a given node fail. Scanning of the diagram begins at a designated entry point and proceeds until reaching an exit node or a dead end (no successful match on the paths from a given node). A semantic action may be associated with any path; traversal of the path causes the action to occur.

One of the strong advantages favoring transition diagrams as a specification scheme is that they satisfy the often conflicting goals of precision and comprehensibility. Furthermore, a separate diagram can be made for each subconversation, making it possible for the designers and the users to focus upon small parts of the interactive dialogue. A BNF-based specification tends to group all user syntax together; its primary advantage is the relative ease of machine representation.

As a simple example, consider the transition diagram shown in Figure 3. The entry point is shown by the node labeled E, the exit point is shown by the node labeled X, subconversations, i.e., other diagrams, are shown within boxes along a traversed path, and output message names are shown within nodes. Thus, the input string "HOP" would result in the semantic action 1 and the output message MSG; the input string "SKIP" would initiate the subconversation named HOWFAR (another diagram). In this example, an illegal input, such as "GOTO", would cause the diagram to fail to reach an exit point; we shall take up this matter in more detail in the longer example below.

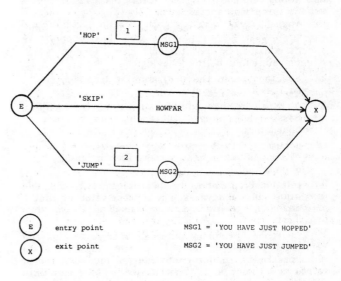

Figure 3 -- Sample transition diagram;
Message names shown in circles;
Semantic actions are numbers in
small rectangles;
Subconversations are names in boxes

Data Base Definition

The next aspect of the specification is to define the data base, since IIS operations are generally tied to the logical structure of the data base.

Many approaches to modeling data bases have been advanced [11,12,13,14] and issues of database design are currently a topic of great debate and extensive research within the database community [15,16]. Much of the debate centers around the amount of "real world

265

knowledge" that is captured in the data model. In current practice, though, data base design is closely tied to specification of the operations upon the data base for a variety of reasons, including optimization of the data organization, understanding of relationships among data elements, and efforts to check the validity of the data base operations.

One approach, the ANSI/SPARC framework [17], is based upon three levels of data model: the conceptual model, the external model, and the internal model. The conceptual model attempts to capture the semantics of the data; it is mapped through two levels into a logical data base design compatible with machine representation and processing.

The internal model, which is primarily concerned with how the data is stored, is not relevant at the specification stage. The external model, a subset of the conceptual model, defines the view of the data for each class of user, making it possible to provide shared access to the data base for different user classes with different access rights and different operations. Thus, a given system may include several external models reflecting different views of a single conceptual model; these are all mapped into a single internal model. In the specification of an IIS, an external model, combined with the operations defined for that user class, requires a separate user view specification.

The first step is to identify the data elements and, to the largest extent possible at an early stage, to specify constraints upon the data items. Various kinds of constraints include the following:

1   a data type in the programming language sense, such as integer or string

2   a range for acceptable values of that object, possibly a numeric subrange or a number of characters

3   access rights for the object, designating which classes of users may access and/or modify that object

4   relationships among the data objects, e.g., that one value must always exceed another value or that a change in one item necessitates a change in another item

We then produce external models using the relational model of data [11], analyzing the data elements to define, for each external model, a set of relations that are "normalized" to eliminate dependencies among attributes with a given relation and hence to prevent various anomalies from occurring within the data base [18,19]. A similar approach is taken in the Structured Systems Analysis method for software development [20].

The data base is defined as a set of relations, where each relation may be viewed as a two-dimensional table having an arbitrary number of rows *(tuples)* with a fixed number of columns *(attributes)*, each of which has values from a specified domain. Each tuple is unique, with the uniqueness determined by a subset of the attributes known as the *key* attributes.

Although we are continuing to investigate several data models, for now we have adopted the relational model of data as a data base specification tool for a number of reasons, including the following:

1   it is based upon the mathematical theory of relations and therefore has a sufficiently formal definition for purposes of testing and verification

2   both procedural (algebra-like) and non-procedural (predicate calculus-like) operations are defined

upon relations, so that one can precisely specify the data base operations in terms of the defined relations

3   numerous implementations of relational data base management systems are in existence [21,22], making it possible in some instances to proceed directly from the specification to an operational system

4   relations are easily mapped into other kinds of storage structures, including hierarchically and network organized data bases, inverted files, and B-trees

For all of these reasons, relations seem to be the best method of specifying the content and structure of the data base. We shall present an example of such a definition below.

Operations

It is now apparent that the structure of an IIS is based upon user input causing various operations to be carried out. Also, the maintenance and routine use of the system will require that other actions be carried out. Among the many different possible kinds of operations are the following:

1   IIS initiation and termination

2   online assistance

3   data base access

4   data base modification

5   usage statistics

In short, some of the operations may involve conversational access to the data base, while others may not, and some of the operations may be the result of user input, while others with be performed directly by the IIS, independent of user input. From the standpoint of specification, however, it is important to describe *all* of the operations as carefully, completely, and precisely as possible.

Each defined operation upon the data base can then be associated with a user class. The set of operations defined for a given class helps to achieve the mapping from the conceptual model to the particular external model for that class and to the relational database organization defined in the database specification phase.

It is important to distinguish between the user view of an operation and the internal view of an operation. A user operation typically results in a number of system-level operations. We will use the term "structured operation" to refer to the user's view of an operation; this notion encompasses the idea of a "transaction" upon a data base, as well as other logical operations requested by the user of an IIS [23].

As an example, consider a teller information system in a bank (described in greater detail below). One of the user level operations requests that a customer with a given account number make a withdrawal. The steps in the structured operation would include the following:

1) check validity of the account number
2) determine the amount to be debited
3) check the balance in the given account to make sure that sufficient funds are available
4) update the balance in the account to reflect the debited amount
5) record the transaction on a transaction log

This example is typical in that a structured operation includes, but is not limited to, a step involving data base access and/or modification. If we consider the example further, we see that the five steps constitute a specification for what is to be done in the structured operation. (Note that steps 3,4, and 5 are imprecise here since we have not defined the database organization.)

For a given IIS, if we specify the actions for each of the structured operations, the result is a complete specification of the operations. In combination with the data base specification and the user interface definition, the product is a complete specification of the IIS, our desired goal.

The definition of the structured operations forms the link between the user interface and the data base. It is necessary to define the semantic actions, i.e., a structured operation, for each path on the transition diagrams designating such an action. The specification of the actions contains the operations on the data base, using a relational algebra or calculus-like notation to define formally the retrieval or update operation(s). Any relationally complete language can be used effectively in this role; we have used PLAIN [24] in the example below.

In early stages of the specification, one can be less precise about the data base operations, as in the example above, tightening the specification when the database design is determined. In this way, there is an iteration between pure specification and architectural design, as well as between process and data specification.

The entire process of specifying these structured operations can rely heavily upon notions of data abstraction, as applied to data base management [25,26,27,28], extending the work on algebraic specification of data types [3,29]. From the user perspective, the logical operation to be performed as a result of the user input is independent of both the representational detail of the data (physical level) and the data base organization (logical level). In other words, what appears to be a transaction to the user is mapped into a set of lower-level operations, the details of which are hidden from the user. Furthermore, different data abstractions can be developed for different user classes, providing each class with a different "view" of the system, corresponding very closely to the ANSI/SPARC notion of multiple external models.

There are a number of advantages to using the data abstraction approach to the design of operations. First, as noted above, it is possible to achieve a high degree of data independence, since information about data base organization may be effectively hidden from large parts of the IIS. Second, necessary checks on data validity and semantic integrity [30] can be incorporated within each operation, thereby gaining additional control over correctness. Third, some security measures may be achieved by limiting the set of abstract operations available to a given user class, thereby offering some protection against malicious users.

It is important to note here that this approach to operations definition is workable for those systems where a large percentage of the operations upon the data can be determined in advance. Such is the case for most IIS's used by computer-naive users. In general, however, it is also necessary to provide an alternative mechanism for retrieval from the data base, e.g., a query language, to handle special "one-time" user requests. Our specification methodology concentrates on the routine structured operations with relatively little consideration given to the unstructured special requests.

An Example

In this section, we will present an application of the specification technique described here. Space limitations prohibit a complete specification; thus, we show just enough to give the flavor of the method and to convince the reader of its practicality in serving the needs of the three different views of the specification.

Requirements Definition

An on-line computer system is needed to improve the speed and accuracy of the tellers' transactions with bank customers. It must allow the teller to carry out the routine transactions of opening, closing, crediting and debiting accounts, and determining account balances easily and quickly. All transactions involving changes to an account must be recorded on a transaction log.

At the time that an account is opened, each authorized signer for that account must supply a signature for a signature card. The type of account (personal checking, Key Account, commercial checking, limited service, student account, senior citizen account) must be selected and checks must be ordered. Each cosigner on an account must provide name, address, telephone number, and mother's maiden name. One of the cosigners is designated as the primary account holder for the purpose of mailing statements and other documents.

The system maintains an account record for each account that contains an account number, the account type, identifying information for the primary account holder, a list of transactions, and a current balance. For each transaction, an identification number, the account number, a date, a transaction type, and an amount must be recorded on a transaction log.

The system must provide prompt and reliable responses to all interactions. The system shall be capable of interfacing with a system that will print regularly scheduled statements for customers.

User View Specification

System Commands

Each of the system's commands and their operations are defined in this section. The proper usage of each command is defined by means of a simple notation. Uppercase letters are used to denote the actual command entry while lowercase letters indicate that the user should substitute a value of the type listed. For example, the general structure of the credit command is defined as:

CR accountnumber dollaramount

This command can be used to credit $25.00 to account number 1234567 by entering:

CR 1234567 25.00

The definition is followed by the sequence of steps that are performed when the command is given. In addition, the system checks that the account number is valid and that all dollar amounts typed in are positive amounts containing a decimal point and two places after the decimal point.

CREDIT: CR accountnumber dollaramount
Operations:
- Add 'dollaramount' to current balance of 'accountnumber'
- Enter transaction on transaction log
- Display 'accountnumber', transaction type, 'dollaramount', and new balance for teller verification

DEBIT: DB accountnumber dollaramount

Operations:
- Check 'accountnumber' for sufficient funds
- Subtract 'dollaramount' from current balance in 'accountnumber'
- Enter transaction on transaction log
- Display 'accountnumber', transaction type, 'dollaramount', and new balance for teller verification

BALANCE: BAL accountnumber

Operations:
- Display 'accountnumber' and current balance for 'accountnumber'

NEW: NEW

Operations:
- System prompts teller to
  - enter name, address, telephone number and mother's maiden name for each cosigner
  - select type of account
  - order checks for printing
- Generate new account number for chosen account type
- Display customer identification and account type for teller verification
- Enter account information into set of account records

CLOSE: CLOSE accountnumber

Operations:
- If account type of 'accountnumber' is Key Account and balance is negative, collect funds owed (manual operation)
- Request closing statement for 'accountnumber' (manual operation)
- Remove account and associated information from system

HELP: HELP

Operations:
- Display message listing all legal commands and a summary of their function and use

QUIT: QUIT

Operations:
- Display signoff message
- Log user (teller) off system

System Data Base

The data items included in the data base are described in Table 1, showing their domains and the constraints upon their values.

(Additional user view specification is omitted here.)

Design/Verification View Specification

The transition diagram for the user interface to the banking system is shown in Figure 4. Messages named in circles in the diagram are shown at the bottom of the page. NEWACCT is a diagram, not shown here, that carries on the subconversation to handle the 'NEW' command, obtaining the needed information from the customer, checking its validity, and guiding the user through the steps to open the account. When the values ACCTNO and AMOUNT are entered by the user, the system checks them syntactically and semantically against their characteristics specified in Table 1 and determines the validity of ACCTNO.

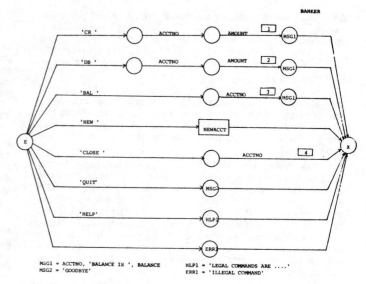

MSG1 = ACCTNO, 'BALANCE IS ', BALANCE HLP1 = 'LEGAL COMMANDS ARE ....'
MSG2 = 'GOODBYE' ERR1 = 'ILLEGAL COMMAND'

Figure 4 -- **Transition Diagram for Simple Banking System Version 1**

Table 1. Data Items for Teller Information System Example

User Name	System Name	Domain	Constraints
Account Number	ACCT	Integer	7 digits; first digit matches account type
Name	NAME	String	
Address	ADDRESS	String	
Telephone Number	PHONE	String	7 to 10 numerics
Mother's Maiden Name	MMNAME	String	
Account Type	ACCTTYPE	1..6	1=personal checking; 2=commercial checking; 3=student account; 4=senior citizen account; 5=Key Account; 6=limited
Primary Signer	PRIMARY	Boolean	
Transaction Number	IDENT	0..9999	
Transaction Date	DATE	Char[6]	6 numerics; format YYMMDD
Transaction Type	TTYPE	1..4	1=check; 2=deposit; 3=service charge; 4=loan payment
Transaction Amount	AMT	0..999999.99	2 digits after decimal
Current Balance	BALANCE	0..999999.99	2 digits after decimal
Next Account Number	NUM	Integer Array	1 element per account type; values are 7 digits; first digit matches account type

The relational data base organization is shown in Figure 5. A summary of the relations, with the key attributes shown in bold face, is shown at the top of the figure, while a more precise definition, using PLAIN syntax, appears at the bottom. The semantic actions 1 through 4 denoted in boxes on paths of the transition diagram are shown in Figure 6, using information about the database organization.

268

INFO (ACCT, NAME, ADDRESS, PHONE, MMNAME, PRIMARY, ACCTTYPE)

CHECK (ACCT, BALANCE)

CHECKTRANS (ACCT, IDENT, DATE, TTYPE, AMT)

NEXTNUM (ACCTTYPE, NUM)

Figure 5 --   Relational database organization
for simple banking system

These two diagrams, together with the semantic
actions shown in Figure 6, and the semantic actions of
the other diagram, constitute a complete specification of
the system, showing that the actions are driven by user
input.

1

imports CHECK, CHECKTRANS: **modified**;

CHECK% := CHECK [acctno];
CHECK%.BALANCE := CHECK%.BALANCE + dollaramount;
CHECKTRANS :+ [<acctno, id, today, 2, dollaramount>];
write acctno, ' credit $', dollaramount, \n,
    'new balance $', CHECK%.BALANCE

2

imports CHECK, CHECKTRANS: **modified**;

CHECK% := CHECK [acctno];
if CHECK%.BALANCE < 0
then
    write 'insufficient funds', \n
else
    CHECK%.BALANCE := CHECK%.BALANCE - dollaramount;
    CHECKTRANS :+ [<acctno, id, today, 1, dollaramount>];
    write acctno, ' debit $', dollaramount, \n,
        'new balance $', CHECK%.BALANCE

3

imports CHECK: **readonly**

bal := CHECK [acctno].BALANCE

4

imports CHECK, INFO: **modified**

bal := CHECK [acctno].BALANCE;
if bal < 0 & ACCTTYPE = 5
then
    {collect funds owed};
{request closing statement};
CHECK :- CHECK [acctno];
temp := INFO where ACCT = acctno;
INFO := INFO - temp

Figure 6 --   Semantic actions for simple
banking system of Figure 4

Revising the Specification

Study of the transition diagram shown in Figure 4
indicates that the resulting system would be most
intolerant of user errors, a common occurrence in an
IIS. The only diagnostic message shown is ERR1, telling
the user that the given command was illegal. No
recovery measures are shown for erroneous values for
ACCTNO or AMOUNT; by the rules for transition diagrams,

all that we know is that the diagram "fails." The
implication of such a failure is that the IIS would abort at
the point of failure, forcing the user to begin again.
Such failure is clearly undesirable, and every effort
should be made to specify a *robust* system, one that will
accommodate errors in user input and, to as large an
extent as possible, to prevent system or hardware errors
from destroying the IIS or its data base.

The strategy for achieving robustness in user input
is to construct diagrams that are less likely to fail. This
goal can be achieved by specifying additional points at
which the user can request help, as well as by providing
diagnostic messages keyed to the specific error made by
the user, in much the same way that one attempts to
isolate the errors and provide meaningful diagnostics in
use of a programming language.

Considerable added effort is required to provide this
degree of "user-friendliness", since each node of the
transition diagram must be revised to include a path for
those inputs that do not conform to the expected input,
as well as to designate the failure exits from a diagram
in addition to the normal exit.

Figures 7, 8, and 9 are part of the revised
specification for the banking example. The main
diagram (Figure 7) now provides for subconversations for
five of the operations, those requiring more than one
item of input. Figure 8 shows the subconversation for
the 'CR' command. Note that the word HELP can be
recognized at most points and that semantic action 3

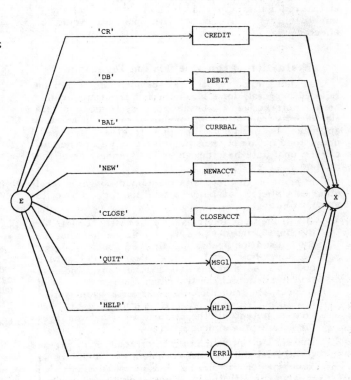

BANKER

MSG1 = 'GOODBYE'
HLP1 = 'LEGAL COMMANDS ARE ....'
ERR1 = 'ILLEGAL COMMAND'

Figure 7 --   Transition diagram for Simple Banking System
Version 2

keeps track of the number of times the user has failed to provide correct input at a given point, leading to diagram failure only when the user has failed three consecutive times. It can be shown that the diagram always terminates, returning either success (X) or failure (F) that can be used as a branch point in the calling diagram. Figure 9, containing the semantic actions for the subconversation of Figure 8, also relies on the data base design of Figure 5.

It should be noted that semantic action [1] checks the validity of ACCTNO, since its validity cannot be checked by syntax alone. An invalid ACCTNO causes an *exception* to be raised, denoting the occurrence of this exceptional condition. The exception must be treated by an "exception handler", a separate action to deal with the condition. In interactive information systems, it is important to prevent typical user errors, such as an invalid account number, from causing system failure. In this case, the exception can be trapped, an appropriate error message can be generated, and the user can be asked to repeat the command.

Ideally, one should also strive to minimize the amount of backup in user input. In this example, though, the input line required both an account number and an amount. An alternative approach would rely upon item-by-item prompting of user input, with the resulting increase in interaction serving to simplify the error checking. This strategy could potentially entail a separate subconversation for each class of input item if maximum system robustness were required.

Another likely change would be redesign of the data base organization. Such a change would affect those semantic actions that access or modify any of the redefined relations. Note that the user view of the structured operation would probably remain unchanged, but that the realization of the operation would be affected.

Evaluation of the Specification Technique

As one would expect, a specification technique tailored expressly for a given class of programs, in this case interactive information systems, differs significantly from other approaches to specification. Our approach is synthetic, bringing together the well-understood notion of transition diagrams with principles of relational data base design as the foundations of the method.

In addition to the points mentioned above, several other advantages can be cited for this approach to IIS specification:

1   The transition diagrams may be easily coded for machine processing, using techniques similar to those used for processing directed graphs. Figure 10 shows how the transition diagram of Figure 8 could be coded in this way. Furthermore, since the representation of the transition diagram is a set of records, the transition diagrams for a given system could be managed with a relational data base system, potentially the same system that manages the data for the implemented IIS.

2   The ease of implementing the transition diagrams greatly simplifies the problem of building a "mockup" of the IIS, so that potential users can experiment with the interface, making any desired changes in the form of input or output messages, gaining an early idea of how the IIS will appear in operation. Revised text can be placed directly on the transition diagram. For the most part, such a prototype system can be built in the absence of the

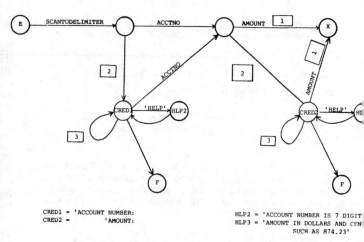

CRED1 = 'ACCOUNT NUMBER:
CRED2 =   'AMOUNT:

HLP2 = 'ACCOUNT NUMBER IS 7 DIGIT
HLP3 = 'AMOUNT IN DOLLARS AND CEN
            SUCH AS 874.23'

Figure 8 --   Transition diagram for Credit Command subconversation of Simple Banking System

[1]

```
exception badacct;
imports CHECK, CHECKTRANS: modified

if exists (CHECK [acctno])
then
    CHECK% := CHECK [acctno];
    CHECK%.BALANCE := CHECK%.BALANCE + dollaramount;
    CHECKTRANS :+ [ <acctno, id, today, 2, dollaramount> ];
    write acctno, ' credit $', dollaramount, \n,
        'new balance $', CHECK%.BALANCE
```

[2]

```
errcount := 1
```

[3]

```
if errcount ≥ 3
then
    {fail}
else
    errcount := errcount + 1
```

Figure 9 --   Semantic actions for transition diagram of Figure 8

Node	Transition	Target	Action	Message
E	SCANTODELIMITER	CR1		
CR1	ACCTNO	CR2		
CR1	<ANY>	CR3	2	CRED1
CR2	AMOUNT	X	1	
CR2	<ANY>	CR4	2	CRED2
CR3	ACCTNO	CR2		
CR3	'HELP'	CR5/CR3		HLP2
CR3	<ANY>	CR3	3	CRED1
CR4	AMOUNT	X	1	
CR4	'HELP'	CR6/CR4		HLP3
CR4	<ANY>	CR4	3	CRED2

Note: Transition is diagram name or string literal; Action may be numbered semantic action or named subconversation

Figure 10 -- Machine processable encoding of transition diagram of Figure 8

semantic actions, but then can be used as the actions are implemented.

3 The semantic actions resulting from the construction of transition diagrams are typically quite simple, providing a workable decomposition of the problem and leading to the definition of module interfaces and functions.

Although, on balance, this specification method seems to be quite effective, there are a couple of weaknesses that should be observed:

1 The comprehensibility of the transition diagrams decreases as the number of diagrams and the number of error-handling cases increases. One can easily ascertain that various error conditions are treated at the appropriate points in the dialogue, but the required volume of error-handling semantic actions can overwhelm the visibility of the "normal" semantic actions. This result is, of course, a mixed blessing.

   A particularly unpleasant cause of loss of comprehensibility is the desire to provide for multiple levels of skill among users. Experienced users would like terse commands and shorter system messages, while novice users require explanations and are willing to give input in a lengthier format until they are comfortable with use of the IIS. The result is that two (or more) different sets of user/IIS interface must be designed and incorporated into transition diagrams.

2 Although the specification method is based upon formalizable concepts of grammars (transition diagrams) and relations, it is sufficiently different from other specification techniques that new techniques for testing, validation, and verification are required. This area has not been adequately explored.

3 As with other specification methods that attempt to assist in design and verification of the resulting software system, there is no explicit way to tie the design/verification view of the specification to the user view. This, too, is an area in need of further study.

If this specification method is examined against the goals for specifications listed in the introduction, it can be seen that the method is quite effective in meeting those goals. Testability and unambiguity are achieved by the precise syntax definition and data base design, combined with the formal language used for data base operations. Some informality, however, is present in the remainder of the semantic actions. This potential deficiency could be overcome by adopting a formal specification language such as SPECIAL, SSL, or AXES as a means of defining the actions.

Implementability is also fairly easy to check, since the transition diagrams can be directly encoded and since the data base design could also be directly implemented. However, the method does not provide assistance in tying performance metrics to the specification.

Consistency is achieved in a couple of ways. First, there is a complete set of diagrams that represent the entire system structure. Naming conventions can be used to give each message, each subconversation, and each token a unique name; this can be mechanically checked. Furthermore, the definitions of the semantic actions must use a single data base design so that the data base operations are internally consistent.

Traceability, comprehensibility, and completeness are harder to assess. As noted, there is no explicit way to tie the design/verification view of the specification to the user view specification or to the requirements, implying that traceability must be accomplished through a review process, such as a walkthrough. From the example presented above, though, one can easily see how the process could be carried out, linking specific pieces of the User View Specification to the appropriate transition diagram(s) and data base definitions and operations. We plan to develop some procedures for assisting in this activity.

Comprehensibility is also a subjective measure. However, the decomposition of the dialogue achieved through the construction of separate diagrams for subconversations is a powerful aid in understanding the specification. Furthermore, the relatively high-level notation used for the data base operations is considerably less formidable for the reader than is an algebraic specification.

There does not appear to be a foolproof method to guarantee completeness of the specification for this kind of system. It is to be expected that the user will identify additional features and functions throughout the development process and during the operational lifetime of the system. What is important, then, is that the system be able to accommodate those changes with a minimum of maintenance effort, as indicated by the goal of modifiability.

Finally, writeability of specifications using this method has a mixture of strengths and weaknesses. Its greatest strength is that it provides for the assemblage of all parts of the specification within a single framework. Its most significant weakness is the necessary maintenance of the transition diagrams, a problem shared with some other tools that employ pictorial representations, e.g., SADT. It would appear, subjectively at least, that this method is average in this respect.

The Software Development Environment

The specification technique presented here is part of the USE (User Software Engineering) methodology being developed at the University of California, San Francisco. The aim of the USE project is to devise techniques and automated tools in support of the design and development of reliable, economical, user-centered information systems. This specification technique is just one aspect of the total methodology, which is intended to span the entire software life cycle [31].

Programs specified in this setting are to be implemented in the programming language PLAIN (Programming LAnguage for INteraction) [24]. PLAIN is a Pascal-like language intended to meet the specific needs of interactive information systems, while adhering to the goals of a systematic approach to software development. PLAIN provides strong support for modularity and for abstraction, but also contains such features as strings with associated operations, a rudimentary pattern specification and pattern matching capability, exception-handling, and a relational data base definition and manipulation facility.

Thus, it can be seen that the specification method presented here is intended to ease the transition between the specification and the programs written in PLAIN, as well as to simplify comparison of the PLAIN program with the previous specification. This approach should be contrasted with that of Gypsy [32], where a single language serves for both specification and implementation. Our belief is that the formal specification notions, as embedded in Gypsy, are not suitable for many users and that an alternative notation is needed. This belief is based upon experience in trying to specify interactive information systems with such a formal notation and in presenting formal specifications to computer-naive end users. Nonetheless, it is most beneficial if the specification notation can be easily transformed into a programming language.

Conclusions and Future Work

The development of specifications for interactive information systems combines techniques used for program specifications with those used for database design. The user view specification is a natural language, informal description of a system. The design view specification relies upon design representation aids, particularly transition diagrams. The verification view, combined with the design view, uses the formalisms inherent in the transition diagrams, combined with assertions and data integrity constraints. Together, they provide an integrated approach to the development of specifications that can be tied to all other areas of the software development life cycle.

Experience with the techniques discussed above are still extremely limited and it will be necessary to gain more knowledge about the relative strengths and weaknesses of this approach, particularly with larger systems. Work is presently underway at UCSF to apply this approach to the specification and design of a significant medical application. An automated tool for processing transition diagrams has already been built and successfully applied in the implementation of a language translator [33].

The effectiveness of the method cannot be ultimately determined until several systems have been specified, implemented, and tested using the methodology. In this respect, the availability of the PLAIN language processor will be a major milestone. From preliminary indications, though, it appears that this specification method is of considerable assistance in the initial phases of constructing an IIS and that it is better suited for this class of programs than other extant methods.

Acknowledgments -- Computing support was provided by National Institutes of Health grant RR-1081. Peter Freeman and the referees provided valuable comments on earlier drafts of this paper.

References

[1] Boehm, B.W., "Software and its Impact: a Quantitative Assessment," *Datamation*, vol. 19, no. 5 (May, 1973), pp. 48-59.

[2] Boehm, B.W., "Software Engineering," *IEEE Transactions on Computers*, vol. C-25, no. 12 (December, 1976), pp. 1226-1241.

[3] Liskov, B. and S.N. Zilles, "Specification Techniques for Data Abstractions," *IEEE Transactions on Software Engineering*, vol. SE-1, no. 1 (March, 1975), pp. 7-19.

[4] Roubine, O. and L. Robinson, "SPECIAL Reference Manual," SRI International, Technical Report CSG-45, Menlo Park, CA, 1976.

[5] Austin, S.L., B.P. Buckles, and J.P. Ryan, "SSL -- a Software Specification Language," Science Applications Inc., Report SAI-77-537-HU, Huntsville, AL, 1976.

[6] Hamilton, M. and S. Zeldin, "AXES Syntax Description," Technical Report TR-4, Higher Order Software, Cambridge, MA, 1976.

[7] Johnson, S.C., "YACC — Yet Another Compiler-Compiler," Bell Laboratories, Murray Hill, NJ, June, 1977.

[8] Conway, M.E., "Design of a Separable Transition-Diagram Compiler," *Comm. ACM*, vol. 6, no. 7 (July, 1963), pp. 396-408.

[9] MUMPS Development Committee, *American National Standard MUMPS Language Standard*. ANSI X11.1-1977.

[10] Parnas, D.L., "On the Use of Transition Diagrams in the Design of a User Interface for an Interactive Computer System," *Proc. 24th National ACM Conference*, 1969, pp. 379-385.

[11] Codd, E.F., "A Relational Model of Data for Shared Data Banks," *Comm. ACM*, vol. 13, no. 6 (June, 1970), pp. 377-387.

[12] CODASYL Data Base Task Group. *April 71 Report*.

[13] Chen, P.P.S., "The Entity-Relationship Model: Toward a Unified View of Data," *ACM Transactions on Database Systems*, vol. 1, no. 1 (March, 1976), pp. 9-36.

[14] Nijssen, G.M. (ed.) *Architecture and Models in Data Base Management Systems*. Amsterdam: North-Holland, 1977.

[15] Sundgren, B., "Data Base Design in Theory and Practice," *Proc. 4th Int'l Conf. on Very Large Data Bases*, 1978, pp. 3-16.

[16] Wiederhold, G. *Database Design*. New York: McGraw-Hill, 1977.

[17] ANSI/X3/SPARC Study Group on Data Base Management Systems: Interim Report 75-02-08, *FDT*, vol. 7, no. 2 (1975).

[18] Codd, E.F., "Further Normalization of the Database Relational Model," in *Data Base Systems*, ed. R. Rustin. Englewood Cliffs: Prentice-Hall, 1972, pp. 35-63.

[19] Fagin, R., "Multivalued Dependencies and a New Normal Form for Relational Databases," *ACM Transactions on Database Systems*, vol. 2, no. 3 (September, 1977), pp. 262-278.

[20] Gane, C. and T. Sarson. *Structured Systems Analysis: Tools and Techniques*. New York: Improved System Technologies, Inc., 1977.

[21] Astrahan, M.M. *et al.*, "System R: Relational Approach to Database Management," *ACM Transactions on Database Systems*, vol. 1, no. 2 (June, 1976), pp. 97-137.

[22] Stonebraker, M., "The Design and Implementation of INGRES," *ACM Transactions on Database Systems*, vol. 1, no. 3 (September, 1976), pp. 189-222.

[23] Gray, J., "Notes on Data Base Operating Systems," IBM San Jose Research Laboratory, Research Report RJ2188, February, 1978.

[24] Wasserman, A.I., D.D. Sherertz, and E.F. Handa, "Report on the Programming Language PLAIN," University of California San Francisco, Laboratory of Medical Information Science, Technical Report No. 34, 1978.

[25] Weber, H., "A Software Engineering View of Data Base Systems," *Proc. 4th Int'l Conf. on Very Large. Data Bases*, 1978, pp. 36-51.

[26] Smith, J.M. and D.C.P. Smith, "Database Abstractions: Aggregation and Generalization," *ACM Transactions on Database Systems*, vol. 2, no. 2 (June, 1977), pp. 105-133.

[27] Lockemann, P. *et al.*, "Data Abstractions for Data Base Systems," Universitat Karlsruhe, Institut fur Informatik, Interner Bericht Nr. 6/78, April, 1978. (To appear in *ACM Transactions on Database Systems*)

[28] Wasserman, A.I., "The Extension of Abstract Data Types to Data Base Management," submitted for publication, 1979.

[29] Guttag, J.V., "Abstract Data Types and the Development of Data Structures," *Comm. ACM*, vol. 20, no. 6 (June, 1977), pp. 396-404.

[30] Brodie, M.L., "Specification and Verification of Data Base Semantic Integrity," University of Toronto, Computer Systems Research Group, Technical Report CSRG-91, April, 1978. (Ph.D. dissertation)

[31] Wasserman, A.I., "USE: a Methodology for the Design and Development of Interactive Information Systems," *Proc. IFIP WG 8.1 Working Conference on Formal Models and Practical Tools for Information System Design*, April, 1979.

[32] Ambler, A.L. *et al.*, "Gypsy: a Language for Specification and Implementation of Verifiable Programs," *Proc. of ACM Conf. on Language Design for Reliable Software, ACM SIGPLAN Notices*, vol. 12, no. 3 (March, 1977), pp. 1-10.

[33] Wasserman, A.I. and D.D. Sherertz, "Implementation of the MUMPS Language Standard," University of California San Francisco, Laboratory of Medical Information Science, Technical Report No. 14, 1975.

Client-Centered Design: Concepts and Experience [1]

Linda Milburn Rudawitz
Manager, Systems Engineering, Holmes & Narver, Inc.,
999 Town and Country Road, Orange, California 92668,
USA

and

Peter Freeman

Associate Professor, Department of Information and
Computer Science, University of California, Irvine, Irvine,
California 92717, USA

Although software engineering has been concerned primarily with large-scale software efforts, there is a critical need for the tools and techniques of software engineering on smaller projects. We have been concerned with application of good software engineering practices to industrial consulting situations. This paper discusses the concepts we have found helpful and illustrates them by reference to a specific project. The project we discuss is the development and expansion, over a five year period, of a cost analysis program for the *United States Postal Service.*

Keywords: Client-Centered Design, Modular Design, Information Presentation, Programming Style, Software Engineering, User Interaction.

Linda Milburn Rudawitz is manager of Systems Engineering for Holmes & Narver, a United States Filter Company. She is responsible for cost analysis, cash flow, and risk analysis for major Holmes & Narver projects, as well as direct development of software solutions for clients in government and industry.

Peter Freeman is Associate Professor of Information and Computer Science at the University of California, Irvine. He has been involved in the analysis, design, and construction of advanced computer applications and the training of software engineers since 1961.

[1] This paper is based in part on the M.S. Thesis of the first author.

© North-Holland Publishing Company
Systems, Objectives, Solutions 1 (1981) 21–32

1. Introduction

We have been concerned with the application of good software engineering practices in situations that we characterize as *"client-centered"*. These are situations in which a consultant (an individual, an external consulting firm, or a consulting department within a larger organisation) serves as the agent for uniting a client (someone with a problem to be solved) with the appropriate computing power.

Although client-centered projects may involve several people (analysts, programmers, functional specialists), we have focused on the role of the *system analyst/programmer* in the context of small to medium scale industrial consulting projects. This role is neither that of a vendor attempting to make large or general purpose systems for subsequent sale, nor that of the end user out to solve a specific problem of personal interest. The consultant's goal is to meet the client's needs in whatever manner seems most appropriate. The consultant must be fully capable of developing a computerized system, but must also be prepared to use manual methods wherever they are appropriate. Above all, the consultant must keep sight of the client's needs and avoid falling into the trap of implementation for its own sake.

The consultant must be concerned with three separate problems:

1. The client's needs and how they can best be met;
2. User-oriented design considerations for whatever computerized systems are to be developed;
3. Power and extensibility factors in the internal design of the computer program(s).

The consultant is concerned with somewhat different problems from those involved in design of large-scale computer-based systems. The client is not primarily interested in buying a computer program. The client wants his problem solved but may not care about the actual computer program used to solve it. He is, however, very concerned with the details of the analysis. Explaining the computerized solution to the client is a very real part of the consultant's job.

In a similar manner, the system analyst on a consulting project is not concerned with the problems of machine efficiency and minimum execution time that concern the machine-oriented designer. The final product will not be used for regular production runs and the execution cost will be minimal when compared to the cost of analysis and program development. Meeting the client's needs on-time and within-budget is much more important than elegance and execution efficiency.

This paper discusses a set of concepts we have found to be effective in client-centered design and describes their application to a specific project. We suggest that this paper be read as an *indication* of an approach to client-centered design and the results that may follow; it is neither a proof of the approach nor a description of all possible client-centered techniques.

2. Experience

The particular project we shall discuss is the development of an on-line cost analysis tool for use by *United States Postal Service* management for evaluation of bulk mail processing and rate design questions.

2.1. Development History

Late in 1973, Holmes & Narver, Inc., was awarded a contract to study the *"Effects of the National Bulk Mail System on Bulk Mail Costs"*. The National Bulk Mail System (NBMS) is a nation-wide network of bulk processing facilities (Bulk Mail Centers or BMCs). This system was under construction at that time and represented a major departure from previous

Table 1
Cost model development history

Development events	Dates	Total number of modules	Approx. lines of Fortran Code	Memory Usage	Comments
1. Manual System	12/73–6/74	N/A			
2. Computerized, BMC only	7/74	12	900		
3. Add Non-NBMS	8/74	20			Phase I –
4. Add National Summary	9/74	25	2500	Overlay	Initial Development
5. Add Cost Adjustment Factors	9/74–12/74			Data By	
6. Add Data Base Change	9/74–2/75	50	4000	Mail Class	
7. Expand Dimensions	5/75–8/75				
8. Change transportation	6/75–6/76			4 Segment	Phase II –
9. Update Change Sections	8/75–12/76	80	5000	Program	Expansion
10. Apply to different data	6/76–12/76			Overlay	Application to
11. Create Air Model	8/76–12/76				new problem
12. Add acceptance/delivery	4/78–6/78				
13. Make 21 Distinct BMC models	6/78–8/78			Change	Phase III –
14. Change transportation	7/78–9/78	100	7000	Overlay	Expansion,
15. Add Selected Data Summary	5/78–10/78			Structure	addition of acceptance
16. Add Data Base Display	6/78–1/79				and delivery
17. Update Interfaces to Match	9/78–3/79				Data collection
Finished Project	5/79	130	9000	3 Level, 10 Segment Overlay	In use

United States Postal Service (USPS) ways of handling bulk mail.

Our assignment was to estimate the effects that this large mechanized system would have on the cost of mail processing. A computerized model was not originally anticipated, but it soon became obvious that some sort of computer assistance would be required because of the large amounts of data that were being generated (Table 1, Event 1). At that time neither the client (USPS) nor the consultant (Holmes & Narver) had any firm ideas of what might be required from the computer in terms of calculations or reports.

A somewhat limited program was developed to predict costs based on engineering time standards (Table 1, Events 2 through 6). The USPS technical contract monitor was closely involved in the development of this computerized model and was able to interact with the project team to develop a tool that presented information in ways that were clear and useful to him.

This early model was used primarily to present the information that was developed under this contract. The original model consisted of about fifty program modules and was small enough to run without program overlays. Table 1 illustrates the way the model grew during subsequent development phases.

As a result of the experience with this initial Cost Model, the contract monitor became convinced that the tool we were developing had potential for a supporting. role in the development of cost information for proposed mail classifications and for use in the rate cases.

In mid-1975, a contract was granted to expand the Cost Model to consider mail processing outside the BMCs and to develop a more detailed model of transportation between BMCs (Events 7 through 9). This model would be able to trace the cost of handling bulk mail all the way from the origin post office, through the NBMS, to the destination post office. Throughout model expansion, it was necessary to be ready to provide the most up-to-date information to the client on a moment's notice. It was essential that a working model be retained throughout the modification process. Detailed analysis of the transportation problem resulted in enlarging the program to the point that overlays were required in order to run on the required system.

In mid-1976, as the model expansion was being completed, the Postal Service decided to use the model to provide cost information for a new mail classification that was being considered (Event 10). The consultant was asked to apply the model to this new type of mail and to generate an air transportation model to supplement the surface transportation network already included in the model (Event 11).

Several Postal Service employees were trained in the use of the model and the actual program was turned over to the Postal Service by the end of 1976. Over the next year the people involved in the project went their separate ways. Most of the Postal Service people who were involved with the Cost Model were assigned to other jobs within the USPS. The consultant's involvement with the model was limited to answering occasional questions about the data sources and results of the study.

Early in 1978, the Postal Service formed a special Parcel Post Task Force to study possible changes to the rate structure for parcel mail. The task force decided that the Cost Model, expanded to include acceptance and delivery as well as mail processing, was the tool they needed for their study. Since the Bulk Mail System was fully operational by this time, actual costs could be collected to replace the engineering standards originally used in the model.

A data collection effort took place in mid-1978 while the model was once more being expanded (Event 12). That data was coded, reduced and entered into the model by early August in time to provide support to an important rate filing. Since actual operating data was gathered for each BMC, the program had to be modified to accept 21 independent BMC data sets rather than a single data set with a few variables that differed by BMC (Event 13). In addition to those changes, well over 1000 lines of new code had to be entered and tested over a period of less than six weeks to meet the USPS deadlines.

The Parcel Post Task Force continued with its study (Events 14–17) after the pressure of the rate filing and presented a set of recommendations to the Postmaster General. The Cost Model was used extensively in preparation of those recommendations. The model is still being used (mid-1980) for evaluation of proposed parcel processing alternatives and rate structures.

The model grew over a period of about five years.

In most cases the design decisions made this growth easier. From the very beginning it was clear that the program would have to evolve with the changing needs of the client. Although greatly expanded, in some ways the current model is very similar to the original model. The interface with the user remains essentially the same although the specific options have been changed or expanded many times. The calculations and reports have changed and the current model does many more things than it did originally, but the basic design and organization remain as clean and straight-forward as the original.

2.2. Program Characteristics

All programs were written in Computer Sciences Corporation Fortran V, to execute on their Univac 1108 based INFONET System. All development and usage was via interactive terminals. The model was built to work with any type of terminal. It has been used with at least 10 types, including GE Terminet, TI Silent 700, CDI Miniterm, DECwriter, IBM 2741, Sorok IQ 120, and ADM 3.

2.3. Usage Characteristics

The model was built as a tool for USPS personnel and is primarily run (via timesharing terminals) directly by the people who need the answers (not by *"computer"* people). These include the contract monitor, operating personnel from several locations across the country, and headquarters personnel from three different departments. In addition to the analyst that built the model, several of the contractor's personnel have used the model including both managers and clerks.

The remainder of this paper will present a set of concepts for client-centered design and illustrate them with examples from our experience with the USPS Cost Model project (More detail can be found in [4]).

3. Concepts and Illustrations

Client-centered design is a collection of project and program organization techniques that help to achieve three objectives:

1. maximization of the information the client receives;
2. generation of flexible and extendible programs;
3. minimization of the danger that the client's real needs and goals will be lost in the process of creating a computer program.

Although it focuses on the design activity, considerable amounts of analysis and plain old programming are involved. Client-centered design has three aspects: external design features; internal design features; and project organization features.

3.1. External Design Features

The external program design features we have used can be characterized as being user-centered [2]. Those aspects of a program that are visible to the client (such as output formats, input requirements, and operational features) are carefully designed to cater to his or her human nature. Some of the major concerns we have dealt with are information presentation, user interaction, and user protection.

3.1.1. Information Presentation

Any information generated must be easily understood by the client. This rule extends to human-generated information as well as computer output. User manuals, option lists, program specifications, computer output, or anything else presented to the client must be well organized, clearly written, and cleanly presented.

Although output should not be voluminous, excessive use of abbreviations or jargon should be avoided. Titles and headings should serve as a guide to permit the user to locate the desired information quickly and easily. Enough space should be allowed on tables to make them easy to read and visually pleasing.

The method used to achieve these results is straight-forward:
1. design output formats early;
2. show mockups to the client and other non-experts;
3. use their feedback for refinement;
4. spend sufficient time to do the job correctly.

For example, at the beginning of the Cost Model project, it was not clear what sort of reports would be needed. We knew that reports would be required about processing within a single BMC and that national summaries would also be required but the

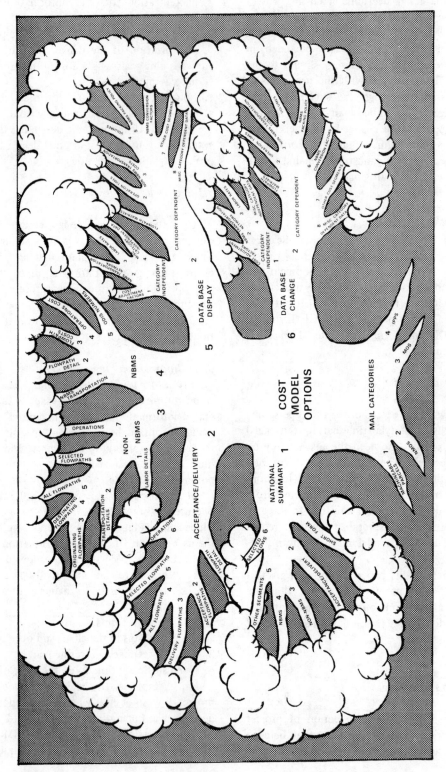

Fig. 1. Cost Model Tree.

exact form and content of those reports was unknown. Several possible report formats were generated and presented to the client for his comments. As a result of this, several additional requirements were made clear and valuable suggestions were given on ways to make the reports more understandable.

This process of generating initial reports and then modifying them was followed during all phases of model development. As the model was used, many other needs surfaced and features to meet those needs were added to the model. The concept of a flowpath (a sequence of operations that a type of mail undergoes), for example, is essential to the analysis the program performs. Reference to a flowpath number corresponding to a paper description was inadequate. It soon became obvious that the program would need to be able to display the text description as well as the costs for flowpaths.

3.1.2. User Interaction

Programs written in the client-centered environment are often interactive. As such, the way in which they interact with the user is an important area of external design. *Programs should make the client's experience with the computer as comfortable and stress-free as possible.*

Programmers often forget that most people communicate primarily with other people. If the client is part of management, even the typewriter keyboard may be unfamiliar. For them, communication with the computer may be difficult if considerable thought is not given to the form and content of the person-computer dialogue.

As in the case of information presentation, there is a wide variety of things to consider (see example [3]). However, we found the following general characteristics useful:

1. the person should feel in ultimate control;
2. responses should be meaningful;
3. a minimum amount of effort should be required of the user;
4. verbosity as well as extreme brevity should be avoided;
5. as much flexibility as possible should be used.

Some simple approaches can go a long way toward achieving these objectives. State diagrams or some other device can be used to build a simple model of the conversation to insure that the response set is complete (see, for example, [5]). Mode settings can be provided to permit the client to use concise or full forms of responses. Program responses and messages can use terms that the client is familiar with. A *"help"* function can be incorporated for use in any situation to gain immediate explanation of commands or messages that the client doesn't understand.

In the case of the Cost Model, a number chosen from a list of options proved more acceptable than a text response since the typewriter keyboard was almost as foreign as the computer itself to some of the users. A visual representation of the program was provided to the user as a guide (see Figure 1). The simplicity of the responses and the visibility of the program logic that this approach provided gave the user a comfortable feeling of being in control of the program at all times. Several print modes were provided to allow users with more experience to run the program without waiting for the terminal to print large amounts of output. Tables could be sent to a high speed printer while option tables, prompts and error messages came to the terminal. Sophisticated users could suppress all instructions and receive only one line prompts at the terminal. A *"help"* feature was incorporated through use of the escape key (since it is effectively full duplex on a normally half duplex system). Activation of the escape key at any point causes the program to stop what it is doing and re-print the last option table before prompting for a new option.

These and other similar ways of achieving good user interaction boil down to three simple rules:
1. understand the user;
2. understand the nature of the conversations between the user and the program;
3. make sure the program caters to the client within the constraints of the expected conversations.

3.1.3. User Protection

The user should not have to deal with aspects of the computer that are not directly related to the results he or she requires. The user should not be burdened with anything that it is not absolutely necessary for him to know. This includes operating and file system parameters as well as internal program details. If something deals with the machine or the system software and has no bearing on the problem that the client is trying to solve, protect him or her from it.

Table 2
External Design Features

Technique	Application	Benefits	Drawbacks
Permit user to give feedback on output format before final coding	All output tables	1. Reveals misinterpretations 2. Helps determine what is important to client 3. Makes sure output is understandable	1. Additional computer time to generate samples and revisions 2. Elapsed time required for review by client
Limit number of required types of user response	User input requests	1. Eliminate confusion over what is required of the user 2. Standardized coding	Limiting the types of user responses may require the user to respond a larger number of times than would be required with more flexible responses
Use of option tables	Control of user movement within the program	1. User satisfaction 2. Uniform responses 3. Standard control sequence for all of program 4. Flexibility to add and subtract options	Fairly large amounts of time are required to print option tables on low speed user terminal
Graphic illustration of program structure	Program "tree" illustration (Figure 2)	1. Guides user 2. Easy to use 3. Helps user to understand the program	1. Time required to generate diagram 2. Necessity for finding an appropriate illustration for a particular project

How that is done must depend to a large extent on the nature of the environment in which the program runs, but the general solution is clear: Conditions which the user must be protected from must be identified and program structures devised to either handle the conditions without the knowledge of the user or to serve as a filter between the user and the system.

User protection also extends to shielding the user from his own mistakes. It is very frustrating to be running a program and then have a simple mistake cause the program to terminate without supplying the intended results. All Cost Model input responses are protected by branch points in case of error. The user remains under control of the program unless he terminates it normally or does something over which the program *cannot* maintain control (such as hanging up the telephone). The response to input errors is, thus, very different in a client-centered project than in the traditional batch program where error termination may be the desirable response.

Some of the concepts discussed in this section are summarized in Table 2.

3.2. Internal Design Features

The internal design of programs on a client-centered project can impact the success of the project as much as the external design that the client sees and deals with. One of the characteristics of this type of project is that frequent changes in objectives are the rule rather than the exception. The ability of the analyst/programmer to react effectively to such changes is largely dependent on the internal design of the programs.

Internal program design is the focus of a large amount of current research. A given project must choose design features appropriate to the application. However, the internal design features that we have to be the most useful in a client-centered environment are applicable to most projects.

3.2.1. Modular Design
The most important tool one has for making a client-centered program modifiable is modularity. Small well-defined modules that are loosely coupled

to other modules are the goal. Where possible, the internal structure of the program should mirror the problem structure as seen by the client; this will make small changes in the problem domain translate into small changes in the program domain in most cases. For example, the modules in the Cost Model mirror the options the user sees so that adding or deleting user options corresponds directly to adding or deleting modules.

In our experience, changes to a client-centered program usually are one of three types: control; calculation; or display. Making sure that these aspects are separated into separate modules (for example, having each major report or display generated by different module) permits the analyst/programmer to respond effectively to the changes that must be expected in a client-centered situation.

For example, the major calculation sections of the Cost Model are separated from the display sections. When changes were made to the way calculations were handled for the BMCs, only the single affected calculation module had to be changed rather than the dozen or so display modules that use the results of that calculation.

3.2.2. Avoidance of Obscure Language Features

One of the ways to make a program easier to understand and modify is *to restrict the code to straight-forward and well understood language features*. Programmers often like to use special features because they are interesting and seem to provide additional capabilities. The main objection to the use of obscure features is that they may not work the way the programmer thought they would.

Poring over manuals to locate exciting features and spending hours at a terminal experimenting with them is not what the client intended to pay for. The client wants results, not cute program features. If standard features can solve the problem, there is very little excuse for experimenting with unfamiliar and exotic features.

The point is that programmers working on a consulting project should use features that they understand, that others understand, and that will work on as many different systems as possible. Projects are not budgeted for experimentation. The goal is to produce suitable output in the least amount of programming time and for the least amount of computer money.

Use of obscure features usually requires more debugging time and can cost excessive amounts of money. If an unfamiliar language feature is necessary for an essential program result, then it should be used. But, if some simpler means would accomplish the same end, it should be used instead.

3.2.3. Careful Documentation

It is essential that programs be well documented. Documentation of programs is often considered a boring and distasteful part of the project. The unfortunate thing is that it may also be the most important part. If the documentation is not clear and complete, the program may become useless because no one understands exactly what it should do or how to use it.

Creating sufficient documentation need not be an odious task and can, indeed, be an important part of the debugging and verification process. Several things can contribute to easing the documentation process while at the same time producing a system that can be understood and used by others. Modularity, proper data communication, and mapping of user visible structures onto internal structures can help make documentation easier. We have found the following specific documentation techniques useful:

1. writing the code itself to be as clear as possible;
2. including much of the documentation in the program code;
3. carefully describing variable and subroutine interactions.

3.2.4. Programming Style

The programmer's style and selection of language features can have a tremendous effect on the readability of the code. Many suggestions have been presented elsewhere (see, for example, [1]) for language structures and usage that make programs clearer and less prone to error.

Specific stylistic measures should be chosen and used consistently on a client-oriented project. The pressures of time and the demands for results are no excuse for using poor style. The positive benefits of using good style will more than pay off in most cases.

On the Cost Model project, several ground rules were established before coding began.

1. Module and variable names would be selected with initial characters that correspond to the section of the model where they would be used (i.e. B for

BMC, R for regional, C for data base changes, and P for data base print modules).

2. Line numbers would be chosen in an organized fashion:

   1–99 – driver sections of modules;
   100–199 – the first sub-section in a module;
   200–299 – the second sub-section in a module, etc.;
   1000 + related line number – format statements.

3. Parameters would be passed explicity rather than as flags in common.

4. Data base variables would not be modified except

Table 3
Internal design features

Technique	Application	Benefits	Drawbacks
Separation of control, calculation and display	Breakdown into modules	1. Each function can be modified without changing other code 2. Makes addition and deletion of features easy 3. Makes code easier to understand	1. Somewhat longer code 2. Many small modules
Echo structure the client sees	Relationship of internal structure to external interface	1. Client's understanding of capabilities is more likely to match actual capabilities 2. When changes are required, the amount of effort is usually in proportion to the amount of change the user sees	Internal organization can sometimes be more efficient if not restricted by user's view of program
Avoidance of obscure language features	Detail coding	1. Obscure features often don't work 2. Much time can be wasted trying to get features to work 3. Special features restrict the program to a single system 4. Operating system updates can destroy special features 5. Faster, more error free coding with well understood features	1. Special features may be required to generate a particular needed result 2. Special features can be interesting to the programmer
Don't take advantage of special data cases	Calculation sections	1. Special cases are likely to change as the project progresses 2. Special assumptions are easy to violate or forget 3. Code will handle more general problems	1. Calculations may be less efficient 2. Tests may need to be added to take care of pathological cases (divide by zero, etc.)
Avoid unnecessarily intricate algorithms	Calculation sections	1. Easier to program 2. Easier to understand later 3. Less debugging	1. Perhaps less efficient 2. Less 'fun' to program
Plan for changes	Design for overlays before they become necessary Allow for any number of additional options	1. Makes changes easier when they are required 2. Imposes better structure on current code	1. Additional initial planning 2. Requires provisions for things that may not happen
Don't hesitate to throw out code	Replace entire sections of code as needs change	1. It is often easier to start a section over again than to modify an existing section 2. User requests can be met with more flexibility if existing code is not considered 'sacred'	A lot of work may have to be thrown out and then done over again slightly differently

in the data initialization and data base change sections.

5. The number of entry points, exit points, and GOTO statements would be kept to a minimum within modules.

These rules contributed to a style of coding that was easy to read and modify.

Some of the concepts presented in this section are summarized in Table 3.

3.3. Project Organization

Using the best internal and external design approaches will fail to produce satisfactory results unless they are properly applied. The need for management and technical procedures to be synergistic is perhaps even more important in a client-oriented environment than on a large project because of the close working relationship between the client and the analyst/programmer.

Good project planning and management is a must. In addition we have found three things that can contribute significantly to the success of a client-oriented project:

1. focus on the client's needs;
2. be sensitive to the relationship with the client;
3. take a system view.

3.3.1. Focus on the Client's Needs

The central and most critical aspect of client oriented design is the realization that the client and his needs are the only reason for the existence of the project. Elegant and powerful computer programs may be nice, but if they don't do what the client *needs* then they do not belong in the project.

It is very easy to become involved in the programming process to the extent that you lose track of the reasons for undertaking the project in the first place. Before getting involved in some intricate algorithm or powerful but obscure language feature, the analyst should ask himself some very basic questions.

1. *"Is this something I really need to do?"*
2. *"Is there a simpler, but perhaps not as elegant way to accomplish the same goal?"*
3. *"Is the additional development and debugging time required for the use of certain features justified by the benefits that will be obtained?"*

In the context of consulting projects the answers to these questions are often *"no"*. Since the program will not become a production program and may be restricted by user input (in the case of an on-line program), additional programming and debugging cost is unlikely to be offset by reduced execution cost.

The goal of client-centered design is to meet the client's needs. Those needs and the client's perception of them will change as the project progresses. Something that seemed to be exactly what the client needed will become inadequate and require change when he sees the actual results. Preliminary results will suggest other areas of investigation and other computer program requirements. Intricate and obscure coding will be difficult to modify. Clever algorithms are often impossible to modify to meet even slightly different goals. The end result is that the extra programming effort is wasted because goals and needs change.

Before the consultant can begin to satisfy the client's needs, he must be able to understand them. This can be a much more difficult task than it seems because the client himself may not clearly understand his needs and requirements. A large part of the consultant's job is to help the client clarify the desired results of the project.

This focus on the client's needs must constantly be used to choose problems to work on, technical solutions to apply to them, and project organization to guide the project to a successful conclusion.

3.3.2. The Client/Consultant Relationship

Sensitivity to the client/consultant relationship must be maintained. In a consulting project, the client often has no previous direct experience with computers and their capabilities and limitations. He may have a very limited view of capabilities in some areas and unrealistic expectations in other areas. As he sees what can be done, other possibilities surface and the client may radically change his perception of what the final result of the analysis and development effort should be.

This changing perception on the part of the client can be either a trap or an opportunity. The choice between trap and opportunity depends heavily on three factors:

1. the relationship between the consultant and the client;
2. the contractual restraints on the project;

3. the consultant's capabilities and the flexibility of his design methodology.

If the project team has built up a good communication link with the client, it is possible to discuss the alternatives and to examine each possibility in terms of its cost, benefits, and side effects on the rest of the project. Changes that seem simple to the client may actually require extremely expensive and time consuming modification. On the other hand, a good relationship permits the client to voice ideas that may seem difficult to him but may be relatively easy to implement within the existing structure of the model.

Even a client sometimes gets involved in the grandeur of the computer model and tends to forget that the study originally had certain goals and a finite amount of resources. A good client/consultant relationship helps smooth things when the time comes to draw a line and say only so much can be done in the context of this contract. Other studies may be required to follow-up the leads uncovered during the initial project.

3.3.3. System View

In a client-oriented situation the primary deliverable is a solution to a problem. It is essential to keep in mind that a solution to a client's problem will usually be more than just a program. It may consists of intermediate results, exploratory studies, manually produced answers, as well as a program which is able to produce further answers.

In some cases, the most valuable result for the client may not be a program or any given set of answers but rather introduction to a new problem-solving approach. For example, if the client has never used simulation before because it seemed too complex, then a successful client-oriented project that introduces the client to the power of simulation may be far more important in the long run to that client (as well as to the consultant!) than the specific simulation undertaken.

Organizationally this means that the consultant must organize his/her time and resources into a system capable of delivering a total solution to the client. This view is used to balance manual and automatic processes, assign staff, and undertake sub-projects.

4. Conclusion

This case study has been presented as an example of a successful project. None of the concepts or techniques are presented as the only way to accomplish these goals. Instead, they are intended to illustrate an attitude and a way of thinking about a project. Remembering that service is foremost and that the client's needs are the reason for the project's existence are far more important than remembering any specific techniques.

Several questions about why this project was successful come to mind. As with any case study, we can only speculate on the answers; nonetheless, we feel the following are quite defensible and thus should be taken seriously by others wishing to improve their performance in similar projects.

4.1. How Did Client-Centered Design Lead to Client Satisfaction?

As reported above, the client was satisfied with the answers obtained from the Cost Model and the whole process of developing it. To us, the critical factor in bringing about this satisfaction was the mix of external and internal design features and the interaction with the consultant.

All three factors were necessary. Without appropriate external features, the model would have been difficult for the client to use. Without the internal features, the model would have been impossible for the consultant to change rapidly in response to client needs. Without a consultant who was sensitive to the client and to his relationship with the computer, the appropriate design features would never have been brought into existence.

4.2. Why Did the Computer Come to be Seen as a Tool for Further Work?

The computer is clearly a powerful tool for this type of problem solving. It is rarely the case that a computer cannot assist a manager in analyses such as were handled by the model in this case study. When the computer is seen by the manager as not being helpful, it is usually because that power has not been applied to the right aspect of the problem or because usage of the computer becomes such an odious task that the manager is repulsed.

In this case both technical and organizational factors were carefully adjusted to make sure that the client's experience with the computer was helpful along both *quantitative* (amount of answers provided) and *behavioral* (ease of usage) lines. The result was that the client came to think of the computer as a partner when similar problem-solving situations arose.

4.3. Are the Technical Design Features Simply Facilitating Factors?

No. The technical design features (internal and external) we have described are a prerequisite to successful client-centered projects. The most sensitive analyst, who pays careful attention to the informational needs of the client, cannot rapidly change a poorly structured program nor explain a cryptic error message printed out on the client's terminal on a Saturday when the consultant is unavailable. Conversely, behavioral considerations must be taken into account or the good technical features will be misapplied and thus end up being done for the sake of the programmer rather than the client.

If the analyst/programmer can approach a project with the goal of helping someone solve a problem, rather than with the intention of doing some interesting programming the project will be half way to a successful conclusion already. The consultant cannot afford to forget the client. The service aspect of the job is the most important of all. A client who is satisfied with the results and understands the program will be much more receptive to the application of computers to other problems.

The industrial consulting project is by no means the only situation where needs are more important then elegance. Computer technology has advanced to the point where it infringes on every aspect of our lives. Far too often the effects on people have been frustrating and dehumanizing. *It is time to worry about the problem of making computers serve their users in ways that are comfortable and satisfying as well as fast and cost effective.*

References

[1] B.W. Kerninghan and P.J. Plauger, Elements of Programming Style, (McGraw Hill, 1974).

[2] Rob Kling, "The Organizational Context of User-Centered Design", MIS Quarterly, Dec. 1977, pp. 41–52.

[3] James Martin, Design of Man-Computer Dialogues (Prentice-Hall, 1973).

[4] Linda Milburn, Client Oriented Design: A Case Study, Master's Thesis (University of California, Irvine, 1976).

[5] A.I. Wasserman and Susan K. Stinson, "A Specification Method for Interactive Information Systems", Proceedings of the Conference on Specifications for Reliable Software, IEEE Computer Society, 1979.

Case Study

Participative Systems Design: Structure and Method

Enid Mumford

Professor of Organisational Behaviour, Manchester Business School, University of Manchester, Booth Street West, Manchester M15 6PB, UK

Participative Systems Design: Structure and Method Abstract

This paper describe how a form of participative systems design was used in *Rolls Royce Aero-Engine Division*, Derby (England) for the design of an on-line computer-based suppliers accounts system. A steering committee and a design group were formed from the management, trade union and clerks of the departments that would be affected. Increases in job satisfaction and efficiency were made system objectives and all clerical staff were involved in the decision processes. The design group analysed the job satisfaction and efficiency needs of the departments and discussed then with their departmental colleagues. They then produced *three* alternative Organizational designs for task structures to be associated with the new technical system. The choice of which of these to implement was made by all the affected staff. The paper discusses how the selected socio-technical system was implemented and its consequences for management and clerks.

Keywords: System, Design, Consensus Design, Organizational Change, Job Satisfaction, Efficiency.

Enid Mumford is Professor of Organizational Behaviour at the Manchester Business School and Director of its MBA programme. She started her career in the aircraft industry as a Personnel Manager at Rotol Ltd., Gloucester, later moving to J.D. Francis Ltd, a manufacturer of alarm clocks, as Superintendent of Assembly, a post which gave her valuable experience of running a production department. She next joined the Department of Social Science at Liverpool University where she investigated industrial relations problems on the docks and in coal mining. Her career at Liverpool was interrupted by a one-year programme of research at the University of Michigan, Ann Arbor. She joined the Manchester Business in 1966. Her current research focusses on problems associated with the introduction of new technology. She is particularly interested in systems design and in helping users to acquire the skills and knowledge which will enable them to play a design role when new technology is being introduced. She is the author of fifteen books.

© North-Holland Publishing Company
Systems. Objectives, Solutions 1 (1981) 5–19

1. Participative System Design: Its Rationale

Participative systems design means *handing responsibility for the design of a new work system to the employees who eventually will have to operate it.* Its acceptance as an efficient and ethical approach appears to be growing as the values of western society become more democratic. There are *four* principal arguments for the use of such an approach when new computer systems are being designed. These are, *first*, an argument based on values which states that people have a moral right to control their own destinies and that this applies as much in the work situation as elsewhere[5]. In many countries, including Britain, this philosophy is now part of the policy of the main political parties, although there is still argument over how it shall be achieved. The *second* is an expediency argument and states that activities are ultimately controlled by those who perform them, and that people who do not have a say in decisions may decide to repeal the decisions of others as soon as those others leave the scene [3,9]. The *third* relates to the location of knowledge and states that the experts on operational factors such as task design are the people who do the jobs [2]. The *fourth* argument is that involvement acts as a motivator and will lead to more productivity and efficiency [11]. Those managers and trade unions who support this kind of participation probably do so for mixed motives which may include some or all of the above. However from the employee's point of view it is the consequences of a participative philosophy for his own work and work situation that are important rather than the motives that lie behind the enthusiasm of either side in industry to subscribe to it.

2. Participative Systems Design: Different Approaches

Participation in systems design can take a number of different forms and the author calls the three approaches which she has used *'Consultative'* Design, *'Representative'* Design and *'Consensus'* Design. Each approach requires a higher level of participation than the last and their development has been the result of an evolution of thinking and practice. To date the author has used participative design methods in seven organisations as follows: Consultative Design in the first, Representative Design in the next two and Consensus Design in the last four. *'Consultative' design* leaves the bulk of design decisions with the traditional systems design group, although the objectives they set and the eventual form the system takes is greatly influenced by the needs, particularly the job satisfaction needs, of the user department. With this approach the technical system design group will make considerable efforts to diagnose accurately what kind of new system will give the user, including here subordinates and supervisors, a more satisfying and efficient work environment.

With *'representative' design* a design group is formed representing all grades of users and all functions in a particular department or departments. The task of this 'representative' group is to design a new system of work to fit with the new technology. This work system must provide both high job satisfaction and high efficiency.

'Consensus' systems design is a higher level of participation in that it attempts to involve all members of user departments continuously throughout the systems design process. There is still a representative design group but this group communicates and consults continuously with its colleagues.

By making organisational efficiency and job satisfaction joint objectives, the design group is using what is often called a *socio-technical* approach. By socio-technical we mean a design philosophy that produces productivity, quality, coordination and control; but also provides a work environment and task structure in which people can achieve personal development and satisfaction.

In this paper the author will describe the methodology and group processes associated with the use of a consensus approach for the design of a new computer system and its organisational context. The firm involved was the aero-engine division of *Rolls Royce Ltd.* Here a new on-line computer system to handle suppliers accounts was being introduced into two departments: Purchase Invoice which cleared the accounts, and a Treasure's Unit which passed and signed cheques for payment. These two departments together had a staff of fifty, the majority located in Purchase Invoice.

A representative design group of eight people was formed, drawn from the staff of the two user departments and including the two systems analysts responsible for the design of the technical part of the system. Management decided to select the members of this design group itself although in the author's view it would have been preferable to have had the group democratically elected, and in other companies this has been the normal practice.

Because a consensus design approach was used the design group not only had to come up with a new form of work organisation for the department, incorporating the use of a computer; it also had to feedback its ideas to department colleagues on the alternative forms this new work system could take, and allow the final decision to be made by the department as a whole. In order to do this the design group required information on user job satisfaction and efficiency needs, and also job design skills. In addition it needed communication and consultation skills so that it could keep constantly and effectively in touch with the views of all clerks in the department. Experience to date suggests that the latter skills are more difficult to acquire than the former.

3. Structure and Procedures for Consensus Design

The first and most essential step in any form of participative systems design, whether *'consultative'*, *'representative'* or *'consensus'* is to get the agreement of management, the trade unions and user department employees to this approach. Departmental management must be enthusiastic rather than merely acceptive as to some extent they are handing over some of their traditional responsibilities to their subordinates.

In *Rolls Royce Ltd,* once management and the trade union had given their approval, the proposition was discussed with all the clerks in small groups and it was their decision on whether or not a participative approach should be tried. They agreed to try the consensus model. The next step was to set up two participative structures; a design group and a steering group.

The Rolls Royce *Design Group* was not elected by its collegeagues but the members did adequately represent the different grades, functions and sexes in the two user departments. The two professional systems analysts were members of the Group but the departmental supervisors decided not to join it in case their presence inhibited the discussions of their subordinates. They asked that they should be kept in touch with its thinking and decisions and this was complied with.

Any new design group is likely to have two major problems. One, of ensuring the continuing interest and sanction of top management and the trade unions; two, of not producing design solutions that are likely to be unacceptable to the organisation because they conflict with some important aspect of company policy. The answer to these problems is the creation of a *steering group*. In Rolls Royce Ltd this consisted of the senior managers responsible for the user departments, the head of management services, the chairman of the trade union branch, the systems manager responsible for the user computer system, the factory medical officer, the author and, at a later stage the clerk who acted as the chairman of the Design Group. The Steering Group had two important roles. One of giving the Design Group support and encouragement. The second of acting as an arbitrator if the Design Group was uncertain whether a particular design solution would conflict with company policy. In the event the Steering Group never imposed any constraints on the Design Group. Their message was always *'You design the best system from your point of view and we will support you'*.

4. The Design Task

If employees are to contribute to the design of their own work systems when new technology is introduced they need a set of analytical tools to enable them to identify their own job satisfaction and efficiency needs, to set specific objectives, to redesign

the organisation of their department around the new technology and to contribute to the design of the technical part of the system. This paper describes a number of analytical and diagnostic procedures, developed by the author and others, which can assist any participative design process. It shows how these tools were used in the Rolls Rouce context to enable the Design Group to proceed from an initial state of confusion, to clarification of the nature of their design role and competence in carrying this out.

5. Step 1 – Analysis of the Required System

5.1. Describing the Essential [1] Organisational System

Many firms introduce new technology by imposing it on an existing organisational structure which is not altered to accommodate it. However the implementation of new technology provides an opportunity for taking a fresh look at departmental organisation, and for establishing clearly the primary objectives and essential functions of the departments accepting the new technology. This preliminary examination of key objectives and functions is called essential systems analysis. It consists of the following:

1. Specifying in detail the nature of the *presenting problem or opportunity*. Why should an existing system or systems be redesigned?

In Rolls Royce Ltd the problem which a new computer based work system could help solve was the slow payment of suppliers' accounts. This in turn led to poor relationships between the firm and its suppliers.

2. Identifying those groups with an *interest* in how the problem is solved.

The groups with most interest in how this problem was solved were the employees of the Purchase Invoice and Treasurers' Departments, including both clerks and managers; the Management Services staff involved in the design of any new computer based work system, and the Rolls Royce suppliers. Some employees in departments where work linked to that

---

[1] By *'essential'* organisation is meant those functions which a system must cater for if it is to achieve its principal goal or goals.

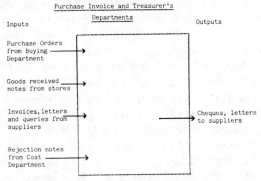

Fig. 1. System Boundary.

of Purchase Invoice and the Treasurers' Departments would also be slightly affected and their opinions were sought when that part of the system was being designed.

3. Defining the *boundaries* of the system with which the design exercise is concerned. A simple input–output model can be of use here showing what inputs enter the system and where they come from, and what outputs leave the system and where they go to. If the system is an information one which will cross many functional boundaries a tracer approach which identifies the paths taken by information and the senders and receipients may be a useful preliminary.

Fig. 1 shows very simply the boundaries of the Rolls Royce system and the inputs and outputs to and from the two internal departments. The boundaries indicate where the new system design was concentrated although, as we have noted, departments contingent to Purchase Invoice and the Treasurer's Department were also slightly affected.

4. Specifying the *primary objectives* of the system –

the principal reasons for its existence. It is important to establish that there is a consensus view on primary objectives before proceeding further.

In Rolls Royce Ltd, the Design Group had little difficulty in agreeing that the primary objectives of the Purchase Invoice and Treasurers' Departments were:

The control and motivation of suppliers.

A fast, accurate, economic and enthusiastic service from suppliers.

A steady cash flow resulting from the rapid and regular payment of suppliers' accounts.

A high quality of working life for the clerks and managers in the Purchase Invoice and Treasurers' Departments.

5. Identifying principal *unit operations* [2] (subsystems) associated with each objective or set of objectives. By unit operation is meant an integrated set of activities which are attached to a major system function. This set of activities is separated from other sets of activities by some kind of boundary – a change of input, time, location etc.

This notion of a unit operation has value at both the diagnostic and design stages of a new system. At the diagnostic stage, which is what we are concerned with here, it helps a design group to free themselves from focussing on the existing organisation of work and assists them in the task of logically thinking through the basic activities which their department must carry out if it is to achieve its primary objectives. Basic unit operations will tend to remain the same irrespective of the level of technology or the nature of work procedures.

At the design stage a good job design principle is to ensure that unit operations are not split up. A work group should be given responsibility for one or more unit operations if its task activities are to have logic and purpose.

The unit operations associated with the objectives of the Purchase Invoice and Treasurers' Departments were:

a) The receipt, opening, checking and distribution of mail-letters, invoices, credit notes etc.

b) The passing of invoices for payment.

[2] The notion of a unit operation has been developed by practitioners of the socio-technical design approach. See [10].

c) Dealing with rejected goods. This often involved asking suppliers to send a credit note.

d) The payment of cheques.

Unit operations b), c) and d) each had an important problem solving component, that of dealing with suppliers' queries. These were usually related to dealyed or non-payment of invoices.

Each of these unit operations can be logically separated from the others.

The principal inputs for a) are a mail receiving system, a communication system, adding and photocopying machines and clerical workers. To control the mail distribution activity the unit operation requires accurate information on the Sections to which mail should be delivered. The principal output is the arrival of checked mail at the correct Purchase Invoice Section.

The principal inputs for b) are invoices and goods received notes which have to be matched with each other. Accurate information on suppliers is also required. The output is the notification by Purchase Invoice to the Treasurer's Department that an invoice has been passed for payment.

The inputs for c) are a notification from the Stores that goods received are not of the required quality. Control of this situation will require careful testing and checking of goods inwards in the stores. The output is the request to a supplier for a credit note to cover any payments already made.

The inputs to d) are invoices passed for payment. The output is a signed cheque sent to the supplier.

Once unit operations have been identified the next level of analysis is to establish the nature of the activities associated with each unit operation. The method is as follows:

Describe each unit operation in detail, concentrating on its essential activities and requirements rather than existing technology, procedures or organisational shape. Many of these will be changed in the redesigned phase. Unit operation descriptions will cover the following activities [3].

One – operational activities. Necessary activities associated with the unit operation's principal objective and function. For example unit operation a) will involve receiving, checking and distributing mail, and

ensuring that this mail arrives at each section speedily and regularly.

Two – problem avoidance or correction activities; variances which must ideally be avoided, or rapidly corrected if they occur. A variance is defined as a tendency for a system or subsystem to deviate from some desired norm or standard [10]. These problems should be described in the following way:

In terms of the systems *sensitivity* to the problem; i.e., the problem is likely to be expensive or difficult to correct. Its occurrence will cause a major disturbance in the functioning of the unit operation. At this level of analysis only variances which tend to occur because of the nature of the systems goals or essential functions should be recorded. Variances which are a result of an existing set of procedures or organisation of work will be examined later.

Problems to which the system is most sensitive are called *'Key'* variances. It is important to note any feedback loops between one Key variance and another. See Fig. 2.

An example of a variance to which the system is sensitive in unit operation a) is the time taken to check and distribute mail to the sections. Non-arrival of mail greatly increased the peaks and troughs of the working day.

The following information will be relevant to an understanding of system and sensitivity:

the nature of the problem

the cause of the problem

the likelihood of its occurrence

the nature of its impact on the unit operation or adjoining systems

The nature of the resources required for problem avoidance or recovery

the cost of avoidance

the cost of recovery – in time, money or other important resources.

Three – coordination activities. These are activities within a unit operation or between unit operations which must be coordinated if the subsystem is to function efficiently. For example, in the Rolls Royce example the payment of cheques to suppliers by the Treasurer's Department had to be carefully coordinated with the passing of invoices by the Purchase Invoice sections.

Four – development activities. These are of two kinds as follows:

[3] This is an adaptation of a cybernetic model developed by Stafford Beer. See [1].

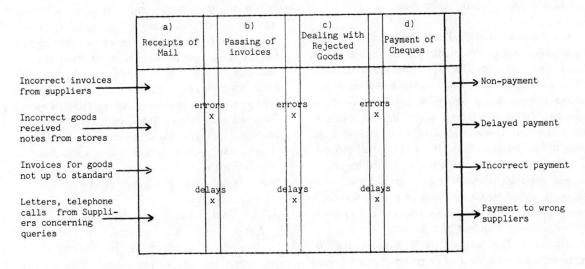

Unit Operations in Purchase Invoice and Treasurers' Departments

Variances are particularly likely to occur at the boundaries of
the system and at the interface between one unit operation and
another

Fig. 2. Examples of Key Variances to which the Rolls Royce System was sensitive.

(a) *to improve efficiency.* Assuming that the unit operation is not operating at optimal efficiency, the technical, procedural, organisational and resource changes that could bring it closer to an optimal state (N.B. skill and knowledge are always important resources).

(b) *to adapt to change.* Assuming that the environment in which the unit operation occurs is not completely static; the technical, procedural, organisational and resource developments that will be required to cope with environmental changes. Forecasts of the nature of these changes and an estimate of the time period over which predicted changes are likely to occur are important aspects of what the authors call *'future analysis'.*

Five – control activities. The nature of the controls required to establish that the unit operation and the total system are operating at high efficiency. These will include standards, monitoring systems and methods for identifying when new variances are beginning to occur. It is usual to find management

problems at the boundaries between unit operations and at the boundary between the system and its environment.

If an information system is being designed, the information requirements to ensure control and motivation at each of these levels — system operation, problem avoidance or correction, coordination, development and control — and at the boundaries between them, can be broadly specified at this stage. They will be set out in detail when the description of unit operations and diagnosis of organisational and human needs have been completed and objectives for the new system have been set.

This analysis is quite independent of any technology that is being used or will be used in the future. The nature and level of technology is merely and aid to assisting the department to more effectively achieve its primary goals and essential functions. There will of course be a feedback loop here with new technical possibilities enabling new objectives and functions to be attained.

5.2. Identifying Job Satisfaction Needs

The approach described in the paper always makes an improvement in job satisfaction an important system design objective. This means that job satisfaction needs and expectations must be made explicit as part of the system description. This involves individuals associated with the system specifying the kinds of satisfaction they would ideally like to receive from their work environment. Unless a very small group is involved this information is best collected by asking system users to complete questionnaires and using the data collected on this way as a basis for small group discussion in how these job satisfaction needs and expectations can best be achieved.

Job satisfaction, defined by Mumford as the *'fit' between what an individual or group is seeking from the work situation and what they are receiving,* is seen as being achieved when three kinds of needs are met in the work situation [12]. These are personality needs, competence and efficiency needs and needs associated with personal values. Therefore any description of a system prior to its redesign should include the following information on job satisfaction.

5.2.1. Needs Associated with Personality

Knowledge needs. How, ideally, would each individual or group forming part of the system like their existing skills and knowledges to be used? What opportunities would they like for these to be developed further?

Psychological needs. What are their needs for responsibility, status, esteem, security and advancement and how do they define these needs?

5.2.2. Needs Associated with Competence, Control and Efficiency in the Work Role and the Successful Performance of Work Activities.

Support/control needs. The kind of support services which users at every level believe would enable them to carry out their work responsibilities more efficiently.. These support services will include the information and materials necessary to work at a high level of competence as well as supervisory support and good working conditions.

The kind of control systems that users believe would assist their motivation and efficiency. The level and structure of wages and salaries is an important part of any control system.

Task needs. The kinds of task structure that different groups of users will find motivating, interesting and challenging. For example, to what extent do users want jobs that include elements of all our five system levels. ie. opportunities for self management, for developing new methods, services or products, for coordinating their own activities and taking organisational decisions, for solving their own problems and monitoring their own progress, as well as the level one tasks of producing a product or service.

5.2.3. Needs Associated with Employee Values

Ethical needs. How do users at every level want to be treated by management. Do the organisation's policies on communication, consultation and participation meet employee expectations. Do other kinds of policy also meet these expectations?

In the Rolls Royce Purchase Invoice and Treasurers' Departments the job satisfaction needs expressed most forcibly were the following:

Needs Associated with Personality. 74% of clerks wanted better opportunities to use their skill and knowledge. 59% wanted to have more responsibility. By this they meant larger, more important jobs.

Needs Associated with competence, control and efficiency. 36% of clerks wanted more work freedom. By this they meant to be less subjected to management imposed work controls. 72% wanted to get a sense of achievement more often. The ability to feel achievement was related to the challenge and interest of work. 56% wanted to do a whole job. Instead of doing a few small, specialised and routine tasks, many clerks expressed a preference for much larger jobs in which they could carry out all the tasks associated with servicing a group of suppliers. These would include passing invoices, ensuring cheques were paid and answering suppliers' queries. 49% wanted more opportunity to take decisions and use judgement. The ability to do this was related to the size and importance of a clerk's job.

The lists above provided guidance to the Rolls Royce Design Group on those job satisfaction objectives that must be attained through the new computer based work system and the way it was designed.

6. Step 2 – Analysis of the Existing System

6.1. Discrepancy Analysis

Once system essentials have been described following the analytical model above, it is useful to establish the extent to which existing organisational arrangements are meeting or failing to meet efficiency and job satisfaction objectives and needs.

This provides information on the extent to which the existing system diverges from the required or *'closer to ideal'* system. A word of warning is needed here, however. Too great a concentration on the weaknesses of the existing system may lead to a superficial remedying of these weaknesses via a minor reorganisation plus the intervention of a new technical system. A more fundamental re-thinking of organisational needs is required so that any redesign is based on a clear identification of organisational objectives and purposes, and an analysis of staff job satisfaction needs which incorporates a philosophy of personal development and is based on what can be made to happen rather than on an improvement of what happens now.

Discrepancy analysis covers an identification of *variances* which are a product of existing procedures and organisation of work, or availability of resources. Many of these kinds of variances will interact with each other and travel through the work system. A variance matrix will show the pervasiveness of a problem (i.e., if it occurs it leads to, or interacts with, other problems in the unit operation or adjoining systems); an example from Rolls Royce Ltd, is given in Fig. 3.

It can be seen, for example, how variance 1 (invoices wrongly addressed by supplier) affects variance 3 (invoice has to be returned to supplier); this in turn affects variances 5, 6, 8, 9 and 10. If variance 1 can be eliminated or rapidly controlled then it will reduce the impact of variances further down the system. Variances 2, 3 and 5 have a similar pervasive impact on the system.

Discrepancy analysis will also involve an examination of existing task structures and work flows to establish the extent to which there is a good or bad fit between these and efficiency requirements, and a survey of the extent to which existing organisational arrangements are meeting employee job satisfaction

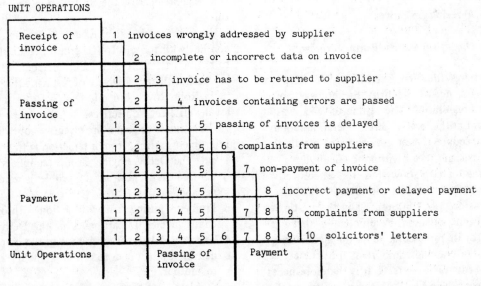

Fig. 3. Variance Matrix. Variances are numbered 1, 2, 3 etc. on the right hand side of the matrix with the nature of the variances written beside them. The numbers in adjoining boxes on the same line are variances which interact with the right hand side variances.

needs. This job satisfaction information can be collected in the same questionnaire as that used to establish the kinds of satisfaction that employees would ideally like to receive from their work situation. Both *'fact'* (now) and *'preference'* (the future) questions can be included.

Discrepancy analysis will assist an identification of systems areas where there is already a good fit between efficiency and job satisfaction needs, and work organisation and technology. It will also help identify those areas where the fit is poor and the variances or dissatisfaction are prone to occur. It should only be used as a guide to areas which do not require redesign because they are working effectively if the existing system is clearly geared to achieving efficiency and job satisfaction goals in these areas.

In Rolls Royce the information collected on efficiency and job satisfaction needs by Analysis-Steps 1 and 2 was then fed back to all staff in the user departments and discussed in small groups. This was done to check its accuracy and to establish improvement priorities. All user staff were asked to contribute suggestions on how both sets of needs might be met through a reorganisation of the work of the department and the use of a computer based information system.

7. Step 3 – Agreeing Objectives

7.1. Setting Objectives and Evaluating Strategies

In describing the first system analysis step we referred to the need to identify the primary objectives of the organisation. The setting of objectives at that level and at the level of actual operation requires a formal procedure if user groups are to handle this stage of the design process without difficulty.

The design group now has to set objectives intended to reduce discrepancies between the essential system as described in Step 1 and the existing or predicted future situation. A problem is that each user group (or its representative on the design group) will tend to rate as most important those objectives which further its own interests. It is therefore necessary to recognise and deal with this potential conflict of goals. An ideal solution is to find a design which meets each group's most important objectives, but

this is not always possible, and conflicting situations often arise. If these are brought out into the open early enough, they can be discussed by all concerned and it may be possible to reach agreement on priority objectives.

The procedure has also to assist the design team to choose a strategy that will assist the attainment of priority objectives. One method is first, to assess the extent to which each strategy contributes to the achievement of priority objectives related to the interests of particular user groups.

The detailed, sequential steps to be taken by the design group are as follows:

Identify interest groups which are not already represented in the design group (buying, stores, production departments etc.), paying particular attention to any subgroups that might suffer from proposed changes. If a representative of an interest group cannot join the objective setting meetings then a member of the design group, in addition to acting for his own constituents, will also assume responsibility for one of these unrepresented groups.

List the objectives which are most important to each interest group; including here groups which have direct representation on the design team and those which have indirect representation. The techniques of variance analysis and job satisfaction analysis will provide a great deal of the information required to do this.

Note if the objectives of any interest group are in conflict with those of other groups. When this proves to be the case the design group members will need to establish if there is any way of resolving this conflict.

In Rolls Royce Ltd, the Design Group set the following efficiency objectives.

To estimate or gain more effective control over:
1. Problems arising from interaction with groups outside the Derby Engine Group (suppliers and subcontractors). These are the problems set out in the variance matrix.
2. Problems arising from interaction with other Purchase Invoice Departments in the Derby Engine Group and with other groups in the company eg. deliveries of supplies to one area which are invoiced to another.
3. Problems arising from the interaction of the Purchase Invoice and Treasurer's Departments with other departments at Rolls Royce Ltd, eg. with

the Purchase Department and with Stores.

4. Problems arising from the interaction between Purchase Invoice and the Treasurer's Department, eg. nonclearance of invoices, overlapping work responsibilities.

5. Problems arising from interaction between groups in the Purchase Invoice Department.

The efficiency of any new form of work organisation, once implemented, would be tested by checking that these problems had either been eliminated or more effectively controlled, without the introduction of any new problems.

In addition, in Rolls Royce, job satisfaction objectives were set directed at giving the clerks the following:

Better opportunities to use their skills and knowledge

More work responsibility

More work freedom

A greater sense of achievement

The opportunity to do a whole job

More opportunity to take decisions and use judgement.

Once specific efficiency and job satisfaction objectives have been set for the new computer based work system than a number of alternative system design strategies must be developed for comparison with the current system. This is the beginning of the sociotechnical design phase.

It must be emphasised that setting objectives and evaluating strategies will become a negotiating process as the different interests represented in the design group press for priority to be given to those goals and strategies most likely to further the needs and expectations of their constituents. One advantage of the method described here is that these issues are brought into the open [4].

8. Step 4 – Designing the Organisational System

8.1. Socio-technical System Design

A participative approach to work design means that the employees of a department or their represen-

[4] System analysis, Step 3, – Setting Objectives and Evaluating Strategies – was developed by John Hawgood of *Durham University* and Frank Land of *London School of Economics*.

tatives construct a new form of work organisation which is based on a diagnosis by them of their own needs. There are a number of philosophical approaches to work design which such design groups may want to consider. The two most frequently used are *'job enrichment'* and the *'socio-technical'* approach. Job enrichment focusses on the job of the individual worker and tries to build up this job in such a way that it increases in interest, responsibility and challenge. The job may be extended by adding to it preliminary activities such as setting it up and acquiring the necessary materials, or completion activities such as final quality inspection and the rectification of errors, tasks which previously have been carried out by other individuals. The aim of job enrichment is to improve the relationship between the individual and his work.

The socio-technical method was originally developed by the *Tavistock Institute* in the United Kingdom, and this takes a very different approach. The concept of a socio-technical system is derived from the premise that any production system requires both a technology or process for transforming raw materials into output, and a social structure linking the human operators both with the technology and with each other. A socio-technical system is any unit in the organisation composed of a technological and a social subsystem having a common task or goal to accomplish. If we are concerned with clerical systems based on the use of a computer, the technical system will consist of the tools, techniques and procedures used for processing the raw materials of information. The social structure is the network of roles, relationships and tasks which interact with the technical system. The purpose of the socio-technical system approach is to produce technical and social structures which have a high capacity to achieve technical and social goals and which reinforce each other in the achievement of these goals.

Socio-technical analysis incorporates a logical analysis of the technical components of the work system (machines, procedures, information) and the grouping of these into 'unit operations'. Unit operations, as we have seen, are logically integrated sets of tasks, one set being separated from the next by a change of state in the input or product. For example, in the Purchase Invoice Department, the tasks of preparing accounting data for the computer, putting the data into the computer, and correcting errors will be a logically different set of activities from matching accounts with goods-received notes and investigating discrepancies. Work design which uses a socio-technical approach identifies unit operations and allocates one or more unit operations to each work group. The work group then has the responsibility for allocating tasks amongst its members and for training its members so that eventually each individual is competent to carry out all tasks.

The Rolls Royce Design Group developed three alternative strategies for reorganising the Purchase Invoice and Treasurers' Departments around the new computer system. Redesign concentrated on Purchase Invoice as the Treasurer's Department contained only a small number of staff.

Alternative 1 was to split the Purchase Invoice Department into a number of autonomous or self-managing groups. Each group would take responsibility for all the activities associated with handling the accounts and problems of a group of suppliers. A group would consist of six clerks, each of whom would be able to perform all the tasks for which the group was responsible. The existing grading structure of the department would be eliminated and all clerks would eventually become the same grade. Grading would in effect be based on job knowledge and everyone who wished to do so would be able to acquire this knowledge.

Alternative 2 was a more conservative approach and a modification of the existing work system. The organisation of the Purchase Invoice Department would not be greatly altered from its pre-computer form but there would be an enrichment of the jobs of the lower-grade clerks. In the job satisfaction survey this group had expressed least job satisfaction.

Alternative 3 was a complete compromise between alternatives 1 and 2. The majority of staff in the Purchase Invoice Department would be organised in self-managing groups as in 1. But, in addition there would be a service group with responsibility for handling mail and for other activities which were common to all groups. The work of the Service Group would be routine but the Design Group knew that a small number of staff in the department did not want the responsibility of more complex tasks. Some variety could be introduced into this work through job rotation. There would also be a small specialist group of higher grade clerks who would look after specialist supplies and activities. This would meet the needs of a group of senior clerks who were extremely reluctant to change their present role and responsibilities.

Alternatives 1 and 3 would both achieve the efficiency and job satisfaction objectives set by the Design Group (see Table 1). Alternative 2 would be much less effective in doing this.

After each of these three alternative organisational designs had been formulated a description of it was fed back to their departmental colleagues by the members of the design group, with a request for comment and criticism. Alternative 1 had been seen by the Design Group as assisting the clerks to become multi-skilled, as giving them more control over their work and as providing opportunities for problem solving which did not exist with the present functional organisation of work. However this solution met with considerable hostility from a group of senior clerks who saw the opportunity for all clerks to become multi-skilled as threatening their own status.

Alternative 2 had focussed on enriching the most routine jobs but this was criticised on the basis that it did not greatly alter the existing organisation of work.

Alternative 3 received the most favourable response from the clerks as a whole.

In retrospect these alternative organisational designs should have been presented to, and discussed with, the Purchase Invoice and Treasurer's Clerks at one and the same time. The sequential reporting generated some conflict in the department as each solution was viewed as a possible final one.

This conflict was overcome through explanation and a guarantee that the final design solution would be chosen by all the clerks and not management or the Design Group alone.

The three alternative designs were then presented to the Steering Group by the Design Group members themselves. At this stage they had all been carefully documented and their advantages and disadvantages thought through in detail. The Steering Group was most impressed by the competence of the Design Group and somewhat amazed that a group of clerks could do such an excellent design job. They indicated that any of the three design solutions would be acceptable to them, although they preferred the first

Table 1
Perceived advantages of Alternatives 1 and 3

Job satisfaction advantages (ability of work system to meet job satisfaction objectives)	Efficiency advantages (ability of work system to control system variances)
1. Many clerks wanted to be able to see a job through from start to finish. The proposed autonomous group structure of the Purchase Invoice department would permit this.	1. The proposed systems would provide better control of variances. Clerks would be able to deal with the problems and queries of the suppliers for which their work group was responsible.
2. Clerks wanted more self management opportunities. They would have the opportunity to organise themselves in different ways within their groups.	2. The learning opportunities of the autonomous group structure would mean a greater spread of knowledge between clerks and therefore greater employee flexibility.
3. Clerks wanted more responsibility. The autonomous group structure would enable clerks to take responsibility for all matters relating to a supplier's account, including dealing with all queries.	3. More interesting, challenging work should increase labour stability and reduce labour turnover costs.
4. Clerks said their existing work was too routine. The proposed work systems would provide more interest and flexibility.	4. Greater work efficiency would make the department a more desirable and attractive place of work. Clerks would be able to demonstrate their own competence.
5. Clerks wanted an opportunity to increase their skills and knowledge. The proposed systems provided excellent learning opportunities. Clerks could move up the department grading structure as they become able to handle all the tasks for which their work group was responsible.	5. Greater work efficiency should mean more slack in the work system and therefore more time for training.

or third. The three solutions were then once again presented by the Design Group to all their clerical colleagues in the user department at a meeting chaired by the Chairman of the Trade Union Branch. All the clerks voted on the three design options and the third solution was chosen by a large majority.

Although a consensus decision had been taken the Design Group's task was by no means over. They now had to specify the selected solution in considerable detail and develop the framework for the new autonomous group structure. They had to create a strategy for implementation which would include training and the physical layout of the reorganised department. They also had to work with the technical systems designers and decide how the clerks would interact with the new computer terminals.

9. Step 5 – Implementing the System

9.1. Systems Implementation and Operation

Once a system has been designed it has to be implemented and this involves a set of change processes in which an existing system is assisted to move smoothly and successfully from one organisational state to another. The new work structure and level of technology have to be established in such a way that they fit well with employee expectations and values so that a set of social, technical and administrative relationships is developed which both leads to greater efficiency and provides job satisfaction and opportunities for personal development. This relationship between tasks, technology, human needs and organisational goals needs to be stable but it should not be static. A department must be able to respond to new demands from its customers or from other departments with which it has to interact, while at the same time maintaining a state of internal equilibrium. An ability to accept and adjust easily to new pressures will assist the avoidance of stress and conflict.

A system that has been participatively designed can still encounter serious problems if the way it is introduced does not fit with the users' ideas of what is an acceptable implementation strategy. All groups concerned with the change processes, including senior and departmental management, the design team, the clerks as a group and, if they are affected, the external group of customers or suppliers, must understand the nature and logic of the change consequences, must approve and like the change strategies that are adopted and must regard the results of these as beneficial to their own interests. Implementation involves providing the user with a commitment to the new work system, with an understanding of how it functions and with the skills to operate it efficiently. Commitment is facilitated by involvement in the design processes and by a belief that the system will increase job satisfaction and provide an improvement on previous work methods. This belief must not be jeopardised through poor implementation, as change will only prove successful if groups which experience it can adapt easily to the new situation and feel comfortable with it.

Implementation in Rolls Royce Ltd was held up for some months due to a combination of circumstances. The design of the technical part of the system, in particular the change to an interactive on-line terminal system, had to be completed. Also the newly created job structure had to be subjected to the normal job evaluation procedures and the job evaluation officers had a heavy programme of work in other departments at the time. This delay was frustrating for the clerks and caused a drop in morale and some suspicion that the democratically chosen new work system would not be introduced.

When implementation did begin the Purchase Invoice Department was faced with the problem of changing from groups with specialist activities, for example, sections that dealt only with production invoices, raw material invoices, or commercial invoices, etc. to groups that would deal with all types of invoice for a set of suppliers' accounts. This change required a great deal of tranining to enhance the knowledge of those involved and at the same time a new office layout and new social groups would be required. In addition there were the problems of how to implement the new work method without too much disruption of the day-to-day workload, and how the ensure that the new groups were structurally and socially viable.

The first strategy considered was to begin implementation by forming a single group under the leadership of one of the most experienced section leaders in the department. The group would be structurally representative of the groups to be formed later but would consist of the best clerks in each grade. This group would act as the nucleus of future groups and would eventually, after its members had mastered the new work methods, split and form two groups. The same process would then take place until the desired number of groups had been reached. It was thought that this method of implementation would allow 'on the job training' by the most experienced clerks and that it could be implemented over a time period and at a pace which would fit with the existing workload of the clerks. It also allowed time to calculate the allocation of suppliers across the groups, which was no easy task. It was not sufficient merely to split the alphabet into equal sections because the complexity of some accounts had to be taken into consideration as well as the numbers of invoices. An incremental approach of this kind would permit a gradual introduction and evaluation of the new method of work.

This approach also had a disadvantage however. The bringing together in one group of all the best clerks in the department would denude the rest of the department of expertise. It was therefore decided to make a clean-cut changeover and to move from the old structure to the new virtually overnight. A number of sections were formed, with six in each, and these were to become the multi-skilled groups specified in the chosen work design solution. Some clerks moved into this new group structure with initial doubts but most people setteled down easily and quickly and the general view was that the new system was a success. Job titles were changed so that everyone was now called *'Accounts Clerk'* instead of *'Junior'* or *'Senior'* clerk.

Once the new multi-skilled group structure had settled down both the clerks and their managers regarded the change as an organisational success. Efficiency and job satisfaction had considerably improved and there was more staff mobility. Clerks were no longer trapped in a rigid hierarchical grading structure with promotion only possible if someone in a higher grade left the company. New clerks now entered the department and were able to move up from one job grade to the next as their knowledge increased and they became multi-skilled.

The advantages of the new work system could be summed up as:

298

More flexibility

More job satisfaction

More efficiency, (an important factor here was that each work group now solved its own problems and corrected its own mistakes).

An ability to attract high quality staff, (clerks now wanted to work in the department whereas previously it had had serious recruitment difficulties).

But there were also some unexpected disadvantages. As the accounts clerks became multi-skilled they were much sought after by other departments and were offered higher job grades than they could attain in their own department. Many moved up and then out of Purchase Invoice into other departments in the company. This was beneficial for the firm as a whole but the manager of the Purchase Invoice Department complained that he was now training his staff to benefit other departments and that he would like to have more staff stability. One way of securing this was to ensure that his clerks could move on to even higher grades within their own department. Efforts were therefore made to increase the skill content of the clerks' work even further so that it would merit a higher grade on the job evaluation scale.

This grading problem also caused some dissatisfaction with the firm's job evaluation policies. The clerks wanted their more skilled jobs to be recognised in higher grades and higher pay and although this had happened to some extent they believed that the firm should have given more. There was no disappointment with the new multi-skilled task structure however. Clerks and managers regarded it as a great improvement on the previous system of work.

The author returned to Rolls Royce some twelve months after the system had become operational and settled down, and discussed its effects with senior and departmental management and with the clerk who had been Chairman of the Design Group. All three believed the selected solution to have been effective in increasing efficiency and job satisfaction and meeting design objectives. The pre-change problems of inability to attract staff, routine work and poor promotion prospects had gone. The new problem of staff moving up the departmental hierarchy and then out into other departments which could provide higher grades and salaries was seen as a short term one. This would be solved through attaching a higher grade

to the multi-skilled jobs associated with the autonomous group structure.

In order to diffuse the design approach described in this paper into other parts of Rolls Royce, the author organised a course on participative design for Rolls Royce systems analysts and user managers.

10. The rationale behind the approach

Participation, as *Mary Parker Follett* once pointed out, is not just voting. It also requires thinking, knowledge and competence. It is more than joint discussion; it is joint problem solving. Participative systems design requires a design group, which is probably new to the design task, to identify organisational efficiency problems and human job satisfaction needs; to set organisational objectives which will meet these two sets of needs; to create alternative design strategies, incorporating new technology, as a means for achieving these objectives, and to implement the selected system. A major learning process is therefore involved in which a design group has to move from an initial state of confusion; to a clarification of its task, and to competence in carrying out this task.

This complex design and change process, when carried out participatively, requires a means to assist participation and a means to assist learning and the development of competence. In the authors view, participative systems design therefore requires a humanistic value system, a methodology that assists the acquisition of knowledge on how to design good human and organisational systems and a democratic structure that enables effective participation to be realised. She believes that the approach described in this paper contributes to both of these. The participative structure of design group and steering group assists the bringing together of interest groups at different organisational levels. The steering group with its representatives of senior management and senior trade union officials will set the parameters within which the design group has freedom to design. It will also act as a helper and guide whenever the design group seeks its assistance on questions of policy. The author's experience in Rolls Royce Ltd and other firms has been that Steering Groups are more likely to offer encouragement and freedom than control and constraints. The lower level design group is then able to analyse its own needs, set its own objectives and create its own future, *providing* it knows how to do this.

It is here that the methodology becomes important as an aid to the development of this competence. The different analysis and design steps described in this paper provide a systematic route along which a design group can proceed. Each step is a learning opportunity but also a means for achieving further progress towards the completion of the design task. Clearly, the steps described here are not the only means for achieving this design competence, but they are an example of useful tools that assist learning.

Critics of the approach usually see it as too complex, too time consuming and too expensive. In reality it appears to be none of these things. It is a way of simplifying the design task and enabling people who are not experts to contribute to this. The time involved is usually about six months with a design group meeting once a week or once a fortnight. Invariably the design of the organisational part of the system is completed before the design of the technical part. The costs of the approach are low and related to the time of those involved. The savings may be great as systems are implemented which are understood, liked and contribute to an improvement in the quailty of working life.

References

[1] S. Beer, The Brain of the Firm (Allan Lane. The Penguin Press, 1972).

[2] A. Edstrom and L. Nauges, "The Implementation of Computer Based Information Systems under Varying Structural Conditions", Paper presented to Altorg Conference, Gothenburg, May 1974.

[3] B. Hedberg, P. Nystrom and W. Starbuck, "Camping on See-Saws, Prescription for a Self-Designing Organisation", Administrative Science Quarterly, Vol. 21, (1), (1976), 41–62.

[4] E. Mumford, "Job Satisfaction: A Method of Analysis", Personnel Review, Vol 1, (3), (1972), 49–87.

[5] E. Mumford, "Human Values and the Introduction of Technical Change", in Moneta (ed), Information Technology. North Holland. Proceedings of the 3rd Jerusalem Conference on Information Technology (1978).

[6] E. Mumford, F. Land and J. Hawgood, "A Participative Approach to the Design of Computer Systems". Impact of Science on Society. Vol 28, (3) (1978), 235–253.

[7] E. Mumford and D. Henshall, The Participative Design of Computer Systems, (Associated Business Press, 1978).

[8] E. Mumford and M. Weir, Systems Design:The Ethics Method. (Associated Business Press, 1979).

[9] P.C. Nystrom, (1975), "Registers, Adapters and Innovators: On the Implementation of Managerial Goal Setting Systems". Working Paper. University of Wisconsin, Milwaukee (1975).

[10] J.C. Taylor (1978), "The socio-technical approach to work design", in ref. [13].

[11] J.K. White and R.A. Ruh, "The Effects of Personal Values on the Relationship between Participation and Job Attitudes". Administrative Science Quarterly, Vol 18, (4) (1973) 295–333.

[12] E. Mumford, "Job Satisfaction: A Method of Analysis", in ref. [13].

[13] K. Legge and E. Mumford (Eds.), Designing Organisations for Satisfaction and Efficiency (Gower Press, 1978).

Part V

Architectural Design Techniques: Process View

Once the information processing problem to be solved is understood and a set of functional specifications has been written, the next step in software development is to establish the structure of the system that will be built. This activity, often called architectural or general design, involves the external definition of subparts of the system (subsystems, facilities, and modules) and the interfaces between them. While this activity can be (and often is) carried out informally, there are numerous methods that can be systematically used to assist in establishing system structure.

We divide these architectural design methods into two groups: those providing a process or functionally based architecture and those yielding an architecture focused on data objects, treating the former in this Part and the latter in the next Part. It should be noted that the methods used for analysis and specification often strongly influence the choice of an architecture and that it is often easiest to create an architecture based on the structure of the problem as determined in the earlier work stages.

Furthermore, it should be noted that many different architectures can work successfully for the same problem, in much the same way that different architectures could fulfill the requirements for an office building. Indeed, application of the methods described in this Part and the succeeding Part to a single problem would yield many different possibilities.

There is, however, one key concept that can be found in virtually all of the architectural design methods, whether process-oriented or data-oriented: modularization. This concept is at the heart of problem solving, programming methodology, and design. Solution of a complex problem requires successful decomposition of the problem into a number of smaller problems where each problem can be addressed independently and where the interfaces between each of the pieces is well defined. In software design, an important form of this concept is information hiding, in which the internal details of an algorithm or data structure are hidden within a single module, making those details unavailable outside the module.

The idea of modularization in software design was clearly stated by Parnas in his classic paper "On the Criteria to be Use in Decomposing Systems into Modules." He shows how modules can be defined and used to hide design decisions, thus making changes easier and making the relationship between parts of the system clearer.

Much of Parnas' subsequent work on software specification and design proceeds along a natural course from the ideas expressed in that paper. His award-winning paper on designing software for ease of extension and contraction shows some techniques for designing flexible software, again based on the ideas of modularization.

We have noted that the first step of software design is to create an architecture for the system to be built. In terms of modularization, the task is to define the modules and the way(s) in which they are connected. While there is a concern with the function to be performed by each module, there is often less concern at this stage with the details of *how* the module will carry out the function. Such matters are part of the *detailed design* activity, as treated in Part VI.

Issues of module structure are treated by DeRemer and Kron in their paper "Programming-in-the-Large Versus Programming-in-the-Small." DeRemer and Kron effectively distinguish the tasks of architectural design from detailed design, pointing out that there are a different set of concerns in the two activities. They suggest the need for a Module Interconnection Language (MIL) that describes the module structure and linkages. In their framework, architectural design is a process of programming with modules. The idea of a MIL has been accepted by many development organizations, and it is now possible to point not only to specific MIL's, but also to the incorporation of those concepts in a variety of design languages and programming languages.

Modularity is also at the heart of "Structured Design," as described here by Stevens, Myers, and

EHO205-5/83/0000/0301$01.00 © 1983 IEEE

Constantine. Structured design is especially concerned with two aspects of modularity: module strength (or cohesion) and module connectivity. Ideally, each module should perform a single well-defined function (maximum cohesion) rather than carrying out several (possibly related) functions. Similarly, each module should be connected to other modules by data passing, e.g., parameters, without having one module control another by passing control information or having one module need to know anything of the internal details of another module.

Structured Design has been extensively used as a software design technique. In combination with Structured Systems Analysis (as described in the paper by Gane in Part II), structured programming, and appropriate management control, Structured Design is at the heart of several complete software development methodologies.

The paper here is the earliest published description of Structured Design, predating the development of Structured Systems Analysis and the establishment of a complete software development methodology. Nonetheless, the key ideas and a good example of the use of Structured Design may be found in this paper, and it provides a good starting point for the lengthier descriptions of Structured Design cited in the bibliography.

An increasing number of software systems involve aspects of concurrency and/or real-time control. Such systems, including operating systems, air traffic control, and communications switching systems, have existed for many years and are now joined by microprocessor-based embedded systems, distributed systems, and transaction-based systems.

Design and development of these complex systems require a set of analysis and design tools capable of representing the control and concurrency aspects of the problem. In earlier Parts, we saw methods, such as SADT and RSL, that support the analysis and specification of such systems. Here we examine some other possible approaches.

The R-net technique used in RSL is based on Petri nets. Petri nets are a general purpose modelling technique that have been applied to a wide variety of applications. They have been used for both hardware and software models; within software, they have been used for analysis, architectural design, and dialogue modelling. The paper by Agerwala is a tutorial introduction to the concepts and use of Petri nets.

The System ARchitect's Apprentice (SARA) is an interactive collection of tools to be used for multilevel design of concurrent hardware/software computer systems. In other words, SARA is a tool set that supports an approach, termed the UCLA design methodology, for the design of concurrent systems.

The SARA project, under the direction of Gerald Estrin, dates from 1975, but the underlying ideas may be traced back to Estrin's Graph Model of Computation developed in the early 1960's. (Estrin's model bears a very strong resemblance to Petri nets, developed concurrently and independently.) SARA supports both a bottom-up composition (abstraction) procedure and a top-down partitioning (refinement) approach to software design.

The design methodology proceeds from behavioral modelling (using the Graph Model of Behavior -- based on the earlier Graph Model of Computation) through module interface definitions and the generation of code skeletons. Three structural primitives are used: modules, sockets, and interconnections, where a socket encapsulates behavior related to the interface between a module and its environment, and an interconnection connects modules at their sockets.

The two papers reprinted in this book describe some of the important concepts of SARA, but by no means do they tell the entire story. The first paper, by Campos and Estrin, describes the methodology and the modelling primitives, showing the application of the ideas to a message-transmitting example. The reader should note, though, that the methodology as depicted in Figure 1 of the paper has since been revised to include evaluation phases subsequent to the Partition and Composition steps.

The second paper, by Razouk, Vernon, and Estrin, appears in Part VIII. The interested reader will find that the UCLA design methodology and its tools are well documented in published papers and technical reports. Additional references are given in the bibliography.

Hoare's paper proposes parallel composition of communicating sequential processes as a fundamental program structuring method. He develops a small programming language that includes nondeterministic control structures (as developed by Dijkstra), a command for concurrent execution of processes, and input and output commands to allow communication between the sequential processes. Hoare uses this small language to display the solution to many small examples. These ideas are still in the research stage.

The language developed by Hoare, while not intended as a production programming language, could serve reasonably well as a design language for applications exhibiting real time control and/or concurrency. The modelling approach of Jackson as described in the article on JSD in Part III is also based on sequential processes, so one could formulate a methodology for software development based on these ideas.

Finally, the paper by Riddle describes some of his work on DREAM, involving the production of tools that will aid the designer in developing and assessing the quality of a design at the architectural level. Riddle's approach is based on the concept of a monitor, as defined by Hoare. A monitor not only hides internal representation of data objects and the details of the operations on those objects but also includes a semaphore-like synchronization mechanism. These ideas are central to Riddle's more recent work with the Joseph software development environment.

On the Criteria To Be Used in Decomposing Systems into Modules

D.L. Parnas
Carnegie-Mellon University

This paper discusses modularization as a mechanism for improving the flexibility and comprehensibility of a system while allowing the shortening of its development time. The effectiveness of a "modularization" is dependent upon the criteria used in dividing the system into modules. A system design problem is presented and both a conventional and unconventional decomposition are described. It is shown that the unconventional decompositions have distinct advantages for the goals outlined. The criteria used in arriving at the decompositions are discussed. The unconventional decomposition, if implemented with the conventional assumption that a module consists of one or more subroutines, will be less efficient in most cases. An alternative approach to implementation which does not have this effect is sketched.

Key Words and Phrases: software, modules, modularity, software engineering, KWIC index, software design

CR Categories: 4.0

Introduction

A lucid statement of the philosophy of modular programming can be found in a 1970 textbook on the design of system programs by Gouthier and Pont [1, ¶10.23], which we quote below:[1]

> A well-defined segmentation of the project effort ensures system modularity. Each task forms a separate, distinct program module. At implementation time each module and its inputs and outputs are well-defined, there is no confusion in the intended interface with other system modules. At checkout time the integrity of the module is tested independently; there are few scheduling problems in synchronizing the completion of several tasks before checkout can begin. Finally, the system is maintained in modular fashion; system errors and deficiencies can be traced to specific system modules, thus limiting the scope of detailed error searching.

Usually nothing is said about the criteria to be used in dividing the system into modules. This paper will discuss that issue and, by means of examples, suggest some criteria which can be used in decomposing a system into modules.

A Brief Status Report

The major advancement in the area of modular programming has been the development of coding techniques and assemblers which (1) allow one module to be written with little knowledge of the code in another module, and (2) allow modules to be reassembled and replaced without reassembly of the whole system. This facility is extremely valuable for the production of large pieces of code, but the systems most often used as examples of problem systems are highly-modularized programs and make use of the techniques mentioned above.

[1] Reprinted by permission of Prentice-Hall, Englewood Cliffs, N.J.

Author's address: Department of Computer Science, Carnegie-Mellon University, Pittsburgh, PA 15213.

"On the Criteria To Be Used in Decomposing Systems into Modules" by David L. Parnas from *Communications of the ACM*, December 1972, pages 1053–1058. Copyright 1972, Association for Computing Machinery, Inc., reprinted by permission.

Expected Benefits of Modular Programming

The benefits expected of modular programming are: (1) managerial—development time should be shortened because separate groups would work on each module with little need for communication: (2) product flexibility—it should be possible to make drastic changes to one module without a need to change others; (3) comprehensibility—it should be possible to study the system one module at a time. The whole system can therefore be better designed because it is better understood.

What Is Modularization?

Below are several partial system descriptions called *modularizations*. In this context "module" is considered to be a responsibility assignment rather than a subprogram. The *modularizations* include the design decisions which must be made *before* the work on independent modules can begin. Quite different decisions are included for each alternative, but in all cases the intention is to describe all "system level" decisions (i.e. decisions which affect more than one module).

Example System 1: A KWIC Index Production System

The following description of a KWIC index will suffice for this paper. The KWIC index system accepts an ordered set of lines, each line is an ordered set of words, and each word is an ordered set of characters. Any line may be "circularly shifted" by repeatedly removing the first word and appending it at the end of the line. The KWIC index system outputs a listing of all circular shifts of all lines in alphabetical order.

This is a small system. Except under extreme circumstances (huge data base, no supporting software), such a system could be produced by a good programmer within a week or two. Consequently, none of the difficulties motivating modular programming are important for this system. Because it is impractical to treat a large system thoroughly, we must go through the exercise of treating this problem as if it were a large project. We give one modularization which typifies current approaches, and another which has been used successfully in undergraduate class projects.

Modularization 1

We see the following modules:

Module 1: Input. This module reads the data lines from the input medium and stores them in core for processing by the remaining modules. The characters are packed four to a word, and an otherwise unused character is used to indicate the end of a word. An index is kept to show the starting address of each line.

Module 2: Circular Shift. This module is called after the input module has completed its work. It prepares an index which gives the address of the first character of each circular shift, and the original index of the line in the array made up by module 1. It leaves its output in core with words in pairs (original line number, starting address).

Module 3: Alphabetizing. This module takes as input the arrays produced by modules 1 and 2. It produces an array in the same format as that produced by module 2. In this case, however, the circular shifts are listed in another order (alphabetically).

Module 4: Output. Using the arrays produced by module 3 and module 1, this module produces a nicely formatted output listing all of the circular shifts. In a sophisticated system the actual start of each line will be marked, pointers to further information may be inserted, and the start of the circular shift may actually not be the first word in the line, etc.

Module 5: Master Control. This module does little more than control the sequencing among the other four modules. It may also handle error messages, space allocation, etc.

It should be clear that the above does not constitute a definitive document. Much more information would have to be supplied before work could start. The defining documents would include a number of pictures showing core formats, pointer conventions, calling conventions, etc. All of the interfaces between the four modules must be specified before work could begin.

This is a modularization in the sense meant by all proponents of modular programming. The system is divided into a number of modules with well-defined interfaces; each one is small enough and simple enough to be thoroughly understood and well programmed. Experiments on a small scale indicate that this is approximately the decomposition which would be proposed by most programmers for the task specified.

Modularization 2

We see the following modules:

Module 1: Line Storage. This module consists of a number of functions or subroutines which provide the means by which the user of the module may call on it. The function call $CHAR(r,w,c)$ will have as value an integer representing the cth character in the rth line, wth word. A call such as $SETCHAR(r,w,c,d)$ will cause the cth character in the wth word of the rth line to be the character represented by d (i.e. $CHAR(r,w,c) = d$). $WORDS(r)$ returns as value the number of words in line r. There are certain restrictions in the way that these routines may be called; if these restrictions are violated the routines "trap" to an error-handling subroutine which is to be provided by the users of the routine. Additional routines are available which reveal to the caller the number of words in any line, the number of lines currently stored, and the number of characters in any word. Functions *DELINE* and *DELWRD* are provided to delete portions of lines which have already been stored. A precise specification of a similar module has been given in [3] and [8] and we will not repeat it here.

Module 2: INPUT. This module reads the original lines from the input media and calls the line storage module to have them stored internally.

Module 3: Circular Shifter. The principal functions provided by this module are analogs of functions provided in module 1. The module creates the impression that we have created a line holder containing not all of the lines but all of the circular shifts of the lines. Thus the function call $CSCHAR(l,w,c)$ provides the value representing the cth character in the wth word of the lth circular shift. It is specified that (1) if $i < j$ then the shifts of line i precede the shifts of line j, and (2) for each line the first shift is the original line, the second shift is obtained by making a one-word rotation to the first shift, etc. A function *CSSETUP* is provided which must be called before the other functions have their specified values. For a more precise specification of such a module see [8].

Module 4: Alphabetizer. This module consists principally of two functions. One, *ALPH*, must be called before the other will have a defined value. The second, *ITH*, will serve as an index. $ITH(i)$ will give the index of the circular shift which comes ith in the alphabetical ordering. Formal definitions of these functions are given [8].

Module 5: Output. This module will give the desired printing of set of lines or circular shifts.

Module 6: Master Control. Similar in function to the modularization above.

Comparison of the Two Modularizations

General. Both schemes will work. The first is quite conventional; the second has been used successfully in a class project [7]. Both will reduce the programming to the relatively independent programming of a number of small, manageable, programs.

Note first that the two decompositions may share all data representations and access methods. Our discussion is about two different ways of cutting up what *may* be the same object. A system built according to decomposition 1 could conceivably be identical *after assembly* to one built according to decomposition 2. The differences between the two alternatives are in the way that they are divided into the work assignments, and the interfaces between modules. The algorithms used in both cases *might* be identical. The systems are substantially different even if identical in the runnable representation. This is possible because the runnable representation need only be used for running; other representations are used for changing, documenting, understanding, etc. The two systems will not be identical in those other representations.

Changeability. There are a number of design decisions which are questionable and likely to change under many circumstances. This is a partial list.

1. Input format.
2. The decision to have all lines stored in core. For large jobs it may prove inconvenient or impractical to keep all of the lines in core at any one time.
3. The decision to pack the characters four to a word. In cases where we are working with small amounts of data it may prove undesirable to pack the characters; time will be saved by a character per word layout. In other cases we may pack, but in different formats.
4. The decision to make an index for the circular shifts rather that actually store them as such. Again, for a small index or a large core, writing them out may be the preferable approach. Alternatively, we may choose to prepare nothing during *CSSETUP*. All computation could be done during the calls on the other functions such as *CSCHAR*.
5. The decision to alphabetize the list once, rather than either (a) search for each item when needed, or (b) partially alphabetize as is done in Hoare's FIND [2]. In a number of circumstances it would be advantageous to distribute the computation involved in alphabetization over the time required to produce the index.

By looking at these changes we can see the differences between the two modularizations. The first change is confined to one module in both decompositions. For the first decomposition the second change would result in changes in every module! The same is true of the third change. In the first decomposition the format of the line storage in core must be used by all of the programs. In the second decomposition the story is entirely different. Knowledge of the exact way that the lines are stored is entirely hidden from all but module 1. Any change in the manner of storage can be confined to that module!

In some versions of this system there was an additional module in the decomposition. A symbol-table module (as specified in [3]) was used within the line storage module. This fact was completely invisible to the rest of the system.

The fourth change is confined to the circular shift module in the second decomposition, but in the first decomposition the alphabetizer and the output routines will also know of the change.

The fifth change will also prove difficult in the first decomposition. The output module will expect the index to have been completed before it began. The alphabetizer module in the second decomposition was designed so that a user could not detect when the alphabetization was actually done. No other module need be changed.

Independent Development. In the first modularization the interfaces between the modules are the fairly complex formats and table organizations described above. These represent design decisions which cannot be taken lightly. The table structure and organization are essential to the efficiency of the various modules and must be designed carefully. The development of those formats will be a major part of the module development and that part must be a joint effort among the several development groups. In the second modularization the interfaces are more abstract; they consist primarily in the function names and the numbers and types of the parameters. These are relatively simple decisions and the independent development of modules should begin much earlier.

Comprehensibility. To understand the output module in the first modularization, it will be necessary to understand something of the alphabetizer, the circular shifter, and the input module. There will be aspects of the tables used by output which will only make sense because of the way that the other modules work. There will be constraints on the structure of the tables due to the algorithms used in the other modules. The system will only be comprehensible as a whole. It is my subjective judgment that this is not true in the second modularization.

The Criteria

Many readers will now see what criteria were used in each decomposition. In the first decomposition the criterion used was to make each major step in the processing a module. One might say that to get the first decomposition one makes a flowchart. This is the most common approach to decomposition or modularization. It is an outgrowth of all programmer training which teaches us that we should begin with a rough flowchart and move from there to a detailed implementation. The flowchart was a useful abstraction for systems with on the order of 5,000–10,000 instructions, but as we move beyond that it does not appear to be sufficient; something additional is needed.

The second decomposition was made using "information hiding" [4] as a criterion. The modules no longer correspond to steps in the processing. The line storage module, for example, is used in almost every action by the system. Alphabetization may or may not correspond to a phase in the processing according to the method used. Similarly, circular shift might, in some circumstances, not make any table at all but calculate each character as demanded. Every module in the second decomposition is characterized by its knowledge of a design decision which it hides from all others. Its interface or definition was chosen to reveal as little as possible about its inner workings.

Improvement in Circular Shift Module

To illustrate the impact of such a criterion let us take a closer look at the design of the circular shift module from the second decomposition. Hindsight now suggests that this definition reveals more information than necessary. While we carefully hid the method of storing or calculating the list of circular shifts, we specified an order to that list. Programs could be effectively written if we specified only (1) that the lines indicated in circular shift's current definition will all exist in the table, (2) that no one of them would be included twice, and (3) that an additional function existed which would allow us to identify the original line given the shift. By prescribing the order for the shifts we have given more information than necessary and so unnecessarily restricted the class of systems that we can build without changing the definitions. For example, we have not allowed for a system in which the circular shifts were produced in alphabetical order, *ALPH* is empty, and *ITH* simply returns its argument as a value. Our failure to do this in constructing the systems with the second decomposition must clearly be classified as a design error.

In addition to the general criteria that each module hides some design decision from the rest of the system, we can mention some specific examples of decompositions which seem advisable.

1. A *data structure*, its internal linkings, *accessing procedures and modifying procedures* are part of a single module. They are not shared by many modules as is conventionally done. This notion is perhaps just an elaboration of the assumptions behind the papers of Balzer [9] and Mealy [10]. Design with this in mind is clearly behind the design of BLISS [11].
2. *The sequence of instructions necessary to call a given routine and the routine itself are part of the same module.* This rule was not relevant in the Fortran systems used for experimentation but it becomes essential for systems constructed in an assembly language. There are no perfect general calling sequences for real machines and consequently they tend to vary as we continue our search for the ideal sequence. By assigning responsibility for generating the call to the person responsible for the routine we make such improvements easier and also make it more feasible to have several distinct sequences in the same software structure.
3. The *formats of control blocks* used in queues in operating systems and similar programs *must be hidden* within a "control block module." It is conventional to make such formats the interfaces between various modules. Because design evolution forces frequent changes on control block formats such a decision often proves extremely costly.
4. *Character codes, alphabetic orderings, and similar data should be hidden* in a module for greatest flexibility.
5. The sequence in which certain items will be processed should (as far as practical) be hidden within a single module. Various changes ranging from equip-

ment additions to unavailability of certain resources in an operating system make sequencing extremely variable.

Efficiency and Implementation

If we are not careful the second decomposition will prove to be much less efficient than the first. If each of the functions is actually implemented as a procedure with an elaborate calling sequence there will be a great deal of such calling due to the repeated switching between modules. The first decomposition will not suffer from this problem because there is relatively infrequent transfer of control between modules.

To save the procedure call overhead, yet gain the advantages that we have seen above, we must implement these modules in an unusual way. In many cases the routines will be best inserted into the code by an assembler; in other cases, highly specialized and efficient transfers would be inserted. To successfully and efficiently make use of the second type of decomposition will require a tool by means of which programs may be written as if the functions were subroutines, but assembled by whatever implementation is appropriate. If such a technique is used, the separation between modules may not be clear in the final code. For that reason additional program modification features would also be useful. In other words, the several representations of the program (which were mentioned earlier) must be maintained in the machine together with a program performing mapping between them.

A Decomposition Common to a Compiler and Interpretor for the Same Language

In an earlier attempt to apply these decomposition rules to a design project we constructed a translator for a Markov algorithm expressed in the notation described in [6]. Although it was not our intention to investigate the relation between compiling and interpretive translators of a langugage, we discovered that our decomposition was valid for a pure compiler and several varieties of interpretors for the language. Although there would be deep and substantial differences in the final running representations of each type of compiler, we found that the decisions implicit in the early decomposition held for all.

This would not have been true if we had divided responsibilities along the classical lines for either a compiler or interpretor (e.g. syntax recognizer, code generator, run time routines for a compiler). Instead the decomposition was based upon the hiding of various decisions as in the example above. Thus register representation, search algorithm, rule interpretation etc. were modules and these problems existed in both compiling and interpretive translators. Not only was the decomposition valid in all cases, but many of the routines could be used with only slight changes in any sort of translator.

This example provides additional support for the statement that the order in time in which processing is expected to take place should not be used in making the decomposition into modules. It further provides evidence that a careful job of decomposition can result in considerable carryover of work from one project to another.

A more detailed discussion of this example was contained in [8].

Hierarchical Structure

We can find a program hierarchy in the sense illustrated by Dijkstra [5] in the system defined according to decomposition 2. If a symbol table exists, it functions without any of the other modules, hence it is on level 1. Line storage is on level 1 if no symbol table is used or it is on level 2 otherwise. Input and Circular Shifter require line storage for their functioning. Output and Alphabetizer will require Circular Shifter, but since Circular Shifter and line holder are in some sense compatible, it would be easy to build a parameterized version of those routines which could be used to alphabetize or print out either the original lines or the circular shifts. In the first usage they would not require Circular Shifter; in the second they would. In other words, our design has allowed us to have a single representation for programs which may run at either of two levels in the hierarchy.

In discussions of system structure it is easy to confuse the benefits of a good decomposition with those of a hierarchical structure. We have a hierarchical structure if a certain relation may be defined between the modules or programs and that relation is a partial ordering. The relation we are concerned with is "uses" or "depends upon." It is better to use a relation between programs since in many cases one module depends upon only part of another module (e.g. Circular Shifter depends only on the output parts of the line holder and not on the correct working of *SETWORD*). It is conceivable that we could obtain the benefits that we have been discussing without such a partial ordering, e.g. if all the modules were on the same level. The partial ordering gives us two additional benefits. First, parts of the system are benefited (simplified) because they use the services of lower[2] levels. Second, we are able to cut off the upper levels and still have a usable and useful product. For example, the symbol table can be used in other applications; the line holder could be the basis of a question answering system. The existence of the hierarchical structure assures us that we can "prune" off the upper levels of the tree and start a new tree on the old trunk. If we had designed a system in which the "low level" modules made some use of the "high level" modules, we would not have the hierarchy, we would find it much harder to remove portions of the system, and "level" would not have much meaning in the system.

[2] Here "lower" means "lower numbered."

Since it is conceivable that we could have a system with the type of decomposition shown in version 1 (important design decisions in the interfaces) but retaining a hierarchical structure, we must conclude that hierarchical structure and "clean" decomposition are two desirable but *independent* properties of a system structure.

Conclusion

We have tried to demonstrate by these examples that it is almost always incorrect to begin the decomposition of a system into modules on the basis of a flowchart. We propose instead that one begins with a list of difficult design decisions or design decisions which are likely to change. Each module is then designed to hide such a decision from the others. Since, in most cases, design decisions transcend time of execution, modules will not correspond to steps in the processing. To achieve an efficient implementation we must abandon the assumption that a module is one or more subroutines, and instead allow subroutines and programs to be assembled collections of code from various modules.

Received August 1971; revised November 1971

References

1. Gauthier, Richard, and Pont, Stephen. *Designing Systems Programs*, (C), Prentice-Hall, Englewood Cliffs, N.J., 1970.
2. Hoare, C. A. R. Proof of a program, FIND. *Comm. ACM 14*, 1 (Jan. 1971), 39–45.
3. Parnas, D. L. A technique for software module specification with examples. *Comm. ACM 15*, 5 (May, 1972), 330–336.
4. Parnas, D. L. Information distribution aspects of design methodology. Tech. Rept., Depart. Computer Science, Carnegie-Mellon U., Pittsburgh, Pa., 1971. Also presented at the IFIP Congress 1971, Ljubljana, Yugoslavia.
5. Dijkstra, E. W. The structure of "THE"-multiprogramming system. *Comm. ACM 11*, 5 (May 1968), 341–346.
6. Galler, B., and Perlis, A. J. *A View of Programming Languages*, Addison-Wesley, Reading, Mass., 1970.
7. Parnas, D. L. A course on software engineering. Proc. SIGCSE Technical Symposium, Mar. 1972.
8. Parnas, D. L. On the criteria to be used in decomposing systems into modules. Tech. Rept., Depart. Computer Science, Carnegie-Mellon U., Pittsburgh, Pa., 1971.
9. Balzer, R. M. Dataless programming. Proc. AFIPS 1967 FJCC, Vol. 31, AFIPS Press, Montvale, N.J., pp. 535–544.
10. Mealy, G. H. Another look at data. Proc. AFIPS 1967 FJCC, Vol. 31, AFIPS Press, Montvale, N.J., pp. 525–534.
11. Wulf, W. A., Russell, D. B., and Habermann, A. N. BLISS, A language for systems programming. *Comm. ACM 14*, 12 (Dec. 1971), 780–790.

Designing Software for Ease of Extension and Contraction

DAVID L. PARNAS

Abstract—Designing software to be extensible and easily contracted is discussed as a special case of design for change. A number of ways that extension and contraction problems manifest themselves in current software are explained. Four steps in the design of software that is more flexible are then discussed. The most critical step is the design of a software structure called the "uses" relation. Some criteria for design decisions are given and illustrated using a small example. It is shown that the identification of *minimal* subsets and *minimal* extensions can lead to software that can be tailored to the needs of a broad variety of users.

Index Terms—Contractibility, extensibility, modularity, software engineering, subsets, supersets.

Manuscript received June 7, 1978; revised October 26, 1978. The earliest work in this paper was supported by NV Phillips Computer Industrie, Apeldoorn, The Netherlands. This work was also supported by the National Science Foundation and the German Federal Ministry for Research and Technology (BMFT). This paper was presented at the Third International Conference on Software Engineering, Atlanta, GA, May 1978.

The author is with the Department of Computer Science, University of North Carolina, Chapel Hill, NC 27514. He is also with the Information Systems Staff, Communications Sciences Division, Naval Research Laboratory, Washington, DC.

I. INTRODUCTION

THIS paper is being written because the following complaints about software systems are so common.

1) "We were behind schedule and wanted to deliver an early release with only a <proper subset of intended capabilities>, but found that that subset would not work until everything worked."

2) "We wanted to add <simple capability>, but to do so would have meant rewriting all or most of the current code."

3) "We wanted to simplify and speed up the system by removing the <unneeded capability>, but to take advantage of this simplification we would have had to rewrite major sections of the code."

4) "Our SYSGEN was intended to allow us to tailor a system to our customers' needs but it was not flexible enough to suit us."

After studying a number of such systems, I have identified some simple concepts that can help programmers to design software so that subsets and extensions are more easily obtained. These concepts are simple if you think about software in the way suggested by this paper. Programmers do not commonly do so.

II. Software As a Family of Programs

When we were first taught how to program, we were given a specific problem and told to write one program to do that job. Later we compared our program to others, considering such issues as space and time utilization, but still assuming that we were producing a single product. Even the most recent literature on programming methodology is written on that basis. Dijkstra's *A Discipline of Programming* [1] uses predicate transformers to specify *the* task to be performed by *the* program to be written. The use of the definite article implies that there is a unique problem to be solved and but one program to write.

Today, the software designer should be aware that he is not designing a single program but a family of programs. As discussed in an earlier paper [2], we consider a set of programs to be a program family if they have so much in common that it pays to study their common aspects before looking at the aspects that differentiate them. This rather pragmatic definition does not tell us what pays, but it does explain the motivation for designing program families. We want to exploit the commonalities, share code, and reduce maintenance costs.

Some of the ways that the members of a program family may differ are listed below.

1) They may run on different hardware configurations.

2) They may perform the same functions but differ in the format of the input and output data.

3) They may differ in certain data structures or algorithms because of differences in the available resources.

4) They may differ in some data structures or algorithms because of differences in the size of the input data sets or the relative frequency of certain events.

5) Some users may require only a subset of the services or features that other users need. These "less demanding" users may demand that they not be forced to pay for the resources consumed by the unneeded features.

Engineers are taught that they must try to anticipate the changes that may be made, and are shown how to achieve designs that can easily be altered when these anticipated changes occur. For example, an electrical engineer will be advised that the world has not standardized the 60-cycle 110-V current. Television designers are fully aware of the differing transmission conventions that exist in the world. It is standard practice to design products that are easily changed in those aspects. Unfortunately, there is no magic technique for handling unanticipated changes. The makers of conventional watches have no difficulty altering a watch that shows the day so that it displays "MER" instead of "WED," but I would except a long delay for redesign were the world to switch to a ten day week.

Software engineers have not been trained to design for change. The usual programming courses neither mention the need to anticipate changes nor do they offer techniques for designing programs in which changes are easy. Because programs are abstract mathematical objects, the software engineers' techniques for responding to anticipated changes are more subtle and more difficult to grasp than the techniques used by designers of physical objects. Further, we have been led astray by the other designers of abstract objects—mathematicians who state and prove theorems. When a mathematician becomes aware of the need for a set of closely related theorems, he responds by proving a more general theorem. For mathematicians, a more general result is always superior to a more specialized product. The engineering analogy to the mathematician's approach would be to design television sets containing variable transformers and tuners that are capable of detecting several types of signals. Except for the U.S. armed forces stationed overseas, there is little market for such a product. Few of us consider relocations so likely that we are willing to pay to have the generality present in the product. My guess is that the market for calendar watches for a variable length week is even smaller than the market for the television sets just described.

In [2] I have treated the subject of the design of program families rather generally and in terms of text in a programming language. In this paper I focus on the fifth situation described above; families of programs in which some members are subsets of other family members or several family members share a common subset. I discuss an earlier stage of design, the stage when one identifies the major components of the system and defines relations between those components. We focus on this early stage because the problems described in the introduction result from failure to consider early design decisions carefully.

III. How Does the Lack of Subsets and Extensions Manifest Itself?

Although we often speak of programs that are "not subsetable" or "not extensible," we must recognize that phrase as inaccurate. It is always possible to remove code from a program and have a runable result. Any software system can be extended (TSO proves that). The problem is that the subsets and extensions are not the programs that we would have designed if we had set out to design just that product. Further, the amount of work needed to obtain the product seems all out of proportion to the nature of the change. The obstacles commonly encountered in trying to extend or shrink systems fall into four classes.

A. Excessive Information Distribution

A system may be hard to extend or contract if too many programs were written assuming that a given feature is present or not present. This was illustrated by an operating system in which an early design decision was that the system would support three conversational languages. There were many sections of the system where knowledge of this decision was used. For example, error message tables had room for exactly three entries. An extension to allow four languages would have required that a great deal of code be rewritten. More surprisingly, it would have been difficult to reduce the system to one that efficiently supported only two of the languages. One could remove the third language, but to regain the table space, one would have had to rewrite the same sections of code that would be rewritten to add a language.

B. A Chain of Data Transforming Components

Many programs are structured as a chain of components, each receiving data from the previous component, processing it

311

(and changing the format), before sending the data to the next program in the chain. If one component in this chain is not needed, that code is often hard to remove because the output of its predecessor is not compatible with the input requirements of its successor. A program that does nothing but change the format must be substituted. One illustration would be a payroll program that assumed unsorted input. One of the components of the system accepts the unsorted input and produces output that is sorted by some key. If the firm adopts an office procedure that results in sorted input, this phase of the processing is unnecessary. To eliminate that program, one may have to add a program that transfers data from a file in the input format to a file in the format appropriate for the next phase. It may be almost as efficient to allow the original SORT component to sort the sorted input.

C. Components That Perform More Than One Function

Another common error is to combine two simple functions into one component because the functions seem too simple to separate. For example, one might be tempted to combine synchronization with message sending and acknowledgment in building an operating system. The two functions seem closely related; one might expect that for the sake of reliability one should insist on a "handshake" with each exchange of synchronization signals. If one later encounters an application in which synchronization is needed very frequently, one may find that there is no simple way to strip the message sending out of the synchronization routines. Another example is the inclusion of run-time type-checking in the basic subroutine call mechanism. In applications where compile-time checking or verification eliminates the need for the run-time type-check, another subroutine call mechanism will be needed. The irony of these situations is that the "more powerful" mechanism could have been built separately from, but *using*, simpler mechanisms. Separation would result in a system in which the simpler mechanism was available for use where it sufficed.

D. Loops in the "Uses" Relation

In many software design projects, the decisions about what other component programs to use are left to individual systems programmers. If a programmer knows of a program in another module, and feels that it would be useful in his program, he includes a call on that program in his text. Programmers are encouraged to use the work of other programmers as much as possible because, when each programmer writes his own routines to perform common functions, we end up with a system that is much larger than it need be.

Unfortunately, there are two sides to the question of program usage. Unless some restraint is exercised, one may end up with a system in which nothing works until everything works. For example, while it may seem wise to have an operating system scheduler use the file system to store its data (rather than use its own disk routines), the result will be that the file system must be present and working before any task scheduling is possible. There are users for whom an operating system subset without a file system would be useful. Even if

one has no such users, the subset would be useful during development and testing.

IV. Steps Towards a Better Structure

This section discusses four parts of a methodology that I believe will help the software engineer to build systems that do not evidence the problems discussed above.

A. Requirements Definition: Identifying the Subsets First

One of the clearest morals in the earlier discussion about "design for change" as it is taught in other areas of engineering is that one must anticipate changes before one begins the design. At a past conference [3] many of the papers exhorted the audience to spend more time identifying the actual requirements before starting on a design. I do not want to repeat such exhortations, but I do want to point out that the identification of the possible subsets is part of identifying the requirements. Treating the easy availability of certain subsets as an operational requirement is especially important to government officials who purchase software. Many officials despair of placing strict controls on the production methods used by their contractors because they are forbidden by law to tell the contractor how to perform his job. They may tell him what they require, but not how to build it. Fortunately, the availability of subsets may be construed as an operational property of the software.

On the other hand, the identification of the required subsets is not a simple matter of asking potential users what they could do without. First, users tend to overstate their requirements. Second, the answer will not characterize the set of subsets that might be wanted in the future. In my experience, identification of the potentially desirable subsets is a demanding intellectual exercise in which one first searches for the *minimal* subset that might conceivably perform a useful service and then searches for a set of *minimal* increments to the system. Each increment is small—sometimes so small that it seems trivial. The emphasis on minimality stems from our desire to avoid components that perform more than one function (as discussed in Section III-C). Identifying the minimal subset is difficult because the minimal system is not usually a program that anyone would ask for. If we are going to build the software family, the minimal subset is useful; it is not usually worth building by itself. Similarly, the maximum flexibility is obtained by looking for the smallest possible increments in capability: often these are smaller increments than a user would think of. Whether or not he would think of them before system development, he is likely to want that flexibility later.

The search for a minimal subset and minimal extensions can best be shown by an example. One example of a minimal subset is given in [4]. Another example will be given later in this paper.

B. Information Hiding: Interface and Module Definition

In an earlier section we touched upon the difference between the mathematician's concept of generality and an engineer's approach to design flexibility. Where the mathematician wants his product, a theorem or method of proof, to be as general as possible, i.e., applicable, without change, in as many situations as possible, an engineer often must tailor his product to the situation actually at hand. Lack of generality is necessary to make the program as efficient or inexpensive as possible. If he must develop a family of products, he tries to isolate the changeable parts in modules and to develop an interface between the module and the rest of the product that remains valid for all versions. The crucial steps are as follows.

1) Identification of the items that are likely to change. These items are termed "secrets."

2) Location of the specialized components in separate modules.

3) Designing intermodule interfaces that are insensitive to the anticipated changes. The changeable aspects or "secrets" of the modules are not revealed by the interface.

It is exactly this that the concept of information hiding [5], encapsulation, or abstraction [6] is intended to do for software. Because software is an abstract or mathematical product, the modules may not have any easily recognized physical identity. They are not necessarily separately compilable or coincident with memory overlay units. The interface must be general but the contents should not be. Specialization is necessary for economy and efficiency.

The concept of information hiding is very general and is applicable in many software change situations—not just the issue of subsets and extensions that we address in this paper. The ideas have also been extensively discussed in the literature [5]-[9]. The special implications for our problem are simply that, as far as possible, even the presence or absence of a component should be hidden from other components. If one program uses another directly, the presence of the second program cannot be fully hidden from its user. However, there is never any reason for a component to "know" how many other programs use it. All data structures that reveal the presence or number of certain components should be included in separate information hiding modules with abstract interfaces [10]. Space and other considerations make it impossible to discuss this concept further in this paper; it will be illustrated in the example. Readers for whom this concept is new are advised to read some of the articles mentioned above.

C. The Virtual Machine (VM) Concept

To avoid the problems that we have described as "a chain of data transforming components," it is necessary to stop thinking of systems in terms of components that correspond to steps in the processing. This way of thinking dies hard. It is almost certain that your first introduction to programming was in terms of a series of statements intended to be executed in the order that they were explained to you. We are goal oriented; we know what we start with and what we want to produce. It is natural to think in terms of steps progressing towards that goal. It is the fact that we are designing a family of systems that makes this "natural" approach the wrong one.

The viewpoint that seems most appropriate to designing soft-

ware families is often termed the virtual machine approach. Rather than write programs that perform the transformation from input data to output data, we design software machine extensions that will be useful in writing many such programs. Where our hardware machine provides us with a set of instructions that operate on a small set of data types, the extended or virtual machine will have additional data types as well as "software instructions" that operate on those data types. These added features will be tailored to the class of programs that we are building. While the VM instructions are designed to be generally useful, they can be left out of a final product if the user's programs do not use them. The programmer writing programs for the virtual machine should not need to distinguish between instructions that are implemented in software and those that are hardware implemented. To achieve a true virtual machine, the hardware resources that are used in implementing the extended instruction set must be unavailable to the user of the virtual machine. The designer has traded these resources for the new data elements and instructions. Any attempt to use those resources again will invalidate the concept of virtual machine and lead to complications. Failure to provide for isolation of resources is one of the reasons for the failure of some attempts to use macros to provide a virtual machine. The macro user must be careful not to use the resources used in the code generated by the macros.

There is no reason to accomplish the transformation from the hardware machine to a virtual machine with all of the desired features in a single leap. Instead we will use the machine at hand to implement a few new instructions. At each step we take advantage of the newly introduced features. Such a step-by-step approach turns a large problem into a set of small ones and, as we will see later, eases the problem of finding the appropriate subsets. Each element in this series of virtual machines is a useful subset of the system.

D. Designing the "Uses" Structure

The concept of an abstract machine is an intuitive way of thinking about design. A precise description of the concept comes through a discussion of the relation "uses" [11], [12].

1) The relation "uses": We consider a system to be divided into a set of programs that can be invoked either by the normal flow of control mechanisms, by an interrupt, or by an exception handling mechanism. Each of these programs is assumed to have a specification that defines exactly the effect that an invocation of the program should have.

We say of two programs A and B that A *uses* B if correct execution of B may be necessary for A to complete the task described in its specification. That is, A *uses* B if there exist situations in which the correct functioning of A depends upon the availability of a correct implementation of B. Note that to decide whether A *uses* B or not, one must examine both the implementation *and* the specification of A.

The *"uses"* relation and "invokes" very often coincide, but *uses* differs from *invokes* in two ways:

a) Certain invocations may not be instances of *"uses."* If A's specification requires only that A *invoke* B when certain conditions occur, then A has fulfilled its specification when it has generated a correct call to B. A is correct even if B is incorrect or absent. A proof of correctness of A need only make assumptions about the way to invoke B.

b) A program A may use B even though it never invokes it. The best illustration of this is interrupt handling. Most programs in a computer system are only correct on the assumption that the interrupt handling routine will correctly handle the interrupts (leave the processor in an acceptable state). Such programs use the interrupt handling routines even though they never call them. *"Uses"* can also be formulated as *"requires the presence of a correct version of."*

Systems that have achieved a certain "elegance" (e.g., T.H.E. [5], Venus [6]) have done so by having parts of the system *"use"* other parts in such a way that the "user" programs were simplified. For example, the transput stream mechanism in T.H.E. *uses* the segmenting mechanism to great advantage. In contrast, many large and complex operating systems achieve their size and complexity by having "independent" parts. For example, there are many systems in which "spooling," virtual memory management, and the file system all perform their own backup store operations. Code to perform these functions is present in each of the components. Whenever such components must share a single device, complex interfaces exist.

The disadvantage of unrestrained "usage" of each others facilities is that the system parts become highly interdependent. Often there are no subsets of the system that can be used before the whole system is complete. In practice, some duplication of effort seems preferable to a system in which nothing runs unless everything runs.

2) The uses hierarchy: By restricting the relation *"uses"* so that its graph is loop free we can retain the primary advantages of having system parts *"use"* each other while eliminating the problems. In that case it is possible to assign the programs to the levels of a hierarchy by the following rules:

a) level 0 is the set of all programs that *use* no other program;

b) level i (i $\geqslant$ 1) is the set of all programs that *use* at least one program on level i - 1 and no program at a level higher than i - 1.

If such a hierarchical ordering exists, then each level offers a testable and usable subset of the system. In fact, one can get additional subsets by including only parts of a level. The easy availability of these subsets is very valuable for the construction of any software systems and is vital for developing a *broad* family of systems.

The design of the "uses" hierarchy should be one of the major milestones in a design effort. The division of the system into independently callable subprograms has to go on in parallel with the decisions about *uses*, because they influence each other.

3) The criteria to be used in allowing one program to use another: We propose to allow A *"uses"* B when all of the following conditions hold:

a) A is essentially simpler because it uses B;

b) B is not substantially more complex because it is not allowed to use A;

c) there is a useful subset containing B and not A;

d) there is no conceivably useful subset containing A but not B.

During the process of designing the "uses" relation, we often find ourselves in a situation where two programs could obviously benefit from using each other and the conditions above cannot be satisfied. In such situations, we resolve the apparent conflicts by a technique that we call "sandwiching." One of the programs is "sliced" into two parts in a way that allows the programs to "use" each other and still satisfy the above conditions. If we find ourselves in a position where A would benefit from using B, but B can also benefit from using A, we may split B into two programs: B1 and B2. We then allow A to use B2 and B1 to use A. The result would appear to be a sandwich with B as the bread and A as the filling. Often, we then go on to split A. We start with a few levels and end up with many.

An earlier report [11] introduced many of the ideas that are in this paper and illustrated them by proposing a "uses" relation for a family of operating systems. It contains several examples of situations where "sandwiching" led us from a "T.H.E.-like structure" [14] to a structure with more than twice as many levels. For example, the virtual memory mechanism was split into address translation and dynamic allocation of memory areas to segments.

The most frequent instances of splitting and sandwiching came because initially we were assuming that a "level" would be a "module" in the sense of Section IV-B. We will discuss this in the final part of this paper.

4) Use of the word "convenience": It will trouble some readers that it is usual to use the word "convenience" to describe a reason for introducing a certain facility at a given level of the hierarchy. A more substantial basis would seem more scientific.

As discussed in [11] and [13], we must assume that the hardware itself is capable of performing all necessary functions. As one goes higher in the levels, one can lose capabilities (as resources are consumed)—not gain them. On the other hand, at the higher levels the new functions can be implemented with simpler programs because of the additional programs that can be used. We speak of "convenience" to make it clear that one could implement any functions on a lower level, but the availability of the additional programs at the higher level is useful. For each function we give the lowest level at which the features that are useful for implementing that function (with the stated restrictions) are available. In each case, we see no functions available at the next higher level that would be useful for implementing the functions as described. If we implemented the program one level lower we would have to duplicate programs that become available at that level.

V. EXAMPLE: AN ADDRESS PROCESSING SUBSYSTEM

As an example of designing for extensibility and subsets, we consider a set of programs to read in, store, and write out lists of addresses. This example has also been used, to illustrate a different point, in [10] and has been used in several classroom experiments to demonstrate module interchangeability. This

The following items of information will
be found in the addresses to be processed
and constitute the only items of relevance
to the application programs:

- Last name
- Given names (first name and possible
  middle names)
- Organization (Command or Activity)
- Internal identifier (Branch or Code)
- Street address or P.O. box
- City or mail unit identifier
- State
- Zip code
- Title
- Branch of service if military
- GS grade if civil service

Each of the above will be strings of
characters in the standard ANSI alphabet,
and each of the above may be empty or blank.

Fig. 1.

example is intended as an integral part of this paper; several statements in the final summation are supported only in this section.

A. Our Basic Assumptions

1) The information items discussed in Fig. 1 will be the items to be processed by all application programs.

2) The input formats of the addresses are subject to change.

3) The output formats of the addresses are subject to change.

4) Some systems will use a single fixed format for input and output. Other systems will need the ability to choose from several input or output formats at run-time. Some systems will be required in which the user can specify the format using a format definition language.

5) The representation of addresses in main storage will vary from system to system.

6) In most systems, only a subset of the total set of addresses stored in the system need be in main storage at any one time. The number of addresses needed may vary from system to system, and in some systems the number of addresses to be kept in main memory may vary at run-time.

B. We Propose the Following Design Decisions

1) The input and output programs will be table driven: the table will specify the format to be used for input and output. The contents and organization of these format tables will be the "secrets" of the input and output modules.

2) The representation of addresses in core will be the "secret" of an address storage module (ASM). The implementation chosen for this module will be such that the operations of changing a portion of an address will be relatively inexpensive, compared to making the address table larger or smaller.

3) When the number of addresses to be stored exceeds the capacity of an ASM, programs will use an address file module (AFM). An AFM can be made upward compatible with an ASM; programs that were written to use ASM's could operate using an AFM in the same way. The AFM provides additional

commands to allow more efficient usage by programs that do not assume the random access properties of an ASM. These programs are described below.

4) Our implementation of an AFM would use an ASM as a submodule as well as another submodule that we will call block file module (BFM). The BFM stores blocks of data that are sufficiently large to represent an address, but the BFM is not specialized to the handling of addresses. An ASM that is used within an AFM may be said to have two interfaces. In the "normal interface" that an ASM presents to an outside user, an address is a set of fields and the access functions hide or abstract from the representation. Fig. 2 is a list of the access programs that comprise this interface. In the second interface, the ASM deals with blocks of contiguous storage and abstract from the contents. There are commands for the ASM to input and output "addresses" but the operands are storage blocks whose interpretation as addresses is known only within the ASM. The AFM makes assumptions about the association between blocks and addresses but not about the way that an address's components are represented as blocks. The BFM is completely independent of the fact that the blocks contain address information. The BFM might, in fact, be a manufacturer supplied access method.

C. Component Programs

1) Module: Address Input

INAD: Reads in an address that is assumed to be in a format specified by a format table and calls ASM or AFM functions to store it.

INFSL: Selects a format from an existing set of format tables. The selected format is the one that will be used by INAD. There is always a format selected.

INFCR: Adds a new format to the tables used by INFSL. The format is specified in a "format language." Selection is *not* changed (i.e., INAD still uses the same format table).

INTABEXT: Adds a blank table to the set of input format tables.

INTABCHG: Rewrites a table in the input format tables using a description in a format language. Selection is not changed.

INFDEL: Deletes a table from the set of format tables. The selected format cannot be deleted.

INADSEL: Reads in an address using one of a set of formats. Choice is specified by an integer parameter.

INADFO: Reads in an address in a format specified as one of its parameters (a string in the format definition language). The format is selected and added to the tables and subsequent addresses could be read in using INAD.

2) Module: Address Output

OUTAD: Prints an address in a format specified by a format table. The information to be printed

315

MODULE: ASM

NAME OF ACCESS PROGRAM*	INPUT PARAMETERS						OUTPUT	
*ADDTIT:	asm	X	integer	X	string	→	asm	•
ADDGN:	asm	X	integer	X	string	→	asm	•
ADDLN:	asm	X	integer	X	string	→	asm	•
ADDSERV:	asm	X	integer	X	string	→	asm	•
ADDBORC:	asm	X	integer	X	string	→	asm	•
ADDCORA:	asm	X	integer	X	string	→	asm	•
ADDSORP:	asm	X	integer	X	string	→	asm	•
ADDCITY:	asm	X	integer	X	string	→	asm	•
ADDSTATE:	asm	X	integer	X	string	→	asm	•
ADDZIP:	asm	X	integer	X	string	→	asm	•
ADDGSL:	asm	X	integer	X	string	→	asm	•
SETNUM:	asm	X	integer	→	asm	•		
FETTIT:	asm	X	integer	→	string			
FETGN:	asm	X	integer	→	string			
FETGN:	asm	X	integer	→	string			
FETLN:	asm	X	integer	→	string			
FETSERV:	asm	X	integer	→	string			
FETBORC:	asm	X	integer	→	string			
FETCORA:	asm	X	integer	→	string			
FETSORP:	asm	X	integer	→	string			
FETCITY:	asm	X	integer	→	string			
FETSTATE:	asm	X	integer	→	string			
FETZIP:	asm	X	integer	→	string			
FETGSL:	asm	X	integer	→	string			
FETNUM:	asm	→	integer					

*These are abbreviations: ADDTIT = ADD TITLE; ADDGN = ADD GIVEN NAME, etc.

Fig. 2. Syntax of ASM functions.

is assumed to be in an ASM and identified by its position in an ASM.

OUTFSL: Selects a format table from an existing set of output format tables. The selected format is the one that will be used by OUTAD.

OUTTABEXT: Adds a "blank" table to the set of output format tables.

OUTTABCHG: Rewrites the contents of a format table using information in a format language.

OUTFCR: Adds a new format to the set of formats that can be selected by OUTFSL in a format description language.

OUTFDEL: Deletes a table from the set of format tables that can be selected by OUTFSL.

OUTADSEL: Prints out an address using one of a set of formats.

OUTADFO: Prints out an address in a format specified in a format definition language string, which is one of the actual parameters. The format is added to the tables and selected.

3) Module: Address Storage (ASM)

FET: (Component Name): This is a set of functions used to read information from an address store. Returns a string as a value. See Fig. 2.

ADD: (Component Name): This is a set of functions used to write information in an address store. Each takes a string and an integer as parameters. The integer specifies an address within the ASM. See Fig. 2.

0BLOCK: Takes an integer parameter, returns a storage block as a value.

1BLOCK: Accepts a storage block and integer as parameters. Its effect is to change the contents of an address store—which is reflected by a change in the values of the FET programs.

ASMEXT: Extends an address store by appending a new address with empty components at the end of the address store.

ASMSHR: "Shrinks" the address store.

ASMCR: Creates a new address store. The parameter specifies the number of components. All components are initially empty.

ASMDEL: Deletes an existing address store.

4) Module: Block File Module

BLFET: Accepts an integer as a parameter and returns a "block."

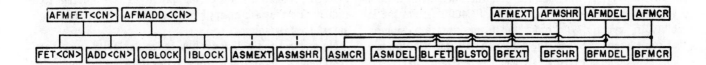

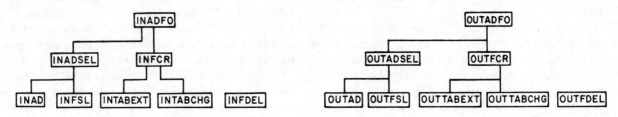

Fig. 3.

BLSTO : Accepts a block and an integer and stores the block.

BFEXT : Extends BFM by adding additional blocks to its capacity.

BFSHR : Reduces the size of the BFM by removing some blocks.

BFMCR : Creates a file of blocks.

BFMDEL : Deletes an existing file of blocks.

5) Module: Address File Module

This module includes implementations of all of the ASM functions except OBLOCK and IBLOCK. To avoid confusion in the diagram showing the uses hierarchy we have changed the names to:

AFMADD (Component Name) defined as in Fig. 2
AFMFET (Component Name) defined as in Fig. 1
AFMEXT defined as in BFM above
AMFSHR defined as in BFM above
AFMCR defined as in BFM above
AFMDEL defined as in BFM above.

D. Uses Relation

Fig. 3 shows the *uses* relation between the component programs. It is important to note that we are now discussing the implementation of those programs, not just their specifications. The *uses* relation is characterized by the fact that there are a large number of relatively simple, *single-purpose* programs on the lowest level. The upper level programs are implemented by means of these lower level programs so that they too are quite simple. This *uses* relation diagram characterizes the set of possible subsets.

E. Discussion

To pick a subset, one identifies the set of upper level programs that the user needs and includes only those programs that those programs use (directly or indirectly). For example, a user who uses addresses in a single format does not need the component programs that interpret format description lan-

guages. Systems that work with a small set of addresses can be built without any BFM components. A program that works as a query system and never prints out a complete address would not need any Address Output components.

The system is also easily extended. For example, one could add a capability to read in addresses with self-defining files. If the first record on a file was a description of the format in something equivalent to the format description language, one could write a program that would be able to read in that record, use INTABCHG to build a new format table, and then read in the addresses. Programs that do things with addresses (such as print out "personalized" form letters) can also be added using these programs and selecting only those capabilities that they actually need.

One other observation that can be made is that the upper level programs can be used to "generate" lower level versions. For example, the format description languages can be used to generate the tables used for the fixed format versions. There is no need for a separate SYSGEN program.

We will elaborate on this observation in the conclusion.

VI. SOME REMARKS ON OPERATING SYSTEMS: WHY GENERALS ARE SUPERIOR TO COLONELS

An earlier report [11] discusses the design of a "uses" hierarchy for operating systems. Although there have been some refinements to the proposals of that report, its basic contents are consistent with the present proposals. This section compares the approach outlined in this paper and the "kernel" approach or "nucleus" approach to OS design [18]-[20]. It is tempting to say that the suggestions in this paper do not conflict with the "kernel" approach. These proposals can be viewed as a refinement of the nucleus approach. The first few levels of our system could be labeled "kernel," and one could conclude that we are just discussing a fine structure within the kernel.

To yield to that temptation would be to ignore an essential difference between the approaches suggested in this paper and the kernel approach. The system kernels known to me are such that some desirable subsets cannot be obtained without major surgery. It was assumed that the nucleus must be in every system family member. In the RC4000 system the inability to separate synchronization from message passing has led some users to bypass the kernel to perform teletype handling functions. In Hydra as originally proposed [19], "type checking" was so intrinsic to the call mechanism that it appeared impossible to disable it when it was not needed or affordable.[1]

Drawing a line between "kernel" and the rest of the system, and putting "essential" services of "critical programs" in the nucleus yields a system in which kernel features cannot be removed and certain extensions are impractical. Looking for a *minimal* subset and a set of *minimal* independent incremental function leads to a system in which one can trim away unneeded features. I know of no feature that is always needed. When we say that two functions are *almost* always used together, we should remember that "almost" is a euphemism for "not."

VII. SUMMATION

This paper describes an approach to software intended to result in systems that can be tailored to fit the needs of a broad variety of users. The points most worthy of emphasis are as follows.

1) The Requirements Include Subsets and Extensions: It is essential to recognize the identification of useable subsets as part of the preliminaries to software design. Flexibility cannot be an afterthought. Subsetability is needed, not just to meet a variety of customers' needs, but to provide a fail-safe way of handling schedule slippage.

2) Advantages of the Virtual Machine Approach: Designing software as a set of virtual machines has definite advantages over the conventional (flowchart) approach to system design. The virtual machine "instructions" provide facilities that are useful for purposes beyond those originally conceived. These instructions can easily be omitted from a system if they are not needed. Remove a major box from a flowchart and there is often a need to "fill the hole" with conversion programs.

3) On the Difference Between Software Generality and Software Flexibility: Software can be considered "general" if it can be used, *without change*, in a variety of situations. Software can be considered flexible, if it is *easily changed* to be used in a variety of situations. It appears unavoidable that there is a run-time cost to be paid for generality. Clever designers can achieve flexibility without significant run-time cost, but there is a design-time cost. One should incur the design-time cost only if one expects to recover it when changes are made.

Some organizations may choose to pay the run-time cost for generality. They build general software rather than flexible software because of the maintenance problems associated with maintaining several different versions. Factors influencing this decision include a) the availability of extra computer resources,

[1] Accurate reports on the current status and performance of that system are not available to me.

b) the facilities for program change and maintenance available at each installation, and c) the extent to which design techniques ease the task of applying the same change to many versions of a program.

No one can tell a designer how much flexibility and generality should be built into a product, but the decision should be a conscious one. Often, it just happens.

4) On the Distinction Between Modules, Subprograms, and Levels: Several systems and at least one dissertation [14]-[17] have, in my opinion, blurred the distinction between modules, subprograms, and levels. Conventional programming techniques consider a subroutine or other callable program to be a module. If one wants the modules to include all programs that must be designed together and changed together, then, as our example illustrates, one will usually include many small subprograms in a single module. If does not matter what word we use; the point is that the unit of change is not a single callable subprogram.

In several systems, modules and levels have coincided [14], [15]. This had led to the phrase "level of abstraction." Each of the modules in the example abstract from some detail that is assumed likely to change. In our approach there is no correspondence between modules and levels. Further, I have not found a relation, "more abstract than," that would allow me to define an abstraction hierarchy [12]. Although I am myself guilty of using it, in most cases the phrase "levels of abstraction" is an abuse of language.

Janson has suggested that a design such as this one (or the one discussed in [11]) contain "soft modules" that can represent a breach of security principles. Obviously an error in any program in one of our modules can violate the integrity of that module. All module programs that will be included in a given subset must be considered in proving the correctness of that module. However, I see no way that allowing the component programs to be on different levels of a "uses" hierarchy makes this process more difficult or makes the system less secure. The boundaries of our modules are quite firm and clearly identified.

The essential difference between this paper and other discussions of hierarchically structured designs is the emphasis on subsets and extensions. My search for a criterion to be used in designing the *uses* hierarchy has convinced me that if one does not care about the existence of subsets, it does not really matter what hierarchy one uses. Any design can be bent until it works. It is only in the ease of change that they differ.

5) On Avoiding Duplication: Some earlier work [21] has suggested that one needs to have duplicate or near duplicate modules in a hierarchically structured system. For example, they suggest that one needs one implementation of processes to give a fixed number of processes at a low level and another to provide for a varying number of processes at a user's level. Similar ideas have appeared elsewhere. Were such duplication to be necessary, it would be a sound argument against the use of "structured" approaches. One can avoid such duplication if one allows the programs that vary the size of a data structure to be on a higher level than the other programs that operate on that data structure. For example, in an operating system, the programs to create and delete processes need not be on the same level as the more frequently used scheduling operations. In designing software, I regard the need to code similar functions in two separate programs as an indication of a fundamental error in my thinking.

6) Designing for Subsets and Extensions Can Reduce the Need for Support Software: We have already mentioned that this design approach can eliminate the need for separate SYSGEN programs. We can also eliminate the need for *special-purpose* compilers. The price of the convenience features offered by such languages is often a compiler and run-time package distinctly larger than the system being built. In our approach, each level provides a "language extention" available to the programmer of the next level. We never build a compiler; we just build our system, but we get convenience features anyway.

7) Extension at Run-Time Versus Extension During SYSGEN: At a later stage in the design we will have to choose data structures and take the difference between run-time extension and SYSGEN extension into consideration. Certain data structures are more easily accessed but harder to extend while the program is running; others are easily extended but at the expense of a higher access cost. These differences do not affect our early design decisions because they are hidden in modules.

8) On the Value of a Model: My work on this example and similar ones has gone much faster because I have learned to exploit a pattern that I first noticed in the design discussed in [11]. Low level operations assume the existence of a fixed data structure of some type. The operations on the next level allow the swapping of a data element with others from a fixed set of similar elements. The high level programs allow the creation and deletion of such data elements. This pattern appears several times in both designs. Although I have not designed your system for you, I believe that you can take advantage of a similar pattern. If so, this paper has served its purpose.

ACKNOWLEDGMENT

The ideas presented in this paper have been developed over a lengthy period and with the cooperation and help of many collaborators. I am grateful to numerous Philips employees for thought provoking comments and questions. Price's collaboration was invaluable at Carnegie-Mellon University. The help of W. Bartussek, G. Handzel, and H. Wuerges at the Technische Hochschule Darmstadt led to substantial improvements. Heninger, Weiss, and J. Shore at the Naval Research Laboratory helped me to understand the application of the concepts in areas other than operating systems. B. Trombka and J. Guttag both helped in the design of pilots of the address process system. Discussions with P. J. Courtois have helped me to better understand the relation between software structure and run-time characteristics of computer systems. Dr. E. Britton, H. Rettenmaier, L. Belady, Dr. D. Stanat, G. Fran, and Dr. W. Wright made many helpful suggestions about an earlier draft of this paper. If you find portions of this paper helpful, these people deserve your thanks.

REFERENCES

[1] E. W. Dijkstra, *A Discipline of Programming.* Englewood Cliffs, NJ: Prentice-Hall, 1976.

[2] D. L. Parnas, "On the design and development of program families," *IEEE Trans. Software Eng.,* vol. SE-2, pp. 1-9, Mar. 1976.

[3] 2nd Int. Conf. Software Engineering, Oct. 13-15, 1976; also, *IEEE Trans. Software Eng.,* (Special Issue), vol. SE-2, Dec. 1976.

[4] D. L. Parnas, G. Handzel, and H. Würges, "Design and specification of the minimal subset of an operating system family," presented at the 2nd Int. Conf. Software Engineering, Oct. 13-15, 1976; also, *IEEE Trans. Software Eng.,* (Special Issue), vol. SE-2, pp. 301-307, Dec. 1976.

[5] D. L. Parnas, "On the criteria to be used in decomposing systems into modules," *Commun. Ass. Comput. Mach.,* Dec. 1972.

[6] T. A. Linden, "The use of abstract data types to simplify program modifications," in *Proc. Conf. Data: Abstraction, Definition and Structure,* Mar. 22-24, 1976; also, *ACM SIGPLAN Notices* (Special Issue), vol. II, 1976.

[7] D. L. Parnas, "A technique for software module specification with examples," *Commun. Ass. Comput. Mach.,* May 1972.

[8] ——, "Information distribution aspects of design methodology," in *1971 Proc. IFIP Congr.* Amsterdam, The Netherlands: North-Holland, 1971.

[9] ——, "The use of precise specifications in the development of software," in *1977 Proc. IFIP Congr.* Amsterdam, The Netherlands: North-Holland, 1977.

[10] ——, "Use of abstract interfaces in the development of software for embedded computer systems," Naval Res. Lab., Washington, DC, NRL Rep. 8047, June 1977.

[11] ——, "Some hypotheses about the 'uses' hierarchy for operating systems," Technische Hochschule Darmstadt, Darmstadt, West Germany, Tech. Rep., Mar. 1976.

[12] ——, "On a 'buzzword': Hierarchical structure," in *1974 Proc. IFIP Congr.* Amsterdam, The Netherlands: North-Holland, 1974.

[13] D. L. Parnas and D. L. Siewiorek, "Use of the concept of transparency in the design of hierarchically structured systems," *Commun. Ass. Comput. Mach.,* vol. 18, July 1975.

[14] E. W. Dijkstra, "The structure of the "THE"-multiprogramming system," *Commun. Ass. Comput. Mach.,* vol. 11, pp. 341-346, May 1968.

[15] B. Liskov, "The design of the Venus operating system," *Commun. Ass. Comput. Mach.,* vol. 15, pp. 144-149, Mar. 1972.

[16] P. A. Janson, "Using type extension to organize virtual memory mechanisms," Lab. for Comput. Sci., M.I.T., Cambridge, MA, MIT-LCS-TR167, Sept. 1976.

[17] ——, "Using type-extension to organize virtual memory mechanisms," IBM Zurich Res. Lab., Switzerland, Res. Rep. RZ 858 (#28909), August 31, 1977.

[18] P. Brinch Hansen, "The nucleus of the multiprogramming system," *Commun. Ass. Comput. Mach.,* vol. 13, pp. 238-241, 250, Apr. 1970.

[19] W. Wulf, E. Cohen, A. Jones, R. Lewin, C. Pierson, and F. Pollack, "HYDRA: The kernel of a multiprocessor operating system," *Commun. Ass. Comput. Mach.,* vol. 17, pp. 337-345, June 1974.

[20] G. J. Popek and C. S. Kline, "The design of a verified protection system," in *Proc. Int. Workshop Prot. In Oper. Syst.,* IRIA, pp. 183-196.

[21] A. R. Saxena and T. H. Bredt, "A structured specification of a hierarchical operating system," in *Proc. 1975 Int. Conf. Reliable Software.*

David L. Parnas received the B.S., M.S., and Ph.D. degrees in electrical engineering—systems and communications sciences from the Carnegie Institute of Technology, Pittsburgh, PA.

He held the position of Assistant Professor of Computer Science at the University of Maryland and at Carnegie-Mellon University. During the period 1969-1970 he was employed by Philips-Electrologica, Apeldoorn, The Netherlands, and at the MBLE Research Laboratory, Brussels, Belgium. He then returned to Carnegie-Mellon

University where he held the rank of Associate Professor until 1973. In June of 1973 he was appointed Professor and Head of the Research Group on Operating Systems I at the Technical University of Darmstadt, Germany, where he remained through August 1976. He is presently Professor in the Department of Computer Science, University of North Carolina, Chapel Hill. He is also with the Information Systems Staff, Communications Sciences Division, at the Naval Research Laboratory, Washington, DC. He has published papers in the areas of computer design languages and simulation techniques. His current interests are in the field of software engineering methods, computer system design, abstract specification for programs, verification that a program meets its specifications, and cooperating sequential processes.

Programming-in-the-Large
Versus
Programming-in-the-Small

FRANK DeREMER AND HANS H. KRON

Abstract—We distinguish the activity of writing large programs from that of writing small ones. By large programs we mean systems consisting of many small programs (modules), usually written by different people.

We need languages for programming-in-the-small, i.e., languages not unlike the common programming languages of today, for writing modules. We also need a "module interconnection language" for knitting those modules together into an integrated whole and for providing an overview that formally records the intent of the programmer(s) and that can be checked for consistency by a compiler.

Index Terms—Accessibility, external name, information hiding, linking, module interconnection language, project management tool, protection, scope of definition, system hierarchy, virtual machine, visibility.

I. INTRODUCTION

PROGRAMMING a large system in any typical programming language available today is an exercise in obscuration. We work hard at discovering the inherent structure in a problem and then structuring our solution in a compatible way. Research into "structured programming" [2] tells us that this approach will lead to readable, understandable, provable, and modifiable solutions. However, current languages discourage the accurate recording of the overall solution structure; they force us to write programs in which we are so preoccupied with the trees that we lose sight of the forest, as do the readers of our programs!

Manuscript received September 19, 1975; revised December 1, 1975. The work reported herein was supported in part by the National Science Foundation under Grant GJ 36339. This paper was presented at the International Conference on Reliable Software, Los Angeles, CA, April 1975.

F. DeRemer is with the Board of Studies in Information Sciences, University of California, Santa Cruz, CA.

H. H. Kron was with the Board of Studies in Information Sciences, University of California, Santa Cruz, CA. He is now with the Technische Hochschule Darmstadt, Fachbereich Informatik, Darmstadt, Germany.

Let us refer to typical languages as "languages for programming-in-the-small" (LPS's). Let us use the term "module" to refer to a segment of LPS code defining one or more named resources to be used in other modules. Each "resource" is a variable, constant, procedure, data structure, mode, or whatever is definable in the LPS. Preferably a module is one to a few pages long and is easily comprehensible by a single person who understands the intended environment and function of the module.

We argue that structuring a large collection of modules to form a "system" is an essentially distinct and different intellectual activity from that of constructing the individual modules. That is, we distinguish programming-in-the-large from programming-in-the-small. Correspondingly, we believe that essentially distinct and different languages should be used for the two activities. We refer to a language for describing system structure as a "module interconnection language" (MIL); it is one necessity for supporting programming-in-the-large.

A byproduct of using a separate language for describing module interconnectivity is that the modules themselves may more easily be programmed in distinct languages. This can be an important need. For example, in writing a compiler one typically desires rather different languages for writing the scanner, parser, semantic analyzer, and code generator.

II. OBJECTIVES OF ANY MODULE INTERCONNECTION LANGUAGE (MIL)

An MIL should provide a means for the programmer(s) of a large system to express their *intent* regarding the overall program structure in a concise, precise, and checkable form. Where an MIL is not available, module interconnectivity information is usually buried partly in the modules, partly in an often amorphous collection of linkage-editor instructions, and partly in the informal documentation of the project. Aside

Reprinted from *IEEE Transactions on Software Engineering*, Volume SE-2, Number 2, June 1976, pages 80–86. Copyright © 1976 by The Institute of Electrical and Electronics Engineers, Inc.

from the issue that each of these three areas is ill-suited to express interconnectivity, the smearing of the relevant information over disjoint media is highly unreliable. Even more unsatisfactory are the facilities for specifying and enforcing module *disconnectivity* via information hiding, limiting access to resources, establishing protection layers, closing off subsystems, etc. The lack of such facilities invites undisciplined or even unsocial programming, as shown by one of Weinberg's case studies [17], since there is no automated means of enforcing the surface consensus of the programming team.

That current languages fail to support the global task of composing large systems was well argued by Wulf and Shaw in their paper entitled "Global variables considered harmful" [20]. A responding paper [3] proposed a scheme of declarations to augment block structure as a solution to the problems associated with global variables. The scheme provided mechanisms to protect variables from violations of various sorts by contained blocks, and to allow limited access to certain variables by selected internal blocks. Similar approaches have been suggested by others [1], [18], [7]. We believe that some of the mechanisms proposed were appropriate, but that they were inappropriately placed in the LPS.

Linkage: One may regard an MIL as being a higher-level language for specifying how a "linker" is to prepare for "loading" a program comprised of separately compiled segments [15]. Roughly, the linker must resolve static references to "external" names, i.e., names defined externally to each separately compiled module. A distinction, however, is that we do not expect the linkage to happen after compilation but rather as part of it.

Tradeoff: One cost of this approach will be a more complex compiling system than has been necessary heretofore. However, the compiler can be more helpful to us by providing more feedback at early stages of system development. The cost should be more than offset by the increased speed and accuracy with which we will be able to construct and maintain large systems.

In summary, then, an MIL should serve as:

1) a *project management tool*, encouraging and recording the stepwise refinement of a system by a project manager [17], chief programmer [12], or modularizer [11], thus encouraging structuring before starting to program the details;

2) a *design tool* for, and actual *means of establishing* overall program structure, including the composition of new systems by combining subsystems of existing software, and encouraging information hiding [13] and the construction of virtual machines [2], i.e., subsystems whose internal structure is hidden, but which provide desired resources;

3) a *means of communication* between members of a programming team, such that a disciplined intercommunication among subsystems results, encouraging system hierarchy while allowing flexible, if disciplined connections among modules; and

4) a *means of documenting* system structure in a clear, concise, formal, and checkable way. The latter leads to proving-in-the-large, i.e., in addition to establishing the correctness of the modules (proving-in-the-small), we should prove on the MIL level that correct modules work together correctly.

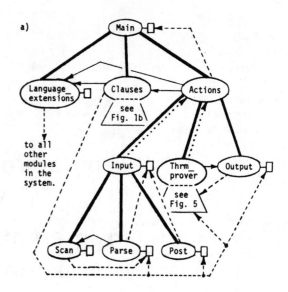

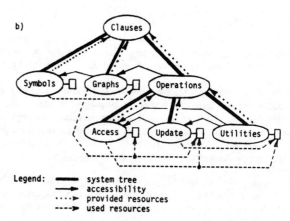

Legend:
———— system tree
——▶ accessibility
·····▶ provided resources
----▶ used resources

Fig. 1. System structure for a theorem proving program.

III. AN EXAMPLE

To demonstrate the use of an MIL we graphically display a sample program structure in Fig. 1. The particular system illustrated is a theorem proving program written in Algol/W [19] by Prof. Sharon Sickel at the University of California, Santa Cruz. The program was written without the aid of an MIL; we tediously reviewed it after it was complete and factored out the overall structure. The exercise suggested some ways to improve the structure; in fact, what is presented here is the improved version.

The missing part of Fig. 1 is developed in Section V, culminating in Fig. 5. In that section, we also define the concepts that are only sketched next.

Graphical representation: Any system structure is represented as follows.

1) *Nodes* and *bold edges* constitute the "system tree"; each edge connects a "parent" (system) to one of its "children" (subsystems).

2) *Dotted lines* going upward along the tree edges from a child to its parent indicate that resources "provided" by the child are also "provided" by the parent. In other words, some of the resources provided by the child are passed via the parent to siblings and/or ancestors of the parent.

3) *Solid arrows*, always between siblings, denote "sibling accessibility links." These are established by the parent (chief programmer) so that the siblings may use each other's resources as necessary.

4) *Rectangular boxes* attached to the nodes indicate LPS modules. Every leaf has a module. In our sample system, each module attached to a non-leaf serves the purpose of being the "driver" of its (sub-) system.

5) *Dashed arrows* indicate that some resources provided by the node at the tail of the arrow are used by the module at the head of the arrow. The global aspects of the flow of resource names are addressed in detail in Section V.

Refinements: Fig. 1 represents the program at a high level of abstraction. As the diagram is further developed, specific resource names would start to appear and refinements would be made to accessibility. For examples, a parent might give a child accessibility to only a subset ("group") of the resources provided by siblings of the child, or the parent might hide some or all of its environment from the child.

IV. The Universe of Discourse of MIL 75

We now present a particular language, MIL 75, for describing interconnections among modules. Being quite new, it has received little use thus far, so we expect it to evolve further toward an optimally useful language for describing system structure.

The universe of discourse of MIL 75 consists of three sets: recourses, modules, and systems. Resources are atomic, as regards MIL 75; they are the nameable entities in the LPS's used to program the modules, e.g., variables, constants, procedures, data types, etc. The formalism below associates a set of resources with each module. Names of resources, modules, and systems are used in an MIL 75 program to establish system structure.

External scope: An MIL 75 program addresses the question of who knows whom within a collection of modules. It defines the scopes of definitions of names across module and subsystem boundaries. It has nothing to say about the scopes of definitions *within* modules, these being defined by block structure, and other constructs in the LPS's.

Static, not dynamic: We emphasize that the interconnections addressed in MIL 75 are *static* ones, just as the names used to establish the connections are *statically known*, rather than being computed at run time. In effect, the MIL program structures a global region through which the modules communicate. Thus, for example, MIL 75 could be used as a high-level language for programming the "global" declarations that are included in the compilation of each BCPL module [16]. However, MIL 75 admits of rather less restricted implementations, as may be deduced from Section V.

No loading: Furthermore, it is to be stressed that MIL 75 does not address the problem of loading. That is, it has nothing to say about when modules or subsystems are to be loaded, nor does it say what, if any, overlay scheme is to be used. Perhaps we need, in addition to an MIL, a "subsystem loading language" to address exactly those issues. Presumably, the MIL program provides many of the right points of reference for describing loading and overlay strategies.

No functional specification: An MIL 75 program does not specify the nature of resources. Of course, the functional specification of modules and subsystems is important, but that is a separate issue not dealt with in this paper. A good solution may be to coalesce an MIL and a "function specification language." Perhaps the latter would be a language of axioms [14], [5], [4].

No types: Similarly, MIL 75 does not provide any ways of specifying the type of an object or defining language extensions. Rather it is used to specify *paths* for transmitting relevant information from one module to another. Such paths may be defined for any named entity that has its defined and applied occurrences distributed over different modules.

It is assumed that the total LPS + MIL compiling system will do as much bookkeeping as necessary to do all static checking as soon as the necessary information is available. Clearly, this will require a nontrivial file system so that the compiler may keep summaries of each module and its external connections for the compiler's own use in subsequent compilations and recompilations. A modification of Liskov's "description units" [10] seem to be appropriate for such bookkeeping.

Accessibility: Finally, an MIL 75 program gives a particular module either unrestricted access to an object or none at all. We assume that any restrictions such as "read only," "write only," "read before write," "execute only," and other more general monitorings, are appropriate to the domain of, and programmable in, the LPS's.

V. The Semantics of MIL 75

The module interconnection language MIL 75 can be defined via attribute grammars [8]; essentially, an MIL 75 program specifies a tree whose nodes are augmented by attributes. The latter are sets of resource names. In this section, however, we define the language by starting with a simple algebraic structure (a tree) and refining it stepwise. Simultaneously, the language concepts are presented and motivated by the stepwise development of the subsystem, Thrm_prover, which is to become part of the system in Fig. 1.

A. System Hierarchy

We concentrate on the overall system structure first. Since MIL 75 is intended to encourage structured programming, it imposes a tree structure on the system under construction. This "system tree" expresses nothing but the hierarchical relation between systems and subsystems. For now, we do not contemplate modules or resources at all. This will happen later, possibly forcing us to refine the system tree during the development of an actual system. Fig. 2 shows the tree of the system Thrm_prover.

Our guideline for the rough decomposition of the project into a tree is that each node should finally encompass an intellectually manageable part of the whole problem, assuming that adequate support is provided by other nodes. Conceptually, there is for each system tree node a designer who is

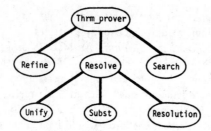

Fig. 2. Sample system tree.

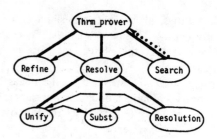

Fig. 3. Sibling accessibility links.

responsible for the programming associated with "his" node and who supervises the designers of its children.

Definition: A "system tree" is a tuple $T = (N, S, Pa, Sn, t)$ where

1) N is a finite set of "nodes";

2) t is a distinguished member of N called the "root";

3) $Pa: (N - \{t\}) \rightarrow N$ is a total function, called the "parent function," such that for any node n_1 in N there is a sequence of nodes $n_1, n_2, \cdots, n_k$ $(k \geqslant 1)$ with $n_k = t$ and $Pa(n_i) = n_{i+1}$ $(1 \leqslant i < k)$.

The terms "child," "sibling," etc., are defined in the obvious manner. Finally,

4) S is a finite set of "system names"; and

5) $Sn: N \rightarrow S$ is a bijection, i.e., each node in N is associated with a unique system name.

When preexisting subsystems are used in a new system, or when a very large system is constructed, the uniqueness of system names may prove difficult to achieve. Therefore, the syntax of MIL 75 allows "qualified names" (e.g., Resolve. Unify) for unambiguity and "aliases" for renaming.

B. Provided and Derived Resources

The next decisions to be made during the development presumably concern the function of each subsystem. As the function of a subsystem can be completely described in terms of the resources it uses and provides, we now consider the association of resources with system tree nodes.

Ultimately, resources will originate in the modules. Pursuing a top-down approach, however, the designer of any system tree node p states the set of resources provided by p. Then the question is where these resources come from. Some might originate in a module later to be attached to the node p, and thus are the direct responsibility of the designer of p. All other resources must come from any children of p. Therefore, the designer of p states the set of resources each child q *must provide*. This statement specifies the desired function of q, provided that all resources are adequately specified.

As seen from the node p, the resources it demands from its children are called "derived resources." The node p may derive resources from a child q and provide them to its own parent, in turn. In diagrams, such a case is indicated by a dotted arrow from q to p (cf. Fig. 3).

Definition: A "resource-augmented system tree" is a tuple $T_R = (T, R, Pr, Mp)$ where

1) $T = (N, S, Pa, Sn, t)$ is a system tree;

2) R is a finite set of "resources";

3) Pr: $N \rightarrow 2^R$ is a total function (2^R denotes the powerset of R); we say that "n provides r" iff $r \in \text{Pr}(n)$;

4) $Mp: N \rightarrow 2^R$ is a total function; we say that "n must provide r" iff $r \in Mp(n)$;

5) $Mp(n) \subseteq \text{Pr}(n)$ for all n in N; and

6) $Mp(p) \cap Mp(n) = \phi$ for all pairs of siblings p, n.

Naturally, it is a task of an MIL compiler to check that conditions 5) and 6) are satisfied, i.e., that the upward flow of derived resources is consistent. We allow set inclusion in 5) for facilitating a bottom-up approach, where preexisting subsystems are used in a new parent system.

C. Accessibility

The next refinement is concerned with the interaction between siblings. The power and the responsibility to establish channels for transmitting resources between siblings rests solely with their parent. Here we follow Parnas' policy of a "designer controlled information distribution" [13]. Consider Fig. 3, where the "sibling accessibility links" are drawn as solid arrows between siblings.

These links do not represent individual connections between modules and resources. Rather, they allow the sibling at the tail of the arrow to access any resource provided by the sibling at the arrow head. In Fig. 3, for example, Search has access to (any resource provided by) Resolve. For reliability reasons, access rights are nontransitive; for instance, Search has no access to Refine. Also, the children of Resolve are invisible to Search. Thus, Search can access a resource provided by Unify if and only if this resource is also provided by Resolve. In short, the substructure of one sibling is not apparent to another.

The accessibility links between a set of siblings may form any directed graph. Thus, the parent may allow mutual recursion between resources (e.g., procedures, coroutines, or data structures) of its children.

Inherited access: Typically, the access rights granted to a node are also useful for most of its children. In MIL 75, a child inherits *by default* all access rights that have been granted to its parent. In Fig. 3, Resolution inherits access to its "uncle" Refine; in Fig. 1(a), Parse inherits access to its "granduncle" Clauses.

Alternatively, any parent may "will" a child nothing or an explicitly specified subset of its own access rights, thus making the child less "privileged" and formally asserting that the child and all its descendants cannot exploit or disturb certain resources. If a child is to be partially disinherited, the parent

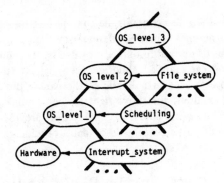

Fig. 4. Privileged nodes at the bottom.

must list all access rights left to the child. Thus, if the parent later obtains additional access rights to vulnerable resources, they do not inadvertently shine through to the less privileged child.

Derived access: Naturally, a parent has access to the resources that it demands from any of its children. However, all descendants of its children are invisible to the parent. Thus, we can build layers of virtual machines as in Fig. 4, where the most privileged nodes are at the bottom.

Definition: An "access-augmented system tree" is a tuple $T_A = (T, \text{Sac}, \text{Iac})$ where

1) $T = (N, S, Pa, Sn, t)$ is a system tree;

2) Sac and Iac are relations on $N - \{t\}$;

3) p Sac n (pronounced "p has sibling-access to n") implies that p and n are siblings;

4) p Iac n (pronounced "p inherits access to n") implies that either $Pa(p)$ Sac n or $Pa(p)$ Iac n.

Definition: A node p "has access to" a node n iff either p Sac n, p Iac n, or $p = Pa(n)$.

D. Module Placement

We proceed to place modules into the system tree. With each node, we may associate at most one module, as indicated by the following.

1) With each leaf n, we must associate a module, the "leaf module" at n. A leaf without module is not allowed, since it cannot provide any resources.

2) A module associated with a non-leaf n may act as a "driver" or "monitor" of the system named $Sn(n)$. Such a "root module" at n must define all resources in $\text{Pr}(n)$ that are not derived from the children of n.

3) A non-leaf without root module serves as a structural entity only, making an integrated whole out of its subsystems and establishing a single interface to the outside.

Origin and usage of resources: For each module m at a node n, there must be two statements in the MIL 75 program: 1) the "statement of origin," listing the resources defined in m, and 2) the "statement of usage," listing the resources that are used, but not defined, in m. For clarity, the latter statement is divided into a list of the "derived resources" provided by children of n, and a list of all others, i.e., those obtained through sibling or inherited access.

The compiling system must check that 1) the actual usage of resources by module m conforms to the access rights granted

to node n, and that 2) any resource provided by n either comes from a child or originates in module m. No node may provide a resource that is obtained through sibling access or inherited access; such a flow of resources would probably have deleterious effects on reliability.

Usage links: The compiling system can now derive and graphically display the "usage links," drawn as dashed arrows in Figs. 1 and 5. If a node n has access to a node p, and the module m at n uses a resource provided by p, then a usage link points from the node p to the module m. Fig. 6 shows the three possible cases. Recall that the resource(s) provided by p might not originate in the module at p, if any. However, this is irrelevant to, and hidden from, the module m.

Fig. 6 also suggests a graphical check on consistency: we can always form a cycle by traversing the usage link, zero or more tree edges upward, and finally one sibling accessibility link [Fig. 6a) and 6b)], or by traversing the usage link and one tree edge downward [Fig. 6c)].

Definition: A "module interconnection structure" is a tuple $T_M = (T, T_R, T_A, M, \text{Mod}, \text{Or}, \text{Ud}, \text{Und})$ where

1) $T = (N, S, Pa, Sn, t)$ is a system tree, $T_R = (T, R, \text{Pr}, Mp)$ is a resource-augmented system tree, and $T_A = (T, \text{Sac}, \text{Iac})$ is an access-augmented system tree;

2) M is a finite set of "modules";

3) Mod: $N \to M$ is a *partial*, injective function, such that $\text{Mod}(q)$ is defined for every leaf q; we say that $\text{Mod}(n)$ is the "module at n";

4) Or, Ud, and Und are total functions $N \to 2^R$, such that $\text{Or}(n) = \text{Ud}(n) = \text{Und}(n) = \phi$ if $\text{Mod}(n)$ is undefined; we say that $r \in \text{Or}(n)$ is a "resource originating in $\text{Mod}(n)$," $r \in \text{Ud}(n)$ is a "derived resource used in $\text{Mod}(n)$," and $r \in \text{Und}(n)$ is a "nonderived resource used in $\text{Mod}(n)$";

5) for every p, n in N: $\text{Or}(p) \cap \text{Or}(n) = \phi$;

6) we define for all $p \in N$ the set of "derived resources" $D(p) = \{r \in R | \exists q \in N: Pa(q) = p \text{ and } r \in Mp(q)\}$; then, for all $p \in N$,

7) $\text{Pr}(p) \subseteq \text{Or}(p) \cup D(p)$;

8) $\text{Ud}(p) \subseteq D(p)$; and

9) $r \in \text{Und}(p)$ implies $(\exists n) [(p \text{ Sac } n \text{ or } p \text{ Iac } n) \text{ and } r \in Mp(n)]$.

E. Programming in MIL 75

A complete MIL 75 program consists of a sequence of "system descriptions." Each is assumed to be (re-) compilable alone, or with any others. Put together, they must define a module interconnection structure T_M.

A system description for a node p consists of statements specifying

1) $Sn(p)$, the designer's name, and a relevant date;

2) $\text{Pr}(p)$;

3) $\text{Mod}(p)$, $\text{Or}(p)$, $\text{Ud}(p)$, and $\text{Und}(p)$;

and for each child q of p:

4) $Sn(q)$, $Mp(q)$, and $\{n \in N | q \text{ Sac } n\}$; and

5) the set $W = \{n \in N | q \text{ Iac } n\}$ either by enumeration (such that $W \subseteq I$ is satisfied) or by default (then $W = I$ is assumed), where $I = \{n \in N | p \text{ Iac } n \text{ or } p \text{ Sac } n\}$.

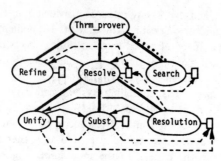

Fig. 5. Module placement and usage links.

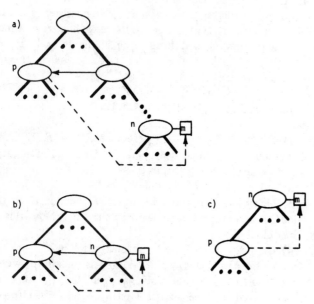

a)

b)

c)

Fig. 6. Usage links.

Phrases specifying empty sets in 3) and 4) above may be omitted. Also, the name of Mod(p) may be left out if it is identical with the system name $Sn(p)$. There follows a sample system description.

```
system Input
    author      'Sharon Sickel'
    date        'July, 1974'
    provides    Input_parser
    consists of
        root module
            originates       Input_parser
            uses derived     Parser, Post_processor
            uses nonderived  Language_extensions
        subsystem Scan
            must provide Scanner
        subsystem Parse
            must provide Parser
            has access to Scan
        subsystem Post
            must provide Post_processor
```

Groups: To increase the compactness of MIL 75 programs and to encourage an even more refined granting of access rights, MIL 75 also contains the concept of grouping (cf. [3]). The designer of a parent can define named subsets or "groups" of the set of derived resources provided by its children. Then, the parent can grant its children access rights to these groups. A group acts as a virtual child of the parent, but has neither module, children, nor access rights. The compiler must check that no child q has access to a group that provides a resource also provided by q, lest the descendants of q inherent access to that resource.

VI. CONCLUSIONS: THE GAIN IN RELIABILITY

A module interconnection language embodies a design methodology for reliable software. It provides much needed forms of abstraction, expression, and verification, vis-a-vis programming-in-the-large. Reliability is enhanced during system design, the actual programming, system testing, and maintenance and modification.

System Design: Modularization, as a forethought rather than an afterthought, helps in finding reliable solutions to complex problems by applying the traditional method of "divide and conquer." The advantages of modularization, however, are often apparently offset by added complexity in the connections among modules [9]. This is not surprising; our problems are not solved by design methodologies that concentrate only on issues of programming-in-the-small. We will obtain more reliable software only if programming-in-the-large is recognized as a separate activity that relies, as heavily as does programming-in-the-small, on a language providing abstraction, structure, and style.

Programming: The results of the system design phase must be communicated to and among the members of the programming team or project. Such communication concerns, among other things, the modules that constitute the system, the position of each module in the hierarchy, the resources each module must provide, and the access rights with which each module is endowed. It is unreasonable to expect that this information can be reliably transmitted via anything but a formal language, or enforced by anything less than a rigorous compiling system.

Testing: A substantial amount of testing can be done by independently exercising each module. However, there is a wide gap between testing individual modules and testing the system as a whole. Performing only these two kinds of tests involves too big a jump in levels of abstraction and results in a gap in confidence. The hierarchical subsystem concept of an MIL suggests a more gradual bottom-up development of the testing phase. Also, the MIL program states clearly, for each subsystem, the connections to other subsystems and who is responsible for testing. In short, the MIL supports "structured testing."

Maintenance and modification: Each connection and dependency between modules is durably documented in the MIL program. No link between modules can be left out of the documentation and be forgotten—the compiling system will complain. Furthermore, the hierarchical structure imposed by the MIL makes it easy to replace modules and/or subsystems; and the compiler can support system modification by providing cross-references and graphs of system structure, accessibility links, and usage links. Finally, the modified system structure is automatically checked for consistency.

Outlook: It is obvious that we need languages for programming-in-the-large. An MIL is but a first approximation to such a language, since it does not include facilities for the specification of the *function* of modules. An MIL may be regarded as only a "language feature" in the sense of Hoare [6]. It seems, however, powerful enough to increase software reliability, even in the absence of other needed extensions to current languages.

ACKNOWLEDGMENT

We are grateful to F. Frazier, N. Habermann, J. Horning, J. Ichbiah, B. Lorho, W. McKeeman, D. Michels, D. Ross, S. Sickel, B. Wulf, and the referees for many helpful comments and stimulating discussions.

REFERENCES

[1] B. L. Clark and J. J. Horning, "The system language for project SUE," *SIGPLAN Notices,* vol. 6, Oct. 1971.

[2] E. W. Dijkstra, "Notes on structured programming," in *Structured Programming,* O.-J. Dahl, E. W. Dijkstra, and C. A. R. Hoare, Ed. New York: Academic, 1972.

[3] J. E. George and G. R. Sager, "Variables—Bindings and protection," *SIGPLAN Notices,* vol. 8, Dec. 1973.

[4] J. Guttag, "The use of type for the definition of abstract data objects," Dept. Comput. Sci., Univ. Toronto, Ont., Canada, Mar. 1974.

[5] C. A. R. Hoare, "Proof of correctness of data representations," *Acta Informatica,* vol. 1, pp. 271–281, 1972.

[6] ——, "Hints on programming language design," Memo AIM-224, Comput. Sci. Dept., Stanford University, Dec. 1973; also in *Proc. Symp. Principles of Programming Languages,* Boston, Oct. 1973.

[7] J. D. Ichbiah, "Visibility and separate compilations," in *Proc. IFIP WG 2.4,* La Grande Motte, France, May 1974.

[8] D. E. Knuth, "Semantics of context-free languages," *Mathematical Systems Theory,* vol. 2, 1968.

[9] B. H. Liskov, "A design methodology for reliable software systems," in *1972 Fall Joint Comput. Conf., AFIPS Conf. Proc.,* vol. 41. Montvale, NJ: AFIPS Press, 1972, pp. 191–199.

[10] B. H. Liskov and S. Zilles, "Programming with abstract data types," in *Proc. Symp. Very High Level Languages, SIGPLAN Notices,* vol. 9, Apr. 1974.

[11] J. Maynard, *Modular Programming.* New York: Petrocelli Books, 1972.

[12] H. D. Mills, "Chief programmer teams: Techniques and procedures," IBM Internal Rep., Jan. 1970.

[13] D. L. Parnas, "Information distribution aspects of design methodology," Tech. Rep., Dept. Comput. Sci., Carnegie-Mellon University, Feb. 1971.

[14] ——, "A technique for software module specifications with examples," *Commun. Ass. Comput. Mach.,* vol. 15, May 1972.

[15] L. Presser and J. R. White, "Linkers and loaders," *ACM Comput. Surveys,* vol. 4, Sept. 1972.

[16] M. Richards, "The BCPL reference manual," Memo 69/1, The University Mathematical Laboratory, Cambridge, England, Jan. 1969.

[17] G. M. Weinberg, *The psychology of computer programming.* New York: Van Nostrand Reinhold, 1971, pp. 71–75.

[18] J. R. White, and L. Presser, "A tool for enforcing system structure," Rep. CS-11, Dept. Elec. Eng., Univ. California, Santa Barbara, Apr. 1972.

[19] N. Wirth and C. A. R. Hoare, "A contribution to the development of ALGOL," *Commun. Ass. Comput. Mach.,* vol. 6, June 1966.

[20] W. Wulf and M. Shaw, "Global variables considered harmful," *SIGPLAN Notices,* vol. 8, Feb. 1973.

Frank DeRemer received the B.S. and M.S. degrees in electrical engineering and the Ph.D. degree in computer science from the Massachusetts Institute of Technology, Cambridge, MA, in 1965, 1966, and 1969, respectively.

He has worked for the RCA Research Laboratories, Princeton, NJ, the NASA Research Center, Cambridge, MA, the Digital Systems Laboratory at the University of Illinois, Urbana, and the Boeing Scientific Research Laboratories, Seattle, WA. He is currently Assistant Professor of Information Sciences at the University of California, Santa Cruz. His teaching and research interests are in programming linguistics and methodology, and computational models. This includes translator writing systems based on $LR(k)$ grammars, subtree transformational grammars, attribute and affix grammars, as well as programming language design, program verification, software engineering, and models of automata theory.

Dr. DeRemer is a member of the IEEE Computer Society, the Association for Computing Machinery, Special Interest Group on Programming Languages, Sigma Xi, Tau Beta Pi, and Eta Kappa Nu.

Hans H. Kron was born in Rockenhausen, W. Germany, on January 20, 1949. He received the Vordiplom in Informatik from the Technische Hochschule Darmstadt, Darmstadt, Germany, in 1972. He transferred to the University of California at Santa Cruz in 1973, and received the M.S. and Ph.D. degrees in information sciences in 1974 and 1975, respectively.

He is now with the Technische Hochschule Darmstadt, Fachbereich Informatik, Darmstadt, Germany. His current interests include subtree transformational grammars, tree templates, tree automata, formal definitions of programming languages, and programming language design.

Dr. Kron is a member of the Association for Computing Machinery and SIGPLAN.

Considerations and techniques are proposed that reduce the complexity of programs by dividing them into functional modules. This can make it possible to create complex systems from simple, independent, reusable modules. Debugging and modifying programs, reconfiguring I/O devices, and managing large programming projects can all be greatly simplified. And, as the module library grows, increasingly sophisticated programs can be implemented using less and less new code.

Structured design

by W. P. Stevens, G. J. Myers, and L. L. Constantine

Structured design is a set of proposed general program design considerations and techniques for making coding, debugging, and modification easier, faster, and less expensive by reducing complexity.[1] The major ideas are the result of nearly ten years of research by Mr. Constantine.[2] His results are presented here, but the authors do not intend to present the theory and derivation of the results in this paper. These ideas have been called *composite design* by Mr. Myers.[3-5] The authors believe these program *design* techniques are compatible with, and enhance, the *documentation* techniques of HIPO[6] and the *coding* techniques of structured programming.[7]

These cost-saving techniques always need to be balanced with other constraints on the system. But the ability to produce simple, changeable programs will become increasingly important as the cost of the programmer's time continues to rise.

General considerations of structured design

Simplicity is the primary measurement recommended for evaluating alternative designs relative to reduced debugging and modification time. Simplicity can be enhanced by dividing the system into separate pieces in such a way that pieces can be considered, implemented, fixed, and changed with minimal consideration or effect on the other pieces of the system. Observability (the ability to easily perceive how and why actions occur) is another useful consideration that can help in designing programs that can be changed easily. Consideration of the effect of reasonable changes is also valuable for evaluating alternative designs.

Mr. Constantine has observed that programs that were the easiest to implement and change were those composed of simple, independent modules. The reason for this is that problem solving is faster and easier when the problem can be subdivided into pieces which can be considered separately. Problem solving is hardest when all aspects of the problem must be considered simultaneously.

The term *module* is used to refer to a set of one or more contiguous program statements having a name by which other parts of the system can invoke it and preferably having its own distinct set of variable names. Examples of modules are PL/I procedures, FORTRAN mainlines and subprograms, and, in general, subroutines of all types. Considerations are always with relation to the program statements *as coded*, since it is the programmer's ability to understand and change the *source* program that is under consideration.

While conceptually it is useful to discuss dividing whole programs into smaller pieces, the techniques presented here are for designing simple, independent modules originally. It turns out to be difficult to divide an existing program into separate pieces without increasing the complexity because of the amount of overlapped code and other interrelationships that usually exist.

Graphical notation is a useful tool for structured design. Figure 1 illustrates a notation called a *structure chart*,[8] in which:

1. There are two modules, A and B.
2. Module A *invokes* module B. B is *subordinate* to A.
3. B receives an input parameter X (its name in module A) and returns a parameter Y (its name in module A). (It is useful to distinguish which calling parameters represent data passed *to* the called program and which are for data to be *returned* to the caller.)

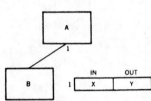

Figure 1   A structure chart

Coupling and communication

To evaluate alternatives for dividing programs into modules, it becomes useful to examine and evaluate types of "connections" between modules. A connection is a reference to some label or address defined (or also defined) elsewhere.

The fewer and simpler the connections between modules, the easier it is to understand each module without reference to other

Table 1 Contributing factors

	Interface complexity	Type of connection	Type of communication
low	simple, obvious	to module by name	data
COUPLING			control
high	complicated, obscure	to internal elements	hybrid

modules. Minimizing connections between modules also minimizes the paths along which changes and errors can propagate into other parts of the system, thus eliminating disastrous "ripple" effects, where changes in one part cause errors in another, necessitating additional changes elsewhere, giving rise to new errors, etc. The widely used technique of using common data areas (or global variables or modules without their own distinct set of variable names) can result in an enormous number of connections between the modules of a program. The complexity of a system is affected not only by the number of connections but by the degree to which each connection couples (associates) two modules, making them interdependent rather than independent. Coupling is the measure of the strength of association established by a connection from one module to another. Strong coupling complicates a system since a module is harder to understand, change, or correct by itself if it is highly interrelated with other modules. Complexity can be reduced by designing systems with the weakest possible coupling between modules.

The degree of coupling established by a particular connection is a function of several factors, and thus it is difficult to establish a simple index of coupling. Coupling depends (1) on how complicated the connection is, (2) on whether the connection refers to the module itself or something inside it, and (3) on what is being sent or received.

Coupling increases with increasing complexity or obscurity of the interface. Coupling is lower when the connection is to the normal module interface than when the connection is to an internal component. Coupling is lower with data connections than with control connections, which are in turn lower than hybrid connections (modification of one module's code by another module). The contribution of all these factors is summarized in Table 1.

When two or more modules interface with the same area of storage, data region, or device, they share a common environment. Examples of common environments are:

interface
complexity

• A set of data elements with the EXTERNAL attribute that is

330

copied into PL/I modules via an INCLUDE statement or that
is found listed in each of a number of modules.

- Data elements defined in COMMON statements in FORTRAN modules.
- A centrally located "control block" or set of control blocks.
- A common overlay region of memory.
- Global variable names defined over an entire program or section.

The most important structural characteristic of a common environment is that it couples every module sharing it to every other such module without regard to their functional relationship or its absence. For example, only the two modules XVECTOR and VELOC might actually make use of data element X in an "included" common environment of PL/I, yet changing the length of X impacts *every* module making any use of the common environment, and thus necessitates recompilation.

Every element in the common environment, whether used by particular modules or not, constitutes a separate path along which errors and changes can propagate. Each element in the common environment adds to the complexity of the total system to be comprehended by an amount representing all possible pairs of modules sharing that environment. Changes to, and new uses of, the common area potentially impact all modules in unpredictable ways. Data references may become unplanned, uncontrolled, and even unknown.

A module interfacing with a common environment for some of its input or output data is, on the average, more difficult to use in varying contexts or from a variety of places or in different programs than is a module with communication restricted to parameters in calling sequences. It is somewhat clumsier to establish a new and unique data context on each call of a module when data passage is via a common environment. Without analysis of the entire set of sharing modules or careful saving and restoration of values, a new use is likely to interfere with other uses of the common environment and propagate errors into other modules. As to future growth of a given system, once the commitment is made to communication via a common environment, any new module will have to be plugged into the common environment, compounding the total complexity even more. On this point, Belady and Lehman,[9] observe that "a well-structured system, one in which communication is via passed parameters through defined interfaces, is likely to be more growable and require less effort to maintain than one making extensive use of global or shared variables."

The impact of common environments on system complexity may be quantified. Among M objects there are M $(M-1)$ ordered pairs of objects. (Ordered pairs are of interest because A and B sharing a common environment complicates both, A being coupled to B and B being coupled to A.) Thus a common environment of N elements shared by M modules results in $NM(M-1)$ first order (one level) relationships or paths along which changes and errors can propagate. This means 150 such paths in a FORTRAN program of only three modules sharing the COMMON area with just 25 variables in it.

It is possible to minimize these disadvantages of common environments by limiting access to the smallest possible subset of modules. If the total set of potentially shared elements is subdivided into groups, all of which are *required* by some subset of modules, then both the size of each common environment and the scope of modules among which it is shared is reduced. Using "named" rather than "blank" COMMON in FORTRAN is one means of accomplishing this end.

The complexity of an interface is a matter of how much information is needed to state or to understand the connection. Thus, obvious relationships result in lower coupling than obscure or inferred ones. The more syntactic units (such as parameters) in the statement of a connection, the higher the coupling. Thus, extraneous elements irrelevant to the programmer's and the modules' immediate task increase coupling unnecessarily.

type of connection

Connections that address or refer to a module as a whole by its name (leaving its contents unknown and irrelevant) yield lower coupling than connections referring to the internal elements of another module. In the latter case, as for example the use of a variable by direct reference from within some other module, the entire content of that module may have to be taken into account to correct an error or make a change so that it does not make an impact in some unexpected way. Modules that can be used easily without knowing anything about their insides make for simpler systems.

Consider the case depicted in Figure 2. GETCOMM is a module whose function is getting the next command from a terminal. In performing this function, GETCOMM calls the module READT, whose function is to read a line from the terminal. READT requires the address of the terminal. It gets this via an externally declared data element in GETCOMM, called TERMADDR. READT passes the line back to GETCOMM as an argument called LINE. Note the arrow extending from *inside* GETCOMM to *inside* READT. An arrow of this type is the notation for references to internal data elements of another module.

Figure 2 Module connections

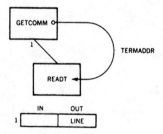

Now, suppose we wish to add a module called GETDATA, whose function is to get the next data line (i.e., not a command) from a

Figure 3 Improved module
connections

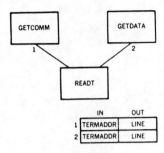

Figure 4 Control-coupled
modules

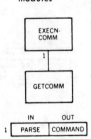

(possibly) different terminal. It would be desirable to use module READT as a subroutine of GETDATA. But if GETDATA modifies TERMADDR in GETCOMM before calling READT, it will cause GETCOMM to fail since it will "get" from the wrong terminal. Even if GETDATA restores TERMADDR after use, the error can still occur if GETDATA and GETCOMM can ever be invoked "simultaneously" in a multiprogramming environment. READT would have been more usable if TERMADDR had been made an input argument to READT instead of an externally declared data item as shown in Figure 3. This simple example shows how references to internal elements of other modules can have an adverse effect on program modification, both in terms of cost and potential bugs.

Modules must at least pass data or they cannot functionally be a part of a single system. Thus connections that pass data are a necessary minimum. (Not so the communication of control. In principle, the presence or absence of requisite input data is sufficient to define the circumstances under which a module should be activated, that is, receive control. Thus the explicit passing of control by one module to another constitutes an additional, theoretically inessential form of coupling. In practice, systems that are *purely* data-coupled require special language and operating system support but have numerous attractions, not the least of which is they can be fundamentally simpler than any equivalent system with control coupling.[10])

Beyond the practical, innocuous, minimum control coupling of normal subroutine calls is the practice of passing an "element of control" such as a switch, flag, or signal from one module to another. Such a connection affects the execution of another module and not merely the data it performs its task upon by involving one module in the internal processing of some other module. Control arguments are an additional complication to the essential data arguments required for performance of some task, and an alternative structure that eliminates the complication always exists.

Consider the modules in Figure 4 that are control-coupled by the switch PARSE through which EXECNCOMM instructs GETCOMM whether to return a parsed or unparsed command. Separating the two distinct functions of GETCOMM results in a structure that is simpler as shown in Figure 5.

The new EXECNCOMM is no more complicated; where once it set a switch and called, now it has two alternate calls. The sum of GETPCOMM and GETUCOMM is (functionally) less complicated than GETCOMM was (by the amount of the switch testing). And the two small modules are likely to be easier to comprehend than the one large one. Admittedly, the immediate gains here may appear marginal, but they rise with time and the number of alternatives in the switch and the number of levels over which it is passed. Control coupling, where a called module "tells" its caller what to do, is a more severe form of coupling.

Modification of one module's code by another module may be thought of as a hybrid of data and control elements since the code is dealt with as data by the modifying module, while it acts as control to the modified module. The target module is very dependent in its behavior on the modifying module, and the latter is intimately involved in the other's internal functioning.

Cohesiveness

Coupling is reduced when the relationships among elements *not* in the same module are minimized. There are two ways of achieving this—minimizing the relationships among modules and maximizing relationships among elements in the same module. In practice, both ways are used.

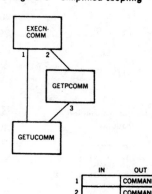

Figure 5   Simplified coupling

The second method is the subject of this section. "Element" in this sense means any form of a "piece" of the module, such as a statement, a segment, or a "subfunction". Binding is the measure of the cohesiveness of a module. The objective here is to reduce coupling by striving for high binding. The scale of cohesiveness, from lowest to highest, follows:

1. Coincidental.
2. Logical.
3. Temporal.
4. Communicational.
5. Sequential.
6. Functional.

The scale is not linear. Functional binding is much stronger than all the rest, and the first two are much weaker than all the rest. Also, higher-level binding classifications often include all the characteristics of one or more classifications below it *plus* additional relationships. The binding between two elements is the highest classification that applies. We will define each type of binding, give an example, and try to indicate why it is found at its particular position on the scale.

When there is no meaningful relationship among the elements in a module, we have coincidental binding. Coincidental binding might result from either of the following situations: (1) An existing program is "modularized" by splitting it apart into modules. (2) Modules are created to consolidate "duplicate coding" in other modules.

coincidental binding

As an example of the difficulty that can result from coincidental binding, suppose the following sequence of instructions appeared several times in a module or in several modules and was put into a separate module called X:

```
A = B + C
GET CARD
PUT OUTPUT
IF B = 4, THEN E = 0
```

Module X would probably be coincidentally bound since these four instructions have no apparent relationships among one another. Suppose in the future we have a need in one of the modules originally containing these instructions to say GET TAPERECORD instead of GET CARD. We now have a problem. If we modify the instruction in module X, it is unusable to all of the other callers of X. It may even be difficult to *find* all of the other callers of X in order to make any other compatible change.

It is only fair to admit that, independent of a module's cohesiveness, there are instances when any module can be modified in such a fashion to make it unusable to all its callers. However, the *probability* of this happening is very high if the module is coincidentally bound.

logical binding
Logical binding, next on the scale, implies some logical relationship between the elements of a module. Examples are a module that performs all input and output operations for the program or a module that edits all data.

The logically bound, EDIT ALL DATA module is often implemented as follows. Assume the data elements to be edited are master file records, updates, deletions, and additions. Parameters passed to the module would include the data and a special parameter indicating the type of data. The first instruction in the module is probably a four-way branch, going to four sections of code — edit master record, edit update record, edit addition record, and edit deletion record.

Often, these four functions are also intertwined in some way in the module. If the deletion record changes and requires a change to the edit deletion record function, we will have a problem if this function is intertwined with the other three. If the edits are truly independent, then the system could be simplified by putting each edit in a separate module and eliminating the need to decide which edit to do for each execution. In short, logical binding usually results in tricky or shared code, which is difficult to modify, and in the passing of unnecessary parameters.

Temporal binding is the same as logical binding, except the elements are also related in time. That is, the temporally bound elements are executed in the same time period.

The best examples of modules in this class are the traditional "initialization", "termination", "housekeeping", and "clean-up" modules. Elements in an initialization module are logically bound because initialization represents a logical class of functions. In addition, these elements are related in time (i.e., at initialization time).

Modules with temporal binding tend to exhibit the disadvantages of logically bound modules. However, temporally bound modules are higher on the scale since they tend to be simpler for the reason that *all* of the elements are executable at one time (i.e., no parameters and logic to determine which element to execute).

A module with communicational binding has elements that are related by a reference to the same set of input and/or output data. For example, "print and punch the output file" is communicationally bound. Communicational binding is higher on the scale than temporal binding since the elements in a module with communicational binding have the stronger "bond" of referring to the same data.

When the output data from an element is the input for the next element, the module is sequentially bound. Sequential binding can result from flowcharting the problem to be solved and then defining modules to represent one or more blocks in the flowchart. For example, "read next transaction and update master file" is sequentially bound.

Sequential binding, although high on the scale because of a close relationship to the problem structure, is still far from the maximum—functional binding. The reason is that the procedural processes in a program are usually distinct from the *functions* in a program. Hence, a sequentially bound module can contain several functions or just part of a function. This usually results in higher coupling and modules that are less likely to be usable from other parts of the system.

Functional binding is the strongest type of binding. In a functionally bound module, all of the elements are related to the performance of a single function.

A question that often arises at this point is what is a function? In mathematics, $Y = F(X)$ is read "Y is a function F of X." The function F defines a transformation or mapping of the independent (or input) variable X into the dependent (or return) variable Y. Hence, a function describes a transformation from some

STRUCTURED DESIGN

input data to some return data. In terms of programming, we broaden this definition to allow functions with no input data and functions with no return data.

In practice, the above definition does not clearly describe a functionally bound module. One hint is that if the elements of the module all contribute to accomplishing a single goal, then it is probably functionally bound. Examples of functionally bound modules are "Compute Square Root" (input and return parameters) "Obtain Random Number" (no input parameter), and "Write Record to Output File" (no return parameter).

A useful technique in determining whether a module is functionally bound is writing a sentence describing the function (purpose) of the module, and then examining the sentence. The following tests can be made:

1. If the sentence *has* to be a compound sentence, contain a comma, or contain more than one verb, the module is probably performing more than one function; therefore, it probably has sequential or communicational binding.

2. If the sentence contains words relating to time, such as "first", "next", "then", "after", "when", "start", etc., then the module probably has sequential or temporal binding.

3. If the predicate of the sentence doesn't contain a single specific object following the verb, the module is probably logically bound. For example, Edit All Data has logical binding; Edit Source Statement may have functional binding.

4. Words such as "initialize", "clean-up", etc. imply temporal binding.

Functionally bound modules *can* always be described by way of their elements using a compound sentence. But if the above language is unavoidable while still completely describing the module's function, then the module is probably not functionally bound.

One unresolved problem is deciding how far to divide functionally bound subfunctions. The division has probably gone far enough if each module contains no subset of elements that could be useful alone, and if each module is small enough that its entire implementation can be grasped all at once, i.e., seldom longer than one or two pages of source code.

Observe that a module can include more than one type of binding. The binding between two elements is the highest that can be applied. The binding of a module is lowered by every element pair that does not exhibit functional binding.

Predictable modules

A predictable, or well-behaved, module is one that, when given the identical inputs, operates identically each time it is called. Also, a well-behaved module operates independently of its environment.

To show that dependable (free from errors) modules can still be unpredictable, consider an oscillator module that returns zero and one alternately and dependably when it is called. It might be used to facilitate double buffering. Should it have multiple users, each would be required to call it an even number of times before relinquishing control. Should any of the users have an error that prevented an even number of calls, all other users will fail. The operation of the module given the same inputs is not constant, resulting in the module not being predictable even though error-free. Modules that keep track of their own state are usually not predictable, even when error-free.

This characteristic of predictability that can be designed into modules is what we might loosely call "black-boxness." That is, the user can understand what the module does and use it without knowing what is inside it. Module "black-boxness" can even be enhanced by merely adding comments that make the module's function and use clear. Also, a descriptive name and a well-defined and visible interface enhances a module's usability and thus makes it more of a black box.

Tradeoffs to structured design

The overhead involved in writing many simple modules is in the execution time and memory space used by a particular language to effect the call. The designer should realize the adverse effect on maintenance and debugging that may result from striving just for minimum execution time and/or memory. He should also remember that programmer cost, is, or is rapidly becoming, the major cost of a programming system and that much of the maintenance will be in the future when the trend will be even more prominent. However, depending on the actual overhead of the language being used, it is very possible that a structured design can result in less execution and/or memory overhead rather than more due to the following considerations:

For memory overhead

1. Optional (error) modules may never be called into memory.

Figure 6 Definitions of symbols used in structure charts

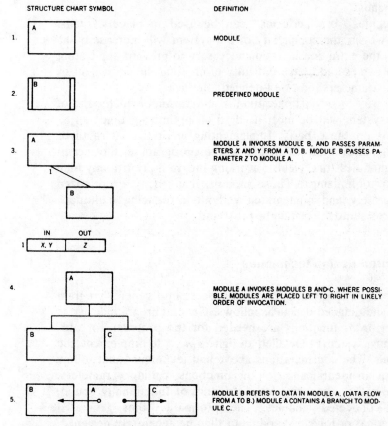

STRUCTURE CHART SYMBOL — DEFINITION

1. MODULE

2. PREDEFINED MODULE

3. MODULE A INVOKES MODULE B, AND PASSES PARAMETERS X AND Y FROM A TO B. MODULE B PASSES PARAMETER Z TO MODULE A.

IN OUT
1 | X, Y | Z

4. MODULE A INVOKES MODULES B AND C. WHERE POSSIBLE, MODULES ARE PLACED LEFT TO RIGHT IN LIKELY ORDER OF INVOCATION.

5. MODULE B REFERS TO DATA IN MODULE A. (DATA FLOW FROM A TO B.) MODULE A CONTAINS A BRANCH TO MODULE C.

THE MORE COMPREHENSIVE "PROPOSED STANDARD GRAPHICS FOR PROGRAM STRUCTURE," PREFERRED BY MR. CONSTANTINE AND WIDELY USED OVER THE PAST SIX YEARS BY HIS CLASSES AND CLIENTS, USES SEPARATE ARROWS FOR EACH CONNECTION, SUCH AS FOR THE CALLS FROM A TO B AND FROM A TO C, TO REFLECT STRUCTURAL PROPERTIES OF THE PROGRAM. THE CHARTING SHOWN HERE WAS ADOPTED FOR COMPATIBILITY WITH THE HIERARCHY CHART OF HIPO.

2. Structured design reduces duplicate code and the coding necessary for implementing control switches, thus reducing the amount of programmer-generated code.
3. Overlay structuring can be based on actual operating characteristics obtained by running and observing the program.
4. Having many single-function modules allows more flexible, and precise, grouping, possibly resulting in less memory needed at any one time under overlay or virtual storage constraints.

For execution overhead

1. Some modules may only execute a few times.
2. Optional (error) functions may never be called, resulting in zero overhead.
3. Code for control switches is reduced or eliminated, reducing the total amount of code to be executed.

STEVENS, MYERS, AND CONSTANTINE and IBM SYST J

STEVENS, MYERS, AND CONSTANTINE   IBM SYST J

4. Heavily used linkage can be recompiled and calls replaced by branches.

5. "Includes" or "performs" can be used in place of calls. (However, the complexity of the system will increase by at least the extra consideration necessary to prevent duplicating data names and by the difficulty of creating the equivalent of call parameters for a well-defined interface.)

6. One way to get fast execution is to determine which parts of the system will be most used so all optimizing time can be spent on those parts. Implementing an initially structured design allows the testing of a working program for those critical modules (and yields a working program prior to any time spent optimizing). Those modules can then be optimized separately and reintegrated without introducing multitudes of errors into the rest of the program.

Structured design techniques

It is possible to divide the design process into general program design and detailed design as follows. General program design is deciding *what* functions are needed for the program (or programming system). Detailed design is *how* to implement the functions. The considerations above and techniques that follow result in an identification of the functions, calling parameters, and the call relationships for a structure of functionally bound, simply connected modules. The information thus generated makes it easier for each module to then be separately designed, implemented, and tested.

The objective of general program design is to determine what functions, calling parameters, and call relationships are needed. Since flowcharts depict *when* (in what order and under what conditions) blocks are executed, flowcharts unnecessarily complicate the general program design phase. A more useful notation is the structure chart, as described earlier and as shown in Figure 6.

structure charts

To contrast a structure chart and a flowchart, consider the following for the same three modules in Figure 7 — A which calls B which calls C (coding has been added to the structure chart to enable the proper flowchart to be determined; B's code will be executed first, then C's, then A's). To design A's interfaces properly, it is necessary to know that A is responsible for invoking B, but this is hard to determine from the flowchart. In addition, the structure chart can show the module connections and calling parameters that are central to the consideration and techniques being presented here.

Figure 7 Structure chart compared to flowchart

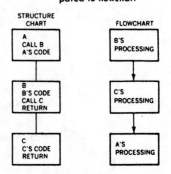

The other major difference that drastically simplifies the nota-

Figure 8 Basic form of low-cost implementation

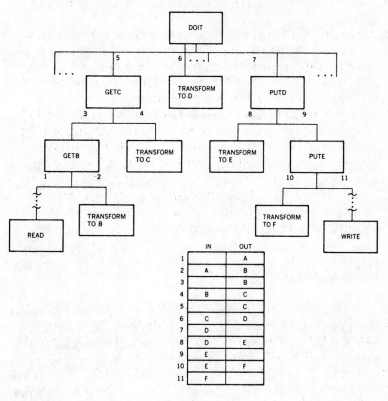

	IN	OUT
1		A
2	A	B
3		B
4	B	C
5		C
6	C	D
7	D	
8	D	E
9	E	
10	E	F
11	F	

Figure 9 Transaction structure

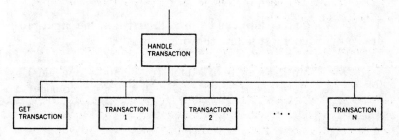

tion and analysis during general program design is the absence in structure charts of the decision block. Conditional calls can be so noted, but "decision designing" can be deferred until detailed module design. This is an example of where the *design* process is made simpler by having to consider only part of the design problem. Structure charts are also small enough to be worked on all at once by the designers, helping to prevent suboptimizing parts of the program at the expense of the entire problem.

common structures A shortcut for arriving at simple structures is to know the general form of the result. Mr. Constantine observed that programs of the general structure in Figure 8 resulted in the lowest-cost

Figure 10   Rough structure of simulation system

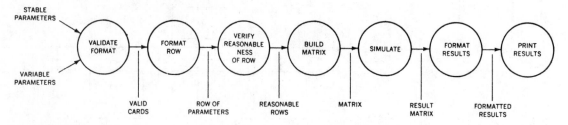

implementations. It implements the input-process-output type of program, which applies to most programs, even if the "input" or "output" is to secondary storage or to memory.

In practice, the sink leg is often shorter than the source one. Also, source modules may produce output (e.g., error messages) and sink modules may request input (e.g., execution-time format commands.)

Another structure useful for implementing parts of a design is the transaction structure depicted in Figure 9. A "transaction" here is any event, record, or input, etc. for which various actions should result. For example, a command processor has this structure. The structure may occur alone or as one or more of the source (or even sink) modules of an input-process-output structure. Analysis of the transaction modules follows that of a transform module, which is explained later.

The following procedure can be used to arrive at the input-process-output general structure shown previously.

designing
the structure

Step One. The first step is to sketch (or mentally consider) a functional picture of the problem. As an example, consider a simulation system. The rough structure of this problem is shown in Figure 10.

Step Two. Identify the external conceptual streams of data. An *external* stream of data is one that is external to the system. A *conceptual* stream of data is a stream of related data that is independent of any physical I/O device. For instance, we may have several conceptual streams coming from one I/O device or one stream coming from several I/O devices. In our simulation system, the external conceptual streams are the input parameters, and the formatted simulation the result.

Step Three. Identify the *major* external conceptual stream of data (both input and output) in the problem. Then, using the diagram of the problem structure, determine, for this stream, the points of "highest abstraction" as in Figure 11.

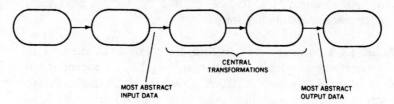

Figure 11 Determining points of highest abstraction

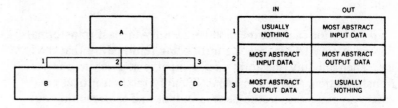

Figure 12 The top level

	IN	OUT
1	USUALLY NOTHING	MOST ABSTRACT INPUT DATA
2	MOST ABSTRACT INPUT DATA	MOST ABSTRACT OUTPUT DATA
3	MOST ABSTRACT OUTPUT DATA	USUALLY NOTHING

The "point of highest abstraction" for an input stream of data is the point in the problem structure where that data is farthest removed from its physical input form yet can still be viewed as coming in. Hence, in the simulation system, the most abstract form of the input transaction stream might be the built matrix. Similarly, identify the point where the data stream can first be viewed as going out — in the example, possibly the result matrix.

Admittedly, this is a subjective step. However, experience has shown that designers trained in the technique seldom differ by more than one or two blocks in their answers to the above.

Step Four. Design the structure in Figure 12 from the previous information with a source module for each conceptual input stream which exists at the point of most abstract input data; do sink modules similarly. Often only single source and sink branches are necessary. The parameters passed are dependent on the problem, but the general pattern is shown in Figure 12.

Describe the function of each module with a short, concise, and specific phrase. Describe what transformations occur when that module is called, not how the module is implemented. Evaluate the phrase relative to functional binding.

When module A is called, the program or system executes. Hence, the function of module A is equivalent to the problem being solved. If the problem is "write a FORTRAN compiler," then the function of module A is "compile FORTRAN program."

Module B's function involves obtaining the major stream of data. An example of a "typical module B" is "get next valid source statement in Polish form."

Module C's purpose is to transform the major input stream into the major output stream. Its function should be a nonprocedural description of this transformation. Examples are "convert Polish form statement to machine language statement" or "using keyword list, search abstract file for matching abstracts."

Module D's purpose is disposing of the major output stream. Examples are "produce report" or "display results of simulation."

Step Five. For each source module, identify the last transformation necessary to produce the form being returned by that module. Then identify the form of the input just prior to the last transformation. For sink modules, identify the first process necessary to get closer to the desired output and the resulting output form. This results in the portions of the structure shown in Figure 13.

Repeat Step Five on the new source and sink modules until the original source and final sink modules are reached. The modules may be analyzed in any order, but each module should be done completely before doing any of its subordinates. There are, unfortunately, no detailed guidelines available for dividing the transform modules. Use binding and coupling considerations, size (about one page of source), and usefulness (are there subfunctions that could be useful elsewhere now or in the future) as guidelines on how far to divide.

During this phase, err on the side of dividing too finely. It is always easy to recombine later in the design, but duplicate func-

Figure 13 Lower levels

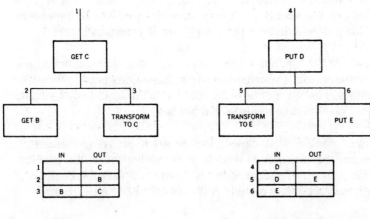

STRUCTURED DESIGN

Figure 14   Design form should follow function

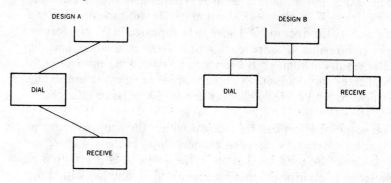

tions may not be identified if the dividing is too conservative at this point.

Design guidelines

The following concepts are useful for achieving simple designs and for improving the "first-pass" structures.

match program to problem

One of the most useful techniques for reducing the effect of changes on the program is to make the structure of the design match the structure of the problem, that is, form should follow function. For example, consider a module that dials a telephone and a module that receives data. If receiving immediately follows dialing, one might arrive at design A as shown in Figure 14. Consider, however, whether receiving is part of dialing. Since it is not (usually), have DIAL's caller invoke RECEIVE as in design B.

If, in this example, design A were used, consider the effect of a new requirement to transmit immediately after dialing. The DIAL module receives first and cannot be used, or a switch must be passed, or another DIAL module has to be added.

To the extent that the design structure does match the problem structure, changes to single parts of the problem result in changes to single modules.

scopes of effect and control

The *scope of control* of a module is that module plus all modules that are ultimately subordinate to that module. In the example of Figure 15, the scope of control of B is B, D, and E. The *scope of effect* of a decision is the set of all modules that contain some code whose execution is based upon the outcome of the decision. The system is simpler when the scope of effect of a decision is in the scope of control of the module containing the decision. The following example illustrates why.

Figure 15   Scope of control

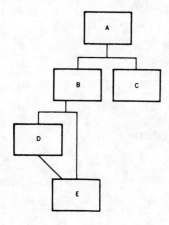

If the execution of some code in A is dependent on the outcome of decision X in module B, then either B will have to return a flag to A or the decision will have to be repeated in A. The former approach results in added coding to implement the flag, and the latter results in some of B's function (decision X) in module A. Duplicates of decision X result in difficulties coordinating changes to both copies whenever decision X must be changed.

The scope of effect can be brought within the scope of control either by moving the decision element "up" in the structure, or by taking those modules that are in the scope of effect but not in the scope of control and moving them so that they fall within the scope of control.

module size

Size can be used as a signal to look for *potential* problems. Look carefully at modules with less than five or more than 100 executable source statements. Modules with a small number of statements may not perform an entire function, hence, may not have functional binding. Very small modules can be eliminated by placing their statements in the calling modules. Large modules may include more than one function. A second problem with large modules is understandability and readability. There is evidence to the fact that a group of about 30 statements is the upper limit of what can be mastered on the first reading of a module listing.[11]

error and end-of-file

Often, part of a module's function is to notify its caller when it cannot perform its function. This is accomplished with a return error parameter (preferably binary only). A module that handles streams of data must be able to signal end-of-file (EOF), preferably also with a binary parameter. These parameters should not, however, tell the caller what to do about the error or EOF. Nevertheless, the system can be made simpler if modules can be designed without the need for error flags.

intialization

Similarly, many modules require some initialization to be done. An initialize module will suffer from low binding but sometimes is the simplest solution. It may, however, be possible to eliminate the need for initializing without compromising "black-box-ness" (the same inputs *always* produce the same outputs). For example, a read module that detects a return error of file-not-opened from the access method and recovers by opening the file and rereading eliminates the need for initialization without maintaining an internal state.

selecting modules

Eliminate duplicate functions but not duplicate code. When a function changes, it is a great advantage to only have to change it in one place. But if a module's need for its own copy of a random collection of code changes slightly, it will not be necessary to change several other modules as well.

Figure 16 Outline of problem structure

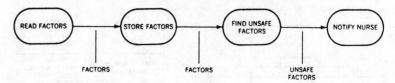

Figure 17 Points of highest abstraction

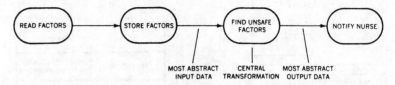

If a module seems almost, but not quite, useful from a second place in the system, try to identify and isolate the useful subfunction. The remainder of the module might be incorporated in its original caller.

Check modules that have many callers or that call many other modules. While not always a problem, it may indicate missing levels or modules.

isolate specifications

Isolate all dependencies on a particular data-type, record-layout, index-structure, etc. in one or a minimum of modules. This minimizes the recoding necessary should that particular specification change.

reduce parameters

Look for ways to reduce the number of parameters passed between modules. Count every item passed as a separate parameter for this objective (independent of how it will be implemented). Do not pass whole records from module to module, but pass only the field or fields necessary for each module to accomplish its function. Otherwise, all modules will have to change if one field expands, rather than only those which directly used that field. Passing only the data being processed by the program system with necessary error and EOF parameters is the ultimate objective. Check binary switches for indications of scope-of-effect/scope-of-control inversions.

Have the designers work together and with the complete structure chart. If branches of the chart are worked on separately, common modules may be missed and incompatibilities result from design decisions made while only considering one branch.

Figure 18   Structure of the top level

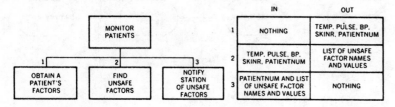

	IN	OUT
1	NOTHING	TEMP. PULSE. BP, SKINR. PATIENTNUM
2	TEMP. PULSE. BP, SKINR. PATIENTNUM	LIST OF UNSAFE FACTOR NAMES AND VALUES
3	PATIENTNUM AND LIST OF UNSAFE FACTOR NAMES AND VALUES	NOTHING

Figure 19   Structure of next level

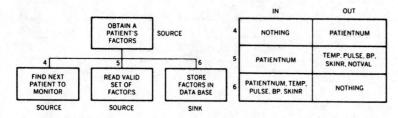

	IN	OUT
4	NOTHING	PATIENTNUM
5	PATIENTNUM	TEMP. PULSE. BP, SKINR. NOTVAL
6	PATIENTNUM. TEMP. PULSE. BP. SKINR	NOTHING

An example

The following example illustrates the use of structured design:

A patient-monitoring program is required for a hospital. Each patient is monitored by an analog device which measures factors such as pulse, temperature, blood pressure, and skin resistance. The program reads these factors on a periodic basis (specified for each patient) and stores these factors in a data base. For each patient, safe ranges for each factor are specified (e.g., patient X's valid temperature range is 98 to 99.5 degrees Fahrenheit). If a factor falls outside of a patient's safe range, or if an analog device fails, the nurse's station is notified.

In a real-life case, the problem statement would contain much more detail. However, this one is of sufficient detail to allow us to design the structure of the program.

The first step is to outline the structure of the problem as shown in Figure 16. In the second step, we identify the external conceptual streams of data. In this case, two streams are present, factors from the analog device and warnings to the nurse. These also represent the major input and output streams.

Figure 17 indicates the point of highest abstraction of the input stream, which is the point at which a patient's factors are in the form to store in the data base. The point of highest abstraction of the output stream is a list of unsafe factors (if any). We can now begin to design the program's structure as in Figure 18.

STRUCTURED DESIGN

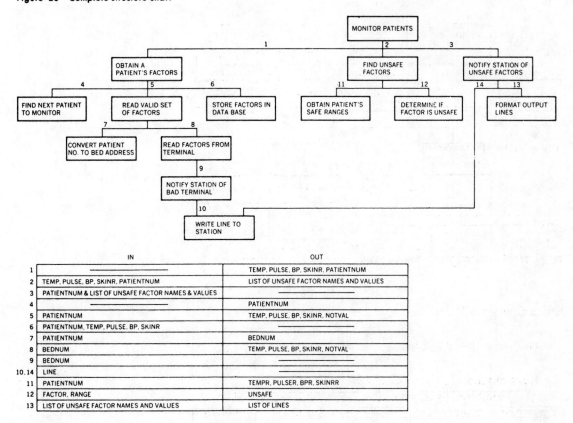

Figure 20 Complete structure chart

	IN	OUT
1		TEMP, PULSE, BP, SKINR, PATIENTNUM
2	TEMP, PULSE, BP, SKINR, PATIENTNUM	LIST OF UNSAFE FACTOR NAMES AND VALUES
3	PATIENTNUM & LIST OF UNSAFE FACTOR NAMES & VALUES	
4		PATIENTNUM
5	PATIENTNUM	TEMP, PULSE, BP, SKINR, NOTVAL
6	PATIENTNUM, TEMP, PULSE, BP, SKINR	
7	PATIENTNUM	BEDNUM
8	BEDNUM	TEMP, PULSE, BP, SKINR, NOTVAL
9	BEDNUM	
10,14	LINE	
11	PATIENTNUM	TEMPR, PULSER, BPR, SKINRR
12	FACTOR, RANGE	UNSAFE
13	LIST OF UNSAFE FACTOR NAMES AND VALUES	LIST OF LINES

In analyzing the module "OBTAIN A PATIENT'S FACTORS," we can deduce from the problem statement that this function has three parts: (1) Determine which patient to monitor next (based on their specified periodic intervals). (2) Read the analog device. (3) Record the factors in the data base. Hence, we arrive at the structure in Figure 19. (NOTVAL is set if a valid set of factors was not available.)

Further analysis of "READ VALID SET OF FACTORS", "FIND UNSAFE FACTORS" and "NOTIFY STATION OF UNSAFE FACTORS" yields the results shown in the complete structure chart in Figure 20.

Note that the module "READ FACTORS FROM TERMINAL" contains a decision asking "did we successfully read from the terminal?" If the read was not successful, we have to notify the nurse's station and then find the next patient to process as depicted in Figure 21.

Modules in the scope of effect of this decision are marked with an X. Note that the scope of effect is *not* a subset of the scope

STEVENS, MYERS, AND CONSTANTINE   IBM SYST J

Figure 21 Structure as designed

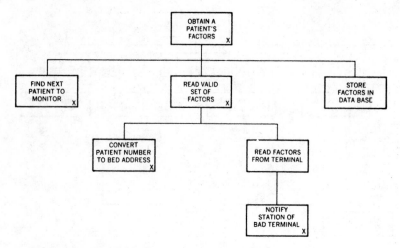

Figure 22 Scope of effect within scope of control

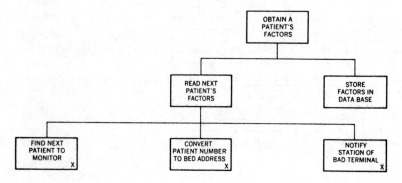

of control. To correct this problem, we have to take two steps. First, we will move the decision up to "READ VALID SET OF FACTORS." We do this by merging "READ FACTORS FROM TERMINAL" into its calling module. We now make "FIND NEXT PATIENT TO MONITOR" a subordinate of "READ VALID SET OF FACTORS." Hence, we have the structure in Figure 22. Thus, by slightly altering the structure and the function of a few modules, we have completely eliminated the problem.

Concluding remarks

The HIPO Hierarchy chart is being used as an aid during general systems design. The considerations and techniques presented here are useful for evaluating alternatives for those portions of the system that will be programmed on a computer. The charting technique used here depicts more details about the interfaces than the HIPO Hierarchy chart. This facilitates consideration during general program design of each individual connection and its associated passed parameters. The resulting design can be documented with the HIPO charts. (If the designer decides to have more than one function in any module, the structure chart should show them in the same block. However, the HIPO Hierarchy chart would still show all the functions in separate blocks.) The output of the general program design is the input for the detailed module design. The HIPO input-process-output chart is useful for describing and designing each module.

Structured design considerations could be used to review program designs in a walk-through environment.[12] These concepts are also useful for evaluating alternative ways to comply with the requirement of structured programming for one-page segments.[7]

Structured design reduces the effort needed to fix and modify programs. If all programs were written in a form where there was one module, for example, which retrieved a record from the master file given the key, then changing operating systems, file access techniques, file blocking, or I/O devices would be greatly simplified. And if *all* programs in the installation retrieved from a given file with the same module, then one properly rewritten module would have *all* the installation's programs working with the new constraints for that file.

However, there are other advantages. Original errors are reduced when the problem at hand is simpler. Each module is self-contained and to some extent may be programmed independently of the others in location, programmer, time, and language. Modules can be tested before all programming is done by supplying simple "stub" modules that merely return preformatted results rather than calculating them. Modules critical to memory or execution overhead can be optimized separately and reintegrated with little or no impact. An entry or return trace-module becomes very feasible, yielding a very useful debugging tool.

Independent of all the advantages previously mentioned, structured design would *still* be valuable to solve the following problem alone. Programming can be considered as an art where each programmer usually starts with a blank canvas—techniques, yes, but still a blank canvas. Previous coding is often not used because previous modules usually contain, for example, *at least* GET and EDIT. If the EDIT is not the one needed, the GET will have to be recoded also.

Programming can be brought closer to a science where current work is built on the results of earlier work. Once a module is written to get a record from the master file given a key, it can be used by all users of the file and need not be rewritten into each succeeding program. Once a module has been written to do a table search, anyone can use it. And, as the module library grows, less and less new code needs to be written to implement increasingly sophisticated systems.

Structured design concepts are not new. The whole assembly-line idea is one of isolating simple functions in a way that still produces a complete, complex result. Circuits are designed by connecting isolatable, functional stages together, not by designing one big, interrelated circuit. Page numbering is being increasingly sectionalized (e.g., 4–101) to minimize the "connections" between written sections, so that expanding one section does not require renumbering other sections. Automobile manufacturers, who have the most to gain from shared system elements, finally abandoned even the coupling of the windshield wipers to the engine vacuum due to effects of the engine load on the performance of the wiping function. Most other industries know well the advantage of isolating functions.

It is becoming increasingly important to the data-processing industry to be able to produce more programming systems and produce them with fewer errors, at a faster rate, and in a way that modifications can be accomplished easily and quickly. Structured design considerations can help achieve this goal.

CITED REFERENCES AND FOOTNOTES

1. This method has not been submitted to any formal IBM test. Potential users should evaluate its usefulness in their own environment prior to implementation.
2. L. L. Constantine, *Fundamentals of Program Design*, in preparation for publication by Prentice-Hall, Englewood Cliffs, New Jersey.
3. G. J. Myers, *Composite Design: The Design of Modular Programs*, Technical Report TR00.2406, IBM, Poughkeepsie, New York (January 29, 1973).
4. G. J. Myers, "Characteristics of composite design," *Datamation* 19, No. 9, 100–102 (September 1973).
5. G. J. Myers, *Reliable Software through Composite Design*, to be published Fall of 1974 by Mason and Lipscomb Publishers, New York, New York.
6. HIPO—Hierarchical Input-Process-Output documentation technique. Audio education package, Form No. SR20-9413, available through any IBM Branch Office.
7. F. T. Baker, "Chief programmer team management of production programming," *IBM Systems Journal* 11, No. 1, 56–73 (1972).
8. The use of the HIPO Hierarchy charting format is further illustrated in Figure 6, and its use in this paper was initiated by R. Ballow of the IBM Programming Productivity Techniques Department.
9. L. A. Belady and M. M. Lehman, *Programming System Dynamics or the Metadynamics of Systems in Maintenance and Growth*", RC 3546, IBM Thomas J. Watson Research Center, Yorktown Heights, New York (1971).
10. L. L. Constantine, "Control of sequence and parallelism in modular programs," *AFIPS Conference Proceedings, Spring Joint Computer Conference* 32, 409 (1968).
11. G. M. Weinberg, *PL/I Programming: A Manual of Style*, McGraw-Hill, New York, New York (1970).
12. *Improved Programming Technologies: Management Overview*, IBM Corporation, Data Processing Division, White Plains, New York (August 1973).

Concurrent Software System Design
Supported by SARA at the Age of One*

by

Ivan M. Campos** and Gerald Estrin

Computer Science Department (BH 3732)
University of California at Los Angeles
(213) 825-2786

ABSTRACT

This paper presents a multilevel modeling method suitable for the design of concurrent hardware or software systems. The methodology is requirement driven and uses tools incorporated in a programming system called SARA (Systems ARchitect's Apprentice). Both top down refinement and bottom up abstraction are supported. The design of an asynchronous sender receiver illustrates the key steps in going smoothly from programming in the large to programming in the small or actual code. The same methodology can be used to design hardware systems by applying different pragmatics than those proposed for software systems. SARA consists of a set of interactive tools implemented both at UCLA and also on the MIT-Multics system. Although SARA continues in long-term development, completed design tools are accessible for experimentation by authorized users at either location via the ARPANET.

Introduction

Analysis of software system errors has shown that most bugs are "born" in the design phase, i.e., the design itself is usually faulty [DIJ72], and when a bug is uncovered some changes in the basic design are likely to occur. Whenever such modification is made, it is generally difficult to keep track of all consequences that it may provoke. Ill-designed systems often display a high degree of connectivity among subsystems [PA72b], [YCO76]. Many interconnections

*This research was supported by the U.S. Department of Energy, Cont No. EY-76-S-03-0034, PA214.

**Presently at: Ivan Moura Campos, Departamento De Ciencia Da Computacao, Universidade Federal De Minas Gerais, Pampulha, Belo Horizonte - MG, 30 000 Brasil

KEYWORDS: CONCURRENT, SOFTWARE DESIGN, TOP-DOWN, BOTTOM-UP.

may be "hidden", i.e. they represent unstated assumptions that a subsystem makes about other subsystems and lead to unforseen side effects when seemingly harmless changes are made [PAR75], [THO76].

In an attempt to progress towards producing better software, extra effort tends to be invested in design. Data abstraction concepts have been introduced into languages such as CLU [LIZ74], EUCLID [POP78], and ALPHARD [WUL74] which it is hoped will most effectively lead to better design. At the same time active research continues to uncover more effective methods for analysis and synthesis of verified programs [CRO77].

At UCLA, Estrin and his colleagues have been involved in the development of models of computational algorithms, models of interpreters, and procedures for mapping one on the other since the early 1960's. The UCLA Graph Model of Computation [EST63], [ME67], [GCE72], [CER72], [WIN72], [POS74], [YAV74]; the development of a methodology (DCDS) for design of hierarchical hardware and firmware systems [PTA69]; and the revelation of difficulties in evaluation of unstructured computer systems [EMU72] led this UCLA group to concentrate on synthesis of structured systems, in which one might manage complexity from the outset and prepare for further analysis.

The major current thrust of work at UCLA on methodology of synthesis is consolidation of these results by completing a set of tools which support a structured multilevel design procedure for software or hardware development [EST78]. This interactive computer-aided system called SARA (Systems ARchitect's Apprentice) is one year old and provides languages to help a designer form useful abstractions which can be manipulated and tested in a disciplined way [GAR75], [FEN77], [CAM77], [PAL77] and which may be forced to retain good properties [OVE77].

SARA supports both a bottom-up composition (abstraction) procedure and a

Reprinted from *Proceedings of the Third International Conference on Software Engineering*, 1977, pages 230–242. Copyright © 1977 by The Institute of Electrical and Electronics Engineers, Inc.

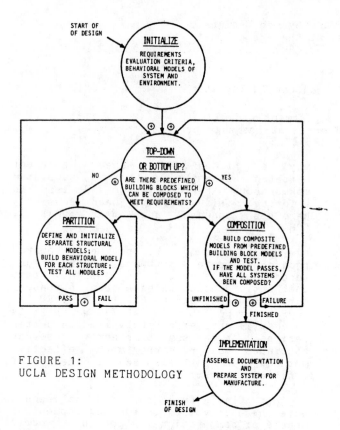

FIGURE 1:
UCLA DESIGN METHODOLOGY

top-down partitioning (refinement) procedure as illustrated in Figure 1. In both cases, however, the procedures are requirement-driven so that attention can be focused on the gap between a designer's declared intent and the current approximation of the system's behavior.

Models are built using a small number of primitives (Tables 1,2) whose creation and manipulation are supported by SARA interactive translators and a simulator.

The authors chose not to provide, in this paper, the full detail of syntax and semantics implemented in SARA. The interested reader can find such information in [FEN77]. We have tried to include enough detail to follow examples. Note that the "@" symbol is used for many purposes: to identify a socket name or a declaration or language processor.

Modules, sockets and interconnections are structural modeling primitives which allow creation of a hierarchical name space for a fully nested system. Named modules permit interaction only through sockets. Socket names are known both inside and outside of modules, thus supporting declarations of interfaces. Named interconnections support interaction among modules.

Explicit control flow behavior can be expressed by control nodes, which span initiation and termination of associated processes, and by directed control arcs, which are used to express precedence conditions. Control conditions and thresholds can be prescribed to condition process initiation. Control consequences can be prescribed to take effect following process completion. Tokens mark the state of control flow and a token machine governs progress of the state of a model. Data flow is described by graphs composed of controlled processors, uncontrolled processors, datasets and data arcs.

All of the above primitives are currently used to form models which are static in the sense that the topology currently does not change during execution. Interpretations can be associated with the data flow primitives (processors and datasets) and provide the semantics for modeling of dynamics. Currently, a pre-processed PL/I (PLIP) is

TABLE 1: MODELING PRIMITIVES

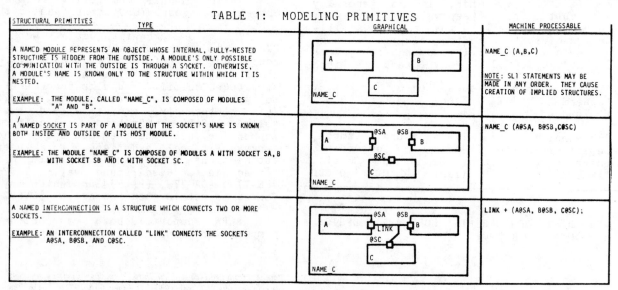

STRUCTURAL PRIMITIVES / TYPE	GRAPHICAL	MACHINE PROCESSABLE
A NAMED MODULE REPRESENTS AN OBJECT WHOSE INTERNAL, FULLY-NESTED STRUCTURE IS HIDDEN FROM THE OUTSIDE. A MODULE'S ONLY POSSIBLE COMMUNICATION WITH THE OUTSIDE IS THROUGH A SOCKET. OTHERWISE, A MODULE'S NAME IS KNOWN ONLY TO THE STRUCTURE WITHIN WHICH IT IS NESTED. EXAMPLE: THE MODULE, CALLED "NAME_C", IS COMPOSED OF MODULES "A" AND "B".		NAME_C (A,B,C) NOTE: SL1 STATEMENTS MAY BE MADE IN ANY ORDER. THEY CAUSE CREATION OF IMPLIED STRUCTURES.
A NAMED SOCKET IS PART OF A MODULE BUT THE SOCKET'S NAME IS KNOWN BOTH INSIDE AND OUTSIDE OF ITS HOST MODULE. EXAMPLE: THE MODULE "NAME C" IS COMPOSED OF MODULES A WITH SOCKET SA, B WITH SOCKET SB AND C WITH SOCKET SC.		NAME_C (A@SA, B@SB,C@SC)
A NAMED INTERCONNECTION IS A STRUCTURE WHICH CONNECTS TWO OR MORE SOCKETS. EXAMPLE: AN INTERCONNECTION CALLED "LINK" CONNECTS THE SOCKETS A@SA, B@SB, AND C@SC.		LINK + (A@SA, B@SB, C@SC);

TABLE 2: BEHAVIORAL MODELING PRIMITIVES

BEHAVIORAL PRIMITIVES TYPE	GRAPHICAL	MACHINE PROCESSABLE

A NAMED <u>CONTROL NODE</u> REPRESENTS A STEP IN A PROCESS BEING MODELED. A CONTROLLED DATA PROCESSOR (SEE BELOW) MAY BE ASSOCIATED WITH A NODE TO PROVIDE INTERPRETATION OF THE PROCESS.
 	
<u>EXAMPLE</u>: A NODE N1 HAS A SINGLE ENTRY ARC S AND A SINGLE EXIT ARC X.
		`@CONTROL GRAPH;`
		`  @NODES N1;`
		`  @ARCS S,X;`
		`  N1 (S:X);`
		`@END;`

A NAMED DIRECTED <u>CONTROL ARC</u> REPRESENTS NON-VOLATILE PRECEDENCE RELATIONS BETWEEN SETS OF NODES. IF THERE IS MORE THAN ONE SOURCE OR DESTINATION NODE THE ARC IS CALLED COMPLEX; OTHERWISE IT IS CALLED SIMPLE. AN ENABLING TOKEN IS PLACED ON AN ARC EITHER AS A STARTING STATE OR UPON TERMINATION OF ANY OF ITS SOURCE NODES. WHEN A NODE IS INITIATED, ITS ENABLING TOKENS ARE ABSORBED.
 	
<u>EXAMPLE</u>: A2 AND X ARE SIMPLE CONTROL ARCS. A1 IS A COMPLEX CONTROL ARC WHOSE SOURCE SET IS NODES N1, N2 and N4 AND WHOSE DESTINATION SET IS N5. S IS AN INCOMING COMPLEX ARC WHOSE DESTINATION SET IS N1, N2, AND N3. IF THERE WERE AN INITIAL TOKEN ON S, THE TOKEN MACHINE MECHANISM WOULD NON-DETERMINISTICALLY ENABLE N1 OR N2 OR N3 AND THE TOKEN WOULD BE ABSORBED.
		`@CONTROL GRAPH:`
		`  @NODES N1,N2,N3,N4,N5;`
		`  @ARCS S,A1,A2,X;`
		`  N1 (S:A1);`
		`  N2 (S:A1);`
		`  N3 (S:A2);`
		`  N4 (A2:A1);`
		`  N5 (A1:X);`
		`@END;`

<u>INPUT CONTROL LOGIC</u>
A LOGICAL RELATION AMONG THE INPUT ARCS TO A NODE SPECIFIES THE PRECEDENCE CONDITIONS THAT MUST BE SATISFIED BY TOKEN STATES FOR THE NODE TO BE INITIATED. TOKENS FROM THE INITIATING ARCS WHICH SATISFY THE INPUT RELATIONS ARE ABSORBED BY THE TOKEN MACHINE. TOKENS ARE ABSORBED FROM ONE OF AN INITIATING ARC SET GOVERNED BY AN OR RELATION IN A MANNER ESTABLISHED IN THE TOKEN MACHINE AND FROM ALL MEMBERS OF AN INITIATING ARC SET GOVERNED BY AN <u>AND</u> RELATION.
 	
<u>EXAMPLE</u>: IF ENABLING TOKENS EXIST ON EITHER A1 OR A2 AND ON EITHER A3 OR A4 THEN N1 CAN BE INITIATED.
 	
<u>OUTPUT CONTROL LOGIC</u>
A LOGICAL RELATION AMONG THE OUTPUT ARCS SPECIFIES WHICH ARCS HAVE TOKENS PLACED UPON THEM WHEN A CONTROL NODE IS TERMINATED. WHEN AN EXCLUSIVE OR OUTPUT RELATION HOLDS, A DATA PROCESSOR INTERPRETATION MUST DECIDE WHICH ARC RECEIVES A TOKEN. WHEN AN AND RELATION HOLDS ALL OUTPUT ARCS RECEIVE TOKENS.
 	
<u>EXAMPLE</u>: WHEN N1 TERMINATES, ITS ASSOCIATED CONTROLLED DATA PROCESSOR WILL HAVE DECIDED WHETHER TOKENS ARE TO BE PLACED ON B1 AND B2 OR ON B3 AND B4.
		<u>INPUT: OUTPUT CONTROL LOGIC</u>
		`@CONTROL GRAPHS;`
		`  @NODES N1;`
		`  @ARCS A1,A2,A3,A4,B1,B2,B3,B4;`
		`  N1((A1+A2) * (A3+A4);`
		`     (B1+B2) * (B3+B4));`
		`@END;`

A NAMED <u>CONTROLLED DATA PROCESSOR</u> REPRESENTS A DATA TRANSFORMATION OBJECT WHICH IS ACTIVATED WHEN AN ASSOCIATED CONTROL NODE IS INITIATED. E.G., PROCESSOR P1 IS INITIATED WHENEVER EITHER N1 OR N2 IS INITIATED. WHEN PROCESSOR P1 TERMINATES IT CAUSES TOKENS TO BE PLACED ON OUTPUT ARCS OF THE CONTROL NODE WHICH INITIATED IT. AN INTERPRETATION OF THE DATA TRANSFORMATION AND OTHER PARAMETERS SUCH AS TIME DELAY OR RESOURCE REQUIREMENTS CAN BE ASSOCIATED WITH THE DATA PROCESSOR.
 	
<u>EXAMPLE</u>: PROCESSOR P1 HAS A RANDOM DELAY ASSOCIATED WITH IT. IRAND IS A BUILT-IN FUNCTION. THE CONTROL GRAPH CARRIES THE BURDEN OF GUARANTEEING THAT N1 AND N2 ARE ENABLED IN A DESIRED SEQUENCE. OTHERWISE THEY WILL BE ACTIVATED IN A NON-DETERMINISTIC ORDER AND THE SIMULATOR WILL SHOW POSSIBLE CONTENTION.
		`@DATA GRAPH;`
		`  @PROCESSOR P1 (N1,N2);`
		`@END;`
		
		`PLIP INTERPRETATION`
		`@PROCESSOR P1;`
		`  DCL IRAND ENTRY(FIXED BIN(31)`
		`       FIXED BIN(31))RETURNS`
		`       (FIXED BIN(31));`
		`       /*RANDOM # GENERATOR*/`
		`  DCL NUMBER FIXED BIN(31);`
		`  NUMBER=IRAND(1,2)`
		`       /*PICK AN INTEGER: 1 OR`
		`       2*/`
		`  IF NUMBER=1 THEN @OUTPUT_ARCS=`
		`       'B1,B2';`
		`       ELSE @OUTPUT_ARCS='B3,B4';`
		`  @DELAY=IRAND (10,100);`
		`       /*PICK RANDOM DELAY FROM`
		`       10 TO 100*/`
		`@END PROCESSOR;`

A NAMED <u>UNCONTROLLED DATA PROCESSOR</u> REPRESENTS A DATA TRANSFORMER WHICH PROVIDES, AT ITS OUTPUT, STATED FUNCTIONS OF ITS INPUTS INDEPENDENT OF CONTROL NODE STATES. IN THE DATA GRAPH AN UNCONTROLLED PROCESSOR IS IDENTIFIED BY PROVIDING AN EXPLICIT DECLARATION. AN INTERPRETATION OF THE DATA TRANSFORMATIONS AND OTHER PARAMETERS MAY BE ASSOCIATED WITH IT IN AN IDENTICAL MANNER TO THE CONTROLLED PROCESSOR.		`@DATA GRAPH;`
		`  @UNCONTROLLED_PROCESSORS U1;`
		`@END;`

A NAMED <u>DATA SET</u> REPRESENTS A PASSIVE COLLECTION OF DATA. DATA STRUCTURE MAY BE ASSOCIATED WITH A DATASET. ALL PL/1 DECLARATIONS NOT CONTAINING SCOPE OR STORAGE CLASS ATTRIBUTES ARE ACCEPTED AS DEFINITIONS OF DATA SETS. CHARACTER STRINGS CANNOT HAVE THE VARYING ATTRIBUTE.
 	
<u>EXAMPLE</u>: THE DATASET D1 IS A SIX-DECIMAL-DIGIT COMPLEX FLOATING POINT NUMBER.
		`@DATA GRAPH;`
		`  @DATASETS D1;`
		`@END;`
		
		`PLIP INTERPRETATION`
		`@DATASET D1 COMPLEX`
		`  FLOAT DECIMAL(6);`

A NAMED <u>DATA ARC</u> STATICALLY BINDS DATA PROCESSORS AND DATASETS. A DATA PROCESSOR HAS READ OR WRITE ACCESS TO A DATA SET IF THE ARROW POINTS TO OR FROM THE DATA PROCESSOR RESPECTIVELY.
 	
<u>EXAMPLE</u>: PROCESSOR P1 IS INITIATED BY CONTROL NODE N1. P1 READS DATA FROM DATASETS D2 AND D3 AND WRITES THEIR SUM INTO DATASET D1.
		`@DATA GRAPH;`
		`  @PROCESSORS P1(N1);`
		`  @DATASETS D1, D2, D3;`
		`  @ARCS DA1, DA2, DA3;`
		`     DA3 (D3:P1);`
		`     DA2 (D2:P1);`
		`     DA1 (P1:D1);`
		`@END;`
		`PLIP INTERPRETATION`
		`@DATASET D1 FIXED BIN(31);`
		`@DATASET D2 FIXED BIN(31);`
		`@DATASET D3 FIXED BIN(31);`
		`@PROCESSOR P1;`
		`  @READ(D3); @READ(D2);`
		`  D1 = D2+D3;`
		`  @WRITE(D1);`
		`@END PROCESSOR;`

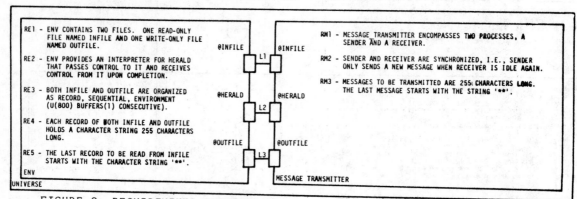

SL1 CODE FOR STRUCTURAL MODEL OF UNIVERSE

```
UNIVERSE(ENV,MESSAGE_TRANSMITTER); ENV(@INFILE,@HERALD,@^UTFILE); MESSAGE_TRANSMITTER(@INFILE,@HERALD,@OUTFILE);
UNIVERSE(L1+(ENV@INFILE,MESSAGE_TRANSMITTER@INFILE)); UNIVERSE(L2+(ENV@HERALD,MESSAGE_TRANSMITTER@HERALD));
UNIVERSE(L3+(ENV@OUTFILE,MESSAGE_TRANSMITTER@OUTFILE));
```

RE1 - ENV CONTAINS TWO FILES. ONE READ-ONLY FILE NAMED INFILE AND ONE WRITE-ONLY FILE NAMED OUTFILE.

RE2 - ENV PROVIDES AN INTERPRETER FOR HERALD THAT PASSES CONTROL TO IT AND RECEIVES CONTROL FROM IT UPON COMPLETION.

RE3 - BOTH INFILE AND OUTFILE ARE ORGANIZED AS RECORD, SEQUENTIAL, ENVIRONMENT (U(800) BUFFERS(1) CONSECUTIVE).

RE4 - EACH RECORD OF BOTH INFILE AND OUTFILE HOLDS A CHARACTER STRING 255 CHARACTERS LONG.

RE5 - THE LAST RECORD TO BE READ FROM INFILE STARTS WITH THE CHARACTER STRING '**'.

ENV

@INFILE @INFILE
L1
@HERALD @HERALD
L2
@OUTFILE @OUTFILE
L3

RM1 - MESSAGE_TRANSMITTER ENCOMPASSES TWO PROCESSES, A SENDER AND A RECEIVER.

RM2 - SENDER AND RECEIVER ARE SYNCHRONIZED, I.E., SENDER ONLY SENDS A NEW MESSAGE WHEN RECEIVER IS IDLE AGAIN.

RM3 - MESSAGES TO BE TRANSMITTED ARE 255 CHARACTERS LONG. THE LAST MESSAGE STARTS WITH THE STRING '**'.

MESSAGE TRANSMITTER

UNIVERSE

FIGURE 2: REQUIREMENTS SUPERIMPOSED ON ENV AND MESSAGE_TRANSMITTER

the interpretation language. An interactive simulator supports experiments on models. Extensive discussion of SARA modeling may be found in the references noted above.

The objective of this paper is to expose the SARA methodology as applied to software. We make use of a classical example of cooperating asynchronous processes. The central problem is the set of tools and procedures to be brought to bear on building possibly concurrent software systems which reliably carry out the designer's intent.

We also wish to propose a role of SARA models not only as design and evaluation tools, but also as the basis for a superstructure to be overlaid on the actual code of a designed product as redundant information for the operating system. One consequence of imposing such a superstructure on source code modules is that it provides its operating system and its user with a "live" documentation whose objective is to enforce consistency between requirements, structure, function and behavior of the software system.

In the body of the paper below, we take the reader through the key steps of an example design and try to generalize the procedure through commentary. We chose the design of an asynchronous sender-receiver process. It is a relatively simple example which is of some importance and serves to bring out many properties of our design method and the SARA system.

Following an informal statement of need, the design universe is partitioned into the system to be designed and its environment. An initial behavioral model (of the system and of the environment) fixes all assumptions under which the design is to proceed. Requirements

establish evaluation criteria for the system. Following "top-down" levels of designer-created behavior, there is a final composition step to produce PL/I code. In the models below, comments will highlight SARA conventions. In all other cases PL/I conventions will be assumed to hold.

A Design Example

The informal statement of our design problem is "design a system whereby a process SENDER produces and sends a sequence of data to another process, RECEIVER, which receives and consumes them asynchronously. In order to smooth speed variations between the two processes, and to occasionally permit the SENDER to be ahead of the RECEIVER, the system should use a shared temporary storage area as a MESSAGE BUFFER".

Defining the Structure

The initial design steps in the SARA design procedure [EST78], [CAM77] lead us to partition our UNIVERSE into two SL1 modules, MESSAGE TRANSMITTER, the system to be designed, and ENV, its environment. The machine processable SL1 code, its graphical representation and the requirements for both ENV and MESSAGE TRANSMITTER are shown in Figure 2. Parentheses establish nesting level so that the second line of SL1 code is read "ENV is composed of three sockets, called @INFILE, @HERALD, and @OUTFILE". Identifiers starting with the character '@' are socket names. The symbol '+' indicates that the system to its left is an interconnection which connects the sockets whose names appear between the parentheses that follow it. Thus the third SL1 statement says that "within UNIVERSE there is an interconnection named SL1 which connects the socket ENV @INFILE to MESSAGE TRANSMITTER @INFILE".

DESCRIPTION OF UNINTERPRETED GMB

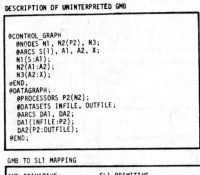

```
@CONTROL_GRAPH
    @NODES N1, N2(P2), N3;
    @ARCS S(1), A1, A2, X;
    N1(S:A1);
    N2(A1:A2);
    N3(A2:X);
@END,
@DATAGRAPH;
    @PROCESSORS P2(N2);
    @DATASETS INFILE, OUTFILE;
    @ARCS DA1, DA2;
    DA1(INFILE:P2);
    DA2(P2:OUTFILE);
@END;
```

INTERPRETATION OF DATA GRAPH

PLIP

```
@DATASET INFILE FILE RECORD SEQUENTIAL INPUT
    ENVIRONMENT(U(800) BUFFERS(1) CONSECUTIVE);
@DATASET OUTFILE FILE RECORD SEQUENTIAL OUTPUT
    ENVIRONMENT (U(800) BUFFERS(1) CONSECUTIVE);
@PROCESSOR P2;
    DCL MESSAGE CHAR (255);
    OPEN FILE(INFILE);
    OPEN FILE(OUTFILE);
    /* SENDER PROCESS */
LOOP:  READ FILE(INFILE) INTO(MESSAGE);
    @READ(INFILE);
    /* RECEIVER PROCESS */
    WRITE FILE(OUTFILE) FROM(MESSAGE);
    @WRITE(OUTFILE);
    /* TEST FOR COMPLETION */
    IF SUBSTR(MESSAGE,1,2)¬= '**'
        THEN GO TO LOOP;
    CLOSE FILE(INFILE);
    CLOSE FILE(OUTFILE);
@ENDPROCESSOR;
```

GMB TO SL1 MAPPING

| GMB PRIMITIVE | | SL1 PRIMITIVE | |
NAME	TYPE	NAME	TYPE
S	C_ARC	ENV	MODULE
N1	C_NODE	ENV	MODULE
A1	C_ARC	ENV@HERALD	SOCKET
A2	C_ARC	ENV@HERALD	SOCKET
N3	C_NODE	ENV	MODULE
X	C_ARC	ENV	MODULE
INFILE	DATASET	ENV	MODULE
DA1	D_ARC	ENV@INFILE	SOCKET
DA2	D_ARC	ENV@OUTFILE	SOCKET
OUTFILE	DATASET	ENV	MODULE
A1	C_ARC	L2	INTERC
A2	C_ARC	L2	INTERC
DA1	D_ARC	L1	INTERC
DA2	D_ARC	L3	INTERC
A1	C_ARC	MESSAGE_TRANSMITTER@HERALD	SOCKET
A2	C_ARC	MESSAGE_TRANSMITTER@HERALD	SOCKET
N2	C_NODE	MESSAGE_TRANSMITTER	MODULE
DA1	D_ARC	MESSAGE_TRNASMITTER@INFILE	SOCKET
P2	PROCESSOR	MESSAGE_TRANSMITTER	MODULE
DA2	D_ARC	MESSAGE_TRANSMITTER@OUTFILE	SOCKET

SOCKET ATTRIBUTES

SL1 SOCKET	ATTRIBUTES
ENV@INFILE	DATA OUTPUT
	CHARACTER (255)
	NONVARYING UNALIGNED
	STATIC EXTERNAL
ENV@HERALD	CONTROL INPUT-OUTPUT
ENV@OUTFILE	DATA INPUT
	CHARACTER (255)
	NONVARYING UNALIGNED
	STATIC EXTERNA'
MESSAGE_TRANSMITTER@INFILE	DATA INPUT
	CHARACTER (255)
	NONVARYING UNALIGNED
	STATIC EXTERNAL
MESSAGE_TRANSMITTER@HERALD	CONTROL INPUT-OUTPUT
MESSAGE_TRANSMITTER@OUTFILE	DATA OUTPUT
	CHARACTER (255)
	NONVARYING UNALIGNED
	STATIC EXTERNAL

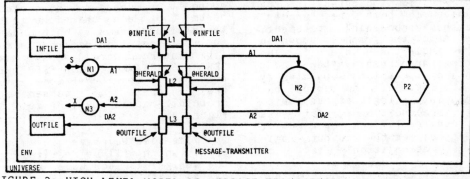

FIGURE 3: HIGH LEVEL MODEL OF MESSAGE TRANSMITTER AND ITS ENVIRONMENT

The MESSAGE TRANSMITTER requirements, R4, R5, R6, and R7, explicitly refer to the message buffer and the associated synchronization constraints. We can state them more formally as follows:

(R4) size(MESSAGE BUFFER) = MAX &
    (forall i, o<=i<=MAX - 1) (BUFFER (i) is CHAR (255))
Let
r = number of messages already received at a given instant.
s = number of messages already sent at a given instant.
#messages = total number of messages transmitted (unknown until halting);
S(i) = the ith message sent; and
R(i) = the ith message received; then

(R5) $0<=s-r<=MAX$,
(R6) $0<=r<=s$
(R7) (forall r, $1<=r<=\#messages$)
(forall i, $1<=i<=r$)
    $(R(i) = S(i))$.

The Behavioral Model GMB (Graph Model of Behavior)

Figure 3 contains the graphical representation of the GMB model of the interaction between ENV and MESSAGE TRANSMITTER, its machine processable representation (upper left), the PLIP interpretation associated with the datasets and the processor of the data graph (upper right), the explicit mapping of GMB primitives into the structure (lower left) and the list of attributes

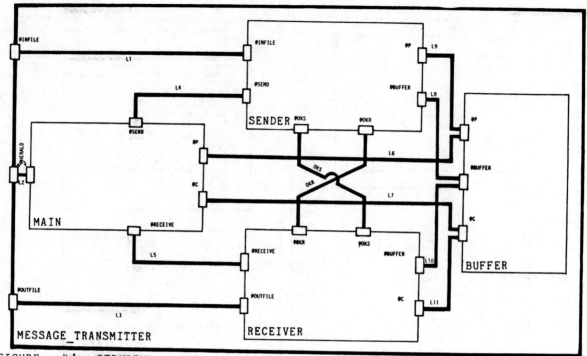

FIGURE   4:   STRUCTURAL MODEL OF MESSAGE_TRANSMITTER PARTIONED INTO FOUR SUBSYSTEMS

for each socket (lower right). Notice that the correspondence between node N2 and processor P2 is indicated in the source GMB code in both the "@nodes" statement and the "@processor" statement. The initial state of the graph is shown to consist of a single token on arc S. The expressions in parentheses after node names contain arc expressions separated by a colon. To the left of the colon one specifies the input logic expression to the node (precondition for its activation); conversely to the right of the colon one specifies the output logic expression (postcondition to its deactivation). Any well-formed logic expression can be used. If the designer is restricted to using the operators AND ("*") and OR ("+") then analysis [GOS72] of control graph properties is made easier.

The above model is read by the SARA translator and simulated, even at this high level, by providing messages in INFILE and observing at the end of simulation that they appear in OUTFILE. MESSAGE TRANSMITTER requirements R6 to R9 could be shown to be satisfied at this level of design. MESSAGE TRANSMITTER requirements R1 to R5 cannot yet be readily satisfied using this high level design and another more detailed level of design is needed.

Designing Message Transmitter

If we had a library of building block programs whose models indicated that they might be linked together to produce a trial solution, we would use such a composition procedure and evaluate it. We assume not and therefore go top down in the design process. We choose to start out by partitioning the structure into four interconnected subsystems: MAIN, SENDER, RECEIVER, and BUFFER. The machine processable structural model is omitted in the interest of terseness but its graphical representation is depicted in Figure 4.

The idea we have in mind at this point (which will be realized as we finish the design) is to have a main program called HERALD and two external procedures, SEND and RECEIVE, plus a shared storage area containing the message buffer.

Statement of Subsystem's Functions

We now develop a list of functional specs for each one of MESSAGE TRANSMITTER's subsystems. At the end of each subsystem requirement we indicate (enclosed in parentheses) the mapping of each one of them into a subset of MESSAGE TRANSMITTER's overall requirements (defined above). We note that all of MESSAGE TRANSMITTER's requirements have been covered. The functional specs are shown mapped onto their subsystem modules in Figure 5.

The Behavioral Model - Level 2

We now refine node N2 and its

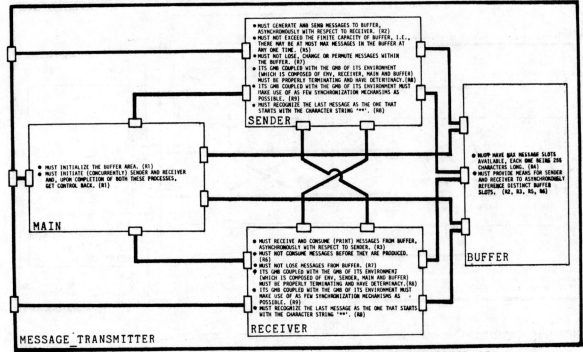

SENDER
- MUST GENERATE AND SEND MESSAGES TO BUFFER, ASYNCHRONOUSLY WITH RESPECT TO RECEIVER. (R2)
- MUST NOT EXCEED THE FINITE CAPACITY OF BUFFER, I.E., THERE MAY BE AT MOST MAX MESSAGES IN THE BUFFER AT ANY ONE TIME. (R5)
- MUST NOT LOSE, CHANGE OR PERMUTE MESSAGES WITHIN THE BUFFER. (R7)
- ITS GMB COUPLED WITH THE GMB OF ITS ENVIRONMENT (WHICH IS COMPOSED OF ENV, RECEIVER, MAIN AND BUFFER) MUST BE PROPERLY TERMINATING AND HAVE DETERMINACY. (R8)
- ITS GMB COUPLED WITH THE GMB OF ITS ENVIRONMENT MUST MAKE USE OF AS FEW SYNCHRONIZATION MECHANISMS AS POSSIBLE. (R9)
- MUST RECOGNIZE THE LAST MESSAGE AS THE ONE THAT STARTS WITH THE CHARACTER STRING '**'. (R8)

MAIN
- MUST INITIALIZE THE BUFFER AREA. (R1)
- MUST INITIATE (CONCURRENTLY) SENDER AND RECEIVER AND, UPON COMPLETION OF BOTH THESE PROCESSES, GET CONTROL BACK. (R1)

BUFFER
- MUST HAVE MAX MESSAGE SLOTS AVAILABLE, EACH ONE BEING 256 CHARACTERS LONG. (R4)
- MUST PROVIDE MEANS FOR SENDER AND RECEIVER TO ASYNCHRONOUSLY REFERENCE DISTINCT BUFFER SLOTS. (R2, R3, R5, R6)

RECEIVER
- MUST RECEIVE AND CONSUME (PRINT) MESSAGES FROM BUFFER, ASYNCHRONOUSLY WITH RESPECT TO SENDER. (R3)
- MUST NOT CONSUME MESSAGES BEFORE THEY ARE PRODUCED. (R6)
- MUST NOT LOSE MESSAGES FROM BUFFER. (R7)
- ITS GMB COUPLED WITH THE GMB OF ITS ENVIRONMENT (WHICH IS COMPOSED OF ENV, SENDER, MAIN AND BUFFER) MUST BE PROPERLY TERMINATING AND HAVE DETERMINACY. (R8)
- ITS GMB COUPLED WITH THE GMB OF ITS ENVIRONMENT MUST MAKE USE OF AS FEW SYNCHRONIZATION MECHANISMS AS POSSIBLE. (R9)
- MUST RECOGNIZE THE LAST MESSAGE AS THE ONE THAT STARTS WITH THE CHARACTER STRING '**'. (R8)

MESSAGE_TRANSMITTER

FIGURE 5: STRUCTURAL MODEL OF MESSAGE TRANSMITTER OF
FIGURE 3 WITH REQUIREMENTS FOR EACH SUBSYSTEM

associated processor P2 (Figure 3), thus producing the Graph Model of Behavior depicted in Figure 6 (control graph) and Figure 7 (data graph). These graphs are shown mapped onto their respective structures. The attributes for each of the sockets of MESSAGE TRANSMITTER's subsystems and the source GMB code corresponding to Figure 6 and 7 are omitted to conserve space.

We notice that in order to synchronize the shared use of the message buffer by the two processes (SENDER and RECEIVER) we create two control arcs (semaphores), OKS and OKR, which indicate to the appropriate process whether or not it is "ok" to send or "ok" to receive messages.

The initial state of the graph is as follows. There is one token on the input arc A1 and MAX (= size of the circular buffer, in messages) tokens on arc OKS. This initial condition guarantees that the only process that can start at the very beginning is the SENDER process. The SENDER process has tokens on each of its required input arcs. The RECEIVER process requires tokens on each of its input arcs and there is initially no token on OKR.

As SENDER places messages in the shared buffer, it places tokens on OKR, thus enabling RECEIVER to receive and consume them asynchronously. Conversely, as RECEIVER consumes messages by taking them out of the buffer, it places tokens (one for each consumed mesage) on OKS.

Evaluation of Subsystem's Behavior

At this point we develop a PLIP interpretation (see Figure 8) associated with the GMB of each of the newly created subsystems (MAIN, SENDER, RECEIVER, BUFFER) and evaluate their behavior against the requirements set for each one of them.

For purposes of validation, a model has been run in the SARA interactive GMB simulator and its behavior satisfied all requirements. As shown in [CAM77], a validated model such as has been developed here can be made to function as an "invariant" specification for any lower level models derived from it.

Code Synthesis --- Bottom-Up Composition

The specification of each of MESSAGE TRANSMITTER's subsystems is completely defined. All four subsystems are simple enough to be directly synthesized from the information gathered so far in the models, and we go bottom-up in the design process.

A few observations are in order. The fact that PLIP is an extension to PL/I via a preprocessor places us in a privileged position to directly synthesize PL/I code. In this case we cannot do it directly because the "standard" PL/I does not support counting semaphores and the associated SIGNAL and WAIT operations. For purposes of this modeling study, let us assume the existence of an extended PL/I machine which does support such data

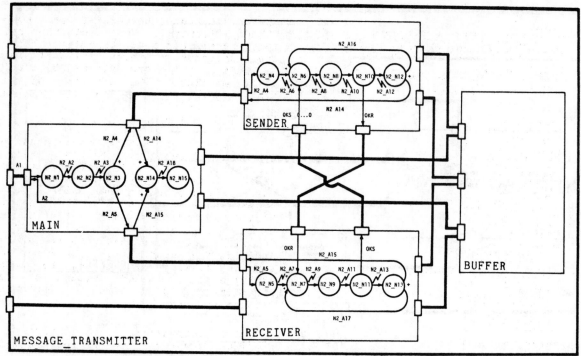

FIGURE 6: CONTROL GRAPH MODELS OF ALL SUBSYSTEMS IN MESSAGE TRANSMITTER SUPERIMPOSED ON THEIR RESPECTIVE STRUCTURAL MODELS

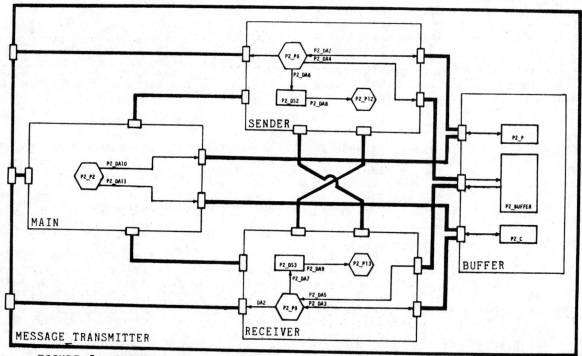

FIGURE 7: DATA GRAPH MODELS OF ALL SUBSYSTEMS IN MESSAGE TRANSMITTER SUPERIMPOSED ON THEIR RESPECTIVE STRUCTURAL MODULES

types. We will try to treat each PL/I statement as a building block model of the corresponding PL/I statement.

In order to be consistent with the overall statement of the design procedure though, we must validate the modeled behavior of MESSAGE TRANSMITTER against the overall requirements set for it during the initial design steps, before we go from model to actual code.

360

```
/*PLIP*/
&dataset INFILE FILE SEQUENTIAL INPUT EXTERNAL
         ENVIRONMENT(U(800) BUFFERS(1) CONSECUTIVE);
&dataset OUTFILE FILE SEQUENTIAL OUTPUT EXTERNAL
         ENVIRONMENT(U(800) BUFFERS(1) CONSECUTIVE);
&dataset P2_DS2 bit(1);
&dataset P2_DS3 bit(1);
&dataset P2_BUFFER(0:MAX-1) character(255);
&dataset P2_F fixed binary(15);
&dataset P2_C fixed binary(15);

&processor P2_P2;
  P2_F = 0;
  P2_C = 0;
&write(P2_F, P2_C);
&endprocessor;

&processor P2_P8;
  dcl MESSAGE character(255);
  get file(INFILE) into(MESSAGE);
  P2_BUFFER(P2_P) = MESSAGE;
&write(P2_BUFFER(P2_P));
  P2_P = mod(P2_P +1, MAX);
&write(P2_P);
  if substr(MESSAGE,1,2) = '**'
    then P2_DS2 = '1'B;
    else P2_DS2 = 'C'B;
&write(P2_DS2);
&endprocessor;

&processor P2_P9;
  dcl MESSAGE character(255);
  &read(P2_BUFFER(P2_C));
  MESSAGE = P2_BUFFER(P2_F);
  write file(OUTFILE) from(MESSAGE);
  P2_C = mod(P2_C +1, MAX);
&write(P2_C);
  if substr(MESSAGE,1,2) = '**'
    then P2_DS3 = '1'B;
    else P2_DS3 = 'C'B;
&write(P2_DS3);
&endprocessor;

&processor P2_P12;
  &read(P2_DS2);
  if P2_DS2 = '0'B
    then &output_arcs = 'P2_A16';
    else &output_arcs = 'P2_A14';
&endprocessor;

&processor P2_P13;
  &read(P2_DS3);
  if P2_DS3 = '0'B
    then &output_arcs = 'P2_A17';
    else &output_arcs = 'P2_A15';
&endprocessor;
```

FIGURE 8

PLIP INTERPRETATIONS FOR DATA GRAPH MODEL
OF MESSAGE_TRANSMITTER IN FIGURE 7

As stated above, we have already validated each of MESSAGE TRANSMITTER's subsystems with respect to their individual subrequirements. It so happens that in this validation process the "driver" that was available to use for evaluation of each subsystem was the model of each subsystem's environment,i.e. the rest of the GMB/PLIP model. As a consequence, in a single simulation session evaluating each of the subsystems, we evaluated the behavior of MESSAGE TRANSMITTER against the requirements set for it in the initial design steps. We are therefore ready to directly synthesize the code (which can be seen as a "fabricated phase" after the modeling has been completed, and we assume that future development of SARA might make this process automatic).

The structural model and the socket attributes of each of MESSAGE TRANSMITTER's subsystems suggest the templates for the code shown in Figure 9 (left). The bodies of HERALD, SEND and RECEIVE are drawn directly from the GMB/PLIP models already developed and validated. All sequential portions of the code are simply appended to each other in the appropriate procedure, as shown in Figure 9 (center). What would then remain to be done would be to transfer to each of the procedures those flow-of-control mechanisms which are provided by the SARA token machine. The effects of such transfers are shown in Figure 9 (right).

Synthesis of HERALD

The interpretation associated with the sub-GMB that has been mapped into the structural model MAIN constitutes the body HERALD. The statements to initialize the buffer are present in the PLIP code for processor P2_P2 (Figure 7). The fact that MAIN gives control concurrently at node N2_N3 (Figure 6) (to the SENDER and RECEIVER processes) and gets it back at node N2_N14 after both processes have terminated will be implied by a pair "cobegin........coend" within the main procedure. This can also be implemented with semaphores.

The activation of the SENDER and RECEIVER processes can be implemented by procedure calls such as
CALL SEND; CALL RECEIVE;

Synthesis of SEND and RECEIVE

The synthesis of the code for both the sender and receiver processes brings out some interesting points. We shall discuss the sender process. The synthesis of the receiver process is, mutatis mutandis, equivalent. Let us analyze node N2_N6 in Figure 6. It is initiated when there is at least one token on OKS and at least one token on either N2_A6 or N2_A16. Given that OKS is a semaphore (notice its absence from the data graph), the need to have at least one token on OKS can be directly satisfied by the statement
WAIT(OKS);

The loop indicated by the control arc N2_A16 is implemented by simply labeling the WAIT(OKS) statement, which becomes
N2_A16: WAIT(OKS);

This is the first executable statement in the body of SEND. Let us now compose the remainder of SEND by declaring as internal variables all those datasets that have been mapped into SENDER in the GMB-to-SL1 mapping (in this case P2_DS2). We concatenate them with the declarations of the internal variables found in the PLIP code of those processors which were also mapped into SENDER. In this case the processors are P2_P8 and P2_P12 and the only internal variable is MESSAGE, declared in processor P2_P8.

We now append all executable statements whithin the PLIP code for processor P2_P8 to those of processor

```
HERALD:PROCEDURE;
    DCL SEND ENTRY EXTERNAL;
    DCL RECEIVE ENTRY EXTERNAL;
    DCL P2_P REAL FIXED BINARY (15,0)
        UNALIGNED STATIC EXTERNAL;
    DCL P2_C REAL FIXED BINARY (15,0)
        UNALIGNED STATIC EXTERNAL;
    ........................
    ........................
    ........................
END HERALD;
```

```
HERALD:PROCEDURE;
    DCL SEND ENTRY EXTERNAL;
    DCL RECEIVE ENTRY EXTERNAL;
    DCL P2_P REAL FIXED BINARY (15,0)
        UNALIGNED STATIC EXTERNAL;
    DCL P2_C REAL FIXED BINARY (15,0)
        UNALIGNED STATIC EXTERNAL;
    P2_P = 0;
    P2_C = 0;
    @WRITE (P2_P,P2_C);
    COBEGIN;
        CALL SEND;
        CALL RECEIVE;
    COEND;
END HERALD;
```

```
HERALD:PROCEDURE;
    DCL SEND ENTRY EXTERNAL;
    DCL RECEIVE ENTRY EXTERNAL;
    DCL P2_P REAL FIXED BINARY (15,0)
        UNALIGNED STATIC EXTERNAL;
    DCL P2_C REAL FIXED BINARY (15,0)
        UNALIGNED STATIC EXTERNAL;
    P2_P = 0;
    P2_C = 0;
    COBEGIN;
        CALL SEND;
        CALL RECEIVE;
    COEND;
END HERALD;
```

```
SEND:PROCEDURE;
    DCL INFILE FILE RECORD SEQUENTIAL INPUT EXTERNAL
        ENVIRONMENT (U(800) BUFFERS(1) CONSECUTIVE);
    DCL OKR SEMAPHORE INITIAL (0) EXTERNAL;
    DCL OKS SEMAPHORE INITIAL (MAX) EXTERNAL;
    DCL P2_BUFFER (0 : MAX-1) CHARACTER (255)
        UNALIGNED STATIC EXTERNAL;
    DCL P2_P REAL FIXED BINARY (15,0)
        UNALIGNED STATIC EXTERNAL;
    ........................
    ........................
    ........................
END SEND;
```

```
SEND:PROCEDURE;
    DCL INFILE FILE RECORD SEQUENTIAL INPUT EXTERNAL
        ENVIRONMENT (U(800) BUFFERS(1) CONSECUTIVE;
    DCL OKR SEMAPHORE INITIAL (0) EXTERNAL;
    DCL OKS SEMAPHORE INITIAL (MAX) EXTERNAL;
    DCL P2_BUFFER (0 : MAX-1) CHARACTER (255)
        UNALIGNED STATIC EXTERNAL;
    DCL P2_P REAL FIXED BINARY (15,0)
        UNALIGNED STATIC EXTERNAL;
    DCL P2_DS2 BIT (1);
    DCL MESSAGE CHARACTER (255);
N2_A16:  WAIT(OKS);
        GET FILE(INFILE) INTO(MESSAGE);
        P2_BUFFER(P2_P) = MESSAGE;
        @WRITE(P2_BUFFER(P2_P));
        P2_P = MOD(P2_P + 1,MAX);
        @WRITE(P2_P);
        SIGNAL(OKR);
        IF SUBSTR (MESSAGE,1,2) = '**'
            THEN P2_DS2 = '1'B;
            ELSE P2_DS2 = '0'B;
        @WRITE(P2_DS2);
        @READ(P2_DS2);
        IF P2_DS2 = '0'B
            THEN @OUTPUT_ARCS = 'N2_A16';
            ELSE @OUTPUT_ARCS = 'N2_A14';
END SEND;
```

```
SEND:PROCEDURE;
    DCL INFILE FILE RECORD SEQUENTIAL INPUT EXTERNAL
        ENVIRONMENT(U(800) BUFFERS(1) CONSECUTIVE);
    DCL OKR SEMAPHORE INITIAL(0) EXTERNAL;
    DCL OKS SEMAPHORE INITIAL(MAX) EXTERNAL;
    DCL P2_BUFFER(0 : MAX-1) CHARACTER(255)
        UNALIGNED STATIC EXTERNAL;
    DCL P2_P REAL FIXED BINARY(15,0)
        UNALIGNED STATIC EXTERNAL;
    DCL P2_DS2 BIT(1);
    DCL MESSAGE CHARACTER(255);
N2_A16: WAIT(OKS);
        GET FILE(INFILE) INTO(MESSAGE);
        P2_BUFFER(P2_P) = MESSAGE;
        P2_P = MOD(P2_P+1,MAX);
        SIGNAL(OKR);
        IF SUBSTR(MESSAGE,1,2) = '**'
            THEN P2_DS2 = '1'B;
            ELSE P2_DS2 = '0'B;
        IF P2_DS2 = '0'B;
            THEN GO TO N2_A16
            ELSE RETURN;
END SEND;
```

```
RECEIVE:PROCEDURE;
    DCL OUTFILE FILE RECORD SEQUENTIAL OUTPUT EXTERNAL
        ENVIRONMENT (U(800) BUFFERS(1) CONSECUTIVE);
    DCL OKR SEMAPHORE INITIAL (0) EXTERNAL;
    DCL OKS SEMAPHORE INITIAL (MAX) EXTERNAL;
    DCL P2_BUFFER (0 : MAX-1) CHARACTER(255)
        UNALIGNED STATIC EXTERNAL;
    DCL P2_C REAL FIXED BINARY (15,0)
        UNALIGNED STATIC EXTERNAL;
    ........................
    ........................
    ........................
END RECEIVE;
```

```
RECEIVE:PROCEDURE;
    DCL OUTFILE FILE RECORD SEQUENTIAL OUTPUT EXTERNAL
        ENVIRONMENT (U(800) BUFFERS(1) CONSECUTIVE);
    DCL OKR SEMAPHORE INITIAL (0) EXTERNAL;
    DCL OKS SEMAPHORE INITIAL (MAX) EXTERNAL;
    DCL P2_BUFFER (0 : MAX-1) CHARACTER (255)
        UNALIGNED STATIC EXTERNAL;
    DCL P2_C REAL FIXED BINARY (15,0)
        UNALIGNED STATIC EXTERNAL;
    DCL P2_DS3 BIT (1);
    DCL MESSAGE CHARACTER (255);
N2_A17:  WAIT(OKR);
        @READ(P2_BUFFER (P2_C));
        MESSAGE = P2_BUFFER(P2_P);
        WRITE FILE(OUTFILE) FROM(MESSAGE);
        P2_C = MOD(P2_C+1,MAX);
        @WRITE(P2_C);
        IF SUBSTR(MESSAGE,1,2) = '**'
            THEN P2_DS3 = '1'B;
            ELSE P2_DS3 = '0'B;
        @WRITE(P2_DS3);
        @READ(P2_DS3);
        IF P2_DS3 = '0'B
            THEN @OUTPUT_ARCS = 'N2_A17';
            ELSE @OUTPUT_ARCS = 'N2_A15';
END RECEIVE;
```

```
RECEIVE: PROCEDURE;
    DCL OUTFILE FILE RECORD SEQUENTIAL OUTPUT EXTERNAL
        ENVIRONMENT(U(800) BUFFERS(1) CONSECUTIVE);
    DCL OKR SEMAPHORE INITIAL(0) EXTERNAL;
    DCL OKS SEMAPHONE INITIAL(MAX) EXTERNAL;
    DCL P2_BUFFER(0 : MAX-1) CHARACTER(255)
        UNALIGNED STATIC EXTERNAL;
    DCL P2_P REAL FIXED BINARY(15,0)
        UNALIGNED STATIC EXTERNAL;
    DCL P2_DS3 BIT(1);
    DCL MESSAGE CHARACTER(255);
N2_A17: WAIT(OKS);
        MESSAGE = P2_BUFFER(P2-P);
        WRITE FILE(OUTFILE) FROM(MESSAGE);
        P2_C = MOD(P2_C+1,MAX);
        SIGNAL(OKS);
        IF SUBSTR(MESSAGE,1,2) = '**'
            THEN P2_DS3 = '1'B;
            ELSE P2_DS3 = '0'B;
        IF P2_DS3 = '0'B
            THEN GO TO N2_A17;
            ELSE RETURN;
END RECEIVE;
```

FIGURE 9:   TEMPLATES(left), TEMPLATES WITH CONCATENATED CODE
            BODIES(center), FINAL CODE(right)

P2_P12. The result of these operations is shown in figure 9 (center).

The next "cleaning-up" step consists of deleting all the @READ and @WRITE statements from the code, since they are only used by the SARA GMB simulator. What remains to be done now is simply substitute the flow-of-control implied by the "@OUTPUT ARCS='arcname'" by PL/I constructs. The PLIP statement
@OUTPUT ARCS = 'N2_A16'; is replaced by
GO TO N2_A16;
and the PLIP statement
@OUTPUT ARCS = 'N2_A14';
is replaced by

RETURN;
The final code for HERALD, SEND and RECEIVE is shown in Figure 9 (right).

Summary and Conclusions

Structural Modeling

The SARA structural model has the objective of naming the components of hierarchical modular systems and defining the interconnections among these components.

There is no semantic information explicitly communicated by a SARA structural model, and even when the identifiers used to name components might suggest what their intended function is, no behavior can be deduced from it. The structural model simply defines interconnected modules at the various levels of abstraction, thus creating a name space to serve as a basis for the synthesis of behavioral models of a system.

Each of the components of a structural model is ultimately named as responsible for contributing to carrying out at least one of the requirements which drive the design of a particular system, but again, only the behavioral models shall have the power to describe how or when a component performs its intended function. Therefore, no particular flow of resources of any kind can be deduced from a structural model. Only the potential for resource flow between two structures can be deduced from the existence of an interconnection between them.

A structural model may be created by both top-down and bottom-up design strategies. At any given level, it allows for graph representation of communication between components. In a structural model a designer declares conception of a system with regard to the number of components, their names and the allowable communication paths between them.

Behavioral Modeling

Flow of Control

When modeling software systems, the flow-of control graph shows an uninterpreted model of the execution of possibly concurrent processes. These processes are modeled by the nodes in a control graph. Potential concurrency is shown by the control logic expresions involving inbranching and outbranching control arcs.

Flow of Data

The objective of the flow of data model is to show potential activations of data paths between processors and datasets. With the mapping of the behavioral model (both flow of control and flow of data) onto the structural model, SARA gathers information about visibility of resource names among the structural elements of a system. The term resource name is used here to denote that class of names which can actually be made available for reference in a program i.e., which actually define a modules environment.

In PL/I, for example, the class of names which can actually be made available for reference between components of a multiple-module system is composed of procedure entry-point names and external identifiers representing variable names. Similar constructs are available in most high-level algorithmic programming languages at current use.

As a superstructure to be imposed upon the final code or software systems, the structural and behavioral models have the following objectives:
-- To show the potential flow of resource names between the structural components of a software system.

-- To give a designer complete control over the distribution of information betwen modules. Sockets are the place where one states one's intent with regards to identifier visibility and access rights among modules at any level. The sharing of resource names is facilitated, without unwanted spread of accessibility, that is, different types of access are distinguishable (read-only, read-write), and access to different subsets of a set of ressources can be specified. The idea here is to enforce the specifications over the source code at compile/link time.
-- Both top-down and bottom-up design strategies are supported by multilevel modeling facilities.
-- Hierarchical organization is enforced, and the structural model, in conjunction with the flow-of-control and flow-of-data models, can keep around conceptual entities that would otherwise vanish in the design process. The whole design tree is kept, not just the leaves, thus making the final product comprehensible both top-down and bottom-up. The SL1 model and the list of attributes associated with each of its sockets encompass what has been proposed in the literature [DKR75], [THO76] as a MIL (Module Interconnection Language). Our approach is more general in that we can define and enforce interface commitments among concurrent software systems.
-- To increase the validity of the final product, all mappings and checks for completeness and consistency can be done with machine assistance through SARA.

With respect to flow-of-control, for example, SARA provides analysis facilities to check for proper-termination. A properly terminating flow-of-control model is reentrant, deadlock-free and has determinacy, i.e., regardless of the relative order of execution of the subprocesses involved, the result is always the same.

The main contribution of the SARA system for software synthesis is the fact that it offers a continuous path from programming-in-the-large all the way down to programming-in-the-small of possibly concurrent systems, while providing a designer with interactive tools and checking procedures to enforce consistency between requirements, structure, function and behavior.

There are a number of issues which require further study:

-- The statement of requirements of a design is the cornerstone of the use of the design methodology. So far the English language description of this set is used in SARA. A more formal scheme for describing requirements is needed, as well as the associated criteria to evaluate whether or not a given design satisfies the previously stated set of requirements.

-- The structural and behavioral models cited in this paper (SL1 and GMB) are restricted to representing static topologies. We currently handle any dynamic behavior in the interpretation associated with the data graph (i.e., in PLIP).

-- Refinement and abstraction rules for GMB primitives are proposed in [CAM77], but they are fairly restrictive, in the sense that only single-entry/single-exit control graphs can be abstracted into a single primitive, and conversely.

-- Many interesting asynchronous systems, especially in the process-control area are interrupt-driven. The modeling of interrupts in a GMB generates at least two control arcs per interrupt, which tends to overcrowd the control graph.

-- We have mentioned above that the SL1 model together with the list of attributes of each of its sockets encompass what has been proposed in the literature as a Module Interconnection Language (MIL). An interesting project is to couple this information with the linkage editor of some computing system and provide users with the ability to specify and machine-check the consistency of bindings at various levels of abstraction.

-- Currently, the only way two GMB processors can transfer information between them is through the use of datasets, which act as external (global) variables for the processors involved.

REFERENCES

[CAM77] Campos, I.M., "Multilevel Modeling for Synthesis of Reliable Concurrent Software Systems", Ph.D. Dissertation, Computer Science Department, University of California, Los Angeles, 1977.

[CER72] Cerf, V.G., "Multiprocessors, Semaphores, and a Graph Model of Computation", Report UCLA-ENG-7223, Computer Science Department, UCLA, April 1972.

[CRO77] Crocker, Stephen D., "State Deltas: A Formalism for Representing Segments of Computation," Ph.D. in Computer Science, University of California, Los Angeles, August 1977.

[DDH72] Dahl, O.J., E.W. Dijkstra and C.A.R. Hoare, Structured Programming, Academic Press, London, 1972.

[DEN73] Dennis, J.E., "Modularity", in F.L. Bauer (ed.) Advanced Course on Software Engineering, Springer-Verlag, New York, 1973.

[DIJ72] Dijkstra, E.W., "The Humble Programmer", 1972 ACM Turing Award Lecture, CACM 15:10 (October 1972), pp. 859-866.

[DRK75] DeRemer, F. and H.H. Kron, "Programming-in-the-Large versus Programming-in-the-Small", Proceedings of International Conference on Reliable Software in SIGPLAN Notices 10:6 (June 1975), pp. 114-121.

[EMU72] Estrin, G., R.R. Muntz and R. Uzgalis, "Modeling, measurement and Computer Power", AFIPS Conference Proceedings, Vol. 40, pp.725-738, Spring Joint Computer Conference, 1972.

[EST63] Estrin, G. and R. Turn, "Automatic Assignment of Computations in a VAriable Structure Computer System", IEEE Transactions on Electronic Computers, Vol. EC 12, No. 5, December 1963.

[EST78] Estrin, Gerald "A Methodology for Design of Digital Systems - Supported by SARA at the Age of One". AFIPS Conference Proceedings, Vo. 47, 1978 National Computer Conference.

[FEN77] Fenchel, R.S., "System Architect's Apprentice (SARA) System Reference Manual", Computer Science

Department, University of California, Los Angeles, May 1977.

[GAR75] Gardner, Jr., R.I., "A Methodology for Digital System Design Based on Structural and Functional Modelilng", Report UCLA-ENG-7488, University of California, Los Angeles, CA., January 1975.

[GCE72] Gostelow, K.P., V.G. Cerf, G. Estrin and S. Volansky, "Proper Termination of Flow-of-Control in Programs Involving Concurrent Processes", Proceedings of the ACM Annual Conference, Boston, August 1972, pp.742-754.

[LIZ74] Liskov, B.H. and S.N. Zilles "Programming with Abstract Data Types", Proceedings of a Symposium on Very High Level Languages, in SIGPLAN Notices 9:4 (April 1974), pp. 50-59.

[ME67] Martin, D.F. and G. Estrin, "Experiments on Models of Computations and Systems", IEEE Transactions on Electronic Computers, Vol. EC-16, No. 1, Feb. 1967, pp. 59-69.

[MGK75] McGowan, C.L. and J.R. Kelly, Top-Down Structured Programming Techniques, Petrocelli/Charter, New York, N.Y. 1975.

[OVE77] Overman, W.T., "Formal Verification of GMBs", Internal Memorandum, Computer Science Department, University of California, Los Angeles, July 1977.

[PAL77] Proceedings of Symposium on Design Automation and Microprocessors, Palo Alto, CA., Feb. 24-25.

[PAR75] Parnas, D.L., "The Influence of Software Structure on Reliability", SIGPLAN Notices 10:6 (June 1975).

[PA72a] Parnas, D.L., "A Technique for Software Module Specificationns with Examples", CACM 15:5 (May 1972), pp. 330-336.

[PA72b] Parnas, D.L., "On the Criteria to be Used for Decomposing Systems into Modules", CACM 15:12 (December 1972), pp. 1053-1058.

[PBH73] Brinch-Hansen, P., Operating Systems Principles, Prentice-Hall, Englewood Cliffs, N.J. 1973

[POP76] Popek, G., J.J. Horning, B.W. Lampson, R. London, J. Mitchell, "Notes on the Design of Euclid", Proceedings of the ACM Conference on Language Design for Reliable Software, Raleigh, North Carolina, March 28-30, 1978.

[POS74] Postel, J.B., "A Graph Model Analysis of Computer Communications Protocols", Ph.D. Dissertation in Computer Science, UCLA, 1974.

[PTA69] Potash, H.A. Tyrill, D. Allen, S. Joseph and G. Estrin, "DCDS digital simulating system", AFIPS conference Proceedings, Vol. 35, Fall Joint Computer Conference, 1969.

[THO76] Thomas, J.W., "Module Interconnection in Programming Systems Supporting Abstraction", Computer Science Program Technical Report No. CS-16, Brown University, Providence, R.I., April 1976.

[WIN72] Wingfield, M.A., "The Design of an Extensible Processor", Ph.D. in Engineering, University of California, Los Angeles, CA., June 1970.

[WIR71] Wirth, N., "Program Development by Stepwise Refinement", CACM 14:4 (April 1971), pp. 221-227.

[WUL74] Wulf, W.A., "ALPHARD: Toward a Language to Support Structured Programs", Technical Report, Carnegie-Mellon University, April 1974.

[YAV74] Yavne, M. "Synthesis of Properly Terminating Graphs", Report UCLA-ENG-7434, Computer Science DEpartment, UCLA, May 1974.

[YCO76] Yourdon, E. and L.L. Constantine, Structured Design, Yourdon Inc., New York 1976.

"Communicating Sequential Processes" by C.A.R. Hoare from *Communications of the ACM*, August 1978, pages 666–677. Copyright 1978. Association for Computing Machinery, Inc., reprinted by permission.

Programming   S. L. Graham, R. L. Rivest
Techniques   Editors

Communicating Sequential Processes

C.A.R. Hoare
The Queen's University
Belfast, Northern Ireland

This paper suggests that input and output are basic primitives of programming and that parallel composition of communicating sequential processes is a fundamental program structuring method. When combined with a development of Dijkstra's guarded command, these concepts are surprisingly versatile. Their use is illustrated by sample solutions of a variety of familiar programming exercises.

Key Words and Phrases: programming, programming languages, programming primitives, program structures, parallel programming, concurrency, input, output, guarded commands, nondeterminacy, coroutines, procedures, multiple entries, multiple exits, classes, data representations, recursion, conditional critical regions, monitors, iterative arrays

CR Categories: 4.20, 4.22, 4.32

1. Introduction

Among the primitive concepts of computer programming, and of the high level languages in which programs are expressed, the action of assignment is familiar and well understood. In fact, any change of the internal state of a machine executing a program can be modeled as an assignment of a new value to some variable part of that machine. However, the operations of input and output, which affect the external environment of a machine, are not nearly so well understood. They are often added to a programming language only as an afterthought.

Among the structuring methods for computer pro-

This research was supported by a Senior Fellowship of the Science Research Council.

Author's present address: Programming Research Group, 45, Banbury Road, Oxford, England.

grams, three basic constructs have received widespread recognition and use: A repetitive construct (e.g. the **while** loop), an alternative construct (e.g. the conditional **if..then..else**), and normal sequential program composition (often denoted by a semicolon). Less agreement has been reached about the design of other important program structures, and many suggestions have been made: Subroutines (Fortran), procedures (Algol 60 [15]), entries (PL/I), coroutines (UNIX [17]), classes (SIMULA 67 [5]), processes and monitors (Concurrent Pascal [2]), clusters (CLU [13]), forms (ALPHARD [19]), actors (Hewitt [1]).

The traditional stored program digital computer has been designed primarily for deterministic execution of a single sequential program. Where the desire for greater speed has led to the introduction of parallelism, every attempt has been made to disguise this fact from the programmer, either by hardware itself (as in the multiple function units of the CDC 6600) or by the software (as in an I/O control package, or a multiprogrammed operating system). However, developments of processor technology suggest that a multiprocessor machine, constructed from a number of similar self-contained processors (each with its own store), may become more powerful, capacious, reliable, and economical than a machine which is disguised as a monoprocessor.

In order to use such a machine effectively on a single task, the component processors must be able to communicate and to synchronize with each other. Many methods of achieving this have been proposed. A widely adopted method of communication is by inspection and updating of a common store (as in Algol 68 [18], PL/I, and many machine codes). However, this can create severe problems in the construction of correct programs and it may lead to expense (e.g. crossbar switches) and unreliability (e.g. glitches) in some technologies of hardware implementation. A greater variety of methods has been proposed for synchronization: semaphores [6], events (PL/I), conditional critical regions [10], monitors and queues (Concurrent Pascal [2]), and path expressions [3]. Most of these are demonstrably adequate for their purpose, but there is no widely recognized criterion for choosing between them.

This paper makes an ambitious attempt to find a single simple solution to all these problems. The essential proposals are:

(1) Dijkstra's guarded commands [8] are adopted (with a slight change of notation) as sequential control structures, and as the sole means of introducing and controlling nondeterminism.

(2) A parallel command, based on Dijkstra's *parbegin* [6], specifies concurrent execution of its constituent sequential commands (processes). All the processes start simultaneously, and the parallel command ends only when they are all finished. They may not communicate with each other by updating global variables.

(3) Simple forms of input and output command are introduced. They are used for communication between concurrent processes.

(4) Such communication occurs when one process names another as destination for output *and* the second process names the first as source for input. In this case, the value to be output is copied from the first process to the second. There is *no* automatic buffering: In general, an input or output command is delayed until the other process is ready with the corresponding output or input. Such delay is invisible to the delayed process.

(5) Input commands may appear in guards. A guarded command with an input guard is selected for execution only if and when the source named in the input command is ready to execute the corresponding output command. If several input guards of a set of alternatives have ready destinations, only one is selected and the others have *no* effect; but the choice between them is arbitrary. In an efficient implementation, an output command which has been ready for a long time should be favored; but the definition of a language cannot specify this since the relative speed of execution of the processes is undefined.

(6) A repetitive command may have input guards. If all the sources named by them have terminated, then the repetitive command also terminates.

(7) A simple pattern-matching feature, similar to that of [16], is used to discriminate the structure of an input message, and to access its components in a secure fashion. This feature is used to inhibit input of messages that do not match the specified pattern.

The programs expressed in the proposed language are intended to be implementable both by a conventional machine with a single main store, and by a fixed network of processors connected by input/output channels (although very different optimizations are appropriate in the different cases). It is consequently a rather static language: The text of a program determines a fixed upper bound on the number of processes operating concurrently; there is no recursion and no facility for process-valued variables. In other respects also, the language has been stripped to the barest minimum necessary for explanation of its more novel features.

The concept of a communicating sequential process is shown in Sections 3–5 to provide a method of expressing solutions to many simple programming exercises which have previously been employed to illustrate the use of various proposed programming language features. This suggests that the process may constitute a synthesis of a number of familiar and new programming ideas. The reader is invited to skip the examples which do not interest him.

However, this paper also ignores many serious problems. The most serious is that it fails to suggest any proof method to assist in the development and verification of correct programs. Secondly, it pays no attention to the problems of efficient implementation, which may be particularly serious on a traditional sequential computer. It is probable that a solution to these problems will require (1) imposition of restrictions in the use of the proposed features; (2) reintroduction of distinctive no-

tations for the most common and useful special cases; (3) development of automatic optimization techniques; and (4) the design of appropriate hardware.

Thus the concepts and notations introduced in this paper (although described in the next section in the form of a programming language fragment) should not be regarded as suitable for use as a programming language, either for abstract or for concrete programming. They are at best only a partial solution to the problems tackled. Further discussion of these and other points will be found in Section 7.

2. Concepts and Notations

The style of the following description is borrowed from Algol 60 [15]. Types, declarations, and expressions have not been treated; in the examples, a Pascal-like notation [20] has usually been adopted. The curly braces { } have been introduced into BNF to denote none or more repetitions of the enclosed material. (Sentences in parentheses refer to an implementation: they are not strictly part of a language definition.)

```
<command> := <simple command>|<structured command>
<simple command> := <null command>|<assignment command>
    |<input command>|<output command>
<structured command> := <alternative command>
    |<repetitive command>|<parallel command>
<null command> := skip
<command list> := {<declaration>; |<command>;} <command>
```

A command specifies the behavior of a device executing the command. It may succeed or fail. Execution of a simple command, if successful, may have an effect on the internal state of the executing device (in the case of assignment), or on its external environment (in the case of output), or on both (in the case of input). Execution of a structured command involves execution of some or all of its constituent commands, and if any of these fail, so does the structured command. (In this case, whenever possible, an implementation should provide some kind of comprehensible error diagnostic message.)

A null command has no effect and never fails.

A command list specifies sequential execution of its constituent commands in the order written. Each declaration introduces a fresh variable with a scope which extends from its declaration to the end of the command list.

2.1 Parallel Commands

```
<parallel command> := [<process>{||<process>}]
<process> := <process label> <command list>
<process label> := <empty>|<identifier> ::
    |<identifier>(<label subscript>{,<label subscript>}) ::
<label subscript> := <integer constant>|<range>
<integer constant> := <numeral>|<bound variable>
<bound variable> := <identifier>
<range> := <bound variable>:<lower bound>..<upper bound>
<lower bound> := <integer constant>
<upper bound> := <integer constant>
```

Each process of a parallel command must be *disjoint* from every other process of the command, in the sense that it does not mention any variable which occurs as a target variable (see Sections 2.2 and 2.3) in any other process.

A process label without subscripts, or one whose label subscripts are all integer constants, serves as a name for the command list to which it is prefixed; its scope extends over the whole of the parallel command. A process whose label subscripts include one or more ranges stands for a series of processes, each with the same label and command list, except that each has a different combination of values substituted for the bound variables. These values range between the lower bound and the upper bound inclusive. For example, $X(i:1..n) :: CL$ stands for

$$X(1) :: CL_1 || X(2) :: CL_2 || ... || X(n) :: CL_n$$

where each CL_j is formed from CL by replacing every occurrence of the bound variable i by the numeral j. After all such expansions, each process label in a parallel command must occur only once and the processes must be well formed and disjoint.

A parallel command specifies concurrent execution of its constituent processes. They all start simultaneously and the parallel command terminates successfully only if and when they have all successfully terminated. The relative speed with which they are executed is arbitrary.
Examples:

(1) [cardreader?cardimage||lineprinter!lineimage]

Performs the two constituent commands in parallel, and terminates only when both operations are complete. The time taken may be as low as the longer of the times taken by each constituent process, i.e. the sum of its computing, waiting, and transfer times.

(2) [west :: DISASSEMBLE||X :: SQUASH||east :: ASSEMBLE]

The three processes have the names "west," "X," and "east." The capitalized words stand for command lists which will be defined in later examples.

(3) [room :: ROOM||fork(i:0..4) :: FORK||phil(i:0..4) :: PHIL]

There are eleven processes. The behavior of "room" is specified by the command list ROOM. The behavior of the five processes fork(0), fork(1), fork(2), fork(3), fork(4), is specified by the command list FORK, within which the bound variable i indicates the identity of the particular fork. Similar remarks apply to the five processes PHIL.

2.2 Assignment Commands

```
<assignment command> ::= <target variable> := <expression>
<expression> ::= <simple expression>|<structured expression>
<structured expression> ::= <constructor>(<expression list>)
<constructor> ::= <identifier>|<empty>
<expression list> ::= <empty>|<expression>{,<expression>}
<target variable> ::= <simple variable>|<structured target>
<structured target> ::= <constructor>(<target variable list>)
<target variable list> ::= <empty>|<target variable>
    {,<target variable>}
```

An expression denotes a value which is computed by an executing device by application of its constituent operators to the specified operands. The value of an expression is undefined if any of these operations are undefined. The value denoted by a simple expression may be simple or structured. The value denoted by a structured expression is structured; its constructor is that of the expression, and its components are the list of values denoted by the constituent expressions of the expression list.

An assignment command specifies evaluation of its expression, and assignment of the denoted value to the target variable. A simple target variable may have assigned to it a simple or a structured value. A structured target variable may have assigned to it a structured value, with the same constructor. The effect of such assignment is to assign to each constituent simpler variable of the structured target the value of the corresponding component of the structured value. Consequently, the value denoted by the target variable, if evaluated *after* a successful assignment, is the same as the value denoted by the expression, as evaluated *before* the assignment.

An assignment fails if the value of its expression is undefined, or if that value does not *match* the target variable, in the following sense: A *simple* target variable matches any value of its type. A *structured* target variable matches a structured value, provided that: (1) they have the same constructor, (2) the target variable list is the same length as the list of components of the value, (3) each target variable of the list matches the corresponding component of the value list. A structured value with no components is known as a "signal."

Examples:

(1) $x := x + 1$ — the value of x after the assignment is the same as the value of $x + 1$ before.

(2) $(x, y) := (y, x)$ — exchanges the values of x and y.

(3) $x := cons(left, right)$ — constructs a structured value and assigns it to x.

(4) $cons(left, right) := x$ — fails if x does not have the form $cons(y, z)$; but if it does, then y is assigned to left, and z is assigned to right.

(5) $insert(n) := insert(2*x + 1)$ — equivalent to $n := 2*x + 1$.

(6) $c := P()$ — assigns to c a "signal" with constructor P, and no components.

(7) $P() := c$ — fails if the value of c is not P(); otherwise has no effect.

(8) $insert(n) := has(n)$ — fails, due to mismatch.

Note: Successful execution of both (3) and (4) ensures the truth of the postcondition $x = cons(left, right)$; but (3) does so by changing x and (4) does so by changing left and right. Example (4) will fail if there is *no* value of left and right which satisfies the postcondition.

2.3 Input and Output Commands

```
<input command> ::= <source>?<target variable>
<output command> ::= <destination>!<expression>
<source> ::= <process name>
```

```
<destination> ::= <process name>
<process name> ::= <identifier>|<identifier>(<subscripts>)
<subscripts> ::= <integer expression>{,<integer expression>}
```

Input and output commands specify communication between two concurrently operating sequential processes. Such a process may be implemented in hardware as a special-purpose device (e.g. cardreader or lineprinter), or its behavior may be specified by one of the constituent processes of a parallel command. Communication occurs between two processes of a parallel command whenever (1) an input command in one process specifies as its source the process name of the other process; (2) an output command in the other process specifies as its destination the process name of the first process; and (3) the target variable of the input command matches the value denoted by the expression of the output command. On these conditions, the input and output commands are said to *correspond*. Commands which correspond are executed simultaneously, and their combined effect is to assign the value of the expression of the output command to the target variable of the input command.

An input command fails if its source is terminated. An output command fails if its destination is terminated or if its expression is undefined.

(The requirement of synchronization of input and output commands means that an implementation will have to delay whichever of the two commands happens to be ready first. The delay is ended when the corresponding command in the other process is also ready, or when the other process terminates. In the latter case the first command fails. It is also possible that the delay will never be ended, for example, if a group of processes are attempting communication but none of their input and output commands correspond with each other. This form of failure is known as a deadlock.)

Examples:

(1) cardreader?cardimage	from cardreader, read a card and assign its value (an array of characters) to the variable cardimage
(2) lineprinter!lineimage	to lineprinter, send the value of lineimage for printing
(3) $X?(x, y)$	from process named X, input a pair of values and assign them to x and y
(4) DIV!($3*a + b$, 13)	to process DIV, output the two specified values.

Note: If a process named DIV issues command (3), and a process named X issues command (4), these are executed simultaneously, and have the same effect as the assignment: $(x, y) := (3*a + b, 13)$ ($\equiv x := 3*a + b; y := 13$).

(5) console(i)?c	from the ith element of an array of consoles, input a value and assign it to c
(6) console($j - 1$)!"A"	to the $(j - 1)$th console, output character "A"
(7) $X(i)$?V( )	from the ith of an array of processes X, input a signal V( ); refuse to input any other signal
(8) sem!P( )	to sem output a signal P( )

2.4 Alternative and Repetitive Commands

```
<repetitive command> ::=*<alternative command>
<alternative command> ::= [<guarded command>
      {[]<guarded command>}]
<guarded command> ::= <guard> → <command list>
      |(<range>{,<range>})<guard> → <command list>
<guard> ::= <guard list>|<guard list>;<input command>
      |<input command>
      <guard list> ::= <guard element>{;<guard element>}
<guard element> ::= <boolean expression>|<declaration>
```

A guarded command with one or more ranges stands for a series of guarded commands, each with the same guard and command list, except that each has a different combination of values substituted for the bound variables. The values range between the lower bound and upper bound inclusive. For example, $(i:1..n)G \rightarrow CL$ stands for

$$G_1 \rightarrow CL_1[]G_2 \rightarrow CL_2[]...[]G_n \rightarrow CL_n$$

where each $G_j \rightarrow CL_j$ is formed from $G \rightarrow CL$ by replacing every occurrence of the bound variable i by the numeral j.

A guarded command is executed only if and when the execution of its guard does not fail. First its guard is executed and then its command list. A guard is executed by execution of its constituent elements from left to right. A Boolean expression is evaluated: If it denotes false, the guard fails; but an expression that denotes true has no effect. A declaration introduces a fresh variable with a scope that extends from the declaration to the end of the guarded command. An input command at the end of a guard is executed only if and when a corresponding output command is executed. (An implementation may test whether a guard fails simply by trying to execute it, and discontinuing execution if and when it fails. This is valid because such a discontinued execution has no effect on the state of the executing device.)

An alternative command specifies execution of exactly one of its constituent guarded commands. Consequently, if all guards fail, the alternative command fails. Otherwise an arbitrary one with successfully executable guard is selected and executed. (An implementation should take advantage of its freedom of selection to ensure efficient execution and good response. For example, when input commands appear as guards, the command which corresponds to the earliest ready and matching output command should in general be preferred; and certainly, no executable and ready output command should be passed over unreasonably often.)

A repetitive command specifies as many iterations as possible of its constituent alternative command. Consequently, when all guards fail, the repetitive command terminates with no effect. Otherwise, the alternative command is executed once and then the whole repetitive command is executed again. (Consider a repetitive command when all its true guard lists end in an input guard. Such a command may have to be delayed until either (1) an output command corresponding to one of the input

369

guards becomes ready, or (2) all the sources named by the input guards have terminated. In case (2), the repetitive command terminates. If neither event ever occurs, the process fails (in deadlock.)
Examples:

(1) $[x \geq y \rightarrow m := x [] y \geq x \rightarrow m := y]$

If $x \geq y$, assign x to m; if $y \geq x$ assign y to m; if both $x \geq y$ and $y \geq x$, either assignment can be executed.

(2) $i := 0; *[i < \text{size}; \text{content}(i) \neq n \rightarrow i := i + 1]$

The repetitive command scans the elements content(i), for $i = 0, 1, \ldots$, until either $i \geq$ size, or a value equal to n is found.

(3) $*[c:\text{character}; \text{west}?c \rightarrow \text{east}!c]$

This reads all the characters output by west, and outputs them one by one to east. The repetition terminates when the process west terminates.

(4) $*[(i:1..10)\text{continue}(i); \text{console}(i)?c \rightarrow X!(i, c); \text{console}(i)!\text{ack}();$
$\quad \text{continue}(i) := (c \neq \text{sign off})]$

This command inputs repeatedly from any of ten consoles, provided that the corresponding element of the Boolean array continue is true. The bound variable i identifies the originating console. Its value, together with the character just input, is output to X, and an acknowledgment signal is sent back to the originating console. If the character indicated "sign off," continue(i) is set false, to prevent further input from that console. The repetitive command terminates when all ten elements of continue are false. (An implementation should ensure that no console which is ready to provide input will be ignored unreasonably often.)

(5) $*[n:\text{integer}; X?\text{insert}(n) \rightarrow \text{INSERT}$
$\quad []n:\text{integer}; X?\text{has}(n) \rightarrow \text{SEARCH}; X!(i < \text{size})$
$\quad]$

(Here, and elsewhere, capitalized words INSERT and SEARCH stand as abbreviations for program text defined separately.)
On each iteration this command accepts from X either (a) a request to "insert(n)," (followed by INSERT) *or* (b) a question "has(n)," to which it outputs an answer back to X. The choice between (a) and (b) is made by the next output command in X. The repetitive command terminates when X does. If X sends a nonmatching message, deadlock will result.

(6) $*[X?V() \rightarrow \text{val} := \text{val} + 1$
$\quad []\text{val} > 0; Y?P() \rightarrow \text{val} := \text{val} - 1$
$\quad]$

On each iteration, accept *either* a V() signal from X and increment val, *or* a P() signal from Y, and decrement val. But the second alternative cannot be selected unless val is positive (after which val will remain invariantly nonnegative). (When val > 0, the choice depends on the relative speeds of X and Y, and is not determined.) The repetitive command will terminate when both X and Y are terminated, or when X is terminated and val $\leq$ 0.

3. Coroutines

In parallel programming coroutines appear as a more fundamental program structure than subroutines, which can be regarded as a special case (treated in the next section).

3.1 COPY
Problem: Write a process X to copy characters output by process west to process east.
Solution:

$X :: *[c:\text{character}; \text{west}?c \rightarrow \text{east}!c]$

Notes: (1) When west terminates, the input "west?c" will fail, causing termination of the repetitive command, and of process X. Any subsequent input command from east will fail. (2) Process X acts as a single-character buffer between west and east. It permits west to work on production of the next character, before east is ready to input the previous one.

3.2 SQUASH
Problem: Adapt the previous program to replace every pair of consecutive asterisks "**" by an upward arrow "↑". Assume that the final character input is not an asterisk.
Solution:

$X :: *[c:\text{character}; \text{west}?c \rightarrow$
$\quad [c \neq \text{asterisk} \rightarrow \text{east}!c$
$\quad []c = \text{asterisk} \rightarrow \text{west}?c;$
$\quad\quad [c \neq \text{asterisk} \rightarrow \text{east}!\text{asterisk}; \text{east}!c$
$\quad\quad []c = \text{asterisk} \rightarrow \text{east}!\text{upward arrow}$
$\quad]] \ ]$

Notes: (1) Since west does not end with asterisk, the second "west?c" will not fail. (2) As an exercise, adapt this process to deal sensibly with input which ends with an odd number of asterisks.

3.3 DISASSEMBLE
Problem: to read cards from a cardfile and output to process X the stream of characters they contain. An extra space should be inserted at the end of each card.
Solution:

$*[\text{cardimage}:(1..80)\text{character}; \text{cardfile}?\text{cardimage} \rightarrow$
$\quad i:\text{integer}; i := 1;$
$\quad *[i \leq 80 \rightarrow X!\text{cardimage}(i); i := i + 1]$
$\quad X!\text{space}$
$]$

Notes: (1) "(1..80)character" declares an array of 80 characters, with subscripts ranging between 1 and 80. (2) The repetitive command terminates when the cardfile process terminates.

3.4 ASSEMBLE
Problem: To read a stream of characters from process X and print them in lines of 125 characters on a lineprinter. The last line should be completed with spaces if necessary.

Solution:

```
lineimage:(1..125)character;
i:integer; i := 1;
*[c:character; X?c →
     lineimage(i) := c;
     [i ≤ 124 → i := i + 1
     []i = 125 → lineprinter!lineimage; i := 1
]  ];
[i = 1 → skip
[]i > 1 → *[i ≤ 125 → lineimage(i) := space; i := i + 1];
     lineprinter!lineimage
]
```

Note: (1) When X terminates, so will the first repetitive command of this process. The last line will then be printed, if it has any characters.

3.5 Reformat

Problem: Read a sequence of cards of 80 characters each, and print the characters on a lineprinter at 125 characters per line. Every card should be followed by an extra space, and the last line should be completed with spaces if necessary.

Solution:

```
[west::DISASSEMBLE||X::COPY||east::ASSEMBLE]
```

Notes: (1) The capitalized names stand for program text defined in previous sections. (2) The parallel command is designed to terminate after the cardfile has terminated. (3) This elementary problem is difficult to solve elegantly without coroutines.

3.6 Conway's Problem [4]

Problem: Adapt the above program to replace every pair of consecutive asterisks by an upward arrow.

Solution:

```
[west::DISASSEMBLE||X::SQUASH||east::ASSEMBLE]
```

4. Subroutines and Data Representations

A conventional nonrecursive subroutine can be readily implemented as a coroutine, provided that (1) its parameters are called "by value" and "by result," and (2) it is disjoint from its calling program. Like a Fortran subroutine, a coroutine may retain the values of local variables (*own* variables, in Algol terms) and it may use input commands to achieve the effect of "multiple entry points" in a safer way than PL/I. Thus a coroutine can be used like a SIMULA class instance as a concrete representation for abstract data.

A coroutine acting as a subroutine is a process operating concurrently with its user process in a parallel command: [subr::SUBROUTINE||X::USER]. The SUBROUTINE will contain (or consist of) a repetitive command: *[X?(value params) → ... ; X!(result params)], where ... computes the results from the values input. The subroutine will terminate when its user does. The USER will call the subroutine by a pair of commands: subr!(arguments);

... ; subr?(results). Any commands between these two will be executed concurrently with the subroutine.

A multiple-entry subroutine, acting as a representation for data [11], will also contain a repetitive command which represents each entry by an alternative input to a structured target with the entry name as constructor. For example,

```
*[X?entryl(value params) → ...
[]X?entry2(value params) → ...
]
```

The calling process X will determine which of the alternatives is activated on each repetition. When X terminates, so does this repetitive command. A similar technique in the user program can achieve the effect of multiple exits.

A recursive subroutine can be simulated by an array of processes, one for each level of recursion. The user process is level zero. Each activation communicates its parameters and results with its predecessor and calls its successor if necessary:

```
[recsub(0)::USER||recsub(i:1..reclimit)::RECSUB].
```

The user will call the first element of

```
recsub: recsub(1)!(arguments); ... ; recsub(1)?(results);.
```

The imposition of a fixed upper bound on recursion depth is necessitated by the "static" design of the language.

This clumsy simulation of recursion would be even more clumsy for a mutually recursive algorithm. It would not be recommended for conventional programming; it may be more suitable for an array of microprocessors for which the fixed upper bound is also realistic.

In this section, we assume each subroutine is used only by a *single* user process (which may, of course, itself contain parallel commands).

4.1 Function: Division With Remainder

Problem: Construct a process to represent a function-type subroutine, which accepts a positive dividend and divisor, and returns their integer quotient and remainder. Efficiency is of no concern.

Solution:

```
[DIV::*[x,y:integer; X?(x,y) →
     quot,rem:integer;quot := 0; rem := x;
     *[rem ≥ y → rem := rem − y; quot := quot + 1];
     X!(quot,rem)
     ]
||X::USER
]
```

4.2 Recursion: Factorial

Problem: Compute a factorial by the recursive method, to a given limit.

Solution:

```
[fac(i:1..limit)::
*[n:integer;fac(i − 1)?n →
     [n = 0 → fac(i − 1)!1
```

371

```
[]n > 0 → fac(i + 1)!n − 1;
    r:integer;fac(i + 1)?r;fac(i − 1)!(n ∗ r)
  ]]
]|fac(0)::USER
]
```

Note: This unrealistic example introduces the technique of the "iterative array" which will be used to a better effect in later examples.

4.3 Data Representation: Small Set of Integers [11]

Problem: To represent a set of not more than 100 integers as a process, S, which accepts two kinds of instruction from its calling process X: (1) S!insert(n), insert the integer n in the set, and (2) S!has(n); ... ; S?b, b is set true if n is in the set, and false otherwise. The initial value of the set is empty.

Solution:

```
S::
content:(0..99)integer; size:integer; size := 0;
*[n:integer;X?has(n) → SEARCH;X!(i < size)
[]n:integer;X?insert(n) → SEARCH;
    [i < size → skip
    []i = size; size < 100 →
        content (size) := n; size := size + 1
]   ]
```

where SEARCH is an abbreviation for:

```
i:integer; i := 0;
*[i < size; content(i) ≠ n → i := i + 1]
```

Notes: (1) The alternative command with guard "size < 100" will fail if an attempt is made to insert more than 100 elements. (2) The activity of insertion will in general take place concurrently with the calling process. However, any subsequent instruction to S will be delayed until the previous insertion is complete.

4.4 Scanning a Set

Problem: Extend the solution to 4.3 by providing a fast method for scanning all members of the set without changing the value of the set. The user program will contain a repetitive command of the form:

```
S!scan( ); more:boolean; more := true;
*[more;x:integer; S?next(x) → ... deal with x ....
[]more; S?noneleft( ) → more := false
]
```

where S!scan( ) sets the representation into a scanning mode. The repetitive command serves as a **for** statement, inputting the successive members of x from the set and inspecting them until finally the representation sends a signal that there are no members left. The body of the repetitive command is *not* permitted to communicate with S in any way.

Solution: Add a third guarded command to the outer repetitive command of S:

```
... []X?scan( ) → i:integer; i := 0;
            *[i < size → X!next(content(i)); i := i + 1];
            X!noneleft( )
```

4.5 Recursive Data Representation: Small Set of Integers

Problem: Same as above, but an array of processes is to be used to achieve a high degree of parallelism. Each process should contain at most one number. When it contains no number, it should answer "false" to all inquiries about membership. On the first insertion, it changes to a second phase of behavior, in which it deals with instructions from its predecessor, passing some of them on to its successor. The calling process will be named S(0). For efficiency, the set should be sorted, i.e. the ith process should contain the ith largest number.

Solution:

```
S(i:1..100)::

*[n:integer; S(i − 1)?has(n) → S(0)!false
[]n:integer; S(i − 1)?insert(n) →
    *[m:integer; S(i − 1)?has(m) →
        [m ≤ n → S(0)!(m = n)
        []m > n → S(i + 1)!has(m)
        ]
    []m:integer; S(i − 1)?insert(m) →
        [m < n → S(i + 1)!insert(n); n := m
        []m = n → skip
        []m > n → S(i + 1)!insert(m)
] ] ]
```

Notes: (1) The user process S(0) inquires whether n is a member by the commands S(1)!has(n); ... ; [(i:1..100)S(i)? b → skip]. The appropriate process will respond to the input command by the output command in line 2 or line 5. This trick avoids passing the answer back "up the chain." (2) Many insertion operations can proceed in parallel, yet any subsequent "has" operation will be performed correctly. (3) All repetitive commands and all processes of the array will terminate after the user process S(0) terminates.

4.6 Multiple Exits: Remove the Least Member

Exercise: Extend the above solution to respond to a command to yield the least member of the set and to remove it from the set. The user program will invoke the facility by a pair of commands:

```
S(1)!least( ); [x:integer;S(1)?x → ... deal with x ...
                []S(1)?noneleft( ) → ...
                ]
```

or, if he wishes to scan and empty the set, he may write:

```
S(1)!least( );more:boolean; more := true;
        *[more; x:integer; S(1)?x → ... deal with x ... ; S(1)!least( )
        []more; S(1)?noneleft( ) → more := false
        ]
```

Hint: Introduce a Boolean variable, b, initialized to true, and prefix this to all the guards of the inner loop. After responding to a !least( ) command from its predecessor, each process returns its contained value n, asks its successor for its least, and stores the response in n. But if the successor returns "noneleft( )," b is set false and the inner loop terminates. The process therefore returns to its initial state (solution due to David Gries).

372

5. Monitors and Scheduling

This section shows how a monitor can be regarded as a single process which communicates with more than one user process. However, each user process must have a different name (e.g. producer, consumer) or a different subscript (e.g. $X(i)$) and each communication with a user must identify its source or destination uniquely.

Consequently, when a monitor is prepared to communicate with *any* of its user processes (i.e. whichever of them calls first) it will use a guarded command with a range. For example: $*[(i:1..100)X(i)?(\text{value parameters})$ $\rightarrow ... ; X(i)!(\text{results})]$. Here, the bound variable i is used to send the results back to the calling process. If the monitor is not prepared to accept input from some particular user (e.g. $X(j)$) on a given occasion, the input command may be preceded by a Boolean guard. For example, two successive inputs from the same process are inhibited by $j = 0$; $*[(i:1..100)i \neq j; X(i)?(\text{values}) \rightarrow ... ; j := i]$. Any attempted output from $X(j)$ will be delayed until a subsequent iteration, after the output of some other process $X(i)$ has been accepted and dealt with.

Similarly, conditions can be used to delay acceptance of inputs which would violate scheduling constraints—postponing them until some later occasion when some other process has brought the monitor into a state in which the input can validly be accepted. This technique is similar to a conditional critical region [10] and it obviates the need for special synchronizing variables such as events, queues, or conditions. However, the absence of these special facilities certainly makes it more difficult or less efficient to solve problems involving priorities—for example, the scheduling of head movement on a disk.

5.1 Bounded Buffer

Problem: Construct a buffering process X to smooth variations in the speed of output of portions by a producer process and input by a consumer process. The consumer contains pairs of commands $X!\text{more}( )$; $X?p$, and the producer contains commands of the form $X!p$. The buffer should contain up to ten portions.
Solution:

```
X::
buffer:(0..9) portion;
in,out:integer; in := 0; out := 0;
comment 0 ≤ out ≤ in ≤ out + 10;
    *[in < out + 10; producer?buffer(in mod 10) → in := in + 1
    []out < in; consumer?more( ) → consumer!buffer(out mod 10);
        out := out + 1
    ]
```

Notes: (1) When out < in < out + 10, the selection of the alternative in the repetitive command will depend on whether the producer produces before the consumer consumes, or vice versa. (2) When out = in, the buffer is empty and the second alternative cannot be selected even if the consumer is ready with its command $X!\text{more}( )$.

However, after the producer has produced its next portion, the consumer's request can be granted on the next iteration. (3) Similar remarks apply to the producer, when in = out + 10. (4) X is designed to terminate when out = in and the producer has terminated.

5.2 Integer Semaphore

Problem: To implement an integer semaphore, S, shared among an array $X(i:1..100)$ of client processes. Each process may increment the semaphore by S!V( ) or decrement it by S!P( ), but the latter command must be delayed if the value of the semaphore is not positive.
Solution:

```
S::val:integer; val := 0;
    *[(i:1..100)X(i)?V( ) → val := val + 1
    [](i:1..100)val > 0; X(i)?P( ) → val := val − 1
    ]
```

Notes: (1) In this process, no use is made of knowledge of the subscript i of the calling process. (2) The semaphore terminates only when all hundred processes of the process array X have terminated.

5.3 Dining Philosophers (Problem due to E.W. Dijkstra)

Problem: Five philosophers spend their lives thinking and eating. The philosophers share a common dining room where there is a circular table surrounded by five chairs, each belonging to one philosopher. In the center of the table there is a large bowl of spaghetti, and the table is laid with five forks (see Figure 1). On feeling hungry, a philosopher enters the dining room, sits in his own chair, and picks up the fork on the left of his place. Unfortunately, the spaghetti is so tangled that he needs to pick up and use the fork on his right as well. When he has finished, he puts down both forks, and leaves the room. The room should keep a count of the number of philosophers in it.

Fig. 1.

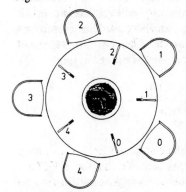

Solution: The behavior of the ith philosopher may be described as follows:

```
PHIL = *[... during ith lifetime ... →
    THINK;
    room!enter( );
    fork(i)!pickup( ); fork((i + 1) mod 5)!pickup( );
    EAT;
    fork(i)!putdown( ); fork((i + 1) mod 5)!putdown( );
    room!exit( )
    ]
```

The fate of the ith fork is to be picked up and put down by a philosopher sitting on either side of it

```
FORK =
    *[phil(i)?pickup( ) → phil(i)?putdown( )
    []phil((i − 1)mod 5)?pickup( ) → phil((i − 1) mod 5)?putdown( )
    ]
```

The story of the room may be simply told:

```
ROOM = occupancy:integer; occupancy := 0;
    *[(i:0..4)phil(i)?enter( ) → occupancy := occupancy + 1
    [](i:0..4)phil(i)?exit( ) → occupancy := occupancy − 1
    ]
```

All these components operate in parallel:

```
[room::ROOM||fork(i:0..4)::FORK||phil(i:0..4)::PHIL].
```

Notes: (1) The solution given above does not prevent all five philosophers from entering the room, each picking up his left fork, and starving to death because he cannot pick up his right fork. (2) Exercise: Adapt the above program to avert this sad possibility. Hint: Prevent more than four philosophers from entering the room. (Solution due to E. W. Dijkstra).

6. Miscellaneous

This section contains further examples of the use of communicating sequential processes for the solution of some less familiar problems; a parallel version of the sieve of Eratosthenes, and the design of an iterative array. The proposed solutions are even more speculative than those of the previous sections, and in the second example, even the question of termination is ignored.

6.1 Prime Numbers: The Sieve of Eratosthenes [14]
Problem: To print in ascending order all primes less than 10000. Use an array of processes, SIEVE, in which each process inputs a prime from its predecessor and prints it. The process then inputs an ascending stream of numbers from its predecessor and passes them on to its successor, suppressing any that are multiples of the original prime. Solution:

```
[SIEVE(i:1..100)::
    p,mp:integer;
    SIEVE(i − 1)?p;
    print!p;
    mp := p; comment mp is a multiple of p;
    *[m:integer; SIEVE(i − 1)?m →
        *[m > mp → mp := mp + p];
        [m = mp → skip
        []m < mp → SIEVE(i + 1)!m
    ]    ]
||SIEVE(0)::print!2; n:integer; n := 3;
        *[n < 10000 → SIEVE(1)!n; n := n + 2]
||SIEVE(101)::*[n:integer;SIEVE(100)?n → print!n]
||print::*[(i:0..101) n:integer; SIEVE(i)?n → ...]
]
```

Note: (1) This beautiful solution was contributed by David Gries. (2) It is algorithmically similar to the program developed in [7, pp. 27–32].

6.2 An Iterative Array: Matrix Multiplication
Problem: A square matrix A of order 3 is given. Three streams are to be input, each stream representing a column of an array IN. Three streams are to be output, each representing a column of the product matrix IN $\times$ A. After an initial delay, the results are to be produced at the same rate as the input is consumed. Consequently, a high degree of parallelism is required. The solution should take the form shown in Figure 2. Each of the nine nonborder nodes inputs a vector component from the west and a partial sum from the north. Each node outputs the vector component to its east, and an updated partial sum to the south. The input data is produced by the west border nodes, and the desired results are consumed by south border nodes. The north border is a constant source of zeros and the east border is just a sink. No provision need be made for termination nor for changing the values of the array A.

Fig. 2.

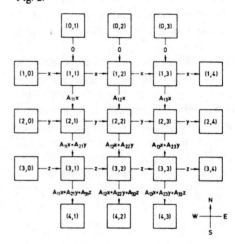

Solution: There are twenty-one nodes, in five groups, comprising the central square and the four borders:

```
[M(i:1..3,0)::WEST
||M(0,j:1..3)::NORTH
||M(i:1..3,4)::EAST
||M(4,j:1..3)::SOUTH
||M(i:1..3,j:1..3)::CENTER
]
```

The WEST and SOUTH borders are processes of the user program; the remaining processes are:

```
NORTH = *[true → M(1,j)!0]
EAST = *[x:real; M(i,3)?x → skip]
CENTER = *[x:real; M(i,j − 1)?x →
        M(i, j + 1)!x; sum:real;
        M(i − 1, j)?sum; M(i + 1,j)!(A(i,j)•x + sum)
    ]
```

7. Discussion

A design for a programming language must necessarily involve a number of decisions which seem to be fairly arbitrary. The discussion of this section is intended to explain some of the underlying motivation and to mention some unresolved questions.

7.1 Notations

I have chosen single-character notations (e.g. !,?) to express the primitive concepts, rather than the more traditional boldface or underlined English words. As a result, the examples have an APL-like brevity, which some readers find distasteful. My excuse is that (in contrast to APL) there are only a very few primitive concepts and that it is standard practice of mathematics (and also good coding practice) to denote common primitive concepts by brief notations (e.g. $+, \times$). When read aloud, these are replaced by words (e.g. plus, times).

Some readers have suggested the use of assignment notation for input and output:

```
<target variable> := <source>
<destination> := <expression>
```

I find this suggestion misleading: it is better to regard input and output as distinct primitives, justifying distinct notations.

I have used the same pair of brackets ([...]) to bracket all program structures, instead of the more familiar variety of brackets (**if..fi, begin..end, case...esac**, etc.). In this I follow normal mathematical practice, but I must also confess to a distaste for the pronunciation of words like **fi, od**, or **esac**.

I am dissatisfied with the fact that my notation gives the same syntax for a structured expression and a subscripted variable. Perhaps tags should be distinguished from other identifiers by a special symbol (say #).

I was tempted to introduce an abbreviation for combined declaration and input, e.g. $X?(n:\text{integer})$ for n:integer; $X?n$.

7.2 Explicit Naming

My design insists that every input or output command must name its source or destination explicitly. This makes it inconvenient to write a library of processes which can be included in subsequent programs, independent of the process names used in that program. A partial solution to this problem is to allow one process (the *main* process) of a parallel command to have an empty label, and to allow the other processes in the command to use the empty process name as source or destination of input or output.

For construction of large programs, some more general technique will also be necessary. This should at least permit substitution of program text for names defined elsewhere—a technique which has been used informally throughout this paper. The Cobol COPY verb also permits a substitution for formal parameters within the copied text. But whatever facility is introduced, I would recommend the following principle: Every program, after assembly with its library routines, should be printable as a text expressed wholly in the language, and it is this printed text which should describe the execution of the program, independent of which parts were drawn from a library.

Since I did not intend to design a complete language, I have ignored the problem of libraries in order to concentrate on the essential semantic concepts of the program which is actually executed.

7.3 Port Names

An alternative to explicit naming of source and destination would be to name a *port* through which communication is to take place. The port names would be local to the processes, and the manner in which pairs of ports are to be connected by channels could be declared in the head of a parallel command.

This is an attractive alternative which could be designed to introduce a useful degree of syntactically checkable redundancy. But it is semantically equivalent to the present proposal, provided that each port is connected to exactly one other port in another process. In this case each channel can be identified with a tag, together with the name of the process at the other end. Since I wish to concentrate on semantics, I preferred in this paper to use the simplest and most direct notation, and to avoid raising questions about the possibility of connecting more than two ports by a single channel.

7.4 Automatic Buffering

As an alternative to synchronization of input and output, it is often proposed that an outputting process should be allowed to proceed even when the inputting process is not yet ready to accept the output. An implementation would be expected automatically to interpose a chain of buffers to hold output messages that have not yet been input.

I have deliberately rejected this alternative, for two reasons: (1) It is less realistic to implement in multiple disjoint processors, and (2) when buffering is required on a particular channel, it can readily be specified using the given primitives. Of course, it could be argued equally well that synchronization can be specified when required by using a pair of buffered input and output commands.

7.5 Unbounded Process Activation

The notation for an array of processes permits the same program text (like an Algol recursive procedure) to have many simultaneous "activations"; however, the exact number must be specified in advance. In a conventional single-processor implementation, this can lead to inconvenience and wastefulness, similar to the fixed-length array of Fortran. It would therefore be attractive to allow a process array with no a priori bound on the number of elements; and to specify that the exact number of elements required for a particular execution of the program should be determined dynamically, like the maximum depth of recursion of an Algol procedure or the number of iterations of a repetitive command.

However, it is a good principle that every actual run of a program with unbounded arrays should be identical to the run of some program with all its arrays bounded in advance. Thus the unbounded program should be defined as the "limit" (in some sense) of a series of bounded programs with increasing bounds. I have chosen to concentrate on the semantics of the bounded case—which is necessary anyway and which is more realistic for implementation on multiple microprocessors.

7.6 Fairness
Consider the parallel command:

$[X:: Y!\text{stop}(\ )|| Y::\text{continue:boolean; continue} := \text{true;}$
$\quad *[\text{continue}; X?\text{stop}(\ ) \rightarrow \text{continue} := \text{false}$
$\quad \quad [\!]\text{continue} \rightarrow n := n + 1$
$\quad \quad]$
$].$

If the implementation always prefers the second alternative in the repetitive command of Y, it is said to be *unfair*, because although the output command in X could have been executed on an infinite number of occasions, it is in fact always passed over.

The question arises: Should a programming language definition specify that an implementation must be *fair*? Here, I am fairly sure that the answer is NO. Otherwise, the implementation would be obliged to successfully complete the example program shown above, in spite of the fact that its nondeterminism is unbounded. I would therefore suggest that it is the programmer's responsibility to prove that his program terminates correctly—without relying on the assumption of fairness in the implementation. Thus the program shown above is incorrect, since its termination cannot be proved.

Nevertheless, I suggest that an efficient implementation should try to be reasonably fair and should ensure that an output command is not delayed unreasonably often after it first becomes executable. But a proof of correctness must not rely on this property of an efficient implementation. Consider the following analogy with a sequential program: An efficient implementation of an alternative command will tend to favor the alternative which can be most efficiently executed, but the programmer must ensure that the logical correctness of his program does not depend on this property of his implementation.

This method of avoiding the problem of fairness does not apply to programs such as operating systems which are intended to run forever because in this case termination proofs are not relevant. But I wonder whether it is ever advisable to write or to execute such programs. Even an operating system should be designed to bring itself to an orderly conclusion reasonably soon after it inputs a message instructing it to do so. Otherwise, the *only* way to stop it is to "crash" it.

7.7 Functional Coroutines
It is interesting to compare the processes described here with those proposed in [12]; the differences are most

striking. There, coroutines are strictly deterministic: No choice is given between alternative sources of input. The output commands are automatically buffered to any required degree. The output of one process can be automatically fanned out to any number of processes (including itself!) which can consume it at differing rates. Finally, the processes there are designed to run forever, whereas my proposed parallel command is normally intended to terminate. The design in [12] is based on an elegant theory which permits proof of the properties of programs. These differences are not accidental—they seem to be natural consequences of the difference between the more abstract applicative (or functional) approach to programming and the more machine-oriented imperative (or procedural) approach, which is taken by communicating sequential processes.

7.8 Output Guards
Since input commands may appear in guards, it seems more symmetric to permit output commands as well. This would allow an obvious and useful simplification in some of the example programs, for example, in the bounded buffer (5.1). Perhaps a more convincing reason would be to ensure that the externally visible effect and behavior of every parallel command can be modeled by some sequential command. In order to model the parallel command

$Z :: [X!2 || Y!3]$

we need to be able to write the sequential alternative command:

$Z :: [X!2 \rightarrow Y!3 [\!] Y!3 \rightarrow X!2]$

Note that this *cannot* be done by the command

$Z :: [\text{true} \rightarrow X!2; Y!3 [\!] \text{true} \rightarrow Y!3; X!2]$

which can fail if the process Z happens to choose the first alternative, but the processes Y and X are synchronized with each other in such a way that Y must input from Z before X does, e.g.

$\quad Y :: Z?y; X!\text{go}(\ )$
$|| X :: Y?\text{go}(\ ); Z?x$

7.9 Restriction: Repetitive Command With Input Guard
In proposing an unfamiliar programming language feature, it seems wiser at first to specify a highly restrictive version rather than to propose extensions—especially when the language feature claims to be primitive. For example, it is clear that the multidimensional process array is not primitive, since it can readily be constructed in a language which permits only single-dimensional arrays. But I have a rather more serious misgiving about the repetitive command with input guards.

The automatic termination of a repetitive command on termination of the sources of all its input guards is an extremely powerful and convenient feature but it also involves some subtlety of specification to ensure that it is implementable; and it is certainly not primitive, since the required effect can be achieved (with considerable inconvenience) by explicit exchange of "end()" signals. For example, the subroutine DIV(4.1) could be rewritten:

```
[DIV :: continue:boolean; continue := true;
 *[continue; X?end() → continue := false
 []continue; x,y:integer; X?(x,y) → ... ; X!(quot,rem)
||X :: USER PROG; DIV!end()
 ]
```

Other examples would be even more inconvenient.

But the dangers of convenient facilities are notorious. For example, the repetitive commands with input guards may tempt the programmer to write them without making adequate plans for their termination; and if it turns out that the automatic termination is unsatisfactory, reprogramming for explicit termination will involve severe changes, affecting even the interfaces between the processes.

8. Conclusion

This paper has suggested that input, output, and concurrency should be regarded as primitives of programming, which underlie many familiar and less familiar programming concepts. However, it would be unjustified to conclude that these primitives can wholly replace the other concepts in a programming language. Where a more elaborate construction (such as a procedure or a monitor) is frequently useful, has properties which are more simply provable, and can also be implemented more efficiently than the general case, there is a strong reason for including in a programming language a special notation for that construction. The fact that the construction can be defined in terms of simpler underlying primitives is a useful guarantee that its inclusion is logically consistent with the remainder of the language.

Acknowledgments. The research reported in this paper has been encouraged and supported by a Senior Fellowship of the Science Research Council of Great Britain. The technical inspiration was due to Edsger W. Dijkstra [9], and the paper has been improved in presentation and content by valuable and painstaking advice from D. Gries, D. Q. M. Fay, Edsger W. Dijkstra, N. Wirth, Robert Milne, M. K. Harper, and its referees. The role of IFIP W.G.2.3 as a forum for presentation and discussion is acknowledged with pleasure and gratitude.

Received March 1977; revised August 1977

References

1. Atkinson, R., and Hewitt, C. Synchronisation in actor systems. Working Paper 83, M.I.T., Cambridge, Mass., Nov. 1976.
2. Brinch Hansen, P. The programming language Concurrent Pascal. *IEEE Trans. Software Eng. 1*, 2 (June 1975), 199–207.
3. Campbell, R.H., and Habermann, A.N. The specification of process synchronisation by path expressions. *Lecture Notes in Computer Science 16*, Springer, 1974, pp. 89–102.
4. Conway, M.E. Design of a separable transition-diagram compiler. *Comm. ACM 6*, 7 (July 1963), 396–408.
5. Dahl, O-J., et al. SIMULA 67, common base language. Norwegian Computing Centre, Forskningveien, Oslo, 1967.
6. Dijkstra, E.W. Co-operating sequential processes. In *Programming Languages*, F. Genuys, Ed., Academic Press, New York, 1968, pp. 43–112.
7. Dijkstra, E.W. Notes on structured programming. In *Structured Programming*, Academic Press, New York 1972 pp. 1–82.
8. Dijkstra, E.W. Guarded commands, nondeterminacy, and formal derivation of programs. *Comm. ACM 18*, 8 (Aug. 1975), 453–457.
9. Dijkstra, E.W. Verbal communication, Marktoberdorf, Aug. 1975.
10. Hoare, C.A.R. Towards a theory of parallel programming. In *Operating Systems Techniques*, Academic Press, New York, 1972, pp. 61–71.
11. Hoare, C.A.R. Proof of correctness of data representations. *Acta Informatica 1*, 4 (1972), 271–281.
12. Kahn, G. The semantics of a simple language for parallel programming. In *Proc. IFIP Congress 74*, North Holland, 1974.
13. Liskov, B.H. A note on CLU. Computation Structures Group Memo. 112, M.I.T., Cambridge, Mass, 1974.
14. McIlroy, M.D. Coroutines. Bell Laboratories, Murray Hill, N.J., 1968.
15. Naur, P., Ed. Report on the algorithmic language ALGOL 60. *Comm. ACM 3*, 5 (May 1960), 299–314.
16. Reynolds, J.C. COGENT. ANL-7022, Argonne Nat. Lab., Argonne, Ill., 1965.
17. Thompson, K. The UNIX command language. In *Structured Programming*, Infotech, Nicholson House, Maidenhead, England, 1976, pp. 375–384.
18. van Wijngaarden, A. Ed. Report on the algorithmic language ALGOL 68. *Numer. Math. 14* (1969), 79–218.
19. Wulf, W.A., London, R.L., and Shaw, M. Abstraction and verification in ALPHARD. Dept. of Comptr. Sci., Carnegie-Mellon U., Pittsburgh, Pa., June 1976.
20. Wirth, N. The programming language PASCAL. *Acta Informatica 1*, 1 (1971), 35–63.

Formal Models and Practical Tools
for Information Systems Design
H.-J. Schneider, Editor
North-Holland Publishing Company
© *IFIP, 1979*

AN EVENT-BASED DESIGN METHODOLOGY
SUPPORTED BY DREAM

William E. Riddle

Department of Computer Science
University of Colorado at Boulder
Boulder, Colorado 80309

A methodology for the architectural design of software systems is composed of three interrelated facilities. First, there must be some means of capturing the requirements for the system in some primarily non-procedural specification. Second, there must be some means for describing potential modularizations of the system in some primarily pseudo-procedural design which captures the essential detail concerning the modules' interfaces and their interactions. Finally, there must be some means of determining whether a system design appropriately meets the system specification. In this paper, we present a design methodology based on the use of event and event sequence descriptions. We first give a brief definition of the Design Realization, Evaluation And Modelling (DREAM) system and its description language as they relate to an event-based design method. Then we define the design method and give a simple example.

INTRODUCTION:

Many methodologies have recently been advanced for the disciplined, orderly development of software systems. Each has as its basis a development method (or process for the gradual, evolutionary development of a software system) which serves to decompose the overall synthesis task into a sequence of smaller, more manageable steps. Many methodologies lend additional help to software developers in the form of guidelines, maxims or techniques that serve to support the method which they provide. A few offer help for the analysis which must be done to assure that the developed system delivers the functional capabilities which are required and does so within the performance and economic constraints which have been levied against the system.

A particularly effective way in which a development methodology may be delivered to software design practitioners is as a computerized support system. Systems of this type (e.g., [1], [2], [3], [4], [5], [6], [7], [8], [9], [10], [11], [12], [13], [14], [15], [16]) provide a language for the precise, but abstract, description of systems at intermediate points in their development when completely detailed descriptions cannot be given. This language then allows the definition of various development techniques and the provision of computerized aids supporting these techniques.

In our own development support system, called the Design Realization, Evaluation And Modelling (DREAM) system [12], we have focused upon providing help for the development of concurrent software systems (that is, those systems having parts which may be perceived as operating asynchronously and in parallel, even if the system actually executes in a uniprocessor environment). We have additionally focused upon providing analysis aid which is highly integrated with a top-down design method, so that system developers may gradually develop their confidence in the appropriateness of a system in tandem with developing the system itself.

In this paper we discuss the DREAM system and one of the development methods which it supports. In the next section, we narrow the scope of consideration to that phase of the software development life-cycle for which DREAM has been developed. We then discuss description languages in general and the DREAM description language in particular. Then, after outlining the DREAM system and discussing the types of computerized aid it provides, we outline a variant of the traditional top-down design method which the DREAM system provides and give a short example of its use.

ARCHITECTURAL DESIGN PHASE:

The software system development process may be divided into three major phases.[1] Chronologically first among these is the requirements definition phase during which the users' requirements are expressed in terms of the system's expected functional capabilities as well as in terms of performance and economic constraints upon the system. Chronologically last is a phase which may be called the algorithm design phase, during which the system's processing algorithms and internal data structures are developed to the level of detail needed to permit compilation.

Intermediate to these two phases is a phase which we call architectural design. During this phase the system's gross organization is specified in terms of a hier- archically structured collection of modules, each of which plays some well-defined role in the delivery of the system's functional capabilities. In addition to the delineation of the modules, their interfaces and interactions are defined in order to specify the coordination needed to assure the delivery of the expected func- tional capabilities and the observance of the constraints which have been levied upon the system.

The synthesis task during design[2] is therefore the development of a modularization for the system and the definition of strategies for interactions among the modules. The associated analysis task is to assess the strategies with respect to the sys- tem's requirements with the intent of certifying that if the modules operate and interact as specified then the requirements will be satisfied.

SOFTWARE DESIGN DESCRIPTION LANGUAGES:

The description task during architectural design is a modelling task that is only superficially similar to the traditional programming task encountered during the algorithm design phase. Modelling shares with programming the need to specify some details concerning the processing performed by the system. But this specifi- cation should be abstract with respect to specific mechanisms for implementing the processing. Stated differently, the specification should be expressed in require- ments-oriented terms which reflect the effect of system operation rather than im- plementation-oriented terms reflecting the system's actual operation and, there- fore, the cause of the observable effects. There is the need, therefore, for lan- guages which are considerably different from programming languages and, in this section, we discuss the attributes of such design description languages.

Because of the need to highlight module boundaries and interactions, a design de- scription language needs to be behavior-oriented rather than operation-oriented. A behavior-oriented language supports the abstraction of a module by allowing the description of the effect of the module's operation without the description of the manner in which this effect is caused. One approach to abstraction is to al- low descriptions that are projections of the actual modules within the system. In a projection, the operational details of the module are suppressed, resulting in a description which focuses upon the module's overall behavioral characteristics. Another approach to abstraction is to allow a description which is orthogonal to the system's implementation description in the sense that the description may form associations among the elements of the system that are completely different from those formed by the system's internal, physical organization. Thus, the modules may be merely logical entities rather than physical entities. A final approach to behavioral abstraction is to allow descriptions that are non-procedural in that they describe the effect of the module's processing without specifying an algorithm for achieving the effect.

> Example: Assertions [15] are non-procedural projections of the modules they describe. They are orthogonal to the implementations of the modules in that they do not necessarily imply that one procedure must exist for each set of input/output relations defined by an assertion -- one generalized module could conceivably implement many sets of input/output relations.

The need to be able to investigate the interactions among the modules and the interplay among the various strategies implies that design description languages should be analysis-oriented. An obvious criterion is that descriptions be unambiguous, so that formal analysis techniques may be defined which derive information about the overall operation of a collection of interacting modules. Descriptions should also be outward-directed, specifying the characteristics of a module that are pertinent to its interactions with other modules, again so that characteristics of the overall operation of a collection of modules may be uncovered. Finally, descriptions should be redundant, specifying a behavior either from different points of view -- for instance, from the point of view of both the supplier or user of some processing facility -- or with respect to different sets of concerns -- for instance, with respect to desired properties of the overall operation as well as with respect to the operation of the individual modules.

> Example: Several recently defined programming languages -- such as Euclid [19], CLU [20], and Alphard [21] -- satisfy many of these criteria. They each have a well-defined semantics and hence lead to unambiguous descriptions. Redundancy is allowed either through the incorporation of assertions which allow formal verification, such as in Alphard, or the use of data abstractions and strict typing which lead to useful compile-time checks, as in CLU. Outward-directed descriptions are generally allowed through axioms, as in Alphard and Euclid, which allow the effect of a sequence of operations to be deduced.

Design description languages should also be modification-oriented so that descriptions may be easily augmented, as new decisions are made, or returned to a previous state should decisions be reversed. Descriptions should be modular so that self-contained descriptions of different aspects of the system may be separately specified. They should also be hierarchical so that the descriptions may be iteratively elaborated. It is also usually desirable to allow incremental descriptions so that fragments of the overall description may be prepared in an arbitrary order. This is sometimes contradictory with the desire to have hierarchical descriptions, but only when it is required (sometimes unnecessarily) that the order in which portions of the description are developed corresponds to the nesting structure of the hierarchy.

> Example: Algolic programming languages admit hierarchical, modular descriptions and the current trend toward incorporating data abstraction constructs, as for example in CLU, enhances programming languages with respect to these criteria. Incremental descriptions are not easily achieved in block-structured languages (and are somewhat inconsistent with the idea of structured programming), but can be achieved in languages which use the idea of guarded commands [22].

Finally, design description languages should be guidance-oriented in that they should allow descriptions which help guide the further design (and eventual implementation) of the system but do not overly constrain the design (or implementation) decisions remaining to be made. Descriptions should therefore be non-prescriptive such that they capture the decisions already made but do not prescribe the manner in which the resulting properties of the system should be achieved. Although non-prescriptive, descriptions should also be inward-directed, helping the designers to discover the options that are possible and feasible for ensuing decisions. It is sometimes beneficial to allow attribute descriptions in which various properties of the system are described positively by indicating the values that they may assume or negatively by indicating the values that are not to be allowed.

> Example: Assertions are non-prescriptive and frequently inward-directed since they describe a procedure's function as the conjunction of constraints and can therefore indicate different cases which should be handled. Assertions could also be used to give attribute descriptions which specify the range of permissible values for each attribute.

The examples have indicated that contemporary programming languages have moved in the direction of design description. Partially this is because programming is also algorithm design; partially, it is in recognition of the need to perform analysis in order to produce reliable programs. But programming languages are rarely acceptable design languages because they are inherently operation-oriented and specify behavior only implicitly through procedures for achieving the behavior.

THE DREAM DESIGN LANGUAGE:

As a basis for the DREAM system, which we discuss in the next section, we have developed a design description language called the DREAM Design Notion (DDN) which possesses many of the characteristics delineated in the last section. In this section, we discuss the major facilities available in DDN and indicate how these give rise to the various characteristics. The discussion here is brief and without examples. Some brief examples are given later -- others and more detailed discussions of the DDN facilities are given in the cited references.

DDN descriptions are of classes of components within a system [23]. Class-oriented descriptions were introduced in the SIMULA language [24] and have been incorporated in a wide variety of computer-oriented description schemes ([14], [20], [21], [25], [26], [27], [28]). DDN allows parameterized descriptions so that some of the details of a member (or instance) of the class may be specified when the member is created. This facility allows the specification of many different types of variation among members of a class. For example, it allows the description of system components which have a variable number of subcomponents (such as the class of multiple-task programs), a variable number of output linkages (such as the class of message transmitters in a computer network), or variable types of subcomponents (such as the class of stacks).

Class definition constructs facilitate the hierarchical definition of a software system since the designers are encouraged to think of the system as decomposible into subcomponents which are members of a set of classes and which are themselves decomposible into subcomponents which are members of other classes. They also facilitate projection and orthogonality since a class serves to collect together all of the information pertinent to a collection of components and hence leads to descriptions which highlight those characteristics common to the collection rather than particular to its members. Finally, class definition facilities allow modular descriptions which may be incrementally developed since fragments of a class definition may be prepared in any order. In sum, class definition facilities primarily enhance the modification orientation of the language.

As implied above, a system must be hierarchically decomposed into its subcomponents to be described in DDN -- components are composed of sub-components which are composed of sub-subcomponents, etc. The tree-like system organization which results is often natural in describing the details of a system's algorithmic processing as indicated by the usefulness of structured programming ([29], [30]) for program description. The tree-like organization is not appropriate, however, in situations in which sharing occurs either because of the nature of the system (as in shared database systems such as online reservation systems) or because of a desire to layer the system into levels of virtual machines (as in many current operating systems).

To allow non-tree-like organizations, DDN contains instantiation control constructs [23]. Using these constructs, the designers may specify that components which are described, for clarity of description, as distinct are actually a single component in the final system configuration. These constructs are similar in effect to equivalencing constructs such as found in the Fortran programming language, but do not allow components of differing types to be "overlaid". They are also similar in effect to the aliasing constructs typically provided by parameter passing mechanisms and capability-based addressing schemes, but are not intended to be effected by the transmission of addresses at run-time. Thus, the constructs provide for the description of sharing relationships that are determinded by the system's configuration and which do not vary during system operation.

The instantiation control constructs contribute primarily to the inward-directedness of DDN since they allow explicit description of the system's eventual physical configuration. They also contribute by allowing the implicit description of all of the contexts in which a given component is to function, thus leading the designer of the component to consider how the component should be implemented so as to efficiently and effectively function in the various contexts.

The instantiation control constructs also lead to orthogonal, modular descriptions since logically different parts of the system may be separately described even though they share common subparts. The constructs may then be used to separately describe the sharing relationships among the parts. This also tends to lead to incremental descriptions.

Components in a DDN description are considered to execute concurrently and asynchronously and there are two major types of components [11]. Subsystems are those components which (logically at least) operate concurrently, interact freely but in a way acceptable to both parties to any interaction, and collectively provide the system's functional capabilities ([31], [32]). Monitors also operate concurrently, but provide data storage capabilities and possess built-in mechanisms that may be used to synchronize the potentially conflicting demands placed by other components [50]. The DDN view of a system is therefore that it is composed of hierarchically organized collections of sequential processes which interact through shared data objects which individually contain the necessary synchronization code.

This parallel-world view of systems enhances the clarity of system descriptions in the following way. It is generally recognized that complex systems may be more easily comprehended if they can be broken into simpler, smaller parts which interact in well-defined ways [33]. When this is done, then an understanding of the system's operation may be obtained by first understanding the parts and then understanding the interactions among the parts. As evidenced by recent texts on operating systems ([34], [35]) and recently developed methods for structuring artificial intelligence systems [35], decomposition of a complex software system is easier when the parts operate concurrently and interact asynchronously.

In terms of the characteristics delineated in the previous section, the parallel-world view primarily facilitates modularization. It also allows abstractions to be more easily constructed, since it facilitates projection of the intermodule interactions and the overall effect of the interactions by allowing the suppression of detail concerning how the interaction is accomplished. Finally, it allows outward-directed descriptions which focus upon overall properties of the system which derive from the interactions among the components.

In collections of concurrently operating components which interact via shared data structures, it is common for the shared data structures to be used for message exchange. This form of interaction is distinguished in DDN and constructs are provided for explicitly describing the message generation and utilization characteristics of subsystems and the message flow among the subsystems. This message transfer view leads to descriptions which are orthogonal, projective and outward-directed, allowing as it does focus upon the logical characteristics of module interdependencies and interactions.

The final set of DDN description facilities are those for the non-procedural specification of overall system operation through the definition of behavior by the algebraic specification of sets of sequences of events [37]. Arbitrary events may be defined such as "program added to schedule queue" or "legal access made to database" and sequences of events which the designer wishes to allow may be specified by constructs ([38], [37]) which are extensions to those found in regular expressions and similar to those defined for path expressions ([39], [40]) and flow expressions [41].

The event sequence expression constructs of DDN have been included primarily to allow analysis. They provide a redundant, outward-directed description which may be checked for consistency against the operational descriptions of the component interactions [42]. As a descriptive scheme, however, they also provide for the non-procedural, non-prescriptive, projective and orthogonal description of the operation of collections of subsystems.

THE DREAM DESIGN SUPPORT SYSTEM:

Precisely-defined design description languages of the sort discussed in the previous section can serve as a basis for the delivery of several types of aid to software design practitioners. Tools, or computerized techniques providing this aid, are most effectively delivered as a set of coherent, integrated facilities within a design support system. These tools may be classified as follows:

> bookkeeping tools provide aid in recording the current state of the development, in modifying and augmenting this record, and in returning it to a previous state if decisions are reversed

> supervisory tools provide aid in assuring that practices and procedures that are deemed beneficial are actually followed

> management tools provide aid in assessing progress and making resource allocation decisions

> feedback tools provide aid in measuring the characteristics of the system under development for the purpose of detecting errors, gaining confidence in the appropriateness of the decisions that have been made, and guiding the further development of the system

The DREAM system is organized as depicted in Figure 1. (This organization has been patterned after that developed for the Tools for Program Development (TOPD) system [8].) Central to the system is a database in which information is stored in textual form, organized into textual units or fragments of description which individually specify different aspects of the system. Textual units are organized hierarchically -- for example, a textual unit describing a class of subsystems is composed of textual units which describe the subcomponents comprising each subsystem, the interfaces through which messages flow, the message transmission

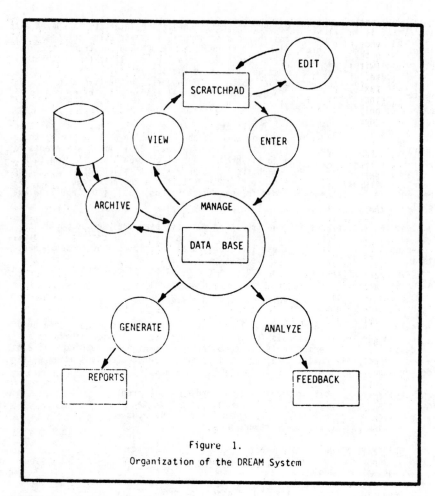

Figure 1.
Organization of the DREAM System

activities performed, and other aspects.

Several bookkeeping tools are provided as information insertion and retrieval mechanisms. Mechanisms for augmenting and modifying the information in the database on a textual unit basis facilitate the gradual evolution of the system's design while the current description is constantly available. Textual units which are to be added to the database (using ENTER) are prepared with the aid of a text editing facility (EDIT) and may be altered versions of units which have been copied from the database (using VIEW). Modifications to the database never result in the deletion of textual units which were previously entered -- thus designers have all of the previous versions of the design available and may back up to any previous point merely by retrieving the description which corresponds to that point and re-entering it, thus making it the current description. Problems caused by having an ever-expanding database are eliminated by an archiving mechanism (ARCHIVE) which may be used to copy the database to external, offline storage, retaining only the latest version of each textual unit in the database itself.

DREAM does not currently provide any supervisory aids since one of the intents of the system is to allow the experimental determination of the efficacy of various aids and hence none were pre-defined in the system. DREAM has, however, been de-signed with the aim of allowing these aids to be easily added to the system as mechanism (within MANAGE) which control the flow of information into and out of the database. For example, documentation standards can be enforced by requiring that each textual unit be accompanied by a documentation unit when it is entered. Or, the principle of information hiding could be enforced by permitting designers access to only some of the information regarding components which they did not personally design. Or, a particular design method could be enforced by requiring that items in a design description be entered in a particular order.

Nor does DREAM currently provide any management aids, primarily because it is not clear what these aids should be. DREAM does provide a basis for management aids (such as GENERATE) as long as they can be formulated in terms of summary reports concerning the completeness or rates of change of the information in the database.

It is in the area of analysis aid that DREAM has been developed to provide the most aid. The analysis aids (such as ANALYZE) that are under development provide feedback analysis [43] in which information concerning the characteristics and properties of the system under design is derived and presented to the designers to be used in formulating rigorous arguments about the design's correctness or in-correctness. The only aid of this sort provided in the current DREAM system is a syntax checking mechanism, providing a check that is a necessary pre-requisite to any other analysis. The aids that are contemplated will span a broad spectrum (discussed in detail in [44]), from simple ones such as cross-reference generators to sophisticated ones which derive predictions of run-time characteristics by either analytic [42] or simulation [45] techniques.

AN EVENT-BASED DESIGN METHOD:

With the DREAM design support system and the DDN design description language, we have attempted to lend support to a variety of design styles rather than enforce our own style. A major reason is that we wish to be able to use the DREAM system to quantitatively measure the differences among various approaches to design. An equally important reason, however, is that we are not confident that we could de-fine a method that was universally applicable across the full spectrum of systems which may be addressing using the DREAM system.

Our predilection toward top-down design methods is, however, quite evident in DREAM and DDN. We feel that these methods are the most effective to use since they allow designers the opportunity to introduce detail as warranted by considera-tion of a system's requirements rather than by consideration of aspects of the processing domain.

In using DDN to describe a variety of existing software systems ([46], [47], [48], [49], [50], [51]), we have found that it admits an interesting and novel variation of the traditional top-down design method. We call this variation the event-based design method and it is the purpose of this section to describe it in some detail and make some observations as to its value.

As with most design methods, the event-based design method consists of a design step which is applied iteratively. This basic step is graphically represented in Figure 2. The first task is to identify, on the basis of the partial design pre-pared by previous steps, events which are pertinent to the aspect of the system which is to be addressed at this design step. Then, the partial design is used to develop constraints upon the occurrences of these events which are necessary to assure that the system operates as required or intended. The next task is then to define system components which can produce the delineated events, and the final

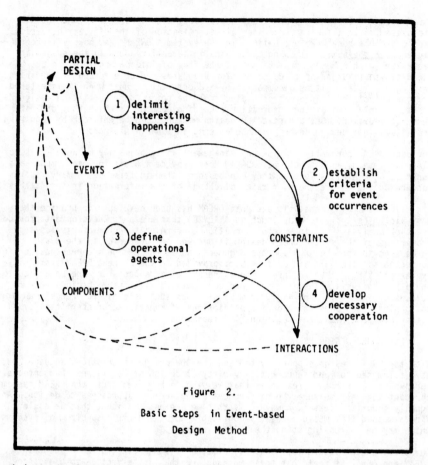

Figure 2.

Basic Steps in Event-based
Design Method

task is to develop the interactions among the components which lead to the observance of the constraints.

Each design step therefore consists of the initial specification of the required behavior to be exhibited by the part of the system under consideration at this step. After this specification is prepared, the step is then completed by defining modules and module interactions which produce this required behavior.

As an example, consider the design of an on-board system for the in-flight monitoring of an aircraft's engines, and specifically that step at which we detail the interactions needed to call the attention of the pilot to the heating up of one of the engines. We hypothesize a partial design that includes the requirements of interest at this step, namely: there are four engines; a hot engine is to be signalled to the pilot by sounding an audio-alarm device; and signalling the existence of one hot engine should not block the recognition of another engine heating up and the signalling of this to the pilot. Notice that at this step we cannot focus exclusively on only the software parts of the system but must also consider non-software parts.

The events identified at this design step are defined, using the DDN language, in Figure 3. They correspond to four interesting "happenings" of concern at this step

```
EVENT DEFINITION;
    heat up: DESCRIPTION; temperature of an engine becomes greater
                than or equal to 150 degrees F END;,
    ring: DESCRIPTION; audio-alarm device sounds END;,
    notice: DESCRIPTION; monitor recognizes that engine has heated
                up END;,
    handle_hot_engine: SEQUENCE(heat up, notice, ring)
    END EVENT DEFINITION;
```

Figure 3.

and reflect aspects of the system that an external agent could observe during system operation. In addition to three "primitive", undecomposed events, we have defined the overall event of handling a hot engine as a sequence of instances of the three primitive events.

The constraints of interest at this point are recorded in Figure 4, again using

```
DESIRED BEHAVIOR;
    SEQUENCE(heat_up, notice, ring),
    POSSIBLY 4 CONCURRENT
      (SEQUENCE(heat_up, notice, ring))
    END DESIRED BEHAVIOR;
```

Figure 4.

the DDN description technique. First, we have established that every time an engine heats up, this is noticed by the monitoring system and the alarm is sounded. The second constraint reflects the requirement that the handling of hot engines be able to be carried out concurrently in the case that another engine heats up when one hot engine is being handled. In this description, the constraints are expressed in terms of desirable properties of the sequences of the sequences of events which occur during system operation. In approaching the description task this way, the desired effect is non-procedurally and non-prescriptively being specified.

Figure 5 gives a DDN definition of the components suggested by the events that have been defined. Notice the components are ones which operate concurrently and that both hardware and software components are specified.

The interactions among the components are defined, in message transmission terms, in Figure 6. Parts are defined and "plugged" together to establish the communication pathways, and the control process models specify the message transfer among the components. It should be emphasized that message transmission is being used to model the interactions among the components and that the interactions may actually take place using some other mechanism. Note that programming-language-like

```
SUBCOMPONENTS;
    engines ARRAY[1::4] OF [engine],
    monitors ARRAY[1::4] OF [engine_monitor],
    alarm OF [audio_device]
    END SUBCOMPONENTS;
```

Figure 5.

```
[engine_monitor]: SUBSYSTEM CLASS;
    request_status: OUT PORT;  END OUT PORT;
    receive_status: IN PORT;
        BUFFER SUBCOMPONENTS; signal OF [status_signal]
            END BUFFER SUBCOMPONENTS;
        END IN PORT;
    sound_alarm: OUT PORT;  END OUT PORT;
    observe: CONTROL PROCESS;
        MODEL;
            ITERATE SEND request_status;
                    RECEIVE receive_status;
                    IF signal = is_hot
                        THEN notice: NULL;
                                        SEND sound_alarm;
                        END IF;
                    END ITERATE;
            END MODEL;
        END CONTROL PROCESS;
    END SUBSYSTEM CLASS;

[status_signal]: MONITOR CLASS;
    STATE SUBSETS;  is_ok, is_hot  END STATE SUBSETS;
    END MONITOR CLASS:

[engine]: SUBSYSTEM CLASS;
    status_request: IN PORT;  END IN PORT;
    status_report: OUT PORT;
        BUFFER SUBCOMPONENTS; signal OF [status_signal]
            END BUFFER SUBCOMPONENTS;
        END OUT PORT;
    report: CONTROL PROCESS;
        MODEL;
            ITERATE RECEIVE status_request;
                    MAYBE heatup: SET signal TO is_hot;
                        ELSE        SET signal TO is_ok;
                        END MAYBE;
                    END ITERATE;
            END MODEL;
        END CONTROL PROCESS;
    END SUBSYSTEM CLASS;
```

```
[alarm]: SUBSYSTEM CLASS;
   ring_request: IN PORT;  END IN PORT;
   ringer: CONTROL PROCESS;
      MODEL;
         ITERATE RECEIVE ring_request;
               ring: NULL;
                  END ITERATE;
         END MODEL;
      END CONTROL PROCESS;
   END SUBSYSTEM CLASS;

CONNECTIONS;
   FOR ALL i IN [1::4];
      PLUG (engines[i]|status_request, monitors[i]|request_status);
      PLUG (engines[i]|status_report, monitors[i]|receive_status);
      PLUG (engines[i]|sound_alarm,   alarm|ring_request);
      END FOR;
   END CONNECTIONS;
```

Figure 6.

constructs are used to define the interactions. Also note that models of the hardware are specified to record the capabilities that are required -- the engines, for
example, must have sensors and be able to "send out" status signals upon demand.
Finally, note that the events identified at the beginning of this design step have
been related to specific points during the operation of the system by labelling
statements with the event identifiers.

We feel that the event-based design method outlined in the previous discussion
formalizes the general practices of many software designers and that this formalization leads to several benefits. The greatest benefit comes from the provision
of an important additional facility -- the definition of events and constraints.
This facility allows the gradual reduction of requirements to precise statements
oriented to the system's evolving modularization.

Another benefit, which we only briefly argue here, is the ability to verify the design as it evolves. The constraints developed at each step provide a redundant
specification against which the newly designed operation of (part of) the system
may be checked. In our example, we could use the pseudo-procedural descriptions
given in Figure 6 as input to a simulator and thereby derive sequences of event
occurrences. These sequences may then be compared to the desired sequences as
stated in Figure 4. Of course, simulation is not in general sufficient since one
needs to know all possible sequences of events that may arise. It is possible to
derive a description of all possible sequences but the comparison is not, in general, feasible [42]. We are continuing our research in this area, seeking
algorithms for subcases which span a wide variety of naturally occurring situations.

CONCLUSION

We have described a variation of the traditional top-down design method that utilizes the concepts of event and event sequence definition. At each step, criteria
for system modules being elaborated at that step are extracted from the existing
design and precisely stated using the event and event sequence constructs. The
step is then completed by detailing the interactions among newly-designed and existing modules necessary to satisfy the criteria. The opportunity then exists to
analyze the new, partial design to assure that the criteria are met before proceeding to the next design step.

The event-based design method arose in the process of our assessment of the effectiveness of the DREAM development support system and its description language, DDN. We have not extensively used it in design experiments, but have conducted two simple experiments in order to refine its definition. We have found it natural and easy-to-use, and feel that it both formalizes the practices of design practitioners and provides a basis for the integration of analysis with synthesis during software system design.

REFERENCES:

[1] Ambler, A.1., Good, D.I., Browne, J.C., Burger, W.F., Cohen, R.M., Hock,C.G., and Wells, R.E. Gypsy: A language for specification and implementation of verifiable programs. Software Engineering Notes, 2, 2 (March 1977), 1-10.

[2] Baker, J.W., Chester, D., and Yeh, R.T. Software development by step-wise evaluation and refinement. SDBEG-2, Software and Data Base Engineering Group, Dept. of Computer Sci., Univ. of Texas, Austin, January 1978.

[3] Campos, I., and Estrin, G. SARA aided design of software for concurrent systems. Proc. 1978 National Computer Conf., Anaheim, Calif., June 1978, pp. 325-336.

[4] Davis, C.G., and Vick, C.R. The software development system. IEEE Trans. on Software Engineering, SE-3, 1 (January 1977), 69-84.

[5] Estrin, G., and Campos, I. Concurrent software system design, supported by SARA at the age of one. Proc. 3rd International Conf. on Software Engineering, Atlanta, Georgia, May 1978, pp. 230-242.

[6] Estrin, G. Application of machine descriptions to design of concurrent systems. In Moneta, J. (ed.), Information Technology, JCIT3/North-Holland Pub. Co., 1978.

[7] Good, D.I. Constructing verified and reliable communications systems. Software Engineering Notes, 2, 5 (October 1977), 8-13.

[8] Henderson, P., Snowdon, R.A., Gorrie, J.D., and King, I.I. The TOPD System. Tech. Report 77, Computing Laboratory, Univ. of Newcastle upon Tyne, England, September 1975.

[9] Moriconi, M.S. A system for incrementally designing and verifying programs. ICSCA-CMP-9, Certifiable Minicomputer Project, Inst. for Computing Sci. and Computer Applications, Univ. of Texas, Austin, December 1977.

[10] Pearson, D.J. CADES - Computer aided design and evaluation system. Computer Weekly, (July/August 1973).

[11] Riddle, W.E., Wileden, J.C., Sayler, J.H., Segal, A.R. and Stavely, A.M. Behavior modelling during software design. IEEE Trans. on Software Engineering, SE-4, 4 (July 1978), 283-292.

[12] Riddle, W.E., Sayler, J.H., Segal, A.R., Stavely, A.M., and Wileden, J.C. DREAM - A software design aid system. In Moneta, J., (ed.), Information Technology, JCIT-3/North-Holland Pub. Co., August 1978.

[13] Robinson, L., Levitt, K., Neumann, P., and Saxena, A. A formal methodology for the design of operating systems software. In Yeh, R.T. (ed.) Current Trends in Programming Methodology, Vol.I, Prentice-Hall Inc., Englewood Cliffs, N.J., 1977.

[14] Snowdon, R. Interactive use of a computer in the preparation of structured programs. Thesis, Univ. of Newcastle upon Tyne, England, 1976.

[15] Teichroew, D., and Hershey, E.A. PSL/PSA: A computer-aided technique for structured documentation and analysis of information processing systems. IEEE Trans. on Software Engineering, SE-3, 1 (January 1977), 41-48.

[16] Van Horn, E.C. Software evolution using the SEER data base. Digital Equipment Corp., Maynard, Massachusetts, June 1978.

[17] Peters, L.J., and Tripp, L.L. A model of software engineering. Proc. 3rd International Conf. on Software Engineering, Atlanta, May 1978, pp. 63-70.

[18] Manna, Z. Mathematical Theory of Computation. McGraw-Hill, New York, 1974.

[19] Popek, G.J., et al. Notes on the design of Euclid. Software Engineering Notes, 2, 2 (March 1977), 11-18.

[20] Liskov, B., Snyder, A., Atkinson, R., and Schaffert, C. Abstraction mechanisms in CLU. Comm. ACM, 20, 8 (August 1977), 564-576.

[21] Wulf, W.A., London, R.L., Shaw, M. Abstraction and verification in Alphard. In Schuman, S.A. (ed.), New Directions in Algorithmic Languages, IRIA (1975).

[22] Dijkstra, E. A Discipline of Programming. Prentice-Hall, Englewood Cliffs, N.J., 1976.

[23] Riddle, W.E. Hierarchical description of software system organization. RSSM/40, CU-CS-120-77, Dept. of Computer Sci., Univ. of Colorado at Boulder, November 1977.

[24] Dahl, O., and Nygaard, K. SIMULA - An Algol-based simulation language. Comm. A.C.M., 9, 9 (September 1966), 671-678.

[25] Henderson, P. Finite state modelling in program development. Proc. 1975 International Conf. on Reliable Software, Los Angeles, April 1975.

[26] Liskov, B.H., and Zilles, S.N. Specification techniques for data abstractions. IEEE Trans. on Software Engineering, SE-1, 1 (March 1975), 7-19.

[27] Parnas, D.L. A technique for software module specification with examples. Comm. ACM, 15, 5 (May 1972), 330-336.

[28] Wirth, N. The programming language PASCAL. Acta Informatica, 1, (1971), 35-63.

[29] Dahl, O., Dijkstra, E., and Hoare, C.A.R. Structured Programming, Academic Press, N.Y., 1973.

[30] Wirth, N. Program development by step-wise refinement. Comm. ACM, 14, 4 (April 1971), 221-227.

[31] Riddle, W.E. Abstract process types. RSSM/42, CU-CS-121-77, Dept. of Computer Sci., Univ. of Colorado at Boulder, December 1977 (revised July 1978).

[32] Riddle, W.E., Sayler, J.H., Segal, A.R., Stavely, A.M., and Wileden, J.C. A description scheme to aid the design of collections of concurrent processes. Proc. 1978 National Computer Conf., Anaheim, Calif., June 1978, pp. 549-554.

[33] Simon, H.A. The architecture of complexity. Proc. Am. Phil. Soc., 106, (December 1962), pp. 467-482. Also in Simon, Sciences of the Artificial, MIT Press, Cambridge, 1969.

[34] Brinch Hansen, P. The Design of Concurrent Processes. Prentice-Hall, Englewood Cliffs, N.J., 1977.

[35] Habermann, A.N. Introduction to Operating System Design. SRA, Chicago, 1976.

[36] Fennel, R., Lesser, V.R. Parallelism in artificial intelligence problem solving: A case study of HEARSAY II. IEEE Trans. on Computers, C-26, 2 (February 1977).

[37] Wileden, J.C. Behavior specification in a software design system. RSSM/43, COINS Tech. Rep. 78-14, Dept. of Computer and Info. Sci., Univ. of Massachusetts, Amherst, July 1978.

[38] Riddle, W.E. An approach to software system behavior description. To Appear: J. of Computer Languages.

[39] Campbell, R.A., and Habermann, A.N. The specification of process synchronization by path expressions. In Lecture Notes in Computer Science, 16, Springer Verlag, Heidelberg, 1974.

[40] Habermann, A.N., Path expressions. Computer Sci. Dept., Carnegie-Mellon Univ., Pittsburg, June 1975.

[41] Shaw, A.C. Software descriptions with flow expressions. IEEE Trans. on Software Engineering, SE-4, 3 (May 1978), 242-254.

[42] Riddle, W.E. An approach to software system modelling and analysis. To appear: J. of Computer Languages.

[43] Riddle, W.E. A formalism for the comparison of software analysis techniques. RSSM/29, Dept. of Computer and Comm. Sci., Univ. of Michigan, Ann Arbor, July 1977.

[44] Stavely, A.M. Design feedback and its use in software design aid systems. Proc. Software Quality Assurance Workshop, San Diego, November 1978.

[45] Sanguinetti, J.W. Performance prediction in an operating system design methodology. RSSM/32 (Ph.D. Thesis), Dept. of Computer and Comm. Sci., Univ. of Michigan, Ann Arbor, May 1977.

[46] Cuny, J. A DREAM model of the RC 4000 multiprogramming system. RSSM/48, Dept. of Computer and Comm. Sci., Univ. of Michigan, Ann Arbor, July 1977.

[47] Cuny, J. The GM terminal system. RSSM/63, Dept. of Computer and Comm. Sci., Univ. of Michigan, Ann Arbor, August 1977.

[48] Riddle, W.E. DREAM design notation example: The T.H.E. operating system. RSSM/50, Dept. of Computer Sci., Univ. of Colorado at Boulder, April 1978.

[49] Segal, A.R. DREAM design notation example: A multiprocessor supervisor. RSSM/53, Dept. of Computer and Comm.Sci., Univ. of Michigan, Ann Arbor, August 1977.

[50] Riddle, W.E., Sayler, J.H., Segal, A.R., Stavely, A.M. and Wileden, J.C. Abstract monitor types. Proc. of Specification of Reliable Software Conf., Boston, April 1979.

[1] The distinction of phases which we use here is a simplified version of the many, diverse distinctions that have been made by others, for example by [17].

[2] For the remainder of this paper we use the term design to refer to architectural design.

Part VI

Architectural Design Techniques: Data View

Part V focuses primarily on process decomposition and structure in creating a software architecture. The papers in this Part, by contrast, give primary attention to the data design component of software systems and to techniques for deriving the data design. To some extent, this distinction is artificial, since every software design activity must eventually address both the process design and data design. However, we have made the distinction on the basis of whether process aspects or data aspects *drive* the design process.

On a historical basis, the process-oriented approach is considerably older than the data- (or object-) oriented approach. The data-oriented approach derives from two separate streams of work: formal specifications of abstract data objects and conceptual modeling of database and information systems. The articles reprinted here illustrate both of these approaches.

Much of the work in formal specification of data objects is closely related to work in program verification. To prove a program correct, one must be able to give a mathematical proof that a program conforms to its specification. In the absence of a formal mathematically based specification of the system, it is impossible to give such a proof. By describing systems in terms of the objects (or object classes) used in a system and the operations that are performed upon those objects, one is able to specify and verify each operation separately.

The paper by Liskov and Zilles describes some of these techniques for algebraic specification of data objects, laying out the important concepts of this idea. This topic has been pursued by many groups since the mid-1970's and is found to be an important issue in software specification and design, program verification, and programming language design. Many of the programming languages designed since then incorporate a mechanism for supporting the implementation of such data objects.

Approaches to information system design methodologies, such as TAXIS (described in Part III) and User Software Engineering (described in Part IX), have extended the ideas to objects beyond the stacks and queues described in this paper. The paper by Leveson, Wasserman, and Berry shows the use of such behavioral abstraction for the specification of information systems. The five-step process described in the paper permits formal specification and verification of such systems. It is important to note that the formalization is not given in axioms, as is done by Liskov/Zilles and other workers in abstract data types, but rather in preconditions and postconditions. The pre- and post-condition approach was found to be more compatible with assertions in programming languages and in the expression of the complex relationships among objects and operations in an information system.

The importance of formal specification of data types can be seen from Gehani's paper, where he describes the successful use of formal specification to detect some specification problems and to improve the design. As noted in the Introduction to Part III, formal specifications alone are not sufficient for the specification of a system, and informal specifications are useful and necessary, especially for persons who are unfamiliar with the mathematical notation. Gehani's experience supports this observation and he shows further that formal specifications are useful in improving the quality of the informal specification.

Grady Booch's paper, "Object-Oriented Design," adapted from his book *Software Engineering with Ada* (Benjamin, 1983) and contributed to this volume, shows how to use the object-oriented ideas in the context of module development *and* implementation using Ada[TM] packages. The steps of his approach involve identifying the objects, identifying the operations on the objects, establishing the interfaces, and programming the operations. He shows these steps through an example of counting leaves on a binary tree.

The use of object-oriented approaches and/or formal specifications of data types implies that an

---

[TM]Ada is a trademark of the US Department of Defense (Ada Joint Program Office).

EHO205-5/83/0000/0393$01.00 © 1983 IEEE

analysis activity has preceded the specification. Indeed, in Booch's method, he assumes previous specification of an entire system and application of the object-oriented design ideas to a small piece of the system. A typical system would have many objects and many operations, so it would be necessary to apply these ideas repeatedly. However, by using the decomposition and modularization ideas described previously, it would be possible to apply such a "divide and conquer" approach.

The two remaining papers in this Part each propose a multistage methodology for database design. Because they are oriented toward database design, they should be used in conjunction with some of the other analysis, specification, and design ideas presented elsewhere in this collection.

The Smiths' approach is based on the use of three kinds of abstraction -- classification, aggregation, and generalization -- to understand the problem and to design the database. These abstraction methods are at the heart of a "conceptual data model," a high-level view of objects and their interrelationships. The conceptual data model can be mapped in several ways, such as to one or more external data models revealing some particular aspect of the conceptual model (as might be seen by a particular user group) or to a physical data model, representing the realization of part or all of that conceptual model with a particular database management system.

It should be noted that the conceptual data model hides information about the internal representation of the data and its physical structures and that the external data model may hide information from users that is present in the conceptual model. In other words, many of the concepts of data modeling and database design are very similar to those we have seen in the process-oriented view.

The Smiths' conceptual data model, called the Semantic Hierarchy Model, is a strong influence in TAXIS and RMF, as described by Greenspan, Mylopoulos, and Borgida in Part III. One can also easily see the way in which a conceptual data model fits within the framework established by Bubenko in Part II.

Another approach to system design is shown in the Yao, Navathe, and Weldon paper, in which they model a number of disparate user views of a database (external views) and then proceed through view restructuring and view integration to yield a single workable design. The resulting design may be a conceptual design or a lower level design constrained by some database management system. If we assume that the product is a conceptual design, though, we see that the Smiths' approach starts with a conceptual design and yields external views (top down) and that the Yao, Navathe, and Weldon approach is bottom-up.

In summary, we are seeing a unification of the ideas from the process-oriented and data-oriented approaches. Whether one starts from the "top" or the "bottom," it is necessary to fill in the details from top to bottom. Similarly, starting with the data objects yields the required operations, and initial identification of the operations must result in recognition of the objects upon which the operations are performed.

Specification Techniques for Data Abstractions

BARBARA H. LISKOV AND STEPHEN N. ZILLES, MEMBER, IEEE

Reprinted from *IEEE Transactions on Software Engineering*, Volume SE-1, Number 1, March 1975, pages 7–19. Copyright © 1975 by The Institute of Electrical and Electronics Engineers, Inc.

Abstract—The main purposes in writing this paper are to discuss the importance of formal specifications and to survey a number of promising specification techniques. The role of formal specifications both in proofs of program correctness, and in programming methodologies leading to programs which are correct by construction, is explained. Some criteria are established for evaluating the practical potential of specification techniques. The importance of providing specifications at the right level of abstraction is discussed, and a particularly interesting class of specification techniques, those used to construct specifications of data abstractions, is identified. A number of specification techniques for describing data abstractions are surveyed and evaluated with respect to the criteria. Finally, directions for future research are indicated.

Index Terms—Data abstractions, programming methodology, proofs of correctness, specifications, specification techniques.

I. INTRODUCTION

IN THE past, the advantages of formal specifications have been outweighed by the difficulty of constructing them for practical programs. However, recent work in programming methodology has identified a program unit, supporting a data abstraction, which is both widely useful, and for which it is practical to write formal specifications. Some formal specification techniques have already been developed for describing data abstractions. It is the promise of these techniques, some of which are described later in this paper, which leads us to believe that formal specifications can soon become an intrinsic feature of the program construction process. By writing this paper, we hope to encourage research in the development of formal specification techniques, and their application to practical program construction.

In the remainder of the introduction we discuss what is meant by formal specifications, and then explain some advantages arising from their use. In Section II a number of criteria are presented which will permit us to judge techniques for constructing formal specifications. Section III identifies the kind of program unit, supporting a data abstraction, to which the specification techniques described later in this paper apply. Section IV discusses properties of specification techniques for data abstractions and in Section V some existing techniques for providing specifications for data abstractions are surveyed and compared. Finally, we conclude by pointing out areas for future research.

Manuscript received December 4, 1974; revised February 5, 1975. This work was supported in part by the IBM funds for research in computer science.

B. H. Liskov is with the Department of Electrical Engineering and Computer Science, Massachusetts Institute of Technology, Cambridge, Mass.

S. N. Zilles is with IBM Corporation, San Jose, Calif.

Proofs of Correctness

Of serious concern in software construction are techniques which permit us to recognize whether a given program is correct, i.e., does what it is supposed to do. Although we are coming to realize that correctness is not the only desirable property of reliable software, surely it is the most fundamental. If a program is not correct, then its other properties (e.g., efficiency, fault tolerance) have no meaning since we cannot depend on them.

Techniques for establishing the correctness of programs may be classified as to whether they are formal or informal. All techniques in common use today (debugging, testing, program reading) are informal techniques; either the investigation of the properties of the program is incomplete, or the steps in the reasoning place too much dependence on human ingenuity and intuition. The continued existence of errors in software to which such techniques have been applied attests to their inadequacy. Formal techniques, such as the verification condition [1], [2] and fixed-point [3] methods, attempt to establish properties of a program with respect to all legitimate inputs by means of a process of reasoning in which each step is formally justified by appeal to rules of inference, axioms and theorems. Unfortunately, these techniques have been very difficult to apply, and have therefore not yet been of much practical interest. However interest in formal techniques can be expected to increase in the future; economic pressure for reliable software is growing [4] and the domain of applicability of formal techniques is also growing because of the development of programming methodologies leading to programs to which formal techniques are more readily applied. Indeed, application of proof techniques to practical programs is being attempted in the area of operating system security [5]–[7], where the need for absolute certainty about the correct functioning of software is very great.

To study techniques which establish program correctness, it is interesting to examine a model of what the correctness of a program means. What we are looking for is a process which establishes that a program correctly implements a *concept* which exists in someone's mind. The concept can usually be implemented by many programs—an infinite number, in general—but of these only a small finite number are of practical interest. This situation is shown in Fig. 1. In current practice, the concept is stated informally and, regardless of the technique used to demonstrate the correctness of a program (usually testing), the result of applying the technique can be stated only in informal terms.

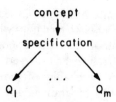

Fig. 1.   Concept and all the programs which implement the concept correctly.

Fig. 2.   Concept, its formal specification, and all programs which can be proved equivalent to the specification.

With formal techniques, a *specification* is interposed between the concept and the programs. Its purpose is to provide a mathematical description of the concept, and the correctness of a program is established by proving that it is equivalent to the specification. The specification will be provably satisfied by a class of programs (again, often an infinite number of which only a small finite number are of interest). This situation is shown in Fig. 2.

Proofs of large programs do not consist of a single monolithic proof with no interior structure. Instead, the overall proof is divided into a hierarchy of many smaller proofs which establish the correctness of separate program units. For each program unit, a proof is given that it satisfies its specification; this proof makes use of the specifications of other program units, and rests on the assumption that those program units will be proved consistent with their specifications.[1] Thus a specification is used in two ways: as a description against which a program is proved correct, and as a set of axioms in the proof of other programs. At the top of the proof hierarchy is a program unit which corresponds to the entire program. At the bottom is the programming language, and the hierarchy is based on the axioms for the programming language and its primitives.

The proof methodology can fail in two ways. First, a proof may incorrectly establish some program (or program unit) P as equivalent to the specification when, in fact, it is not. This is a problem which can be eliminated by using a computer as, at least, a proof checker. (Observe that one advantage of using formal specifications is that such specifications can be processed by a computer.)

The second way the methodology can fail is if the specification does not correctly capture the meaning of a concept. We will say a specification *captures* a concept if every Q_i in Fig. 2 is some P_j in Fig. 1. There is no formal way of establishing that a specification captures a concept, but we expect to have gained from using the proof methodology

because (hopefully) a specification is easier to understand than a program, so that "convincing oneself" that a specification captures a concept is less error prone than a similar process to a program. Furthermore, any distinction between concept and specification may be irrelevant because of the hierarchical nature of the proof process. If a program P is proven equivalent to its specification, and every program using P is proven correct using that specification, then the concept which P was intended to implement can safely be ignored.

Advantages of Formal Specifications

Proving the correctness of programs is described above as a two step process: first, a formal specification is provided to describe the concept, and second, the program is proven equivalent to the specification by formal, analytic means. Formal techniques are not necessarily limited to axiomatic methods. For example, it may also be possible to develop testing methodologies that are based on a comparison of the formal specification and the implementation. The output of a methodology would be a set of critical test cases which, if successfully executed, establish that the program correctly implements the specification. The formality of the specification means that the computer can aid in the proof process, for example, by checking the steps of a program proof, or by automatically generating test cases.

Clearly, the specification must be present before a proof can be given. However, formal specifications are of interest even if not followed by a formal proof. Formal specifications are very valuable in conjunction with the idea of making code "public" [8] in order to encourage programmers to read one another's code. In the absence of a formal specification, a programmer can only compare a program he is reading with his intuitive understanding of what the program is supposed to do. A formal specification would be better, since intuition is often unreliable. With the addition of formal specifications, code reading becomes an informal proof technique; each step in the proof process now rests on understanding a formal description rather than manipulating the description in a formal way.[2] As such, it can be a powerful aid in establishing program correctness.

Formal specifications can also play a major role while a program is being constructed. It is widely recognized that a specification of what a program is intended to do should be given before the program is actually coded, both to aid understanding of the concept involved, and to increase the likelihood that the program, when implemented, will perform the intended function. However, because it is difficult to construct specifications using informal techniques, such as English, specifications are often omitted, or are

---

[1] Special techniques [3] must be used if the program units are mutually recursive.

[2] The relationship between proofs and understanding is a major motivating factor in structured programming. For example, the "go to" statement is eliminated because the remaining control structures are each associated with a well-known proof technique, and therefore the programs are intellectually manageable [9].

given in a sketchy and incomplete manner. Formal specification techniques, like the ones to be described later in this paper, provide a concise and well-understood specification or design language, which should reduce the difficulty of constructing specifications.

Formal specifications are superior to informal ones as a communication medium. The specifications developed during the design process serve to communicate the intentions of the designer of a program to its implementors, or to communicate between two programmers: the programmer implementing the program being specified, and the programmer who wishes to use that program. Problems arise if the specification is ambiguous: that is, fails for some reason to capture the concept so that two programs with different conceptual properties both satisfy the specification. Ambiguities can be resolved by mutual agreement, provided those using the specification realize that an ambiguity exists. Often this is not realized, and instead the ambiguity is resolved in different ways by different people. Formal specifications are less likely to be ambiguous than informal ones because they are written in an unambiguous language. Also, the meaning of a formal specification is understood in a formal way, and therefore ambiguities are more likely to be recognized.

The above paragraphs have sketched a program construction methodology that could lead to programs which are correct by construction. Formal specifications play a major role in this methodology, which differs from standard descriptions of structured programming [9] primarily in the emphasis it places on specifications.[3] Specifications are first introduced by the designer to describe the concepts he develops in a precise and unambiguous way. Each concept will be supported by a program module. The specifications are used as a communication medium among the designers and the implementors to insure both that an implementor understands the designer's intentions about a program module he is coding, and that two implementors agree about the interface between their modules. Finally, the correctness of the program is proved in the hierarchical fashion described earlier. The method of proof may be either formal or informal, and the proofs can be carried out as the modules are developed, rather than waiting for the entire program to be coded. Progress in developing formal specification techniques will enhance the practicality of applying this methodology to the construction of large programs.

II. CRITERIA FOR EVALUATING SPECIFICATION METHODS

An approach to specification must satisfy a number of requirements if it is to be useful. Since one of the most important goals of specification techniques is to permit the writing of specifications for practical programs, the criteria described below include practical as well as theoretical considerations.

[3] See the paper by Hoare [10] for a structured programming example in which specifications are emphasized.

We consider that the first criterion must be satisfied by any specification technique.

1) Formality: A specification method should be formal, that is, specifications should be written in a notation which is mathematically sound. This criterion is mandatory if the specifications are to be used in conjunction with proofs of program correctness. In addition, formal specification techniques can be studied mathematically, so that other interesting questions, such as the equivalence of two specifications, may be posed and answered. Finally, formal specifications are capable of being understood by computers, and automatic processing of specifications should be of increasing importance in the future.

The next two criteria address the fundamental problem with specifications—the difficulty encountered in using them.

2) Constructibility: It must be possible to construct specifications without undue difficulty. We assume that the writer of the specification understands both the specification technique and the concept to be specified. Two facets of the construction process are of interest here: the difficulty of constructing a specification in the first place, and the difficulty in knowing that the specification captures the concept.

3) Comprehensibility: A person trained in the notation being used should be able to read a specification and then, with a minimum of difficulty, reconstruct the concept which the specification is intended to describe. Here (and in criterion 2) we have a subjective measure in mind in which the difficulty encountered in constructing or reading a specification is compared with the inherent complexity (as intuitively felt) of the concept being specified. Properties of specifications which determine comprehensibility are size and lucidity. Clearly small specifications are good since they are (usually) easier to understand than larger ones. For example it would be nice if a specification were substantially smaller than the program it specifies. However, even if the specification is large, it may still be easier to understand than the program because its description of the concept is more lucid.

The final three criteria address the flexibility and generality of the specification technique. It is likely that techniques satisfying these criteria will meet criteria 2 and 3 as well.

4) Minimality: It should be possible using the specification method to construct specifications which describe the interesting properties of the concept and *nothing more.* The properties which are of interest must be described precisely and unambiguously but in a way which adds as little extraneous information as possible. In particular, a specification must say *what* function(s) a program should perform, but little, if anything, about *how* the function is performed. One reason this criterion is desirable is because it minimizes correctness proofs by reducing the number of properties to be proved.

5) Wide Range of Applicability: Associated with each specification technique there is a class of concepts which the technique can describe in a natural and straightforward fashion, leading to specifications satisfying criteria 2 and 3. Concepts outside of the class can only be defined with difficulty, if they can be defined at all (for example, concepts involving parallelism will not be describable by any of the techniques discussed later in the paper). Clearly, the larger the class of concepts which may be easily described by a technique, the more useful the technique.

6) Extensibility: It is desirable that a minimal change in a concept results in a similar small change in its specification. This criterion especially impacts the constructibility of specifications.

III. THE SPECIFICATION UNIT

The quality of a specification (the extent to which it satisfies the criteria of the preceding section) is dependent in large part on the program unit being specified. If a specification is attached to too small a unit, for example, a single statement, what the specification says may be uninteresting, and furthermore there will be more specifications than can conveniently be handled. (The specification could express no more than the following comment, sometimes seen in programs:

$$x := x + 1; \quad \text{``increase } x \text{ by 1.''})$$

A specification of too small a unit does not correspond to any useful concept. What is wanted is a specification unit which corresponds naturally to a concept, or abstraction, found useful in thinking about the problem to be solved.

The most commonly used kind of abstraction is the functional or procedural abstraction in which a parameterized expression or collection of statements is treated as a single operation. The specification for a functional abstraction is normally given by an *input–output specification* which describes the mapping of the set of input values into the set of output values.

Recent work in the area of programming methodology, however, has identified another kind of abstraction, the *data abstraction.* This comprises a group of related functions or operations that act upon a particular class of objects, with the constraint that the behavior of the objects can be observed only by applications of the operations [11].[4] A typical example of a data abstraction is a "push down stack"; the class of objects consists of all possible stacks, and the group of operations includes the ordinary stack operations, like push and pop, an operation to create new stacks, and an operation to test whether a stack is empty.

Data abstractions are widely used in large programs, although the constraint on observable object behavior has not always been followed.[5] Some examples are segments, processes, files, and abstract devices of various sorts, in addition to the more ordinary stacks, queues, and symbol tables. In each case the implementation of

the abstraction is given in the form of a multiprocedure module [14]. Each procedure in the module implements one of the operations; the module as a whole may provide a single object (for example, there is a single system data base), some fixed maximum number of objects (for example, there is a fixed maximum number of segments), or as many objects as users require (for example, a new stack is provided whenever a user asks for one).

The realization that a multiprocedure module is important in system design preceded the identification of the multiprocedure module as an implementation of a data abstraction.[6] It is illuminating to examine the arguments in favor of the multiprocedure module as an implementation unit. The procedures are grouped together because they interact in some way: they share certain resources (for example, a data base which only they use, and possibly some real resource, like the real-time clock owned by the process abstraction in [15]); and they also share information (for example, about the format and meaning of the data in the shared-data base, and the meaning of the states of the shared resource). Considering the entire group of procedures as a module permits all information about the interactions to be hidden from other modules [16]: other modules obtain information about the interactions only by invoking the procedures in the group [14]. The hiding of information simplifies the interface between modules, and leads directly to simpler specifications because it is precisely the interface which the specifications must describe.

As an example of the problems which arise when the data abstraction is ignored and the operations in the group are given input–output specifications independently of one another, consider the following specification for the operation push. Assuming the push operation is a function,

$$\text{push: stack} \times \text{integer} \rightarrow \text{stack}$$

the input–output specification must define the information content of the output value of push (the stack object returned by push) in terms of the input values of push (a stack object and an integer). This can be done by defining a structure for stack objects, and then describing the effect of push in terms of this structure. A typical stack structure might be (in PASCAL [17])

<u>type</u> stack = <u>record</u> top: <u>integer</u>,
data: <u>array</u> [1···100] of <u>integer</u>
<u>end</u>

and then the meaning of

$$t := \text{push } (s,i)$$

could be stated (using notation developed by Hoare [2])[7]

---

[4] Morris has discussed some criteria for determining what constitutes a sufficient set of operations [12].
[5] The constraint has been followed in the Venus system [13].

[6] It is an open question whether every multiprocedure module implements a data abstraction. We believe that the correspondence holds. In the Venus system [13], which was built entirely from such modules, every module did correspond to a data abstraction.
[7] This specification ignores the behavior of push if the stack is full, that is if s.top = 100.

true $\{t := \text{push } (s,i)\} \; \forall j[1 \le j \le s.\text{top}$

$$\supset t.\text{data}[j] = s.\text{data}[j]$$

$$\& \; t.\text{data}[t.\text{top}] = i$$

$$\& \; t.\text{top} = s.\text{top} + 1].$$

A similar specification could be given for pop.

There are several things wrong with such a specification. A serious flaw is that it does not describe the concept of stack-like behavior, but instead specifies a lot of extraneous detail. Concepts of stack-like behavior—for example, a theorem stating that pop returns the value most recently pushed on the stack—can only be inferred from this detail. The inclusion of extraneous detail is undesirable for two reasons. First, the inventor of the concept must get involved in the detail (which is really implementation information), rather than stating the concept directly. Second, the inclusion of the detail detracts from the minimality (as defined in the criteria) of the specification, and it is likely that a correctness proof of an implementation of push and pop based on a different representation for stack objects would be difficult. Another problem is that the independence of the specifications of push and pop is illusory; a change in the specification of one of them is almost certain to lead to a change in the specification of the other. For example, in addition to being related through the structure chosen for stack objects, the specifications of push and pop are also related in their interpretation of this structure: the decision to have the selector "top" point to the topmost piece of data in the stack (rather than to the first available slot).

If a data abstraction such as stack is specified as a single entity, much of the extraneous detail (concerning the interactions between the operations) can be eliminated, and the effects of the operations can be described at a higher level. Some specification techniques for data abstractions as a unit use input–ouput specifications to describe the effects of the operations, but these specifications are expressed in terms of abstract objects with abstract properties instead of the very specific properties used in the example above. In other techniques, it is not even necessary to describe the individual operations separately, but instead, the effects of the operations can be described in terms of one another. As an example, just to convey a feeling for the latter approach, the effect of pop might be defined in terms of push by

$$\text{pop } (\text{push } (s,v)) = v$$

which states that pop returns the value most recently pushed.

In the remainder of the paper, we will concentrate on specification techniques for data abstractions. In doing this we will not ignore input–output specifications since these form a part of some of the techniques we will discuss, but we will also discuss techniques, like the one illustrated above, that are applicable only to data abstractions. We limit our attention in this way because the specification techniques for data abstractions are all fairly recent, and have received relatively little attention so

Fig. 3. Operations of the stack abstraction and their functionality.

far. Also, the information-hiding aspect of data abstractions, discussed above, promises that specification techniques focused on such units will satisfy the criteria very well.

IV. PROPERTIES OF SPECIFICATIONS OF DATA ABSTRACTIONS

Although the specification techniques to be described in the next section differ from one another in many particulars, there are also ways in which they are similar. All the techniques must convey the same information—information about the meaning of data abstractions—and this information is conveyed in a mathematical way. In this section, we discuss a mathematical view of the specification techniques, and the information contained in the specifications. We also discuss some of the problems arising from discrepancies between the mathematical and programming views of data abstractions.

All the specification techniques for data abstractions can be viewed as defining something very like a mathematical *discipline*; the discipline arises from the specification of the data abstraction in a manner not unlike the way in which number theory arises from specifications, like Peano's axioms, for the natural numbers. The *domain* of the discipline—the set on which it is based—is the class of objects belonging to the data abstraction, and the operations of the data abstraction are defined as mappings on this domain. The theory of the discipline consists of the theorems and lemmas derivable from the specifications.

The information contained in a specification of a data abstraction can be divided into a semantic part and a syntactic part. Information about the actual meaning or behavior of the data abstraction is described in the semantic part; the description is expressed using a vocabulary of terms or symbols defined by the syntactic part.

The first symbols which must be defined by the syntactic part of a specification identify the abstraction being defined and its domain or class of objects. Usually, an abstraction has a single class of defined objects, and, in this case, it is conventional to use the same symbol to denote both the abstraction and its class of objects. Thus the objects belonging to the data abstraction, stack, are referred to as stacks. (It is possible for an abstraction to have more than one class of defined objects, but this presents no mathematical difficulties, and we will not consider it further [18].)

The remaining symbols introduced by the syntactic part name the operations of the abstraction, and define their functionality—the domains of their input and output values. An example is shown in Fig. 3, where the functionality of the operations of the data abstraction, stack, is described. (In Fig. 3, the operation, TOP, returns the value in the top of the stack without removing it; POP removes the value without returning it.)

Several interesting observations can be made about this example. First, more than one domain appears in the specification in Fig. 3. In practice, the specifications for almost all interesting data abstractions include more than one domain. Normally, only one of these (the class of stacks in the example) is being defined; the remaining domains (integer in the example) and their properties are assumed to be known. Of course, the specifications must clearly distinguish between the domains assumed to be known and the ones to be defined.

A second observation is that, given this distinction, the group of operations can be partitioned into three blocks. The first block, the *primitive constructors*, consists of those operations that have no operands which belong to the class being defined, but which yield results in the defined class. This block includes the constants, represented as argumentless operations (for example, the CREATE operation for stacks). The second block, the *combinational constructors*, consists of those operations (PUSH and POP in the example) which have some of their operands in and yield their results in the defined class. The third block consists of those operations (TOP for stacks) whose results are not in the defined class.

A third observation is that the mathematical description of the functionality of an operation does not necessarily correspond to the way the operation would be programmed. One difference is that the functions in the example have only one output value, while in practice it is often desirable for a program to return more than one result. For example, one might define a stack operation

POP2: STACK $\rightarrow$ STACK $\times$ INTEGER

which removes a value from a stack, and returns both the new stack and the value. This operation can be modeled mathematically by a pair of operations, one for each result. For example, the result of POP2 can be defined as the pair of results from POP and TOP, where both are applied simultaneously to the same stack value. When such an association is made, the specification must clearly indicate the relationship between the operation symbols.

A more serious discrepancy is that the operations are viewed by the specification as acting on time-invariant, mathematical values, but the objects found in most programming languages can be modified in some way. These modifications are the result of side effects in some of the applicable operations. For example, although the PUSH operation used above is purely functional, it would more likely be implemented so that no result is returned, and PUSH modifies (has a side effect upon) an existing stack object.

The now conventional solution to this difficulty is to factor a modifiable object into two components: an object identity (unique for each distinct object) and a current state. The modifications affect only the state component, so a given object (over time) is represented by a sequence of pairs of values in which the object identity is always the same. Each operation with a side effect is defined by a mapping which yields a new pair of values representing the same object and a new state.

There are two frequently occurring cases in which the identity component of an object can be omitted in the specifications. First, if there is only one object, such as in the KWIC index example described by Parnas [19], then the identity component is obviously redundant. Second, if, as is the case in certain programming languages, the identity of an object is uniquely given by the symbolic name of identifier that denotes the object, then a separate identity component is unnecessary. The symbolic name of an object becomes its identity, and the use of a new symbolic name implies that a new object is introduced.[8] This approach is unsatisfactory for the many languages in which a given object may have two or more distinct symbolic names; for example, an object may be accessible both via a parameter and a global name. Then the approach fails because side effects will not appear under both names (see for example, [20]).

The semantic part of the specification uses the symbols defined in the syntactic part to express the meaning of the data abstraction. Two different approaches are used in in capturing this meaning: either an abstract model is provided for the class of objects and the operations defined in terms of the model, or the class of objects is defined implicitly via descriptions of the operations.

In following the abstract model approach, the behavior is actually defined by giving an abstract implementation in terms of another data abstraction or mathematical discipline, one whose properties are well understood. The data abstraction being used as the model also has a number of operations, and these are used to define the new operations. The complexity of the descriptions depends on how closely the new operations match the old ones. Sometimes they match very closely; at other times the descriptions can be arbitrarily complex.

The approach of defining the objects implicitly via descriptions of the operations is much closer to the way mathematical disciplines are usually defined. The domain or class of objects is determined inductively. Usually it is the smallest set closed under the operations. Only those operations identified above as constructors are used in defining this closure. The closure is the smallest set which contains the results of the primitive constructors and the results of the combinational constructors when the appropriate operands are drawn from the set. For example, with stacks, the only primitive constructor is the constant operation CREATE which yields the empty stack, and the class of stacks consists of the empty stack and all stacks that result from applying sequences of PUSH's and POP's to it. One difficulty with the implicit definition approach is that if the specifications are not sufficiently complete, in the sense that all the relationships among the operations are indicated, several distinct sets

---

[8] See, for example, Hoare's rule of assignment [2].

may be closed under the operations. The distinct sets result from different resolutions of the unspecified relationships.

In the next section, specification techniques employing both the abstract model and the implicit definition approaches will be discussed.

V. SPECIFICATION TECHNIQUES

In this section we present a survey of selected techniques for giving formal specifications of data abstractions. This survey is not complete, but it is intended to be illustrative. We do not describe the techniques in enough detail for the reader to be able to immediately apply them; indeed, achieving such a description is a matter of research for at least some of the techniques. Rather, our intention is to introduce the most promising formal techniques, to indicate their strengths and weaknesses, and to provide pointers into the literature so that more information can be obtained.

Of the many techniques by which a data abstraction can be specified, most do not meet the criteria set forth in Section II because they are either too informal, or too low level. Thus, textual (English) specifications and specifications in terms of an implementation, such as the class definitions of SIMULA 67 [21], will not be considered. In addition, a number of techniques developed for specifying the semantics of programming languages—though relevant in varying degree—are not considered because of their specialized use. The techniques that are discussed and which seem most promising are those which use some form of abstraction to reduce the complexity of the specifications.

The techniques fall into five categories which are (in order of increasing abstractness of the specifications): use of a fixed domain of formal objects, such as sets or graphs; use of an appropriate, but otherwise arbitrary, known formal domain; use of a state machine model; use of an implicit definition in terms of axioms; and use of an implicit definition in terms of algebraic relations. Techniques in the first two categories use the abstract model approach, while those in the remaining categories use the implicit definition approach. Each of the categories is illustrated by one particular technique chosen to be typical of the category and, where possible, to be accessible in the literature. Following the description of the example, the technique is evaluated with respect to the criteria of Section II. Finally, we summarize the evaluations, and compare the categories with one another.

Use of a Fixed Discipline

We begin by discussing specification techniques in which a fixed language—that of some established mathematical discipline—is used for all specifications. The given discipline is used to provide a high-level (abstract) implementation or model of the desired data abstraction. The class of objects is represented by a subset of the mathematical domain and the operations are defined in terms of the

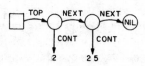

Fig. 4. *V*-graph representation for a stack.

Fig. 5. *V*-graph representing the initial stack configuration.

operations on that domain. Although any mathematical discipline (number theory, analysis) might be used, practical usage has been restricted primarily to graphs [22]–[24], sets [25]–[27], and the theory developed around the Vienna Definition Language [28].

As an example of using a fixed discipline, we will consider Earley's use of graphs in describing data structures [22]. Each instance of a data structure is represented by a graph or, as he called it, a *V*-graph. These are constructed from atoms, nodes, and links. Atoms represent data with no substructure. Links are given labels, called selectors, and are directed from nodes to nodes or atoms; the only requirement on links is that two links with the same selector can not emanate from the same node. The selectors can be any node or atom (strings, integers). Nodes have no significance other than as place holders in the structure being described; in our discussion, we will display nodes as circles, except that header nodes will be displayed as boxes. For example, a representation of a stack holding the integers 2 and 25 is shown in Fig. 4; the structure has a single header node, and the node labeled NIL is a special terminator. The values stored in the stack are accessible via the selector, CONT.

Once a *V*-graph representation has been chosen, two methods are available for defining the operations. First, operations may be defined by expressions written in terms of primitive *V*-graph operations. These operations provide the ability to use the selectors to access and modify the links and nodes. Thus, the stack operation TOP can be defined directly to access the contents of the node selected by the selector TOP.

A second definition method is used to describe operations which modify the structure of the representing *V*-graphs. These operations are defined by means of pictures of *V*-graph transformations. The operations could be described by complicated expressions in terms of the primitive operations; however by using pictures, a more minimal description, containing less extraneous detail, can be achieved. For example, the stack operations PUSH, POP, and CREATE are defined via transformations. First, an initial configuration is defined to represent the empty stack produced by CREATE; this is shown in Fig. 5. Then, PUSH and POP are defined by giving before and after pictures for the corresponding transformations. The left-hand *V*-graph dis-

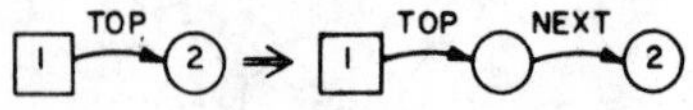

Fig. 6.   V-graph specification for PUSH.

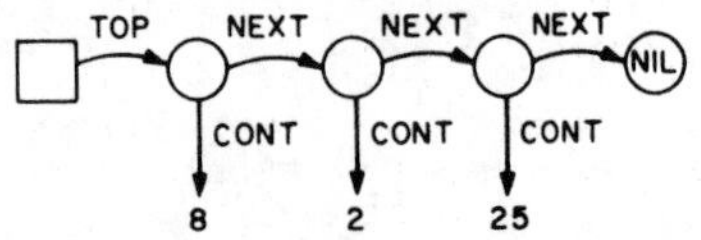

Fig. 7.   V-graph resulting from PUSHing 8 onto the stack shown in Fig. 4.

plays a pattern, in the form of a path of selectors from a header node to other nodes, to match against the operands of the transformation. Some of the nodes in the left-hand V-graph are given labels which can be used to identify the new position of these nodes in the rearrangement defined by the right-hand V-graph, which represents the result of the transformation. For example, Fig. 6 describes the operation PUSH as follows: for any arbitrary stack object, PUSH causes a new node to be inserted between the header node and the node previously connected to it via the link labeled TOP; the value being PUSHed will be on the CONT link of the newly added node. Fig. 7 displays the result of PUSHing 8 onto the stack shown in Fig. 4. A similar definition can be given for POP; it would show POP to be the inverse of PUSH (the arrow in Fig. 6 would be reversed).

The technique of using a fixed discipline to express the specifications satisfies many of the criteria set forth in Section II. Certainly, it can be made sufficiently formal. For someone familiar with the given discipline, the specifications are usually easily understood and easily constructed if they describe concepts within the range of applicability of the chosen discipline. Extensibility presents no problem provided that the representation selected for the class of objects of the abstraction is adequate to express the properties of the extension. Even proofs of correctness of the uses of the specifications are simplified by using the multitude of theorems which exist for established disciplines.

However, techniques using a fixed discipline are deficient with respect to the criteria of minimality and range of applicability. Using such a technique to express specifications is similar to writing programs in a programming language which provides a single data structuring method;[9] although a single method can be powerful enough to implement all user-defined data structures, it does not follow that all data structures are implemented with equal facility. Similarly, we cannot expect that all data abstractions can be specified equally well in terms of a fixed discipline. For example, the graphical representation is very suitable for showing the paths by which the content of a data structure can be accessed. But, if the access path is not relevant, such as when testing whether an object is in a given set,

then the graphical representation over-specifies the desired structure; that is, the abstract representation introduces details which need not be preserved in an implementation capturing the specifier's intentions. The use of extra details violates the criterion of minimality and places a practical limit on the range of applicability of a fixed discipline.

Use of an Arbitrary Discipline

The unwanted representational detail which results from using a fixed discipline can be reduced by allowing the specifications to be written in any convenient discipline. This approach is particularly useful when the class of objects of the desired data abstraction is a subset of some established mathematical domain. Hoare has used this approach to specify sets [29], [30] and certain subsets of the integers [30]. The operations on the data abstraction are defined by expressions in the chosen discipline. For example, an operation to insert an integer in a set might be defined by

$$\text{insert } (s,i) \equiv s := s \cup i$$

where assignment is used to show that s is updated with a side effect.

Many of the properties of specifications in which an arbitrary discipline is chosen are the same as when a fixed discipline is used. Allowing the specifier to choose a convenient discipline removes some of the limitations of a fixed discipline, but not all. Actually, the number of disciplines available for use is not large, and, in addition, if a completely free choice of discipline could be made it is doubtful that the resulting specifications would be comprehensible. Thus, in reality, the specifier must choose among a small number of disciplines; some of these might be existing mathematical disciplines, while others would be disciplines developed especially for use in specifications. This situation is analogous to writing programs in a language providing several data structuring facilities; programming experience indicates that there will always be (problem oriented) abstractions which cannot be ideally represented by any of the data structuring methods. Thus, it appears unlikely that all data abstractions can be given minimal specifications by choosing among a number of disciplines.

Use of a State Machine Model

As was noted in Section IV, the class of objects can be defined implicitly rather than by means of an explicit model. If the class of objects is viewed as states of an abstract (and not necessarily finite) state machine,[10] then the class can be defined implicitly by characterizing the states of the machine. Parnas [31] has developed a technique and notation for writing such specifications. The basic idea is to separate the operations into two groups: those which do not cause a state change but allow some aspect

---

[9] In fact, Earley defined a programming language, VERS, in which V-graphs were the data structuring method [22].

[10] In this case, the set of states of the state machine is the set of time-invariant mathematical values that we discussed in Section IV.

402

```
V - operation : TOP
possible values : integer ; initially undefined
parameters : none
effect : error call if 'DEPTH' = 0

O - operation : PUSH (a)
possible values : none
parameters : integer a
effect : error call if 'DEPTH' = MAX
            else ( TOP = a ; DEPTH = 'DEPTH' + 1 )
```

Fig. 8. Partial state-machine specification for the stack abstraction.

```
1  CREATE (STACK)
2  STACK(S) & INTEGER (I) ⊃ STACK (PUSH(S,I)) &
                      [POP(S) ≠ STACKERROR ⊃ STACK (POP(S))] &
                      [TOP(S) ≠ INTEGERERROR ⊃ INTEGER (TOP(S)]
3  (∀A) [A(CREATE) &
          (∀S)(∀I) [STACK(S) & INTEGER (I) & A(S)
                ⊃ A(PUSH (S,I) & [S ≠ CREATE ⊃ A(POP(S))]]
          ⊃ (∀S) [STACK (S) ⊃ A(S)]]
4  STACK(S) & INTEGER (I) ⊃ PUSH (S,I) ≠ CREATE
5  STACK(S) & STACK (S') & INTEGER(I)
                ⊃ [PUSH(S,I) = PUSH (S',I) ⊃ S = S']
6  STACK(S) & INTEGER(I) ⊃ TOP(PUSH(S,I)) = I
7  TOP(CREATE) = INTEGERERROR
8  STACK(S) & INTEGER(I) ⊃ POP (PUSH (S,I)) = S
9  POP(CREATE) = STACKERROR
```

Fig. 9. Axiomatic specification of the stack abstraction.

of the state to be observed—the value returning or *V*-operations—and those which cause a change of state—the operate or *O*-operations. The *O*-operations correspond to the constructors of Section IV. The specifications are given by indicating the effect of each *O*-operation on the result of each *V*-operation. This implicitly determines the smallest class of states necessary to distinguish the observable variations in the values of the *V*-operations. It also determines the transitions among these states caused by the *O*-operations.

We again use the integer stack data abstraction as an example, and consider the operations TOP and PUSH. TOP is a *V*-operation which is defined as long as the stack is not empty, and PUSH is an *O*-operation which affects the result of TOP. Looking at just these two operations, the state machine specifications might read as shown in Fig. 8, where DEPTH is another *V*-operation whose definition is not shown here, but which is intended to reflect the number of integers on the stack, and MAX represents the maximum number of integers which can be stored on the stack. Quotes around an operation name are used to indicate its value before the *O*-operation is executed.

This type of specification is different from those previously considered because it is free of representational details. No extra information is introduced if the specifications are expressed entirely in terms of the names of operations, types, and possibly some initial values (like MAX in the definition of PUSH). Thus, one might expect to achieve quite reasonable minimality. In practice, however, it is not always easy to build a simple description of the effect of an *O*-operation. The problem is that certain *O*-operations may have "delayed effects" on the *V*-operations: some property of the state will be observable by the *V*-operation only after some other *O*-operation has been applied. For example PUSH has a delayed effect on TOP, in that the former top-of-stack element is no longer directly observable by TOP, but will again be observable after POP is applied. Parnas used an informal language to describe this delayed effect [31]. Delayed effects can be described formally by introducing "hidden functions" to represent aspects of the state which are not immediately observable. Users of the state-machine model [6], [7] have made extensive use of such hidden functions. However, adding hidden functions can also add representational detail, and thus detract from the minimality of the specification.

The state-machine specifications are slightly deficient with respect to the other criteria of Section II. Because of

the problem of delayed effects noted above, they are sometimes difficult to construct. Because the *O*-operations which change the result of a *V*-operation are totally separated from that *V*-operation, the specifications are sometimes difficult to read. The separation also affects extensibility since adding a new *V*-operation may require updates to a large portion of the *O*-operation specifications.

With respect to the criterion of formality, we expect that state-machine specifications can be given an adequate formalization but much work remains to be done. In particular, it is necessary to develop a formal (not necessarily effective) construction for the state machine specified by a given set of specifications. This will necessitate defining the language which can be used to describe the effects of an *O*-operation. In addition, work on developing the proof methodology to use with state-machine specifications is needed. Price [6] has proven a number of properties of a particular data abstraction, but the methodology for proving the correctness of an implementation still needs to be developed. Some of the needed formalization is being done in an ongoing project at SRI [7], [32].

Use of Axiomatic Descriptions

An alternative to using state machines to implicitly determine a data abstraction is to give a list of properties possessed by the objects and the operations upon them. This approach can be formalized by expressing the properties as axioms for the data abstraction. Axiomatization has been used by Hoare [2], [33] to define the built-in data types of a programming language. The technique can also be used to give specifications for user-created data abstractions.

An axiomatization of the integer stack abstraction in which popping the top element off the stack (POP) and examining the top element (TOP) are separate operations, is given in Fig. 9. In this example, STACK and INTEGER are predicates; STACK is being defined, but INTEGER is assumed to be defined elsewhere. The axioms are written in a form analogous to Peano's axioms for the natural numbers. Axioms 1 and 2 define the range of the applicable operations. Axiom 3 is the induction axiom which limits the class of stacks to those that can be constructed with the given operations. Axioms 4 and 5 insure the distinctness of the results of the PUSH operation. Axioms 6 and 7 define the result of the TOP operation and Axioms 8 and 9 define the result of POP. Axioms 7 and 9 capture the fact that neither TOP nor POP may be legally applied to an empty stack (the result of CREATE).[11]

The axioms determine an abstract representation for stacks in the following manner. Consider the set of all legal expressions that can be constructed from the given operations. This set of expressions names every possible member of the class of stacks. Some pairs of expressions may name the same stack, however; for example, both

PUSH (CREATE, 7) and

POP (PUSH (PUSH (CREATE, 7), 25))

denote the same stack. Therefore, the class of stack objects is represented by equivalence classes over the set of all expressions. These equivalence classes are determined (noneffectively, in general) by the axioms.

If the axioms are sufficiently well chosen, the equivalence classes are unique. If not, then several sets of equivalence classes may satisfy the axioms. If, for example, Axiom 4 is omitted, then two distinct sets of equivalence classes—one in which the result of PUSH is always distinct from the empty stack and one in which it is not—would both satisfy the axioms.

The axiomatic specifications can almost always be minimal and widely applicable, in part because there are so few limitations on the form of the axioms. In addition, the approach seems to support extensibility, since, in most cases, it suffices to add new axioms to describe the extended concept, or at most, to modify a few existing axioms. The formalization of the axiomatic technique is borrowed directly from existing mathematics. Proving the correctness of an implementation of a data abstraction specified by axioms means showing that the implementation is a model of the axioms.

The axiomatic approach is most seriously deficient with respect to the criteria of comprehensibility and constructibility. As discussed in Section IV, the approach does not directly define a model for the class of objects; instead the class is defined only implicitly. It is sometimes difficult to see that the axioms really define the set of values of interest. In addition, the possibility that several very different sets of values may satisfy the axioms is disturbing.

Use of Algebraic Definitions

It is reasonable to expect that all data abstractions one might be interested in implementing on a computer would have finitely constructible, countable domains. In view of this, the first three axioms in Fig. 9 can be omitted, providing suitable notation is developed to indicate the group of applicable operations and their functionality. Algebraic specifications [18] provide such a notation.

[11] In these axioms, we are using the standard mathematical technique for making a partial function total: the output domain of the function is extended by one special, recognizable value which will be the result of the function in all cases where it was previously undefined.

```
Functionality:
    CREATE :                      → STACK
    PUSH   :      STACK X INTEGER → STACK
    TOP    :      STACK → INTEGER U INTEGERERROR
    POP    :      STACK → STACK U STACKERROR

Axioms:

    1'  TOP(PUSH(S,I)) = I
    2'  TOP(CREATE) = INTEGERERROR
    3'  POP(PUSH(S,I)) = S
    4'  POP(CREATE) = STACKERROR
```

Fig. 10. Algebraic specification of the stack abstraction.

The algebraic specification technique is based on a generalization of the algebraic construction known as a *presentation*. A presentation of the stack abstraction is shown in Fig. 10. Only four axioms are now needed (labeled with primes to avoid confusion with the axioms in Fig. 9). Axioms 1–3 are replaced by the definition of functionality; this is sufficient to define the set of legal, finitely constructible expressions in these operations. In the usual algebraic terminology, the legal expressions are called *words*. Next, it is necessary to specify which of these expressions are to yield equivalent results, through a set of defining axioms referred to as *relations* or relation schemata: this is done by Axioms 1'–4' (which correspond to Axioms 6–9 in Fig. 9). The construction which gives meaning to a presentation automatically forces all expression pairs which cannot be shown to be equivalent to be distinct. This simplifies the expression of the specifications and is why Axioms 4 and 5 are not needed.

Almost all the comments about how axiomatic definitions satisfy the criteria apply equally well to algebraic definitions. Algebraic and axiomatic definitions are equally good with respect to the criteria of minimality, wide range of applicability, and extensibility. (Algebraic definitions are shorter than axiomatic ones, but they are not more minimal because they express the same information.) The algebraic approach can be easily formalized by borrowing from existing mathematics; most results carry over in a straightforward manner, although some generalization is needed to treat several existing domains simultaneously. For algebraic specifications, proving the correctness of an implementation means showing that it defines an isomorphic image of the presented algebra. This isomorphism can be established implicitly by showing that the defining axioms hold in the implementation and that the mapping is one–one [18], [34].

The algebraic approach is superior to the axiomatic approach with respect to the criteria of constructibility and comprehensibility, because the approach is more structured. However, algebraic specifications are still deficient with respect to these criteria. Although use of the algebraic approach precludes the possibility of more than one set of values satisfying the axioms, it is still possible that the set of values defined is not the one intended. We believe this difficulty can be eased if a methodology is developed which can be applied to constructing and understanding such specifications. Some progress in this direction has been made [18], [35], but more work is needed.

The analyses given in this section indicate that there is no single specification technique that is universally better than the others. One major difference among the techniques is the extent to which they exhibit a *representational bias*, that is, the extent to which the specifications suggest a representation or implementation for the abstractions being defined. The representational bias of a technique determines, in large measure, its range of applicability. Techniques having a representational bias will be limited primarily to those abstractions which are naturally expressed in the representation; however, within the range, specifications will be fairly easy to construct and comprehend, and reasonably minimal. Those techniques which make use of an existing mathematical discipline to specify an abstract model for the class of defined objects have a representational bias. Such techniques will be preferred for abstractions which fit nicely into the discipline (for example, where the objects of the abstraction are elements of an existing domain).

The techniques providing an implicit definition of the class of objects have no representational bias, and will clearly be preferable for those abstractions not well matched to an existing discipline. They may sometimes be preferred even when one of the abstract model approaches could be used. The abstract model approaches tend to suggest an implementation for the abstraction, and this may be undesirable, not because it precludes very different implementations, but because it may be hard for the implementor to find a different but better implementation.

All the implicit definition techniques, with their lack of representational bias, have a wide range of applicability, but they vary in the extent to which they satisfy the criteria of minimality, constructibility, and comprehensibility. The difficulty in the state-machine approach of coping with delayed effects reduces the minimality and constructibility of the specifications, though not necessarily the comprehensibility. The introduction of hidden V-functions may impact the free choice of an implementation, since the implementor may feel the need to implement these hidden functions, which is not necessary. Algebraic and axiomatic specifications are more minimal than state-model specifications, but they may be more difficult to construct and understand.

The state-machine technique appears to be least satisfactory with respect to the criterion of extensibility, because introducing a new V-operation is likely to necessitate changes to the definitions of many O-operations. However, the criterion of extensibility, based on the notion of a "small" change to the concept, is really quite vague. Perhaps a small change is one requiring only a minor modification to the specification. Also, the different specification techniques may tolerate different kinds of changes, and this could be a factor in choosing a technique.

The criterion of formality is not entirely satisfied by any of the techniques, although the state-machine model is the least formalized. There are two important aspects to formalization. First, the syntax and semantics of the language in which the specifications are written must be fully defined. Defining the semantics involves more than just defining the meaning of each symbol; a construction (it may be noneffective) of the defined class of objects from the specification must also be provided. This is only difficult in the implicit definition approaches; in the abstract model approaches the specification describes the objects explicitly. Second, a methodology for proving that an implementation satisfies a specification must be provided. Additional work on formalization would expand the usefulness of the techniques. Unless a technique is adequately formalized, it will be difficult, if not impossible, to train people to use it correctly and coherently.

We conclude by discussing one previously unmentioned aspect of specification techniques: the extent to which they capture all interesting properties of a data abstraction. For example, consider the treatment of errors in the various specification techniques. In some techniques, errors are completely ignored. In others, notably the axiomatic and algebraic techniques, the presence of errors is acknowledged, but not in a particularly illuminating way. The solution of adding an extra error element to the output domain, while mathematically sound, does not provide the kind of information that a user of the abstraction requires. A more realistic approach is taken by the state-machine technique; here, error cases are prominently displayed, different errors can be given meaningful names (although this was not shown in the example), and even the order in which errors will be recognized by a given operation can be specified. It is noteworthy that this technique is based on a model of the way errors will be handled in running programs; such a model may be necessary if errors are to be specified in a realistic manner. The treatment of errors is not the only example where the specification techniques are deficient (e.g., performance requirements are also missing). Much more work is needed to identify the interesting properties of data abstractions, and to develop the specification techniques to express those properties.

VI. CONCLUSIONS

A major premise of this paper has been that formal specifications should come to play a fundamental role in the construction of reliable software. Two reasons were given for this: 1) The growing economic pressure for reliable programs indicates that increased effort in this direction is justified, and 2) the recognition of a new kind of module— the multiprocedure module—has led to the identification of a specification unit for which specifications are practical. This kind of module is helpful in the construction of software, because it permits data abstractions to be used in building programs. Since data are the fundamental concern of programs, we can expect the use of data abstractions to be widespread.

To indicate the form such specifications might take, Section V discussed several specification techniques. The techniques discussed were promising in that they did succeed in describing data abstractions at a reasonably abstract level. However, none of the techniques are ready to be applied to practical programs. Some techniques have not yet been put on a firm mathematical basis (although we believe that all the techniques surveyed are capable of being adequately formalized). Other techniques ignore a fundamental aspect of data abstractions: how to cope with errors and exceptions. Finally, none of the techniques has been applied widely enough that its expressive power can be evaluated. Recent uses of the state-machine technique of Parnas to specify operating systems [7] or parts thereof [6] may indicate that that technique is suitable for systems of interesting size, but the complexity of at least one of those specifications [6] indicates the specification technique requires further refinement. It is reasonable to expect deficiencies in the other specification techniques to emerge when they are likewise applied to large programs.

Some deficiencies in the techniques are already apparent. The range of applicability of the various techniques is often smaller than we would like; examples were discussed in Section V. Since the range of applicability is different for the different techniques, we may expect that using a combination of techniques when describing a large program would be a profitable approach. However, there are programs whose meaning cannot be captured by any of the described techniques. For example, specifications using the techniques cannot be given for programs involving parallel activity. We chose not to survey work going on in developing specification techniques to handle parallelism because the work is very recent and quite preliminary. However, one promising approach uses data abstractions as the specification units [36].

The specification techniques discussed in this paper can adequately describe modules—the blocks out of which systems are built—but it is not clear that they can describe the entire system. For example, Parnas has shown how a KWIC sytem can be modularized [16], and each module was described using his specifications, but the specification of the system as a whole was given in English. It seems unlikely that an entire system can be viewed as a single, top-level module, so perhaps a different kind of specification technique is desirable here.

Even if we are not able to describe an entire system using the specification techniques, the ability to define most of the modules used in constructing a system in a precise, formal way would be a major advance in the construction of reliable software. The specification techniques discussed in this paper are all quite recent; much is being accomplished by concentrating on the data abstraction as a specification unit. This general area appears to be a very promising one for further study: work in applying existing techniques to large programs, in extending and formalizing existing techniques, and in proposing new techniques, for both sequential and parallel programs, is of the utmost importance.

ACKNOWLEDGMENT

The authors greatfully acknowledge the helpful suggestions made by J. Dennis and the referees.

REFERENCES

[1] R. W. Floyd, "Assigning meanings to programs," in *Proc. Symp. Applied Mathematics*, vol. XIX, Mathematical Aspects of Computer Science, American Mathematical Society, Providence, R.I., 1967, pp. 19–32.

[2] C. A. R. Hoare, "An axiomatic basis for computer programming," *Commun. Ass. Compt. Mach.*, vol. 12, pp. 576–580, 583, Oct. 1969.

[3] Z. Manna, S. Ness, and J. Vuilemin, "Inductive methods for proving properties of programs," *Commun. Ass. Comput. Mach.*, vol. 16, pp. 491–502, Aug. 1973.

[4] B. Boehm, "Software and its impact: A quantitative assessment," *Datamation*, vol. 19, pp. 48–59, May 1973.

[5] M. Schroeder, "Certification of computer systems," Mass. Inst. Technol., Cambridge, Project MAC Progress Rep. 11, to be published.

[6] W. R. Price, "Implications of a virtual memory mechanism for implementing protection in a family of operating systems," Dep. Comput. Sci., Carnegie-Mellon Univ., Pittsburgh, Pa., 1973.

[7] P. G. Neumann *et al.*, "On the design of a provably secure operating system," in *Proc. Int. Workshop on Protection in Operating Systems*, IRIA, Rocquencourt, France, 1974, pp. 161–175.

[8] F. T. Baker, "Chief programmer team management of production programming," *IBM Syst. J.*, vol. 2, pp. 56–73, Jan. 1972.

[9] E. W. Dijkstra, "Notes on structured programming," in *Structured Programming* (APIC Studies in Data Processing, no. 8). New York: Academic, 1972, pp. 1–81.

[10] C. A. R. Hoare, "Proof of a program: FIND," *Commun. Ass. Comput. Mach.*, vol. 14, pp. 39–45, Jan. 1971.

[11] B. H. Liskov and S. Zilles, "Programming with abstract data types," in *Proc. Ass. Comput. Mach. Conf. Very High Level Languages*, SIGPLAN Notices, vol. 9, Apr. 1974, pp. 50–59.

[12] J. H. Morris, "Toward more flexible type systems," in *Proc. Programming Symp.*, Paris, France, Apr. 9–11, 1974, *Lecture Notes in Computer Science*, vol. 19. New York: Springer-Verlag, pp. 377–384.

[13] B. H. Liskov, "The design of the Venus operating system," *Commun. Ass. Comput. Mach.*, vol. 15, pp. 144–149, Mar. 1972.

[14] ——, "A design methodology for reliable software systems," in *1972 Fall Joint Comput. Conf., AFIPS Conf. Proc.*, vol. 41. Montvale, N.J.: AFIPS Press, 1972, pp. 191–199.

[15] E. W. Dijkstra, "The structure of the 'THE'—multiprogramming system," *Commun. Ass. Comput. Mach.*, vol. 11, pp. 341–346, May 1968.

[16] D. L. Parnas, "Information distribution aspects of design methodology," in *Proc. Int. Fed. Inform. Processing Congr.*, Aug. 1971.

[17] N. Wirth, "The programming language PASCAL," *Acta Informatica*, vol. 1, pp. 35–63, 1971.

[18] S. N. Zilles, "Data algebra: A specification technique for data structures," Ph.D. dissertation (forthcoming), Project MAC, Mass. Inst. Technol., Cambridge, 1975.

[19] D. L. Parnas, "On the criteria to be used in decomposing systems into modules," *Commun. Ass. Comput. Mach.*, vol. 15, pp. 1053–1058, Dec. 1972.

[20] R. M. Burstall, "Some techniques for proving correctness of programs which alter data structures," in *Machine Intelligence*, D. Michie, Ed., vol. 7. New York: Elsevier, 1972.

[21] O. J. Dahl, B. Myhrhaug, and K. Nygaard, "The SIMULA 67 common base language," Norwegian Computing Center, Oslo, Publication S-22, 1970.

[22] J. Earley, "Toward an understanding of data structures," *Commun. Ass. Comput. Mach.*, vol. 14, pp. 617–627, Oct. 1971.

[23] A. W. Holt, "Mem-theory, a mathematical method for the description and analysis of discrete finite information systems," Applied Data Research, Inc., 1965.

[24] C. Christensen, "An example of the manipulation of directed graphs in the AMBIT/G programming language," in *Interactive Systems for Applied Mathematics*, Klerer and Reinfelds, Ed. New York: Academic, 1968.

[25] J. Earley, "Relational level data structures for programming languages," *Acta Informatica*, vol. 2, pp. 293–309, 1973.

[26] J. B. Morris, "A comparison of madcap and SETL," Los Alamos Sci. Lab., Univ. of California, Los Alamos, N. Mex., 1973.

[27] J. Schwartz, "On programming, an interim report on the SETL project," Dep. Comput. Sci., Courant Inst. Math. Sci., New York Univ., New York, 1973.

[28] A. Birman, "On proving correctness of microprograms," *IBM J. Res. Develop.*, vol. 18, pp. 250–267, May 1974.

[29] C. A. R. Hoare, "Proof of a structured program: 'The sieve of Eratosthenes'," *Comput. J.* vol. 15, pp. 321–325, Nov. 1972.

[30] ——, "Proof of correctness of data representations," *Acta Informatica*, vol. 1, pp. 271–281, 1972.

[31] D. L. Parnas, "A technique for the specification of software modules with examples," *Commun. Ass. Comput. Mach.*, vol. 15, pp. 330–336, May 1972.

[32] P. G. Neumann, "Toward a methodology for designing large systems and verifying their properties," Gesellschaft fur Informatik, Berlin, Germany, 1974.

[33] C. A. R. Hoare and N. Wirth, "An axiomatic definition of the programming language PASCAL," *Acta Informatica*, vol. 2, pp. 335–355, 1973.

[34] S. N. Zilles, "Algebraic specification of data types," Mass. Inst. Technol., Cambridge, Project MAC Progress Rep. 11, to be published.

[35] J. Donahue, J. D. Gannon, J. V. Guttag, and J. J. Horning, "Three approaches to reliable software: Language design, dyadic specification, complimentary semantics," Comput. Sci. Res. Group, Univ. of Toronto, Toronto, Ont., Canada, Tech. Rep. 45, Jan. 1975.

[36] C. Hewitt and I. Greif, "Actor semantics of PLANNER-73," in *Proc. 2nd Ass. Comput. Mach. Symp. Principles of Programming Languages*, Palo Alto, Calif., Jan. 20–22, 1975, pp. 67–77.

Barbara H. Liskov received the B.A. degree in mathematics from the University of California, Berkeley, and the M.S. and Ph.D. degrees in computer science from Stanford University, Stanford, Calif.

From 1968 to 1972 she was associated with the Mitre Corporation, Bedford, Mass., where she participated in the design and implementation of the Venus Machine and the Venus Operating System. She is presently Assistant Professor of Electrical Engineering and Computer Science at the Massachusetts Institute of Technology, Cambridge. Her research interests include programming methodology and the design of languages and systems to support structured programming.

Stephen N. Zilles (S'71–M'73) was born in Toledo, Ohio, on July 1, 1941. He received the S.B. degree in economics and politital science in 1963 and in mathematics in 1967 from the Massachusetts Institute of Technology, Cambridge. In 1970, he received the S.M. and E.E. degrees in electrical engineering, also from the Massachusetts Institute of Technology.

From 1963 to 1968 he was employed by the IBM Corporation, San Jose, Calif., where he worked on the compilation of PL/I, an interactive system for building large programs and Formac, a system for algebraic manipulation. While completing the M.S. and E.E. degrees at the Massachusetts Institute of Technology he was a Teaching Assistant, and a Research Assistant in Programming Linguistics at MIT Project MAC. Upon returning to IBM in 1970 he was Advanced Programming Manager responsible for implementing a prototype language interpreter. Since 1971 he has been active in the design and evaluation of programming and command languages at IBM. His current interests are in the semantics and design of programming languages with particular emphasis on the description and representation of data types.

Mr. Zilles is the Secretary–Treasurer of the Association for Computing Machinery SIGPLAN and a member of the Association for Computing Machinery Board on Special Interest Groups and Committees. He is a member of Sigma Xi and the Association for Computing Machinery.

SOFTWARE—PRACTICE AND EXPERIENCE, VOL. 12, 433–444 (1982)

Specifications: Formal and Informal—A Case Study

NARAIN GEHANI*

Bell Laboratories, 6 Corporate Place, Piscataway, N.J. 08854, U.S.A.

SUMMARY

Formal specifications (algebraic) are given for an informally specified small subsystem of the Change Management Automatic Build System. A comparison of the two specifications shows that although informal specifications are easier to read, the formal specifications are clearer, specify operation domains precisely, define the interaction between the operations, show the incompleteness of the informal specifications and are devoid of implementation details. The formal specifications pointed to the need of a function not in the subsystem whose inclusion would improve the system design. This inclusion is now being considered. However, the use of algebraic specifications requires practice and experience. Although the formal specification of large systems is somewhat impractical at the moment, experience in using formal specifications can lead to better informal specifications.

KEY WORDS   Formal specifications   Informal specifications

INTRODUCTION

Informal specifications of systems, while easy to read, tend to be ambiguous, incomplete, imprecise and overspecific. Formal specifications alleviate these problems, and may be used to show the correctness of system implementation and the equivalence of different implementations. They also offer potential for the development of automated aids for the detection of the above problems. Reference 1 is an excellent introduction to formal specifications and their advantages.

Guttag's[2] algebraic specification technique is favoured by many computer scientists. Having seen and used this specification technique on fairly well studied examples such as stacks, queues, lists, symbol tables, etc., I decided to compare the informal specifications of some real system with its algebraic specifications.

For the comparison I selected the EVENT LOG subsystem of the Change Management Automatic Build system for which the informal specifications[3] were available. The EVENT LOG subsystem was selected because it was small, part of a working system with clear informal specifications available, and because members of its design team are accessible. The intent of this paper is not to criticize the informal specifications of the EVENT LOG subsystem, but to compare informal specifications with formal specifications.

---

*Current address: Bell Laboratories, Murray Hill, NJ 07974, U.S.A.

0036–0644/82/050433–12$01.20

Received 20 May 1980

The Change Management Automated Build System (CM ABS), a successful software management system, supports the manufacture of software products that generally are

(a) diverse in their use of language processors, program libraries and software construction methods,

(b) too large to be recompiled in their entirety for every release or every version, and

(c) large enough to constitute a significant engineering records problem.

CM ABS imposes only a minimal set of conventions on software products and is adaptable for use by individual software projects for software construction.

The manufacture of the release of a software product is envisioned as building a series of versions (called builds) of the product. The final version is designated to be the release which is then sent out to the customers. Associated with each release is the EVENT LOG subsystem, a record of the status of the versions of the software product developed in building the release.[4, 5]

THE ALGEBRAIC SPECIFICATION TECHNIQUE

Algebraic specifications have two parts:

(i) the syntax—the operations of the system are specified indicating the number of arguments, the argument types and the result type;

(ii) the semantics—algebraic equations (axioms) are given that relate the values created by the operations.

In the basic notation, the operations are functions without side effects; none of the arguments are changed. Guttag[6] has extended the notation to allow for changes in arguments, that is, to allow procedures.

The algebraic specification technique is illustrated by specifying a rather high level and abstract version of a relational database.[7] A relational database consists of a set of relations. Relations are identified by their names. They can be added, deleted and retrieved from a database. Additionally one can check for the membership of a relation in a database. The informal specifications for the operations of a relational database are:

new	returns as its result an empty database.
add(d, n, r)	returns a database which is the result of adding the relation r with the name n to the database d. If a relation with the name n was previously in the database then an error occurs.
delete(d, n)	returns a database d which is the same as d but with the relation named n deleted. If such a relation did not exist then an error occurs.
empty(d)	returns **true** if the database d is empty and **false** otherwise.
in(d, n)	returns **true** if the relation named n is in the database d and **false** otherwise.
get(d, n)	returns the relation with name n if one exists in the database d; otherwise an error is indicated.

In writing the formal specifications an additional operation *insert* is needed. This operation is similar to *add* except that it does not check to see if the relation being added is present or not in the database. It is an internal operation not available to the users of the relational database.

The formal specifications are:

1. **type** *database*

2. **external operations** *new, add, delete, empty, in, get*
3. **internal operation** *insert*

4. **syntax**

5.   *new*: $->database$
6.   *add*: $database \times name \times relation -> database \cup \{\text{ERROR}\}$
7.   *empty*: $database -> boolean$
8.   *in*: $database \times name -> boolean$
9.   *delete*: $database \times name -> database \cup \{\text{ERROR}\}$
10.   *insert*: $database \times name \times relation -> database$
11.   *get*: $database \times name -> relation \cup \{\text{ERROR}\}$

12. **semantics**

13.   **var** *d*: *database*; *n, m, name*: *r*: *relation*

14.   **axioms**

15.   *empty(new)* = **true**
16.   *empty(insert(d, n, r))* = **false**

17.   *in(new, n)* = **false**
18.   *in(insert(d, m, r), n)* = **if** $n = m$ **then true else** *in(d, n)*

19.   *delete(new, n)* = ERROR
20.   *delete(insert(d, m, r), n)* = **if** $n = m$
                                then *d*
                                else *insert(delete(d, n), m, r)*

21.   *get(new, n)* = ERROR
22.   *get(insert(d, m, r), n)* = **if** $n = m$ **then** *r* **else** *get(d, n)*

23.   *add(d, n, r)* = **if** *in(d, n)* **then** ERROR **else** *insert(d, n, r)*
24. **end** *database*.

In the definition of the above database, the types *name* and *relation* have been used but not defined. Some explanatory notes on the above formal specifications are given below:

Line 2:   specifies the operations available to users of the database.
Line 3:   specifies an operation internal to the database and not available to the user.
Line 5:   specifies the syntax of the operation *new*. Operation *new* takes no arguments and returns a value of type *database*.

Line 6:   specifies that *add* takes 3 arguments—a database, a name and a relation. It returns either a database or an error as its result.

Line 13:   variable *d* is declared to be type *database*, *n* and *m* to be of type *name*, and *r* of type *relation*.

Line 15:   the result of applying the operation *empty* on a database that contains no relations (the operation *new* returns such a database) is **true.**

Line 16:   *empty* returns **false** if any relation has been inserted into a database.

Line 17:   the operation *in* returns **false** when one tries to see if a relation is present in an empty database.

Line 18:   operation *in* checks to see if the relation named *n* is in the database by recursively looking at the relations inserted.

Line 19:   deleting a relation from an empty database results in an error.

Line 20:   a relation named *n* is deleted by recursively looking at all the relations inserted to see if it is present.

Line 23:   the operation of adding a relation *r* named *n* to a database *d* results in an error if *n* is already present in *d*; otherwise *add* is equivalent to *insert*.

By convention, any operation that has an ERROR value for an argument returns ERROR as its result. Instead of using one kind of error value, i.e. ERROR, we could have used different error values, i.e. ERROR$_1$, ERROR$_2$, etc. to differentiate error classes.

The use of the axioms in determining the result of applying an operation to the database is now illustrated by means of examples.

Examples

1. *new* represents the empty database

2. We add a relation *r*1 named SUPPLIER to an empty database. We have

    add(new, SUPPLIER, *r*1)
      = *insert(new*, SUPPLIER, *r*1)—by axiom on line 23,
    i.e. a database with one relation named SUPPLIER

3. To the database in (2) we add the relation *r*2 with the name PARTS. We get

    add(insert(new, SUPPLIER, *r*1), PARTS, *r*2)
      = *insert(insert(new*, SUPPLIER, *r*1), PARTS, *r*2)—by axiom on line 23

4. We check to see if a relation named SALES is in the above database, i.e.

    in(insert(insert(new, SUPPLIER, *r*1), PARTS, *r*2), SALES)
      = *in(insert(new*, SUPPLIER, *r*1), SALES)—by axiom on line 18
      = *in(new*, SALES)—by axiom on line 18
      = **false**—by axiom on line 17

    The relation SALES is not in the database.

5. We try to delete the relation named SALES from the database of (3), i.e.

    delete(insert(insert(new, SUPPLIER, *r*1), PARTS, *r*2), SALES)
      = *insert(delete(insert(new*, SUPPLIER, *r*1), SALES), PARTS, *r*2)—by axiom on line 20
      = *insert(insert(delete(new*, SALES), SUPPLIER,), PARTS, *r*2)—by axiom on line 20
      = *insert(insert(ERROR, SUPPLIER, *r*1), PARTS, *r*2)—by axiom on line 19

$= insert(\text{ERROR}, \text{PARTS}, r2)$—convention about error arguments

$= \text{ERROR}$—convention about error arguments

Deletion of the relation named SALES leads to an error as it is not in the database.

6. Let us try to retrieve the relation named SUPPLIER, i.e.

$get(insert(insert(new, \text{SUPPLIER}, r1), \text{PARTS}, r2), \text{SUPPLIER})$

$= get(insert(new, \text{SUPPLIER}, r1), \text{SUPPLIER})$—by axiom on line 22

$= r1$—by axiom on line 22

It is interesting to note that no axioms were given for the operations *new* and *insert*. As long as the effects of these operations (i.e. 'properties') are known in terms of the behaviour of the other operations, further specification of behaviour of these operations is not required. They may be implemented in any way as long as their effect on the other operations is as specified by the axioms. This should not surprise us too much. Similar examples can be found in other disciplines. For example, when building a bridge we do not care what materials are used as long as they satisfy certain properties. The materials should have a certain elasticity, tensile stress, resistance to corrosion, price, etc. These properties are stated explicitly while in case of the operations *new* and *insert*, the 'properties' are implicitly stated by the axioms.

The operations *new* and *insert* are called 'constructor' operations. For details of 'constructor' operations and how to construct algebraic specifications see References 2, 6 and 8. Some limitations of the algebraic specification technique are discussed by Majster.[9, 10]

INFORMAL SPECIFICATIONS OF THE EVENT LOG SUBSYSTEM

In this section, the informal specifications of the EVENT LOG subsystem, as given by Lyons,[3] are summarized. Only the essentials are included.

Associated with each release of a product is an eventlog in which status information is entered about all versions (called builds) of a release. The manufacture of a new release of the product is envisioned as building a series of versions starting from the old release. The final version is designated to be the new release. The eventlog is updated and queried by means of the following operations:

create(r)   creates a null eventlog *r*.

newbuild(r)   updates the eventlog *r* to allow the recording of modifications to build the next version (i.e. *build*. *Note* several versions are associated with a release). The new build number is written out on to the standard file. New build numbers range between 1 and 999.

append(r, b, e, t)   text *t* is associated with event *e* of build *b* in the eventlog *r*. Previous text associated with the event *e* is not affected.

extract(r, b, le)   retrieves the text corresponding to the events in the list *le* associated with build *b* of eventlog *r*. The text is prefixed by the corresponding event. The retrieval order is identical to the order in which these events were entered. If the event list *le* is left out then the event list is assumed to be all the list of the events associated with the build *b*.

delete(r, b, e)   the event *e* of build *b* and the text associated with it are deleted from eventlog *r*.

Destruction of an eventlog is accomplished by destroying its underlying representation which is supposed to be a file.

FORMAL SPECIFICATIONS FOR THE EVENT LOG SUBSYSTEM

The eventlog as specified by the formal specifications differs from the informally specified eventlog in the following ways:

(i) An operation *destroy* is included to eliminate an eventlog.

(ii) An operation *lastbuild* # which returns the latest build number (i.e. version number) is included. The operation *newbuild* is now modified so that it does not return a build number. This build number can be determined via the operation *lastbuild* # .

(iii) In the simplest form of the algebraic technique, the operations must be functions and not procedures since no side effects are allowed. Consequently all the operations are defined as functions in the formal specifications. In contrast all operations except *extract* are defined as procedures in the informal specifications.

The formal specification of the EVENT LOG subsystem also includes some operations that are not available to the user. These are necessary for the specification of the above system. The operations are:

nbuild   this is similar to new-build but it does not check to see if the last build number was 999. Only build numbers up to 999 are allowed.

add   is similar to *append* except that it does not check to see if the build number being referenced is legal.

extractall   this is a special case of the operation *extract*. It retrieves text associated with all events of a build.

extractlist   this is also a special case of the operation *extract*. It retrieves text only for the events specified.

1.   **type** *eventlog*

2.   **external operations** *create, newbuild, lastbuild* # *, append, extract, delete, destroy*

        internal operations *newbuild, add, extractall, extractlist*

3.   **syntax**

4.   *create*: $\rightarrow eventlog$

5.   *newbuild*: $eventlog \rightarrow eventlog \cup \{\text{ERROR}\}$

6.   *nbuild*: $eventlog \rightarrow eventlog$

7.   *lastbuild* # : $eventlog \rightarrow build \text{\#} \cup \{0\} \cup \{\text{ERROR}\}$

8.   *add*: $eventlog \times build \text{\#} \times event \times text \rightarrow eventlog$

9.   *append*: $eventlog \times build \text{\#} \times event \times text \rightarrow eventlog \cup \{\text{ERROR}\}$

10.   *extract*: $eventlog \times build \text{\#} \times eventlist \rightarrow text \cup \{\text{ERROR}\}$

11.   *extractall*: $eventlog \times build \text{\#} \rightarrow text \cup \{\text{ERROR}\}$

12.   *extractlist*: $eventlog \times build\# \times eventlist \rightarrow text \cup \{\text{ERROR}\}$
13.   *delete*: $eventlog \times build\# \times event \rightarrow eventlog \cup \{\text{ERROR}\}$
14.   *destroy*: $eventlog \rightarrow text$

15.   **semantics**

16.   **var** *r*:*eventlog*; *b*, *b*1:*build*#;
     elist:*eventlist*; *e*,*e*1:*event*;
     t:*text*

17.   **axioms**

18. $lastbuild\#(create) = 0$
19. $lastbuild\#(nbuild(r)) = 1 + lastbuild\#(r)$
20. $lastbuild\#(add(r, b, e, t)) = lastbuild\#(r)$

21. $append(r, b, e, t) = $ **if** $lastbuild\#(r) \geqslant b$
         then $add(r, b, e, t)$
         else ERROR

22. $newbuild(r) = $ **if** $lastbuild\#(r) = 999$
         then ERROR
         else $nbuild(r)$

23. $extract(r, b, elist) = $ **if** $null(elist)$
         then $extractall(r, b)$
         else $extractlist(r, b, elist)$

24. $extractall(create, b) = empty$
25. $extractall(nbuild(r), b) = extractall(r, b)$
26. $extractall(add(r, b1, e, t), b) = $ **if** $b = b1$
         then $extractall(r, b) \parallel attach(e, t)$
         else $extractall(r, b)$

27. $extractlist(create, b, elist) = empty$
28. $extractlist(newbuild(r), b, elist) = extractlist(r, b, elist)$
29. $extractlist(add(r, b1, e, t), b, elist) = $
         if $b1 = b$ **and** $in(e, elist)$
            then $extractlist(r, b, elist) \parallel attach(e, t)$
            else $extractlist(r, b, elist)$

30.   *delete(create, b, e) = create*

31.   *delete(nbuild(r), b, e) = nbuild(delete(r, b, e))*

32.   *delete(add(r, b1, e1), b, e) =* **if** *b = b1* **and** *e = e1*
                                    then *delete(r, b, e)*
                                  else *add(delete(r, b, e), b1, e1)*

33.   *destroy(r) = empty*

34.   **end** *eventlog*

In defining the type eventlog we have used, but not specified, other types and their operations. They are:

(a) *build#*—subrange of integers from 1 to 999
(b) *text*—sequence of lines;
      empty denotes a null sequence of lines
      ‖ used for text concatenation
(c) *line*—character string
(d) *eventlist*—list of events with operations
      in(e, L) returns **true** if event *e* is in eventlist *L* and **false** otherwise
      null(L) returns **true** if eventlist *L* is null and **false** otherwise
(e) *event*—character string
      attach(e, t) prefixes the text *t* by a line containing the event *e* for identification.

The formal specifications define two operations, *lastbuild#* and *destroy*, which are not included in the informal specifications. Their inclusion is explained in the comparison. Some notes to help in understanding the formal specification of the EVENT LOG subsystem are provided below.

Line 2:   specifies the external operations which are available to eventlog users and internal operations which are hidden from the user. The internal operations are necessary for the specifications.

Lines 4–14:   Specify the syntax of all the operations defined in the specifications. for example:

      (i) *create*—an operation with no arguments which returns a new eventlog.
      (ii) *newbuild*—takes as argument an eventlog and returns either an eventlog or an error.
      (iii) *nbuild*—takes as input an eventlog and returns an eventlog.
      (iv) *extract*—takes as input an eventlog, a build number and an eventlist and returns as result either text or an error.

Line 16:   Declares the types of variables used in the axioms defining the semantics of eventlog's operations.

Lines 18–20:   Define the behaviour of the operation *lastbuild#*. Line 18 specifies that the *lastbuild#* of a new eventlog is 0, line 19 specifies that operation *nbuild* increases the value of *lastbuild#* by 1, and line 20 specifies that operation *add* does not change the *lastbuild#*.

Line 21:   Specifies that the operation *append* is the same as *add* provided *lastbuild#(r)* $\geqslant b$ where *r* is the eventlog to which we are adding information about build number *b*; otherwise we get an error as a result of append.

Line 22:   Specifies that performing the operation *newbuild* on an eventlog r when the *lastbuild* $\#(r) = 999$ leads to an error; otherwise, *newbuild* is the same as performing *nbuild*.

Line 23:   Specifies that the operation *extract* is the same as *extractall* if the event list is null; otherwise it is the same as *extractlist*. Operation *extractall* retrieves all information about a build while *extractlist* only retrieves information about the specified events. So if information about all events of a build is desired, the user does not specify any events when using the operation *extract*.

Line 26:   This line is one of the axioms for *extractall*. It says that if the last operation we did on an eventlog r was to add information t about build number $b1$, then check to see if $b1$ is equal to build number b. If b is equal to $b1$ then perform *extractall* on r and concatenate the information retrieved to t; otherwise just perform extractall on r.

Line 33:   The result of destroying an eventlog is a null sequence of lines, viz. *empty*. Since a destoyed eventlog is not an object of type eventlog, no further operations can be performed on it. This restriction is clear from the syntactic definitions of the operations.

Note that we have again not given any axioms for operations *create*, *nbuild* and *add*. Instead, the other operations are defined in terms of them.

COMPARISON OF THE INFORMAL AND FORMAL SPECIFICATIONS

In comparing the formal specifications with the informal specifications (those given in Reference 3, the following points were noted:

(i) Readability

The informal specifications are easier to read but formal specifications are clear and precise. The algebraic specification technique is easy to learn for people with some mathematical background.

(ii) Missing operation

This observation was the most surprising of all and was possible because formal specifications lead me to a better understanding of the EVENT LOG subsystem. In the specifications for *append*, a check has to be made to ensure that the build number being referenced is less than the last build number. It was observed that no operation is provided in the EVENT LOG subsystem to determine the last build number. The last build number is written out to the standard file by the operation *newbuild*. The user has to keep track of the last build number manually. This seemed to be a serious deficiency and was confirmed by Muenzer.[11] For example, one cannot write a program that retrieves all the text associated with the last build (i.e. version). The inclusion of an operation *lastbuild* $\#$ for the EVENT LOG subsystem is now under consideration.

(iii) 'Manual' operation

For some reason, it was decided that destruction of an eventlog will be accomplished manually, one would destroy the eventlog by deleting the file that represented it. I feel that destroying an eventlog should be an operation like *create*, *add*, etc. and have therefore included it in the formal specifications. Having done this, the effect of applying operations on a destroyed eventlog can be defined.

(iv) Clarity, interaction between operations

The syntactic part of the formal specifications is clearly separated from the semantic part. The operation domains are clearly specified in the Formal Specifications. Interaction between operations is easily discernible. For example performing a *delete* operation before or after a successful *newbuild* operation has the same result.

(v) Implementation details

Specifications should not include implementation details. They should specify what is to be done and not how. The informal specifications contains implementation details, e.g. 'eventlog is represented by a file'; the eventlog will be eliminated by 'deleting the file that represents it', lines of text associated with a key are to be stored as one unit, etc. If it is desirable to suggest an implementation then the implementation details should be provided but kept clearly separated from the specifications. The informal specifications do have a section on representation details. However, not all the implementation details are isolated here; some of them are mixed with the specifications of the subsystem.

There are situations where it is essential that a system must be implemented in a certain way. Then specifications detailing the implementation should be provided both for informal specifications and formal specifications[8]—whichever is being used.

(vi) Errors and boundary conditions

The informal specifications did not specify what would happen in case operations were applied to an eventlog that had been destroyed, the initial build number, the effect of applying the newbuild operation more than 999 times, extracting information about a build number greater than the last build number or a build number that has no information associated with it, what the initialization of the eventlog is supposed to be, etc.

(vii) Imprecision

The eventfield is defined by the informal specification to be a character string of 'moderate' length. What is a moderate length? Such vague specifications will lead to incompatibilities and cannot be used for reference by the user and the implementor.

(viii) Incompleteness

For the append operation 'Lines of text are read from the standard file ...'. It is not specified how this text is terminated.

(ix) Procedures versus functions

All operations in the formal specifications have been defined as functions. Implementation of these operations as functions will lead to inefficient implementations. As mentioned before, the algebraic specification technique has been extended to allow for defining operations that are procedures.

(x) Miscellaneous

The informal specifications are interspersed with environmental details, e.g. version restrictions, the version of the system that maintains it, write permission in the release directory, etc. These are important, but they should be specified separately.

CONCLUSIONS

All the points listed in the comparison except for the one about the missing operation were in a sense expected. It took me about a day to understand the EVENT LOG subsystem and its context, and about an hour to write the formal specifications. There was an error in the specifications relating to the definition of the destroy function. This was pointed out by Lyons.[12] Such an error would probably have not been detected had the specifications been informal. It was fairly easy to modify the axioms to eliminate this error. Although formal specifications may be hard, if not impossible, to write for huge systems such as OS 360, experience in the use of formal specifications and understanding their advantages can lead to the development of better informal specifications.

Formal specifications cannot replace informal specifications—they are complementary. Ideally, system specifications should include both formal and informal specifications. The informal specifications are easier to read and understand while the formal specifications tend to be clearer, precise, unambiguous, etc. Whenever there are any doubts about the informal specifications, the formal specifications should be used to resolve doubts. Additionally, if it is desirable to suggest an implementation, then the implementation details should be specified separately from the specifications—formal or informal.

Liskov[13] points out that formal specifications can also be used in conjunction with automated tools for detection of certain kinds of inconsistency and incompleteness. In addition, formal specifications can sometimes be used to generate implementations automatically although these implementations may not be as efficient as manual ones.

Formal specifications, such as the algebraic specifications, do not allow the specification of the behavioural characteristics of systems such as storage requirements or input and output characteristics. According to Winograd[14] programming in the future will depend more and more on specifying behaviour.

Musa[15] points out that, in software development, specification defects are the most costly to fix and have the greatest impact on schedules. The larger the system, the larger the proportion of defects due to specifications. Consequently, one must be careful in writing specifications. The use of formal specifications is an effort in this direction.

ACKNOWLEDGEMENTS

Thanks are due to T. B. Muenzer for helping me understand the EVENT LOG subsystem, and R. H. Canaday, F. L. Dalrymple, P. V. Guidi, B. W. Kernighan, J. R. Kliegman, T. G. Lyons, D. A. Nowitz and C. S. Wetherell for their comments.

REFERENCES

1. B. Liskov, 'Specification techniques for data abstractions', *IEEE Conference on Reliable Software Engineering*, Vol. 1, No. 1 (March 1975).
2. J. V. Guttag, 'The algebraic specification of abstract data types', *Acta Informatica* **10**, 27–52 (1978).
3. T. G. Lyons, *Change Management Automated Build System EVENT LOG Sub-System Design Specification*, Bell Labs, November 1977.

4. T. G. Lyons and T. B. Muenzer, *Proposal for the Field Trial of the Change Management Automated Build System (CM ABS) by the Division of Revenues Processing (DRP) Project*, Bell Labs, November 1977.
5. T. B. Muenzer, *Change Management Automated Build System*, Bell Labs, March 1977.
6. J. V. Guttag, E. Horovitz and D. R. Musser, 'Some extensions to algebraic specifications', *Proc. Language Design for Reliable Software*, March 1977, pp. 63–67.
7. C. J. Date, *An Introduction to Data Base Systems*, Addison-Wesley, Mass., 1975.
8. J. V. Guttag, E. Horovitz and D. R. Musser, 'Abstract data types and software validation', *CACM* 21, (12), 1048–1064 (1978).
9. M. E. Majster, 'Limits of the algebraic specification of data types', *SIGPLAN Notices*, 12, 37–41 (1977).
10. M. E. Majster, 'Treatment of partial operations in the algebraic specification technique', *Proc. of Specifications of Reliable Software*, April 1979.
11. T. B. Muenzer, *Private communication*, June 1979.
12. T. G.Lyons, *Private communication*, 30 August, 1979.
13. B. Liskov and.V. Berzins, 'An appraisal of program specifications' in Peter Wegner (ed.), *Research Direction in Software Technology*, The MIT Press, 1979.
14. T. Winograd, 'Beyond programming languages', *CACM*, 22, 391–401 (1979).
15. J. Musa, *Program Specifications: A Mini-Tutorial*, TM 79–3725–1, Bell Labs, June 1979.

OBJECT—ORIENTED DESIGN

Grady Booch

Abstract: Our ability to manage complexity is a fundamental human limitation in the creation of large software systems that are reliable, maintainable, efficient, and understandable. Traditionally, we have applied design methodologies that are primarily functional in nature, but such methodologies have their deficiencies, particularly in light of the development of high order languages, such as Ada*, that offer support for data abstraction and information hiding. In this paper, we present an object—oriented design methodology that is declarative, rather than imperative, and examine its theoretical roots, its benefits, and its application in an object—oriented programming style using the Ada language.

No matter what the particular application, our problem space is rooted somewhere in the real world, and the solution space is implemented by a combination of software and hardware. H. Ledgard developed a model to describe a typical programming task, as shown in Figure 1. As this figure illustrates, in the problem space we have some real—world objects, each of which has a set of appropriate operations. These objects may be as simple as a checkbook ledger or as complex as an interplanetary spacecraft. Also in the problem space we have some real—world algorithm that operates on these objects and provides transformed objects as results. For example, a real—world result may be a balanced checkbook or a course change for a spacecraft.

Whenever we develop a software system, we either model a real—world problem entirely in software or, in the case of an embedded computer system, take real—world objects and transform them in software and hardware to produce real—world results. No matter what the implementation, our solution space parallels the problem space. First, programming languages provide tools for a programmer to represent the real—world objects; in essence, the programmer abstracts the objects in the problem space and implements the abstraction in software. Next, some computer algorithm that transforms these software objects is applied. Again, the programmer uses his or her logical abstraction of the operations in the real world. Finally, these algorithms produce some form of output data, which are either mapped physically to some real—world action, such as the movement of a control surface, or are interpreted by humans in non—real time.

----

* Ada is a trademark of the U. S. Department of Defense (Ada Joint Program Office)

Adapted with permission from *Software Engineering with Ada*, Benjamin/Cummings Publishing Co., Menlo Park, CA, 1983.

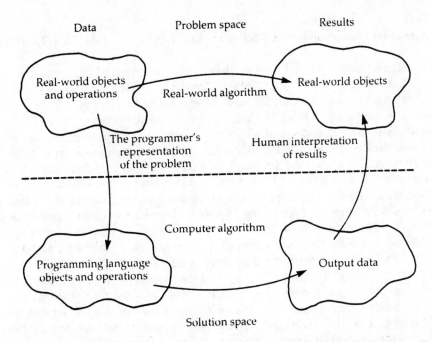

Figure 1: Model for a typical programming task [1].

Intuitively, it is clear that the closer the solution space maps to our concept of the problem space, the better we can achieve our goals of modifiability, efficiency, reliability, and understandability. All the things we know in the real world are abstractions, and, if our solutions are distant from the problem space, we must make a mental or physical transformation to the real-world abstractions, thus increasing the complexity of our solution.

If we examine human languages, we find that they all have two primary components, noun phrases and verb phrases. There exists a parallel structure in programming languages, since they provide constructs for implementing objects (noun phrases) and operations (verb phrases). However, most of the languages developed prior to the introduction of Ada are primarily imperative, that is, they provide a rich set of constructs for implementing operations, but are generally weak when it comes to abstracting real-world objects. Furthermore, the topologies of these languages indicate that they all have a relatively flat structure [2]. However, the real world is neither flat nor sequential but is instead multidimensional and often highly parallel. Thus, the first three generations of programming languages (including FORTRAN, COBOL, and Pascal), and especially assembly languages, widen the gap between the problem space and the solution space.

LIMITATIONS OF FUNCTIONAL METHODOLOGIES

Software engineering principles cannot be applied haphazardly. We must structure our systems in a disciplined manner. Most importantly, as we divide systems into modules, we must apply consistent criteria for the decomposition.

Traditionally, there are basically three design methodologies that provide such criteria, namely:

* Top-down structured design

* Data-structure design
* Parnas decomposition criterion

A full discussion of these design methodologies is beyond the scope of this paper, but in the next few paragraphs we will provide the essential details of each criterion.

Top-down structure design, as described by E. Yourdon, suggests that we decompose a system by making each step in the process a module [3]. This leads us to program modules that are highly functional, and so is well suited to sequential problems. At the highest levels of the solution, we define the highest level of algorithmic abstraction (the 'what' of the process), and lower levels provide primitive operations that implement these higher-level actions.

D. Jackson and P. Warnier provided an alternative design methodology, called *data-structure design*, that has proved very effective in COBOL-type applications [4, 5]. Using this technique, we first define our data structures, and then structure the program units based on the data structure. In this way, we attempt to clearly define the implementation of the objects in our solution space, and them make their structure visible to the necessary functional units that provide the operations on the objects.

In the *Parnas decomposition criterion*, we decompose our system so that each module in the solution hides a design [6]. In this manner, we explicitly capture our design structure in the software at the level at which we made the design decision. If we then need to modify our solution, we should easily be able to localize the effects of the modification.

Now, there is nothing inherently evil about any of these design methodologies; each is quite appropriate for a particular class of problems. However, we suggest that each of these methodologies has some weaknesses relative to the creation of large, complex software systems.

Top-down design techniques are imperative in nature, that is, they force us to concentrate on the operations in the solution space, with little regard for the design of the data structures. As Yourdon states, "Certain consequences result from this approach. The sequential, procedural, methodological aspects of programs are further emphasized. In this description, the effort is concentrated on two things - on finding a computational method and on the sequential statement-by-statement translation of the method" [7]. In this methodology, the subprogram becomes the fundamental unit of decomposition; we should also note that the subprogram is the only structural unit in most early generation programming languages. However, as Guttag reports, "Unfortunately, the nature of the abstractions that may be conveniently achieved through the use of subroutines is limited. Subroutines, while well suited to the description of abstract events (operations), are not particularly well suited to the description of abstract objects. This is a serious drawback, for in a great many applications, the complexity of the data objects to be manipulated contributes substantially to the overall complexity of the problem" [8].

Data-structure design techniques are at the other end of the spectrum. They concentrate on the objects and treat the operations in a global fashion. Yourdon reports that "...the data-structure approach seems to work best on relatively small system. On larger system, the designer must work with several sets of data. In such a situation, there is an excellent chance that one or more structure clashes will occur...if the designer is forced to deal with the entire problem and with all of the structure classes at once, it usually will be difficult for him to see how to decompose the problem into smaller, separately solvable problems" [9].

In some sense, these first two design methodologies do not aid the programmer in managing the complexity of the overall solution, and in fact may add to the complexity of the problem. As a reaction to this situation, the Parnas criterion applies the principle of information hiding to reduce the amount of detail that the designer must work with at each level of the solution [10]. In addition, this approach encapsulates design decisions that are likely to change, thereby easing the maintenance problem since the scope of effect of such a design decision can be well-defined. We believe, and our experience supports it, that this is absolutely the correct approach. Unfortunately, this methodology offers little guidance in selecting what design decisions to hide, nor how to best layer or group them; furthermore, as Plum notes, it is not clear how to translate "from design units and design interfaces into programmable, interconnected modules" [11].

Using these first two design methodologies, we may, on the one hand, have a solution that is totally functional, and thus avoids a reasonable implementation of our real-world object abstraction, or, on the other hand, we may end up with clear data structures, but the operations will be obscure. The effect is somewhat like trying to communicate in English using just verbs or just nouns. At the very least, we shall have to make a mental transformation from the solution space to the problem space, and, in the worst case, we must make a physical transformation. In any case, these methodologies may leave us with a solution that is removed from the problem space. In addition, all of these methodologies force us into a sequential way of thinking and do not provide any tools for identifying parallelism inherent in the problem space.

AN OBJECT-ORIENTED DESIGN METHODOLOGY

What we desire, then, is a methodology that lets us map solutions directly to our view of the problem. In addition, much like human languages, we seek a balanced treatment between the objects and operations in our solution. We shall call this an *object-oriented* design methodology to emphasize the fact that it is not a purely functional design technique. Instead, this approach recognizes the importance of software objects as actors, each with its own set of applicable operations.

We do not claim to have 'invented' the concept of object-oriented design, but rather we have tried to build upon the work of others. In particular, object-oriented design is founded upon the principles of abstraction, as first defined by Dijkstra [12], and information hiding, as presented by Parnas [13]. We have also been influenced by the research on abstract data types by B. Liskov and J. Guttag of the Massachusetts Institute of Technology, and Robinson and K. Leavitt of Stanford Research Institute. In addition, this methodology follows the object orientation encouraged by the languages SIMULA and SMALLTALK. The particular technique we present for designing object-oriented software was first introduced by R. Abbott of California State University, Northridge. Our contribution has been to continue Dr. Abbott's work, with our research and application of a mapping of object-oriented principles into Ada, particularly for complex, concurrent systems.

Before we study this particular methodology, it is important that we establish some object-oriented concepts first, the most important of which is the notion of an *object* itself. Actually, the idea of an object should not be anything new to us; intuitively, in the real world, an object is simply an entity that is visible or otherwise tangible; we can do things to an object (like throw a rock) or objects can have a 'life' of their own (for example, as in a stream flowing down a mountainside). In our software, an object is also any entity that acts or can be acted upon; in a sense, objects are the computational resources of our system that parallel (abstract) the objects from the real world. Furthermore, as MacLennan observes, "objects exist in time and hence can be created, destroyed, copied, shared, and updated" [14].

Every object is an instance of some type; a type characterizes a set of values and a set of operations applicable to objects of that type. We may apply primitive data types (such as integers), so called because they are inherent in the particular implementation language, and thus have a predefined set of operations (such as assignment, addition, multiplication, comparison, etc.). We may also define abstract data types, built by extending the subject language, and defined by a unique set of values and operations for all instances of the type. An instance of such an abstract type can be viewed from two perspectives; from the 'outside,' as characterized by its state (values) and visible operations, and from the 'inside,' which is the implementation of the object itself [15]. In the spirit of the Parnas criterion, we effectively shield the user of the object from the details and design decisions made by the implementor of the object. In so doing, we effectively reduce the complexity the object user must deal with.

In purely functional design methodologies, the basic decomposition criterion is that each step in the process represents a module. In an object-oriented design methodology, we take a different approach, namely:

Each object in the system represents a module

In general, the operations in a system are associated with the definition of each abstract object. However, we may identify the basic flow of control in the system using a top-down structured design technique, but only after we have architected the objects in our system.

To guide the design process, we next present the steps in our methodology:

```
Define the problem
Develop an informal strategy
Formalize the strategy
    Identify objects and their attributes
    Identify operations on the objects
    Establish the interfaces
    Implement the operations
```

In the remainder of this section, we provide further details of this methodology, including the rationale for each step. In a following section, we provide an application of this methodology using the Ada programming language.

Before we proceed, however, there is one important point we must make: just as structured programming doesn't mean simply writing 'goto-less' programs, applying these steps doesn't necessarily mean that one is using object-oriented design. Rather, an object-oriented style is more of a *philosophy* to be applied during the creation of a system; it is a perspective that emphasizes the significance of software objects over traditionally functional abstractions. These steps offer guidance in the identification of such objects during the design and implementation of a system, using the principles of abstraction and information hiding in an attempt to improve program reliability, maintainability, and understandability.

Define the Problem

Just as in any other problem-solving process, we start our methodology by defining the problem. This step is no different from how we traditionally analyze problems. In fact, tools such as SADT or data flow diagrams are appropriate at this point. However, no matter what tool is used, the important point is that we gain an understanding of the structure of the problem space.

Of course, we recognize that we cannot expect perfect knowledge of the problem. Rather, our understanding is an iterative process, and, as we go deeper into the design of the solution, we shall most likely uncover new aspects of the problem that we did not recognize before. However, since our ultimate solution should map directly to the problem, this new-found understanding of the problem space should not greatly affect our design. We should be able to limit the scope of the change to a module in the solution space that parallels an entity in the problem. In real-world projects, we usually describe the problem space in some type of formal specification; for our example, we shall only introduce the features of the problem necessary to completely design and implement a given level of the solution.

Develop an Informal Strategy

Once we have an understanding of at least the highest levels of the problem, the second step is to create an informal strategy that parallels our view of the world. Starting with an informal strategy may seem contrary to contemporary thought, but the human though process is not usually formal. Instead, when developing a solution, we first have an intuitive feel for the problem and then tighten up our understanding by evolving more formal descriptions. In regard to understanding the problem itself, R. Balzer, N. Goldman, and D. Wile note that "...it should be recognized that informality will always exist during the formulation of a specification" [16].

Eventually, formality will be necessary if we are to communicate our understanding to other people or computers with any degree or completeness or consistency, and our approach will lead us to such a formal treatment. For the moment, however, we shall exploit the existence of our informal understanding. Using our object-oriented methodology, we shall express our informal strategy, using natural English descriptions, in terms of the concepts from the problem space. In fact, at this level, it is best that the designer place no restrictions on the form of the text. If we are to develop a solution that maps to our view of the real world, then now is not the time to limit our ability to think about the problem. Neither do we need concern ourselves with the structure of the solution. As we shall see, the implementation will naturally evolve.

Formalize the Strategy

The third step in the process involves formalizing our strategy, using some simple rules. Within this step, we first identify the objects and their attributes. Earlier we mentioned that programming languages contain constructs for describing objects, which in turn parallel the noun phrases in human languages. To implement this step in the process, we simply return to our informal strategy and extract the nouns which represent objects, along with any qualifying adjectives which represent attributes of each object. This is a relatively mechanical process that could probably be automated using some artificial intelligence technique.

As we select the noun phrases from our strategy, we uncover several types of nouns, including [17]:

* *Common nouns.* Name a class of entities (e.g., table, terminal, sensor, switch)
* *Mass nouns and units of measure.* Name a quality, activity, or substance, or a quantity of the same (e.g., water, matter, fuel)
* *Proper nouns and nouns of direct reference.* Name of a specific being or entity (e.g., nozzel-pressure sensor, my table, abort switch)

The first two categories, common and mass nouns, along with units of measure, do not identify specific objects but rather imply abstract data types. From these types of nouns, we may identify specific objects as instances of these data types. Additionally, the proper nouns and nouns of direct reference map to specific real-world objects from the problem space.

As we select the adjectives appropriate to each object, we identify the attributes, or qualities, of that particular object. These attributes may identify constraints upon a given object (such as a range of possible values) or may even give us an indication of timing relationships. Thus if we select adjectives such as "asynchronous," "concurrent," or "independent," we begin to expose the parallel nature of the problem space, even at this early point in the design process.

In the next step, we repeat our mechanical process, this time underlining the verb phrases that are in our informal strategy. In this manner, we begin to extract any real-world operations. As we step through this process, we must associate each operation with a particular object. In addition, we select the adverb phrases associated with each action. In this manner, we identify attributes of the operations, such as timing relationships, sequence of control, and number of iterations. Just as before, we may expose some operations that execute concurrently with other processes.

We are now ready to formalize our strategy even further. In this step, we must establish the relationships among the objects. What this means is that we formally describe the visible interfaces to each object, using Ada as the design language. In this manner, we form a contract between a user of the object and the object itself, explicitly defining the operations we may perform. Of course, we determined what these operations were in the previous step. Through its packaging and generic facilities, Ada not only permits us to easily describe such a contract but, in addition, enforces the contract by preventing us from violating our logical abstraction. Since a given object in the real world will not interact with all other objects, we must also formally describe the scope and visibility of each entity. We can derive this information directly from our informal strategy. In the next section, we will use some symbols that graphically portray the scope and visibility relationships.

As the next step in the process, we take the operations previously identified for each object and implement them in our programming language. In this way, we develop the design of our solution in a form that is also executable. Again, we refer to our informal strategy to assist us in designing the operations in the proper sequence of control, as identified by the adverbial phrases. Furthermore, if our strategy implies that any of these operations are to execute concurrently with other processes, we may now implement such operations as parallel tasks.

Our process in not quite complete since, as we begin to implement the operations, we shall certainly uncover other objects and operations that form part of the current level of implementation. Thus, we must repeat the process, at this different level, and again identify the objects and operations applicable to this point in the design. We repeat our methodology until we reach the point where our level of decomposition is understandable without further modularity.

This approach supports the principles of software engineering. Clearly, the object-oriented design methodology supports abstraction and information hiding, since we directly implement our abstractions from the problem space. In addition, with Ada as our target language, we can physically hide the details of our operations and even the representation of our objects.

This approach provides a purposeful strategy for decomposing a system into modules, in which we localize our design decisions to match our view of the real world. Furthermore, we now have a uniform notation for selecting the objects and operations that are part of our design.

DESIGNING INTO ADA

Any language, human or computer, does two things for the user: First, it provides a *range of expression.* For example, a certain Eskimo dialect has over 30 words for "snow." Similarly, an APL programmer is permitted to think in terms of vectors. Second, it *constrains* a user's thinking. For example, notice how rich the English language is in expressing action, while many other European languages have a richer set of nouns; think also about a FORTRAN programmer, and ask him or her to solve a problem using recursion.

Within any given language, sufficient tools must be provided to allow us to express a problem solution. Ideally, we would like to use a language that lets us directly reflect our view of the problem space. With languages from the early generations, we too often have to fit the solution to the language, rather than adapting the language to the solution. As a result, our tools get in the way of the primary goal — solving the problem. In the case where programming from the problem space into a language directly reflects our structure of the problem space, we are presented with an implementation that is understandable and therefore helpful in managing the complexity of the larger system. Such a language must provide tools for expressing primitive objects and operations and must, in addition, be extensible so that we may build our own abstract objects and operations. In the best case, we also need our language to enforce these abstractions.

Ada is such a programming language. It provides a rich set of constructs for describing primitive objects and operations and, in addition, offers a packaging construct with which we may build and enforce our own abstractions. Note that the object-oriented design methodology is only one model with which to apply Ada. We may apply any traditional design methodology with it. However, Ada provides the programmer some unique features not found in most production languages, including tasking, exception handling, and packaging. As a result, the capabilities of Ada demand that we break ourselves from the flat, sequential mind-set into which other languages force us and instead think in the broader terms of the problem space. Our object-oriented design methodology offers such a conceptual model.

APPLYING THE METHODOLOGY

To illustrate the application of this object-oriented design methodology using Ada, we will apply it to the problem of counting the leaves on a binary tree [18]. This example was first presented by Abbott, and we have reworked the solution and completed the Ada implementation. This may seem like a rather academic exercise to start with, however it is complex enough to be non-trivial, and simple enough to serve as a gentle first venture into object-oriented design. We should add that we have successfully applied this methodology to vastly larger problems, including those that require the use of concurrency [see also 19].

Define the Problem

A binary tree is a simple data structure often found in compilers, gaming programs, and data base systems. As Figure 2 indicates, a binary tree consists of *nodes* (nonterminals A .. D) and *leaves* (terminals 1 .. 5). In a complete binary tree, each node has two branches. Thus, a given node is either a leaf or consists of two subtrees. If a tree is just a leaf, then:

NUMBER_OF_LEAVES(TREE) = 1

If it consists of two subtrees:

NUMBER_OF_LEAVES(TREE) = NUMBER_OF_LEAVES(RIGHT_SUBTREE) +
NUMBER_OF_LEAVES(LEFT_SUBTREE)

This *recursive* definition still applies if one of the subtrees is empty (a null tree).

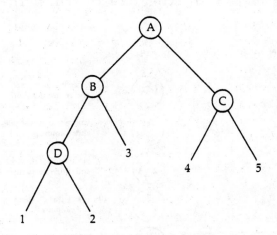

Figure 2: A binary tree.

Our goal is to develop a system that counts the leaves of a given tree.

Develop an Informal Strategy

There are many ways to count the leaves of a binary tree. For example, we could start at one node and traverse the tree until all of the leaves have been visited. However, this is an imperative method that requires high-level knowledge of how the elements of a tree are physically connected (an implementation detail). Instead, we shall use an algorithm that appeals to an intuitive approach. In this manner, if our representation of the tree changes physically, perhaps for efficiency reasons, then the logical structure of our system should remain invariant. We will assume that the language used to express our algorithm has the three basic control structures (sequential, conditional, and iterative) and that it has no predefined objects or operations. However, we will also assume that we have a facility for defining objects and their operations for our abstract world (extensibility). Given these constraints, we can present our informal strategy:

> Keep a pile of the parts of the tree that have not yet been counted. Initially, get a tree and put it on the empty pile; the count of the leaves is initially set to zero. As long as the pile is not empty, repeatedly take a tree off the pile and examine it. If the tree consists of a single leaf, then increment the leaf counter and throw away that tree. If the tree is not a single leaf but instead consists of two subtrees. split the tree into its left and right subtrees and put them back on the pile. Once the pile is empty, display the count of the leaves.

Figure 3 gives an example of the use of this informal strategy.

	LEAF_COUNT	TREE	PILE		LEAF_COUNT	TREE	PILE
1. Initially:	0			7. Since it is a tree, split it and return the subtrees.	1		
2. Take a tree off the pile and examine it.	0			8. Take a tree off the pile and examine it.	1	.3	
3. Since it is a tree, split it and return the subtrees.	0			9. Since it is a leaf, count it and throw away the tree.	2		
4. Take a tree off the pile and examine it.	0	1		10. Take a tree off the pile and examine it.	2	2	
5. Since it is a leaf, count it and throw away the tree.	1			11. Since it is a leaf, count it and throw away the tree.	3		
6. Take a tree off the pile and examine it.	1			12. Since the pile is empty, we can display the count.	3		

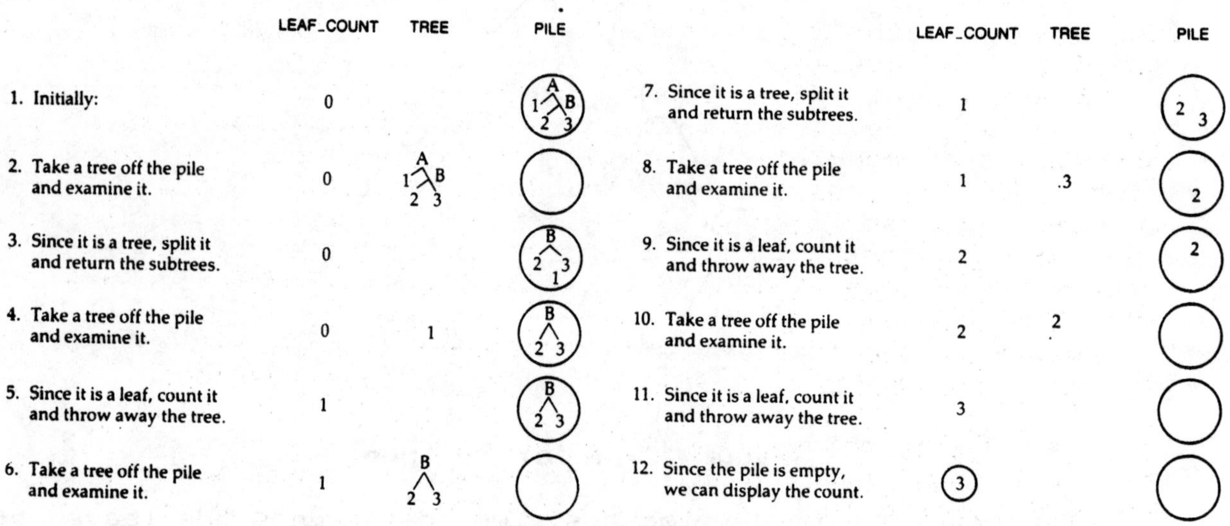

Figure 3: Example of counting the leaves.

Formalize the Strategy

The next step in our design is to take this informal strategy and express it formally using Ada.

Identify the Objects and their Attributes
This is a simple task. We repeat our informal strategy, this time underlining the nouns and adjectives:

> Keep a pile of the parts of the tree that have not yet been counted. Initially, get a tree and put it on the empty pile ; the count

of the <u>leaves</u> is initially set to zero. As long as the <u>pile</u> is not empty, repeatedly take a <u>tree</u> off the <u>pile</u> and examine <u>it</u>. If the <u>tree</u> consists of a <u>single leaf</u>, then increment the <u>leaf counter</u> and throw away that <u>tree</u>. If the <u>tree</u> is not a <u>single leaf</u> but instead consists of <u>two subtrees</u>, split the <u>tree</u> into its <u>left and right subtrees</u> and put <u>them</u> back on the <u>pile</u>. Once the <u>pile</u> is empty, display the <u>count of the leaves</u>.

From this evaluation, we can see that our basic objects are:

* LEAF_COUNT
* PILE
* LEFT_SUBTREE, RIGHT_SUBTREE, TREE

These are all abstract objects; they are a logical part of this problem space. Note the the LEFT_SUBTREE, RIGHT_SUBTREE, and the TREE are all just instances of the same type of object, which we shall call TREE_TYPE. Similarly, we will assume that the LEAF_COUNT and the PILE are both objects of the type COUNTER_TYPE and PILE_TYPE, respectively.

At this point, it is important that we distinguish between a type and an object. Basically, an object is the instance of some (possibly anonymous) type. We may not operate upon a type, but rather we may only operate upon an instance of a type. In this example, we chose to explicitly identify the type of each object, although we do not always have to do so. In the case where we uncover only one instance of a particular object (such as the LEAF_COUNT), we may chose to hide the name of that object's type to prevent a user from declaring multiple objects, since that may in fact violate our abstraction of the problem space.

<u>Identify Operations on the Objects</u>
This too is a simple task. We repeat our informal strategy, this time underlining the verbs and adverbs:

Keep a pile of the parts of the tree that have not yet been counted. <u>Initially, get</u> a tree and <u>put</u> it <u>on</u> the empty pile; the count of the leaves is <u>initially set to zero</u>. As long as the pile <u>is not empty</u>, <u>repeatedly take</u> a tree <u>off</u> the pile and <u>examine</u> it. If the tree <u>consists of a single leaf</u>, then <u>increment</u> the leaf counter and <u>throw away</u> that tree. If the tree <u>is not a single leaf</u> but instead consists of two subtrees, <u>split</u> the tree into its left and right subtrees and <u>put</u> them <u>back</u> on the pile. Once the pile <u>is empty, display</u> the count of the leaves.

Note that the verbs implying existence (e.g., *keep*) are not underlined. This is because declaration of an object (PILE, in this example) already implies its existence.

As we step through our informal strategy this second time, we must associate each operation with its object. Furthermore, any adverbs that we encounter act as modifiers to the basic operations, indicating the time of an event (INITIAL) or the conditions under which an event occurs (while the pile IS_NOT_EMPTY). From this evaluation, we can observe that the operations applicable to our objects are:

* LEAF_COUNT
  -- DISPLAY
  -- INCREMENT
  -- ZERO
* PILE
  -- IS_NOT_EMPTY
  -- PUT
  -- PUT_INITIAL
  -- TAKE
* LEFT_SUBTREE, RIGHT_SUBTREE, TREE
  -- GET_INITIAL
  -- IS_SINGLE_LEAF
  -- SPLIT
  -- THROW_AWAY

As noted earlier, since the LEFT_SUBTREE, RIGHT_SUBTREE, and TREE are all instances of the same abstract type, we group the applicable operations together.

Establish the Interfaces

Given the objects in our world plus the operations we may perform upon them, we can now describe the relationships among them. Using a notation that defines a symbol for each class of Ada program units (packages, subprograms, tasks, and generic units), we visualize the design of our solution as shown in Figure 4 [20]. In particular, note that the main action of our solution is indicated by a subprogram, and the objects are represented by the three packages. The packages encapsulate the definition of the underlying types of each object; we export the name of each type, along with the specification for each of the applicable operations. (by *export*, we mean "make available outside the package definition.") The arrows indicate what program unit can see other program units. Thus, the main subprogram can see all three packages, but not the reverse. The PILE_PACKAGE must see the TREE_PACKAGE, however, since the PILE must understand the structure of what is being PUT or TAKEn.

Given this design, we can next describe the interface of each package. This interface will establish a contract between the package and its user; we hide the details of each entity, and make visible only the interfaces. Furthermore, we enforce our logical abstraction of the objects in the solution by revealing the specification of only the applicable operations. It is not important for the package user to understand how these operations are implemented, it is only important that a user be able to apply these operations.

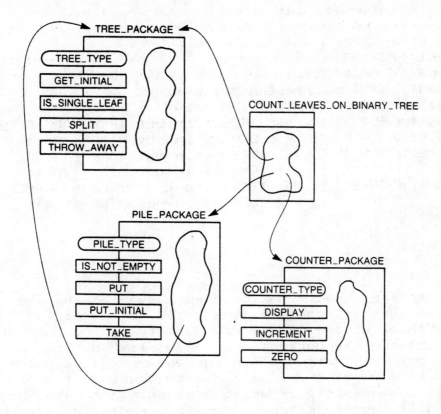

Figure 4: Design of COUNT_LEAVES_ON_BINARY_TREE

Using Ada as our design language, we can formally declare the interfaces of the entities in our solution. A package specification provides the visible part of our interfaces, while a package body, which is separately compilable, provides the implementation of the operations. These package specifications provide the definition of our abstract data types.

For the LEAF_COUNT, which is an instance of a COUNTER_TYPE, we can implement the interface as:

```
package COUNTER_PACKAGE is
   type COUNTER_TYPE is limited private;
   procedure DISPLAY    (COUNTER : in      COUNTER_TYPE);
   procedure INCREMENT (COUNTER : in out COUNTER_TYPE);
   procedure ZERO      (COUNTER : out     COUNTER_TYPE);
private
   ...
end COUNTER_PACKAGE;
```

In this package specification, we can name the operations with procedures. The **in, in out,** and **out** reserved words are known as modes and indicate the direction of data flow relative to the subprogram. We have declared the COUNTER_TYPE as **limited private**, which indicates that the structure of the type is not visible (and thus not usable) outside the package. We omit the implementation of each private part in this paper for simplicity.

For the PILE, which is an instance of a PILE_TYPE, we

implement the interface as:

```
with TREE_PACKAGE;
package PILE_PACKAGE is
   type PILE_TYPE is limited private;
   function  IS_NOT_EMPTY (PILE : in      PILE_TYPE) return BOOLEAN;
   procedure PUT          (TREE : in out TREE_PACKAGE.TREE_TYPE;
                           ON   : in out PILE_TYPE);
   procedure PUT_INITIAL  (TREE : in out TREE_PACKAGE.TREE_TYPE;
                           ON   : in out PILE_TYPE);
   procedure TAKE         (TREE : out    TREE_PACKAGE.TREE_TYPE;
                           OFF  : in out PILE_TYPE);
private
   ...
end PILE_PACKAGE;
```

In this package specification, we have again used a limited
private type, but for the moment we will not complete the private
part. Note that, with a limited private type, the only operations
available outside the package are those listed in the package
specification; operations of assignment or the test for equality
or inequality are not even available to users of the package. We
have applied the style of using procedures to name the abstract
actions, while the function names a predicate (that is, an
expression that evaluates TRUE or FALSE).

   Within this PILE_PACKAGE, we must know the form of the things
we can keep on the PILE. To indicate a dependency among program
units, we use a **with** clause; in our case, we make the
TREE_PACKAGE visible, and thus usable throughout the
PILE_PACKAGE. Once it is visible, we can name the services of the
TREE_PACKAGE using dot notation, as in TREE_PACKAGE.TREE_TYPE.

   To complete the definition of our interfaces, we can describe
the TREE_TYPE as:

```
package TREE_PACKAGE is
   type TREE_TYPE is private;
   procedure GET_INITIAL   (TREE       : out    TREE_TYPE);
   function  IS_SINGLE_LEAF (TREE       : in     TREE_TYPE)
                             return BOOLEAN;
   procedure SPLIT          (TREE       : in out TREE_TYPE;
                             LEFT_INTO  : out    TREE_TYPE;
                             RIGHT_INTO : out    TREE_TYPE);
   procedure THROW_AWAY     (TREE       : in out TREE_TYPE);
private
   ...
end TREE_PACKAGE;
```

In this declaration, we have again deferred the implementation of
the **private** part. In several of the procedure declarations, note
that we have used the **in out** mode, and for good reason. For
example, in SPLIT, we want to take one TREE and break it into its
composite parts, returning only those parts and a null value for

the original TREE. If we did not export the original TREE, we would have CLONED the tree, not SPLIT it.

Implement the Operations

Now that we have declared the specifications for the COUNTER_TYPE, PILE_TYPE, and TREE_TYPE, we have a set of tools available to employ in the solution to our problem. The final step in the solution process is to implement our informal strategy, along with the operations we defined earlier. We work from the top down, starting with the informal strategy itself. The Ada solution that follows is highly readable, since it matches the problem space very closely:

```
with COUNTER_PACKAGE, PILE_PACKAGE, TREE_PACKAGE;
use  COUNTER_PACKAGE, PILE_PACKAGE, TREE_PACKAGE;
procedure COUNT_LEAVES_ON_BINARY_TREE is
   LEAF_COUNT    : COUNTER_TYPE;
   LEFT_SUBTREE  : TREE_TYPE;
   PILE          : PILE_TYPE;
   RIGHT_SUBTREE : TREE_TYPE;
   TREE          : TREE_TYPE;
begin
   GET_INITIAL(TREE);
   PUT_INITIAL(TREE, ON => PILE);
   ZERO(LEAF_COUNT);
   while IS_NOT_EMPTY(PILE)
     loop
        TAKE(TREE, OFF => PILE);
        if IS_SINGLE_LEAF(TREE) then
           INCREMENT(LEAF_COUNT);
           THROW_AWAY(TREE);
        else
           SPLIT(TREE,
                 LEFT_INTO  => LEFT_SUBTREE,
                 RIGHT_INTO => RIGHT_SUBTREE);
           PUT(LEFT_SUBTREE, ON => PILE);
           PUT(RIGHT_SUBTREE, ON => PILE);
        end if;
     end loop;
   DISPLAY(LEAF_COUNT);
end COUNT_LEAVES_ON_BINARY_TREE;
```

The first part of this procedure uses the **with** clause to name the packages it needs to see. This clause formally implements the relationships indicated in Figure 4. Following the name of the main procedure itself are the declarations for the objects as we named them. Finally, the implementation of our algorithm follows the **begin** of a block. Notice how the Ada code reads just like our informal strategy.

The final part of our implementation would include the completion of the package bodies along with the private parts. However, we omit these details since they do not add to our discussion of object-oriented design.

SUMMARY

Rentsch observes that "object-oriented programming will be in the 1980's what structured programming was in the 1970's. Everyone will be in favor of it. Every manufacturer will promote his products as supporting it. Every manager will pay lip service to it. Every programmer will practice it (differently). And no one will know just what it is" [21]. In this paper, we have attempted to define "just what it is" with our presentation of the rationale for and essential concepts of an object-oriented style. Traditionally, an object orientation was practical only in languages such as SMALLTALK. With the introduction of Ada, we believe, and our experience bears this out, that it is not only appropriate but very desirable to apply these object-oriented concepts to the creation of large, complex systems.

REFERENCES

[1] H. Ledgard and M. Marcotty, *The Programming Language Landscape* (Chicago: Science Research Associates, 1981), p. 166.

[2] G. Booch, *Software Engineering with Ada* (Menlo Park: Benjamin/ Cummings, 1983), pp. 33-36.

[3] E. Yourdon and L. Constantine, *Structured Design: Fundamentals of a Discipline of Computer Program and System Design* (Englewood Cliffs, N.J.: Prentice-Hall, 1979), p. 106.

[4] Ibid., p. 246.

[5] M. Jackson, *Principles of Program Design*, (New York: Academic Press, 1975).

[6] D. Parnas, "On the Criteria to be Used in Decomposing a System into Modules," CMU-CS-71-101, *Communications of the ACM*, Vol 15, No. 12 (December 1972).

[7] Yourdon, p. 31.

[8] J. Guttag, "Abstract Data Types and the Development of Data Structures," *Communications of the ACM*, (June 1977), p. 206.

[9] Yourdon, p. 250.

[10] Parnas, p. 232.

[11] Yourdon, p. 253.

[12] B. Liskov, "A Design Methodology for Reliable Software Systems," Proceedings, Fall Joint Computer Conference, AFIPS, 1972, p.67.

[13] Parnas, p. 232.

[14] B. J. MacLennan, "Values and Objects in Programming Languages," SIGPLAN Notices, Vol 17, No. 12 (December 1982), p. 70.

[15] T. Rentsch, "Object-oriented Programming, SIGPLAN Notices, December 1982, p. 52.

[16] R. Balzer, N. Goldman, and D. Wile, "Informality in Program Specifications," *IEEE Transactions on Software Engineering*, Vol SE-4, No. 2 (March 1978), p. 94.

[17] Ada Style Guide, Ada Joint Program Office, 1982, pp. 137-146.

[18] G. Booch, "Object-oriented Design," *Ada Letters*, Vol. 1, No. 3:56. *See also* R. J. Abbott, "Report on Teaching Ada," Technical Report SAI-81-313-WA, Science Applications, Inc., McLean, Virginia, December 1980.

[19] Booch, *Software Engineering with Ada*.

[20] G. Booch, "Describing Software Design with Ada," SIGPLAN Notices, September 1981.

[21] Rentsch, p. 51.

CONCEPTUAL DATABASE DESIGN

D C P and J M Smith

Computer Corporation of America

D and J SMITH are co-directors of the Computer Science Research Department at the Computer Corporation of America. They were both formerly on the Computer Science Faculty at the University of Utah. Their research interests include semantic data models, database design, database machines, distributed database management and query optimisation. Diane Smith is vice-chairman of the ACM Special Interest Group on the Management of Data (SIGMOD).

First appeared in *Infotech State of the Art Report on Data Design*, 1980

CONCEPTUAL DATABASE DESIGN

ABSTRACT

The decision to implement a database is motivated by the need to share data among a variety of diverse applications and to integrate data for supporting more sophisticated applications. Both of these requirements complicate the already difficult task of providing safe and efficient access to computerised data. The database designer is responsible for developing an integrated design that can realistically be implemented in existing computer environments. His task can be eased by breaking the design process into separate stages of requirements analysis, conceptual design and physical design. This paper focuses on the development of conceptual designs. It itemises what must be specified in conceptual designs, presents language and diagrammatic tools for their specification, demonstrates a methodology for using these tools and discusses the evaluation of the final design.

INTRODUCTION

Database Management Systems (DBMSs) have evolved from file systems to answer two critical needs: support for more inter-related data and support for sharing data among many diverse applications. These goals are being achieved, in part, by providing DBMS software to physically link related data into complex structures using such mechanisms as pointer chains, indices and sequential positioning. They are also being achieved by the development of database design methodologies and rules - such as the practice of storing information in a non-redundant fashion so that changes by one application to the single copy of the data are seen by all its users.

To reduce the complexity of using DBMSs, designers have developed special interfaces to these systems that decompose their use into easy to understand phases. Thus, most DBMSs have Data Description Languages (DDLs), Data Manipulation Languages (DMLs) and Query Languages (QLs). The DDL is used to specify the design of the database. The DML is used to write application programs that access the database in terms of the objects specified using the DDL. And the QL is used for more 'casual' database accesses. The DML is oriented toward the development of database access programs that are efficient to execute while QLs are oriented towards ease in writing such programs.

It is the database design process that is the topic of this paper and in particular the design of the *conceptual level* of a database. We will begin by explaining conceptual design and where it fits into the overall design process. We will consider, in detail, exactly what should appear in a good conceptual design, as well as how it should be specified. We will describe tools for assisting the design and specification processes and outline a methodology for using these tools and evaluating the final design.

THE LEVELS OF DATABASE DESIGN

A database design must encompass all aspects of the data to be stored - beginning with
details of how it is presented to different users and ending with how it is to be
represented on the hardware of a particular installation. To achieve this in an
orderly and correct fashion, the design process has been structured into the three
distinct phases shown in Figure 1. (These three phases correspond to the three levels
in the ANSI/SPARC DBMS model (001).) The first phase, which may be called 'view design',
is the identification and design of interfaces for the different end-user groups.
Each end user requires a particular 'view' of the database to support his own application idiosyncrasies. A view should present data in the structure which is most effective for the user. This may be reports, computer generated 3-D images, graphs or
natural language text. The view must provide tailored update facilities for the user
to manipulate the database.

The next phase which may be called 'conceptual design' is the integration of all the
concepts which are necessary to support the various application views. In effect,
conceptual design is the production of a 'community' model in which the idiosyncrasies
of the individual views are resolved. At the conceptual level, data should appear in
a structure which is most perspicuous for concept integration. It should explicitly
define how concepts are related one to another; it should not contain any implementation
detail; and it should be locally modifiable. Update primitives at the conceptual
level must be explicitly designed to preserve the community view. End-user update

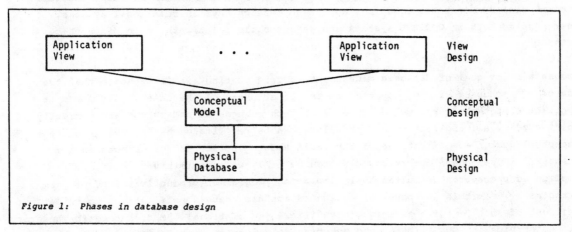

Figure 1: Phases in database design

facilities must be written in terms of these primitives, so that they also preserve
the community view.

The final phase, 'physical design', is the mapping of the conceptual model on to
physical computing devices. In this phase, performance considerations must be
analysed and shown compatible with application requirements. With most database
management systems, the physical mapping is partially hidden and 'tuning' is allowed
on only a fixed set of parameters.

This paper is concerned only with an *idealisation* of the conceptual design phase.
This idealisation assumes the availability at one time of the set of concepts which
are to be integrated. These concepts are further assumed to be 'clean'; in the
sense that they all have distinct meanings which are perfectly understood by the

conceptual designer. These concepts take the form of noun phrases (which will become object names) and verb phrases (which will become operation names). In practice it will take several iterations through the three phases to produce a fixed set of clean concepts.

THE CONTENTS OF A CONCEPTUAL DESIGN

The conceptual design of a database serves two functions. It is used in interactions with applications programmers to verify the correctness of the programs being developed. It is also used as a guideline for the physical designers - specifying to them what must be implemented without constraining how it is implemented. To achieve these objectives the following kinds of information must be determined by the design process:

- The structure of the database's conceptual objects,
- The structure of its basic functions and update procedures, and
- Integrity constraints on the database.

The conceptual objects of a database are all of the individuals important to the running of an enterprise whether they be people, products, events or the inter-relationships among these. Such individuals must be grouped into types which identify their significant attributes and processing constraints. These types can then be implemented on commercial DBMSs as tuples, records or segments, for example (given that the system is relational, CODASYL or hierarchic (002), respectively). These types, in turn, are then grouped so as to identify their inter-relationship structure. In commercial DBMSs, these groupings appear as foreign keys in relational systems, owner-coupled sets in CODASYL systems and parent-child relationships in hierarchic systems.

Because a major goal of database management is data sharing, it is expected that the updates of each user will be apparent to the other users of the data. This makes it important that the necessary side effects of such changes be understood and correctly implemented by all application groups. This can be facilitated by including in the conceptual design specifications of the basic update operations for objects in the database. These update operations can then be utilised as primitives in more complicated procedures (simultaneously improving programmer productivity and program correctness). In this way physical designers can use these specifications to guide their use of such features as unique identifiers in relational DBMSs, automatic/mandatory set memberships in CODASYL DBMSs and sub-tree deletions in hierarchic systems.

It is also useful for the conceptual design to include, via function and procedure specifications, conventions for naming individuals that exhibit a correct sensitivity to updates. For example, it may be useful to name an individual in such a way that he will still be accessed whether or not changes have been made to some selected set of his attributes.

In addition to the integrity constraints maintained by the primitive update operations and those enforced by type declarations, there may be many more sophisticated constraints that must be maintained for the database. For example, a constraint may involve several different types of individuals and many individuals of each type. For example, a payroll database may be constrained to have no employee earn more than his manager. Reducing a manager's salary will typically require that the salary of many employees be checked. Since such constraints could be impacted by many arbitrary application groups it is important that they be specified as part of the conceptual design.

EVALUATING A CONCEPTUAL DESIGN

To understand what makes a good conceptual design, we can most easily find this out by examining the impact of a bad design on database usage, accessibility and performance. We begin this examination by pointing out that a bad design can be irreversible. Having designed a database, loaded it with data and written programs to run against it, we may find that we have invested too much time and programming effort to discard. A design may be bad in several different ways. It may be incomplete: data needed to support some applications may not be derivable from the data stored in the database. It may increase the difficulty of writing application programs and reduce their efficiency: data items may be grouped together in inconvenient and inappropriate ways. It may be too inflexible in a rapidly evolving environment: it may inhibit changes either to the structure of the database or to its (software or hardware) systems support.

On the basis of these problems we can itemise a useful set of properties that characterise a 'good' conceptual design as follows:

● Concept complete: derivable concepts should be included

● Unbiased toward applications: groupings which favour one application at the expense of others should be identified and removed when possible

● Evolvable: it should be locally modifiable and it should be flexible in supporting user interpretations

● Independent of existing installation and DBMS constraints.

Concept completeness guarantees not only that no useful objects are left out of the database but also that physical database designers are not inappropriately constrained. It is true that for many derived concepts the derivation can only be made in one direction. An average can be computed from a set of salaries. The individual salaries cannot be computed from the average. However, when the derivation is reversible (for example, given today's date, age can be computed from birthdate and *vice versa*), there may be a performance reason for choosing one object to be the base and the other to be 'derived' when there is no conceptual basis for making this decision.

'Biased' groupings of database objects *should* be designed for application views. Here they facilitate the development of programs written against those views. Keeping these groupings 'unbiased' at the conceptual level produces a design that is independent of user priorities and performance demands. Once such a design that is concept complete and unbiased has been produced it may then be necessary to apply efficiency producing transformations to it in generating the physical design. Performance and cost limitations may require that some of the concepts specified for the sake of completeness may need to be eliminated. Some user priorities may be so significant as to justify biasing the physical design to support them. By performing this analysis in a separate phase we create the environment for doing it in a more systematic and disciplined way.

The significance of having a conceptual design that is 'locally modifiable' lies in the fact that it is typically produced by many iterations through the design process.

If each modification requires a significant re-design, the process becomes unnecessarily difficult and time-consuming. This property of a database design is comparable to the property of program modularity in software engineering. Flexibility of interpretation is another property that facilitates the design process in that new applications may be added with potentially little impact on the existing design.

The impact of system independence is obvious in light of the current rate at which hardware changes are being made and the difference between vendors' implementations of the same DBMS family. Initially tailoring a design to fit the limitations of the current state of its intended support system makes it difficult to separate out these restrictions when the support system changes or is replaced. The better approach is to develop the design independent of such limitations and conventions first and then tailor it to the system. When changes occur the original design will be available to facilitate system update or conversion.

DESIGN TOOLS AND METHODOLOGIES

Having considered the importance and difficulty of achieving a good conceptual design we now look to see what assistance is available to produce such a design. The primary tool in database design is the language used to specify the design. Such a specification language, called a *data model* by the database community, is a tool in the sense that its vocabulary and syntax shapes the way designers perceive the application they are modelling. A model too primitive in its vocabulary requires more complicated concepts to be built up, producing a specification that is difficult to understand and therefore to use and to verify. A model that makes certain nuances of an application easy to express and others difficult, guides its users to recognise the former in their applications and to miss the latter. Thus, an important step in producing a good conceptual design is selecting a good data model.

Each of the following properties contribute to the value of a good data model:

1 *It should be expressive*

A data model that is sensitive to important distinctions will guide its users to include the concepts and objects necessary to a good design.

2 *It should not overconstrain implementors*

Because a conceptual design is the mechanism used to instruct physical database implementors the model on which it is based should not imply particular implementation strategies. Its vocabulary should be at a high enough level to be free of implementation connotations.

3 *A data model should have a formal basis*

This eliminates the danger of ambiguity and provides the physical designers and implementors with a sound foundation for verifying their work.

4 *A data model should be widely applicable*

A conceptual design for an extensive enterprise may need to encompass applications that are very dynamic in terms of interactions among the different objects of interest and that are relatively static. It may need to encompass applications that are very scientific and others that are very commercial in their orientation. If a different data model is necessary for each such situation there will be no hope of producing an integrated design that can be checked for internal consistency. Using more than one data model also imposes an unnecessary learning and selection burden on the designer.

5 *A data model should be understandable*

A conceptual design for an extensive enterprise can be both very large and very complex. To show even a part of a specification to an end user to check its correctness it is necessary that the data model in which it is expressed provides some kind of non-technical presentation mode. Preferably there should be a pictorial mode which utilises as labels in some effective way the terminology and linguistic constructs of the end user.

6 Finally and most fundamentally, *a data model must reflect and support human concept formation and understanding*

If the composition rules (syntax) of the data model force its users to assemble objects in ways that differ from how they would naturally assemble them, they will resist the imposition of the data model or misuse it in an effort to make it more habitable. Humans have innate mechanisms for coping with complexity. It is important and necessary that a data model exploit them.

The utility of a data model depends not just on the properties described above, but also on the existence of a set of rules or a methodology for using it. Without such guidance many designs may be produced even using a good data model before an acceptable one is achieved. A particular data model and its associated design methodology will be presented in the remaining sections of this paper.

THE SEMANTIC HIERARCHY DATA MODEL

To specify a conceptual design, the data model to be presented here provides the following, (see (003) for a more formal presentation of this model):

- A way of capturing the notion of *individual* and the important relationships in which individuals participate; it permits the specification of a *data space*

- A mechanism for specifying the constraints imposed on individuals and their relationships by virtue of their being grouped into *types*

- A predicate language for naming individuals in terms of their semantic properties

- Primitive operations for manipulating individuals

- Statements for controlling the sequencing of operations (control structures).

The method for modelling the individuals pertinent to an enterprise and their inter-relationships is based on mechanisms that humans use for thinking about such things. It is the premise of this data model that we as human beings succeed in understanding complex systems by creating *abstractions* from them that can be named and conceived of as a whole. Thus, an abstraction of a system is a collection of details that can be treated as a whole. For example, a 'book' names a collection of typed pages which are bound together; a 'room' names a set of walls, a floor, a ceiling and possibly some furniture; 'run' names a collection of movements which can be applied to an animal body; 'job type' names a collection including the types 'secretary', 'engineer' and 'trucker'. In each of these cases, the abstractions focused on the details of interest and ignored any other details. The abstractions that we employ appear to have two forms: abstractions of the *state* of a system and abstractions of the *transformation* of a system. The former are abstract *objects* while the latter are abstract *operations*. We will consider abstract objects first and integrate operations into our data model later.

The terms 'concept' and 'abstract object' will be used interchangeably. One goal of conceptual design is to define the relative structure of objects. A database does not usually consist of independent objects; normally, some objects can be formed from other objects. There seem to be three important methods, each a different abstraction mechanism, for object formation: *classification*, *generalisation* and *aggregation*.

Classification forms an object by suppressing details about individuals and emphasising properties of the class to which they belong. It collects *instances* to form a new *type*. Generalisation forms a new type by merging existing types. Aggregation forms an object as a relationship among other objects. Formally, classification, generalisation and aggregation correspond to the set theoretic operations of 'membership', 'union' and 'cartesian product', respectively.

Figure 2 illustrates the idea of classification. In the first line, Mary, Jane and Jack are classified as having type 'secretary'. Similarly, Jack and Judy are classified as having type 'engineer'. This is pictorially represented in Figure 3 at the instance level by connecting each individual to its type by an arrow labelled 'ϵ'. The head of the arrow points to the type. Both 'secretary' and 'engineer' are database objects in their own right and have the type 'employee type'. Thus, 'employee type' is a higher-order type. These 'instance-of' relationships generate a hierarchic structure of the kind depicted in the instance diagram of Figure 3.

Figure 4 illustrates the idea of generalisation. For example, the class of types '{secretary, trucker}' can be generalised to the new type employee. This means that any instance of secretary is also an instance of employee and that any instance of trucker is also an instance of employee. This is depicted in Figure 5 for some of the individuals of Figure 2. In generalisation, individual differences between secretaries and truckers are ignored (for example, secretaries have typing speeds and truckers have special licenses). Common traits are emphasised. So all instances of employee will have social security numbers while only instances of employee who are also secretaries will have typing speeds. In general, if the class {O_1, ... , O_n} can be generalised to O, then O_i is said to be a *category* of O. For example, 'dog' is a category of 'animal'.

Figure 6 illustrates the idea of aggregation. Consider the four object types 'person', 'room', 'hotel' and 'date'. A relationship involving these types may be expressed as 'a *person* reserves a *room* in a *hotel* for a *date*'. This relationship can be abstracted as the single object 'reservation'. In this aggregation, details about the participating objects are ignored and the relationship is named as a whole. The same observation applies to the other example in Figure 6. In general, if the relationship $R(O_1, ..., O_n)$ is aggregated to O then type O_i is said to be a *component* of type O. For example, 'room' is a component of 'reservation' and 'instructor' is a component of 'class'.

```
    Collection of instances                    New type

    {Mary, Jane, Jack}                          secretary
        {Jack, Judy}                            trucker
{secretary, trucker, engineer}               employee type
    {I_1, ..., I_n}                                O


    -   $I_i$ is an instance of O


    -   classification suppresses details of instances and emphasises properties of
        a class as a whole


Figure 2:   Classification examples
```

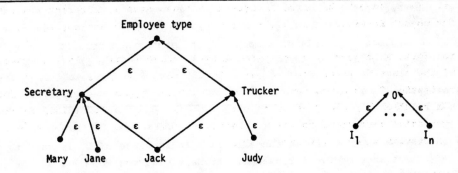

Figure 3: Pictorial representation of Figure 2

```
    Collection of types                        New type

{secretary, trucker}                          employee
{car, truck, bicycle}                        road-vehicle
{dog, cat, elephant}                           animal
  {O_1, ..., O_n}                                 O


  -   $O_i$ is a category of O


  -   generalisation suppresses the differences between categories and emphasises
      common properties


Figure 4:   Generalisation examples
```

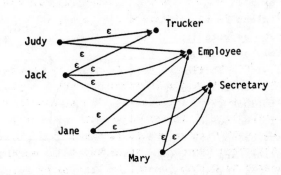

Figure 5:   Pictorial representation of first generalisation example in Figure 4

```
Relationship among types                    New type

a person reserves a room
in a hotel for a date                        reservation

an instructor offers a
course during a semester                      class

a vehicle hauls a load
to a destination from a                       haulage
source

R(O₁, ..., Oₙ)                                O

-  Oⱼ is a component of O

-  Aggregation suppresses details of components and emphasises details of the
   relationship as a whole
```

Figure 6: Aggregation examples

We use different terminology at the instance level. An instance of O_i is said to be an *attribute* of an instance of O. For example, if Mary reserves Room 212 at the Sheraton for May 12th then Mary is the 'person' attribute of this reservation. The attributes of an individual must have a separate existence before they are related by the creation of the individual itself. For example, Mary must exist before she can make a reservation. Note that it is not sufficient simply to say that Mary is an attribute of the relation. Consider as an example a marriage relationship among a parson, a groom and a bride. Mary could be either the bride or the parson. In cases like this it is important not to lose such distinctions. We represent these notions pictorially by connecting an object and its type to an aggregate object with a line labelled with the symbol 'π'. This is illustrated for the marriage example in Figure 7 where Mary is shown to be the bride in one marriage 'M1' and the parson in another marriage 'M2'.

The three mechanisms we have discussed above (classification, generalisation and aggregation) are the basic ways we have of structuring information. They each contribute important guidelines to the development of a database design. Classification in producing higher order types (such as the type 'employee type') identifies opportunities to collect summary data for management applications. For example, an attribute of 'secretary' might be the fact that a company has 100 secretaries. This count is appropriately associated with 'secretary' but *not* with a particular secretary, say Mary. Generalisation encourages the designer to look for special cases. Aggregation encourages the analysis of the impact of updates on structures. These guidelines are codified into a methodology in the penultimate section entitled 'Design methodology'.

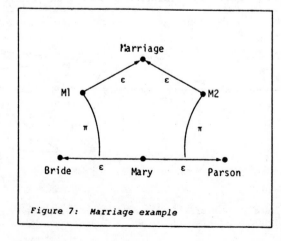

Figure 7: Marriage example

The objects resulting from classification, aggregation and generalisation are not special in any way. A type (or class) may also have attributes; in which case it is an aggregate object. An aggregate object may also be the generalisation of some class of object types; in which case it will also be a generic object. A generic object may be the aggregation of some relationship between objects; in which case it will also be an aggregate object. In general, each object is a type, an aggregate object and a generic object. However, some components and/or categories of the object may not be of interest and thus need not appear in the conceptual model. An object will be called *primitive* when it has no instances, components or categories of interest.

SPECIFYING THE STRUCTURE OF OBJECTS

When classification, generalisation and aggregation are repeatedly applied to objects, hierarchies of objects are formed. ('Hierarchy' is used here in its mathematical sense as an acyclic directed graph. A 'tree' is a restricted hierarchy with only a single root and no shared nodes.) Figure 8 illustrates a classification hierarchy involving concepts related to vehicles. 'Boat B1' and 'glider G1' are instances of the type 'wind-powered vehicle'. 'Wind-powered vehicle' and 'motor vehicle' are instances of the type 'propulsion category'. Note that 'glider G1' is an instance of two types. The object 'motor vehicle' is cross-hatched because it will be used as a common object throughout several examples.

Figure 9 illustrates a generalisation hierarchy over various categories of vehicle. The class {VW truck, Ford truck, GM truck} is generalised to 'truck'. The class {truck, liner, plane} is generalised to 'motor vehicle'. The class {road vehicle,

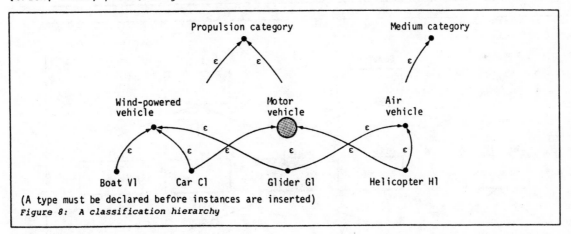

(A type must be declared before instances are inserted)
Figure 8:   A classification hierarchy

motor vehicle, air vehicle} is generalised to 'vehicle'. There are two important things to observe about the structure of generalisation hierarchies. First, notice that some categories are shared between several objects. For example, 'truck' is shared between 'road vehicle' and 'motor vehicle', and 'plane' is shared between 'motor vehicle' and 'air vehicle'. Second, a generalisation hierarchy may have several roots, not just a single root. While the hierarchy in Figure 9 only has one root, if this root is removed, the resulting hierarchy has three roots, namely 'road vehicle', 'motor vehicle' and 'air vehicle'.

Figure 10 shows an aggregation hierarchy which involves 'motor vehicle'. This hierarchy will be described by working from top to bottom. A 'haulage' has three components: the 'motor vehicle' which did the hauling, the 'site' to which the haulage was made, and the 'load' being hauled. A 'service' also has three components: the 'mechanic' who performed the service, the 'date' of the service, and the 'motor

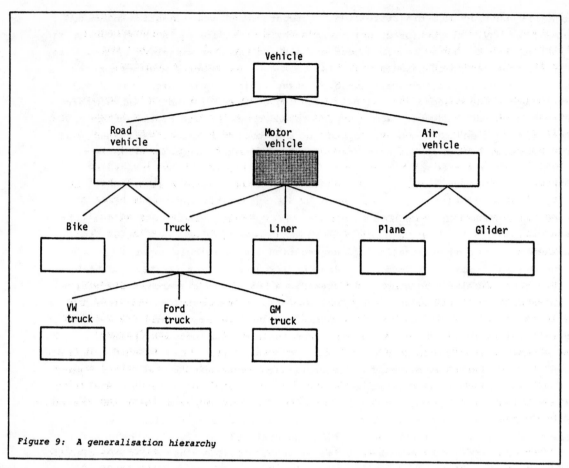

Figure 9: A generalisation hierarchy

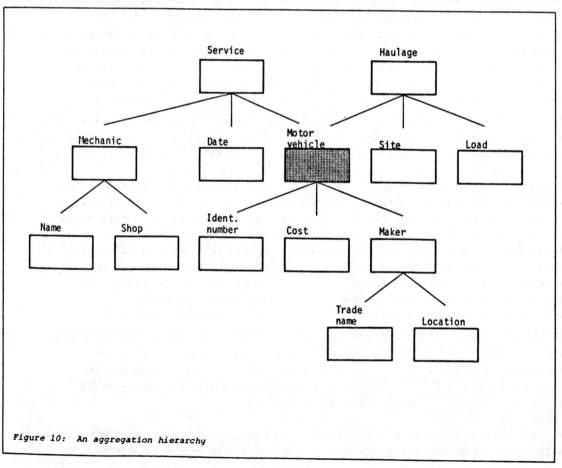

Figure 10: An aggregation hierarchy

vehicle' receiving the service. Notice that 'motor vehicle' is a component which is shared between 'service' and 'haulage'. A 'motor vehicle' has its own components: its 'ident(ification) number', the 'cost' of its purchase, and the 'maker' who produced it. The components of 'mechanic' and 'maker' are self-explanatory.

The previous description of Figure 10 is neutral with respect to a user's viewpoint. Suppose, instead, the viewpoint of a user interested in motor vehicles is taken. This user will regard 'motor vehicle' as an entity, 'service' as a relationship (i e, a mechanic services a motor vehicle on a date), 'haulage' as a relationship (i e, a motor vehicle hauls a load to a site), and 'ident.number', 'cost' and 'maker' as components. On the other hand, a user interested in makers would regard 'maker' as an entity, 'motor vehicle' as a relationship (i e, a chassis), and 'trade name' and 'location' as components. Finally, a user who is interested in services as entities (for example, the service manager) would regard 'mechanic', 'date' and 'motor vehicle' as components.

There is a very important conclusion which can be drawn from the previous paragraph. It is inappropriate to assign a *fixed* interpretation of relationship, entity or component to an object. Such an interpretation should only be *relative* to the viewpoint of a particular user. If a user views an object as an entity then its 'parent' objects appear as relationships and its 'child' objects appear as components. Different users may view different objects as entities. A representation for conceptual models which requires a fixed interpretation will artificially constrain concept integration. Artificial constraints usually manifest themselves in increased complexity and anomalous update properties.

It is worthwhile comparing Figures 8, 9 and 10 to note the different structural contexts in which the object 'motor vehicle' appears. Figure 8 is concerned with types only. As a type 'motor vehicle' has instances 'car C1' and 'helicopter H1'. 'Car C1' is neither a component nor a category of 'motor vehicle'. Figure 9 is concerned with categories only - a 'motor vehicle' is a category of 'vehicle', not a component nor an instance. Figure 10 is concerned with components only - a 'cost' is a component of 'motor vehicle', not a category. If we want to interpret the edges in these hierarchies then we do it as follows. An edge in a classification hierarchy may be read as '*is-one-of*'. An edge in a generalisation hierarchy may be read as 'is-a' and an edge in an aggregation hierarchy is 'is-part-of'. For example, 'car C1' '*is-one-of*' a car, a 'motor vehicle' *is-a* 'vehicle' and a 'cost' 'is-part-of' a 'motor vehicle'.

A conceptual design must include the classification, aggregation and generalisation hierarchies for all concepts needed to support the application views. In principle, these hierarchies for a conceptual design could be defined separately. However, more modularity is achieved if the structure of each object is defined as a single unit. To distinguish the components from the categories in this structure, it is helpful to place the components in the plane of the paper, the categories in the plane perpendicular to the paper and to connect the classification structure along the diagonal. For example, Figure 11 presents the structure of 'motor vehicle' in this way.

Such three dimensional diagrams can be extended recursively to include the structure of types, components and categories. This is often a very clear way to present conceptual structure and will be used in later sections. However, since *any* two objects can (in principle) be generalised or aggregated, conceptual models do not always fit neatly onto a three dimensional grid system.

To specify such structures we use a simple type declaration language. It lists for each type in the structure its component types and sub-types (sub-categories). For

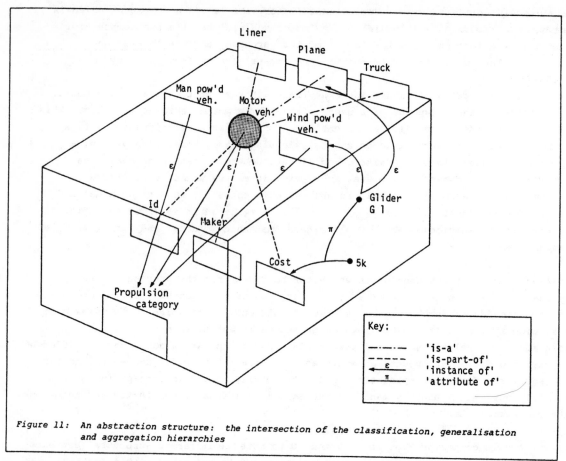

Figure 11: *An abstraction structure: the intersection of the classification, generalisation and aggregation hierarchies*

example, the type structure of 'motor vehicle' as depicted in Figures 8, 9 and 10 is specified as follows:

```
def motor vehicle:   sub
                    truck, liner, plane
               com
                    inden.no, cost, maker
               end
```

To establish its 'instance of' relationship to 'propulsion category' we must use a create operation. This and other primitive operations will be discussed in the next section.

A type specification of the kind described above is meant to place constraints on the data space. The first constraint requires that every primitive object has a type. The second requires that if a type has a sub-type, then an instance of the sub-type is also an instance of the type. The final constraint ensures that an individual has an attribute only if its type has as a component type the type of the attribute. These constraints capture the generally accepted semantics of the notions of classification, generalisation and aggregation.

SPECIFYING THE BEHAVIOUR OF OBJECTS

When the data space of a database is initially created, it contains as individuals only the types given in the type definitions. To describe changes to the space we can

450

use the primitive operations *create*, *destroy* and *modify*. These operations apply to single individuals. Their syntax is given in Figure 12.

CREATE

       create n: *types*
                A, B
             attributes
                c: C, d_1: D, d_2: D
             end

  where n is a name for the individual being created,
      A and B are the types of the individual named n,
      c is the C attribute of n,
      d_1 is a D attribute of n and
      d_2 is another D attribute of n.

DESTROY

       destroy n;
  where n is the name, of the individual to be removed from the database.

MODIFY

       modify n: *types*
               remove A
               add B, C
             attributes
               removed d: D, e: E
               add f: F
             end

  where n is the name of the individual to be modified,
      A is a type to which it is to be added,
      B and C are types from which n is to be removed,
      d is a D attribute and e is an E attribute which
        are to be removed from n
      f is an F attribute which is to be added to n.

Figure 12

When a (primitive) individual is created, it may be given a name, and its type and attributes must be specified. The name is optional since an unnamed individual can still be identified via a predicate. The semantics of the *create* operation are to form the new individual, to implement its memberships in the specified types and its attribute relationships, and to verify that all type constraints as specified by the appropriate type declarations are satisfied. When an individual is destroyed, it is removed from the data space and from any type memberships and attribute relationships in which it had participated. The modification of an individual may involve removals or additions to its type memberships and attribute relationships. The modify operation can be applied to individuals that are types as well as to primitive individuals. In fact, this is how the classification structure of a data space is created. To specify that the relationship depicted in Figure 8 that 'motor vehicle' is an instance of the type 'propulsion category' we must specify the following operation:

    modify motor vehicle: *types*
                    add propulsion category
               end

To use each of these operations it is necessary to name in some way the individuals being affected by them. The predicate language is provided for naming individuals in terms of their structure - their attributes, categories, and types. It is a first order language with the three special predicates:

```
x is the y attribute of z,
x is of type y, and
x is equivalent to y (x = y).
```

Figure 13 gives some examples of naming individuals in an employee data space.

```
def employee type:  end
def employee:  sub

                manager,  managee, janitor,  engineer
            com
               salary
            end
def manager:  end              def janitor:  com
                                                broom closet
def managee:  com                            end
              manager
            end                def engineer:  com
                                                office
                                              end


P1(x):  x is the office of the engineer 'Tom'.
    :  x is the 'office' attribute of 'Tom'.

P2(x):  x is the employee type of Joe.
    :  x is of type 'employee-type'
       and 'Joe' is of type x.

P3(x):  x is an attribute of Jim.
    :  For some y, x is a y attribute of 'Jim'.

P4(x):  x is a managee who earns the same as his manager.
    :  x is of type managee and for some s and some y, s
       is the 'salary' attribute of s and s is the 'salary'
       attribute of y and y is the 'manager' attribute of
       x.
```

Figure 13: A type definition and some predicates for a data space

Using these primitive operations, naming capabilities and simple control structures such as the *if-then-else* construct of standard programming languages, functions and procedures can be constructed that describe the behaviour of the enterprise being modelled. Predicates may be used for the purpose of *function definition*. A function F, which takes as a parameter an instance x of a type X and which returns a *single* instance y, may be defined in terms of a predicate P(x, y) as follows:

$$F(x: X) \equiv y \mid P(x, y).$$

On the other hand, if the function returned a *set* of instances, it would be defined as:

F(x: X) ≡ {y} ¦ P(x, y).

Relative to the type definition in Figure 13, functions to return the manager of a managee and the salary of an employee could be defined as:

MANAGER(x: managee) ≡ y ¦ y is the 'manager' attribute of x.
SALARY(x: employee) ≡ y ¦ y is the 'salary' attribute of x.

Function applications may be used in place of individual symbols in a predicate. Such usage can often reduce the number of variables and quantifiers in a predicate. For example, the predicate P4(x) in Figure 13 could be written as:

P4(x): x is of type 'manager' and
        SALARY(MANAGER(x)) ≡ SALARY(x).

Function definitions may be recursive. For example, a function which returns the chain of managers above a particular managee may be defined as:

MNGRCHN(x: managee) ≡
     {y}   y ≡ MANAGER (x) or
           y is of type MNGRCHN(MANAGER(x))

In addition to predicates, the *create* operation may also be used for function definition. A function F with parameter x of type X may be defined as:

F(x: X) ≡   *create : types*
                    Y, ...
                attributes
                    x: X, ...
                end

In this case an individual, whose types include Y and whose attributes include x: X, is created and returned as the value of the function application. This facility is extremely useful as it allows nameless individuals to be identified by a function application.

Database procedures can be specified in a similar way. As an example, consider a procedure which raises to $1000 the salary of a janitor if he currently receives $800 and otherwise fires him.

RAISE/FIRE(x: janitor):
      if SALARY (x) ≡ 800
      then modify x: *attributes*
                        remove 800: salary
                        add 1000: salary
                    end
      else destroy x;

It is often useful to apply procedures to all individuals in a given set. For this purpose a '*for each*' iterator is provided. For example, to process all janitors in a set S, it is only necessary to write:

PROCESS(S: *set* janitor): *for each* x ε S *do* RAISE/FIRE(x).

The *behavioural* semantics of a type are characterised by its operations in much the same way as its *structural* semantics are characterised by its sub-types and component types. Type definitions are therefore extended to allow the inclusion of operators for each type. A *function* is associated with a type if the function can be applied to, or can identify, *any* instance of that type.

Some operations may be associated with several types. For example, if a type has sub-types then any operation associated with the type is also associated with each sub-type. Further, if a function requires parameters of several types and identifies instances of yet another type, then the function is associated with all these types. To avoid pointless duplication of definitions, only operation *names* will be associated with types. Definitions of operations will remain global to all types.

As an example, the association of the previously defined operations MANAGER, SALARY, MNGHCHN, RAISE/FIRE, PROCESS with the types 'employee' and 'janitor' is shown below:

```
def employee : sub
                manager, managee,
                janitor, engineer
            com
                salary
            functions
                SALARY
            end
def janitor  : com
                broom closet
            functions
                SALARY
            procedures
                RAISE/FIRE, PROCESS
            end
```

Notice that SALARY is associated with both 'employee' and 'janitor' since it can be uniformly applied to any instance of these types. However, MANAGER is not associated with either 'employee' or 'janitor' since the function is only defined for instances of 'managee'. The procedure RAISE/FIRE is associated with 'janitor' but not with 'employee' for similar reasons. Using these primitive operations, naming capabilities and simple control structures such as the *if-then-else* construct of standard programming languages, functions and procedures can be constructed that describe the behaviour of the enterprise being modelled.

DESIGN METHODOLOGY

The previous three sections of this paper described a data model as a basis for developing conceptual designs. We can summarise the basic ideas underlying this model as two principles. The first one, which is concerned with the structure of objects, we call the principle of 'object relativity':

relationship, entity, component, category, attribute and instance are just different interpretations of the same abstract objects.

This principle is critical if concepts are to be integrated into a single conceptual design in a simple and natural way. The second principle is concerned with the behaviour of objects as they are manifested in user updates and is called the principle of 'individual preservation':

every user-invokable update operation must preserve the integrity of individuals.

This principle motivates the way the primitive update operations have been defined.

In this section we embody these principles and the data model in a 'methodology' for producing a conceptual design. Figure 14 outlines the methodology. Its simplicity is a direct result of the above stated principles. Because we permit objects to assume

---

Assumption

The names of all objects which are treated (by some user) as a type or an action are supplied by requirements analysis.

1 *Classification*

    - Determine immediate type/instance relationships between names.

2 *Generalisation*

    - Determine immediate object/category correspondences between names.
    - Determine if categories should generate new (higher-order) types.

3 *Aggregation*

    - Determine immediate object/component correspondences between names.

    - Determine whether all important aggregate relationships between objects have been identified.

    - Determine whether any components of an object are the basis for refining it further into new categories.

4 *Object suppression*

    - Suppress 'uninteresting' types, categories and aggregate objects.

5 *Naming*

    - Determine important naming conventions.

6 *Behaviour*

    - Identify the conditions for updating the objects specified in steps 1-4.

7 *Specification*

    - For each object specify its types, categories, components, its names as functions and its behaviour as procedures.

Figure 14: A design methodology

---

simultaneously the different roles of type, instance, category, etc, there are no complicated rules for determining and resolving any role conflicts. Because the primitive update operations have been defined in terms of individuals, it is unnecessary to develop more complicated mechanisms to capture the side effects of updating individuals. To illustrate the methodology, it will be applied to the collection of concepts given in Figure 15. These concepts are assumed to be supplied by requirements analysis. However, in presenting the methodology we do not assume that all names have been generated at the beginning. There are intermediate steps for capturing concepts that were missed.

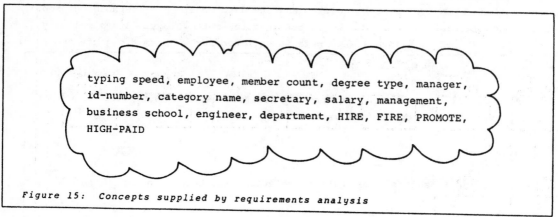

typing speed, employee, member count, degree type, manager, id-number, category name, secretary, salary, management, business school, engineer, department, HIRE, FIRE, PROMOTE, HIGH-PAID

Figure 15: *Concepts supplied by requirements analysis*

In applying step 1 to these concepts we find that there are no type/instance relationships. The result of applying the first instruction of step 2 to these concepts is the generalisation hierarchy of Figure 16. This hierarchy is based on the observation that 'secretary', 'engineer' and 'manager' are different categories of 'employee'. The second instruction of step 2 suggests that we might want to treat the three categories of 'employee' as instances of a type 'employee category'. This generates the classification hierarchy of Figure 17.

The result of applying the first instruction of step 3 is the aggregation hierarchy of Figure 18. Only a few highlights of this hierarchy will be discussed.

'Management' relates an 'employee' to his 'manager'. Notice that Figure 16 expresses the fact that a 'manager' is also an 'employee'. 'Employee', 'secretary', 'engineer' and 'manager' share the components 'id-number', 'salary' and 'department' but also have additional components of their own. 'Employee category' relates a 'category name' to the count of members in that category (i e, 'member count'). If the concept 'employee category' had not been generated by step 2 it would have been generated by the second instruction of step 3 in determining that 'category name' and 'member count' are related.

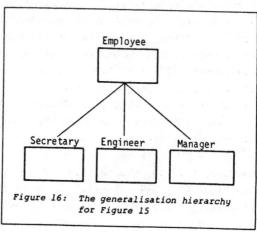

Figure 16: *The generalisation hierarchy for Figure 15*

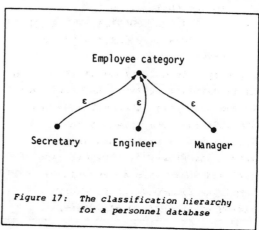

Figure 17: *The classification hierarchy for a personnel database*

456

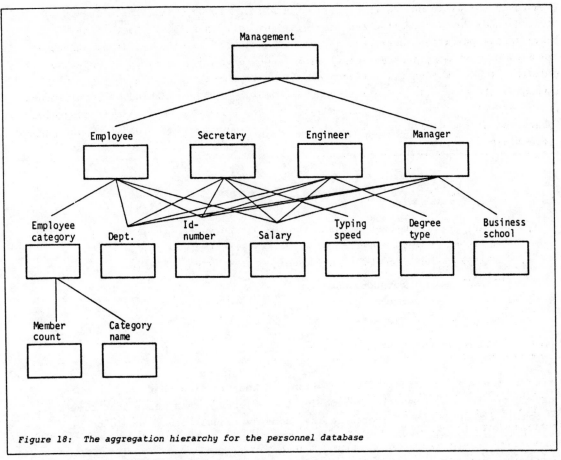

Figure 18:   *The aggregation hierarchy for the personnel database*

This instruction also suggests, for example, that we might want to make the relation-ship between 'employee' and 'department' more explicit. This is depicted in Figure 19. Instruction 3 of step 3 suggests, for example, that we could further refine engineer into sub-categories on the basis of degree type, or manager into sub-categories by business school. However, in step 4 we must question whether these extensions are of interest to any end users. Since these new categories and the new aggregate object 'assignment' of Figure 19 do not have any additional components of interest (note that the generated object 'employee type' had two components of interest) then we might conclude that they are not worth including in our final conceptual design.

Applying step 5 to our hierarchies and the names of Figure 15 results in associating the name HIGH-PAID with employee and each of its three categories and defining it appropriately. For example, it could be defined as:

HIGH-PAID (x: employee) = {y}   (z)
            (z is the 'salary' attrib-
            ute of y and z > $20 000).

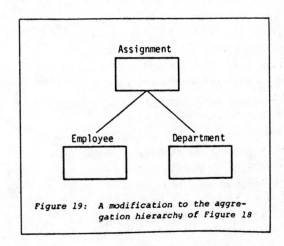

Applying step 6 to this state of the design results in definitions for HIRE, FIRE, and PROMOTE and associates them with the app-ropriate objects. The three of these procedures would be associated with 'employee', 'secretary', 'engineer' and 'manager' and would also be associated with 'employee category' since their application to an individual affects

Figure 19:   *A modification to the aggre-gation hierarchy of Figure 18*

457

the 'member count' for the appropriate instances. Specifications for 'employee' and 'employee category' are given below.

```
def employee:   sub
                    manager, secretary
                    engineer
                com
                    id number, name,
                    department
                functions
                    HIGH-PAID
                procedures
                    HIRE, FIRE, PROMOTE
                end


def employee category:   com
                             category name,
                             member count
                         procedures
                             HIRE, FIRE, PROMOTE
                         end
```

In looking at the specifications it is important to keep in mind that they do not imply any particular implementation scheme for the objects. This means that some objects could be implemented as stored tables, some by ranges, others could be 'virtual' (in the CODASYL sense).

SUMMARY AND CONCLUSIONS

This paper has attempted to present not just a data model and methodology for conceptual design but to develop an understanding of why these tools are needed and how they come to take the forms they do. These forms are currently at some distance from the DDLs, DMLs and QLs provided by available DBMSs. As their value becomes more apparent to database practitioners we would expect to see DBMSs evolve in the directions that have been described. This follows the trends already established within DBMS development to facilitate specification in ever more human compatible terms.

———————

REFERENCES

001   YORMARK B
      The ANSI/X3/SPARC/SGDBMS architecture
      In *The ANSI/SPARC DBMS model* D A
      Jardine (ed) North-Holland Publ Co
      New York (1977)

002   ACM
      ACM Computing Surveys
      vol 8 no 1 (March 1976)

003   SMITH J M and SMITH D C P
      A database approach to software specification

Proc Software Development Tools
Workshop (May 1979) and CCA Tech
Rep (1979)

004 BACHMAN C and DAYA M
The role concept in data models
Proc VLDB III Japan (1977)

005 BRODIE M L
Specification and verification of
database semantic integrity
University of Toronto Computer
Systems Research Group Tech Rep
CSRG-91 (April 1978)

006 CHEN P S
The entity-relationship model:
toward a unified view of data
ACM Trans on Database Syst pp 9-36
(March 1976)

007 COPELAND G P
Language requirements for a database
kernel
Tektronix Beaverton Ore (1978)

008 GUTTAG J V
Abstract data types and the develop-
ment of data structures
CACM vol 20 no 6 pp 396-404 (June
1977)

009 HAMMER M
Data abstractions and databases
Proc Conf on *Data: abstraction,*
definition and structure FDT (Bull-
etin of ACM SIGMOD) vol 8 no 2 pp
58-59 (1976)

010 HAMMER M and McLEOD D
The semantic data model: a model-

ling mechanism for database applica-
tions
Proc ACM SIGMOD pp 26-35 (1978)

011 KENT W
Data and reality
North-Holland Publ Co Amsterdam
(1978)

012 LISKOV B H and ZILLES S N
Programming with abstract data types
ACM SIGPLAN Notices vol 9 no 4 pp
50-60 (April 1974)

013 MYLOPOULOS J, BERNSTEIN P and WONG H
A language facility for designing
interactive database - intensive
applications
Proc ACM SIGMOD (1978) (to be published
in full in ACM Trans on Database
Syst (1979))

014 SCHMIDT J W
Some high-level constructs for data
of type relation
ACM Trans on Database Syst vol 2 no 3
pp 247-261 (Sept 1977)

015 SHIPMAN D W
The functional data model and the
data language DAPLEX
To appear in ACM Trans on Database
Syst (1979)

016 SMITH J M and SMITH D C P
Database abstractions: aggregation
CACM pp 405-413 (June 1977)

017 SMITH J M and SMITH D C P
Database abstractions: aggregation
and generalisation

ACM Trans on Database Syst pp 105–
133 (June 1977)

018   SMITH J M and SMITH D C P
Principles of database design
NYU Symp on Database design (1978)

019   SMITH J M
Comments on the papers: *A software
engineering view of database management* by A I Wasserman and *A software
engineering view of database systems*
by H Weber Proc VLDB IV Berlin
(Sept 1978)

AN INTEGRATED APPROACH TO LOGICAL DATABASE DESIGN

S. B. Yao
Purdue University

Shamkant B. Navathe and Jay-Louise Weldon
New York University

This paper provides an integrated approach for research related to the problem of logical database design. The process of logical database design is classified into five phases: requirements analysis, view modeling, view integration, view restructuring, and schema analysis and mapping. The input, processing steps, and output for each phase are briefly described. The problems associated with each phase are pointed out. Existing approaches to database design are described and related to these five phases. The significance of this integrated approach for the development of computer-aided methodologies for logical database design is discussed.

1. INTRODUCTION

At the current state-of-the-art, the methods used in the design of database applications are essentially trial-and-error, supported by neither a scientific foundation nor an engineering discipline. The ad hoc approach to design frequently leads to inflexible solutions that do not meet the prescribed requirements. Costly remedial measures often produce more delay in operation without a tangible improvement. Much of the existing information on system design is presented in the form of individual analyses. These analyses do provide valuable insight, but they can hardly be adequate substitutes for a systematic design discipline.

It is generally accepted that there are two levels in the design of a database a) the logical design, defining and combining the views of many applications into a centrally controlled and maintained logical databases, with provisions for data sharing and security; and b) the physical design, including all the implementational details and considerations of a particular database system.

In this paper, we will address mainly the design issues which apply at the logical design level. Since realistic databases involve thousands of data elements, and the evaluation of an enormous amount of structured information is implied (e.g. see Raver and Hubbard 1977), it is desirable to develop computer aided tools to aid the design. In what follows, a conceptual framework is presented within which current research in logical database design is reviewed. It is also suggested as to how these seemingly unrelated approaches may be integrated into a computer aided design system.

2. THE LOGICAL DATABASE DESIGN PROCESS

The problem of logical database design is rich; it ranges from system-independent analysis to system-dependent optimization. Existing research tends to concentrate on only a few aspects of the design process. Consequently, each approach has its own view of the design process. It is desirable to define a general logical design process in order to compare and integrate existing approaches.

The process of logical database design can be divided into five general steps:

1) Requirement Analysis. The problem or environment in the real world must be analyzed to make the necessary components of the database explicit and to elicit both the data and processing needs of all potential database users.

2) View Modeling. Using the results of step 1 as input, abstract representations must be developed that correspond with each user's view of the real world. This step both verifies the previous step and lays a basis for the next.

3) View Integration. The several (and perhaps conflicting) user views must be integrated into one global or community view of the database. This global view must continue to support all user views.

4) View Restructuring. If the target system is known, a given community view can be mapped into alternate logical structures in the particular system. This step takes as input the canonical representation of a community view and restructures it into multiple structures in the target system.

5) Schema Analysis and Mapping. This step arrives at the storage level representation of data in the given target system. An analysis of physical implementation alternatives is performed and optimal storage structures are chosen.

If a target database management system has not been selected, steps 4 and 5 must be repeated for each candidate target system. The final selection among alternatives would then be across all systems.

It is important to note the following:

1) It is observed that the requirement analysis provides input to all other design steps, since the information extracted from applications is relevant to all design stages.

2) Each design step produces not a unique solution but a set of solutions associated with measures which represent various properties of the particular solution.

Reprinted with permission from *Proceedings of New York University Symposium on Database Design*, May 1978. Copyright © 1978 by New York University Graduate School of Business Administration.

3) The designer should interact with the design process to select an appropriate solution as the input to the next design step. A selection criterion must be stated.

4) Since the design requirements collected by the requirement analysis may be incomplete and inconsistent, the designer must be consulted to resolve ambiguities.

5) The design is usually not a single-pass process. Various conditions discovered by the designer may force a re-design and iterate to an earlier design step.

Although there exists a large amount of work in the literature which relates to logical database design, there is no existing approach which is comprehensive enough to address all the steps of the logical design process mentioned above. In the following sections we will describe the inputs, processes and outputs of each step. Existing design methods will be discussed under the above framework. Problems yet to be addressed will be pointed out.

3. REQUIREMENT ANALYSIS

Requirement analysis (r.a.) provides initial input to the database design process. This step seeks to identify each user (application) of the database and, for each, analyzes the user's requirements regarding the content and use of the database. Ideally the r.a. step should provide input which is both an accurate representation of the users' views and also a complete specification of the required database (i.e. all succeeding steps will be able to draw the data they require from the r.a. output). Further, r.a. output should be in a form which is both usable by the succeeding steps and also amenable to review and verification by the users of the database. Thus, to be effective, a methodology for r.a. should include:

- a specification of the data to reside in the database
- suggested techniques for data collection (e.g., analysis of oral or narrative descriptions, document review, accumulation of performance statistics).
- a language or format for data collection and review
- an output specification which is compatible with the input to one or more view modeling techniques.

A specification of necessary data has been proposed by Kahn (1976) which classifies the information structure and the process structure. Some typical design inputs following this classification are shown in Figure 1. A major shortcoming of existing approaches to database design has been that they consider either the information structure oriented input or the process structure oriented input, but fail to incorporate both.

Requirement analysis for database design may be considered a special case of the general problem of gathering and specifying requirements for information systems. Little work has been reported in the literature which focuses on the requirement

A. The information-structure-oriented design input:

-for each entity:	entity name
	cardinality
-for each attribute:	attribute name
	repeating factor
	length of data value
	value set size
	probability of existence
-for each intra-entity relationship:	relationship name
	attributes related
	cardinality of multi-valued dependency
-for each inter-entity relationship:	relationship name
	relationship type (aggregation/ generalization)
	entities related
	cardinality ratio
	probability of existence
	whether used for identification of of instances

B. The process-structure-oriented design input:

-for each process:	frequency of occurrence
	priority and weight
	precedence
	volume of data processed
	data items required
-for each access operation:	type of operation
	mode of access (random/ sequential)
	hit ratio
	frequency of occurrence
	frequency of data items accessed
	frequency of intra-entity relationship path accessed
	frequency of inter-entity relationship path accessed

Figure 1: Database Design Input

analysis for database design per se. However, there is a large body of literature devoted to the more general problem as evidenced by a special issue of IEEE Transactions in Software Engineering (IEEE TSE 1977). The work in this area consists of development of high level languages to specify, store and retrieve the description of a proposed information system. Some facility for analysis, report generation, cross referencing, and selective display is present in each system.

The PSL/PSA technique developed by the University of Michigan ISDOS project (Teichroew and Hershey 1977) uses the Problem Statement Language to describe the following attributes of a system: input/output flows, structure between system components, size and volume, system dynamics. The data structure aspect of system description includes all the relationships which exist among data used and/or manipulated by the system as seen by the users of the system. The ELEMENT, ENTITY, ATTRIBUTE, GROUP, SET are some of the PSL statement-types used to describe a data structure.

The data derivation aspect of the system description specifies which data objects are involved in particular PROCESSES in the system. It is concerned with what information is used, updated and/or derived, how this is done and by which processes. The PSL/PSA system has a command language facility which a designer uses to retrieve and display parts of the database containing the system description. A number of reference, summary and analysis reports can be produced. If PSL/PSA were to be used for view modeling/integration, each view would either have to be described in PSL syntax or extracted from the central PSL/PSA database.

The CASCADE system at University of Trondheim, Norway is another system which has the objective of developing formal tools of information system analysis and design. The system specification and system presentation modules in CASCADE store a description of the information system. The information objects are related to other objects, variables, and elements. Processing is represented in the form of a tree structure. The coded representations of information and process structures would constitute an input to logical database design (Solvberg 1974).

Hammer et al (1977) have developed a very high level language called BDL which a designer could use to develop transaction processing programs for business applications. The basic data structure of this language is a document, or form, composed of fields of data items or data groups. Homogenenous collections of documents may be defined as files. BDL addresses the implementation of individual applications. As such the only provision for data sharing is redundancy, i.e. one document flowing through more than one step or application.

The design methodology of Bubenko et al (1976) starts with a knowledge of the queries which will be used against the database (all the queries which will ever be used, not just a minimal set which must be supported), and derives two schemas: a response-oriented schema and a storage-oriented schema. The storage-oriented schema corresponds to what might be called the normal logical database design, as it stores each item of information once and does not have redundant set-types or links. The response-oriented schema is designed so that each query will have to access as few record types as possible when ordering and other constraints of the design procedure are taken into account. The design procedure then derives the final design as a compromise between the two schema alternatives.

The existing approaches to view modeling or to logical database design in general have not addressed the collection and analysis of information and processing requirements in detail. For example, IBM's DBDA (IBM 1975) is initiated by a list of data items and inter-item relationships culled from input/output documents while Smith & Smith (1977) assume that the designer can name and assign attributes to the objects in the abstraction structure. CINCOM Systems, Inc. (Sheppard 1977) has a more general requirements analysis plan that utilizes tabular checklists to collect information on both entities and processes.

An integrated approach to database design requires that the r.a. step provide data which is both accurate and complete. In other words, the user views should not be misrepresented by inadequate document sampling or incorrect formulation of required processes. However, redundant relationships and even inconsistent data groupings should not be eliminated at this step. Implicit decisions on such issues may freeze that design too early and result in artificial design constraints. The view integration and schema analysis steps will address these questions explicitly and the designer can then make a more informed choice. The level and nature of this tolerable uncertainty in r.a. has yet to be determined.

As mentioned in the overview of the design process, r.a. provides input to every step of the process. The designer and the users interact to develop the specification and refine it as the design progresses. Thus the full extent of r.a. will be determined by the input requirements of the succeeding steps.

4. VIEW MODELING

The objective of the view modeling step is to represent each user's view of the database using a common modeling technique. Once the views are represented, the designer can compare and integrate them. Figure 2 shows a schematic for the View Modeling step. Inputs to this step consist of information and processing requirements as determined by the requirement analysis step, as well as semantic information about the application which is known by the user or designer of the data base. The View Modeling process includes a modeling subprocess and a verification process. In the modeling subprocess inputs are analyzed and formal representations of user views are developed In the verification subprocess these representations are evaluated by the designer and the users in light of their requirements and a representation is selected for each view. The output of View Modeling is therefore a formal representation of each user's view.

The view modeling step is most clearly addressed by database design methods which are explicitly concerned with data modeling. Data models of Bachman (1969), Codd (1970), Senko et al. (1973) and Chen (1976) all accept as input, descriptions and attributes of entities and the relationships among these entities. Using the primitives of the target data model, a representation is developed which embodies the semantics of these entities and relationships. Bachman represents entities as record types and relationships as owner-member set types. Loops and m:n relation-ships are then eliminated to produce a network data model. Codd represents both entities and rela-tionships as relations. Using the data semantics in the form of functional dependencies relations are normalized.

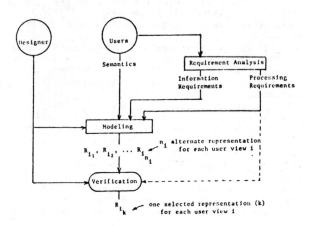

Figure 2: The View Modeling Step

The DIAM (Senko et al. 1973) incorporates four successive models of data, starting at a high-ly abstract level and going down to the level of encoding on physical devices. The Entity Set Model (ESM) and the string model are of interest in view modeling since they deal with logical data struc-tures. In ESM the basic item of information is an entity which corresponds to some real-world-object or concept, and appears as a collection of attri-bute values. The string model is used to represent attribute grouping and relationships among entities.
    Chen's entity-relationship model is a simple extension to the data structure diagram. It is simple and easy to conceptualize, and claimed to be semantically richer than the relational and the entity set model. The entity-relationship model represents a view by means of entities, relation-ships, and the attributes of each of them. However, it does not allow the representation of relation-ships between two relationships, or between an entity and a relationship.

The database abstraction methodology (Smith & Smith 1977) represents both entities and rela-tionships as objects. This method distinguishes between two different types of relationships: association of similar entities (generalization) and association of related entities (aggregation). The semantic processes of aggregation and generali-zation are used to build a multi-dimensional hier-archicy of objects which represents the user's view

Navathe and Schkolnick (1978) draw from the data abstraction model of Smith and Smith and pro-pose a technique for view representation to achieve a better modeling of the usage perspective and to incorporate the relationshops among data instances,

especially those which are used for identification purposes. The objective is to obtain a vehicle which represents a user view as explicitly as possible in the following sense:

Information Structure Perspective

-distinction among different kinds of asso-ciations between entities;
-allowing associations in which entities or associations or a combination of the two can participate;
-incorporation of the dependence of entities on one another for the sake of identifi-cation.

Usage Perspective

-effect of insertion and deletion of enti-ties and associations on one another at schema and instance levels;
-incorporation of user-defined rules about instances of data.

In all of the methods described above the "objects" of the view representation produced are data groups. The contents of these groups are either unspecified (Bachman), or specified directly by the designer (Chen, Codd, Navathe & Schkolnick, Senko et al, Smith & Smith). Codd, Senko et al and Smith & Smith allow the designer to determine identifying data elements (keys) for each object whereas Navathe and Schkolnick expli-citly model the identification of instances.

In database design methods oriented toward producing implementation level schemas, the view modeling step is less distinct: it is more tightly bound to the requirements analysis or view integration steps. In general, these methods are process-oriented and define a view as data used in a process. Most take descriptions of data items, item relationships and usage of data elements as input to the view modeling step.

The CINCOM method (Dyba 1977; Sheppard 1977) relies on descriptions of data elements, processing specifications and policy constraints on events and data as input. Each process is then documented as a series of events and data elements are asso-ciated with the events in which they are used. Each view, or function, is represented by a flow diagram of events, annotated with associated data elements. These diagrams become the input to an analysis of frequency-of-use which groups elements, determines keys, and synthesizes a community view. (This analysis is described further in Secion 5.)

To Gerritsen (1975), each view is described by the queries that must be supported. These queries in the HI-IQ language, names of entities, and data item descriptions are the input to view modeling. Gerritsen's automated designer derives relationships between items and between items and entities from the queries. The information struc-ture needed to support the view is then represented by a series of assertions governing the location of items and entities in the final DBTG schema. The cardinality ratios of the relationships described are implicit in these assertions, since in a DBTG schema a record type placed "above" another one implies a 1:m relationship.

In DBDA (IBM 1975, Raver & Hubbard 1977) views are represented by directed graphs of data items and their relationships on which the cardinality of each relationship is recorded. These diagrams are produced by recording data items from existing input/output documents and analyzing their interrelationships. Nodes which are the source of relationships, but not the target of any are implicitly regarded as keys.

Mitoma also uses data item descriptions and item interrelationships as input to view modeling (Mitoma 1975; Mitoma & Irani 1975). He defines data relations (or binary relationships) for each pair of items to be used together. The items and data relations are recorded using a non-directed graph, in which each node is an item and each edge, a data relation. Unlike the other methods,

Mitoma's view representation contains explicit and det led instance level information. The cardinality of each data relation (the number of instances of item pairs) is recorded. In addition, the cardinality ratio for each relation is recorded specifically in terms of its average and maximum values, e.g. 2:5 or 1:250 instead of m:n or 1:n.

The process-oriented methods described above address the problem of data grouping during view integration rather than during view modeling. Key determination is similarly postponed until view integration, except in the case of DBDA.

Table 1 summarizes the characteristics of the view modeling step for the several design methodologies discussed in this Section.

Table 1: CHARACTERISTICS OF VIEW MODELING IN SEVERAL DATABASE DESIGN METHODOLOGIES

CHARACTERISTICS	Chen	CINCOM	Codd	DBDA (Hubbard)	DBTG (Bachman)	Gerritsen	Mitoma	Navathe & Schkolnick	Senko	Smith
Input:										
info. requirements										
objects	x		x		x	x		x	x	x
items		x		x		x	x		x	
processing requirements		x		x		x	x	x		
Processing:										
semantic analysis	x		x	x				x	x	x
item analysis		x		x		x	x		x	
data grouping	x		x						x	x
key determination/ identification analysis		x		x				x	x	x
Output:										
representation										
objects	x		x		x	x		x	x	x
items		x		x		x	x		x	
explicit cardinality ratios of instances				x			x			
explicit cardinality of instances				x			x			

5. VIEW INTEGRATION

The objective of the view integration step is to merge the several view representations produced in view modeling into an integrated canonical structure. This output structure represents the community view and must satisfy the following:

a) it must be internally consistent
b) it must reflect accurately each of the original views
c) it must support the processing requirements specified in the requirements analysis step.

As with view modeling, the integration step may actually produce several candidate structures, all of which would then be verified against processing or specifications and those satisfying the process requirements will be regarded as community structures (see Figure 3).

View integration initially involves some editing to remove inconsistencies. Inconsistencies and redundancies may arise at the data-element, data-group or data-relationship level, in the form of one name referring to different components (homonyms), or different names referring to the same component (synonyms). These could be reported and subsequently corrected after designer intervention. This editing is handled internally by the DBDA system.

When no inconsistencies or redundancies remain to be resolved the view integration is complete. However, a process verification is required to determine which of the alternate structures satisfy processing requirements. The process specification may be either in terms of queries or procedures. Verification will consist of insuring i) that keys used in processing may be found, ii) that data items required are available and iii) that the relationships needed to associate data items or groups are represented. Efficiency related characteristics such as access path length and access frequencies, will be considered in the Schema Analysis and mapping step, following.

View integration approaches can be broadly classified into three categories:

(i) Item level synthesis using frequency information,
(ii) Item level synthesis using items and functional dependencies,
(iii) Merging of object-level structures.

5.1. Synthesis using items and frequencies

In this approach a user view is modeled in terms of items, associations between items and frequency information about the use of these associations by processes. Integration follows the rationale that items most frequently accessed must get priority in the structure by being placed nearest to the entry points in the structure.

This approach is followed in a method developed by CINCOM Systems, Inc. (Dyba 1977; Sheppard 1977) and in another method described by Mitoma (Mitoma 1975; Mitoma & Irani 1975).

In the CINCOM method, user views are repre-

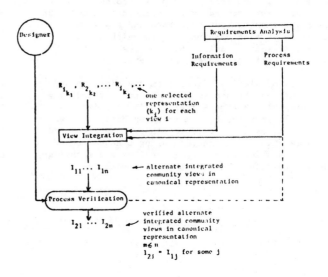

Figure 3: The View Integration Step

sented by flow diagrams of processes. The data items which are required for each processing step, or event, are noted on the diagrams. Using this information three statistics are computed for each data item:

1) the number of events in which it is used
2) the number of other data items with which it is used
3) the percentage of data items with which it is used often (i.e. for which the frequency of use exceeds a specified threshold).

For example, suppose a data item A is used by 10 events, is used with 6 other data elements, and in 4 of these 6 cases, the frequency of use exceeds a threshold of 70%. The three statistics for A would then be: 10,6 and 67%, respectively.

A classification scheme (see Table 2) is used to classify data elements into (a) keys, (b) attributes with one key, and (c) attributes with 2 or more keys. (These categories correspond to TOTAL control keys, master file elements, and variable file elements, respectively. See CINCOM (1976)). After this determination, a diagram linking attributes and keys is produced which represents the community view of the database.

In Mitoma's method data items are named and described, and binary relationships between data items (called data realtions) are defined. Each

	No. of Events (#1)	No. of Other Data Elements (#2)	% of Data Elements with a High Data Usage (#3)
Entity Key	Used by HIGH No.	Used with a HIGH No.	Used a LOW % of Time
Attribute to 1 Key	Used by LOW No.	Used with a LOW No.	Used a HIGH % of Time
Attribute to 2 or more Keys	Used by AVERAGE No.	Used with an AVERAGE No.	Used an AVERAGE % of Time

Table 2: Item classification in CINCOM method (Dyba 1977)

binary data relation is characterized by its cardinality (number of item pair occurences) and frequency ratios describing the number of values of one item related to a single value of the other tiem. For each data relation a set of implementations is generated, where an implementation is a DBTG-compatible structured collection of item occurrences that instantiate the relation in the database. Schemas are then built by combining implementations for each data relation specified. The resulting schemas are examined in the light of various feasibility conditions (such as consistency, minimum redundancy, and other DBTG constraints). Those schemas which are feasible are selected as alternate community views.

Both CINCOM and Mitoma use additional process-oriented information during an analysis phase which follows integration to select the best community view as the schema.

5.2 Synthesis using items and functional dependencies

In this method, a user view is modeled in terms of items, functional dependencies between items and one-to-many and "conditonal associations" between items. The database design aid (DBDA) of IBM (IBM 1975; Raver and Hubbard 1977) and Wang and Wedekind's (1975) approach fall into this category. Items are grouped together and keys are assigned so that the non-key items in each group are functionally dependent on the key items. The resulting set of groups is analogous to a minimum cover of relations.

In DBDA, the associations among items are divided into simple (one-to-one), complex (one-to-many) and conditional. One-to-one associations represent functional dependencies. During integration keys are defined such that they are not functionally dependent on any items and segments are defined by collecting with a key all the items functionally dependent on it. The associations which do not represent a functional dependency are candidates for logical relationships in IMS.

Wang and Wedekind's approach goes through the following steps:

i) Collect all functional dependencies for a pertinent set of applications.

ii) Obtain a minimum cover of functional dependencies by a minimum cover algorithm.

iii) Partition the minimal cover into disjoint subsets so that within each subset all functional dependencies have identical left hand side attribute domains.

iv) Combine each partition to generate a third normal form relation. This represents an optimal set of 3NF relations.

v) The 3NF relations are combined into logical segments according to prescribed performance requirements and projected information activities. The relations corresponding to the resulting segments could be 1NF or 2NF.

Other work on minimum cover algorithms such as Delobel and Casey (1973) and normal form synthesis algorithms (Bernstein 1976) are relevant to this approach.

5.3 Merging of object-level structures

In this method a user view is modeled in terms of data objects, groups or associations rather than items. Chen's (1976) entity-relationship diagram, Smith and Smith's (1977) aggregation and generalization hierarchies and Navathe and Schkolnick's (1978) view diagrams are of this type. In general, these views are in the form of networks or acyclic graphs. Integration of such views involves superimposing the views, matching identical components, resolving the differences between unmatched components, detecting and resolving redundancies, etc.

467

Figure 4 shows two separate views in the view representation method of Navathe and Schkolnick (1978). An oval represents an entity, a data object, or a simple data association whereas a rectangle represents an identifying association. A # sign by an oval indicates that it is fully internally identified. (See Navathe (1977) for definitions.) Merging of the two views is accomplished by superimposing the entity "Course".

Identical entities can always be merged. Otherwise, suppose E and E' are two entities for which

$E \subseteq E'$, (in terms of their decriptor sets)

id(E) = id(E'), for every internal id of E and E'

tid(E) = t i d(E'), i.e., the total identifiers are the same then the result of merging E and E' may be regarded as E'. It however implies that descriptors in the set E'-E receive null values in the instances of E after merging.

While operating on binary associations which are functional in nature, if one of the associations is a composition of two others, the former may be eliminated with designer approval.

In general, existing methods have not directly addressed the following porblems which occur during view integration using this approach:

i) Key determination: Given the groups of data elements with individual identifiers, the problem is to assign global keys. (Global refers to that which holds for an instance of the group across the entire database.) The existing approach in DBDA is quite arbitrary in that the keys are assigned by the designer as part of the input. Using identifying versus non-identifying relationships, the paths in a network which are used for

identification purposes may be defined (Navathe 1977). Once the identifying paths are found, the global keys can be obtained.

ii) Detection and resolution of inconsistencies and redundancies among entities and among associations: When two entities or associations are in partial agreement, the situation may be resolved in several ways:
   a) by merging them so that the integrated view can still support the source views
   b) by carrying them unchanged, treating them separately and imposing constraints on their processing (e.g., updating in multiple instances)
   c) by splitting them, merging the common parts and leaving the different parts unchanged.

In order to minimize redundancy, etc. additional schema operations may be required to be performed on the component views. Although some work of Navathe (1976) is directly applicable to this issue, the problem needs further research. Designer interaction could be used to mitigate the incorporation of the complete semantic information about each view. Criteria need to be developed for evaluating alternate regroupings.

The process of view integration when a DBMS and a Data Directory/Dictionary system is already in place can be greatly simplified by the use of the data dictionary system. The interface between it and the design process needs to be further investigated.

6. VIEW RESTRUCTURING

This phase and the next one (schema analysis and mapping) are target system dependent. If a target database management system has already been selected the restructuring, analysis and mapping is governed by the logical and physical data modeling features available in that system.

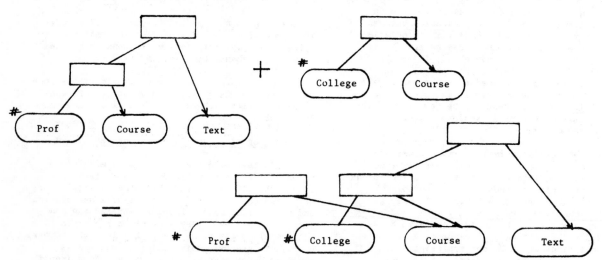

Figure 4: Merging of Views (Navathe and Schkolnick 1978)

Otherwise, the two phases are reiterated for every candidate target system being considered.

Figure 5 shows the view restructuring step. The input to view restructuring is twofold:

i) Integrated community views in a canonical representation. These are previously verified to ensure that all specified processing is feasible against each of them.

ii) A description of the target system: it is highly unlikely that all facilities of a database management system can be conveyed to the restructurer as a set of parameters. The following types of features may be parameterized.
—Number of relations in which a group may participate as a member. The two extremes are one for purely hierarchical systems, and some finite limit for network systems. A system like IMS allows both physical and logical relations and must be dealt with specially.
—Maximum number of levels of hierarchy allowed
—Maximum number of group types (record types or segment types) allowed
—Maximum number of elements in a group
—Maximum number of relations for which a group can be a member.

The features which do not lend themselves to parameterization will have to be "hard-coded" into a version of the restructurer for a particular target system. For example, relations are implemented differently in IMS, DBTG and TOTAL even at the logical level.

The processing in this phase involves the mapping of a view in canonical representation into a data structure in the target system. Equivalent target views must satisfy two constraints:

a) there is no loss of information
b) the original processing specification is satisfied

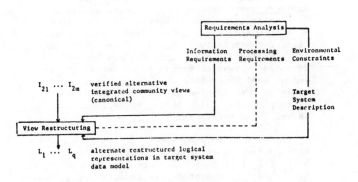

Figure 5: View Restructuring

A very simple example is shown in Figure 6.

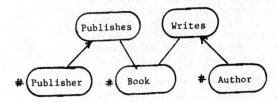

(a) Community View in Canonical Representation (Navathe & Schkolnick 1978)

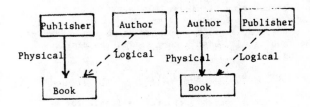

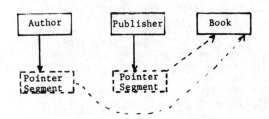

(b) Restructured Views in IMS

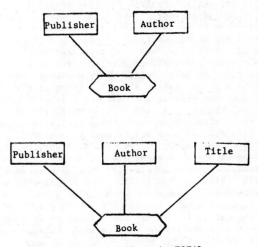

(c) Restructured Views in TOTAL

Figure 6: A simple example of view restructuring

469

The community view shows three entities which are fully internally identified (signified by the # sign). Publishes (Publisher, Book) and Writes (Author,Book) are two associations. The structure may be mapped into IMS in the different ways shown by incorporating different combinations of physical and logical pointers and pointer segments. In TOTAL the choice is between assigning an entity to a master file or a variable file.

In general, view restructuring should be able to map a network-like community view into any data model as dictated by a target system. This general problem has not been fully addressed yet but the work of the data translation project at the University of Michigan (Navathe 1976; Swartwout et al 1977) or XPRS project at IBM Research (Shu et al 1975; Shu et al 1977) can be applied to restructuring of views. The above research was originally intended to apply to restructuring of schemas of already populated databases. However the mapping of views is very similar to restructuring schemas.

7. SCHEMA ANALYSIS AND MAPPING

Given a logical structure suitable for a particular system, the next step in the design is to select appropriate access structures available within a system. (See Figure 7.) For example, given a DBTG logical structure represented in terms of a network, it is essential to select the location mode for record types and set types as well as the implementation method for the set types (such as 'pointer array' or 'chain'). Most of the analysis performed in this stage involves the physical properties of the database system and is sometimes classified as part of the 'physical database design'. Independent of a particular system, the design decisions that must be made can be summarized as follows:

1. Determination of file structures. The basic problem in physical database design is the selection of an appropriate file structure. This decision must be made before any secondary design issues may be considered. Since each application has its particular data and processing requirements, they generally require specific file structures to be designed. This obviously requires a great deal of effort. Alternatively, the designer may examine the existing file structures and select one to implement. However, if the target system allows many possible file structure configurations, many models must be analyzed. In order to systematically examine file structures for selection or design, a modeling approach is useful. The file models developed by Severance (1975, 1976) and Yao (1976, 1977) are capable of representing a number of common file structures in terms of a set of parameters which allow for subsequent analysis. In fact, there exist some preliminary results on the 'optimal' selection of file structures (Yao & Merten 1975). A good design guide for practitioners can also be found in Severance and Duhne (1976).

2. Access path selection. The file structure selection above is applicable to database structures involving only one file. The situation where more than one file is involved is far more

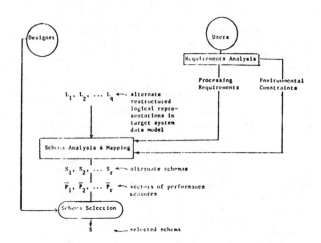

Figure 7: Schema Analysis and Mapping Step

complex since we must also consider a) the link structures among files, b) the algorithm for accessing, and c) secondary access structures.

The "link" structures refer to the access structures defined between different files for the purpose of cross references. The link structures usually exist for one-to-many or one-to-one relationships. The set implementations in DBTG are examples of links.

There are usually a limited number of ways in which a single file structure can be accessed. For a given type of file structure, usually a "standard" access algorithm is used (Lefkovitz 1969). When the structure involves multiple files however, numerous access paths are possible (e.g. Blasgen & Eswaren 1977). The problem of selecting access paths for queries was recently studied (Rothnie 1975; Smith & Chang 1975; Wong & Youssefi 1976). The approach has been to decompose a complex access requirement that involves many files into a series of simpler accesses that involve at most two files, and efficient access algorithms can be found for the latter (Wong & Youssefi 1976; Yao 1978).

The secondary access structure is that structure which is used in combination with a basic file structure. It includes the use of CALC (i.e. hashing) and secondary indexes. The problem of index selection has been extensively studied under some constraints. (See references under Index selection.) If the number of candidate indexes is small, then an enumeration approach is possible (Anderson & Berra 1977). If the access activities against different attributes are independent, then an efficient algorithm can be used to locate the optimal index set (Schkolnick 1975). If more detailed model and larger problem size are to be considered, then heuristic procedures such as developed by Hammer (1976) should be used. The existing methods are still far from reality since only single-file access is considered. An extension for multiple-files is necessary when the index selection is incorporated in a design system.

3. **Data Allocation.** If attributes of a file have different access activity, then it may be advantageous to partition the record into subsets and store them in different files. This can be visualized as "vertical" partition of files. Most of the techniques developed on the problem involve mathematical programming. A good summary is given by March and Severance (1978). Record clustering is a concept similar to segmentation, except the former attempts to perform a "horizontal" partitioning of files. Records with high likelihood of being accessed together are grouped in one partition. Since in a database system, it is possible for some applications to access records in different files, the grouping of records should extend to consider different files. A restructed class of problems to partition and group records in IMS-type hierarchical structure was studied by Schkolnick (1977), and a fast algorithm for this type of record clustering is available. The extension of this method to network databases is also reported (Schkolnick 1978).

While the above surveys the problems associated with physical design and their solutions, it is our major goal to integrate these available techniques into a design system to aid the designer. A "decision support" system for database design was developed by Gambino and Gerritsen (1977). The system allows the designer to specify design choices which are then checked against the given logical structure for feasibility and consistency. This allows the designer to explore the alternatives in design with some estimate of their performance. The system, however, does not attempt to perform any optimization or heuristic procedure in searching for a good solution. Since the space of all alternative solutions is usually quite large, we propose to integrate existing techniques into the design system to restrict the search space to a manageably smaller size.

8. AUTOMATING THE LOGICAL DATABASE DESIGN PROCESS

Real world experience with database design (see Raver & Hubbard 1977) indicates that no set of manual techniques will suffice for this process. The size and complexity of these problems require computer support. On the other hand, a fully automatic design system in which a human is not actively involved may generate schemas which are not acceptable to the users. A computer-aided approach allowing interaction between the designer and the system appears most desirable.

Tasks which could benefit from computer support exist in all five phases of the design process. Automated approaches to requirements analysis (e.g. Teichroew et al 1975; Hammer et al 1977) have been extensively explored. (These approaches were discussed in Section 3 above.) Computerization of the rest of the database design process is less common.

Existing database design methodologies may be classified into four categories based on the degree of formality of their procedures: manual, design guidelines or rules, computer aided, or automatic. Methods classified as manual (e.g. Bachman, Codd, Senko et al, Chen, Smith & Smith) rely heavily on the designer's skill. Using interviews and other systems analysis techniques the designer becomes conversant with the application semantics, and designs a model. This approach can be both inefficient and unreliable.

Methodologies such as the CINCOM method and those described by Palmer (1978) and Curtice and Jones (1978) include detailed guidelines and rules for the designer to follow. These approaches treat database design as a step-by-step process and utilize such aids as forms for data collection, specialized notation and quantitative criteria for data grouping and key determination. They remain, however, manual methods.

To date the only computer-aided system approach to logical database design is that of the Data Base Design Aid (DBDA). However, it mainly performs view integration with little consideration to other steps. It also suffers from the following drawbacks:

1) Arbitrary decisions are made using only the information structure perspective, e.g. elimination of "implied associations", determination of keys, and grouping of elements.

2) The input to the system is prepared on the basis of input documents and reports which may give an incomplete specification of the user views.

There are other less elaborate design aids. Mitoma's system (1975) automatically generates candidate schemas from data relations defined on data item pairs. The system is also used to select an optimal schema based on the criteria of storage and costs. This approach is predicated on the assumption that all statistics related to the processing of data are already available; they go through the solution of an optimization problem to yield a DBTG data structure. No consideration is given to local views and their integration, or the the determination of keys. Gerritsen's Data Base Designer (DBD) derives item and entity relationships from queries and synthesizes a network schema from assertions describing these relationships.

Computer-based systems have also been proposed to solve physical design problems, e.g. the selection of file structures or minimum cost configurations. Teorey and Das (1976) developed a file design analyzer to select optimal file organizations based on Yao's (1974) analytical model. Hoffer (1975) has developed a system that groups data items so as to minimize access times and storage size. Berelian and Irani (1977) have extended Mitoma's schema optimization procedure to consider the constraints of a paging environment.

Three phases of the logical database design

process show the greatest need for further development of computer aids:

i) View modeling. As mentioned above, no computer support exists for this step, yet the complexity of the process for even a moderate size application is unwieldy for manual methods. The authors are currently developing an interactive system to aid the process of database abstraction. This system will build, verify, and maintain abstraction structures at the request of the designer. Verification will be performed with respect to the syntactic and semantic rules for well-defined abstraction structures. While the syntactic portion of the verification process could be entirely automatic, the semantic portion will generate assertions about the structure which must be affirmed by the designer. The system will also produce structure descriptions, on request, at any point in the design process.

ii) View integration. Needed are interactive tools for the detection and resolution of redundancies and inconsistencies, perhaps linked to a data dictionary; tools for applying minimum cover algorithms to simplify integrated views; and tools incorporating operators for matching and merging object level view representations.

iii) View restructuring. Systems are needed here to generate and analyze candidate schemas for various target systems. This support is required for full consideration of the large number of possible solutions.

9. SUMMARY

Existing work on logical database design varies in the types of tasks addressed (data modeling versus schema optimization), the level of detail (e.g. object versus item level), and the ultimate result (e.g. a system independent data model versus a detailed, system dependent schema). In this paper we have proposed a framework for logical database design which integrates existing methodologies. While describing our approach we have cited relevant research and noted useful results. The main purpose of this effort has been to identify areas of the logical design process for further research. In particular, the need for computer-aided design tools in all phases of the design process has been emphasized. While a truly comprehensive computer-aided design system does not yet exist, we believe that such a system could be developed in the not-too-distant future.

REFERENCES

Design Methodology

Curtice, R. M. and P.E. Jones, Jr. "Key Steps in the Logical Design of Data Bases," Proc. NYU Symposium on Database Design, (May 1978).

Dyba, Jerome E. "Principles of Data Element Identification," Auerbach Data Base Management Services, Portfolio #23-01-03, 1977.

Palmer, I. R. "Practicalities in Applying a Formal Methodology to Data Analysis," Proc. NYU Symposium on Database Design, (May 1978).

Sheppard, D. "Data Base Design Methodology - Parts I & II," Auerbach Data Base Management Series, Portfolios #23-01-01,02, 1977.

Requirement Analysis

Bubenko, J. A. Jr. and S. Berild, E. Lindencrona-Ohlin and S. Nachmens. "From Information Structures to DBTG Data Structures," Proc. Conference on Data, SIGMOD FDT, Vol. 8, No. 2, 1976.

Hammer, M., W. G. Howe, V. J. Kruskal and I. Wladawsky. "A Very High Level Programming Language for Data Processing Applications," Comm. ACM, Vol. 20, No. 11, November 1977.

IEEE Transactions on Software Engineering, Vol. SE-3, No. 1 (January 1977).

Kahn, B. K. "A Method for Describing Information Required by the Database Design Process," Proc. 1976 ACM SIGMOD International Conference on Management of Data, June 1976, ACM, New York.

Solvberg, A. Computer Aided Systems Construction and Design Evaluation, University of Trondheim, Norway, 1974.

Teichroew, D. and E. A. Hershey III. "PSL/PSA: A Computer-Aided Technique for Structured Documentation and Analysis of Information Processing Systems." IEEE Transactions on Software Engineering, January 1977.

View Modeling

Bachman, C. W. "Data Structure Diagrams," Data Base, Vol. 1, No. 2 (Summer 1969).

Chen, P. P. S. "The Entity-Relationship Model - Toward a Unified View of Data," ACM Transactions on Database Systems, Vol. 1, No. 1 (March 1976).

Codd, E. F. "A Relational Model of Data for Large Shared Data Banks," Comm. ACM, Vol. 13, No. 6 (June 1970).

Navathe, S. B. and M. Schkolnick. "View Representation in Logical Database Design," Proc. ACM-SIGMOD International Conference on Management of Data, June 1978.

Senko, M. E., E. B. Altman, M. M. Astrahan and P. L. Fehder. "Data Structures and Accessing in Data-Base Systems," IBM Systems Journal, Vol. 12, No. 1, 1973.

Smith, J. M. and D. C. P. Smith. "Database Abstractions: Aggregation and Generalization," ACM Transactions on Database Systems, Vol. 2, No. 2, June 1977.

View Integration

Bernstein, P. A. "Synthesizing Third Normal Form Relations from Functional Dependencies," _ACM Transactions on Data Base Systems_, Vol. 1, No. 4 (December 1976).

Delobel, C. and R. G. Casey, "Decomposition of a Data Base and the Theory of Boolean Switching Functions," _IBM J. Res. Develop._, Vol. 17, No. 5 (September 1973).

Wang, D. P. and H. H. Wedekind. "Segment Synthesis in Logical Data Base Design," _IBM J. of Research and Development_, January 1975.

View Restructuring

Navathe, S. B. _A methodology for generalized database restructuring_. Ph.D. Dissertation, University of Michigan (1976). Available from University Microfilms, Ann Arbor, MI, Order No. TSZ 7627,557.

Navathe, S. B. "Schema Analysis for Database Restructuring," presented at the Third VLDB, Tokyo, Japan, September 1977; to appear in _ACM Transactions on Database Systems_.

Shu, N. C. and B. C. Housel and V. Y. Lum. "CONVERT: a high-level translation definition language for data conversion," _CACM_, Vol. 18, No. 10 (October 1975), pp. 557-567.

Shu, N. C. and B. C. Housel, R. W. Taylor, S. P. Ghosh, V. Y. Lum. "EXPRESS: A Data Extraction, Processing, and Restructuring System," _ACM Transactions on Database Systems_, Vol. 2, No. 2 (June 1977).

Swartwout, D. E., and M. E. Deppe, J. P. Fry. "Operational software for restructuring network databases," _Proc. AFIPS 1977 National Computer Conference_.

Physical Design (General)

Berelian, E. and K. B. Irani. "Evaluation and Optimization of Database Design in a Paging Environment," Proc. 3rd VLDB, Tokyo, Japan, October 1977.

Blasgen, M. W. and K. P. Eswaren, "Storage access in relational data bases," _IBM Systems J._, No. 4, 1977, pp. 363-377.

Gambino, T. J. and R. Gerritsen, "A Database Design Decision Support System, " _Proc. 3rd VLDB_, Tokyo, Japan, October 1977.

Hoffer, J. A. _A Clustering Approach to the Generation of Subfiles for the Design of a Computer Data Base_, Ph.D. Dissertation, Cornell University, 1975.

Lefkovitz, D. _File Structures for On-Line Systems_, Spartan Books, New York, 1969.

March, S. T. and D. G. Severance. "A Mathematical Modelling Approach to the Automatic Selection of Database Design," _Proc. SIGMOD 1978_, Austin, Texas.

Rothnie, J. B. "Evaluating inter-entry retrieval expressions in a relational data base management system," _Proc. AFIPS 1975 NCC_, Vol 44, Montvale, NJ: AFIPS, pp. 417-423.

Schkolnick, M. "A Clustering Algorithm for Hierarchical Structures," _ACM TODS_, Vol. 2, No. 1, March 1977, pp. 27-44.

Schkolnick, M. "A Model of Internal Accesses in Network Databases," in preparation. 1978.

Severance, D. G. "A Parametric Model of Alternative File Structures," _Information Systems_, Vol. 1, No. 2, 1975.

Severance, D. G. and R. Duhne. "A Practitioner's Guide to Addressing Algorithms," _Comm. ACM_, Vol. 19,6 (June 1976), pp. 314-326, 1061-1072.

Smith, J. M. and P. Y. T. Chang. "Optimizing the performance of a relational algebra and database interface," _Comm. ACM_, Vol. 18, No. 10, October 1975, pp. 568-579.

Wong, E. and K. Youssefi. "Decomposition--a strategy for query processing," _ACM Trans. on Database Systems_, Vol 1, No. 3, September 1976, pp. 223-241.

Yao, S. B. _Evaluation and optimization of file organization through analytic modeling_, Ph.D. Thesis, Univerisity of Michigan, Ann Arbor, Michigan, 1974.

Yao, S. B. "Modeling and performance evaluation of physical data base structures," _Proc. ACM 1976 Annual Conf._, October 1976, pp. 303-

Yao, S. B. "An attribute based model for data base access cost analysis," _ACM Trans. Database Systems_, Vol. 2, No. 1, March 1977, pp. 45-67.

Yao, S. B. "Optimal Evaluation of Two-Variable Queries," unpublished manuscript, 1978.

Yao, S. B. and A. Merten. "Selection of file organization through analytic modeling," _Proc. Int. Conf. on VLDB_, Framingham, MA, September 1975, pp. 255-267.

Physical Design (Index Selection)

Anderson, H. D. and P. B. Berra. "Minimum cost selection of secondary indexes for formatted filed, _ACM Trans. Database Systems_, Vol. 2, No. 1, March 1977, pp. 68-90.

Hammer, M. and A. Chan. "Index selection in a self-adaptive data base management system," _ACM SIGMOD_, 1976.

Lum, V. Y., and H. Ling. "An optimization problem on the selection of secondary keys," _Proc. ACM Nat. Conference_, 1971, pp. 349-356.

Schkolnick, M. "The optimal selection of secondary indices for files," _Information Systems_, Vol. 1, pp. 141-146, 1975.

Yue, P. C. and C. K. Wong. "Storage cost considerations in secondary index selection," _Int. Jr. of Computer and Information Sciences_, Vol. 4, No. 4, 1975.

Automated Design Methodology

Gerritsen, R. "A Preliminary System for the Design of DBTG Data Structures," _Comm. ACM_, Vol. 18, No. 10, October 1975.

IBM, _Database Design Aid General Information Manual and Designer's Guide_, Publication Nos. GH20-1626-0 and GH20-1627-0, 1975.

Mitoma, M. F. _Optimal Data Base Schema Design_, Ph.D. Dissertation, University of Michigan, 1975.

Mitoma, M. F. and K. B. Irani. "Automatic Data Base Schema Design and Optimization," _Proc. First Conf. on VLDB_, September 1975.

Raver, N. and G. U. Hubbard. "Automated Logical Data Base Design: Concepts and Applications," _IBM Systems J._, Vol. 16, No. 3, 1977.

Teorey, T. J. and K. S. Das. "Application of an analytical model to evaluate storage structures," _Proc. ACM SIGMOD Conf._, June 1976, pp. 9-19.

Miscellaneous

CINCOM Systems, _OS/TOTAL Application Programmer's Guide_, Publ. No. PO2-1236-00, CINCOM Systems, Cincinnati, OH, 1976.

CODASYL, _Data Base Task Group Report_, ACM, New York, 1971.

0306–4379/83/010015–09$03.00/0
Pergamon Press Ltd.

BASIS: A BEHAVIORAL APPROACH TO THE
SPECIFICATION OF INFORMATION SYSTEMS

Nancy G. Leveson

Information and Computer Science, University of California, Irvine, Irvine, CA 92717, U.S.A.

Anthony I. Wasserman

Medical Information Science, University of California, San Francisco, San Francisco CA 94143, U.S.A.

and

Daniel M. Berry

Computer Science Department, University of California, Los Angeles, Los Angeles, CA 90024, U.S.A.

(*Received 6 October* 1982)

Abstract—This paper is an overview of BASIS (Behavioral Approach to the Specification of Information Systems),
a multi-step formal method used for information systems design and development. The steps include information
analysis, semantic specification, verification of the specification, concrete implementation, and verification of the
implementation. In this way, BASIS can be used to provide a formal basis for information systems development.
We provide an example showing how BASIS can be used in conjunction with implementation in the programming
language PLAIN.

Information systems have traditionally been developed
in an *ad hoc* manner, growing as the need for new
capabilities becomes apparent. This lack of preplanning
and disciplined development has led to systems that are
unstructured, hard to use, and difficult to maintain.
Recognition of this problem has led to extensive efforts
to create methodologies for information system
design[28]. Such methodologies provide technical
methods, organizational approaches, and automated tools
covering the entire development life cycle, from analysis
through specification, design, implementation, testing
and/or verification, and operation.

In the field of information systems, particular attention
has been given to information modelling and database
design[8, 18, 19, 24, 35, 36]. Although many requirements
analysis methods and data models[9, 25] have been proposed and described for data base systems, there are
currently few techniques that "bridge the gap" between
system requirements and data base design. That is, there
is no way to determine whether the complex data structures of the data model actually satisfy the needs of the
users of the system. Continuing along the path of
defining more and more structural ("semantic") models
does not appear to promise any progress on this problem.

While most data models have focused on the abstraction of data structures, other models have introduced the notion of behavioral abstraction and have
emphasized the need for including the operations on the
data within the abstraction[1, 4, 10, 12, 15, 20, 23, 33].
This latter approach appears to hold promise for linking
the system requirements and the data base design into
one methodology for information system design.

Behavioral abstraction is a key component of the User
Software Engineering (USE) methodology[27, 30] for the
specification and development of information systems.
This paper describes BASIS (Behavioral Approach to
the Specification of Information Systems), a formal
specification method which provides the link between
system requirements and data base design in USE.

INFORMATION SYSTEM DESIGN

Informally, an information system may be viewed as
consisting of a database and some operations (transactions) to be executed on the data. Different sets of
transactions are normally available to the different classes of users of the information system, i.e. different
"views" of the data are provided. Thus the analysis
which precedes the design of the information system
should include the identification of the operations
(transactions) to be executed on the data, as well as the
data elements themselves. (We distinguish here between
an information system, where the transactions can be
specified in advance, and a generalized database system
where arbitrary sets of retrieval and update operations are
required.) Thus, the concern is not purely with data base
design, but with the data base in an information system
context where there is some understanding of the ways in
which the data will be used.

This paper assumes that some requirements analysis
technique has been used to identify the transaction
requirements of the system prior to the use of BASIS.
There are many possible methods, including Structured
Systems Analysis[3, 5], SADT†[21], or some of the
modelling techniques noted above.

The order in which decisions are made in designing an
information system affects the structure and flexibility of

---

†SADT is a trademark of SofTech, Inc.

the final system because early design decisions influence and often determine or constrain later decisions. BASIS imposes discipline and structure on the order of design decisions and provides a context in which to make these decisions. Implementation decisions are postponed until the design specification is complete and the information relevant to these decisions have been recorded. The system designer then performs database design and implementation with some knowledge of expected usage patterns. This strategy can have a major impact on the ease of data access and the logical complexity of the code needed to retrieve data.

Not only is the order of decisions important in information system design, but it must be possible to provide a record of these decisions as they are made, to support evolvability so that changes can be made with the least impact, and to provide for the verification of the design decisions as they are made. This verification process, involving the formal demonstration of equivalence between the system and its specification, requires a formal specification that is precise and unambiguous. BASIS provides such a specification.

The rest of this paper presents the details of the five major steps in designing an information system using BASIS: information analysis, semantic specification, verification of the design specification, implementation, and verification of the implementation.

The first step (information analysis) involves the analysis of the desired objectives of the information system and the specification of the objects and transactions involved in the system to be built. These objectives may not all be computerized immediately and new activities may be added at a later time.

The second step (semantic specification) includes the specification of the logical rules or properties (constraints) of the real world information system which the computerized information system must reflect. The semantics of an information system include not only the operations and activities of the system, but also the legal states of the data. If the data starts out in a legal or accurate state and only legal operations are applied, then the data will be guaranteed to have semantic integrity. As opposed to most prior approaches, the approach taken here is to use *both* a static and a dynamic specification of the semantics of the data.

The third step involves verification of the formal specification developed by the first two steps. This includes verifying that the requirements have been correctly specified and that the semantic integrity (correctness) of the data as specified cannot be violated by the transactions of the information system.

Once the formal specification has been verified, the system can be implemented. Although the implementation could be accomplished using a wide variety of languages, it is most convenient to use a language with many of the required facilities built-in. PLAIN[29] is such a language. Since PLAIN has been extensively described elsewhere, only the major features are presented.

Finally, it is necessary to verify that the implementation actually satisfies the specification. Since the BASIS specification is a formal one based on standard axiomatic semantics, standard verification techniques and tools can be used to accomplish this final step.

Each of these steps is now described in more detail.

INFORMATION ANALYSIS

A behavioral specification contains a description of the objects of the information system and the operations defined on these objects. These operations are determined from the systems requirements procedure which precedes the design of the information system. In USE, for example, the analysis leads to the specification of the system as a set of transition diagrams describing the user/program dialogue along with the operations performed as a result of inputs, combined with a database model[31].

The results of the requirements specification will be a set of objectives or views of the information system by the users or groups of users along with a set of user/information system transactions. For example, the objectives in a University enrollment system might be to create a master schedule, to keep track of enrollment of students in classes, and to maintain information on students and teaching personnel. This information in turn is used to determine the objects of the information system used by each view. As an example:

> view *Scheduling*
>   *transactions*
>   schedule-class
>   *uses* class, schedule
>   delete-class
>   *uses* class, schedule
>   is-scheduled
>   *uses* schedule
>
> view *enrollment*
>   *transactions*
>   enroll-student
>   *uses* student, class, schedule.

In the above, the view "scheduling" might use the objects class and schedule, the view "enrollment" use the objects class, schedule, etc.

The set of objects determined to be required by the views will comprise the schema objects of the data base system underlying the information system. After objects are identified, it is necessary to specify the abstract operations to be defined on each schema object. As an example, a university information system might have such objects as students, professors, classrooms, etc. In particular, the abstract object professor might have the operations "hire," "promote", "change address," and "department?" defined on it in addition to a create operation which acts as a generator for instances of the abstract object.

Note that not all possible update operations need be predefined, but only a characterizing or minimal set. This characterizing set must be such that any other operations on the data may be achieved by a combination of operations from the set. This is not really as difficult as it may first appear, and, furthermore, operations can easily be added later.

The necessity for pre-defined abstract schema operations arises from the desire to protect the integrity and security of the data. Integrity and security problems are the result of providing users with freedom of use of operations on the underlying data model used to implement the abstraction, e.g. the relational algebra operations of the relational model or tree and graph traversal operations of the hierarchical and network models respectively. In order for the information system to then exercise control over the integrity and security of the data, complex procedures such as integrity constraint specification and enforcement procedures as well as access right and authorization schemes are necessary. These schemes, for the most part, require such high overhead to be complete that they reach the point of being impractical, unrealistic, and inflexible. Another approach to semantic integrity enforcement is to provide a data model which incorporates all the semantics of the data within the structures of the model. This also appears to be unrealistic. But by specifying integrity and access rights at the transaction level, security and semantics can be defined at a conceptually higher level so that definition and checking of access privileges and integrity violations is simplified. Note that this transaction-oriented approach places no inherent restrictions on the range of operations that can be performed. Even corrections to erroneous data values can be made into pre-defined operations and the authority to use these operations restricted.

Each object may also have exception-handling operations defined for it. These operations are essentially responses to attempts to violate the semantic integrity of the data. They may be responsible for ensuring that the integrity of the data is intact before informing the user of the problem (especially if the problem is due to a user error), or may attempt to resolve the problem without user intervention.

In order to provide control over the use of an abstract object, it is convenient to specify the operations one object may perform on another object. As an example, the operation "enroll" may *import* separate rights for each parameter of the operation, e.g.

enroll (student⟨verify⟩, class⟨is-full⟩)

which states that enroll may invoke the verify operation defined on the abstract object student and also check to see if the class is full.

Furthermore, it is possible to define selectors on objects which allow more *ad hoc* retrieval than is possible with a pure transaction-oriented system. Examples of selectors are "FIRST STUDENT," "NEXT STUDENT," "FIRST STUDENT SUCH THAT...", etc. The use of a selector allows selective retrieval or iteration over objects of the data base without tying the user's program to a particular data structure or data model. In order to provide a truly secure information system environment, however, such facilities can be provided only on a highly restrictive basis[32].

The complete view specification in BASIS is similar to that of the schema objects, i.e. specification of the schema objects visible to the view, the transactions on these objects, the semantics of the transactions, exception-handling operations, and the imported operations and selectors on each object which the view can legally invoke.

Most data base design methodologies define first the data base objects, then the views, and finally the transactions. Each of these steps is based on some type of structural abstraction (data model). In the USE methodology this process is reversed. The transactions are first defined (thus defining the views), then the schema objects, and last any underlying data model. By proceding in this fashion, i.e. top-down from the requirements, it can be guaranteed that the resulting system will satisfy the requirements. The opposite bottom-up strategy provides no such guarantee.

SEMANTIC INTEGRITY SPECIFICATION

The data base can be correct or not only with respect to the semantics of the information system being modelled, so to ensure integrity it is necessary first to have a specification of the rules or invariants that the data base must reflect. An integrity system cannot be expected to guarantee the correctness of every value in the data base, but only to enforce the constraints which have been made explicitly. The system being proposed allows complete flexibility in constraint enforcement. If it is decided that the checking of certain constraints during particular operations is not worth the extra run-time overhead, then the designer has the flexibility of omitting these checks. In fact, the designer has complete control over which constraints are checked in which operations—although if some checking is omitted, then the complete integrity of the data base cannot be guaranteed.

The specification should allow the expression of any consistency or validity constraint. Formality is important, but the specification should also be in terms used by the application specialists. In BASIS, it was decided that constraints would be specified both in predicate calculus and in narrative text.

The question now arises as to the type of constraints that should be specified. In specifications focusing on structural abstraction, the specification of the integrity constraints usually includes the static characteristics of the data[6]. On the other hand, in some behavioral approaches to data base specification, only the operations or behavioral characteristics are specified[15, 33]. Both of these approaches have drawbacks[11]. A static specification leads to enforcement problems, and a purely operational specification leads to difficulty in verifying the accuracy, consistency, and completeness of the specification, in modifying the integrity rules, and in communicating necessary information to the users of the data base. In order to overcome these difficulties, an integrity specification in BASIS includes both the static characteristics of the data (semantic invariants of the objects) and the changes or operations allowed. A verification procedure is provided for the specification to ensure that the operations preserve the semantic invariant.

Figure 1 is a BASIS specification of an abstract object "class." In order to simplify the example, only the parts of the specification which are relevant to semantic integrity are included. A complete BASIS specification of a university information system may be found in [11].

object class
  abstract image
    id: 00000 . . . 99999
    cname: name
    prof: professor
    loc: room
    ctime: time
    max_enroll: 10 . . . 300
    students: *set of* students

  abstract invariant
    [number of students enrolled in less than
    or equal to the maximum allowed]
    $0 \leqslant$ cardinality(students) $\leqslant$ max_enroll

  operations
    create-class (cid: 00000 . . . 99999, *n*: name,
    p: professor, *r*: room, *t*: time, max: 0 . . . 300)
    returns c: class
      post
        id = cid
        cname = *n*
        prof = *p*
        loc = *r*
        ctime = *t*
        max_enroll = max
        students = { }
    assign-professor (*c*: class, *p*: professor)
      post c. prof = *p*
    add-student (*c*: class, *s*: student)
      pre $0 \leqslant$ cardinality(*c*. students) $<$ *c*.max_enroll
        & is-enrolled(*c*, *s*) = *false*
      post c.students = *c*.students' *union* {*s*}
    delete-student (*c*: class, *s*: student)
      pre is-enrolled(*c*, *s*) = *true*
      post c.students = *c*.students'-{*s*}
    is-enrolled(*c*: class, *s*: student) *returns b*: boolean
      post b = *s in c*.students
    change-room (*c*: class, *r*: room)
      post c.room = *r*
    change-time (*c*: class, *t*: time)
      post c.time = *t*

Fig. 1. Specification of the object "class".

There are three main parts to a BASIS specification of semantic integrity: the abstract image, the invariant, and input and output constraints for each operation defined on the abstract object.

The abstract image of an object is a list of the attributes associated with the object along with constraints on the values of these attributes for instances of the abstract object. Note that although an abstract image is defined in the specification, the implementation of the information system is not constrained by the abstract image. That is, to describe the properties of an abstract object, it is convenient to imagine a specific image, but this image is only hypothetical and does not describe any real implementation.

The invariant is composed of the inter-attribute constraints, i.e. the constraints on the relationships between the components of the abstract image. It is possible to write a specification in BASIS without an abstract invariant. The abstract invariant is eliminated by including the constraints specified by the abstract invariant in the input and output constraints for the operations. This is analogous to saying that a static specification of integrity can be replaced by a dynamic specification. However, the specifications required to do so become quite complicated and have the drawbacks noted above, and therefore is discouraged in BASIS.

The abstract operations are defined, in BASIS, by the input and output constraints which characterize the effects of the operations. In Hoare's notation, this is written

$$C_{\text{pre}_j}\{S_j\}C_{\text{post}_j}$$

where C_{pre_j} and C_{post_j} are the preconditions and postconditions, respectively, for operation j, and S_j is the code for operation j.

The pre and post constraints specify the legal manipulations on the abstract object. The integrity of the data can be violated in two ways: (1) illegal changes in values, and (2) legal changes which are made in an illegal order. Specifying the legal sequence of operations is important when the set of legal operations depends on the characteristics of the database such as the occurrence or non-occurrence of certain operations in the past, at the same time, or in the future [15]. The specification of the pre and post constraints is important for three reasons: (1) the checking of particular constraints is tied to particular operations, (2) the pre and post constraints for the operations act as a guide for the implementor, and (3) they are used to prove that the specification and implementation are correct.

VERIFICATION

Verification of integrity is defined as proving that the behavioral specification is consistent, i.e. that the operations preserve the invariant. Thus verifying the integrity of the data involves induction—first prove that the abstract objects have the specified properties (satisfy the abstract invariant) when they are first created, and then show that all operations which change the object preserve these properties. The proof procedure is derived from Hoare's technique for proving the correctness of data representations [7]. More formally, prove that:

(1) The create operations establishes the abstract invariant I_a

$$C_{\text{pre}_i}(a) \ \& \ C_{\text{post}_i}(a) \rightarrow I_a(a)$$

where C_{pre} and C_{post} are the pre and post conditions, respectively, on the create operation, and a is an abstract object.

(2) Show that each operation j preserves the abstract invariant,

$$C_{\mathrm{pre}_j}(a') \ \& \ I_a(a') \ \& \ C_{\mathrm{post}_j}(a) \rightarrow I_a(a)$$

where a' is the abstract object prior to the execution of the operation.

Using the class example in Fig. 1, the proof would consist of the following steps:

(1) Prove that the abstract invariant, I_a, holds after the creation of the abstract object class:

Show: $0 < \max \leqslant 300$ & $c.\max\_enroll = \max$ & $c.students = \{ \}$ & ...

$\rightarrow 0 \leqslant \mathrm{cardinality}(c.students) \leqslant c.\max\_enroll$

Proof: $0 \leqslant \max\_enroll \leqslant 100$

$\rightarrow 0 = \mathrm{cardinality}(\{ \}) < c.\max\_enroll \leqslant 300$

$\rightarrow 0 \leqslant \mathrm{cardinality}(c.students) \leqslant c.\max\_enroll$.

(2) Prove that the abstract invariant holds after each abstract operation. The only two operations for which the proof is not trivial are add-student and delete-student.

(a) for add-student

Show: $0 \leqslant \mathrm{cardinality}(c.students') < c.\max\_enroll$ & is-enrolled$(c', s) = false$ &

$c.students = c.students'$ union $\{s\}$ &

$0 \leqslant \mathrm{cardinality}(c.students) \leqslant c.\max\_enroll$

$\rightarrow 0 \leqslant \mathrm{cardinality}(c.students) \leqslant c.\max\_enroll$

Proof: $\mathrm{cardinality}(c.students')$ union $\{s\} = \mathrm{cardinality}(c.students') + 1$

Since $0 \leqslant \mathrm{cardinality}(c.students') < c.\max\_enroll$

then $0 \leqslant \mathrm{cardinality}(c.students) \leqslant c.\max\_enroll$

(b) for delete-student

Show: is-enrolled$(c', s) = true$ &

$0 \leqslant \mathrm{cardinality}(c.students') \leqslant c.\max\_enroll$ &

$c.students = c.students'\text{-}\{s\}$

$\rightarrow 0 \leqslant \mathrm{cardinality}(c.students) \leqslant c.\max\_enroll$

Proof: $\mathrm{cardinality}(c.students') = \mathrm{cardinality}(c.students) - 1$

Since $\mathrm{cardinality}(c.students') \leqslant c.\max\_enroll$

then $\mathrm{cardinality}(c.students) \leqslant c.\max\_enroll$.

Also, since is-enrolled$(c', s) = true$,

then $0 < \mathrm{cardinality}(c.students')$ and

therefore $0 \leqslant \mathrm{cardinality}(c.students)$.

Mechanical aids can simplify this verification process. A complete BASIS specification of a university information system has been proven correct using the SDC Ina Jo System[2]. It is interesting to note that several errors in the specification of integrity constraints were discovered during the verification process although the original specification had been independently reviewed by several people (including all three authors of this paper).

IMPLEMENTATION

The abstract specification acts as a guide for constructing the information system. The implementation must have the same behavior as the abstract specification, but is not constrained to using the same representations and algorithms for realizing that behavior. In fact, the implementation can be based on any data model and use any programming language. It is, however, most convenient to use a language specifically designed for implementing information systems such as PLAIN[29] or RIGEL[22].

The programming language PLAIN has been developed explicitly to support the systematic implementation of interactive information systems. PLAIN is a Pascal-based language that brings together modern programming language concepts with data base management by providing relations as a built-in type, along with a relational algebra-like set of operations. In addition, the PLAIN *module* feature makes it possible to create data abstractions; since relations are a builtin type and the PLAIN *external* declaration makes it possible to access existing data bases and modules, it is relatively easy to follow the BASIS methodology through to implementation using PLAIN. In addition, PLAIN contains an *assert* statement that can be used to check the preconditions, postconditions, and invariants. If an assertion evaluates to false during program execution, an exception is raised, making it possible to interrupt an operation before any violation of semantic integrity or protection.

Finally, PLAIN contains a procedure-oriented exception-handling mechanism. One may associate a *handler* for any exception with statements or compound statements. PLAIN includes predefined exceptions for any of the potentially harmful situations in the interactive information system system environment. Thus, the type checking features of the language can check for many kinds of errors at translation time, while the exception handling features can check for and take action upon runtime errors.

For the class example above, a module declaration might be of the form:

```
type class = module
  exports
    procedure create-class ( ... );
    procedure assign-professor ( ... );
    procedure add-student ( ... );
    procedure delete-student ( ... );
    procedure is-enrolled ( ... );
    procedure change-room ( ... );
    procedure change-time ( ... );
  imports student, professor, ...: readonly;
  rep relation [key class-id]
      class-id: string;
      class-name: string;
      prof-name: string;
      ...

  ops
    {here follows the procedure declarations and
    bodies, each of which may have exceptions, and
    any number of assertions; the language features
    available in the procedures permit database
    manipulation, string handling, and various forms
    of computation.}
end module
```

In general, each schema object will be represented by a relation in PLAIN while the views will import the schema objects which the view can read or modify. For efficiency of implementation, new relations may also be declared at the view level. If one creates a *module* providing authorization checking for various users and user classes, one can provide a high degree of security as well[32].

ENFORCEMENT OF INTEGRITY

Enforcement of integrity requires checking that the implemented update operations do not violate the abstract specification. Integrity problems can occur from an illegal sequence of legal operations or from faulty operations that make updates which violate integrity rules. Preconditions on operations can eliminate illegal sequences of operations, and verification techniques can prove that the operations preserve the abstract invariant as described above.

Verifying the correctness of the implementation includes proofs of the correctness of the representation of the objects and the implementations of the operations with respect to their pre and post constraints using assertions for run-time checks. Programmer control over the placement of assertions within the operations allows for flexibility in where the run-time checks are actually done.

This verification can be accomplished using standard methods. For example, using the Alphard proof procedure[34], it is necessary to specify an implementation invariant I_{rep} on the representation, an abstraction function "abs" (mapping between the implementation representation and the abstract image), and input and output constraints, C_{in_j} and C_{out_j}, for each of the implementations of the abstract operations.

Given that x is an object, x' is the object before the operation is performed, S_j is the code which implements operation j, and I_a, C_{pre} and C_{post} are the invariant and the pre and post constraints of the abstract specification, the proof consists of the following three steps:

(1) Show that the data structures used in the implementation constitute a valid representation of the abstract concept, i.e.

$$I_{rep}(x) \rightarrow I_a(abs(x)).$$

(2) Show that each operation body satisfies its input and output constraints and preserves the representation invariant, i.e.

$$C_{in_j}(x) \ \& \ I_{rep}(x)\{S_j\}C_{out_j} \ \& \ I_{rep}(x).$$

(3) Establish the relationship between the implementation input and output constraints and the abstract pre and post constraints, i.e.

$$C_{pre_j}(abs(x)) \ \& \ I_{rep}(x) \rightarrow C_{in_j}(x)$$
$$C_{pre_j}(abs(x')) \ \& \ I_{rep}(x') \ \& \ C_{out_j}(x) \rightarrow C_{post}(abs(x)).$$

Examples of this type of proof can be found in the literature (e.g. [16]).

VIEWS AND SHARED DATA OBJECTS

A user does not interact directly with a data base, but instead interacts with a view of it. The view becomes in effect a virtual data base. A number of views of a data base will usually exist because a data base is shared, and different users may need to view the data in logically different ways since they are using the data base for different purposes. This situation is shown in Fig. 2.

In BASIS, a view is an abstraction which is determined by the set of transactions that can be performed by the class of users. These transactions are specific to the view of the data base with which the user interacts. Different views may then incorporate different subsets of objects, may have both nonoverlapping objects and objects in common, may import only certain rights to execute operations on objects, and may see the object they share involved in different relationships.

The view specification, like the object specification, includes an abstract image which lists the objects the view can access, an invariant which specifies the inter-object constraints, pre and post constraints on each transaction, imported rights, and exception-handling procedures.

For the most part, different classes of users are given different and nonoverlapping views that have a very small, and possibly empty, intersection of data objects. In cases where the views involve disjoint portions of the data, they may be specified and verified in the same manner as the schema objects.

However, if the views are allowed to manipulate shared objects (and not just copies of the same data), the views must agree, at least to some extent, on the semantics of the shared objects. Otherwise, integrity may be lost when one view alters an object in a way which makes the integrity constraints of another view no longer true. Proof procedures developed for verifying abstract data types cannot be applied without alterations since they assume that objects are not shared, that each program creates its own objects, and that the objects are destroyed when the program finishes executing.

There are two ways of ensuring this consistency—through the specification of a shared "intermediate view" or by methods for ensuring the consistency of separate abstractions.

Using the first method, a view or "composed object" is defined in the usual way. If another view needs to alter a shared object, it must do so by invoking transactions defined on the composed object. Thus, if a shared object d_1 is in some relationship with another object d_2, then this relationship (composed object) may be defined as a separate abstract object d_s where the relationship is specified in the abstract invariant of the specification of the composed object. All operations allowed on the composed object must, of course, be defined in the specification of the object, and thus, must preserve the invariant, i.e. the relationship. Views or abstractions which contain the composed object need not see it identically. It is possible to control how an object is shared by using access rights as described above. Thus one view may only have the right to invoke operations i and j on the shared object, while another may have the right to issue calls to operations j and k.

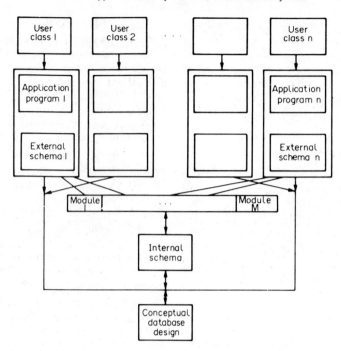

Fig. 2. Multilevel information system model.

A second way to ensure consistency between views involving shared data is to ensure that the implementations of the abstract specification are *compatible*, i.e. ensure the properties of the shared objects. The question then is what relationship must hold between the two implementations in order for the types to be considered compatible.

The implementation representation of an abstract object will consist of several variables $c_1, c_2, \ldots, c_n$ where $n > 0$ and is related to an abstract object, A, by the abstraction function such that $A = \mathrm{abs}(c_1, c_2, \ldots, c_n)$. The representation invariant, I_{rep}, defines the relationship between the variables $c_1, c_2, \ldots, c_n$ to ensure that they fall within the domain of abs. That is, I_{rep} is the characteristic function of the domain of abs:

$$\mathrm{domain(abs)} = \{c_1, c_2, \ldots, c_n ! I_{\mathrm{rep}}(c_1, c_2, \ldots c_n)\}.$$

If the same implementation participates in the construction of multiple views, then an abstraction function will be required for each view where the domain of each abs is the same (although their ranges may obviously differ), i.e.

$$\mathrm{domain(abs_1)} = \mathrm{domain(abs_2)} = \cdots = \mathrm{domain(abs_n)} = \{c_1, \ldots, c_n ! I_{\mathrm{rep}}(c_1, \ldots, c_n)\}.$$

If each abstract view has a different implementation, then each implementation must preserve the properties of and relationships among the shared variables. That is, the invariants must place the same constraints on the possible combinations of values that shared variables may take. Here shared variables must include not only the variables in the intersection of the domains of the abstraction functions, but also all variables which are related to these variables.

Formally, let k implementations share the objects $c_1, c_2, \ldots, c_n$ for $i, k > 0$. The k implementations will be said to be *compatible* if and only if the intersection of the domains of the abs function for each implementation is $\{c_1, \ldots, c_i ! I_{\mathrm{srep}}(c_1, \ldots, c_i)\}$ where I_{srep} is the characteristic function of the shared objects. For implementations which have no shared variables, the intersection will be empty, and the implementations will be trivially compatible.

In order to prove that several implementation are compatible, it is necessary to define an invariant I_{cs} which specifies the constraints on the shared object and to show that:

$$I_{cj}(c_1, \ldots, c_i) \rightarrow I_{cs}(c_1, \ldots, c_i)$$

for each implementation j.

As an example, assume that a relation student exists in the data base with domains $D = \{D_1, D_2, \ldots, D_n\}$, and that three views are defined on this relation:

(1) View 1 defined operations only on lower-division students, e.g.

$$I_{c1} = 0 \leq \#\mathrm{units} < 60 \ \& \ldots$$

(2) View 2 operates only on upper division students, e.g.

$$I_{c2} = 60 \leq \#\mathrm{units} \ \& \ldots$$

(3) View 3 sees all students but not all of the domains of the relation,

$$I_{c3} = 0 \leq \#\text{units} \ \& \ \ldots$$

To prove that the views are compatible, it is necessary to define the invariant of the relation "student"

$$I_{\text{stud}} = 0 \leq \#\text{units} \ \& \ \ldots$$

and then to show that I_{c1}, I_{c2}, and I_{c3} imply I_{stud}. If a new view which uses the relation student is added in the future, then it will be necessary only to show that the invariant of the added view implies I_{stud} in order to be sure that it is compatible with all other views.

Since the implementations of the operations preserve the implementation invariant I_{rep}, and thus the shared invariant I_{srep}, these operations must maintain the integrity of the shared object.

SUMMARY

BASIS is a design methodology for information systems based on formal behavioral specifications. All aspects of the system are specified using one uniform notation. This specification is machine processable, is useful for formal verification and for incorporating future modifications, and serves as documentation not only for the system designers and implementors, but for the users as well. The proposed methodology provides for the complete specification, verification, and enforcement of semantic integrity. Operations are pre-specified and pre-verified with assertions added for those constraints which cannot be proved to always hold.

Essentially, the semantic integrity of the data base is preserved by restricting the transactions to those which are meaningful and integrity-preserving. Even if the system is never formally verified, integrity constraints are associated with particular operations so that programmers are aware of them when implementing the abstract operations (hopefully increasing the likelihood that they are not violated) and ensuring that a minimum of constraints must be checked at execution time. Further, there is complete control over when the assertions are checked, thus providing the possibility of selective enforcement based on cost and need. Finally, proofs are broken down into a sequence of small, easy to manage steps, and when changes are made, only a small portion of the specification will be likely to require reverification. Since the user is unable to make use of any details of the implementation, the resulting user programs will probably also be easier to validate as correct, and changes to the implementation will not require revalidation of user programs.

BASIS has been extended to include the design of distributed information systems[13]. Current work is focusing on extending the specification to include the specification and modelling of concurrency controls and protocols[12].

REFERENCES

[1] V. D. Antonellis and B. Zonta: Modelling events in data base applications design. *Proc. 7th Int. Conf. on VLDB*, Cannes, pp. 23–31 (1981).

[2] D. M. Berry, The application of the formal development methodology to data base design and integrity verification. *Proc. Comput. Sci. Conf.*, Santiago, Chile (1981).

[3] T. De Marco: *Structured Analysis and System Specification*. Prentice-Hall, Englewood Cliffs, New Jersey (1979).

[4] H. Ehrig, H. J. Kreowski and H. Weber: Algebraic schemes for data base systems. *Proc. 4th Int. Conf. on VLDB*, Berlin, pp. 427–440 (1978).

[5] C. Gane and T. Sarson: *Structured Systems Analysis: Tools and Techniques*. Prentice-Hall, Englewood Cliffs, New Jersey (1979).

[6] M. M. Hammer and D. J. McLeod: Semantic integrity in a relational data base system. *Proc. Int. Conf. on VLDB*, Boston, pp. 25–47 (Sept. 1975).

[7] C. A. R. Hoare: Proof of correctness of data representation. *Acta Informatica* 1, pp. 271–281 (1972).

[8] B. K. Kahn: A method for describing information required by the database design process. *Proc. ACM SIGMOD Conf.*, pp. 53–64 (1976).

[9] L. Kerschberg, A. Klug and D. Tsichritzis: A taxonomy of data models, In *Modelling and Database Management Systems* (Edited by G. Nijssen) North-Holland, (1976).

[10] M. Leonard and B. T. Luong: Information systems design approach integrating data and transactions. *Proc. 7th Int. Conf. on VLDB*, Cannes, pp. 235–246 (1981).

[11] N. G. Leveson: Applying behavioral abstraction to information system design and integrity. Ph.D. Thesis, Computer Science Department, University of California Los Angeles, March 1980. (Also published as Technical Rep. 47, Laboratory of Medical Information Science, University of California San Francisco, 1980.)

[12] N. G. Leveson and R. R. Razouk: Behavioral modelling in the design of distributed information systems. *Proc. 2nd IEEE Comput. Sci. Conf.* Santiago, Chile, Aug. 1982.

[13] N. G. Leveson and A. I. Wasserman: Logical decentralization and semantic integrity in a distributed information system, In *Distributed Data Sharing Systems*, (Edited by R. P. van de Riet and W. Litwin) North Holland, Amsterdam, pp. 243–253 (1982).

[14] N. G. Leveson and A. I. Wasserman: A methodology for information systems design based on formal specifications. Submitted for publication.

[15] P. C. Lockemann, H. C. Mayr, W. H. Weil and W. H. Wohlleber: Data abstraction for database systems. *ACM Trans. on Database Systems* 4, 60–75 (1979).

[16] R. L. London, M. Shaw and W. A. Wulf: Abstraction and verification in Alphard: a symbol table example. In *ALPHARD: Form and Content* (Edited by M. Shaw) Springer Verlag, New York, pp. 161–190 (1981).

[17] J. Mylopoulos, P. A. Bernstein and H. K. T. Wong: A language facility for designing database-intensive applications. *ACM Trans. on Database Systems* 5, pp. 185–207 (1980).

[18] G. M. Nijssen, F. J. van Assche and J. J. Snijders: End-user tools for information systems requirements definition. In *Formal Models and Practical Tools for Information Systems Design*, (Edited by H. J. Schneider). North-Holland, Amsterdam, pp. 125–148 (1979).

[19] T. W. Olle, H. G. Sol and A. A. Verrijn-Stuart (Eds): *Information System Design Methodologies—A Comparative Review*. North Holland, Amsterdam (1982).

[20] P. Paolini: Abstract data types and data bases. Ph.D. Dissertation, Computer Science Department, University of California Los Angeles, (1981).

[21] D. T. Ross and K. Schoman: Structured analysis for requirements definition. *IEEE Trans. Software Engng*, **SE-3**, pp. 6–15 (1977).

[22] L. Rowe and K. A. Shoens: Data abstraction, views, and updates in RIGEL. *Proc. ACM SIGMOD Conf.*, Boston, pp. 71–81 (1979).

[23] H. Sakai: A method for defining information structures and transactions in conceptual schema design. *Proc. 7th Int. Conf. on VLDB*, Cannes, pp. 225–234 (1981).

[24] A. Sølvberg: A contribution to the definition of concepts for expressing users information systems requirements. *Proc. Int. Conf. on Entity-Relationship Approach to Systems Analysis and Design*, Los Angeles (Dec. 1979).

[25] D. C. Tsichritzis and F. H. Lochovsky: *Data Models*. Prentice-Hall, Englewood Cliffs, New Jersey (1981).

[26] R. P. van de Riet, M. L. Kersten and A. I. Wasserman: A module definition facility for access control in communicating data base systems. In *Distributed Data Sharing Systems*. (Edited by R. P. van de Riet and W. Litwin) North-Holland, Amsterdam, pp. 255–272 (1982).

[27] A. I. Wasserman: USE: A methodology for the design and development of interactive information systems. *Formal Models and Practical Tools for Information Systems Design* (Edited by H. J. Schneider). North Holland, Amsterdam, pp. 31–50 (1979).

[28] A. I. Wasserman: Information system design methodology: *J. Am. Soc. Information Sci.* **31**, 5–24 (1980).

[29] A. I. Wasserman *et al.*: Revised report on the programming language PLAIN. *ACM SIGPLAN Notices* **16**(5), 59–80 (1981).

[30] A. I. Wasserman: The user software engineering methodology—an overview. *Information System Design Methodologies—A Comparative Review* (Edited by T. W. Olle, H. G. Sol and A. A. Verrijn-Stuart). North Holland, Amsterdam, pp. 589–628 (1982).

[31] A. I. Wasserman and S. K. Stinson: A specification method for interactive information systems. *Proc. Specifications of Reliable Software*, Cambridge, MA, pp. 68–79 (April 1979).

[32] A. I. Wasserman, R. P. van de Riet, M. L. Kersten and N. G. Leveson: A formal, integrated approach to data and usage integrity in health information systems. *Data Protection in Health Information Systems*, (Edited by K. Sauter *et al.*). North Holland (1983).

[33] H. Weber: A software engineering view of data base systems. *Proc. 4th Int. Conf. on VLDB*. Berlin, pp. 36–51 (1978).

[34] W. A. Wulf, R. L. London and M. Shaw: An introduction to the construction and verification of Alphard programs. *IEEE Trans. on Software Engng*, **SE-2**, 263–265 (1976).

[35] S. B. Yao, S. B. Navathe and J. L. Weldon: An integrated approach for logical database design. *Proc. NYU Symp. on Database Design*, pp. 1–14 (May 1978).

[36] R. T. Yeh, N. Roussopoulos and P. Y. T. Chang: Systematic derivation of software requirements through structured analysis. Infotech State of the Art Report, *Data Design*, Infotech Limited, Maidenhead, England, pp. 87–106 (1980).

Part VII

Detailed Design Techniques

Detailed design is the activity that immediately precedes code production. At this stage, all of the details and decisions have to be made so that implementation can proceed in a straightforward way. To use the terms of DeRemer and Kron, detailed design deals with "programming-in-the-small," making decisions that typically affect only a single module.

Thus, detailed design involves selection of algorithms, selection of logical data structures, and evaluation of other design alternatives. The detailed design, as well as the architectural design, can be reviewed according to management guidelines (see Part VIII) to determine the quality of the design. One wants to make certain that an implementation of the detailed design will lead to a system that satisfies the functional specification.

The papers in this Part may be divided into two categories: techniques for expanding upon the detail of an architectural design using one of the architectural design techniques described in Part V or Part VI, and techniques for constructing architectural and detailed design concurrently. The first three papers fall into the first category, while the last three papers fit the second category.

A "program design language" is a programming language-like notation to describe the inputs, outputs, local data, and algorithm for a module. Such languages have been used informally for a long time and have been called metacode, Structured English, and other similar names. In general, a program design language expresses the structure of the system defined in architectural design, and permits additional details to be filled in. When the program design language for a system is completed, it can be reviewed, and used as a basis for coding.

PDL (Program Design Language), an instance of such a language, was developed by Caine, Farber, and Gordon in the mid-1970's. The language and its associated processor support the detailed design of a system prior to its being coded in PL/I. The processor is used to check the PDL for consistency of interfaces, as well as to produce reports on the design structure. The PDL language was designed to facilitate the transformation of PDL code to PL/I.

Such program design languages, even without a processor, have proved to be extremely successful for describing the logical flow of a program or program unit, and they have totally replaced traditional flowcharts in many organizations. The advantages cited for program design languages include ease of machine processing, readability, and ease of transformation to well-structured program code.

One can see that the module definitions and structure provided by a method such as Structured Design are well complemented by a program design language allowing the functions of each module to be more fully defined. Privitera's paper shows how this can be done in conjunction with the Ada programming language. His idea is that one can use Structured Design, and then use Ada both as a system design language and as an implementation language. He shows that Ada provides the concepts (especially *packages*) to represent the design.

Recent work with program design languages has linked them to data dictionaries and report writing tools. For example, the version of PDL described by Caine and Gordon has been superseded by a newer tool named PDL/81, which provides such capabilities.

Another alternative to traditional flowcharts is structured flowcharts. Rather than permitting unconstrained flow of control, a structured flowchart is limited to the control structures recommended for structured programming: composition, if-then-else, while-do, and call. These structured flowcharts, as developed by Nassi and Shneiderman, rely upon a graphical notation for describing program logic. Yoder and Schrag describe their successful experience with this technique.

The remaining three papers are less closely tied to specific methods for architectural design. For small problems, they can be used alone, yielding both the design decisions and executable code. In addition, they can be used to work out the details of part or all of a system that has been decomposed into a software architecture.

Michael Jackson's original design method, now termed JSP (Jackson Structured Programming) has gained widespread acceptance in both Europe and the United States. It is based on the idea that the structure of the system closely follows the structure of the problem domain, and it provides an algorithmic approach for mapping a set of input and output structures into a program structure, and then semi-automatically into code. While JSP was primarily intended for common commercial data processing applications, it has been used for a broad range of applications. It should be noted that the JSP method can be used either together with or independently of the JSD modelling ideas described in Part III.

Wirth's classic paper on stepwise refinement was one of the first papers to effectively make the point that program design and data design must occur jointly. Furthermore, gradual elaboration of detail allows the programmer to address one design decision at a time and to make certain that each successive refinement of the program maintains program correctness. This method is particularly appropriate for relatively small, well-defined problems (possibly part of larger systems), and it may be seen as an intuitive, top-down approach to program construction.

PDL—A tool for software design

by STEPHEN H. CAINE and E. KENT GORDON

Caine, Farber & Gordon, Inc.
Pasadena, California

INTRODUCTION

During the past several years, industry has seen an explosion in the cost of software production coupled with a decline in the quality and reliability of the results. A realization that structured programming, top-down design, and other changes in techniques can help has alerted the field to the importance of applying advanced design and programming methods to software production.[1,2]

For the past four years, Caine, Farber & Gordon, Inc. has used such advanced techniques as structured programming, top-down design and system implementation, centralized program production libraries, and egoless programming teams for all of its programming.[3-8] With these techniques we have achieved a level of productivity comparable to that recently reported by others employing similar techniques.

However, within the last year, we greatly refined these techniques, applying them to design as well as to programming. This has resulted in increased productivity, greatly decreased debugging effort, and clearly superior products. On recent complex projects we have achieved production rates, over the full development cycle, of 60-65 lines of finished code per man-day and computer utilization of less than 0.25 CPU hours per thousand lines of finished code. For comparison, these production rates are approximately half again better than our best efforts using just structured programming techniques and 4-6 times better than average industrial experience using classical techniques. Computer usage was four times smaller than our experience with just structured programming techniques and more than 10 times smaller than classical industrial averages.

As an example, consider the two CFG projects shown in Table 1. Project "A" is a major component of a seismic data processing system for oil exploration. It was produced using "classical" structured programming techniques and production rates compare favorably to other projects[3] which used similar techniques. Project "B" is a system for the automatic restructuring of Fortran programs.[9] It was developed using the latest CFG methods. Production rates were 50 percent better than for project "A" and the amount of computer time used in development was approximately one quarter of that used for the first project. In each case, a "line" of code was taken to be one 80-column source card with common data definitions counted only once. Both projects were developed using an IBM 370/158.

In order to achieve the results that we are currently experiencing, we have developed a comprehensive software production methodology which places its greatest emphasis on design. Before *any* code is written, a complete design is produced which contains:

- all external and internal interface definitions
- definitions of all error situations
- identification of all procedures
- identification of all procedure calls
- definition of all global data
- definition of all control blocks
- specification of the processing algorithms of all procedures

The design is produced and presented top-down and is oriented toward understandability by people. While in no sense is our design process automated, it is supported by a series of tools—both computerized and procedural.

This paper is not intended to present our complete design and implementation methodology. Rather, it discusses one of the design tools—the "Program Design Language" (PDL) and its computerized processor. Both of these have been in extensive use since the autumn of 1973.

THE PURPOSE OF PDL

PDL is designed for the production of structured designs in a top-down manner. It is a "pidgin" language in that it uses the vocabulary of one language (i.e., English) and the overall syntax of another (i.e., a structured programming language). In a sense, it can be thought of as "structured English."

While the use of pidgin languages is also advocated by others, we have taken the additional steps of imposing a degree of formalism on the language and supplying a processor for it. Input to the processor consists of control information plus designs for procedures (called "segments" in PDL). The output is a working design document which can, if desired, be photo-reduced and included in a project development workbook.

The output of the processor completely replaces flowcharts since PDL designs are easier to produce, easier to change, and easier to read than are designs presented in flowchart form.

TABLE 1—Production Comparisons

	PROJECT "A"	PROJECT "B"
DEVELOPMENT METHOD	CLASSICAL STRUCTURED	LATEST CFG
PROGRAMMING LANGUAGE	PL/I DIALECT	PL/I
SIZE OF PROGRAM (LINES)	32,000	27,000
SIZE OF TEAM	3–6	3–5
ELAPSED TIME (MONTHS)	9	6
LINES PER MAN-DAY	40	65
CPU HOURS PER 1000 LINES (IBM 370/158)	0.90	0.16

DESIGNING FOR PEOPLE IN PDL

Like a flowchart, and unlike a program, PDL can be written with whatever level of detail is appropriate to the problem at hand. A designer can start with a few pages giving the general structure of his system and finish, if necessary, with even more precision than would exist in the corresponding program.

In our experience, the purpose of a design is to communicate the designer's idea to other people—not to a computer. Figure 1 shows a sample design "segment" for a simple exchange sort. Note that we are *not* attempting to illustrate efficient sorting methods. Rather, having decided to use this particular sorting method, we wish to present the algorithm in a way that it can be easily comprehended. Given that the "DO UNTIL" construct represents a loop whose completion test occurs at the *end* of the loop, the operation of the algorithm is apparent. It is clearly better, from the viewpoint of understandability, than either the flowchart of Figure 2 or the translation of the algorithm into PL/I as shown in Figure 3.

A virtue of PDL is that a rough outline of an entire problem solution can be quickly constructed. This level of design can be easily understood by people other than the designer. Thus, criticisms, suggestions, and modifications can be quickly incorporated into the design, possibly resulting in complete rewrites of major sections. When the design has stabilized at this level, more detail can be added in successive passes through the design with decisions at each point affecting smaller and smaller areas.

```
SORT (TABLE, SIZE OF TABLE)

IF SIZE OF TABLE > 1
   DO UNTIL NO ITEMS WERE INTERCHANGED
      DO FOR EACH PAIR OF ITEMS IN TABLE (1-2, 2-
      3, 3-4, ETC.)
         IF FIRST ITEM OF PAIR > SECOND ITEM OF
         PAIR
            INTERCHANGE THE TWO ITEMS
         ENDIF
      ENDDO
   ENDDO
ENDIF
```

Figure 1—PDL design of a simple sorting algorithm

THE FORM OF A DESIGN IN PDL

A design produced in PDL consists of a number of "flow segments," each corresponding roughly to a procedure in the final implementation. A sample of a high-level flow segment from a large design is shown in Figure 4. If a statement in a segment references another flow segment,

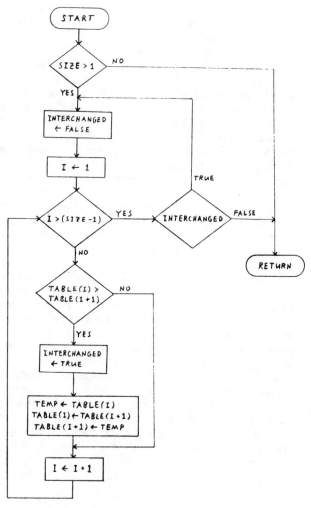

Figure 2—Flowchart for sorting algorithm of Figure 1

```
SORT:
  PROCEDURE(TABLE);
  DECLARE TABLE(*) FIXED BIN;
  DECLARE INTERCHANGED BIT(1);
  DECLARE TEMP FIXED BIN;
  IF DIM(TABLE,1) > 1 THEN
    DO;
      INTERCHANGED = '1'B;
      DO WHILE (INTERCHANGED);
        INTERCHANGED = '0'B;
        DO I = LBOUND(TABLE,1) TO
        HBOUND(TABLE,1)-1;
          IF TABLE(I)>TABLE(I+1) THEN
            DO;
              INTERCHANGED = '1'B;
              TEMP = TABLE(I);
              TABLE(I) = TABLE(I+1);
              TABLE(I+1) = TEMP;
            END;
        END;
      END;
    END;
END SORT;
```

Figure 3—PL/I procedure for sorting algorithm

the page number of the referenced segment is shown to the left of the referencing statement. A sample low-level segment is shown in Figure 5.

The statements which compose a flow segment are entered in free form. The PDL processor automatically underlines keywords, indents statements to correspond to structure nesting levels, and provides automatic continuation from line to line.

Design information may also be entered in "text seg-

ments." These contain purely textual information such as commentary, data formats, assumptions, and constraints.

The document output by the PDL processor is in a form ready for photo-reduction and publication. It contains:

- a cover page giving the design title, data, and processor identification
- a table of contents (Figure 6)
- the body of the design, consisting of flow segments and text segments
- a "reference tree" showing how segment references are nested (Figure 7)
- a cross-reference listing showing the page and line number at which each segment is referenced (Figure 8)

DESIGN CONSTRUCTS

What goes into a design segment is generally at the discretion of the designer. In choosing the form of presentation, he is guided by a compendium of style which has been developed through extensive experience. However, the language and the processor have been defined to encourage and support design constructs which relate directly to the constructs of structured coding. The two primary constructs are the IF and the DO.

The IF construct

The IF construct provides the means for indicating conditional execution. It corresponds to the classical IF ... THEN ... ELSE construct of Algol-60[10] and PL/I,

```
CFG, INC.    AIL CEVELCPMENT WCRKBCCK (14.90)                                    06 JUL 74   PAGE 39
             EXPRESSION AND REFERENCE PRCCESSING


       PRCCESS EXPRESSICN


  REF
  PAGE ******************************************************************************************************
       *                                                                                                   *
       *  1    PUSH "SCE" (START CF EXPRESSICN) CNTC CPERATOR STACK                                         *
  40 * 2      PRCCESS OPERANC                                                                               *
       *  3    DC WHILE NEXT TOKEN IS AN CPERATCR                                                           *
       *  4      DO WHILE OPERATCR IS NOT SAME AS CPERATCR CN TCF CF OPERATOR STACK AND ITS PRECEDENCE IS LESS  *
       *           THAN OR ECUAL TC PRECECENCE CF CPERATCR CN THE TOP OF THE OPERATOR STACK                 *
  42 * 5        BUILD TOP NCCE                                                                              *
       *  6        PCP OPERATOR STACK                                                                       *
       *  7      ENDDO                                                                                      *
       *  8    IF NEW OPERATOR IS SAME AS TCP OPERATCR CN CPERATCR STACK                                    *
       *  9        INCREMENT OPERAND CCUNT IN TCF CF CPERATCR STACK BY CNE                                  *
       * 10    ELSE                                                                                         *
       * 11        PUSH NEW OPERATOR ANC OPERAND CCUNT CF 2 CNTC OPERATCR STACK                             *
       * 12    ENDIF                                                                                        *
  40 * 13     PROCESS OPERANC                                                                               *
       * 14    ENDDO                                                                                        *
       * 15    DO WHILE TCP OF OPERATOR STACK IS NCT "SCE"                                                  *
  42 * 16       BUILD TGP NODE                                                                              *
       * 17       POP CPERATOR STACK                                                                        *
       * 18    ENDDO                                                                                        *
       * 19    PCP OPERATOR STACK                                                                           *
       * 20    (TCP OF OPERANC STACK CCNTAINS TCP NCCE IN EXPRESSION)                                       *
       *                                                                                                   *
       ******************************************************************************************************
```

Figure 4—Sample of a high-level PDL flow segment

```
           AVERAGE OVER POINTS (RADIUS)

  REF
  PAGE  ***************************************************************************************
        *                                                                                    *
        *    1      IF DEBUGGING                                                              *
  29  *  2         START LINE (CURRENT CYCLE)                                                 *
  28  *  3         PRINT POINTS IN BUFFER (CURRENT BUFFER)                                    *
        *    4      ENDIF                                                                     *
        *    5      POINTS <- 0                                                               *
        *    6      SX <- 0                                                                   *
        *    7      SY <- 0                                                                   *
        *    8      BUFFER <- PREVIOUS OF PREVIOUS BUFFER                                     *
        *    9      DO FOR 5 BUFFERS                                                          *
  22  *  10         MOVE GOOD POINTS TO WORK BUFFER (BUFFER,RADIUS)                           *
        *   11         IF DEBUGGING                                                           *
  28  *  12            PRINT POINTS IN BUFFER (WORK BUFFER)                                   *
        *   13         ENDIF                                                                  *
        *   14         IF POINT COUNT OF WORK BUFFER > 0                                      *
        *   15            DO FOR POINTS IN WORK BUFFER                                        *
        *   16               ADD X TO SX                                                      *
        *   17               ADD Y TO SY                                                      *
        *   18            ENDDO                                                               *
        *   19            ADD POINT COUNT OF WORK BUFFER TO POINTS                            *
        *   20         ENDIF                                                                  *
        *   21         BUFFER <- NEXT BUFFER                                                  *
        *   22      ENDDO                                                                     *
        *   23      IF POINTS > 0                                                             *
        *   24         AX <- SX/POINTS                                                        *
        *   25         AY <- SY/POINTS                                                        *
        *   26      ELSE (NO DATA FOR POINT)                                                  *
        *   27         AX <- NEGATIVE                                                         *
        *   28         AY <- 0                                                                *
        *   29      ENDIF                                                                     *
        *                                                                                    *
        ***************************************************************************************
```

Figure 5—Sample low-level PDL flow segment

augmented by the ELSEIF of languages such as Algol-68.[11] The latter is used to prevent excessive indentation levels when cascaded tests are used.

The general form of the construct is shown in Figure 9. Any number (including zero) ELSEIF's are allowed and at most one ELSE is allowed.

The DO construct

This construct is used to indicate repeated execution and for case selection. The reasons for the dual use of this construct are historic in nature and closely map several of the in-house implementation languages we frequently use. It may be effectively argued that a separate construct for case selection would be better.

The iterative DO is indicated by:

> DO iteration criteria
> > one or more statements
> ENDDO

The "iteration criteria" can be chosen to suit the problem. As always, bias toward human understandability is preferred. Statements such as:

DO WHILE THERE ARE INPUT RECORDS
DO UNTIL "END" STATEMENT HAS BEEN

PROCESSED
DO FOR EACH ITEM IN THE LIST EXCEPT
THE LAST ONE

occur frequently in actual designs.

Our experience, and that of others,[7] has shown that a provision for premature exit from a loop and premature repetition of a loop are frequently useful. To accomplish this, we take the statement

> UNDO

to mean that control is to pass to the point following the ENDDO of the loop. Likewise,

> CYCLE

is taken to mean that control is to pass to the loop termination test.

Since we may wish that an UNDO or CYCLE apply to an outer loop in a nest of loops, any DO may be labelled and the label may be placed after the UNDO or CYCLE.

Case selection is indicated by

> DO CASE selection criteria

Again, we advocate the use of understandable selection criteria such as

DO CASE OF TRANSACTION TYPE
DO CASE OPERATOR TYPE
DO CASE OF CONTROL CARD VERB

Generally, we use labels in the body of the DO to indicate where control passes for each case. This is illustrated in Figure 10.

FUTURE DIRECTIONS

The results we have achieved with PDL have exceeded our original expectations. However, it is clear that further development is both possible and desirable. The areas which we are currently exploring include:

- *handling of data*: The current PDL presents a procedural design—a design of control flow and processing actions. It would be very desirable to have a similar mechanism for the design of data structures and data flow. A method for integrating the data and procedural designs and performing mutual cross-referencing would be very powerful, indeed.
- *interactive versions*: the current PDL processor is

STOW

LN	DEF	SEGMENT
1	4	STOW
2	11	SET DEFAULTS
3	35	FIND STARTING SECTOR
4	6	WRITE ON TAPE
5	38	CONVERT TO TANK ID
6	19	BUILD PROCESSED DATA ARRAY
7	24	INITIALIZE INPUT BUFFERS
8	31	GET POINTS
9	34	GET BATCH
10	36	READ DISK
11	32	MOVE AND COUNT POINTS
12	26	MOVE TO BUFFER
13	20	PROCESS A POINT
14	21	AVERAGE OVER POINTS
15	29	START LINE
16	28	PRINT POINTS IN BUFFER
17	22	MOVE GOOD POINTS TO WORK BUFFER
18	28	PRINT POINTS IN BUFFER
19	25	ADVANCE INPUT BUFFERS
20	31	GET POINTS
21	34	GET BATCH
22	36	READ DISK
23	32	MOVE AND COUNT POINTS
24	26	MOVE TO BUFFER
25	17	BUILD COMPRESSED DATA ARRAY
26	10	DISPLAY COMPRESSED POINTS
27	5	EXECUTE A COMMAND
28	6	WRITE ON TAPE
29	38	CONVERT TO TANK ID
30	19	BUILD PROCESSED DATA ARRAY
31	24	INITIALIZE INPUT BUFFERS
32	31	GET POINTS
33	34	GET BATCH
34	36	READ DISK
35	32	MOVE AND COUNT POINTS
36	26	MOVE TO BUFFER
37	20	PROCESS A POINT
38	21	AVERAGE OVER POINTS
39	29	START LINE
40	28	PRINT POINTS IN BUFFER
41	22	MOVE GOOD POINTS TO WORK BUFFER
42	28	PRINT POINTS IN BUFFER
43	25	ADVANCE INPUT BUFFERS
44	31	GET POINTS
45	34	GET BATCH
46	36	READ DISK
47	32	MOVE AND COUNT POINTS
48	26	MOVE TO BUFFER

Figure 7—Sample of a segment reference tree

batch oriented. The ability to compose and, more importantly, to modify a design on-line in a manner specifically planned for interactive use would be of great assistance. This would be particularly advantageous during the early stages of a project when design changes are often frequent and extensive.

- *total design system*: an integrated computer system for software design, such as the DES system of Professor R. M. Graham,[12] is a natural outgrowth of our work with PDL. Such a system would act as an information management system maintaining a data base of designs. Designs could be entered and modified; questions about a design and the inter-relations of its parts could be asked and answered; reports on design status and completeness could be prepared. Provision for simulation of a design for performance estimation and a mechanism for transition from design to code are also important.

CONCLUSIONS

In the autumn of 1973, we integrated the use of PDL and its processor into our software design and implementation methodology. Since then, it has been used on a number of

TABLE OF CONTENTS

Figure 6—Sample table of contents from a PDL design

489

```
CFG, INC.-  AIL DEVELOPMENT WORKBOOK (20.90)
            INDEX TO GROUPS AND SEGMENTS

     3   GP   MAIN PHASE FLOW

     8   SG   MAKE SUCCESSOR EDGE
                  7:08    7:11    7:19

    31   SG   MARK LOOP ENTRY BLOCKS
                 30:02

    39   SG   MARK LOOP MEMBERSHIP
                 37:13

    32   SG   MARK ONE LOOP ENTRY BLOCK
                 31:13

     4   SG   OPTIMIZE

    54   SG   PERFORM BACKWARD MOVEMENT
                 37:17

    45   SG   PERFORM LOCAL CSE ELIMINATION
                 44:01

    36   SG   PERFORM TRANSFORMATIONS
                  4:06

    47   SG   PROCESS ASSIGNMENT FOR CSE
                 45:07   51:10   52:16

    48   SG   PROCESS CALL FOR CSE
                 45:09   51:12   52:18

    46   SG   PROCESS COMPUTATIONAL TRIPLE FOR CSE
                 45:05

    17   SG   PROCESS FETCH INFORMATION
                 16:05   16:08   16:10   16:12   16:13   16:15   16:18

    18   SG   PROCESS STORE INFORMATION
                 16:06

    56   SG   REDUCE STRENGTH
                 37:18

    65   SG   REDUCE STRENGTH OF ONE TRIPLE
                 56:07

    27   SG   RESOLVE TENTATIVE BACK DOMINATORS
                 25:09

    55   GP   STRENGTH REDUCTION PART OF TRANSFORMATIONS SUBPHASE

    22   SG   TRACE CALLS
                  4:03

    23   SG   TRACE ONE NODE
```

Figure 8—Part of an index to a design

projects of varying sizes. The results have been comparable to those discussed earlier.

PDL is not a "panacea" and it is certainly possible to produce bad designs using it. However, we have found that our designers and programmers quickly learn to use PDL effectively. Its emphasis on designing for people provides a high degree of confidence in the correctness of the design. In our experience, it is almost impossible to "wave your hands" in PDL. If a designer doesn't really yet see how to solve a particular problem, he can't just gloss over it

```
IF condition
  one or more statements
ELSEIF condition
  one or more statements
  .
  .
  .
ELSEIF condition
  one or more statements
ELSE
  one or more statements
ENDIF
```

Figure 9—General form of IF construct

```
    DO CASE OF TRANSACTION TYPE
ADD:
      CREATE INITIAL RECORD
DELETE:
      IF DELETION IS AUTHORIZED
        CREATE DELETION RECORD
      ELSE
        ISSUE ERROR MESSAGE
      ENDIF
CHANGE:
      INCREMENT CHANGE COUNT
      CREATE DELETION RECORD
"OTHER":
      ISSUE ERROR MESSAGE
    ENDO
```

Figure 10—Example of DO CASE construct

without the resulting design gap being readily apparent to a reader of the design. This, plus the basic readability of a PDL design, means that clients, management, and team members can both understand the proposed solution and gauge its degree of completeness.

We have also found that PDL works equally well for large and small projects. Because it is so easy to use, persons starting to work on even a "quick and dirty" utility will first sketch out a solution in PDL. In the past, such programs were usually written with little or no design preceding the actual coding.

REFERENCES

1. Boehm, B. W., "Software and its Impact: A Quantitative Assessment," *Datamation*, May 1973, pp. 48-59.
2. Goldberg, J., (editor), *Proceedings of a Symposium on the High Cost of Software*, Stanford Research Institute, 1973.
3. Baker, F. T., "Chief Programmer Team Management of Production Programming," *IBM Sys. J.*, Vol. 11, No. 1, 1972, pp. 56-73.
4. Bohm, C. and G. Jacopini, "Flow Diagrams, Turing Machines and Languages With Only Two Formation Rules," *Comm. ACM*, May 1966, pp. 366-371.
5. Dijkstra, E., "GO TO Statements Considered Harmful," *Comm. ACM*, March 1968, pp. 147-148.
6. Mills, Harlan D., "On the Development of Large Reliable Programs," *IEEE Symp. Computer Software Reliability*, 1973, pp. 155-159.
7. Peterson, W. W., T. Kasami and N. Tokura, "On the Capabilities of WHILE, REPEAT and EXIT Statements," *Comm. ACM*, August 1973, pp. 503-512.
8. Stevens, W. P., G. J. Myers and L. L. Constantine, "Structured Design," *IBM Sys. J.*, Vol. 13, No. 2, 1974, pp. 115-139.
9. De Balbine, G., *Better Manpower Utilization Using Automatic Restructuring* Caine, Farber & Gordon, Inc., 1974 (in publication).
10. Naur, P. et al., "Report on the Algorithmic Language ALGOL 60," *Comm. ACM*, May 1960, pp. 299-314.
11. Van Wijngaarden, A. et al., "Report on the Algorithmic Language ALGOL 68," *Numerische Mathematik*, 14, 1969, pp. 79-218.
12. Graham, R. M., G. J. Clancy and D. B. Devaney, "A Software Design and Evaluation System," *Comm. ACM*, February 1973, pp. 110-116.

ADA DESIGN LANGUAGE FOR THE STRUCTURED DESIGN METHODOLOGY

Dr. J. P. Privitera

Ford Aerospace and Communications Corporation

ABSTRACT

It is shown how Ada can be used to good advantage as a design language in conjunction with the structured analysis and design methodology.

1. INTRODUCTION

One of the uses envisioned for Ada is as a *system design language*, a language in which preliminary sketches of a system can be expressed, checked, and refined. Since Ada is so new and so little tested in this capacity, several questions arise concerning this proposed usage:

- At which stage in the progression from requirements to detailed design should Ada enter the design process?

- How adequate are Ada program units for expressing the properties of typical system modules?

- What design aids (e.g.s, stylistic conventions, automated tools) might be used with Ada to better suit it for use as a design language?

- Does the process of refinement change Ada designs? Would it be simply a matter of filling in more and more details, or are structural changes likely to occur?

The questions have been phrased as if there were one answer for each of them, but answers will vary from methodology to methodology and from system design to system design. To take only one example, Ada program units may be fine for expressing the kind of system modules one gets via methodology X, but inappropriate for ones derived via methodology Y. Or, keeping the methodology fixed, we may find that Ada program units express well the modules in real time systems, but poorly express modules in business data processing systems.

1.1 Purpose and Results of the Paper

The **purpose** of this paper is to demonstrate that the structured analysis and design methodology (SADM) is compatible with both Ada (used as a design language) and problems forming an important part of Ada's application domain, namely, real time systems. In so demonstrating, each of the questions above will be answered *for this methodology.*

Let us clarify what we mean by asserting that SADM is compatible with Ada used as a design language.

1. The first point to clarify is the combination in which SADM and Ada (the design language) are claimed to be compatible. We shall argue that the proper arrangement of Ada with a design methodology is to have Ada *express* designs generated via the methodology.

2. By 'compatible' we mean that SADM produces system designs that make good use of Ada's most advanced features, and that Ada expresses well the sorts of designs one gets from SADM.

3. We mean 'compatible in their present forms'. We do not advocate any drastic changes either to SADM or to Ada. The modifications we propose for SADM amount to changes in viewpoint, and those we propose for Ada are also minimal, being confined to some commenting conventions and the addition of some useful Ada-definable entities.

4. To demonstrate compatibility we offer an annotated example of a real time system designed using SADM and expressed in Ada.

In showing the compatibility of Ada and SADM, there are two traps to be avoided. The first is triviality. The progression

1. System Requirements (from a customer)

2. Structured Analysis (products: data flow diagrams, data dictionary, etc.)

3. Structured Design (product: structure chart)

4. PDL (product: pseudocode)

5. Implementation (product: running system)

is well known. A trivial way that Ada could be used with SADM is to substitute it for a PDL. This would make use of the Algol subset of Ada, but little more.

We shall show how to make the progression

1. Requirements

2. Structured Analysis

3. Structured Design

4. Ada

5. Implementation

in such a way that Ada's modern features are used.

The second trap is irrelevance. It is well known that Ada can be used to express data flow diagrams. Thus, it may be worthwhile to skip the design phase of structured analysis and design and go from data flow diagrams directly to Ada, thereby making structured analysis (SA) a design methodology in its own right. We shall show that the structured design (SD) phase *can* be skipped, but also that there are good reasons not to.

1.2 The Example

In September of 1981 the British Department of Industry issued the *Report on the Study of an Ada Based System Development Methodology* [2], the purpose of which was to give guidance to early practitioners of system design in Ada. The study examined in depth four system development methodologies from the point of view of their suitability for use in conjunction with Ada. To provide a basis for comparison, each of the four methodologies was applied to the same problem, that of designing a (simplified) aircraft monitoring system. We examine this same example, adding our perspectives to those of the participants in the *Study*.

1.3 Outline of the Paper

The rest of the paper is structured as follows. Numbers refer to section numbers.

2 Discusses in general terms the project of fitting Ada and a methodology together.

3 Overview of the relevant features of Ada, SA, and SD.

4 Discusses how Ada could be used to express designs derived via the SA methodology (i.e., data flow diagrams).

''Ada Design Language for the Structured Design Methodology'' by J.P. Privitera from *Proceedings of the AdaTEC Conference,* October 1982, pages 76–90. Copyright © 1982, Association for Computing Machinery, Inc., reprinted by permissions.

5 Discusses how Ada could be used to express designs derived via the SD methodology (i.e., structure charts).
6 Introduces the aircraft monitoring system example.
7 Applies SA to the example.
8 Applies SD to the example.
9 Expresses the design from section 8 in Ada.
10 Conclusions.

2. COMBINING ADA WITH METHODOLOGIES

The purpose of this section is to answer the questions,

- Why is it desirable to combine Ada with a methodology?

- What are the issues to be addressed if we do?

- Why combine Ada with the structured methodologies?

2.1 Why Combine Ada With A Methodology?

Ada includes many features for programming-in-the-large. One may speculate that Ada might be all that is required for system design or, in other words, that Ada is, or nearly is, a methodology in its own right.

In our experience, Ada does not satisfy the requirements of a methodology. It certainly provides no insight on how problems are to be analyzed and, while there is guidance of a sort in the desire to use Ada's system structuring features effectively, Ada alone says nothing about *how* to structure a system hierarchically, only that hierarchy can be expressed; it says nothing about *where* we should look to find our system modules, only that, once found, they may be conveniently written as program units; and it says nothing about *what* parts of a module belong in its interface and what parts in its implementation, only that, once identified, these parts can be kept separate.

2.2 What are the Issues?

Assume that you want to join Ada to methodology X.

- Where do you fit Ada in the X design process?

- How can you judge if the union is successful?

We will answer the first question for the structured methodologies, but only after gaining some experience with a worked example (see section 10.2). The first question is addressed now.

2.2.1 Criteria for Success. Suppose that methodology X has some notation for expressing system designs (e.g., data flow diagrams). Let D be a design expressed in the notation.

Informational Equivalence. It should be possible to express in Ada all and only the information present in D. One should not be forced to delete information present in D, as this is obviously wasteful, but neither should one be forced to add information to D, since this means making decisions that one might rather defer.

Respecting the Design. The Ada representation of D should respect D's structure. Those portions of modules identified by X as belonging to interfaces should go in program unit specifications; those portions that X relegates to implementations should be put in program unit bodies.

Caveats. How seriously should we take these strictures? There are situations where a design notation (e.g., data flow diagrams, see section 4.1.3) may not allow one to express all one knows about a system. In such a situation it would be silly to refrain from expressing what one knows in Ada just to copy a deficient design. We do not advocate slavishly copying designs in Ada down to the last detail.

Rather, what we do argue is that there should be a set of heuristics to aid one in translating from the design notation (e.g., structure charts) into Ada, whether or not one makes use of these heuristics very often, for three reasons:

- The existence of a uniform way to translate from a design notation into Ada opens the possibility of machine translation.

- Large systems will be built by teams of programmers at varying levels of experience both with the design methodology and with Ada. For novices in one or both areas, it is useful to have simple

rules to follow as they gain experience.

- Design reviews are made much easier if there is a close and uniform correspondence between the original design notation and the Ada expression of the design.

2.3 Ada and the Structured Methodologies

Our concern is not with arbitrary methodologies X, Y, or Z, but with the 'structured methodologies', structured analysis (SA) and structured design (SD). These methodologies are well suited for use with Ada since they are pictorial where Ada is formal. Their strengths lie in the ability to express informal and intuitive ideas about a system in a terse but readily understandable way. In contrast, part of Ada's strength as a design language lies in providing a formal notation for expressing designs, one that can be subjected to mechanical checks. Ada and the structured methodologies thus complement each other.

When we combine Ada with SA and SD in sections 4 and 5, respectively, informational equivalence will be preserved and design structure respected.

3. DESIGN FEATURES OF ADA AND THE METHODOLOGIES

This section summarizes the features of Ada and the structured methodologies that are pertinent to using them in conjunction.

3.1 Ada Design Features

Ada was designed to incorporate the best software engineering research of the late 1960s and the 1970s. Issues such as strong typing, encapsulation, concurrency, abstract data types, separation of concerns (e.g., specificification from implementation, levels of detail at the appropriate level of abstraction), and many others find concrete embodiment in the syntax and semantics of Ada. We assume that the reader is familiar with these concepts.

In the following subsections we provide a brief discussion of those Ada design features that have special relevance to this paper.

3.1.1 Program Units in Ada. There are three kinds of program units in Ada: packages, tasks, and subprograms. Each has a distinct purpose, but there are some important common aspects. In all three cases, there is a distinction between the specification of the unit, and its implementation. The syntax and semantics of a specification varies depending upon which type of program unit one is dealing with (and likewise for an implementation). Nonetheless, the general purpose of a specification of any type of program unit is to describe the interface presented by that unit to the external environment.

Various stylized uses of packages can be employed to utilize different software engineering design techniques. Examples are abstract data types (described further below), finite state machines, factorization of shared definitions, and software components used as building blocks.

The implementation of the three types of program units specify the details of how the visible interface of the specification is achieved. For subprograms, the implementation provides the algorithmic details of how the subprogram realizes its required behavior. For tasks, the implementation provides various 'accept' statements corresponding to the 'entry' statements of the specification. The combinatation of the task body being at an accept statement, and some outside caller of the task having invoked an entry call, is required for task rendezvous to occur. For packages, the implementation provides further detail about the entities mentioned in the package specifications.

3.1.2 Types in Ada. A type in Ada characterizes a set of values that a variable of that type may assume, and a set of operations applicable to the values. The use of Ada's typing features allows the designer to impose structuring or partitioning on a problem space, preventing the inadvertent mixing of apples and oranges, such as adding together a telephone number with a social security number.

3.1.3 Abstract Data Types. By using the package constructs in a well-defined way, the designer can specify various types of objects and the operations allowable on those objects, without having to worry that the particular *representation* of those objects will be destroyed by outside users. For example, the designer can specify a symbol table as an abstract data type, and can specify the (parameterized) operations allowable on any particular symbol table. Such operations would normally include making an entry in the symbol table, looking up a key in the symbol table, checking if the table if full, etc.

By making available only the above sorts of operations on symbol tables, the designer does not have to worry that users of the symbol table package will inadvertently (or perhaps deliberately, through a misguided sense of optimization) exploit some coincidental feature of the representation of the symbol table.

3.2 Deferred Decisions

In design, and even coding, there are often many decisions that one would like to postpone. This section describes some conventions that allow decisions to be deferred and yet still produce legal Ada. They all add certain 'TBD' declarations to the package STANDARD (hence making them globally visible).

What kinds of decisions are commonly deferred? We present the kinds of decisions we found it useful to defer in the design example.

Types. Often one doesn't want to write out the entire definition of a type, but instead let it be represented by just its name. If TYPE__TBD were the name of some private type added to STANDARD we can simply declare

    type T **is new** TYPE__TBD;

for a type T that will be refined later.

Assignments. One often wants to show that a variable is being assigned a new value but not specify what that value is. If the declaration

    VALUE__TBD : TYPE__TBD;

exists in STANDARD, then we can legally write

    X := VALUE__TBD;

in Ada designs, with appropriate comments, as long as the type of X is a type derived from TYPE__TBD, or is TYPE__TBD itself.

Often, however, the type of X is known and is not derived from TYPE__TBD. To handle these cases we can add an overloaded function, still called VALUE__TBD, of every introduced type, to STANDARD.

Processing. It is often preferable to describe processing by a comment, rather than give its Ada statements, but nevertheless leave a placeholder for the statements to be filled in. If the declaration

    procedure PROCESSING__TBD;

is added to STANDARD, then we can legally write

    PROCESSING__TBD;

in Ada designs, with appropriate comments.

Addresses. We found it useful to defer the decision of what address to use for a hardware interrupt. If

    ADDRESS__TBD : INTEGER;

were added to STANDARD we could legally write

    task INTERRUPT__HANDLER **is**
      entry INTERRUPT;
      for INTERRUPT
        use at ADDRESS__TBD;
      end INTERRUPT__HANDLER;

for example.

3.3 Annotations

Devices for expressing deferred decisions are used when Ada would normally require us to express more than we actually know. The opposite situation can also occur: we may know more than Ada allows us to express, or at least express conveniently. In these situations we usually rely upon comments. However, there are situations that recur with such regularity that they should be handled by uniform methods.

These methods employ structured Ada comments, called *annotations*, that could have significance to an Ada design language processor (though obviously not to an Ada compiler).

For example, requirements tracing is an important part of design validation, but Ada includes no mechanism for relating system modules to the requirements they are meant to satisfy. If we had a 'requirements' annotation, to be used as in

package P
-- **req** 12, 46, 80;
is
    -- specification of P
end P;

(where requirements are assumed to have been numbered), then requirements tracing could be made accessible to automated design aids.

3.3.1 Implementing the Additions to Ada. We have already explained how the TBD mechanisms could be implemented. Annotations are Ada comments, of course, but they can be made recognizable to an Ada design language processor either by the use of reserved keywords, as we have shown here, or by special delimiters. '{' and '}' are used for this purpose in Ford Aerospace's 'Ada Design Language' [3], which also implements the TBD mechanisms.

3.4 The Structured Methods in Overview

In recent years several methodologies for structuring the design process have emerged in the literature. This paper is concerned with two of them, 'structured analysis' (SA) and 'structured design' (SD). Yourdon and Constantine [5] demonstrate that there is much to be gained by using these two methodologies together, and they refer to the composite methodology as 'structured analysis and design' (SADM). For our purposes, it is convenient to distinguish between the two. Before giving separate descriptions of each we will dwell briefly on an important feature they share.

3.4.1 Black Box Modularity. Both SA and SD represent systems in terms of 'black box modules', that is, entities which are characterized by

- Interface: the externally visible behavior of a module; *what* services it provides to its users.

and

- Implementation: the means by which a module's behavior is determined; *how* it provides its services.

The similarity to Ada is obvious. However, the specifics of what belongs in a module interface and what belongs in a module implementation differ from structured analysis to structured design to Ada.

3.5 Structured Analysis

Structured analysis evolved out of the analysis of information flow in typical office situations. It is a technique of describing pictorially the flow of information between a collection of separate 'information processors'. Structured analysis expresses the flow of information between the processors by a data flow diagram (DFD), a diagram comprising 'bubbles' which represent the information processors, and labeled arrows between them identifying the type of information flowing from one bubble to another.

Data flow diagrams have since found widespread acceptance in a variety of design situations. They provide a number of features that are pleasing and convenient in a design methodology. First, the data flow diagrams are pictures, and it is, humanly speaking, much pleasanter and easier to deal with a picture, than it is to deal with a complex, if precise description, expressed in textual form. Second, data flow diagrams express inherent concurrency in a problem in a natural manner. The bubbles in a data flow diagram are most conveniently thought of as concurrent information processors working asynchronously. Thus, data flow diagrams have been found to be useful in the design of real time systems such as those which are of interest to the defense contractor community. Finally, data flow diagrams are informal. This can be regarded as a strength or a weakness. If this feature is not abused, a data flow diagram can sketch out the essential solution of a problem without cluttering it up with details. On the other hand, if abused, it is possible to elide many important factors in a design and come up with an oversimplified view of a problem.

Here is a brief dictionary of the most important DFD entities we will encounter.

bubbles are places where data is processed. These are the modules of SA.

boxes are data sources or sinks. Think of boxes as special sorts of bubbles, ones where data is created *ex nihilo* or destroyed, as the case may be.

arrows are data flows. An arrow's label names the type of data that flows across the arrow.

open boxes are data stores.

the data dictionary is where the data types labeling the arrows are defined.

the mini-specs are where the functions of nonrefinable bubbles are defined.

Bubbles, arrows, etc. are the atomic building blocks of data flow diagrams. From the opposite perspective, DFD's have five global properties:

Data Locality. In a data flow diagram a given data type will usually have significance over a very small collection of contiguous bubbles. In fact, for a data type T in a data flow diagram, there can often be found one bubble B such that either T only labels arrows entering B, or T only labels arrows leaving B. (All the data flows of Figure 5 provide examples of this phenomenon.) There is no law that says this must be so, but good design practice tends to encapsulate decisions (in this case, the decision about how to define a type), in single modules.

Black Box Modularity. A bubble is a black box module, so it has a visible interface and an invisible (to its users) implementation. The interface makes visible:

1. The types of data imported to the bubble.

2. The types of data exported from the bubble.

3. The relation between the imported data and the exported data.

The black box hides the mechanism by which the imported data is transformed into the exported data, but details about the bubble implementation can be found (by the implementor) in two places:

- In the data flow diagrams that refine complex bubbles.

- In the mini-specs of the bubbles that will not be further refined.

Connections. The way bubbles are connected is quite explicit, there being a connection between two bubbles if an arrow joins them.

Nonprocedurality. In a data flow diagram the movement of data is nonprocedural; the diagram does not express the flow of control. The absence of control flow can be a definite advantage since data flow diagrams are typically produced at a stage in the design process when control considerations are premature.

Concurrency. Data flows are conceptually concurrent.

3.6 Structured Design

While data flow diagrams came a long way towards representing the information flow between information processors as a solution to a design problem, the implementation of a data flow diagram in sequential computers was still unsolved. Structured design made up for this lack. It enabled a designer to prepare the solution of the information flow problem for computer implementation in a sequential language.

In the process of structured design, the solution to an information flow problem is expressed as a structure chart, essentially a call-graph of active procedures which are hierarchically arranged. Any procedure in the structure chart is represented as a box which calls procedures "below" it to provide it with certain services, and is called by procedures above it providing certain services. The information flowing along a procedure call is clearly identified in the structure chart.

The structure chart also has much to recommend as a design notation. It too is a pictorial solution to the design problem. Furthermore, it is straightforward to implement a structure chart in any sequential programming language that supports a procedure and function call mechanism.

Structured design did, however, have a problem in that it was not always easy to directly derive the structure chart representing the solution to an information flow problem. Yourdon's structured analysis and design methodology proposes a two phase approach. First the data flow diagram solution to the problem is derived. Then using a process called 'transform and transaction analysis', the data flow diagram is converted into a structure chart.

In this process, the modules of data flow diagrams (bubbles) become modules of the structure chart (*boxes* -- not to be confused with the source/sink boxes of a data flow diagram), and other boxes may also be added.

Figure 6 is an example of a structure chart. The hierarchy of boxes in the figure is immediately obvious. Perhaps less obvious is the fact that the hierarchy implies a separation between interfaces and implementations: all the lines impinging on a box from above belong to its interface; *what* services it provides to its users (who are above the box). All those impinging on it from below belong to its implementation; *how* it provides its services (by calling lower boxes).

3.7 Overview of Our Argument

Having established the groundwork, we pick up the main thread of our argument in the following sections. Recall that our twin goals are to demonstrate that structure charts can be informatively expressed in Ada, and to defend ourselves against the claim that with Ada one need design no further than DFD's.

Our method proceeds in three steps. First, we will show how to express DFD's in Ada, so we have something to compare a structured design approach against. Second, we will show how to express structure charts in Ada. In doing so, most of what we learn about expressing DFD's in Ada will come in handy. Finally, we will defend the SD methodology against the rival claims of stand-alone SA, by evaluating their results when applied to an example (sections 7.1, 10).

4. ADA AND STRUCTURED ANALYSIS

The purpose of this section is to show how data flow diagrams may be faithfully translated into Ada.

Recall the five global characteristics of data flow diagrams from section 3.5:

1. Black box modularity of bubbles.

2. Data locality.

3. Explicit connections among bubbles.

4. Nonprocedural data flow.

5. Concurrency of data flow.

By trying to ensure that these properties are preserved under translation to Ada, a scheme for representing DFD's in Ada will emerge.

4.1 Black Box Modularity

A bubble interface shows three things:

1. The types of data imported into the bubble.

2. The types of data exported from the bubble.

3. The relation between the imported and exported data.

The interface of a bubble describes it as an amalgam of two kinds of data types, imported and exported, and an operation that changes imported into exported data.

Since we want to respect DFD structure, bubble interfaces should map into Ada program unit specifications, and implementations into bodies. Thus the Ada specification of a bubble should mention the imported and exported data and the operation that changes the one into the other. Data type transforming operations are represented in Ada by procedures, functions, and tasks, so these entities will appear as all or parts of bubble specifications.

4.1.1 Data Locality. According to data locality, a data type is usually relevant to a small number of bubbles, indeed, it may often be specially linked with a single bubble, that bubble being either its sole source or sole destination. In this case, the type definition should reside in the bubble for the sake of *cohesiveness* ([4], Ch. 7). The most convenient way to specify both data and an operation together in one Ada program unit is, of course, to package them, so a bubble's interface would take the form

```
package BUBBLE is
   -- imported and/or
   -- exported data
   -- declarations

   -- operation declaration
end BUBBLE;
```

In the other case (when some type is equally related to a number of bubbles), the type definition could be part of a package that is accessible only to those bubbles that need the type. This situation will have no bearing on the issue of translating structure charts into Ada.

4.1.2 Concurrency. The bubbles of a DFD are conceptually concurrent processes, hence we can be more specific about the form of their operations:

```
package BUBBLE is
   -- imported and/or
   -- exported data
   -- declarations

   -- task declaration
end BUBBLE;
```

Now, as we said before, there are times when one knows more than a DFD shows, for example, that certain bubbles actually bear a sequential relation to each other. In such cases it naturally makes sense to use procedures and functions instead of tasks. We are here making the least number of assumptions about what the designer knows.

4.1.3 Nonprocedurality. A data flow between two bubbles A and B

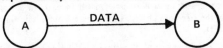

is usually implemented in one of two ways:

1. A can pass the DATA to B by calling a procedure or entry of B having DATA as an **in** parameter. In this situation A is called the *user* bubble and B is called the *server*.

2. The situation can be reversed and B can be the user (and A the server) by having B call a procedure or entry of A having DATA as an **out** parameter.

Often we know what the user/server relationship is between pairs of bubbles, but user/server relationships are not specified in a DFD, since the notion of an operation *calling* another operation is procedural. Could we represent the data flow from A to B if we haven't decided the user/server relationship?

Ada is a procedural language and data flow in Ada must eventually come down to calls, but we can arrange matters so that bubble packages are nonprocedural, in the sense that no bubble package calls another, by a simple device. In the data flow shown above we could let A have a server task,

```
package A is
   type DATA is ...;
   task PRODUCER is
      entry GIVE (DATUM :
         out DATA);
   end PRODUCER;
end A;
```

and B have a server task

```
with A;
package B is
   -- type declarations
   task CONSUMER is
      entry TAKE (DATUM :
         in A.DATA);
   end CONSUMER;
end B;
```

and let the arrow between them be represented by a user procedure

```
with A, B;
procedure A__TO__B is
   DATUM : A.DATA;
begin
   loop
      A.PRODUCER.GIVE (DATUM);
      B.CONSUMER.TAKE (DATUM);
   end loop;
end A__TO__B;
```

4.1.4 Import/Export. Information about the data imported by a package can be found

1. in its **with** clauses, where at least we learn from where it *might* be importing data,

2. in its specification part, specifically in those places where procedures or task entries having **in** parameters are declared, and

3. in its body part, specifically in those calls to procedures or task entries in other bubble packages having **out** parameters.

The same statements hold true for exported data, if we interchange 'in' and 'out'.

Now consider bubble packages, and let us assume that some user/server relationships have been decided, so that 3 is relevant. Of all the locations above 3 is clearly the most inconvenient. We simply do not wish to have to scan a package body to find all the places where it calls procedures or tasks in other packages, since these are likely to be scattered throughout the body. Moreover, it is simply bad software engineering form to place information pertinent to a bubble's interface with its implementation details.

We are led to invent a '**calls**' annotation, used analogously to procedure and task entry specifications. It tells explicitly, in the specification, which entries and procedures in other bubble packages are called from this one. For example, a **calls** annotation could be used to highlight imported data as in the figure:

```
with B;
package A is

   -- type declarations

   task TRANSFORM is
      -- An entry point for
      -- imported data:
      entry IMPORT (B__DATUM :
         in B.DATA);
      -- Another entry point
      -- for imported data:
   --   calls B.EXPORT (B__DATUM :
   --      out B.DATA);
   end TRANSFORM;

end A;
```

Figure 1. The **calls** Annotation

The **calls** annotation recapitulates procedure, function, or entry specifications *in the called package* although, as in the figure, it may need to use selected component notation.

It is now possible to read off the imported and exported data types by examining the parameter modes appearing in parameter lists following the keywords **entry** and **procedure**, and in **calls** annotations.

Of course, creation of the calling tree of Ada program units is something that can be (and should be) done by an automated design aid. However, the **calls** annotation is useful in design situations where the designer knows something about the calling structure of his design text, but program unit bodies have not been filled in to the point where a meaningful calling tree is constructible.

4.1.5 Bubble Connections. Ada intends program units to be usable as *library units*, hence they cannot name their users. A program unit has no control over who may use its services, other than the very weak control implied by the scope rules. On the other hand, a data flow diagram limits very sharply the users of a bubble; they are all the other bubbles connected to it by an arrow. This is valuable information which we do not wish to discard when expressing a DFD in Ada.

Unembellished Ada cannot express the kind of information so readily apparent in a data flow diagram, so to permit a bubble package's connections to be more readily discerned we can add a 'from' annotation, to be used with procedure specifications and task entries as in the figure:

```
with B;
package A is
  -- type declarations
  task TRANSFORM is
      entry INPUT (B__DATUM :
          in B.DATA);
--      from B, C
  end TRANSFORM;
end A;
```

Figure 2. The **from** Annotation

The annotation specifies that A.TRANSFORM.INPUT is called from within package B and also C.

5. ADA AND STRUCTURED DESIGN

Because of the way they have been used in the past, structure charts are often associated with sequential code based upon the procedure as the fundamental program unit. If it were true that structure charts led inevitably to such code, they would be unsuitable for use with Ada. This section refutes the perception by giving a method for translating structure charts into Ada that uses the modern features of Ada to good advantage. In section 9 we will put the method to a practical test.

5.1 Transform Analysis

The purpose behind converting DFD's into structure charts is to introduce a hierarchy into the system structure. *Transform analysis* is one process whereby a data flow diagram may be converted into a structure chart; it is the sole method considered in this paper. The hierarchy it introduces is based upon a hierarchy of data ordered by *abstractness*.

In a transform analysis of a DFD one does six things:

1. *Identify* the central transforms. These are groups of bubbles that deal with the most abstract data types.

2. *Select* 'boss' bubbles. For each central transform, see if there is one bubble that looks like it coordinates the activities of its neighbors. Such a bubble is a good candidate for promoting to be the 'boss' of its neighbors.

3. *Hire* boss bubbles. If a central transform has no obvious boss candidate, then invent a bubble to coordinate the activities of the central transform bubbles.

4. *Lift* boss bubbles and let all other bubbles hang down.

5. Remove the arrowheads from the arrows, putting them with the data labels, and *collapse* all arrows (now just lines) having common source and destination (so now two bubbles can have at most one line between them).

6. *Turn* bubbles into boxes.

All these steps will be illustrated when we work the aircraft monitoring system example.

Step 1 makes the connection between the bubbles and the hierarchy of data. Steps 2 and 3 locate a unique bubble for each of the most abstract data types, either by selection or invention. Steps 4 and 5 display the hierarchy that has just been introduced into the design. When in step 4 a boss bubble is lifted, it becomes the superior of the bubbles around it in the hierarchy. When in step 5 lines with common sources and destinations are collapsed, the lines cease to represent only data flows, but now also represent ordering in the hierarchy. Step 6 is just cosmetic.

There are some differences between the way we have explained transform analysis and the way it is usually explained, e.g., in [4].

- Usually the relationship between the hierarchy of the structure chart and the data abstraction hierarchy is not so explicitly drawn.

- [4] writes as if there were always one central transform, whereas in the aircraft monitoring system example there were several unrelated data types of equal abstraction.

- Most importantly, perhaps, lines usually represent the *calling structure*, whereas here they represent hierarchy pure and simple, *and say nothing about user/server relationships*.

5.2 Structure Charts in Ada

The reader may have observed that at this point no obvious differences have emerged between DFD's and structure charts that would necessitate having to make the representations of boxes and bubbles different. The most that has happened is that the DFD has been cast in a hierarchical form.

However, hierarchy *does* have consequences that make box packages different from bubble packages, as we will see. Boxes will still be represented by packages having specifications

```
package BOX is
  -- data declarations

  -- task declaration
end BOX;
```

but the data that is declared will be different, annotations will be differently placed, and we will be able to fill in parts of box package bodies from the structure chart, as we were not able to do for bubbles from the DFD.

5.2.1 Black Box Modularity. Structure chart boxes are still black box modules, but because of the hierarchy in a structure chart, their interfaces differ from those of DFD bubbles. The interface of a box describes it as it looks to its users, who are all the boxes *above* it that are connected to it by a line. This description comprises:

- The types of data imported into the box *from above*.

- The types of data exported *upwards* from the box.

- The relation between the upward-imported data and the upward-exported data.

These facts cause box package specifications to have the typical form

```
package BOX is
  -- upward-imported and/or
  -- upward-exported
  -- data declarations

  -- task declaration
end BOX;
```

A box has two parts, its interface and its implementation, of which we have just discussed the former. As for implementations, whereas for DFD's one looks at the mini-spec of a bubble or a data flow refinement of it for its implementation (that is, one looks *elsewhere* than the DFD), a structure chart displays some implementation information on its face: a box is implemented in terms of the boxes to which it is connected from below. These considerations do not as yet allow us to write down a general form for box package bodies. That will come shortly.

5.2.2 Calling Structure. We mentioned earlier that structure charts are typically thought to display the calling structure of the system, but that this is not so to our way of thinking. We will now see how calling structure does fall out of the structure chart, but the fact that it does will not be a consequence of the methodology, but of Ada!

Suppose that box B is a subordinate of box A in a structure chart. Then there is a line from A down to B and data may flow along this line in either or both directions. Suppose that data of type DATA flows along the line. What would happen if B were the user for this data flow and A the server?

If A were the server, then A's package specification would have to specify some function, procedure, or task entry, call it OPERATION, for B to call. OPERATION's specification would have to mention DATA as a parameter. But B is part of the implementation of A, as is DATA. Hence OPERATION is an artifact of A's implementation and does not belong in A's specification. Neither does DATA, for the same reason.

The consequence of all this is that a box may never call up, it can only call down. It follows that a box package should have the general form

package BOX **is**
    -- upward-imported and
    -- upward-exported
    -- data declarations

    task OPERATION **is**
        -- entries for calls
        -- from above
    end OPERATION;
end BOX;

package body BOX
-- **calls** <entries in lower boxes>
is
    -- local declarations
    task body OPERATION **is**
        -- calls to lower boxes
    end OPERATION;
end BOX;

Figure 3. General Form of a Box in Ada

Notice how the **calls** annotation now resides in the box package body, unlike bubble packages, where it resided in the specification.

Is it always possible to cast system modules in the form of Figure **3**? That is, can the user/server relationships of modules always be made to conform to the dictum that modules may never call up, but only down? In fact, while it it sometimes inconvenient to adhere to this rule, user/server relationships rarely turn out to be defined by the problem itself. That is, they are not God-given, and we can usually switch the roles of user and server with impunity, as the aircraft monitoring example will illustrate (see especially section 9.4.1).

Finally, it must be remembered that everything we have said about how boxes should be represented is to be taken as recommendations, not immutable laws, so user/server relationships, in particular, can be adjusted to suit a designer's fancy. In the design example we are about to consider, these recommendations were adhered to often enough, but we did not make a fetish of them.

6. DESCRIPTION OF THE EXAMPLE

The aircraft monitoring system (AMS), which is illustrated in Figure 4, performs various aircraft monitoring and recording functions.

6.1 Sensors

The aircraft has four engines, each fitted with temperature and pressure sensors, and the fuel tank is fitted with a sensor to provide information on the quantity of fuel remaining. These sensors are to be polled by the system at regular one second intervals. All sensor readings are fed to dials, one for each sensor. All readings are also tested

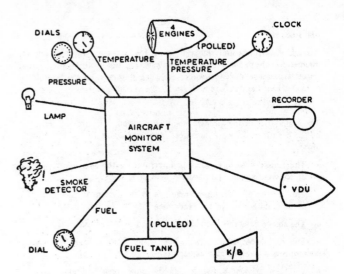

Figure 4. The Aircraft Monitoring System

to be within a safe working range. After three consecutive out of range readings a light corresponding to the sensor is changed from green to red by the system to warn the pilot. The system switches a warning light from green to red when only 10% of the full fuel load remains in the tank. Three consecutive out of range readings are taken to prevent intermittent transmission failures causing an alarm sequence. Any sensor which fails to respond to a poll sequence is timed out and treated as if it had supplied an out of range reading. Three consecutive time outs also cause the warning light to switch from green to red.

Conversely, three consecutive in range readings will cause a sensor's warning light to glow green if it has been previously been glowing red.

6.2 Smoke Detectors

The aircraft is fitted with a number of smoke detectors. Two types of interrupts can be generated by the smoke detectors:

    a. when smoke is first detected;

    b. when smoke is subsequently no longer detected.

There is a smoke warning light. On receipt of any smoke detected interrupt the system switches the light from green to red. When no smoke is detected the smoke warning light glows green.

In order to test the detectors it is possible for the system to act as if smoke had been detected, i.e., a 'smoke' interrupt will be generated followed by a 'no smoke' interrupt. It is anticipated that this test will be performed as part of the flight preparation sequence but could be repeated at any time.

6.3 VDU

The system supports a video display unit (VDU) and a keyboard. The keyboard can be used to request that the VDU display new sensor data (e.g., latest readings or a recent history of readings) or certain values calculated from the data (e.g., rate of change of pressure, rate of fuel consumption).

In addition, any out of limit readings from sensors, smoke interrupts, etc. which cause warning lights to be illuminated will cause messages to be displayed on the VDU. These warning messages take precedence over requested displays and will persist until acknowledged via the keyboard. When all warning messages have been acknowledged the last requested display will be displayed.

The keyboard can be used to request the smoke detectors to simulate smoke detection.

The VDU echoes keyboard inputs.

6.4 Recorder

All sensor readings and smoke detector interrupts are recorded on a magnetic medium for subsequent analysis, together with all keyboard requests and acknowledgements. All such data are tagged with the time at which the data are received by the system.

6.5 Hardware/Software Interface

The boundaries of the aircraft monitoring system software are defined by the hardware/software interface. The interface is abstracted as follows:

- The smoke detectors generate interrupts to the system upon the detection of smoke and its subsequent disappearance.

- The sensors provide sensor readings to the system in the form of numeric data when polled (and when they do not time out).

- The smoke detectors individually respond to test commands.

- The dials accept integers in the range from 1 to 360. These numbers are interpreted as degrees.

- The lights respond to two commands, 'glow green' and 'glow red'.

- The VDU accepts data of type 'updates'. Each update is an instruction in the VDU command language. These instructions tell the VDU how to change its screen.

- The recorder accepts data of type 'recorder data' (about which we will not be more specific).

- The keyboard has a button for each of the allowed pilot commands. Thus, there is a TEST button (for testing the smoke detectors), a DISPLAY MOST RECENT SENSOR READINGS button (for causing the most recent sensor readings to be displayed on the VDU, an ACKNOWLEDGE ENGINE PRESSURE button to acknowledge warnings concerning the engine pressures, and so forth.

- Has it just been out of range or timed out three times consecutively after having been previously in range? (If so, alarms should be posted.)

- Has it just been in range three times consecutively after having been functioning abnormally? (If so, its warning light should turn from red to green.)

- Is it functioning as before? (No actions taken.)

'Pilot's info' names the four different types of information that are displayed for the pilot on the VDU in non-emergency situations:

- most recent sensor readings

- values calculated from recent sensor readings

- rates of change of sensor readings

- recent history of sensor readings.

Looking now at the bubbles, the ALARM HANDLER determines the appropriate alarms to post based on the sensor status, smoke status, and acknowledgements received.

For further definitions of the data types and bubbles the reader is referred the Appendices, where Figure 5's *data dictionary* and *mini-specs* are given.

If the AMS were a real world problem then the bubbles in Figure 5 would be further analyzed, yielding several levels of data flow diagrams. However, the top level alone suffices for the purpose of illustrating the uses of structured analysis with Ada.

7.1 Evaluation of the Data Flow Design

Before even seeing the result of SD applied to the AMS we can make some judgements as to the quality of the design SA has given us.

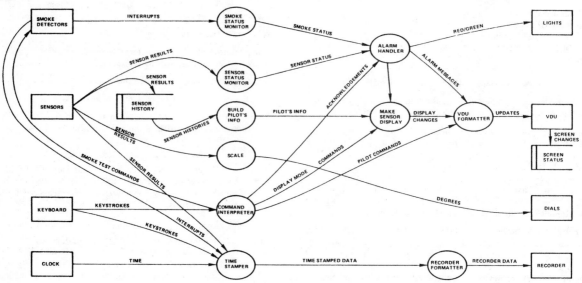

Figure 5. Top Level Data Flow Diagram

7. STRUCTURED ANALYSIS OF THE AMS

Figure 5 shows the top level data flow diagram that we developed for the AMS. Some of the data types and bubbles are not immediately apparent from the requirements: A sensor result is a sensor reading, or an indication that a sensor has timed out. A sensor history is a history of recent sensor readings. The 'smoke status' is the global smoke situation of the aircraft, i.e., is it on fire or not? The 'sensor status' for a particular sensor tells whether that sensor is changing its functioning mode:

7.1.1 Strengths. On the plus side, the data flow design has been produced with a minimum of effort. This may be useful to applications requiring a rapidly developed prototype system. In such situations, converting a DFD into Ada may provide a way to do this.

7.1.2 Weaknesses. Figure 5 imposes no hierarchy on its arrows or bubbles. They are all at the 'top level' and hence of equal importance. This is typical of data flow diagrams. Upon reflection, though, one realizes that the AMS exists to provide its users (the pilot and crash investigator) with certain types of data (pilot's info, smoke and sensor status, time stamped data) and certain capabilities (to test the smoke

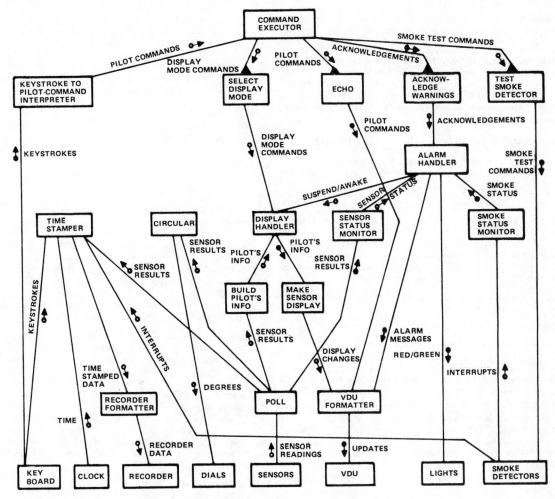

Figure 6. AMS Structure Chart

detectors, choose display modes, acknowledge warnings). All else is secondary and exists to support these functions.

Thus, there is a natural hierarchy inherent in the AMS, one that Figure 5 does not reveal: the data types and capabilities that constitute the *raison d'etre* of the AMS form the top level of the system, the rest belong to implementations at a lower level. Further distinctions are possible, and we see that Figure 5 comprises at least four levels of data:

1. A level corresponding to the pilot's commands.

2. A level corresponding to the five users' information data types.

3. An intermediate level containing such types as alarm messages and display changes.

4. A level corresponding to the hardware interfaces of the source and sink boxes.

However, while Figure 5 shows all the data types at the four levels, it does not separate the levels, nor distinguish them in any way.

This is a pity, since it leads to a system design that is difficult to comprehend in small pieces; one must grasp it all at once. To impose hierarchy, and thereby separate the system into levels, we use structure charts.

8. STRUCTURED DESIGN OF THE AMS

The structure chart in Figure 6 is the result of a straightforward application of *transform analysis* ([4], Ch. 9) to the data flow diagram of Figure 5. Seven processes occurred during the analysis:

1. The central transforms were identified. For examples, the SENSOR STATUS MONITOR deals with the high level sensor

status data type and the TIME STAMPER deals with time stamped data, so these are in central transforms. Where possible, boss bubbles were selected from the central transforms. For example, TIME STAMPER becomes a boss.

2. Some boss boxes were invented to oversee the handling of certain data types. For examples, the structure chart box called DISPLAY HANDLER was invented to manage the handling of pilot's information. It becomes the superior of the two bubbles BUILD PILOT'S INFO and MAKE SENSOR DISPLAY. COMMAND EXECUTOR was invented to oversee the execution of pilot commands. It becomes the superior of the entire system. ACKNOWLEDGE WARNINGS was invented to handle warning acknowledgements. It is the superior of the ALARM HANDLER. POLL was invented to oversee the handling of sensor results (in fact, we have let POLL create sensor results from its attempts to gather readings from the sensors).

3. The boss bubbles were lifted above their undistinguished neighbors.

4. Some bubbles were renamed. The bubble SCALE became the box CIRCULAR (for the way its output is displayed on a circular dial). COMMAND INTERPRETER was elaborated to KEYSTROKE TO PILOT-COMMAND INTERPRETER.

5. All bubbles of Figure 5 turned into boxes; all arrows became lines with the directionality of the data flows now indicated by little arrows next to the data types on the lines.

6. The stores disappeared, being absorbed into appropriate boxes.

7. Some boxes (four, to be exact) were absorbed into the COM-
MAND EXECUTOR box, as is indicated by the little hats they
wear.

There is one difference to note between this and the usual structure
charts one sees. In Figure 6 not all boxes have superiors (e.g., TIME
STAMPER), whereas in standard structure charts, only the root box
has no superior. This reflects the concurrency of the AMS; the TIME
STAMPER operates independently of and in parallel with the rest of
the system.

9. EXPRESSING THE STRUCTURE CHART IN ADA

The system design is embodied in Figure 6, together with Figure 5's
data dictionary and mini-specs. In this section the heuristics from section 5 are employed to translate this design into Ada.

9.1 Preview of Some Features

- In the Ada that follows, we often found it difficult to keep *all*
  implementation details out of a box's specification. The problem
  almost invariably was that coherency considerations often made it
  desirable to define data exported from a box in the box's specification, even if that data was only being exported to lower level boxes.
  In these situations we always favored coherence.

- To avoid inessential details, the design below assumes only one sensor and one smoke detector.

- We have not considered the issue of system shutdown.

- The presentation order is *not* the compilation order.

9.2 Topmost System Modules

Figure 6 shows COMMAND EXECUTOR to be the topmost box of
the system, deriving its inputs from the KEYBOARD TO PILOT-
COMMAND INTERPRETER. To be able to name component data
types and procedures mnemonically, we have shortened the names of
the boxes to EXECUTE and PILOT, respectively. This choice of
names also conforms to the fact that PILOT exports a data type,
namely PILOT.COMMANDS, which is at the level of the pilot's
comprehension of the system, so that PILOT may be regarded as the
system's image of the actual pilot (with KEYBOARD as his 'implementation'.)

PILOT exports the type PILOT.COMMANDS to EXECUTE and
contains a procedure PILOT.COMMAND__IS which EXECUTE
calls to obtain new PILOT.COMMANDS. Both boxes could have
been represented by packages containing tasks (as in Figure 3), but
some extra considerations about how EXECUTE should work (section
9.2.2) allow us to use procedures instead.

9.2.1 PILOT. PILOT.COMMANDS has three subtypes:

TESTS   Test commands. In this system there is only one, namely,
the smoke system test.

MODES   The four choices of display modes.

ACKS   Warning acknowledgements.

```
package PILOT is

    type COMMANDS is
        -- test command:
        (SMOKE__TEST,
        -- display mode commands:
        MOST__RECENT__READINGS,
        CALCULATED__VALUES,
        RATES__OF__CHANGE,
        SENSOR__HISTORIES,
        -- acknowledgements:
        ENGINE__PRESSURE__WARNING__ACK,
        ENGINE__TEMP__WARNING__ACK,
        FUEL__LEVEL__WARNING__ACK);

    subtype TESTS is COMMANDS
        range SMOKE__TEST .. SMOKE__TEST;
```

```
    subtype MODES is COMMANDS
        range MOST__RECENT__READINGS ..
            SENSOR__HISTORIES;

    subtype ACKS is COMMANDS
        range ENGINE__PRESSURE__WARNING__ACK ..
            FUEL__LEVEL__WARNING__ACK;

    procedure COMMAND__IS (COMMAND :
        out COMMANDS);
    -- from EXECUTE

end PILOT;
```

Notice how the **from** annotation has been used to show that
PILOT.COMMAND__IS is called by EXECUTE.

PILOT's implementation relies on the KEYBOARD specification,
neither of which will be shown. It suffices to say that when
PILOT.COMMAND__IS is called, it calls on KEYBOARD for a new
keystroke. If none have been made, PILOT.COMMAND__IS waits
(for the pilot to press a key). If a keystroke was made, then it is the
KEYBOARD that has been waiting, perhaps locked, for the previous
keystroke to be serviced. With the new keystroke, whenever it arrives,
PILOT.COMMAND__IS consults a dictionary (possibly implemented
by a table) to see which PILOT.COMMAND it signifies, then passes
the PILOT.COMMAND on to EXECUTE.

9.2.2 EXECUTE. EXECUTE could be represented by a package
containing a task, following the general form of box packages. However, it is a degenerate case of the usual sort of box. It creates no
data, being responsible for handling PILOT.COMMANDS, so it
would be a task sitting alone inside a package, useful only for separate
compilation purposes. We can make the task a procedure, and discard
the package shell altogether, since EXECUTE will only be called once
(from outside the system) at system startup (we are ignoring shutdown), so we need not guard against several invocations of EXECUTE
being in existence at the same time. (If this were a danger, then we
would want EXECUTE to be a task so we could rendezvous with it.)

```
with PILOT;
procedure EXECUTE is
-- calls PILOT.COMMAND__IS (COMMAND :
--     out PILOT.COMMANDS);

    procedure SELECT (MODE :
        in PILOT.MODES)
    is separate;

    procedure ECHO (COMMAND :
        in PILOT.COMMANDS)
    is separate;

    procedure ACKNOWLEDGE (WARNING :
        in PILOT.ACKS)
    is separate;

    procedure SMOKE__TEST
    is separate;

    COMMAND : PILOT.COMMANDS;
    MODE    : PILOT.MODES;
    WARNING : PILOT.ACKS;

begin
    loop
        -- Get the next user command:
        PILOT.COMMAND__IS (COMMAND);
        -- Service it:
        if
            COMMAND in PILOT.TESTS
        then -- do a
            SMOKE__TEST;
        elsif
            COMMAND in PILOT.MODES
```

```
then
    MODE := COMMAND;
    SELECT (MODE);
elsif
    COMMAND in PILOT.ACKS
then
    WARNING := COMMAND;
    ACKNOWLEDGE (WARNING);
end if;
ECHO (COMMAND);
end loop;
end EXECUTE;
```

Notice how the **calls** annotation was used to give a synopsis at the beginning of the body of the calls EXECUTE makes.

9.3 Mid-level System Modules

The next subsections present some of the mid-level modules.

9.3.1 ALARM HANDLER. The ALARM HANDLER is responsible for posting alarms to the LIGHTS and VDU, when this is called for.

There is a conflict between defining alarm messages in the ALARM HANDLER module, where the type is created, and defining it in the VDU FORMATTER, where it is bound. Cohesion favors the first choice: the creation of alarm messages is the reason there is an ALARM HANDLER, but to the VDU FORMATTER, alarm messages are just one of several kinds of data to be displayed on the VDU. In favor of the second choice is the fact that according to the structure chart, alarm messages are part of the implementation of the ALARM HANDLER module, and hence should not appear in its specification. We sided with cohesion, thereby sacrificing the design structure.

The ALARM HANDLER is represented in Ada by a package named ALARM encapsulating a type named ALARM.MESSAGES and a task named ALARM.HANDLER:

```
with PILOT;
package ALARM
-- Keeps track of which alarms,
-- if any, should be posted to
-- the LIGHTS and VDU.
is

    type MESSAGES is new TYPE_TBD;

    task HANDLER is
        entry ACKNOWLEDGE (WARNING :
            in PILOT.WARNINGS);
--      from EXECUTE.ACKNOWLEDGE
    end HANDLER;

end ALARM;
```

Notice the use of TYPE_TBD to defer the decision of how to define ALARM.MESSAGES and notice also that ALARM has the normal form of box packages (Figure **3**).

The specification shows that as far as its superiors (there is only one, namely ACKNOWLEDGE) are concerned, ALARM exists solely to acknowledge warnings.

ALARM's body, shown next, reveals it to be a server as far as ACKNOWLEDGE is concerned, and a user as far as SENSOR, SMOKE, etc. are concerned. But SENSOR and SMOKE provide intermittent data to the ALARM.HANDLER; it is more natural to consider them the users and ALARM the server. For example, whenever a new sensor status is generated, SENSOR could actively attempt to send it to the ALARM.HANDLER. However, with the 'conditional entry' device, the ALARM.HANDLER can be made the user. Periodically it checks to see whether SENSOR is ready to accept a call, using a conditional entry to make the check. SENSOR is only ready to do so if it has a new sensor status to report.

```
with DISPLAY, LIGHTS, VDU_FORMAT,
    SENSOR, SMOKE;
package body ALARM
-- calls
--      SENSOR.STATUS_MONITOR.REPORT
--          (STATE : out SENSOR.STATUS),
--      SMOKE.STATUS_MONITOR.REPORT
--          (STATE : out SMOKE.STATUS),
--      DISPLAY.HANDLER.SUSPEND,
--      DISPLAY.HANDLER.RESUME,
--      VDU_FORMAT.THE (ALARM_MESSAGE :
--          in ALARM.MESSAGES),
--      LIGHTS.TURN_GREEN,
--      LIGHTS.TURN_RED;
is

    SENSOR_STATE : SENSOR.STATUS;
    SMOKE_STATE  : SMOKE.STATUS;

task body HANDLER is

    ALARM_MESSAGE : MESSAGES;

begin
    loop
        -- ALARM.HANDLER is a server
        -- for ACKNOWLEDGE:
        select
            -- if there is an acknowledgement,
            accept ACKNOWLEDGE (WARNING :
                in PILOT.ACKS)
            from ACKNOWLEDGE;
            do -- acknowledge it,
                -- Start normal display:
                DISPLAY.HANDLER.RESUME;
                -- Remove the warning
                -- from the VDU:
                ALARM_MESSAGE := VALUE_TBD;
                VDU_FORMAT.THE
                    (ALARM_MESSAGE);
            end;
        else -- no acknowledgements, so
            null; -- do something else
        end select;


        -- ALARM.HANDLER is
        -- a user to SENSOR:
        select -- conditional entry:
            SENSOR.STATUS_MONITOR.
                REPORT (SENSOR_STATE);
            case SENSOR_STATE is
                when TURNED_BAD =>
                    LIGHTS.TURN_RED;
                    -- Stop normal display:
                    DISPLAY.HANDLER.SUSPEND;
                    -- Send warning to VDU:
                    ALARM_MESSAGE := VALUE_TBD;
                    VDU_FORMAT.THE
                        (ALARM_MESSAGE);
                when TURNED_GOOD =>
                    LIGHTS.TURN_GREEN;
                    -- Nothing goes to VDU
                when NO_CHANGE =>
                    null;
            end case;
        else;
            null;
        end select;
```

```
        -- ALARM.HANDLER is
        -- user to SMOKE:
        select -- conditional entry:
                SMOKE.STATUS__MONITOR.
                    REPORT (SMOKE__STATE);
                case SMOKE__STATE is
                    when PRESENT =>
                            LIGHTS.TURN__RED;
                            -- Stop normal display:
                            DISPLAY.HANDLER.SUSPEND;
                            -- Send warning to VDU:
                            ALARM__MESSAGE := VALUE__TBD;
                            VDU__FORMAT.THE
                            (ALARM__MESSAGE);
                    when ABSENT
                            LIGHTS.TURN__GREEN;
                            -- Nothing goes to VDU
                end case;
            end select;
        end loop;
    end HANDLER;

end ALARM;
```

Note the use of VALUE__TBD's to indicate an assignment to ALARM__MESSAGE that we are unable at this stage to further specify.

The reason why there are two conditional entries and not one like:

```
select
    SENSOR.STATUS__MONITOR.REPORT (SENSOR__STATE);
    ...
else
    SMOKE.STATUS__MONITOR.REPORT (SMOKE__STATE);
    ...
end select;
```

is that the latter arrangement favors the first entry, only attempting the second entry if the first rendezvous is impossible. We want the two entries to be of equal standing.

With ALARM specified we can implement one of EXECUTE's subprocedures, namely, ACKNOWLEDGE:

```
with PILOT, ALARM;
separate (EXECUTE)
procedure ACKNOWLEDGE (WARNING :
    in PILOT.ACKS)
is
begin
    ALARM.HANDLER.ACKNOWLEDGE (WARNING);
end ACKNOWLEDGE;
```

9.3.2 SMOKE STATUS MONITOR. The SMOKE STATUS MONITOR is represented by an Ada package SMOKE containing a type SMOKE.STATUS and a task SMOKE.STATUS__MONITOR.

The requirements state that the smoke detectors communicate with the system via interrupts. In our design, the portions of the system with which the smoke detectors are in communication are the SMOKE and TIME STAMPER modules. We have chosen to implement these interrupts in the most straightforward manner possible, having them go directly to SMOKE and TIME STAMPER. However, this implementation causes the high level modules SMOKE and TIME STAMPER to be servers for the low level DETECTORS module. The high level modules must then contain entries for the low level interrupts in their specifications, something we have been trying to avoid. So in this case, the principle that the Ada representation should reflect the structure of the design is violated. Still, SMOKE very nearly has the form of Figure 3.

```
package SMOKE is

    type STATUS is (FOUND, GONE);

    task STATUS__MONITOR is
        entry REPORT (STATE :
            out STATUS);
--      from ALARM.HANDLER
        -- The following are
        -- low level entries:
        entry SMOKE__FOUND;
            for SMOKE__FOUND
            use at ADDRESS__TBD;
--      from DETECTORS.SMOKE
        entry SMOKE__GONE;
            for SMOKE__GONE
            use at ADDRESS__TBD;
--      from DETECTORS.SMOKE
    end STATUS__MONITOR;

end SMOKE;
```

Notice the use of the annotation ADDRESS__TBD to defer the decision of which addresses should be used for the two interrupts.

9.3.3 SENSOR STATUS MONITOR. This module has been implemented as a package called SENSOR exporting the type SENSOR.STATUS and encapsulating the task SENSOR.STATUS__MONITOR. Its form follows Figure 3 exactly.

```
package SENSOR
-- Abstracts away all features
-- of the sensors except that
-- they are continuously running
-- mechanisms that can be
-- starting to function normally,
-- starting to function abnormally,
-- or functioning as before.
is
    type STATUS is
        (TURNED__GOOD, TURNED__BAD, NO__CHANGE);

    task STATUS__MONITOR is
        entry REPORT (STATE :
            out STATUS);
--      from ALARM.HANDLER
    end STATUS__MONITOR;

end SENSOR;
```

SENSOR's implementation employs a function EVALUATE to make the three-in-a-row tests. As implementing EVALUATE is routine it will not be done here. Note that the SENSOR.STATUS__MONITOR attempts to rendezvous with POLL. We will have more to say about this when POLL is discussed.

```
with POLL;
package body SENSOR is
    SENSOR__RESULT : POLL.SENSOR__RESULTS;
    task body STATUS__MONITOR is
        STATE : STATUS;
        function EVALUATE (SENSOR__RESULT :
            in POLL.SENSOR__RESULTS)
            return STATUS
            -- Makes the 3-in-a-row tests
        is separate;
```

502

```
      begin
          loop
              -- Wait for the latest SENSOR__RESULT:
              POLL.CYCLE.MONITOR (SENSOR__RESULT);
              STATE := EVALUATE (SENSOR__RESULT);
              accept REPORT (STATE :
                  out STATUS);
--              from ALARM.HANDLER;
          end loop;
      end STATUS__MONITOR;

end SENSOR;
```

9.3.4 DISPLAY HANDLER.

The DISPLAY HANDLER module is represented in Ada by a package named DISPLAY encapsulating a type DISPLAY.CHANGES (to be sent to VDU__FORMAT) and a task DISPLAY.HANDLER.

The conflict between cohesion and design structure arose here as well. Should we define display changes in DISPLAY for the sake of cohesion, or define them in VDU__FORMATTER for the sake of keeping implementation details out of the specification? As always, we chose cohesion.

```
with PILOT;
package DISPLAY is

    type CHANGES is new TYPE__TBD;

    task HANDLER is
        entry SUSPEND;
--      from ALARM.HANDLER;
        entry RESUME;
--      from ALARM.HANDLER;
        entry SWITCH__TO (NEW__MODE :
            in PILOT.MODES);
--      from EXECUTE.SELECT
    end HANDLER;

end DISPLAY;
```

The body of DISPLAY is too long to write out, even at the shallow level of analysis it has been subjected to so far.

9.4 A Low Level Module

The low (but not lowest) level modules are POLL, VDU__FORMAT, and RECORDER__FORMAT. We will only present POLL, as it is by far the most interesting.

9.4.1 POLL.

The POLL module is responsible for getting sensor readings to their various consumers. In addition, it determines whether a sensor has timed out (but not whether it is in range).

The first way it might occur to someone to implement POLL is by a task that once every second polls the SENSORS and then makes entry calls to TIME STAMPER, CIRCULAR, BUILD PILOT'S INFO, and SENSOR STATUS MONITOR to give them the latest sensor results. However, to do so would make POLL the user and the others the servers, even though POLL is subordinate to them all in the structure chart. So we make POLL the server and SENSOR, TIME STAMPER, etc. the users. These consumers of sensor readings spend most of their time waiting to rendezvous with POLL for the latest sensor result. If POLL were the user, they would spend most of their time waiting for POLL to attempt a rendezvous with them, which amounts to much the same thing.

```
with SENSORS;
package POLL
-- Polls the sensors, determines time
-- outs, and distributes the results.
is

    type STATUS
    -- a discriminant for the
    -- SENSOR__RESULTS type,
    is
        (RETURNED, TIMED__OUT);
    type SENSOR__RESULTS
        (STATE : STATUS := RETURNED)
    is
    -- the sensor reading or an
    -- indication that it has timed out
    record
        case STATE is
            when RETURNED =>
                SENSOR__READING : SENSORS.READINGS;
            when TIMED__OUT =>
                null;
        end case;
    end record;

    task CYCLE is
        entry PROCESS (RESULT :
            out SENSOR__RESULTS);
--      from BUILD.PILOT__INFO;
        entry CONVERT (RESULT :
            out SENSOR__RESULTS);
--      from CIRCULAR
        entry MONITOR (RESULT :
            out SENSOR__RESULTS);
--      from SENSOR.STATUS__MONITOR;
        entry STAMP (RESULT :
            out SENSOR__RESULTS);
--      from TIME.STAMPER;
    end CYCLE;

end POLL;
```

The body of POLL reveals that a delay statement is used to keep the POLL.CYCLE running at one second intervals:

```
with SENSORS;
package body POLL
-- calls SENSORS.GENERATE.FOR__POLL (READING :
--      out SENSOR.READINGS);
is

    READING : SENSORS.READINGS;

    task body CYCLE is

        RESULT : SENSOR__RESULTS;
        INTERVAL : constant DURATION := 1.0;
        NEXT__TIME : CALENDAR.TIME := CALENDAR.CLOCK;

    begin
        loop
            -- How much longer to wait before
            -- the polling cycle starts again:
            delay NEXT__TIME - CALENDAR.CLOCK;
            -- A conditional entry:
            select
                -- Is the READING ready?
                SENSORS.GENERATE.FOR__POLL
                    (READING);
                -- If yes, then:
                RESULT :=
                    (STATE  => RETURNED,
                     SENSOR__READING => READING);
            else -- sensor has timed out
                RESULT :=
                    (STATE => TIMED__OUT);
            end select;

            -- Now follows the distribution
            -- of the RESULT.
```

```
      --
      -- BUILD.PILOT__INFO has
      -- been waiting for the latest
      -- RESULT. Give it to him:
      accept PROCESS (RESULT :
            out SENSOR__RESULTS);
--        from BUILD.PILOT__INFO;
      -- The SENSORS.STATUS__MONITOR
      -- has been waiting for the latest
      -- RESULT. Give it to him:
      accept MONITOR (RESULT :
            out SENSOR__RESULTS);
--        from SENSOR.STATUS__MONITOR;
      -- The CIRCULAR.DISPLAY has
      -- been waiting for the latest
      -- RESULT. Give it to him:
      accept CONVERT (RESULT :
            out SENSOR__RESULTS);
--        from CIRCULAR.DISPLAY;
      -- Give the RESULT
      -- to the TIME.STAMPER:
      accept STAMP (RESULT :
            out SENSOR__RESULTS);
--        from TIME.STAMPER;
        -- Set the time for the next
        -- polling cycle to start:
        NEXT__TIME := NEXT__TIME + INTERVAL;
      end loop;
    end CYCLE;

end POLL;
```

9.5 Some Hardware Interface Modules

The hardware interface modules are SENSORS, KEYBOARD, RECORDER, LIGHTS, DIALS, VDU, and SMOKE DETECTORS. We present a sampling of some of their specifications. No bodies are given as the modules are presumed to be hardware-implemented.

9.5.1 LIGHTS. The LIGHTS module is represented by the package LIGHTS:

```
package LIGHTS is

  procedure TURN__RED;
-- from ALARM.HANDLER

  procedure TURN__GREEN;
-- from ALARM.HANDLER

end LIGHTS;
```

When the design is refined to take the multiplicity of lights into account, both procedures will be parameterized by sensor names.

9.5.2 RECORDER. The RECORDER module is somewhat more interesting than LIGHTS in having, besides an operation, a type:

```
package RECORDER is

  type DATA
      -- will not be further refined
  is new TYPE__TBD;

  procedure TAPE (INCOMING__DATA :
      in DATA);
  is separate;

end RECORDER;
```

10. CONCLUSIONS

We have presented a scheme for expressing structure charts in Ada that we believe makes the structured analysis and design methodology a useful predecessor to expressing a design in Ada.

In section 7.1 we noticed certain deficiencies a purely data flow design for the AMS. None of these occur in the structure chart design, and no flaws of such a large character are evident to me. It is on these grounds that we recommend applying the full structured analysis and design methodology, rather than stopping at data flow diagrams.

10.1 Refining the Design

The design has been taken to a point where the kinds of changes that would have to be made to have a running AMS are mostly refinements. Stubs and TBD's of various sorts have to be filled in and, of course, we have not written down several of the modules, but the most serious change is upgrading the design to allow for a multiplicity of sensors and smoke detectors. Nevertheless, this too is a refinement of the design, in a certain sense. Broad structural changes should not occur.

We believe that this is as it should be: design steps that require the wholesale modification of Ada code are fraught with peril. The experience of having worked several versions of the AMS in Ada (and trying to modify the designs we got) has convinced us that Ada is too rigid, too formal, and too detailed a notation to permit the kind of restructuring that is carried out so simply in a transform analysis.

10.2 The Place of Ada in the Design Process

After what we have just said, it follows that we believe that designs should be expressed in Ada when they have reached a stage where they will require no more restructuring, but only refinements. For the structured analysis and design methodology, this stage is achieved after structure charts have been developed, but not before. Had we expressed the DFD of Figure 5 in Ada, and then attempted to restructure the Ada design to get to the design we finally achieved, the restructuring would have been far more painful than the simple rearrangement of bubbles in a picture that transform analysis requires.

11. ACKNOWLEDGEMENTS

It is a pleasure to acknowledge the aid provided by members of the Ford Aerospace Ada Technology group. Special thanks go to Mark Sadler and Dr. Larry Yelowitz for extensive editorial suggestions. Dr. Yelowitz and Dr. R. Krishnaswamy also made contributions to the text. Jeremy Holden provided a valuable sounding board for design ideas, and David Goddard was invaluable in an earlier design experiment.

12. REFERENCES

[1] Booch, G. *Software Engineering With Ada.* Benjamin/Cummings, to appear.

[2] Dept. of Industry, UK. *Report on the Study of an Ada Based System Development Methodology.* September 1981.

[3] Ford Aerospace & Comm. Corp. *Reference Manual for Design in Ada.* April 1982.

[4] Page-Jones, M. *The Practical Guide to Structured Systems Design.* Yourdon Press, 1980.

[5] Yourdon, E. and L. Constantine. *Structured Design.* Yourdon Press, 1978.

APPENDIX 1: DATA DICTIONARY

We define the data types labeling the arrows of Figure 5. The conventions of [ ] are observed. Thus, the vertical bar '|' indicates alternatives, the plus sign '+' indicates concatenation, the brackets '[' and ']' are used for grouping, and the braces '{' and '}' indicate repetition. Thus an item '$a : b+[c|d]+\{e\}$' indicates that a has three components, a b followed by one of c or d, followed by several e's.

sensor result   : sensor reading + timeout

sensor reading
: [temperature reading
| pressure reading
| fuel reading]
These are real numbers in certain ranges (which will not be further specified), coupled with sensor numbers (so we know where the reading came from).

sensor number
: An integer in the range 1 to 9.

timeout
: sensor number
+ timeout flag

sensor history
: {sensor result}
A recent history of sensor results, e.g., the last 10 results of each of the sensors.

degree
: [An integer in the range 1 to 360]
+ sensor name

keystroke
: A signal resulting from the depression of a key.

interrupt
: [smoke | no smoke]
+ detector number

time
: Time of day to the nearest second.

red/green
: Commands to the lights.

display mode command
: most recent readings
| calculated values
| rates of change
| sensor histories

smoke test command
: Command to a smoke detector to test itself.

acknowledgement
: pressure warning acknowledgement
| temperature warning acknowledgement
| fuel level warning acknowledgement

pilot command
: display mode command
| smoke test command
| acknowledgement

suspend/awake
: Command to the Sensor Display Creator to stop/start creating sensor displays for the VDU. Used to allow warning messages to preempt normal displays.

alarm message
: sensor warning message
| smoke warning message

time stamped datum
: time + [sensor result
| interrupt | keystroke]

display change
: A new line of characters for display on the VDU.

update
: An instruction in the VDU's command language telling it how to update its sensor display.

screen change
: An instruction internal to the VDU having the effect of changing the screen display.

smoke status
: smoke present | smoke absent
The global smoke situation in the aircraft.

sensor status
: sensor number +
[timing out | normal
| out of range]

pilot's info
: [most recent readings
| calculated values
| rates of change
| sensor histories]

recorder data
: Some form of data appropriate to the RECORDER.

APPENDIX 2: MINI-SPECS

Here are the mini-specs for Figure 5:

SENSORS

Input   None.
Output   Sensor results (i.e., readings or timeouts).
Function Yield sensor results when polled.

SMOKE DETECTORS

Input   Smoke test commands.
Output   Smoke /no smoke interrupts.
Function Perform self-test on command; generate appropriate interrupts when smoke first detected or subsequently absent.

CLOCK

Input   None.
Output   The time accurate to the nearest second.
Function Generates time.

KEYBOARD

Input   None.
Output   Keystrokes.
Function Generates keystrokes.

DIALS

Input   Degrees.
Output   None.
Function Positions dial hand to the input degree.

LIGHTS

Input   Red/green commands.
Output   None.
Function Glow red or green on command.

RECORDER

Input   Recorder data.
Output   None.
Function Records the data on a magnetic medium.

VDU

Input   Updates (to the screen).
Output   None (the Screen Status store is internal to the VDU as are the screen change instructions).
Function Performs updates to the screen status, echos pilot commands.

SENSOR STATUS MONITOR

Input   Sensor results.
Output   Sensor status.
Function Determines whether a sensor has begun to behave normally, abnormally (timing out or out of range three times in succession), or exhibits no change.

BUILD PILOT'S INFO

Input   Sensor histories.
Output   Pilot's info.
Function Builds pilot's info from sensor histories.

MAKE SENSOR DISPLAY

Input   Pilot's info, display mode commands, and suspend/awake signals.
Output   Display changes.
Function Creates sensor display changes according to the latest display mode command received, if not suspended.

COMMAND INTERPRETER

Input   Keystrokes.
Output   Pilot commands, i.e., smoke test commands, display mode commands, and acknowledgements.
Function Interprets the keystrokes as commands.

DISPLAY WARNINGS

Input   Warning messages and acknowledgements.
Output   Warning updates and suspend/awake signals.
Function Preempts sensor display for warnings, issues warning updates, and removes acknowledged warnings.

SMOKE STATUS MONITOR

Input   Interrupts.
Output   Warning messages and red/green commands.
Function Keeps track of the global smoke situation on the aircraft, issues warning messages and red/green commands.

TIME STAMPER

Input   Sensor results, keystrokes, interrupts, and time.
Output   Time stamped data.
Function Time stamps incoming data.

VDU FORMATTER

Input   Alarm messages, display changes, and pilot commands.
Output   VDU updates.
Function Changes the input character data into instructions (updates) to the VDU telling it how to change its screen.

RECORDER FORMATTER

Input   Time stamped data.
Output   Recorder data.
Function Change time stamped data into a form (recorder data) that can be input to RECORDER.

NASSI-SHNEIDERMAN CHARTS
AN ALTERNATIVE TO FLOWCHARTS FOR DESIGN

by
Cornelia M. Yoder and Marilyn L. Schrag
IBM Corporation
System Products Division
Endicott, New York 13760

ABSTRACT

In recent years structured programming has emerged as an advanced programming technology. During this time, many tools have been developed for facilitating the programmer's use of structured programming. One of these tools, the Structured Flowcharts developed by I. Nassi and B. Shneiderman in 1972, is proving its value in both the design phase and the coding phase of program development.

Several programming groups in System Products Division, Endicott, New York, have used the Nassi-Shneiderman charts as replacements for conventional flowcharts in structuring programs. The charts have been used extensively on some projects for structured walk-throughs, design reviews, and education.

This paper describes the Nassi-Shneiderman charts and provides explanations of their use in programming, in development process control, in walk-throughs, and in testing. It includes an analysis of the value of Nassi-Shneiderman charts compared to other design and documentation methods such as pseudo-code, HIPO charts, prose, and flowcharts, as well as the authors' experiences in using the Nassi-Shneiderman charts.

The paper is intended for a general data processing audience and although no special knowledge is required, familiarity with structured programming concepts would be helpful. The reader should gain insight into the use of Nassi-Shneiderman charts as part of the total development process.

INTRODUCTION

The search for a good design method and a good documentation method to use in conjunction with structured programming has resulted in several widely varying yet very useful techniques. One of these is the Structured Flowcharts of I. Nassi and B. Shneiderman.

The Nassi-Shneiderman Charts have many features to recommend them for use in top-down structured programming environment, not the least of which is the difficulty of designing unstructured programs using the charts. The authors were introduced to this charting technique in 1973 and have been using it successfully on their respective projects since that time. The use of Nassi-Shneiderman Charts has spread to almost everyone who has been exposed to their use as the need to express and verify the design and documentation of programs has increased.

Nassi-Shneiderman Charts or N-S Charts is not the only design language that has been developed recently; for example, pseudo-code is another excellent technique. Nor is N-S Charting the only documentation method; pseudo-code can be used for program documentation, and HIPO charting also has many advocates.

One of the purposes of this paper will be to compare N-S Charts to other design and documentation methods in a constructive way - each of the different techniques has its advantages and disadvantages, and each is useful in certain situations. Before these comparisons, there is a brief introduction to Structured Programming followed by a description of the Nassi-Shneiderman Charts.

STRUCTURED PROGRAMMING CONCEPTS

Structured programming, contrary to some programmers' beliefs, is not a set of coding rules and restrictions. Structured programming is a style, an attitude toward programming that starts with fundamental goals of the programming process. Classically, programming goals were correctness, efficiency, and creativity. Of these, correctness is the only valid programming goal remaining today. Efficiency has become of minor importance with the advent of very high speed computers and virtual memories. Creativity, not bad itself, was classically directed toward cleverness and obscurity, with frequently detrimental results.

In today's programming environment new goals have been set. Correctness remains of primary importance; however, maintainability (the ease of fixing errors), modifiability (the ease of making changes), and readability (the clarity of the program) have replaced program efficiency and abstruseness as desirable program characteristics. The programmer who sacrifices modifiability to save a few bytes or who gleefully hands over a program saying, "I'll bet you can't guess what this one does!" is finally receiving the disdain so long deserved.

Once these new programming goals were set, it was inevitable that many programming techniques would be developed to achieve them. One of the best techniques has been structured code. (The distinction in terms is clear. Structured coding is the set of standard coding methods for accomplishing the goals of structured programming.) Structured coding is a set of program structures sufficient for writing any proper program (one entry point and one exit point) together with some rules for segmentation and indentation. The required set of program structures is not unique; one minimum set consists of structures titled SEQUENCE, IFTHENELSE, and DOWHILE. Frequently, other structures such as DOUNTIL and CASE are included. These structures are diagrammed using conventional flowchart symbols in Figure 1.

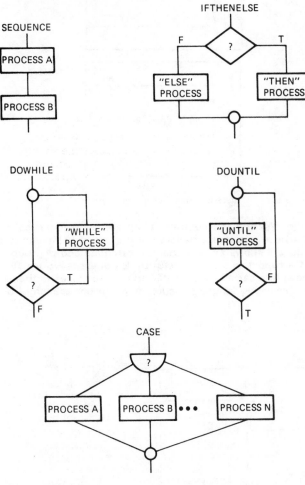

Figure 1. Required Set of Program Structures

NASSI-SHNEIDERMAN CHARTS

In SIGPLAN Notices of the ACM, August, 1973, Messrs. Nassi and Shneiderman published a new flowcharting language with a structure closely akin to that of structured code. The advantages they claimed for their charts have proven correct; they are as follows:

1. The scope of iteration is well-defined and visible.

2. The scope of IFTHENELSE clauses is well-defined and visible; moreover, the conditions or process boxes embedded within compound conditions can be seen easily from the diagram.

3. The scope of local and global variables is immediately obvious.

4. Arbitrary transfers of control are impossible.

5. Complete thought structures can and should fit on no more than one page (i.e. no off-page connectors).

6. Recursion has a trivial representation.

The authors have added another advantage to those listed above:

7. These charts are adaptable to the peculiarities of the system or language they are used with.

By combining and nesting the basic structures, all of which are rectangular, a programmer can design a structured, branch-free program. Figure 2 shows

Figure 2. Process Symbol

the basic PROCESS symbol - a rectangle representing assignments, calls, input/output statements, or any other sequential operations. In addition, a PROCESS symbol may contain other symbols nested within it. The PROCESS symbol may be of any chosen dimensions provided the symbol fits on one page. The symbol used to represent a decision is shown in Figure 3.

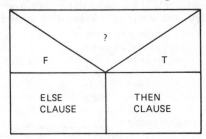

Figure 3. Decision Symbol

This IFTHENELSE symbol contains the test or decision in the upper triangle and the possible outcomes of the test in the lower triangles. "Yes" and "No" may be substituted for "True" and "False," and there is no particular objection to switching them right and left, although consistency is desirable. The rectangles contain the functions to be executed for each of the outcomes. Notice the ELSE and THEN clause boxes are actually PROCESS symbols and may contain any valid PROCESS statements or nested structures.

Repeating processes are represented by an iteration symbol. One of three symbols may be used depending on whether loop termination is at the beginning or the end of the loop. Figure 4 shows a DOWHILE symbol, used for loops which test a condition at the beginning.

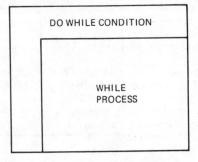

Figure 4. DOWHILE Symbol

Figure 5 is a DOUNTIL symbol, for loops which test for termination at the end. Figure 6 is a combination for loops with compound tests and may also be used for special constructs such as DO FOREVER or for setting off BEGIN/END blocks.

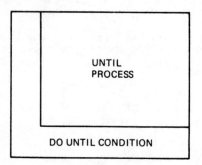

Figure 5. DOUNTIL Symbol

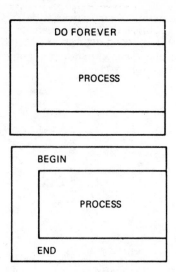

Figure 6. Other Acceptable Symbols

The CASE structure is represented by the symbol in Figure 7. This form of CASE requires the setting of a variable to an integer value, and the choice of path is based on the value of that variable. Figure 8 depicts a more powerful form of CASE, but one that requires the designer to be certain the conditions chosen are mutually exclusive and cover all necessary condition testing.

Nesting of structures to create programs should now be an obvious extension of the use of basic symbols. Figure 9 shows an N-S chart to calculate and print an FICA report in a style useful to designers. Figure 10 shows the same chart written in a style closer to the programming language, such as programmers might use.

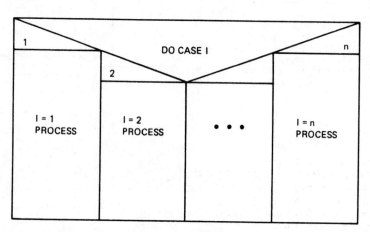

Figure 7. CASE Symbol

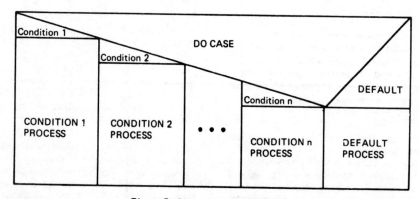

Figure 8. Alternative CASE Symbol

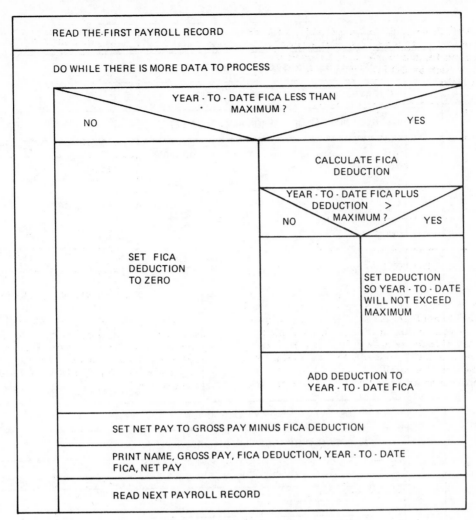

Figure 9. Example of N - S Chart Used For Design

USING NASSI-SHNEIDERMAN CHARTS

The practical use of N-S charts requires some basic techniques for optimum benefits. The major uses of N-S charts fall into three categories: Creating the logic design, programming from the charts, and writing program documentation. In addition, the N-S charts can be used for higher level design and procedural documentation; they have also been very well received for walkthroughs and design reviews.

I. CREATING THE LOGIC DESIGN

Nassi-Shneiderman charts were developed as a better way than traditional flow charts to describe the logic of a structured program. Drawing the chart and developing the logic go hand-in-hand, with the constraints of N-S charts (single page, no branch symbols) forcing the development of a structured design, that will in turn lead to structured code.

How to Start

Let us assume that functional design for a project has been completed, and that a modular design technique was used to determine function, input, and output for each module to be programmed. The programmer is now ready to design logic for structured coding.

The N-S chart starts with a rectangle drawn at the top of the page. This block might be any of the N-S symbols, depending on the module's function. If the module requires initialization of some variables, the first block is probably a processing symbol. If the module's function is performed repeatedly, a block with an iterative symbol will be close to the top of the page. If the function to be performed is conditional, a decision symbol will be used initially.

Arranging the N-S Structure

When a block is drawn symbolizing a decision, the programmer must make an actual decision about the assignment of processing paths on the chart (see Figure 11). An effective technique is to locate on the right the path which in coding would be equivalent to the 'then' clause of an 'if' statement, and to locate on the left the path equivalent to the 'else' clause (see Figure 12). A consistent technique for path assignment makes the chart easier to draw and to read.

Suppose repeated decisions must be made. It is possible that much of the page would be taken up by blank paths (corresponding to null ELSE statements), or by paths with little processing. Very little room would then be left for describing the main processing path of the program (see Figure 13).

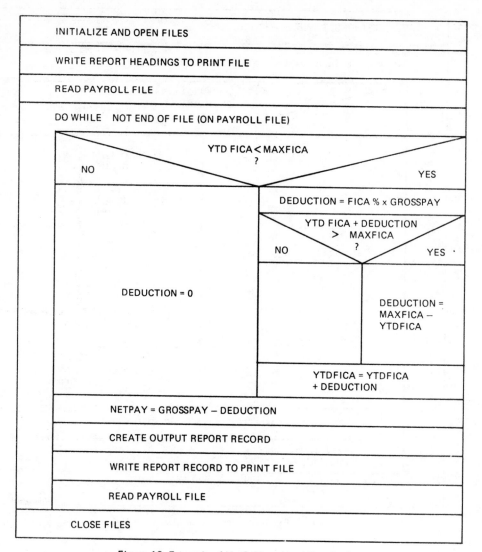

Figure 10. Example of N - S Chart Used For Coding

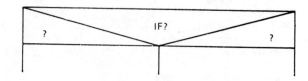

Figure 11. Choice of Path Assignment

Figure 12. IF A THEN Process B ELSE Process C

When to Segment

As the programmer continues to draw the chart and develop the design, nested iteration and decision symbols will cause the blocks to get increasingly smaller. If the programmer did not give some thought initially to segmentation of the module, he or she may find that space has run out on the chart before the design is complete. Any rectangular position of an N-S chart can be removed from the main routine, replaced by a processing block, and made a separate segment or internal subroutine with its own N-S chart. Figure 15 shows in dark lines three of the possible segments which could be removed from the main routine. The choice should depend on the extent to which the portion that is removed constitutes a single function.

Differences in N-S Structure

The N-S chart for a module will visually reflect the design of the module. It may be large or small, complex or simple, depending on the function to be performed. A module at the top of the modular design hierarchy will consist mainly of calls to lower-level modules and evaluation of return codes. Its chart will probably have a diagonal look as can be seen in Figure 16.

A module at the lowest level will perform the actual processing of the data. Figure 17 shows such a module, with a single call to a service module to write an error message.

510

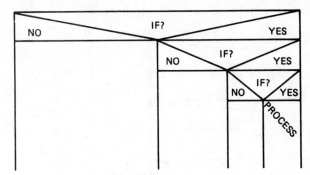

Figure 13. Unskewed N - S Chart

To allow more room on the chart for describing the processing paths, the decision triangle can be skewed, as in Figure 14, allocating space as it is needed.

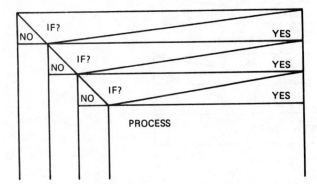

Figure 14. Skewed N - S Chart

II. PROGRAMMING FROM N-S CHARTS

Once the logic design for the module is completed, coding and testing of the module can begin. In both coding and testing, the N-S chart serves as a guide.

Coding

Translating from the N-S chart to code, especially in a high level language, is very easy; this ease is one reason why N-S charts have been accepted enthusiastically by programmers who have tried them.

The code will be structured; there is no possibility of a branch, and the coded segments will be small. IFTHENELSE statements are well defined by the chart, as are the limits of DO structures.

Testing

The N-S chart can be used as a guide while testing the module. The number of test cases which will be required may be readily determined by counting decision blocks (count 2 per decision) and iteration blocks (count 2 or 3 per loop, depending on boundary conditions of the loop).

The precise test cases needed and data required may be developed directly from the charts, and the tested paths may be checked off on the charts as tests are executed.

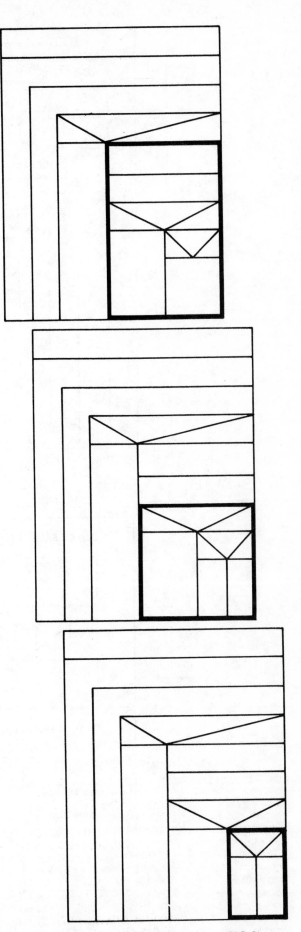

Figure 15. Possible Choices for Segmenting an N-S Chart

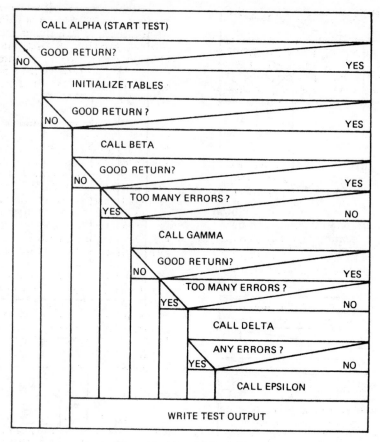

Figure 16. Diagonal N - S Chart

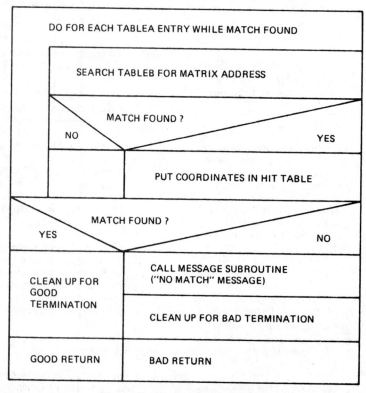

Figure 17. Nondiagonal N - S Chart

III. N-S CHARTS AS PROGRAM DOCUMENTATION

The Nassi-Shneiderman chart is a graphic representation of a module's logic design and a blueprint for the code. This makes it an excellent tool to use in educating other programmers on the function of the module. An N-S chart provides a maintenance programmer with a quick reference for finding the code performing any logical function.

IV. OTHER USES

Other parts of this paper described the use of N-S charts to design and program structured code. The high acceptance level of the charts by programmers who have used them indicates that use of the symbols may expand to other areas.

For example, a possible use may be in functional design. Process blocks can be described in general terms, rather than at the detailed level used for logic design.

As usage of N-S symbols extends beyond programmers to people in other technical areas, as have the symbols of traditional flowcharts, they can become a part of user's procedural documentation.

An area where use of N-S charts has already expanded beyond initial expectations is for presentations at walkthroughs and review. The graphic, visually descriptive qualities of the charts make them easy to use as presentation aids when describing program function to users and other nonprogramming people. Code inspections are significantly easier when a corresponding N-S chart is available to graphically depict the code being inspected. If N-S charts are used for design inspections, then code may be inspected directly against them.

CONCLUSIONS

Many design/documentation methods are in use today; some of these methods have existed for many years, and some methods were recently developed. Among the former are prose, the writing of specifications and documentation in English paragraphs, and conventional flowcharting. The latter includes N-S charts, pseudo-code, and HIPO Charts. None of these methods is bad in itself; for a particular use, one is often better than another.

For example, a program design at a high level, such as a functional specification, may lend itself to prose and to HIPO Charts. Yet, neither of these is much good for detailed logic specifications; prose is often ambiguous and seldom possible to use for coding. HIPO Charts have no facilities for structuring program logic and are also very difficult to use in coding.

Flowcharting has been the method to get from prose or HIPO Charts to code; however, flowcharting is quickly giving way to pseudo-code and Nassi-Shneiderman charts. The latter items have structuring ability built into the technique, and both can be easily translated directly into code. Pseudo-code has the advantage of depicting graphically the logic and also clearly and visually identifying processes within compound conditionals.

For education of users and for walkthroughs or reviews, a combination of HIPO Charts for input/function/output and N-S charts for logical flow has proven extremely useful. Flowcharts and pseudo-code are too strongly programming-oriented for use by nonprogrammers. Pseudo-code might also be useful for code inspections particularly if coded into the programs as comments.

Program documentation has traditionally been separate from programs. One of the hoped-for benefits of structured code was self-documenting programs. To some extent, this benefit has been realized; yet, in many cases supplementary documentation is required. Pseudo-code provides one excellent way of including this supplementary explanation of code within the program as comments. Modification of documentation then requires exactly the same mechanism as modification of the code, and as a result, it aids in maintaining the documentation at a current level.

However, if external program documentation is required, a graphical representation of the code (something impossible to code into the program) can be significantly better. The success of HIPO Charts has demonstrated this fact for overview and function documentation. For displaying logic, N-S charts are much better than HIPO Charts and far better than flowcharts and prose.

SUMMARY

Nassi-Shneiderman Charts have proven to be useful in nearly all phases of program development from early design through walk-throughs, coding, testing, and user education. An excellent graphic technique, the N-S charts provide a simple, yet elegant language that, intentionally, is compatible with structured programming goals and methods. As Nassi and Shneiderman wrote,

"Programmers who first learn to design programs with these symbols never develop the bad habits which other flowchart notation systems permit...Since no more than fifteen or twenty symbols can be drawn on a single sheet of paper, the programmer must modularize his program into meaningful sections. The temptation to use off-page connectors, which lead only to confusion, is eliminated. Finally, the ease with which a structured flowchart can be translated into a structured flowchart can be translated into a structured program is pleasantly surprising."[1]

Because Nassi-Shneiderman charts are only now becoming known, the method has not been fully exploited. There is potential in many areas for expanding on the usage of such structured charts and if the logical thinking we are now insisting on in programming can be spread to other disciplines, we cannot lose.

BIBLIOGRAPHY

1. I. Nassi and B. Shneiderman, "Flowchart Techniques for Structured Programming," SIGPLAN Notices of the ACM, v. 8, n. 8, 12-26 (August 1973).

CONSTRUCTIVE METHODS OF PROGRAM DESIGN

M. A. Jackson

Abstract Correct programs cannot be obtained by attempts to test or to prove incorrect programs: the correctness of a program should be assured by the design procedure used to build it.

A suggestion for such a design procedure is presented and discussed. The procedure has been developed for use in data processing, and can be effectively taught to most practicing programmers. It is based on correspondence between data and program structures, leading to a decomposition of the program into distinct processes. The model of a process is very simple, permitting use of simple techniques of communication, activation and suspension. Some wider implications and future possibilities are also mentioned.

1. Introduction

In this paper I would like to present and discuss what I believe to be *a more constructive method of program design*. The phrase itself is important; I am sure that no-one here will object if I use a LIFO discipline in briefly elucidating its intended meaning.

'Design' is primarily concerned with structure; the designer must say what parts there are to be and how they are to be arranged. The crucial importance of modular programming and structured programming (even in their narrowest and crudest manifestations) is that they provide some definition of what parts are permissible: a module is a separately compiled, parameterized subroutine; a structure component is a sequence, an iteration or a selection. With such definition, inadequate through they may be, we can at least begin to think about design: what modules would make up that program, and how should they be arranged? Should this program be an iteration of selections or a sequence of iterations? Without such definitions, design is meaningless. At the top level of a problem there are P^N possible designs, where P is the number of distinct types of permissible part and N is the number of parts needed to make up the whole. So, to preserve our sanity, both P and N must be small: modular programming, using tree or hierarchical structures, offers small values of N; structured programming offers, additionally, small values of P.

'Program' or, rather 'programming' I would use in a narrow sense. Modeling the problem is 'analysis'; 'programming' is putting the model on a computer. Thus, for example, if we are asked to find a prime number in the range 10^{50} to 10^{60}, we need a number theorist for the analysis; if we are asked to program discounted cash flow, the analysis calls for a financial expert. One of the major ills in data processing stems from uncertainty about this distinction. In mathematical circles the distinction is often ignored altogether, to the detriment, I believe, of our understanding of programming. Programming is about computer programs, not about number theory, or financial planning, or production control.

'Method' is defined in the Shorted OED as a 'procedure for attaining an object'. The crucial word here is 'procedure'. The ultimate method, and the ultimate is doubtless unattainable, is a procedure embodying a precise and correct algorithm. To follow the method we need only execute the algorithm faithfully, and we will be led infallibly to the desired result. To the extent that a putative method falls short of this ideal it is less of a method.

To be 'constructive', a method must itself be decomposed into distinct steps, and correct execution of each step must assure correct execution of the whole method and thus the correctness of its product. The key requirement here is that the correctness of the execution of a step should be largely verifiable without reference to steps not yet executed by the designer. This is the central difficulty in stepwise refinement: we can judge the correctness of a refinement step only be reference to what is yet to come.

Reprinted with permission from *Proceedings of the First Conference of the European Cooperation in Informatics,* Volume 44, 1976, pages 236-262. Copyright © by Springer-Verlag, Heidelberg.

and hence only by exercising a degree of foresight to which few people can lay claim.

Finally, we must recognize that design methods today are intended for use by human beings: in spite of what was said above about constructive methods, we need, now and for some time to come, a substantial ingredient of intuition and subjectivity. So what is presented below does not claim to be fully constructive - merely to be 'more constructive'. The reader must supply the other half of the comparison for himself, measuring the claim against the yardstick of his own favored methods.

2. Basis of the Method

The basis of the method is described, in some detail, in (1). It is appropriate here only to illustrate it by a family of simple example problems.

Example 1

A cardfile of punched cards is sorted into ascending sequence of values of a key which appears in each card. Within this sequence, the first card for each group of cards with a common key value is a header card, while the others are detail cards. Each detail card carries an integer amount. It is required to produce a report showing the totals of amount for all keys.

Solution 1

The first step in applying the method is to describe the structure of the data. We use a graphic notation to represent the structures as trees:

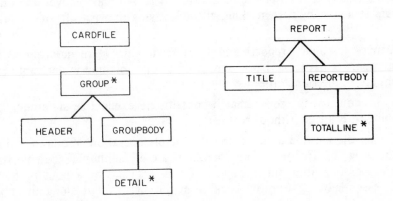

The above representations are equivalent to the following (in BNF with iteration instead of recursion):

$$<\text{cardfile}> ::= \{<\text{group}>\}_0^\infty$$
$$<\text{group}> ::= <\text{header}><\text{groupbody}>$$
$$<\text{groupbody}> ::= \{<\text{detail}>\}_0^\infty$$
$$<\text{report}> ::= <\text{title}><\text{reportbody}>$$
$$<\text{reportbody}> ::= \{<\text{totalline}>\}_0^\infty$$

The second step is to compose these data structures into a program structure:

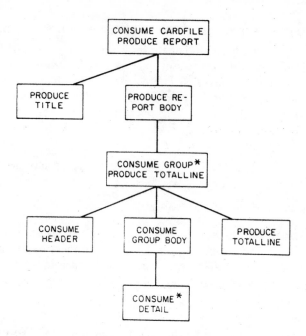

This structure has the following properties:

- It is related quite formally to each of the data structures. We may recover any one data structure from the program structure by first marking all nodes lying in a path from a marked node to the root.

- The correspondences (cardfile : report) and (group : totalline) are determined by the problem statement. One report is derivable from one cardfile; one totalline is derivable from one group, and the totallines are in the same order as the groups.

- The structure is vacuous, in the sense that it contains no executable statements: it is a program which does nothing; it is a tree without real leaves.

The third step in applying the method is to list the executable operations required and to allocate each to its right place in the program structure. The operations are elementary executable statements of the programming language, possibly after enhancement of the language by a bout of bottom-up design; they are enumerated, essentially, by working back from output to input along the obvious data-flow paths. Assuming a reasonably conventional machine and a line printer (rather than a character printer), we may obtain the list:

1. write title

2. write totalline (groupkey, total)

3. total := total + detail.amount

4. total := 0

5. groupkey := header.key

6. open cardfile

7. read cardfile

8. close cardfile

Note that every operation, or almost every operation, must have operands which are data objects. Allocation to a program structure is therefore a trivial task if the program structure is correctly based on the data structures. This triviality is a vital criterion of the success of the first two steps. The resulting program, in an obvious notation, is:

516

```
CARD-REPORT sequence
    open cardfile;
    read cardfile;
    write title;
    REPORT-BODY iteration until cardfile.eof
        total := 0;
        groupkey := header.key;
        read cardfile;
        GROUP-BODY iteration until cardfile.eof
                        or detail.key ≠ groupkey
            total := total + detail.amount;
            read cardfile;
        GROUP-BODY end
        write totalline (groupkey, total);
    REPORT-BODY end
    close cardfile;
CARDFILE-REPORT end
```

Clearly, this program may be transcribed without difficulty into any procedural programming language.

Comment

The solution has proceeded in three steps: First, we defined the data structures; second, we formed them into a program structure; third, we listed and allocated the executable operations. At each step we have criteria for the correctness of the step itself and an implicit check on the correctness of the steps already taken. For example, if at the first step we had wrongly described the structure of cardfile as

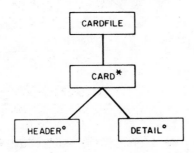

(that is: $<\text{cardfile}> ::= \{<\text{card}>\}_0^\infty$

$<\text{card}> ::= <\text{header}> | <\text{detail}>$),

we should have been able to see at the first step that we had failed to represent everything we knew about the cardfile. If nonetheless we had persisted in error, we would have discovered it at the second step, when we would have been unable to form a program structure in the absence of a cardfile component corresponding to a totalline in report.

The design has throughout concentrated on what we may think of as a static rather than a dynamic view of the problem: on maps, not on itineraries, on structures, not on logic flow. The logic flow of the finished program is a by-product of the data structures and the correct allocation of the 'read' operation. There is an obvious connection between what we have done and the design of a very simple syntax analysis phase in a compiler: the grammar of the input file determines the structure of the program which parses it. We may observe that the 'true' grammar of the cardfile is not context-free: within one group, the header and detail cards must all carry the same key value. It is because the explicit grammar cannot show this that we are forced to introduce the variable groupkey to deal with this stipulation.

Note that there is no error-checking. If we wish to check for errors in the input we must elaborate the structure of the input file to accommodate those errors explicitly. By defining a structure for an input file we define the domain of the program: if we wish to extend the domain, we must extend the input file structure accordingly. In a practical data processing system, we would always define the structure of primary input (such as decks of cards, keyboard messages, etc) to encompass all physically possible files: it would be absurd to construct a program whose operation is unspecified (and therefore, in principle, unpredictable) in the event of a card deck being dropped or a wrong key depressed.

Example 2

The cardfile of example 1 is modified so that each card contains a card-type indicator with possible values 'header', 'detail' and other. The program should take account of possible errors in the composition of a group: there may be no header card and/or there may be cards other than detail cards in the group body. Groups containing errors should be listed on an errorlist, but not totaled.

Solution 2

The structure of the report remains unchanged. The structure of the errorlist and of the new version of the cardfile are:

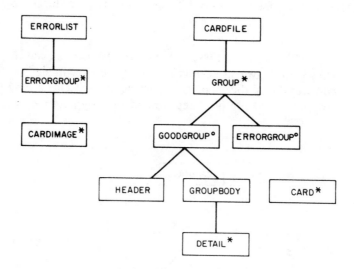

The structure of cardfile demands attention. Firstly, it is ambiguous: anything which is a goodgroup is also an errorgroup. We are forced into this ambiguity because it would be intolerably difficult - and quite unnecessary - to spell out all of the ways in which a group may be in error. The ambiguity is simply resolved by the conventions we use: the parts of a selection are considered to be ordered, and the first applicable part encountered in a left-to-right scan is chosen. So a group can be parsed as an errorgroup only if it has already been rejected as a goodgroup. Secondly, a goodgroup cannot be recognized by a left-to-right parse of the input file with any predetermined degree of lookahead. If we choose to read ahead R records, we may yet encounter a group containing an error only in the R+1'th card.

Recognition problems of this kind occur in many guises. Their essence is that we are forced to a choice during program execution at a time when we lack the evidence on which the choice must be based. Note that the difficulty is not structural but is confined to achieving a workable flow of control. We will call such problems 'backtracking' problems, and tackle them in three stages:

- Ignore the recognition difficulty, imagining that a friendly demon will tell us infallibly which choice to make. In the present problem, he will tell us whether a group is a goodgroup or an errorgroup. Complete the design procedure in this blissful state of confidence, producing the full program text.

518

- Replace our belief in the demon's infallibility by a sceptical determination to verify each 'landmark' in the data which might prove him wrong. Whenever he is proved wrong we will execute a 'quit' statement which branches to the second part of the selection. Those 'quit' statements are introduced into the program text created in stage a.

- Modify the program text resulting from stage b to ensure that side-effects are repealed where necessary.

The result of stage a, in accordance with the design procedure used for example 1, is:

```
CFILE-REPT-ERR sequence
    open cardfile;
    read cardfile;
    write title;
    REPORT-BODY iteration until cardfile.eof
        groupkey := card.key;
        GROUP-OUTG select goodgroup
            total := 0;
            read cardfile;
            GOOD-GROUP iteration until cardfile.eof
                    or detail.key ≠ groupkey
                total := total + detail.amount;
                read cardfile;
            GOOD-GROUP end
            write totalline (groupkey, total);
        GROUP-OUTG or errorgroup
            ERROR-GROUP iteration until cardfile.eof
                    or card.key ≠ groupkey
                write errorline (card);
                read cardfile;
            ERROR-GROUP end
        GROUP-OUTG end
    REPORT-BODY end
    close cardfile;
CFILE-REPT-ERR end
```

Note that we cannot completely transcribe this program into any programming language, because we cannot code an evaluable expression for the predicate goodgroup. However, we can readily verify the correctness of the program (assuming the infallibility of the demon). Indeed, if we are prepared to exert ourselves to punch an identifying character into the header card of each goodgroup - thus acting as our own demon - we can code and run the program as an informal demonstration of its acceptability.

We are now ready to proceed to stage b, in which we insert 'quit' statements into the first part of the selection GROUP-OUTG. Also, since quit statements are not present in a normal selection, we will replace the words 'select' and 'or' by 'posit' and 'admit' respectively, thus indicating the tentative nature of the initial choice. Clearly, the landmarks to be checked are the card-type indicators in the header and detail cards. We thus obtain the following program:

```
CFILE-REPT-ERR sequence
    open cardfile;
    read cardfile;
    write title;
    REPORT-BODY iteration until cardfile.eof
        groupkey := card.key;
        GROUP-OUTG posit goodgroup
            total := 0;
            quit GROUP-OUTG if card.type ≠ header;
            read cardfile;
            GOOD-GROUP iteration until cardfile.eof
                    or card.key ≠ groupkey
                quit GROUP-OUTG if card.type ≠ detail;
                total := total + detail.amount;
                read cardfile;
            GOOD-GROUP end
            write totalline (groupkey, total);
        GROUP-OUTG admit errorgroup
            ERROR-GROUP iteration until cardfile.eof
                    or card.key ≠ groupkey;
                write errorline (card);
                read cardfile;
            ERROR-GROUP end
        GROUP-OUTG end
    REPORT-BODY end
    close cardfile;
CFILE-REPT-ERR end
```

The third stage, stage c, deals with the side-effects of partial execution of the first part of the selection. In this trivial example, the only significant side-effect is the reading of cardfile. In general, it will be found that the only troublesome side-effects are the reading and writing of serial files; the best and easiest way to handle them is to equip ourselves with input and output procedures capable of 'noting' and 'restoring' the state of the file and its associated buffers. Given the availability of such procedures, stage c can be completed by inserting a 'note' statement immediately following the 'posit' statement and a 'restore' statement immediately following the 'admit'. Sometimes side-effects will demand a more ad hoc treatment: when 'note' and 'restore' are unavailable there is no alternative to such cumbersome expedients as explicitly storing each record on disk or in main storage.

Comment

By breaking our treatment of the backtracking difficulty into three distinct stages, we are able to isolate distinct aspects of the problem. In stage a we ignore the backtracking difficulty entirely, and concentrate our efforts on obtaining a correct solution to the reduced problem. This solution is carried through the three main design steps, producing a completely specific program text: we are able to satisfy ourselves of the correctness of that text before going on to modify it in the second and third stages. In the second stage we deal only with the recognition difficulty: the difficulty is one of logic flow, and we handle it, appropriately, by modifying the logic flow, and we handle it, appropriately, by modifying the logic flow of the program with quit statements. Each quit statement says, in effect, 'It is supposed (posited) that this is a goodgroup; but if, in fact, this card is not what is ought to be then this is not, after all, a goodgroup'. The required quit statements can be easily seen from the data structure definition, and their place is readily found in the program text because the program structure perfectly matches the data structure. The side-effects arise to be dealt with in stage c because of the quit statements, producing discontinuities in the context of the computation and hence side-effects. The side-effects are readily identified from the program text resulting from stage b.

Note that it would be quite wrong to distort the data structures and the program structure in an attempt to avoid the dreaded four-letter word 'goto'. The data structures shown, and hence the program structure, are self-evidently the correct structures for the problem as stated: they must not be abandoned because of difficulties with the logic flow.

3. Simple Programs and Complex Programs

The design method, as described above, is severely constrained: it applies to a narrow class of serial file-processing programs. We may go further, and say that if defines such a class - the class of 'simple programs'. A 'simple program' has the following attributes:

- The program has a fixed initial state; nothing is remembered from one execution to the next.

- Program inputs and outputs are serial files, which we may conveniently suppose to be held on magnetic tapes. There may be more than one input and more than one output file.

- Associated with the program is an explicit definition of the structure of each input and output file. These structures are tree structures, defined in the grammar used above. This grammar permits recursion in addition to the features shown above; it is not very different from a grammar of regular expressions.

- The input data structures define the domain of the program, the output data structures its range. Nothing is introduced into the program text which is not associated with the defined data structures.

- The data structures are compatible, in the sense that they can be combined into a program structure in the manner shown above.

- The program structure thus derived from the data structures is sufficient for a workable program. Elementary operations of the program language (possibly supplemented by more powerful or suitable operations resulting from bottom-up designing) are allocated to components of the program structure without introducing any further 'program logic'.

A simple program may be designed and constructed with the minimum of difficulty, provided that we adhere rigorously to the design principles adumbrated here and eschew any temptation to pursue efficiency at the cost of distorting the structure. In fact, we should usually discount the benefits of efficiency, reminding ourselves of the mass of error-ridden programs which attest to its dangers.

Evidently, not all programs are simple programs. Sometimes we are presented with the task of constructing a program which operates on direct-access rather than on serial files, or which processes a single record at each execution, starting from a varying internal state. As we shall see later, a simple program may be clothed in various disguises which give it a misleading appearance without affecting its underlying nature. More significantly, we may find that the design procedure suggested cannot be applied to the problem given because the data structures are not compatible: that is, we are unable at the second step of the design procedure to form the program structure from the data structures.

Example 3

The input cardfile of example 1 is presented to the program in the form of a blocked file. Each block of this file contains a card count and a number of card images.

Solution 3

The structure of blockedfile is:

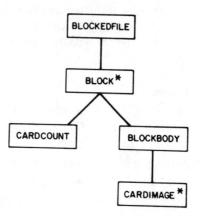

This structure does not, of course, show the arrangement of the cards in groups. It is impossible to show, in a single structure, both the arrangement in groups and the arrangement in blocks. But the structure of the report is still:

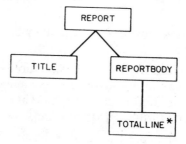

We cannot fit together the structures of report and blockedfile to form a program structure; nor would we be in better case if we were to ignore the arrangement in blocks. The essence of our difficulty is this: the program must contain operations to be executed once per block, and these must be allocated to a 'process block' component; it must also contain operations to be executed once per group, and these must be allocated to a 'process group' component; but it is impossible to form a single program structure containing both a 'process block' and a 'process group' component. We will call this difficulty a 'structure clash'.

The solution to the structure clash in the present example is obvious: more so because of the order in which the examples have been taken and because everyone knows about blocking and deblocking. But the solution can be derived more formally from the data structures. The clash is of a type we will call 'boundary clash': the boundaries of the blocks are not synchronized with the boundaries of the groups. The standard solution for a structure clash is to abandon the attempt to form a single program structure and instead decompose the problem into two or more simple programs. For a boundary clash the required decomposition is always of the form:

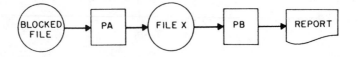

The intermediate file, file X, must be composed of records each of which is a cardimage, because cardimage is the highest common factor of the structures blockedfile and cardfile. The program PB is the program produced as a solution to example 1; the program PA is:

```
PA sequence
    open blockedfile;
    open fileX;
    read blockedfile;
    PABODY iteration until blockedfile.eof
        cardpointer := 1;
        PBLOCK iteration until cardpointer > block.cardcount
            write cardimage (cardpointer);
            cardpointer := cardpointer + 1;
        PBLOCK end
        read blockedfile;
    PABODY end
    close fileX;
    close blockedfile;
PA end
```

The program PB sees file X as having the structure of cardfile in example 1, while program PA sees its structure as:

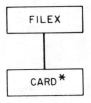

Comment

The decomposition into two simple programs achieves a perfect solution. Only the program PA is cognizant of the arrangement of cardimages in blocks; only the program PB of their arrangement in groups. The tape containing file X acts as a cordon sanitaire between the two, ensuring that no undesired interactions can occur: we need not concern ourselves at all with such questions as 'what if the header record of a group is the first cardimage in a block with only one cardimage?', or 'what if a group has no detail records and its header is the last cardimage in a block'; in this respect our design is known to be correct.

There is an obvious inefficiency in our solution. By introducing the intermediate magnetic tape file we have, to a first approximation, doubled the elapsed time for program execution and increased the program's demand for backing store devices.

Example 4

The input cardfile of example 1 is incompletely sorted. The cards are partially ordered so that the header card of each group precedes any detail cards of that group, but no other ordering is imposed. The report has no title, and the totals may be produced in any order.

Solution 4

The best we can do for the structure of cardfile is:

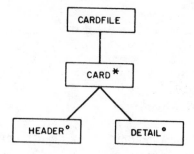

which is clearly incompatible with the structure of the report, since there is no component of cardfile corresponding to totalline in the report. Once again we have a structure clash, but this time of a different type. The cardfile consists of a number of groupfiles, each one of which has the form:

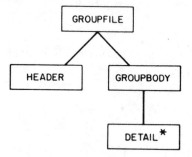

The cardfile is an arbitrary interleaving of these groupfiles. To resolve the clash (an 'interleaving clash') we must resolve cardfile into its constituent groupfiles:

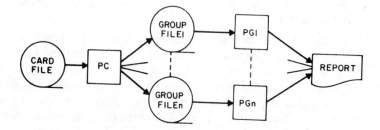

Allowing, for purposes of exposition, that a single report may be produced by the n programs PG1, ... PGn (each contributing one totalline), we have decomposed the problem into n+1 simple programs; of these, n are identical programs processing the n distinct groupfiles groupfile1, ... groupfilen; while the other, PC, resolves cardfile into its constituents.

Two possible versions of PC are:

```
PC1 sequence
    open cardfile;
    read cardfile;
    open all possible groupfiles;
    PC1BODY iteration until cardfile.eof
        write record to groupfile(record.key);
        read cardfile;
    PC1BODY end
    close all possible groupfiles;
    close cardfile;
PC1 end
```

and

```
PC2 sequence
    open cardfile;
    read cardfile;
    PC2BODY iteration until cardfile.eof
        REC-INIT select new groupfile
            open groupfile(record.key);
        REC-INIT end
        write record to groupfile(record.key);
        read cardfile;
    PC2BODY end
    close all opened groupfiles;
    close cardfile;
PC2 end
```

Both PC1 and PC2 present difficulties. In PC1 we must provide a groupfile for every possible key value, whether or not cardfile contains records for that key. Also, the programs PG1, ... PGn must be elaborated to handle the null groupfile:

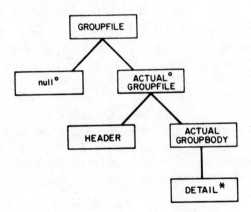

In PC2 we must provide a means of determining whether a groupfile already exists for a given key value. Note that it would be quite wrong to base the determination on the fact that a header must be the first record for a group: such a solution takes impermissible advantage of the structure of groupfile which, in principle, is unknown in the program PC; we would then have to make a drastic change to PC if, for example, the header card were made optional:

525

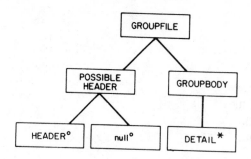

Further, in PC2 we must be able to run through all the actual key values in order to close all the groupfiles actually opened. This would still be necessary even if each group had a recognizable trailer record, for reasons similar to those given above concerning the header records.

Comment

The inefficiency of our solution to example 4 far outstrips the inefficiency of our solution to example 3. Indeed, our solution to example 4 is entirely impractical. Practical implementation of the designs will be considered below in the next section. For the moment, we may observe that the use of magnetic tapes for communication between simple programs enforces a very healthy discipline. We are led to use a very simple protocol: every serial file must be opened and closed. The physical medium encourages a complete decoupling of the programs: it is easy to imagine one program being run today, the tapes held overnight in a library, and a subsequent program being run tomorrow; the whole of the communication is visible in the defined structure of the files. Finally, we are strengthened in our resolve to think in terms of static structures, avoiding the notoriously error-prone activity of thinking about dynamic flow and execution-time events.

Taking a more global view of the design procedure, we may say that the simple program is a satisfactory high level component. It is a larger object than a sequence, iteration or selection; it has a more precise definition than a module; it is subject to restrictions which reveal to us clearly when we are trying to make a single program out of what should be two or more.

4. Programs, Procedures and Processes

Although from the design point of view we regard magnetic tapes as the canonical medium of communication between simple programs, they will not usually provide a practical implementation.

An obvious possiblity for implementation in some environments is to replace each magnetic tape by a limited number of buffers in main storage, with a suitable regime for ensuring that the consumer program does not run ahead of the producer. Each simple program can then be treated as a distinct task or process, using whatever facilities are provided for the management of multiple concurrent tasks.

However, something more like coroutines seems more attractive (2). The standard procedure call mechanism offers a simple implementation of great flexibility and power. Consider the program PA, in our solution to example 3, which writes the intermediate file X. We can readily convert this program into a procedure PAX which has the characteristics of an input procedure for file X. that is, invocations of the procedure PAX will satisfactorily implement the operations 'open file X for reading', 'read file X' and 'close file X after reading'.

We will call this conversion of PA into PAX 'inversion of PA with respect to file X'. (Note that the situation in solution 3 is symmetrical: we could equally well decide to invert PB with respect to file X, obtaining an output procedure for file X.) The mechanics of inversion are a mere matter of generating the appropriate object coding from the text of the simple program: there is no need for any modification to that text. PA and PAX are the same program, not two different programs. Most practicing programmers seem to be unaware of this identity of PA and PAX, and even those who are familiar with coroutines often program as if they supposed that PA and PAX were distinct things. This is partly due to the baleful influence of the stack as a storage allocation device: we cannot jump out of an inner block of

PAX, return to the invoking procedure, and subsequently resume where we left off when we are next invoked. So we must either modify our compiler or modify our coding style, adopting the use of labels and go to statements as a standard in place of the now conventional compound statement of structured programming. It is common to find PAX, or an analogous program, designed as a selection or case statement: the mistake is on all fours with that of the kindergarten child who has been led to believe that the question 'what is 5 multiplied by 3?' is quite different from the question 'what is 3 multiplied by 5?'. At a stroke the poor child has doubled the difficulty of learning the multiplication tables.

The procedure PAX is, of course, a variable state procedure. The value of its state is held in a 'state vector' (or activation record), of which a vital part is the text pointer; the values of special significance are those associated with the suspension of PAX for operations on file X—open, write and close. The state vector is an 'own variable' par excellence, and should be clearly seen as such.

The minimum interface needed between PB and PAX is two parameters: a record of file X, and an additional bit to indicate whether the record is or is not the eof marker. This minimum interface suffices for example 3: there is no need for PB to pass an operation code to PAX (open read or close). It is important to understand that this minimum interface will not suffice for the general case. It is sufficient for example 3 only because the operation code is implicit in the ordering of operations. From the point of view of PAX, the first invocation must be 'open', and subsequent invocations must be 'read' until PAX has returned the eof marker to PB, after which the final invocation must be 'close'. This felicitous harmony is destroyed if, for example, PB is permitted to stop reading and close file X before reaching the eof marker. In such a case the interface must be elaborated with an operation code. Worse, the sequence of values of this operation code now constitutes a file in its own right: the solution becomes:

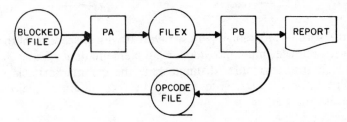

The design of PA is, potentially, considerably more complicated. The benefit we will obtain from treating this complication conscientiously is well worth the price: by making explicit the structure of the opcode file we define the problem exactly and simplify its solution. Failure to recognize the existence of the opcode file, or, just as culpable, failure to make its structure explicit, lies at the root of the errors and obscurities for which manufacturer's input-output software is deservedly infamous.

In solution 4 we created an intolerable multiplicity of files—groupfile1,... groupfilen. We can rid ourselves of these by inverting the programs PG1,...PGn with respect to their respective groupfiles: that is, we convert each of the programs PGi to an output procedure PGFi, which can be invoked by PC to execute operations on groupfilei. But we still have an intolerable multiplicity of output procedures, so a further step is required. The procedures are identical except for their names and the current values of their state vectors. So we separate out the pure procedure part—PGF—of which we need keep only one copy, and the named state vectors SVPGF1, ... SVPGFn. We must now provide a mechanism for storing and retrieving these state vectors and for associating the appropriate state vector with each invocation of PGF; many mechanisms are possible, from a fully-fledged direct-access file with serial read facilities to a simple arrangement of the state vectors in an array in main storage.

5. Design and Implementation

The model of a simple program and the decomposition of a problem into simple programs provides some unity of viewpoint. In particular, we may be able to see what is common to programs with widely different implementations. Some illustrations follow.

a.   A conversational program is a simple program of the form:

The user provides a serial input file of messages, ordered in time; the conversation program produces a serial file of responses. Inversion of the program with respect to the user input file gives an output procedure 'dispose of one message in a conversation'. The state vector of the inverted program must be preserved for the duration of the conversation: IBM's IMS provides the SPA (Scratchpad Area) for precisely this purpose. The conversation program must, of course, be designed and written as a single program: implementation restrictions may dictate segmentation of the object code.

b.   A 'sort-exit' allows the user of a generalized sorting program to introduce his own procedure at the point where each record is about to be written to the final output file. An interface is provided which permits 'insertion' and 'deletion' of records as well as 'updating'.

We should view the sort-exit procedure as a simple program:

To fit it in with the sorting program we must invert it with respect to both the sortedfile and the final output. The interface must provide an implementation of the basic operations: open sortedfile for reading; read sortedfile (distinguishing the eof marker); close sortedfile after reading; open finaloutput for writing; write finaloutput record; close finaloutput file after writing (including writing the eof marker).

Such concepts as 'insertion' and 'deletion' of records are pointless: at best, they serve the cause of efficiency, traducing clarity; at worst, they create difficulty and confusion where none need exist.

c.   Our solution to example 1 can be seen as an optimisation of the solution to the more general example 4. By sorting the cardfile we ensure that the groups do not overlap in time: the state vectors of the inverted programs PGF1, ... PGFn can therefore share a single area in main storage. The state vector consists only of the variable total; the variable groupkey is the name of the currently active group and hence of the current state vector. Because the records of a group are contiguous, the end of a group is recognizable at cardfile.eof or at the start of another group. The individual groupfile may therefore be closed, and the totalline written, at the earliest possible moment.

We may, perhaps, generalize so far as to say that an identifier is stored by a program only in order to give a unique name to the state vector of some process.

d.   A data processing system may be viewed as consisting of many simple programs, one for each independent entity in the real world model. By arranging the entities in sets we arrange the corresponding simple programs in equivalence classes. The 'master record' corresponding to an entity is the state vector of the simple program modelling that entity.

The serial files of the system are files of transactions ordered in time: some are primary transactions, communicating with the real world, some are secondary, passing between simple programs of the system. In general, the real world must be modelled as a network of entities or of entity sets; the data processing system is therefore a network of simple programs and transaction files.

Implementation of the system demands decisions in two major areas. First a scheduling algorithm must be decided; second, the representation and handling of state vectors. The extreme cases of the first are 'real-time' and 'serial batch'. In a pure 'real-time' system every primary transaction is dealt with as soon as it arrives, followed immediately by all of the secondary and consequent transactions, until the system as a whole becomes quiet. In a pure 'serial batch' system, each class (identifier set) of primary transactions is accumulated for a period (usually a day, week or month). Each simple program of that class is then activated (if there is a transaction present for it), giving rise to secondary transactions of various classes. These are then treated similarly, and so on until no more transactions remain to be processed.

Choosing a good implementation for a data processing system is difficult, because the network is usually large and many possible choices present themselves. This difficulty is compounded by the long-term nature of the simple programs: a typical entity, and hence a typical program, has a lifetime measured in years or even decades. During such a lifetime the system will inevitably undergo change: in effect, the programs are being rewritten while they are in course of execution.

e. An interrupt handler is a program which processes a serial file of interrupts, ordered in time:

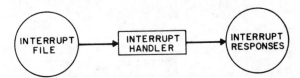

Inversion of the interrupt handler with respect to the interrupt file gives the required procedure 'dispose of one interrupt'. In general, the interrupt file will be composed of interleaved files for individual processes, devices, etc. Implementation is further complicated by the special nature of the invocation mechanism, by the fact that the records of the interrupt file are distributed in main storage, special registers and other places, and by the essentially recursive structure of the main interrupt file (unless the interrupt handler is permitted to mask off secondary interrupts).

f. An input-output procedure (what IBM literature calls an 'access method') is a simple program which processes an input file of access requests and produces an output file of access responses. An access request consists of an operation code and, sometimes, a data record; an access response consists of a result code and, sometimes, a data record. For example, a direct-access method has the form:

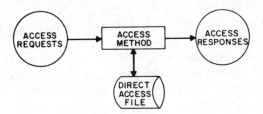

By inverting this simple program with respect to both the file of access requests and the file of access responses we obtain the desired procedure. This double inversion is always possible without difficulty, because each request must produce a response and that response must be calculable before the next request is presented.

The chief crime of access method designers is to conceal from their customers (and, doubtless, from themselves) the structure of the file of access requests. The user of the method is thus unable to determine what sequences of operations are permitted by the access method, and what their effect will be.

g. Some aspects of a context-sensitive grammar may be regarded as interleaved context-free grammars. For example, in a grossly simplified version of the COBOL language we may wish to stipulate that any variable may appear as an operand of a MOVE statement, while only a variable declared as numeric may appear as an operand of an arithmetic (ADD, SUBTRACT, MULTIPLY or DIVIDE) statement. We may represent this stipulation as follows:

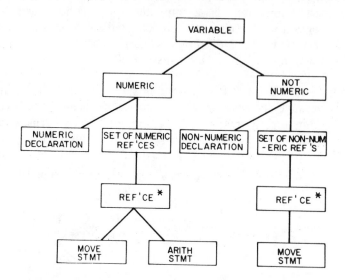

The syntax-checking part of the compiler consists, partly, of a simple program for each declared variable. The symbol table is the set of state vectors for these simple programs. The algorithm for activating and suspending these and other programs will determine the way in which one error interacts with another both for diagnosis and correction.

6. A Modest Proposal

It is one thing to propose a model to illuminate what has already been done, to clarify the sources of existing success or failure. It is quite another to show that the model is of practical value, and that it leads to the construction of acceptable programs. An excessive zeal in decomposition produces cumbersome interfaces and pointlessly redundant code. The "Shanley Principle" in civil engineering (3) requires that several functions be implemented in a single part; this is necessary for economy both in manufacturing and in operating the products of engineering design. It appears that a design approach which depends on decomposition runs counter to this principle: its main impetus is the separation of functions for implementation in distinct parts of the program.

But programs do not have the intractable nature of the physical objects which civil, mechanical or electrical engineers produce. They can be manipulated and transformed (for example, by compilers) in ways which preserve their vital qualities of correctness and modifiability while improving their efficiency both generally and in the specialized environment of a particular machine. The extent to which a program can be manipulated and transformed is critically affected by two factors: the variety of forms it can take, and the semantic clarity of the text. Programs written using today's conventional techniques score poorly on both factors. There is a distressingly large variety of forms, and intelligibility is compromised or even destroyed by the introduction of implementation-orientated features. The justification for these techniques is, of course, efficiency. But in pursuing efficiency in this way we become caught in a vicious circle: because our languages are rich the compilers cannot understand, and hence cannot optimize, our programs; so we need rich languages to allow us to obtain the efficiency which the compilers do not offer.

Decomposition into simple programs, as discussed above, seems to offer some hope of separating the considerations of correctness and modifiability from the considerations of efficiency. Ultimately, the objective is that the first should become largely trivial and the second largely automatic.

The first phase of design would produce the following documents:

- a definition of each serial file structure for each simple program (including files of operation codes!);
- the text of each simple program;
- a statement of the communication between simple programs, perhaps in the form of identities such as

$$\text{output } (p_i, f_r) \equiv \text{input } (p_j, f_s).$$

It may then be possible to carry out some automatic checking of self-consistency in the design—for instance, to check that the inputs to a program are within its domain. We may observe, incidentally, that the 'inner' feature of Simula 67 (4) is a way of enforcing consistency of a very limited case. More ambitiously, it may be possible, if file-handling protocol is exactly observed, and read and write operations are allocated with a scrupulous regard to principle, to check the correctness of the simple programs in relation to the defined data structures.

In the second phase of design, the designer would specify, in greater or lesser detail:

- the synchronization of the simple programs;
- the handling of state vectors;
- the dissection and recombining of programs and state vectors to reduce interface overheads.

Synchronization is already loosely constrained by the statements of program communication made in the first phase: the consumer can never run ahead of the producer. Within this constraint the designer may choose to impose additional constraints at compile time and/or at execution time. The weakest local constraint is to provide unlimited dynamic buffering at execution time, the consumer being allowed to lag behind the producer by anything from a single record to the whole file, depending on resource allocation elsewhere in the system. The strongest local constraints are use of coroutines or program inversion (enforcing a single record lag) and use of a physical magnetic tape (enforcing a whole file lag).

Dissection and recombining of programs becomes possible with coroutines or program inversion; its purpose is to reduce interface overheads by moving code between the invoking and invoked programs, thus avoiding some of the time and space costs of procedure calls and also, under certain circumstances, avoiding replication of program structure and hence of coding for sequencing control. It depends on being able to associate code in one program with code in another through the medium of the communication data structure.

A trivial illustration is provided by solution 3, in which we chose to invert PA with respect to file X, giving an input procedure PAX for the file of cardimages. We may decide that the procedure call overhead is intolerable, and that we wish to dissect PAX and combine it with PB. This is achieved by taking the invocations of PAX in PB (that is, the statements 'open fileX', 'read fileX' and 'close fileX') and replacing those invocations by the code which PAX would execute in response to them. For example, in response to 'open fileX' statement in PB can be replaced by the statement 'open blockedfile'.

A more substantial illustration is provided by the common practice of designers of 'real-time' data processing systems. Suppose that a primary transaction for a product gives rise to a secondary transaction for each open order item for that product, and that each of those in turn gives rise to a transaction for the open order of which it is a part, which then gives rise to a transaction for the open order of which it is a part, which then gives rise to a transaction for the customer who placed the order. Instead of having separate simple programs for the product, order item, order and customer, the designer will usually specify a 'transaction processing module': this consists of coding from each of those simple programs, the coding being that required to handle the relevant primary or secondary transaction.

Some interesting program transformations of a possibly relevant kind are discussed in a paper by Burstall and Darlington (5). I cannot end this paper better than by quoting from them:

"The overall aim of our investigation has been to help people to write correct programs which are easy to alter. To produce such programs it seems advisable to adopt a lucid, mathematical and abstract programming style. If one takes this really seriously, attempting to free one's mind from considerations of computational efficiency, there may be a heavy penalty in program running time; in practice it is often necessary to adopt a more intricate version of the program, sacrificing comprehensibility for speed. The question then arises as to how a lucid program can be transformed into a more intricate but efficient one in a systematic way, or indeed in a way which could be mechanized."

"...We are interested in starting with programs having an extremely simple structure and only later introducing the complications which we usually take for granted even in high level language programs. These complications arise by introducing useful interactions between what were originally separate parts of the program, benefiting by what might be called 'economies of interaction'." ∎

References

1. Principles of Program Design; M A Jackson; Academic Press 1975.

2. Hierarchical Program Structures; O-J Dahl; in Structured Programming; Academic Press 1972.

3. Structured Programming with *go to* Statements; Donald E Knuth; in ACM Computing Surveys Vol 6 No 4 December 1974.

4. A Structural Approach to Protection; C A R Hoare; 1975.

5. Some Transformations for Developing Recursive Programs; R M Burstall & John Darlington; in Proceedings of 1975 Conference on Reliable Software; Sigplan Notices Vol 10 No 6 June 1975.

Program Development by Stepwise Refinement

Niklaus Wirth
Eidgenössische Technische Hochschule
Zürich, Switzerland

The creative activity of programming—to be distinguished from coding—is usually taught by examples serving to exhibit certain techniques. It is here considered as a sequence of design decisions concerning the decomposition of tasks into subtasks and of data into data structures. The process of successive refinement of specifications is illustrated by a short but nontrivial example, from which a number of conclusions are drawn regarding the art and the instruction of programming.

Key Words and Phrases: education in programming, programming techniques, stepwise program construction
CR Categories: 1.50, 4.0

1. Introduction

Programming is usually taught by examples. Experience shows that the success of a programming course critically depends on the choice of these examples. Unfortunately, they are too often selected with the prime intent to demonstrate what a computer can do. Instead, a main criterion for selection should be their suitability to exhibit certain widely applicable *techniques*. Furthermore, examples of programs are commonly presented as finished "products" followed by explanations of their purpose and their linguistic details. But active programming consists of the design of *new* programs, rather than contemplation of old programs. As a consequence of these teaching methods, the student obtains the impression that programming consists mainly of mastering a language (with all the peculiarities and intricacies so abundant in modern PL's) and relying on one's intuition to somehow transform ideas into finished programs. Clearly, programming courses should teach methods of design and construction, and the selected examples should be such that a gradual *development* can be nicely demonstrated.

This paper deals with a single example chosen with

these two purposes in mind. Some well-known techniques are briefly demonstrated and motivated (strategy of preselection, stepwise construction of trial solutions, introduction of auxiliary data, recursion), and the program is gradually developed in a sequence of *refinement steps*.

In each step, one or several instructions of the given program are decomposed into more detailed instructions. This successive decomposition or refinement of specifications terminates when all instructions are expressed in terms of an underlying computer or programming language, and must therefore be guided by the facilities available on that computer or language. The result of the execution of a program is expressed in terms of data, and it may be necessary to introduce further data for communication between the obtained subtasks or instructions. As tasks are refined, so the data may have to be refined, decomposed, or structured, and it is natural to *refine program and data specifications in parallel*.

Every refinement step implies some design decisions. It is important that these decision be made explicit, and that the programmer be aware of the underlying criteria and of the existence of alternative solutions. The possible solutions to a given problem emerge as the leaves of a tree, each node representing a point of deliberation and decision. Subtrees may be considered as *families of solutions* with certain common characteristics and structures. The notion of such a tree may be particularly helpful in the situation of changing purpose and environment to which a program may sometime have to be adapted.

A guideline in the process of stepwise refinement should be the principle to decompose decisions as much as possible, to untangle aspects which are only seemingly interdependent, and to defer those decisions which concern details of representation as long as possible. This will result in programs which are easier to adapt to different environments (languages and computers), where different representations may be required.

The chosen sample problem is formulated at the beginning of section 3. The reader is strongly urged to try to find a solution by himself before embarking on the paper which—of course—presents only one of many possible solutions.

2. Notation

For the description of programs, a slightly augmented *Algol 60* notation will be used. In order to express repetition of statements in a more lucid way than by use of labels and jumps, a statement of the form

repeat ⟨statement sequence⟩
until ⟨Boolean expression⟩

is introduced, meaning that the statement sequence is to be repeated until the Boolean expression has obtained the value **true**.

3. The 8-Queens Problem and an Approach to Its Solution[1]

Given are an 8×8 chessboard and 8 queens which are hostile to each other. Find a position for each queen (a configuration) such that no queen may be taken by any other queen (i.e. such that every row, column, and diagonal contains at most one queen).

This problem is characteristic for the rather frequent situation where an analytical solution is not known, and where one has to resort to the method of trial and error. Typically, there exists a set A of candidates for solutions, among which one is to be selected which satisfies a certain condition p. Thus a solution is characterized as an x such that $(x \in A) \wedge p(x)$.

A straightforward program to find a solution is:

repeat Generate the next element of A and call it x
until $p(x) \vee$ (no more elements in A);
if $p(x)$ then x = solution

The difficulty with this sort of problem usually is the sheer size of A, which forbids an exhaustive generation of candidates on the grounds of efficiency considerations. In the present example, A consists of $64!/(56! \times 8!) \doteq 2^{32}$ elements (board configurations). Under the assumption that generation and test of each configuration consumes 100 μs, it would roughly take 7 hours to find a solution. It is obviously necessary to invent a "shortcut," a method which eliminates a large number of "obviously" disqualified contenders. This *strategy of preselection* is characterized as follows: Find a representation of p in the form $p = q \wedge r$. Then let $B_r = \{x \mid (x \in A) \wedge r(x)\}$. Obviously $B_r \subseteq A$. Instead of generating elements of A, only elements of B are produced and tested on condition q instead of p. Suitable

---

[1] This problem was investigated by C. F. Gauss in 1850.

candidates for a condition r are those which satisfy the following requirements:

1. B_r is much smaller than A.
2. Elements of B_r are easily generated.
3. Condition q is easier to test than condition p.

The corresponding program then is:

repeat Generate the next element of B and call it x
until $q(x) \vee$ (no more elements in B);
if $q(x)$ then x = solution

A suitable condition r in the 8-queens problem is the rule that in every column of the board there must be exactly one queen. Condition q then merely specifies that there be at most one queen in every row and in every diagonal, which is evidently somewhat easier to test than p. The set B_r (configurations with one queen in every column) contains "only" $8^8 = 2^{24}$ elements. They are generated by restricting the movement of queens to columns. Thus all of the above conditions are satisfied.

Assuming again a time of 100 μs for the generation and test of a potential solution, finding a solution would now consume only 100 seconds. Having a powerful computer at one's disposal, one might easily be content with this gain in performance. If one is less fortunate and is forced to, say, solve the problem by hand, it would take 280 hours of generating and testing configurations at the rate of one per second. In this case it might pay to spend some time finding further shortcuts. Instead of applying the same method as before, another one is advocated here which is characterized as follows: Find a representation of trial solutions x of the form $[x_1, x_2, \cdots, x_n]$, such that every trial solution can be generated in steps which produce $[x_1], [x_1, x_2], \cdots, [x_1, x_2, \cdots, x_n]$ respectively. The decomposition must be such that:

1. Every step (generating x_j) must be considerably simpler to compute than the entire candidate x.
2. $q(x) \supset q(x_1 \cdots x_j)$ for all $j \leq n$.

Thus a full solution can never be obtained by extending a partial trial solution which does not satisfy the predicate q. On the other hand, however, a partial trial solution satisfying q may not be extensible into a complete solution. This method of *stepwise construction of trial solutions* therefore requires that trial solutions failing at step j may have to be "shortened" again in order to try different extensions. This technique is called *backtracking* and may generally be characterized by the program:

$j := 1$;
repeat trystep j;
  if successful then advance else regress
until $(j < 1) \vee (j > n)$

In the 8-queens example, a solution can be constructed by positioning queens in successive columns starting with column 1 and adding a queen in the next column in each step. Obviously, a partial configuration not satisfying the mutual nonaggression condition may never be extended by this method into a full solution. Also, since during the jth step only j queens have to be considered and tested for mutual nonaggression, finding a partial solution at step j requires less effort of inspection than finding a complete solution under the condition that all 8 queens are on the board all the time. Both stated criteria are therefore satisfied by the decomposition in which step j consists of finding a safe position for the queen in the jth column.

The program subsequently to be developed is based on this method; it generates and tests 876 partial configurations before finding a complete solution. Assuming again that each generation and test (which is now more easily accomplished than before) consumes one second, the solution is found in 15 minutes, and with the computer taking 100 μs per step, in 0.09 seconds.

4. Development of the Program

We now formulate the stepwise generation of partial solutions to the 8-queens problem by the following first version of a program:

```
variable board, pointer, safe;
considerfirstcolumn;
repeat trycolumn;
    if safe then
    begin setqueen; considernextcolumn
    end else regress
until lastcoldone ∨ regressoutoffirstcol
```

This program is composed of a set of more primitive instructions (or procedures) whose actions may be described as follows:

considerfirstcolumn. The problem essentially consists of inspecting the safety of squares. A pointer variable designates the currently inspected square. The column in which this square lies is called the currently inspected column. This procedure initializes the pointer to denote the first column.

trycolumn. Starting at the current square of inspection in the currently considered column, move down the column either until a safe square is found, in which case the Boolean variable *safe* is set to **true**, or until the last square is reached and is also unsafe, in which case the variable *safe* is set to **false**.

setqueen. A queen is positioned onto the last inspected square.

considernextcolumn. Advance to the next column and initialize its pointer of inspection.

regress. Regress to a column where it is possible to move the positioned queen further down, and remove the queens positioned in the columns over which regression takes place. (Note that we may have to regress over at most two columns. Why?)

The next step of program development was chosen to refine the descriptions of the instructions *trycolumn* and *regress* as follows:

```
procedure trycolumn;
repeat advancepointer; testsquare
until safe ∨ lastsquare

procedure regress;
    begin reconsiderpriorcolumn
    if − regressoutoffirstcol then
        begin removequeen;
            if lastsquare then
```

```
        begin reconsiderpriorcolumn;
            if ¬ regressoutoffirstcol then
                removequeen
        end
    end
end
```

The program is expressed in terms of the instructions:

considerfirstcolumn
considernextcolumn
reconsiderpriorcolumn
advancepointer
testsquare   (sets the variable *safe*)
setqueen
removequeen

and of the predicates:

lastsquare
lastcoldone
regressoutoffirstcol

In order to refine these instructions and predicates further in the direction of instructions and predicates available in common programming languages, it becomes necessary to express them in terms of data representable in those languages. A decision on how to represent the relevant facts in terms of data can therefore no longer be postponed. First priority in decision making is given to the problem of how to represent the positions of the queens and of the square being currently inspected.

The most straightforward solution (i.e. the one most closely reflecting a wooden chessboard occupied by marble pieces) is to introduce a Boolean square matrix with $B[i, j] = $ **true** denoting that square (i, j) is occupied. The success of an algorithm, however, depends almost always on a suitable choice of its data representation in the light of the ease in which this representation allows the necessary operations to be expressed. Apart from this, consideration regarding storage requirements may be of prime importance (although hardly in this case). A common difficulty in program design lies in the unfortunate fact that at the stage where decisions about data representations have to be made, it often is still difficult to foresee the details of the necessary instructions operating on the data, and often quite impossible to estimate the advantages of one possible representation over another. In general, it is therefore advisable to delay decisions about data representation as long as possible (but not until it becomes obvious that no realizable solution will suit the chosen algorithm).

In the problem presented here, it is fairly evident even at this stage that the following choice is more suitable than a Boolean matrix in terms of simplicity of later instructions as well as of storage economy.

j is the index of the currently inspected column; (x_j, j) is the coordinate of the last inspected square; and the position of the queen in column $k < j$ is given by the coordinate pair (x_k, k) of the board. Now the variable declarations for pointer and board are refined into:

integer j $(0 \leq j \leq 9)$
integer array $x[1:8]$ $(0 \leq x_i \leq 8)$

and the further refinements of some of the above instructions and predicates are expressed as:

procedure *considerfirstcolumn*;
   begin $j := 1$; $x[1] := 0$ **end**

procedure *considernextcolumn*;
   begin $\cdots j := j+1$; $x[j] := 0$ **end**

procedure *reconsiderpriorcolumn*; $j := j-1$

procedure *advancepointer*;
   $x[j] := x[j] + 1$

Boolean procedure *lastsquare*;
   $lastsquare := x[j] = 8$

Boolean procedure *lastcoldone*;
   $lastcoldone := j > 8$

Boolean procedure *regressoutoffirstcol*;
   $regressoutoffirstcol := j < 1$

At this stage, the program is expressed in terms of the instructions:

testsquare
setqueen
removequeen

As a matter of fact, the instructions *setqueen* and *removequeen* may be regarded as vacuous, if we decide that the procedure *testsquare* is to determine the value of the variable *safe* solely on the grounds of the values $x_1 \cdots x_{j-1}$ which completely represent the positions of the $j-1$ queens so far on the board. But unfortunately the instruction *testsquare* is the one most frequently executed, and it is therefore the one instruction where considerations of efficiency are not only justified but essential for a good solution of the problem. Evidently a version of *testsquare* expressed only in terms of $x_1 \cdots x_{j-1}$ is inefficient at best. It should be obvious that *testsquare* is executed far more often than *setqueen* and *removequeen*. The latter procedures are executed whenever the column (j) is changed (say m times), the former whenever a move to the next square is undertaken (i.e. x_j is changed, say n times). However, *setqueen* and *removequeen* are the only procedures which affect the chessboard. Efficiency may therefore be gained by the method of *introducing auxiliary variables* $V(x_1 \cdots x_j)$ such that:

1. Whether a square is safe can be computed more easily from $V(x)$ than from x directly (say in u units of computation instead of ku units of computation).
2. The computation of $V(x)$ from x (whenever x changes) is not too complicated (say of v units of computation).

The introduction of V is advantageous (apart from considerations of storage economy), if

$$n(k-1)u > mu \quad \text{or} \quad \frac{n}{m}(k-1) > \frac{v}{u},$$

i.e. if the gain is greater than the loss in computation units.

A most straightforward solution to obtain a simple version of *testsquare* is to introduce a Boolean matrix B such that $B[i, j] =$ **true** signifies that square (i, j)

is not taken by another queen. But unfortunately, its recomputation whenever a new queen is removed (v) is prohibitive (why?) and will more than outweigh the gain.

The realization that the relevant condition for safety of a square is that the square must lie neither in a row nor in a diagonal already occupied by another queen, leads to a much more economic choice of V. We introduce Boolean arrays a, b, c with the meanings:

$a_k =$ **true** : no queen is positioned in row k
$b_k =$ **true** : no queen is positioned in the $/$-diagonal k
$c_k =$ **true** : no queen is positioned in the $\backslash$-diagonal k

The choice of the index ranges of these arrays is made in view of the fact that squares with equal sum of their coordinates lie on the same $/$-diagonal, and those with equal difference lie on the same $\backslash$-diagonal. With row and column indices from 1 to 8, we obtain:

Boolean array $a[1:8]$, $b[2:16]$, $c[-7:7]$

Upon every introduction of auxiliary data, care has to be taken of their *correct initialization*. Since our algorithm starts with an empty chessboard, this fact must be represented by initially assigning the value **true** to all components of the arrays a, b, and c. We can now write:

procedure *testsquare*;
   $safe := a[x[j]] \wedge b[j+x[j]] \wedge c[j-x[j]]$
procedure *setqueen*;
   $a[x[j]] := b[j+x[j]] := c[j-x[j]] :=$ **false**
procedure *removequeen*;
   $a[x[j]] := b[j+x[j]] := c[j-x[j]] :=$ **true**

The correctness of the latter procedure is based on the fact that each queen currently on the board had been positioned on a safe square, and that all queens positioned after the one to be removed now had already been removed. Thus the square to be vacated becomes safe again.

A critical examination of the program obtained so far reveals that the variable $x[j]$ occurs very often, and in particular at those places of the program which are also executed most often. Moreover, examination of $x[j]$ occurs much more frequently than reassignment of values to j. As a consequence, the principle of introduction of auxiliary data can again be applied to increase efficiency: a new variable

integer i

is used to represent the value so far denoted by $x[j]$. Consequently $x[j] := i$ must always be executed before j is increased, and $i := x[j]$ after j is decreased. This final step of program development leads to the reformulation of some of the above procedures as follows:

```
procedure testsquare;
    safe := a[i] ∧ b[i+j] ∧ c[i−j]
procedure setqueen;
    a[i] := b[i+j] := c[i−j] := false
procedure removequeen;
    a[i] := b[i+j] := c[i−j] := true
procedure considerfirstcolumn;
    begin j := 1;  i := 0 end
procedure advancepointer;  i := i+1
procedure considernextcolumn;
    begin x[j] := i;  j := j+1;  i := 0 end
Boolean procedure lastsquare;
    lastsquare := i = 8
```

The final program, using the procedures

```
testsquare
setqueen
regress
removequeen
```

and with the other procedures directly substituted, now has the form

```
j := 1;  i := 0;
repeat
    repeat i := i+1;  testsquare
    until safe ∨ (i=8);
    if safe then
    begin setqueen;  x[j] := i;  j := j+1;  i := 0
    end else regress
until (j > 8) ∨ (j < 1);
if j > 8 then PRINT(x) else FAILURE
```

It is noteworthy that this program still displays the structure of the version designed in the first step. Naturally other, equally valid solutions can be suggested and be developed by the same method of stepwise program refinement. It is particularly essential to demonstrate this fact to students. One alternative solution was suggested to the author by E. W. Dijkstra. It is based on the view that the problem consists of a stepwise extension of the board by one column containing a safely positioned queen, starting with a null-board and terminating with 8 columns. The process of extending the board is formulated as a procedure, and the natural method to obtain a complete board is by *recursion* of this procedure. It can easily be composed of the same set of more primitive instructions which were used in the first solution.

```
procedure Trycolumn(j);
    begin integer i;   i := 0;
        repeat i := i+1;   testsquare;
            if safe then
            begin setqueen;   x[j] := i;
                if j < 8 then Trycolumn (j+1);
                if ¬ safe then removequeen
            end
        until safe ∨ (i=8)
    end
```

The program using this procedure then is

```
Trycolumn(1);
if safe then PRINT(x) else FAILURE
```

(Note that due to the introduction of the variable i local to the recursive procedure, every column has its own pointer of inspection i. As a consequence, the procedures

```
testsquare
setqueen
removequeen
```

must be declared locally within *Trycolumn* too, because they refer to the i designating the scanned square in the *current* column.)

5. The Generalized 8-Queens Problem

In the practical world of computing, it is rather uncommon that a program, once it performs correctly and satisfactorily, remains unchanged forever. Usually its users discover sooner or later that their program does not deliver all the desired results, or worse, that the results requested were not the ones really needed. Then either an extension or a change of the program is called for, and it is in this case where the method of stepwise program design and systematic structuring is most valuable and advantageous. If the structure and the program components were well chosen, then often many of the constituent instructions can be adopted unchanged. Thereby the effort of redesign and reverification may be drastically reduced. As a matter of fact, the *adaptability* of a program to changes in its objectives (often called **maintainability**) and to changes in its environment (nowadays called portability) can be measured primarily in terms of the degree to which it is neatly structured.

It is the purpose of the subsequent section to demonstrate this advantage in view of a generalization of the original 8-queens problem and its solution through an extension of the program components introduced before.

The generalized problem is formulated as follows:

Find *all* possible configurations of 8 hostile queens on an 8×8 chessboard, such that no queen may be taken by any other queen.

The new problem essentially consists of two parts:

1. Finding a method to generate further solutions.
2. Determining whether all solutions were generated or not.

It is evidently necessary to generate and test candidates for solutions in some *systematic manner*. A common technique is to find an *ordering of candidates* and a condition to identify the last candidate. If an ordering is found, the solutions can be mapped onto the integers. A condition limiting the numeric values associated with the solutions then yields a criterion for termination of the algorithm, if the chosen method generates solutions strictly in increasing order.

It is easy to find orderings of solutions for the present problem. We choose for convenience the mapping

$$M(x) = \sum_{j=1}^{8} x_j 10^{j-1}$$

An upper bound for possible solutions is then

$$M(x_{\max}) = 88888888$$

and the "convenience" lies in the circumstance that our earlier program generating one solution generates the minimum solution which can be regarded as the starting point from which to proceed to the next solution. This is due to the chosen method of testing squares strictly proceeding in increasing order of $M(x)$ starting with 00000000. The method for generating further solutions must now be chosen such that starting with the configuration of a given solution, scanning proceeds in the same order of increasing M, until either the next higher solution is found or the limit is reached.

6. The Extended Program

The technique of extending the two given programs finding a solution to the simple 8-queens problem is based on the idea of modification of the global structure only, and of using the same building blocks. The global structure must be changed such that upon finding a solution the algorithm will produce an appropriate indication—e.g. by printing the solution—and then proceed to find the next solution until it is found or the limit is reached. A simple condition for reaching the limit is the event when the first queen is moved beyond row 8, in which case regression out of the first column will take

place. These deliberations lead to the following modified version of the nonrecursive program:

```
considerfirstcolumn;
  repeat trycolumn;
    if safe then
    begin setqueen;   considernextcolumn;
      if lastcoldone then
      begin PRINT(x); regress
      end
    end else regress
  until regressoutoffirstcol
```

Indication of a solution being found by printing it now occurs directly at the level of detection, i.e. before leaving the repetition clause. Then the algorithm proceeds to find a next solution whereby a shortcut is used by directly regressing to the prior column; since a solution places one queen in each row, there is no point in further moving the last queen within the eighth column.

The recursive program is extended with even greater ease following the same considerations:

```
procedure Trycolumn(j);
begin integer i;
  ⟨declarations of procedures testsquare, advancequeen,
  setqueen, removequeen, lastsquare⟩
  i := 0;
  repeat advancequeen;   testsquare;
    if safe then
    begin setqueen;   x|j| := i;
      if ¬ lastcoldone then Trycolumn(j+1) else PRINT(x);
      removequeen
    end
  until lastsquare
end
```

The main program starting the algorithm then consists (apart from initialization of a, b, and c) of the single statement $Trycolumn(1)$.

In concluding, it should be noted that both programs represent the same algorithm. Both determine 92 solutions in the *same* order by testing squares 15720 times. This yields an average of 171 tests per solution; the maximum is 876 tests for finding a next solution (the first one), and the minimum is 8. (Both programs coded in the language Pascal were executed by a CDC 6400 computer in less than one second.)

7. Conclusions

The lessons which the described example was supposed to illustrate can be summarized by the following points.

1. Program construction consists of a sequence of *refinement steps*. In each step a given task is broken up into a number of subtasks. Each refinement in the description of a task may be accompanied by a refinement of the description of the data which constitute the means of communication between the subtasks. Refinement of the description of program and data structures should proceed in parallel.

2. The degree of *modularity* obtained in this way will

determine the ease or difficulty with which a program can be adapted to changes or extensions of the purpose or changes in the environment (language, computer) in which it is executed.

3. During the process of stepwise refinement, a *notation* which is natural to the problem in hand should be used as long as possible. The direction in which the notation develops during the process of refinement is determined by the language in which the program must ultimately be specified, i.e. with which the notation ultimately becomes identical. This language should therefore allow us to express as naturally and clearly as possible the structures of program and data which emerge during the design process. At the same time, it must give guidance in the refinement process by exhibiting those basic features and structuring principles which are natural to the machine by which programs are supposed to be executed. It is remarkable that it would be difficult to find a language that would meet these important requirements to a lesser degree than the one language still used most widely in teaching programming: Fortran.

4. Each refinement implies a number of *design decisions* based upon a set of design criteria. Among these criteria are efficiency, storage economy, clarity, and regularity of structure. Students must be taught to be conscious of the involved decisions and to critically examine and to reject solutions, sometimes even if they are correct as far as the result is concerned; they must learn to weigh the various aspects of design alternatives in the light of these criteria. In particular, they must be taught to revoke earlier decisions, and to back up, if necessary even to the top. Relatively short sample problems will often suffice to illustrate this important point; it is not necessary to construct an operating system for this purpose.

5. The detailed elaborations on the development of even a short program form a long story, indicating that careful programming is not a trivial subject. If this paper has helped to dispel the widespread belief that programming is easy as long as the programming language is powerful enough and the available computer is fast enough, then it has achieved one of its purposes.

Acknowledgments. The author gratefully acknowledges the helpful and stimulating influence of many discussions with C.A.R. Hoare and E. W. Dijkstra.

References

The following articles are listed for further reference on the subject of programming.

1. Dijkstra, E. W. A constructive approach to the problem of program correctness. *BIT 8* (1968), 174–186.
2. Dijkstra, E. W. Notes on structured programming. EWD 249, Technical U. Eindhoven, The Netherlands, 1969.
3. Naur, P. Programming by action clusters. *BIT 9* (1969) 250–258.
4. Wirth, N. Programming and programming languages. Proc. Internat. Comput. Symp., Bonn, Germany, May 1970.

Part VIII

Design Validation

Two of the primary reasons for identifying design as a separate phase of a software development methodology are

(1) the ability to focus on specific design problems and evaluate alternative solutions to these problems, either singly or in combination and

(2) the ability to assure the quality of the emerging system prior to its implementation.

There is extensive evidence showing that the costs of finding and fixing errors increase sharply throughout a software development project. These costs are caused both by the number of steps that must be repeated to recover from the error and by the cascading effect of making subsequent decisions based on that error. Thus, whenever a software development methodology identifies a project phase and a visible work product associated with that phase, the use of that methodology should include a process to assure the quality of that product and to validate it against earlier products.

In the case of software design, poor design decisions can result in bad structure, unhandled cases, inefficient programs, undesired side effects, clumsy user interfaces, and/or erroneous results. Clearly, it is worth considerable effort to validate designs and to remove as many of these defects as possible.

Furthermore, it is important to learn from each software development project and to build up a body of design knowledge. Such knowledge is particularly useful on future similar projects where an understanding of previous decisions and the basis on which they were made can save time and prevent bad decisions.

The papers in this section point to some of the issues and steps of design validation. The paper by Freeman investigates the nature of the review process used in software design and proposes a technique for improving reviews. This technique, design rationalization, basically involves capturing the reasoning that goes into a design along with the actual design, thus providing a richer base for review.

Fagan's paper describes design and code inspections, a systematic procedure for error detection and removal developed and used within IBM. Inspection teams are trained to study designs or code for certain common types of errors, and carry out these inspections on software at specific times in the development process. Fagan notes that the third inspection, following unit testing, had been shown to be unproductive. Subsequently, though, IBM has discovered that the third inspection may be valuable if the result of unit testing has caused numerous changes to be made in the program code.

The paper by Razouk, Vernon, and Estrin focuses on the test environment for SARA models, and the way in which the SARA approach supports system testability during the design process. Unlike the previous two papers, the emphasis here is on tool support for the design evaluation process, involving execution of a model of the design. This paper has been selected for its extensive example, including the transcript of a SARA session. It is a companion to the Campos and Estrin paper published in Part V. Further information on the SARA project is given in the Overview for Part V.

EHO205-5/83/0000/0541$01.00 © 1983 IEEE

Toward improved review of software designs*

by PETER FREEMAN

University of California, Irvine
Irvine, California

INTRODUCTION

A good deal of effort has been invested in recent years to improve both the form of programs and the processes used to create them.[2,9,10] As the payoffs from this work become apparent and more widespread,[3] attention is turning to the form of designs and the processes used to create them.[1,5]

One aspect of software design, *reviewability*, has received scant attention. In this paper, we want to stress the importance of making designs reviewable and suggest an operational technique for aiding in their review. Underlying our discussions is the principle (perhaps obvious) that designs which can be easily reviewed have a better chance of meeting the expectations of their purchasers and users.

A methodology being developed by the author, *design rationalization*, provides a means for making software designs more reviewable before they are actually implemented. The body of this paper develops this idea.

Before we begin, three important points must be made. First, what we are proposing here is an *approach* to the improvement of design practice. It is not an algorithm. It cannot be applied to a situation without some thought and study. It certainly cannot be guaranteed to work in all situations. If you demand instant success, then look elsewhere! But, if you are concerned with improving design practice in your organization, especially with respect to reviewability, then we believe the idea presented here merits your study and experimentation.

Second, we must stress that there are already well-specified procedures for reviewing designs, but that in spite of their good intentions, they fail in some important respects. Much of the procurement of software by the government is now controlled by standards (promulgated by the Defense Department and other parts of the government) that spell out elaborate review procedures that must be carried out during the design phase (for example, Reference 11). Additionally, some organizations are experimenting with their own review standards aimed at improving the reviewability of software designs. (For example, good success has been informally reported by TRW at recent technical meetings with their usage of "unit development folders.") What these standards do not stress and what we consider essential to good review, is the recording of the reasoning behind design decisions, both local and global. It is this fact that our technique addresses most strongly and which we will stress in this paper.

The third point is that not all design situations are equal. We differentiate between *discovery design* and *routine design*. In the former, a great deal of creativity is required since the right structure (and even functions) for the software must be discovered during the course of the design. In the latter, the system being designed is similar to others which are well understood; thus routine design is more a process of choosing the right values for a set of parameters. Design of a program to prepare the payroll for an organization is clearly routine design. Design of a complex system to provide managers with real-time summary information automatically is discovery design, given our current understanding of such systems. In this paper we restrict ourselves to consideration of routine design situations.

We will describe and illustrate the design rationalization methodology and then show how it can be used to improve the reviewability of software designs. Because new methods are usually adopted slowly (and rightfully so), we close with some suggestions for experimentation with this technique.

DESIGN REVIEWS

Routine software designs are typically reviewed several times in different ways. Before we propose a way of improving design reviews, we want to consider some of their characteristics.

First, look at the range of review formats. An important part of the design process is a constant, but informal, review and iteration of the design by the designers themselves. When the preparation of a design is a large undertaking and/or is supported by a highly structured organization (such as the Federal government), formal design reviews are often specified (as in Reference 11) at which people other than the designers determine if the proposed design is acceptable (by whatever standards have been set up). Finally, the ultimate user of the

* This work was supported by National Science Foundation Grant GJ-36414.

software will review the design informally through usage and sometimes formally in preparation for requesting changes or a new design.

Our concern in this paper is the *reviewability* of a design—that is, the ease with which it can be compared to objectives. Designs cannot be executed directly as can programs, but it is still essential to compare them to desired criteria as early as possible in the development process.

While review of a design must necessarily mean different things to different people (depending on the methodology used, what is expected of the reviews, the stage of the process at which it is performed, and so on), let us be more explicit.

We see four possible components of any design review:

- checking for functional completeness;
- comparison of the design to operational goals and constraints;
- comparison of the design to non-operational goals and constraints;
- performance prediction.

"Operational" goals clearly and unambiguously spell out what is desired, while "non-operational" goals do not. For example,

Operational: "The system should provide a distinct error code for each error discovered."

Non-operational: "The system should handle errors cleanly."

It may be possible to characterize design reviews differently, but these four aspects capture most of what we see happening in the review of a software design.

The most prevalent question asked in a review is, "Will the system do what it is supposed to do?" The normal techniques of reading a design, perhaps aided by a structured walkthrough,[8] will generally suffice for answering this question. Because a design is typically stated in functional terms, most of it speaks directly to the question of what the system will do. While existing techniques do permit review for the completeness of major functions, it is still difficult to ascertain from a design whether small or unwanted functions are present.

Likewise, for explicitly stated structural goals or constraints, existing design formats permit at least a passable review. For example, if certain data structures or interfaces are part of the design requirements, then it is usually possible to determine if these requirements have been met by inspecting the design.

It is when we come to the last two components of a design review—comparison to non-operational requirements and performance prediction—that the need for improvement becomes most apparent. Even though it may be possible to make some design goals more operational (that is, detailed and open to objective evaluation), reviewers will still be asked to evaluate designs with respect to non-operational goals. For instance, consider the following design goals:

"The system should be tolerant of user mistakes."

"Only state-of-the-art techniques should be used."
"Output formats should be neat and readable."
"The system should be maintainable."

Determining whether these goals have been met or not requires the reviewer to interpret or infer information from the design and to provide a good deal of external information. Typically, the information provided in a design document is not the right type and/or is in the wrong form to permit such goals to be evaluated directly (if at all). The reviewer usually must proceed unaided.

Finally, designs provide almost no help at all for performance prediction. *Ad hoc* comparisons of parts of the design to previous designs (for which performance is known) may provide some meaningful predictions of resource usage. But even if the parts can be identified from the design, determining which are critical to performance and what the interactions between parts will be is very difficult. The information needed is simply not present in most designs.

Cutting across all aspects of design reviewing is the need for knowing the reasoning behind decisions. Rarely, if ever, in current practice does design documentation record the alternatives that were considered and the reasons for rejecting some of them. Yet, this information can greatly aid the reviewer in understanding the design and in evaluating it against stated objectives.

This brief look at the nature of design reviews certainly does not exhaust what can be said about them, but it should set the stage for considering how to improve them.

DESIGN RATIONALIZATION

There is no argument that software designs should be more reviewable and that if they were the resulting implementations could be improved. This is especially true in the case of routine designs where the form of the result is pretty well known in advance. We will outline below how design rationalization can be used to improve the

---

DESIGN PROBLEM 3: How should an error detected in a command string be handled?

    ALTERNATIVE 3-1: Abort the program when an error is found.
        EVALUATION 3-1: Easy to implement.
        Provides the user very little information.
        Wastes resources if the error occurs after much processing.
    ALTERNATIVE 3-2: Ask the user to re-enter the command string.
        EVALUATION 3-2: Must reset the state of the program.
        Makes the system "softer" on the user.
        Takes more processing time, even if no error encountered.
        May prevent waste of resources if trivial error.
    ALTERNATIVE 3-3: Try to correct the user's mistake.
        EVALUATION 3-3: Maximally useful to user.
        Substantial resources needed to try correction.
        Interaction with user more complex (must specify correction and allow override).
DECISION 3: Alternative 3-2, because it provides a balance between our goal to make the system easy on the user and the constraint that it be fast.

    Figure 1—Information contained in a typical rationalization

reviewability of designs, especially in the area of recording the rationale for decisions.

The basis for design rationalization is the belief that designs can be improved by making them more rational. That is, design decisions should be based on logical reasoning, be supported by facts, and be recorded. The cornerstone of this technique is the *explicit* recording of design information in the form of design problems, alternative solutions, and the evaluations or arguments leading to the choice of a particular alternative.

The basic operation is the identification and recording of the information essential to a rational design. While variation in format is appropriate, the information shown in Figure 1 is fundamentally what goes into a rationalized design. The example shown there involves a single, rather low-level decision. In an actual rationalization we would record information pertaining to the entire design, both locally and globally.

If the information is collected and recorded as the design decisions are being made, we are doing a *synthesis rationalization*. If the information is primarily recorded after the design decisions are made, then we are doing an *analysis rationalization*. In either case, there are several important parameters: what features or decisions of the design shall be rationalized, how do we generate alternatives, what criteria shall be used for evaluating them, and on what basis should a decision be made.

Note that this methodology does not specify in what order decisions should be made. Neither does it spell out criteria for making decisions, except to specify that they should be made by considering alternatives and presenting evidence for and against each alternative. In this sense, design rationalization is more of a framework or forcing function within which particular decision strategies such as top-down or bottom-up can be used.

We must stress that the important aspect of design rationalization is its insistence on the *explicit* capture and recording of design information including the reasoning used. Without this, we have nothing but motherhoods about the importance of making rational decisions—which everyone already believes. With the explicit recording of information underlying decisions, however, we have a technique for increasing the rationality of designs.

With this brief introduction, let us look at how design rationalization can be used to improve the reviewability of designs.

A SCENARIO

The characteristics of a design review discussed above can be observed whenever a design is evaluated. For definiteness, though, let us focus here on the use of rationalization to improve formal reviews of routine designs. Consider the following scenario:

1. *Initial specifications are prepared.* Assuming the specs are at a functional level, they are rationalized by providing explicit alternatives for critical specifications. Reasoning, based on facts is then spelled out for choosing a particular set of specifications.

2. *Specifications review.* The rationalizations permit the potential designers to understand more readily some of the specifications. They also permit those with funding responsibility to consider alternative forms of the system and to evaluate whether the system being specified is what is needed.

3. *Initial Design.* Once the specifications are finalized, an initial design is prepared, using the synthesis rationalization technique. Design decisions to be rationalized will include the overall organization of the system (control and data), choice of implementation language, choice of hardware, and other high-level decisions made at this stage. In addition, more detailed considerations of internal structure of the system may be documented by explicit lists of alternatives and evaluations.

4. *Internal Review.* When a design phase is completed, an internal review (such as the design walk throughs practiced by some organizations) and an analysis rationalization is performed by the designers and others in their immediate organization. This review may prompt changes to the design. The system's features are more thoroughly explained, additional alternatives are provided, and the evaluations of alternatives are strengthened. Some evaluations can only be made on the basis of global considerations after the entire design has taken shape. For example, choice of a data structure may depend on its usage by several different modules. This internal review has the effect of catching some design errors in-house while at the same time improving the explicitness of the rationalization.

5. *External review.* The initial design, augmented by the rationalization, is thoroughly reviewed by whatever outside agency has been designated to monitor progress. Rejected choices are explicitly spelled out in the rationalization along with the reasoning used to reject them. This permits reviewers to assess better the quality of the design and its fit to the specifications. Rejected alternatives may be recognized by the reviewers as important to some of the goals even though the designers felt they were not.

6. *Iteration and design refinement.* After any design review, changes to the design may be needed. After these have been made the design process continues by refining the design (or extending it, depending on the approach being used). Using the techniques outlined in 3, 4, and 5, the design and review iterative cycle will continue until a complete design ready for implementation is obtained.

7. *Implementation.* It is rare that the implementors of a system can proceed without making any changes or additions to a design. Typically, many decisions (hopefully, low-level) concerning the structure of the programs being built must still be made. The rationalizations now play a role in a different form of

design review. As the implementors seek to carry out the design, they must review it from the standpoint of understanding the intent of the designers when that is not clear and of making sure that decisions being made during implementation are not changing critical features of the design. The rationalization contains much of the reasoning information needed for this type of review.

8. *Redesign.* After a system is in use, more information is available on how well it fulfills its intended purpose. If the need for an improved system becomes clear then a major modification of the existing system or specification of a new system may become necessary. In this case, review of the design of the existing system to determine how it can be improved will be an important part of the design of the new system. This redesign process can profit from the rationalization by recovering rejected alternatives from the initial design.

This scenario illustrates the more important forms of formal design reviews often called for in the context of routine software design projects in large organizations. The use of design rationalization in these different review situations has been informally indicated, but the crux of the method—the explicit capture of design information otherwise lost and its presentation in a form convenient for review and comparison to goals—should be clear.

As a limited example of the usage of design rationalization, we performed a rather thorough analysis rationalization on a small system which had been designed and implemented as an improvement on an earlier system. The new system had several stated goals, including making it maintainable. The language used in the new system and some of the obvious features of the new design indicated that indeed this goal might have been achieved. The rationalization we produced, however, indicated that most of the effort in the redesign had been spent on local reorganizations of the system, with little thought given to overall control and code organization of the system. The careful analysis of the system that the rationalization supported convinced us that maintainability had been improved only marginally because of the lack of attention to overall structure. We were thus able to assess more accurately both the system and the techniques used to design it. This is illustrative of one type of benefit we would expect to reap from using design rationalization.

DISCUSSION

Our interest is in seeing design rationalization used to improve the practice of software design. To facilitate this, we will discuss some of its advantages and disadvantages in this section.

Advantages

One advantage comes from helping a reviewer identify alternatives. If one is knowledgeable in the area of the design, then alternatives may spring to mind easily. However, many reviewers will not be experts and will have difficulty knowing what alternatives (if any) might have been chosen for the design. Even for the expert, generating alternatives is often not easy.

The value of a rationalization in this respect is twofold. First, actual alternatives that have been rejected will be readily available for the reviewer to consider. Information that has been generated during the course of the design will not have been lost, but will be available for the reviewer. Perhaps even more importantly, the rationalization can serve as a pump-primer to get the reviewer started to thinking about feasible alternatives for the question at hand.

We are all familiar with the effect of being presented with a problem situation and of seeing at first only one solution. Unless one is familiar with the content area and has thought about the problem previously, it takes some effort to seek out alternatives. However, if someone suggests an alternative, even if it is not a good one, then we often can come up with additional suggestions much more easily. This is similar to one of the techniques suggested by De Bono[4] for facilitating lateral thinking—that is, of finding new ways of looking at an old situation.

Fundamentally, a reviewer is asked to certify that the decisions made by the designer are good decisions with respect to the goals and constraints of the design task. If the reviewer knows only the results of the designer's reasoning and not the steps by which the decisions were made, then the biases and knowledge limitations of the reviewer may seriously affect his or her judgments as to the quality of the design decisions. If the design is supported by explicit information in the form of a rationalization, however, then the reviewer can assess more easily the factual evidence and logical reasoning used by the designer.

This situation has an analogy in mathematics. If one is presented with a theorem, the truth or falsity of it may not be immediately evident and we may or may not be prepared to accept it as true. Given a step-by-step proof of the theorem, however, we can convince ourselves not only of its truth but also of why it is true (in terms of axioms and reasoning).

While the evaluations in a design rationalization are nowhere near as orderly as a mathematical proof, they do present the reasoning that has been used so that others can decide for themselves whether that reasoning is complete and valid. In addition, where the reasoning used to make a decision involves assumptions, exposing this reasoning will permit the reviewers to discover and assess the validity of the assumptions (since many of them may be related to the user environment which the reviewer knows more about anyway).

The advantages discussed here have touched on what we believe to be the basic advantage of design rationalization for improving reviewability: It forces the explicit recording of decision reasoning information which is otherwise lost.

Disadvantages

It should be clear that producing a rationalized design will, in general, take more effort than producing an rationalized design. At a minimum, the effort needed to record alternatives and evaluations, even if otherwise generated, is added effort. However, we have typically found that generating the explicit lists of alternatives and evaluations also requires a good deal of effort. Finding meaningful evaluations, that relate the decision under consideration to the goals and constraints of the problem, is often difficult in the absence of an underlying theoretical basis or quantitative evaluation technique. The advantages of design rationalization (both for reviewability and quality of a design) must be weighed against this added cost.

At present we cannot offer explicit suggestions for choosing the design problems/features to rationalize nor sure-fire methods of generating alternatives and evaluations. It is clear that one cannot rationalize every single decision in a program of any significant size. Further, important decisions in one design may have no major role in another. Choosing the important ones (those for which the choice of a solution has some definite effect on the resulting design or its use) is difficult.

A more subtle problem that may not be immediately evident concerns the level at which decisions are made. The thrust of design rationalization as we have presented it above is to make decisions at a local level. Basically, the question asked is, "What is the best alternative, and why, for this particular decision?" This leads to local optimization, which in many cases will not be optimal. That is, sometimes we must make decisions taking into account the alternatives for other decisions which have not yet been resolved. It is to help alleviate this concentration on the local context that we have suggested in the scenario above that some rationalization be done after the initial design is completed.

Research

We are continuing our investigations of design rationalization both to provide additional evidence of its advantages and to find ways of reducing its disadvantages. Included in this work are some informal investigations of design situations in which some designers use rationalization and others do not, development of techniques to make easier the choice of problems and generation of alternatives and evaluations, and the construction of tools to help in recording the information. These studies are described in References 6 and 7 and other working papers available from the author.

SOME SUGGESTIONS FOR USING DESIGN RATIONALIZATION

Any methodology not based on formal techniques is open to interpretation by those using it. Such interpreta-

tions are, in fact, required in most cases to make methodology useful in the context of a particular organization or a particular type of task.

Thus, we understand that design rationalization must be adapted to your particular organizational task context. While it is difficult to predict the difficulties you will encounter, our limited experience with helping others use it does suggest some guidelines.

Remembering that we are concerned here with formal reviews of routine designs, we suggest the following:

1. Choose a small, but realistic design problem on which to try out the technique. Make sure the design is of a system of which the designer has some knowledge.
2. Use a design project that is "real" (not done just for experimentation).
3. Make sure sufficient time and resources are allocated to the project so that the designers are not under pressure.
4. Use at least two designers (but probably not more than three) so that they can work as a group when generating alternatives and evaluations.
5. Use your normal design techniques augmented by the use of rationalizations as suggested in the scenario above.
6. Carefully choose some criteria by which you can judge whether the rationalization assists in design review. Some suggestions are: number of design flaws discovered relative to similar projects, level of detail of design flaws discovered, perceived ease of review by reviewers, time taken to review design documents.
7. Maintain careful observations of the use of rationalization to permit later analysis of the trial.
8. Assess the trial when completed. If rationalization seems to help in your situation, even a little, try to find ways to improve the technique for your situation.
9. Try it again.

These suggestions can be boiled down to a simple statement: Approach the use of design rationalization from the standpoint of an experimental fitting of an idea to your situation and expect to make changes.

CONCLUSION

Development of techniques for the review of software designs has been largely neglected. We have described a methodology, design rationalization, which has characteristics that will help improve the reviewability of designs. We have given a scenario for its usage and discussed some of its advantages and disadvantages. Suggested guidelines for trying it out were given.

We have stressed that the strength of design rationalization lies in its forcing *explicit* recording of design information, especially that which explains the reasons behind features of the design. The existence of this information in a form that permits independent review of design choices and the reasoning leading up to them should assist in most situations.

We have not spelled out an explicit technique for one to follow. Rather, we have described an idea, assessed its use for improving the current practice of design review, and suggested ways in which it can be adapted to varied organizational settings. As with much of software engineering today, the application of this idea in large-scale situations must ultimately be carried out by those with software creation problems to solve.

While our research continues into the ramifications of this idea and the techniques for using it, others can profit from trying it in their contexts. We recognize the difficulty of changing one's patterns of doing something and the difficulties in forcing oneself into the discipline of design rationalization. Yet, only through trial and error usage of this and other proposed methodologies can we gradually develop the tools necessary for the routine design of large and important classes of software.

REFERENCES

1. Brown, R. R., "1974 Lake Arrowhead Workshop on Structured Programming," *Computer*, October, 1974, pp. 61-63.
2. Dahl, O. J., E. W. Dijkstra, and C. A. R. Hoare, *Structured Programming*, Academic Press, 1973.
3. *Datamation*, special issue on structured programming, December 1973.
4. De Bono, Edward, *New Think*, Basic Books, 1972.
5. Freeman, Peter, "Automating Software Design," *Computer*, April 1974.
6. Freeman, Peter, *Reliable Software Through Rational Design*, ICS Technical Report #55, University of California, Irvine, October 1974.
7. Freeman, Peter, *Design Rationalization*, ICS Technical Report #57, University of California, Irvine, November 1974.
8. IBM, *Structured Walkthroughs*, training brochure.
9. Mills, H. D., "Top Down Programming in Large Systems," in *Debugging Techniques in Large Systems*, R. Rustin (ed.), Prentice-Hall, 1971.
10. Parnas, D. L., "On the Criteria to the Used in Decomposing Systems into Modules," *Comm. ACM*, December 1972.
11. U.S. Air Force MIL-STD 1521, *Technical Reviews and Audits for Systems Engineering and Computer Programming*, available from National Technical Information Service, Springfield, VA., September 1972.

Substantial net improvements in programming quality and productivity have been obtained through the use of formal inspections of design and of code. Improvements are made possible by a systematic and efficient design and code verification process, with well-defined roles for inspection participants. The manner in which inspection data is categorized and made suitable for process analysis is an important factor in attaining the improvements. It is shown that by using inspection results, a mechanism for initial error reduction followed by ever-improving error rates can be achieved.

Reprinted with permission from *IBM Systems Journal*, Volume 15, Number 3, 1976, pages 219–248. Copyright © 1976 by International Business Machines Corporation.

Design and code inspections to reduce errors in program development

by M. E. Fagan

Successful management of any process requires planning, measurement, and control. In programming development, these requirements translate into defining the programming process in terms of a series of operations, each operation having its own exit criteria. Next there must be some means of measuring completeness of the product at any point of its development by inspections or testing. And finally, the measured data must be used for controlling the process. This approach is not only conceptually interesting, but has been applied successfully in several programming projects embracing systems and applications programming, both large and small. It has not been found to "get in the way" of programming, but has instead enabled higher predictability than other means, and the use of inspections has improved productivity and product quality. The purpose of this paper is to explain the planning, measurement, and control functions as they are affected by inspections in programming terms.

An ingredient that gives maximum play to the planning, measurement, and control elements is consistent and vigorous *discipline*. Variable rules and conventions are the usual indicators of a lack of discipline. An iron-clad discipline on all rules, which can stifle programming work, is not required but instead there should be a clear understanding of the flexibility (or nonflexibility) of each of the rules applied to various aspects of the project. An example of flexibility may be waiving the rule that all main paths will be tested for the case where repeated testing of a given path will logically do no more than add expense. An example of necessary inflexibility would be that *all* code must be

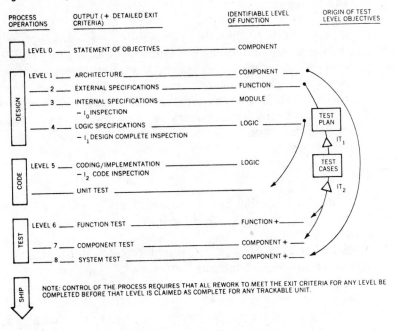

Figure 1 Programming process

PROCESS OPERATIONS	OUTPUT (+ DETAILED EXIT CRITERIA)	IDENTIFIABLE LEVEL OF FUNCTION	ORIGIN OF TEST LEVEL OBJECTIVES
LEVEL 0	STATEMENT OF OBJECTIVES	COMPONENT	

DESIGN

- LEVEL 1 — ARCHITECTURE — COMPONENT
- 2 — EXTERNAL SPECIFICATIONS — FUNCTION
- 3 — INTERNAL SPECIFICATIONS — MODULE — I_0 INSPECTION
- 4 — LOGIC SPECIFICATIONS — LOGIC — I_1 DESIGN COMPLETE INSPECTION

TEST PLAN

IT_1

CODE

- LEVEL 5 — CODING/IMPLEMENTATION — LOGIC — I_2 CODE INSPECTION
- UNIT TEST

TEST CASES

IT_2

TEST

- LEVEL 6 — FUNCTION TEST — FUNCTION +
- 7 — COMPONENT TEST — COMPONENT +
- 8 — SYSTEM TEST — COMPONENT +

SHIP

NOTE: CONTROL OF THE PROCESS REQUIRES THAT ALL REWORK TO MEET THE EXIT CRITERIA FOR ANY LEVEL BE COMPLETED BEFORE THAT LEVEL IS CLAIMED AS COMPLETE FOR ANY TRACKABLE UNIT.

inspected. A clear statement of the project rules and changes to these rules along with faithful adherence to the rules go a long way toward practicing the required project discipline.

A prerequisite of process management is a clearly defined series of operations in the process (Figure 1). The miniprocess within each operation must also be clearly described for closer management. A clear statement of the criteria that must be satisfied to exit each operation is mandatory. This statement and accurate data collection, with the data clearly tied to trackable units of known size and collected from specific points in the process, are some essential constituents of the information required for process management.

In order to move the form of process management from qualitative to more quantitative, process terms must be more specific, data collected must be appropriate, and the limits of accuracy of the data must be known. The effect is to provide more precise information in the correct process context for decision making by the process manager.

In this paper, we first describe the programming process and places at which inspections are important. Then we discuss factors that affect productivity and the operations involved with inspections. Finally, we compare inspections and walk-throughs on process control.

The process

A process may be described as a set of operations occurring in a definite sequence that operates on a given input and converts it to some desired output. A general statement of this kind is sufficient to convey the notion of the process. In a practical application, however, it is necessary to describe the input, output, internal processing, and processing times of a process in very specific terms if the process is to be executed and practical output is to be obtained.

In the programming development process, explicit requirement statements are necessary as input. The series of processing operations that act on this input must be placed in the correct sequence with one another, the output of each operation satisfying the input needs of the next operation. The output of the final operation is, of course, the explicitly required output in the form of a verified program. Thus, the objective of each processing operation is to receive a defined input and to produce a definite output that satisfies a specific set of exit criteria. (It goes without saying that each operation can be considered as a miniprocess itself.) A well-formed process can be thought of as a continuum of processing during which sequential sets of exit criteria are satisfied, the last set in the entire series requiring a well-defined end product. Such a process is not amorphous. It can be measured and controlled.

Unambiguous, explicit, and universally accepted exit criteria would be perfect as process control checkpoints. It is frequently argued that universally agreed upon checkpoints are impossible in programming because all projects are different, etc. However, *all* projects do reach the point at which there is a project checkpoint. As it stands, any trackable unit of code achieving a clean compilation can be said to have satisfied a universal exit criterion or checkpoint in the process. Other checkpoints can also be selected, albeit on more arguable premises, but once the premises are agreed upon, the checkpoints become visible in most, if not all, projects. For example, there is a point at which the design of a program is considered complete. This point may be described as the level of detail to which a unit of design is reduced so that one design statement will materialize in an estimated three to 10 source code instructions (or, if desired, five to 20, for that matter). Whichever particular ratio is selected across a project, it provides a checkpoint for the process control of that project. In this way, suitable checkpoints may be selected throughout the development process and used in process management. (For more specific exit criteria see Reference 1.)

The cost of reworking errors in programs becomes higher the later they are reworked in the process, so every attempt should be made to find and fix errors as early in the process as possible. This cost has led to the use of the inspections described later and to the description of exit criteria which include assuring that all errors known at the end of the inspection of the new "clean-compilation" code, for example, have been correctly fixed. So, rework of all known errors up to a particular point must be complete before the associated checkpoint can be claimed to be met for any piece of code.

Where inspections are not used and errors are found during development or testing, the cost of rework as a fraction of overall development cost can be suprisingly high. For this reason, errors should be found and fixed as close to their place of origin as possible.

Production studies have validated the expected quality and productivity improvements and have provided estimates of standard productivity rates, percentage improvements due to inspections, and percentage improvements in error rates which are applicable in the context of large-scale operating system program production. (The data related to operating system development contained herein reflect results achieved by IBM in applying the subject processes and methods to representative samples. Since the results depend on many factors, they cannot be considered representative of every situation. They are furnished merely for the purpose of illustrating what has been achieved in sample testing.)

The purpose of the test plan inspection IT_1, shown in Figure 1, is to find voids in the functional variation coverage and other discrepancies in the test plan. IT_2, test case inspection of the test cases, which are based on the test plan, finds errors in the test cases. The total effects of IT_1 and IT_2 are to increase the integrity of testing and, hence, the quality of the completed product. And, because there are less errors in the test cases to be debugged during the testing phase, the overall project schedule is also improved.

A process of the kind depicted in Figure 1 installs all the intrinsic programming properties in the product as required in the statement of objectives (Level 0) by the time the coding operation (Level 5) has been completed—except for packaging and publications requirements. With these exceptions, all later work is of a verification nature. This verification of the product provides no contribution to the product during the essential development (Levels 1 to 5); it only adds error detection and elimination (frequently at one half of the development cost). I_0, I_1, and I_2 inspections were developed to measure and influence intrinsic

Figure 2 A study of coding productivity

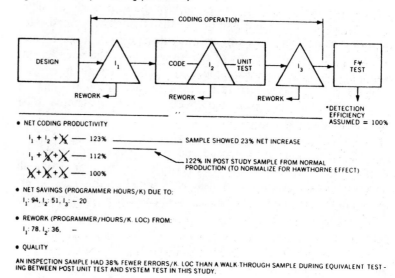

quality (error content) in the early levels, where error rework can be most economically accomplished. Naturally, the beneficial effect on quality is also felt in later operations of the development process and at the end user's site.

An improvement in productivity is the most immediate effect of purging errors from the product by the I_0, I_1, and I_2 inspections. This purging allows rework of these errors very near their origin, early in the process. Rework done at these levels is 10 to 100 times less expensive than if it is done in the last half of the process. Since rework detracts from productive effort, it reduces productivity in proportion to the time taken to accomplish the rework. It follows, then, that finding errors by inspection and reworking them earlier in the process reduces the overall rework time and increases productivity even within the early operations and even more over the total process. Since less errors ship with the product, the time taken for the user to install programs is less, and his productivity is also increased.

The quality of documentation that describes the program is of as much importance as the program itself for poor quality can mislead the user, causing him to make errors quite as important as errors in the program. For this reason, the quality of program documentation is verified by publications inspections (PI_0, PI_1, and PI_2). Through a reduction of user-encountered errors, these inspections also have the effect of improving user productivity by reducing his rework time.

A study of coding productivity

A piece of the design of a large operating system component (all done in structured programming) was selected as a study sample (Figure 2). The sample was judged to be of moderate complexity. When the piece of design had been reduced to a level of detail sufficient to meet the Design Level 4 exit criteria[2] (a level of detail of design at which one design statement would ultimately appear as three to 10 code instructions), it was submitted to a design-complete inspection (100 percent), I_1. On conclusion of I_1, all error rework resulting from the inspection was completed, and the design was submitted for coding in PL/S. The coding was then done, and when the code was brought to the level of the first clean compilation,[2] it was subjected to a code inspection (100 percent), I_2. The resultant rework was completed and the code was subjected to unit test. After unit test, a unit test inspection, I_3, was done to see that the unit test plan had been fully executed. Some rework was required and the necessary changes were made. This step completed the coding operation. The study sample was then passed on to later process operations consisting of building and testing.

The inspection sample was considered of sufficient size and nature to be representative for study purposes. Three programmers designed it, and it was coded by 13 programmers. The inspection sample was in modular form, was structured, and was judged to be of moderate complexity on average.

Because errors were identified and corrected in groups at I_1 and I_2, rather than found one-by-one during subsequent work and handled at the higher cost incumbent in later rework, the overall amount of error rework was minimized, even within the coding operation. Expressed differently, considering the inclusion of *all* I_1 time, I_2 time, and resulting error rework time (with the usual coding and unit test time in the total time to complete the operation), a *net* saving resulted when this figure was compared to the no-inspection case. This net saving translated into a 23 percent increase in the productivity of the coding operation alone. Productivity in later levels was also increased because there was less error rework in these levels due to the effect of inspections, but the increase was not measured directly.

An important aspect to consider in any production experiment involving human beings is the Hawthorne Effect.[3] If this effect is not adequately handled, it is never clear whether the effect observed is due to the human bias of the Hawthorne Effect or due to the newly implemented change in process. In this case a *control sample* was selected at random from many pieces of work *after the I_1 and I_2 inspections were accepted as commonplace.* (Previous experience without I_1 and I_2 approximated the net cod-

(marginal notes)
inspection sample

coding operation productivity

ing productivity rate of 100 percent datum in Figure 2.) The difference in coding productivity between the experimental sample (with I_1 and I_2 for the first time) and the control sample was 0.9 percent. This difference is not considered significant. Therefore, the measured increase in coding productivity of 23 percent is considered to validly accrue from the only change in the process: addition of I_1 and I_2 inspections.

control sample
The control sample was also considered to be of representative size and was from the same operating system component as the study sample. It was designed by four programmers and was coded by seven programmers. And it was considered to be of moderate complexity on average.

net savings
Within the coding operation only, the net savings (including inspection and rework time) in programmer hours per 1000 Non-Commentary Source Statements (K.NCSS)[4] were I_1: 94, I_2: 51, and I_3: -20. As a consequence, I_3 is no longer in effect.

If personal fatigue and downtime of 15 percent are allowed in addition to the 145 programmer hours per K.NCSS, the saving approaches one programmer month per K.NCSS (assuming that our sample was truly representative of the rest of the work in the operating system component considered).

error rework
The error rework in programmer hours per K.NCSS found in this study due to I_1 was 78, and 36 for I_2 (24 hours for design errors and 12 for code errors). Time for error rework must be specifically scheduled. (For scheduling purposes it is best to develop rework hours per K.NCSS from history depending upon the particular project types and environments, but figures of 20 hours for I_1, and 16 hours for I_2 (*after the learning curve*) may be suitable to start with.)

quality
The only comparative measure of quality obtained was a comparison of the inspection study sample with a fully comparable piece of the operating system component that was produced similarly, except that walk-throughs were used in place of the I_1 and I_2 inspections. (Walk-throughs[5] were the practice before implementation of I_1 and I_2 inspections.) The process span in which the quality comparison was made was seven months of testing beyond unit test after which it was judged that both samples had been equally exercised. The results showed the inspection sample to contain 38 percent less errors than the walk-through sample.

Note that up to inspection I_2, no machine time has been used for debugging, and so machine time savings were not mentioned. Although substantial machine time is saved overall since there are less errors to test for in inspected code in later stages of the process, no actual measures were obtained.

Table 1 Error detection efficiency

Process Operations	Errors Found per K.NCSS	Percent of Total Errors Found
Design		
I_1 inspection ⎫		
Coding ⎬	38*	82
I_2 inspection ⎭		
Unit test ⎫		
Preparation for ⎬	8	18
acceptance test ⎭		
Acceptance test	0	
Actual usage (6 mo.)	0	
Total	46	100

*51% were logic errors, most of which were missing rather than due to incorrect design.

In the development of applications, inspections also make a significant impact. For example, an application program of eight modules was written in COBOL by Aetna Corporate Data Processing department, Aetna Life and Casualty, Hartford, Connecticut, in June 1975.[6] Two programmers developed the program. The number of inspection participants ranged between three and five. The only change introduced in the development process was the I_1 and I_2 inspections. The program size was 4,439 Non-Commentary Source Statements.

An automated estimating program, which is used to produce the normal program development time estimates for all the Corporate Data Processing department's projects, predicted that designing, coding, and unit testing this project would require 62 programmer days. In fact, the time actually taken was 46.5 programmer days including inspection meeting time. The resulting saving in programmer resources was 25 percent.

The inspections were obviously very thorough when judged by the inspection error detection efficiency of 82 percent and the later results during testing and usage as shown in Table 1.

The results achieved in Non-Commentary Source Statements per Elapsed Hour are shown in Table 2. These inspection rates are four to six times faster than for systems programming. If these rates are generally applicable, they would have the effect of making the inspection of applications programs much less expensive.

inspections in applications development

Table 2 Inspection rates in NCSS per hour

Operations	I_1	I_2
Preparation	898	709
Inspection	652	539

Inspections

Inspections are a *formal*, *efficient*, and *economical* method of finding errors in design and code. All instructions are addressed

Table 3. Inspection process and rate of progress

Process operations	Rate of progress*(loc/hr) Design I_1	Code I_2	Objectives of the operation
1. Overview	500	not necessary	Communication education
2. Preparation	100	125	Education
3. Inspection	130	150	*Find errors*
4. Rework	20 hrs/K.NCSS	16 hrs/K.NCSS	Rework and re-solve errors found by inspection
5. Follow-up	–	–	See that all errors, prob-lems, and concerns have been resolved

*These notes apply to systems programming and are conservative. Comparable rates for applications programming are much higher. Initial schedules may be started with these numbers and as project history that is keyed to unique environments evolves, the historical data may be used for future scheduling algorithms.

at least once in the conduct of inspections. Key aspects of inspections are exposed in the following text through describing the I_1 and I_2 inspection conduct and process. I_0, IT_1, IT_2, PI_0, PI_1, and PI_2 inspections retain the same essential properties as the I_1 and I_2 inspections but differ in materials inspected, number of participants, and some other minor points.

the people involved

The inspection team is best served when its members play their particular roles, assuming the particular vantage point of those roles. These roles are described below:

1. *Moderator* – The *key person* in a successful inspection. He must be a competent programmer but need *not* be a technical expert on the program being inspected. To preserve objectivity and to increase the integrity of the inspection, it is usually advantageous to use a moderator from an unrelated project. The moderator must manage the inspection team and offer leadership. Hence, he must use personal sensitivity, tact, and drive in balanced measure. His use of the strengths of team members should produce a synergistic effect larger than their number; in other words, *he is the coach*. The duties of moderator also include scheduling suitable meeting places, reporting inspection results within one day, and follow-up on rework. *For best results the moderator should be specially trained.* (This training is brief but very advantageous.)
2. *Designer* – The programmer responsible for producing the program design.
3. *Coder/Implementor* – The programmer responsible for translating the design into code.
4. *Tester* – The programmer responsible for writing and/or executing test cases or otherwise testing the product of the designer and coder.

556

If the coder of a piece of code also designed it, he will function in the designer role for the inspection process; a coder from some related or similar program will perform the role of the coder. If the same person designs, codes, and tests the product code, the coder role should be filled as described above, and another coder—preferably with testing experience—should fill the role of tester.

Four people constitute a good-sized inspection team, although circumstances may dictate otherwise. The team size should not be artificially increased over four, but if the subject code is involved in a number of interfaces, the programmers of code related to these interfaces may profitably be involved in inspection. Table 3 indicates the inspection process and rate of progress.

scheduling inspections and rework

The total time to complete the inspection process from overview through follow-up for I_1 or I_2 inspections with four people involved takes about 90 to 100 people-hours for systems programming. Again, these figures may be considered conservative but they will serve as a starting point. Comparable figures for applications programming tend to be much lower, implying lower cost per K.NCSS.

Because the error detection efficiency of most inspection teams tends to dwindle after two hours of inspection but then picks up after a period of different activity, it is advisable to schedule inspection sessions of no more than two hours at a time. Two two-hour sessions per day are acceptable.

The time to do inspections and resulting rework must be scheduled and managed with the same attention as other important project activities. (After all, as is noted later, for one case at least, it is possible to find approximately two thirds of the errors reported during an inspection.) If this is not done, the immediate work pressure has a tendency to push the inspections and/or rework into the background, postponing them or avoiding them altogether. The result of this short-term respite will obviously have a much more dramatic long-term negative effect since the finding and fixing of errors is delayed until later in the process (and after turnover to the user). Usually, the result of postponing early error detection is a lengthening of the overall schedule and increased product cost.

Scheduling inspection time for modified code may be based on the algorithms in Table 3 *and on judgment.*

Keeping the objective of each operation in the forefront of team activity is of paramount importance. Here is presented an outline of the I_1 inspection process operations.

I_1 inspection process

Figure 3 Summary of design inspections by error type

VP Individual Name		Missing	Wrong	Extra	Errors	Error %
CD	CB Definition	16	2		18	3.5 ⎫
CU	CB Usage	18	17	1	36	6.9 ⎬ 10.4
FS	FPFS	1			1	.2
IC	Interconnect Calls	18	9		27	5.2
IR	Interconnect Reqts	4	5	2	11	2.1
LO	Logic	126	57	24	207	39.8 ←
L3	Higher Lvl Docu	1		1	2	.4
MA	Mod Attributes	1			1	.2
MD	More Detail	24	6	2	32	6.2
MN	Maintainability	8	5	3	16	3.1
OT	Other	15	10	10	35	6.7
PD	Pass Data Areas		1		1	.2
PE	Performance	1	2	3	6	1.2
PR	Prologue/Prose	44	38	7	89	17.1 ←
RM	Return Code/Msg	5	7	2	14	2.7
RU	Register Usage	1	2		3	.6
ST	Standards					
TB	Test & Branch	12	7	2	21	4.0
		295	168	57	520	100.0
		57%	32%	11%		

Figure 4 Summary of code inspections by error type

VP Individual Name		Missing	Wrong	Extra	Errors	Error %
CC	Code Comments	5	17	1	23	6.6
CU	CB Usage	3	21	1	25	7.2
DE	Design Error	31	32	14	77	22.1 ←
F1			8		8	2.3
IR	Interconnect Calls	7	9	3	19	5.5
LO	Logic	33	49	10	92	26.4 ←
MN	Maintainability	5	7	2	14	4.0
OT	Other					
PE	Performance	3	2	5	10	2.9
PR	Prologue/Prose	25	24	3	52	14.9 ←
PU	PL/S or BAL Use	4	9	1	14	4.0
RU	Register Usage	4	2		6	1.7
SU	Storage Usage	1			1	.3
TB	Test & Branch	2	5		7	2.0
		123	185	40	348	100.0

1. *Overview* (whole team) — The designer first describes the overall area being addressed and then the specific area he has designed in detail — logic, paths, dependencies, etc. Documentation of design is distributed to all inspection participants on conclusion of the overview. (For an I₂ inspection, no overview is necessary, but the participants should remain the same. Preparation, inspection, and follow-up proceed as for I₁ but, of course, using code listings *and* design specifications

FAGAN

as inspection materials. Also, at I_2 the moderator should flag for special scrutiny those areas that were reworked since I_1 errors were found *and other design changes* made.)

2. *Preparation* (individual) — Participants, using the design documentation, literally do their homework to try to understand the design, its intent and logic. (Sometimes flagrant errors are found during this operation, but in general, the number of errors found is not nearly as high as in the inspection operation.) To increase their error detection in the inspection, the inspection team should first study the ranked distributions of error types found by recent inspections. This study will prompt them to concentrate on the most fruitful areas. (See examples in Figures 3 and 4.) Checklists of clues on finding these errors should also be studied. (See partial examples of these lists in Figures 5 and 6 and complete examples for I_0 in Reference 1 and for I_1 and I_2 in Reference 7.)

3. *Inspection* (whole team) — A "reader" chosen by the moderator (usually the coder) describes how he will implement the design. He is expected to paraphrase the design as expressed by the designer. Every piece of logic is covered at least once, and every branch is taken at least once. All higher-level documentation, high-level design specifications, logic specifications, etc., and macro and control block listings at I_2 must be available and present during the inspection.

Now that the design is understood, *the objective is to find errors.* (Note that an error is defined as any condition that causes malfunction or that precludes the attainment of expected or previously specified results. Thus, deviations from specifications are clearly termed errors.) The finding of errors is actually done during the implementor/coder's discourse. Questions raised are pursued only to the point at which an error is recognized. It is noted by the moderator; its type is classified; severity (major or minor) is identified, and the inspection is continued. Often the solution of a problem is obvious. If so, it is noted, but no specific solution hunting is to take place during inspection. (The inspection is *not* intended to redesign, evaluate alternate design solutions, or to find solutions to errors; it is intended just to find errors!) A team is most effective if it operates with only one objective at a time.

Within one day of conclusion of the inspection, the moderator should produce a written report of the inspection and its findings to ensure that all issues raised in the inspection will be addressed in the rework and follow-up operations. Examples of these reports are given as Figures 7A, 7B, and 7C.

Figure 5 Examples of what to examine when looking for errors at I_1

I_1 Logic

Missing

1. Are All Constants Defined?
2. Are All Unique Values Explicitly Tested on Input Parameters?
3. Are Values Stored after They Are Calculated?
4. Are All Defaults Checked Explicitly Tested on Input Parameters?
5. If Character Strings Are Created Are They Complete, Are All Delimiters Shown?
6. If a Keyword Has Many Unique Values, Are They All Checked?
7. If a Queue Is Being Manipulated, Can the Execution Be Interrupted; If So, Is Queue Protected by a Locking Structure; Can Queue Be Destroyed Over an Interrupt?
8. Are Registers Being Restored on Exits?
9. In Queuing/Dequeuing Should Any Value Be Decremented/Incremented?
10. Are All Keywords Tested in Macro?
11. Are All Keyword Related Parameters Tested in Service Routine?
12. Are Queues Being Held in Isolation So That Subsequent Interrupting Requestors Are Receiving Spurious Returns Regarding the Held Queue?
13. Should any Registers Be Saved on Entry?
14. Are All Increment Counts Properly Initialized (0 or 1)?

Wrong

1. Are Absolutes Shown Where There Should Be Symbolics?
2. On Comparison of Two Bytes, Should All Bits Be Compared?
3. On Built Data Strings, Should They Be Character or Hex?
4. Are Internal Variables Unique or Confusing If Concatenated?

Extra

1. Are All Blocks Shown in Design Necessary or Are They Extraneous?

4. *Rework* — All errors or problems noted in the inspection report are resolved by the designer or coder/implementor.

5. *Follow-Up* — It is imperative that every issue, concern, and error be entirely resolved at this level, or errors that result can be 10 to 100 times more expensive to fix if found later in the process (programmer time only, machine time not included). It is the responsibility of the moderator to see that all issues, problems, and concerns discovered in the inspection operation have been resolved by the designer in the case of I_1, or the coder/implementor for I_2 inspections. If more than five percent of the material has been reworked, the team should reconvene and carry out a 100 percent reinspection. Where less than five percent of the material has been reworked, the moderator at his discretion may verify the quality of the rework himself or reconvene the team to reinspect either the complete work or just the rework.

commencing inspections In Operation 3 above, it is one thing to direct people to find errors in design or code. It is quite another problem for them to find errors. Numerous experiences have shown that people have to be taught or prompted to find errors effectively. Therefore, it

Figure 6 Examples of what to examine when looking for errors at I₂

INSPECTION SPECIFICATION

I₂ *Test Branch*

Is Correct Condition Tested (If X = ON vs. IF X = OFF)?
Is (Are) Correct Variable(s) Used for Test
(If X = ON vs. If Y = ON)?
Are Null THENs/ELSEs Included as Appropriate?
Is Each Branch Target Correct?
Is the Most Frequently Exercised Test Leg the THEN Clause?

I₂ *Interconnection (or Linkage) Calls*

For Each Interconnection Call to Either a Macro, SVC or Another Module:
Are All Required Parameters Passed Set Correctly?
If Register Parameters Are Used, Is the Correct Register Number Specified?
If Interconnection Is a Macro,
Does the Inline Expansion Contain All Required Code?
No Register or Storage Conflicts between Macro and Calling Module?
If the Interconnection Returns, Do All Returned Parameters Get Processed
Correctly?

is prudent to condition them to seek the high-occurrence, high-cost error types (see example in Figures 3 and 4), and then describe the clues that usually betray the presence of each error type (see examples in Figures 5 and 6).

One approach to getting started may be to make a preliminary inspection of a design or code that is felt to be representative of the program to be inspected. Obtain a suitable quantity of errors, and analyze them by type and origin, cause, and salient indicative clues. With this information, an inspection specification may be constructed. This specification can be amended and improved in light of new experience and serve as an on-going directive to focus the attention and conduct of inspection teams. The objective of an inspection specification is to help maximize and make more consistent the error detection efficiency of inspections where

Error detection efficiency

$$= \frac{\text{Errors found by an inspection}}{\text{Total errors in the product before inspection}} \times 100$$

reporting inspection results

The reporting forms and form completion instructions shown in the Appendix may be used for I₁ and I₂ inspections. Although these forms were constructed for use in systems programming development, they may be used for applications programming development with minor modification to suit particular environments.

The moderator will make hand-written notes recording errors found during inspection meetings. He will categorize the errors

1. PR/M/MIN Line 3:   the statement of the prologue in the REMARKS section needs expansion.
2. DA/W/MAJ Line 123: ERR–RECORD–TYPE is out of sequence.
3. PU/W/MAJ Line 147: the wrong bytes of an 8-byte field (current–data) are moved into the 2-byte field (this year).
4. LO/W/MAJ Line 169: while counting the number of leading spaces in NAME, the wrong variable (1) is used to calculate "J".
5. LO/W/MAJ Line 172: NAME–CHECK is PERFORMED one time too few.
6. PU/E/MIN Line 175: In NAME–CHECK, the check for SPACE is redundant.
7. DE/W/MIN Line 175: the design should allow for the occurrence of a period in a last name.

Figure 7B Example of module detail report

DATE_____

CODE INSPECTION REPORT

MODULE DETAIL

MOD/MAC:____CHECKER_____SUBCOMPONENT/APPLICATION_____

SEE NOTE BELOW

PROBLEM TYPE:	MAJOR*			MINOR		
	M	W	E	M	W	E
LO: LOGIC		9			1	
TB: TEST AND BRANCH						
EL: EXTERNAL LINKAGES						
RU: REGISTER USAGE						
SU: STORAGE USAGE						
DA: DATA AREA USAGE		2				
PU: PROGRAM LANGUAGE		2				1
PE: PERFORMANCE						
MN: MAINTAINABILITY					1	
DE: DESIGN ERROR					1	
PR: PROLOGUE				1		
CC: CODE COMMENTS						
OT: OTHER						
TOTAL:	13			5		

REINSPECTION REQUIRED?____Y_____

*A PROBLEM WHICH WOULD CAUSE THE PROGRAM TO MALFUNCTION. A BUG. M = MISSING, W = WRONG, E = EXTRA
NOTE: FOR MODIFIED MODULES, PROBLEMS IN THE CHANGED PORTION VERSUS PROBLEMS IN THE BASE SHOULD BE SHOWN IN THIS MANNER: 1(2), WHERE 1 IS THE NUMBER OF PROBLEMS IN THE CHANGED PORTION AND 2 IS THE NUMBER OF PROBLEMS IN THE BASE

and then transcribe counts of the errors, by type, to the module detail form. By maintaining cumulative totals of the counts by error type, and dividing by the number of projected executable source lines of code inspected to date, he will be able to establish installation averages within a short time.

Figures 7A, 7B, and 7C are an example of a set of code inspection reports. Figure 7A is a partial list of errors found in code inspection. Notice that errors are described in detail and are classified by error type, whether due to something being missing,

Figure 7C   Example of code inspection summary report

CODE INSPECTION REPORT
SUMMARY   Date___11/20/–___

To: Design Manager_____KRAUSS_____ Development Manager_____GIOTTI_____
Subject: Inspection Report for_____CHECKER_____ Inspection date_____11/19/–_____
           System/Application_____ Release_____Build_____
           Component_____ Subcomponents(s)_____

Mod/Mac Name	New or Mod	Full or Part Insp.	Programmer	Tester	ELOC Added, Modified, Deleted									Inspection People-hours (X.X)				Sub-component
					Pre-insp			Est Post			Rework			Prep	Insp Meetg	Re-work	Follow-up	
					A	M	D	A	M	D	A	M	D					
	N		McGINLEY	HALE	348			400			50			9.0	8.8	8.0	1.5	
				Totals														

Reinspection required?___YES___ Length of inspection (clock hours and tenths)___2.2_____
Reinspection by (date)___11/25/–___ Additional modules/macros?___NO_____
DCR #'s written___C-2_____
Problem summary: Major___13_____ Minor___5_____ Total___18_____
Errors in changed code: Major_____Minor_____ Errors in base code: Major_____Minor_____
___LARSON___   ___McGINLEY___   ___HALE___
   Initial Desr   Detailed Dr   Programmer   Team Leader   Other   Moderator's Signature

wrong, or extra as the cause, and according to major or minor
severity. Figure 7B is a module level summary of the errors contained in the entire error list represented by Figure 7A. The
code inspection summary report in Figure 7C is a summary of
inspection results obtained on all modules inspected in a particular inspection session or in a subcomponent or application.

Inspections have been successfully applied to designs that are
specified in English prose, flowcharts, HIPO, (Hierarchy plus
Input-Process-Output) and PIDGEON (an English prose-like
meta language).

**inspections
and
languages**

The first code inspections were conducted on PL/S and Assembler. Now, prompting checklists for inspections of Assembler,
COBOL, FORTRAN, and PL/1 code are available.[7]

One of the most significant benefits of inspections is the detailed
feedback of results on a relatively real-time basis. The programmer finds out what error types he is most prone to make and
their quantity and how to find them. This feedback takes place
within a few days of writing the program. Because he gets early
indications from the first few units of his work inspected, he is
able to show improvement, and usually does, on later work even
during the same project. In this way, feedback of results from
inspections must be counted for the programmer's use and benefit: *they should not under any circumstances be used for programmer performance appraisal.*

**personnel
considerations**

Skeptics may argue that once inspection results are obtained,
they will or even must count in performance appraisals, or at

Figure 8 Example of most error-prone modules based on I_1 and I_2

Module name	Number of errors	Lines of code	Error density. Errors/K. Loc
Echo	4	128	31
Zulu	10	323	31
Foxtrot	3	71	28
Alpha	7	264	27 ← Average
Lima	2	106	19 Error
Delta	3	195	15 Rate
.	.	.	.
.	.	.	.
.	67	.	.

least cause strong bias in the appraisal process. The author can offer in response that inspections have been conducted over the past three years involving diverse projects and locations, hundreds of experienced programmers and tens of managers, and so far he has found no case in which inspection results have been used negatively against programmers. Evidently no manager has tried to "kill the goose that lays the golden eggs."

A preinspection opinion of some programmers is that they do not see the value of inspections because they have managed very well up to now, or because their projects are too small or somehow different. This opinion usually changes after a few inspections to a position of acceptance. The quality of acceptance is related to the success of the inspections they have experienced, the *conduct of the trained moderator*, and the *attitude demonstrated by management*. The acceptance of inspections by programmers and managers as a beneficial step in making programs is well-established amongst those who have tried them.

Process control using inspection and testing results

Obviously, the range of analysis possible using inspection results is enormous. Therefore, only a few aspects will be treated here, and they are elementary expositions.

most error-prone modules A listing of either I_1, I_2, or combined $I_1 + I_2$ data as in Figure 8 immediately highlights which modules contained the highest error density on inspection. If the error detection efficiency of each of the inspections was fairly constant. the ranking of error-prone modules holds. Thus if the error detection efficiency of inspection is 50 percent, and the inspection found 10 errors in a

Figure 9 Example of distribution of error types

	Number of errors	%	Normal/usual distribution, %
Logic	23	35	44
Interconnection/Linkage (Internal)	21	31 ?	18
Control Blocks	6	9	13
—	·	8	10
—	·	7	7
—	·	6	6
—	·	4	2
		100%	100%

module, then it can be estimated that there are 10 errors remaining in the module. This information can prompt many actions to control the process. For instance, in Figure 8, it may be decided to reinspect module "Echo" or to redesign and recode it entirely. Or, less drastically, it may be decided to test it "harder" than other modules and look especially for errors of the type found in the inspections.

distribution of error types

If a ranked distribution of error types is obtained for a group of "error-prone modules" (Figure 9), which were produced from the same Process A, for example, it is a short step to comparing this distribution with a "Normal/Usual Percentage Distribution." Large disparities between the sample and "standard" will lead to questions on why Process A, say, yields nearly twice as many internal interconnection errors as the "standard" process. If this analysis is done promptly on the first five percent of production, it may be possible to remedy the problem (if it is a problem) on the remaining 95 percent of modules for a particular shipment. Provision can be made to test the first five percent of the modules to remove the unusually high incidence of internal interconnection problems.

inspecting error-prone code

Analysis of the testing results, commencing as soon as testing errors are evident, is a vital step in controlling the process since future testing can be guided by early results.

Where testing reveals excessively error-prone code, it may be more economical and saving of schedule to select the most error-prone code and inspect it before continuing testing. (The business case will likely differ from project to project and case to case, but in many instances inspection will be indicated). The selection of the most error-prone code may be made with two considerations uppermost:

Table 4. Inspection and walk-through processes and objectives

	Inspection		Walk-through	
Process Operations	Objectives	Process Operations	Objectives
1. Overview	Education (Group)	—	—
2. Preparation	Education (Individual)	1. Preparation	Education (Individual)
3. Inspection	Find errors! (Group)	2. Walk-through	Education (Group) Discuss design alternatives Find errors
4. Rework	Fix problems	—	
5. Follow-up	Ensure all fixes correctly installed	—	

Note the separation of objectives in the inspection process.

Table 5 Comparison of key properties of inspections and walk-throughs

Properties	Inspection	Walk-Through
1. Formal moderator training	Yes	No
2. Definite participant roles	Yes	No
3. Who "drives" the inspection or walk-through	Moderator	Owner of material (Designer or coder)
4. Use "How To Find Errors" checklists	Yes	No
5. Use distribution of error types to look for	Yes	No
6. Follow-up to reduce bad fixes	Yes	No
7. Less future errors because of detailed error feedback to individual programmer	Yes	Incidental
8. Improve inspection efficiency from analysis of results	Yes	No
9. Analysis of data → process problems → improvements	Yes	No

1. Which modules head a ranked list when the modules are rated by test errors per K.NCSS?
2. In the parts of the program in which test coverage is low, which modules or parts of modules are most suspect based on $(I_1 + I_2)$ errors per K.NCSS and programmer judgment?

From a condensed table of ranked "most error-prone" modules, a selection of modules to be inspected (or reinspected) may be made. Knowledge of the error types already found in these modules will better prepare an inspection team.

The reinspection itself should conform with the I_2 process, except that an overview may be necessary if the original overview was held too long ago or if new project members are involved.

Inspections and walk-throughs

Walk-throughs (or walk-thrus) are practiced in many different ways in different places, with varying regularity and thoroughness. This inconsistency causes the results of walk-throughs to vary widely and to be nonrepeatable. Inspections, however, having an established process and a formal procedure, tend to vary less and produce more repeatable results. Because of the variation in walk-throughs, a comparison between them and inspections is not simple. However, from Reference 8 and the walk-through procedures witnessed by the author and described to him by walk-through participants, as well as the inspection process described previously and in References 1 and 9, the comparison in Tables 4 and 5 is drawn.

Figure 10A describes the process in which a walk-through is applied. Clearly, the purging of errors from the product as it passes through the walk-through between Operations 1 and 2 is very beneficial to the product. In Figure 10B, the inspection process (and its feedback, feed-forward, and self-improvement) replaces the walk-through. The notes on the figure are self-explanatory.

effects on development process

Inspections are also an excellent means of measuring completeness of work against the exit criteria which must be satisfied to complete project checkpoints. (Each checkpoint should have a clearly defined set of exit criteria. Without exit criteria, a checkpoint is too negotiable to be useful for process control).

Inspections and process management

The most marked effects of inspections on the development process is to change the old adage that, "design is not complete until testing is completed," to a position where a very great deal must be known about the design before even the coding is begun. Although great discretion is still required in code implementation, more predictability and improvements in schedule, cost, and quality accrue. The old adage still holds true if one regards inspection as much a means of verification as testing.

Observations in one case in systems programming show that approximately two thirds of all errors reported during development are found by I_1 and I_2 inspections prior to machine testing.

percent of errors found

Figure 10 (A) Walk-through process, (B) Inspection process

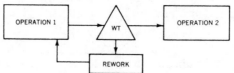

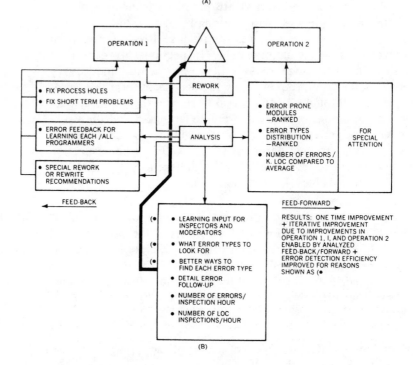

The error detection efficiencies of the I_1 and I_2 inspections separately are, of course, less than 66 percent. A similar observation of an application program development indicated an 82 percent find (Table 1). As more is learned and the error detection efficiency of inspection is increased, the burden of debugging on testing operations will be reduced, and testing will be more able to fulfill its prime objective of verifying quality.

effect on cost and schedule

Comparing the "old" and "new" (with inspections) approaches to process management in Figure 11, we can see clearly that with the use of inspection results, error rework (which is a very significant variable in product cost) tends to be managed more during the first half of the schedule. This results in much lower cost than in the "old" approach, where the cost of error rework was 10 to 100 times higher and was accomplished in large part during the last half of the schedule.

process tracking

Inserting the I_1 and I_2 checkpoints in the development process enables assessment of project completeness and quality to be

568

Figure 11　Effect of inspection on process management

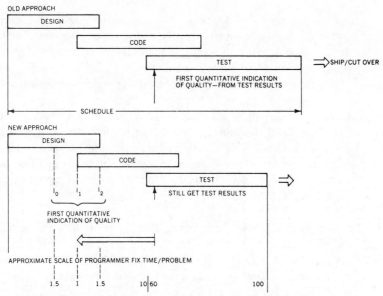

POINT OF MANAGEMENT CONTROL OVER QUALITY IS MOVED UP MUCH EARLIER IN SCHEDULE.

ERROR REWORK AT THIS LEVEL IS 1/10 AS EXPENSIVE.

made early in the process (during the first half of the project instead of the latter half of the schedule, when recovery may be impossible without adjustments in schedule and cost). Since individually trackable modules of reasonably well-known size can be counted as they pass through each of these checkpoints, the percentage completion of the project against schedule can be continuously and easily tracked.

effect on product knowledge

The overview, preparation, and inspection sequence of the operations of the inspection process give the inspection participants a high degree of product knowledge in a very short time. This important side benefit results in the participants being able to handle later development and testing with more certainty and less false starts. Naturally, this also contributes to productivity improvement.

An interesting sidelight is that because designers are asked at pre-I_1 inspection time for estimates of the number of lines of code (NCSS) that their designs will create, and they are present to count for themselves the actual lines of code at the I_2 inspection, the accuracy of design estimates has shown substantial improvement.

For this reason, an inspection is frequently a required event where responsibility for design or code is being transferred from one programmer to another. The complete inspection team is convened for such an inspection. (One-on-one reviews such as desk debugging are certainly worthwhile but do not approach the effectiveness of formal inspection.) Usually the side benefit of finding errors more than justifies the transfer inspection.

inspecting modified code

Code that is changed in, or inserted in, an existing module either in replacement of deleted code or simply inserted in the module is considered modified code. By this definition, a very large part of programming effort is devoted to modifying code. (The addition of entirely new modules to a system count as new, not modified, code.)

Some observations of errors per K.NCSS of modified code show its error rate to be considerably higher than is found in new code; (i.e., if 10.NCSS are replaced in a 100.NCSS module and errors against the 10.NCSS are counted, the error rate is described as number of errors per 10.NCSS, not number of errors per 100.NCSS). Obviously, if the number of errors in modified code are used to derive an error rate per K.NCSS for the whole module that was modified, this rate would be largely dependent upon the percentage of the module that is modified: this would provide a meaningless ratio. A useful measure is the number of errors per K.NCSS (modified) in which the higher error rates have been observed.

Since most modifications are small (e.g., 1 to 25 instructions), they are often erroneously regarded as trivially simple and are handled accordingly; the error rate goes up, and control is lost. In the author's experience, *all* modifications are well worth inspecting from an economic and a quality standpoint. A convenient method of handling changes is to group them to a module or set of modules and convene the inspection team to inspect as many changes as possible. But all changes must be inspected!

Inspections of modifications can range from inspecting the modified instructions and the surrounding instructions connecting it with its host module, to an inspection of the entire module. The choice of extent of inspection coverage is dependent upon the percentage of modification, pervasiveness of the modification, etc.

bad fixes

A very serious problem is the inclusion in the product of bad fixes. Human tendency is to consider the "fix," or correction, to a problem to be error-free itself. Unfortunately, this is all too frequently untrue in the case of fixes to errors found by inspections and by testing. The inspection process clearly has an operation called Follow-Up to try and minimize the bad-fix problem, but the fix process of testing errors very rarely requires scrutiny of fix quality before the fix is inserted. Then, if the fix is bad, the whole elaborate process of going from source fix to link edit, to test the fix, to regression test must be repeated at needlessly high cost. The number of bad fixes can be economically reduced by some simple inspection after clean compilation of the fix.

Summary

We can summarize the discussion of design and code inspections and process control in developing programs as follows:

1. Describe the program development process in terms of operations, and define exit criteria which must be satisfied for completion of each operation.
2. Separate the objectives of the inspection process operations to keep the inspection team focused on one objective at a time.:

Operation	Objective
Overview	Communications/education
Preparation	Education
Inspection	Find errors
Rework	Fix errors
Follow-up	Ensure all fixes are applied correctly

3. Classify errors by type, and rank frequency of occurrence of types. Identify *which types* to spend most time looking for in the inspection.
4. Describe *how* to look for presence of error types.
5. Analyze inspection results and use for constant process improvement (until process averages are reached and then use for process control).

Some applications of inspections include function level inspections I_0, design-complete inspections I_1, code inspections I_2, test plan inspections IT_1, test case inspections IT_2, interconnections inspections IF, inspection of fixes/changes, inspection of publications, etc., and post testing inspection. Inspections can be applied to the development of system control programs, applications programs, and microcode in hardware.

We can conclude from experience that inspections increase productivity and improve final program quality. Furthermore, improvements in process control and project management are enabled by inspections.

ACKNOWLEDGMENTS
The author acknowledges, with thanks, the work of Mr. O. R. Kohli and Mr. R. A. Radice, who made considerable contributions in the development of inspection techniques applied to program design and code, and Mr. R. R. Larson, who adapted inspections to program testing.

Figure 12 Design inspection module detail form

DATE_____

DETAILED DESIGN INSPECTION REPORT

MODULE DETAIL

MOD/MAC:_____SUBCOMPONENT/APPLICATION_____

SEE NOTE BELOW

PROBLEM TYPE:	MAJOR*			MINOR		
	M	W	E	M	W	E
LO: LOGIC						
TB: TEST AND BRANCH						
DA: DATA AREA USAGE						
RM: RETURN CODES/MESSAGES						
RU: REGISTER USAGE						
MA: MODULE ATTRIBUTES						
EL: EXTERNAL LINKAGES						
MD: MORE DETAIL						
ST: STANDARDS						
PR: PROLOGUE OR PROSE						
HL: HIGHER LEVEL DESIGN DOC.						
US: USER SPEC.						
MN: MAINTAINABILITY						
PE: PERFORMANCE						
OT: OTHER						
TOTAL:						

REINSPECTION REQUIRED?_____

*A PROBLEM WHICH WOULD CAUSE THE PROGRAM TO MALFUNCTION: A BUG. M = MISSING, W = WRONG, E = EXTRA.
NOTE: FOR MODIFIED MODULES, PROBLEMS IN THE CHANGED PORTION VERSUS PROBLEMS IN THE BASE SHOULD BE SHOWN IN THIS MANNER: 3(2), WHERE 3 IS THE NUMBER OF PROBLEMS IN THE CHANGED PORTION AND 2 IS THE NUMBER OF PROBLEMS IN THE BASE.

CITED REFERENCES AND FOOTNOTES

1. O. R. Kohli, *High-Level Design Inspection Specification*, Technical Report TR 21.601, IBM Corporation, Kingston, New York (July 21, 1975).
2. It should be noted that the exit criteria for I_1 (design complete where one design statement is estimated to represent 3 to 10 code instructions) and I_2 (first clean code compilations) are checkpoints in the development process through which every programming project must pass.
3. The Hawthorne Effect is a psychological phenomenon usually experienced in human-involved productivity studies. The effect is manifested by participants producing above normal because they know they are being studied.
4. NCSS (Non-Commentary Source Statements), also referred to as "Lines of Code," are the sum of executable code instructions and declaratives. Instructions that invoke macros are counted once only. Expanded macroinstructions are also counted only once. Comments are not included.
5. Basically in a walk-through, program design or code is reviewed by a group of people gathered together at a structured meeting in which errors/issues pertaining to the material and proposed by the participants may be discussed in an effort to find errors. The group may consist of various participants but always includes the originator of the material being reviewed who usually plans the meeting and is responsible for correcting the errors. How it differs from an inspection is pointed out in Tables 2 and 3.
6. *Marketing Newsletter*, Cross Application Systems Marketing, "Program inspections at Aetna," MS-76-006, S2, IBM Corporation, Data Processing Division, White Plains, New York (March 29, 1976).

7. J. Ascoly, M. J. Cafferty, S. J. Gruen, and O. R. Kohli, *Code Inspection Specification*, Technical Report TR 21.630, IBM Corporation, Kingston, New York (1976).

8. N. S. Waldstein, *The Walk-Thru—A Method of Specification, Design and Review*, Technical Report TR 00.2536, IBM Corporation, Poughkeepsie, New York (June 4, 1974).

9. Independent study programs: *IBM Structured Programming Textbook*, SR20-7149-1, *IBM Structured Programming Workbook*, SR20-7150-0, IBM Corporation, Data Processing Division, White Plains, New York.

GENERAL REFERENCES

1. J. D. Aron, *The Program Development Process: Part 1: The Individual Programmer*, Structured Programs, 137–141, Addison-Wesley Publishing Co., Reading, Massachusetts (1974).

2. M. E. Fagan, *Design and Code Inspections and Process Control in the Development of Programs*, Technical Report TR 00.2763, IBM Corporation, Poughkeepsie, New York (June 10, 1976). This report is a revision of the author's *Design and Code Inspections and Process Control in the Development of Programs*, Technical Report TR 21.572, IBM Corporation, Kingston, New York (December 17, 1974).

3. O. R. Kohli and R. A. Radice, *Low-Level Design Inspection Specification*, Technical Report TR 21.629. IBM Corporation, Kingston, New York (1976).

4. R. R. Larson, *Test Plan and Test Case Inspection Specifications*, Technical Report TR 21.586, IBM Corporation, Kingston, New York (April 4, 1975).

Appendix: Reporting forms and form completion instructions

Instructions for Completing Design Inspection Module Detail Form

This form (Figure 12) should be completed for each module/ macro that has valid problems against it. The problem-type information gathered in this report is important because a history of problem-type experience points out high-occurrence types. This knowledge can then be conveyed to inspectors so that they can concentrate on seeking the higher-occurrence types of problems.

1. MOD/MAC: The module or macro name.
2. SUBCOMPONENT: The associated subcomponent.
3. PROBLEM TYPE: Summarize the number of problems by type (logic, etc.), severity (major/minor), and by category (missing, wrong, or extra). For modified modules, detail the number of problems in the changed design versus the number in the base design. (Problem types were developed in a systems programming environment. Appropriate changes, if desired, could be made for application development.)

Figure 13 Design inspection summary form

DESIGN INSPECTION REPORT
SUMMARY   Date

To: Design Manager............................ ....Development Manager.
Subject: Inspection Report for ....Inspection date
System Application.. .. .. Release ....   Build
Component............. .... Subcomponents(s).

Mod Mac Name	New or Mod	Full or Part Insp.	Detailed Designer	Programmer	ELOC Added, Modified, Deleted									Inspection People-hours (X.X)				Sub-component
					Est. Pre			Est. Post			Rework			Over-view & Prep	Insp Meetg	Re-work	Follow up	
					A	M	D	A	M	D	A	M	D					
			Totals															

Reinspection required? ....Length of inspection (clock hours and tenths)
Reinspection by (date). ....Additional modules/macros?
DCR #'s written...
Problem summary: Major .... Minor.............. .... Total
Errors in changed code: Major ..... .Minor.......... ....Errors in base code: Major.... Minor

Initial Desr   Detailed Dr   Programmer   Team Leader   Other   Moderator's Signature

4. REINSPECTION REQUIRED?: Indicate whether the module/macro requires a reinspection.

All valid problems found in the inspection should be listed and attached to the report. A brief description of each problem, its error type, and the rework time to fix it should be given (see Figure 7A, which describes errors in similar detail to that required but is at a coding level).

Instructions for Completing Design Inspection Summary Form

Following are detailed instructions for completing the form in Figure 13.
1. TO: The report is addressed to the respective design and development managers.
2. SUBJECT: The unit being inspected is identified.
3. MOD/MAC NAME: The name of each module and macro as it resides on the source library.
4. NEW OR MOD: "N" if the module is new; "M" if the module is modified.
5. FULL OR PART INSP: If the module/macro is "modified," indicate "F" if the module/macro was fully inspected or "P" if partially inspected.
6. DETAILED DESIGNER: and PROGRAMMER: Identification of originators.
7. PRE-INSP EST ELOC: The estimated executable source lines of code (added, modified, deleted). Estimate made prior to the inspection by the designer.

Figure 14   Code inspection module detail form

DATE_____

CODE INSPECTION REPORT

MODULE DETAIL

MOD/MAC:_____ SUBCOMPONENT/APPLICATION_____

SEE NOTE BELOW

PROBLEM TYPE:	MAJOR*			MINOR		
	M	W	E	M	W	E
LO: LOGIC						
TB: TEST AND BRANCH						
EL: EXTERNAL LINKAGES						
RU: REGISTER USAGE						
SU: STORAGE USAGE						
DA: DATA AREA USAGE						
PU: PROGRAM LANGUAGE						
PE: PERFORMANCE						
MN: MAINTAINABILITY						
DE: DESIGN ERROR						
PR: PROLOGUE						
CC: CODE COMMENTS						
OT: OTHER						
TOTAL:						

REINSPECTION REQUIRED?_____

*A PROBLEM WHICH WOULD CAUSE THE PROGRAM TO MALFUNCTION: A BUG. M = MISSING, W = WRONG, E = EXTRA.
NOTE: FOR MODIFIED MODULES, PROBLEMS IN THE CHANGED PORTION VERSUS PROBLEMS IN THE BASE SHOULD BE SHOWN IN THIS MANNER: 3(2), WHERE 3
IS THE NUMBER OF PROBLEMS IN THE CHANGED PORTION AND 2 IS THE NUMBER OF PROBLEMS IN THE BASE.

8. POST-INSP EST ELOC: The estimated executable source lines of code. Estimate made after the inspection.

9. REWORK ELOC: The estimated executable source lines of code in rework as a result of the inspection.

10. OVERVIEW AND PREP: The number of people-hours (in tenths of hours) spent in preparing for the overview, in the overview meeting itself, and in preparing for the inspection meeting.

11. INSPECTION MEETING: The number of people-hours spent on the inspection meeting.

12. REWORK: The estimated number of people-hours spent to fix the problems found during the inspection.

13. FOLLOW-UP: The estimated number of people-hours spent by the moderator (and others if necessary) in verifying the correctness of changes made by the author as a result of the inspection.

14. SUBCOMPONENT: The subcomponent of which the module/macro is a part.

15. REINSPECTION REQUIRED?: Yes or no.

16. LENGTH OF INSPECTION: Clock hours spent in the inspection meeting.

17. REINSPECTION BY (DATE): Latest acceptable date for reinspection.

575

Figure 15 Code inspection summary form

CODE INSPECTION REPORT
SUMMARY   Date _____

To   Design Manager _____ Development Manager _____
Subject   Inspection Report for _____ Inspection date _____
          System Application _____ Release _____ Build ____
          Component _____ Subcomponents(s) _____

Mod Mac Name	New or Mod	Full or Part Insp	Programmer	Tester	ELOC Added, Modified, Deleted									Inspection People-hours (X X)				Sub-component
					Pre-insp			Est Post			Rework			Prep	Insp Meetg	Re-work	Follow up	
					A	M	D	A	M	D	A	M	D					
			Totals															

Reinspection required? _____ Length of inspection (clock hours and tenths) _____
Reinspection by (date) _____ Additional modules/macros? _____
DCR #'s written _____
Problem summary: Major _____ Minor _____ Total _____
    Errors in changed code: Major ____ Minor ____ Errors in base code: Major ____ Minor ____

Initial Desr   Detailed Dr   Programmer   Team Leader   Other   Moderator's Signature

18. ADDITIONAL MODULES/MACROS?: For these subcomponents, are additional modules/macros yet to be inspected?

19. DCR #'S WRITTEN: The identification of Design Change Requests, DCR(s), written to cover problems in rework.

20. PROBLEM SUMMARY: Totals taken from Module Detail forms(s).

21. INITIAL DESIGNER, DETAILED DESIGNER, etc.: Identification of members of the inspection team.

Instructions for Completing Code Inspection Module Detail Form

This form (Figure 14) should be completed according to the instructions for completing the design inspection module detail form.

Instructions for Completing Code Inspection Summary Form

This form (Figure 15) should be completed according to the instructions for the design inspection summary form except for the following items.

1. PROGRAMMER AND TESTER: Identifications of original participants involved with code.

2. PRE-INSP. ELOC: The noncommentary source lines of code (added, modified, deleted). Count made prior to the inspection by the programmer.

3. POST-INSP EST ELOC: The estimated noncommentary source lines of code. Estimate made after the inspection.

4. REWORK ELOC: The estimated noncommentary source lines of code in rework as a result of the inspection.

5. PREP: The number of people hours (in tenths of hours) spent in preparing for the inspection meeting.

Reprint Order No. G321-5033.

EVALUATION METHODS IN SARA—
THE GRAPH MODEL SIMULATOR

Rami R. Razouk

Mary Vernon

Gerald Estrin

Computer Science Department
University of California
Los Angeles, California 90024

ABSTRACT

The supported methodology evolving in the SARA (System ARchitects' Apprentice) system creates a design framework on which increasingly powerful analytical tools are to be
grafted. Control flow analyses and program verification tools
have shown promise. However, in the realm of the complex
systems which interest us there is a great deal of research·
and development to be done before we can count on the use
of such powerful tools. We must always be prepared to
resort to experiments for evaluation of proposed designs.

This paper describes a fundamental SARA tool, the graph
model simulator. During top-down refinement of a design,
the simulator is used to test consistency between the levels
of abstraction. During composition, known building blocks
are linked together and the composite graph model is tested
relative to the lowest top-down model. Design of test environments is integrated with the multilevel design process.
The SARA methodology is exemplified through design of a
higher level building block to do a simple FFT.

INTRODUCTION

Advances in LSI technology have made available complex
hardware components at low costs. Consequently there is increased interest in designing systems using ensembles of
these elements. providing speed through concurrency and reliability through redundancy. This trend makes it difficult to
verify behavior of programs and raises costs of design and
testing for both hardware and software systems. Many
veterans of the first three generations of computer system
development fear that lessons learned about the value of
structured design will be put aside by the multitude of new
designers. Computer aided structured design is needed to
avoid high costs of development and the disasters caused by
failing systems.

Computer aided design is based on the development of
machine processable models and the use of computer tools to
evaluate the models. Modeling and analysis of complex systems which exhibit concurrent behavior requires highly sophisticated analytical tools. Control flow analyses and program verification tools have shown promise [1]. However, in
the realm of the complex systems which interest us there is a
great deal of research and development to be done before we
can count on the use of such analytical power. We must always be prepared to resort to experiments for evaluation of
proposed designs.

The supported methodology evolving in the SARA (Sys-

tem ARchitects' Apprentice) system builds a design framework on which increasingly powerful analytical tools are to be
grafted. This paper describes a fundamental SARA tool, the
graph model simulator. During top-down refinement of a
design, the simulator is used to test consistency between the
levels of abstraction. During composition, known building
blocks are linked together. The composite graph model can
then be tested relative to the lowest top-down model and,
when desired, can be evaluated with respect to the original
system requirements.

The design of experiments using SARA tools is a critical
part of the design process and is the focus of the discussions
presented here. Section 1 describes the SARA design
methodology. Section 2 discusses the graph model (GMB)
used to represent the behavior of systems being designed.
Section 3 introduces the GMB simulator and its capabilities.
Section 4 discusses guidelines for designing a *test environment*
which can be used to check the consistency of models of a
system at different levels of abstraction. Finally, Section 5
shows, through an example, how a test environment is used
in the design process to increase confidence that a design
satisfies its requirements.

1 THE SARA METHODOLOGY

The SARA methodology is a requirement-driven, top-
down and bottom-up design methodology [2]. Each step of a
design starts with the establishment of an *invariant* [3] which
includes requirements on the system and assumptions about
its environment. The system is designed by modeling its
structure and behavior. A top-down design strategy can be
applied by refining structural and behavioral models of the
system. A bottom-up design strategy can be applied by composing structural and behavioral models of existing building
blocks (BBMs). When composition is successful SARA intends to support replacement of BBMs by physical building
blocks. Below we discuss the concept of the invariant and
the design process in the SARA methodology.

1.1 The Design Invariant

· We define a SARA design invariant to consist of the following:

a. A design universe structurally partitioned into a named
   system and its named environment, connected by named
   interconnections through named interfaces.

b. A set of functional requirements to be met by the system
   to be designed, and a set of evaluation criteria to be used
   to determine the satisfaction of these requirements.

c. A set of design constraints imposed on the design, and a
   corresponding set of evaluation criteria.

† This research was supported by the Department of Energy,
contract no. EY-76-S-03-0034, PA214.

577

d. A set of assumptions about the behavior of the environment to which the system must interface.

e. A highest level *abstract* behavioral model of the system and its environment.

f. A behavioral model of a removable test environment.

A *well conceived* invariant will leave room for design decisions to be made, while pinning down the design at its interface with other systems (i.e. the environment). The highest level invariant is derived from the needs of some *customer*. Invariants at lower levels may inherit parts of higher level invariants with more detail being introduced at each level. For example, requirements at the top level of design filter down to lower levels, but at each level new requirements, which reflect new knowledge, are introduced. The reader may find it strange to accept the notion of *changing invariants* but so long as any higher level model is a proper abstraction of a lower level model the invariant is not contradicted.

1.2 The Design Process

Once an invariant has been established, one of two design strategies may be used:

• Bottom-up design:

The system may be synthesized from existing Building Block models. This step is limited by the availability of suitable BBMs. When such BBMs are found any proposed composite model must at least be tested for consistency with the abstract structural and behavioral model. This may be done by running the same test data through both models and comparing the results of the two levels of abstraction. Such testing is prerequisite to fabrication.

• Top-down refinement:

If no suitable set of BBMs is found, the behavioral models may be refined and partitioned into subsystems [4]. The refined model must also satisfy the system requirements and must therefore be tested for consistency with respect to the abstract model. Such testing serves to increase confidence that the ensemble of subsystems interacts in such a way as to satisfy the requirements. This is an important step before design attention can be focussed on any subsystem. Refinement of the model of a system may imply some refinement of the model of the test environment. The idea of designing a system and its test environment in parallel is important to the SARA methodology.

Once validation of the refined model is complete, each subsystem can be considered individually. An invariant is established for each subsystem before the design can proceed. By establishment of a new invariant, the design of each subsystem can be viewed as an independent design task. It is recognized that the task of establishing an invariant and determining that it does not contradict a higher level invariant may involve considerable interaction between designers as well as some partial exploratory design of some of the subsystems.

There is a large overhead involved in specifying an invariant and in validating the models with respect to that invariant. This cost generally motivates designers to compose a design at the earliest possible point. Knowledge of available building blocks is critical, as is the availability of a rich library of BBMs.

2 THE GRAPH MODEL OF BEHAVIOR

The Graph Model of Behavior (GMB) allows designers to model various aspects of a system in three modeling domains: control, data and interpretation. The control graph is based on the Graph Model of Control (GMC) developed at UCLA [5-17], and has been shown to be equivalent to Petri Nets [14]. The data graph and interpretation were introduced by Gardner [18], drawing on work by Potash [19] and the LOGOS group [20] at Case-Western Reserve.

In the GMB, all parts of a design can be modeled in the data and interpretation domains. It is up to the designer whether to explicitly model control aspects of a system. The trade-offs are:

a. Aspects of the system which are explicitly modeled as control can be analyzed and tested for deadlock freeness and other interesting control properties.

b. Control graphs may get unmanageably complex if too much detail is introduced into them at an early stage of design. Analysis and testing of such complex graphs may not be feasible.

In SARA the control and data graphs are processed by the GMB Translator while the interpretation is processed by the SARA PL/I Preprocessor (PLIP). The processed models can be simulated using the GMB Simulator. We now examine in detail the three modeling domains of the GMB.

2.1 Control Domain

The control graph consists of nodes which represent events, and arcs which describe precedence relationships among the events.

Each node has an input logic expression which dictates the conditions under which that node is to be initiated. An "OR" (+) in the input logic means a node may be initiated through any one of a set of designated arcs. An "AND" (·) in the input logic means that both arcs must pass control before the node is initiated. A node input logic expression may be an arbitrary function of its input arcs using "AND" and "OR" operators.

Each node has an output logic expression which dictates the arcs through which the node passes control upon its termination. An "OR" implies a decision to be made among designated arcs. An "AND" implies the passage of control through more than one arc. As is the case with input logic expressions, output logic expressions may be complex functions.

A control graph is a static description of possible control sequences. The control state of such a graph is represented by the distribution of *tokens* on control arcs. When a node is initiated the tokens which enabled it are absorbed. Upon node termination, tokens are created and placed on output arcs. The semantics of a control graph are carried out by underlying machinery: the *token machine*. This token machine performs state-to-state transformations dictated by the graph, starting from the initial token distribution, and terminating when no further transformations are possible. When considering the problem of taking designs to fabrication the semantics hidden in the token machine must be considered.

As an example of the modeling power of the control graph Figure 1 shows the use of multisource-multidestination arcs with initial tokens to model resource sharing. The example graph models three concurrent processes (n2,n3, and n4) sharing two instances of a resource. The resource is modeled by the two initial tokens on arc R. Sharing of the resource is modeled by the multiple sources and multiple destinations of arc R. Figure 2 shows the machine processable form of the control graph. Note that arcs R and S are designated as initially having two and one tokens respectively. All other control arcs have no tokens initially.

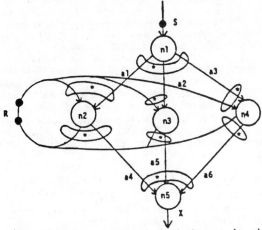

Figure 1. Modeling resourse sharing in the control graph

```
@control_graph
    @nodes n1,n2,n3,n4
    @arcs S(1),a1,a2,a3,a4,a5,a6,
          X,R(2)
    n1(S : a1*a2*a3)
    n2(a1*R : a4*R)
    n3(a2*R : a5*R)
    n4(a3*R : a6*R)
    n5(a4*a5*a6 : X)
@end
```

Figure 2. GMB source for control graph

2.2 Data Domain

The data graph describes data transformations, some of which are triggered by the control graph. The data graph primitives are:

a. Datasets

b. Controlled processors

c. Uncontrolled processors

d. Dataarcs

Datasets model static collections of data. Controlled processors are data transformers whose activation depends on the initiation of control nodes to which they are mapped. Termination of controlled processors causes termination of their initiating control nodes. Uncontrolled processors are data transformers whose control is independent of the control graph. They are triggered by changes to any of their input datasets. Data arcs model data paths and access paths between datasets and processors. Figure 3 shows the data graph part of the GMB shown in Figure 1. Figure 4 shows the machine processable form of the data graph including the mapping between control nodes and controlled processors. The semantics of both controlled and uncontrolled processors are carried out by the token machine.

2.3 Interpretation Domain

The interpretation is used to define formats of data stored in datasets and transported through data arcs. It is also used to define transformations on data performed by data processors.

The format of the data is specified in the form of PL/I declarations associated with data arcs and datasets. The example below shows the definition of a *template* which is associated with arcs da0, da1, da2, da3 and which is implicitly associated with dataset ds1.

@*template* (da0, da1, da2, da3) t1 (2) char(10);

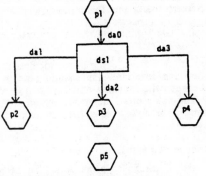

Figure 3. Data graph for Figure 1

```
@data_graph
    @controlled_processors p1(n1),p2(n2),
                           p3(n3),p4(n4),p5(n5)
        @datasets ds1
        @arcs da0,da1,da2,da3
        da0(p1 : ds1)
        da1(ds1 : p2)
        da2(ds1 : p3)
        da3(ds1 : p4)
@end
```

Figure 4. GMB source for data graph

Timescale definition commands are used to define time units used in a model, and relationships among them. The example below shows the definition of the default timescale used in the absence of a user-defined timescale.

```
@timescale ;
@smallest_time_unit = @ns;
      @us = 1000 @ns;
      @ms = 1000 @us;
      @sec = 1000 @ms;
@endtimescale ;
```

The processor interpretation consists of PL/I code augmented with the following PLIP (PL/I Preprocessor) features needed to communicate information to the token machine:

a. @*read* and @*write* commands which are needed to control data access through input and output data arcs. A read from an input data arc makes available to the processor a local copy of data stored in the dataset which is in the source set of the data arc. A write to a data arc causes a copy of some local storage to be sent, via the data arc, to a dataset in the destination set of the data arc. Below are examples of read and write commands. The @*after* option used to delay the effect of write commands will be discussed in more detail in a later section.

```
@read local_var @from da1;
@write local_var @to da2 @after 100 @ms;
```

b. @*output_arcs* command which is used in the interpretation for controlled processors to effect decisions in the flow of control whenever an "OR" appears in the output logic of the corresponding control node. In the example below a control flow decision between arcs x and a is made based on the contents of the dataset accessible through arc da5.

```
@processor p5;
@read flag @from: da5;
if flag
    then @output_arcs = "x";
    else @output_arcs = "a";
@endprocessor ;
```

c. Some timing constructs which are used to effect delays in the control and data transformations dictated by the interpretations of processors. Timing can be modeled in GMB using two timing constructs: processor delays and dataset-write delays.

The *simplest* of the two is the processor delay. It is used to indicate the amount of simulation time which is to elapse between the initiation and termination of the processor. The value of the delay may be an arbitrary PL/1 expression. The following is the syntax of this timing construct:

@ *delay* — 200 @ms;

In the case of controlled processors, that delay dictates the time when tokens appear on the output arcs of the corresponding control node. During that delay period the processor and its control node are said to be *active* and may not be initiated a second time.

In the case of uncontrolled processors, the delay dictates the maximum frequency at which a processor may perform its data transformation. If the input datasets change faster than the maximum frequency allows, warnings are issued at simulation time.

As shown in the example in 2.3a the value of the delay may be followed by a time unit specification.

The *second timing construct* is used in conjunction with dataset-write commands. The delay dictates the amount of simulation time to elapse before the dataset is updated. In a controlled processor the delay is relative to the initiation time of the processor. In an uncontrolled processor the delay is relative to the time the input datasets change. In the example below the dataset connected to arc da1 will be updated 200 nanoseconds (in simulation time) after the processor is initiated.

@ *write* local_var @ *to* da1 @ *after* 200 @ns;

The delays used in write statements of controlled processors are restricted to be less than or equal to the processor delay. This restriction arises from the fact that a controlled processor can only affect the state of the data during its *active* period. Uncontrolled processors, since they are not controlled by the control graph, do not have that restriction.

2.4 Extended Primitives

Sections 2.1 and 2.2 describe the primitives currently accepted by the GMB Translator. These primitives are well suited for modeling concurrency and elementary synchronization mechanisms. New, well-structured synchronization primitives have been proposed by Ruggiero [21] and Van Mierop [22]. These primitives are aimed at better designs of distributed interacting processes. Interest in other primitives stems from their direct mapping to fabrication or their current use in existing computer-aided design systems.

The ability to incorporate new primitives into the SARA simulation and analysis environment is of great importance. The first step has been taken to define the semantics of new primitives in terms of the existing control and data primitives and the current interpretation language. The addition of an automatic translation mechanism between the new primitives and the simulatable GMB primitives will substantially increase the power of the SARA simulation and analysis environment.

One example of such translations was proposed by Ruggiero in [23] where he defines Dennis' Data-flow primitives in terms of existing GMB primitives.

2.5 Other Interpretation Languages

The ability to add new interpretation languages to the SARA models is important for the same reasons outlined for new primitives. A mechanism for the addition of new languages has been tested through the use of Fortran subroutines within the framework of PLIP. Similar mechanisms should make it possible for designers to write interpretations for models in a target language or in a language more suitable for modeling the system being designed. Even with the capability of modeling in a target language, it is always necessary to understand any difference between the simulation environment and the environment in which the real system will be expected to function.

3 THE GMB SIMULATOR

The GMB Simulator is an interactive, discrete-event simulator which allows designers to perform experiments on models which have been defined and processed by the GMB Translator and PLIP. It is designed to allow experiments to be performed before a system is completely designed. A simulation may be run using the bare control graph to detect control flow anomalies, using the control graph and data graph to detect resource contention, and using the completely interpreted GMB to validate the complete design.

The simulator starts from an initial control and data state and performs the state-to-state transitions dictated by the GMB. As with all discrete-event simulators an event list is maintained, and at every step in a simulation experiment the simulation clock is advanced to the time of the next predicted event. The following events characterize a GMB simulation:

a. Control node initiations (controlled processor activations).

b. Uncontrolled-processor initiations

c. Control node terminations.

d. Dataset writes.

Each of these events alters the control and/or data states of the GMB and can potentially trigger other events.

• **Control node initiations:**

A node is initiated only if its input logic is satisfied. Upon initiation tokens are removed from its input arcs according to the logic expression. Removal of tokens from arcs may prevent the initiation of other nodes currently scheduled for initiation. The controlled processor to which the initiated node is mapped is activated. Based on the interpretation, the following subsequent events are scheduled:

— dataset writes are scheduled at the times specified in the interpretion of the processor.

— termintion of the node and placement of tokens on the output arcs are scheduled according to the processor delay.

• **Uncontrolled processor initiations:**

Uncontrolled processors are initiated by changes in their input datasets and may cause the scheduling of dataset writes.

• **Control node terminations:**

Upon termination of a node tokens are placed on its output arcs based on the @ *output_arcs* command in the interpretation for its processor. The release of these tokens makes nodes in the destination sets of the output arcs candidates for initiation.

● **Dataset writes:**

When a dataset is updated and its value changes, it causes the scheduling of the initiation of all uncontrolled processors to which it is connected.

The scheduling of events starts from the initial states of both the control graph and the data graph. The initial token distribution specifies all candidate nodes for initiation. In the data graph, all uncontrolled processors are initially active. The processing of events proceeds from the initial states as described above until no events remain.

3.1 Simulator Commands

The simulator allows designers to:

a. Control initiation (@*start*, @*restart*), resumption (@*continue*) and termination (@*end*) of simulation experiments. The @*load* command is used to load a new model.

b. Set breakpoints at various points in the graph. Breakpoints can be set at node initiations and terminations (@*node_start*, @*node_end*). Breakpoints can be triggered by the activation of a node a specified number of times (@*node_count*) or by the number of tokens on an arc (@*token_max*, @*token_min*). Breakpoints can be set at given simulation times or may be repeated every simulation time interval (@*break_time*, @*break_time_int*). Breakpoints can also be triggered by the updating of a dataset or by the initiation of an uncontrolled processor (@*dataset_write*, @*processor_initiation*).

c. Set the control state and/or the data state of the GMB using the @*state* and/or the @*set_ds* commands.

d. Examine the state of the simulation including:

- Listing the current GMB model being simulated (@*list_model*).

- Listing breakpoints (@*list_breaks*).

- Listing the token distribution on control arcs (@*list_arcs*).

- Listing contents of datasets (@*list_ds*).

- Listing active nodes and processors (@*list_nodes*, @*list_processors*).

- Listing the simulation time in a unit determined by the @*set_default_time_unit* command (@*list_time*).

- Listing all of the above (@*list_state*).

The syntax of these commands can be easily obtained, by typing "?", through the SARA help system. A more complete description of the syntax and semantics of these commands can be found in [24,25].

3.2 Built-in Checks

Along with these user-controlled commands there are some basic checks which have been built into the simulator to aid a designer in detecting design flaws. They are:

a. Processor and dataset contention:

If two nodes are mapped to the same processor and they are both initiated the simulator issues a warning that the controlled processor has been activated twice in parallel. Similarly, if two processors have access to the same dataset and their periods of activity overlap the simulator issues a warning that a potential memory accessing conflict exists. Data arc contention may also exist but is lumped under dataset contention since no data arc contention can exist without a dataset contention.

b. Uncontrolled processor re-initiation

If any inputs to an uncontrolled processor change before the processor delay since the last change has elapsed, a warning is issued.

c. Improper termination of the control graph:

If the control state reaches a terminal state which is not *proper* a warning is issued. A *proper* terminal state is one which is identical to the initial state except that tokens have been removed from the entry arcs and have been placed on the exit arcs of the control graph. Deadlocks in the flow of control always lead to improper termination.

4 DESIGNING THE TEST ENVIRONMENT

A primary goal of the SARA methodology is to encourage the design of *testable* systems. Experience has shown that non-invasive testing of systems, not originally designed with that purpose in mind, may be infeasible [26,27]. A testable system must at least include *hooks* for anticipated measurements. It is sometimes desirable to integrate testers which can generate test data, observe a system's behavior and report failures. Such integration permits systems to test their own state of health.

Testability of systems is supported in the SARA methodology by including a model of the test environment in the design invariant. The test environment includes test data generation and measurements. It carries any evaluation criteria used in validating the system. In the absence of more powerful analyses test measurements may provide the only indicator of a system's correctness.

Two approaches are generally applicable when performing measurements on models of systems. The first approach is to develop more powerful measurement tools. In the case of the SARA system, and specifically GMB models, it is possible to build measurement capabilities into the simulator. This has already been done for the built-in checks discussed in Section 3.2. The second approach, and the one recommended here, is to explicitly model measurements in the test environment. This approach generally leads to the design of testable systems. The use of the same primitives to model the test environment and the system itself makes it possible for both to be taken to fabrication. We seek to perform the same measurements on the model and on the eventual real system. Placing a testing mechanism in the environment forces designers to create systems which can be tested through their interface elements. Although test systems may be removed in fabrication, explicit modeling of measurements forces designers to deal with the perturbations often introduced by the measuring mechanisms themselves.

This section deals with the design of test environments. Section 4.1 discusses the types of measurements which need to be carried out in order to validate hardware and software designs. Section 4.2 presents the differences between a test environment and the assumed environment. Section 4.3 states general requirements imposed on all test environments and section 4.4 presents guidelines for the design of a test environment.

4.1 Testing Software and Hardware Systems

The SARA models and tools are intended to aid design and test of both hardware and software systems. When validating software systems the measurements involve: contention for resources, timing, memory requirements and bottlenecks (queue lengths). Similar observations are needed when validating hardware with the following key differences:

a. Functional modeling is generally at a more detailed level when dealing with hardware.

b   Timing measurements play a critical role in the validation of hardware systems and must therefore be more precise.

When testing hardware systems the emphasis generally shifts from the more abstract problems of resource contention and bottlenecks to more detailed problems of timing. Designers must be aware of this shift and design test environments accordingly.

4.2 Test Environment vs. Assumed Environment

A model of the assumed environment should reflect any behavior which can significantly affect the designed system. A test environment model should be completely consistent with the assumed environment at the interface to the system. It generally varies elsewhere because of the role it plays in validation. The following are some key differences between the assumed environment and the test environment.

a. While the assumed environment models general behavior, the test environment focuses on particular behavior selected to cover data flow paths and ranges of data. This process of focussing, which involves test data selection, is very important to the successful evaluation of a design but is beyond the scope of this paper [28-34].

b. The test environment is required to support all measurements which must be made to evaluate the design. These measurements are not necessarily part of the assumed environment.

c. Integral to the SARA design methodology is the recommendation that the same tests be run on both abstract and detailed levels of any design. The test environment interfaces to these two levels of abstraction and it must therefore undergo refinement reflecting increased detail in stimuli and responses. The refinement must be consistent with the invariant assumed environment.

We now examine the process of designing the test environment. The starting point of the design is a set of requirements imposed on all test environments.

4.3 Requirements On Test Environment

a. A test environment must be capable of generating all specified input control and data signals to the system. Actual inputs should be derived from designer-selected test cases and must be consistent with behavior prescribed for the environment.

b. A test environment must receive all output control and data signals from the system.

c. A test environment must observe the quantities specified in the evaluation criteria. Whenever possible, the measurements should be evaluated directly by the test environment to verify that the requirements are met.

d. If measurements cannot be evaluated directly, the test environment must record the relevant raw data when testing the abstract model. In such cases, when testing the detailed model, the test environment must compare currently generated data with previously recorded results.

e. Comparison of results of two tests must tolerate some disagreement due to the increased precision (detail) introduced by refinement.

f. A test environment must detect failures to pass evaluation criteria and disagreements between test results at the two levels of abstraction. It must also include some mechanism for recovering from test failures. The minimal recovery mechanism is to abort the testing sequence and to report the nature of the failure.

g. A test environment must stop a simulation run when test data is exhausted. Data which has been generated for future evaluation must be made available to the designer. A final report on the completed tests should be generated.

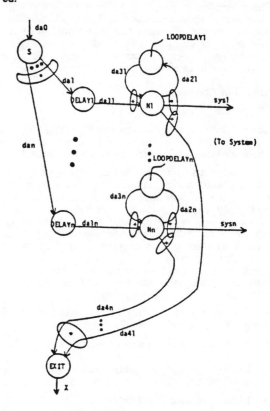

Figure 5. Generating control inputs

4.4 Guidelines For Design Of Test Environments

The guidelines shown here are intended to assist a designer in creating a test environment. Our goal is for the guidelines to evolve into a systematic way of translating system requirements and evaluation criteria into test environments. The discussion below refers to the requirements listed in Section 4.3.

a. Generating control and data inputs (Requirement a):

In order to correctly generate *control inputs* each control signal is generated by a control node. Signals which are required to be simultaneous can be generated by a single node. Generating a sequence of control signals can be accomplished by putting each control node in a loop. The delay in such a loop can be derived from the required frequency of the particular control signal. For example, Figure 5 shows the control graph needed to generate n control signals. Node S is used to initiate the testing sequence. Nodes DELAY1 through DELAYn are used to stagger initiation of the loops. Such staggering depends on required relationships between control signals. Nodes N1 through Nn generate the control signals and terminate the loops when testing is completed. The processors mapped to nodes LOOPDELAY1 through LOOPDELAYn hold the delays which govern the time behavior of the signals.

A control signal generated in the manner described above can be used to drive a system directly if there are no control dependencies between it and other input/output control signals. A control node with an appropriate input logic expression can be added to express such control dependencies. Figure 6 shows an example of an input signal which is conditional on the receipt of an output signal.

Data inputs must be generated in a way consistent with assumptions on the environment. Inputs are divided into synchronously-generated and asynchronously-generated data [35].

Synchronously-generated data inputs can be modeled in the test environment using the general construct shown in Figure 7. The timing relationship between the input data and the synchronizing control signal determines the delays of processors CONTROL_GENP and DATA_GENP.

Asynchronously generated data inputs can be generated by uncontrolled processors. Sequences of asynchronous inputs are generated by looping uncontrolled processors as shown in Figure 8. The loop delay is the write-delay to the loop dataset.

b. Receiving control and data outputs (Requirement b):

Each *control output* must be received by an individual control node. Since there may be assumptions on the environment as to how fast it can receive these output signals, a loop may be needed to constrain re-initiation of the node. Figure 9 shows an example of one of a set of n control outputs received by the test environment. The delay of node DELAY1 determines the speed with which the output control signal can be received. If the environment can receive it as fast as it is generated the delay becomes zero and the loop can be eliminated. For output signals which are subsequently used to control inputs, a token must be passed back to the input generators. An example is shown in Figure 10. The delay in node DELAY2 can be used to model anticipated delays in the environment.

Synchronously-generated *data outputs* are received by controlled processors mapped to the control nodes receiving the synchronizing control outputs. Asynchronously generated data outputs are received by uncontrolled processors.

c. Performing measurements needed for evaluation (Requirement c):

The types of measurements which need to be performed during validation of designs have been presented in section 4.2. These measurements require some basic mechanisms:

* Clocks.
* Counters.
* Accumulators.

Clocks are used for timing measurements; counters and accumulators are used for queue length measurements and resource utilization measurements. The difference between counters and accumulators is that counters are incremented and decremented by fixed quantities while accumulators are incremented and decremented by variable quantities. Below we focus on timing measurements through explicit modeling of a clock in the test environment. The same ideas can be applied to other measurements.

Figure 11 shows how an uncontrolled processor can be used to model a clock. The particular write-delay to TIME determines the granularity of the clock. A control graph and a controlled processor can model the same mechanism. Unless a set of correlated clocks is needed, explicit modeling of control gains us no analytical power and only complicates the control flow.

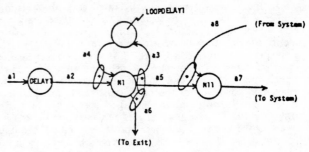

Figure 6. Modeling input control dependencies

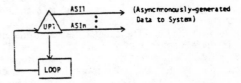

Figure 7. Synchronously generating data inputs

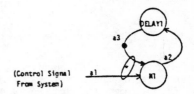

Figure 8. Asynchronously generating data inputs

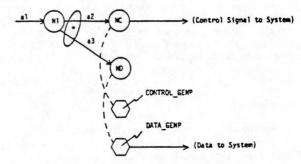

Figure 9. Receiving control outputs

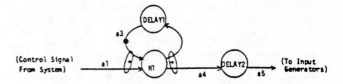

Figure 10. Modeling output control dependencies

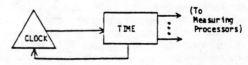

Figure 11. Modeling a clock using an uncontrolled processor

A timing measurement usually involves a time relationship between two or more signals. The time of generation of each signal must therefore be recorded. When all measurements needed to evaluate a requirement are available, the evaluation is performed. Figure 12 shows how an evaluation criterion involving a timing relationship between two control signals may be included in the test environment. The evaluation involves two control signals: S1 and S2. The time of generation of control signal S1 is recorded by a control node which intercepts it as it is generated, before passing it on to the system. A control node intercepts the output control signal S2, then reads the current clock value and initiates the test.

The above example is particularly simple because it is restricted to handling the case when signal S1 is generated only once before each generation of S2. To handle the case where several inputs can be generated before corresponding outputs are received, the single data item used to store the time of generation of the input signal must be replaced by a circular buffer, with a maximum buffer size estimated by the designer. Figure 13 shows the declaration of one such dataset and shows interpretations of the sending and receiving processors.

d. Storing and retrieving test results (Requirement d):

During testing of an abstract model a test environment must permanently store test results. The values stored can act as reference values to check the consistency of the two levels of abstraction. The test environment must interface to a file system to record and access test results. In cases where the behavior of the system is deterministic each processor making a measurement which needs to be recorded simply writes it to a results file. The detailed test environment then reads a result whenever a measurement is made. The task becomes difficult when non-determinism is introduced. In such cases the results must be temporarily stored in datasets and then written out in a specific format at the end of the testing. The file can then be used to initialize datasets in the test environment during testing of lower level models. Whenever a comparison needs to be made, the dataset containing the expected results of that particular measurement can be read.

e. Allowing for error tolerances in measurements (Requirement e):

In general, detailed models should yield test results which are more *accurate* than abstract models. *Accurate*, in this context, means closer to the behavior of the designed system. The detailed model reflects added knowledge gained during the refinement process. When dealing with timing measurements, for example, the detailed model usually requires a finer grained clock. When dealing with numerical data, increased accuracy may imply greater precision. Error tolerances can be set by processors in the test environment as part of the initialization of a test sequence. Tolerances can be stored internally to the processors or can be explicitly model as datasets. Explicit modeling of error tolerances allows them to be modified during simulation.

f. Detecting and reporting test failures (Requirement f):

Two modes of operation are possible when failures are detected: Simulation can continue as failure data is accumulated, or it can be interrupted as failures are encountered. In the first mode failure data is recorded the same way correct data is recorded. In the second mode test failures should be signaled by setting a flag. All input generators should examine the flag and be able to stop generating inputs when it is set. Any measured quantities should be recorded because the state of the data may change by the time the simulation comes to a halt. Any processor detecting a failure should re-

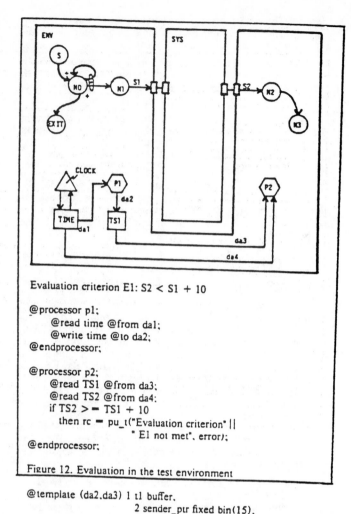

Evaluation criterion E1: S2 < S1 + 10

```
@processor p1;
    @read time @from da1;
    @write time @to da2;
@endprocessor;

@processor p2;
    @read TS1 @from da3;
    @read TS2 @from da4;
    if TS2 >= TS1 + 10
        then rc = pu_t("Evaluation criterion" ||
                    " E1 not met", error);
@endprocessor;
```

Figure 12. Evaluation in the test environment

```
@template (da2,da3) 1 t1 buffer,
                2 sender_ptr fixed bin(15),
                2 receiver_ptr fixed bin(15),
                2 times(0:max-1) float bin(53);

@processor p1;
    @read time @from da1;
    @read buffer @from da2;
    sender_ptr = mod(sender_ptr+1, max);
    times(sender_ptr) = time;
    @write buffer @to da2;
@endprocessor;

@processor p2;
    @read TS1_buffer @from da3;
    @read TS2 @from da4;
    receiver_ptr = mod(receiver_ptr+1, max);
    if TS2 >= TS1_buffer.times(receiver_ptr) + 10
        then rc = pu_t("Evaluation criterion" ||
                    " E1 not met", error);
    @write TS1_buffer @to da3;
@endprocessor;
```

Figure 13. Buffering measurements

port whether the failure involves a direct measurement in an evaluation criterion or a dissagreement between the two levels of abstraction. Figure 13 shows how the interpretation in a test processor can make use of the SARA I/O system to report the failure to the designer.

Some test failures are difficult to detect and require the addition of complex recovery mechanisms in the environ-

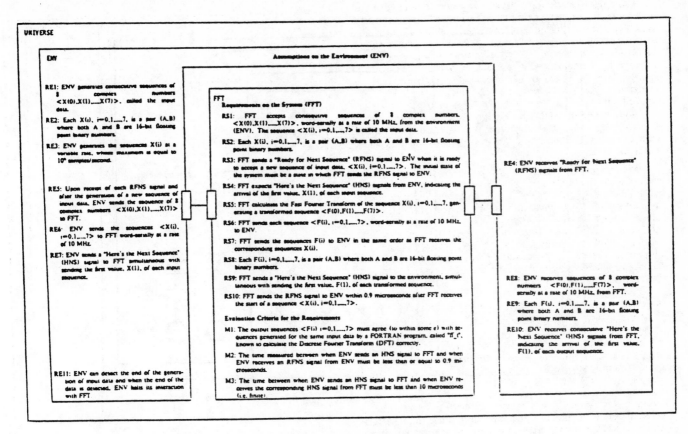

Figure 14. Initial partitioning and requirements

ment. One example of such a failure is the *loss* of an expected control signal. The detection of this type of failure requires the addition of alternate control paths which act as *time-outs*.

g. Terminating a simulation (Requirement g):

Termination of a test sequence occurs when the end of the input data is encountered. All processors which read the input data file must detect the end of the data. Controlled processors terminate a test sequence by placing a token on the exit arc instead of generating a stimulus to the system. Uncontrolled processors terminate a test sequence by ceasing dataset-writes to the loop variables which would normally cause their triggering.

5 FFT EXAMPLE

In this section we present a design example and demonstrate the use of a test environment to establish that the design meets its requirements. The example we have chosen is the design of a system to calculate the Fast Fourier Transform (FFT) of consecutive sets of 2^n data points. We choose $n = 3$ for simplicity. This problem is a well-defined problem in signal processing and its solutions are widely published in the literature [36-39]. Previous treatments of the FFT design example in relation to the SARA design methodology are also contained in the literature [40, 41].

We begin in Section 5.1 by describing the FFT design invariant. In Section 5.2, the design of a test environment for the abstract and detailed models is discussed in more depth. In Section 5.3, the design of the detailed FFT is briefly described. Finally, in Section 5.4, the simulation and measurement of the models at both levels of abstraction is introduced. The transcript of a simulation session is included in Appendix A.

5.1 The FFT Design Invariant

The requirements and associated evaluation criteria for the system (FFT), mapped onto an initial partitioning of the design universe, are presented in Figure 14. These requirements may be viewed in the context of a larger (signal processing) design problem which has been partitioned, leading to the specification shown in the figure. We can assume that we are designing a high level FFT building block which would be considered for use in composing more complex systems. The timing specifications in the requirements reveal the hardware context of the design. In a software context, an analogous set of requirements with appropriate timing specifications can be formulated.

The functional requirements for FFT (RS1 through RS8) specify that the system must accept serial input of 8 data values, as well as a control signal communicating the arrival of the input data; that the system must produce 8 data out-

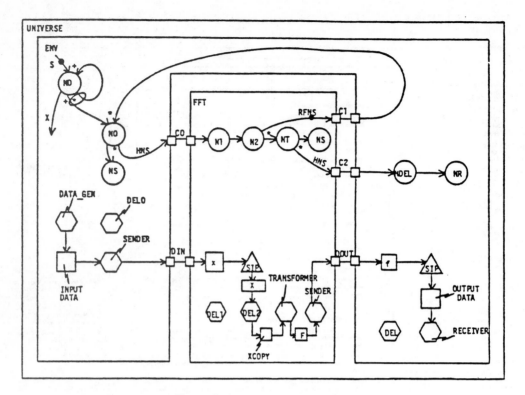

Figure 15a. The abstract model of FFT

puts, as well as a control signal communicating the transmission of the output data; and that the system must produce a control signal indicating when it is ready to receive new input data. In addition, RS10 imposes a timing constraint on FFT.

Three evaluation criteria (M1,M2,M3) are specified for determining whether the design will satisfy the stated requirements. Results of a design evaluation using these criteria will indicate whether or not all the requirements are satisfied by the design for the given test data. For example, if FFT does not accept the input data (RS1), then either the output data will be incorrect (M1 fails), or the time until the output data is received will be infinite (M3 fails). The value of ϵ which is a measure of the tolerance associated with M1, is dealt with in the design of the test environment.

The requirements have been carefully selected so as to completely specify the interface between the environment and the system, yet not impose any pre-conceived notions of a desirable design. One assurance we have that these preferred qualities characterize the requirements is that all specified measurements can be made in the environment. The measurements are discussed in relation to a test environment in the next section.

The assumptions on the environment (ENV), which essentially mirror the requirements for the system, are also presented in Figure 14. Assumption RE3 dictates that ENV generate input sequences at a maximum rate of 1 M samples/second, and also at slower rates, requiring proper system behavior at below maximum operation. From the assumptions, requirements, and evaluation criteria, we can (creatively) construct initial abstract structural and behavioral models for the design. These initial models are shown in Figure 15. The interpretation associated with the behavioral model is described below.

The structural model provides interconnections (DIN, DOUT) between the system (FFT) and the environment (ENV) to allow for serial input of 8 data values and serial output of 8 data values, in addition to interconnections

```
@template (da5 da6) data(8) complex float bin(16);

@processor TRANSFORMER;
    declare n fixed bin(35) init(8);
    declare (temp_x, temp_f) (8) float bin(27) complex;
    declare ff_t entry((•) float bin(27) complex,
                        (•) float bin(27) complex,
                        fixed bin(35));

    @delay = (700 + 100) @ns; /•nanoseconds•/
    @read x @from da5;
    temp_x = x;
    call ff_t(temp_x,temp_f,n);
    f = temp_f;
    @write f @to da6 @after (700 + 100) @ns;
@endprocessor;

subroutine ff_t(input,output,n)
    dimension input(n),output(n)
    integer n
    doubleprecision pi
    complex input,output,alpha
    pi = 3.1415927
    x = 2•pi/n
    alpha = —cmplx(0.,x)
    alpha = cexp(alpha)
    do 10 i=1,n
    output(i) = (0.,0.)
    do 20 j=1,n
    output(i) = output(i) + (alpha↑((i—1)•(j—1))) • input(j)
    20 continue
    10 continue
end
```

Figure 15b. PLIP source for TRANSFORMER and FORTRAN source for ff_t

(C0,C1,C2) for sending and receiving the control signals specified by RE7, RS3, and RS9.

The abstract behavioral model for the system contains five processors. SIP (Serial Input Processor) buffers the input data values for use by DEL2. At this level of abstraction, the delay for this buffering is assumed to be zero. DEL1 delays the initiation of N2 by 0.7 microseconds, the time required to receive an input sequence serially from ENV. DEL2 makes a copy of the input data for TRANSFORMER and terminates after 0.2 microseconds. The abstract model for FFT has an initial token on the RFNS control arc, and will generate each subsequent RFNS signal upon the termination of node N2. DEL2, therefore, models the delay between receiving the last value in an input sequence and sending a RFNS signal to ENV. Here we also model the anticipated return of the RFNS signal before the transform calculations are complete. The combined delay specified for DEL1 and DEL2 is the maximum allowable delay, according to RS10.

TRANSFORMER, controlled by the delayed HNS control signal from ENV, calculates the Fourier transform of the input data. The calculations are implemented as a FORTRAN program ("ff_t"), which is based on a published algorithm [42]. "ff_t" has been thoroughly tested independently, resulting in a high degree of confidence in the correctness of the calculations. SENDER sends the transformed data values serially to ENV. The transform calculations may overlap the input and/or output of data in a more detailed model. At the abstract level, we isolate those delays in DEL1 and SENDER and associate a delay (0.7 microseconds) with TRANSFORMER which we believe will satisfy the requirements.

The abstract model for FFT has been constructed such that all of the measurable behavior of FFT is isolated in the control-node/processor pairs: N1/DEL1, N2/DEL2, and NT/TRANSFORMER. TRANSFORMER calculates the Fourier transform of the input data using the FORTRAN

program specified in M1 as a measure of output data correctness. M2 implies a measure of the delay between activation of FFT/N1 and termination of FFT/N2 in the abstract model. This delay, associated with DEL1 and DEL2, satisfies M2. Similarly, the combined delay for DEL1, DEL2, and TRANSFORMER (1.6 microseconds) satisfies M3. For these reasons, we expect that the evaluation criteria will be met by the abstract model of FFT as long as the system behaves properly (provides outputs when given inputs) at the interface with ENV.

The behavioral model for the environment contains five controlled processors. DATA_GEN generates sequences of input data at a variable rate, as specified by RE3. In the test environment, DATA_GEN generates test data, which is read from a file. This file is assumed to have been previously designed and is *created* during initialization of the model. SENDER, indirectly controlled by the RFNS signal from FFT and by the generation of a sequence by DATA_GEN, sends the input data to FFT. SENDER uses @*write* delays to model the serial input rate given in RE6. RECEIVER, controlled by a delayed HNS signal from FFT, receives and *consumes* the transformed data which has been buffered by the uncontrolled processor ENV/SIP. The control constructs for ND (DATA_GEN), NS (SENDER) and NR (RECEIVER) are examples of the constructs recommended in Section 4.4 (Figures 5, 6, 7, and 9). Additional primitives must be included in the model of the environment (forming the test environment), in order to perform the measurements on the system.

5.2 The Design of the Test Environment

A test environment for FFT which is consistent with the *assumed* environment modeled in Figure 15 and which is capable of performing the measurements specified in Figure 14, is presented in Figure 16. The test environment has been derived from the assumed environment following the guidelines presented in Section 4.

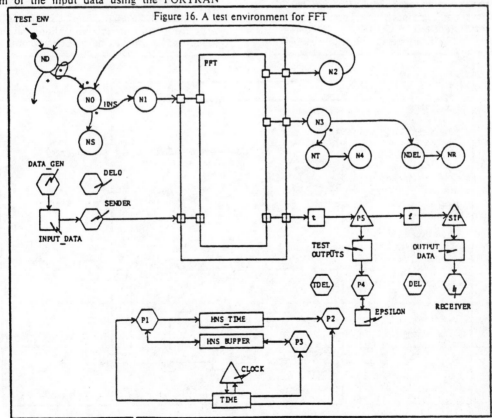

Figure 16. A test environment for FFT

Five controlled processors (P1,P2,P3,TDEL,P4) and one uncontrolled processor (P5), which are not part of the assumed environment, have been included in the test environment. The control signals relevant for the measurements are *intercepted* at the interface to the system by the nodes (N1,N2,N3). Processor P5 intercepts the data values relevent for the measurements, storing a copy of the values in TEST_OUTPUTS. Zero delay is associated with each of the processors (P1,P2,P3,P5), since the test environment will not be taken to fabrication and we want to reduce the amount of artifact induced by our model. As described in Section 4.4, an uncontrolled processor (CLOCK), which records the simulation clock time (TIME) for use in the measurements, is also included in the test environment.

The timing relationships between control signals and the values of the data signals are inspected by the processors (P1, P2, P3, P4). Processor P1 reads and records the time when each HNS control signal is sent to FFT. This time is recorded by P1 in HNS_TIME (read by processor P2), and in HNS_BUFFER (read by P3). Node N2 is initiated by each RFNS signal received by ENV. Processor P2 performs measurement M2 by computing the elapsed time between HNS_TIME and the initiation of N2. The assumptions on the environment state that the sending of the HNS control signal is conditional on the receipt of the RFNS signal. This guarantees that N2 is activated after a particular HNS_TIME is recorded but before a new HNS_TIME is registered.

Processor P3 performs measurement M3 by computing the time elapsed between the *oldest* entry in HNS_BUFFER and the initiation of N3. Since the assumptions on ENV do not specify that the input HNS signal is conditional on the output HNS signal, the recorded HNS input times must be buffered. The buffering is accomplished using the construct presented in Figure 13 of Section 4.4.

Measurements M2 and M3 will be performed on both levels (abstract and detailed) of the FFT model as described in the preceding paragraphs. Measurement M1, on the other hand, will be performed by comparing the output data values from the two levels of the model. Processor P4 in the test environment for the abstract model records the output data values in a file ("results"). Processor P4 in the test environ-

ment for the detailed model compares the values recorded in the file with the values observed during simulation of the detailed model. TDEL in the test environment delays the activation of P4 until all eight values of the output sequence are available. P4 in the detailed test environment prompts the designer upon its first activation during the simulation, for a value of ϵ to be used for the data comparisons. The value of ϵ entered by the designer is stored in a dataset which can be modified during the course of the simulation. Any failures reported by P4 are with respect to the current value of ϵ.

The test environment presented here does not halt when data errors are detected, nor does it detect the absence of expected control signals. These features can be built into the test environment by providing a data path from P4 to DATA_GEN, and an alternate control path (a *timeout*) from N1 to N2 and N3. For simplicity, we choose to leave the error recovery from these test failures up to the designer during simulation.

As the final step in establishing the invariant, the test environment must be composed with the abstract model of FFT. The resulting composite model must be simulated to verify that the abstract model satisfies the evaluation criteria M2 and M3, and to collect the outputs for verifying M1 in the detailed model. This is presented in Appendix A along with the simulation and testing of the detailed model.

5.3 The Detailed Level Design

Given the design invariant described in Section 5.1, we seek to compose the system (FFT) from known Building Block Models. In the absence of suitable BBMs, the design must be further partitioned. The composite model of the system resulting from either course of action must be tested for consistency with the invariant, using the test environment described in Section 5.2. In this case, we construct FFT out of existing hardware BBMs for a unit known as a butterfly (Figure 17).

A butterfly takes two complex numbers (X,Y) as inputs, performs a multiplication, an addition, and a subtraction, and produces two complex numbers as outputs. The delays asso-

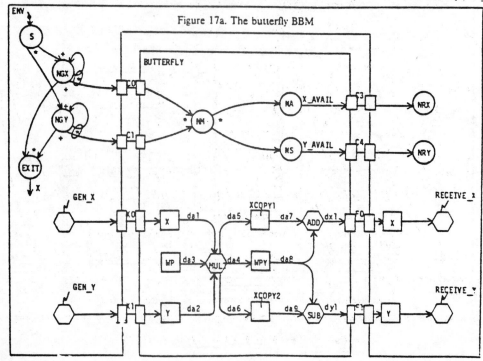

Figure 17a. The butterfly BBM

```
@template (dx0,dy0,dx1,dy1) i_o complex float decimal(16);
@template  (da1,da2,da5,da6,da7,da9)  x_y  complex  float  de-
cimal(16);
@template (da3) wp complex float decimal(16) initial(1);
@template (da4,da8) wpy  complex float decimal(16);

@processor MULT;
    @read Y @from da2;
    @read W @from da3;
    z  =  Y • W;
    @delay = 250 @ns;  /•nanoseconds•/
    @write z @to da4 @after 250 @ns;
    @read X @from da1;
    @write X @to da5;
    @write X @to da6;
@endprocessor;
@processor ADD;
    @read X @from da7;
    @read factor @from da8;
    sum  =  X + factor;
    @write sum @to dx1 @after 50 @ns;
    @delay = 50 @ns;
@endprocessor;
@processor SUB;
    @read X @from da9;
    @read factor @from da8;
    Y  =  X − factor;
    @write Y @to dy1 @after 50 @ns;
    @delay = 50 @ns;
@endprocessor;
```

Figure 17b. PLIP source for butterfly

ciated with each of the processors, which model the arithmetic operations, reflect the speeds of the high performance hardware being modeled. Twelve of these butterfly units can be composed to form a system which will calculate the FFT of sequences of 8 data inputs [39], as shown in Figures 18a and b. We have pipelined the model by returning the RFNS signal to ENV as soon as the first column of butterflies is ready for new input data.

Three additional BBMs are used to construct the detailed model: FAN_OUT, SYNCH, and DEMUX. FAN_OUT behaves as a token multiplier, having zero delay in our model. SYNCH is a synchronizing BBM which takes (8) control signal/data value pairs as inputs. When all 8 control signals have been received, SYNCH sends one output control signal and a serial stream of (8) output data values at 10 MHz. DEMUX takes serial (mutiplexed) input data values at a maximum rate of 10 MHz, and routes the values along (8) separate output paths. The generation of a data value along each of the output paths is accompanied by the generation of a control output, signaling the availability of the data. The initiation of DEMUX is accomplished by an input control signal which arrives simultaneous with receipt of the first input data value. The reader may observe some apparent artifact in the redundancy of inputs to each of the butterfly models in the first column (B11, B21, B31, B41) in Figure 18a. The ANDing of the control inputs is redundant because they are sequenced by the DEMUX control graph. This arises in the model because of the generality of the BBMs and does no harm. It is consistent with the BBM environment in Figure 17.

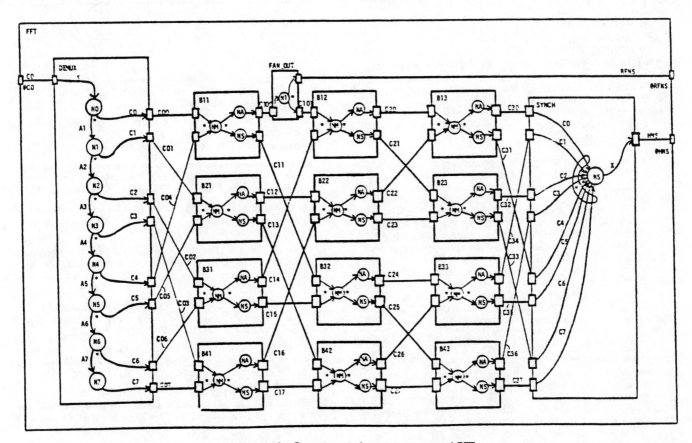

Figure 18a. Control graph for detailed model of FFT

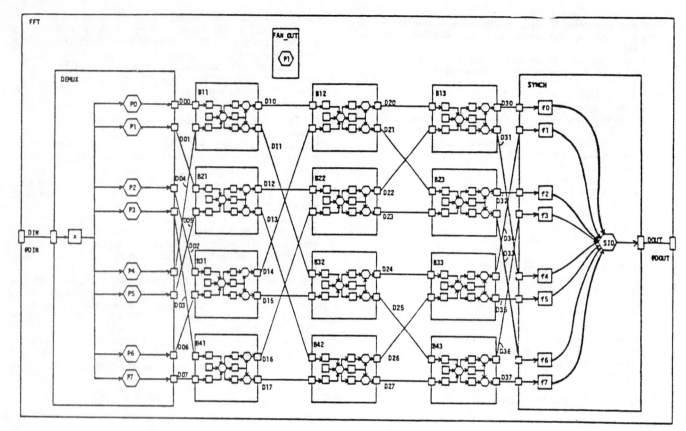

Figure 18b. Data graph for detailed model of FFT

5.4 Simulation of the Models

A transcript of a SARA session during which the models presented in this section are entered and simulated, is presented in Appendix A. Particular attention should be paid to the warnings issued by the simulator and the test failures reported by the test environment. The session includes comments which describe these and other events as they occur.

CONCLUSION

This paper has described key properties of the SARA graph model simulator. We have focussed particular attention on a methodology for developing a test environment as part of the design process. The test environment is used during simulation to check for consistency between different levels of a mutilevel design. The designer can plan to carry the test environment to fabrication with the rest of the system or to discard it. In the former case appropriate choices of delays in the models permit exploration of artifact introduced by the test measurement process itself. As exemplified in Section 4.4, one can expect to see evolution of many instrumentation mechanisms for use in testing. We have concentrated on measurement during design but past experience [43, 44] shows that such work is also applicable to analysis of existing computer systems.

In a manner consistent with previous work of the SARA group, our investigations are carried out in public. The work in this paper is exemplified by the simple FFT design described in Section 5 and in Appendix A. Any researcher with an account at MIT-Multics or RADC-Multics can gain access to SARA, check our work and explore extensions. We take pride in what we believe is a well designed and well implemented system which is comfortable for the user. However, our charter is to explore new powerful design methods and so we cannot promise to maintain the system responsively. We will be pleased to hear of weaknesses which you may uncover.

REFERENCES

1. Overman, W. T. "Formal Verification of GMB's", Internal Memorandum 176. Computer Science Department, UCLA, Los Angeles, CA, July 1977.

2. Estrin, G. "A Methodology for design of digital systems - supported by SARA at the age of one", *AFIPS Conference Proceedings*, National Computer Conference, 1978.

3. Campos, I. "Multilevel Modeling for Synthesis of Reliable Concurrent Software Systems", Ph.D. dissertation, Computer Science Department, University of California, Los Angeles, 1977.

4. Gardner, R.I. "Multi-level Modeling in SARA", *Proceedings of the Symposium on Design Automation and Microprocessors*, Palo Alto, CA, pp. 63-66, February 1977.

5. Estrin, G. and R. Turn, "Automatic Assignment of Computations in a Variable Structure Computer System," *IEEE Transactions on Electronic Computers*, Vol. EC-12, No.5, December 1963.

6. Martin, D.F. and G. Estrin, "Experiments on Models of Computations and Systems," *IEEE Transactions on Electronic Computers*, Vol. EC-16, No. 1, pp. 59-69, February 1967.

7. Martin, D. and G. Estrin, "Models of Computational Systems-Cyclic to Acyclic Graph Transformations," *IEEE Transactions on Electronic Computers*, Vol. EC-16, No. 1, pp. 70-79, February 1967.

8. Baer, J.L.E., and G. Estrin, "Bounds for Maximum Parallelism in a Bilogic Graph Model of Computation." *IEEE Transactions on Computers*, Vol. C-18, No.11, November 1969.

9. Martin, D.F. and G. Estrin, "Path Length Computations on Graph Models of Computations." *IEEE Transactions on Computers*, Vol. EC-18, pp. 530-536, June 1969.

10. Russell, E. and G. Estrin, "Measurement based automatic analysis of FORTRAN programs", *AFIPS Conference Proceedings*, Spring Joint Computer Conference, Vol. 34, pp. 723-732, 1969.

11. Bovet, D. and G. Estrin, "A Dynamic Memory Allocation Algorithm," *IEEE Transactions on Computers*, Vol. C-19, No. 5, pp. 403-411, May 1970.

12. Bovet, D. and G. Estrin, "On Static Memory Allocation in Computer Systems," *IEEE Transactions on Computers*, Vol. C-19, No. 6, pp. 492-503, June 1970.

13. Volansky, S.A. "Graph Model Analysis and Implementation of Computational Sequences", Ph.D. dissertation, UCLA-ENG-7048, June 1970.

14. Gostelow, K.P. "Flow of Control, Resource Allocation and the Proper Termination of Programs", Ph.D Dissertation, Computer Science Department, University of California, Los Angeles, CA, 1971.

15. Cerf, V., "Multiprocessors, Semaphores, and a Graph Model of Computation", Ph.D. dissertation, UCLA-ENG-7223, April 1972.

16. Gostelow, K., V. Cerf, and G. Estrin, "Proper Termination of Flow of Control in Programs Involving Concurrent Processes," *Proceedings of the ACM*, Vol.11, Boston, August 1972.

17. Yavne, M. "Synthesis of Properly Terminating Graphs," Computer Science Department, University of California, Los Angeles, Ca, UCLA-ENG-7434, May 1974.

18. Gardner, R. I. "A Methodology for Digital System Design Based on Structural and Functional Modeling", Technical Report, UCLA-ENG-7488, January 1975.

19. Potash, H., A. Tyrrill, D. Allen, S. Joseph and G. Estin, "DCDS Digital Simulating System," *AFIPS Conference Proceedings*, 1969 Fall Joint Computer Conference, Vol. 35, pp. 707-720.

20. Rose, C.W., F.T. Bradshaw, and S.W. Katzke, "The LOGOS Representation System". *Proceedings Sixth annual IEEE Computer Conference* (CompCon 72), San Fransisco, September 1972, pp. 187-190.

21. Ruggiero, W. "A distributed data and control driven machine: programming and architecture", Ph.D. dissertation, Computer Science Department, University of California, Los Angeles, CA, 1978.

22. VanMierop, D. "Design and Verification of Distributed Interacting Processes," Ph.D. dissertation, UCLA-ENG-7920, March 1979.

23. Ruggiero, W. et.al. "Analysis of Data Flow Models Using the SARA Graph Model of Behavior," *AFIPS Conference Proceedings*, National Computer Conference, June 1979.

24. Razouk, R., and G. Estrin, "The Graph Model of Behavior Simulator," *Proceedings of Symposium on Design Automation and Microprocessors*, Palo Alto, CA, February 1977.

25. Razouk, R. "GMB Simulator System Reference Manual", Computer Science Department, University of California, Los Angeles, CA, January 1977.

26. Estrin, G., D. Hopkins, B. Coggan and S.D. Crocker, "SNUPER COMPUTER, Instrumentation Automation," *AFIPS Conference Proceedings*, Vol. 30, pp. 645-656, Spring Joint Computer Conference, April 1967.

27. Estrin, G., R.R. Muntz and R.C. Uzgalis, "Modeling, Measurement and Computer Power," *AFIPS Conference Proceedings*, Vol. 40, pp.725-738, Spring Joint Computer Conference, 1972.

28. Proceedings of the Software Quality and Assurance Workshop, *ACM Special Interest Group on Measurement and Evaluation*, Vol. 7, No. 3 and 4, Novermber 1978.

29. Clarke, L.A. "A system to generate test data and symbolically execute programs," *IEEE Transactions on Software Engineering*, Vol SE-2, pp. 215-228, Sept. 1976.

30. Howden, W.E. "Reliability of the path analysis testing strategy," *IEEE Transactions on Software Engineering*, Vol SE-2, pp. 208-215, Sept. 1976.

31. Ramamoorthy, C.V., S.F. Ho, and W.T. Chen, "On the Automated Generation of Program Test Data," *IEEE Transactions on Software Engineering*, Vol. SE-2, December 1976.

32. Gabow, H.N., S.N. Maheshwari and L.J. Osterweil, "On two Problems in the Generation of Program Test Paths," *IEEE Transactions on Software Engineering*, Vol SE-2, pp. 227-231, Sept. 1976.

33. Howden, W.E. "Symbolic Testing and the Dissect Symbolic Evaluation System," *IEEE Transactions on Software Engineering*, Vol SE-3, pp. 266-278, July 1977.

34. Lundstrom, S. "Adaptive Random Data Generation for computer software testing," *AFIPS Conference Proceedings*, National Computer Conference, pp. 505-512, 1978.

35. Drobman, J. "A Model-Based Design System and Methodology for Composition of Microprocessor-Based Digital Systems", Dissertation Prospectus, May 1977.

36. Cooley, J.W. and J.W. Tukey, "An algorithm for the machine calculation of complex Fourier series," *Mathematics of Computation*, Vol. 19, pp. 297-301, April 1965.

37. Cochran, W.T., et.al. ,"What is the Fast Fourier Transform," *Proceedings of the IEEE*, Vol. 55, No. 10, pp. 1664-1674, October 1967.

38. Bergland, G.D., "FFT Hardware Implementations - A Survey," *IEEE Transactions on Audio Electroacoustics*, Vol. AV-17, No.2, pp. 104-108, June 1969.

39. Allen, J., "Computer Architecture for Signal Processing," *Proceedings of IEEE*, Vol. 63, No. 4, pp. 624-633, April 1975.

40. Campos, I., and G. Estrin, "SARA aided design of software for concurrent systems", *AFIPS Conference Proceedings*, National Computer Conference, pp. 325-336, 1978.

41. Fenchel, R. S. and R.R. Razouk, "UCLA SARA (System ARchitects' Apprentice) Demonstration," Computer Science Department, University of California, Los Angeles, June 1979.

42. Macnaghten, A.M. and C.A.R. Hoare, "Fast Fourier Transform Free From Tears," *The Computer Journal*, Vol. 20, No.1, pp. 78-83, February 1977.

43. Noe, J. D., "A Petri Net Description of the CDC 6400," *Proceedings, ACM Workshop on System Performance Evaluation*, Harvard University, pp. 362-378, 1971.

44. Noe, J. D. and G. J. Nutt, "Validation of a Trace-driven CDC 6400 Simulation," *AFIPS Conference Proceedings*, Spring Joint Computer Conference, Vol. 40, pp. 749-757, 1972.

/* The following is a transcript of a SARA session.
/* All user input is preceded by the SARA system prompt ">".
/* PL/I-like comments are entered during the session to
/* explain the inputs and outputs as they appear.
/* In order to conserve space, less pertinent sections
/* of the session have been omitted. These are marked with "..".
/* The following Multics command starts a SARA session
ec >udd>SARA>SARA_system>ec>sara
SARA Selector March 11, 1979
New or modified news:
no news changes
>/* Files containing descriptions of the models reside in the
>/* following Multics directory
>&library >udd>SARA>SARA_library>fft
working library now >udd>SARA>SARA_library>fft
>/* The first step is the specification of the graph for
>/* the abstract model of FFT and the test environment.
>/* The following steps invoke the GMB Translator.
>@behavior; @gmb
SARA.Behavior
SARA.Behavior.GMB
>@translator 2 /* Estimated size of the model is 2
SARA.Behavior.GMB.Translator
gmbplex size factor = 2
GMB Translator V. 15m June 1977
>/* This is the GMB Translator. The source code for
>/* the test environment resides in the file "test_env.gmb".
>/* Source for the abstract model of FFT resides in
>/* "abstract.gmb". These files will be read in using
>/* the "&input" system command. It is necessary to
>/* request that all input be echoed to the terminal in
>/* order to view the input from the files.
>&output * +input_echo
output destination * for message warning error listing trace prompt
input_echo classes
>&input test_env.gmb
input source is >user_dir_dir>SARA>SARA_library>fft>test_env.gmb
/* TEST_ENV */
@control_graph
@nodes env_nd, env_n0, env_ns, env_ndel, env_nr,
        env_n1, env_n2, env_n3, env_nt, env_n4
@arcs env_s(1), env_x, env_a1, env_a2, env_a3,
        env_hns, env_a4, env_a5, env_a6,
        ac0, hns, rfns(1), env_a7, env_a8
env_nd(env_s + env_a1 : env_x + (env_a1 * env_a2))
        .
        .
@end
@data_graph
@controlled_processors env_data_gen(env_nd), env_del0(env_n0),
        .
        .
@end
>&input abstract.gmb
input source is >user_dir_dir>SARA>SARA_library>fft>abstract.gmb

/* ABSTRACT FFT */
.@control_graph
@nodes fft_n1, fft_n2, fft_nt, fft_ns
        .
        .
@end
@data_graph
@controlled_processors fft_del1(fft_n1), fft_del2(fft_n2),
        fft_transformer(fft_nt), fft_sender(fft_ns)
@uncontrolled_processors fft_sip
@datasets fft_x, fft_X, fft_xcopy, fft_F
@arcs fft_da1, fft_da2, fft_da3, fft_da4, fft_da5, fft_da6, fft_da7,
        dadin, dadout
fft_da1(fft_x : fft_sip)
        .
        .
@end
>&output * -input_echo
output destination * for message warning error listing trace prompt classes
>@store abstract /* Store the processed model
model stored
>@end
percentage of gmbplx tables used = 62.0%
end of GMB translation
no translation errors
SARA.Behavior.GMB
>/* Next we use PLIP to define the interpretation for the graph
>@plip abstract
SARA.Behavior.GMB.PLIP
GMB PL1 Preprocessor May 19, 1979
Current model: abstract
>/* As with the graph, the source code for PLIP resides in two previously
>/* generated files: "abstract_test_env.plip" and "abstract.plip"
>&output * +input_echo
output destination * for message warning error listing trace prompt
input_echo classes
>&input abstract_test_env.plip
input   source   is
>user_dir_dir>SARA>SARA_library>fft>abstract_test_env.plip
@template (env_da1 env_da2 env_da5 env_da6)
        data_sequence (0:7) complex float binary(16);
        .
        .
@processor env_data_gen;
declare counter fixed binary(15) static init(0);
declare (infile, results) file;
declare endfile condition;
on endfile(infile) begin;
                close file(infile);
                @output_arcs="env_x";
                go to done;
                end;
get file(infile) list(sequence);
if counter < 5
    then do; /* max frequency for 5 test sequences */
        @delay = 1 @us;
        @write sequence @to env_da1 @after 1 @us;
        end;
    else do; /* less than max frequency for 5 test sequences */
        @delay = 2 @us;
        @write sequence @to env_da1 @after 2 @us;
        end;
counter = mod(counter+1,10);
@output_arcs="env_a1, env_a2";
done: return;
@endprocessor;
@processor env_del0;
@delay = 100 @ns;
@endprocessor;

```
@processor env_sender;
@read data @from env_da2;
value = data(0);
@write value @to dadin;
value = data(1);
@write value @to dadin @after 100 @ns;

@endprocessor
      .
      .
      .
@processor env_p4;
declare results file;
@read test_outputs @from env_da9;
put file(results) list(test_outputs);
@endprocessor;
>&input abstract.plip
input source is >user_dir_dir>SARA>SARA_library>fft>abstract.plip
      .
      .
      .
>&output * -input_echo
output destination * for message warning error listing trace prompt classes
>/* We must store the PLIP and request a PL/I compilation
>@store
***   0 errors
***   1 warnings
Do you want to compile the PLIP output? (y or n)>y
PL/I compilation in progress
PL/I 24c
Current model: abstract
>@end   /* Model compiled successfully
End of GMB PL1 Preprocessor
SARA.Behavior.GMB
>/* The abstract model may now be simulated.
>@sim abstract   /* This command invokes the simulator
SARA.Behavior.GMB.Simulator
GMB Simulator March 25, 1979
>/* The two files used by the test environment (for generating
>/* test data and for storing test results) must be bound to
>/* storage segments in the library.
>&setios infile infile
>user_dir_dir>SARA>SARA_library>fft>infile allocated to infile
>&setios results results
>user_dir_dir>SARA>SARA_library>fft>results allocated to results
>@token_max env_hns rfns hns /* Set breakpoints
>/* Set a breakpoint at node env_n4 which stores test results
>@node_end env_n4
>@start 0 ns /* Start the simulation
token_max breakpoint.
arc name: env_hns, number of tokens:   1
>@list_time /* Examine the time first ENV_HNS signal generated
Time = 1100 ns
>/* Examine the clock time which is used to perform measurements
>@list_ds env_time
env_time = 1.100000000000000e+003;
>@list_ds env_input_data /* Examine first sequence of test data
env_input_data(0) = 1.0000e+000+1.0000e+000i
env_input_data(1) = 1.0000e+000+1.0000e+000i
env_input_data(2) = 1.0000e+000+1.0000e+000i
env_input_data(3) = 1.0000e+000+1.0000e+000i
env_input_data(4) = 1.0000e+000+1.0000e+000i
env_input_data(5) = 1.0000e+000+1.0000e+000i
env_input_data(6) = 1.0000e+000+1.0000e+000i
env_input_data(7) = 1.0000e+000+1.0000e+000i;
>@continue
warning: two or more processors may simultaneously access dataset
env_input_data
token_max breakpoint.
arc name: rfns, number of tokens:   1
>/* Examine the time of generation of RFNS signal. Comparison of this
>/* time with the time ENV_HNS was generated shows that
>/* M2 is satisfied. (This comparison is performed by env_p2)
```

```
>@list_time
Time = 2000 ns
>@continue
token_max breakpoint.
arc name: env_hns, number of tokens:   1
>@list_time /* Second HNS signal generated by TEST_ENV
Time = 2100 ns
>@continue
warning: two or more processors may simultaneously access dataset
env_input_data
token_max breakpoint.
arc name: hns, number of tokens:   1
>/* First HNS signal generated by FFT. Comparison of
>/* the current simulation time with the time the first
>/* ENV_HNS was generated shows that M3 is satisfied.
>@list_time
Time = 2800 ns
>@list_ds env_hns_buffer
env_hns_buffer.sender_ptr =      2
env_hns_buffer.receiver_ptr =      0
env_hns_buffer.times(0) = 0.000000000000000e+000
env_hns_buffer.times(1) = 1.100000000000000e+003
env_hns_buffer.times(2) = 2.100000000000000e+003
      .
      .
      .
>@token_max   /* Remove token_max breakpoints
>&output * -warning   /* Supress warnings of dataset contention
output destination * for message error listing trace prompt classes
>@continue
node_end breakpoint.
node name: env_n4
>@list_ds env_test_outputs /* First sequence of test results
env_test_outputs(0) = 8.0000e+000+8.0000e+000i
env_test_outputs(1) = 1.0431e-007+1.6391e-007i
env_test_outputs(2) = -7.4506e-009+2.0862e-007i
env_test_outputs(3) = -1.1921e-007+2.3097e-007i
env_test_outputs(4) = -2.8312e-007-2.6822e-007i
env_test_outputs(5) = -4.7684e-007+2.0862e-007i
env_test_outputs(6) = -8.1211e-007+4.4703e-008i
env_test_outputs(7) = -1.6093e-006-5.2899e-007i;
>@node_end   /* Remove breakpoint from node env_n4
>@token_max env_x   /* Continue until end of test data generation
>@continue
token_max breakpoint.
arc name: env_x, number of tokens:   1
>@token_max rfns   /* continue until RFNS is received from FFT
>@continue
token_max breakpoint.
arc name: rfns, number of tokens:   1
>/* continue until test results are received by TEST_ENV
>@node_end env_n4
>@continue
node_end breakpoint.
node name: env_n4
>@list_ds env_test_outputs /* Last sequence of test results
env_test_outputs(0) = 6.2000e-001+6.8000e-001i
env_test_outputs(1) = -4.1607e-001+2.9636e+001i
env_test_outputs(2) = -1.7000e-001-3.3000e+001i
env_test_outputs(3) = 4.2513e+000-4.3223e+000i
env_test_outputs(4) = 1.0000e+001+1.8000e+001i
env_test_outputs(5) = -2.0393e-001+4.2364e+001i
env_test_outputs(6) = -5.1000e+001-1.7000e+001i
env_test_outputs(7) = 5.3749e+001-3.9678e+001i;
>@list_time
Time = 17502 ns
>/* End simulation
>&clrios results
results cleared
>@end
End of GMB Simulator
```

SARA.Behavior.GMB
>/* Now we will follow the same steps with the detailed model
> @translator 8 /* Larger size estimate
    .
    .
    .
> @plip detailed
    .
    .
    .
>/* Now we simulate the detailed model
> @sim detailed /* Size estimate of 8 carried over
SARA.Behavior.GMB.Simulator
GMB Simulator March 25, 1979
>/* Attach file "results". "infile" is still attached
> &setios results results
> user_dir_dir>SARA>SARA_library>fft>results allocated to results
> @token_max env_hns rfns hns /* Same breakpoints as in abstract model
> @node_end env_n4
> @start 0 ns
token_max breakpoint,
arc name: env_hns, number of tokens: 1
> @list_time /* Generation time of first HNS signal
Time = 1100 ns
> @list_ds env_input_data /* first test input sequence
env_input_data(0) = 1.0000e+000+1.0000e+000i
env_input_data(1) = 1.0000e+000+1.0000e+000i
env_input_data(2) = 1.0000e+000+1.0000e+000i
env_input_data(3) = 1.0000e+000+1.0000e+000i
env_input_data(4) = 1.0000e+000+1.0000e+000i
env_input_data(5) = 1.0000e+000+1.0000e+000i
env_input_data(6) = 1.0000e+000+1.0000e+000i
env_input_data(7) = 1.0000e+000+1.0000e+000i;
> @continue
warning: two or more processors may simultaneously access dataset
env_input_data
warning: two or more processors may simultaneously access dataset
demux_x
    .
    .
    .
token_max breakpoint,
arc name: rfns, number of tokens: 1
> @list_time
Time = 1901 ns
> @continue
warning: two or more processors may simultaneously access dataset
b21_wpy
warning: two or more processors may simultaneously access dataset
b31_wpy
warning: two or more processors may simultaneously access dataset
b41_wpy
token_max breakpoint,
arc name: env_hns, number of tokens: 1
> &output * -warning
output destination * for message error listing trace prompt classes
> @continue
    .
    .
    .
token_max breakpoint,
arc name: hns, number of tokens: 1
> @list_time /* Time FFT generates first HNS signal
Time = 3402 ns
> @list_ds env_hns_buffer /* Generation time of all HNS signals
env_hns_buffer.sender_ptr =   3
env_hns_buffer.receiver_ptr =   0
env_hns_buffer.times(0) = 0.000000000000000e+000
env_hns_buffer.times(1) = 1.100000000000000e+003
env_hns_buffer.times(2) = 2.100000000000000e+003
env_hns_buffer.times(3) = 3.100000000000000e+003
    .
    .
> @token_max /* Clear token_max breakpoints

> @continue
Enter `epsilon` for comparison of results> .005
node_end breakpoint,
node name: env_n4
>/* The absence of an error message indicates that M1
>/* is satisfied for the first set of test data.
> @list_ds env_test_outputs
env_test_outputs(0) = 8.0000e+000+8.0000e+000i
env_test_outputs(1) = 0.0000e+000+0.0000e+000i
env_test_outputs(2) = 0.0000e+000+0.0000e+000i
    .
    .
env_test_outputs(7) = 0.0000e+000+0.0000e+000i;
> @continue
    .
    .
node_end breakpoint,
node name: env_n4
> @list_ds env_test_outputs /* Last test result
env_test_outputs(0) = 6.2000e+001+6.8000e+001i
env_test_outputs(1) =-4.1607e+001+2.9636e+001i
env_test_outputs(2) =-1.7000e+001-3.3000e+001i
    .
    .
env_test_outputs(7) = 5.3749e+001-3.9678e+001i;
> @list_time
Time = 18103 ns
> @end /* End simulation
End of GMB Simulator
SARA.Behavior.GMB
> &clrios results
results cleared
> &setios results results
> user_dir_dir>SARA>SARA_library>fft>results allocated to results
>/* restart simulation with smaller epsilon
> @sim detailed
SARA.Behavior.GMB.Simulator
GMB Simulator March 25, 1979
> @node_end env_n4
> @start 0
Enter `epsilon` for comparison of results> .00001
node_end breakpoint,
node name: env_n4
> @continue /* First test sequence passes test. Continue.

Evaluation criterion M1 is NOT satisfied for element 1 in sequence
Evaluation criterion M1 is NOT satisfied for element 3 in sequence
Evaluation criterion M1 is NOT satisfied for element 5 in sequence
Evaluation criterion M1 is NOT satisfied for element 7 in sequence
node_end breakpoint,
node name: env_n4
>/* Second test sequence fails. End simulation
> @end
End of GMB Simulator
SARA.Behavior.GMB
> @quit
End of SARA Selector

Today's modeling tools, appropriate for conventional sequential systems, will be inadequate for the complex concurrent systems of the 80's. Petri nets may offer a solution.

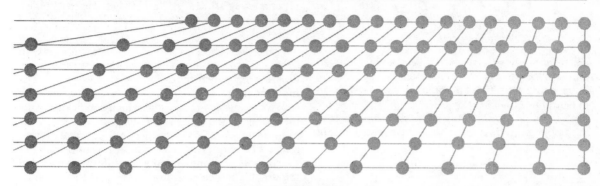

Special Feature:

Putting Petri Nets to Work

Tilak Agerwala*
IBM

Petri nets have developed over the last decade into a suitable model for representing and studying concurrent systems. Petri nets can be viewed as a special structure to be studied as an intellectual exercise, as another automaton capable of accepting or generating formal languages, or as a representation scheme for describing, analyzing, and synthesizing different kinds of "real" systems. This paper brings together a large body of work on useful applications of Petri nets.

Modeling a system using (interpreted) Petri nets has three potential advantages: First, the overall system is often easier to understand due to the graphical and precise nature of the representation scheme. Secondly, the behavior of the system can be analyzed using Petri net theory,[1] which includes tools for analysis such as marking trees and invariants, and established relationships between certain net structures and dynamic behavior. Techniques developed for the verification of parallel programs[2-4] can also be applied. Finally, since Petri nets can be synthesized using bottom-up and top-down approaches, it is possible to systematically design systems whose behavior is either known or easily verifiable.

It is expected that many future computer-based systems will incorporate multiple, communicating units. Such systems can exhibit very complex interactions and behaviors. Tools for modeling, representing, and analyzing conventional sequential systems will be totally inadequate. Future computer system designers and users will require new conceptual mechanisms and theories to deal with their

*This work was performed while the author was at the University of Texas at Austin.

systems. Petri nets incorporate the fundamental concepts which can be used as a basis for these models and theories.

What are Petri nets?

A Petri net may be identified as a bipartite, directed graph $N=(T,P,A)$ where

$T=\{2_1 t_2, \ldots, t_n\}$ is a set of *transitions*
$P=\{p_1 p_2, \ldots, p_m\}$ is a set of *places*
$\quad (T \cup P$ form the nodes of $N)$
$A \subseteq \{T \times P\} \cup \{P \times T\}$ is a set of directed arcs.

A *marking* M of a Petri net is a mapping:

$$M: P \to I$$

where $I = \{0, 1, 2, \ldots\}$. M assigns *tokens* to each place in the net. Where convenient M can also be viewed as a vector whose ith component $(M)_i$ represents the number of tokens M assigns to p_i. A Petri net $N = (T,P,A)$ with marking M is a *Marked Petri Net* $C = (T,P,A,M)$.

Pictorially, places are represented by circles, transitions by bars, and tokens by small black dots. Figure 1 presents an example of a Petri net.

The above definition of a marked Petri net may be viewed as the *syntax* of a language for system representation. The *semantics* of the language (which give the behavior of the system) are specified by defining certain *simulation rules:* The set of *input places* of a transition t is given by $I(t) = \{p \mid (p,t) \varepsilon A\}$. The set of *output places* of a transition t is given by $O(t) = \{p \mid$

December 1979

Reprinted with permission from *Computer*, December 1979, pages 85–94.
Copyright © 1979 by The Institute of Electrical and Electronics Institute, Inc.

$(t,p) \varepsilon A$ }. A transition t is said to be *enabled* in a Petri net $N = (T,P,A)$ with marking M if $M(p) > 0$ for all $p \varepsilon I(t)$. An enabled transition can *fire* by removing a token from each input place and putting a token in each output place. This results in a new marking M' where

$$M'(p) = \begin{cases} M(p) + 1 & \text{if } p \varepsilon O(t), p \not\in I(t) \\ M(p) - 1 & \text{if } p \varepsilon I(t), p \not\in O(t) \\ M(p) & \text{otherwise} \end{cases}$$

Tokens are indivisible—i.e., a token can be removed from a place by only one transition. Except for the above restrictions, firing of transitions proceeds in an asynchronous manner.

In Figure 1a, t_1 is the only transition that can fire. On completion, p_1 is empty and p_2 and p_3 each contain a token. At this stage t_2 and t_3 are both enabled and can fire *concurrently* since they do not share any input places. When these two firings are completed, p_4 and p_5 are the only places containing tokens. (See Figure 1b.) This situation represents a *conflict:* Both t_4 and t_5 are enabled, but firing of either disables the other. In such a case, the decision as to which one fires is completely arbitrary. The ability to represent both concurrency and conflict makes Petri nets very powerful.

Transitions in a Petri net could represent events in a real system. A marked net then represents the coordination or synchronization of these events. The movement of tokens clearly shows which conditions cause a transition to fire and which conditions come into being on the completion of firing. Moreover, the nets are not based on any concept of a central system state. The nets provide a natural representation of systems where control and state information is distributed. The use of finite state machines in such cases often leads to unmanageably large single states.

Additional concepts. A marking M' is *immediately reachable* from M if the firing of some t in M yields M'. M' is *reachable* from M if it is immediately reachable from M or is reachable from any marking which is immediately reachable from M or is M itself. The *reachability set* $R(M)$ of a marked Petri net (T,P,A,M) is the set of all markings reachable from M. A place in a marked Petri net (T, P, A, M) is *k-bounded* if and only if there exists a fixed k such that $M'(p) \leqslant k$ for all $M' \varepsilon R(M)$. A marked Petri net is *k*-bounded if for some fixed k each place is *k*-bounded. A place is safe if it is l-bounded and a marked Petri net is safe if each place in it is safe. A transition t in a marked Petri net (T,P,A,M) is *live* if for each $M' \varepsilon R(M)$ there exists a marking reachable from M' in which t is enabled. A marked Petri net is live if each transition is live. Boundedness and liveness are important net properties.

Petri nets find their basis in a few simple rules yet can exhibit very complex behavior. This paper will introduce some analysis techniques later. Analysis in general requires some knowledge about the reachability set and can often be quite complex. As a result, restricted classes of Petri nets have been introduced and their properties studied. Two important subclasses are marked graphs and free choice nets. A *marked graph* is a Petri net in which each place is an input place of at most one transition and the output place of at most one transition. Marked graphs can represent concurrency but not conflict. A *free choice* Petri net is a Petri net where every place p is either the only input place of a transition or there is at most one transition which has p as an input place. Analysis of such substructures have provided relationships between structure and marking on the one hand and dynamic behavior (liveness, safeness, etc.) on the other.

For a more comprehensive study of Petri nets the reader is referred to Peterson.[1]

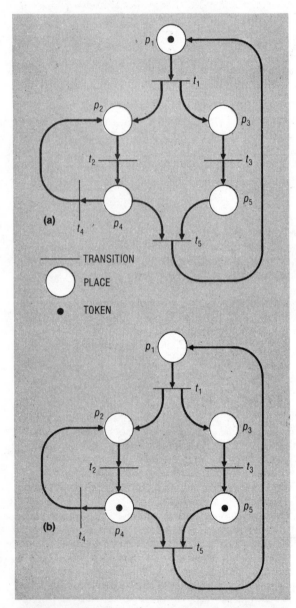

Figure 1. An example of a Petri net showing the ability to represent both concurrency (a) and conflict (b).

Interpretation

Petri nets, as defined in the previous section, are an abstract model. A net represents a system when a meaning or interpretation is assigned to various entities in the net—namely, the places, transitions, and tokens. Petri nets can be used in many different environments by using appropriate interpretations. Figure 2 represents a computer system where a processor is devoted to servicing two devices that are gathering data from the outside world. The cycle on the left represents device I_1 and the cycle on the right I_2. Device I_1 obtains new data (firing of t_1) only when the previous data has been transmitted (token in p_1). Completion of this activity is signaled by a token in p_2. Under these conditions, if a processor is available, it executes the service routine for I_1 and signals that the transmission is complete by placing a token in p_1. The whole cycle for I_1 can then repeat. The cycle for I_2 is quite similar. Notice that the net represents both concurrency and conflict.

Interpretations do not have to be computer related. A net could represent a chemical process where input places represent reacting chemicals, transitions represent reactions, output places the results of a reaction, and tokens the number of molecules of a given type. Figure 3 represents a particular reaction. Other novel interpretations will be discussed later.

Within the same field of application, different degrees of interpretation can be used. Thus, for a net representing parallel computation the interpretation may be minimal, such as simply assigning an operation name to each transition. A complete interpretation can also be used where for each transition, the exact transformation, the input and output memory locations, and the initial memory contents are specified. The degree of interpretation depends on the type of information to be obtained. Complete interpretation is required, for example, to establish that data integrity is maintained in a given parallel computation. For the derivation of general properties such as liveness and safeness, a partial interpretation should be used.

Based on the interpretations provided, Petri nets can be used to represent systems in a top-down fashion at various levels of abstraction and detail. For example, a single transition at a higher level such as "floating point add" may be expanded at a lower level into a series of transitions, "extract exponents," "compare exponents," "shift mantissa," etc. Petri nets have been used to model the CDC 6400 operating systems using this approach.[5] The approach is extremely useful in systems analysis where high-level descriptions which provide good perspective can be used, for example, to identify potential bottlenecks which may then be analyzed in detail using lower-level descriptions.

Operating systems and compilers

Petri nets can represent, in a straightforward manner, the flow of control in programs containing constructs such as IF-THEN-ELSE, DO-WHILE, GOTO, and PARBEGIN-PAREND (see Figure 4). The net is uninterpreted: A token in place p indicates initiation of the IF-THEN-ELSE statement; it is not specified whether S_1 will execute or S_2. The representation is straightforward and will not be elaborated on further. Petri nets can clearly and explicitly represent the interaction between concurrent processes coordinated using P and V operations on semaphores.[6]* Such processes are frequently found in operating systems. As an example consider a system of two processes: (1) a producer (input process or device) that obtains data and places it in a bounded buffer (of size B); (2) a consumer (computing process or device) that removes data from the buffer and operates on it. The processes are asynchronous but must be prevented from accessing the buffer simultaneously; buffer overflow and underflow must also be prevented. Figure 5 gives the programs of the two processes coordinated using P and V primitives. (E represents the number of empty buffer positions, F the number of full buffer positions, and M is used for mutual exclusion.) Figure 6 gives a compact net for the system. As an example of system verifications, this net will be analyzed in two different ways.

*P and V operations are indivisible, operate only on special variables called semaphores, and can be logically defined as follows:

$$P(S) \equiv \text{if } S > 0 \text{ then } S: = S-1 \text{ else wait}$$
$$V(S) \equiv S: = S+1$$

A waiting process can be scheduled at some later time when $S > 0$. At this time S is decremented and the process continues.

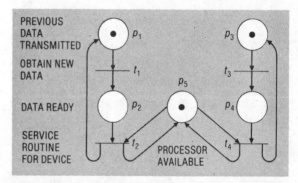

Figure 2. The processor in this system services two devices that are gathering data from the outside world.

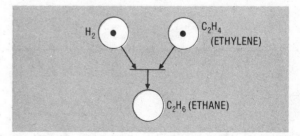

Figure 3. Petri nets can also be used to model chemical reactions.

Net invariants are used in the first approach. An invariant is a set of places, I, such that

$$\sum_{p \,\varepsilon\, I} M(p)$$

is a constant for each reachable marking M, and I does not have any proper subsets that are invariants. Let $N = (T,P,A)$ be a Petri net. The incidence matrix C of N is defined as $C = (C(t,p))$ where $t \,\varepsilon\, T$ and $p \,\varepsilon\, P$ such that

$$C(t,p) = \begin{cases} -1 \text{ if } (p,t) \,\varepsilon\, A, \ (t,p) \,\&\, A \\ +1 \text{ if } (t,p) \,\varepsilon\, A, \ (p,t) \,\&\, A \\ 0 \quad \text{otherwise} \end{cases}$$

Let y be a solution of the system of equations

$$C \cdot y = 0$$

where each element of y is either 0 or 1 and y cannot be obtained additively from other solutions. The set of places corresponding to the non-zero elements of y is an invariant.[7] For the net in Figure 6, the system of equations (above) is equivalent to:

$$\begin{array}{c} \\ t_1 \\ t_2 \\ t_3 \\ t_4 \end{array} \begin{array}{cccccccc} p_1 & p_2 & p_3 & p_4 & p_5 & p_6 & p_7 \\ \left[\begin{array}{ccccccc} -1 & 1 & 0 & 0 & 0 & 0 & 0 \\ 1 & -1 & 0 & 0 & -1 & 0 & 1 \\ 0 & 0 & -1 & 1 & 1 & 0 & -1 \\ 0 & 0 & 1 & -1 & 0 & 0 & 0 \end{array}\right] \end{array} \begin{bmatrix} y_1 \\ y_2 \\ y_3 \\ y_4 \\ y_5 \\ y_6 \\ y_7 \end{bmatrix} = \begin{bmatrix} 0 \\ 0 \\ 0 \\ 0 \\ 0 \\ 0 \\ 0 \end{bmatrix}$$

The corresponding equations are:

$$\begin{aligned} -y_1 + y_2 &= 0 \\ y_1 - y_2 - y_5 + y_7 &= 0 \\ -y_3 + y_4 + y_5 - y_7 &= 0 \\ y_3 - y_4 &= 0 \end{aligned}$$

The solutions which cannot be additively obtained from other solutions are:

$$[1 \ 1 \ 0 \ 0 \ 0 \ 0 \ 0]$$
$$[0 \ 0 \ 0 \ 0 \ 1 \ 0 \ 1]$$
$$[0 \ 0 \ 1 \ 1 \ 0 \ 0 \ 0]$$
$$[0 \ 0 \ 0 \ 0 \ 0 \ 1 \ 0]$$

The invariants are:

$$\{p_1,p_2\}, \{p_3,p_4\}, \{p_5,p_7\}, \{p_6\}$$

Given the set of invariants, some properties about the dynamic behavior of the net can be deduced.[7,8] Assume M_0, the initial marking, is as shown in Figure 6 with $B > 0$. Let NP_i represent the total number of tokens in p_i.

Boundedness. Since each place is in some invariant and the net starts with a bounded marking, the net is bounded.

L: So
Do while P_1
  if P_2 then
    S_1
  else
    S_2
  end if
  par begin S_3,S_4,S_5
  par end
end do
go to L

Figure 4. Example of a Petri net used to represent the flow of control in programs containing certain kinds of constructs.

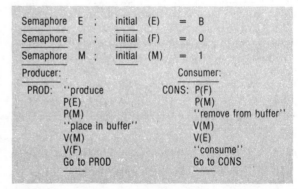

```
Semaphore E ;    initial (E)  = B
Semaphore F ;    initial (F)  = 0
Semaphore M ;    initial (M)  = 1

Producer:                      Consumer:

  PROD: "produce              CONS: P(F)
        P(E)                        P(M)
        P(M)                        "remove from buffer"
        "place in buffer"          V(M)
        V(M)                        V(E)
        V(F)                        "consume"
        Go to PROD                  Go to CONS
```

Figure 5. Programs of two concurrent processes coordinated using P and V primitives.

Conservativeness. Since the set of places can be partitioned into disjoint subsets each of which is an invariant, the net is conservative and the total number of tokens in the net remains constant.

Mutual exclusion. If an input or output place of a transition t is contained in an invariant I, t is said to be a transition of I. If two transitions are transitions of the same invariant and the initial marking is such that the sum of the tokens in the places of the invariant is 1, then the transitions are mutually exclusive and cannot fire simultaneously. Thus, the initial marking and invariant $\{p_6\}$ guarantee that t_2 and t_3 are mutually exclusive.

No buffer underflow. Buffer underflow is impossible since t_3 cannot fire if the buffer is empty ($NP_7 = 0$).

No buffer overflow. Since $\{p_5, p_7\}$ is an invariant, the initial marking guarantees that $NP_5 + NP_7$ is always B. Therefore, $NP_7 \leqslant B$ and buffer overflow cannot occur.

No deadlock. A deadlock will be said to have occurred if the net reaches a marking where no transition can fire. If the net is deadlocked, t_2 cannot fire. This implies that $NP_5 = 0$ or $NP_2 = 0$. In the former case, from the initial marking M_0 and invariant $\{p_5, p_7\}$ it can be concluded that $NP_7 > 0$; if $NP_3 = 0$ then $NP_4 = 1$ (from invariant $\{p_3, p_4\}$) and t_4 can fire, else $NP_3 = 1$ and t_3 can fire. In the latter case, $NP_2 = 0$, from invariant $\{p_1, p_2\}$ and M_0 it can be concluded that $NP_1 = 1$ and t_1 can fire. Thus, if t_2 cannot fire, then either t_4 or t_3 or t_1 can and the net can never be deadlocked.

Invariants are a useful aid to verifying the behavior of Petri nets. Rather than solving a system of equations, all the invariants can be systematically obtained by following certain rules during the construction of a net.[9]

A basic approach to analyzing Petri nets is to use the *reachability tree*. The nodes of a reachability tree of a marked Petri net represent reachable markings of the net. Let $N = (T, P, A, M_0)$ be a marked Petri net. Let ω be a special quantity such that $\omega \pm x = \omega, x < \omega$ and $\omega \leqslant \omega$ for every integer x. M is considered to be a vector below. The reachability tree for N is constructed as follows:

Let the initial marking be the root node and tag it "new."

While new markings exist *do*

Select a new marking M.

If M is identical to another node in the tree which is not new, then tag M to be "old" and stop processing M.

If no transition is enabled in M, tag M to be "terminal."

For every transition t enabled in M

(1) Obtain the marking M' which results from firing t in M.

(2) If there exists a path from the root to M containing a marking M'' such that $M' > M''$, then replace $(M')_i$ by ω wherever $(M')_i > (M'')_i$.

(3) Introduce M' as a node, draw an arc from M to M' labeled t, and tag M' to be "new."

End

It can be shown that the above procedure always terminates in a finite number of steps resulting in a finite tree. Also, a place p_i is unbounded if and only if the tree contains a marking with $(M)_i = \omega$. For bounded nets, each node is a reachable marking and the tree contains all reachable markings. The reachability tree for Figure 6 and $B = 1$ is given in Figure 7. Analysis of this tree yields some useful in-

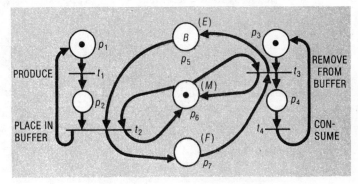

Figure 6. A compact net for the two-process system.

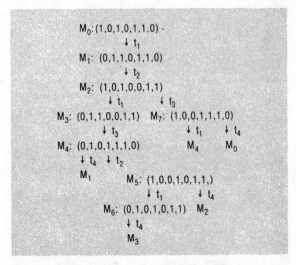

Figure 7. Reachability tree for Figure 6 and B = 1.

formation. It indicates exactly the set of reachable markings. Since no node contains an ω, the net is bounded. In fact, the net is safe since no reachable marking assigns more than one token to any place. The net is conservative: the sum of tokens in each marking is 4. There is no buffer overflow since no marking assigns more than 1 token to p_7. An analysis of the tree indicates that from any marking in the tree any transition can be enabled by an appropriate firing sequence. The net is thus live. With $B = 1$, t_2 and t_3 are never enabled simultaneously and they are therefore mutually exclusive. Detailed information about a system's behavior can be obtained from an analysis of its reachability tree. The major disadvantage is that the reachability tree can easily become complex, large, and unmanageable. This would be true for our example if B was chosen to be greater than 1.

Resource allocation is a major activity of operating systems. Consider a system of N processes each of which requires exclusive access to a subset of m resources R_1, R_2,...R_m.[10] Processes are granted access without any consideration of priorities. If two processes use disjoint subsets of resources they may execute simultaneously. On completion, each process voluntarily releases its acquired resources. The reader is invited to construct a Petri net for a particular system where there are three processes X, Y, and Z competing for a card reader, printer, and tape. Process X requires the reader and printer, process Y the reader and tape, and process Z the printer and tape. This problem has also been referred to as the "Cigarette Smoker's Problem."[11]

Petri nets have been applied to compiler modeling to determine whether existing compilation algorithms are suitable for parallel processing.[12,13] An XPL/S compiler was first directly modeled (using an extension of Petri nets) resulting in a net that had little concurrency; the application of known methods for the automatic detection of parallelism yielded poor results. However, it was noticed that the compilation process could be modeled as a three-stage software pipeline. The net representation facilitated the subsequent restructuring of the compiler and its associated data structures. The three-stage pipeline was simulated assuming a three-processor system, and the results indicated that a speedup of 2:1 could be obtained over the sequential case. Different degrees of interpretation were used at different stages: initial analysis required relatively little interpretation; for detailed simulation, complete interpretation was used. In general, the Petri net-based model was found to be a useful tool.

Distributed data bases and communication protocols

The applicability of Petri nets to distributed data base systems is demonstrated below by modeling a duplicate file update protocol. A copy of the data base exists at each site in the distributed system. Requests to update the data base can originate at any site. The update protocol must guarantee that all copies are identical except for transient update times (mutual consistency).

Centralized and decentralized control schemes have been described by Ellis[14] and by Noe and Nutt using E-nets.[15] A data base controller is associated with each site, and it is the only entity allowed to update the local data base. An update request by a user is channeled through the local controller to a central supervisor. If some other update could be in progress the supervisor rejects the request; the user is informed of this and may request the update at a later time. Otherwise, permission is granted to the local controller and the update is performed by all controllers in the system.

A Petri net representing the local controller is given in Figure 8. A user request for update is signaled by a token in IR. The local controller is notified of acceptance (rejection) by the supervisor by a token in ACCEPT (DENY). "Broadcase update" causes a token to appear in place UPD in each controller. Each "transmit ACK" causes a token to appear in place ACK in the originating controller. A slight generalization has been introduced in this net: "Transmit 'done' to supervisor and user" occurs only when the controller is waiting for an acknowledgement and place ACK contains n-1 tokens (n-1

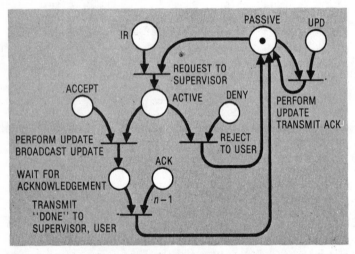

Figure 8. Petri net representing the local controller in a distributed system.

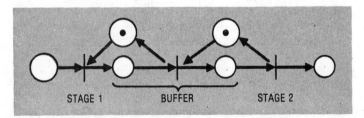

Figure 9. Simple two-stage pipeline with a buffer of size 2 between stages.

acknowledgements received from the n-1 remote controllers).

Petri net analysis tools can be used to verify the protocol. Invariants can establish that the sum of tokens in "ACTIVE," "PASSIVE," "Wait for acknowledgement" is always 1. Thus, even though there could be more than one token in IR, only one request at a time is serviced. Detailed analysis of the entire system can be used to establish that all data bases perform the same sequence of updates; mutual consistency is guaranteed. In the absence of failures the net can be shown to be live, thus ruling out the presence of "hang-up states." A supervisor crash could prevent tokens from ever being placed in ACCEPT or DENY, and this could soon halt all activity in the system. By assigning further interpretation (such as transition execution times) the net can be simulated to obtain throughput and response times. The applicability of other related models such as E-nets and RESQ for distributed data base modeling has been informally discussed by Chandy.[16]

Petri nets can be used to model and analyze communication protocols.[17, 18] Analysis can be performed using a token machine (TM) which is a directed graph whose nodes represent unique markings. An arc (m_i, m_j) labeled t indicates that m_j is reachable from m_i by firing transition t. A well-behaved protocol (WBP) can be defined as one whose TM satisfies certain conditions: (1) the number of states is finite; (2) from any state there is a directed path to the initial state; (3) there is no directed loop containing only exceptional states; (4) etc. The following validation methodology is then applicable: Model the protocol as a Petri net. Obtain the TM and analyze it for WBP properties. If the protocol is not well-behaved, determine whether the model is incorrect or the protocol is inherently not well-behaved. If the former condition holds, adjust the Petri net and continue iteratively. This methodology was proposed by Merlin and applied to a telephone signaling protocol.[17] A similar approach was taken by Postel and Farber[18] to analyze computer communication protocols using the UCLA graph model.[19]

Computer hardware

Though computer hardware modeling has not been discussed explicitly, the application of Petri nets in this area should be evident. Figure 9 represents a simple two-stage pipeline with a buffer of size two between stages. Pipelines have frequently been used in high-performance computer systems such as the Texas Instruments Advanced Scientific Computer, the IBM 360/91, and the CRAY-1. A multiple functional unit computer resembling the CDC 6600 has also been modeled.[20] Shapiro and Saint[21] used Petri nets to generate efficient CDC 6600 programs: An algorithm originally expressed in a conventional high-level language is represented as a net to remove incidental sequencing constraints imposed by the language. The sequencing constraints required by the target hardware are then introduced into the net.

All sequences of which this net is capable are realizable on the target hardware and perform the desired functional mapping.

Speed-independent circuit design

A circuit in which the presence of arbitrary delays in elements and connections has no effect upon circuit operation is called a speed-independent circuit. Such designs have been used where speed is critical since the circuit is not constrained by a clock but operates "as fast as possible." An example is the design of a processor for the synthesis of music.[22] A conventional processor cannot approach the necessary speed in this application, which requires a very large number of computations.

One of the major problems with speed-independent circuit design in the past was the lack of a formal model to represent, analyze, and synthesize such circuits. A suitable model should have the following characteristics: (1) the model should provide a clear and understandable representation of the circuit; (2) there should be a direct correlation between elements of the model and circuit realizations; and (3) the model should not serve only as a description scheme but should be accompanied by mathematical tools which allow analysis and synthesis. Clearly, Petri nets have a potential for being useful in this environment: places, tokens, and transitions could represent wires, signals, and actions.

For direct implementation as a speed-independent circuit, a Petri net should be live, safe, and persistent (in any reachable marking an enabled transition can be disabled only by being fired). A non-safe net would be difficult to implement since the circuit would have to keep track of the number of tokens present. Also, non-safeness and non-persistence can lead to critical races and will generally not result in speed-independence.[22] A live net guarantees that all parts of the corresponding circuit realization are utilized.

Speed-independent circuits were modeled by Patil and Dennis using Petri nets.[23] The hardware is represented as two structures: the control structure which is a Petri net and the data flow structure which consists of registers, operation units, decision elements, and data links. Firing of a transition in the control structure corresponds to the execution of an operation in the data flow structure. The sequence of steps is (1) remove tokens from input places; (2) send a ready signal to the operator over a control link; (3) execute the operation; (4) receive acknowledge signal from operator on the control link; (5) put tokens in output places.

In addition to the work on modeling, the implementation of Petri nets has also been studied.[22-25] The approach where circuit modules are directly substituted for places and transitions[24] usually leads to fairly complex circuit realizations. Misunas[22] uses an alternative approach to reduce complexity: a basic collection of Petri net functions and their corresponding speed-independent hardware implementation have ben developed. Complete circuits can be obtained either directly from the circuit modules or a Petri net can first be synthesized using the net modules and directly translated into the circuit realization. The latter has the advantage that the circuit can be analyzed and verified using the Petri net description. A transistor level implementation which has desirable fault properties has also been studied.[25]

Speed-independent circuits have some useful properties: they operate at maximum speed, are insensitive to delays in circuit elements and connections (these delays could vary based on environmental conditions such as humidity and temperature or with aging), and do not exhibit races and hazards. In addition, the circuits have advantages with respect to design verification, simulation, and fault detection.[25] Design verification of ordinary circuits which may exhibit races and hazards requires five-valued simulation: 0(true logical zero), 1(true logical one), X(unknown), U(rising signal), and D (falling signal). Such simulators use complex timing analysis and involved data structures. A simulator that uses only the first three values is much simpler but useful only for logic verification in conventional circuits. For speed-independent circuits, a simple three-valued simulator, which performs the simulation assuming a unit delay in each element and zero delay in the interconnections, is adequate for both logic and design verification. Also, speed-independent implementations of live, safe, and persistent Petri nets are inherently fail-secure[25]: most failures cause circuit operation to cease and fault propagation is prevented. This property is useful in highly secure computer systems and circuits that interface with expensive peripherals or sophisticated weapons systems.

Some major problems with speed-independent circuits are that testing is not fully understood and fault detection and isolation require the use of timing information. More significant, however, is the fact that the development of Petri net theory has provided impetus to research in the important area of speed-independent circuits.

Petri nets as a uniform design language

It should be clear from the preceding discussion that in addition to being a very suitable model for concurrent systems, Petri nets exhibit two other useful properties. First, the nets are equally suited for the representation of hardware and software systems. This is particularly useful given today's microprocessor technology wherein a large number of conventional hardware systems now contain an intimate mix of hardware and software. Secondly, Petri nets can be used at all levels including network, PMS, register-transfer, functional, and gate. The interpretation can be varied to suit the particular requirements of each level and the nets can be analyzed or simulated. The nets thus have an advantage over existing design languages which are generally not applicable across the entire spectrum. In conventional approaches different languages, simulators, and analytical tools have to be used at different levels.

The best example of the utility and feasibility of the Petri net approach as a design language is provided by the powerful LOGOS system,[26] which is Petri net-based. Another example of the use of Petri nets for design verification is described by Azema et al.[27]

In this context, it is important to note that Petri nets can be designed in a top-down manner so that certain properties are preserved.[28] Consider a net, N, which is live and safe with respect to an initial marking M_0. Let there be a place p (called an idle place) which has exactly one input transition and one output transition, which is the only place marked in M_0, and which is not marked in any other marking. Let M_0 be reachable from every marking in its reachability set. Under these conditions, N is said to be a well-behaved net. (Necessary and sufficient conditions for a net to be well-behaved can easily be given with respect to the corresponding token machine.) Let N_1 and N_2 be well-behaved nets. Let t be a transition in N_1, p the idle place in N_2, and t_1 and t_2 the corresponding input and output transitions of p. Substitute N_2 for t as follows: delete place p and arcs (t_1, p) and (p, t_2) from N_2. Delete t and its input and output arcs from N_1. Cause the input (output) places of t to become input (output) places of t_2 (t_1). The resulting net N can be shown to be well-behaved. The substitution preserves precedence and independence relationships between activities represented by transitions at the previous level of abstraction. Thus, important properties can be established during synthesis without the necessity of complex a posteriori verification.

A design methodology (for speed-independent systems) has been developed.[25] This methodology incorporates a common description language, a top-down synthesis procedure which preserves important properties, and a procedure for direct translation into hardware implementations. The work establishes the potential of Petri nets in this area.

Novel interpretations of nets

Since a live system is free from deadlock, the property of liveness has received much attention in net literature. On the other hand, a dead transition (not enabled in any reachable marking) can be viewed as an invariant assertion about the modeled system's behavior.[29] Using this interpretation, a net calculus, isomorphic to propositional calculus, has been derived by Thieler-Mevissen.[30] In this approach a transition is enabled only if each of its input places contains a token and all its output places are empty. A single transition with input and output places (an elementary net) can then represent an elementary disjunction of literals (a clause), as shown in Figure 10. An assignment of truth values to literals is called a case, and a correspondence between markings and cases can be established as follows: $M(p) = 1$ if and only if p is True. The transition t in Figure 10 is enabled when $M(a) = M(b) = M(c) = 1$ and $M(d) = M(e) = 0$. The corresponding assignment of truth values is $a = b = c =$ True and $d = e =$ False, and the clause C is False. Any marking other than M causes transition t to be dead; the corresponding case makes clause C True.

The union of two elementary net $N_1 = (T_1, P_1, A_1)$ and $N_2 = (T_2, P_2, A_2)$ is defined as $(T_1 \cup T_2, P_1 \cup P_2, A_1 \cup A_2)$. If N_1 and N_2 represent clauses C_1 and C_2 respectively, then $N_1 \cup N_2$ represents $C_1 \wedge C_2$. The net in Figure 11 represents the proposition $(\bar{a} \vee \bar{b} \vee c) \wedge (\bar{c} \vee \bar{d} \vee e)$. Since every proposition can be expressed in conjunctive normal form, every proposition can be represented as a Petri net and every Petri net represents a proposition. When interpreted as a proposition a Petri net is called a fact net. If the proposition holds in a set of cases S, the net is a fact concerning S. To complete the calculus of fact nets and establish its isomorphism to propositional calculus, two net transformation rules can be shown to be consistent and complete[30]—i.e.,

(1) If a net is a fact concerning a set of cases S, then all derived nets N^* are also facts concerning S.
(2) If a proposition B follows (in propositional logic) from proposition A, then the net for B is derivable from the net for A by the rules.

Petri nets have also been used to represent mathematical knowledge.[31] Each token in a place has a definite structure and represents a well-defined construct of mathematics: a set, a group, etc. The transitions represent specifications which generate new constructs. Used in this manner the nets can be a valuable teaching and working tool for mathematics.

A subclass of Petri nets, free choice nets, have been found useful for modeling industrial production environments.[32] An "assembly line," for example, can be represented by a net similar to that in Figure 9. Necessary and sufficient conditions for a free choice net to be live and safe can be used to analyze production systems which are modeled using these nets. The nets have even been used in the representation of legal systems.[33]

The modeling power of Petri nets

It has been established that Petri nets cannot model certain priority situations.[34] Many extensions to Petri nets have been proposed, some of which yield no increase in power but do facilitate modeling.[35] A fundamental extension is to allow a special arc from a place p to a transition t such that t can fire only if p is empty.[8] This extension not only allows a more natural representation in many situations but also leads to Turing completeness.[35,36] Other extensions such as switches,[12] constraint sets,[24] and external firing priorities[37] are equivalent to zero-testing.[36] If nets are restricted to be bounded then all extensions are equivalent to finite state machines, and different extensions are merely better suited for different applications.

Conclusions

Petri nets can be used in many disciplines as a tool for representation, analysis, and synthesis. However, Petri nets are difficult to analyze. Bounded systems can be completely analyzed using marking trees, but these can rapidly become unmanageable. For general Petri nets the reachability problem, though decidable, has been shown to be exponentially time- and space-hard. However, if analysis problems are encountered, this reflects on the complexity of the system being modeled and should not be considered to be a disadvantage of the Petri nets. ∎

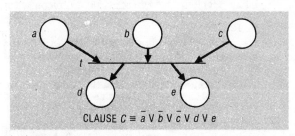

Figure 10. A Petri net representation of an elementary disjunction.

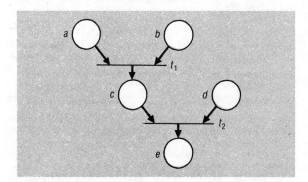

Figure 11. A Petri net representation of the proposition $(\bar{a} \vee \bar{b} \vee c) \wedge (\bar{c} \vee \bar{d} \vee e)$.

References

1. J. Peterson, "Petri Nets," *Computing Surveys*, Vol. 9, No. 3, Sept. 1977, pp. 223-252.

2. C. A. R. Hoare, "Parallel Programming, an Axiomatic Approach," Tech. Report C5-73-394, Stanford University, Oct. 1973.

3. R. M. Keller, "Formal Verification of Parallel Programs," *Comm. ACM*, Vol. 19, No. 7, July 1976, pp. 371-384.

4. S. Owicki and D. Gries, "Verifying Properties of Parallel Programs: An Axiomatic Approach," *Comm. ACM*, Vol. 19, No. 5, May 1976, pp. 279-285.

5. J. D. Noe, "A Petri Net Model of the CDC 6400," Report 71-04-03, Computer Science Dept., University of Washington, 1971; also in *Proc. ACM SIGOPS Workshop on System Performance Evaluation*, N. Y., 1971, pp. 362-378.

6. E. W. Dijkstra, "Cooperating Sequential Processes," *Programming Languages*, F. Genuys (ed.), Academic Press, N. Y., 1968, pp. 43-112.

7. K. Lautenbach and H. A. Schmid, "Use of Petri Nets for Proving Correctness of Concurrent Process Systems," *Proc. IFIP Congress 74*, North-Holland Pub. Co., Amsterdam, The Netherlands, 1974, pp. 184-191.

8. T. Agerwala and M. Flynn, "Comments on Capabilities, Limitations and 'Correctness' of Petri Nets," *Proc. First Ann. Symp. Computer Architecture*, ACM, N. Y., 1973, pp. 81-86.

9. T. Agerwala and Y. Choed-Amphai, "A Synthesis Rule for Concurrent Systems," *Proc. 15th Design Automation Conf.*, Las Vegas, June 1978, pp. 305-311.

10. T. Agerwala, "Some Extended Semaphore Primitives," *Acta Informatica*, Aug. 1977, pp. 201-220.

11. S. S. Patil, "Limitations and Capabilities of Dijskstra's Semaphore Primitives for Coordination Among Processes," Computation Structures Group Memo 57, Project MAI, MIT, Cambridge, Mass., Feb. 1971.

12. J. L. Baer, "Modeling for Parallel Computation: a Case Study," *Proc. 1973 Sagamore Computer Conf. Parallel Processing*, Springer-Verlag, N. Y., 1973, pp. 13-22.

13. J. L. Baer and C. S. Ellis, "Model, Design, and Evaluation of a Compiler for a Parallel Processing Environment," *IEEE Trans. Software Eng.*, Vol. SE-3, No. 6, Nov. 1977, pp. 394-405.

14. C. A. Ellis, "A Robust Algorithm for Updating Duplicate Data Bases," *Second Berkeley Workshop on Distributed Data Management*, 1977.

15. J. D. Noe and G. J. Nutt, "Macro E-Nets for Representation of Parallel Systems," *IEEE Trans. Computers*, Vol. C-22, No. 8, Aug. 1973, pp. 718-727.

16. K. M. Chandy, "Models of Distributed Systems," *Proc. 1977 Int'l Conf. on Very Large Data Bases*, pp. 105-120.

17. P. M. Merlin, "A Methodology for the Design and Implementation of Communication Protocols," *IEEE Trans. Communications*, Vol. COM-24, No. 6, June 1976, pp. 614-621.

18. J. B. Postel and D. Farber, "Graph Modeling of Computer Communication Protocols," *Proc. Fifth Texas Conf. on Computing Systems*, Univ. of Texas, Austin, Oct. 1976, pp. 66-77.

19. K. P. Gostelow, "Flow of Control, Resource Allocation and the Proper Termination of Programs," PhD diss., Computer Science Dept., UCLA, Dec. 1971.

20. J. B. Dennis, "Modular Asynchronous Control Structures for a High Performance Processor," *Record of the Prohect MAC Conf. Concurrent Systems and Parallel Computation*, ACM, N. Y., 1970, pp.55-80.

21. R. M. Shapiro and H. Saint, "A New Approach to Optimization of Sequencing Decisions," *Ann. Review of Automatic Programming*, Vol. 6, No. 5, 1970, pp. 257-288.

22. D. Misunas, "Petri Nets and Speed Independent Design," *Comm. ACM*, Vol. 16, No. 8, Aug. 1973, pp. 474-481.

23. S. S. Patil and J. B. Dennis, "The Description and Realization of Digital Systems," *Digest of Papers, COMPCON 72*, IEEE Computer Society, San Francisco, 1972, pp. 223-226.

24. S. S. Patil, "Coordination of Asynchronous Events," MAC TR-72, Project MAC, MIT, June 1970.

25. E. Pacas-Skewes, "A Design Methodology for Digital Systems Using Petri Nets," PhD diss., University of Texas at Austin, 1979.

26. C. W. Rose and M. Albarran, "Modeling and Design Description of Hierarchical Hardware/Software Systems," *Proc. 12th Design Automation Conf.*, Boston, Mass., June 1975, pp. 421-430.

27. P. Azema et al., "Petri Nets as a Common Tool for Design Verification and Hardware Simulation," *Proc. 13th Design Automation Conf.*, San Francisco, June 1976, pp. 109-116.

28. R. Valette and R. Prajoux, "A Model for Parallel Control Systems and Communication Systems," *Proc. 1976 Conf. on Information Sciences and Systems*, The Johns Hopkins University, Baltimore, Md., pp. 313-318.

29. C. A. Petri, "Interpretations of Net Theory," Interner Bericht 75-07, Gesellschaft fur Mathematik und Datenverabeitung, Bonn, W. Germany, July 1975.

30. G. Thieler-Mevissen, "The Petri Net Calculus of Predicate Logic," Interner Bericht ISF-76-09, Institut fur Informationssystemforschung, Gesellschaft fur Mathematic und Datenverabeitung, Birlinghoven, W. Germany, Dec. 1976.

31. H. J. Genrich, "The Petri Net Representation of Mathematical Knowledge," GMD-ISF Internal Report 75-06, Institut fur Informationssystemforschung, Gesellschaft fur Mathematik und Datenverabeitung, Birlinghoven, W. Germany, 1975.

32. M. Hack, "Analysis of Production Schemata by Petri Nets," MAC TR-94, Project MAC, MIT, Feb. 1972.

33. J. A. Meldman and A. W. Holt, "Petri Nets and Legal Systems," *Jurimetrics J.*, Vol. 12, No. 2, Dec. 1971, pp. 65-75.

34. S. R. Kosaraju, "Limitations of Dijkstra's Semaphore Primitives and Petri Nets," Tech. Report 25, The Johns Hopkins University, May 1973; also in *Operating Systems Review*, Vol. 7, No. 4, Oct. 1973, pp. 122-126.

35. T. Agerwala, "Towards a Theory for the Analysis and Synthesis of Systems Exhibiting Concurrency," PhD diss., The Johns Hopkins University, 1975.

36. T. Agerwala and M. Flynn, "On the Completeness of Representation Schemes for Concurrent Systems," *Conf. on Petri Nets and Related Methods*, MIT, 1976.

37. M. Hack, "Petri Net Languages," Computation Structures Group Memo 124, Project MAC, MIT, Cambridge, Mass., June 1975.

Tilak Agerwala is a research staff member at the IBM T. J. Watson Research Center in Yorktown Heights, New York. From April 1975 to January 1979 he was an assistant professor in the Departments of Electrical Engineering and Computer Sciences and a faculty affiliate of the Electronics Research Center at the University of Texas at Austin. During the summer of 1977 he was a member of the technical staff at Bell Telephone Laboratories, Murray Hill, New Jersey. His research interests are in the areas of computer architecture, distributed and parallel computer systems, operating systems, microprocessors, and Petri nets.

A member of ACM, IEEE, and Sigma Xi, Agerwala received a B. Tech. degree in 1971 from the Indian Institute of Technology at Kanpur, and his PhD in 1975 from The Johns Hopkins University.

Part IX

Software Development Methodologies

We now return to the fundamental notion of a software development methodology linking together all of the various methods for analysis, specification, design, implementation, testing, evolution, and all of the other aspects of software development, along with related issues of management, automated tools, and the development environment.

If we simply define "methodology" as a set of steps by which one carries out a software development effort, from beginning to end, then it is apparent that *everyone* has some kind of methodology, whether good or bad. The nature of the methodology is dependent upon a multitude of factors, including the nature of the software being built (size, criticality, etc.), the nature of the organization in which the software is specified or built, the requirements of the customer(s) for the software, the qualifications and training of the software development staff and management, and available computing equipment.

With this definition of methodology, the common goal of software development organizations is simply to *improve* the process by which software is created, leading to better quality software and to better control over the development process, with the important objective of reducing the cost of any modifications to the software subsequent to the original development.

In addition to this broad definition of methodology, there is a narrower definition as well. This narrower definition of methodology is a (predominantly technical) set of steps that can be followed from the beginning to the end of a software development. In this sense, issues of management are complementary; there is a distinction between the methodology itself (the technical steps) and the application of the methodology on a particular project.

The papers in this section use both of these definitions. The first paper, on concepts and requirements for Ada methodologies, uses methodology in its broadest sense, while the other papers use the more restrictive meaning.

"Ada Methodologies: Concepts and Requirements" is a first effort to identify and organize the issues associated with creating software development methodologies that are suitable for use with the Ada programming language. We have seen already in this tutorial volume that many of the issues in software specification and design are largely independent of the target programming language, although knowledge of the target language begins to have significant influence in some design decisions.

The software technology effort within the Department of Defense proceeded from design of a high-level programming language suitable for the construction of embedded systems (Ada) through requirements for a set of tools to support the development and execution of Ada programs to requirements for a methodology. Just as the Ada programming language and the Ada Programming Support Environment started with a set of requirements, the identification of suitable Ada-linked methodology steps starts with these requirements.

The requirements are quite general, pointing to the importance of covering all phases of software development, supporting transitions between phases, supporting validation and verification of the intermediate work products, and facilitating communication among all interested persons on a software development project, to name just some of the major points. The paper illustrates the relationship between the technical steps of a methodology and related issues of management and automated support.

An important area of future methodology development is evaluation. There are many ways in which methodologies many be evaluated, including technical, usage, management, and economic characteristics. It is clear, though, that much work is needed both in defining criteria for methodology evaluation and in applying those criteria to specific methodologies.

The remaining three papers describe the technical aspects of three methodologies: the Ballistic Missile Defense (BMD) Software Development System, Higher Order Software, and User Software

Engineering. As with other methodologies, these methodologies are evolving rapidly as experience is gained in their use and as better tools are developed to support their use. Indeed, the BMD approach is presently evolving into a new methodology for development of distributed systems.

The paper by Davis and Vick on the Software Development System complements the paper by Bell, Bixler, and Dyer on SREM (in Part III). The Davis and Vick paper describes the entire software development system and shows how different tools and techniques were used for different aspects of the software life cycle. Within the past couple of years, these tools have been modified and implemented on smaller computers, so that the methodology can be applied to systems other than the BMD project. This advance should make it possible to use the methodology for the creation of systems less complex than is BMD.

Higher Order Software (HOS), developed by Margaret Hamilton and Saydean Zeldin, is also a set of steps supported by automatic tools. The paper here discusses not only some aspects of software development methodologies but also the HOS methodology. Hamilton and Zeldin identify some desirable properties for a methodology -- note that there is some overlap, but there are also some significant differences, with the list in "Ada Methodologies: Concepts and Requirements." Hamilton and Zeldin also point to some important aspects of standardizing a methodology and using it effectively.

The HOS methodology is based on a set of axioms that allows the definition of modular, hierarchically structured systems in a functional notation. The system definition can be expressed in a formal specification language AXES, which may then be used with other tools for resource allocation and code generation. As with the Davis and Vick paper, this paper is already several years old and development of the methodology and tools has progressed well beyond the stage described in this paper.

Finally, User Software Engineering, developed by Wasserman, is a methodology for the design and development of interactive information systems, primarily those systems involving conversational access to data. User Software Engineering gives particular attention to the role of the user interface and to involvement of the user community in designing one or more appropriate interfaces. Thus, external design of the system is done very early, from which a prototype of the user/program dialogue can be easily and quickly constructed.

User Software Engineering also combines informal methods for specification with a formal method using operational specifications, making it possible to apply program verification techniques to this class of system. As with the other methodologies described in this section, the User Software Engineering tools are essential to effective use of the methodology.

It seems safe to observe that evaluation of methodologies will place increasing weight on the availability of automated tools that *specifically* support the methodology, as we have seen in this volume not only with the three methodologies described in this Part, but also with SARA and TAXIS.

Department of Defense

Ada Joint Program Office

Ada™ Methodologies:
Concepts and Requirements

November 1982

™Ada is a trademark of the U.S. Department of Defense (Ada Joint Program Office).

PREFACE

As I observed in Ada® Letters ("The Need for a Programming Discipline to Support the APSE", Vol. I, No. 4, pp 21-23, May/June 82), we will not realize the full potential of Ada until we are able to define a software development methodology complete with management practices which can in turn be supported by automated tools. I announced in that paper that Professors Freeman and Wasserman had agreed to prepare a first draft of a "Methodman". This document is the promised draft.

Although I believe that Professors Freeman and Wasserman have done a superb job of defining the desirable characteristics of a methodology to support the software development process, we recognize that it is incomplete and must be refined. Just as Strawman was refined to produce Steelman, and Pebbleman was refined into Stoneman, this document is being circulated for comment that will assist in the refinement process.

Many software activities (both technical and managerial) are independent of the programming language. Indeed, although the Ada language and the APSE provide a basis for better support for a software discipline, the development of a total life-cycle methodology expands the scope of the Ada Program. On October 8, 1982, Dr. Edith W. Martin, Deputy Under Secretary of Defense for Research and Advanced Technology, announced plans for a DoD Software Initiative. This initial version of "Methodman" may be viewed as an initial function of the initiative. It demonstrates the essential role that the Ada Program will play in the initiative and concurrently, the need for the initiative to press for technology innovation beyond Ada.

The Ada Program has received substantial benefit from public interaction. The distribution of this draft is another important step in continuing that interaction. It is also indicative of the professionalism of Peter Freeman and Tony Wasserman that they consent (as did Dave Fisher and John Buxton) to subject their work for public scrutiny and comment.

Constructive comments should be sent to the Ada Joint Program Office, Suite 1210, 801 N. Randolph St. Arlington, VA 22203.

Larry E. Druffel, Lt. Colonel, USAF
Director
Ada Joint Program Office

UNIVERSITY OF CALIFORNIA

BERKELEY · DAVIS · IRVINE · LOS ANGELES · RIVERSIDE · SAN DIEGO · SAN FRANCISCO

SANTA BARBARA · SANTA CRUZ

November, 1982

This document has benefited greatly from the many valuable comments that we have received on its previous drafts. We are thankful to everyone who gave us both written and verbal comments during the preliminary review process, and appreciate their contributions. These people include: B.N. Barnett, L.A. Belady, M. Brodie, R. Bruno, G. Estrin, R. Fairley, H. Fischer, R.L. Glass, S. Gutz, H. Hart, H. Hess, R. Houghton, C.A. Irvine, M.A. Jackson, L. Johnson, E. Koskela, J. Lancaster, J. Larcher, B. Liskov, P.C. Lockemann, I. Macdonald, J.B. Munson, E.J. Neuhold, D.L. Parnas, L. Peters, K.T. Rawlinson, D.J. Reifer, W. Riddle, C. Rolland, T. Standish, H.G. Stuebing, W. Tichy, R. Van Tilburg, L. Tripp, C. Tully, J. Wileden, M. Zelkowitz, and N. Zvegintzov.

We included a selected bibliography in an earlier draft, but have decided against its inclusion in this report, since a bibliography would have recognized the work of some while omitting that of others. It should be apparent that our ideas have been shaped by a vast amount of work both inside and outside DoD over the past 15 years, and that our role here was to consolidate this body of work and to establish a framework from which methodologies could be developed and enhanced. We gratefully acknowledge this debt to our colleagues who have contributed to the present understanding of software development methodologies.

We especially wish to thank Lt. Col. Larry Druffel, who sponsored this effort, and provided the framework in which we could accomplish the work. Finally, we appreciate the assistance of USC Information Sciences Insitute for handling the administrative aspects of this work.

Anthony I. Wasserman
Medical Information Science
University of California, San Francisco

Peter Freeman
Information and Computer Science
University of California, Irvine

1. INTRODUCTION

This document rationalizes the need for the use of coherent software development methodologies in conjunction with Ada and its programming support environments (APSE's) and describes the characteristics that such methodologies should possess. It is recognized that software development, particularly for embedded systems, is increasingly done in the context of overall systems development, including hardware and environmental factors. While there is a strong need for integrated systems engineering, this document focuses on the software issues only.

Emphasis is thus given to the *process* by which software is developed for Ada applications, not just with the language or its automated support environment. The development activity yields a collection of work products (including source and object versions of Ada programs). These work products are valuable not only through the development phase, but also through the entire lifetime of the system as modifications and enhancements are made to the system.

The analysis, design, and development of complex systems, such as those to be programmed in Ada, must be controlled through a collection of management procedures and technical methods. Differences in organizational structures, applications, and existing approaches, however, make it impractical to prescribe a single methodology that can be uniformly followed.

Accordingly, this paper identifies requirements for software development methodologies, as was done in the sequences of documents leading to the "Steelman" and "Stoneman" reports. A preliminary version of these requirements has been used to evaluate some existing methodologies for software development. These requirements can serve as a basis for evolving methodologies and for creating new ones oriented to the special problems of embedded systems to be implemented in Ada. The emphasis, then, is on the conceptual basis for software development methodologies.

As with the work leading to the design of Ada and the specifications for Ada Programming Support Environments, this work builds upon, but is not constrained by, the current set of methodologies and development practices. Instead, this document sets down some underlying principles. Thus, there are no references to specific techniques or to existing standards, based on the belief that improved methodologies can be developed from the foundation established here. Of course, such standards and techniques have influenced the requirements identified here.

An important assumption throughout this document is that the methodology used for creating systems should be preeminent over the tools used in it. In other words, tools should support a methodology, and not the other way around.

There is also very little emphasis on Ada itself, except in the discussion of implementation. Other aspects of the development methodology are described on the assumption that Ada is the target programming language. However, most of the concepts are based on currently understood notions of software engineering and programming methodology, and are therefore not tightly coupled to the programming language. Indeed, many of the requirements for a software development methodology are largely independent of the target programming language.

2. RATIONALE

A key assumption of modern software development practices is that increased effort in the earlier stages of development will be reflected in reduced costs for testing and evolution* (maintenance). Such effort is intended both to prevent errors from being introduced into the system, and to detect any such errors at the earliest possible time. The resulting software will

---

*The word "evolution" is used rather than "maintenance" throughout this document to refer to the three activities of repair, adaptation, and enhancement that may occur after initial development. The term "evolution" is intended to better describe the actual situation without the traditionally negative connotation of "maintenance."

be of higher quality and will be more likely to fulfill the needs of its users.

The unifying notion is that of a *coherent methodology*, a system of technical methods and management procedures that covers the entire development activity. A methodology can be supported by automated tools; the collection of available tools provides a "programming support environment," which can, among other things, aid developer communication and productivity. Within a methodology, it is important to be able to review the progress of the work at various intermediate checkpoints. In this manner, it becomes possible to identify problems in projects at earlier stages and to take corrective action.

An important concept in discussing methodologies is the "life cycle", a model of the activities that comprise the software development and evolution of a system. There are numerous life cycle models in use, with still others described in the literature. Each of these models forms a framework for describing the steps of system development and the products that are produced at each step. Rather than adhere to a *single* existing model, this document follows a model that is *representative* of many (but not all) of the models, so that one can easily relate it to others.

The specific phases and names vary from one model to another, but typically include analysis, functional specification, design, implementation, validation, and evolution, defined as follows:

Analysis - a step concerned with understanding the problem and describing the activities, data, information flow, relationships and constraints of the problem; the typical result is a requirements definition;

Functional specification - the process of going from the statement of the requirements to a description of the functions to be performed by the system to process the required data; functional specification involves the *external* design of the software;

Design - the process of devising the *internal* structure of the software to provide the functions specified in the previous stage, resulting in a description of the system structure, the architecture of the system components, the algorithms to be used, and the logical data structures;

Implementation - the production of executable code that realizes the design specified in the previous stage;

Validation - the process of assuring that *each* phase of the development process is of acceptable quality and is an accurate transformation from the previous phase +;

Evolution - the ongoing modifications (repair, adaptation to new conditions, enhancement with new functions) to a system caused by new requirements and/or the discovery of errors in the current version of a system.

This sequence of phases separates analysis and functional specification activities, based on the observation that the product of analysis is a functional specification, but that the functional specification may only address a portion of the problem that has been analyzed. (Note that "specification" is used both as a verb to denote a process and as a noun to denote a work product.)

Throughout development and evolution, there are aspects of management and communication, including documentation, validation, budgeting, personnel deployment, project review, scheduling. and configuration management, that serve to tie the stages together and provide the organizational environment in which the technical procedures can be made effective.

+ Note that validation is not simply a single phase, but rather a step performed as part of each phase. Thus, validation of design is the process of determining that the design is a valid transformation from the functional specification.

The combination of technical procedures with management techniques should create a synergistic effect in which the resulting process provides significantly greater improvement in the production of software than would be provided by either the technical or the management elements alone.

In short, one cannot choose a tool, a management practice, or any other element of the total environment without considering that element in its relation to the other parts of the development system. This concept is illustrated by Figure 1.

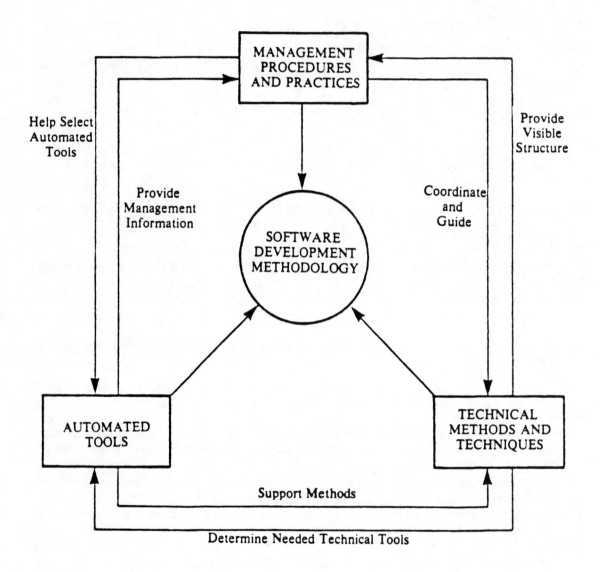

Figure 1   SOFTWARE DEVELOPMENT METHODOLOGY

It is essential that management and technical elements be synergistic. It can be seen from Figure 1 that management methods provide guidance in the use of technical methods, while the technical methods serve to provide the intermediate results that make management possible. The importance of this concept in the context of a methodology is that one cannot look at technical or management elements alone, but rather must look at their combination. Before proceeding with the requirements for a methodology to support Ada, it is useful to describe the roles of various development phases in somewhat greater detail.

2.1 Analysis

Analysis of the problem at hand is the essential first step of any software development activity. Without such analysis, it is impossible to proceed; furthermore, an inadequate job of analysis is virtually certain to lead to project failure, since poor understanding of the problem makes it impossible to produce a good specification.

Successful analysis involves communication with users and customers for the system, who can describe their needs. Analysis also involves communication with the eventual developers of the system, who must be able to evaluate implementation feasibility and to describe any design or implementation constraints.

Because of the complexity of systems, key tools for analysis must support problem decomposition, through any of a variety of schemes, including: procedural decomposition, data abstraction, data flow, processing sequence, or transaction modeling. Graphical notations are especially helpful in showing the interrelationships of system components to one another and in facilitating the communication process.

A particularly effective method for analysis is *modeling*, representing the problem and/or the real world situation in a formal (mathematical or graphical) notation. The evolving model can be used as the basis for communication and for understanding the tasks that will comprise the system. In some instances, an *executable* model, or a prototype of some part of the system, may be built to assist in the analysis process. In others, properties of the model may be exploited to learn more about the subject (for example, whether certain activities may occur in parallel).

2.2 Functional Specification

A functional specification is a description of "what" the system will do. Whereas analysis serves to describe the problem and to identify requirements, the functional specification is the first statement of the system's intended behavior. Thus, it contains a statement of the system functions, the external interfaces, the required data items, and requirements upon performance, design, and implementation.

Functional specifications have many different roles within the software life cycle, including the following:

- The functional specification is a means for precisely stating the software system requirements. At this stage, the technical realization of the system model is documented in as much detail as possible. The functional specification can be compared against the requirements definition to ascertain the correspondence between the specification and the needs.

- The functional specification provides insight into the problem structure and is used during the design phase as a checkpoint against which to validate the design. Typically, there will be an iteration between specification and design, as insight into some of the system construction problems help to clarify the functional specification.

- The functional specification is the basis against which validation is performed. Clearly, one cannot validate a program in the absence of an unambiguous functional specification. Such a functional specification is essential whether validation is carried out through acceptance testing or through formal proof of program correctness.

- Modifications and enhancements to a system throughout its operational lifetime require an understanding of the system functions, as documented in the functional specification.

During evolution, the functional specification can help to locate those system functions that must be changed, and can then be revised accordingly.

The implication of this multifaceted role is that a functional specification must be able to serve (to some degree) each of these four different functions. In practice, this means that functional specifications must have both a formal and an informal component.

Throughout the remainder of this paper, the term "specification" refers to a functional specification. This usage should be distinguished from a more general usage in which each stage is a "specification" of what is to be done in the subsequent stage. In that usage, a detailed description of the logic of a sorting algorithm would be considered as a specification for Ada code to be written. Thus, this document refers to "the design" where others might use the term "the design specification."

2.3 Design

The process of software design permits the developer to determine more precisely the feasibility of implementing the functional specification, to analyze alternative system structures, to develop algorithms for the solution of the problem, and to define detailed constraints upon the implementation. In summary, it is a stage at which the primary concern is with the internal structures from which the software will be built.

The internal design activity can be separated into two phases: architectural design and detailed design. (In very large systems, one can separate design into more than two phases.) Architectural design is concerned with recognition of the overall software structure and the interconnection of program pieces, while detailed design is more concerned with the selection of algorithms and data structures that are appropriate to the fulfillment of specific system functions.

One of the key goals of the design process is to simplify the subsequent stages of coding and testing. At the end of the design phase, virtually all of the key decisions concerning program organization, logical data structures, and processing algorithms will have been made, with the intent of making code production into a straightforward transformation of the design into an executable representation.

The output of the design activity is a *software blueprint* that can be used by the Ada programmer(s) to implement the system without having to refer back to the functional specification and without having to make unwarranted assumptions about the requirements.

2.4 Implementation

Implementation of systems, in this instance, involves the production of executable Ada code. The code should reflect the structure of the design and perform the function(s) specified for the system. The code should adhere to the precepts of structured programming, with emphasis on comprehensibility of code. It is important to note that coding is only a small portion of the overall software development activity; good coding cannot make up for poor analysis or design.

In general, the comprehensibility of programs written in a high-level language can be achieved through uniformity of programming style, use of mnemonic names for procedures and data, judicious inclusion of comments, and avoidance of unrestricted control flow. Comprehensibility of Ada programs is further enhanced by use of the information hiding properties of modules (*package*), minimization of interaction between tasks and exceptions, minimization of the different choices for *digits* and for *delta* in a single program, and careful use and documentation of tasking statements such as guarded *select, delay* and *terminate*.

2.5 Validation and Verification

Validation is the process of determining that a system correctly performs those functions described in the functional specification. Verification is a process to ensure that each phase of the development process correctly carries out the intent of the previous step. One must verify the code against the system design, which in turn has been verified against the functional specification for the system. Together, they provide assurance of system quality.

Validation of programs (code) may be done through either testing or formal proof of correctness. Although there has been much work on mathematical proofs of program correctness, most code is verified and validated through testing, which may be described as a series of controlled experiments to provide empirical evidence that a program behaves properly (and provides the desired results for broad classes of anticipated inputs).

Testing is normally done in three stages: module testing, integration testing, and acceptance testing. In module testing, individual program units are tested for correctness. In integration testing, two or more modules are joined and tested together, to see if they work properly together and to make certain that the interfaces mesh. Finally, acceptance testing determines whether the system conforms to its functional specification.

In general, errors found in module and integration testing reflect errors made during design or implementation, while errors found during acceptance testing reflect specification errors -- incomplete, inconsistent, incorrect, or ambiguous statements of what the system was to do. The most serious aspect of this situation is that the errors that were made first are detected last! An error in the requirements definition may not be caught until the entire system has been constructed and tested; such an error may require massive changes in the system design and implementation. It is for this reason that analysis and design errors are the most expensive kind of errors, and that efforts such as formal reviews of design and code have a significant payoff in terms of development costs.

2.6 Management Procedures

As noted earlier, a software development methodology is actually a blend between a collection of technical procedures and a set of management techniques that can result in effective deployment of project personnel, predictability of project schedule, budget, and outcome, accurate estimation of software properties, and the final result of a high-quality system that meets the needs of its users throughout the lifetime of the system.

Management of software development involves both management of people and management of the software product. The former involves issues of supervision of individual and project progress, and selection of appropriate team organizations and individual assignments. The latter focuses on deciding when a system is ready to be released and controlling the means by which it (and its subsequent versions) are released and modified. Furthermore, the management activity includes selection and revision of the technical procedures that are to be used by the systems organization.

The discipline provided by software development techniques leads to an environment in which management becomes possible, primarily because these techniques require the creation of intermediate products, e.g., specifications and designs, that can be reviewed and used to measure progress. Discipline refers to the adherence to a systematic procedure for the process of software production, a procedure that can be followed and repeated for a large class of software projects.

3. REQUIREMENTS FOR A SOFTWARE DEVELOPMENT METHODOLOGY

The goal of a software development activity is the effective creation of a set of work products, comprising an operational system and its supporting documents. For every software system, there are desirable qualities, such as reliability, correctness, evolvability, and efficiency, just to name several of the most common. A software development methodology should assure, to the greatest extent possible, that these system qualities are achieved. Furthermore, the methodology should make it possible to decide among different system qualities, rather than restricting the choice.

Many approaches have been proposed and used for creating systems. There is every indication that these approaches will be refined and that new approaches will be introduced in the future. Furthermore, it seems clear that many of these approaches can be successfully used to develop systems implemented in Ada. Our notion of a methodology is that of a *system* of methods and tools, carefully chosen and integrated to support both the development and evolution processes.

The purpose of this section, then, is to establish a framework for development methodologies through a set of requirements for a methodology. The list of requirements is given first, and each requirement is then discussed at greater length.

A methodology should:

1. cover the *entire* development process, simplifying transitions between project phases;

2. enhance communication among all interested persons at all stages of development;

3. support problem analysis and understanding;

4. support both top-down and bottom-up approaches to software development;

5. support software validation and verification through the development process;

6. facilitate the capture of design, implementation, and performance constraints in the system requirements;

7. support the software development organization;

8. support the evolution of a system throughout its existence;

9. be supported by automated aids;

10. make the evolving software product visible and controllable at all stages of development;

11. be teachable and transferable;

12. be open-ended.

3.1. ENTIRE DEVELOPMENT PROCESS

A methodology should cover the *entire* development process. It does little good to have a methodology for software design if there is no systematic procedure to produce the functional specification used for the design and the Ada program(s) that must be created from the design. In other words, it should address all of the phases discussed in Section 2, from analysis through evolution.

The methodology should facilitate transitions between phases of the development cycle. When a developer is working on a particular phase of a project (other than requirements analysis), it is important to be able to refer to the previous phase and to trace one's work. At the design stage, for example, one must make certain that the architecture of the software system provides for all of the specified functions; one should be able to identify the software module(s) that fulfill each system function. During implementation, it should be easy to establish a correspondence between modules in the system design and program units, and between the logical data objects from the design stage and the physical data objects in the program.

It is important to note that one must be able to proceed not only forward to the next phase of the life cycle, but also backward to a previous phase so that work can be checked and any necessary corrections can be made. This phased approach to software development makes it clear that information lost at a particular phase is generally lost forever, with an impact on the resulting system. For example, if an analyst fails to document a requirement, it will not appear in the functional specification. Eventually, during acceptance testing (or perhaps during system operation), that failure will be recognized and it will be necessary to make modifications to the system.

3.2 ENHANCE COMMUNICATION AMONG INTERESTED PARTIES

A methodology should enhance communication among all of the different persons involved in a software development project at all of the different stages of development. Among the paths of communication that should be supported are those among developers and users, developers and customers, developers and their managers, and among developers themselves.

Written documents serve to support this communication by providing a record of decisions and agreements. At times, such documents may be informal, simply recording a piece of information or an agreement. This approach is particularly useful when a document is intended for someone without specialized knowledge of software development. However, precise communication among technically knowledgeable individuals is enhanced by the use of formal notations, including graphical representations and specialized languages. Examples of such notations are data flow diagrams, HIPO diagrams, algebraic specification of data types, and Ada. The methodology should prescribe the forms of documentation and representation that will be used for this technical communication at all stages of the development process.

3.3 SUPPORT FOR PROBLEM ANALYSIS AND UNDERSTANDING

A methodology should support effective problem-solving techniques. It should encompass intellectual processes to support problem decomposition.

Modeling is a particularly important aspect of this objective. There exist techniques for activity and data modeling. Formal modeling techniques should be based upon a suitable set of primitives for the application domain. For embedded systems, concepts such as external interfaces and concurrent processes should be included. The resulting model should serve to answer questions about the problem domain and can be used to define the scope of interest for the system. Unless one has suitable tools for analysis of the problem, one cannot easily produce a functional specification or a satisfactory system.

Problem solving techniques are used to decompose the problem and to create the model. Techniques such as data abstraction, data flow diagrams, functional decomposition, transaction modeling, and state machines have been effectively used for this purpose in the past. The goal of this phase is to determine the structure of the problem -- the interrelation of the parts of the problem.

3.4 SUPPORT FOR TOP-DOWN AND BOTTOM-UP DEVELOPMENT

The methodology should support a variety of different approaches to system design and development. While systems are often modeled or analyzed using methods of top-down decomposition, there are typically low-level constraints, such as interface requirements, for which a bottom-up approach is necessary. Efforts to reuse software designs and/or code, including the use of packages, also leads to the use of bottom-up techniques to develop software. Finally, design constraints, such as performance requirements, necessitate the creation and testing of low-level aspects of a system before many of the high-level aspects have been developed.

Thus, the methodology must not constrain the development organization to follow either a pure bottom-up or a pure top-down approach to software development, but should allow any combination of the two in system design and implementation.

3.5 SUPPORT FOR VALIDATION AND VERIFICATION

The methodology must support determination of system correctness throughout the life cycle. System correctness encompasses many issues, including not only the correspondence between the results of one stage of development and the previous stage, but also the extent to which the system meets user needs. Accordingly, the methodology must not only be concerned with techniques for validation of the complete system, but also must give attention to obtaining the most complete and consistent verification of each work product throughout the development. For example, the methods used for analysis and specification of the system should make it possible to trace later system development back to the requirements and functional specification.

The methodology must prescribe a strategy for assurance of system quality. Test planning, document review, design and code walkthroughs and/or inspections should be integrated in the methodology, with emphasis given to early error detection and correction. A test plan should establish standards for test coverage, a means for measuring that coverage, and the acceptable quality criterion.

3.6 SUPPORT FOR CONSTRAINTS

A methodology should facilitate the inclusion of design, implementation, and performance constraints in the system requirements. Embedded systems to be constructed in Ada often have severe requirements on memory utilization, real time response, use of specific machine-dependent features, or integration with other hardware or software systems. Experience has shown that severe constraints have a major detrimental effect on system development.

It should be possible to state these requirements using the methodology. Furthermore, it should allow them to be incorporated into each subsequent stage and verified. This requirement may necessitate the use of analytical tools and/or construction of prototype systems.

3.7 SUPPORT FOR THE SOFTWARE DEVELOPMENT ORGANIZATION

The methodology must, above all, support the intellectual efforts of the designers and other technical people. Beyond this, it should support the software development organization that has been chosen for the project at hand. It must be possible to manage the developers and the developers must be able to work together. This requirement implies the need for effective communication among analysts, developers, and managers, with well-defined steps for making progress visible throughout the development activity. The intermediate products generated by the methods and tools, such as a detailed design or an acceptance test plan, can be reviewed by the organization so that progress can be effectively measured and so that quality can be assured.

The methodology must support the management of the project. It should include methods for cost estimation, project planning (scheduling), and staffing. It should also specify methods for ongoing review of project progress, such as design walkthroughs and code inspections. The management procedures should maintain a project handbook and library, showing project history, project plans, and the evolving software product(s). Finally, the management procedures should identify an evolving set of standards and conventions that can be applied to all projects.

3.8 SUPPORT FOR SYSTEM EVOLUTION

The methodology should support the eventual evolution of the system. Systems typically go through many versions during their lifetimes, which may last eight to ten years or more. New requirements arise from changes in technology, usage patterns, or user needs, and these changes or additional requirements must be reflected in a modified system. In many ways, the evolution activity is a microcosm of the development process itself. The development methodology can assist this evolutionary activity by providing accurate external and internal system documentation, and a well structured software system that is easily prototype and modified by those making the system changes.

3.9 AUTOMATED SUPPORT

Wherever possible, the methodology should be supported by automated tools that improve the productivity of both the individual developer and the development team. This collection of tools, and the way in which they are used, constitute a "programming support environment." (Note that the word programming is not used in the sense of "coding" here, but rather in a more general sense.) A partial set of recommended tools for such an environment are described in the "STONEMAN".

The tools should be integrated so that they may communicate via a common database and so that they can work effectively with one another. Furthermore, these tools should be linked to the methods so that the tools support the management methods and technical practices.

3.10 SOFTWARE CONFIGURATION

The methodology should maintain the visibility of the emerging and evolving software product and its supporting work products. All of these items should be placed in the database of the associated Ada Programming Support Environment.

The underlying notion is that of software configuration management. All of the components of a software development project must be identified, collected, and controlled in order to assure proper distribution of the finished system and its supporting work products, as well as to assist in evolution of the product and version control.

The methodology must be applicable to a large class of software projects. While it is clear that different methodologies will be needed for different classes of systems and for different organizational structures, an organization should be able to adopt a methodology that will be useful for a sizeable number of programs that they will build. Certainly, it makes little sense to develop a methodology for each new system to be built.

3.11 TEACHABILITY AND TRANSFERABILITY

The methodology must be teachable. Even within a single organization, there will be a sizeable number of people who must use the methodology. These people include not only those who are there when the methodology is first adopted, but also those who join the organization at a later time. Each of these people must understand specific techniques that comprise the technical aspects of the methodology, the organizational and managerial procedures that make it effective, automated tools that support the methodology,and the underlying motivations for the methodology.

Transferability of the methodology is greatly aided by teaching materials, including user documentation, organized courses, exercises, and examples.

3.12 OPEN-ENDED

A methodology should be open-ended. It should be possible to introduce new technical and managerial methods, as well as to create new tools, and thereby modify the methodology. Techniques and tools evolve through a process of "natural selection", whereby newer, more effective techniques and tools, supplement or replace existing ones.

4. RELATIONSHIP TO ADA PROGRAMMING SUPPORT ENVIRONMENT (APSE)

The "STONEMAN" Report defines three levels of programming support environment for Ada.

KAPSE - A Kernel APSE supporting basic functions of operating systems, database, and communication support. This Kernel can provide tool portability from one computer system to another.

MAPSE - A Minimal APSE providing a methodology-independent set of essential tools to support the Ada programmer. These tools include language editors, translators, configuration management, loading, linking, and static and dynamic analysis tools.

APSE - fuller support for development of Ada programs, including tools for requirements, specification, design and management. An APSE offers a coordinated and complete set of tools which is applicable at all stages of the system life cycle.

It is the full APSE that provides the linkage to specific methodologies for system development. The APSE exists to support the methodology (not the other way around), since the toolset should be a means to an end and not an end in itself.

Specifically, STONEMAN describes a database as the central feature of an APSE system. (It should be noted that this usage of "database" differs from its more traditional data-processing usage.) The database acts as the repository for all information associated with each project throughout the project life cycle.

The automated tools of the methodology (see 3.8) comprise the APSE. They are used to create, modify, analyze, transform, and display objects in the database. The workproducts produced by the methodology are included in the database for a project.

Thus, the APSE and the methodology have a symmetric relationship. The methodology defines the tools at the APSE level (building upon the MAPSE), while the APSE provides the central repository needed to support teamwork and quality control in the methodology.

The methodology and the tools, in turn, are part of a more general software development environment, as shown in Figure 2. This broader notion of environment includes the software developers, the organization to which they belong, and the physical workspace in which software development takes place.

There are many influences within the workplace that affect the productivity of software developers, including access to computers, privacy and noise levels in working areas, ergonomic considerations of terminals, and availability of reference materials, including books and journals. There is little doubt that such factors can have significant bearing on the productivity of developers, regardless of methodology and tools, and further study must be done on identification and measurement of the most significant factors so that every possible step is taken to enhance the ability of software development organizations to produce the best possible systems in the minimum interval of time.

5. METHODOLOGY EVALUATION

In a strict sense, *every* software development organization already has a methodology for building software systems. While some software is developed according to modern practices of software development, most of it is built in an *ad hoc* way. Accordingly, it is best to view the discussion of software development methodologies from the perspective of *changing* current practices, replacing them with new techniques that improve the process of software development and the quality of the resulting products.

The process of change requires an understanding of the strengths and weaknesses of the existing methodology, as well as an evaluation of the strengths and weaknesses of new methods, techniques, and tools. While the general requirements for methodologies presented in Section 3 provide a framework for modification and evaluation of methodologies, more specific criteria for evaluation can also be identified. Unfortunately, few of these criteria are quantifiable. Furthermore, differences in organizational structures, software development practices, and system characteristics make it difficult to assign relative weights to the criteria. (Individual organizations, considering their own specific needs, may be able to do so, however.)

The criteria are divided into four major categories: technical, usage, management, and economic. Some of the allocations to categories is arbitrary. The ordering within categories has no significance.

5.1 Technical Characteristics

By technical characteristics we mean features that pertain to the support of various technical concepts by the method.

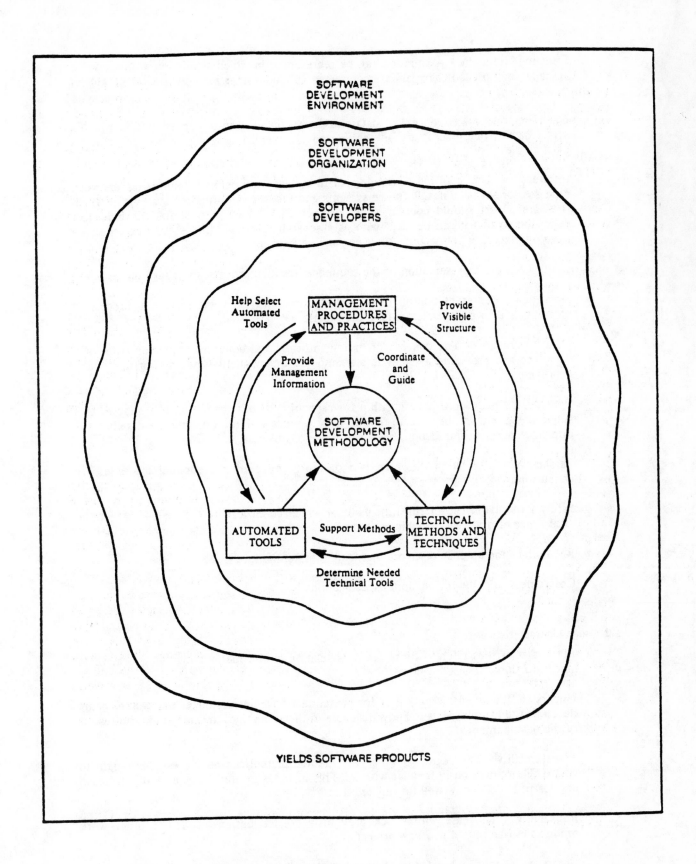

Figure 2 -- Software Development Environment

Function Hierarchy - A situation can be represented in which a function at one level is actually composed of several interconnected functions that exist at a level of greater detail.

Data Hierarchy - The concept of data classes; a situation can be represented in which a set of data at one level is actually composed of several interrelated pieces of data that exist at a level of greater detail.

Interfaces - The concept of having distinct and well-defined boundaries between processes or sets of data. Software systems and the large information systems of which they are a part should contain many distinct parts. Each part should have a clear definition so that it can be dealt with as a separable unit. If this is the case, then we have interfaces, or connections, between the various parts.

Control Flow - Representation of the sequence in which processes will take place.

Data Flow - Representation of the flow of information types between various processing elements and/or storage elements in the system.

Data Abstraction - The concept of hiding information about the implementation of a data type and providing a set of implementation-independent functions for use of the data type.

Procedural Abstraction - an algorithm for carrying out some operation is abstracted to a single name that can be used to invoke to procedure without knowing the details of its implementation. (Transactions are an instance of this case.)

Parallelism - a situation in which two or more cooperating sequential processes are concurrently in execution.

Safety - the avoidance of run-time failures which could lead to the loss of life or the occurrence of other catastrophic consequences.

Reliability - the absence of errors that lead to system failure.

Correctness - fidelity to functional specifications.

5.2 Usage Characteristics

Usage characteristics refer to those features relating to the methodology's application to development situations. These include:

Understandability - How easy it is for someone who is interested in the system being developed, but not especially knowledgeable in the technique, to understand the results of the development.

Transferability - The degree to which the method or tool can be successfully taught to personnel not previously familiar with it. This includes not only how easy it is to teach and learn, but also how well formulated it is.

Reusability - The ease with which previously created designs, code, or other work products can be reused in a new project.

Computer Support - Existence of automated tools which can be easily obtained and which aid in the use of the methodology or some of its steps.

Life-Cycle Range - The span of phases in the development life-cycle over which the tools or method can be usefully applied. This must by necessity be an approximate measure.

Task Range - The span of tasks to which the item may be usefully applied. Traditional classifications of software applications (business, scientific, systems, etc.) are not very useful for this evaluation. There are scientific and business problems that share the same problems while there are other tasks that say, within the business category, are quite dissimilar.

Cohesiveness - The extent to which the technical methods, management procedures, and automated tools may be combined to support the methodology.

Extent of Usage - A judgment as to how widespread the current usage of the methodology is.

Ease of phase transition - The extent to which information developed at one phase of development supports work to be done at a subsequent phase (e.g. from analysis to design).

Decision highlighting -- the ability of a technique to make visible and highlight key technical or project decisions (e.g. choice of data structures, nearness to completion of a project); the ability of a technique to illuminate the consequences of a development decision.

Validation - the extent to which the methodology assists in the determination of system correctness

Repeatability - the extent to which similar results are obtained when the methodology (or an included aspect) is applied more than once to the same problem.

Ease of change to work products - the amount of effort required to modify a work product when some aspect of requirements, specification, or design is changed.

5.3 Management Characteristics

These are the factors that relate to the ability of an aspect of the methodology to enhance the management of software development activities.

Manageability - The degree to which the method or tool permits standard management techniques of estimation, in-process status checking and control to be applied. The evaluations are based on the existence of well-defined steps and intermediate products which make management possible and the existence of management techniques applying specifically to the method at hand.

Teamwork - the extent to which the methodology and the development environment aid, rather than hinder, teamwork.

Phase Definitions - the identification within the methodology of development phases that represent intermediate stages of the development process.

Work products - the documents and systems that result from application of the methodology.

Configuration management - the way in which the methodology and/or its tools provides for organization, tracking, and maintenance of the emerging work products, including control of releases and multiple versions.

Exit criteria - the way in which phases of development and work products are defined to provide explicit stopping or exit criteria for each stage of development.

Scheduling - the methodological support for project scheduling.

Cost estimation - the methodological support for cost estimation.

5.4 Economic Characteristics

Use of a software development methodology should also produce tangible economic benefits in software quality and the productivity of the software development organization, so that one should also consider the following aspects:

Local benefits (with respect to phase) - Compared to informal/traditional ways of carrying out the processes of a given phase, how much improvement can be expected through the use of a given tool or method?

Life cycle benefits - the benefit of a method relative to a particular stage, adjusted for the relative importance of that stage in the overall life cycle.

Cost of acquisition - the cost of obtaining training, tools, rights, etc. to use the methodology or some associated tool or technique.

Cost of use - the operational cost (computer time, forms, etc.) of using the methodology or some associated aspect.

Cost of management - the cost of managing the methodology or some associated technique.

6. CONCLUSION

The purpose of this document is to present the rationale for software development methodologies and to establish a framework for the description and creation of such methodologies in conjunction with embedded systems and Ada Programming Support Environments. To a lesser extent, we have tried to identify areas where additional research and development are needed before full methodological support becomes available.

There are many ways in which systems can be constructed and many tools that can be used. There are many existing methodologies and many more are likely to emerge based on different concepts of problem solving, approaches to system structuring, and organizational structures. The emergence of several widely used methods for analysis, specification, and design, combined with compatible APSE's, should lead to a small set of technical approaches to the specification, design, development, and validation of Ada programs, yielding standardized forms of work products.

Although the management aspects will differ among organizations, the narrowing of alternatives for technical methods and tools can contribute to enhanced maintainability of embedded systems. Subsequent work can recommend and/or develop technical methods that satisfy the framework described in this document. Such work can then aid in identifying tools that can be built in support of methodologically-oriented APSE's. The eventual integration of management procedures with suitable APSE's and Ada Methodologies can thereby further the goals set out when the Ada program was first undertaken.

The Software Development System

CARL G. DAVIS AND CHARLES R. VICK

Abstract—This paper contains a discussion of the Software
Development System (SDS), a methodology addressing the problems
involved in the development of software for ballistic missile defense
systems. These are large real-time, automated systems with a requirement for high reliability. The SDS is a broad approach attacking problems arising in requirements generation, software design, coding, and
testing. The approach is highly requirements oriented and has resulted
in the formulation of structuring concepts, a requirements statement
language, process design language, and support software to be used
throughout the development cycle. This methodology represents a
significant advance in software technology for the development of
software for a class of systems such as BMD. The support software
has been implemented and is undergoing evaluation.

Index Terms—Requirements, software design, software development,
software engineering, specifications, validation, verification.

Manuscript received July 22, 1976; revised September 14, 1976.
The authors are with the U.S. Army Ballistic Missile Defense Advanced Technology Center, Huntsville, AL 35807.

I. INTRODUCTION

THE development of highly reliable software for large
real-time weapons systems on schedule and minimizing
life cycle costs has been recognized as one of the most significant problems confronting the defense community today
[1], [2]. One of these weapons systems having many complexities, unique features, and highly stressing characteristics
is a Ballistic Missile Defense (BMD) system.

BMD systems must be able to detect and defend against
threatening objects, e.g., missile warheads, reentering the
atmosphere at several thousand meters per second with a
reentry phase of only several seconds. The BMD mission is
of strategic importance with the cost of failure being the
potential loss of offensive capability or large loss of life. BMD
systems include large, powerful phased array sensors that must
detect reentering objects and provide information for identification, classification, and guidance of the highly maneuverable

missiles designed to intercept the threat. The systems also contain data processing subsystems which are tightly coupled to the rest of the system, controlling and managing the available resources (radar, missile, and data processing), and making decisions to maximize the probability of a successful defense. The battle must also be capable of being conducted in a nuclear environment, with a high assurance of success.

Operationally, BMD systems possess the following characteristics.

1) They must be highly reliable. High system reliability is translated into data processing hardware and software reliability requirements which will ensure the correct execution of the tens of millions of instructions per second required for response.

2) They cannot be realistically tested except in an operational environment. This imposes the need for an extensive engagement simulation and test program to generate the simulated data and environment required to validate the performance of the system.

3) They are automated due to the short (several seconds) length of an engagement. The engagement consists of rapid sequences of millisecond processing responses to the data generated by sensors. Failures or undesirable system responses cannot be manually modified.

4) They are large and complex. The data processing subsystem must process data received from many incoming objects, allocate resources, control the engagement, and perform command and control functions inherent in a BMD system. Large data bases are created which must be rapidly accessed by complex decision algorithms.

5) They must be extremely flexible in their response. Wide variations in threat characteristics, reentry phenomenology, and nuclear environmental conditions are experienced by these systems.

The developmental problems involved in defining such a system are many and complex. The following are typical of the constraints and interactions which contribute to the complexities of developing such a system.

Environmental: The external environment in which a BMD system must operate is often imprecisely defined. This impreciseness comes about through 1) uncertainties in the definition of the threat against which the system must defend; 2) lack of information characterizing the environment as well as the system sensors perception of that environment; and 3) the effects of offensive and defensive tactics (e.g., blackout due to nuclear bursts) upon the engagement. This unavoidable vagueness in definition forces system performance to be specified over an extensive set of input conditions necessitating a requirement which, for a system of this size, is very difficult to verify.

Field Testing: As was previously mentioned, the inability to field test a BMD system in a tactical situation prior to its actual use forces a heavy reliance upon analysis and simulation as a final validation of system performance. This reliance upon simulation places extremely stressing requirements for successively verifying system performance at each level of description. Interactive system validation further creates developmental problems such as specification of simulation fidelity, achieving the desired simulation flexibility, instrumentation, validation

of test drivers, etc. While the specification and achievement of hardware reliability is reasonably well understood, the associated specification of software reliability remains an area of considerable research.

Solution Complexity: The complexities associated with automated weapons systems contribute significantly to the development problem. These include: the tuning required of the algorithmic solutions which must analyze and base system actions upon the large amounts of data generated; the identification, specification, and implementation of the contingencies (error recovery) involved in system operation; and the time critical aspects which stress computing system capability. The development of a system with this complexity requires the capability to successively structure the system in increasing levels of detail, allowing the system definition to be effectively analyzed and tradeoffs made at each level before proceeding to more detailed descriptions.

Size: The magnitude of the BMD problem translates into large developmental organizations which in turn stress the ability to manage and control such a development. The many solution paths to the problem force any developmental approach to provide for rapid assessment of design decisions, early error detection, and the flexibility to rapidly respond to changes. Problem size and complexity also both contribute to the inability to accurately estimate the computer software size and hence the data processing hardware size, configuration, etc.

Developmental Time: Systems the size of BMD are developed in a rapidly changing environment. The system must react to an ever increasing threat complexity and rapidly improving technology. This forces the requirement for a developmental approach which will ensure rapid deployment but have the flexibility to quickly react to external changes. Lastly, the problems of management visibility and control also plague BMD software development through the lack of well-defined approaches with visible progress measures.

Research and development on the first ballistic missile defense system began in 1957 with the Nike-Zeus system [3]. Special-purpose digital computers were employed with a Nike-Zeus missile making the first intercept of a TITAN ICBM in 1962. The follow-on Nike-X saw the development of another special-purpose digital computer to handle estimated peak loadings of 10 million instructions per second. This special-purpose machine was incorporated into the Sentinel System which preceded the finally deployed SAFEGUARD System. The data processing system design was dominated by the requirements for high throughput and availability/ reliability constraints. The SAFEGUARD System software components consisted of 735 000 real-time software instructions, 580 000 support software instructions, and 830 000 installation and maintenance instructions. These programs identified many needs for BMD weapons systems development such as, the need for a higher order language, the requirements for modular design techniques, the essentiality of providing a clear definition of computing requirements, and the need to design data recording and reduction systems early in the developmental cycle. Design reviews also proved to be an effective means for communicating problems and solutions.

The System Technology Program [4], a successor to SAFE-

GUARD, has gone through a similar progression of studies from initial MDS I and II studies to the Site Defense Program, evolving from a prototype demonstration into a broad system technology program. This program has employed many advanced tools and techniques such as process construction languages, automated test tools, structured programming, automated traceability aids, etc., and successfully applied them to the development of prototype system constructs. With the use of such tools and techniques and more governmental emphasis upon design-to-cost, high reliability, and improved management visibility and control, much additional insight into software development problems was derived. One of the more significant needs identified was the requirement for improved techniques for the generation and transmission of requirements from the early stages of system design through the final stages of software development. The advantages of developmental baselines, structured software development, verification by simulation, and tight control of quality of code through standards and formal procedures were also clearly demonstrated.

The large amount of money and research successfully spent in the SAFEGUARD and System Technology Programs provided evidence that the ability to produce large complex real-time BMD systems was not keeping pace with the increasing complexity and capacity demanded of advanced defense concepts. In recognition of this problem, the ballistic missile defense research community initiated a software research program in the early 1970's to address the issues which had arisen in BMD software development. It became apparent early in this program that any attack upon a problem of this complexity must be of broad scope and yet provide a degree of formalism not currently available nor required for less stressing developments. This resulted in the Software Development System (SDS), which is a software development approach that forces early error detection, allows rapid assessment of design decisions, ensures the capability to respond rapidly to change, and provides visibility and control of the development process. The program has concentrated upon developing a set of defined and measurable procedures supported by special-purpose languages and advanced tools. This methodology has been developed, implemented, and is currently undergoing evaluation. It consists of a defined approach to requirements engineering, software design, coding and testing, and verification and validation. Component parts of the methodology have been used with favorable results. The integrated effect of the overall approach is currently under investigation through a series of proof-of-principle experiments.

The SDS methodology [5] description in this paper will consist of a discussion of overall requirements in terms of the software development cycle followed by detailed descriptions of the solutions used in each phase of software development.

The early aspects of the development cycle concerned with requirements engineering are discussed in Section V, Software Requirements Engineering Methodology (SREM) [6]. This description will include a discussion of the Requirements Statement Language, RSL [7], support software, and other unique features. Three additional approaches toward the generation and unambiguous communication of correct system level requirements upon the data processing subsystem are

then discussed. These approaches include system structuring techniques based upon a Finite State Machine description [8], Petri Net and formal Logic Analysis [9], and formalized graph theory analyses of specifications [10].

The approach to the succeeding activities of software design, coding, and testing are described in Section VII, Process Design Engineering. This approach is described in terms of the Process Design Methodology (PDM) [11], the unique features and characteristics of the Process Design Language PDL2 [12], and automated tools of the Process Design System (PDS). Verification and validation activities in the development cycle are discussed in light of a promising approach toward the adaptive testing of large real-time weapons systems [13], as well as approaches toward a development of a laboratory for development and evaluation of BMD software quality [14].

II. METHODOLOGY REQUIREMENTS

The results from previously mentioned BMD developments and other large-scale weapons systems experience resulted in the identification in the early 1970's of the following set of characteristics which a software development approach for BMD must have. Subsequently, reports by the Applied Physics Laboratory [15] and MITRE [16] have indicated similar sets of problems throughout the Department of Defense and have made similar recommendations. Most recently high level DoD emphasis is being provided by the DoD 5000 series of regulations. The required characteristics include the following.

1) *Data Processing Description Capability:* The system must allow for inclusion of data processing limitations early in the development cycle. This must include the means for assessment of data processing induced system limitations (e.g., processing delays and inaccuracies), as well as the ability to provide accurate estimation of data processing hardware requirements, and support tradeoffs between alternative approaches.

2) *Requirements Orientation:* Requirements approaches must be developed which ensure means for stating the required processing without the inclusion of unwarranted design detail; ensure unambiguous communication of intent; provide a means to validate requirements; ensure their feasibility; and be responsive to the invariable change.

3) *Design:* The software design process must provide a means for early error detection, rapid modification, and designed-in reliability. The approach must ensure the production of a highly reliable modular product which will minimize the life cycle costs.

4) *Automation:* The system must possess as much automation as possible in every phase of software development. The aids should be such that they provide maximum utilization of the thoroughness of the computer to eliminate many sources of human error.

5) *Management:* The system must consist of well-defined phases containing intermediate milestones which provide for measurement and evaluation of progress. Techniques must be devised which allow *a priori* costing and scheduling based upon a defined, structured approach to development.

6) *Testing:* The system must provide means for the allocation of performance to the data processing subsystem, the

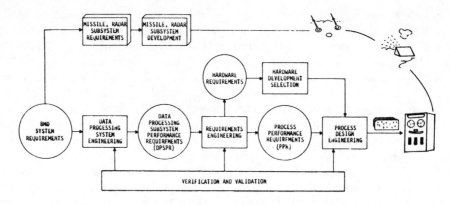

Fig. 1. Software development cycle.

refinement of that allocation and improved means for the testing, verification, and validation of that performance as an integral part of the development cycle.

7) Structured Decomposition and Development: There must be a technology which forces the problem to be stated and structured at a high level, analyzed at that level, and then allows the developer to proceed with the addition of detail in an orderly, defined, and measurable fashion. This must proceed from early system definition through code delivery in a traceable and flexible manner. This technology must assure maximum designed-in reliability in the development cycle.

These characteristics of SDS and its relation to these needs will be discussed in the following sections.

III. THE DEVELOPMENT CYCLE

The phases of the software development cycle which provide a framework within which the research activities have been pursued are shown in Fig. 1. This cycle differs somewhat from the normal development cycle description, reflecting views taken in the implemented approaches. The initial activity, Data Processing System Engineering, is concerned with the development and transformation of a set of system requirements into functional and performance requirements upon the data processing subsystem which will ensure proper system performance. Included are the activities of system design, subsystem definition, interface specification, performance allocation to the data processing subsystem, and identification of normal and contingency system operating rules. This activity would proceed until the data processing subsystem has been identified by its functional and performance requirements and interface definitions. The resulting requirements (Data Processing Subsystem Performance Requirements– DPSPR's) are communicated to the data processing subsystem developers for further decomposition, design, implementation and testing.

Based upon the DPSPR, detailed subsystem requirements are developed for the data processing subsystem in a phase known as Requirements Engineering. In the Requirements Engineering phase the detailed subsystem computational requirements are ·developed in a Software Requirements Engineering (SRE) activity which also forms the basis for data processing hardware requirements. The SRE activity is a process of iterative addition of design detail with the emphasis

upon avoiding unnecessary constraints upon the following process design phase. This activity may include the demonstration of the feasibility of requirements through the development of nonreal-time simulation analysis aids. It should be noted that the term requirements used in this activity is the statement of requirements upon processing to meet system objectives, e.g., the timing, accuracy, and computational requirements for the tracking of a potential target, as opposed to the formal definition of detailed requirements for software modules. Design decisions required in developing computational and functional requirements are those affecting the functional and logical flow of requirements, e.g., a decision to specify whether radar pulses should be synchronously or asynchronously scheduled with respect to data processing inputs. The requirements are also developed with a minimum number of decisions affecting processor configuration, core size, etc., with the resulting Process Performance Requirements (PPR) minimizing any bias for a particular hardware configuration. Since we are dealing with a highly sensitive real-time system, the response time for various computational processes is very critical. The PPR contains performance requirements for each computational path within the process, including interface definitions, suggested candidate algorithms, etc., which are required to meet system performance.

The hardware requirement aspects of Requirements Engineering are concerned with the development of data processing hardware requirements which will ensure that the selected configuration will satisfy and meet system computational requirements of the system. Decisions to be made in this phase include specifications of the various hardware characteristics, such as size, number of processors, performance, etc.

The PPR functional and performance requirements are then analyzed together with the characteristics of the hardware system. This mapping of requirements with the hardware characteristics form the first step of Process Design Engineering. This results in a top level software design and a definition of operating system requirements. From this structure the design proceeds in a structured manner with implementation and testing of each level of definition.

At each step of the SDS methodology, a comprehensive testing procedure, Hierarchical Verification and Validation [17], is used to validate and verify the functional and/or

TABLE I
METHODOLOGY SURVEY

		TAG	ADS	ISDOS	SODA	LOGOS	HIPO	CSC THREADS	TOP DOWN	MODEL DRIVEN	CHIEF PROGRAMMER	SOP	ENGAGEMENT LOGIC	ARDI	AUTASIM
PRODUCT ORIENTATION	SYSTEM TYPE														
	SIMULATION	·	L			H	N	L	M	M	M			M	H
	REAL-TIME SOFTWARE	L		L			L		M	M	M		H	L	
	MANAGEMENT INFO	H	H	H			H	H	M	L	H				M
	BUSINESS APPLICATION	H	H	H	H		H	H	M	M	H	H		H	
	DATA REDUCTION	L	L				M	M	M	M	M			M	
	TELECOMMUNICATION	M	M	M			L	M	M	M	M			L	M
	SYSTEM SIZE														
	LARGE PROG. > 100K	L		M			L	L	M	H	M	L	H	L	
	MEDIUM 10 TO 100K	H	H	H	H	H	H	H	M	H	H	H	H	H	M
	SMALL < 10K	H	H	H	H	H	H	H	H	M		H	H	M	M
PRINCIPLE CONCEPTS															
	IMPROVE CAPABILITY FOR SYSTEM DESIGN	M	M	H	H	H	M	M	M	M	M	M	H		M
	SIMULATE SYSTEM DESIGN AUTOMATICALLY									H					
	AUTOMATE SIMULATOR CONSTRUCTION														H
	IMPROVE COMMUNICATION OF REQT'S	H	H				H			M		M	M		
	SYSTEMATIZE SYSTEM DESIGN		H							H			M	M	
	IMPROVE REQUIREMENTS ANALYSIS	M	H							M		H	M		
	INTRODUCE DISCIPLINE	M	M							H		M	M		
	PROVIDE MODULAR BUILDING BLOCK									H					H
	DESCRIBE INPUTS, PROCESSES, OUTPUTS	H	H	L			H	H				M			

performance characteristics of the software phase. Total system requirements and the specifications derived from them are used as the absolute reference to verify the design and implementation correctness at each level.

IV. REQUIREMENTS ENGINEERING LITERATURE REVIEW

Past work in the area of techniques explicitly addressing the development of requirements has been scarce, however, work which is applicable to requirements development has been extensive. Several high quality surveys by Teichroew [18], Couger [19], Burns et al. [20], and Reifer [21] provide reporting on these methods. Of particular interest is the survey by Burns et al. which provides a review and evaluation of system development methodologies, testing techniques, management techniques, and automated tools to determine whether a methodology existed that was applicable to the development of large-scale real-time software requirements. This survey resulted in three major conclusions.

1) There was no methodology defined in sufficient detail that tackles the problem of real-time software requirements and software development. Those methodologies that are applicable (even though partially) are not completely implemented. Scientific application was deemphasized and intensive real-time computational needs are generally unmentioned.

2) Systems generally had little emphasis on how to state requirements. Those examined were either a concise description of a methodology without any apparent implementation or of a specific implementation of some general ideas never formally stated.

3) Many automated tools were available but were not integrated into a usable system.

Among the systems included in the review were the Accurately Defined System (ADS) [22] by NCR, the Time Automated Grid System (TAG) [23] by IBM, the Hierarchy and Input Output Process System (HIPO) [24] by IBM, as well as the Information System Design and Optimization System (ISDOS) [25] developed at the University of Michigan, LOGOS [26] which had been under development at Case Western Research, AUTASIM [27] developed by General Research Corporation for the U. S. Army, the eclectic Model Driven approach [28] by TRW, and the Systems Optimization and Design Algorithm (SODA) [29]. Management approaches such as CSC Threads [30] and Chief Programmer Team [31] were also included, as well as an additional nineteen languages which were reviewed for their ability to support a requirements methodology. The survey included the state-of-the-art techniques having one or more features desirable in software requirements development.

Burns identified nine concepts which range from the ability to improve the capability for systems design to the capability to describe inputs, processes, and outputs. These were marked with an "H" if the item was highly appropriate, an "M" if it had some applicability without a specific orientation toward the category, an "L" if it had low applicability, and a blank if no capabilities were directly applicable to the category. Applications based on system size and type are also presented (see Table I).

A further comparison between the ISDOS technique surveyed by Burns, the Higher Order Software (HOS) techniques pursued by Hamilton and Zeldin [32], [33] at the C. S. Draper Laboratory, the Structured Analysis and Design Technique (SADT, a trademark of SofTech, Inc.) [34], [35] and the SREM approach is shown in Table II. The comparison is designed to highlight differences in philosophy and approach taken by each of the techniques.

Under the general attributes section of Table II, the term high is used to indicate the ability to provide automated aids for static or dynamic checking of the requirements description as well as the ability to provide computer-aided requirements documentation. The first entry in the methodology section is designed to provide the author's estimate of the degree to which there exists a formalism for proceeding from one level to the next more detailed level of description. A yes is indicative of techniques and procedures which guide this definition, a no indicates that it is felt that this is not addressed to any great degree. The documentation support category is a reflection of the ability of the methodology to support computer-aided generation of documentation. The SREM approach was felt to provide the most flexible approach for

TABLE II
REQUIREMENTS METHODOLOGY COMPARISON

		SREM	ISDOS	HOS	SADT
GENERAL ATTRIBUTES	APPLICATION WITHIN THE DEVELOPMENT CYCLE	SUBSYSTEM/SYSTEM REQUIREMENTS DEFINITION	SYSTEM DEFINITION	SYSTEM/SUBSYSTEM DEFINITION	SYSTEM/SUBSYSTEM DEFINITION
	PRIMARY APPLICATION EMPHASIS	TIME CRITICAL WEAPONS SYSTEMS, BMD	INFORMATION PROCESSING SYSTEMS	INTERFACE CRITICAL SYSTEMS, SPACE APPLICATIONS	MANAGEMENT INFORMATION SYSTEMS
	DEGREE OF AUTOMATION	HIGH	HIGH	PLANNED	MANUAL
	HIGHER ORDER LANGUAGE	RSL	PSL	AXES	ENGLISH
	REQUIREMENTS CAPTURED IN MACHINE PROCESSABLE FORM	YES	YES	PLANNED	NO*
	STATUS	IMPLEMENTED, UNDER EVALUATION	IMPLEMENTED, WIDE VARIETY OF USER EXPERIENCE	CONCEPTUALIZED, UNDER DEVELOPMENT	USED IN WIDE VARIETY OF PROJECTS
METHODOLOGY	DEFINED APPROACH FOR PROCEEDING FROM ONE LEVEL TO ANOTHER	YES	NO	NO	YES
	DOCUMENTATION SUPPORT	AUTOMATED, FLEXIBLE FORMAT	AUTOMATED, FIXED REPORTS	NOT ADDRESSED YET	MANUAL LIBRARIAN*
	MANAGEMENT ASPECTS ADDRESSED	DEFINED, MEASURABLE STEPS. LANGUAGE SUPPORTED.	LANGUAGE SUPPORTED	NOT ADDRESSED YET	DEFINED SET OF REVIEW PROCEDURES
	ANALYSIS AIDS				
	• CONSISTENCY AND COMPLETENESS CHECKING	AUTOMATED ANALYSIS	AUTOMATED REPORTS FOR ANALYSIS	NOT DEFINED YET	MANUAL*
	• SIMULATION SUPPORTED	YES	NO	NO	MANUAL
RQMTS. DESC.	FORMAL STRUCTURING MECHANISM	REQUIREMENTS NETWORKS (R-NETS)	TREES OR NETWORKS OF FUNCTIONS	PROCESS TREE	SADT STRUCTURED DIAGRAMS
	FUNCTIONAL REQUIREMENT FORM	LOGICAL FLOW DESCRIPTION	FUNCTIONAL INTERACTIONS	ABSTRACTIONS OF DATA AND CONTROL STRUCTURE	DATA AND ACTIVITY GRAPHS WITH TEXT
LANGUAGE CHARACTERISTICS	SUPPORTS DESCRIPTION OF				
	• STRUCTURE	YES	YES	YES	ENGLISH DESCRIPTIONS VIA SADT
	• DATA	YES	YES	YES	• DIAGRAMS
	• PERFORMANCE RQMTS.	YES	NO	NO	• TEXTS
	• SIMULATION MODELS	YES	NO	NO	• GLOSSARY
	• TRACEABILITY	YES	YES	YES	

*ISDOS SUPPORT FOR SADT PLANNED.

generation of documentation. The ability of the methodology to supply management information is summarized in the next category with ISDOS and SREM providing language support for the inclusion of management information and SADT providing a well-defined set of review procedures. The ability to analyze requirements statements is described under the analysis aids categories. SREM has considerably more emphasis and detailed capability for automated static and dynamic analysis.

The requirements description categorization is designed to describe the basic approach for describing requirements. The approaches vary widely from the SREM flow-oriented requirements-net which allows description of processing sequences; the input-processing-output functional sequences described in ISDOS; the abstractions of control structure and data required by the HOS approach; and the SADT data and activity graphs which reflect the flow of input and output data, control and processor information.

The language characteristics section is designed to provide a differentiation of the capabilities of the language in its ability to support each of five important categories. The main difference observed is the SREM language capability for the statement of performance requirements and simulation models. It should also be recognized that wide differences are reflected in the language capabilities for expression of structures, data, and traceability information due to the wide variation in requirements structuring approaches.

V. SOFTWARE REQUIREMENTS ENGINEERING METHODOLOGY

The requirements generation phase of software development is one of disconcerting complexity yet extreme importance. Requirements suffer from many ills; they are often designs rather than a statement of need, they are difficult to verify and hence are often incorrect, they conflict within themselves (inconsistencies), they are difficult to test, and when one desires to modify them it is difficult to locate and accurately modify all affected areas.

As a typical example, the errors analyzed in several large software projects by Bell and Thayer [36] indicated greater than 30 percent of the requirements errors were due to the incorrect requirements. Missing and incomplete requirements added an additional 20 percent of the requirements errors with inconsistent and incompatible requirements contributing an additional 10 percent. Unclear requirements, typos, and out-of-scope requirements provided other significant requirements error sources. Their work has shown a surprising correlation between diverse projects in the types and percentages of requirements errors which occur.

Any methodology which will provide the required improvement in the requirements generation phase must be able to 1) ensure the generation of correct requirements through preventing or minimizing error sources, 2) provide an assurance of rapid and accurate modification of requirements, and 3) must be a measurable and manageable process.

The software requirements area has until the last several years suffered from a lack of data. This was due to the fact that data about requirements errors was costly to obtain, was not viewed as having much more than historical value, and was felt to only be a source of embarrassment as a measure of inability to do things correctly. These problems are being overcome by a gradual awareness of the need for requirements data and the willingness to sponsor research into the types and categories of requirements errors. Studies by Bell and Thayer [36], Thayer [37], and LOGICON [38], for example, have provided a much needed quantification of the problems in developing requirements.

The approach to the development of SREM concentrated heavily upon definition of its requirements in the early development phases and then proceeded as a sequential set of proposed approaches backed by empirical verification. The resulting SREM consists of a combination of languages, tools, and procedures which will reduce or eliminate known error

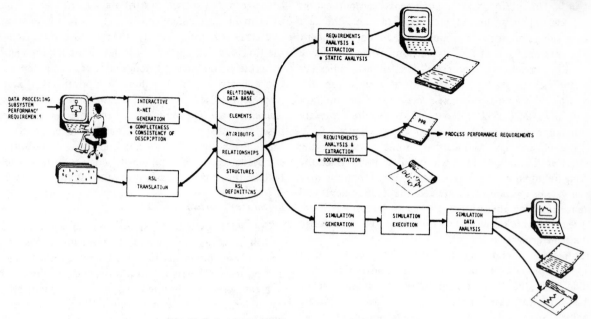

Fig. 2. Software Requirements Engineering Methodology.

sources. As an example, the generation of testable requirements in SREM is addressed in a positive fashion through the development of a structure for statement of requirements which allows the identification of 1) test points in the requirements, 2) the data to be collected at these points, and 3) an executable description of the tests to which the data will be subjected. The requirements statement now contains a clear description of the tests to which the software will be subjected to meet the requirements. Computer-aided simulation generation techniques are also an integral part of the methodology and provide the capability to validate, statically and dynamically, the requirements description. Other examples of positive approaches for error reduction are the techniques used to reduce errors, delays, and frustrations involved in documentation through the development of a set of automated documentation tools based upon the ability to flexibly access information stored in a requirements data base.

Improvements in the ability to produce modular requirements which can be easily and reliably modified is reflected in the need to adequately locate all references to a requirement (traceability) and the ability to modify the requirement without introducing any new errors. Positive approaches in SREM to ensure traceability of requirements are contained in features of the Requirements Statement Language (RSL) which have elements TRACES FROM, TRACES TO to ensure upward and downward traceability of requirements. In addition, the language element DECISION allows requirements affected by a design decision to be later traced to that decision. Flexible data extraction of requirements information stored in a relational data base provides a rapid and reliable means to ensure location of all affected requirements. Accurate modification of requirements is ensured through the ability to rapidly enter and retrieve requirements information, tools which will check for consistency with existing descriptions, and static and dynamic verification through simulation.

The previously mentioned necessity for a manageable and predictable requirements development has resulted in the development of a set of defined and measurable steps for requirements development with criteria for completion and measures of completeness for each step. In addition, interfaces between developing activities and information required to initiate and control activities have been identified.

An overview of the SREM approach is shown in Fig. 2. Requirements descriptions in RSL are entered interactively or in a batch mode and are checked for consistency with previously entered data and completeness of description, via automated analyzers. The requirements description is stored in a relational data base, which is accessed through a flexible retrieval system. Simulations may be built and executed to validate the stated requirements. Upon the completion of static and dynamic validation, the requirements are generated using automated aids. Early structuring and analysis provide for rapid feedback to the system designer.

A. Significant Features

Requirements have been stated in a myriad of forms (e.g., functional flows, engagement logic, control flow, data flow, etc.), with each having a particular advantage suited to the problem under description. Descriptions of data processing subsystem requirements in the SREM approach for BMD have taken an input-processing-output orientation with processing flow through the subsystem being described in terms of required paths through the subsystem. This approach was chosen to clearly specify the highly stringent performance requirements upon the data processing subsystem. Each required path of processing is identified by a message (stimulus), a set or sequence of processing steps (including required decision nodes with decision variables), and response (output message) with data which are local to processing on a path or which must be saved for processing upon a subsequent path being identified. The performance requirements are defined in terms of the timing, accuracies, etc., required across the data processing subsystem for each stimulus, and are not dependent upon the internal form of their expression. When processing order is not a requirement, potential parallelism is indicated.

This approach in stating requirements is a significant departure from the approaches taken in many of the military standards (e.g., MIL STD-490) in which requirements are stated in terms of functions and subfunctions. While a functional system description does have some advantage, the difficulties are such that: 1) it is difficult to easily trace the processing required by an input message; 2) functions may span subsystems and are so interrelated that requirements and acceptance tests for physical entities cannot be easily devised; and 3) requirements stated in this form tend to force a design with the same drawbacks.

Performance requirements in SREM are stated on each path or sequence of paths in terms of "validation points," i.e., identified points in the processing where data must be made available in the software for collection, and "tests" which are executable procedures which define the performance pass-fail criteria which will be imposed upon the software. This path-oriented approach has been tried manually on several projects and found to significantly highlight to the requirements developer the need for each path and the performance requirements the path must meet.

B. Requirements Statement Language (RSL)

Requirements have been stated in a wide variety of languages ranging from English text, equations, and logical expression to machine processable forms such as PSL. Large projects tend to have a predominance of English text with its associated ambiguities and misinterpretations. While some work and progress has been made in the area of machine recognition and analysis of English text, problems are for the most part manually resolved through review meetings, interface control boards, etc., in a lengthy and costly manner. To avoid ambiguity and promote precision and communication of BMD requirements, the Requirements Statement Language (RSL) was developed. RSL supports the statement and documentation of requirements, and along with the Requirements Engineering and Validation System provides a flexible means for statement, verification, and documentation of requirements. The language represents a compromise between the desire for naturalness of expression, unambiguous communication and machine processing. The language requires a minimum of punctuation and when passed through a post processor produces a product very difficult to distinguish from English except for the repetitive nature of the statements.

The concepts for defining requirements are embodied in four language primitives: elements, attributes, relationships, and structures. The elements are the set of objects and ideas used in the requirements description. DATA would be an example of a language element which would describe required elements of information. Relationship is the second language element which describes a binary relation between two elements. An example of such a relationship is INPUT as a description of data items to a processing step. The third

language primitive is the attribute. Attributes are modifiers of elements, e.g., the element DATA would have an attribute of INITIAL VALUE. Finally, the structure primitive is used as the flow-oriented approach for describing requirements. This structure is composed of nodes and processing steps. All RSL concepts are expressed in these four primitives. Extensibility is present in redefinition of relationships, addition of new elements, etc. The requirements are stored in a relational data base, the Abstract System Semantic Model (ASSM), which forms a repository for the requirements. Data in the ASSM are available to the requirements engineer interactively or by batch output via the capabilities of the support software.

C. Support Software

The BMD systems which are being described are so large that it is virtually impossible for humans to ensure that all parts of a requirements specification are complete, consistent, and correct. The rigor and thoroughness of the computer is a great asset in checking requirements specifications. A computer-aided system must enforce some measure of discipline on the creativity of the engineer so that the development process always moves in the direction of reduced ambiguity and increased consistency. For example, the computer can perform static checking of the requirements to illuminate inconsistencies such as conflicting names, improper sequences of processing steps, and conflicting uses of items of information which must be present in the system. With the flow orientation of SREM, information is available which allows the computer to check the dynamic consistency of the system through the use of simulation. The set of support tools is referred to as the Requirements Engineering and Validation System (REVS).

The REVS software includes an interactive graphics package to aid in the specification of flow paths, static consistency checkers which primarily check for consistency in the use of information throughout the system, and an automated simulation generation and execution package which aids in the study of dynamic interactions of the various requirements. In addition, REVS contains an extraction and reporting system which allows for flexible extraction of information from the ASSM as well as documentation software to produce reports and analyses. This system is independent of the extensions to RSL so that new concepts added to the language may be included in queries to the data base.

Also of prime interest and concern in the SREM is the use and development of requirements simulations. Simulation is claimed to be a rapid means of evaluating alternatives or providing a measure of the dynamic correctness of a system being simulated. In reality, for large complex systems, simulations are sometimes more complex than the product being simulated; they are difficult to modify and require significant patching or custom designing in order to operate properly. The time required to modify a simulation in order to evaluate the effects of a proposed change forces delay and additional costs, resulting in simulation providing an after-the-fact verification of an already implemented change. In addition, there is no assurance that the simulation accurately reflects the product being simulated, due to the fact that changes made to the simulator in order to improve its running often fail to be reflected in the requirements. Detailed requirements simulations have not been used extensively on large software development projects, but experience within the BMD Community has shown such a use does provide a significant reduction in errors which are passed on to the software design phase. Simulations supported by SREM may vary in detail from functional descriptions to detailed simulations with candidate algorithms undergoing an assessment as feasible candidates for later real-time optimization.

The approach in SREM was guided by the desire to ensure simulation could be effectively utilized as an "in-line" process for the validation of requirements. This was accomplished through providing a means of preventing the divergence of requirements simulators and the requirements being simulated, and automating an approach for simulation generation. The divergence problem is addressed by restricting the access to the simulator source code and by forcing the simulation generation software to operate only upon ASSM information. Modifications to the simulator may be accomplished only through modification of the ASSM which forces a requirements change.

Simulation construction must be an automated process, be easy to use, and provide rapid access to simulation results. The simulation construction module of REVS obtains the model of simulation structure from the structured definition of the requirements. Information for data files, etc., are obtained from the data hierarchy descriptions. Executable models of the processing steps are described as an integral part of the RSL requirements description. The simulation construction module now provides the simulation executive, initialization, interfacing with driver simulations, link editing, etc., required to complete the simulation generation process.

This approach has significantly reduced the potential sources of error in the use of simulation in the requirements development process. Questions concerning the efficiency of such a mechanical simulation generation approach are an open issue still under investigation. It is felt that potential inefficiencies in run time or core utilization are far outweighed by the benefits of on-line evaluation of requirements through simulation.

D. Methodology Procedures

An integral part of SREM is the development of the steps and procedures required in the generation of the subsystem computational requirements, the PPR. Each step has measurable criteria for its completion to support the scheduling, control, and visibility into the requirements development process. These are not an optimum set of procedures, nor will they ensure an "optimal" solution, but are designed to provide a structured differentiation of necessary activities. Various feedback paths, detailed tool definitions, and additional insight into the methodology steps are provided by Alford [6].

Fig. 3 provides a pictorial overview of the steps of the methodology, which consists of the four activities of translation, decomposition, allocation, and analytical feasibility demonstration.

1) *Translation:* This initial SREP activity develops the requirements baseline essential to subsequent developmental

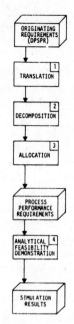

Fig. 3. Overview of SREM.

efforts. Activities in this effort include the establishment of traceability to the DPSPR and generation of the requirements structure with data descriptions and processing steps. This forms a structured review of the initiating specification and as such, through a feedback to the DPSPR developer, ensures a complete, consistent, and correct starting point.

2) *Decomposition:* This activity is concerned with the addition of design detail required for the generation of a complete set of computational requirements. Processing path requirements are constructed from information in the DPSPR. The step is completed when all the messages across the interface have been identified with a data processing subsystem response which has been analyzed for consistency of definition.

3) *Allocation:* In this step of the requirements development process, many of the tradeoffs and sensitivity analyses are performed in order to provide an allocation of performance to each of the processing paths. The simulation generation capabilities of REVS provide efficient means for dynamic validation of the performance allocation. The output of the step is a complete set of the computational requirements of the data processing subsystem which are generated via the data extraction features in the REVS system.

4) *Analytic Feasibility Demonstration:* This step is introduced to aid in reduction of the complexity of the subsequent process design phase. As was previously mentioned, the nonreal-time simulation of critical processing requirements provides a measure of their feasibility, and provides algorithms to the process designer which may be candidates for further optimization to meet timing requirements.

Finally, it should be noted that RSL and REVS are flexible systems, easy to modify. The extension features built into the system allow progressively more complex modification to the language including the ability to change the language definition and generate a new translator through an integral compiler writing system. Software support tools are isolated from the language changes via the ASSM. This type of flexibility is intended to keep the requirements engineering and validation system viable for a much longer period than would otherwise be possible.

The REVS system has been implemented on the Texas Instruments Advanced Scientific Computer at the BMDATC Advanced Research Center in Huntsville, AL. The REVS software consists of 35K lines of Pascal and Fortran code. With the overlay structure, REVS requires approximately 220K words to execute, including I/O buffers, stack and heap space.

VI. Data Processing System Engineering (DPSE)

The generation of initial system level requirements upon the subsequent performance of the data processing subsystem provides the keystone of the development process. Unless the subsystem is accurately defined functionally and performance wise, the subsequent subsystem requirements development, design, coding, and testing will not have a solid and consistent developmental basis from which to work. Experience in large software developments have shown that an inadequate job of subsystem specification results in the software requirements developer or process designer making and implementing the decisions which affect system performance. As a result each person in the development chain is completing the system synthesis effort. This uncontrolled development results in a product which more often than not does not reflect the original intent of the system purchaser and fails to provide an originating document to which the system may be accurately compared. A consistent and correct baseline from which to begin subsystem development will ensure that 1) the customer has a solid basis upon which to base acceptance, 2) the subsystem developer can be assured that by meeting his requirements he will ensure correct system performance, and 3) there will be a structured basis for maintaining and upgrading the system.

This necessitates a technology which will, as a part of system evolution, provide for the development of complete, consistent, and correct subsystem requirements through a structured approach to system synthesis and decomposition as well as a means for verification of the decomposed requirements. Such a technology should provide a decomposition approach which has a mathematical foundation ensuring not only desirable description properties, e.g., completeness, consistency, traceability between levels, but that the system description will contain an abstraction of the desired properties of the end product. This decomposition technology must be embedded in a methodology for system synthesis which supports performance allocation, is highly automated, and is a measurable and manageable process.

Three approaches toward the development of such a technology are the subject of continuing research. These are an approach using the formalized analysis of specifications based upon graph theory designated the Verification Graph Method; system structuring techniques based upon Petri Net and formal logic analysis entitled the Petri Net Method; and thirdly, a

Finite State Machine approach to structuring and defining systems.

The three concepts have been manually applied to the development of a set of system level requirements for a distributed BMD defense system [39]-[40]. Each concept provides a system decomposition structure, with definitions of completeness, consistency, and traceability to provide a measure of increased preciseness in contributing to the generation of correct specifications. Following a description of each approach the advantages and shortcomings of each approach will be discussed.

A. The Verification Graph (VG) Method

This system specification methodology is an approach to assuring correct subsystem specification through a formalized graphical analysis of system level specifications. The methodology described by Belford et al. [10] consists of three sequential phases: 1) decomposition; 2) static analysis; and 3) dynamic analysis. Each phase is applied at each level of requirements description to assure a complete and correct basis for further decomposition. For the first level of requirements, the system specification is decomposed and then statically analyzed. The first two phases are iterated until a consistent set of system requirements exists. Finally, dynamic analysis is performed, and the three phases are iterated until a verified, validated, and complete set of requirements exists.

The decomposition of system requirements is achieved through the specification of the interactions of system functions using the notion of a *decomposition element (DE)*.

The DE represents a functional requirement and the associated performance characteristics from the system specification. A functional requirement includes a description of a function, the information or action input to the function, and the information or action output from the function. This is expressed as:

	Input	Transformation	Output
Functional Requirements =	Stimulus	Functional Argument	Response
		Performance Characteristics	

A stimulus is the initiator of an action and is the input to the functional argument. The functional argument is the action or transformation performed upon or as a result of the initiating action of the stimulus. A response is the output of the functional argument. The performance characteristics from the system specification are associated with each stimulus, functional argument, and response.

The verification graph (VG) can be automatically generated when the DE's are specified. It is represented as a directed arc in the VG representing the stimulus/response pairs of the requirements in the specification as decomposed into DE's. Each functional node of the graph represents functional requirements in the specification. Decisional nodes represent either branching requirements or logical requirements.

The directed graph model is amenable to analyses such as the following.

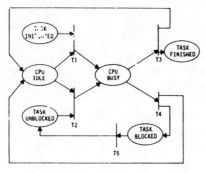

Fig. 4. Example of Petri Net model.

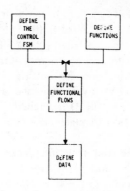

Fig. 5. System Decomposition Methodology.

1) Consistency: Each node in the digraph must be either functional or logical; each dilink in the digraph must be either local or global; and the set of all nodes and dilinks in the digraph must be connected.

2) Traceability: The global stimulus dilink(s) and global response dilink(s) in sublevel digraphs must map one-to-one in quantity, direction, and value to simply connected dilinks in the next-higher-level digraph.

3) Completeness: All sublevel digraphs must be traceable to functional nodes in the next-higher-level digraph, and these functional nodes must exhaust the set at that level.

Besides these static analyses, simulation models are constructed from the specification for analysis of dynamic behavior and performance characteristics.

A mechanical translator of the DE specification and support management software has been developed for the methodology.

B. Petri Net Method

The Petri Net described in detail by Balkovich and Engleberg [9] provides a system structuring technology based upon Petri Nets and formal logic descriptions.

Data processing subsystem requirements development involves, among others, the description of the operating rules of the system as conditions and events. These rules are considered to be best described by the Petri Net model. Fig. 4 illustrates how Petri Nets can be used to express operating rules for a system and how they could be analyzed. A Petri Net is a directed graph that distinguishes two types of vertices: 1) events or transitions (represented by vertical bars), and 2) conditions or places (represented by circles).

An event is said to be enabled if all of its input conditions are satisfied (marked by a token). The behavior implied by the network is derived by a selection rule that specifies the selection of one enabled event. The selected event is then fired (a token is removed from each input place, and a token is put on each output place). Repeated application of the selection rule produces a simulation of possible event sequences.

The design methodology, using the Petri Net, allows for the successive refinement of detail in the performance specifications. This capability introduced the need for techniques to verify that refinements or decomposition of specifications were consistent with earlier high level specifications. Formal verification is made possible by the identification that Petri Nets can be represented as the conjunction of conditional

expressions describing the condition for firing individual transitions. For example, transitions T3 and T4 are captured by:

IF CPU BUSY THEN [(TASK FININISHED AND CPU IDLE) XOR (TASK BLOCKED AND CPU IDLE)]

The formal logic translation of the Petri Net allows automated theorem proving on the consistency of the decomposition.

Although this model is successful with respect to operating rule specification, performance requirements are not adequately described or evaluated by the network models. Constructing a model of the system requires that the Petri Net tokens be assigned "attributes." Attributes can be accessed by "transition procedures" associated with transitions. Thus, in the example of Fig. 4, transitions T1 and T2 would access the attributes of the tokens occupying the "task initiated" and "task unblocked" conditions. For example, if priority is the criterion being modeled by the selection rule, then selection would be based on the token with the highest priority (determined by the transition procedures).

Simulation, as the chief means for performance evaluation, requires a model of the environment and the performance achieved by the implementation of the rules. The designer must select models with greater fidelity than that which may have been employed by the system engineer, but ones that do not go as far as prototype software. The Petri Net serves to relate the models to the specified operating rules to form a simulation. The Petri Net description of the requirements can be connected automatically into the framework for an event-based simulation. The collection of models associated with events and conditions, and the environment simulator, form a simulation of the system that allows the analyst to verify that the stated performance requirements meet system objectives.

C. The FSM Method (Finite State Machine)

The FSM approach deals with the description of a BMD system as a structured finite state machine. This approach as described by Salter [8] identifies four essential elements of a system in the process of decomposing system requirements into data processing requirements. These are the control, functions, data, and functional flows. Each of these is modeled by a structure that allows formal mechanical analysis. The decomposition methodology is illustrated in Fig. 5.

The control of a data processing system is the mechanism

that activates system functions in the desired sequence. Control is modeled as a structured finite state machine (FSM) (a hierarchy of FSM's whose only cycles are loops). This allows automated checks for: 1) consistency—for a given state and any given input, no more than one transition is possible; 2) completeness—for any given state and any given input, a transition is defined; and 3) reachability—there is a path to the FSM from the START state and a path from it to an END state.

System functions and their interdependence are modeled by a directed graph whose nodes represent the functions where an arc from function A to function B indicates that function B requires an input generated by function A (A impacts B). The directed graph model readily lends itself to connectivity and structural analysis. Properties such as reachability and completeness with respect to the system requirements can be verified. This allows one to analyze the system for inherent parallelism, dependencies and cycles, of mutually dependent functions.

A functional flow is the output of one or more states of the control FSM, causing an ordered execution of data processing functions and nondata processing subsystems. Specification of functional flows can be checked for: consistency—if each impact in a functional flow corresponds to an impact in the system function structure; completeness—if each data processing function is contained in at least one functional flow; and reachability—if each functional flow is the output of at least one state in the control FSM.

Data is defined by indicating for each data object the functions to which it is an input and from which it is an output. This is used to relate the several functions within a functional flow, to drive the control mechanism, and to link control to the functional flows.

Data is said to be *consistent* with the function structure if each element of data has both a source and a destination, and if every impact defined by the data is an impact in the system impact relation. Data is said to be *complete* if each impact in the system impact relation is defined by the data. An element of data is said to be *reachable* if its value is defined before being used. Mechanical tests can be provided to measure consistency and completeness of data. An open question is that of how to determine reachability.

It is the intention of the methodology that the integration of these elements with the verification of the properties defined before should guarantee at least a consistent and well-formed definition of the data processing subsystem.

D. DPSE Assessment

Each of the above approaches have addressed the most essential and basic aspects of the problem. However, these methodologies vary in their capability to provide a decomposition technology for large real-time weapons systems. The VG methodology requiring definition of all system requirements in terms of DE's relies upon the capability to describe system functions as the simple stimulus/argument/response format of the DE. With respect to this feature, the FSM system is somewhat more sophisticated in that it recognizes the importance of separately specifying the control, data functions,

and functional flow elements of the system and their interactions and interrelations. However, the discipline of translating system requirements into a model of the various elements, especially control, remains undefined. In addition, there are concerns about the ability to allow partial system descriptions and the retainment of design freedom in such an approach.

All techniques still fail to define their effectiveness in terms of the overall reliability measures of the ultimate product. It is true that all of these techniques check for certain properties of the specifications such as consistency, but currently there is no relation between these attributes and those of direct concern of the end user. In addition, other methodology related needs of performance allocation have been addressed only in an extremely limited sense.

These approaches are undergoing further research and assessment as to their applicability to meet the system level definition requirements for BMD.

VII. PROCESS DESIGN ENGINEERING

A unified and well-defined discipline for all aspects of the software design, coding, and testing of large real-time software projects is a need that is widely recognized. The highly time critical, high reliability environment in a BMD system forces extreme reliance upon a technology which will ensure a manageable approach to producing a high quality subsystem. Software design is described as a "wicked problem" [42] and the development of a methodology to support this is a problem of even greater difficulty. Software design and coding efforts often bear the brunt of problems induced much earlier in the development cycle. Premature hardware selection often results in inadequate capacity forcing a large amount of optimizing to meet system requirements. Inconsistent, infeasible, and missing requirements add to the designer's problems. Changes in requirements complicated by the parallel development of multiple versions of the software cause an extremely difficult management problem.

Any approach toward solving problems encountered in this activity must possess several important characteristics. There should be a language which is matched to the complexity of the problem. For BMD this language should support the ability to describe and model the problem at varying degrees of detail throughout all design phases. The language should support the description of the computational, timing, synchronization, and control aspects of the problem, support a strong degree of error checking, and be easy to use and communicate.

Supporting software should be an integral part of the process design phase of development. A high degree of automation designed to provide the developer with rapid and thorough checking capability, as well as the reduction of error through elimination of many tedious manual tasks, is essential for the development of a reliable software product. Examples of tools which are essential to this task are as follows: tools which keep track and allow reliable modification of the many versions of software which may be under parallel development at the same time (configuration control); tools to ensure interface integrity after modification and reduce the high incidence of interface errors; and tools which ease the development task by providing

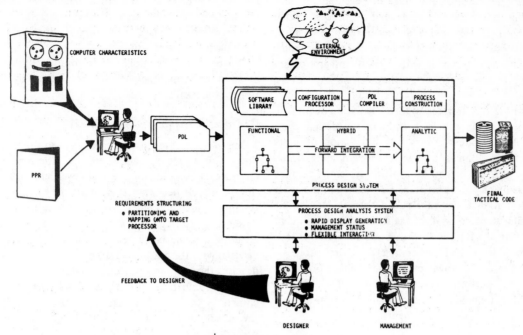

Fig. 6. Process Design Engineering.

the developer the ability to rapidly define, configure, execute, and evaluate a process.

Since General Purpose Operating Systems (GPOS) do not generally give the efficiencies desired, special-purpose operating systems have been an integral part of BMD software development. This necessitates the capability to structure the development of a tactical operating system in a higher order language and provide modeling techniques to allow the tradeoffs required for definition as well as ensuring an orderly and defined transition from execution under the GPOS with a modeled special-purpose or tactical operating system to execution under the tactical operating system.

The complexities and size of the problem under consideration demand an approach to development that will allow proceeding from high level models of the system to the detailed code in an orderly and defined manner. The design methodology must also provide an approach to testing that will ensure that each level of system description is subjected to a realistic environment which will verify the system response. Size of the resulting tactical process usually forces an externally resident environmental simulation for final verification of performance. Lastly, any approach must be manageable. There must be the ability to rapidly obtain the information required for management decisions, as well as a defined sequence of activities which allow accurate scheduling and cost estimating.

A. Approach

The BMD approach to the design, coding, and testing of software is encompassed in the previously mentioned Process Design Methodology (PDM) [11]. This approach consists of a set of process design procedures and techniques supported by software development tools accessed through a single language, PDL2. PDM consists of the following major components.

1) A structuring technology to allow an unambiguous and traceable transformation from computer-independent computational requirements (the PPR) to a top-level process design effectively.

2) Design, implementation, and testing techniques supported by the Process Design System, PDS.

3) A Process Design System consisting of support tools for automating such functions as requirements traceability, configuration management, library management, simulation control, data collection and analysis, and documentation.

4) A set of models and techniques to accurately estimate project costs and schedules, designed to provide information to assist management in the effective control of BMD software development.

The process design engineering approach is depicted in Fig. 6. Initial structuring techniques identify a set of tasks and tradeoffs that must be performed to identify a top level software structure. The Process Design System, through the capabilities of PDL2 and its support software, provide the tools to make the tradeoffs and support evolution to the final code. These tradeoffs not only include the tasking structure but also impact the operating system design.

The design of the software proceeds in an evolutionary manner as each task is further partitioned into a set of computational algorithms that are executed via a prescribed sequencing logic. This approach proceeds in a somewhat top-down manner, seeking to initially describe the sequencing logic of the final process and adding detail through increasingly detailed algorithmic models. The process is thus represented as a mixture of modules at each stage of the development where some modules are detailed code and some are merely skeletons of the tasks to be performed. The Process Design System keeps track of these modules as they evolve through the development steps into final code, executes the process with an environment simulator at any stage of development, and allows rapid analysis of the performance of the process. Since the entire process is represented at any development stage, each module is tested in its complete environment. The interface problems usually associated with software integration are identified early in the design where they can be more easily resolved.

Since this approach is designed to force resolution of control, structure, and interface problems early in the design cycle prior to the major coding efforts, the integration of more detailed algorithms follows a logical "forward integration" sequence, in which the highest level of the system is detailed first, and subsequent processing steps are detailed in the order of processing. In this way, analytic data provided by the initial processing steps are available as an input to subsequent analytic algorithms. Iteration of this implementation, test, and evaluation cycle results in the complete real-time process.

Throughout the development cycle, the evolving process is tested against the performance criteria stated in the Process Performance Requirements to ensure that the real-time software will satisfy the system requirements.

B. Capabilities

The PDS capabilities are provided through the following integrated set of software tools.

1) A software library management subsystem to maintain and control alternate versions of models. This provides a convenient "menu" for selecting and testing various process configurations, and includes a text editing capability for convenient modification of modules (with access keys to prevent unauthorized or accidental changes).

2) A configuration management system to provide name control and a system configuration index which uniquely identifies the specific version of each component selected by the designer.

3) Process construction facilities which automatically collect specified modules and link them together into an executable process. PDS allows for independent module compilation and automatic recompilation of all lower level modules affected by a change in a higher level module.

4) A simulation system to support testing of the process through three levels of simulation of increasing real-time fidelity. The first level uses an internal environment simulator and operates in a batch environment. The second level, again using the internal driver, allows interfacing with the tactical operating system and a simulated radar interface. The third level uses a separate computer for the system environment and threat simulator, interconnected through interface hardware for full-scale system testing.

5) Data collection directives that permit declaring where and when desired data are to be collected. Post-simulation performance analysis is supported by the Process Design Analysis Programs which retrieve the specified performance data, perform analysis, generate reports, and create graphic displays.

6) A single language, PDL2, for definition of process components throughout all phases of design, permitting an increasingly more detailed description of the process components as the design evolves in a top-down manner from a functional to an analytic representation of the process. An important feature of the language is the support of structured programming techniques and syntax.

7) Automatic recompilation without designer intervention of all subservient modules that are affected by the modification of a particular module.

C. Process Design Language (PDL2)

One important research aspect has been the identification of the requirements for and implementation of PDL2. This language is based upon the high-level language, Pascal, with the extensions necessary to support the real-time control and timing required by BMD software. This total capability for developing, testing, and analyzing an experimental process, all using a single language, is essential to provide the process designer with the automated support he needs to systematically develop the real-time process. PDL2 is a dialect of, and its design is compatible with, N. Wirth's Pascal [43]. Pascal was chosen as the base language for PDL2 primarily because of the advanced data structuring facilities which allow for comprehensive compile-time checking of data accessing.

Extensions to basic Pascal [44] were made in the following main areas.

1) *Tasking and Synchronization Primitives*. Processes are likely to be implemented on multiprocessors to obtain necessary computing capacity. Even in the case of a single processor, the need for interrupting tasks by tasks of higher priority will cause a parallelism which must be taken into account in preserving data sanity. The approach chosen was to provide primitives suitable to the implementation of specific schemes of tasking and synchronization. A multitasking operating system is currently under development using PDS2 and PDL2 capabilities.

2) *Variable Length Arrays*. A recognized deficiency of Pascal is the absence of variable length arrays. PDL2 permits the declaration of arrays whose upper dimension is bound when the array is allocated and allows variable length arrays to be passed as procedure parameters.

3) *Vector Operations*. These were added primarily to exploit the vector and parallelism of advanced computer architectures—but may also increase the code efficiency on serial computers. Vector operations also contribute to code readability.

4) *Assertion Statements*. These statements provide optional run-time verification (not proof) of the programmer's proof assertion. Thus, if a program contains:

ASSERT I + J < 100

Code would be output to evaluate the expression I + J < 100 and output an appropriate error message if the expression were false.

5) *Parameterized String Substitutions (MACROS)*. MACROS permit the definition of in-line procedures and functions, allowing the user to make the decisions on trading space for speed. Also, MACROS are intentionally syntactically similar to procedure calls so that conversion from one to the other is facilitated. For example, in the compiler, there was a procedure which returned the next character in the input

string. This procedure was very short and was called frequently but from only a few procedures. Conversion of this procedure to a MACRO resulted in a significant speedup in the compiler because of the elimination of subroutine linkage overhead.

6) An Escape Statement. A frequent criticism of structured programming languages is the inefficiency involved in terminating a loop in which commons are avoided. The common is declared only once at a level such that it is a root of all subtrees which reference the common. Individual procedures which reference the common must explicitly request access to the common with the ACCESS statement.

7) PP Code Generation. The compiler also generates code for the TI ASC peripheral processor to facilitate operating system implementation. Machine specific features are also defined in a general manner for portability. For example, the CR file is definitely a machine-dependent feature, yet it is simply defined as a common. The compiler must know about the CR file and treat it specially, but compilers are always machine specific.

The Process Design System (PDS) has been implemented and is running on the TI ASC at the BMDATC Advanced Research Center. The PDL2 compiler consists of approximately 22K statements of PDL2 code with the rest of PDS consisting of approximately 21K additional PDL2 statements. The compiler processes between 2500 and 4000 PDL2 statements per minute and requires 200K words of core for compilation plus additional data storage area.

The effectiveness of this process design approach has yet to be fully quantified. As a part of the evolution of the approach a real-time software process of significant size (20K lines of PDL1) was developed using this process approach supported by a forerunner language, PDL1. A significant data collection and analysis effort [45] was undertaken. This approach showed a significant increase in the errors detected early in the design phase with the majority of the errors detected prior to the 50 percent completion point in the program. Designer productivity was compared with equivalent real-time developments and found to be considerably better. The productivity was measured at 1.7 man-months/1000 equivalent machine instructions.

VIII. VERIFICATION AND VALIDATION

The testing of large interactive, real-time systems such as BMD provides a set of problems which strongly parallel those of the development of the tactical code. A testing philosophy which provides the maximum assurance of early error detection is essential to provide a highly reliable software product. Significant investigations into testing via nonreal-time interactive and externally resident simulation of all nondata processing components called a System, Environment, and Threat Simulator (SETS) [46] have been conducted. An outgrowth of this program has been the identification of an approach to providing a significant decrease in the time and cost of BMD system testing as well as providing the ability to better define the "performance space" of the software under test and determine a measure of its robustness over wide ranges of input. This problem is being addressed through investigation of automated techniques for the interactive generation of test cases, performance evaluation techniques to allow the assessment of the BMD software response to that threat, and algorithms to intelligently perturb the input space. Preliminary research results based upon experience with SETS have shown that the interactive construction and modification of test cases does provide a significant reduction in the time to develop test variants. Performance measure characterization to allow assessment of the software response to the threat still suffers from the inability to relate data processor subsystem functions to higher level system functions. This activity will result in a feasibility demonstration of achieved capabilities early in 1977.

IX. SUMMARY

The SDS represents the only known completely conceived and integrated methodology designed for the development of software for a class of large real-time weapons systems such as BMD. The SDS development has been the result of much empirical testing and evaluation and is felt to represent a significant advance in software technology. The results obtained from the experiments during SDS development have been very encouraging and the methodology is now entering a phase of intensive evaluation. The program is one of continuing evolution designed to keep pace with the ever increasing demands made upon data processing technology. Every effort will be made to make the results of these research efforts available for use and evaluation by others.

ACKNOWLEDGMENT

The information and concepts presented in this paper summarize the work of many people within the Ballistic Missile Defense Advanced Technology Center (BMDATC) and private industry. Corporations which have participated in this program include TRW Defense and Space Systems Group, Texas Instruments, Computer Science Corporation, Aeronutronics-Ford, General Research Corporation, LOGICON, Science Applications, Inc., and the System Development Corporation.

We also thank C. V. Ramamoorthy and H. H. So for their valuable contributions to the writing of this paper.

REFERENCES

[1] Software Management Conference, abridged proceedings, first series, 1976.
[2] C. R. Vick, "Specifications for reliable software," presented at EASCON '74, Washington, DC, Oct. 1974.
[3] "Safeguard data-processing system," *Bell Syst. Tech. J.*, special supplement, 1975.
[4] R. Williams, "Managing the development of reliable software," presented at the 1975 Int. Conf. Reliable Software, Apr. 1975.
[5] "The BMDATC software development system," BMDATC, vols. I and II, and supplement, July 1976.
[6] M. W. Alford, "A requirements engineering methodology for real-time processing requirements," *IEEE Trans. Software Eng.*, vol. SE-3, pp. 60–69, Jan. 1977.
[7] T. E. Bell, D. C. Bixler, and M. E. Dyer, "An extendable approach to computer-aided software requirements engineering," *IEEE Trans. Software Eng.*, vol. SE-3, pp. 49–60, Jan. 1977.
[8] K. Salter, "A methodology for decomposing system requirements into data processing requirements," in *Proc. 2nd Int. Software Eng. Conf.*, Oct. 1976.

[9] E. Balkovich and G. Engleberg, "Research toward a technology to support the specification of data processing system performance requirements," in *Proc. 2nd Int. Software Eng. Conf.*, Oct. 1976.

[10] P. Belford *et al.*, "Specifications–A key to effective software development," in *Proc. 2nd Int. Software Eng. Conf.*, Oct. 1976.

[11] S. N. Gaulding and J. D. Lawson, "Process design engineering–A methodology for real-time software requirements," in *Proc. 2nd Int. Software Eng. Conf.*, Oct. 1976.

[12] R. Koppang, "Process design system–An integrated set of software development tools," in *Proc. 2nd Int. Software Eng. Conf.*, Oct. 1976.

[13] D. W. Cooper, "Adaptive testing," in *Proc. 2nd Int. Software Eng. Conf.*, Oct. 1976.

[14] J. Benson and R. Melton, "A laboratory for the development and evaluation of BMD software quality enhancement techniques," in *Proc. 2nd Int. Software Eng. Conf.*, Oct. 1976.

[15] "DOD weapons systems software management study," The Johns Hopkins Univ., Applied Physics Lab., May 1975.

[16] "DOD weapons systems software acquisition and management study," vol. I, MITRE Findings and Recommendations, The MITRE Corp., May 1975.

[17] S. J. Werson, D. W. Cooper, and R. L. Stone, "Hierarchical verification and validation software design," General Res. Corp., CR-7-626, vol. 2, Mar. 1976.

[18] D. Teichroew, "A survey of languages for stating requirements for computer-based information systems," in *1972 Fall Joint Comput. Conf., AFIPS Conf. Proc.*, vol. 41. Montvale, NJ: AFIPS Press, 1972, pp. 1203–1224.

[19] J. D. Couger, "Evolution of business systems analysis techniques," *Computing Surveys*, pp. 167–198, Sept. 1973.

[20] F. Burns *et al.*, "Current software requirements engineering technology," TRW Systems Group, Huntsville, AL, Aug. 1974.

[21] D. Riefer, "Software specifications: A tutorial," in *Proc. COMPCOM 76*, Sept. 1976.

[22] B. Langefors, "Information system design computations using generalized matrix algebra," *BIT*, vol. 5, pp. 96–121, 1965.

[23] *The Time Automated Grid System (TAG): Sales and Systems Guide*, IBM, publ. GY20-0358-1, end edition, May 1971.

[24] *HIPO: Design Aid and Documentation Tool*, IBM, SR20-9413-0, 1973.

[25] D. Tiechroew, E. Hershey, and M. Bastarache, "An introduction to PSL/PSA," ISDOS Working Paper 86, Dept. Industrial and Operations Eng., Univ. Michigan, Ann Arbor, Mar. 1974.

[26] C. W. Rose, "LOGOS and the software engineer," in *1972 Fall Joint Comput. Conf., AFIPS Conf. Proc.*, vol. 41. Montvale, NJ: AFIPS Press, 1972, pp. 311–323.

[27] R. T. Burger, "AUTASIM: A system for computerized assembly of simulation models," presented at the Winter Simulation Conf., SIGPLAN Notices, Jan. 1974.

[28] B. W. Boehm, "A concept of model driven software," in *Proc. TRW Symp. Reliable, Cost Effective, Secure Software*, Los Angeles, CA, Mar. 1974.

[29] J. F. Nunnamaker, "A methodology for the design and optimization of information processing systems," in *1971 Fall Joint Comput. Conf., AFIPS Conf. Proc.*, vol. 28. Montvale, NJ: AFIPS Press, 1971.

[30] *A Users Guide to the Threads Management System*, Computer Sciences Corp., Nov. 1973.

[31] F. T. Baker, "Chief programmer team management of production programming," *IBM Syst. J.*, vol. 11, pp. 56–73, 1972.

[32] M. Hamilton and S. Zeldin, "Higher order software–A methodology for defining software," *IEEE Trans. Software Eng.*, pp. 9–32, Mar. 1976.

[33] ——, "The foundations for axes: a specification language based upon completeness of control," The Charles Stark Draper Laboratory, Inc., R-964, Mar. 1976.

[34] D. Ross and K. Shoman, "Structured analysis for requirements definition," in *Proc. 2nd Int. Software Eng. Conf.*, Oct. 1976.

[35] "SADT™ The SofTech Approach to System Development," SofTech, The Software Technology Company, Jan. 1976.

[36] T. Bell and T. Thayer, "Software requirements: Are they really a problem?" in *Proc. 2nd Int. Software Eng. Conf.*, Oct. 1976.

[37] T. Thayer, "Understanding software through analysis of empirical data," TRW Software Series, TRW-SS-75-04, May 1975.

[38] "The Development of a Software Theory to Classify and Detect Software Errors," LOGICON Rep. HR-74012, Mar. 1974.

[39] "DPSPR final report," Contract DASG60-75-C-0123, General Research Corp., Santa Barbara, CA, Apr. 1976.

[40] "Data processing system requirements," Final Rep. DASG60-75-C-0124, Aeronutronic-Ford Corp., Willow Grove, PA, June 1976.

[41] "System decomposition technology," Final Rep., Computer Science Corp., Huntsville, AL, Apr. 1976.

[42] L. Peters and L. Tripp, "Is software design wicked?" *Datamation*, pp. 127–129, May 1976.

[43] K. Jensen and N. Wirth, *PASCAL Users Manual and Report*. New York: Springer-Verlag, 1974.

[44] "Process design methodology," vol. 1, Process Design Language Specifications, Texas Instruments, Huntsville, AL, Dec. 1975.

[45] J. Lawson, "Baseline software process productivity and error analysis," Texas Instruments, Huntsville, AL, Apr. 1976.

[46] D. F. Palmer *et al.*, "SETS 1 software design specifications," General Research Corp., CR-1-516, July 1972.

Carl G. Davis received the B.A.E. degree from the Georgia Institute of Technology, Atlanta, in 1961, the M.S. degree in aerospace engineering in 1966, and the M.S. and Ph.D. degrees in engineering mechanics in 1972, from the University of Alabama.

He has held positions as an Aerospace Engineer with the U.S. Army Missile Command from 1964 to 1969 and as a Research Assistant at the University of Alabama from 1969 to 1972. Since 1972 he has been a member of the Technical Staff of the U.S. Army Ballistic Missile Defense Advanced Technology Center, Huntsville, AL, with primary responsibilities in the area of software engineering. Research programs under his direction have included requirements engineering, process design, and software verification and validation.

Charles R. Vick received the bachelors degree in mathematics from Oklahoma City University in 1965 and has completed graduate work in mathematics at the University of Alabama.

He has worked in the field of real-time data processing research and development for the past twelve years. Areas of application include air defense and more recently ballistic missile defense. Activities in computer science advanced under his leadership over the recent past include parallel processing with associative array architecture and software engineering. He initiated a research program in software engineering in 1969 which has led to a comprehensive first generation software engineering system. He is the Director of the Data Processing Directorate of the Ballistic Missile Defense Advanced Technology Center, Huntsville, AL. The Center is responsible for research and development for the U.S. Army in all technologies supporting advanced ballistic missile defense applications.

The Relationship Between Design and Verification

M. Hamilton and S. Zeldin

Higher Order Software, Inc., Cambridge, Massachusetts

The assumption is made here that a design process, in order to be effective, must include techniques that facilitate the effectiveness of the verification of the target design resulting from that process. The assumption is also made that these techniques can and should be universal in nature. That is, any system designer should be able to use these techniques to benefit his or her own design process and to check for the proper use of these techniques, both statically and automatically, with the aid of a common set of tools.

Once a set of universal techniques has been verified, there is no longer a need to verify such techniques each time a new system is designed. It follows, then, that there is no longer a need to verify or prevent those categories of problems that are known to exist no longer, given the correct use of those system design techniques that eliminates that class of problems.

Verification of a system design includes the identification of redundancies, logical incompleteness, and inconsistencies of a system definition, description, implementation, and execution. If a system design process inherently produces a design that no longer requires certain types of "after the fact" verification, many aspects previously associated with the verification process can be eliminated. We discuss our recent experiences in defining systems where we have attempted to show the relationship between design and verification. An example specification is used to demonstrate the properties of a system definition whose design supports elimination of unnecessary verification, maximum use of static verification, and minimum use of dynamic verification.

INTRODUCTION

A system development process is a system that develops another system. Such a system can be viewed as a process where each instance is continuously receiving requirements as inputs and producing specifications as outputs. In such a development system, *requirements* are those items that are desired or needed and *specifications* are the results that realize those requirements; one engineer's requirements could be another engineer's specifications [1].

There are several disciplines, or combinations thereof, that can occur as a development process. These disciplines include design, implementation, verification, management, and documentation. All of these disciplines also take place throughout a system development process and, depending on point of view, one engineer's design process could be viewed as another engineer's management, implementation, verification, or documentation process. Each of these disciplines is just as interchangeable with respect to each other, depending entirely on a given point of view.

A development process is viewed as a management process when it is considered with respect to its *control* of other disciplines.

A development process is viewed as a *documentation* process when it is considered with respect to its *description* of other disciplines.

A development process is viewed as a *design* process when it is considered with respect to its *definition* of other disciplines.

A development process is viewed as a *resource allocation* process if it is considered in terms of its *implementation* of other disciplines.

A development process is viewed as a *verification* process if it is viewed in terms of its *execution* of other disciplines.

A successful execution of a target system is directly dependent on a successful execution of a development process.

The design process is a focal point for all of the other disciplines. Not only does it determine if a

Address correspondence to M. Hamilton, President, or S. Zeldin, Vice-President, Higher Order Software, Inc., 806 Massachusetts Avenue, Cambridge, Massachusetts 02139.

The Journal of Systems and Software 1, 29–56 (1979)
© Elsevier North Holland, Inc., 1979

system is going to work, but it also directly affects the effectiveness of the other disciplines. A design process, however, is not complete until the process itself or its results have been verified. It follows then that the verification process is a focal point for all the other disciplines as well.

For each step of design, there should be a "counterstep" of verification. This does not mean that for every new thought in the design process it is necessary to have a one-to-one corresponding "thoughtback" for the entire verification process; quite the contrary—not only would such a method be time consuming, but it would also not be reliable. At times, in fact, the process of design could be interpreted as one and the same as the process of verification. This occurs when certain design characteristics are included for the purpose of preventing unnecessary verification. In such a case, some types of verification requirement are designed out of the system. What is left is the second-order verification that guarantees that unnecessary verification requirements with respect to design have been eliminated, and then a need to verify only that which is truly part of the original intent of the design.

Many engineers desire to improve their own design techniques. These design techniques include techniques for producing the design for a solution to a particular problem as well as the design for the process that will verify that solution. More often than not, these engineers appear to be talking about a different design process since they are involved in different types of systems or different phases of development within a given system. Actually, they are applying the same process (i.e., design) in different ways. In the context of a typical system development process, design could be the process of developing concepts, requirements, specifications, code, or computers; likewise, design could be the process of going from a concept to a set of requirements, from requirements to a set of specifications, from specifications to a set of code, or from code to a set of computers. In each of these processes, a designer considers the task of preparing a design to reside eventually in a "machine" environment (e.g., a computer for a software system). One of the problems in a design approach is that the designer either worries unnecessarily about design considerations irrelevant to his own process or bypasses certain design considerations under the impression that they have already been, or will later be, handled by someone else.

A designer should be concerned with the design that is to reside in that designer's development phase, and that design *only*. Each designer goes through the same generic process but should be applying that pro-

cess to a different phase of the overall application. Thus the inputs and outputs of that design process should be both unique and self-contained.

Other than a good deal of insight, a successful designer has necessary and sufficient knowledge about a particular problem, an understanding of the nature of a design process, an understanding of the nature of the reverse of a design process (the verification process), and a means to perform a set of effective implementations.

The verification process exists for the purpose of finding errors in the output of a design process. There are those errors that can always be found by automated means (provided that the design process incorporates proper procedures) and those that cannot always be found by automated means. We divide the former into two kinds. The first is determined by analyzing a system (or a set of subsystems) on a stand-alone basis. For example, if a specification has an inconsistency among its functions or if a computer program has a data conflict, such errors can be found by analyzing only the system in question. In this case, it is possible to design the system in such a way that checks can be made with respect to interface correctness (i.e., logical completeness, consistency, and nonredundancy). The second kind is that which is determined by checking one development layer with the development layer from which it evolved. An example of such a comparison is that of checking a computer program against its specification. Again, checks can be made with respect to interface correctness between layers.

Errors that cannot always be found by automated means are those that are determined by checking a development layer against the intent of the original designer. A small percent of large-system development errors fall into this category [2]. This problem is alleviated by providing both techniques that automatically eliminate other sources of errors and those that support the verification engineer in finding the remaining errors.

An ordering for a verification process then becomes apparent. One first concentrates on eliminating certain types of verification by following design principles that make this possible. This is the *conceptual phase* of the verification process. Then one concentrates on using these principles correctly. A check for correct use of principles can be performed both statically and automatically. This is the *static phase* of the verification process. Finally, one concentrates on verifying only that part of the design which is concerned solely with the performance of a particular algorithm. This is the *dynamic phase* of the verification process.

THE RATIONALE FOR USING A METHODOLOGY

An effective methodology can assist a designer with respect to both the design itself and its verification. There are concerns, however, on the part of some project managers with regard to introducing a new methodology into an organization especially when it affects an ongoing project. Often, unfortunately, methods are never improved because of insufficient time to introduce new methods when, in fact, part of the reason for not having enough time is the methods already being used.

How does one convince project managers of the benefits of introducing a methodology into their organization (excluding success stories about competitors)? Project managers, whose first priority is to deliver items that work, and work on time, are in the majority and must have some proof that the introduction of a methodology will serve their needs better. We have found that an effective way to demonstrate a methodology within a given project is to select a module within that project's environment and to show the differences in definition of that module using the new methodology as opposed to the methods already being used on that particular project. Invariably, the most significant results are those where the use of certain design techniques eliminates some traditional categories of errors. The power of new concepts is often realized when those errors are uncovered in an engineer's own system, especially when that module is thought to be already working!

Once a project manager sees that some methodology can be more effective than none (i.e., no common adopted methodology), an interest develops with respect to other methodologies. Which one is best? How do we choose between one and another? It then becomes apparent that there should be a common set of criteria by which to compare methodologies.

Some project managers are much harder to convince than others, with respect to using an effective methodology, because they are fortunate enough to have all "smart" people. It is true that the smartest person, by definition, would apply an effective methodology. An effective methodology, however, applied in common by several smart people, would far exceed the advantages of each smart person applying techniques in an ad hoc manner, since all the intricacies of a complex system are by nature beyond the grasp of any human being. The designs of all smart people must still be integrated. Thus a manager can be much more effective by defining a standard means to integrate the methods of these people before the fact rather than after.

Once a project manager decides to adopt a certain methodology, the immediate problem becomes how to implement it without impacting deliverable items of an ongoing project. In this case, a project manager can be assisted in using those aspects of the methodology that either make results more visible, find or prevent errors, or do any of these more quickly. Once these incremental techniques are introduced, engineers start feeling more at home with those aspects of the methodology and are much more prepared to start using other aspects when the proper time comes (e.g., the start of a new project).

Some progress has been made with respect to a particular project when the managers say "We are convinced, but how do we convince our engineers?" It often has been the case in such an environment that their engineers say "We are convinced, but how do we convince our management?"

Finally, say, the engineers and their management are convinced of the practical advantages of using an effective methodology but become nostalgic for the old days, thinking that poorer methods left more room for creativity. It is true that an effective methodology provides more constraints for the designers but *only* in the area of preventing the production of errors. As a result, creative designers should be *less* constrained in producing better designs. Once the project manager recognizes this, selection of a methodology is imminent.

DESIRABLE PROPERTIES FOR A METHODOLOGY

A methodology can support but never replace a designer. A tool can be developed to replace some of the designer's functions in general or even all of them for a particular project; however, the designer still has the prerogative to create new designs and design new uses for the same tool or new tools for different uses.

Too often the same problems exist in the development of methodologies as do in the problems the methodologies are intended to address. That is, there are often inconsistencies within a methodology. In addition, improvements to a methodology are often ad hoc, and modifications to a methodology to fix or enhance it are made to already existing modifications. Likewise, in the attempt to select an existing methodology, there is always a risk of comparing (1) techniques addressing very different problems, (2) techniques intending to address a problem, but not effectively addressing it at all, (3) techniques with respect to nonexistent or ill-defined requirements, (4) the "syntax" of methodologies instead of the "semantics" of methodologies, (5) techniques based on unfamiliar paradigms with preconceived notions, (6) techniques addressing the wrong problems or those that are ''in the noise,'' (7) techniques with respect to completion or amount of use rather than to the problems they are solving, and (8) techniques with respect to the algorithms they are being used to define.

There are many methodologies today whose intent is to provide standards and techniques to assist the engineer in the design and verification process [3]. The developers of these methodologies are all proponents of reliable designs, and most methodologies advocate some similar techniques towards this aim. For example, it is commonly accepted that it is beneficial to produce a hierarchical breakdown of a given design in order to provide more manageable pieces with which to work. However, there are variations among methodologies. Some emphasize a concentration of data flow as opposed to functional flow [4–7]; others, just the opposite [8–10], or both functional and data flow equally [11]. Still others emphasize documentation standards [12,13], graphical notation [14], or semantic representation [15].

There are certainly positive aspects in many of these methodologies and, in particular, in what they are trying to obtain. However, to make comparisons among them or to determine the effectiveness of individual ones, it is necessary to determine the properties by which to make those comparisons.

From our own experience in developing large systems, we have determined a checklist of properties by which to analyze the techniques or the methodology being used by a particular project. We believe that these properties are necessary if a methodology is to be effective in the design and verification processes of a large system development.

We make the assumption that a methodology should have techniques for defining systems that are consistent and logically complete; but these techniques are useful only if they are within themselves consistent and logically complete, both with respect to each other and to the system to which they are being applied.

A methodology should have a standard set of definitions that resides in a well-publicized and evolving glossary. In our experience, we discovered that a mere change in the definitions of such terms as *error* and *system* could have far-reaching practical implications on a large system development process [16].

A methodology should have the mechanisms to define *all* of the relationships that exist in a system environment [17]. This includes communication within and among systems and the resource allocation[1] that provides for such communication. Thus, not only must all data, data flow, functions, and functional flow be able to be defined explicitly, but the relationships (and control of the relationships) between data and data, function and function, and data and function must be able to be defined within any given system environment.

A methodology should have the mechanisms to define *all* of the relationships that exist between possible viewpoints (or development layers) of a system. If, for example, one is concerned with a definition of a system, it is viewed with respect to what it is supposed to do. If one is concerned with a description of a system, it is viewed with respect to whether or not the definition is effectively conveyed. If one is concerned with an implementation of a system, it is viewed with respect to whether or not the system is constructed to do what it is supposed to do. If one is concerned with an execution of a system, it is viewed with respect to whether or not the system does what it is supposed to do. Whereas the description and implementation layers of a system represent static views, the definition and execution layers of a system represent dynamic views.

A methodology should have the mechanisms consistently and completely to define an object and its relationships *formally*. That is, every system in the environment of an object system (people, hardware, tools, software) should be able to understand a definition of an object and its relationships the same way.

A methodology should provide for *modularity*. That is, any change should be able to be made locally (with respect to levels and layers of development), and if a change is made, the result of that change should be able to be traced throughout both the system within which that change resides, through-

---

[1] *Resource allocation* is the process (or system) that prepares one system to communicate with another system. (Such a process is, of course, a communication process with respect to the resource allocation of itself.) We define resource allocation in this way because of our finding that various engineers, including numerical analysts, programmers, hardware designers, and others, use ''resource allocation'' to mean very different things that reflect each of their specific interests. A definition was sought that described the process that focused on the fundamental feature of allocating resources, regardless of the characteristics of the specific resource. By having a definition that is concerned with the *general* property of resource allocation, ad hoc formulations are not required. In addition, one can then ask some fundamental questions about the ways in which systems can be constructed, regardless of the specific project. We have sought other definitions as well with the same aim in mind, i.e., to uncover fundamentals on which systems can be designed, constructed, and verified.

out other systems within that system's environment, and throughout all evolutions of the development of that system.

- A methodology should provide a set of *primitive standard mechanisms* that are used both for defining and verifying a system in the form of a hierarchy.

- A methodology should provide for a library of an *evolving* set of more powerful (with respect to simplicity and abstraction) mechanisms based on the standard set of primitive mechanisms. Having an extensible library of mechanisms can serve as management standards as well as save a lot of time for everyone involved in a project. (Why should only one designer have Arabic numerals available to use in performing long division when all the rest are still trying to use Roman numerals [18]?).

- A methodology should allow system engineers to communicate in a language, with common semantic primitives and a *familiar dialect,* that is extensible, flexible, and serves as a "library" of common data and structure mechanisms.

- A methodology should provide for a *development model,* including a set of definitions, tools and techniques, that supports a given system development process.

- Finally, not only must a methodology be effective, but it must also be able to be used as well, and the results of that use should be made available to others.

It is no coincidence that our own methodology has evolved with properties that correspond to those which we consider to be desirable ones for designing and verifying systems, since it was our direct experience with large systems that yielded the basis of the methodology of Higher Order Software (HOS).

SOME PROPERTIES OF HOS IN TERMS OF **AXES**

AXES, a specification language based on HOS, is a formal notation for writing definitions of systems. Although it is not a programming language, AXES is a complete and well-defined language capable of being analyzed by a computer. AXES [19] provides mechanisms to define data types (in order to identify objects), functions (in order to relate objects of types), and structures (in order to relate functions). AXES is the vehicle to define a system so that interface specifications can be automatically checked statically. The foundations of AXES are based on a set of control axioms derived from empirical data of large systems [2] and on the assumption of the existence of a universal set of objects. Figure 1 illustrates the evolvement of the primitive AXES mechanisms from the control axioms and the existence of the objects used to define systems. Each axiom describes a relation of immediate domination with respect to a functional system. We call the union of these relations control. From these axioms a set of three primitive control structures have been derived [20]. The primitive control structures identify control schemata on sets of objects. From the assumption that we can identify an object or a set of objects, a mechanism for defining an algebra for each distinct set of objects is provided in AXES. Each algebra takes the form of a set of axioms that relate operations applied to objects of a type. To form a system, new control structures are defined in terms of the primitive structures (Figure 2), or in terms of other nonprimitive control structures (Figure 3). Operations are defined implicitly by deriving them mathematically from the axioms on a type or explicitly in terms of control structures using already defined operations on a type. When an operation is defined both implicitly and explicitly, the intent of the specification can be cross-checked for correctness.

Once we have a library of control structures, data types, operations, and derived operations, we are ready to form a particular AXES definition using these mechanisms (Figure 4); Figure 5, a graphical illustration of an AXES definition, demonstrates the integration of the concepts illustrated in Figures 1–4. Here the top node of the system is concerned only with the top-level function of defining all predictable systems, whereas the second-level nodes are concerned with

Figure 1. Define primitive AXES mechanisms.

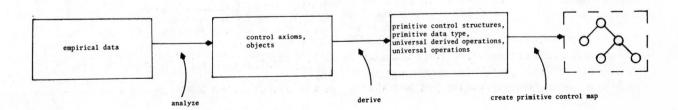

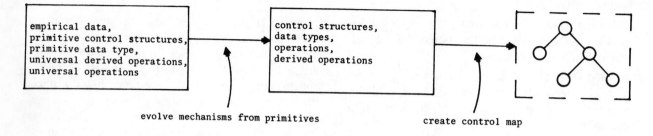

Figure 2. Evolve new AXES derived mechanisms from primitives.

functions such as analyzing the empirical data to produce axioms and objects. These axioms and objects in turn are used as input for deriving primitive control structures, a primitive data type, universal derived operations, and universal operations. These objects are then used as inputs for defining systems. The third level represents the decision "go" or "no go." That is, if there are no empirical data left, all systems in the world are defined. If there are empirical data left, there are more systems in the world to define. The fourth level represents a recursive pass of "define systems" (on the second level) and the whole process of evolvement starts again.

AXES systems are those systems that are defined directly with AXES or with mechanisms defined with AXES. AXES was designed to have a capability for defining both the relationships within a given system environment and between development layers of that system's development process.

Since AXES systems are HOS based and HOS is based on a consistent set of rules or axioms, all AXES systems have a *formal* set of properties. HOS emphasizes completeness of control, where control is defined by axioms that establish the relationships for invocation of functions, input and output, input access rights, output access rights, error detection and recovery, and ordering of functions. Control affects

Figure 3. Evolve new AXES derived mechanisms from existing AXES mechanisms.

an object, the relationships of an object, and the relationships of the development of an object. Everyone defining a module using AXES must follow the same rules in constructing the structure of that module. For example, not only is every object in a system controlled, but every object has a unique controller. The intent is to eliminate ambiguity in understanding either the behavior of an object or the behavior of that object's relationships.

There are many aspects of *modularity* inherent in AXES systems. For example, the definition of the behavior of an object is completely separated from the definition that uses the object; the definition of a development layer is independent from those layers that evolve from it (for example, the specification of a system is independent of its implementation); and AXES provides a way of defining control mechanisms that are functional, as opposed to procedural. (The definition of a control mechanism specifies total ordering among functions, which implies that the description of that definition is order independent. This does not rule out the possibility, however, of describing a procedural process as a functional mechanism.)

AXES systems also display other distinctive properties of modularity:

Both the mechanisms defined with AXES and the systems defined with these mechanisms behave as if they are "instructions"; e.g., a given control structure has no knowledge about a higher-level control structure.

Control, or the chain of command, can be traced directly on a control map. As a result function flow (including both input and output) can be traced di-

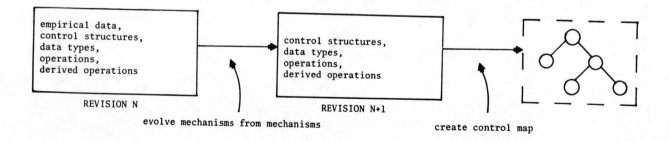

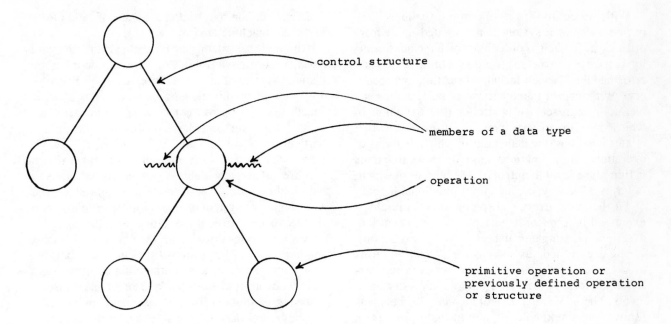

rectly. Changes can be traced and changes can be made locally.

The single-reference, single-assignment property of AXES systems provides for an interesting set of resource allocation alternatives.

An AXES definition can be viewed as a specification that can be directly implemented in terms of a distributed processing environment. Other types of implementations (e.g., multiprogramming and sequential processing) are special cases of a distributed processing environment.

We have found, however, that other aspects of a functional specification should be treated as an integrated

Figure 4. Bird's-eye view of control map constructed from AXES library.

whole and *not* artificially separated for the sake of modularity; for such a separation has often resulted in enhancing the errors in a system. That is, at any node in an AXES hierarchy a user is able to identify an object with respect to an integrated set of *aspects of control* that inherently incorporates *types* of definitional *models* and *viewpoints* of those models.

Figure 5. Axes control map defining system of defining AXES systems.

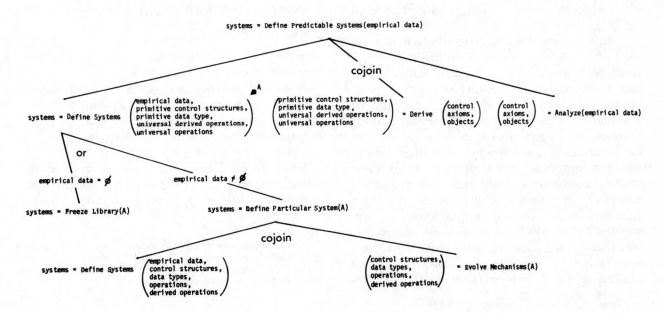

With respect to aspects of control, the input–output behavior of a system is not treated apart from other aspects, such as ordering (which includes priority, degree of concurrency, and synchronization) and error handling (which includes detection and recovery). With respect to models, every node of an AXES hierarchy represents a controller (the definition of which, in terms of structures, is a user model) that relates functions (the definitions of which, in terms of operations, are a functional model). Those functions in turn relate input to output (the definitions of which, in terms of data types, are an informational model).

Furthermore, every node on an AXES hierarchy is expressed in terms of its viewpoints (i.e., definition, description, implementation, and execution). Whereas each node as an object is *defined* in terms of AXES statements, the *description* of each node exists in the form of the "pencil marks" of AXES statements. The *implementation* of an AXES object is performed by using the description of that object as an input in determining an equivalent form of *definition* of that object for purposes of residing on a particular machine environment. An *execution* of an object occurs when that object is assigned to a name. (In AXES an execution for a particular system begins once an object is assigned to one of its names. A system has completely been executed once objects have been assigned to all of its names. Theoretically, then, one could describe, implement, and execute a system by the very fact that its definition exists!)

The fact that aspects of control, types of models, and viewpoints are inherently integrated with respect to each other at a given node significantly simplifies any given system definition. Furthermore, each user in a development process of an AXES system is able to relate to every node in a unique way (the manager with respect to control, the designer with respect to definition, etc.).

With AXES, any system can be defined in terms of a set of *standard primitives*. The primitive control structures provide rules for the definition of dependent functions (e.g., sequential processing), independent functions (e.g., parallel processing), and selection of functions (e.g., reconfiguration). Combinations of primitives form more abstract control structures. It is also possible to tell when a design has been completed since a complete design is one that has been hierarchically decomposed until all terminal nodes of a control structure represent primitive operations or previously defined structures and operations. Since AXES has a common set of specification primitives (i.e., a common specification "machine"), we envision common tools, such as an analyzer to check for correct interfaces and a re-source allocation tool to prepare a specification for a particular machine environment [1].

Although a system can be defined directly with AXES, a more powerful use of AXES can be made by defining systems that are themselves a set of *evolving mechanisms* for defining systems. Thus a set of specification "macros" can collectively form a "language" (or management standards) for defining a particular system or family of systems. It is envisioned that each new system user is able either to use a subset of already defined statements in an AXES based library or to add new statements since the AXES language system provides for extensibility with respect to both structure and data definitions.

AXES provides a user with the capability of using *familiar dialects* for a control structure or data type. Thus, for example, a manufacturing project might have its own set of specification statements to use as a means of standardization, as might an avionics project; but both should be able to intercommunicate since these structures are based on standard primitive mechanisms to which they can both relate.

AXES is intended to provide the mechanisms to define both a *development model* and the management of a system development model, which uses that development model, as systems, since that is, after all, what they both are. Within the context of a complete development process, a means is provided to define management standards, definitions, milestones, disciplines, phases, tools and techniques, and the relationships among all the various components within a development process. A first step in this direction can be found in [1,17].

SOME PRELIMINARIES ON **AXES**

AXES uses the functional notation

$$y = f(x), \tag{1}$$

where x is the input, y is the output, and f is the operation applied to x to produce y.

In attempting to define a system as a function, we assert that for every value of "x"[2] we expect to produce one and only one value for "y." That is, we expect the system to produce predictably the same result each time we apply f to a particular value.

Now, we must incorporate into our definition a means to identify all of the acceptable inputs and outputs. In AXES, each input and output value is

---

[2]To differentiate an object from its name, the "use–mention distinction" is used throughout this paper [35]. That is, to form the name of a given name (or written symbol of any kind) we include that name (or symbol) in quotation marks.

associated with a particular set of values, called a *data type*. The syntax for each algebra, or data type definition, is similar to that used by Guttag [21], but the semantics associated with each algebra is similar to the concepts described by Hoare [22]. The semantics of our algebras assumes the *existence* of objects (see Appendix 1). That is, when we define a system, as in (1), we assume the values x and y to exist and that when f is applied to x, y corresponds to the value x.

In many systems, especially large ones, it is often not readily apparent which input values correspond to the system's intended function until the system is decomposed into smaller pieces. Although we start with a large set of "seemingly" acceptable values, a predictive system must be able to identify "truly" acceptable inputs or to produce an indication that a particular function will not be able to perform its intended function. To identify a system's intended function, we make use of a distinguished value, which we call Reject (Figure 6). This distinguished value is a member of every data type. If an input value corresponds to the value Reject as an output, then the function applied to that input is said to have detected an error. A function applied to an input value of which Reject is a component [e.g., the value (1,3, Reject)] may either assign Reject as an output value, or "recover" from the error by assigning an output value other then Reject.

Once we have identified all acceptable inputs and outputs of our system, we need a means to describe the relationship between the input and output, sometimes called the performance of the function. Relations on a set of operations give rise to a hierarchical structure, like the structure appearing in Figure 7. At each node in our hierarchy we shall put a function, with the intent that at any level of our hierarchy (a level is a set of immediate dominated nodes with respect to a particular node, sometimes called a step of refinement), we can relate the functions at that level to the function at the node immediately dominating them.

We need a set of rules to determine a level, and a set of rules to determine whether we want to create a level. To determine a level, we want all the functions at the nodes of a level to be necessary and sufficient for the replacement of the function at the node directly controlling these functions (Figure 8). This will ensure that we get no more or no less than we want, i.e., that our level is logically complete.

As we continue to build our hierarchy, each level completely replacing the function at the node directly above it, we must be able to define each point at which we want to stop. We stop when we reach a function whose behavior, i.e., its input and output relation, has been defined in terms of other operations on a defined type, and our specification is complete when we determine each stopping point. Now, if we know the behavior of each function at a bottom level and how it relates to the other functions at that same level, we know the behavior of the node directly above it. With the same reasoning, we know the behavior of the functions at each level successively closer to the root, or top node; similarly, we end up knowing the behavior of the root function itself. Thus the behavior of the top node is ultimately determined by the behavior of the collective set of bottom nodes (Figure 9).

Now we also want to assure logical consistency for a level. Since our intent, in the end, is to understand the behavior of the function at the top node, every time we talk about a value of that function we want to assure ourselves that we are talking about the same value at the level directly dominated by that function; that is, we want to be able to determine which values match up with which functions. To talk about a value we use its name, or variable. We want

Figure 6. Acceptable vs intended values of a function.

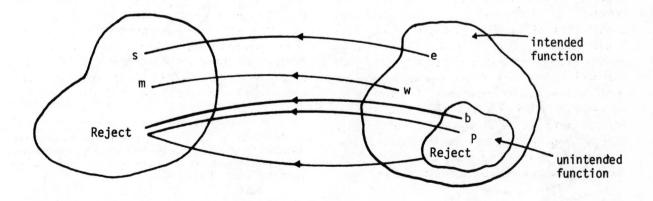

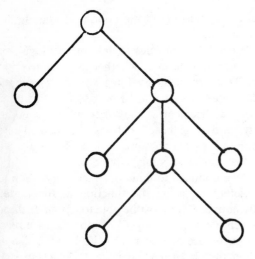

Figure 7. Hierarchical system structure.

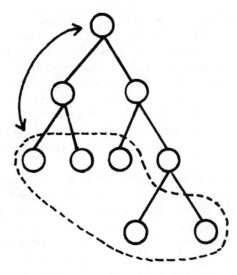

Figure 9. Endpoint completeness.

to be consistent about input variables (Figure 10) and output variables (Figure 11). To avoid specification errors in naming values, a particular name is always associated with the same value as we travel down the hierarchy.

We also want to be able to determine which functions are more important than others. For example, a function is always more important than the functions at the level dominated by that function, and at a particular level each function is assigned an importance with respect to each other function at that level (Figure 12). Among other things, we can use this information to implement specific timing relationships, both relative and absolute, without conflict.

The above concepts, defined in terms of axioms [2], are inherent in every AXES defined mechanism. Now let us see what all this means if we try to specify a particular function. For the purpose of demonstration we select the function that is to produce the greatest common divisor (GCD) of two natural numbers.

To define GCD implicitly, we have the following AXES definition [19, Appendix IV].

Derived Operation: $n_3 = \text{GCD}(n_1, n_2)$;
      where n_1, n_2, n_3, n **are** Naturals;
Factor $(\text{GCD}(n_1, n_2), n_1) = \text{True}$;   (2)
Factor $(\text{GCD}(n_1, n_2), n_2) = \text{True}$;   (3)
Entails (And(And(Factor(n, n_1), Factor(n, n_2)),
   Not(?Equal?(n, Zero))), Factor$(n, \text{GCD}(n_1, n_2)$))
   = True;   (4)
end GCD;

Each operation in terms of which GCD is defined is checked to determine if it has been previously defined. Each defined operation must eventually be able to be traced to a definition of a primitive operation on a defined type (Figure 13). This could be performed automatically. Here, GCD is defined in terms of Factor, an operation on two naturals that

Figure 10. Tracing input names.

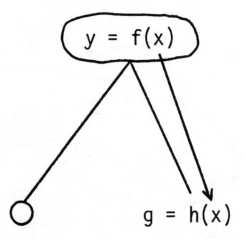

Figure 8. Level completeness.

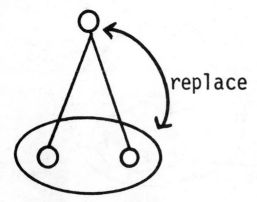

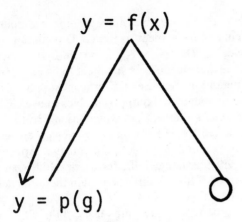

Figure 11. Tracing output names.

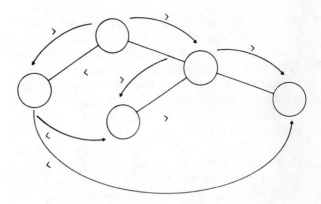

Figure 12. Complete ordering relationships.

produces a Boolean, which tells us when one natural is a factor of another; Entails, an operation on two Booleans that produces a Boolean, provides a notion of entailment; And, an operation on two Booleans that produces a Boolean, and Not, an operation on a Boolean that produces a Boolean, have the usual logical meaning on Booleans; and ?Equal?, which is a primitive operation on two naturals, provides us with a notion of equality for naturals.

Each statement about GCD in the derived operation definition is an assertion about GCD. The set of

statements about GCD must itself be shown to be consistent with the axioms of the type natural from which it is derived. The proof that GCD is consistent with these axioms is performed manually.

The technique of defining derived operations in AXES was introduced to limit the complexity of defining a type. The idea here is to define a type with the *least* number of axioms required to characterize the behavior of the objects of a type; then we can build

Figure 13. Tracing definitions of operations to primitive operations on a type.

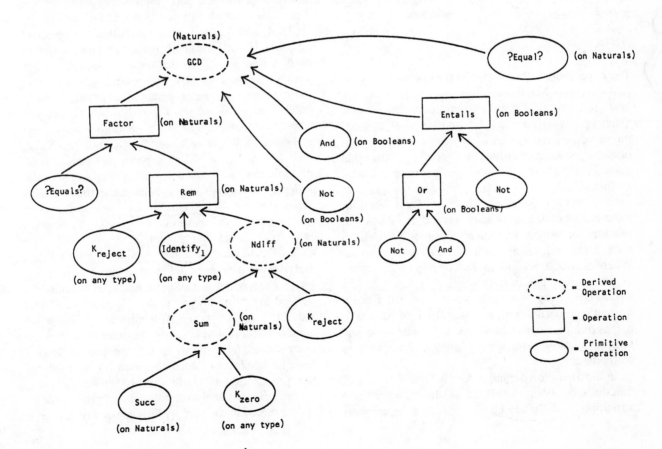

on our basic definitions and simplify our task of proving the consistency of a set of axioms. In a sense, we wind up building a hierarchy of axioms. Without a concept of derived operations we would either have to limit the number of operations allowable on a type, as suggested in languages like CLU [23], which might make a large system specification quite cumbersome to understand, or add a few more axioms to our type definition each time we introduced a new operation, as suggested by Guttag [24], thereby imposing on ourselves the task of proving the consistency of possibly hundreds of axioms in a large system environment.

Operation: $y = \text{GCD}(x_0, y_0)$;

where (x_0, y_0, y) **are** Naturals,
(x_1, y_1) **are** Naturals;

GCD: $y = A(x_0, y_0)\Big|_{x \neq 0 \text{ Or } y \neq 0}$ **or**

$\qquad\qquad y = \text{Reject}\Big|_{x_0 = 0 \text{ And } y = 0}$;

A: $y = y_0\Big|_{x_0 = 0}$ **coor**

$\qquad\qquad y = B(x_0, y_0)\Big|_{x_0 \neq 0}$;

B: $y = A(x_1, y_1)$ **join**

$\qquad\qquad (x_1, y_1) = C(x_0, y_0)$;

C: $(x_1, y_1) = D(x_0, y_0)\Big|_{y_0 \geq x_0}$ **or**

$\qquad\qquad (x_1, y_1) = \text{Xch}(x_0, y_0)\Big|_{y_0 < x_0}$;

D: $x_1 = x_0$ **coinclude**

$\qquad\qquad y_1 = y_0 - x_0$;

end GCD;

The explicit algorithm shown in the operation above, introduced by Manna and Waldinger [25], is defined here in terms of structures that relate operations. Whereas a *structure* is a relation on a set of mappings, i.e., a set of tuples whose members are sets of ordered pairs, an *operation* is a set of mappings that stand in a particular relation. An operation results, mathematically, from taking particular mappings as the arguments (nodes) of a structure. By a *function,* we mean a set of mappings that stand in a particular relation for which particular variables have been chosen to represent their inputs and outputs. Whereas structures and operations can be described as purely mathematical constructs, a function is a hybrid consisting of a mathematical construct and a linguistic construct, i.e., an assignment of particular names of inputs and outputs. Note that our use of the term "function" is slightly different from that in mathematics.

In the operation definition for GCD, a hierarchy of functions is obtained (Figure 14) by using defined structures and "plugging in" particular operations and particular variables to represent the inputs and outputs. With respect to the GCD definition, A, B, Clone$_1$, C, D, Xch, K_{Reject}, and Ndiff are functions. With respect to GCD as an object to be used, GCD is an operation because a user can supply his own particular input and output variables to use GCD as a function for another system definition. [Note that the alternative forms for Clone$_1$ and K_{Reject} are used in the corresponding AXES statements (see Appendix 2) and an alternative infix form for Ndiff using the symbol "–" for "Ndiff" is used in the AXES description.]

The particular structures used in the GCD operation definition are **or, coor, join,** and **coinclude.** The definitions for these structures can be found in Appendix 2. **or** and **join** are two of the three primitive structures. The third primitive structure, which was not used for GCD, is **include,** the definition of which also appears in Appendix 2.

All of the nonprimitive structures used to define GCD explicitly are defined in terms of the primitive structures. For example, in Figure 15 the **coor** structure is built from the **join, or,** and **each** structures. The first level of decomposition for GCD is defined in terms of the primitive **or** structure. In this case the **or** is being used to define the relationship among GCD, A, and K_{Reject}.

In using the set partition control structure (or AXES "**or**" statement) for the relationship among GCD, A, and K_{Reject}, we can check that the input and output to GCD is the same as the input and output to both A and K_{Reject}. In this case, A and K_{Reject} are partial functions of GCD. The control schema for set partition assumes the existence of data type Property (of T) (see [19]), where T is a type. A property is something that maps other things onto truth values. In Figure 14, where **or** is used for GCD, A and K_{Reject} "$x_0 \neq 0$ Or $y_0 \neq 0$" is a particular property on naturals and "$x_0 = 0$ And $y_0 = 0$" is another particular property on naturals. For a set partition, the two properties are mutually exclusive, but one or the other must apply for any value of the input set of a function at the node controlling a level.

To decide whether to decompose functions K_{Reject} and A, we determine whether either function has already been defined. Since K_{Reject} is an already defined operation on any type (it produces a Reject value for any input; see Appendix 2), we know we need not decompose it. A, on the other hand, has not been defined elsewhere, so we proceed to decompose it. The level of decomposition for A is defined in terms of the nonprimitive **coor** structure.

Only B must be decomposed as we proceed down the hierarchy associated with GCD because Clone$_1$ is

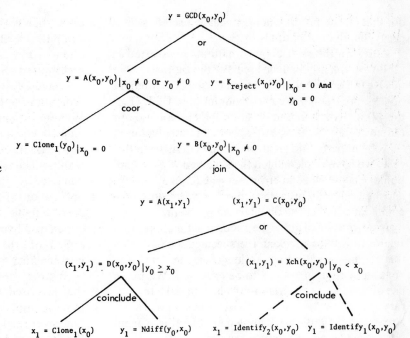

Figure 14. A control map equivalent to the AXES statements for the GCD operation.

a defined operation on any type (it provides a notion of corresponding the same value; see Appendix 2). *B* is related to *A* and *C* by means of an AXES "**join**" statement.

In using the composition control structure (or AXES "**join**" statement) in defining the relationship among functions *B, A,* and *C*, we can check the following: the input to *B* must appear as input to *C*; the output of *C* must appear as input to *A*; and *A* must produce the output for *B*.

In the operation definition of GCD, note that recursive functions are formed by combining control structures (see "*A*" in Figure 14). In this case, the total hierarchy is formed dynamically, where each occurrence of "*A*" requires a different input value. Although we statically check to assure that there is *some* input value that will produce an output, proof that the chosen algorithm will find that input cannot always be checked. A good discussion of this problem can be found in [25]. If an operation has a corresponding derived operation definition, we can use this information to help prove the possibility of termination.

We continue to decompose each function at each level until we reach the point at which a previously defined operation or structure appears. In the GCD case, we check $Clone_1$, Ndiff, K_{Reject}, and Xch. Ndiff has already been mentioned as an operation on naturals. Xch is an operation that exchanges the ordering of an input. Although previously defined [26] in terms of operations $Identify_1$ and $Identify_2$ (whose definitions appear in Appendix 2), we show the Xch

definition in Figure 14 (with dotted lines for information purposes only). A previously defined operation need not be decomposed each time it is used.

The technique of defining structures in AXES was introduced to limit the complexity of interface definitions among systems. Interface correctness can be checked statically by comparing the use of a structure to its definition.

We can extract certain computational properties from the GCD operation definition and use these properties to implement our specification in a programming language. A representative implementation is shown in Figure 16 graphically in terms of an HOS structured design diagram [27], which is now automated as a Universal Flowcharter [28,29]. We shall make the same assumptions as Manna and Waldinger

Figure 15. Tracing definitions of structure to three primitive control structures.

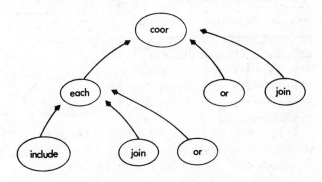

do; that is, the programming language used has integer types, but not naturals.

Although the restriction to naturals is asserted in [25], we explicitly include area 3 of Figure 16 to avoid misuse (an often occurring event during development of large programs). We check our input to GCD (Figure 14) with our input to Program B by area 1 and our output by area 4. If x_0 and y_0 both have the value of "0," then there is no greatest common divisor. In this case, we have implemented the specified K_{Reject} function of Figure 14 as an error message (area 3). Again, leaving area 6 as an assertion in the form only of a comment could cause an interface problem.

Note that each time the recursive function A of Figure 14 is to be invoked, the specification indicates that the initial values are no longer needed once the next invocation of "A" is to be executed. We make use of this fact in Program B by allocating the temporary variables "x" and "y" for each new value. Areas 7–10 of Program B implement function A from our specification of Figure 14.

There are basic assumptions implied in this implementation that may not be correct assumptions for all applications: (1) The expression "$(x, y) \leftarrow (y, x)$" implements the Xch operation. An example of misinterpretation of this expression would be a compiler which would first store the initial value of "y" and "x" and then take the *new* value of "x" and store that in "y." (2) Single statement restart capability is

either not required or, if required, is an inherent compiler capability. This type of ultrareliability is often required, for example, in aerospace real-time applications. Suppose the expression "$(x, y) \leftarrow (y, x)$" were executed and a restart occurred before the program counter advanced to the next statement. Without restart protection, area 10 would be executed over again with the *new* value of "y" and "x" and could, under some conditions, give the incorrect results. These two assumptions would have to be validated as "interface" correct for our particular application. If another implementation is desired for special applications, we start with the *same* specification (of Figure 14) and use the computational *properties* of that specification to derive a new implementation.

We have found that the same design techniques that are used to design a layer, where that design process supports the verification for errors within that layer, can serve the dual purpose of supporting the design and verification processes between development layers (e.g., between specification and the implementation of that specification).

It is in such a process, that of going from one layer to another, that we are made more aware of the significance of the separation of the "what" from the "how." For not only is it the case that the conventional specification process today is more complex than it need be because it confuses the specification with implementation considerations, but it is also the case that the conventional implementation process is more complex than it need be because its specifica-

Figure 16. Graphic description of GCD implementation.

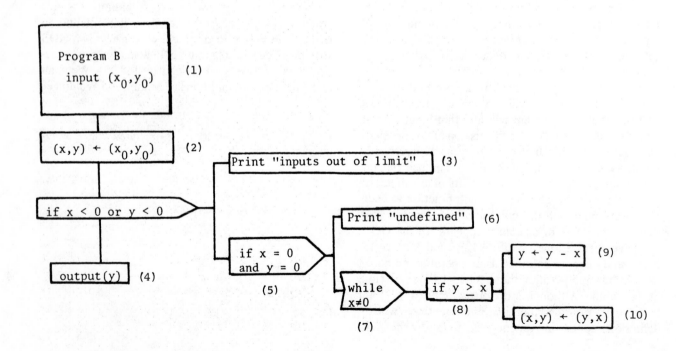

tion is confused with implementation considerations (and, more often than not, considerations that are unrealistic, incompatible with a particular implementation environment, unfeasible, or technologically out of date) or because some specification information is completely missing.

Since an AXES control hierarchy includes all of the information about the objects and the relationships of those objects in a given system, if we wanted to implement a specification in terms of, for example, a software program (such as the GCD one), we could make use of such a specification on a one-to-one basis with any of its possible implementations.

For any implementation, any function on a control map could be implemented as a procedure, a process, or as a set of in-line statements within a procedure or process. One implementation of a given specification could be multiprogrammed, another multiprocessed, and still another sequential. Values, variables, and data types can be directly translated into programming language representations of these objects.

The definition of operations on data types provides not only the set of operations that are allowable in an implementation, but also serves as a basis for checking correctness of intent. If, however, an operation is implemented as a subroutine, decisions affecting data transfer, such as "CALL by name" or "CALL by value," could vary from implementation to implementation.

The layer and level relationships with respect to communication and resource allocation can be used in the assignment of input and output access rights, data flow, functions that are to be invoked, error detection and recovery procedures, and order of execution of implemented modules.

The data flow can be traced directly on the control map in terms of access rights assignments (i.e., input can be traced down and output can be traced up the control map), which suggests, of course, that the access rights themselves can be readily determined for any given implementation. For example, with respect to scope, a variable only needs to be declared at the level where it first appears. That same variable "local" to the level of the controller above it can also be implemented as such.

It is not possible with the use of conventional computers always to maintain a single-assignment, single-reference status when going from a specification to an implementation, but it is possible to resource-allocate more efficiently an implementation when its specification is defined with single-assignment, single-reference properties. This is true since the status of any "location" is *always* known. Thus,

a reuse or a sharing of a particular location can not only be determined, but a location can always be shared when it is safe to do so.

Since every node on the control map explicitly states all input and output variables, it is possible for an implementation to be set up to implement alternative plans in the case of a failure.

Priorities can be determined readily for a particular implementation since there are some very specific rules to be followed. (For example, a controller always has a higher priority than the functions it controls.) Thus, a master sequencer-type of executive, in an implementation, would always be forced to maintain a higher priority than the functions (or processes) it invoked. Other types of ordering considerations and their alternatives, such as timing, are also readily apparent. It is clear, for example, that in the implementation of a primitive composition control structure some data from one function must be computed before the other function is initiated; whereas in a primitive set partition structure, only one of the functions need be processed for a given performance pass. Similarly, a primitive class partition would allow for more than one function to be performed at a given time should it be desirable to do so. These facts are directly translatable to the various ordering options that are available in a specification for the processing of those functions in a given implementation.

A REAL-WORLD EXAMPLE

As an illustration of how AXES can be used to represent functionally a system so as to lead the way towards a reliable and efficient implementation, we include here specifications for a satellite navigation system called **navpak**. This system is intended to update navigational parameters of Earth-referenced satellites with imaging data transmitted to the ground from the satellite. The ultimate aim is to be able to determine the orbit and attitude of the satellite precisely enough so that the imaging data can be used to answer user queries, such as "To what landmark am I pointing?" or "Where is Florida?"

This example is intended to provide a specification of the interaction, or relationship, among system components for the case in which the orbit and attitude of the satellite is not precisely known. In this case, the imaging data is used to determine orbit and attitude state estimations from landmark observations. The feasibility of an approach in which orbit and attitude estimates are obtained from landmark data extracted from Earth images generated by an on-board radiometer has been investigated [30].

The process of determining orbit and attitude can be done with varying degrees of automation. The least automated approach is one in which the landmark observation is obtained manually by displaying the imaging data (retrieved from data available on files) directly on graphics devices. In this case, the correlation function (i.e., correlating the geographic coordinates and the coordinates of the displayed image) is intended to be performed by a human user. The function relating the observation to the state of the satellite is to be performed by a computer. Here, the computer processing includes the computation of the landmark time from the coordinates of the displayed image, integrating the best known orbit–attitude information to the time of the geographic coordinates of the landmark (the time is geometrically computed from known geographic coordinates associated with the center of a given scene, or set of images), computing the uncertainty of the observation, and, upon user request, an orbit–attitude–covariance matrix update based on a classical "weighted least squares" statistical estimation algorithm [31].

A total automation of orbit and attitude determination involves automating the correlation function involved in the landmark registration in which preprocessed landmarks are input to the system and processed automatically one at a time (i.e., sequential state updates). When orbit–attitude information is very imprecise, total automation is not feasible. At these times, manual interaction with the processing system is essential so that a person can make the ultimate decision as to whether a particular observation should be incorporated or not. The system described here is designed for automatic processing with the capability for manual override at crucial processing decisions.

The system structure (or set of functional relationships) is as follows.

Structure: $y = \text{Navpak}(x, s, l, c)$;

  where x, y **are** States (of Satellites),
    s, s' **are** Ordered Sets (of Images),
    l, l' **are** Ordered Sets (of Places),
    c, c' **are** Ordered Sets (of Ordered sets (of Images)),
    θ **is an** Option,
    x', x'' **are** States (of Satellites),
    l_1 **is a** Place,
    l_2 **is an** Ordered Set (of Places);

Navpak: $y = f_1(x, s, l, c, \theta)$ **cojoin**
                                  $\theta = \text{Choose}(x, s, l)$;

f_1: $y = f_2(x, s, l, c)\Big|_{\theta=\text{Enter}}$ **or**

                $y = B(x, s, l, c)\Big|_{\theta=\text{Proceed}}$

coor $y = x\Big|_{\theta=\text{Terminate}}$;

f_2: $y = \text{Navpak}(x', s', l', c)$ **cojoin**
                    $(x', s', l') = \text{Override}(x, s, l)$;

B: $y = f_3(x, s, c, l_1, l_2)$ **cojoin** $l_1 = \text{First}(1)$
                                  coinclude
                                      $l_2 = \text{Second}(1)$;

f_3: $y = \text{Navpak}(x'', s, l_2, c)$ **cojoin**
              $x'' = \textbf{extract/filter}_{\text{Intervene,QA}}(x, s, l_1, c)$
                                  failure $x'' = x$;

syntax: Choose to Override x, s, l, c **and aid automatic correlation by Intervene or qualify with** QA **to obtain** y.

end Navpak;

Figure 17 shows the hierarchy of functions for **navpak**, a projection from the AXES definition.

We begin with an initial estimate of the state of the satellite x; a preselected "scene" or set of images of a portion of Earth s; a set of predetermined landmarks or Earth-based locations l; and a set of image sets that have been previously identified as images of particular Earth landmarks c. The intent is to produce a new state estimate y.

navpak is related to its offspring, f_1 and Choose, by a **cojoin** structure. Choose examines $x, s,$ and l and, based on these values, will produce a value of type Option, which consequently gets used as input to f_1, which in turn produces y. Function f_1 is related to its offspring f_2, B, and Clone$_1$ by **or** and **coor** structures. In AXES, a function can be replaced by its next most immediate level of decomposition by simply inserting the level description appropriately in an AXES statement, as in the decomposition for f_1. In the case of f_1, the determination as to which function is to be performed is dependent on the properties "$\theta = $ Enter," "$\theta = $ Proceed," and "$\theta = $ Terminate." Related to its offspring, **navpak** and Override, by a **cojoin** structure, f_2 provides the opportunity to select new data with Override and then to go through the same procedure recursively until the data are acceptable to "Proceed" to B or "Terminate" accepting the initial state value as the best state estimate. To Proceed at B entails using the first landmark to update the state by **extract/filter** (if **extract/filter** fails, the initial data are salvaged for the next try) and then the remaining set of landmarks, along with the new state estimate x'', is resubmitted to the next recursive instance of **navpak**. The **failure** and **extract/filter** structures, as well as some operation definitions described in this section, can be found in Appendix 2.

Each leaf of **navpak** is either a previously defined AXES operation [in this example, Clone$_1$ is an operation for any type, First and Second are primitive operations on type Ordered Set (of T)], a recursive in-

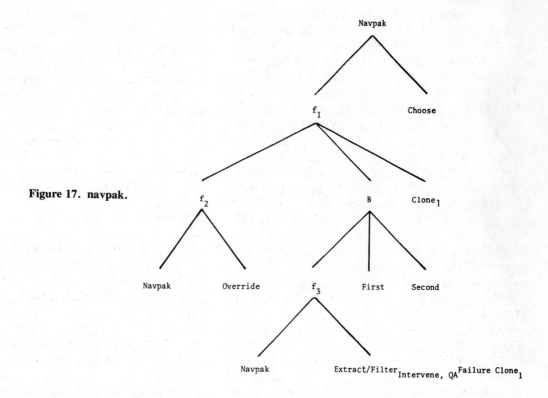

Figure 17. navpak.

vocation (**navpak** itself is recursive), or an unspecified function referred to in the user defined syntax (in this example, Intervene, QA, Choose, and Override are unspecified functions and are referred to in the syntax statement appearing at the end of the AXES definition for **navpak**).

Each variable is identified with a previously defined data type [in this example, we refer each variable to State (of T), Ordered Set (of T), Satellite, Image, Place, or Option]. The **navpak** system requires a large amount of data to be processed. Although much of the data (such as the images and pre-processed landmarks) are intended to be implemented by file representations, this description concentrates on the properties or characteristics of the data, leaving unspecified a particular implementation. Data types used for **navpak** are discussed in Appendix 1.

Once designed and verified, a structure is *used* for an operation definition by identifying particular operations for the unspecified functions and particular variables for those variables mentioned in the user defined syntax. For example, particular operations for Choose, Override, Intervene, and QA and particular variables for x, s, l, and c would be identified when *using* **navpak** for an operation definition.

Particular operations can then be allocated, either manually or automatically, to particular resources. For example, particular Choose and Override oper-

ations would most likely be assigned to human operators in a **navpak** implementation, whereas First and Second would most likely be allocated for computer processing.

We could also use **navpak** to define another structure. In such a case, for example, K_{Constant} operations could be "plugged in" for Choose and Override indicating that the "use" of the use of **navpak** would be the assignment of names of objects. This use of **navpak** would ensure that the ultimate decisions would be accomplished by manual interaction with the processing system.

extract/filter is itself defined as an AXES structure in this example. **extract/filter** determines whether the landmark measurement is suitable to be used to update the estimated state of the satellite. In Figure 18 a projection of the specification for **extract/filter** is shown. Each operation that appears at a leaf node is a specified AXES operation except for the two operations circled by dots, I and Q. These two operations are the unspecified functions of **extract/filter**. The syntax selected here for this structure is not as English in character as it is functional, as compared to the suggested syntax for **navpak**. Different syntactic forms, including those which are graphical, may be chosen for structures, depending on user preference. The **navpak** structure *uses* **extract/filter** by substituting "Intervene" for "I" and "QA" for "Q." (Other structures, such as **or, cojoin,** and **failure** are also used to define **navpak.**) In this case, we are *using* structures to define yet another structure. In a similar way, the **extract/filter** definition uses, for example, the **incorp** structure (see Appendix 2).

The landmark extraction function Lmkrgs (see Figure 18) integrates the vehicle state and covariance matrix to the time of the landmark and defines the uncertainty in the measurement. The landmark extraction function may reject the measurement automatically if it cannot find the landmark in the chosen scene. Lmkrgs is a rather lengthy operation, discussed in terms of the data types vectors, matrices, scalars, time, and angles in [32]. Of interest is the fact that many submodules and groupings of submodules were able to be used over and over again, both within the definition of Lmkrgs itself as well as for various other operations within **navpak**, specifically, operations Final and Update for the **incorp** structure (see Appendix 2).

If the landmark extraction is not successful, the measurement is rejected. If the landmark extraction is successful, the measurement is automatically correlated with a preprocessed image of the landmark (see operation Find in Figure 18 and the expansion of

Figure 18. extract/filter$_{I,Q}$.

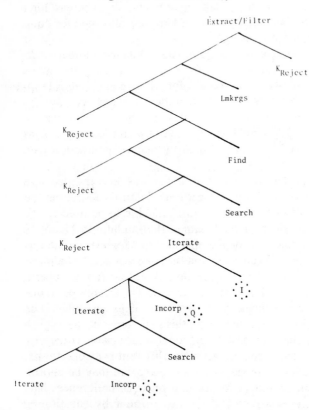

Find in terms of operations on Ordered Sets and Images, Appendix 2) in an attempt to obtain a better measurement time within the uncertainty "window." (See operation Search in Figure 18, in which a region is superimposed on the scene and the chip is matched with the images in the window of the scene.) The correlation is functionally related to the intensity of the image and the intensity of the chip for each particular location in the region being searched. The specification for Search appears in Appendix 2, along with structure definitions used to specify Search. If a negative correlation is found, the measurement is rejected automatically. If a positive correlation is determined (see the operation Iterate, Figure 18), the user has the option to incorporate the measurement immediately by specifying a particular *I* function; if this option is not exercised, automatic processing continues until the region is considered completely searched. If at any step of this process the landmark is rejected, the error filters back up the **extract/filter** structure. Subsequently, if **extract/filter** fails, error recovery is achieved, as seen in the higher-level definition for the **navpak** structure.

At each "better" correlation, the user may decide to incorporate the measurement (see the operation Incorp, Figure 18). When the "best" correlation is determined, the measured landmark is compared to a computed landmark. The computed landmark is used to construct a new region and the measurement is tested to see whether it can be found within the new region. If the measurement is not within the new region, the measurement is rejected. If the measurement is computed to be successful, the user may decide to reject the measurement if not satisfied with the results. This is accomplished by specifying a particular *Q* function. If this option is not exercised, the permanent state is updated, a successful instance of **navpak** has been completed, and the next instance of **navpak** uses the new state for its next measurement.

EXPERIENCES WITH THE APPLICATION OF HOS

HOS has now been employed by our own staff in several different types of application. They include those that were familiar to our engineers as well as some that were not familiar at the beginning of a project. There was direct involvement in some applications whereas in others, involvement only on parallel efforts. Both original designs and redesigns have been prepared. Likewise, in-line verification has been performed on some projects, independent verification on others. In all of these experiences, a conscious attempt has been made to analyze ourselves and others in order to enhance either our own techniques or theirs.

Throughout this process, certain trends, patterns, or common experiences have taken place. Phenomena have been observed, both with respect to the design and verification processes and to the other processes, all of which are directly related to design and verification.

Some Experiences on Specific Projects

One of the first projects was a respecification of the Apollo Guidance Computer (AGC) operating system (OS), an application familiar to us [26]. Unfortunately, we had a great deal of difficulty reconstructing the pieces. This was due mostly to the fact that the AGC OS was poorly documented. Our only solution for completely understanding the system (which included our own results of various design processes, including our own coding and our own verification) was to go back and pour over the original code, which was very clever and difficult to understand. When we began this effort, we thought there was little in the AGC OS upon which we could improve. This attitude was partly a result of the fact that no errors were found for several years within the OS itself. However, when we attempted to respecify the OS, we discovered that many of the development errors that occurred in the application programs using the OS would not have occurred if the AGC OS had certain other inherent properties; for although the AGC OS had properties of hidden data, it did not have properties of hidden timing. From this effort, we therefore determined that the AXES methods were very helpful in demonstrating more reliable design goals with respect to interfaces between application programs and the systems software that executes these programs.

With respect to another project, Position Locator Reporting System (PLRS), our charter was to select the most complex module, specify that module with AXES, and demonstrate the advantages of applying an effective methodology. We did just that. This was the first effort in which we attempted to use AXES in an ongoing project. Not only was our aim to demonstrate its effectiveness, but also to perform this task without impacting schedules or deliverables. In this process, however, we determined that the use of an effective methodology can benefit not only a new project, but also an ongoing project that already employs a different methodology [33].

When our engineers began this effort, the ongoing project engineers were just completing the design of their specifications and were about to embark into a design phase that would result in the implementation of computer code. As a result of our respecification to one module in their system, it was possible to have an understanding of the system and the methods used to develop that system. Recommendations for specific ways of enhancing both their system and the methods to develop that system were made, although this particular system was being developed with methods that were beyond the sophistication of most conventional systems today. In the process of defining standards for the chosen module (i.e., common structures, functions, and data types), it was determined that many of these standards were not only applicable to other modules in the system but to a family of systems within which this one resided (i.e., other communication network systems). During the same respecification process, 16 categories of questionable areas, such as unanswered questions, inconsistencies, incompleteness, and redundancies were determined. This was not only a demonstration of the advantages of using an effective methodology, but this information could be directly applied for the next phase of development. It is our own opinion, however, that many of these problem areas would have been uncovered prior to our involvement had an attempt been made during the specification phase to integrate the top levels of the specification from the beginning. (This same phenomenon was observed in the Navpak project as well, and Navpak had been around a lot longer than PLRS. In fact, a "working" implementation for it already existed. In this case, the integration of specifications was often missing since the problem was too "familiar" to the Navpak engineers.)

One of the more interesting sets of observations made was that involving a project for which a software system was conceptualized and then developed to completion by our staff. This involved the design of the Universal Flowcharter in AXES, which was implemented in PASCAL [28,29]. The programmers, who implemented the flowcharter, determined the design of the code by using AXES specifications as a guide. There were several different engineers on the project. Some of them were involved throughout the project; others only came in during the programming stage. Although our charter was to build a universal flowcharter, we were asked to apply AXES whenever possible. We had the unenviable position of attempting to design something that had never been done before, provide a design in light of continuously changing requirements (this was as a result of both designing a new concept and designing that concept for universal use), deliver and implement that design in terms of well-defined deliverables, and use a methodology (which was our own) throughout all phases of development (when this had never been done before). We were also observing ourselves continuously to see how effectively we were dealing with all of these considerations.

As delivery dates got closer, some designers panicked and decided to start implementing before all of the data types were rigorously defined and therefore before the control maps were completely defined. Others forced themselves to complete the control maps for a particular specification unit before implementation began. Of that set of modules that was completed, some had to be changed after implementation began (e.g., some data types were too specific and were better suited for another machine environment; others needed to be defined in more detail). We did find, however, that any errors that occurred in implementation were in those areas where the specification was *not complete* before implementation. That is, if all changes were negotiated and specified, chances of an error in implementation were almost nonexistent. The other modules (i.e., those that were not completely defined) were not only error prone, but took much longer to debug than those modules whose specifications were completed at least once before implementation.

The Navpak project had the most implementation details embedded in its specifications. A possible reason for this fact was that the Navpak system was already implemented in at least one form, and it is often the case that engineers update specifications further with implementation considerations when more is thought to be known about the implementation. One of the potential problems they would have, therefore, would occur when they wanted to make a change to their existing system; for each time there would be a change, it could be necessary to redesign, or at least retest, the whole system. This could be the case, for example, if a new user option were to be incorporated. This situation is typical of conventional methods and is a good example of how a design problem can affect the verification process in more than one iteration of a particular phase of development. It is for this reason that we chose to discuss a portion of this particular system in more detail.

Although each of these projects has had its own interesting aspects, it has also been quite interesting to observe the commonalities that occur among projects. The process of applying a methodology to each project has certain common elements, and the results of that process also have certain common elements.

For example, the common process of defining AXES modules within each given project produces the common result of identification of commonality between modules in that project. As a result, new structures, functions, and data types are defined and can be added to the general AXES library, as well as to the project specific AXES library. Errors, in particular interface errors, are always found within existing systems, whether they exist as requirements or as completed code. In these projects, a comparison of the old and new versions of a given module is always made. One cumulative result of all these efforts is the list of properties that are recommended for a methodology (discussed in an earlier section) as well as sets of project specific recommendations based upon that list. For every ongoing project, a minimum set of recommendations is always made, if it is not too late to make some incremental changes. For every project just starting up, a more complete set of recommendations is made. An example of one set of recommendations is shown in Table 1.

Certain advantages, as a result of using a more formalized approach, can be directly related to making life easier for the designers and verifiers on a project, as well as for the managers, implementers, and documenters. Some of these will be discussed below.

Acceleration of the Learning Process

The engineers who performed work on these projects needed to go through a learning process of some sort. This varied from learning a new application, to learning about someone else's module on a familiar application, to relearning one's own module after some time had elapsed. On these projects that had applications with which we were most unfamiliar, such as PLRS, we were able to take advantage of such a shortcoming in order to test our methods as a learning technique. Our method of understanding, in this case, was first to attempt to construct a control map; by doing so, we were able to determine existing functions and their relationships. This process not only provided us with an accelerated means of asking the questions that should be asked to construct the definition of a module, but it also became clear that this was a technique for prompting questions that otherwise might never have been asked; for during this process we found that there were areas in the documentation that were either not clear enough, missing, inconsistent, redundant, or not integrated with other areas.

The fact that we were able to use the control map technique as an accelerated learning process for ourselves suggested to us that this same technique could

Table 1. Recommendations of Standards

Definition of design goals: For example, definition of interfaces should be made in the specification phase; i.e., integrate from the beginning.

Rules for design and verification: Specifications should be defined hierarchically, and rules (e.g., those that accompany the control map) should be followed with respect to how one level in the hierarchy relates to the function directly above it. These rules should include ways of defining the invocation of a set of functions, input and output flow, input and output access rights, error detection and recovery, and ordering.

Interface specification document: For every system a standard dictionary (or library) should exist that provides common meanings, ways of saying things, ways of doing things, mechanisms for defining a system, system modules, and support tools and techniques. An evolving dictionary is recommended that includes a set of
definitions of terms
formally defined data types
formally defined control structures
system functions

User manual: A user manual should be provided that contains checklists and explains (1) how users interpret the standards in the interface specification document; (2) how designers design modules to add to the "library" of the interface specification document; and (3) how managers define new standards for system development that in turn can be converted, by the designers, to modules for incorporation into the interface specification document.

User guide to implementation: If specifications contain certain consistent properties, one can take advantage of these properties by understanding their consequences with respect to implementation. Given that there are standards for specifying, it would expedite the implementation process if standards for specifying were defined to go from a specification to an implementation. The user guide should include standards for (1) going from the specification (e.g., a control map) to a computer allocation; (2) reallocating functions to a computer, and (3) providing for reconfiguration of functions in real time.

Definition of development model: The definition of a development model is most helpful to the manager, who is responsible for integrating all the phases of development. In addition to the above recommendations, the development model should define phases of development and how to integrate them; disciplines (such as management, design, verification, implementation, and documentation); and an integrated application of tools and techniques that are to be used, and how and when they are to be used throughout the development process.

be used as a learning tool, for example, for those people new to a project; a manager learning about the work of the people in his project; designers and verifiers learning about each other's modules in the same project; implementers learning about the specification from which they are building; and users, such as maintenance people, learning about the system they are using or changing.

Acceleration of the Specification Process

In the process of constructing various specifications, we found that the control map technique was quite effective in expediting what are often considered to be design processes. In those projects for which we were given the task of defining an alternative module to an existing specification, the existing specification was, for all practical purposes, thought to be complete. But it was necessary for us to design more explicitly function definitions, including data definitions, as well as the integration of these functions. We were able to determine, for example, types of design trade-offs; design decisions with respect to interface correctness (i.e., verification before the fact); common use of specification modules (data types, operations, and structures); more powerful and simpler ways of conveying specifications; when each specification module was complete; how to integrate modules safely; common rules (or management standards) of communication between modules; methods of de-

fining a system so that changes could be made safely; and the effects of those changes traceable within the design and during the design process.

Our findings were that these methods not only supported a designer in providing designs more quickly, but also helped to point out things that might otherwise have been completely forgotten.

Verification and Validation Aid

Within our various efforts for which there was an existing module with which to start, several errors were discovered by the two-step process of formal definition of (1) the data types that were used and (2) the structure (or organization) of the existing module. Because problematic areas were detected early, later development phases were able to benefit: those problems that had not been forestalled were not only able to be detected sooner, but were also prevented from surfacing later or propagating into worse problems.

Establishment of Design Goals

In the process of understanding a module on an existing project, especially a large or complex one, it would always have been helpful if the specification had been concerned more with the definition of the relationships of specified functions (particularly at the top level). The control map technique forced us to consider integration of the functions in the system from the very beginning. Such a design philosophy, if applied, not only aids in understanding a design but eliminates integration problems that would subsequently show up in later development stages. Thus, if a specification were integrated, its implementation would be able to be an evolvement rather than a "redo," as is usually the case, especially in the development of a conventional system.

Enhancement of Existing Techniques

We found that it was possible to indicate certain problem areas or demonstrate ways of making certain improvements to an ongoing project and do so without impacting schedules or milestones if necessary (it always was in our case). Those types of improvement included enhanced methods of error location, the actual discovery of errors, and off-line methods for providing the engineer greater (or more quickly obtained) visibility. (An automated graphics tool would be an example of an add-on feature that would not necessarily have to halt progress during a system development.)

Management Visibility

In those projects in which we were asked to look at a part of a system, we were able to determine a "feel" for the state or health of the specifications of the system in general. For example, a better idea could be formed of the types of interface problem that needed to be resolved before a specification could be successfully implemented. Those steps were determined that would be necessary before a specification could be called complete, and certain recommendations were determined that were thought to be helpful in providing a more reliable specification more efficiently in the future.

The Need for Constructive Standardization

Put simply, the most urgent need on any large-system development process is that of *constructive* standardization. Some standardization, if it is effective, is certainly better than none at all; but if a project is already in development, it is not usually possible to apply an ideal and complete set of standards. However, it is possible to use incrementally those standards that would enhance the development process either by finding errors or by accelerating remaining phases of development. We did this on one very large software effort with uncompromising schedules. For example, we discovered that many in-

terface errors took place in the implementation phase when programmers would use instructions in an unstructured language, such as "GOTO + 3." Errors would creep in when someone would come along, often the same programmer, and inadvertently insert a card between the GOTO instruction and the location at which it should have gone. Once we discovered the amount of errors that resulted, we enforced by standardization the use of instructions such as "GOTO A" rather than "GOTO + 3." As a result, such errors never happened again. The same sort of introduction of standards could take place in any project. We have found that it is too easy to want to hurry the design process in order to meet deliverables. As a result, we too often hesitate to introduce additional standards into a system development process. But hindsight and recent experience, both of our own and of others, have demonstrated that in the end it pays to organize first and build later, especially when involved in the development of large and complex systems.

SUMMARY

In order to change to new and standard techniques, there is always the initial investment that is necessary for defining and developing a model, or subsets thereof for systems in general. We believe that a step in this direction has already been accomplished.

Given AXES and the AXES library as a first step, a second step is to define a set of additional structures, operations, and data types that are necessary for defining a particular family of systems. Once the initial investment has been made to establish what in essence is a way of organizing the development of a system with standards and mechanisms to accomplish that organization, the payoffs should be quite apparent. Design time during the requirements/specifications phase should be no greater than (in fact, we suspect, much less than) with conventional techniques. Implementation designs should take considerably less time than with conventional practices since it is possible to perform such a process on an almost one-for-one basis. We suspect that the largest savings will be realized within the verification processes since most of the recommended techniques provide standards that should eliminate errors before the fact, and it is just these very types of error for which one spends so much time looking today.

APPENDIX 1. Some Data Type Definitions

The following universal primitive operations are defined for any type *T* and can be assumed to apply to each new type definition:

Boolean = Equals (t_1, t_2);
   (t_1, t_2) = Clone$_2$ (t);
t_3 = Identify$_1$ (t_1, t_2);
t_4 = Identify$_2$ (t_1, t_2);

The axioms that characterize these operations and therefore apply to any type are

$$\text{where } t_1, t_2, t_3, t \text{ are } T\text{s};$$

Equals (t, t) = True;   (1)
Equals (t_1, t_2) = Equals (t_2, t_1) (2)
Entails ((Equals (t_1, t_2) And Equals (t_2, t_3)),
   Equals (t_1, t_3)) = True;   (3)
Equals (Identify$_1$ (t_1, t_2), t_1) = True;   (4)
Equals (Identify$_2$ (t_1, t_2), t_2) = True;   (5)
Identify$_1$ (Clone$_2$ (t)) = t;   (6)
Identify$_2$ (Clone$_2$ (t)) = t;   (7)

The first three axioms characterize "equality" as an equivalence relation in terms of type Boolean, which was characterized by Cushing [19 (Appendix 4)]. The fourth property of equality, replaceability, is already fixed simultaneously with the introduction of a type T (e.g., this allows us to use the "=" in each axiom definition), assuming that equality can be defined for a particular type by defining a particular equivalence relation [this must, of course, satisfy axioms (1–3) on any type] on an already known type (one that presupposes equality).

Axioms (4) and (5) characterize the ability to choose, or identify, a particular object. Axioms (6) and (7) characterize the Clone$_2$ operation, which provides for the ability to rename the same object.

We often make use of a special case of the Identify$_1$ operation, which we call the K_{constant} operation. When the first argument of Identify$_1$ is a constant, Identify$_1$ can be viewed as an operation on one argument of type T.

$$K_{\text{constant}}(t) = \text{Identify}_1(\text{constant}, t)$$

An alternative way of writing any K_{constant} operation in AXES is simply to use the constant itself. For example,

"$y = K_1(t)$" is equivalent to "$y = 1$."

This alternative form appears often in the AXES definitions throughout this paper.

Type Ordered Set (of T) makes possible the selection of values from a set of objects in a particular order. The property we want to characterize here is simply the ability to distinguish which is first from "all the rest." Ordered sets can be implemented as files, lists, or arrays, for example.

Data Type: Ordered Set (of T);
primitive operations:
   t = First(ordered set$_1$);
   ordered set$_2$ = Second(ordered set$_1$);
   Boolean = OEquals(ordered set$_1$, ordered set$_2$);
axioms:
      where t **is a** T,
        (a, b) **are** Ordered Sets (of T),
        Nullo **is a** constant Ordered Set (of T);
   First(Nullo) = Reject;
   Second(Nullo) = Reject;

OEquals(a, b) = Equals(First(a), First(b))
         And OEquals(Second(a), Second(b));
end Ordered Set (of T);

The first two axioms define the error conditions for an Ordered Set (of T), and the third axiom provides a concept of equality for Ordered Sets (of T). Ordered Set (of T) is a parameterized type in that, in its use, "T" can be replaced with the name of a particular type. In the Navpak specification, for example, we used Ordered Set (of State (of T)) as a particular use of this type.

The algebra associated with State (of T), itself a parameterized type, is a heterogeneous algebra in terms of types Time and Boolean. Time was characterized in [26].

Having a specification for Time and Boolean, we can now define State (of T) as follows:

Data Type: State (of T);
primitive operations:
   time = Stime(state);
   t = Correspondent(state);
   state$_2$ = Ssucc(state$_1$);
   Boolean = Sequals(state$_1$, state$_2$);
axioms:
      where (s_1, s_2) **are** States (of T),
          time **is a** Time,
           t **is a** T;
   Precedes?(Stime(s_1), Stime(Ssucc(s_1))) = True;
   Equals(Correspondent(s_1), Correspondent(s_2))
     = False $\subset$ Stime(s_1) $\neq$ Stime(s_2) = True;
   Sequals(s_1, s_2) = Equals(Stime(s_1), Stime(s_2))
     And Equals(Correspondent(s_1), Correspondent(s_2));
end State (of T);

The first of these axioms characterizes the time dependence of each State (of T), in terms of the previously defined AXES operation, Precedes?. Precedes? is an operation on two values of type time that produces a Boolean. It provides the notion of being able to determine if one time precedes another. The second axiom imposes a functional relationship between time dependence and the particular t of a State (of T) in that two different states cannot be associated with the same time. The third axiom characterizes equality of a State (of T) in terms of its components. In the Navpak example we used State (of Satellite) as a particular State (of T).

Satellite itself, then, must be defined as a type. The type definition given for Satellite is more analogous to a data structure definition than a behavioral definition in that it only says that two Satellites are equal if their components are equal and that there are four components of a Satellite that will characterize the type. To make this type more useful, the primitive operations specified (and perhaps a few additional ones that would have to be defined) would have to be related by means of the particular approximation to the equations of motion to be used for Navpak.

Data Type: Satellite;
primitive operations:
   vector = Position(satellite);
   vector = Velocity(satellite);

vector = Attitude(satellite);
matrix = Covariance(satellite);
Boolean = Stequals(satellite$_1$, satellite$_2$);
axioms:

        where (s_1, s_2) **are** Satellites;
Stequals(s_1, s_2) = Equals(Positions(s_1), Position(s_2))
        And Equals(Velocity(s_1), Velocity(s_2))
        And Equals(Attitude(s_1), Attitude(s_2))
        And Equals(Covariance(s_1),
          Covariance(s_2));

end Satellite;

Types Vector and Matrix are discussed in [32]. The same sort of data structure definition is supplied for type Image since the only characteristics we were able to abstract from the information we had on hand at the time of this project was that an image was an object that had a particular intensity and associated location.

Data Type: Image;
primitive operations:
  scalar = Intensity(image);
  place = Location(image);
  Boolean = Iequals(image$_1$, image$_2$);
axioms:

        where i_1, i_2 **are** images;
IEquals(i_1, i_2) = Equals(Intensity(i_1), Intensity(i_2))
        And Equals(Location(i_1), Location(i_2));

end Image;

Type Scalar is defined in [32]. Type Place was defined as part of a project now in progress for Defense Civil Preparedness Agency (DCPA) [35], where it was necessary to define a geographic coordinate system in order to distribute food, fuel, and other resources to various regions within the United States.

APPENDIX 2. Some Structure and Operation Definitions

Specifications for the specific Navpak structures **extract/filter, incorp**, and the operations Find and Search appear in this appendix. More general AXES structure definitions, which were used to define these specifications, are also included.

    The primitive control structures form the basis for defining other control structures in AXES. The use of AXES syntax and associated rules for the primitive control structures follow:

For composition, if $y = f_0(x)$,
        f_0: $y = f_2(g)$ **join** $g = f_1(x)$;

(See Figure A1.)

1. One and only one offspring (specifically, f_1 in this example) receives access rights to the input data x from f_0.
2. One and only one offspring (specifically, f_2 in this example) has access rights to deliver the output data y for f_0.
3. All other input and output data that will be produced by offspring, controlled by f_0, will reside in *local* variables (specifically, "g" in this example). Local variable "g" provides communication between the offspring f_2 and f_1.

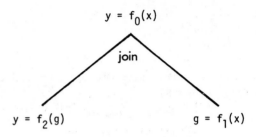

Figure A1. Composition.

4. Every offspring is specified to be invoked once and only once in each process of performing its parent's corresponding function.
5. Every local variable must exist both as an input variable for one and only one function and as an output variable for one and only one different function on the same level.

For Class partition, if (y_1, y_2) = $f_0(x_1$, x_2),
        f_0: $y_1 = f_1(x_1)$ **include** $y_2 = f_2(x_2)$;

(See Figure A2.)

1. All offspring of f_0 are granted permission to receive input values taken from a partitioned variable in the set of the parent's corresponding function domain variables, such that each offspring's set of input variables collectively represents the parent's corresponding function input variables.
2. All offspring of f_0 are granted permission to produce output values for a partitioned variable in the set of the parent's corresponding function range variables, such that the sets of each offspring's output variables collectively represent the parent's corresponding function variables.
3. Each offspring is specified to be invoked per input value received for each process of performing its parent's corresponding function.
4. There is no communication between offspring.

For set partition, if $y = f_0(x)$,
        f_0: $y = f_2(x)\big|_{\text{property}}$ **or** $y = f_1(x)\big|_{\text{Pnot(property)}}$;

(See Figure A3.)

Figure A2. Class partition.

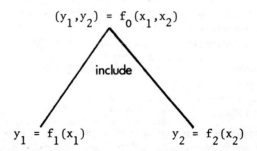

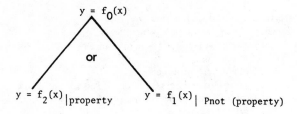

$y = f_0(x)$

or

$y = f_2(x) \big|_{\text{property}}$ $y = f_1(x) \big|_{\text{Pnot (property)}}$

Figure A3. Set partition.

1. Every offspring of the parent at f_0 is granted permission to produce output values of "y."
2. All offspring of the parent at f_0 are granted permission to receive input values from the variable "x."
3. Only one offspring is specified to be invoked per input value received for each process of performing its parent's corresponding function.
4. The values represented by the input variables of an offspring's function comprise a proper subset of the domain of the function of the parent.
5. There is no communication between offspring.

In the above definitions x, y, y_1, y_2, x_1, x_2 are ordered sets of variables; f_0, f_1, f_2 are functions; property is of type Property (of T) [19]; and Pnot is a primitive operation on type property whose result is a property exclusive of its input argument.

One structure, the **each** structure, is intended to be able to perform the same operation on each member of an ordered set of objects. Similar structures have been useful on other projects, such as [33] and [28].

Structure: $y = \text{Each}(x, b)$;
  where x, y are Ordered Sets(of T),
    b is of some type;
Each: $y = \text{Nullo} \big|_{\text{First}(x)=\text{Reject}}$ or $y = f_1(x, b) \big|_{\text{First}(x)\neq\text{Reject}}$;
f_1: $y = \text{Combine}(y_1, y_2)$ join $(y_1, y_2) = f_2(x, b)$;
f_2: $(y_1, y_2) = f_3(a_1, b_1, a_2, b_2)$ join $(b_1, b_2) = \text{Clone}_2(b)$
      include $(a_1, a_2) = \text{Clone}_2(x)$;
f_3: $y_1 = F(a', b')$ include $y_2 = \text{Each}(a'', b'')$
        join $a' = \text{First}(a_1)$
        include $a'' = \text{Second}(a_2)$
        include $b' = \text{Clone}_1(b_1)$
        include $b'' = \text{Clone}_1(b_2)$;
syntax: $y = F([x], b)$;
end Each;

The **each** structure has one unspecified operation F. First and Second are primitive operations on type Ordered Set (of T), defined in Appendix 1. Clone$_2$ is a primitive operation on any type and is also defined in Appendix 1. Combine is a derived operation on type Ordered Set (of T), the specification of which follows:

Derived Operation: $y = \text{Combine}(a, b)$;
  where a is a T,
    (b, y) are Ordered Sets (of T);
First(Combine(a, b)) = a;
Second(Combine(a, b)) = b;
end Combine;

The **each** structure can be used to define the **cojoin** structure, which provides the ability to select components of an input set of a function that serves as common input for dependent subfunctions; similarly, the **coinclude** structure provides the same ability for independent subfunctions, and the **coor** structure provides the same capability for a selection among subfunctions. In each of the following definitions, some type is an ordered set of variables. The notation "$\text{id}_{[b]}(x)$" is an alternative form for the notation "$\text{id}([b], x)$" used to indicate that the user of the structure is to supply the value for "b" as a constant, thereby specifying particular id functions as mappings associated with "x" only. An implicit specification of "a" or "b" occurs when the id function is "performed" by simply replacing "$x_{[a]}$" or "$x_{[b]}$," respectively, by a particular subset of variables of "x" in the use of this structure.

Structure: $y = \text{Cojoin}(x)$;
  where $x, y, g, x_{[a]}, x_{[b]}, x_1, x_2$ **are of some type,**
    a, b **are** Ordered Sets (of Naturals);
  Cojoin: $y = A(x_{[b]}, g)$ **join** $(x_{[b]}, g) = f_1(x)$;
  f_1: $(x_{[b]}, g) = f_2(x_1, x_2)$ **join** $(x_1, x_2) = \text{Clone}_2(x)$;
  f_2: $x_{[b]} = \text{id}_{[b]}(x_1)$ **include** $g = B(x_{[a]})$
        join $x_{[a]} = \text{id}_{[a]}(x_2)$;
syntax: $y = A(x_{[b]}, g)$ **cojoin** $g = B(x_{[a]})$;
end Cojoin;

The specification of id, which is a derived operation on Ordered Set (of T) and Naturals, follows:

Derived Operation: $t = \text{id}_n(\theta)$;
    where n is a Natural,
      θ is an Ordered Set (of T),
      t is a T;
  $\text{id}_n(\theta) = \text{id}_{n-1}(\text{Second}(\theta \big|_{n>1}))$ or First$(\theta \big|_{n=1})$ or Reject $\big|_{n=0}$;
end id;

Structure: $(y_1, y_2) = \text{Coinclude}(x)$;
  where $x, x_1, x_2, y_1, y_2, x_{[a]}, x_{[b]}$ **are of some type,**
    a, b **are** Ordered Sets (of Naturals);
  Coinclude: $(y_1, y_2) = f_1(x_1, x_2)$ **join** $(x_1, x_2) = \text{Clone}_2(x)$;
  f_1: $y_1 = A(x_{[a]})$ **join** $x_{[a]} = \text{id}_{[a]}(x_1)$
        include $y_2 = B(x_{[b]})$
        join $x_{[b]} = \text{id}_{[b]}(x_2)$;
syntax: $y_1 = A(x_{[a]})$ **coinclude** $y_2 = B(x_{[b]})$;
end Coinclude;

Structure: $y = \text{Coor}(x)$;
  where $x_1, y_1, x_{[a]}, x_{[b]}$ **are of some type,**
    property **is a** Property (of T),
    (a, b) **are** Ordered Sets (of Naturals);
  Coor: $y = f_1(x) \big|_{\text{Has(property},x)=\text{True}}$ **or**
        $y = f_2(x) \big|_{\text{Has(property},x)=\text{False}}$;
  f_1: $y = A(x_{[a]})$ **join** $x_{[a]} = \text{id}_{[a]}(x)$;

  f_2: $y = B(x_{[b]})$ **join** $x_{[b]} = \text{id}_{[b]}(x)$;
syntax: $y = A(x_{[a]}) \big|_{\text{property}}$ **coor**
        $y = B(x_{[b]}) \big|_{\text{Pnot(property)}}$;
end Coor;

Has is a primitive operation on type property [19] that provides a notion of associating a particular property with a value.

The **failure** structure, the definition of which follows,

provides for the ability to "recover" from a "detected" error. The definition uses the **cojoin, coor, join,** and **each** structures.

Structure: $y = \text{Failure}(x)$;
   where $(x, g, y, x_{[a]})$ **are of some type,**
     a **is an** Ordered Set (of Naturals);

Failure: $y = f_1(x, g)$	**cojoin** $g = E(x)$;
$f_1\colon y = \text{Clone}_1(g)\Big\|_{g \neq \text{Reject}}$	**coor** $y = f_2(x)\Big\|_{g=\text{Reject}}$;
$f_2\colon y = F(x_{[a]})$	**join** $x_{[a]} = \text{id}_{[a]}(x)$;
syntax: $y = E(x)$	**failure** $y = F(x_{[a]})$;

end Failure;

The operation definition for Clone$_1$, which is also used to define the **failure** structure, is defined in terms of the **join** structure and primitive operations on any type.

Operation: $u' = \text{Clone}_1(u)$;
   where u_1, u_2, u, u' **are** Ts;
  Clone$_1$: $u' = \text{Identify}_1(u_1, u_2)$ **Join** $(u_1, u_2) = \text{Clone}_2(u)$;
end Clone$_1$;

An alternative way of writing the Clone$_1$ operation in AXES is simply to omit writing the operation itself; e.g.,

"$y = \text{Clone}_1(x)$" is equivalent to "$y = x$."

This alternative form appears often in AXES definitions throughout this paper.

every is a structure that requires at least two members of an Ordered Set (of T) as input and successively performs the same operation on the result of the operation performed on the first two members and the next member, as in the sum of a set of naturals or the product of a set of rationals.

Structure: $y = \text{Every}(x)$;
   where $x, x_1, x_2', x_2, g, y, x_2''$ **are of some type;**

Every: $y = \text{Reject}\Big\|_{x_2=\text{Reject}}$	**or**	$y = f_0(x_1, x_2\Big\|_{x_2 \neq \text{Reject}})$
	join $(x_1, x_2) = S(x)$;	
$f_0\colon y = F(x_1, x_2'\Big\|_{x_2''=\text{Reject}})$	**coor**	$y = f_1(x_1, x_2', x_2''\Big\|_{x_2'' \neq \text{Reject}})$
	cojoin $(x_2', x_2'') = S(x_2)$;	
$f_1\colon y = F(x_1, g)$	**cojoin** $g = f_0(x_2', x_2'')$;	

syntax: $y = f<x>$;
end Every;

The **every** structure uses operation S, which produces the first and second component of an Ordered Set, the specification of which follows:

Operation: $(x_1, x_2) = S(x)$;
   where (x_1, x_2) **are** Ordered Sets (of T),
    x_1 **is a** T;
  S: $x_1 = \text{First}(x)$ **coinclude** $x_2 = \text{Second}(x)$;
end S;

The **extract/filter** structure, discussed in the main text of this paper, is specified using structures (of which **cojoin, coor,** and **coinclude** have been specified above and **incorp** is specified below), data types previously defined (see Appendix 1), and operations (of which Find and Search are specified here and Lmkrgs is discussed in length in [32] and in summary in the main text of this paper).

Structure: $y = \text{Extract/Filter}(x, s, m, c)$;
  where x, y, x_m **are** States (of Satellites),
   x, chip **are** Ordered Sets (of Images),
   m **is a** place,
   c, ellipse, ellipse', ellipse''
    are Ordered Sets (of Ordered Sets (of Images)),
   s **is an** Ordered Set (of Images),
   p_1, p_2 **are** Scalars;
   θ **is an** Option;

Extract/Filter: $y = f_1(x, s, m, c\Big\|_{m \neq \text{Reject}})$ **coor**
        $y = \text{Reject}\Big\|_{m=\text{Reject}}$;

f_1: $y = f_2(x_m, s, m, c, \text{ellipse})$ **cojoin**
     $(x_m, \text{ellipse}) = \text{Lmkrgs}(x, s, m)$;

f_2: $y = \text{Reject}\Big\|_{x_m=\text{Reject}}$ **coor**
     $y = f_3(x_m, s, m, c, \text{ellipse}\Big\|_{x_m \neq \text{Reject}})$;

f_3: $y = f_4(x_m, s, m, \text{chip}, \text{ellipse})$ **cojoin**
     $\text{chip} = \text{Find}(m, c)$;

f_4: $x' = \text{Reject}\Big\|_{\text{chip}=\text{Reject}}$ **coor**
    $x' = f_5(x_m, s, m, \text{chip}, \text{ellipse}\Big\|_{\text{chip} \neq \text{Reject}})$;

f_5: $y = f_6(x_m, s, m, \text{chip}, \text{ellipse}', p_1)$ **cojoin**
     $(p, \text{ellipse}') = \text{Search}(\text{chip}, \text{ellipse})$;

f_6: $y = \text{Reject}\Big\|_{p_1 \leq 0}$ **coor**
    $y' = \text{Iterate}(x_m, s, m, \text{chip}, \text{ellipse}', p_1\Big\|_{p_1>0})$;

Iterate: $y = N(x_m, s, m, \text{chip}, \text{ellipse}', p_1, \theta)$ **cojoin**
      $\theta = I(p_1)$;

N: $y = \text{Iterate}(x_m, s, m, \text{chip}, \text{ellipse}', p_1\Big\|_{\theta=\text{Enter}})$ **coor**
  $y = R(x_m, s, m, \text{chip}, \text{ellipse}', p_1\Big\|_{\theta=\text{Proceed}})$
      coor
   $y = \textbf{incorp}_Q(x_m, s, m, \text{ellipse}'\Big\|_{\theta=\text{Terminate}})$;

R: $y = W(x_m, s, m, \text{chip}, \text{ellipse}'', p_1, p_2)$ **cojoin**
    $(\text{ellipse}'', p_2) = \text{Search}(\text{chip}, \text{ellipse}')$;

W: $y = \text{Iterate}(x_m, s, m, \text{chip}, \text{ellipse}'', p_2\Big\|_{p_2-p_1 \leq 0})$ **coor**
   $y = \textbf{incorp}_Q(x_m, s, m, \text{ellipse}''\Big\|_{p_2-p_1>0})$;

syntax: $x' = \textbf{extract/filter}_{I,Q}(x, s, m, c)$;
end Extract/Filter;

Structure: $x' = \text{Incorp}(x, s, m, e)$;
  where x, x', x_t **are** States (of Satellites),
   e, e' **are** Ordered Sets (of Ordered Sets (of Images)),
   θ **is an** Option,
   m **is a** Place,
   s **is an** Ordered Set (of Images);

Incorp: $x' = f_1(x_t, e, e')$ **cojoin**
     $(x_t, e') = \text{Final}(x, s, m, e)$;

f_1: $x' = \text{Reject}\Big\|_{\text{Test}(e,e') \leq 0}$ **coor**
   $x' = \text{Assure}(x_t, e, e')\Big\|_{\text{Test}(e, e')>0}$;

Assure: $x' = f_2(x_t, e, e', \theta)$ **cojoin** $\theta = F(e, e')$;

f_2: $x' = \text{Assure}(x_t, e, e'\Big\|_{\theta=\text{Enter}})$ **coor**
   $x' = \text{Update}(x, e, e'\Big\|_{\theta=\text{Proceed}})$
   coor
    $x' = \text{Reject}\Big\|_{\theta=\text{Terminate}}$;

syntax: $x' = \textbf{incorp}_F(x, s, m, e)$;
end Incorp;

incorp is a structure intended to incorporate a measurement and update the estimated state of a satellite.

In **incorp**, Test is a scalar valued operation that checks the quality assurance of the measurement based on predetermined criteria [32], and operation F is a user supplied operation that may impose additional quality assurance checks. F could be allocated to a human operator, for example, whose "better judgment" would be the additional quality assurance function.

Operation: Chip = Find(m, c);
  where m **is a** place,
      c_2, c **are** Ordered Sets (of Ordered Sets (of Images)),
      l_2, c_1, chip **are** Ordered Sets (of Images),
      l_1 **is an** Image,
      g **is a** place,
      b, b' **are** Booleans;

Find: chip = $f_1(m_1, c_1, c_2)$ **cojoin** $(c_1, c_2) = S(c)$;
f_1: chip = Reject$\big|_{c_1=\text{Reject}}$ **coor** chip = $f_2(m, c_1, c_2\big|_{c_1\neq\text{Reject}}$);

f_2: chip = $f_3(m, c_1, c_2, b)$ **cojoin** b = Locate(m, c_1);
f_3: chip = $c_1\big|_{b=\text{True}}$ **coor** chip = Find(m, $c_2\big|_{b=\text{False}}$);

Locate: $b = f_4(m, l_1, l_2)$ **cojoin** $(l_1, l_2) = S(c_1)$;
f_4: b = False$\big|_{l_1=\text{Reject}}$ **coor** $b = f_5(m, l_1, l_2\big|_{l_1\neq\text{Reject}}$);

f_5: $b = f_6(m, l_2, b')$ **cojoin** b' = Equals(m, g)
                      cojoin g = Location(l_1);
f_6: b = True$\big|_{b'=\text{True}}$ **coor** b = Locate(m, $l_2\big|_{b'=\text{False}}$);

end Find;

Find is an operation that "finds" the set of images that contains place m in a set of sets of images c.

Operation: (p, e') = Search(chip, e);
  where chip **is an** Ordered Set (of Images),
      R, e, e' **are** Ordered Sets (of Ordered Sets (of Images)),
      p, p' **are** Scalars,
      ξ, χ **are** Ordered Sets (of Scalars);

Search: $(p, e') = f_1($chip, $e\big|_{\text{First}(e)\neq\text{Reject}}$)
              coor $p = 0$
              coinclude $e' = e\big|_{\text{First}(e)=\text{Reject}}$;

f_1: $(p, e' = f_2($chip, R, $p'))$
              cojoin $(R, p') = f_3($chip, e);

f_2: (p, e') = Search(chip, $R\big|_{p'\leq 0}$)
              coor $p = p'$
              coinclude $e' = R\big|_{p'>0}$;

f_3: R = Second(e)   **coinclude** $p' = f_4(\xi, \chi)$
              join ξ = Intensity[First (e)]
              include χ = Intensity[chip];

f_4: $p' = \dfrac{\Sigma<[\xi * \chi]>}{\Sigma<[\xi * \xi]> * \Sigma<[\chi * \chi]>}$;
end Search;

Search is an operation that matches a preselected set of images with a component of a set of sets of images when a positive correction p is found. The **each** and **every** structures are used to define p. In the definition of Search, "Σ" is an alternative symbol for the sum operation on Scalars and "$*$" is an alternative symbol for the product operation on Scalars.

ACKNOWLEDGMENT

We would like to thank Barry Boehm of TRW for a most helpful review of this paper.

REFERENCES

1. M. Hamilton and S. Zeldin, Integrated Software Development System/Higher Order Software Conceptual Description, TR-3, Higher Order Software, Inc., Cambridge, Massachusetts, November 1976.

2. M. Hamilton and S. Zeldin, Higher Order Software— A Methodology for Defining Software, *IEEE Trans. on Software Engineering* SE-2 (1), 9–32 (1976).

3. C. V. Ramamoorthy and H. H. So, Appendix to Requirements Engineering Research Recommendations, *Software Requirements and Specifications: Status and Perspectives* (August 1977).

4. M. A. Jackson, *Principles of Program Design,* Academic Press, New York, 1975.

5. R. F. Bridge and E. W. Thompson, A Module Interface Specification Language, Information Systems Research Laboratory, University of Texas at Austin, Technical Report No. 163, December, 1974.

6. J. E. Horowitz Guttag and D. Musser, The Design of Data Structure Specifications, *Proc. 2nd International Conference on Software Engineering,* October 1976, pp. 414–420.

7. L. Robinson and R. C. Holt, Formal Specifications for Solutions to Synchronization Problems, Computer Science Group, Stanford Research Institute, 1975.

8. Computer Sciences Corporation, A Users Guide to the Threads Management System, City, State, November 1973.

9. M. W. Alford, *R*-Nets: A Graph Model for Real-Time Software Requirements, *Proc. MRI Symposium on Computer Software Engineering,* April 1976, pp. 97–108.

10. C. G. Davis and C. R. Vick, The Software Development System, *Proc. 2nd International Conference on Software Engineering,* October 1976, Addendum pp. 27–43.

11. Hughes Aircraft Company, 1975 IR&D Structured Design Methodology, Vol. II: Structured Design, FR 76-17-289, Fullerton, California, 1975.

12. D. Teichroew and E. A. Hershey III, PSL/PSA: A Computer-Aided Technique for Structured Documentation and Analysis of Information Processing Systems, *IEEE Trans. on Software Engineering* SE-3 (1), 41–48 (1977).

13. IBM, HIPO: Design Aid and Documentation Tool, IBM SR20-9413-0, Bethesda, Maryland, 1973.

14. D. Ross, Structured Analysis (SA): A Language for Communicating Ideas, *IEEE Trans. on Software Engineering* SE-3 (1) 16–34 (1977).

15. M. L. Wilson, The Information Automat Approach to Design and Implementation of Computer-Based Systems, Report IBM-FSD, IBM, Bethesda, Maryland, June 1975.

16. M. Hamilton and S. Zeldin, Reliability in Terms of Pre-

dictability, *Proceedings, COMPSAC '78,* Chicago, Illinois, IEEE Computer Society Cat. No. 78CH1338-3C, November, 1978.

17. M. Hamilton and S. Zeldin, The Manager as an Abstract Systems Engineer, *Digest of Papers, Fall COMPCON 77,* Washington, D.C., IEEE Computer Society Cat. No. 77CH1258-3C, September 1977.

18. M. W. Cashman, An Interview with Prof. Edsger W. Dijkstra, *Datamation* 23 (5), 164–166 (1977).

19. M. Hamilton and S. Zeldin, AXES Syntax Description, TR-4, Higher Order Software, Inc., Cambridge, Massachusetts, December 1976.

20. M. Hamilton and S. Zeldin, The Foundations of AXES: A Specification Language Based on Completeness of Control, Doc. R-964, Charles Stark Draper Laboratory, Inc., Cambridge, Massachusetts, March 1976.

21. J. Guttag, The Specification and Application to Programming of Abstract Data Types, Univ. of Toronto Technical Report CSRG-59, September 1975.

22. C. A. R. Hoare, An Axiomatic Approach to Computer Programming, *CACM* 12, 576–580 (1969).

23. B. H. Liskov and S. N. Zilles, Specification Techniques for Data Abstractions, *IEEE Trans. on Software Engineering* 1 (1), 7–9 (1975).

24. J. V. Guttag, E. Horowitz, and D. Musser, Some Extensions to Algebraic Specifications, in *Proc. of an ACM Conference on Language Design for Reliable Software* (D. B. Wortman, ed.), Raleigh, North Carolina, Association for Computing Machinery, New York, March 1977.

25. Z. Manna and R. Waldinger, The Logic of Computer Programming, *IEEE Trans. on Software Engineering* SE-4 (3) 199–229 (1978).

26. Higher Order Software, Inc., Techniques for Operating System Machines, TR-7, Cambridge, Massachusetts, July 1977.

27. M. Hamilton, and S. Zeldin, Top–Down/Bottom–Up, Structured Programming and Program Structuring, Rev. 1. Doc. E-2728, Charles Stark Draper Laboratory, Inc., December 1972.

28. D. Harel and R. Pankiewicz, The Universal Flowcharter, TR-11, Higher Order Software, Inc., Cambridge, Massachusetts, November 1977.

29. J. Rood, T. To, and D. Harel, A Universal Flowcharter, *Proceedings of the NASA/AIAA Workshop on Tools for Embedded Computer Systems Software,* Hampton, Virginia, November 7–8, 1978, pp. 41–44.

30. A. F. Fuchs, C. E. Velez, and C. C. Goad, Orbit and Attitude State Recoveries from Landmark Data, *The Journal of Astronautical Sciences* XXIII (4), 369–381 (1975).

31. Computer Sciences Corporation, Navpak Design for Landsat and Kalman Filter Applications, CSC/TM-77/6012, Arlington, Virginia, January 1977.

32. Higher Order Software, Inc., A Demonstration of AXES for Navpak, TR-9, Cambridge, Massachusetts, September 1977.

33. Higher Order Software, Inc., The Application of HOS to PLRS, TR-12, Cambridge, Massachusetts, November 1977.

34. S. Cushing, Geographically Distributed Systems in Higher Order Software, DCPA Memo No. 7, Higher Order Software, Inc., Cambridge, Massachusetts (in preparation).

35. J. R. Searle, review of J. M. Sadock, *Towards a Linguistic Theory of Speech Acts, Language* 52, 1976.

INFORMATION SYSTEMS DESIGN METHODOLOGIES: A Comparative Review
T.W. Olle, H.G. Sol, A.A. Verrijn-Stuart (editors)
North-Holland Publishing Company
© *IFIP, 1982*

THE USER SOFTWARE ENGINEERING METHODOLOGY:
AN OVERVIEW

Anthony I. Wasserman

Medical Information Science
University of California, San Francisco
San Francisco, CA 94143 USA

The User Software Engineering Methodology is a collection of
methods and tools to support the systematic development of
interactive information systems. The methodology focuses
equally on aspects of systematic software development and user
participation in system specification. The USE methodology is
supported by a set of tools in the Unix^{TM} environment
specifically directed to the needs of interactive information
systems. This paper provides an overview of the methodology and
tools, with emphasis on the innovative aspects of the USE
methodology. Attention is also given to some of the decisions
made in the evolution of the methodology. The USE methodology
is demonstrated through the example of creating an interactive
information system to support the management of IFIP Working
Conferences.

INTRODUCTION

Many computer-based systems may be described as interactive information systems
(IIS), providing their users with conversational access to data. Such users are
frequently unfamiliar with the technical details of computer hardware and software
and view the computer system only as a tool that may be of help to them (or may
possibly be required) in doing their jobs. Trends toward distributed systems,
lower hardware costs, and the criticality of user/program interfaces all indicate
the importance of developing tools and techniques specifically for this class of
systems.

Accordingly, the User Software Engineering project was undertaken in 1975 with the
objective of creating a methodology to support the specification, design, and
implementation of interactive information systems, including the construction of
tools that would support the developer of such systems. Attention was
specifically focused on the application program developer, who had been
traditionally squeezed between the realistic needs of users and the lack of
suitable tools for meeting those needs. At that time, virtually all interactive
systems were being developed in a haphazard, ad hoc manner, and the emerging
techniques for software engineering did not adequately address this very important
class of programs. The goals of the project combined notions of software
engineering and systematic program development with those of user involvement in
the early stages of the software development process.

After considerable study of the state-of-the-art in interactive information systems and tools for their construction, it became possible to identify some requirements for the methodology and tools. These requirements included the following key points:

1. Specification of user/program interaction -- a tool was needed for specifying the user/program dialogue; furthermore, this tool should produce a representation of the dialogue that was both comprehensible to the user and sufficiently precise for the developer

2. Design guidelines for user/program dialogue -- guidelines could assist the application developer in creating a dialogue between the user and the program; ideally, it should be possible to identify several types of dialogues, where the appropriate dialogue type for a given application can be determined from a study of user, organization, and hardware characteristics

3. Experimentation with user/program dialogue -- users needed the chance to work with a "breadboard" of the system to help create a hospitable user interface before full-scale development of the production version of the system was begun; availability of such a tool would assist the user in thinking more carefully about how the system would work and how it would be used; this tool could thus also serve as an effective analysis tool, leading to a better specification and eventually to a better system

4. Language for implementation of interactive information systems -- available programming languages either lacked support for the needs of interactive programs or for the objectives of structured programming (or both!) [1]

5. Assistance in maintenance of program production library -- an automated tool could help keep track of the documentation associated with the specification, design, implementation, and testing of interactive information systems; such a tool could also help keep track of versions of the system and its individual modules

6. Orientation to small and medium-sized machines -- the methodology and tools should take advantage of hardware trends toward distributed systems and mini- and microcomputers; it was assumed that application programs would probably run on such computers and that the development would take place on such computers, regardless of the target machine

7. Integration of tools into a suitable development environment -- these new tools should be built on top of other tools for common tasks such as program editing, text formatting, language development, and other common software development activities, since it was not sensible to undertake to build these tools from scratch

These seven requirements were above and beyond more general requirements for a software development methodology, which includes the following points:

1. The methodology should cover the entire software development cycle. It does relatively little good to have a methodology for software design if there is no systematic procedure to produce the specification used for the design and/or the executable program that must be created from the design. Thus, a methodology must assist the developer at each of the stages of the development cycle.

2. The methodology should facilitate transitions between phases of the development cycle. When a developer is working on a particular phase of a project (other than requirements analysis), it is important to be able to refer to the previous phase and to trace one's work. At the design stage, for example, one must make certain that the architecture of the software system provides for all of the specified functions; one should be able to identify the software module(s) that fulfill each system requirement. During implementation, it should be easy to establish a correspondence between

modules in the system design and program units, and between the logical data objects from the design stage and the physical data objects in the program. It is important to note that one must be able to proceed not only forward to the next phase of the life cycle, but also backward to a previous phase so that work can be checked and any necessary corrections can be made. This phased approach to software development makes it clear that information lost at a particular phase is generally lost forever, with an impact on the resulting system. For example, if an analyst fails to document a requirement, it will not appear in the specification. Eventually, during acceptance testing (or perhaps during system operation), that failure will be recognized and it will be necessary to make modifications to the system.

3. The methodology must support determination of system correctness throughout the development cycle. System correctness encompasses many issues, including not only the correspondence between the system and its specifications, but also the extent to which the system meets the user needs. Accordingly, the methodology must not only be concerned with techniques for validation of the complete system, but must give attention to obtaining the most complete and consistent description of user needs during the early stages of the project. For example, the methods used for analysis and specification of the system should aid problem understanding by the developers, the users, and other concerned parties.

4. The methodology must support the information system development organization. It must be possible to manage the developers, and the developers must be able to work together. This requirement implies the need for effective communication among analysts, developers, and managers, with well-defined steps for making progress visible throughout the development activity. The intermediate products generated by the methods and tools, such as a detailed design or an acceptance test plan, can be reviewed by the organization so that progress can be effectively measured and quality assured.

5. The methodology must be repeatable for a large class of software projects. While it is clear that different methodologies will be needed for different classes of systems and for different organizational structures, an organization should be able to adopt a methodology that will be useful for a sizeable number of programs that they will build. Certainly, it makes little sense to develop a methodology for each new system to be built.

6. The methodology should support the eventual evolution of the system. Systems typically go through many versions during their lifetimes, which may last eight to ten years or more. New requirements arise from changes in technology, usage patterns, or user needs, and these changed or additional requirements must be reflected in a modified system. The development methodology can assist this evolutionary activity by providing accurate external and internal system documentation and a well-structured software system that is easily comprehended and modified by those making the changes to the system.

7. The methodology must be supported by automated tools that improve the productivity of both the individual developer and the development team.

These objectives led to development of the User Software Engineering methodology for the creation of interactive information systems and to the creation of tools that support the methodology. Four principal tools have been developed to date:

1. TDI (Transition Diagram Interpreter) -- a tool for encoding transition diagrams that permits the rapid construction and modification of prototype user/program interfaces, as well as the creation of system prototypes

2. PLAIN (Programming LAnguage for INteraction) -- a procedural programming language derived from Pascal that contains features for building interactive information systems, including strings, patterns and pattern-matching operations, exception-handling, and relations, with a set of operations to support definition and manipulation of relational data bases

3. Troll -- a tool that provides a relational algebra-like interface to a small relational database system, used both as the runtime support of PLAIN and as the "backend" of TDI in the construction of system prototypes

4. Module Control System -- a tool that supports a modular organization of the software system, provides version control, and automatically logs developer activities

OVERVIEW OF THE USE METHODOLOGY

An important initial consideration in developing the User Software Engineering methodology was to support a systematic approach to software development. The potential benefits of such an approach include:

1. improved reliability;

2. verifiability, at least in an informal sense;

3. improved evolvability, including portability and adaptability;

4. system comprehensibility, as a result of improved structure;

5. more effective management control of the development process;

6. higher user satisfaction.

In general, a systematic approach to software development increases effort in requirements analysis, specification, and design. This increase is balanced by expected lower costs for testing and system evolution, since the implemented system will represent a better fit to the user's needs and will operate more reliably than would otherwise be the case.

We found much to commend such a systematic approach to software design and development, but also found one extremely serious flaw: when developing information systems, there may be a long period of time between the early stages of analysis and specification and the actual availability of the system while the systematic procedure is followed. During this time, the user's needs may change significantly, and the user has no system to use in the interim. When the system finally becomes operational, it may do what was originally specified, but user experience with the system may show that what is needed is quite different. As a result, a large part of the systematic development effort may have been wasted as it becomes necessary to redesign and reimplement a system that meets the newly identified needs of the user.

In short, we found some merit to the traditional idea of "let's build one of these and see how it works". If such a system is conceived as a "throwaway" system, intended only to identify user needs or to serve those needs during an interim period while development of a production system is in progress, and it can be built quickly and inexpensively, then there is ample justification for proceeding with this approach, which we shall term the experimental approach. A key aspect of the experimental approach to software development is to be able to build and modify prototype versions of the system very quickly. (Indeed, much of the success of programming systems such as INTERLISP [2] and SMALLTALK [3] may be attributed to the ease with which one can produce an executable system.)

Our approach to the system life cycle has been to introduce prototypes as an aid to analysis and specification. Integration of prototyping into a methodology seems to strike a good balance between the needs of the user and the desire to proceed in a well-disciplined way. This integration of prototyping, combined with a unique method for specifying interactive information systems, plays an important role in the USE methodology.

The interactive information system is modelled and specified using a combination of formal and informal methods. A prototype of the dialogue is built using TDI, and functionality is provided in the prototype by coupling TDI with Troll. The system is then implemented in PLAIN, with the entire development and evolution process controlled by the Module Control System.

The remainder of this paper describes the User Software Engineering development methodology and tools in greater detail, giving an historical perspective on the project. We also show the application of the methodology and tools to the design and development of an interactive information system for the management of a technical conference.

REQUIREMENTS ANALYSIS IN THE USE METHODOLOGY

Requirements analysis and specification are the first steps in the software life cycle. As such, they are a principal determinant of system quality, including reliability, usability, and fit to user needs. Errors introduced at the early stages are often not caught until acceptance testing, if then. Similarly, functions not requested during this process are likely to be omitted from the operational system.

As a result, many methods for requirements analysis and specification have been developed during the past few years. Among these techniques are Structured Systems Analysis (SSA) [4,5], SADT[TM] [6], Information Systems and Analysis of Change (ISAC) [7], and many, many others. A lengthy desription of such techniques is beyond the scope of this paper; some of them are briefly described in [8].

In short, requirements analysis deals with problems of understanding the problem and of communicating that understanding among the concerned individuals and organizations. These requirements are then incorporated into a system specification, which also includes information on the planned use of the system, development constraints, cost constraints, and user considerations.

The analysis and specification process typically also results in the creation of user documentation, based upon design of the user/program "dialogue." This dialogue may be interactive, or may simply be batch-oriented, with a deck of user input producing a file of program output. The input and output may be alphanumeric characters, or may involve a variety of non-alphanumeric characters and devices, such as light pens, graphics, plotters, and audio.

The biggest difficulty with analysis and specification of interactive information systems is that the user (or user representative) and developer must reach agreement on system capabilities and operation at a very early stage. If the user has little or no previous experience with computer-based systems, the user is not likely to have a good understanding of what a computer system can do, let alone be able to decide upon a suitable form of user/program interaction or even to specify a complete set of desired system capabilities.

The likely outcome of this situation is that the user and the developer are unable to communicate effectively with one another and that the user is unable to convey to the developer the information that would result in a totally satisfactory system. The resulting system will then be at best partly satisfactory, necessitating an ongoing process of evolution, as the user comes to understand the functions of the system as compared to the evolving information processing needs of his organization.

Accordingly, any assistance that can be provided in the requirements analysis and specification activity is likely to have a large payoff in terms of reducing the need for maintenance activities and in reducing the cost of the information system over its lifetime. In particular, a means for involving the user in the analysis phase and in the design of the user/system interaction can provide a significant amount of this necessary assistance [9,10,11,12,13]. User involvement in the USE methodology is enhanced through the use of prototypes of the user/program dialogue, and, where feasible, the system itself.

The analysis process is iterative, with the first iteration attempting to reach a reasonable (definitely not perfect) understanding of the problem from the user's perspective. The goal here is to gather enough information about the problem and expected usage patterns to be able to construct a prototype of the user interface to the system. Thus, the analyst must understand the kinds of functions (or transactions) to be performed by the user (or by each class of users) and must use this information to create a user/program dialogue that allows the user to request these functions, with any needed options, as easily as possible.

One or more of the above mentioned analysis techniques can be used for this analysis process. In this regard, we have been extremely pragmatic, and have not chosen to develop our own analysis methods, relying instead on effective use of techniques created by others. Furthermore, we have found that it is possible to be flexible concerning the use of a process-oriented versus a data-oriented approach to analysis.

Indeed, we view these approaches as being complementary. If one identifies operations (process-oriented approach), one cannot then help but identify the objects upon which the operations are performed. Conversely, using principles of data abstraction, identification of operations must follow directly from identification of data objects.

We have been most successful using Structured Systems Analysis and the principles of conceptual database design and data abstraction as put forth by Smith and Smith [14,15]. Structured Systems Analysis not only provides a way of modelling systems through data flow, but also leads to a relational data base design and the creation of a data dictionary. The data abstraction ideas help to refine the data base design, as well as providing a framework for formalizing the specification at a later stage and establishing different views of the system.

Our approach to data base design, carried out informally at the early stages, is to follow a multi-level approach, along the lines of the ANSI/SPARC framework. The conceptual model is intended to capture the semantics of the data. The external model defines the view of the data for different classes of users, so that a given system may contain several external models reflecting a single conceptual model; these are all mapped into a single internal model. We create a conceptual model of the application database objects and their relationships, then define a set of "views" of the database, corresponding to the external models for each user class, and then later define a set of normalized relations as the internal model.

The overall structure of our analysis procedure can then be described as a sequence of five steps.

1. Identify system objectives and constraints, including conflicts of interest among user groups, based upon the problem statement

2. Model the existing system using a requirements analysis method (Structured Systems Analysis)

3. Construct a conceptual model of the data base, using the Semantic Hierarchy Model of Smith and Smith

4. Produce a system dictionary containing the names of all operations, all data items, and all data flows

5. Review the analysis results within the development group and, insofar as possible, with the user(s) and/or customer(s)

At this point, we can either carry out additional analysis based upon the review, proceed to build a prototype of the user/program dialogue, or proceed with the complete system specification. It should be noted that the latter alternative is taken only if the prototype stage is omitted. Our presentation of the methodology will, of course, include the role of prototypes.

Before proceeding further, though, we can examine the application of these analysis ideas to a particular problem.

THE IFIP WORKING CONFERENCE PROBLEM

The problem that we will use to exemplify the USE methodology has been proposed by IFIP Working Group 8.1 (Design and Evaluation of Information Systems) as a standard problem to compare various methodologies for information system design. Briefly summarized, it calls for the development of an information system to support the organization of a small technical conference, providing primarily for the activities of the technical program committee, but also for the general organizing activities. The information system requirements are shown in Figure 1.

> The information system that is to be designed shall support the activities of both the Programme Committee and the Organizing Committee for an IFIP Working Conference, excluding activities of conference budgeting, hotel arrangements, and production of the conference proceedings.
>
> The following Programme Committee activities shall be supported:
>
> 1. Preparing a list of persons to whom the Call for Papers is to be sent.
>
> 2. Registering the letters of intent received in response to the Call.
>
> 3. Registering the contributed papers on receipt.
>
> 4. Distributing the papers among referees.
>
> 5. Collecting the referee reports and selecting the papers for inclusion in the conference program.
>
> 6. Grouping selected papers into sessions for presentation and selecting a chairman for each session
>
> The following Organizing Committee activities shall be supported:
>
> 1. Preparing a list of people to invite to the conference.
>
> 2. Issuing priority invitations to national representatives, Working Group members, and members of associated working groups.
>
> 3. Ensuring all authors of each selected paper receive an invitation.
>
> 4. Ensuring authors of rejected papers receive an invitation.
>
> 5. Avoiding sending duplicate invitations to any individual.
>
> 6. Registering acceptance of invitations.
>
> 7. Generating final list of attendees.

Figure 1 -- Summary of IFIP Working Conference Problem

We have followed the User Software Engineering methodology to the greatest extent possible (some of the automated tools were not operational) in specifying, designing, and developing an interactive information system that met the requirements for this system. We were encouraged to build such a system to support the organizing activities of another IFIP Working Conference for which the author is Chairman of the Technical Programme Committee. In fact, the ongoing conference organizing activities served to identify problems that might not have been found if treating the problem abstractly. It should also be noted, though, that the requirements for the particular Working Conference were slightly different from those of the general problem statement, and we amended the requirements slightly to serve our purposes more directly. Specifically, we ignored the second requirement for the Programme Committee, since our previous conference planning experience had shown relatively little correlation between the letters of intent and the actual papers received.

It should be noted at the outset that our mode of work for this particular problem is not entirely representative of the way in which the author would expect the USE methodology to be applied in the future. This difference occurs for three reasons:

1. Much of the design and development was done by students who were in the process of learning the various information system development techniques and then applying them to this particular problem;

2. The tools (described below) were not all implemented, so it was necessary to limit some activities to hand-coding.

3. The author served as the customer for the system, the developer of the USE methodology, and instructor for the students. Despite efforts to separate the three roles, they could not help but become occasionally intertwined. It would have been ideal to have the problem undertaken and solved by an organization having no direct connection to the author.

Nonetheless, every effort was made to follow the methodology and to provide the best possible example of its application to this problem.

ANALYSIS OF THE IFIP CONFERENCE PROBLEM

Beginning with the brief problem statement, the analysis effort focused on achieving a deeper understanding of the connections between the various activities, the reporting and communication requirements of the various organizers, and, to a lesser extent, the relationship between the aspects of conferences addressed in the problem and the broader aspects of conference organization.

Because the students had only a slight familiarity with problems of conference organization, they were forced to follow the methodology to uncover the details properly. Their approach was multifaceted, involving reading of books on technical conferences to obtain general background [16,17], reading of professional society (ACM and IEEE Computer Society) guidelines for conference organization, interviews with the customer for the system, and personal experience as attendees at such conferences.

Throughout this analysis process, though, the goal was to produce a model of the conference organization activity, using Structured Systems Analysis, and a conceptual data base design. As with most analysis activities, there was some difficulty in bounding the scope of the problem and in understanding the details that distinguished the IFIP conference problem from other conference organization problems. This effect may have been exaggerated in our experience, since early efforts at building an SSA model were far too broad.

Eventually, though, a model of the conference organizational structure was produced. A small excerpt of this model is depicted in Figure 2.

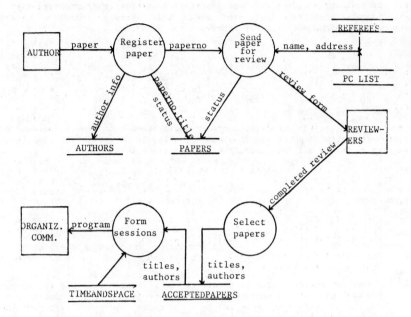

Figure 2. SSA overview diagram of Programme Committee activities.

A system dictionary (not shown) was also made as part of these **analysis** activities. It should be noted that the model is regarded as preliminary and highly subject to change at this point in the development cycle. From this point, though, the next step involves the construction of a prototype of the user/program dialogue. Prototype construction requires design of the dialogue itself, which necessitates making numerous assumptions about program functions and the way in which they will be used, then experimenting with those assumptions and making changes as necessary.

THE ROLE OF PROTOTYPES

In our earlier development of the USE methodology, as described in [18] for example, we went directly from our analysis to a system specification, as described below. While that approach worked successfully on a couple of applications, the potential users didn't really seem to get a true sense of how the system would actually work in practice.

Accordingly, we sought a way to provide the user with that necessary understanding, and identified a prototype of the user/system dialogue as an effective way to achieve that goal. There were four reasons for building such a prototype:

1. it would enable to user to evaluate the interface in practice and to suggest changes to the interface;

2. it would enable the developer to evaluate user performance with the interface and to modify it so as to minimize user errors and improve user satisfaction;

3. it would facilitate experimentation with a number of alternative interfaces and modification of interfaces without having to redraw the diagrams, a potentially tedious and time-consuming process; furthermore, it would be possible to generate the dialouge quickly and to make minor revisions in a matter of minutes;

4.   it would give the user a more immediate sense of the proposed system and thereby encourage users to think more carefully about the needed and desirable characteristics of the system.

This last goal was seen as being particularly significant. In typical development environments, there is a long interval of time between the analysis of the problem and the construction of an operational system. At the outset, the user may have a very limited idea as to what the IIS should do, often as a result of limited knowledge as to what computer systems can do or of intellectual distance from the system itself. In other words, it is often hard for a user to deal with an IIS in abstract terms and to be able to describe needs and possible uses.

With an automated tool, though, the user would be able to simulate the interaction at a very early stage in the development cycle. Even though the functionality of the system is minimal, the user is still forced to think more closely about the task being automated and about the way in which operations will be requested. The result of that thinking should be a more accurate understanding of the problem and improved communication between the user and the analyst/developer.

An even more significant result of this process would be that the original IIS would be a better fit to user needs than was previously possible. The user interface would have been thoroughly tested, and a larger set of desired operations would have been implemented. Thus, the amount of needed system evolution would be reduced, with a corresponding reduction in the cost of the IIS over its lifetime.

The construction of such a prototype then alters the traditional software life cycle, adding this prototype construction as an intermediate step between the requirements analysis and specification.

To see how this prototyping construction method works in practice, it will first be necessary to discuss guidelines for the construction of user/program dialogues, then the method for specification of these dialogues, and then their automation in a prototype. That discussion will, in turn, lead to a lengthier discussion of the specification method and prototypes of an entire system rather than just prototypes of the dialogue.

DESIGN AND MODIFICATION OF USER/PROGRAM DIALOGUE

In many respects, creation of user/program dialogue is the most critical aspect of designing an IIS, since the user's satisfaction with the system will be strongly determined by the ease with which it is possible to request operations. If it is difficult to interact with the IIS, then the user will be less likely to use it and may reject it entirely.

Of course, the user interface is determined not only by the dialogue itself, but also be diverse environmental factors such as terminal type, output speed, readability of user input, hard vs. soft copy, noise level, terminal placement, and input mode (keyboard vs. non-keyboard). These human factors have been the subject of a significant amount of recent research [19,20,21,22,23,24] involving psychologists, industrial engineers, computer scientists, and others, and the discussion of this research is beyond the scope of this paper.

Our approach has been to glean from this research and from our own empirical observations a set of guidelines that we can follow in making a preliminary user/program dialogue. We are aided in this process by the requirements analysis process, which has provided us with information on user characteristics, environmental considerations, legal constraints (e.g., the need for a hard copy), and application needs.

The actual dialogue design process, though, remains largely ad hoc, with only our general guidelines to aid the design process. These guidelines, discussed at greater length in [25], may be summarized as follows:

1. Interactive systems should be interactive, and should not require the user to input lengthy strings conforming to a precise syntax.

2. Underlying aspects of the computer system should be hidden as fully as possible.

3. Users should not be able to cause abnormal program termination.

4. Users should be notified if any request can have major consequences.

5. Systems should provide online assistance.

6. Input requirements should be tailored to user characteristics.

7. Output messages should be tailored to characteristics of terminals.

8. Different user skill levels should be distinguished.

9. User errors should not require a large amount of additional user effort.

10. Response time should be consistent for the same request, and meaningful feedback should be provided to the user.

In many interactive information systems, the permissible operations (transactions) are defined in the specification, so that it is frequently possible to build such systems around a series of user commands. Even so, the process of determining the desired set of operations and then the appropriate commands is not well defined.

The process of dialogue design is basically an iterative one and involves a certain necessary amount of experimentation before developing a set of commands (or other dialogue format) that both provides the desired set of operations and satisfies the user's requirements for ease of use. In many system developments, though, it is difficult to iterate and to experiment with various possible dialogues, for two major reasons. First, the modification of the dialogue may involve major structural changes to the software system, particularly where the addition of new transactions is involved. Second, the interaction may not be testable until the entire IIS has been built, making the cost of experimentation and subsequent modification inordinately high.

Because of the criticality of the user/program dialogue in the overall design of an IIS, though, such iteration and experimentation is essential. Thus, we have given attention to the development of tools and techniques to facilitate the design of the user interface, and to the creation of program development methods that simplify the evolution of that interface.

We have developed a user-centered technique for the specification of an IIS that treats the user/program dialogue as a key component of the system specification and as a starting point for system decomposition [26]. As noted, an interactive program may be viewed as a set of transactions between a user and the program. Each transaction consists of a set of messages transmitted between a user and the program. Furthermore, each transaction results in some "operation", typically involving retrieval from or modification to data in a data base. Thus the specification method consists of specifying the data base, the operations, and the dialogue that comprises each transaction.

From this standpoint, it can be seen that these operations can be organized (perhaps aggregated) to form transactions. Then, appropriate dialogue can be defined for each of these transactions. Such an approach permits separation of the program structure from the particulars of the user/program dialogue, but also makes the dialogue a cornerstone of the specification process, rather than relegating it to a secondary role.

The IIS user interface provides the user with a language for communicating with the system. The interface can take many forms, including multiple choice (menu selection), a command language, a database query language, or natural language-like input. In all cases, however, the normal action of the program is determined by user input, and the program may respond in a variety of ways, including results, requests for additional input, error messages, or assistance in the use of the IIS.

The critical observation, though, is that the semantics of the IIS, i.e., its actions, are driven by raw or transformed user input. As with programming languages, the user language in its runtime context determines the semantic actions to be performed; the resemblance between such a user language and an interpreted programming language is quite strong.

Accordingly, an effective specification technique for programming languages can be used effectively for specifying user interfaces. One can write down the grammar of the user input, and associate program actions with the successful recognition of "words" or "phrases" in the grammar.

A variety of language definition techniques are applicable in this setting. One of the key goals for defining the dialogue was the ability to associate the actions with specific inputs. Thus, some of the highly formal language definition schemes or the report format used for Algol 60 and Pascal were not ideal. Two techniques seemed equally useful: language specification as given to a translator writing system such as YACC [27] and transition diagrams [28]. We chose the latter primarily because of its pictorial representation.

Transition diagrams have been used for a variety of language translators, and are used as the formal specification of the MUMPS programming language [29]. Our own experience has indicated that they are well suited to the construction of interpreters and that they make the sequence of language processing quite visible. In short, they are useful both to the implementers who can build an interpreter directly from the diagram and to the computer-naive users who can easily see what actions will result from the recognition of specific inputs.

A transition diagram is a network of nodes and directed paths. Each path may contain a token, corresponding to a character string in the primitive alphabet (such as ASCII), or the name of another diagram. If the path is blank, it will be traversed as the default case, i.e., if all other paths leaving a given node fail. Scanning of the diagram begins at a designated entry point and proceeds until reaching an exit node or a dead end (no successful match on the paths from a given node). A semantic action may be associated with any path; traversal of the path causes the associated action to occur.

As a brief example, consider Figure 3, showing part of a transition diagram. The diagram is initially in state START, as shown by the double circle. The message associated with START is displayed. If the input string is 'quit', the path from START to BYE will be traversed and the associated action 1 (not specified here) will be taken. Also, the message associated with the node BYE will be displayed. Similarly, if the input string is 'help', the path from START to INFO will be traversed, and the message associated with the node INFO will be displayed. If the input string is 'enter', the subconversation NEWENTRY, represented by another transition diagram (not shown here), will be invoked. NEWENTRY may return with the value good or bad, which then determine the path followed and the action to be taken next.

Intuitively, one can see that paths may contain arbitrary strings, and that the state transitions can invoke arbitrary actions. The distinguished inputs then lead to different states from which other input symbols may cause yet additional actions.

In this manner, one may specify the user/program dialogue. Indeed, one may specify an entire IIS, showing the dialogue and associated actions as a set of transition diagrams, accompanied by specifications of the actions and a conceptual data base design. The user may review these diagrams and see the valid inputs and the actions that occur as a result of those inputs.

Experience with this technique showed that users were indeed able to review the transition diagrams and to observe the nature of the user interface. Furthermore, the diagrams served as a good basis for system design and subsequent implementation. However, it seemed that the users did not really get a true sense of how the system would actually work from the diagrams alone.

We originally tried to incorporate all of the error handling and all of the online assistance information in the transition diagrams. Although that approach worked, it could lead to extremely complicated diagrams, particularly if one wanted to provide extensive diagnostic messages and to support a user-oriented dialogue. For example, if one wanted to give a user three tries at providing some input, and wanted to then take some default action or wanted to provide different messages for each occurrence of the error, it would be necessary to add extra nodes to the diagrams above those needed for "normal" processing. It can be seen that such diagrams could easily become unwieldy.

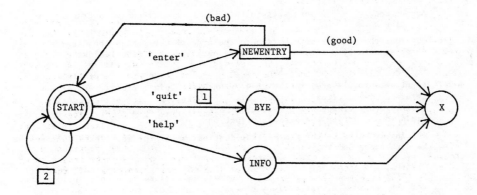

```
START = "Please type a command"
BYE   = "Byebye"
INFO  = "Valid commands are ..."
```

Figure 3 -- Sample transition diagram

As a result, the diagrams that are shown to the user for review only contain the "normal" case, that of providing "correct" input. This approach represents a compromise between showing the entire dialogue with its possible complexities and showing a subset of the dialogue, with increased comprehensibility. (It is, of course, necessary to specify the entire dialogue for the developer.)

Accordingly, we sought to automate the transition diagrams. The primary intent of such automation was to be able to encode the diagrams quickly and to generate the user interface so that the prospective user could interact with it. Another advantage would be the ability to encode the error-handling and online assistance parts of the more-detailed diagrams so that the users could gain experience with those aspects of the dialogue.

THE TRANSITION DIAGRAM INTERPRETER

These goals motivated the design and implementation of the Transition Diagram Interpreter (TDI). The TDI accepts the encoding of one or more transition diagrams as input and produces an executable program simulating the specified interface. An action can be associated with each arc on the transition diagram, so that it would be theoretically possible to implement the entire IIS in this manner. In practice, such an implementation strategy is not likely to be used; however, it is very useful to provide a sample of the user interface or a rapidly built prototype of the system.

Input to the TDI is specified in five sections:

1. Conversation name definition section -- identifies the diagram and its starting point

2. Variable definition section -- permits the specification of names corresponding to lexical elements that may be described as strings of alphanumeric or numeric characters

3. Node message section -- associates a message with a node in the diagram

4. Body section -- describes the structure of the diagram and its transition conditions (see below)

5. Action section -- defines actions that may be associated with transitions in the diagram.

The body section contains information on the arcs of the transition diagram. Each arc is represented by a line of text, where each line has five fields:

1. source name -- the name of the source of the arc

2. input selector -- one of the following: a "Unix regular expression", a returned value from a subconversation (another transition diagram), a variable name defined in a variable definition declaration, or an empty field, representing the default situation;

3. destination name -- the name of the destination of the arc (possibly the same as the source node)

4. action -- if supplied, this item causes the execution of a Unix command prior to entry to the destination. This command is treated as a Unix shell command and thus enables a wide variety of semantic actions, including the display of a message and the invocation of an executable program module

5. return -- can be associated with terminal nodes in a diagram (those from which there are no exit arcs) as a value that can be passed back to the invoking diagram. This facility permits error conditions to be transmitted, and permits the invoking diagram to proceed along different paths depending on events in the subconversation.

In this way, the set of diagrams can be encoded, and a running prototype produced. The encoding of the transition diagram of Figure 3 is shown in Figure 4. (For purposes of clarity and readability, the notation shown here differs slightly from the actual TDI input.)

In addition to providing a "mockup" of the user/program dialogue that serves to familiarize the user with the functions of the system, the TDI can provide some other useful capabilities. First, it can check the encoded diagrams for consistency, making sure, for example, that there is a path from each node. (The problem of checking to see that there is a path from entry to exit becomes combinatorially large as the number of nodes and paths increase.)

```
Diagram     Start Node
```

Figure_3   START


```
Node      Message

START     "Please type a command"
BYE       "Byebye"
INFO      "Valid commands are ... "
X         " "
```

Source node	input selector	destination	action	returns
START	'enter'	<NEWENTRY>		
START	'quit'	BYE	1	
START	'help'	INFO		
START		START	2	
<NEWENTRY>	(good)	X		
<NEWENTRY>	(bad)	START		
BYE		X		
INFO		X		


```
Action Number    Action

1                Close files
2                echo 'illegal command'
```

Figure 4 -- Encoding of transition diagram of Figure 3

Second, it can be used to _measure_ user performance with the interface. It is a very straightforward task to capture information on keystrokes, errors, and other aspects of use to determine the ease of use, the error rates for various user classes, and other key measures of user performance with the system.

One can easily extend this notation to support a variety of input devices in conjunction with the TDI. The input selector, for example, could be defined for graphics primitives, such as the selection of alternatives with a light pen. Such a selection could cause a state transition in much the same way as is done here with characters and character strings.

Furthermore, a more sophisticated positioning of output messages can be supported. In simplest form, the output is simply produced beginning at the point where the output device cursor is positioned. As another example, though, one could associate a line number and a column number with any output to be placed on a screen oriented device. Thus, the message "(12,30)'Hello'" would put the word 'Hello' on line 12 of the display beginning at column 30. Similar kinds of control can be devised for other kinds of output devices.

DIALOGUE DESIGN FOR THE IFIP CONFERENCE EXAMPLE

The conference management system, named CONMAN, would support two classes of end user: a Programme Committee chairman and an Organizing Committee Chairman. (Of course, those individuals could authorize others to use the system in the same capacities.)

Our approach, in this case, was to define two similar command language based dialogues. In both cases, the user would request a given kind of operation with a command, and the program would then elicit any additional information. We have found this approach to be successful in the past, and it can do an excellent job of meeting our general guidelines for dialogue design.

We begin, then, by creating a transition diagram for the "top" level of the dialogue, the command level, as shown for the Programme Committee in Figure 4. From this diagram, it can be seen that the Programme Committee chairman has the following transaction types available:

1. Invite someone to submit a paper.

2. Receive a paper

3. Add a name to referee list

4. Assign a paper to a referee for review
       Figure 4. Transition diagrams for Programme Chairman dialogue

5. Form a conference session

6. Provide help in the use of the system

7. Quit

Each of these transaction types is shown in a rectangular box, designating a subconversation, shown by another transition diagram. In most cases, the path leading to the subconversation is not a string literal, but is rather a name, again designating the name of another transition diagram. If there were simply a single string to cause the transition to the subconversation, this could be shown without using another diagram. However, our desire to support both novice and expert users has led to providing several ways to make the transition, and it is more convenient to show this situation with the additional diagram. Furthermore, this approach makes the top level diagram almost entirely independent of the actual input text, thereby isolating the design decisions concerning the dialogue to the greatest extent possible. The disadvantage to this approach is that it creates additional diagrams that must be reviewed and incorporated into the prototype.

Now, the diagrams shown in Figure 5 may be encoded for the TDI. This encoding is shown in Figure 5.

It can be seen from the transition diagram named receipt that three different inputs, 'np', 'new paper', and 'receive', are treated similarly, causing the initiation of the subconversation <new_paper>. Experienced users can use the terse notation, while other users can use one of the other two equivalently. Numerous alternatives can be provided to accommodate different user preferences as long as there is no conflict in the grammar.

The flavor of this dialogue can also be seen from the diagrams in Figure 5. The system begins by typing

    Welcome to CONMAN
    $

The user then types a response. If the response is 'quit', the program will reply with the message 'Byebye', carry out semantic action 3 of closing the database, and quit. If the response causes one of the subconversations to begin, the CONMAN system will prompt the user for input. Thus, in the <new_paper> subconversation, the system will respond first with

    Enter paper title:

It will subsequently prompt for author names and mailing addresses, then assign a paper number and display this information to the user for confirmation.

It can be seen from the structure of the transition diagrams and the TDI input that it is very easy to alter the diagrams and the input as the users work with the prototype and show their preferences for specific input formats and output messages.

Figure_5

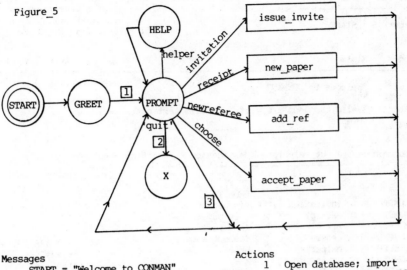

Messages
    START = "Welcome to CONMAN"
    PROMPT = "$"
    HELP = "Valid commands are ..."
    X = "Byebye

Actions
    1   Open database; import
         relations needed by PC
    2   Close database
    3   write 'illegal command'

Figure 5a -- Transition diagram for "transaction level"
        of CONMAN for Programme Committee

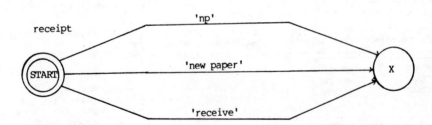

Figure 5b -- Transition diagram showing valid inputs
        to cause transition receipt in Figure 5a

```
Diagram    Start Node
------------------------------
Figure_5   START


Node       Message
------------------------------------------------------------------

GREET      "Welcome to CONMAN"
PROMPT     "$"
HELP       "Valid commands are ..."    {entire text not shown}
X          "Byebye"


Source node    input selector    destination    action    returns
------------------------------------------------------------------------

START                            GREET
GREET                            PROMPT         1
PROMPT         invitation        <issue_invite>
PROMPT         receipt           <new_paper>
PROMPT         newreferee        <add_ref>
PROMPT         choose            <accept_paper>
PROMPT         helper            HELP
PROMPT         'quit'            X              2
PROMPT                           PROMPT         3
HELP                             PROMPT


Action Number    Action
------------------------------------------------------------------------
1                Open database; import relations needed by Programme Committee
2                Close database
3                write 'illegal command'


Diagram    Start Node
------------------------------
receipt    START


Node    Message
------------------------------



Source node    input selector   destination    action    returns
------------------------------------------------------------------

START          'np'             X
START          'new paper'      X
START          'receive'        X


Action Number    Action
------------------------------
```

Figure 6 -- Encoding of diagrams in Figure 5 for TDI

SPECIFICATION OF INTERACTIVE INFORMATION SYSTEMS

The results of analysis, including use of the prototype dialogue, is used to develop the specification for the interactive information system. As the first detailed statement of system functions, specifications play a critical role in the development activity, providing a foundation for future work and a link between the user's concept of the system and its actual implementation.

Specifications are of critical importance in the USE methodology, since:

1. The specification is a means for precisely stating the system requirements. The specification can be compared against the requirements definition to ascertain the correspondence between the specification and the user's needs.

2. The specification provides insight into the system structure and is used during the design phase as a checkpoint against which to validate the design. Typically, there will be an iteration between specification and design, as insight into some of the system construction problems helps to clarify the specification.

3. The specification is the basis against which testing and verification are performed. Clearly, one cannot prove that a program is correct in the absence of a clear understanding of the program's behavioral characteristics. Similarly, although certain kinds of testing can locate clerical errors and other low-level problems, system testing and acceptance testing require comparison of the system against an objective specification.

4. Modifications and enhancements to a system throughout its operational lifetime require an understanding of the system functions, as documented in the specification. During this phase, the specification can help to locate those system functions that must be changed, and can then be revised accordingly.

The implication of this multifaceted role for specifications is that a specification must be able to serve (to a greater or lesser degree) each of these four different functions. We identified some desirable goals for specifications, including:

1. completeness -- capturing all of the features of the system

2. comprehensibility -- ensuring that the specification can be understood by those who must approve it and work with it

3. testability -- attempting to quantify system requirements and to be sufficiently precise so that the correctness of the implemented system can be tested and/or verified

4. traceability -- ensuring that the system specification meets the requirements, and writing the specification in such a way that it can be used to check the subsequent design

5. consistency -- determining that different parts of the system description do not impose inherently conflicting requirements, and that consistent nomenclature is used in the description

6. unambiguity -- assuring that the specification has a unique interpretation in order to eliminate any confusion

7. writeability -- providing a scheme that simplifies the process of expressing the specification, and encouraging its production

8. modifiability -- structuring the specification so that the system functions can be changed to fit changing user requirements

9. implementability -- determining that the system can be feasibly, i.e., within technological and economic boundaries, built

TWO VIEWS OF A SPECIFICATION

The USE approach to specification attempts to address these goals and to provide
for the diverse uses of the specification. We produce a <u>user view</u> and a <u>developer
view</u> of the specification. Our model is depicted in Figure 6 and shows that the
user view is intended for the computer-naive user while the developer view is
intended for the computer-knowledgeable user.

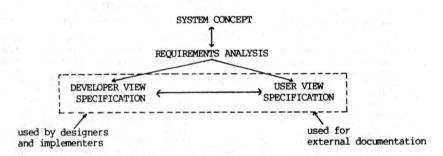

Figure 7. The USE model of specifications.

The <u>user view</u> specification is a detailed, but informal, description of the system
function formulated by the developer working closely with the user. This informal
description can serve as a contract between the developer and the users, and can
also serve as the starting point for more formal specifications. It is often the
case that more than one class of user will have access to a given information
system, frequently with different privileges and operations. In such a case, it
is necessary to specify a separate view for each user class.

The user view specification is aimed at meeting the specification goals of
comprehensibility for the reader and completeness of the system description. It
is written using the terminology of the application environment, reflecting the
user's view of the problem.

The need for comprehensibility implies the need to impose some structure upon the
user view specification. As we have seen, a system can typically be decomposed
into a number of functions, which can in turn be decomposed into subfunctions, and
so on. Such a hierarchical decomposition, combined with gradual refinement of the
system requirements, is a particularly effective way to present the narrative
portion of such a specification.

The <u>developer view</u> specification provides a view of the system functions for a
computer-knowledgeable reader. It is intended to aid the system designers, and
those who are responsible for testing and/or verifying the implemented system.
This view defines a high level program structure, identifies program modules to
the greatest extent possible, and shows the logical data flow between the modules.
Note that there will frequently be a correspondence between the hierarchical
decomposition achieved in the user view specification and the design view
specification.

The developer view specification is used to aid the software designer in
implementing the system, easing the transition between the specification and
design phases of the software life cycle. This specification describes the
behavior of the system and its modules without overly constraining the activities
of the system designers and implementers, who fill in the detail and produce the
algorithms and storage structures. The developer view is primarily addressed to
the specification goals of implementability and consistency.

The developer view also concentrates on the correctness issues of the specification, making it possible to establish testing and verification procedures for the implemented system. The developer view uses a formal notation that is amenable to rigorous checking so that one may, in fact, prove formally or informally the correspondence between the specification and its realization.

The formal notations used for this view makes it possible to utilize automated aids for consistency checking. Names, value ranges, and module interfaces can all be checked from such a specification approach.

Thus, there is a balance between these views of a specification, intended to meet the diverse needs to which specifications are put. We are able to link the two views of the system to one another so that it is possible to achieve "traceability," linking the appropriate part of each specification view to the requirements.

COMPONENTS OF THE IIS SPECIFICATION

Our discussion of interactive information systems to this point makes it clear that an IIS consists of three components: the user interface to the system, the operations upon the data objects, and the database used by the system. The USE specification method leads to a specification of each of these components. We have already seen the use of transition diagrams for specifying the user interface. We specify the database as a set of normalized relations.

There are several reasons for this decision:

1. Relations have a underlying mathematical theory and therefore support formal defintion of systems for purposes of testing and verification;

2. Both procedural (algebra-like) and non-procedural (predicate calculus-like) operations are defined upon relations, so that one can precisely specify the data base operations in terms of the defined relations

3. The existence of several relational database management systems (including Troll) simplifies the implementation of prototype systems;

4. Relations are conceptually straightforward and users can easily understand their structure and use with minimal training.

5. Structured Systems Analysis leads to a set of relations, and we use the Semantic Hierarchy approach to data modelling to define a hierarchy of relations. Use of relations in the specification therefore simplifies the transition between analysis and specification.

For all of these reasons, then, relations seem to be the best method of specifying the content and structure of the database.

The relations for the IFIP Working Conference problem are shown in Figure 7. Note that each attribute has a defined domain showing the set of values that it may assume and that some of these domains are defined along with the relations themselves.

The final step of the specifications is to create a tie between the semantic actions of the transition diagrams and the operations on the data base. Each semantic action must be specified and the method of specification may be chosen from a variety of alternatives. Our preference is to use a narrative form for the user view specification, and then to use a more formal approach for the developer view specification. The specification language can include the semantic actions, including the data base operations.

The specification of the semantic actions in this way is a powerful tool for several reasons:

(1) Each of the semantic actions is quite small, since it is associated with the traversal of a single arc of a transition diagram. Thus, an effective decomposition of the system is produced in this way.

(2) One may continually rework the individual semantic actions, beginning with a prose description and proceeding through a specification language, a program design language, and finally code. Comparison and tracing from one stage of the software life cycle to another is simplified in this way.

(3) The relational data base definition and the syntax of the paths on the transition diagram are extremely well suited to implementation in PLAIN, so that the transformation from the specification of an interactive information system to its realization in a PLAIN program is as straightforward as possible.

```
domain paperrange: integer (1..100);

domain sessionrange: integer (1..30);

domain weekday: scalar (Mon, Tue, Wed, Thu, Fri);

domain clock: integer (800..2000);

domain date: integer (0..3112);

domain money: float (0.00..200.00);

domain paperstatus: scalar (received, inreview, accepted, insession, rejected);

domain person: string;



relation accepted_papers [key paperno] of
     paperno: paperrange;
     title: string;
     sessionnum: sessionrange;
end;

relation attendance [key name] of
     name: person;
     amtpaid: money;
end;

relation author_list [key name, paperno] of
     name: person;
     paperno: paperrange;
end;


relation mailing_list [key name] of
     name: person;
     affiliation: string;
     detail_address: string;
     postcode: string;
     city: string;
     country: string;
end;
```

Figure 8 -- Relational database design for IFIP Working Conference problem

```
relation papers [key paperno] of
     paperno: paperrange;
     title: string;
     resp_pc_member: person;
     status: paperstatus;
end;

relation pc_list [key name] of
     name: person;
     papercount: integer (0..10);   {no PC member handles more than 10 papers}
end;

relation priority_list [key name] of
     name: person;
     role: string;
end;

relation referee_list [key name] of
     name: person;
     number_assigned: integer (0..6);   {limit on papers to be refereed}
end;


relation reviewing [key refname, paperno] of
     refname: person;
     paperno: paperrange;
     datesent: date;
     dateofreply: date;
end;

relation sessions [key sessionnumber] of
     sessionnumber: sessionrange;
     title: string;
     timeslot: sessionrange;
end;

relation session_chair [key sessionnumber] of
     sessionnumber: sessionrange;
     chairman: person;
end;

relation times [key timeslot, room] of
     timeslot: sessionrange;
     room: string;
     day: weekday;
     starttime: clock;
end;
```

Figure 8 (cont.) -- Relational database design for IFIP Working Conference problem

The user view and the developer view of the specifications for each semantic action are easily tied together, as it is possible to describe the user view with text, and then to provide the more precise formal specification as well.

The formal specification method that we have chosen to use is based on the axiomatic approach developed for Alphard [30] and extended to information systems by Leveson [31]. Leveson's methodology supports the specification and verification of information systems, and permits the enforcement of semantic integrity constraints on a data base. The formal specification, termed an operational specification, gives a description of the _behavior_ of the system, including a complete description of the semantics. The semantics include the names of the objects, the operations defined on each object, and the effect of each operation.

The notions of data abstraction are used to define the objects, so that the permissible operations are defined upon each object. As with a narrative text description of the semantics, there is no statement of _how_ the operations will actually be carried out, but only a description of _what_ will be done.

The method involves specifying the pre and post conditions of each operation, using the first-order predicate calculus. In the context of the IFIP Working Conference problem, one object is a paper. We may thus write

```
object paper
    abstract image
            <title, authorlist, papernumber, ...>
    abstract invariant
    abstract operations
            receive paper...
                pre
                post
            review paper
            accept paper
            assign paper to session
            reject paper
            accepted?
            change paper title
            change authorship
```

If we consider the operation "assign paper to session", we can identify some preconditions on the operation, including:

-- the session name is valid
-- the paper has not already been assigned to another session
-- the session does not have more than some maximum number of papers

Postconditions might specify:

-- the session is noted as containing that paper
-- the paper is noted as having been assigned to a session

More formally, the above conditions might be specified as:

```
abstract operations
    assign_paper_to_session (paper, session)
        pre   valid_session_name (session) & ~assigned (paper)
                        & paper_count (session) < MAXPAPERS
        post  assigned (paper) & contains (session, paper)
```

This segment of the example shows that the operational specification must include not only updating operations but also retrieval operations and iterators or generators that permit access to individual pieces of an abstract object.

The preconditions, postconditions, and invariants make it possible to enforce integrity constraints, a set of rules that determine which configurations of the data base are reasonable. There are two major types of semantic invariants: value constraints and inter-object constraints. The value constraints are the set of legal values of instances of the object. We have already seen how the domain definitions of our relations above serve to enforce value constraints.

The inter-object constraints define constraints on the relationships allowed between objects. An example of an inter-object constraint in the IFIP Conference problem is that no paper may be assigned to more than one session. As another example, a particular conference organizing committee could impose the constraint that no person who is a member of the Programme Committee shall be the author of a paper.

In order to prevent integrity violations, it is necessary that all operations defined on the abstract objects preserve the invariants. Integrity problems can arise from faulty operations or from illegal sequences of legal operations. The preconditions are aimed at eliminating illegal sequences of operations, and verification techniques can be used to show the truth of the postconditions.

These formal specifications for "assign paper to session" would be used in conjunction with a narrative description of the operation, which would be as follows:

> "An accepted paper should be assigned to one and only one session.
> An effort should be made to place the paper in a session dealing
> with the major theme of the paper. The paper should not be
> assigned to a session that already has a full set of papers."

We are just beginning to gain some experience with the use of this formalism in conjunction with the decomposition provided by the transition diagram specification method, and have initially had some difficulty in relating the operations defined from this data abstraction approach with those defined as semantic actions in the transition diagrams. We have also been working to improve the method of relating the "data stores" identified through Structured Systems Analysis with the "abstract image" of the formal specification method, using them with a conceptual modelling approach to produce the set of relations that are in the specification.

However, the method works well at the highest level (the "transaction level") of the diagrams, and it is also possible to associate the preconditions and postconditions with those semantic actions that involve database operations.

We are, however, finding the discipline of the formal specification to be extremely helpful as another way of looking at the problem, and have seen that it helps in defining database attributes and the necessary checks that must be made to assure integrity of the operations.

In summary, then, our specification includes the user/program dialogue, shown with transition diagrams including the semantic actions, the data base design, expressed as a set of normalized relations with domain definitions, and the operations, shown in both narrative text and, where appropriate, with a formal specification based on axioms and verification conditions.

Note that the dialogue serves to determine the operations that can be performed by a given user. With reasonable kinds of login and database authorization mechanisms, this predetermination of operations is extremely valuable for protection and security of the IIS. Furthermore, this process of enumerating operations, combined with the specification of the relations in the database, makes it possible for the system designer to define relations and secondary indexes upon those relations that make the most critical operations execute efficiently.

This complete specification then serves as the basis for system design and implementation, as well as for user/customer approval. In the past, we have found this specification technique (even in the absence of the formal specification part) to be satisfactory for this purpose and have used it to specify several medical information systems [32].

ADDING FUNCTIONALITY TO PROTOTYPES

Even with this specification technique, though, we had the impression that the written specification alone was not sufficient for complete understanding by computer-naive users. We sensed that this was particularly true with respect to completeness of IIS functions, and that there was a strong chance that useful functions would be omitted.

Also, we wanted to be able to produce more realistic messages as sample output when users worked with the TDI. Although, it is possible to program all of the system through the action part of the TDI input, the intended use of the TDI was to simulate the user/program dialogue and not to perform the functions. We normally created some fixed messages that would be typical of the expected system output, which could be output as actions associated with the traversal of a path on the transition diagram. Although this approach is an adequate first approximation to reality, it falls short of providing a greater degree of functionality in the prototype.

In particular, since many of the operations involve access to and modification of data in a database, it is possible to provide this desired functionality by using the TDI in conjunction with a database management system. As noted above, one can add functionality to the TDI by providing those functions as actions in the TDI; these actions can be <u>any</u> program that the user of the TDI is allowed to execute. By writing actions that call a database management system, it becomes possible to store either actual or typical data in the database so that the user input can cause actual operations to be performed. In that way, the prototype mechanism becomes much more realistic.

The high-level data definition and manipulation facilities provided by the Troll relational database management system in the USE environment makes it possible to construct such a prototype quite easily. The relations defined in the database design stage of the specification can be defined for the database, and sample data may either be added as part of the prototype construction or directly by the user of the prototype system.

The prototype consists of two tools, TDI and Troll, connected via the Unix pipe mechanism, which permits the output of one process to be given directly as input to another process. The prototype uses two such pipes, one as input from TDI to Troll and another as output from Troll to TDI. This organization is shown in Figure 9.

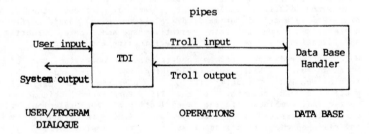

Figure 9. Organization of functional prototype system

The database manipulation facilities in Troll are similar to those of the relational algebra, and include:

1. Formation of data base expressions using the following relational algebra-like operations:

    -selection of a set of tuples satisfying a certain constraint

    -projection on some attributes

    -joining two relations on attributes of the same type

    -set operations: union, intersection, and difference

2. Assignment of a data base expression to a variable

3. Individual tuple operations: - associative access using key-attribute values - insertion/deletion of tuples - modification of non-key attribute values

4. Iteration through the set of tuples with a foreach clause

5. Aggregation operations count, sum, min, max, and avg

Troll also provides some transaction support, including the ability to back out of an unsuccessful transaction. These operations, along with some examples, are described further in Reference 33.

The addition of this functionality seems to have several significant advantages over the non-functional prototype approach:

1. it permits a rapid implementation of a significant portion of the IIS specification with tools that provide a close match to the specification method itself

2. it allows the database design to be evaluated experimentally in much the same way as the dialogue is evaluated, using a prototype database design as the first step in the design of the production version of the database schema

3. it can give the user a far more accurate picture of the actual behavior of the production system

4. it can serve as a workable system version while the production version is being designed, implemented, and tested. (Indeed, we are curious to determine whether the use of this prototype mechanism will obviate the need to construct a production version of the system in some cases.)

An important difference between this prototype method and the rapid construction of systems using a programming system such as MUMPS is that these tools are non-procedural and that one must only do "programming" for the database manipulation operations. Furthermore, the prototype consists of thoroughly tested components, the TDI and Troll, thereby reducing the number of errors that one would normally expect to find in a prototype version of a system.

One potential disadvantage with the functional prototype scheme is that the user may not understand the reasons for proceeding with a carefully designed and systematically implemented production version which can perform the complete set of integrity checks, provide more extensive diagnostics and online assistance, and optimize the format of system output. An associated potential disadvantage is that too much effort might be put into the prototype construction effort, to the point of diminishing returns. There appears to be a limit at which the effort to provide functions with the TDI and Troll exceeds the additional benefits to be gained. The developer must recall that the goal is only to build a prototype and not a production version, with the intent of aiding the user in evaluating the suitability of the specification.

We do not yet have sufficient experience with the use of functional prototypes to determine the extent to which they are an improvement over interface prototypes for the purpose of identifying necessary system functions. Because we have used the USE methodology prior to the addition of this step, we are certain that functional prototypes are not <u>essential</u> to the methodology. However, we strongly believe that they will provide a significant advantage for the user and the developer, particularly for larger systems and for those applications being automated for the first time.

The use of the functional prototype may be seen for the IFIP Working Conference example. We may assume that the relations defined above are stored in a database named conference. For purposes of explanation, we shall simplify the semantic actions somewhat and simply assume that user input has been stored in appropriate variables; in practice, we use the standard Unix parameter passing rules. In the subsequent example, we shall show these variables preceded by a dollar sign ("$"). Following standard Troll practice, comments are enclosed in braces.

The operation of adding a name to the referee list could be achieved as follows:

```
open conference;
import referee_list;
import mailing_list;
insert referee_list [<$refname,0>];
   {initially referee has no papers to review}
   {must also obtain information for mailing_list relation}
if ~exists (mailing_list [$refname]) then
    insert mailing_list [<$refname,$refaffil,$refadress,$refpostcode,
                          $refcity,$refcountry>];
end if;
export referee_list, mailing_list;
quit;
```

As another example, showing the power of the associative addressing facility, consider the action of accepting the paper with paper number $N.

```
open conference;
import papers;
import accepted_papers;
papers [$N].status := accepted;
insert accepted_papers [<$N, papers[$N].title, 0>];
      {initially not assigned to a session}
export accepted_papers, papers;
quit;
```

ARCHITECTURAL AND DETAILED DESIGN

The specification is followed by two stages of design, termed architectural design and detailed design. The process of design involves developing a program structure and logic that describes <u>how</u> to build the system described in the specification subject to any stated constraints. The stage of architectural design involves the creation of an overall program structure and the logical data design. This stage leads to the decomposition of the system into a set of modules with well-defined input and output interfaces and accurately specified functions.

The stage of detailed design involves working out the details of the logic for each module, as well as performing any further needed refinements on the data design. After these design steps have been completed and reviewed, the implementation can be undertaken.

Design may be treated as an implicit part of the specification process or as an explicit phase of the overall system development process. Although we follow the latter approach, it is clear that much of the work in system decomposition and data base design has been carried forth as part of the system specification activity.

The process of architectural design is extremely straightforward in the USE methodology, since much of the necessary work has been accomplished at earlier stages. We follow the general ideas of Structured Design [34], constructing a structure chart to show the overall design. It is normally quite easy to construct the top levels of the structure charts, since the top level of the transition diagram maps almost directly into the transaction model of Structured Design. Alternatively, one could create a structure chart from the SSA Data Flow Diagrams, but that approach seems to be less effective for us, since it tends to obscure the interactive nature of the system.

The major contribution of the structure chart is that it makes the program structure and the module interconnections explicit. We feel, though, that Structured Design is not ideal for our purposes, since it is relatively weak for showing operations on databases. However, the strengths of the method seem to outweigh the weaknesses, particularly since our design is quite apparent from the specification. We would like to improve or extend the structure chart approach, though, to cover the database aspects of architectural design more completely.

In the IFIP Conference problem, we decided to create two separate programs, one for the Programme Committee Chairman and one for the Organizing Committee Chairman, using a shared database. We could alternatively have made a single program, using login information to determine the user class, and hence the appropriate dialogue. We decided that the two program approach was more realistic, given the fact that the Programme Committee Chairman and the Organizing Committee Chairman are generally at different sites.

We also noted that the relations could be split quite well between the two different programs, and that the amount of sharing was very limited, with only the relation mailing_list being subject to update by both chairmen. The relations pc_list, author_list, papers, referee_list, reviewing, accepted_papers, sessions, session_chair, and times are all created and updated by the Programme Committee Chairman, while relations organizers and attendance are exclusively modified by the Organizing Committee Chairman. In addition, the relations are extremely stable, with very few modifications, so that it would be feasible to transfer information between two separate programs running on two different machines at low frequency and at low speed, perhaps even by magnetic tape through the mail. (Indeed, the amount of activity for this problem is sufficiently low that the students analyzing the problem came to the conclusion that it was probably not economically feasible to design and implement an IIS for conferences the size of the IFIP Working Conferences.)

The top levels of the structure chart for the Program Committee Chairman are shown in Figure 9.

The USE approach to detailed design is to use a program design language, similar to that described by Caine and Gordon [35]. A program design language may be viewed as a "very-high-level" programming language, intended to express the logic of a program module in narrative form, following a format that makes them easily comprehensible to other designers. Program design languages have been widely used with great success as a means of describing the detailed logic of a module, and we have likewise had excellent experience with this approach, finding it preferable to strcuctured flowcharts, and far superior to traditional flowcharts. We especially value the fact that program design languages involve linear text, making them machine processable and easily readable.

These characteristics of program design languages are particularly useful for a methodology, since they improve teamwork by making it possible for developers to gain access to everyone's detailed design information as needed and by greatly simplifying the problem of reviewing designs in a structured walkthrough [36].

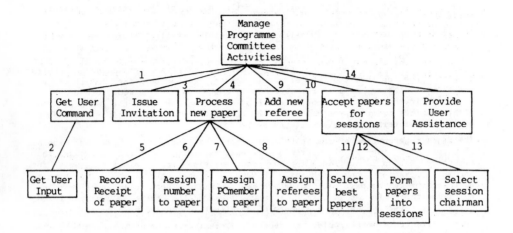

	INPUT	OUTPUT
1		command_id
2		input
3	mailing_list	mailing_list
4	papers, referee_list, reviewing, pc_list, author_list, mailing_list	papers, referee_list, reviewing, pc_list, author_list, mailing_list
5	papers, author_list, mailing_list	papers, author_list, mailing_list
6	papers, author_list	papers, author_list, paper_number
7	papers, pc_list	papers, pc_list
8	papers, referee_list, reviewing, paper_number	papers, referee_list, reviewing
9	referee_list, mailing_list	referee_list, mailing_list
10	papers, accepted_papers author_list, mailing_list, times, sessions, session_chair	papers, accepted_papers, sessions, session_chair
11	papers, accepted_papers	papers, accepted_papers
12	accepted_papers, papers, sessions, times	accepted_papers, papers, sessions
13	session_chair, sessions	session_chair
14	message_number	

Figure 10 -- Partial Structure Chart for Programme Committee system

Because PLAIN is the implementation language of the USE methodology, we have adapted the program design language notation slightly to take advantage of certain features of PLAIN. The major differences between the Caine/Gordon program design language and that used in the USE methodology are the following:

1. Data modules are permitted in addition to procedure modules. In that way, it is possible to incorporate data abstraction more effectively at the detailed design stage, since it is present at both the specification and implementation stages.

2   Each module contains a list of the modules that it calls, as well as a list of the modules that call it.

3. All data objects must have their data types defined.

4. Each module provides for an <u>exception</u> part, showing the exceptional conditions that can arise in the execution of the module

5. The control structures of the <u>algorithm</u> section reflect those of PLAIN, rather than PL/1, as was the case in the Caine/Gordon version.

Program design language is written for each module defined in the structure chart, carrying along the module name and the function description. We are also able to include the calling tree information from the structure chart, along with the input and output information for each module. We have found the use of this information to be of great assistance in tracing backward from the detailed design to the architectural design in checking our design documents.

The detailed design process also provides an additional measure of module size. At the architectural design stage, we expect that the function of a module can be described in one or two declarative sentences, and use that informal rule of thumb as one basis for splitting modules or modifying the design in some other way. At the detailed design stage, though, we begin to be concerned about the eventual size of each module in lines of code. Because we hope to limit the executable code for each module to 60 lines (one page listing), we try to limit the number of lines in the program design language listing of the algorithm to 20. If the detailed design logic for the module exceeds 20 lines, it is likely that the implemented module will be too large, so we attempt to split the module into two or more modules, revising the architectural design as necessary.

The architectural and detailed designs are each reviewed in walkthroughs to try to find and then correct design errors, since the cost of finding errors at the design stage is far lower than finding and correcting them at a later stage. Our experience is that we review the highest three levels of the structure chart most closely at the architectural design stage, and that we are more selective about reviewing modules at the detailed design level. One approach that we have used successfully for selecting modules for review of the detailed design is to ask designers to each select about 20% of their modules for review, giving preference to those that were difficult to design, or critical in terms of execution speed, space utilization, or user interface. If an inordinate number of problems are found in a designer's work, then we will review additional modules designed by that individual. The detailed design for the Assign_Referees module is shown in Figure 10. The end result of the design activity is the production of a <u>representation</u> of the system in a form that simplifies implementation.

We are planning to build a checker to analyze the program design language for all of the modules in an IIS. This tool would be of help in checking the interface descriptions, building data dictionaries, and in building calling trees, all of which are now done manually.

AN INTRODUCTION TO PLAIN

The implementation language of the USE methodology is PLAIN, which was designed specifically to meet the requirements for constructing interactive information systems. PLAIN was the first of the USE tools to be designed, and the design was

```
MODULE Assign_Referees
INPUT
     paperno: paperrange;
     papers, referee_list, reviewing: relation;
OUTPUT
     papers, referee_list, reviewing: relation;
         {all three relations modified by this module}
CALLS
CALLED BY
     new_paper
LOCAL DATA
     input: string;  {user input of name(s)}
     countrefs: integer (0..5);   {number of referees assigned}
FUNCTION
     For the given paper number, Assign_Referees prompts the user to assign
     one or more referees for the paper, accepting names until the user types
     an empty line (<cr> only) or until 5 names have been collected.
     The module increments the count of papers assigned to the referee,
     limiting the number of papers to six, and changes the status of the
     paper after the referees have been assigned.
ALGORITHM
     write  'Select referee(s) for paper number ',  paperno;
     write  papers[paperno].title;
     countrefs := 0;
     write 'Name:';
     read input;
     while  input ~= ""  and countrefs < 5
     loop
         if exists (referee_list [input])
         then
                 if referee_list.number_assigned < 6
                 then
                         referee_list.number_assigned := referee_list.number_assigned + 1;
                         insert reviewing [<input, paperno,100*day+month>];
                         papers.status := inreview;
                         countrefs := countrefs + 1
                 else
                         write 'Referee has too many papers.  Try again.';
                 end if
         else
                 write 'Name not in referee list. Try again.';
                 {***Design problem: note that minor misspellings of
                  referee names or use of last name only may fail to
                  find name in referee_list relation***}
         end if
     end loop
     write countrefs, 'referees assigned';
     if countrefs ~= 0
     then write 'Paper ', paperno, ' in review.'
     else signal noneassigned
     end if;
EXCEPTIONS
     noneassigned
END MODULE
```

Figure 11 -- Program Design Language for "Assign Referee" module

carried out in parallel with the design of many other programming languages, including CLU [37], Alphard [30], Gypsy [38], Euclid [39], and Ada [40]. Of these languages, though, only PLAIN addresses the application area of interactive programs and their need for database management facilities.

From the outset, the contribution was seen to be not so much the introduction of new language features, but rather a synthesis of features whose interrelationships would lead to a useful tool for such application programs. The approach was to make innovations to support interactive programs and to adhere closely to well-understood approaches for other features.

The design goals of PLAIN fall into two categories: those that support systematic programming practices, and those that support the creation of interactive programs. In practice, these goals mesh in the process of language design, but can be separated when examining the design philosophy.

The design goals for systematic programming were:

1. Support for procedural and data abstraction

2. Support for modularity

3. Control structures to encourage linear flow of control within modules

4. Visibility of data flow and data use

5. Prevention of self-modifying programs

6. Program readability

7. Limited language size

Many of the features of PLAIN with respect to systematic programming are derived from Pascal. These goals, and the way that they are addressed in PLAIN, are explained at greater length in Reference 41.

The design goals for supporting the construction of interactive programs were:

1. Features for data base management -- the language must deal with data bases and with operations performed on data bases, as well as with more primitive file concepts

2. Support for strings and string-handling -- interactive programs involve large amounts of text processing, particularly user-program dialogue

3. Facilities for exception-handling -- user errors must be expected, but the user should not be adversely affected

4. Availability of a rudimentary pattern specification and matching facility -- many interactive programs depend on a specific text pattern, e.g., a command, to determine program action

5. Appropriate input/output features

6. Rudimentary timing facilities

With these features, PLAIN programs could be made resilient to user errors, could simplify user interaction with large data bases, and could be made flexible in handling diverse forms of user input. Unlike the case with the systematic programming goals, there were few, if any, languages that had developed a satisfactory solution for achieving the goals for reliable interactive programs. Accordingly, much of the design effort went into the design of features for string handling, exception handling, pattern-matching, and relational data base management.

We now briefly sketch the features of PLAIN that explicitly support interactive programs. The complete language definition is presented in the Revised Report [42].

Data Base Management in PLAIN

A complete set of relational data base management facilities are part of PLAIN. A relation is a built-in data type, and may be seen as a set of records whose storage persistence is separate from the execution time of the programs accessing them. Relations from one or more data bases may be imported into the execution environment of a PLAIN program to perform the desired data base management operations.

One can routinely create and manipulate relations in PLAIN programs. The data base operations in PLAIN are aimed at providing the programmer with some control over the sequence of data base operations, and therefore at incorporating a set of features that permit the programmer to improve the efficiency of the program's database management [43].

The data base management facilities of PLAIN are those that are incorporated into Troll as described above, including the definition of domains and relations, a relational algebra-like set of operations for relational level operations, tuple processing with the for each loop, and item level insertions and modifications.

The Troll interface and the associated PLAIN Data Base Handler were in fact designed and built as part of the PLAIN runtime support system. Thus, the syntax of Troll was strongly influenced by the syntax of the PLAIN data definition and management facilities. We made the decision to separate the Data Base Handler from the remainder of the PLAIN runtime support system, and that decision has made it possible to use the Data Base Handler in conjunction with TDI (as shown above), in conjunction with other programming languages, and as a standalone database management system.

String Handling in PLAIN

The key decision in the inclusion of string handling facilities was to permit the generalized use of variable length strings as well as the more traditional use of fixed length strings. It is permissible in PLAIN to declare a variable of type string, with no stated maximum length: as in Pascal, it is also permissible to declare arrays of characters for those instances where the variable-length facility is not needed.

Additional operators and functions were provided to support the use of this data type. The binary operations of concatenation, string, contains, and string follows (lexical ordering) were introduced, along with functions for string insertion, removal, replacement, and extraction. It is also possible to convert between fixed and variable length strings.

The decision to permit variable length strings, with the necessary implementation overhead associated with heap management, was based on the assumption that string processing would not represent a significant bottleneck in PLAIN programs. Instead, it was felt that most of the execution time would be spent either carrying out database and input/output operations involving secondary storage devices, or in waiting for use input. This decision also made it possible to generalize the Pascal array declaration facility to allow dynamic array (using the same heap management) declarations, thereby overcoming a common criticism of Pascal.

Exception Handling in PLAIN

Events that occur during the execution of a program may cause an exception to be raised as the result of an exceptional condition, such as an arithmetic overflow. Without explicitly handling these exceptions, a program may fail. The interactive user finds such failures to be extremely undesirable, since they may cause the user to lose some work. Instead, it is necessary to handle such situations gracefully. PLAIN incorporates built-in exceptions and permits the programmer to define additional exceptions. All exceptions may be raised by using a signal statement, and the built-in exceptions may be raised automatically by the run-time system.

When an exception is raised, an exception handler is invoked. This handler is a PLAIN procedure, to which parameters may be passed. The handler may clear the active exception and provide for continued program execution, may clear the exception and provide for repetition of the statement that caused the exception to be raised, may notify the invoker of the module that received the exception signal, or may cause the program for fail.

The exception-handling mechanism makes it possible to trap exceptional conditions and to take actions that can prevent situations that may be harmful to the user. In short, it is possible to write extremely robust programs, capable of dealing with virtually every type of user or software error situation. This exception-handling scheme is described at greater length in Reference 44.

Pattern Specification and Matching

The pattern matching facility of PLAIN permits patterns and pattern sets to be declared and used. Pattern matching operators are provided, along with pattern-directed input/output. The pattern declaration facility consists of patterns that are composed of string literals, pattern codes, repetition code, other pattern names, and pattern sets, each consisting of one or more patterns. The pattern codes designate commonly used groupings of characters, such as alphabetic characters or digits. Each pattern code (or group of pattern codes) is preceded by a repetition code, which may be definite or indefinite (0 or more, 1 or more). Pattern specifications are static, similar to those of MUMPS, and unlike the dynamic pattern specifications of SNOBOL4.

The binary pattern matching operators "?=" and "?" test a string to determine if it conforms to a pattern. The keywords match and contains are available for pattern sets to determine if a string matches any pattern in a pattern set. In each case, the former operation tests for an exact match between the target string and the pattern, while the latter looks for any occurrence of the pattern in the string.

The programmer may specify any context-free grammar using the facility. Thus, in the construction of an interactive information system, all of the valid user inputs, such as command strings, may be specified in patterns, and the user input string may be compared with various patterns, with appropriate action taken depending on the success of the string pattern match. The pattern-matching and string handling features of PLAIN are described more completely in Reference 45.

INTERACTIVE SYSTEMS IN PLAIN

It is really the synthesis of these features, rather than any one of them alone, that makes PLAIN a powerful tool for the construction of interactive information systems. For example, relations can be used as the representation mechanism in the declaration of a module (which provides data abstraction facilities) to permit the encapsulation of a set of data base operations that might correspond to a "transaction."

As a more compelling example, consider the scenario of a user of an interactive information system.

1. The user repeatedly types some input, e.g., a command.

2. This input is decoded and parsed; if it is incorrect, a diagnostic message is presented to the user, who then provides alternate input;

3. The input is subjected to various semantic checks, which may also produce diagnostic messages;

4. If the input is validated, then some program action is taken, typically an access to or modification of some item(s) in a database, during which time output messages may be provided to the user.

In general, the main program is a loop that reads user input, branches according to the input, calling the appropriate procedures, and terminating if and when the user issues the command to quit. The legal syntax for the various commands are each specified as patterns, and the patterns are collected into a pattern set. The user input is matched against the pattern set to branch to the appropriate case, including the "illegal command" case. The procedures that are thereby invoked contain data base operations using the data management facilities PLAIN. Any execution time errors result in the signalling of an exception, so that a handler procedure can handle the exceptional condition without causing the program to crash, instead generating an appropriate message and carrying out any necessary recovery activities.

The main program for the Programme Committee Chairman is typical of the main program for interactive systems of this nature, and is shown in Figure 12.

```
program conmanpc;
external
      {declare relations with attributes that are used by conmanpc}
      {these are relations accepted_papers, author_list, mailing_list,
       papers, pc_list, referee_list, reviewing, sessions,
       session_chair, and times}
      {declarations follow those of Figure 8}
var input: string;
      {other global declarations, including exceptions}
pattern cmdset = [invitation, receipt, newreferee, choose, helper, finish];
        invitation = ['i','invite'];
        receipt = ['np','new paper','receive'];
        newreferee = ['nr','referee','add ref'];
        choose = ['a','accept','select'];
        helper = ['h','help','?','H','HELP'];
        finish = ['q','quit','Q','QUIT'];
begin
    write 'Welcome to CONMAN', \n;
    loop
        write '$'; {prompt symbol}
        read input ![ioerr: abort]; {terminate on hardware I/O error}
        case cmdset match input of
            when invitation: issue_invite;
            when receipt: new_paper;
            when newreferee: add_ref;
            when choose: accept_paper;
            when helper: first_aid (1);
            when quit: exit;
            when others: write 'illegal command' {pattern match failed}
        end case;
    repeat;
    write 'byebye'
end conmanpc.
```

Figure 12. PLAIN main program for conmanpc

The program design language segment shown in Figure 11 also converts almost directly into PLAIN. Indeed, the text given for the algorithm is so detailed as to be virtually identical to the PLAIN syntax. The major difference is in the procedure heading, which is shown in PLAIN in Figure 13.

```
procedure Assign_Referees (paperno: paperrange);
exception noneassigned;
imports papers, referee_list, reviewing: modified;
var
    input: string;
    countrefs: 0..5;
begin
        .
        .
        {body of Assign_Referees, following detailed design}
        .
        .
end Assign_Referees;
```

Figure 13. Framework of Assign_Referees procedure in PLAIN

The PLAIN facilities for string handling, pattern matching, exception handling, and data base management make it quite straightforward to write programs that conform to this extremely common scenario. This reason is why PLAIN was designed: to provide the application programmer with an appropriate tool for this important class of software systems. This is not to say that PLAIN is not well suited for other kinds of applications, but simply to observe that PLAIN is addressed to a type of application that is not well treated by other programming languages.

THE USE DEVELOPMENT ENVIRONMENT

As we have noted, the USE methodology is a collection of methods and automated tools for the design and development of interactive information systems. To this point, we have focused on the sequence of steps involved in going from the problem definition to system implementation in a procedural programming language, and have described some of the significant characteristics of some of our tools. We now turn to the software development environment in which systems are designed and implemented in the USE methodology. As before, we shall omit any further discussion of human factors, and concentrate on the collection of tools available to the IIS development organization.

We began by selecting Unix as the best possible existing software support system for the USE methodology. Unix was selected for several reasons, including the following:

1. It was developed to run on small systems, and variants of Unix, Mini-Unix and LSX [46], had been developed to run on even smaller systems.

2. Unix already possessed a good collection of tools that would assist not only the eventual application developer, but would also assist in the construction of the USE tools. Among the most useful of the Unix tools for our purposes are:
    a) the text editor (ex), with the vi option to provide full-screen editing;
    b) the nroff and troff formatting programs, for typewritten and phototypeset output respectively
    c) the tbl program for producing tables, and usable with both nroff and troff
    d) macro packages (me and ms) to simplify the formatting of text, and to permit the standardized formatting of various documents
    e) a fully hierarchical file system, permitting distribution of the various specification, design, and code files into separate directories
    f) a systems programming language (C), along with a type checking program (lint) and a source code debugger (sdb)
    g) a lexical analyzer generator (Lex)
    h) a parser generator (YACC)
    i) a standard I/O library that could be used to implement the I/O operations of PLAIN

j) the "shell" which permits one or more Unix commands to be packaged (in a macro-like way) and executed as if it were a single command

k) a program (make) for combining files and preparing them for execution

l) various programs for checking writing style and spelling (style, diction, spell) in documentation and reports (including this paper)

m) an excellent collection of games, including chess, bridge, and adventure, to occupy the developer during less productive interludes

3. The Unix command language (shell commands) are very easy to learn, and the user of the application programs, as well as the application programmer, would not have to learn a complicated operating system command language; indeed, most of the features of Unix could be made completely invisible to the end user.

4. Unix was in widespread use so that the USE tools could be exported to other organizations.

The basic idea was to build our tools, e.g., TDI, Troll, and the PLAIN system, in the Unix environment, and then to use that environment for the subsequent development of interactive information systems. The only problem with this approach is that we wanted to achieve better integration of the tools and their usage from the standpoint of the developer. We wanted to go beyond the facilities provided by the Programmer's Workbench (PWB) version of Unix [47].

We observed that an additional tool could serve to integrate all of the other tools, as well as to assist in project organization. The specification, design, and development of interactive information systems requires the effort of a group of developers over a period ranging from several months to several years. The resulting IIS may contain hundreds of modules. There will almost certainly be multiple versions of these modules and the IIS itself during the lifetime of the IIS, covering development and evolution of the system, as it is modified and enhanced to accommodate new user and hardware requirements.

These development and evolution activities will generate many documents of different types, including:

- Initial problem statement
- Requirements definition (possibly with analysis reports)
- Software specification
- Project schedule information
- Architectural design, showing overall software structure
- Data dictionary
- Detailed design (in a program design language)
- Source code for each module (perhaps in several versions)
- Object code (or intermediate code) for each module, perhaps in several versions
- One or more versions of the executable program
- Scripts for various common activities, e.g., printing, compiling, and executing the program
- Test data cases and test results
- User documentation
- Trouble reports and change requests

It is apparent from this list that there is a need for some kind of organized information management, not only to keep track of the emerging software product, but also to manage all of the associated documentation. It is this need that motivated the creation of the Module Control System.

We identified requirements for the Module Control System, including the following:

1. Support for versions of modules -- make it possible to maintain two or more versions of the specification, source code, and object code for a given system module

2. Support for versions of systems -- make it possible to maintain two or more versions of a fully linked object version of a software system

3. Simplify the process of compiling, linking, and loading a number of source modules into a single object program

4. Make it possible to maintain information on module interfaces

5. Support the production of a data dictionary

6. Support other important tasks of system development, such as detailed module design and module testing

7. Provide management information, including the status of modules and systems and data on the development process itself

8. Support evolution of existing systems under the Module Control System

9. Permit different users of the Module Control System to encourage or enforce various sets of rules or guidelines concerning the development process

10. Execute on a small computer to support the concept of personal development systems [48,49,50]

11. Utilize, to the greatest extent possible, other tools in the environment of the Module Control System, in order to maximize integration of the Module Control System with those tools and to minimize the size of the running system.

While our other methods and tools are intended to support the technical activities associated with the development of interactive information systems, the Module Control System is aimed more directly at the managerial and organizational issues in software creation. Information on the status of every module can be maintained online so that it is possible to monitor project progress and to identify problems. Furthermore, various members of a project team have access to the information, so that some of the traditional communication and interface problems between members of a group can be overcome.

The Module Control System is a command driven tool that permits the user to create modules and systems, to modify aspects of a module, to compile one or more modules, to examine the status and history of the development, and to run the current version of the system.

Users of the Module Control System may incorporate policies that may be associated with specific commands to permit the execution of an arbitrary program before or after execution of the command. In this way, the Module Control System can be tailored to the needs of specific development environments and can be used to enforce development methodologies, to limit access to parts of a system, and to capture development effort on specific projects.

As the name implies, the basic system building block is the module.* Associated with each module are several "documents":

1. external documentation of the module, possibly a specification;

2. information on the interfaces of the module to other modules in the system;

3. detailed design of the module, possibly written in a program design language [35];

4. source code for the module;

5. object code for the module;

6. test data for the module;

7. a log to record activities involving the module.

Note that, with the exception of the last item, it is necessary to provide for multiple copies of these documents, representing successive versions of the documents.

At the system level, it is necessary to maintain information to govern the system development and to bind the modules together. One may therefore also visualize some system level documents, including:

1. policies governing the development of the system;

2. a log of important system events, such as the creation of a new object version;

3. a directory of modules that comprise the system;

4. directories of versions of modules that comprise each version of the system.

The IIS developer uses the Module Control System throughout the project and can issue various commands that control different functions, including:

1. definition of a system, to have the system establish a directory to hold information about the various modules that comprise the system, along with other administrative information.

2. definition of a module, to have the system create files to store a specification, program design language, source code, object code, and test data for that module. For example, the program design language shown in Figure 11 and the PLAIN code fragment shown in Figure 13 are stored in the Module Control System file hierarchy associated with both the module name "Assign_Referees" and the version number.

3. editing of a file to create or modify some aspect of the information stored about a module; the old version will be saved and the new version will be saved as a set of changes to the old version (except for an object module, where the newest is saved and older versions must be specifically recreated)

4. definition of a version, consisting of a named set of object modules and associated date

5) linking together of a set of object modules to produce an executable load module for Unix

6) display of statistics about the system and the development effort associated with various phases of the system or with specific modules.

The Module Control System may be seen as imposing discipline on the use of the various tools. When one wants to create a new system, one issues either the

    build system

or

    new system

command, depending on whether or not parts of the system already exist. (We used "new system" for conman.pc and conman.oc.)

The Module Control System then prompts for the names of modules, data files, and "include files," creating a hierarchical file system that is used as the project "data base", containing what has been termed the Production Program Library [51].

The Module Control System can be used to assist in tasks of specification, architectural and detailed design, coding, and testing. During specification, the

    modify doc

command is used to edit documentation for modules. There is no required format for such documentation, which can range from narrative text to a formal specification language such as SPECIAL [52]. The documentation may then be displayed using the

    print

command.

The Module Control System provides more assistance at the design stage. Apart from forcing a decomposition into modules, the Module Control System will collect information on module interfaces that can be displayed with the

   make dictionary

command, and provides a template for a Program Design Language that is automatically inserted into the files in the pdl subdirectories for each module. Instead of simply invoking the requested editor, the Module Control System explicitly elicits the interface information so that it can be stored in an easily retrievable format.

Source code is entered through the

   modify src

command, which simply invokes the editor, possibly executing some programs first as a result of existing policies. When one or more modules have been coded, the developer types

   compile

and the Module Control System will ask whether the developer wants to compile the entire system or just a single named module, but the developer will not need to know the details of the system call to the compiler.

When all of the modules have been completed, the developer simply types

   run system

and the Module Control System automatically compiles any files for which there is no current version of the object code, and links all of the object modules with any needed libraries into an executable version of the system. The information needed to carry out these steps is stored in a "make" file, which is generated by the Module Control System and used as input to the Unix Make program. Note that the developer is relieved of the tedious details of remembering which files need to be recompiled, and the need to create a script to carry out the needed compilation and linking.

The Module Control System uses many of the Unix tools directly, as well as giving the user direct access to them through a shell "escape" feature. The details of the Module Control System are described at greater length in Reference [53].

The Unix tools, combined with PLAIN, Troll, the Module Control System, and TDI, form the development environment for the IIS developer. In this way, it can be seen that the Unix tools have been valuable throughout the USE project, and are of further use in system development and future tool building.

CONCLUSIONS AND FUTURE DIRECTIONS

The USE methodology is quite new and has been evolving rapidly as the methods have been used and as the tools have been built. Accordingly, there is relatively little experience with the methods and tools together. To some extent, that situation is a reflection of the rapid changes in the nature of software development and the character of software engineering environments. It is also a characteristic of methodologies in general -- they must evolve and improve as one gains experience in their use.

The development of the USE methodology has been gradual and we have spent considerable time experimenting with our methods and tools, evaluating them informally as we have applied them to specific projects. Indeed, the IFIP Working Conference exercise provided an excellent opportunity to evaluate our approach, and we have made some minor refinements to our approach as a result of work on this problem.

Our efforts in the near future will focus principally on refining the existing tools and on developing new tools to produce a better integrated development environment. We have been exploring the area of personal development systems to provide proper support for these tools. If an IIS developer can be provided with a personal machine that includes these tools, along with suitable facilities for communication with other users and systems, then it becomes much more practical to support high-bandwidth interfaces such as color graphics and audio input/output. The small size of the USE tools and the availability of Unix on several small machines makes it practical to create a "USE development machine".

Although we have identified specific needed improvements for the various tools we have developed, we are especially interested in graphics. Within the USE methodology, several of the methods (SSA, Structure Charts, and transition diagrams) rely upon pictorial representations, and we have observed that system developers in general frequently represent their ideas with pictures, e.g., flow charts, data structures, data base designs. Yet there is almost no automated support for these methods.

In summary, the USE methodology is an attempt to provide the developer of interactive information systems with a method and tools that improve the quality of the systems that are built and the process by which they are built. We regard the present state of the USE methodology as a significant step toward our goals, but feel that there is a great deal of room for further work. Accordingly, we would like to develop graphical tools as part of the USE toolkit, using some of the powerful graphics packages that already exist in the Unix environment.

ACKNOWLEDGMENTS

Many people and organizations have assisted in the development of the USE methodology. The basic ideas underlying the methodology have been strengthed by discussions with Peter Freeman and Nancy Leveson, who, along with Susan Stinson, also provided valuable comments on an earlier draft of this paper. Reind van de Riet, Martin Kersten, Mark Dippe, and David Sherertz played a significant role in the design of PLAIN. Dan Keller and Shu-huar Yeh were of great help in the design and implementation of the Module Control System. Martin Kersten was instrumental in the design of Troll and the implementation of the Data Base Handler. Susan Stinson and David Shewmake have helped in working out the details of the specification method and the TDI. The work of Thomas W. Booster, David S. Goldberg, Esther F. Handa, Karl Lew, Amnon Meyers, Gabriela Novy, Carl Resnikoff, and Harpreet Sandhu has also contributed to the design and development of the USE tools. The efforts of Terrie Cheung, Don Gardner, Klaus-Clemens Schoo, and Phil Strong to apply the USE methods and tools to the IFIP Working Conference problem are also gratefully appreciated. Finally, Tina Walters and Marina Gordillo have been invaluable in keeping the logistical aspects of the project in good order.

This work has been supported by the National Library of Medicine (LM 00153), the National Science Foundation (MCS78-26287), and the Netherlands Organization for the Advancement of Pure Research (ZWO) (grant 62-139). Development of the Module Control System was supported by the National Bureau of Standards under contract NB79KACA1059. Computing facilities have been provided by the Computer Science Division, Electrical Engineering and Computer Sciences Department, University of California, Berkeley, in particular, the VAX-11/780 system supported by the National Science Foundation under grant MCS78-07291, and by a Corporate Research Sponsorship from Digital Equipment Corporation that supported the acquisition of the VAX-11/750 by the Section on Medical Information Science, University of California, San Francisco. Additional computing support was provided by National Institutes of Health grant RR-1081 to the UCSF Computer Graphics Laboratory and by the Vakgroep Informatics, Vrije Universiteit, Amsterdam, the Netherlands.

FOOTNOTES

[1]The Module Control System is completely neutral with respect to the definition of a module, although policies could be used to impose various kinds of size restrictions. The concept of a module within the Module Control System is some fragment of a system that has well defined interfaces (assuming that these are specified by the developer) and that is separately compilable (one or more subprograms).

[TM]SADT is a trademark of SofTech, Inc. Unix is a trademark of Bell Laboratories. Ada is a trademark of the U.S. Department of Defense.

REFERENCES

[1] A.I. Wasserman, "Online Programming Systems and Languages: a History and Appraisal," Technical Report #6, Laboratory of Medical Information Science, University of California, San Francisco, 1974.

[2] W. Teitelman and L. Masinter, "The INTERLISP Programming Environment," Computer, vol. 14, no. 4 (April, 1981), pp. 25-33.

[3] A. Kay and A. Goldberg, "Personal Dynamic Media," Computer, vol. 10, no. 3 (March, 1977), pp. 31-41.

[4] C. Gane and T. Sarson. Structured Systems Analysis. Englewood Cliffs, NJ: Prentice-Hall, 1979.

[5] T. DeMarco. Structured Analysis and System Specification. Englewood Cliffs, NJ: Prentice-Hall, 1979.

[6] D.T. Ross and K.E. Schoman, Jr.. "Structured Analysis for Requirements Definition," IEEE Transactions on Software Engineering, vol. SE-3, no. 1 (January, 1977), pp. 6-15.

[7] M. Lundeberg, G. Goldkuhl, and A. Nilsson, "A Systematic Approach to Information Systems Development," Information Systems, vol. 4, no. 1 (1979), pp. 1-12, and vol. 4, no. 2 (1979), pp. 93-118.

[8] A.I. Wasserman, "Information System Development Methodology," Journal of the American Society for Information Science, vol. 31, no. 1 (1980), pp. 5-24.

[9] A.I. Wasserman, "Some Principles of User Software Engineering for Information Systems," Digest of Papers, COMPCON 75 Spring, IEEE Computer Society, pp. 49-52.

[10] E. Mumford, "Participative Systems Design: Structure and Method," Systems, Objectives, Solutions, vol. 1, no. 1 (January, 1981), pp. 5-19.

[11] L. Rudawitz and P. Freeman, "Client-Centered Design: Concepts and Experience," Systems, Objectives, Solutions, vol. 1, no. 1 (January, 1981), pp. 21-32.

[12] G.M. Nijssen, E.J. van Assche, and J.J. Snijders, "End User Tools for Information System Requirement Definitions," in Formal Models and Practical Tools for Information System Design, ed. H.-J. Schneider. Amsterdam: North-Holland, 1979, pp. 125-148.

[13] M. Lundeberg, "An Approach for Involving the Users in the Specification of Information Systems," in Formal Models and Practical Tools for Information Systems Design, ed. H.-J. Schneider. Amsterdam: North-Holland, 1979, pp. 195-217.

[14] J.M. Smith and D.C.P. Smith, "Database Abstraction: Aggregation and Generalization," ACM Transactions on Database Systems, vol. 2, no. 2 (June, 1977), pp. 105-133.

[15] J.M. Smith and D.C.P. Smith, "Conceptual Database Design," in <u>Tutorial:</u> <u>Software Design Techniques</u>, 3rd edition, ed. P. Freeman and A.I. Wasserman. Los Alamitos, CA: IEEE Computer Society, 1980, pp. 333-356.

[16] R.H. Drain and N. Oakley. <u>Successful Conference and Convention Planning</u>. Toronto: McGraw Hill Ryerson Ltd.. 1978.

[17] H.S. Kindler. <u>Organizing the Technical Conference</u>. New York: Reinhold Publishing Corp.. 1960.

[18] A.I. Wasserman, "USE: a Methodology for the Design and Development of Interactive Information Systems," in <u>Formal Models and Practical Tools for Information System Design</u>, H.-J. Schneider (Ed.), North Holland, Amsterdam, pp. 31-50.

[19] S.K. Card, T.P. Moran, and A. Newell, "The Keystroke-Level Model for User Performance Time with Interactive Systems," <u>Communications of the ACM</u>, vol. 23, no. 7 (July, 1980), pp. 396-410.

[20] <u>IBM Systems Journal</u>, vol. 20, no. 2 (1981).

[21] H.T. Smith and T.R. Green (eds.) <u>Human Interaction with Computers</u>. London: Academic Press, 1980.

[22] B. Shneiderman. <u>Software Psychology</u>. Cambridge, MA: Winthrop Publishers, 1980.

[23] T. Gilb. <u>Humanized Input</u>. Cambridge, MA: Winthrop Publishers, 1977.

[24] S.K. Card, T.P. Moran, and A. Newell. <u>The Psychology of Human-Computer Interaction</u>. Hillsdale, NJ: Erlbaum, 1981, in press.

[25] A.I. Wasserman, "User Software Engineering and the Design of Interactive Systems," <u>Proc. 5th International Conference on Software Engineering</u>, pp. 387-393.

[26] A.I. Wasserman and S.K. Stinson, "A Specification Method for Interactive Information Systems," <u>Proc. IEEE Computer Society Conference on Specifications of Reliable Software</u>, Cambridge, MA, 1979, pp. 68-79.

[27] S.C. Johnson, "Language Development Tools," <u>Bell System Technical Journal</u>, vol 57, no. 6 (July-August, 1978), pp. 2155-2175.

[28] M.E. Conway, "Design of a Separable Transition-Diagram Compiler," <u>Comm. ACM</u>, vol. 6, no. 7 (July, 1963), pp. 396-408.

[29] J.T. O'Neill (Ed.), <u>MUMPS Language Standard</u>, ANSI Standard X11.1, American National Standards Institute. 1977.

[30] W.A. Wulf, R.L. London, and M. Shaw. "An Introduction to the Construction and Verification of Alphard Programs," <u>IEEE Transactions on Software Engineering</u>, vol. SE-2, no. 4 (December, 1976), pp. 253-265.

[31] N.G. Leveson, "Applying Behavior Abstraction to Information System Design and Integrity," Ph.D. dissertation, University of California, Los Angeles, 1980. (Available as Technical Report #47, Laboratory of Medical Information Science, University of California, San Francisco)

[32] A.I. Wasserman and S.K. Stinson, "A Specification Method for Interactive Medical Information Systems," <u>Proc. 3rd Symposium on Computer Applications in Medical Care</u>, Washington, DC, 1980.

[33] A.I. Wasserman, "The Data Management Facilities of PLAIN," <u>Proc. ACM 1979 SIGMOD Conference</u>, Boston, May, 1979, pp. 60-70.

[34] E. Yourdon and L.L. Constantine. <u>Structured Design</u>. Englewood Cliffs, NJ: Prentice-Hall, 1979.

[35] S.H. Caine and E.K. Gordon, "PDL -- a Tool for Software Design", *Proc. AFIPS 1975 NCC*, vol. 44, pp. 271-276.

[36] E. Yourdon. *Structured Walkthroughs*. 2nd ed. Englewood Cliffs, NJ: Prentice-Hall, 1979.

[37] B. Liskov *et al.* *CLU Reference Manual*. Berlin: Springer Verlag, 1981.

[38] D.I. Cood *et al.*. "Report on the Language Gypsy -- Version 2.0," Report ICSCA - CMP -10, Certifiable Minicomputer Project, University of Texas at Austin, 1978.

[39] B.W. Lampson *et al.*. "Report on the Programming Language Euclid," *ACM SIGPLAN Notices*, vol. 12, no. 2 (February, 1977), pp. 1-79.

[40] J.D. Ichbiah *et al.* *Reference Manual for the Ada Programming Language*. Berlin: Springer Verlag, 1981. Arlington, VA, 1980.

[41] A.I. Wasserman, "The Design of PLAIN -- Support for Systematic Programming," *Proc. AFIPS 1980 National Computer Conference*, vol. 49, pp. 731-740.

[42] A.I. Wasserman, D.D. Sherertz, M.L. Kersten, R.P. van de Riet, and M.D. Dippé, "Revised Report on the Programming Language PLAIN," *ACM SIGPLAN Notices*, vol. 16, no. 5 (May, 1981), pp. 59-80.

[43] R.P. van de Riet, A.I. Wasserman, M.L. Kersten, and W. de Jonge, "High-Level Programming Features for Improving the Efficiency of a Relational Database System," *Transactions on Database Systems*, vol. 6, no. 3 (September, 1981), pp. 464-485.

[44] M.D. Dippé, "Exception-Handling in PLAIN," Technical Report #52, Laboratory of Medical Information Science, University of California, San Francisco, 1981.

[45] A.I. Wasserman and T.W. Booster, "String Handling and Pattern Matching in PLAIN," Technical Report #50, Laboratory of Medical Information Science, University of California, San Francisco, 1981.

[46] H. Lycklama, "UNIX on a Microprocessor," *Bell System Technical Journal*, vol. 57, no. 6, part 1 (July, 1978), pp. 2087-2101.

[47] E.L. Ivie, "The Programmer"s Workbench -- A Machine for Software Development," *Communications of the ACM*, vol. 20, no. 10 (October, 1977), pp. 746-753.

[48] S. Cutz, A.I. Wasserman, and M.J. Spier, "Personal Development Systems for the Professional Programmer," *Computer*, vol. 14, no. 4 (April, 1981), pp. 45-53.

[49] N. Wirth, "Lilith: a Personal Computer for the Software Engineer," *Proc. 5th Int'l Conference on Software Engineering*, San Diego, March, 1981, pp. 2-15.

[50] S. Zeigler . *et al.*. "The Intel 432 Ada Programming Environment," *Digest of Papers, COMPCON Spring 81*, IEEE Computer Society, San Francisco, 1981, pp. 405-410.

[51] F.T. Baker, "Structured Programming in a Production Programming Environment," *IEEE Transactions on Software Engineering*, vol. SE-1, no. 2 (June, 1975), pp. 241-252.

[52] O. Roubine and L. Robinson, "SPECIAL Reference Manual", Technical Report CSG-45, SRI International, Menlo Park, CA, 1978.

[53] A.I. Wasserman, S. Yeh, and D.S. Keller, "The Module Control System," submitted for publication, 1981.

Part X
Annotated Software
Design Bibliography

Peter Freeman
Anthony I. Wasserman

This short bibliography presents a selection of references on software design and related topics. The entries cover a range of topics from very practical, narrow pieces to philosophic discussions of the nature of design in other disciplines. The intent is to provide you an entry into the literature, not to list everything that has been published.

We have organized the bibliography into three sections. The first lists references that primarily deal with design topics. The second lists a few of the many references that deal more generally with software engineering. The third lists sources for current information on the topics discussed in this volume.

DESIGN REFERENCES

Alexander, C., *Notes on the Synthesis of Form,* Harvard University Press, Cambridge, Mass., 1964.

In this short book, Alexander presents his analysis of traditional design and the situation we face in designing complex artifacts. He then presents a technique for discovering the important interconnections between parts of the design. Although the method has not proven to be highly successful, his analysis of the design activity contains many insights that are useful for software designers. Recommended for all who are not satisfied with design practice and want to begin to understand why.

Aron, J.D., *The Program Development Process, Part 1: The Individual Programmer,* 1974, *Part 2: The Programming Team,* Addison-Wesley Pub. Co., Reading, Mass.

Aron takes a balanced view of the software development process, focusing concurrently on computer science/programming methodology issues and on management techniques. Part 1 covers problem analysis, program design, coding and debugging. Part 2 covers the system development life cycle, system analysis, and project management techniques, including planning, resource management, and documentation. Aron does not go into great depth on these topics, but manages to raise all of the important points and gives numerous references to other work.

Asimow, M., *Introduction to Design,* Prentice-Hall, Inc., Englewood Cliffs, N.J., 1962.

Intended as a reference source for teachers and students, this book provides a clear exposition of the steps of traditional engineering design. While some of the steps he describes (e.g., planning for distribution) are not directly applicable to software design, it does provide a useful overview of the industrial design process which is becoming increasingly important in software engineering.

Biggs, C.L., E.G. Birks, and W.A. Atkins, *Managing the Systems Development Process,* Prentice-Hall, Inc., Englewood Cliffs, N.J., 1980.

This book presents the methodology for managing system development as practiced by one of the largest accounting/consulting firms. The book covers all phases of the life cycle and includes a number of forms used to record essential information in the development process.

Brooks, F.P., Jr., *The Mythical Man-Month,* Addison-Wesley Pub. Co., Reading, Mass., 1975.

Brooks relates the lessons of his experience as manager of the OS/360 development effort with clarity and wit. Brooks' Law, "Adding people to a late software project makes it later," refers to the non-interchangeability of people and time, thereby motivating the book's title. Brooks also focuses on team organization for software development and the value of documentation. The reader must be careful not to miss the important points hidden among photographs of Babe Ruth, dinosaurs, and Mickey Mouse or the valuable lessons intertwined with pithy quotations from Goethe, Swift, and Ovid. (An excerpt is contained in this volume.)

Dahl, O.J., E.W. Dijkstra, and C.A.R. Hoare, *Structured Programming,* Academic Press, London, 1972.

This book consists of three monographs: "Notes on Structured Programming," by Dijkstra, "Notes on Data Structuring," by Hoare, and "Hierarchical Program Structures," by Dahl and Hoare. Dijkstra's paper was perhaps the single most influential document in the so-called "programming revolution," and typewritten copies were privately circulated for some time before publication here. Dijkstra uses the word "programming" in the broadest possible sense, encompassing the entire problem-solving process, and presents several meticulous examples of systematic program construction. It should be noted that Dijkstra's use of the term "structured programming" does not involve a discussion of the *go to* statement. Hoare's paper is the outline of a theory of data structuring. It contains some elements of his work on axiomatization of computer programming, but is most interesting for the view it gives of the design of PASCAL.

De Marco, T., *Structured Analysis and System Specification,* Prentice-Hall, Inc., Englewood Cliffs, N.J., 1979.

Structured analysis as an explicit technique was almost certainly originated by Doug Ross (see the paper by Ross in this volume). Like many other good approaches and concepts, it has been modified and used in a number of formats. This book by De Marco (who is associated with the Yourdon organization) describes one of the more widely taught variations. (Another variation is described in the paper by Gane in this volume.) The techniques presented here clearly have some strong similarity to SADT, but do not include all of SADT on the one hand and include some important techniques for dealing with data on the other. The book is well written and easy to understand.

Gane, C. and T. Sarson, *Structured Systems Analysis,* Prentice-Hall, Inc., Englewood Cliffs, N.J., 1979.

This book describes Structured Systems Analysis—a collection of techniques intended to strengthen traditional systems analysis. The techniques are similar to those described in De Marco, 1979, and to SADT. The paper in this volume by Gane provides an introduction to them.

Guttag, J., "Abstract Data Types and the Development of Data Structures," *Communications of the ACM,* Vol. 20, No. 6, June 1977.

Abstract data types are an important concept in several of the newer design and programming techniques. This paper, by one of the early researchers in the field, presents and discusses the application of an algebraic technique for specifying abstract data types.

Hice, G.F., W.S. Turner, and L.F. Cashwell, *System Development Methodology,* 2nd ed., North-Holland/American Elsevier Pub. Co., Amsterdam and New York, 1979.

This book contains a wealth of suggestions for project management. The authors have developed a coordinated and well-documented approach to the development of man/machine information systems. Their methodology consists of seven activities: definition study, preliminary design, detail design, program and human job development, testing, data conversion and system implementation, and operations and maintenance. A chapter is devoted to each activity and each includes detailed lists of methods and products for that stage; altogether, a useful book for the serious system developer.

Kent, W., *Data and Reality,* North Holland Pub. Co., Amsterdam, 1978.

This book presents the idea that the traditional methods used for modeling data are inadequate and do not conform well to realistic models of the world. Essentially, present data models are too limited and will need to be improved in the future to reduce their dependence upon computer-based concepts and to incorporate more of the semantic information associated with data objects in the real world.

Jackson, M. *Principles of Program Design,* Academic Press, 1975 and *System Development,* Prentice-Hall International, 1983.

The first book presents the Jackson approach to detailed design and structured programming, including data and problem structure modelling, structure clashes, program inversions, backtracking, and error handling. This technique has been taught and used for the past ten years. The second book presents an essentially expanded version of the method that covers a wider range of problems and a wider aspect of the development lifecycle. In particular it stresses specifications and the process-over-time nature of many of the real-world situations that must be dealt with by computer systems.

Jones, J.C., *Design Methods,* 2nd Edition, Wiley-Interscience, London, 1981.

The two-part book first describes the current state of design methods in the area of architectural and industrial design and then describes briefly a number of new methods that have been developed to improve our ability to design complex artifacts. The analysis of the current status of design is interesting and, although many of the methods are most applicable to other fields, some of them have applications in software.

Liskov, B. and S.N. Zilles, "Programming with Abstract Data Types," *ACM SIGPLAN Notices,* Vol. 9, No. 4, Apr. 1974, pp. 50-59.

When one refines the solution to a problem, it is necessary to refine the data structure along with the procedure. One thinks in terms of "abstract data structures," which are eventually mapped into a physical data structure. An abstract data type is a form of programming language extension whereby one may introduce a new data type into the language, along with the representation of that type and the set of allowable operations on objects of that type. The representation and the set of operations are encapsulated in such a way that the representation of the type is hidden from external modules, which are constrained to use only the given set of operations. The use of abstract types in the programming language CLU is shown.

Lucas, H.C., Jr., *Toward Creative Systems Design,* Columbia University Press, New York, 1974.

Lucas identifies three major problems in the design of information systems: technical, organizational behavior, and project management. In this short treatise he concentrates on the organizational problems (entire organization, groups and individuals) and puts forth a design approach intended to use creatively the inevitable behavior changes that introduction of an information system will bring about. This book provides a good balance to the purely technical aspects of design normally dealt with in courses on design and gives an introduction to the managerial and behavioral aspects.

Myers, G., *Composite/Structured Design*, John Wiley & Sons, Inc., New York, 1978.

Myers was one of the original collaborators in developing structured design (see the paper by Stevens, Myers and Constantine), but takes a somewhat different approach to some aspects of the discipline. This book provides an alternative view to that of Yourdon and Constantine.

Olle, T., H. Sol, and A. Verrijn-Stuart (eds.) *Information System Design Methodology: A Comparative Review*, North-Holland, 1982 and T. Olle, H. Sol, and C. Tully, *Feature Analysis of Information System Design Methodologies*, North-Holland, 1983.

The IFIP Working Group 8.1 is carrying out an extensive review of a number of different design methods under the title Comparative Review of Information System Design Methodologies (CRIS). The first book presents the results of their first public conference, including the results of applying 13 different methods to the same problem. Many of the methods are new and emphasize data modelling and formal specifications; thus, the comparisons may be of interest for some time to come. The second book is essentially a continuation of the results of the WG 8.1 review effort.

Orr, K., *Structured Systems Development*, Yourdon, Inc., New York, 1977.

This book describes Ken Orr's variation on the Warnier approach. It uses the data structure of the output to derive a structured program that computes this output. While very readable, the book is more of an introduction than a complete guide.

Page-Jones, M., *The Practical Guide to Structured Systems Design*, Yourdon Press, 1980.

This is probably the best and most practically-oriented of the several books on structured design. It includes a good introduction to structured analysis, especially the use of data-flow diagrams, and numerous examples.

Parnas, D.L., "A Technique for Software Module Specifications with Examples," *Comm. ACM,* Vol. 15, No. 5, May 1972, pp. 330-336.

Parnas, D.L. and D.P. Siewiorek, "Use of the Concept of Transparency in the Design of Hierarchically Structured Systems," *Comm. ACM,* Vol. 18, No. 7, July 1975, pp. 401-408.

These two papers expand upon the definition and use of modularity beyond the explanations given in the two papers by Parnas in this volume. The earlier paper explains the principle of modularity, stressing that this technique permits one module to be written with little knowledge of the code of other modules and permits modules to be replaced independently of one another. The more recent paper discusses the concept of transparency in system design, applying "levels of abstraction" to both hardware and software.

Peters, L., *Software Design: Methods and Techniques,* Yourdon Press, 1981.

This book provides a survey and thumbnail sketch of a wide range of software design approaches, with special emphasis on the representations used. The author has both a practical background in software design and a research interest in the comparison of methods; he combines these two perspectives in several chapters that explore some of the concepts and issues in software design.

Simon, H.A., *The Sciences of the Artificial,* MIT Press, Cambridge, Mass., 1969.

This book is a written version of the Karl Taylor Compton lectures delivered by Simon in 1968, plus a reprint of one of his earlier papers. It provides very thought-provoking reading on the nature of those activities—such as management science and computer science—that deal with man-made phenomena. A central theme of the lectures is the role of design in these disciplines. His discussion of the necessary skills for design is of particular interest.

Tsichritzis, D. and F. Lochovsky. *Data Models,* Prentice-Hall, 1982.

The authors survey current techniques for developing conceptual data models. Included are relational, network, hierarchial, and entity-relationship models, in addition to others.

Warnier, J., *Logical Construction of Programs,* Van Nostrand Reinhold Books, New York, 1974.

This is an English translation (and not a very good one) of Warnier's L.C.P. approach. It uses the data structure of the output to derive a structured program that computes this output. While very readable, the book is more of an introduction than a complete guide.

Wiederhold, G., *Database Design,* 2nd Edition, McGraw-Hill Book Co., New York, 1983.

This book, which might be more accurately titled "File and Database Design," is a comprehensive study of both analytical models for the evaluation of file and data base designs, as well as a survey of a number of data modeling techniques.

Yeh, R., ed., *Current Trends in Programming Methodology,* Vols. 1, 2, and 4, Prentice-Hall, Inc. Englewood, Cliffs, N.J., 1977, 1978.

Chandy, K. and R. Yeh, eds., *Current Trends in Programming Methodology,* Vol. 3, Prentice-Hall, Inc., Englewood, Cliffs, N.J., 1978.

These four volumes consist of reprints covering a wide range of current research and advanced ideas relevant to design. Volume 1 covers software specification and design, Volume 2 deals with program validation, Volume 3 is on software modeling, and Volume 4 surveys data structuring. The orientation of these volumes is theoretical rather than practical.

Yourdon, E. and L. Constantine, *Structured Design,* Prentice-Hall, Inc., Englewood, Cliffs, N.J., 1979.

This is the primary reference for this method, although there are older and other versions as well (see, for example, Myers 1979, and the paper by Stevens, Myers, and Constantine).

Ample explanation of the basic concepts and their application is given, along with numerous examples. The book is too wordy in many places and some of the crucial steps of creating a structured design are not treated as thoroughly as one would like. But, on the whole, it is a very useful text.

Yourdon, E. *Structured Walkthroughs,* Yourdon Press, 1978.

Walkthroughs are generally acknowledged to be one of the most effective techniques for improving the quality of a design. This book discusses walkthroughs of specifications, designs, and code, explores the role of different actors in the walkthrough process, and discusses the management of the process.

GENERAL REFERENCES

Boehm, B. *Software Engineering Economics,* Prentice-Hall, 1981.

The author, one of the leading workers in software engineering, addresses fundamentals of software engineering economics, provides a quantitative model of the software life-cycle, and discusses the art of software cost estimation. In particular, he discusses a model for cost estimation developed through his industrial experience.

Date, C. *An Introduction to Database Systems,* Third Edition, Addison-Wesley, 1981.

This is one of the most popular, general introductions to current database technology.

Jensen, R.W. and C.C. Tonies, *Software Engineering,* Prentice-Hall, Inc., Englewood, Cliffs, N.J., 1979.

Important software engineering topics including design, programming, verification and validation, security and privacy, management, and legal aspects of software development are treated from the viewpoint of practicing professionals. In addition to the editors, contributing authors include Enos, Van Tilberg, Deutsch, Hascall, and Reddien.

Myers, G.J., *Software Reliability: Principles and Practice,* John Wiley & Sons, Inc., 1976, New York, 1976.

Myers gives an overview of the topics which affect software reliability, giving primary attention to issues of program design and testing, but also touching upon several related topics, including programming languages, verification, and management techniques. Although the book does not contain any exercises, it is the first book which is truly suitable as a text for a software engineering course.

Myers, G., *The Art of Software Testing,* John Wiley & Sons, Inc., New York, 1979.

This short book focuses on the practical aspects of software testing. While good design should reduce the amount of testing effort necessary, a solid understanding of how testing will be carried out is essential for the designer.

Pressman, R. *Software Engineering: A Practitioner's Approach,* McGraw-Hill, 1982.

This general introduction to the practice of software engineering surveys a wide-range of concepts, tools, and techniques applicable across the development life-cycle.

Zelkowitz, M., A. Shaw, and J. Gannon, *Principles of Software Engineering and Design,* Prentice-Hall, Inc., N.J., 1979.

This book contains two chapters of general principles (a good overview of techniques for large-scale software development and a survey of programming methodology topics) and three chapters of examples (a collection of small program design examples and the designs of a small multiprogramming system and of a compiler).

CURRENT INFORMATION SOURCES

Archival Journals
TSE—*IEEE Transactions on Software Engineering*
SPE—*Software Practice and Experience* (John Wiley)
SOS—*Systems, Objectives, Solutions* (North Holland)
JSS—*Journal of Systems and Software* (North Holland)
TOPLAS—*ACM Transactions on Programming Languages and Systems*
TODS—*ACM Transactions on Database Systems*

Other ACM Publications
  Computing Surveys
  Communications
  Computing Reviews
  Software Engineering Notes (SIGSOFT)
  SIGPLAN Notices
  Special conference and workshop proceedings
  Other Special Interest Group (SIG) Publications

Other IEEE Publications
  Computer
  Conference and workshop proceedings (especially the International Conferences of Software Engineering)
  Software

Trade Magazines
  Computerworld
  Software News
  Datamation
  Infosystems

Technical Information Services
  Auerbach Information Management Series (especially Systems Development Management and Computer Programming Management, 6560 North Park Drive, Pennsauken, NJ 08109)
  Datapro Reports, 1805 Underwood Blvd., Delran, NJ 08075
  EDP Analyzer, 925 Anza, Vista, CA 92083

Author Biographies

Peter Freeman is an Associate Professor of Information and Computer Science at the University of California, Irvine, as well as director of a small consulting business. His research interests include the reuse of software designs, and the evaluation of software engineering techniques. He has worked in the computer field since 1961 and has worked as a programmer and participated in various design efforts in addition to his teaching and research.

He holds a Ph.D. in computer science from Carnegie-Mellon University.

Freeman organized the tutorial based on this book (first held at the 2nd International Conference on Software Engineering) and has since presented it and related material in the U.S. and internationally. He has served as an ACM National Lecturer, and as a consultant to the United Nations, the US Government, and various industrial organizations on matters related to software development.

He is the author of more than 30 technical papers, serves on the Editorial Advisory Board of several journals, and is the Consulting Editor for the McGraw-Hill Software Engineering series. He is the author of *Software Systems Principles* (SRA) and co-editor (with A.I. Wasserman) of *Software Engineering Education -- Needs and Objectives*.

Anthony I. Wasserman is a Professor of Medical Information Science at the University of California, San Francisco, and a Lecturer in the Computer Science Division at the University of California, Berkeley. He is the developer of the User Software Engineering methodology for creating interactive information systems. His research interests include programming environments, data base management, and software development methodology.

He holds a Ph.D. degree in computer sciences from the University of Wisconsin -- Madison, and has an AB in mathematics and physics from the University of California, Berkeley.

He is the author of more than 40 technical papers and the editor or co-editor of seven books, including *Tutorial: Software Development Environments* (IEEE Computer Society), *Automated Tools for Information Systems Design* (with H.-J. Schneider) (North Holland), and *Data Protection in Health Information Systems -- Considerations and Guidelines* (with 6 others) (North Holland).

Wasserman has been active in professional organizations, serving as chairman of ACM SIGSOFT, the special interest group on software engineering, from 1976 to 1979, and is presently Vice Chairman of IFIP Working Group 8.1 (Design and Evaluation of Information Systems).

He is Editor-in-Chief of *ACM Computing Surveys*, and a member of the editorial advisory boards of *Information Systems* and *Decision Support Systems*.